MEASUREMENT IN SPORT AND EXERCISE PSYCHOLOGY

EDITORS

Gershon Tenenbaum, PhD
Florida State University

Robert C. Eklund, PhD
Florida State University

Akihito Kamata, PhD
University of Oregon

Human Kinetics

Library of Congress Cataloging-in-Publication Data

Measurement in sport and exercise psychology / editors, Gershon Tenenbaum, Robert Eklund, Akihito Kamata.

     p. ; cm.

  Includes bibliographical references and index.

  ISBN-13: 978-0-7360-8681-3 (hard cover)

  ISBN-10: 0-7360-8681-1 (hard cover)

  I. Tenenbaum, Gershon. II. Eklund, Robert C. (Robert Charles), 1958- III. Kamata, Akihito.

  [DNLM: 1. Athletes--psychology. 2. Exercise--psychology. 3. Psychological Tests. 4. Sports--psychology. QT 260]

  613.7'1--dc23

                       2011035162

ISBN-10: 0-7360-8681-1 (print)

ISBN-13: 978-0-7360-8681-3 (print)

The web addresses cited in this text were current as of May 2011, unless otherwise noted.

Acquisitions Editor: Myles Schrag; **Developmental Editor:** Kevin Matz; **Assistant Editors:** Steven Calderwood, Tyler Wolpert, and Bethany Bentley; **Copyeditor:** Jocelyn Engman; **Indexer:** Betty Frizzéll; **Permissions Manager:** Dalene Reeder; **Graphic Designer:** Bob Reuther; **Graphic Artist:** Kathleen Boudreau-Fuoss; **Cover Designer:** Bob Reuther; **Photographer (cover):** © Human Kinetics; **Art Manager:** Kelly Hendren; **Associate Art Manager:** Alan L. Wilborn; **Illustrations:** © Human Kinetics; **Printer:** Thomson-Shore, Inc.

Printed in the United States of America   10 9 8 7 6 5 4 3 2 1

Human Kinetics

Website: www.HumanKinetics.com

United States: Human Kinetics
P.O. Box 5076
Champaign, IL 61825-5076
800-747-4457
e-mail: humank@hkusa.com

Canada: Human Kinetics
475 Devonshire Road Unit 100
Windsor, ON N8Y 2L5
800-465-7301 (in Canada only)
e-mail: info@hkcanada.com

Europe: Human Kinetics
107 Bradford Road
Stanningley
Leeds LS28 6AT, United Kingdom
+44 (0) 113 255 5665
e-mail: hk@hkeurope.com

Australia: Human Kinetics
57A Price Avenue
Lower Mitcham, South Australia 5062
08 8372 0999
e-mail: info@hkaustralia.com

New Zealand: Human Kinetics
P.O. Box 80
Torrens Park, South Australia 5062
0800 222 062
e-mail: info@hknewzealand.com

E4946

CONTENTS

MEASUREMENT METHODS

9 Idiosyncratic Measures in Sport   81

W. Alex Edmonds, PhD, Michael B. Johnson, PhD, Gershon Tenenbaum, PhD, and Akihito Kamata, PhD

10 Dynamic Assessment in Sport   91

Thomas Schack, PhD

11 Verbal Reports of Cognitive Processes   103

David W. Eccles, PhD

12 Making Sense of Words and Stories in Qualitative Research: Strategies for Consideration   119

Brett Smith, PhD, and Andrew C. Sparkes, PhD

MEASUREMENT ISSUES

PART II Cognition, Perception, and Motivation Measurement . . 177

COGNITION MEASUREMENT

18 Anticipation and Decision Making: Skills, Methods, and Measures   191

Andrew Mark Williams, PhD, and Bruce Abernethy, PhD

19 Measuring Mental Representations   203

Thomas Schack, PhD

SELF-PERCEPTION MEASUREMENT

20 Physical Self-Concept   215

Herbert W. Marsh, PhD, and Jacqueline H.S. Cheng, PhD

21 Exercise and Self-Perception Constructs   227

Catherine Sabiston, PhD, James R. Whitehead, EdD, and Robert C. Eklund, PhD

22 Exercise-Related Self-Efficacy   239

Edward McAuley, PhD, Siobhan M. White, PhD, Emily L. Mailey, MS, and Thomas R. Wójcicki, BS

23 Self-Efficacy and Collective Efficacy 251

Lori Dithurbide, PhD, and Deborah L. Feltz, PhD

24 Effort Perception 265

Selen Razon, MS, Jasmin Hutchinson, PhD, and Gershon Tenenbaum, PhD

MOTIVATION MEASUREMENT

25 Intrinsic and Extrinsic Motivation in Sport and Exercise 279

Robert J. Vallerand, PhD, Eric G. Donahue, BSc, and Marc-André K. Lafrenière, BS

26 Exercise Motivation 293

Philip M. Wilson, PhD

27 Achievement Motivation Processes 303

David E. Conroy, PhD, and Amanda L. Hyde, MS

PART III Emotion, Affect, and Coping Measurement 319

28 Affect, Mood, and Emotion 321

Panteleimon Ekkekakis, PhD

29 Emotional Reactivity 333

Christopher M. Janelle, PhD, and Kelly M. Naugle, PhD

30 Flow 349

Susan A. Jackson, PhD, and Robert C. Eklund, PhD

31 Burnout 359

Robert C. Eklund, PhD, Alan L. Smith, PhD, Thomas D. Raedeke, PhD, and Scott Cresswell, PhD

32 Bayesian Approach of Measuring Competitive Crisis 367

Michael Bar-Eli, PhD, and Gershon Tenenbaum, PhD

33 Psychological Skills   381

Robert Weinberg, PhD, and Samuel Forlenza, MS

34 Coping in Sport and Exercise   393

Ronnie Lidor, PhD, Peter R.E. Crocker, PhD, and Amber D. Mosewich, MSc

PART IV Social and Behavioral Measurement 409

35 Cohesion   411

Albert V. Carron, PhD, Mark A. Eys, PhD, and Luc J. Martin, MA

36 Sequential Analysis of Team Communications and Effects on Team Performance   423

Allan Jeong, PhD

37 Models and Measurement of Leadership in Sport   433

Packianathan Chelladurai, PhD

38 Moral Behavior 443

Maria Kavussanu, PhD, and Ian D. Boardley, PhD

39 Behavioral Measurement in Exercise Psychology 455

Claudio R. Nigg, PhD, Patricia J. Jordan, PhD, and Angela Atkins, MPH

CONTRIBUTORS

Bruce Abernethy, PhD
Professor
School of Human Movement Studies
The University of Queensland
Brisbane, Australia

Soyeon Ahn, PhD
Assistant Professor
Department of Educational and Psychological Studies
University of Miami
Coral Gables, Florida

Angela Atkins, MPH
Teacher
Health, Physical Education, and Leadership
Jarrett Middle School
Honolulu, Hawaii

Michael Bar-Eli, PhD
Professor
Department of Business Administration
Ben-Gurion University of the Negev
Beer-Sheva, Israel
The Zinman College of Physical Education and Sport
  Sciences
Wingate Institute
Netanya, Israel

Betsy Jane Becker, PhD
Mode L. Stone Distinguished Professor of Educational
  Statistics
Department of Educational Psychology and Learning
  Systems
Florida State University
Tallahassee, Florida

Ian D. Boardley, PhD
Lecturer
School of Education
University of Birmingham
Birmingham, United Kingdom

Dirk Büsch, PhD
Vice-Director
Institute for Applied Training Science
Leipzig, Germany

Albert V. Carron, PhD
Professor
School of Kinesiology
University of Western Ontario
London, Canada

Packianathan Chelladurai, PhD
Professor
School of Physical Activity and Educational Services
The Ohio State University
Columbus, Ohio

Jacqueline H.S. Cheng, PhD
Researcher
Department of Education
University of Oxford
Oxford, United Kingdom

David E. Conroy, PhD
Professor
Department of Kinesiology
The Pennsylvania State University
University Park, Pennsylvania

Scott Cresswell, PhD
Research Associate
School of Sport Science, Exercise and Health
University of Western Australia
Crawley, Australia

Peter R.E. Crocker, PhD
Professor
School of Kinesiology
University of British Columbia
Vancouver, Canada

Sarah R. Daniel

Lori Dithurbide, PhD
Research Assistant and Instructor
Department of Kinesiology
Michigan State University
East Lansing, Michigan

Eric G. Donahue, BSc
Doctoral Candidate
Department of Psychology
Université du Québec à Montréal
Montreal, Canada

Travis E. Dorsch, MS
Doctoral Student
Department of Health and Kinesiology
Purdue University
West Lafayette, Indiana

David W. Eccles, PhD
Director, Human Performance Research Center
Learning Systems Institute
Florida State University
Tallahassee, Florida

W. Alex Edmonds, PhD
Program Professor of Applied Research
Applied Research Center
Nova Southeastern University
Fort Lauderdale-Davie, Florida

Panteleimon Ekkekakis, PhD
Associate Professor
Department of Kinesiology
Iowa State University
Ames, Iowa

Ryne Estabrook, PhD
Post-Doctoral Fellow
Virginia Institute for Psychiatric and Behavioral
    Genetics
Virginia Commonwealth University
Richmond, Virginia

Jennifer L. Etnier, PhD
Professor
Department of Kinesiology
University of North Carolina at Greensboro
Greensboro, North Carolina

Edward F. Etzel, EdD
Professor
Department of Sport Sciences
West Virginia University
Morgantown, West Virginia

Mark A. Eys, PhD
Associate Professor
Departments of Kinesiology and Physical Education
    and Psychology
Wilfrid Laurier University
Waterloo, Canada

Deborah L. Feltz, PhD
University Distinguished Professor and Chairperson
Department of Kinesiology
Michigan State University
East Lansing, Michigan

Samuel Forlenza, MS
Graduate Assistant
Department of Kinesiology
Michigan State University
East Lansing Michigan

Kevin J. Grimm, PhD
Associate Professor
Department of Psychology
University of California, Davis
Davis, California

Amanda L. Hyde, MS
Doctoral Student
Department of Kinesiology
The Pennsylvania State University
University Park, Pennsylvania

Jasmin Hutchinson, PhD
Assistant Professor
Department of Exercise Science and Sport Studies
Springfield College
Springfield, Massachusetts

Susan A. Jackson, PhD
Adjunct Senior Lecturer
School of Human Movement Studies
The University of Queensland
St. Lucia, Australia

Christopher M. Janelle, PhD
Professor
Department of Applied Physiology and Kinesiology
University of Florida
Gainesville, Florida

Allan Jeong, PhD
Associate Professor
Department of Educational Psychology and Learning
    Systems
Florida State University
Tallahassee, Florida

Michael B. Johnson, PhD
Assistant Professor
Department of Psychology
University of Tennessee at Chattanooga
Chattanooga, Tennessee

Patricia J. Jordan, PhD
Adjunct Professor
Department of Public Health Sciences
University of Hawaii at Manoa
Honolulu, Hawaii

Maria Kavussanu, PhD
Senior Lecturer
School of Sport and Exercise Sciences
University of Birmingham⁻
Birmingham, United Kingdom

Marc-André K. Lafrenière, BS
Doctoral Candidate
Department of Psychology
Université du Québec à Montréal
Montreal, Canada

Hwa-Young Lee

Ronnie Lidor, PhD
Professor
Wingate Institute
University of Haifa
Haifa, Israel

Emily L. Mailey, MS
Doctoral Student
Department of Kinesiology and Community Health
University of Illinois at Urbana-Champaign
Urbana, Illinois

Herbert W. Marsh, PhD
Professor
Department of Education
University of Oxford
Oxford, United Kingdom

Luc J. Martin, MA
Doctoral Candidate
Department of Kinesiology
University of Western Ontario
London, Canada

Edward McAuley, PhD
Professor
Shahid and Ann Carlson Khan Professor in Applied
    Health Sciences
Departments of Kinesiology and Community Health,
    Psychology, Internal Medicine, and The Beckman
    Institute
University of Illinois at Urbana-Champaign
Urbana, Illinois

Eva V. Monsma, PhD
Associate Professor
Department of Physical Education
University of South Carolina
Columbia, South Carolina

Amber D. Mosewich, MSc
Doctoral Candidate
School of Kinesiology
University of British Columbia
Vancouver, Canada

Kelly M. Naugle, PhD
Post-Doctoral Fellow
Comprehensive Center for Pain Research
University of Florida
Gainesville, Florida

Claudio R. Nigg, PhD
Associate Professor
Department of Public Health Sciences
University of Hawaii at Manoa
Honolulu, Hawaii

Yaacov Petscher, PhD
Director of Research
Florida Center for Reading Research
Florida State University
Tallahassee, Florida

Thomas D. Raedeke, PhD
Associate Professor
Department of Exercise and Sport Science
East Carolina University, –
Greenville, North Carolina

Nilam Ram, PhD
Assistant Professor
Department of Human Development and Family
    Studies
The Pennsylvania State University
University Park, Pennsylvania

Selen Razon, MS
Doctoral Candidate
Department of Educational Psychology and Learning
    Systems
Florida State University
Tallahassee, Florida

Tatiana V. Ryba, PhD
Associate Professor
Department of Public Health
Aarhus University
Aarhus, Denmark

Catherine Sabiston, PhD
Associate Professor
Department of Kinesiology and Physical Education
McGill University
Montreal, Canada

Thomas Schack, PhD
Professor
Faculty of Psychology and Sport Sciences
Center of Excellence: CITEC
Bielefeld University
Bielefeld, Germany

Christopher Schatschneider, PhD
Associate Professor
Department of Psychology
Florida State University
Tallahassee, Florida

Robert J. Schinke, EdD
Professor
School of Human Kinetics
Laurentian University
Greater Sudbury, Canada

Alan L. Smith, PhD
Professor
Department of Health and Kinesiology
Purdue University
West Lafayette, Indiana

Brett Smith, PhD
Senior Lecturer
School of Sport, Exercise, and Health Sciences
Loughborough University
Loughborough, United Kingdom

Andrew C. Sparkes, PhD
Professor
Faculty of Education, Communication, and Leisure
Liverpool John Moores University
Liverpool, United Kingdom

Natalia B. Stambulova, PhD
Professor
School of Social and Health Sciences
Halmstad University
Halmstad, Sweden

Bernd Strauss, PhD
Chair and Professor
Department of Sport Psychology
University of Münster
Münster, Germany

Robert J. Vallerand, PhD
Professor
Department of Psychology
Université du Québec à Montréal
Montreal, Canada

Brandon K. Vaughn, PhD
Professor
Department of Mathematics and Statistics
Everest College
Santa Ana, California
Professor
Department of Business Administration
Baker College
Flint, Michigan

Justine Vosloo, PhD
Assistant Professor
Department of Exercise and Sport Sciences
Ithaca College
Ithaca, New York

Jack C. Watson II, PhD
Professor
Department of Sport Sciences
West Virginia University
Morgantown, West Virginia

Robert Weinberg, PhD
Professor
Department of Kinesiology and Health
Miami University
Miami, Ohio

Siobhan M. White, PhD
Post-Doctoral Fellow
Cancer Prevention Fellowship Program
National Cancer Institute
Bethesda, Maryland

James R. Whitehead, EdD
Associate Professor
Department of Health, Physical Education, and
    Recreation
University of North Dakota
Grand Forks, North Dakota

Andrew Mark Williams, PhD
Professor
Discipline of Exercise and Sports Science
The University of Sydney
Research Institute for Sport and Exercise Sciences
Liverpool John Moores University
Liverpool, United Kingdom

Philip M. Wilson, PhD
Associate Professor
Department of Kinesiology
Brock University
St. Catherines, Canada

Thomas R. Wójcicki, BS
Doctoral Student
Department of Kinesiology and Community Health
University of Illinois at Urbana-Champaign
Urbana, Illinois

Weimo Zhu, PhD
Professor
Department of Kinesiology and Community Health
University of Illinois at Urbana-Champaign
Urbana, Illinois

Introduction

The two chapters included in this section act as an introduction to *Measurement in Sport and Exercise Psychology*. Chapter 1 provides an overview of the material covered in the book and examines the book's overall organization and structure. It also includes a brief introduction to measurement and measurement interpretation and use. Chapter 2 provides a historical review of measurement in sport and exercise, summarizing key developments in psychological and educational measures. It also examines the corresponding developments in sport and exercise psychology and the limitations in current measurement practice.

Introduction to Measurement in Sport and Exercise Psychology

Gershon Tenenbaum, PhD, Robert C. Eklund, PhD, and Akihito Kamata, PhD

Measurement is essential to science. It must be *trustworthy* and *accurate*. It must tell us something about the *persons* being measured and be *conceptually useful* for testing *theoretical contentions* about how people behave in sport and exercise settings. The purpose of *Measurement in Sport and Exercise Psychology* is to provide state-of-the-art knowledge about central issues in measurement in sport and exercise psychology as well as to outline and review existing tools and methods in research areas in the field. This book covers key topics in the field, although not all areas could be presented in this first edition. *Measurement in Sport and Exercise Psychology* targets active and aspiring researchers as well as practitioners in the field. Understanding the measurement methods is crucial for meaningful research and is integral to ethical practice. This book is innovative and creative and fills a gap meriting greater attention in the field. It is designed to serve students who study sport and exercise sciences and psychology worldwide and to become an important resource for researchers, scholars, and practitioners. Measurement is an important issue that is of vital necessity to both academicians and practitioners in the field. This book is a state-of-the-art resource in this domain.

This book begins with a historical review of measurement in sport and exercise and then presents a comprehensive review of measurement theories and issues. These are clustered into four parts:

Part I, Measurement Basics, Methods, and Issues, outlines current psychometric thinking on introspective measurement. Matters such as measurement reliability and validity, classical test theory, item response theory, sampling invariance, modeling change, and Rasch modeling in sport are covered. Part I also introduces unique methods of measurement that were developed in the sport psychology domain as well as in other domains. These include idiographic measurement, dynamic assessment, verbal reports, and making sense of words and stories. Finally, issues such as developmental aspects, cultural issues, ethical considerations, and methods of using meta-analytical techniques to synthesize measurement issues are covered.

Part II, Cognition, Perception, and Motivation, covers measurement issues that relate to cognitive, anticipatory, and mental representation in sport and exercise; self-perception measures such as the physical self, self-perception, self-efficacy, collective efficacy, and effort perception in exercise and sport; and motivation measurements in sport and exercise, a broad concept that is further broken down into achievement motivation processes, intrinsic–extrinsic framework, and exercise-related motivation.

In part III, Emotion, Affect, and Coping Measurement, issues of interest are affect, mood, emotions, flow, burnout, and the psychological skills and coping strategies used for self-regulation and adaptation. A Bayesian approach to measuring psychological crisis is also included in part III.

Part IV, Social and Behavioral Measurement, consists of measurement issues related to team processes. These include team cohesion, leadership, communication, pro- and antisocial behaviors, and behavioral measurements that quantify physical activity.

Parts II, III, and IV of this book relate to specific issues encountered in sport and exercise psychology. The authors of these chapters have followed a common template. Each chapter begins with common definitions of relevant constructs and continues with commentary positioning the constructs within the appropriate theoretical and conceptual framework. Subsequently, commentary is provided on dimensions and sources of confusion and the main measurement tools for construct measurement. Example studies from the literature are highlighted, and recommendations are provided for researchers and practitioners. The end of each chapter presents a tabulated list of measures and sources for website presentation. This conceptual structure aims to

1. link theories to measurement issues,
2. identify limitations and strengths in using measures,
3. introduce the state-of-the-art tools in the field,
4. direct researchers and practitioners to the appropriate use of measures, and
5. introduce future directions and guidance in the field.

Throughout the book, also note the 🖱 that denotes full measures included in the accompanying web resource.

Concepts, Items, and Responses

The development of introspective psychological measures must start with a clear concept about the property intended to be developed. But properties do not stand by themselves; a *theory* provides a framework for starting a process culminating in a measurement product for persons. This measure allows the quantification of thoughts, opinions, attitudes, emotions, personalities, perceptions, cognitions, and behaviors. The theories, as well as the practices and experiences, guide the conceptual framework for the measurement. For example, it is the theory that guides whether a property is a trait (e.g., relatively stable) or a state (e.g., relatively unstable and fluctuating across situations) and

whether a measure should be one-dimensional or multidimensional. Thus, the measurement development process requires us to be theoretically, empirically, and practically knowledgeable about the domain of interest. Indeed, theories do not remain stable across time, and thus measurement must be altered and adjusted accordingly. Measurement develops with the accumulation of knowledge and thus can be seen as a process rather than a final product. This is particularly true in a relatively young discipline such as sport and exercise psychology, where many concepts are new, unique, and not-so-firmly delineated.

Steps in Designing Measures

When designing measures in the form of items or observations, the first step is to define the construct being measured and establish a specification of a test. At the basic level, the construct to be measured in the test must be clearly defined. Without having a good working definition of the construct, the rest of test construction process may not be cohesive. Also, a lack of definition may eventually affect the validity of the interpretation of test scores. One way to establish a clear construct is to develop a construct map (Wilson, 2005). A construct map specifies a definition for the content of the construct on an underlying continuum of the construct. Wilson suggests that an ordering of respondents or an ordering of item responses manifests a construct map. This way, the construct map is likely to be helpful for writing test items.

Ultimately, the test specification is used to decide what test items should be written and what test items should be chosen from the item pool. Therefore, a test specification should contain detailed information about how the test should look, including subdomains and their weights. It serves as a blueprint of the test, and for this reason a test specification is often referred to as a *test blueprint*. In order to establish a test specification, the behaviors representing the construct must be identified and specified. Identifying the behaviors establishes a well-defined population of items. Depending on the test, this process can be straightforward, such as when developing a short assessment instrument (e.g., Abell, Springer, & Kamata, 2009), or very complicated, such as when engaging in large-scale educational testing (e.g., Mehrens & Lehmann, 1991). A typical psychological measure involves extensive literature review and expert judgment to establish a list behavior. This process can be achieved by a well-designed focus group discussion conducted by several content experts.

The next step is to generate statements or behavioral codes that represent the variable we wish to measure in a person. The measure must be sufficient to generate values that represent the property in the person as accurately as possible and, by that, to generate true observations and differences among persons. Theory, empirical knowledge, and practical experience are used as a foundation to generate items and observations. The creation and phrasing of unbiased stems are the starting point of developing the measure. According to Wilson (2005), items should be considered as realizations of the construct to be measured. Therefore, items must be carefully written based on the well-defined construct and the test specification established in the initial step of the test construction.

Once this stage is completed, a response format or an observation scheme is attached to the stems. The format can be open ended or close ended, depending on what we desire to accomplish. Thus, *specific* and *general goals* must guide the measurement process. Responses to attitudinal items can be *affective* or *evaluative* (indicating how much people like or dislike, agree or disagree with a certain issue or opinion), can be *cognitive* (indicating what people think about an issue, topic, or event), or can reveal an *action* (indicating what people do in relation to certain issues and events). Accordingly, the response format can be *comparative* (choosing among alternatives, ranking, rating), *itemized* (use of choices, select one, and rate it), *visual analogue* (graphical), or *numerical ratings* (extent to which the person feels, endorses, agrees). One of the most popular formats in sport and exercise psychology research is the Likert scale. In this format, a statement is provided, and respondents are asked to indicate their degree of agreement with the statement by selecting one of several choices. The number of choices is part of the format design decided by the test developer. For example, if a 5-point scale is chosen, the choices will likely be labeled with "Strongly disagree," "Disagree," "Neutral," "Agree," and "Strongly agree." Taking into consideration the classical test theory principle, it is encouraged that all test items be based on the same format with the same number of scale points. However, item response theory ensures that a mixture of different item formats and different numbers of scale points has no negative effect on deriving test scores (e.g., Embretson & Reise, 2000).

At this stage *response biases* must be considered. These are *social desirability* (wanting to look nice), *acquiescence* (the tendency to endorse or reject all items), *extremity* (selecting extreme responses throughout), *halo* (a very positive stimulus), and *leniency* (overrating, overestimating). Developing introspective measures requires consideration of domain-specific knowledge, item-phrasing knowledge, and psychometric knowledge—all must be integrated and appropriately implemented in the construction process.

Assigning Meaning to Measures

One of the most reviewed topics in measurement is the *meaning* given to the numerical values that constitute the measure of a person. In most cases, measures are used for placing persons or comparing them to a norm (others) established in a reference group (a *norm-referenced measurement*, or *NRM*) or to an expected outcome or performance on a related task (a *criterion-referenced measurement*, or *CRM*). The differences between NRMs and CRMs are in the relativity versus absolute interpretations given to the measure. CRM relates to the chances people have to perform a task given their measured capacity as well as how people perform with respect to some maximal criterion. NRM locates a given measure relative to a norm established on a referenced group, although this lacks the meaning relative to what a person can do or perform given the measure magnitude. Thus, sport and exercise psychologists must be careful in interpreting measures before making judgments about abilities, performances, potentials, selections, and the like.

Introspection and Measurement: Reliability and Validity

In sport and exercise psychology, the major method used for measuring opinions, attitudes, emotions, and perceptions is introspective in nature. There are alternatives to introspective measures, but we cannot replace subjectivity by objectivity, because people behave according to the way they perceive the world. Objective measures allow better understanding of the underlying mechanisms of perception, but such measures are limited in scope as they lack the capacity of *assigning meaning* to the external and internal world. As important as introspective measures are, they must be taken cautiously. People differ in how they perceive the world, but they also differ in the way they express their perceptions, whether expressing in words, pictures, or numbers. Since the birth of psychology, introspective measurement has concerned psychometricians such as Thurstone, Guttman, Angoff, and Rasch. Terms such as *linear continuum, universal (unbiased) unit of measurement, origin* or *zero point, transitivity* (the ability to order people along the continuum), *certainty*, *sufficiency*, and *linearity* have been used and operationalized to advance the new science. At the same time, these concepts allow practitioners to use introspective measure with minimal *measurement error*.

Introspective measures aim to quantify a property or a capacity within a person. In other words, *persons* are the objects of introspective measurement. Measuring a person is possible through the use of *items* that represent the universe of a property. Items constitute measures once they are assigned *values*. When a sufficient number of items constitutes the measure, these items have the potential to become a *sufficient measure*. More specifically, once these items consistently and reliably discriminate among people who vary on a given property, together they constitute a sufficient measure. A sufficient measure consisting of *representative items* or *observations* is one that describes a person as precisely as possible. Once people's properties are described precisely and reliably, we can infer that the measure being used fits its expectations and is reliable. A reliable measure is one that enables us to determine with maximal confidence *how much* one person is *more* or *less* on the measure than another person is on that measure. Such a measure consists of items or observations that remain consistent across samples of persons in parameters indicating their difficulty and *discrimination (fit) level*. A reliable measure is one that produces a value that is free of error. Errors may be generated from internal sources (social desirability, personality, anxiety, and so on) or external or environmental sources (time, space, conditions, climate, inspection, and so on), and their influence on the measurable property must be minimized. Researchers and practitioners should consider seriously the measurement error derived from unreliability estimates. A tendency is to rely heavily on sufficient reliability coefficients such as >.70 or >.80. When these values are converted into measurement error values and the true score of a person is estimated with a 95% or 99% confidence interval, however, we can realize the magnitude of measurement error that is involved. Only then can we decide whether we are ready to tolerate this unreliable portion of the measure. Those who develop measures should consider possible *sources of unreliability* in a way that minimizes, as much as possible, the accumulation of *noise* into the measurement process. Chapter 3 outlines concepts, procedures, and issues regarding reliability.

Along with concerns about reliability issues, there are concerns about validity issues. How confident are we that the measure we develop and use describes the property it is intended to measure?

Validity is a process deserving much thought. To validate a test we must use *external criteria* to demonstrate the measure's *accountability*. Validation depends on the *goal* and the *specific situation* of the measurement. Measures aimed at supporting one decision may be useless in supporting decisions in other situations. Measures must be *decision dependent* as well as *decision directed* for making valid decisions. When we develop a measure, we must outline and follow a sound strategy to collect validity evidence. Such a strategy allows users of measures to decide whether the measure is suitable for their purposes and to what degree they can be confident in using it for making decisions.

As with the process of converting reliability coefficients into measurement error values, we recommend converting validity coefficients into values required for decision making, when possible. For example, the validity of a measure in many cases is aimed at predicting or determining how people will perform (with some probability) on an external task given a score on a measure. Criterion scores predicted by a given measure must consider the standard error of the validity similarly to the standard error of the reliability coefficient. The same idea applies to both coefficients (i.e., the stronger the correlation between the measure and the criterion, the stronger the evidence of the validity). If we wish to determine a cutoff point based on the correlation between the measure and the criterion, we may accept some persons who have a sufficient score on the measure but fail the criterion measure. *Valid acceptance* is evident when people pass the cutting point of both the measure and the criterion. *Valid rejection* occurs when people fail to pass both measures. The two errors possible under such a condition are *valid rejection* and *invalid acceptance*. Both are minimized when the standard error of validity diminishes. Also, note that the concept of validity has been revised in the history of psychometrics, and it is likely to be revised again in the near future. Chapter 4 discusses in detail the concepts and issues regarding validity.

Conclusion

Measurement in Sport and Exercise Psychology is a valuable source of knowledge written by leading scholars in measurement, research, theory, and practice. Readers of this book will be able to

- gain critical knowledge about the existing measurement tools used in the field;
- design new tools to meet specific goals and desires;

- use recommended tools and be cautious about their limitations; and
- comprehend the up-to-date psychometric properties required for designing, modifying, and improving introspective measurement.

Our aspiration is for this book to provide an important contribution for growth and development in the field and to facilitate the efforts of those who strive for the best. Nonetheless, this initial edition of the book does not cover all of the test construction steps mentioned in this chapter. The steps involved in defining and refining constructs to be measured, item writing, and designing the piloting of a preliminary item are not covered. Readers who are interested in the entire process of test construction are referred to excellent textbooks on the subject, including Abell, Springer, and Kamata (2009); Wilson (2005); DeVellis (2003); and Osterlind (2006).

Measurement Practice in Sport and Exercise Psychology

A Historical, Comparative, and Psychometric View

Weimo Zhu, PhD

> ❝ The history of science is largely coextensive with the history of measurement. ❞
> **Warren W. Tryon, 1991**

The opening quote also holds true for the field of sport and exercise psychology. Progress in sport and exercise psychology during the past 100 years, especially since the mid-1960s, has often been associated with advancements in measurement. The history of sport and exercise psychology itself has been described in many excellent reviews and book chapters. Table 2.1 on page 10 summarizes a few of these reviews and chapters. Similarly, the progress, issues, and concerns in measurement have been addressed in many thorough reviews and chapters. Table 2.2 on page 11 summarizes examples in these areas. Instead of repeating content that has already been well addressed, this chapter examines measurement practice in sport and exercise psychology from a unique historical perspective.

First, this chapter summarizes key developments in psychological and educational measurements, mainly those emerging during the past five decades. This is because these fields, although sometimes criticized for their practices (Meier, 1994; Michell, 1999), often serve as the parent fields for sport and exercise psychology. From them, new measurement theories and methods are learned and applied. This chapter then examines the corresponding developments in sport and exercise psychology. Thereafter,

limitations in current measurement practice in sport and exercise psychology, as well as possible causes, are examined. Finally, future directions and recommendations are outlined.

Although the term *measurement* is used throughout this chapter, it is not limited to its commonly used meaning, which is the process of assigning numbers to objects according to agreed-upon rules (Stevens, 1951). Rather, *measurement* represents the full range of measurement practice in sport and exercise psychology, including test and inventory construction, validation, scaling, setting evaluation standards, reporting, and so on. In the literature, *measurement* is often replaced by the term *assessment* when the former has a broader meaning. Both terms, therefore, are used interchangeably in this chapter. Also, *test*, *instrument*, and *inventory* are often used in educational and psychological measurement literature to describe the instrument or device that is used to collect information. These terms are therefore used interchangeably in this chapter. Also, note that this chapter is limited to literature available in English and mainly published in North America. Due to space constraints, this chapter focuses mainly on the quantitative, or psychometric, aspect of measurement. This, however, is not

■ Table 2.1 ■
Selected Publications
on the History of Sport and Exercise Psychology

Authors	Content summary
Landers (1983)	A review focusing on theory testing in sport psychology. After a thorough review on related research studies during three historical periods (1950-1965, 1966-1976, and 1977-1983), the author calls for (a) greater use of meta-analyses to reexamine the past conclusions, (b) avoiding premature commitments to a theory, and (c) becoming less enamored with statistically based null hypothesis testing.
Wiggins (1984)	A review of the history of sport psychology in North America in the book *Psychological Foundation of Sport* edited by Silva III and Weinberg (1984). Periods covered include early history (1890-1920), post–World War II, and formation of the North American Society for the Psychology of Sport and Physical Activity (NASPSPA) and the Canadian Society for Psychomotor Learning and Sport Psychology (CSPLSP).
Lenders, Boutcher, & Wang (1986)	A review of the history and status of the *Journal of Sport Psychology* between 1979 and 1985. The key findings include an increase in female principal authors; a significant increase in experimental studies at the end of this period, throughout which most studies were survey studies; and occasional problems with subject selection and statistical tests. Related methodological problems associated with rejection of manuscripts are discussed.
Singer (1989)	A review on the status and future direction of applied sport psychology in the United States. After a brief review of the history of the field, current professional developments and unique aspects of sport psychology, as well as its interfaces with the practice, its research, and its controversies, are described in detail. Finally, the future of the field is described.
Morgan (1994)	A review on 40 years of progress in sport psychology in exercise science and sport medicine. As part of the American College of Sports Medicine (ACSM) 40th anniversary lectures, the review focuses on advances and future directions in sport psychology within the ACSM.
McCullagh (1995)	A special issue of the *Sport Psychologist* devoted entirely to a historical perspective of sport psychology, in which eight papers address different aspects of sport psychology.
Weinberg & Gould (1995, 1999)	A chapter introducing the history of sport and exercise psychology with many historical photos.
Gill (2000)	A chapter describing in detail the history of sport and exercise psychology, including early roots (1890-1920), Griffith's work (1920-1940), isolated works (1940-1965), emergence (1965-1975), further development (1975-1995), and today (1995-2000).
Weiss & Gill (2005)	A paper in a supplement to celebrate the 75th anniversary of *Research Quarterly for Exercise and Sport* (*RQES*). After reviewing sport and exercise psychology articles published in *RQES*, the authors summarize reemerging themes in the field. Measurement development and validation are noticed as a key emergent issue and interest in the field.
Williams & Straub (2006)	A chapter on the past, present, and future of sport psychology, including an introduction on the history of sport psychology in Eastern Europe.
Smith & Bar-Eli (2007)	A collection of classical papers in sport and exercise psychology. A time line with representative events in the development of sport and exercise psychology is included in the preface.

meant to downplay the critical role of qualitative measurement, including interview, observation, behavioral analysis, and so on, that has also been widely used in measurement practice in sport and exercise psychology (Culver, Gilbert, & Trudel, 2003; Biddle, Markland, Gilbourne, Chatzisarantis, & Sparkes, 2001). Finally, note that the rich history of the development and applications of sport-specific measures is not covered in this chapter since these measures are well described in other chapters in

Selected Publications on Measurement Practice in Sport and Exercise Psychology

Authors	Content summary
Tenenbaum (1986)	An article consisting of critical reflections on measurement issues in sport psychology. This is one of the earliest papers introducing the Rasch model, one of the item response theory models, to the field of sport psychology.
Schutz (1989)	A chapter on new procedures for comparative physical education and sport, including a description of meta-analysis, qualitative research, new statistical procedures such as SEM, log-linear analysis, and all possible subsets regressions. A hypothetical example of SEM is provided.
Ostrow (1990)	A directory of 175 psychological tests in sport and exercise science. The source, purpose, description, construction, reliability, validity, norms, and availability of each test are described. In addition, an extensive review of these tests, including key psychometric information (e.g., content areas, measurement scales employed, test construction procedures, reliability, validity, and norms), is provided in the introduction. Many studies belong to one-shot studies with moderate quality. Nevertheless, this is a great collection of the tests used in sport and exercise psychology.
Dishman (1991)	A criticism of the field of sport psychology for failing as an exercise and sport science, including the following: "lack, or does not use, many of the established measurement technologies, methodologies, and applied theories available to us."
Schutz & Gessaroli (1993)	An excellent and comprehensive review on psychometric issues in sport psychology research, including statistical data analysis and related issues. The key measurement areas are in appropriate usage of factor analysis and internal consistency. The authors call for preparing the new generation of researchers to deal with measurement issues and new dimensions in the coming information age.
Ostrow (1996, 2000)	An update of the 1990 directory that includes 139 new tests. As a result, a total of 314 tests are compiled in the directory. As in the earlier version, each test's purpose, description, reliability, validity, norms, and availability are described. This remains a very useful resource for researchers and practitioners in sport and exercise psychology.
Schutz (1994)	A chapter focusing on methodological issues and measurement problems in sport psychology. Eight pressing problems are described: (1) heuristic versus hypothesis testing research; (2) when the null hypothesis is the research hypothesis; (3) measurement and analysis of change; (4) evaluating the magnitude of an effect; (5) do new statistical procedures clarify or obfuscate; (6) measurement of latent construct; (7) proliferation of sport psychology questionnaires; and (8) validity, reliability, and stability of factor structures. To avoid these problems, the author calls for involving a methodologist at all stages of a research study.
Tenenbaum & Bar-Eli (1995)	A review on contemporary issues in exercise and sport psychology research. A comprehensive literature search and analysis on research issues in sport psychology during three periods (1975-1980, 1981-1985, and 1991). The authors conclude that sport psychology is quite behind other disciplines in applying new methods of measurement and call for developing new measurement devices using both quantitative psychometrics and qualitative methods.
Patterson (1997)	The proceedings of the Eighth Measurement and Evaluation Symposium, Oregon State University, 1996, in which the author responds to Gill (1997). The author believes that a selection of quantitative or qualitative approaches or a combination of both should be made that matches the intent of the study and the measurement need.
Gill (1997)	An extensive description on measurement, statistics, and research design issues in sport and exercise psychology based on a presentation at the Eighth Measurement and Evaluation Symposium, Oregon State University, 1996. The author points out that the current methods cannot deal adequately with the issues and complexity of the measurement models employed in practice and calls for new models and methods.

(continued)

Authors	Content summary
Duda (1998)	An introduction to advances in sport and exercise psychology measurement. There are 29 chapters by a group of experts in (1) sport motivation and perceived competence; (2) sport anxiety and responses to stress; (3) imagery, attention, and psychological skills; (4) group dynamics in sport and exercise; (5) aggression and morality in sport; (6) self-concept and body image; (7) exercise-related cognitions, affect, and motivation; and (8) special considerations and alternative approaches. Measurement issues in these areas are discussed extensively, including a good description on the measurement inventories in related areas.
Marsh (1998)	The foreword for Duda (1998). The author is impressed by the progress made in the previous decade for including more carefully developed instruments; better articulation of the links among instrument design, theory, and practice; and improved application of methodological and statistical techniques. The author, therefore, declares that the heyday of the one-shot instrument seems to have ended. The author also cautions about the overuse of factor analysis since factor analysis itself does not provide a test of the construct validity.
Schutz & Park (2004)	A chapter describing methodological considerations in developmental sport and exercise psychology with a focus on the statistical analysis of change and validity and reliability of the measures.
Andersen, McCullagh, & Wilson (2007)	A study examining the metrics used in sport and exercise psychology and finding many of them to be arbitrary. There is no link between scores from inventories and their actual meaning in terms of real-world behaviors.

this book as well as in an earlier publication edited by Duda (1998).

Key Developments in Educational and Psychological Measurement

The 20th century has been full of exciting developments in educational and psychological measurement theories and methods. While it is impossible to elaborate on all of these developments, the following seem more significant or relevant to sport and exercise psychology: validity evolution, new and rich statistical methods for validation, score reliability and local precision, new testing theories, equating and item banking, computerized adaptive testing (CAT), test fairness and differential item functioning (DIF) procedures, cognitively diagnostic assessment, and technology revolution.

Validity Evolution

There is no doubt that validity is at the heart of any measurement practice. Over the past 70 years there have been major changes in the concept of validity. Very early, validity was simply defined on its commonly used computational method—the *correlation* (Bingham, 1937). In 1949, Cronbach (p. 48) described validity as a property of a test: "the extent to which a test measures what it purports to measure." This definition influenced the view of validity for many

years. In 1954, the American Psychological Association (APA) published the first set of specifications for psychological tests in "Technical Recommendations for Psychological Tests and Diagnostic Techniques," which identified four types of validity: *content*, *predictive*, *concurrent*, and *construct*. Cronbach and Meehl (1955) pointed out that assessors are not interested in the quality of a test but in the inference made through test scores. Thus they proposed the concept of construct validity. The APA revised its recommendation in 1966 and renamed it *Standards for Educational and Psychological Tests and Manuals* (referred to as the *Standards*). In it, the four types of validity were reduced to three—content, criterion, and construct—with the criterion validity encompassing both *predictive* and *concurrent* validity. When the 1966 *Standards* was revised in 1974, the types of validity were changed to aspects, emphasizing that these pieces are part of a larger validity entity. The view of validation, which is a process aimed at collecting evidence to support validity, also changed. No longer was validation an attempt to validate a test; rather, it was an ongoing process of evaluating test scores and the interpretation that can be made from them. Furthermore, validity was considered not as a property that can be measured directly but as a property that must be inferred from the three related aspects of validity. The concept of *unity of validity* was further developed as a unified construct validation in the 1985 *Standards*, which was developed jointly by the American Educational Research Association (AERA), APA, and National Council on Measurement in Education (NCME). Although the three types of validity remained, the term *aspect* was replaced by the term *evidence*. The construct validation of a test was considered to be an effort to accumulate content-, criterion- and construct-related evidence. This view of validity lasted for almost 15 years until the *Standards* was revised again in 1999. This revision brought about two major changes. The first and perhaps most important was that validity was no longer considered to be a property of a test. Rather, it was considered a property of test scores. This change was based on Messick's arguments (1989, 1996a, 1996b) that the traditional view of validity was fragmented and incomplete because it failed to take into account evidence of the value implementation of the meaning of test scores as a basis for action and the social consequences of score use. Because it is the test scores rather than the test that are interpreted and applied by test users, the validity should be the property of the test scores rather than the test. When test scores are used or interpreted in more than one way, each intended interpretation must be validated. Thus the 1999 *Standards* defined validity as follows: "Validity refers to the degree to which evidence and theory support the interpretations of test scores entailed by proposed uses of tests" (AERA, APA, & NCME, 1999, p. 9).

The second change was that validity was no longer considered to be made up of a few distinct types (e.g., factorial validity and content validity). Rather, it was thought that sources of validity evidence are multiple, and validity is a *unitary concept* that reflects the degree to which all the accumulated evidence supports the intended interpretation of test scores—and interpretation of scores are endless. The evidences of validity are classified into five categories (AERA, APA, & NCME, 1999): (1) *based on test content*, (2) *based on response processes*, (3) *based on internal structure*, (4) *based on relationships to other variables*, and (5) *based on consequences of testing*.

In the past, the most common practice was for test developers to conduct a validation study, often in which a single type of validity was collected from a single sample (occasionally split into two for cross-validation). Based on the results, a conclusion was made: "Test is valid" or "Test is not valid." Under the new validity argument framework (Kane, 1992), this kind of practice is not acceptable since a test may not always be valid for all purposes or in all situations, especially when the conclusion is based on a single piece of information. Instead of using a one-shot study design to collect validity evidence,

test developers need to make long-term efforts to continuously collect multiple types of validity evidence, especially when the test is applied to new subgroups and in different contexts. On the other hand, it is almost impossible to collect all the validity evidence at one time, and certain evidences may be more important than others are. Content-based evidence, for example, is important to all kinds of tests and should be treated as the most important evidence to collect. If an inventory is developed to measure a construct or trait, multiple evidences, such as those based on *test content*, *internal structure*, and *response processes*, should be collected simultaneously.

Statistical Methods for Validation

Another notable validity-related change occurring over the past several decades is the richness and sophistication of statistical methods for validation. For a long time, Pearson's correlation was the only method for validation. Gradually, validation of a psychological construct was replaced by factor analysis or similar techniques. The development of factor analysis can be traced back to the beginning of 20th century, when Charles Spearman developed the single-factor model in 1904. In the 1930s and 1940s, Thurstone (1947) extended the model to include more than one factor (see also Thorndike & Lohman, 1990). In the 1970s and 1980s, factor analysis became a major approach for verifying the construct of a new inventory (Cattell, 1978; Child, 1990; Gorsuch, 1983; McDonald, 1985; Mulaik, 1972), and the commonly used statistical software SPSS began including it. Thereafter, factor analysis was extended to many other sophisticated construct or variable modeling techniques, such as path analysis (e.g., Loehlin, 1987), confirmatory factor analysis (CFA; e.g., Bollen, 1989; Hayduk, 1987; Long, 1983), structural equation modeling (SEM; e.g., Byrne, 1998), latent variables analysis (e.g., von Eye & Clogg, 1994), and growth curve modeling (e.g., Duncan, Duncan, Strycker, Li, & Alpert, 1999), just to name a few. Software specific for factor analysis, such as LISREL (Jöreskog & Sörbom, 1984), Amos (Byrne, 2010), and Mplus (Muthén & Muthén, 2007), became commercially available and convenient to use. Meanwhile, many correlation-based validation methods, such as multitrait-multimethod (MTMM) analysis, are still around and active in today's inventory validation process.

Score Reliability, Generalizability Theory, and Local Precision

Like our understanding of validity, our concept of *reliability* has also experienced major changes over time. Three developments are most notable. First, reliability is now considered the property of test scores rather than tests (Thompson, 2003). The rationale behind this change is very similar to that behind the change in validity. Since the inference for an inventory is based on the reliability of scores, which are the interactions between test takers and inventories, the information should not be excluded from the contribution of respondents. For example, the test–retest method is a commonly used research design to determine the reliability of a test. Because the variability of persons (called *person stability*) is confounded with inventory variability (called *instrument reliability*), it is hard to judge which factor is the key contributor to the error, inconsistency, or reliability observed. The situation can be confused further if other factors are introduced, such as when the inventory is administered by different persons or at a different time or when two different forms are used. Thus, to fully understand reliability, *errors* or *variability* must be broken down and controlled in the validation design. The development of generalizability theory (GT) made it possible to design and analyze breakdown errors. This is the second notable development in reliability. GT is based on Lindquist's (1953) text on experimental design based on analysis of variance (ANOVA). However, it was the publication of *The Dependability of Behavioral Measurements: Theory of Generalizability for Scores and Profiles* by Cronbach, Gleser, Nanda, and Rajaratnam (1972) that led to its widespread acceptance. Today, GT has become one of the most popular methods in determining reliability under the framework of classical test theory (CTT; see also Brennan, 1983, 2001). Finally, the third notable change in reliability relates to our understanding and available measures of the local precision of an inventory, which is directly related to the outcome of the reliability. For a long time, the most popular precision measure was the standard error (*SE*) of measurement:

$$SE = SD\sqrt{1-r}, \qquad \textbf{2.1}$$

where *SD* is the standard deviation of scores measured by an inventory and *r* is the reliability of the inventory. It is assumed, however, that the same standard error applies throughout the full range of a scale, which is not true in reality. The development of item response theory (IRT; see the following section) introduced the local standard error (Hambleton & Swaminathan, 1985). The local standard error made possible precision around a specific score, or ability estimate, which is extremely important for individual assessment and diagnosis.

From Classical Test Theory to Item Response Theory

As in other fields, the invention of a new theory and corresponding methods serves as a driving force for new developments in the field of educational and psychological measurement. During the past several decades, the most important testing and measurement theory developed was IRT (Baker, 1985; Hambleton & Swaminathan, 1985; Lord, 1980; Lord & Novick, 1968; Wright & Stone, 1979; Wright & Masters, 1982). Before the 1980s, most tests and inventories were constructed using CTT, which has several noted limitations, including sample dependence in determining item characteristics and an incorrect assumption that the variance of errors of measurement is the same for all examinees (Hambleton & Swaminathan, 1985). IRT eliminated these limitations. More importantly, it made other advanced measurement practices such as item banking and CAT possible or more convenient. Today, all major test agencies use IRT to construct their tests, including the ACT, SAT, Graduate Record Examination (GRE), and Test of English as a Foreign Language (TOEFL). In fact, a specific IRT text was developed for psychologists (Embretson & Reise, 2000), and authors called for new rules of measurement for psychologists (Embretson & Hershberger, 1999). IRT has been applied to commonly used psychological measures such as personality measurement, the Minnesota Multiphasic Personality Inventory (MMPI), Dyadic Adjustment Scale (DAS), and Kaufrnann Adult Intelligence Scale (KAIT) (Embretson & Hershberger, 1999). Besides IRT, another test theory developed in the 1980s was criterion-referenced measurement (Berk, 1980, 1984). In criterion-referenced measurement, the interest changes from comparing a test taker with peers to comparing a test taker with an absolute criterion behavior. For this measurement, a specific cutoff score that determines whether the test taker passes or fails the test has to be developed and validated.

Equating and Item Banking

Multiple inventories, or multiple forms of an inventory, are often used to measure the same construct or trait. To enable comparisons among scores from different inventories or forms, the inventories or forms must be set on the same scale. The statistical process of setting two or more inventories or forms onto the same scale is called *equating*. This method has been refined over the past several decades (Kolen & Brennan, 2004). Based on the theory underlying the test construction, the equating procedure can be classified as traditional equating (e.g., linear equating and equipercentile equating) or IRT equating. Placing inventories on the same scale makes item banking possible. An item bank is a collection of items or questions organized and cataloged to take into account their content and other characteristics (e.g., difficulty and discrimination). With an item bank, test and inventory construction becomes simple and effective since items targeted to a specific group of test takers can be preselected. Most test agencies today construct their test forms using item banks they have developed.

Computerized Adaptive Testing

With an available item bank, CAT also becomes possible. Binet's IQ test was credited as the first adaptive test. In this test, the next set of items to be administered is based on the examinee's performance on the previous set of items. During World War I and II, the military required new procedures for classifying the abilities of a large number of recruits to fit into occupations and to provide individual attention in personnel classification, training, and selection since the old interview-based procedures proved time consuming and inefficient (Drasgow & Olson-Buchanan, 1999; Sands, Waters, & McBride, 1997). The idea of adaptive testing was picked up, and the related algorithm and software were developed in the 1970s and 1980s when computers became more readily available (Weiss, 1983; Wainer et al., 1990). Today, Internet-based CAT is widely used for proficiency tests (e.g., GRE or TOEFL) and many certification and health care tests (Parshall, Spray, Kalohn, & Davey, 2002).

Test Fairness and Differential Item Functioning

Interest in test fairness is most often credited to the 1970s California case of Diana v. State Board of Education. Nine Hispanic children from a farming family were placed in special education classes after testing low on an IQ test administered in English. However, after the children were retested in Spanish, they gained an average of 15 IQ points, and seven of them moved above the cutoff for special education. The court ruled that children should be tested in their native language. Since then, there has been a growing interest in developing procedures that can detect biased items or tests (Berk, 1982). *DIF analysis* is one of these procedures. DIF is based on unequal probabilities of endorsement on an item between two groups of respondents after controlling or matching for ability (Doran & Holland, 1993). The *ability* typically refers to the constructs

or trait levels a test or an instrument is intended to measure (Roussos & Stout, 1996). An item may be a DIF item when two groups of respondents at the same ability level respond to the item differently. DIF is important in educational and psychological testing, medical assessment, and other behavioral science research (e.g., cross-cultural assessment; van de Vijver & Tanzer, 2004). DIF indicates that a test item may be biased to a population subgroup (e.g., minority member, female, elderly person, and so on) and could be a serious threat to the validity of the test or instrument. DIF leads to incorrect explanations of test results and interferes with the selection or classification criterion. Many techniques for DIF detection have been developed in educational and psychological measurement. The four most widely used are the Mantel-Haenszel method, logistic regression, Lord's chi-square test, and simultaneous item bias procedure (Holland & Thayer, 1988; Lord, 1980; Mantel & Haenszel, 1959; Shealy & Stout, 1993; Zumbo, 1999). In addition, DIF, along with other advanced measurement techniques (e.g., factor analysis, growth curve modeling, and residual analysis), has been used for the response shift analysis (Barclay-Goddard, Epstein, & Mayo, 2009). Derived from quality-of-life research, the response shift refers to differences among people or changes within people regarding internal standards, values, or conceptualization of a construct being measured that could lead to ambiguous or paradoxical findings.

Cognitively Diagnostic Assessment

For a long time, psychometric research focused on the *metric* while largely ignoring the *psycho*. As a result, measurement practice centered on assessing the product, rather than the process, of a trait or construct. Starting in the late 1980s, researchers began integrating cognitive psychology into measurement procedures, hoping to learn not only what a person can score on a measure but also how and why a person responds in a certain way and gets a particular score. Factors that may influence the responses, such as level of knowledge and uncertainty, memory processes, and schemas, can also be built into the assessment process. As a result, the theory and methods for a new generation of tests are being developed (Frederiksen, Mislevy, & Bejar, 1993; Tatsuoka, 2009), and cognitively diagnostic assessments are being cultivated (Nichols, Chipman, & Brennan, 1995; Leighton & Gierl, 2007). The major features of these new assessments are (a) focusing on the process (how and why a student responds in a certain way or achieves at a specific level) rather than the product (a student's ability or achievement) and (b) integrating the latest cognitive theory, statistical models, and advanced technology (Frederiksen et al., 1993).

Computers, the Internet, and the Technology Revolution

There is no question that the computer, the Internet, and the whole technology revolution have changed our lives. They have affected assessment practice, too (Tucker, 2009). According to Bennett (2008), technology enabled assessment to reinvent itself in three stages: (1) increasing efficiency by automating existing processes, (2) enabling measurement of new constructs or skills comprehensively using new testing formats (e.g., simulation), and (3) integrating assessment within instruction or intervention. IBM's 805 Test Scoring Machine hit the market in 1938. For a long time afterward, fill-in-the-bubble sheets and scanners were the dominant technologies used in practice. In the 1990s, computer- and Internet-based technologies emerged and online testing and assessment became conventional. The current generation of online testing focuses on three areas: (1) electronic delivery of conventional assessment formats, (2) automation of existing processes, and (3) comparability of scores and interpretation of results across computer-based and paper forms. Among these three areas, automatic scoring, in which the machine (i.e., computer) is trained to score open-ended items, seems the most exciting. According to a recent review by Klein (2008), a variety of methods for machine scoring have proved comparable to human scoring (with human and machine scoring having about .85 score correspondence when compared). Neuroimaging using computed tomography (CT), magnetic resonance imaging (MRI), functional magnetic resonance imaging (fMRI), and positron emission tomography (PET) is another very exciting technology for psychological research (Llewellyn, Hodrien, & Llewellyn, 2008). Using fMRI, for example, O'Craven and Kanwisher (2000) showed that brain imaging allows researchers to tell what a person is thinking. Very recently, Shinkareva and colleagues (2008) used a combination of machine learning and brain imaging to identify the thought processes associated with a single object. It is expected that future technology-enabled assessments will overcome many of the limitations of conventional testing practices and allow us to measure complex and dynamic constructs and skills that were previously impossible to measure directly (Quellmalz & Pellegrino, 2009; Tucker, 2009).

Progress and Status of Measurement in Sport and Exercise Psychology

Because education and psychology are the parent fields of sport and exercise psychology, one obvious question is how the field of sport and exercise psychology is doing when compared with its parent fields. The following section reviews the progress and status of measurement in these fields. First, a concept or theory introduced into the fields of physical education and exercise science, now known as the field of *kinesiology*, is briefly described. A specific review on the progress made and the current status of the measurement in sport and exercise psychology follows. To help the consistency of the evaluation of progress in these areas, a three-level rating scale is employed: (1) Needs catching up, which means little has been done in a specific area and significant efforts should be made to improve the measurement practice; (2) Needs improvement, which means some initial efforts have been made but efforts are still needed to improve the practice; and (3) Keep going, which means that the field of sport and exercise psychology has done well in a specific area but needs continuous updates. These ratings are determined relative to the parent fields of sport and exercise psychology rather than other subdisciplines in kinesiology. To verify the findings described in the review, recent measurement publications in sport and exercise psychology journals were examined. Specifically, all research articles ($n = 98$) published in 2008 in the *Journal of Applied Sport Psychology*, *Journal of Sport and Exercise Psychology*, and *The Sport Psychologist* were screened, and ones that qualified as measurement articles ($n = 27$) were selected and reviewed thoroughly (see table 2.3 for a breakdown by journal and by area). Characteristics of these articles are discussed by area when applicable.

Validity: Still Using the Old Concepts

Validity has long been a key concept described in measurement and research literature in kinesiology. Most of the undergraduate and graduate research method textbooks in the field (e.g., Safrit & Wood, 1995; Morrow, Jackson, Disch, & Mood, 2005; Thomas, Nelson, & Silverman, 2005) include a good introduction or description of validity, and graduate texts on measurement (Safrit & Wood, 1989; Wood & Zhu, 2006) have even more thorough treatments of this topic (see Wood, 1989; Rowe & Mahar, 2006). Most of the updates in validity are covered in these texts. In addition, Schutz and Park (2004) provided a clear description on the evolution

■ **Table 2.3** ■

2008 Measurement-Related Publications in Selected Journals

Journal	Total papers	Measurement papers	CATEGORY Instrument development	Construct and theory modeling	Other
JASP	30	7	1	3	3
JSEP	40	14	4	10	0
TSP	28	6	0	5	1
Total	98	27	7	17	3

JASP = Journal of Applied Sport Psychology; JSEP = Journal of Sport and Exercise Psychology; TSP = The Sport Psychologist. The category labeled *Other* includes papers such as content validity evidence collection and cross-cultural validation.

of type of validity until 1995 in the context of sport and exercise psychology. Yet, most sport and exercise psychology studies still use old concepts and terms. For example, terms such as *factorial validity, construct validity, concurrent validity, external validity, nomological validity,* and *convergent validity* were used to describe the validity evidences in 2008 instrument studies (see Lonsdale, Hodge, & Rose, 2008; Roberts, Callow, Hardy, Markland, & Bringer, 2008). Some of these labels were incorrectly used. For example, Roberts and colleagues (2008) correlated their Vividness of Movement Imagery Questionnaire 2 with the Revised Movement Imagery Questionnaire and labeled the result as *concurrent validity* when it should have been called *convergent validity* (for a discussion regarding the difference between these two types of validity, see Zhu, 1998a). There is a clear need to update the concept of validity in sport and exercise psychology and, more importantly, to use a standardized system to label the validity evidence so that the meaning of the validity evidence can be better communicated and understood. This area is, therefore, rated as Needs improvement (see current views on validity in chapter 4 in this book).

New Validation Methods: Factor Analysis Almost the Only Method

Statistical methods used for validation in sport psychology, including construct and theory modeling, are advanced and sophisticated. For example, all the table 2.3 papers on construct and theory modeling used factor analysis (including both exploratory and confirmatory methods, such as SEM) or other multivariate techniques. This trend is interesting from a historical perspective, with so much progress having been made in this area, since it was only in 1989 when Schutz introduced SEM

and called for the field to employ this advanced technique for instrument development and model and theory testing. Less than 10 years later, Marsh (1998) raised a concern that factor analysis might soon be treated as the validity itself. Current practice confirms Marsh's concern since factor analysis has almost become the only method used in validation studies. Most of the validity studies based on factor analysis provided only partial evidence based on internal structure when other types of evidences (e.g., content, relationship with other variables, response process, and so on) should also have been performed and analyzed. In fact, looking back, some earlier correlation-based MTMM validation studies (e.g., Martens, 1977) are still relevant in today's construct validation. Another positive observation in these measurement papers is that multiple studies, efforts, or samples were often included in a single study report (see Lonsdale et al., 2008; Roberts et al., 2008) or a series of studies were conducted to continue improving the psychometric quality of an instrument (see Jackson, Martin, & Eklund, 2008 for their series effects for the validation of the flow instrument). Finally, as in many other disciplines, in sport psychology $p < .05$ abuse was often observed in many quantitative studies—in other words, determining whether an instrument is valid, a construct is confirmed, or a statistic is significant depended merely on whether the p-value was less than .05. Because p-value can be biased by sample size, many reported valid instruments or significant findings might not be valid or significant due to the large sample employed, thus making the reported findings not wholly reliable. As a result, this area is rated between Keep going (in terms of introducing and applying advanced statistical methods for test construction and construct validation) and Needs improvement (in terms of employing other validation designs and methods and avoiding *p*-value abuse).

Reliability: Focused Only on Internal Consistency

Like validity, reliability and its new methods have been well covered in kinesiology (e.g., Baumgartner, 1989, 2006; Looney, 1989) as well as in sport and exercise psychology (Schutz, 1989). In fact, measurement specialists in kinesiology often have been the ones to introduce the latest measurements and methods to the field. For example, GT was introduced to the field as early as 1976 (Safrit, Atwater, Baumgartner, & West, 1976). Unfortunately, the field of sport and exercise psychology basically ignored these new theories and methods. The Cronbach alpha, a measure of internal consistency, is often the only reliability evidence reported in sport and exercise psychology studies. Rarely, a study employed a test–retest design, which is essential for understanding reliability. Only few, if any, tried to break down the errors related to reliability and use GT methods to analyze it or even paid attention to local precision. To further improve the psychometric quality of sport and exercise psychological assessments, reliability is clearly one area that can be rated as Needs catching up.

New Testing Theory: No Major Application Yet

IRT was introduced to the field more than 20 years ago (Spray, 1987, 1989; Tenenbaum, 1986), and many successful applications have been reported in other subdisciplines in the field (for an overview of IRT in the field, see Zhu, 2006a). Although IRT was believed to have great potential for sport and exercise psychology (Wood, 1987), a number of calls have been made to employ it in measurement practice (Tenenbaum, 1986; Tenenbaum & Bar-Eli, 1995; Fletcher, 1999), and a number of application examples have been reported (Fletcher, 1999; Myers, Wolfe, & Feltz, 2005; Myers, Wolfe, Maier, Feltz, & Reckase, 2006; Myers, Feltz, & Wolfe, 2008; Tenenbaum, 1986; Zhu, Timm, & Ainsworth, 2001), the field of sport and exercise psychology has not taken advantage of this new testing theory and corresponding measurement benefits. A lack of training, a lack of need for mass testing, and the high cost of developing an IRT-based assessment may be the reasons for this neglect. Along the same line, researchers in sport and exercise psychology have also ignored progress in criterion-referenced testing. Criterion-referenced testing and related theories and methods were introduced and described in the 1980s

(Looney, 1989; Safrit, 1989) and were utilized in many other areas (e.g., Fitnessgram fitness testing). Measurements based on criterion-referenced testing, in fact, are critical to many measurement practices in sport and exercise psychology, especially in clinical settings. These practices include identifying and classifying certain traits and conditions such as overtraining, burnout, precompetitive stress, and so on. Yet, no effort has been made to construct sport and exercise psychology criterion-referenced assessments. As a result, scales of most sport and exercise psychology measures are only numerical, with little or no practical or clinical meaning (Andersen, McCullagh, & Wilson, 2007). Clearly, this is another area for sport and exercise psychology that can be rated as Needs catching up.

Equating and Item Banking: No Effort Made

Equating was also introduced to kinesiology more than 10 years ago (see Zhu, 1998b; for an updated review, see also Zhu, 2006b). Although some fitness and physical activity assessment applications (Zhu, 2001; Zhu, Plowman, & Park, 2010) have been reported, the field of kinesiology has not made significant efforts in this area, except for the ongoing PE Metrics project by the National Association for Sport and Physical Education (NASPE) Assessment Task Force (2008), in which items are equated to the same scale for assessing national standards. A lack of equating and item banking also exists in the field of sport and exercise psychology, as no effort has been made to introduce equating and item banking to its measurement practice. As a result, many times numerous instruments are employed to measure the same construct or trait (see Ostrow, 1996, 2002). Since every instrument has its own scale, the scores from the instruments, even those measuring the same constructs, cannot be compared. Since few of these instruments include multiple forms or forms with different difficulty levels, it would be very tricky to avoid the carryover effect when using the instruments to determine a pre- and posttest intervention effect or to measure changes. Sport and exercise psychology is in need of more equating projects, and this area is rated as Needs catching up.

Computerized Adaptive Testing: Just Introduced

CAT was introduced to kinesiology by Spray (1987). Very recently, a more extensive description of CAT was provided (Gershon & Bergstrom, 2006) in a graduate text on kinesiology measurement. However, neither kinesiology nor sport and exercise psychology has taken advantage of CAT. Without IRT-based test calibration or even a ready-to-use item bank, no CAT application is expected. This is another area rated as Needs catching up.

Test Fairness and Differential Item Functioning: Basically Ignored

While fairness is a very important validity issue in instrument development, a related statistical method was not introduced to kinesiology until almost 15 years ago (Looney, Spray, & Castelli, 1996; Zhu & Kurz, 1996). A more extensive description can be found in Cohen (2006). Overall, very little research effort in test fairness and DIF has been made in sport and exercise psychology. A literature search revealed only a few studies (e.g., Asci, Fletcher, & Caglar, 2009; Myers, Wolfe, Feltz, & Penfield, 2006) conducted in this area. Considering that gender, culture, ethnicity, and many other demographic variables may affect how a subject responds to a sport and exercise psychology inventory, a DIF examination should be a must for every inventory in sport and exercise psychology so that any potential bias can be avoided and more accurate scientific information can be generated. This is a key area that Needs catching up.

Cognitively Diagnostic Assessment: Noted and Interest Is Growing

There has long been an interest in measuring cognitive function in sport and exercise psychology. In fact, according to Etnier and colleagues (1997; see also chapter 17 by Etnier in this book on page 179), more than 100 cognitive measures are available, many of which (e.g., reaction time) have been used routinely in sport and exercise psychology. Efforts have also been made to understand cognitive strategies in sport and exercise psychology research (see Morgan, 1978; Morgan & Pollock, 1977) and in designing cognitive appraisals to understand physical achievement outcomes (McAuley & Duncan, 1990). Overall, however, sport and exercise psychology has not taken advantage of new testing theories and methods developed in cognitive diagnostic assessment during the last decade. Most practices in this area are still limited to employing a cognitive measure as a product measure (i.e., a cognitive outcome before and after an exercise intervention) rather than a means to understand the underlying cognitive process. Little effort has been made to design new-generation cognitively diagnostic assessments in sport and psychology. Thus, this area is rated as Needs improvement.

Computer, Internet, and Technology: Beneficial but Not Taken Full Advantage of Yet

The advances in computers, the Internet, and technology have changed our approach to understanding the world, including the process and product of sport and exercise psychology. On the positive side, sport and exercise psychology has taken advantage of progress in computers, the Internet, and technology. Sophisticated technologies, such as eye movement detection (Williams, Davids, Burwitz, & Williams, 1994), electroencephalography (EEG; Hillman et al., 2009), fMRI (Colcombe et al., 2004), and so on, have been used in sport and exercise psychology. On the other side, many technological advances, such as computerized experience sampling (Barrett & Barrett, 2001) and automatic scoring (Shermis & Burstein, 2003), have not been utilized in sport and exercise psychology. Thus, this area is rated as Keep going.

In summary, while the field of sport and exercise psychology is doing well in a few of the reviewed areas, such as using the latest statistical validation methods and technologies, it has not taken advantage of many of the developments in educational and psychological measurements. There are still many areas rated as Needs catching up or Needs improvement.

Conclusion and Recommendations

Almost 20 years ago, Tenenbaum and Bar-Eli (1995) performed a comprehensive review of research literature in sport psychology and concluded that "sport psychology is quite behind other disciplines in applying new methods of measurement" (p. 317). While overall this picture has improved, especially in applying new statistical validation methods and technologies, the field is still somewhat behind. As illustrated in this chapter, there are many areas rated as "Needs catching up" and "Needs improvement." Among them, measurement training, measurement research, improving and encouraging interdisciplinary research, and avoiding one-shot studies may be the most important:

1. Measurement Training. Presently, most undergraduates receive little measurement training. Most sport and exercise psychology books do not cover measurement and most textbooks in kinesiology contain only low-level introductory content concerning measurement. Graduate students in kinesiology are often sent to other departments for statistical and measurement courses, and most of their training remains introductory. Key measurement theories, concepts, and practices of test construction may be mentioned only briefly in these courses. In addition, while some researchers seem to lack fundamental knowledge in measurement and statistics, they are able to produce rather sophisticated statistical analyses with the help of advanced analytical software. The end result, unfortunately, is often statistical misuse. Improving measurement training, especially at the graduate level, must be emphasized. The fundamentals should be in place before advanced techniques are employed, and, in addition to introductory measurement and statistical courses, moderate and advanced measurement (e.g., CTT, GT, IRT) and statistical (e.g., multivariate ANOVA, SEM, hierarchical linear modeling) training should be a part of the graduate curriculum in sport and exercise psychology.

2. Measurement Research. While many advanced measurement methods are used in the field of sport and exercise psychology, few sport and exercise psychology researchers or measurement specialists conduct systematic measurement research in the field. To significantly improve the psychometric quality of sport and exercise measurement, the field must have its own sport psychometricians. In fact, Schutz and Gessaroli (1993) called for similar changes more than 15 years ago.

3. Interdisciplinary Research. Knowledge and technology update quickly, and their rapid change poses serious constraints to knowledge accumulation. To stay abreast with the latest breakthroughs in other fields and take full advantage of them, interdisciplinary teams and research must be developed and conducted to keep up with such advancement. This holds true for sport and exercise psychology research (Weiss, 2008). Training graduate students how to think across disciplines and conduct interdisciplinary research is necessary for the field of sport and exercise psychology to have a successful future.

4. Avoiding the One-Shot Study. As pointed out earlier, in sport and exercise psychology there are still too many one-shot studies, for which poorly constructed measurement inventories are developed, validated only using a convenient sample of college students, and possibly never used again. The accumulation of such measurement tools does not advance measurement practice in sport and exercise psychology. Therefore, the field must move toward a systematic approach for developing a new inventory, which includes the following major steps:

A. Defining the Construct. After the construct to be measured is defined clearly, a table of specification is determined and evaluated by a panel of experts, including practitioners and end users of the inventory.

B. Item and Inventory Construction. The items or questions, including response categories, are developed carefully according to the table of specification. These questions are then piloted and examined using a small convenient sample after a standardized administration instruction is developed.

C. Pilot Testing. After being modified (if needed) based on the information learned in step B, the inventory is administered to a large sample ($N > 200$) from the target population. Item analyses (including DIF analysis), which are often omitted from measurement studies, should be conducted first to ensure each question, including its response category, functions to the target population and its subgroups. If so, the internal structure is then examined using methods related to factor analysis.

D. Modification and Repeat Pilot Testing. Both the items and the inventory are modified according to the information learned from step C. The modified items and inventory are then pilot tested (as done in step C) once more, except when only minimal modification is needed.

E. Validation. The validity and reliability evidences are collected for the modified inventory with multiple samples, including at least one with a large sample size ($N > 400$). Again, the multiple evidences are collected. Examples for validity evidence can include confirming internal structures based on the theoretical construct being measured, relationships with other existing well-established measures, expected response processes and patterns, confirmed group differences, and so on. Examples for reliability evidence might include identifying errors from different facets (e.g., people, time, raters, or contexts), person stability and instrument reliability, overall and local standard error or precision, and so on. In fact, multiple studies should be built in this single step.

F. Cross-Validation. To ensure the generalizability of the measure, collected validity and reliability evidences should be confirmed further by another sample for the same targeted population. If possible, split-sample cross-validation should be avoided since the samples generated from this process are often too similar to each other and findings will likely be generalized to other subsamples. If the inventory is extended to another subpopulation of different age, gender, ethnicity, and so on and items have to be modified, deleted, or added, the cross-validation may return to steps D or E first. If the inventory is extended to other cultures and other languages, steps for cross-validation in these contexts (see Hambleton, Merenda, & Spielberger, 2004) should be followed.

G. Scaling and Reporting. One of the essential goals in developing an inventory is to measure and describe the construct on a numerical scale, upon which scale scores with stable meaning can be compared even if multiple forms of the measure are created. The process of developing a score scale is called *scaling* (for more information, see Zhu, 2006b). As an example, scaled scores of the GRE have a mean of 500 and an *SD* of 100. Even though the contents and items of the GRE differ every year, a score of 800 has the same meaning across years. A stable scale makes it possible to develop the connection between a score and real-life meaning (e.g., to predict performance in graduate school using GRE scores), which is much more important than scaling itself and is the foundation of interpreting findings appropriately and then generating assessment reports. Developing reports with appropriate interpretation scale scores should also be a part of this step.

H. Multiple Forms and Item Banking. After a measurement scale is set up, multiple forms of the measure are considered to meet the repeated assessment needs. Ideally, an item bank eventually is constructed so that new items and questions can be added consistently and new forms with better efficiency and accuracy (but still on the same scale) can be developed to meet the specific needs of new

subgroups. Finally, with such a bank, constructing a CAT-based measure also becomes possible.

I. Revision, Revision, Revision! The psychometric quality of the measure and item bank are continuously monitored, revised, and updated. Only in this way can the quality of the measure be maintained. Development and maintenance of a sound measure are a lifelong commitment!

Acknowledgments

The following colleagues kindly read early drafts of this chapter and provided valuable comments, suggestions, and insights, all of which significantly improved this chapter. Their help is greatly appreciated:

- Dr. Bradley J. Cardinal, Oregon State University
- Dr. Graig Chow, University of California at Los Angeles
- Dr. Deborah L. Feltz, Michigan State University
- Dr. Rainer Martens, Human Kinetics
- Dr. Penny McCullagh, California State University
- Dr. Tara K. Scanlan, University of California at Los Angeles
- Dr. Robert W. Schutz, professor *emeritus* of the University of British Columbia
- Dr. Gershon Tenenbaum, Florida State University, editor of this book
- Dr. Maureen R. Weiss, University of Minnesota

The final version of this chapter, however, does not constitute their endorsement. The author takes the full responsibility for content and presentation.

Measurement Basics, Methods, and Issues

Part I outlines current psychometric thinking on introspective measurement. Matters such as measurement reliability and validity, classical test theory, item response theory, sampling invariance, modeling change, and Rasch modeling in sport are covered. This section also introduces methods of measurement, such as idiographic measurement, dynamic assessment, verbal reports, and making sense of words and stories, that were developed in part in the sport psychology domain. Finally, issues such as developmental aspects, cultural issues, ethical considerations, and methods of using meta-analytical techniques to synthesize measurement issues are covered.

Reliability

Brandon K. Vaughn, PhD, Hwa-Young Lee, and Akihito Kamata, PhD

Reliability is one of the important features in determining a psychometrically sound research instrument. If a measure is *reliable*, test scores for each person should be relatively the same over repeated measurements (assuming that what we are measuring does not change). Thus, characteristics of reliability include consistency, repetition, and reproducibility.

The Theory of Reliability

Simply put, a reliable instrument is one that gives the same measurements when you repeatedly measure the same unchanged objects or events. The theory underlying reliability falls under classical test theory (CTT). CTT postulates linking the observed test score to the sum of the true score (latent unobservable score) and error score:

$$X = T + E, \qquad \text{3.1}$$

where X is the observed score, T is the true score, and E is random measurement error. The following assumptions underlie CTT: (a) True scores and error scores are uncorrelated, (b) the average error score in the population of examinees is 0, and (c) error scores on parallel measures are uncorrelated. Two measures are defined as *parallel* when the two forms have equal true scores and equal error variances. Classical test analysis utilizes traditional item- and sample-dependent statistics. These include item difficulty and item discrimination estimates, distractor analyses, item–test intercorrelations, and a variety of related statistics.

The concept of reliability in CTT relates to the consistency or reproducibility of test scores. In practical terms, this desired quality of test scores essentially means that examinees' test scores will remain relatively consistent over repeated administrations of an instrument. If a measuring instrument were perfectly reliable, then it would have a perfect positive correlation ($r = +1$) with the true scores. *True score* is the true ability of the respondent on that measure. The true score is unknown in practice and considered latent. If we measured an object or event twice with a perfectly reliable measure, and the true score did not change, then we would get the same measurement both times.

We theorize that measurements contain random error but that the mean error is 0. That is, some measurements have errors that make them lower than the true scores, while others have errors that make them higher than the true scores, with the sum of the underestimated errors being equal to the sum of the overestimated errors. Accordingly, random error does not affect the mean of the measurements, but it does increase the variance of the measurements.

If we assume that the true score and error are uncorrelated, so that $\text{Cov}(T, E) = 0$, then the variance of the observed score equals the variance of the true score plus the variance of the error:

$$\sigma_X^2 = \sigma_T^2 + \sigma_E^2 \qquad \text{3.2}$$

From this, we gain the following standard definition of reliability:

$$\rho_{TX}^2 = \frac{\sigma_T^2}{\sigma_X^2} = \frac{\sigma_T^2}{\sigma_T^2 + \sigma_E^2} \qquad \text{3.3}$$

Reliability is defined mathematically as the proportion of the variance in the measurement scores (X) that is due to differences in the true scores (T) rather than random error (E). Also, equation 3.3 states that reliability is equivalent to the squared correlation between the true scores (T) and observed scores (X). The closer the coefficient is to 1, the more the true score variance equals the total variance and thus the more reliable the measure is. In practice, we never know what the reliability of an instrument is because true scores are unknown. In addition, the error component included in observed scores changes randomly from one measurement to the next and this causes scores to change. Therefore, we are unable to calculate reliability exactly from information in the observed test scores and must estimate it instead.

We begin our estimation of reliability by using parallel tests: X and X'. The correlation of the parallel tests is equal to the reliability of the instrument:

$$\rho_{XX'} = \frac{\sigma_{XX'}}{\sigma_X \sigma_{X'}} = \frac{\sigma_T^2}{\sigma_X^2} = \rho_{TX}^2 . \qquad \textbf{3.4}$$

That is, reliability is defined as the correlation between scores from two parallel tests (X and X'). This formulization of reliability is much preferred in practice since the concept of parallel tests at least avoids the issue of latency of the true score. This formulization is the foundation for the most common estimates of reliability. In practice, it is difficult (perhaps impossible) to achieve truly parallel measures. Thus, various methods have been developed to approximate this correlation.

No matter which method is used, there is a common source of error that affects the estimate of reliability. This common source originates from examinees' inconsistent scoring on the same test, which may be referred to as *random measurement error*. However, different additional sources of errors are associated with different methods. Therefore, estimates from different methods are likely to be different from each other. For this reason, many measurement applications see the various estimates as being different types of reliability. However, we would like to emphasize that they are all various attempts at approximating the same quantity— namely, the reliability coefficient.

Before we detail these traditional estimates, we should note that item response theory (IRT) has an equivalent idea to reliability. In the two-parameter logistic (2PL) IRT model, for example, the relationship between examinee ability and a correctly answered, dichotomously scored test item is parameterized as follows:

$$P(U_{ij} = 1 \mid \theta_i, a_j, b_j) = \frac{e^{Da_j(\theta_i - b_j)}}{1 + e^{Da_j(\theta_i - b_j)}} = P_{ij}, \qquad \textbf{3.5}$$

where U_{ij} is the scored response of examinee i to item j, θ_i is the ability level of examinee i, D is a constant equal to 1.7 that provides equivalence to the normal ogive metric, a_j is the discrimination or slope parameter for item j, and b_j is the difficulty or location parameter for item j.

The information function is an important concept in IRT, analogous to the concept of reliability in CTT. The information function for an item indicates the utility of that particular test item for evaluating different levels of examinee ability. That is, the information function is an indicator of the precision with which a given ability level (θ) is measured. In the 2PL IRT model, the function that describes the information of item j with respect to ability θ is as follows:

$$I_j(\theta) = \frac{P_j'^2}{P_j Q_j} = \frac{D^2 a_j^2}{[e^{Da_j(\theta - b_j)}][1 + e^{-Da_j(\theta - b_j)}]^2} \qquad \textbf{3.6}$$

From this function, it can be seen that an item's information increases as (a) the discrimination parameter a_j increases and (b) the value of θ approaches the difficulty parameter. Thus, all things being equal, more discriminating items are more informative. Additionally, easy test items provide more information at lower ability levels than relatively difficult items provide, and difficult test items provide more information at higher ability levels.

Reliability can also be thought of in terms of a factor model. Equation 3.1 can be reformulated as a factor model:

$$X = \lambda F + \sigma, \qquad \textbf{3.7}$$

where X is the observed score, λ is the factor loading (which indicates how the latent factor F affects the observed score X), F is the latent factor, and σ is the error. With this formularization, equation 3.3 can be modified as follows:

$$\rho_{TX}^2 = \frac{\sigma_T^2}{\sigma_X^2} = \frac{\lambda^2 \sigma_F^2}{\sigma_X^2} \qquad \textbf{3.8}$$

Estimating the Reliability Coefficient

As we detail the various ways of estimating reliability, remember that they are all various approaches to estimate the one common reliability coefficient as shown in equation 3.4. Since truly parallel forms are difficult to achieve in practice, various solutions have been proposed to estimate this reliability. These solutions attempt to create the paradigm of parallel forms in various ways. Some solutions are more popular in certain disciplines due to the ease of setting up the approximation.

Random measurement error is always associated with any estimate of reliability. This is to be expected according to equation 3.1, and ideally this random error is the only source of error. However, each approach introduces additional sources of error besides random measurement error. Unfortunately, it is not possible to separate these sources of error unless data are collected from a well-designed experiment. Thus, researchers should be aware that these estimations might have a more exaggerated measurement error because the approximation of parallel forms is not met.

Test–Retest Estimate

The most straightforward method of estimating reliability is to administer a test twice to the same set of subjects and then correlate the two measurements (e.g., compare time 1 with time 2). This method gets closest to the idea of parallel instruments since the same instrument is used both times. Pearson's correlation (r) is the index of correlation most often used in this context. If the test is reliable, and the subjects have not changed from time 1 to time 2, then the value of r should be high. A value of at least .70 is satisfactory for instruments used in research and a value of at least .80 (preferably .90 or higher) is satisfactory for instruments used in practical applications such as making psychiatric diagnoses (traditional rules of thumb are discussed in a later section). In addition, the mean and standard deviation should not change appreciably from time 1 to time 2. On some tests, however, the mean might increase somewhat due to practice effects or change in the trait (e.g., growth). This is an additional error that is confounded with random measurement error by the test–retest estimate. Because of this, some researchers (e.g., Abell, Springer, & Kamata, 2009) caution against its use unless the construct of interest is known to be stable over time or some different gauge of observed scores (which is independent and unbiased) is available. For most constructs dealing with emotional or psychological issues, which have a tendency toward instability across repeated measures, this approach to reliability might yield misleading results.

Alternate Forms Estimate

If there are two or more forms of a test, we may wish to know that the two forms (on means, standard deviations, and correlations with other measures) are equivalent and highly correlated. These alternate forms are sometimes called *parallel forms* in practice, yet we must be careful to differentiate alternates forms from the parallel forms discussed earlier, which have much more stringent requirements. These alternate forms could simply be two versions of an instrument for which subjects have similar (but not exact) scorings. Thus, the r between alternate forms can be used as an estimate of the reliability of the two tests. Unlike test–retest reliability, the two forms of the same test may be administered to the same set of subjects without a time interval so that any practice effect may be controlled. However, in practice, equivalent forms are often difficult to develop, and this nonequivalence adds to the random measurement error. For this reason, the alternate forms estimate of reliability traditionally has been referred to as the *coefficient of equivalency*. However, the degree of equivalency is a separate quantity from random measurement error but is confounded with random measurement error by the alternate forms estimate of reliability. Therefore, the alternate forms estimate in reality does not indicate the degree of equivalence between the two forms. Rather, it is the estimate of reliability, which may have been confounded with the degree of nonequivalence.

Estimates With Internal Consistency

There are several ways to estimate $\rho_{XX'}$ with measures of internal consistency. These are based on intercorrelation among items and assess response consistency across items. One advantage of internal consistency approaches is that they require only one test administration for a group. Several internal consistency approaches are discussed here.

Split-Half Method

One internal consistency approach is to correlate scores on half of the items on the test with the scores on the other half, assuming that the two halves are parallel to each other. That is, we simply divide the test items into two groups, compute each subject's score on each group, and correlate the two sets of scores. If the two groups of items are approximating parallel measures, this method is consistent with the definition of the reliability $\rho_{XX'}$. Also, this method is similar to computing an alternate forms estimate of reliability after producing two alternate forms (the two halves) from a single test. It is common to refer to this coefficient as the *half-test reliability coefficient*, $r_{hh'}$. Since the half-test reliability coefficient is based on alternate forms that comprise only half the number of items on the full test, reducing the number of items on the test reduces reliability. To estimate the reliability of the full test (of the original length), we should apply the Spearman-Brown formula:

$$r_{sb} = \frac{2r_{hh'}}{1 + r_{hh'}},$$ **3.9**

where $r_{hh'}$ is the split-half estimate.

Cronbach Alpha[1]

A problem with the split-half method is that the reliability estimate obtained using one pair of random halves of items is likely to differ from that obtained using another pair of random halves. Which random half is the one we should use? One solution to this problem is to compute the Spearman-Brown corrected split-half reliability coefficient for every one of the possible split halves and then find the mean of those coefficients. Cronbach alpha (also called *coefficient alpha*) represents the average correlation that would be obtained over all possible split halves of the test. It is also an estimate of the reliability, which is derived from the definition of the reliability:

$$\rho_{XX'} = \frac{\sigma_T^2}{\sigma_X^2} \qquad \textbf{3.10}$$

It is the most widely used and reported method for estimating the reliability of test scores.

The way in which coefficient alpha considers interrelatedness of items is by examining the variance that is common among items. Computing coefficient alpha comes from partitioning the variance of the total score into a true component and an error component such that

$$\alpha = 1 - \text{error variance.} \qquad \textbf{3.11}$$

Thus, α is the proportion of a scale's total variance that is attributable to a common source. This common source is the true score of the latent construct being measured. Coefficient alpha can be computed using the following formula:

$$\alpha = \frac{k}{k-1}\left(\frac{\displaystyle\sum_{i=1}^{k}\sum_{\substack{j=1 \\ i\neq j}}^{k}\text{Cov}(X_iX_j)}{\displaystyle\sum_{i=1}^{k}\sum_{\substack{j=1 \\ i\neq j}}^{k}\text{Cov}(X_iX_j)+\sum_{i=1}^{k}\text{Var}(X_i)} \right)$$

$$= \frac{k}{k-1}\left(\frac{\displaystyle\sum_{i=1}^{k}\sum_{\substack{j=1 \\ i\neq j}}^{k}\sigma_{ij}}{\displaystyle\sum_{i=1}^{k}\sum_{\substack{j=1 \\ i\neq j}}^{k}\sigma_{ij}+\sum_{i=1}^{k}\sigma_i^2} \right), \qquad \textbf{3.12}$$

where α is the coefficient alpha, X_i is the measurement for item i, and k is the number of items.

The use of coefficient alpha as an estimate of reliability assumes that items are essentially tau-equivalent, meaning that the true scores for any two items are within a constant of each other for a subject. If this assumption is violated, then the coefficient alpha underestimates reliability. For this reason, it is generally agreed that coefficient alpha is a lower-bound estimate of reliability because perfect essentially tau-equivalence is seldom achieved. Using simulations, Zimmerman and Zumbo (1993) found that violations of this assumption lead to substantive overestimation and underestimation of coefficient alpha. Researchers should be aware of these potential problems when applying coefficient alpha.

Kuder-Richardson Formulas

The method developed by Kuder and Richardson yields an estimate of reliability that is equivalent to the average correlation achieved by computing correlations for all possible split halves for a test. Use of the Kuder-Richardson (K-R) formulas assumes that each test item is scored dichotomously (1 point for a correct answer or endorsing response and 0 points for an incorrect answer or nonendorsing response). The formulas are a special case of coefficient alpha. Therefore, in practice, there is no need to obtain this quantity if a coefficient alpha is obtained.

Interrater Estimate

When estimating the reliability coefficient in which situations involve ratings, approximations for parallel forms can be made by using more than one rater. For essays or other performance-based items that are scored by more than one rater, this estimate also gives evidence on whether all raters are scoring the items in the same way. To use the interrater estimate for reliability, we calculate the percentage of scores that are in absolute agreement when multiple raters rate the same set of papers. Another estimate of reliability that is commonly used from interrater measurements is the average correlation of scores between pairs of raters. In both cases, we might look for percentages above .70.[2] The interrater estimate for reliability is especially important when multiple raters are using a scoring rubric to assess student learning outcomes. Obviously, rater differences add to the overall error in addition to the random error component.

---

[1]Technically, Louis Guttman first detailed the coefficient alpha in 1945. Cronbach's paper in 1951 provided more understanding of this coefficient, and many people insufficiently attribute the coefficient only to Cronbach. *Guttman-Cronbach alpha* might be a better descriptor of this coefficient.

[2]Such values are simple rules of thumb and should not be considered always applicable to all situations. Values should be based on specific research needs as well as on values found commonly in that genre of research (e.g., medical studies might require a more stringent value than educational studies require).

Standard Error of Measurement

The reliability coefficient may not be convenient for interpreting a subject's test score, as the reliability coefficient is in the standardized scale rather than in the observed score scale. For example, suppose a subject receives a score of 29 on 15 items of a sport competitive anxiety test (Mattens, 1977). A score above 30 is considered to be a high level of anxiety. If a test–retest reliability coefficient for a group of people measuring the test is .86, we can conclude that the subject's score might or might not be close to the true score since the estimate of the reliability is not 1.0. In other words, the subject might have either a high anxiety level or an average anxiety level because the instrument is not perfectly reliable, meaning that measurement errors are included in observed scores. If the measurement error is large, the reliability estimate is low. Therefore, test users might be concerned about measurement errors that represent a measure of unreliability in interpreting individual scores. Although we can never know the exact amount of error in a given score, we can estimate the expected variation of observed scores about their true scores. The *standard error of measurement* is the standard deviation of the sampling distribution of the error scores. A single student taking the same test repeatedly will have different test scores due to different levels of error scores. The standard deviation of the distribution of error scores is the standard error of measurement. The standard error of measurement can be used to interpret an examinee's observed score by providing an estimate of the range of scores that would be obtained if examinees were to take the instrument repeatedly. Remember that we calculate the standard error of measurement across an entire sample of people instead of for an individual. In other words, we assume that standard error of measurement is constant for a given instrument, regardless of observed scores (which is also true for reliability estimates).

The standard error of measurement is therefore an index of the unreliability of a test score and is a function of the standard deviation of test scores (σ) and the reliability coefficient ($\rho_{XX'}$) for an instrument. An expression for the standard error of measurement can be derived by using the relationship in equation 3.2. Dividing both sides of this equation by σ_X^2 yields

$$\frac{\sigma_T^2}{\sigma_X^2} + \frac{\sigma_E^2}{\sigma_X^2} = 1 \qquad 3.13$$

Note that the first term in the left-hand expression of equation 3.13 is the definition of $\rho_{XX'}$. This can be solved for σ_E:

$$\frac{\sigma_E^2}{\sigma_X^2} = 1 - \rho_{XX'}, \qquad 3.14$$

so that

$$\sigma_E = \sigma_X \sqrt{1 - \rho_{XX'}}. \qquad 3.15$$

This quantity is the standard error of measurement.

Once the standard error of measurement for a test score is calculated, we can use it to estimate the confidence interval (CI) of the test score. The confidence interval is the estimated range of values likely to include an examinee's true score. Generally, one of three confidence levels are considered (although others might be of interest): 68% (within ±1 SD from the mean), 95% (within ±2 SD from the mean), and 99% (within ±3 SD from the mean). A 95% confidence interval covers 95% of the normal curve, meaning that the probability that a given confidence interval captures the true score is 95%. We can choose the appropriate confidence interval to determine how confident we want to be in our estimation of an examinee's true score, although usually a 95% CI is utilized to estimate a test taker's true score. For example, the confidence intervals at the 68%, 95%, and 99% levels (note that the z-scores corresponding to the 68%, 95%, and 99% probability levels for a normal distribution are 1.00, 1.96, and 2.58, respectively) are obtained as follows:

$$68\%_{ci}: X \pm 1.00 \text{ SEM},$$
$$95\%_{ci}: X \pm 1.96 \text{ SEM, and} \qquad 3.16$$
$$99\%_{ci}: X \pm 2.58 \text{ SEM}.$$

Evaluating the Magnitudes of Reliability Coefficients

Recall that reliability is the ratio of the true score variance to the observed score variance in the population of examinees. The observed score variation is affected by the true score variance and the error variance. So if the error variance is close to 0, the reliability coefficient is close to 1, because the range of the reliability coefficient is between 0 and 1. Consider a measure of intrinsic motivation in which the internal consistency of interest-enjoyment among intrinsic motivation measures, coefficient alpha, equals .78. This means that 78% of the variation in the interest-enjoyment measure is reliable (78% of the obtained score is a true score) and 22% of the variation is due to error.

Yet, how would we interpret this estimate in terms of the actual instrument? There is no exact rule of thumb for an acceptable reliability coefficient. Several researchers (e.g., Abell, Springer, &

Kamata, 2009; Nunnally & Bernstein, 1994) have stated that a reliability coefficient of at least .80 is acceptable to make decisions as a reliable measure. Such research indicates that the traditional value of .70 for acceptable reliability might be too small. However, test users must consider the purpose for using the instrument to determine whether the instrument has adequate reliability. For example, Nunnally and Bernstein (1994) have suggested that a reliability coefficient above .70 may be acceptable for early stages of research. If individual observed scores are aggregated at a group level for data analysis, a low reliability coefficient at the individual level could be acceptable (Abell, Springer, & Kamata, 2009). However, higher values for reliability (above .90) might be more appropriate for high-stakes tests that make important decisions or require more consistent psychometric standards for examinees.

Keep in mind, however, that such suggestions are not meant to be definitive. Traditionally, reliability estimates of .70 have been considered the gold standard. However, in many research situations, higher values are needed. The decision on acceptable values should be based on the research being considered as well as the acceptable values used in the literature of such research.

Improving Reliability

Various factors influence reliability. First, the spread of the scores affects the reliability. The larger the range of the scores, the higher the reliability. There is also a direct connection to the number of items on an instrument. In general, the more items on an instrument, the higher the reliability. Obviously, other factors (e.g., carefully constructed items, objective scoring, and so on) also affect reliability. Thus, reliability can be improved by increasing the spread of the scores, increasing the number of test items and the number and heterogeneity of the students, and using items that are clear and have medium difficulties. Some of these factors are more controllable than others are. The following are recommendations for a researcher concerned with the reliability of an instrument:

■ Use a sufficient number of items or tasks.

■ Use independent raters or observers who have been trained to provide similar scores to the same performances.

■ Construct items and tasks that clearly differentiate students on what is being assessed.

■ Make sure the assessment procedures and scoring are as objective as possible.

■ Continue assessment until results are consistent.

■ Eliminate or reduce the influence of extraneous events or factors.

■ As a post hoc procedure, use software to identify problem items that can be removed from the instrument to increase the reliability coefficient.

■ Use items with reasonable difficulty levels (perhaps between .3 and .8), as questions that have extremely low or high difficulty tend to reduce the variability of scores, and the greater the variability in the measure of the group tested, the greater the reliability of the measure.

Let's look at the use of a post hoc procedure to increase a measure's internal consistency form of reliability. Suppose that we obtain a very low reliability coefficient for a test. If we want to increase the reliability coefficient, we can look at the items measured and delete one or more items that are not highly correlated with the other items being measured. Doing so can improve the reliability because a particular item that is not highly correlated with other items measuring the same concept affects reliability. The SPSS software program will be used in this example. Using the reliability analysis in the SPSS software, we can check the box for "scale mean if item deleted" and then look at the results for "Cronbach's alpha if item deleted" in the item total statistics. If the Cronbach alpha significantly increases when a particular item is deleted (as shown in figure 3.1), we can delete the item to increase the reliability coefficient.

Relationship to Validity

Two essential features of a good instrument are reliability and validity. The goal is to measure people consistently with an instrument that actually measures what it purports to measure. Reliability and validity are not mutually exclusive. Validity is the degree to which a measure actually measures what it states to measure. Cook and Campbell (1979) define it as the "best available approximation to the truth or falsity of a given inference, proposition, or conclusion" (p. 37). Basically, valid instruments usually show signs of reliability, although this is not guaranteed. A reliable instrument does not guarantee a valid measure. For example, if we want to measure a person's intrinsic motivation toward sports, we can choose a test that we think measures intrinsic motivation toward sports. Suppose the reliability coefficient is above .8, meaning that the test measure has acceptable reliability (using the aforementioned

Reliability statistics

Cronbach's alpha	Number of items
.717	4

Item total statistics

	Scale mean if item deleted	Scale variance if item deleted	Corrected item total correlation	Cronbach's alpha if item deleted
var00005	25.5273	4.551	.823	.526
var00006	24.6890	3.697	.746	.490
var00007	25.3840	3.544	.778	.463
var00008	25.0957	6.358	−.012	.950

If one deletes this item, the Cronbach's alpha is increased by .95.

Figure 3.1   SPSS output showing changes in reliability upon item deletion.

guidelines). However, if this inventory tends to measure extrinsic motivation rather than intrinsic motivation, the validity coefficient will be very low. If there are large measurement errors in observed scores due to messy data or a bad test, the results will not be reliable or valid since the test may be measuring a lot of noise. In such a case, the instrument is not capable of measuring what it should be measuring. Thus, a test that is unreliable cannot be valid, yet a test that is valid must be reliable. Reliability is a necessary but not sufficient condition for validity, because reliability sets the upper limit of validity and constrains test validity. The relationship between reliability and validity can be defined as

$$\rho_{xy} \leq \sqrt{\rho_{xx'}}, \qquad \textbf{3.17}$$

where $\rho_{xx'}$) is the reliability of a measure and ρ_{xy} is the validity coefficient. Here, the validity is defined as the correlation between the test scores and a criterion measure, which is considered as one aspect of validity.

Reliability for Multidimensional Instruments

The estimation of reliability assumes that the items come from a unidimensional instrument. What about the reliability of a multidimensional instrument? A common mistake in considering

a multidimensional instrument is to treat it as a unidimensional instrument when calculating reliability. This is often accomplished by summing or averaging item composites. However, research has shown this to be a cautionary way of calculating reliability in such situations (e.g., see Netemeyer, Bearden, & Sharma, 2003; Osburn, 2000).

Obviously, each dimension can be considered separately when computing reliability. For example, in a three-dimensional instrument from which three separate subscale scores are reported, three different coefficient alphas should be computed—one for each of the three constructs. Yet, a common overall reliability for the entire instrument is useful if we are interested in reporting a total summed global score. To achieve this using coefficient alpha, we can compute a stratified coefficient alpha[3] (Cronbach, Shonenman, & McKie, 1965).

The stratified coefficient alpha extends coefficient alpha to the situation where a mixture of subscales appears on a test but the total summed global scores are of interest. In computing the stratified coefficient alpha as an estimate of reliability for global scores, each subscale is treated as a subtest. A separate estimate of reliability is computed for each item group and combined as follows:

$$\alpha_{strat} = 1 - \frac{\sum_{j=1}^{c} \sigma_{X_j}^2 (1 - \alpha_j)}{\sigma_X^2}, \qquad \textbf{3.18}$$

---

[3]Since coefficient alpha is the most commonly used estimate for reliability, its extension for a multidimensional instrument is detailed here. Similar modifications are available for different estimates.

where c is the number of item groups, α_j is the estimate of reliability for each item group, σ_{Xj}^2 is the observed score variance for each item group, and σ_X^2 is the observed score variance for the total score. For components consisting of multiple-choice and open-ended (short answer) items, a standard coefficient alpha (equation 3.12) can be used as the estimate of component reliability. The interrater approach can be used as the estimate of component reliability for item groups with rating scale items.

Misconceptions and Misuses of Reliability

Reliability can be misapplied in practice in a variety of ways. One of the prominent misapplications is treating each estimate of reliability as if it were a separate type of reliability. We must keep in mind that each estimate of reliability (e.g., test–retest, coefficient alpha, and so on) estimates the same thing: the reliability coefficient shown in equation 3.4. As each approach mirrors a true parallel form, each estimate closely approximates the reliability. In the worst-case scenario, the estimates serve as lower bounds to the actual reliability. Yet, they are not different types of reliability. Rather, each is a different attempt at approximating the condition of parallel forms. However, their values typically differ, since each estimation adds different sources of errors to the random measurement error. For this reason, it is possible to approximate the amount of different sources of errors if data are collected effectively under a well-designed study.

Another common misconception is that reliability provides evidence of dimensionality (e.g., unidimensionality). Some people mistakenly believe that a high value of coefficient alpha, for example, is proof that the instrument is unidimensional. However, a multidimensional instrument may indeed yield a high coefficient alpha. Another technique (e.g., factor analysis) must be used to determine dimensionality. Dimensionality and reliability are different concepts that should not be confused (although they are related).

As discussed earlier, there is no single acceptable value for how high a reliability coefficient should be in order to be considered satisfactory. Unfortunately, a reliability estimate of .70 has become the traditional value to deem an instrument reliable. Yet, some situations require a much higher value due to the costs associated with measurement errors. In addition, instruments with estimates below .70 might still be useful in certain circumstances. The actual cutoff value should be chosen with care and should consider the type of research and the relevant literature.

Conclusion

In this chapter we introduced the idea of reliability and the various ways of estimating reliability in practice, most notably coefficient alpha. The standard error of measurement was defined and shown to be of practical importance in the discussion of reliability. We then discussed a variety of ways in which reliability can be improved for an instrument. Next we examined the common misunderstandings and misuses of reliability, including the mistake of viewing the different estimates of reliability as different types of reliability. In essence, all reliability estimates have a common point of estimation. We also discussed how we might approach reliability for multidimensional instruments by using the stratified coefficient alpha.

Conceptualizing Validity

Brandon K. Vaughn, PhD, and Sarah R. Daniel

The phrase *the truthfulness of one's conclusions* encapsulates the general meaning of validity. In the context of measurement theory, there are several ways to view validity, but all are concerned with the confidence we can have regarding conclusions made from measurement instruments. A valid or truthful instrument measures what it is intended to measure. Validity has to do with how assertively we can make inferences or conclusions based on measurement findings. Validity does not refer to the test scores but to the inferences that are made from the scores. An instrument is considered valid if it actually measures the variables it claims to measure and if there are no logical errors in drawing conclusions from the data. Psychologists must be continually vigilant about ensuring that the methods and instruments they employ conform to acceptable criteria of validity. There are multiple ways of assessing validity, including relevant content, soundness of theory or rationale, internal consistency of measures, relatedness of measures to constructs, and generalizability across samples and time. Validity is not an issue that can be investigated by calculating one simple statistic or numerical index. We should not rely on just one way of assessing validity; rather, we must use a multitude of validity evidences. By understanding validity, we not only avoid making critical errors in measurement development or selection (which includes operationalizing constructs, often through scale selection) but also can evaluate the trustworthiness of other research results and conclusions.

Throughout the history of measurement, the partitioning of validity into specific types has become embedded in the measurement field. Measurement validity has been described as being composed of different and sometimes overlapping types of validity, including construct, face, content, predictive, and concurrent validities. Each one of these types addresses an aspect of the quality of assumptions being made. However, the current *Standards for Educational and Psychological Testing* (referred to as the *Standards*) from the AERA, APA, and NCME (1999) emphasizes validity as a unitary concept with no distinct types or kinds. The *Standards* has been revised every 10 to 12 years, and the concept of validity has changed in each revision. The idea of different kinds of validity was emphasized less in the 1985 revision and completely abandoned in the 1999 revision. Today, instead of focusing on defining types of validity (i.e., construct, content, and so on), the *Standards* emphasizes the sources of validity evidence being used to illuminate the quality of the validity assumptions. However, it is useful to have an understanding of the historical types of validity, as they still appear in the measurement literature. Before looking at validity through the lens of evidence sources, let's examine the premodern types of validity.

Validity in the Premodern Era

The traditional view of validity typically included several types of validity. Each type could be seen as independent of the other forms. The following sections discuss some of these traditional perspectives of validity. These perspectives are still important in the modern view of validity, as the modern view simply sees the various types as interrelated instead of independent.

Face Validity

Face validity focuses on the participants in a research study, asking what an average layperson would think that the experiment or test is measuring. Face validity can be viewed as a very rough and superficial assessment of an operational definition: Does it *look like* it is measuring what it claims to measure? For example, a test that claims to measure attitudes toward competition but includes questions such as "Do you like cheese?" has poor face validity. It is important that the questions on a test appear credible to the participants. If participants perceive that questionnaire items don't fit the purpose of the research (as they know it), this disconnect might affect their motivation to answer honestly, their ability to stay focused, and might create feelings of annoyance. Both situations could affect the outcomes of the measure or the study. One way to prevent such scenarios is to conduct a pilot test of proposed questions with persons from the population of interest. Through debriefing, we could gain insight into the participants' thoughts about the items. Sometimes, however, instruments are such that face validity may not be desirable. If an instrument is designed to hide the true purpose of the test from examinees, then strong face validity is not advantageous.

Content Validity

Content validity, like face validity, is subjective. It entails having content experts assess aspects of a questionnaire or operational definition. There are two types of content experts: those who assess the content and those who assess the process. The content is the focus or phenomenon of the measure or study. Content experts, as their name implies, are selected for their expertise in the construct being measured. They assess each item's content and its representativeness of the subject. The experts who assess process provide feedback on test administration or study procedures. These experts take into account things such as the context in which the assessment will take place (e.g., a park versus a classroom) and the population being targeted (e.g., professional athletes versus children). Process experts can help us to plan and effectively deal with specific issues that can arise during data collection. Often, content validity is summarized by the percentage of items matched to objectives or through the use of correlation coefficients.

Construct Validity

Construct validity is the degree to which inferences can be made from study measures and applied to the theoretical constructs upon which those operationalizations are based (Netemeyer, Bearden, & Sharma, 2003). It is the confidence we have that an operational definition faithfully represents the abstract construct it is supposed to represent. Sometimes, the whole purpose of a study is to demonstrate the construct validity of a new measure. Even when this is not the case, construct validity is critically important to any study because a study is only as good as its operational

definitions. We could have a well-designed study with thousands of participants, but if cohesion is operationally defined as family size (which is not correlated with team cohesion), our results would be meaningless. As mentioned previously, abstract concepts are often operationalized with a measure whose score is designed to quantify that construct. For example, Eys, Loughead, Bray, and Carron (2009) developed the Youth Sport Environment Questionnaire (YSEQ). This self-report measure could be used to operationalize the construct of youth cohesion in a study. When selecting such a scale for research, it is important to know if the measure adequately quantifies the concept as theoretically defined. Considering the construct validity of the operational definition helps accomplish this adequacy goal. Traditional ways in which construct validity is considered include the MTMM, construct validity coefficient, convergent and discriminant validity coefficient, and factor analysis.

Convergent Validity

Convergent validity (or criterion validity) is the degree to which the operational definition is correlated with variables it might be expected to be correlated with. If these measures are highly correlated, they are said to converge on the construct of interest (i.e., the operational definition; Hagger & Chatzisarantis, 2009). This form of validation has to do with the relationship of the construct of interest (which has been operationalized through the operational definition) to other chosen constructs that are hypothesized to be related to this construct of interest. The selected constructs are assumed to have a significant amount of shared variance with the construct of interest. For example, let's say that a researcher wants to study the effects of physical activity on executive functioning by using Grant and Berg's (1993) Wisconsin Card Sorting Test (WCST). One way to assess the convergent validity of this measure is to correlate scores on the WCST to outcomes expected to be correlated with executive functioning, such as years of education, grade point average, and IQ. If these variables are positively correlated with the WCST, we can have more faith that it is a legitimate measure of executive functioning. However, it is possible that constructs can have too much in common. If the correlation is substantially high (such as .80 or above), then the construct of interest is not adding anything new to the understanding of the phenomenon as compared with other measures. Kline (2005) states that the ideal correlation range for the construct of interest and constructs chosen for validation purposes is .30 to .50.

Predictive Validity

A special case of convergent validity is predictive validity, or the degree to which an operational definition predicts an outcome that it is designed to predict. For example, let's say a quarterback's executive functioning (as assessed by a measurement instrument) is positively related to his performance during the football season. One measure of predictive validity is the correlation between the quarterback's executive functioning score and his ranking at the end of the season. The logic is that successful quarterbacks have higher levels of executive functioning. Hence, these executive functioning scores provide evidence of predictive validity in the realm of quarterback performance.

Discriminant Validity

Discriminant validity is the degree to which the operational definition is able to discriminate between the target construct and closely related (but conceptually distinct) variables. Whereas convergent validity hopes for high positive correlations between the operational definition and the related variables, discriminant validity hopes for low (or close to 0) correlations between operational definitions (often operationalized with instrument score) and distinct or irrelevant variables. For example, imagine that we comes across a test of mathematical intelligence that includes word problems. A possible concern might be that the test does not adequately discriminate between mathematical ability and verbal ability (i.e., is contaminated by verbal ability). If the correlation between this test of mathematical intelligence and a separate test of verbal ability is close to 0, then we could be much more confident that the math test has discriminant validity with regard to verbal intelligence. If the correlation between the math test and a verbal test is high and positive, then the math test does not adequately discriminate between mathematical ability and verbal ability. There are no hard-and-fast rules for how weak a correlation has to be to confirm discriminate validity. Interpretations of such associations depend on the underlying theory and the source of the observations (Bagozzi, 1981). Hagger and Chatzisarantis (2009) mention guidelines based on Cohen's effect size taxonomy, in which a small effect could be evidence of discriminate validity.

Collecting Evidence of Validity

Typically multiple studies are needed to assess the various sources of validity. When a new measure of an abstract concept is being used as the operational definition, we must do an even more intensive assessment of the various aspects of validity because of the lack of past research to draw upon. Hence the development of an instrument should entail an extensive validity analysis. The YSEQ (Eys et al., 2009) can be used to illustrate the methods that establish the five types of validity. The authors established face validity and content validity for the YSEQ by conducting focus groups, administering open-ended questionnaires, conducting an extensive literature review, and enlisting content experts. As mentioned earlier, these two types of validity are often assessed with more subjective and qualitative methods. The other types of validity (convergent, discriminate, and predictive) are often assessed with statistical methods that appraise relationships among variables (e.g., Pearson product-moment correlation and multiple regression). One way to look at the YSEQ's convergent validity might be to correlate it with Carless and De Paola's (2000) measure of team cohesion. Considering the shared construct of cohesion, a significant, positive, and moderate correlation is expected between these two measures. Discriminate validity could be established by correlating the YSEQ with a measure of mental imagery ability, since no relationship is hypothesized to exist between these two constructs and the correlation is expected to be close to 0. Finally, predictive validity is often assessed using regression techniques that allow for predicative conclusions. We can speculate that YSEQ scores taken at the beginning of a season would have a predictive relationship with the coach's end-of-season assessment of each player's team-building attitude. The regression technique is especially useful if you are interested in the simultaneous relationships among three or more variables. Multiple regression allows for such comparisons.

The methods just discussed assess the validity of making inferences from measurement scores. These approaches include both the subjective methods of asking test takers and experts their opinions about the measure and the statistical methods that use external variables to assess the measure of interest. However, more organized and sophisticated techniques to quantify validity are usually encouraged.

The MTMM approach was originally conceptualized by Campbell and Fiske (1959). It is used for the assessment and verification of convergent and discriminant types of validity of multidimensional psychological constructs. In the Campbell and Fiske version, a model is created in which each of the dimensions (traits) is measured by each of the different methods. The combinations of the observed variables result in the construction of an MTMM matrix, which is then analyzed via the comparison of the magnitude of the respective correlation coefficients. A sample MTMM matrix is shown in figure 4.1.

If the correlations between the same traits that have been measured with different methods are substantially high and positive to allow for further investigation, convergent validity is assumed if these correlations exceed the correlations of other traits that have been measured with the same methods. In order to substantiate construct validity, we have to confirm that the same matrix pattern occurs if the traits are measured with different methods. In contrast, correlations of different traits measured with the same method should be substantially smaller than the correlations of the same trait measured by different methods (discriminant validity). Furthermore, the correlations between cases in which different traits are measured with different methods should be smaller than the correlations between cases in which the same trait is measured with different methods. These criteria, originally set up by Campbell and Fiske (1959), have been criticized by various researchers (e.g., Althauser, Heberlein, & Scott, 1971; Bagozzi, 1978; Marsh, 1989; Widaman, 1985). For instance, researchers have argued that the Campbell and Fiske approach does not allow users to quantify the amount of specific variance in the data.

To overcome these shortcomings, a method called *factor analysis* is frequently used to evaluate construct validity. Factor analysis centers on evaluating the internal structure of an instrument. There are two basic types of factor analysis: exploratory factor analysis (EFA) and confirmatory factor analysis (CFA). Both are employed in the validity appraisal process. A sample CFA model is shown in figure 4.2.

Factor analysis techniques provide information about the interrelationships among the items in the instrument of interest. The interitem correlation or variance–covariance matrix is used for the analysis. Both CFA and EFA are often used during the development of a new instrument. EFA is a data reduction technique; the relationships among items are reduced to one or more possible and as yet unnamed abstract concepts (factors). The reduced set of underlying variables accounts for the variation of the items. This reduced set is the factor solution, which constitutes the construct being measured. Hence, EFA results typically are used to reduce the number of items and to identify underlying dimensions in the measure (Netemeyer et al., 2003). CFA often comes into the picture after an EFA has been run. CFA is seen as an improvement on EFA in that it provides a method for testing the hypothesized relationship of the items to the abstract concept of interest (the measurement model) and statistical tests for how well the data (interitem relationships) fit this measurement model. For a more in-depth discussion of factor analysis in test construction and validation, see Abell, Springer, and Kamata (2009) and Netemeyer and colleagues (2003).

While evaluating the internal structure of a measure developed to tap a construct is an important aspect of establishing validity, this approach alone does not establish construct validity (Kline, 2005). It is important to consider the five types of validity when assessing the truthfulness of an operational definition and resulting measures.

Validity in the Modern Era

Instead of naming specific types of validity evidence (i.e., construct, content, and so on), the 1999 AERA,

	Traits	Method 1			Method 2			Method 3		
		A1	B1	C1	A2	B2	C2	A3	B3	C3
M1	A1	**0.9**								
	B1	0.42	**0.87**							
	C1	0.51	0.39	**0.9**						
M2	A2	0.62	0.16	0.23	**0.86**					
	B2	0.19	0.52	0.21	0.53	**0.8**				
	C2	0.17	0.2	0.45	0.49	0.63	**0.84**			
M3	A3	0.59	0.15	0.26	0.59	0.29	0.19	**0.89**		
	B3	0.26	0.55	0.22	0.18	0.49	0.28	0.41	**0.85**	
	C3	0.17	0.19	0.49	0.19	0.18	0.5	0.39	0.59	**0.9**

Figure 4.1   An MTMM matrix.

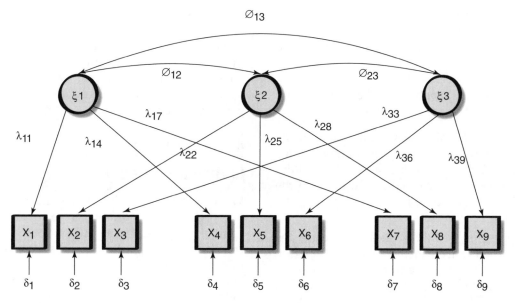

Figure 4.2   A CFA model.

APA, and NCME *Standards* names many sources of validity evidence in order to elucidate the different facets of validity. Accordingly, the idea of different kinds of validity evidence has been abandoned in favor of a unitary concept of validity.

Unlike the earlier paradigm, the modern paradigm views the different aspects of validity as holistic rather than separate. We can think of the types of validity in the traditional view (discussed earlier) as independent tributaries or roadways with little intersections and crossovers. Each tributary (type of validity) is making its own way to the destination of validity. That is, in the past, validity evidence was segmented into independent measures, each encapsulated in a type of validity. Thus, we can consider face validity and predictive validity as two different roadways or tributaries (although both might point in the same direction of validity evidence). In the past, researchers often focused selectively on the aspects of validity important to them (i.e., only traveled down one or two roadways). For example, some researchers might have focused exclusively on the face and predictive tributaries when studying the validity of a given instrument.

The modern view of validity as established in the 1999 AERA, APA, and NCME *Standards* focuses on how all validity is essentially tied into construct validity. In other words, validity should be envisioned as connected attributes (tributaries) that all feed into a commonality of construct validity (as shown in figure 4.3*a*). Thus the modern view abandons the idea that each tributary represents a different kind of validity. As shown in figure 4.3*b*, everything is now viewed as connected. Note that

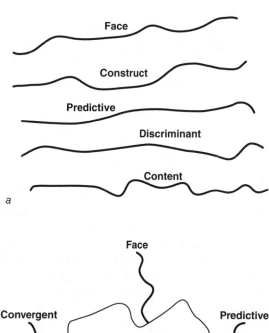

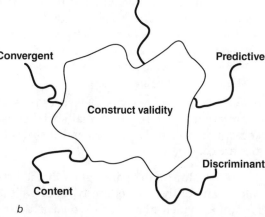

Figure 4.3   The independent and modern view of validity evidence.

not all types of validity evidence are represented in this figure. Each tributary simply focuses on different aspects of the validity evidence rather than on distinct types of validity.

The possible sources of validity evidence (as detailed in the 1999 *Standards*) can be compiled into five categories of evidence based on the following:

1. *Test Content:* This refers to alignment of the standards and the assessment. Researchers must document not only the surface aspects of validity illustrated by a good content match but also the more substantive aspects of validity that clarify the real meaning of a score.

2. *Response Processes:* This takes into account the importance of ensuring that when respondents are taking a measurement instrument they are actually utilizing the skills of interest. In other words, we need to be reasonably certain that respondents completing an instrument designed to assess mathematical reasoning are actually using mathematical reasoning. One of the best opportunities for detecting and eliminating sources of test invalidity occurs during the test development process. Items need to be reviewed for ambiguity, irrelevant clues, and inaccuracy.

3. *Relationships to Other Variables:* This means documenting the validity of an assessment by confirming its positive relationship with other assessments or evidence known or assumed to be valid. It is also useful to gather evidence about what a test does *not* measure.

4. *Internal Structure:* Several statistical techniques have been developed to study the structure of a test. These techniques are used to study both the validity and the reliability of an assessment. Combining several of these statistical techniques can help to ensure a balanced assessment that on the one hand avoids assessing a narrow range of knowledge and skills but still shows very high reliability and on the other hand avoids assessing a very wide range of content and skills, triggering a decrease in the consistency of the results.

5. *Consequences of Testing:* This focuses on score interpretation as well as potential social consequences. Issues of bias, fairness, and distributive justice are considered.

The nice feature of this paradigm is that it incorporates many of the premodern types of validity. For example, evidence based on *test content* borrows from the previous idea of content validity but has a more holistic emphasis. Evidence based on *response processes* is similar to the face validity of the past. Evidence based on *relationships to other variables* is essentially criterion validity, while *internal structure* is more about construct validity. The evidence based on *consequences of testing*, which focuses on the social consequences embedded in testing, was a new addition under the modern view of validity and was largely ignored under the premodern perspective of validity.

Issues of Validity in Research Designs

While the previously discussed issues of validity are of concern when validating a measurement instrument, it is also helpful to be aware of the statistical considerations of validity in the arena of study findings in general, since operational definitions are often operationalized through measurement instruments. These considerations are detailed in the following sections.

Internal Validity

If a study has internal validity, we can be confident that the observed change in the dependent variable (i.e., the score on a measurement instrument) was caused by the independent variable and not some other variable. Thus, a study with high internal validity permits causal conclusions. The major threat to internal validity is a confounding variable, which is a variable other than the independent variable that (1) is often found with the independent variable and (2) may be an alternative cause of the observed change in the dependent variable.

The most common procedure to reduce the risk of confounding variables (and thus increase internal validity) is random assignment of participants to levels of the independent variable. The usual alternative to random assignment is an ex post facto design, also known as a *classificatory design*, in which participants are assigned to levels of the independent variable not randomly but according to some characteristic that they already possess. Randomly assigning participants to levels of the independent variable reduces the risk of any systematic differences between the groups before the study begins. Two groups that have been randomly assigned should, on average, be equal to one another on most potential confounding variables. Random assignment is the defining feature of experiments.

In addition to the confounding variables that may threaten particular studies and jeopardize internal validity, there are several more general threats to internal validity. For instance, participants may discover what the study is about and change their actions (i.e., respond differently on an instrument).

The features of a study that reveal the hypothesis are called *demand characteristics* because they are thought to demand a particular response from participants.

External Validity

External validity is the confidence we have in the generalizability of findings across other people, situations, and times. Before evaluating a study's external validity, we must determine whether the study intended to generalize its *results* (actual numeric estimates of a population, such as voter opinions) or its *findings* (the conclusions it reaches about the relationships between variables, such as the relationship between heat and aggression). Generalizing results requires the study sample to be very representative of the population to which the results will be generalized. Typically, generalizing results requires some kind of probability sampling, which is the process of obtaining participants in which each member of the target population has a known probability of inclusion in the sample.

External validity is often discussed in three contexts: people, situations, and times. A study may have high external validity with regard to people (e.g., a random sample of 1,100 likely voters) but poor external validity with regard to time (e.g., the sample was collected in 1960). Generalizing results across contexts typically requires a probability sample unless the processes under investigation are assumed to be fairly universal. However, the characteristics of the sample should be considered even in the case of probability sampling before assuming the external validity of results

and findings within another population of interest. Thus, researchers must be wary of generalizing results or findings across people (cultures), time (past and future), and situations (changing environments) unless the sample is representative of the applicable context.

External validity, like internal validity and measurement validity, is a matter of degree: All studies have it to some extent. No study is externally invalid; a study is only less generalizable to particular people, settings, or times. In addition, making snap judgments about a study's external validity based on the strategy it employs (lab experiment versus survey) is unwise. Instead, we must consider the claims the researcher is making with regard to generalizing *results* (numeric estimates of population values) versus *findings* (general conclusions) and consider how participants are sampled.

Conclusion

When conducting research, it is important to consider all types of validity (external, internal, and measurement). Failure to consider factors influencing the truthfulness of findings and results can have a serious effect on the quality of research both at the study and application level. The predominant focus of researchers looking at validity is the measurement aspect, as was detailed earlier in this chapter. When focusing on the central measurement question of validity of an instrument, researchers should strive to focus on the holistic approach to validity and not compartmentalize it into separate types of validity evidence.

Validating Scores From New Assessments

A Comparison of Classical Test Theory and Item Response Theory

Yaacov Petscher, PhD, and Christopher Schatschneider, PhD

One of the main purposes of data collection in clinical and research settings is to describe phenomena in a parsimonious manner. Across the social sciences, researchers develop measures that are designed to tap hypothetical constructs such as self-efficacy, motivation, intelligence, and attitude. Because these variables are not directly observable, theory is used about how such constructs manifest across different settings. Such information is used to write sets of items to describe how ability on the tested variables differs among individuals responding to the items. The approach to writing items for an assessment or test varies according the theoretical framework used by the test developer. Similarly, a variety of options exist for formatting items to solicit the appropriate type of information. Items may be oriented toward completion or short answers; however, these formats typically measure a relatively constrained set of skills or knowledge in the area assessed.

The most popular approach to creating assessments and questionnaires in sport and exercise psychology is the use of ordered category items, typically referred to as *Likert-type scaling*, which is a way for respondents to note the degree to which they agree with a statement. Likert-type scales can vary from as few as 2 options (e.g., "Yes" or "No," "Agree" or "Disagree") to as many options as a researcher wishes to provide, although typically 3 to 7 options are provided. The validation of scores from questionnaires and assessments in sport and exercise psychology is a critical task for researchers

interested in describing the theoretical elements pertaining to the psychology of sport performance. Moreover, applied sport psychologists working with athletes not only wish to implement psychological skills training such as mental imagery and relaxation with their clients but also wish to quantify the degree of sport anxiety or motivation, which may assist in applying additional strategies.

Traditionally, the process of validating scores from newly developed measures has been embedded in the context of classical test theory (CTT). This framework has been the cornerstone of measurement since the early 20th century and has remained the most popular approach in psychology and education for assessing the reliability and validity of scores. CTT is easy to apply in most situations due to the relative simplicity of its theoretical model and estimation of item parameters; however, this theoretical approach tends to suffer from relatively weak assumptions that are easy to meet (Hambleton & Jones, 1993). The last 20 years have seen a rise in the application of a different theoretical approach to assessing the psychometrics of new assessments—namely, item response theory (IRT). Although item response theory has been researched for more than 50 years, many psychological measurement instruments and researchers are rooted in classical theories. This chapter is devoted to introducing IRT by discussing methodological approaches to validating new assessments, how these approaches compare with traditional models, and how IRT provides a more comprehensive approach to psychometrics that also rectifies many of the perceived shortcomings associated with classical approaches.

Level of Analysis

Classical Test Theory. One of the most important distinctions between CTT and IRT is the level at which data are analyzed and interpreted. Central to both theories is that the scores must be both reliable and valid; however, *how* reliability and validity are established between the frameworks provides key insights into the test theories. As may be ascertained from the descriptor, CTT focuses on the nature of the total test scores and is rooted in true score theory. True score theory postulates three components: a true score (T), a raw score (X, which is the total score on the assessment or test), and an error score (E). To examine this relationship, let's suppose the Sport Competition Anxiety Test (SCAT; Martens, Vealey, & Burton, 1990) was administered to a pitcher on a baseball team before every game of the regular season. The distribution of all scores would show that during some administrations the anxiety was higher while on other administrations it was lower. The best estimate of the pitcher's true sport competition anxiety would be a function of the average of all of the individual raw scores. If no error existed in the measure ($E = 0$), the total score would be the true score. In reality, the true and error scores are unknown, and we make assumptions about the model. We assume that the errors are normally distributed and that the average of the random error scores around the pitcher's true score is 0: At times it may be positive, such as when pitching against a division rival and anxiety is high, and at other times it may be negative, such as when playing a team that is in last place in the division and anxiety is low. It is also assumed that the true and error scores are uncorrelated, meaning that the pitcher's random errors, whether positive or negative, are not systematically related to the true score. Lastly, we expect that an error score on one form of the test is uncorrelated with an error score on a parallel form of the test.

The most common method to examine error in a test score is to estimate the reliability of scores for the measure. We can do this by administering a test to a group of individuals at one point in time or at multiple points in time (refer to chapter 3 on page 25). A well-known property of reliability in CTT is that it may be increased simply by adding new items, assuming that the new interitem correlations are at the same level of the old. Notwithstanding this mechanism to improve reliability, internal consistency is very sensitive to error sources and is dependent on the sample from which the scores

were obtained. As such, if a questionnaire is administered to multiple samples, the same estimate of reliability is not necessarily to be expected among the different groups. Similarly, the item statistics that exist in the CTT framework (discussed later) are less efficient than the item parameters in IRT, as they depend on the sample from which they are tested. Interestingly enough, when using CTT to validate a set of scores from an assessment, it is important to note the scoring of items. As described by Kline (2005), when responses to items are dichotomous (1, 0), CTT suggests that scores should not be used in the standard factor analysis since it is a linear SEM, and discrete data do not fit in the framework. Although refuted by Kamata and Bauer (2008), this issue has become a problem for researchers who choose to use dichotomous data in a classical framework because of the perceived lack of appropriate analysis, which limits the generalizability of the validity of test scores.

Item Response Theory. IRT is a general framework that examines individual ability based on both individual responses to items and properties of item parameters (i.e., difficulty and discrimination). In this way, IRT focuses on the features of items used to construct reliable scores for an assessment or test. Significant elements of IRT are that item responses are linked to the ability of the individual, and the metrics of the item difficulties and individual ability are the same, typically in *z*-score units. As such, the scores usually range from −3.0 to 3.0, with a score of 0.0 being the average. Positive values in IRT difficulties reflect more difficult items *and* individuals with above-average ability, while negative values indicate easier items *and* individuals with below-average ability. IRT is flexible regarding responses, scoring (dichotomous or polytomous), response categories (ordered or unordered), ability dimensions (one or many), and type of model. In the context of this chapter, it is assumed that one dimension of ability is being measured and that the data are dichotomously scored. These basic assumptions facilitate an introduction to IRT; many other resources exist that discuss the extension of these models (see Hambleton & Swaminathan, 1990; Ostini & Nering, 2006; Van der Linden & Hambleton, 1997). The simplest form of the IRT model is known as a *one-parameter logistic (1PL) model*, or *Rasch model* (see also chapter 8), and is given by the equation

$$P_i(\theta) = \frac{e^{(\theta - b_i)}}{1 + e^{(\theta - b_i)}} \ , \qquad \textbf{5.1}$$

where $P_i(\theta)$ is the probability that a person with an ability level of θ will correctly answer item i and b

is the level of difficulty for item i. This simplistic application of IRT has been used previously to examine item responses which measured the state of flow (Tenenbaum, Fogarty, & Jackson, 1999). Two features of this general equation are worth discussion. First, when the ability score of an individual is equal to the difficulty of an item, the probability of a correct response is always .50. Second, when the value of b is held constant, as θ increases, so does $P_i(\theta)$. These points demonstrate an inherent feature of IRT, which is that items and abilities may be matched (this point is discussed in greater detail in the following section on item difficulty).

A second prevalent model in IRT is the two-parameter logistic (2PL) model, which is a simple extension of the 1PL model in equation 5.1. This model not only estimates the difficulty of the item but also indicates how well the item discriminates among individuals at a particular level of ability. It is estimated with

$$P_i(\theta) = \frac{e^{1.7a_i(\theta-b_i)}}{1+e^{1.7a_i(\theta-b_i)}}, \qquad 5.2$$

where, in addition to the parameters from equation 5.1, a_i represents the discrimination of item i, and 1.7 is a scaling factor. The primary feature of the 2PL model is that it does not assume that all items discriminate at an equal level (as is assumed in the 1PL model), and thus it provides the researcher with more information about the item characteristics.

A final model that is well established but not often applied to questionnaires and surveys is the three-parameter logistic (3PL) model. The additional parameter here is the pseudoguessing parameter (c), which is designed to account for guessing on multiple-choice items (such as academic achievement test items). The 3PL model is described by

$$P_i(\theta) = c_i + (1-c_i)\frac{e^{1.7a_i(\theta-b_i)}}{1+e^{1.7a_i(\theta-b_i)}}. \qquad 5.3$$

Using this equation, it is possible to derive the 1PL and 2PL equations by substituting a value of 0 for the guessing parameter. Because the 1PL and 2PL models are most often used with questionnaires, surveys, and tests where guessing is not a factor, the quantity that multiplies the fraction in equation 5.3 reduces to 1, and the whole equation reduces to equation 5.2. Several other IRT models are available, including Samejima's (1969) graded response model and Bock's (1972) nominal response model, which both handle different structures of the data. Depending on what is being modeled and the question the researcher wishes to handle, a series of flexible item level models can be used

to provide information about item parameters and individual ability.

Item Difficulty

Classical Test Theory. When considering dichotomous items in CTT, difficulty (represented as p) is simply the proportion of individuals who endorse the question in a positive manner. Typical definitions describe item difficulty as the proportion of individuals who answer the question correctly; however, this definition is limited in the social sciences, where dichotomous responses are neither correct nor incorrect but simply a polar choice (e.g., "Yes" or "No," "High" or "Low," "Agree" or "Disagree"). In circumstances where the dichotomous choice is not reduced to correct or incorrect, the data must be properly coded since the percentage of a positive response is based on the item being scored as 1. Item difficulties for dichotomous items can range from 0.00 to 1.00, with higher numbers indicating easier items. As the difficulty is the percentage of respondents endorsing a positive response, items are viewed as easier when a higher proportion of participants select the positive option. One mechanism for viewing the relative difficulty of items on a test is to sort the items by the level of percentage correct. This way we can examine which items have easy, average, and difficult properties.

A more comprehensive approach, developed by George Rasch (1960), is to take the total scores for all individuals and split the data into deciles. Once the data are grouped, the mean p for each group can be plotted for each decile by item. Figure 5.1 provides a sample plot of 3 items. Item 1 shows that as the performance of the groups increases, the difficulty decreases. For individuals who are in the 1st to 10th percentiles when compared with their peers, only 10%, on average, endorse the positive response. This is compared with an average of 90% of those in the 81st to 90th percentiles endorsing the positive response.

Item 2 is an example of where relatively few students in the 1st to 60th percentiles select the positive choice. This is reflected by the low item difficulty of .20 to .30. Students with a total score performance above the 60th percentile have a much higher average percentage of endorsing the positive response, ranging from .60 to .70. Lastly, item 3 demonstrates that regardless of the decile, the mean proportion endorsing the positive response is .80.

When considering just the difficulty of these 3 items, we might conclude that item 1 is of average difficulty, item 2 is hard, and item 3 is easy. Such conclusions, however, are limited by the sample

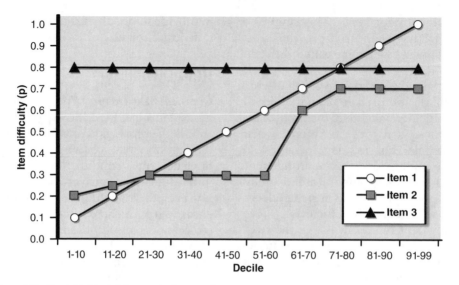

Figure 5.1   Item difficulty plotted by total score decile groupings.

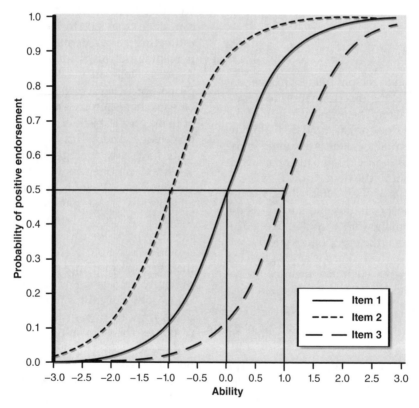

Figure 5.2   IRT item difficulty.

size. If the sample for this study is 200 (a minimally sufficient size in CTT), and we assume that an equal number of individuals is represented in each decile, we would surmise that the individual clusters each represent only 20 students. This number is far too low to allow us to obtain meaningful information about the difficulty of the items across varying total score cluster levels of the students. More impor-

tantly, while some information about differential difficulty across items can be gleaned from figure 5.1, these results are interpretable only for the test or assessment comprising these items.

Item Response Theory. The definition of item difficulty, or the *b* parameter, in the IRT framework requires us to recall two key features of the IRT approach: (1) Models are probabilistic and (2) the metrics of individual ability and item difficulty are the same. Figure 5.2 displays an item characteristic curve (ICC) for 3 items. ICCs are a graphical representation of the relationship between ability and probability of endorsing the correct response. The ICC supplies information about item difficulties, as well as discrimination. The x-axis ranges from −3.0 to +3.0 and simultaneously represents the range of student ability and the range of item difficulty. It represents the 99.9% of the array of expected scores in a population. Negative values describe individuals who perform below average on the assessment or test as well as describe an item that is easy. Positive values indicate above-average ability and difficult items. Values of 0 denote average individual ability and average item difficulty. The y-axis ranges from 0.00 to 1.00 and represents the probability of endorsing a positive response.

Item difficulty under the 1PL and 2PL models can be properly defined as the level of ability where the probability of endorsing a positive response is .50. The three ICCs in figure 5.2 provide an example of an easy, average, and difficult item. The reference line for the y-axis shows the point on the graph where the probability of a positive endorsement is .50. From this point, we can trace across the graph to the three ICCs and then trace down to the x-axis to determine the difficulty of the items. While the three ICCs have the same S-shape, they are differentiated by their location on the graph. Item 1, which is the middle curve, has a b of 0.0, meaning that it is average in difficulty. Because IRT relates item difficulty to ability, an individual with an ability of 0.0 has a .50 probability of a positive endorsement. Item 2 has a b of −1.0, indicating it is an easy item. A person with an ability of −1.0 has a .50 probability of a positive endorsement. However, let's look at what happens when an individual with an ability of 0.0 takes item 2. We can draw a trace line from 0.0 on the x-axis to where it meets a point on the item 2 curve, demonstrating the difficulty of this item for that specific level of ability. In this instance, when the ability is 0.0, the probability of a positive endorsement for item 2 is .80. This makes sense intuitively because the ability of the individual is greater than the difficulty of the item; as such, the probability of a positive endorsement should be higher. Item 3 is considered to be a difficult item, with b = 1.0. Giving this item to a person with an ability of 0.0 is associated with a lower probability of a positive endorsement (i.e., .10) because the individual's ability is less than the difficulty of the item. The probability of a positive endorsement is also less than that for a person with an ability of 1.0.

Item Discrimination

Classical Test Theory. In its simplest form, the discrimination of a dichotomous item is the correlation between the response on an item and the total test score. Typically it is estimated with the D-index, the point biserial correlation, or the biserial correlation. The D-index is calculated by splitting the sample into two groups based on the total test score. Usually the upper group is based on the participants whose total test score is at or above the 75th percentile, while the lower group comprises participants at or below the 25th percentile. Once these groups are created, the difficulty of an item is established for each group, and the difference score between the two groups is calculated to get D. The higher the D-index, the better the item discriminates. Although the biserial correlation and point biserial correlation are computed somewhat similarly, the nuances are such that the calculation is difficult and should be conducted by specialized software (e.g., SAS, SPSS). The choice of which index to use should be based on contextual considerations (Nunnally & Bernstein, 1994); however, most researchers tend to use the point biserial correlation.

Let's refer back to figure 5.1. Though the item plots demonstrate item difficulty, they can be used to discuss discrimination as well. For example, the item 2 curve shows that the item difficulty is relatively low for deciles 1-10 through 51-60. This is followed by a steep slope at the 61-70 decile mark. This increase in slope is a marking point for discrimination and suggests that this item discriminates well; that is, poor performers on the test have a lower percentage correct on this item when compared with high performers, who have a higher percentage correct on this item. By contrasting item 2 with item 3, we observe that item 3 does not discriminate between high and low performers. Regardless of decile, all students had an item difficulty of .80. Thus, this item likely correlates weakly with performance on the rest of the test. Lastly, item 1 demonstrates strong discrimination, as increases in the total test score correspond to increase in the item difficulty. This example is useful, as it provides a natural analogue of how discrimination is described in IRT.

Item Response Theory. Like item discrimination in CTT, item discrimination in IRT, or the *a* parameter, is related to the relationship between responses to an item and performance on the rest of the assessment. In IRT it describes how well an item can differentiate the probability that individuals with different ability levels will endorse the positive response. The values can range from −∞ to +∞ but typically range from 0.0 to +2.0. Item discrimination may formally be described as the degree to which an item discriminates between individuals at different points on the latent continuum of ability. The discrimination parameter assists researchers in examining whether all items in an assessment relate equally to the latent trait being assessed. As previously discussed, the ICCs in figure 5.2 have different levels of difficulty; however, if we now examine their ability to discriminate among individuals with varying ability levels, we can conclude that they all have the same level of discrimination because at no point on the curves do the lines intersect across items. Notice how the slopes of the curves for the 3 items are the same: The upper and lower portions of the curves converge but do not overlap, and for most of the curve, a steep change in the probability of a positive endorsement occurs for small changes in ability. This type of shape is precisely what researchers like to observe in their items because it indicates that an item discriminates well across individuals with different levels of ability.

When discrimination varies across items, we must interpret how that affects the overall item attributes. Figure 5.3 shows ICCs for 3 items with different levels of discrimination but the same level of difficulty. All 3 items have a difficulty of 0.0; however, item 1 has a discrimination of 0.50, item 2 has a discrimination of 1.0, and item 3 has a discrimination of 2.0.

The curves in figure 5.3 intersect, unlike the ones in figure 5.2, and the differences in discrimination can be observed in the slope of the lines. While item 3 is identical to the curves in figure 5.2 and has a

steep slope, item 1 has a very gradual slope. As previously discussed, item discrimination affects the extent to which the probability of a positive endorsement changes across varying levels of ability. It may be observed that item 1, which has a low *a* value, does not have strong discrimination. In fact, an individual with an ability of 0.0 and an individual with an ability of 1.0 have a similar probability of positive endorsement for item 1 (.50 and .58, respectively). In item 3, however, the probability for an ability of 1.0 is .85, and we can observe that slopes assist in producing different conclusions when compared with using item difficulties only.

Item Response Theory Parameter Invariance

The benefit of using IRT in estimating the properties of an item lies not only in the mapping of difficulty onto ability but also in the property of item parameter invariance across ability groups. Because item characteristics do not depend on the group, as they do in CTT, the item parameters should be the same regardless of the ability level of a group. This feature is shown in figure 5.4, in which the solid black line represents the ICC and the distributions reflect different ability groups taking this particular item. Although there are different probabilities of a correct endorsement across the range of ability for the item, the difficulty of the item is 0.0 and is not a function of the three groups. Group 1 is a low-ability group since the mean of the distribution is around −1.0, group 2 is a group of average ability, and group 3 is a high-ability group. If we were to

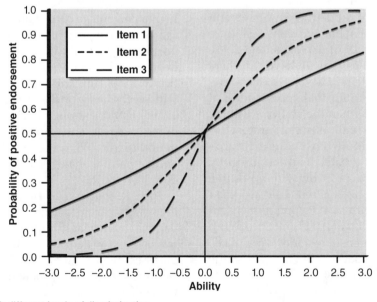

Figure 5.3 ICCs with different levels of discrimination.

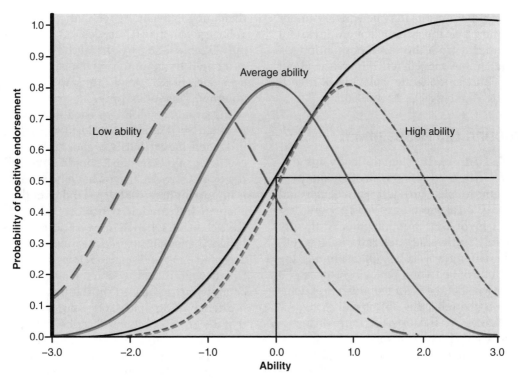

Figure 5.4   Invariance of item difficulty across ability groups.

estimate the item difficulty using CTT, this item would have a low *p*-value in group 1 since the IRT difficulty of 0.0 crosses the distribution at the upper end of the curve. In group 2, this item would have a *p*-value close to 0.50 since the difficulty crosses in the middle of the distribution, and in group 3 this item would be easy since it crosses at the lower end of the curve. Item parameter invariance holds when the specified models fit the data well.

Let's contrast these results with what would be observed if we used IRT to estimate the item parameters in groups of low, average, and high ability, such as those shown in figure 5.4. We can observe that IRT item parameters are invariant across subgroups within a population. Although this demonstration highlights the parameter invariance, it is important to recall that this phenomenon can be observed only when a model fits the data exactly in a population. When this does not occur, the natural log of the probability is not a linear function of ability, and different *a* and *b* parameters may be estimated for the subgroups. Therefore, it is important to check for item invariance in data. One simple procedure for cross-checking results is to use a median split in the sample based on ability and to run the IRT model in both subgroups. Once the item parameters are estimated, they may be plotted for the subsamples to examine the degree of linearity. Item difficulties and discriminations should have

a linear relationship, and the lower the correlation (i.e., the greater the scatter in the plots), the less the invariance. A low correlation may be due to poor item parameter estimation or a misfit of the model to the data, but both may be examined for revisions.

Two final notes on IRT invariance are worth mentioning. First, just as item parameters are invariant across subgroups in a population, so are ability scores. This indicates that ability is unrelated to the administered items. There is a simple method for checking ability invariance that is akin to a split-half method for checking reliability: For a sample of individuals, estimate the participants' ability on the odd items of the test and then the participants' ability on the even items. Then plot the paired ability scores to examine the extent to which ability invariance holds.

Second, item parameter invariance is based on the premise that the distribution of ability scores is the same across samples. If item parameters are estimated in two separate samples with different distributions of scores (e.g., only high-ability individuals compared with only low-ability individuals), we should not expect the parameters to be the same. Although we can test whether the score distributions are the same between two samples simply by estimating the item parameters and comparing, it is more appropriate to conduct an invariance test of the parameters using a multiple group analysis (Muthen & Lehman, 1985). When samples differ, the estimated item parameters may be equated under the assumption that the parameters are invariant between samples from the same population, as research has demonstrated that IRT inferences about ability are robust to moderate violations of invariance (Rupp & Zumbo, 2003, 2004, 2006).

Constructing the Assessment

Classical Test Theory. The item difficulty and discrimination can be used, along with other analyses, to choose items to make up a test with reliable and valid scores. Typical procedures for choosing test items in CTT involve (1) examining item difficulty and removing outliers, (2) determining the reliability of remaining test scores, (3) examining the discriminations of items and removing outliers, (4) determining whether there is a redundancy of items that improves the reliability, (5) repeating steps 2 through 4 as necessary, and (6) testing the relationship between the retained item scores and the latent factor they describe with a factor analysis. Step 1 is conducted by reviewing the p-values of items (assuming items are scored dichotomously) and removing any item that has $p = 0.0$ or $p = 1.0$, given that such values signify that all individuals responded the same way to an item. If an item with one of these values is included in the final set, it will not provide meaningful information for the population because the total score without the item could be known by adding 0 or 1. Many tests and assessments target a particular level of ability; thus, it may be appropriate to choose items for which a low percentage of individuals respond positively. The nature of the assessment should dictate how items are chosen. However, it is common practice to choose items that span the range of difficulty. It should be noted that utilizing this method does not ensure that a range of item difficulties will reflect the range of ability due to the sample-specific nature of the scores. Once the initial item pool is selected, the initial reliability of test scores should be estimated (step 2). Generally speaking, the reliability for an assessment should be at least .80 for research purposes and closer to .90 for clinical decision making (Nunnally & Bernstein, 1994). See also chapter 3 in this volume.

Steps 3 and 4 may be done in tandem by simultaneously examining the discrimination and the item redundancy. Discriminations that are negative or near 0 warrant immediate item removal, as a negative value indicates that individuals who respond positively to the item tend to respond negatively to other items. Likewise, a discrimination of 0 tells us that there is no relationship between how individuals endorse the item and how they respond to the

remaining items in the set. Typically, standardized values greater than 0.3 are desired. Item redundancy may be examined by the alpha-if-deleted index generated by common statistical software packages (e.g., SPSS, SAS, R; refer to chapter 3 in this volume). This index provides an estimated value of the Cronbach alpha for each item as if the item were removed from the model. Items with an alpha-if-deleted index that is higher than the reported coefficient alpha in step 2 should be considered for removal. Once such steps have been completed, it is important to retest the reliability of the scores to evaluate the extent to which coefficient alpha may have changed when items were added or removed. When the reliability reaches a threshold that is acceptable to the researcher, it is then important to test the validity of the scores as they pertain to one or more factors. Based on the theory that guided the item writing, at least one hypothetical construct that the groups of items describe should exist. The SCAT, for example, is unidimensional since all 15 items produce one total score that describes an individual's level of sport competition anxiety. Conversely, the Sport Motivation Scale (SMS) has 28 items but produces seven total scores, each with 4 items, that measure intrinsic motivation to know, intrinsic motivation toward accomplishment, intrinsic motivation to experience stimulation, identified regulation, introjected regulation, external regulation, and amotivation. Analyses such as CFA allow researchers to test the theoretical models of how the written items relate to the hypothetical constructs of interest. Evaluation of model fit allows for further identification of items for possible removal based on the inability of scores to describe the factors. Numerous resources exist to assist individuals in the theoretical and statistical application of factor analysis in the scope of CTT (e.g., Brown, 2006; Kline, 2005).

Item Response Theory. Constructing a new assessment using IRT follows a different set of steps that initially appear to be counterintuitive. While CTT espouses that reliability should be first, the primary assumption of dimensionality must be tested before reliability in IRT. This means that a score from a test can have meaning only if the items measure the intended dimensions. Connected to this assumption is the idea of local independence of items, meaning that responses to a set of items are statistically independent of each other for a given level of individual ability (Hattie, Krakowski, Rogers, & Swaminathan, 1996). The requirement of local independence is quite stringent, requiring that the conditional covariances between pairs of items be 0 and that the product of individual means or variances of items produce higher-order moments

(McDonald, 1979). This rigidity led McDonald to suggest that a weaker principle of independence should be used, one in which the relationship between means and variances does not need to be considered and only the covariances must be 0.

Using the assumption that the test intends to measure only one dimension, Stout (1990) extended the logic of weak local independence to argue for essential unidimensionality rather than ascribing to more stringent standards. Stout argued that a test is essentially unidimensional if, for a given level of ability, the average conditional covariance over pairs of items on the test is *small* in magnitude, as opposed to 0. Essential unidimensionality may be assessed formally by using Stout's Dimtest software program or by examining the ratio of eigenvalues in other statistical modeling software. Once the assumptions have been tested, the process of choosing items to make up the assessment may begin. One of the strong advantages of IRT is that graphs and plots can be used to guide item selection. These graphs and plots typically illustrate variable characteristics of items over a range of trait levels. CTT, on the other hand, largely relies on the numerical indicators of item properties and decision rules that are averaged out over the entire range of trait levels for a given sample. Thus, CTT is limited in that it, for example, assumes the same level of error for all individuals. The basic rules applying to item selection in IRT are similar to those in CTT. Depending on the targeted population, items may be selected to reflect high or low ability or a range of ability. Unlike in classical methods, in IRT methods selecting items across an ability range ensures that the population range of ability is tapped.

In addition to the item difficulty, the item discrimination may be used more comprehensively in IRT than in CTT. Both CTT and IRT use the discrimination index to indicate that higher values communicate a stronger relationship between item response and test performance, but discrimination serves an additional important function in communicating the amount of information an item has in describing the ability range. IRT replaces the traditional concept of reliability with item and test information. Remember that classical theory measures the degree to which scores are free from error and can be described with a single index (i.e., coefficient alpha). This idea is extended in IRT. In IRT, information is indicative of the precision the item has across the entire range of ability and is calculated with

$$I(\theta) = 2.89a^2 P_i(\theta) \times [1 - P_i(\theta)]$$ **5.4**

for the 2PL model; in the 1PL model the a^2 term is dropped. Thus, for a given level of ability, informa-

tion is related to the discrimination of the item and the probability of a positive endorsement and can range from 0 to $+\infty$. Larger values indicate more information at a given level of ability. As the probability of a positive endorsement changes across the range of ability, so does the amount of information.

Consider figure 5.5, which shows information curves for the items in figure 5.3. Items 1, 2, and 3 have discriminations of 0.50, 1.0, and 2.0, respectively, and the difficulty of all items is 0.0. The information curves tell us two important features about our sample items: First, there is a relationship between the magnitude of discrimination and the amount of peak in the curve. Item 1, for example, has a very flat curve with minimal information, so while it contributes an equal amount of information across the range of ability, the amount contributed is a very small amount. The discrimination of item 2 leads to a slightly more peaked distribution of information. Item 2 is equally informative about individuals with an ability of −1.0 to 1.0. Item 3 demonstrates a curve with strong information isolated around a narrow range of ability. The peak of the curve is much higher than those of items 1 and 2, and the amount of information item 3 provides at an ability of −1.0 or 1.0 is the same as that provided by item 2. Furthermore, the amount of information rapidly accelerates with small deviations from those estimates. Second, the highest level of discrimination is found at the level of item difficulty, meaning that items of a particular difficulty that are matched to individuals with the same value in ability are the most informative.

Using the item information and ICCs, we can choose a diverse set of items that provide information across a broad range of abilities. While CTT focuses on the total test score and comparing multiple latent factor models across indexes of fit and standardized item loadings, IRT requires choosing a

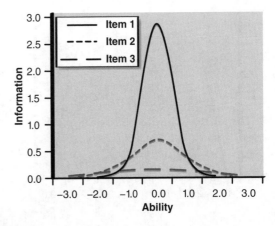

Figure 5.5   Item information curves.

sufficient number of items that are highly informative of a broad range of ability. An important characteristic of item information functions is that they are additive and can become a test information function. The test information function is calculated with

$$TI(\theta) = \Sigma I(\theta) \qquad \textbf{5.5}$$

Thus, at each value in the range of ability, the test information is simply a sum of all the item information at that particular point. The reason why the test information function is a crucial element of item selection is its relationship to the standard error of measurement of each student. IRT student ability is measured with some amount of error that can be quantified. Using the test information for each value of ability, we can calculate the amount of error with

$$SE(\theta) = \frac{1}{\sqrt{TI(\theta)}} \qquad \textbf{5.6}$$

Because error is reciprocally related to information, when a test information curve is plotted, the standard error associated with the information at all points is also available. Figure 5.6 shows this relationship. The test information curve is represented by the solid line and the standard error is the dotted line. Each plotted point on the curve represents the information and error for a specific level of ability. It can be seen that when ability is between −2.0 and 2.0, the information is high and the corresponding standard error is low. Conversely, for ability values outside of this range, the amount of information is low and the standard error is high, indicating that ability levels outside of this range have a high degree of error. Thus scores here are not as reliable as scores within the −2.0 to 2.0 range.

This relationship between information and standard error is significant in that error relates directly to the calculation of a traditional estimate of reliability. While the amount of error related to scores on a scale is considered to be uniform in classical theories, IRT allows for error to vary across the entire range of ability. When the standard error is estimated for θ, it may then be used to determine the marginal level of reliability that exists for any given ability level, with

$$r_{xx'} = 1 - SE(\theta)^2 \qquad \textbf{5.7}$$

The relationship between the standard error in IRT and the reliability in CTT is best illustrated in figure 5.7, which uses the standard error plot from figure 5.6 but truncates the graph to be representative of individuals with $SE \leq 1.0$. Reference lines in the graph represent standard error of CTT reliability where $r_{xx'}$ = .90 (solid line), .85 (dashed line), and .80 (dotted line). By rearranging equation 5.6 to solve for standard error, so that $SE(\theta)$ = $(1 - r_{xx'})^{1/2}$, it can be shown that SE for $r_{xx'}$ = .90 is 0.316, SE for $r_{xx'}$ = .85 is 0.387, and SE for $r_{xx'}$ = .80 is 0.447. Note that these values are based on a standardized value of θ, and they will differ if θ has a different scale.

Figure 5.7 shows that this particular test is most informative (i.e., has low error) for individuals whose ability ranges from −2.0 to 2.0. Since 95% of the data from a normal distribution fall between ability scores of −2.0 and 2.0, at least 95% of students taking this test should have a reliable estimate of their ability of no less than .80. While CTT assumes a constant level of error across all abilities, the standard error in IRT reveals that not all students have the same level of error in their scores. In fact, students with ability scores greater than 2.0 or less than −2.0 have less precision in their scores, and this makes it more difficult to make implications about their ability on the test and its relationship to other scores should a battery of assessments be administered.

Sample Size

An important consideration in both CTT and IRT is the minimum number of participants needed for data analysis. Research currently available to guide this choice is limited; however, several rules of thumb exist to assist in deciding on a sufficient sample. Some have pointed out that a balance may be struck between the sample size and the correlation between items and factors (i.e., standardized loadings). The better a set of items describes a factor, in both CTT and IRT, the smaller the required sample size. For samples <200, items that correlate well with the proposed factor (≥.60) may balance out the small sample size to provide relatively stable

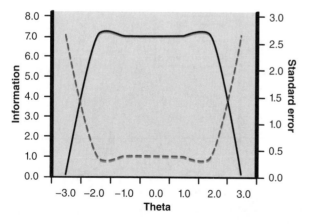

Figure 5.6   Test information and standard error plot.

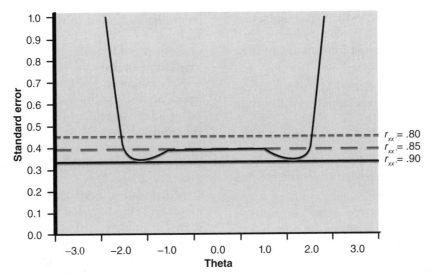

Figure 5.7   IRT standard error compared with CTT standard error at $r_{xx'}$ = .90 (solid line), $r_{xx'}$ = .85 (dashed line), and $r_{xx'}$ = .80 (dotted line).

results (Marsh & Hau, 1999). However, items that relate poorly to the factor necessitate a larger sample size (Thissen, 2003). In the context of IRT, researchers have stated that simple 1PL models may be run with as few as 50 participants (Linacre, 1994) and 2PL models may be run with a minimum of 250 individuals; however, several authors have recommended a sample of 500 for accurate parameter estimates in the 2PL model (Baur & Lukes, 2009; Embretson & Reise, 2000).

Such recommendations must be taken with a grain of salt. Muthen and Muthen (2002) suggested that no rule should be used across all situations since many factors affect the number of individuals needed in a sample, including the type of model (e.g., 1PL or 2PL), the number of factors and observed variables, the distribution of the observed variables, the number of response categories for the items, the amount of missing data, the amount of measurement error in the variables, and the correlations among the observed indicator. With so many variables influencing the sample size decision, it is especially important to view the guidelines as starting points for data collection planning and not as finite rules. While obtaining some information about item performance may be possible in smaller samples, and some information is better than no information, it is important that even minimal criteria are met so that standard errors are unbiased and parameter estimates are accurate.

One approach to determining appropriate sample size given the number of elements that should be considered is to conduct a Monte Carlo simulation study. This technique allows the researcher to specify the model of interest with hypothesized

parameter values that may be used based on previous research. Considerations of normality, missing data, number of factors, and so on may all be manipulated in the simulation. These values are then tested with an initial desired sample size set by the user and are replicated in the simulation a certain number of times. For example, Baur and Lukes (2009) recommended that a sample size of 500 be used to achieve stable results when a 2PL model with 15 items is considered, while McKinley and Mills (1985) recommended a sample size of between 500 and 1,000 when goodness-of-fit index performance was important. When comparing simulation results to recommended sample sizes, it is apparent that simulations provide more information about required sample sizes when particular elements of the analysis are considered. Although some readers may think that such simulations are too complex and intimidating for their needs, the software package Mplus is very user friendly, and the technical manual provides sample syntax for running the simulations.

Conclusion

IRT overcomes many of the reported weaknesses of CTT—namely, that the item and person statistics are dependent on the sample. IRT not only addresses CTT shortcomings but also provides statistics, such as information functions, to assist researchers in choosing reliable items that describe an ability range well. As a way of summarizing the benefits of IRT, we draw from previous research to list the five most important benefits of utilizing IRT when validating scores for new assessments:

1. Since item statistics and individual ability scores are on the same metric, items may be matched to individuals to be most informative of their ability.

2. Even when unrepresentative samples from the population are tested, estimates of the item statistics are applicable.

3. Individual ability scores are not dependent on the difficulty of the test.

4. Shorter tests and assessments can be created with greater reliability.

5. The amount of error across scores is not fixed and fluctuates across levels of the population, providing greater information.

Although CTT is able to address some of its weaknesses through equating procedures or other empirical tests, the robustness of such procedures is not well documented. CTT is an important component of measurement theory that should not be ignored, especially considering the extent to which it is still widely applied in the social sciences. In fact, many current IRT software packages make use of p-values and point biserial correlations as a way for individuals to remove less informative items, or items where the p-values are 0.0 or 1.0. It is critical to be aware of CTT shortcomings, however, and to recognize when other measurement models may be preferred.

An important fact about IRT that many researchers are not yet familiar with is that a CFA with categorical items is the same as IRT, as Kamata and Bauer (2008) have pointed out. This indicates that SEM that contains a measurement model with categorically scored indicators or items is, in fact, an extended IRT model that many researchers may adopt. The advantages of IRT go beyond the examples provided in this chapter. New scaling techniques derived from IRT, such as Mokken scaling, provide insights into traditional scaling methods that are now considered to be outdated (e.g., Guttman scaling [Petscher & Kim, 2011]). IRT applications also include mechanisms for computer adaptive testing (Wainer, 2000), timed and time-limited tests (Van der Linden & Hambleton, 1997), and multidimensional models and instances where items are not dichotomously scored but are Likert type.

Multidimensional IRT models have gained increasing attention due to their ability to measure item parameters and estimate latent ability for items aligned to particular dimensions. There are several models for studying the multidimensional aspects of data, including the multidimensional random coefficient multinomial logit (MRCML) model (Adams, Wilson, & Wang, 1997) and the multidimensional IRT compensatory model (M2PL; Ackerman, 1992). Many assessments and surveys are not scored dichotomously but have a continuum of scores to which the individual may respond. Such examples can also utilize IRT models such as Samejima's (1969) graded response model to account for the differential nature of scoring compared with dichotomous items.

The potential use for IRT in sport and exercise psychology has been studied with some research conducted on how IRT may be applied to psychomotor assessment (Safrit, Cohen, & Costa, 1989) and how DIF models may be used to understand important gender differences in physical self-concept (Fletcher & Hattie, 2005). With greater promotion of these models, researchers in the field will gain a more comprehensive utilization of assessment data to better understand the cognitive and affective attributes of individuals.

Factorial Invariance

Tools and Concepts for Strengthening Research

Ryne Estabrook, PhD

actorial invariance is an important concept for sport and exercise psychology. It is important for making comparisons across gender, race, age groups, and time on the behavioral and psychological constructs commonly used in sport and exercise science. A number of reviews (Bontempo & Hofer, 2007; Schmitt & Kuljanin, 2008; Vandenberg & Lance, 2000) and didactic works for specific disciplines (see Byrne & Stewart, 2006; Horn & McArdle, 1992; Millsap & Meredith, 2007; Widaman & Reise, 1997, among others) have been written on the subject of invariance. The goal of this chapter is to provide an overview of both traditional and novel applications of factorial invariance, focusing on the application of confirmatory factor analysis (CFA) and structural equation modeling (SEM) for applied sport and exercise research.

The importance of factorial invariance is tied to the meaning of latent variables, or lack thereof. Regardless of the method used for the extraction and identification of latent variables or factors, they have no inherent scale or meaning. The interpretation of a latent variable depends on the relationships between that variable and some set of manifest or observed variables. Latent variables are often given names or labels to aid interpretation, but the constitutive meaning of the variable comes from relationships with other manifest and latent variables (Cronbach & Meehl, 1955). When factor analytic models are applied to multiple groups, then factor interpretation must be carried out separately for each group. Researchers who wish to interpret a latent variable in one group as being the same construct as another latent variable in another group must do more than give the two variables the same label. They must estab-

lish that the relationships between that latent variable and the set of manifest variables are the same across groups. Factorial invariance encompasses a set of criteria and accompanying methods for establishing the equivalence of those relationships across groups or models.

The earliest work on factorial invariance pertained exclusively to exploratory factor analysis (EFA). Cattell's (1944) parallel proportional profiles provided a method to rotate a pair of factor analysis solutions, with factor loadings of one sample proportional to the factor loadings of the other. Building on the work of Thomson (1939) and Thurstone (1947), Ahmavaara (1954) showed that simple structure, or the pattern of zero and nonzero factor loadings as described by Thurstone (1947), is preserved regardless of the selection processes underlying sampling. Meredith (1964a, 1964b) later showed that when neither the sample covariances nor the factor variances were standardized, invariance of factor loadings across groups could be achieved in subpopulations selected from a common parent population.

More recent work on invariance has focused on models fit with CFA. Invariance studies based on exploratory models rely on rotation to establish patterns of loadings for comparison across groups. This makes explicit constraints of equality either across groups or to a constant impossible. CFA uses a set of structural equations to model the means, variances, and covariances of a set of manifest variables (hence, structural equation modeling [SEM]). Such models allow for explicit constraints of model parameters to equality across groups as well as for rigorous tests of model fit for the evaluation of these constraints.

Testing of these constraints is of great importance in sport and exercise psychology, when observations are clustered within age groups, schools, and other defined groups. Testing hypotheses related to group comparisons demand invariant measurement structures across these groups.

Factorial Invariance

For the purposes of this discussion, let's consider one specification of a CFA using SEM. There are a number of ways to specify these models, prominently the linear structural relations (LISREL) model (Jöreskog, 1971) and reticular action model (RAM) specification (McArdle, 1980; McArdle & McDonald, 1984). The notation for the following model matches that of Meredith (1993).

Equations 6.1 and 6.2 describe a common measurement model, and figure 6.1 presents an accompanying path diagram. The path diagram has a specific number of manifest variables (three) and latent variables (one), while equations 6.1 and 6.2 may describe any number of manifest and latent variables. The following equations describe the expected means (equation 6.1) and covariances (equation 6.2) for k different groups over which the invariance of some set of model parameters may be tested.

$$\mu_k = \alpha_k + \xi_k \Lambda_k{}' \qquad\qquad \textbf{6.1}$$

$$\Sigma_k = \Lambda_k \Phi_k \Lambda_k{}' + \Theta_k \qquad\qquad \textbf{6.2}$$

Each matrix in equations 6.1 and 6.2 has a specific function, allowing us to refer to an entire class of model parameters with a single symbol. Readers looking to review matrix operations can examine a number of linear algebra texts as well as chapters and appendixes in several multivariate statistics and structural modeling texts (Bollen, 1989; Loehlin, 1998; Raykov & Marcoulides, 2008; Tabachnick & Fidell, 1996, among others). The functions of the matrices described in equations 6.1 and 6.2 are described in the following paragraphs.

Observed Data: μ_k and Σ_k are the observed means and covariances for group k. If the observed data for any group have p variables, then μ_k is a $1 \times p$ matrix of observed means, while Σ_k is a $p \times p$ matrix of observed variances and covariances. In the path diagram presented in figure 6.1, there are three means (a 1×3 matrix) and six variances and covariances (a 3×3 covariance matrix).

Factor Loadings: The Λ_k matrix includes all of the factor loadings, or the regressions of the observed variables on the common factors. The Λ_k matrix is of order $p \times m$ (3×1 in the example), with rows indexing observed variables and columns indexing

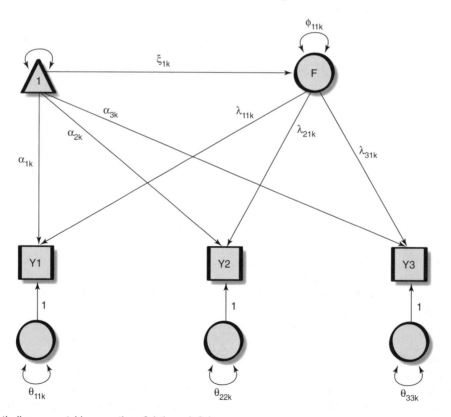

Figure 6.1   Path diagram matching equations 6.1 through 6.4.

latent variables. Thus, the loading of any observed variable on any latent variable is found in the row of the observed variable and the column of the latent variable.

Factor Means: ξ_k is a $1 \times m$ matrix of latent variable means, where m is the number of latent variables (a 1×1 matrix in the example). Latent variables are assumed to have means of 0 in many models, but they may have means in any model where manifest means are somehow constrained.

Intercepts: The α_k vector contains all of the intercepts of the observed variables, conditional on the means of the factors. Many single-group factor analyses do not report these parameters, as they are simply the observed means if the factors have means of 0.

Factor Variances and Covariances: ϕ_k is an $m \times m$ covariance matrix of latent variables (a 1×1 matrix in the example, thus containing only a variance term). While some models constrain factor variances for the purposes of model identification and standardizing the latent variable, this should not be done in studies of factorial invariance unless equivalence of factor variances is of interest.

Unique Factors (Residual Variances or Residual Errors): The unique factors have a $p \times p$ (3×3) covariance matrix Θ_k, with means assumed to be 0. Unless a covariance between unique factors is included (often referred to as *correlated errors*), this matrix is diagonal and contains only 0 in the off-diagonal elements.

The model of three observed variables and one latent variable shown in figure 6.1 has expected means for any group k, as is shown in equation 6.3:

$$[\mu_{1k}\ \mu_{2k}\ \mu_{3k}] = [\alpha_{1k}\ \alpha_{2k}\ \alpha_{3k}] + \qquad \textbf{6.3}$$
$$\xi_{1k}[\lambda_{1k}\ \lambda_{2k}\ \lambda_{3k}]$$

That same model has expected covariances for any group k, as is shown in equation 6.4. While the Λ_k matrix is transposed in parts of equations 6.3 and 6.4, the parameters in those matrices are still indexed first by the observed variable and then by the latent variables.

$$\begin{bmatrix} \sigma_{11k} & \sigma_{12k} & \sigma_{13k} \\ \sigma_{21k} & \sigma_{22k} & \sigma_{23k} \\ \sigma_{31k} & \sigma_{32k} & \sigma_{33k} \end{bmatrix} = \begin{bmatrix} \lambda_{11k} \\ \lambda_{21k} \\ \lambda_{31k} \end{bmatrix}$$
$$[\varphi_{11k}][\lambda_{11k}\ \lambda_{21k}\ \lambda_{31k}] + \qquad \textbf{6.4}$$
$$\begin{bmatrix} \theta_{11k} & 0 & 0 \\ 0 & \theta_{22k} & 0 \\ 0 & 0 & \theta_{33k} \end{bmatrix}$$

In the equations just shown, all groups have both the same number of observed variables p and the same number of latent variables m. In addition, the manifest variables observed in one group must be the same as those observed in all other groups. While there may be differences in other parts of the model (i.e., the scale being tested for invariance is used to predict different variables in different groups), most definitions of invariance require that whatever latent variables are being tested for invariance be indicated by the same set of manifest variables in all groups. Some exceptions to this rule are discussed later in this chapter.

The types or levels of factorial invariance distinguish themselves by placing constraints on the different matrices discussed thus far. In the ensuing sections, these different levels are examined. The matrices and parameters that are free to vary across groups retain the subscript k, while those matrices and parameters constrained to equality across groups are not given a subscript k. For instance, Λ_k refers to the matrix of factor loadings for any single group, while Λ refers to the matrix of factor loadings shared by all groups under investigation, expressed either as $\Lambda_1 = \Lambda_2 = \ldots = \Lambda_k = \Lambda$ or as (more simply) $\Lambda_k = \Lambda$.

Configural Invariance

Configural invariance (Thurstone, 1947; Horn, McArdle, & Mason, 1983) is the form of factorial invariance with the fewest model restrictions. Configural invariance requires only that there be the same number of factors in every group and that the pattern of zero and nonzero or salient factor loadings be identical across groups. There is no restriction on the values of salient loadings. For instance, in an example where six manifest variables indicate two latent variables in two different groups, the factor loadings for the two groups (displayed in the matrices Λ_1 and Λ_2 in equation 6.5) may take the following configurally invariant pattern:

$$\Lambda_1 = \begin{bmatrix} \lambda_{111} & 0 \\ \lambda_{211} & 0 \\ \lambda_{211} & 0 \\ 0 & \lambda_{421} \\ 0 & \lambda_{521} \\ 0 & \lambda_{621} \end{bmatrix}, \Lambda_2 = \begin{bmatrix} \lambda_{112} & 0 \\ \lambda_{212} & 0 \\ \lambda_{212} & 0 \\ 0 & \lambda_{422} \\ 0 & \lambda_{522} \\ 0 & \lambda_{622} \end{bmatrix} \qquad \textbf{6.5}$$

In these matrices, the first factor for either group is indicated by the first three manifest variables, with zero loadings on the other three variables. The second factor is indicated by the last three manifest variables. Notice there are no restrictions on the values of the nonzero loadings, as the factor loadings are free to differ across groups.

In this form of invariance, the latent variables in each group may be interpreted similarly. The meaning of the latent variables comes entirely from the meaning of the manifest variables, and the latent variables are defined by the same manifest variables in all groups. We cannot say that the factors have the same meaning across groups, as the relationships between manifest and latent variables may vary across groups. For this reason, configural invariance has also been termed *non–metric invariance* (Widaman & Reise, 1997), reflecting the inability of this type of invariance to impart constant units for the factor across groups. In the example presented in equation 6.5, the two factors may have different covariances in each group, but this difference could be attributable either to group differences in the strength of the relationship between the factors or to group differences in factor loadings.

Simple structure is a concept related to, but not identical to, configural invariance. Thurstone (1947) created criteria for simple structure, a rotational goal for EFA such that manifest variables have salient loadings on as few factors as possible. Ideally, a model with simple structure has one salient factor loading per variable, with that variable's loadings on all other factors near zero. The example in equation 6.5 is an application of simple structure to a confirmatory model, where some loadings are constrained to a value of 0. If configural invariance is thought of as the invariance of the configuration of latent variables across groups, then simple structure must be present to some degree for this equality to have meaning. Groups constrained to configural invariance can be thought of as having identical simple structures in a confirmatory model.

Metric Invariance

Meredith (1964a, 1964b, 1993) provided the framework for metric invariance in factor analytical models, demonstrating that invariant factor structures should remain invariant under selection and outlining several ordered types of invariance. Whereas factorial invariance refers specifically to the invariance of model parameters in factor models, metric or measurement invariance refers to invariance of measurement. When the observed variables are considered indicators of an unob-

served trait, the factor model takes the form of a measurement model. Meredith (1993) described three ordered levels of metric invariance for latent constructs.

Weak Factorial Invariance

The first type or level of invariance described by Meredith (1993) is weak factorial invariance. Weak factorial invariance constrains the factor loadings to be equal across groups, thus defining the relationships between the manifest and latent variables to be invariant. In matrix terms, the Λ_k matrices for each group are all equal and thus can be represented more simply by Λ (no subscript). The algebraic formulation of models under weak factorial invariance can be found in table 6.1.

When weak factorial invariance can be established, all group differences in covariances between the observed variables can be attributed to group differences in the common and unique factors. This level of invariance does not necessarily imply metric invariance, as the same observed score in a manifest variable does not necessarily correspond to the same level of the latent variable across groups. Additionally, as intercepts (the α matrix) are free to vary across groups, factor means cannot be directly compared. Weak factorial invariance does allow for the testing of relationships involving the latent factor, such that covariances and regressions involving that variable may be analyzed.

Strong Factorial Invariance

The next level of invariance is strong factorial or scalar invariance (Meredith, 1993). This level adds an additional constraint over weak factorial invariance, adding equality constraints to the α matrix as well as the Λ matrix constrained previously. The algebraic formulation of models under strong factorial invariance can be found in table 6.1.

Group differences in observed means can now be attributed entirely to group differences in factor means. In addition to differing in the factors themselves, groups may also differ in the variances (and potentially covariances) of their unique factors. Just as with weak factorial invariance, strong factorial invariance does not always imply metric invariance. However, groups can be compared with respect to their factor means, so questions as to group differences in level of a construct may be answered when strong factorial invariance can be established.

Strict Factorial Invariance

The next level of invariance described by Meredith (1993) is strict factorial invariance. This level adds

■ Table 6.1 ■
Algebraic Definitions of Factorial Invariance

Type	Mean	Covariance
Configural	$\mu_k = \alpha_k + \zeta_k \Lambda_k'$	$\Sigma_k = \Lambda_k \Phi_k \Lambda_k' + \Theta_k$
Weak	$\mu_k = \alpha_k + \zeta_k \Lambda'$	$\Sigma_k = \Lambda \Phi_k \Lambda' + \Theta_k$
Strong	$\mu_k = \alpha + \zeta_k \Lambda'$	$\Sigma_k = \Lambda \Phi_k \Lambda' + T_k$
Strict	$\mu_k = \alpha + \zeta_k \Lambda'$	$\Sigma_k = \Lambda \Phi_k \Lambda' + \Theta$

Model specification for means and covariances across groups under configural, weak, strong, and strict factorial invariance. Subscripted matrices are constrained to equality across groups; matrices without subscripts are estimated independently for each group.

an additional constraint over strong factorial invariance, adding equality constraints to the Θ matrix on top of the constraints to the Λ and α matrices present in strong factorial invariance. The factor model under strict factorial invariance can be found in table 6.1.

Strict factorial invariance necessarily provides metric invariance, as differences in groups constrained to strict factorial invariance are due only to differences in the latent variables. The common factors established by a strict factorially invariant model allow for the clearest attribution of individual and group differences to differences in the constructs of interest.

Relating Levels of Metric Invariance

The invariance types described thus far provide a nested hierarchy, which is presented algebraically in table 6.1 and described in table 6.2. While not sufficient for metric invariance, configural invariance can be considered as nested within weak factorial invariance.

Determining whether metric invariance can be established in empirical data is an important part of factorial invariance. Some argue that only with strict invariance can metric invariance be established (Meredith, 1993), as only then can group differences in the distributions of observed scores be directly attributable to group differences in the distributions of the underlying factors. In many cases, weak or strong factorial invariance may be a sufficient condition for metric invariance. Ultimately, selection of factor models for multiple groups or time points depends both on fit and on the research questions the model is designed to answer. Weak factorial invariance is sufficient for establishing relationships between latent constructs, while strong factorial invariance allows for the comparison of factor means across groups.

■ Table 6.2 ■
Delineating Types of Factorial Invariance

	RESTRICTIONS		
	Factor	Manifest	Residual
Type	Loadings	Intercepts	Variances
	(Λ)	(α)	(Θ)
Configural	Simple	None	None
Weak	Equal	None	None
Strong	Equal	Equal	None
Strict	Equal	Equal	Equal

Equal denotes equality of parameters across groups. *None* denotes no constraints across groups. *Simple* denotes constraint of zero loadings, with no constraints on nonzero loadings.

Alternative Approaches

While Meredith's (1993) work provides a rigorous framework for testing measurement invariance, the Meredith models may provide poor fit or not be appropriate for certain types of data for either practical or conceptual reasons. Several alternatives to weak, strong, and strict factorial invariance have been advanced, each providing distinct solutions to the problem of factorial invariance.

Partial Invariance

The types of factorial invariance described thus far deal with groups of parameters as sets, such that strong factorial invariance necessitates that all factor loadings and all manifest intercepts be invariant. Alternatively, partial factorial invariance describes models in which some, but not all, of the parameters of a particular type (e.g., factor loadings, intercepts, unique factors) are constrained to invariance, while other parameters are free to vary across groups.

The partial invariance approach allows for considerable flexibility in model fitting and better identification of specific rather than global problems in invariance models. Fitting partial invariance models allows for the identification of the specific manifest variables responsible for group differences rather than treats the set of manifest variables as a unit.

However, partial factorial invariance does have several possible problems. Partial invariance models are subject to bias if parameters that are not invariant are constrained to equality. For instance, if a factor loading that should show group differences is constrained to invariance, then factor loadings that should not show group differences may be biased as a result of this misfit. Cheung and Rensvold (1998, 1999; Rensvold & Cheung, 2001) provide a set of methods for dealing with this problem, detailing forward and backward selection criteria to check for parameter bias. Also, how to interpret partial invariance models isn't always clear. For instance, models with fully invariant factor loadings (i.e., weak factorial invariance) and partial invariance of manifest intercepts and unique factor variances may inherit some, all, or none of the interpretation usually associated with strong and strict factorial invariance. Partial invariance is a useful tool and is relevant for describing how, rather than if, factorial invariance is appropriate.

Idiographic Filtering

A necessary component of metric invariance is the requirement that the manifest variables be the same across all groups being compared. However, this requirement may not be appropriate over all types of data. For instance, studies involving child and adolescent development may study what is thought to be the same construct over a variety of ages but may use different measures of that construct for different age groups. Even when the measures are supposed to be the same, individual or group differences in the use and interpretation of certain parts of a measure can create idiosyncratic differences in variables. Although this matter applies to various measurement domains, this is of particular concern for self-report instruments, as individual or group differences in the use of language can alter the use of measures and, by extension, the relationships between the variables that make up a scale.

Idiographic filtering, or higher-order invariance (Nesselroade, Gerstorf, Hardy, & Ram, 2007; Nesselroade & Estabrook, 2008), provides a method for defining factors in terms of their relationships to other constructs rather than their relationships to manifest variables. The invariance constraint in this case does not involve the factor loadings but rather the factor correlations. Latent variables are free to have whatever loadings and variances are appropriate, such that group differences in factor loadings are used to filter out idiosyncratic differences. Idiographic filtering can be achieved by constraining the factor covariance matrix to a correlation matrix. This method provides identification constraints in the form of restricting the factor variances to values of 1, which is sufficient to identify many models. In the more general case, we can describe our factor covariance matrix (denoted Φ in equation 6.2) as consisting of a factor correlation matrix Ψ pre- and postmultiplied by a vector of factor standard deviations, ρ. When higher-order invariance is enforced, the factor correlation matrix Ψ is constrained to invariance, as is shown in equation 6.6:

$$\Phi_k = \rho_k \Psi \rho_{k'} \qquad \qquad 6.6$$

Researchers are then free to apply whatever identification constraints they feel appropriate, using the factor loadings (Λ_k), the factor variances (ρ), or both. Previous use of this method has also included some level of simple structure as an identification constraint (Nesselroade et al., 2007; Nesselroade & Estabrook, 2008). Because the factor correlation matrix is invariant over groups, factor analysis of this matrix yields invariant second-order structures. This method is most appropriate when manifest variables differ, change, or are missing across groups and when the constructs of interest have the same relationships across groups. In the same way that models of partial invariance are susceptible to bias when model parameters that are not invariant are constrained to invariance, idiographic filtering may show bias in factor loading parameters if factor correlations that are not invariant are constrained to equality. The fit of the model to data, however, can be tested by hypothesis.

Fitting Invariance Models

Methods for specifying invariance structures in a confirmatory structural model are relatively straightforward. The invariance models described in this chapter all rely on some set of model constraints, such that some model parameters are constrained to be equal to other parameters. In most of the statistical software used for fitting SEMs, equality constraints are made either by giving multiple model parameters the same label or by using a specific constraint command. Making equality constraints requires that all groups in a multiple-group confirmatory model (or all time points in a longitudinal model) be estimated simultaneously. Simultaneous estimation also allows for easier model comparison.

Let's consider the simple example of three manifest variables and one latent variable presented in figure 6.1 and equations 6.1 through 6.4 as an example of coding models for factorial invariance. This model may be implemented in any SEM package. For this example we will use OpenMx (http://openmx.psyc.virginia.edu), a freely available structural modeling program available as an R package. Paths can be specified in OpenMx using the mxPath function, which defines paths from and to a set of defined variables. The type of path (one- or two-headed arrow), whether the path is freely estimated, the starting values, and the parameter labels are supplied by the user. Putting the following *loadingsFree* object in a multiple-group model specifies the same paths for each group but allows those paths to vary freely across groups:

```
loadingsFree <- mxPath(
    from = "F", to = c("y1","y2", "y3"), arrows = 1,
    free = c(FALSE, TRUE, TRUE), values = 1,
    labels = NA)
```

This function defines one-headed arrows from the latent variable F to the manifest variables y1, y2, and y3. One factor loading is given a fixed value of 1 to scale the latent variable, as is indicated by the single FALSE value in the free argument. All paths are given starting values of 1, and the paths are not given labels. The paths may also be constrained to equality across groups by giving those paths the same label, as shown in the following *loadingsConstrained* object:

```
loadingsConstrained <- mxPath(
    from = "F", to = c("y1", "y2", "y3"), arrows = 1,
    free = c(FALSE, TRUE, TRUE), values = 1,
    labels = c("lambda1", "lambda2", "lambda3"))
```

The paths created in these two pieces of code can then be inserted into the models for each of the groups in the analysis. To constrain to weak factorial invariance, place the loadingsConstrained set of paths in the models for each group (each group is given its own model). To remove this constraint (consistent with a configural invariance model if multiple factors are retained), place the loadingsFree set of paths in the model for each group. OpenMx also allows for matrix specification of the same model:

```
lambdaFree <- mxMatrix(
    type = "Full", nrow = 3, ncol = 1,
    free = c(FALSE, TRUE, TRUE), values = 1,
labels = NA)
```

```
lambdaConstrained <- mxMatrix(
    type = "Full", nrow = 3, ncol = 1,
    free = c(FALSE, TRUE, TRUE), values = 1,
    labels = c("lambda1", "lambda2", "lambda3"))
```

The two versions of the Λ matrix shown here are exact replacements for the path-style representation presented earlier. Regardless of the software or specification used for fitting invariance models, the procedure is the same. The code shown here could easily be applied to means or residual variances simply by changing the variables and types of paths referred to in the code. Fuller examples of weak invariance in both OpenMx and Mplus (Muthén & Muthén, 1998-2007) are presented in appendixes A and B at the end of this chapter.

While the different types of factorial invariance have different uses and interpretations, selecting which parameters to constrain to invariance depends a great deal on model fit. SEMs provide a large number of ways to assess fit, each with certain benefits and drawbacks for the study of invariance.

Congruence

Tucker's congruence coefficient (Burt, 1948; Tucker, 1951) provides a method for assessing the similarity of two sets of factor loadings. Typically it is used with exploratory models. The coefficient is very similar to Pearson's correlation, with similar bounds, interpretation, and insensitivity to scaling. It differs from a correlation in that it does not deal with scores centered around a mean; rather, scores are centered around 0. It also does not have the known distributional properties of the correlation. This provides sensitivity to additive constants, such that sets of loadings [.8, .6, .4] and [.2, 0, −.2] are perfectly correlated but have zero congruence (Lorenzo-Seva & Berge, 2006). The formula for Tucker's congruence coefficient for two sets of loadings x and y (indexed by i) is given in equation 6.7.

$$\varphi = \frac{\sum_{i=1}^{k} x_i y_i}{\sqrt{\sum_{i=1}^{k} x_i^2}\sqrt{\sum_{i=1}^{k} y_i^2}}. \qquad 6.7$$

A number of criteria exist for Tucker's congruence coefficient. Tucker (1951) considered greater than .92 as good to outstanding and greater than .98 as excellent, but criteria of .80 (Horn, Wanberg, & Appel, 1973), .90 (Bentler & Bonett, 1980; Mulaik,

1972), and .95 (Lorenzo-Seva & Berge, 2006) for considering sets of factor loadings equivalent have been used as well. Tucker's congruence coefficient can also be tested for significance differences either from 0, or no relationship (Bentler & Bonett, 1980; Cattell, 1978; Nesselroade, Baltes, & Labouvie, 1971), or from 1, or a perfect relationship (Chan, Ho, Leung, Chan, & Yung, 1999). This statistic is intended for use in exploratory analysis and generally is not used in confirmatory analysis.

Likelihood Ratio Test

The likelihood ratio (LR) test is a very common test statistic for all types of models estimated using maximum likelihood estimation. This statistic compares the estimated likelihoods of two nested models, defined as two models (both fit to the same data) where the smaller model can be considered as a simplification or special case of the larger one. The test statistic is the difference between the -2 log likelihoods ($-2LL$) of the two models and is chi-square distributed with the degrees of freedom equal to the difference in the numbers of parameters in the two models.

The LR test is very useful for tests of factorial invariance due to the nesting inherent in the different levels of invariance. The nested hierarchy of configural, weak, strong, and strict factorial invariance shown in table 6.2 on page 57 lends itself well to the LR test. To use the test, simply fit two models (e.g., models of weak and strong invariance fit to identical multiple-group data) and compute the test statistic as the difference in the $-2LL$ of the two models. If the test statistic is significantly different from 0, then the larger model (weak invariance in this example, as it has more parameters) provides a statistically significant improvement and should be retained. If the difference in fit is not statistically significant, then the simpler model (strong invariance, which has fewer free parameters due to constraints) should be retained. Partial invariance models and idiographic filtering approaches may also be tested using the LR test, but nesting must be evaluated for each comparison.

LR tests for SEMs have been described as being sensitive to sample size (Bollen & Long, 1993; Hu & Bentler, 1993; James, Mulaik, & Brett, 1983), though these usually refer to comparing any model to a fully saturated or perfect fitting model. As sample size becomes large, the LR test becomes powerful enough to detect very small model differences (Satorra & Saris, 1985). This is not a weakness of the test—rather, it is a statement of the statistical power of this test beyond what are commonly thought of as small differences across groups or time points. LR tests are often used in conjunction with more global assessments of model fit in an effort to evaluate the size of the differences in addition to their probability of occurring by chance alone.

Modification Indexes

Modification indexes (or LM tests, after the Lagrange multiplier used to calculate them; Sorbom, 1989) estimate the expected improvement in model fit ($-2LL$) associated with individually freeing or adding all possible parameters not included in a model. Modification indexes aren't often used to test for invariance but are a relevant tool for such analyses. For example, these tests can be very useful for identifying which invariance constraints are responsible for model misfit. However, testing this many parameters creates concerns for multiple testing and may lead to incorrect model specification (MacCallum, 1986). This approach is also subject to the potential problems of any partial invariance model. Modification indexes are a useful exploratory technique for investigating invariance problems in data, but other tests should be used for more global model comparison and for model building.

Global Measures of Model Fit

Numerous articles and texts have been devoted to discussing global fit indexes for SEMs (see Bentler & Bonett, 1980; Hu & Bentler, 1993, among others), with specific investigations of model fit for multiple-group models (Bentler, Lee, & Weng, 1987; Satorra, 1993). Cheung and Rensvold (1998, 1999) have shown that model selection using measures like the Comparative Fit Index (CFI), the Tucker–Lewis Index (TLI), and root mean squared error of approximation (RMSEA) in addition to LR tests is superior to using LR tests in isolation.

Selecting measures of model fit is an important part of assessing factorial invariance. Fortunately, researchers are free to use many fit statistics. This freedom both removes the burden of choosing one method over another and gives a more informative picture of how models truly fit. As the global measures of model fit represent a large class of statistics used for many structural models, many of the measures used in assessing factorial invariance will come in the form of standardized fit indexes (like the aforementioned CFI and TLI), summaries of root mean error (i.e., RMSEA and standardized root mean square residual [SRMR]), and comparisons of model likelihood statistics. These measures should be used jointly to assess fit and to select models, just as in any other SEM.

Ordinal Data

An important component of analyzing psychological data is dealing with ordinal data. Factorial invariance is an important part of establishing measurement, and psychological measurement very often involves binary and ordered categorical data. Using this type of data requires use of alternate specifications of the factor model, typically either a version of SEM that accounts for this feature of the data or some type of item response model.

Changes to Invariance Definitions

The different types or levels of invariance described in this chapter have somewhat different meanings when applied to categorical data. In the simplest case, a binary variable cannot have both a mean (intercept) and a variance, as the mean and variance of binomially distributed data depend on one another by definition. There is no distinction between strong and strict factorial invariance for ordinal data, as only one of the intercept (α_k in equations 6.1 and 6.2) and residual variance (θ_k) terms may be included in any model. By extension, any model consisting entirely of ordinal data constrained to strong factorial invariance is also constrained to strict factorial invariance.

Factor models of ordinal data replace the intercepts relevant to strong and strict factorial invariance with thresholds. Categorical manifest variables are thought to be discrete representations of underlying continuous latent variables. Items with j categories receive $j - 1$ thresholds, which may be constrained to equality across groups. Constraining thresholds of manifest variables across groups necessarily constrains the intercepts and residual variances of the continuous latent variable that underlies the manifest variables, establishing strict factorial invariance as described previously.

Relationships to Item Response Models

Item response models are a large part of the psychological measurement literature (Lord & Novick, 1968; for overviews, see Baker, 2001; Embretson & Reise, 2000; Hambleton, Swaminathan, & Rogers, 1991). Confirmatory factor models are strongly related to item response models and have been shown to be equivalent models for binary data (Kamata & Bauer, 2008; McDonald, 1985; Muthén & Christoffersson, 1981; Muthén, 1981, 1984; Widaman & Reise, 1997). Whereas a large variety of invariance models have been explored in the factor analysis literature, the focus on measurement in item response models has led to modeling approaches that enforce metric invariance through strict factorial invariance. Parameters or individuals that deviate from strict factorial invariance are referred to as *LOI*, an abbreviation for *lack of invariance* (Rupp & Zumbo, 2006).

Differential item functioning (DIF, alternatively studied as *measurement bias*; Drasgow, 1982) is an important concept for item response modeling strongly related to factorial invariance. DIF refers to model parameters that vary across groups in an item response model. There are "a wide variety of statistical procedures for evaluating whether two [item characteristic curves] are different" (Embretson & Reise, 2000, p. 261). Millsap and Everson (1993) provide a review of methods for the analysis of DIF.

Conclusion

Factorial invariance is of considerable importance for rigorous psychological research. Establishing and testing for factorial invariance are an important part of the measurement of latent variables. Understanding the difference between factorial and metric invariance greatly improves the interpretation of all types of factor analysis models. As described in this chapter, factorial invariance refers only to the invariance of parameters from some version of factor analysis, while metric invariance deals with the invariance of measurement. Metric invariance is not specific to the factor model. Establishing invariance of the measurement of various aspects of latent variables improves not only the model fit but also the interpretation and use of latent variables. Having interpretable and meaningful latent variables is key to building sound theory, which is the primary objective of latent variable modeling.

Longitudinal applications of factorial invariance are just as important as (if not more important than) the multiple-group applications discussed in this work. Individuals measured repeatedly on the same scales and constructs are almost certainly undergoing changes of some type—else the repeated measurements are useless. The latent variables under investigation may be changing in mean, variance, and relation to other variables, and the measurement properties that tie the latent variables to the manifest variables may be changing as well. Establishing some amount of factorial invariance is important for the study of change, and the level of factorial invariance established determines what types of change can be investigated in longitudinal analyses.

The proper use of factorial invariance concepts and tools is tied fundamentally to researchers' understanding of statistical methods. All of the methods reviewed in this chapter are multiple-group and longitudinal extensions of single-group and cross-sectional structural equation and item factor models. Factorial invariance is not an alternative set of methods for research and modeling but instead is a part of understanding the data underlying any measurement model. Finding strong evidence for factorial invariance can establish metric invariance and help answer interesting research questions. However, a lack of evidence for factorial invariance is not a weakness of the data but rather an indication that the groups under investigation differ in much more complex (and potentially interesting) ways than previously thought. When this occurs, it is time to dig deeper. A lack of invariance across age, sex, or school in a measure may indicate that these groups differ in more intricate ways than previously thought. Careful application of the tools and concepts of invariance may lead to discovery of these representations in sport and exercise psychology.

Acknowledgments

The author was supported by grant T32 AG20500-08 from the National Institute on Aging and the National Institutes of Health during the writing of this work. The author wishes to thank John Nesselroade for his helpful comments on this work. Correspondence should be addressed to Ryne Estabrook, Virginia Institute for Psychiatric and Behavioral Genetics, Virginia Commonwealth University, PO Box 980126, Richmond, VA, 23298-0126. Email: crestabrook@vcu.edu.

Appendix A: Coding Example for Mplus

```
TITLE: Weak Factorial Invariance Example for Mplus;
DATA: FILE= example.dat;
VARIABLE: NAMES = ID x1-x5 y1-y5 z1-z5 group;
        USEVAR= y1-y3;
        MISSING= .;
        GROUPING = group (0=reference, 1=other);
MODEL:
!Factor Loadings
F BY y1-y3;
!Manifest Intercepts (Labels)
[y1-y3];
!Manifest Residuals (Labels)
y1-y3;
MODEL other:
!Manifest Intercepts (Labels)
[y1-y3];
!Manifest Residuals (Labels)
y1-y3;
```

Appendix B:
Coding Example for OpenMx

```
#Weak Factorial Invariance Example for OpenMx#
library(OpenMx)
loadingsConstrained <- mxPath(
        from = "F", to= c("y1", "y2", "y3"), arrows = 1,
        free = c(FALSE, TRUE, TRUE), values = 1,
        labels = c("lambda1", "lambda2", "lambda3"))
interceptsFree <- mxPath(
        from = "one", to = c("y1", "y2", "y3"), arrows = 1,
        free = c(FALSE, TRUE, TRUE), values = 1, labels = NA)
residualsFree <- mxPath(
        from = c("y1", "y2", "y3"), to = c("y1", "y2", "y3"), arrows = 2,
        free = c(TRUE, TRUE, TRUE), values = 1,
        labels = NA)
factorVar <- mxPath(
        from = "F", to = "F", arrows = 2,
        free = TRUE, values = 1, labels = NA)
factorMean <- mxPath(from = "one", to = "F",
        arrows = 2, free = TRUE, values = 1, labels = NA)
model <- mxModel("Model",
        type = "RAM",
        manifestVars = c("y1", "y2", "y3"),
        latentVars = "F",
        loadingsConstrained, interceptsFree, residualsFree, factorVar, factorMean)
groupOne <- mxModel(model, mxData(groupOneData, type="RAM"))
groupTwo <- mxModel(model, mxData(groupTwoData, type="RAM"))
weakInvariance <- mxModel("Weak Invariance", groupOne, groupTwo)
results <- mxRun(weakInvariance)
```

7

Modeling Change Over Time

Kevin J. Grimm, PhD, and Nilam Ram, PhD

The development of skills, abilities, attitudes, and attributes is best studied by repeatedly testing or observing an individual or collection of individuals over time. Collecting data of this nature allows for the study of the *development process*—examining how much individuals change, when change occurs (e.g., phases), how fast change occurs, whether there are times of discontinuity or transition, and how people differ in these aspects of the developmental (i.e., time-related) process under study. The goal is to understand how change proceeds within an individual—the *individual* developmental process—as well as how individuals differ in their developmental process—the between-person differences in change. The former can be considered a form of data reduction in which the repeated observations are reduced to a smaller number of *change components* (similar to factors in a factor analysis) that adequately describe how the individual changes over time. The latter focuses on whether individuals differ in their scores on the smaller number of *change components*.

Once the developmental process is understood, the question turns to evaluating determinants of the *change components*. Determinants may be personal characteristics (e.g., gender), experimental manipulations, static interindividual differences (e.g., maternal education), or dynamic interindividual differences (e.g., health). The contemporary method for modeling change over time is the latent growth curve (McArdle & Epstein, 1987; Meredith & Tisak, 1990), which can be fit in the SEM or multilevel modeling (MLM) frameworks (see Ferrer, Hamagami, & McArdle, 2004; Ghisletta & Lindenberger, 2004). In this chapter, we review the latent growth curve model and describe the application of various latent growth curve models using data collected as part of a skill acquisition study. In this presentation we focus on individual growth trajectories, model fit and misfit, and interpretation.

Sample Data

The sample data come from a published study comparing modeling and imagery approaches in acquiring and retaining motor skills (experiment 1 from Ram, Riggs, Skaling, Landers, & McCullagh, 2007).[1] The participants, experimental protocol, and measures have been described previously, so here we provide only a brief overview. To begin with, 41 female undergraduate students volunteered to participate in an experimental study evaluating different approaches to learning how to properly execute a squat using free weights.

Participants were assigned to one of four interventions: *imagery*, *modeling*, *combination*, and *control*. In the *imagery* condition, participants listened to an 80 second audiotape of spoken dialogue (in a female voice) that guided them through mental imagery of the squat task before each of four acquisition *blocks*. The dialogue instructed participants to visualize the correct execution of the nine form elements upon which they would be judged (as well as provided information about proper timing). Following the dialogue were 25 seconds of silence during which the participants were instructed to mentally rehearse the movement. In the *modeling* condition, participants watched a 105 second video with front, side, and back views of a woman aged 25 years performing the squat lifts with ideal form. In the *combination* group, participants alternated between

Input and output scripts from Mplus can be found at http://psychology.ucdavis.edu/labs/Grimm/personal/downloads.html.
[1]We would like to thank Penny McCullagh and Sean Skaling for use of these data.

modeling and *imagery* interventions (two each for a total of four). In the *control* condition, participants were offered a newspaper to read during the rests between *blocks*.

Each participant executed four *blocks* of squats on each of 2 days. Two judges rated each squat performance (videotapes) on nine aspects of task execution that were then summed and averaged to obtain *form* scores ranging from 9.5 to 42 (out of a possible 9 to 45) for each of the eight *blocks* (four on day 1 and four on day 2). These *blocks* are of interest to us, as they serve as the repeated measures for modeling individual change. Of further interest is the experimental manipulation—four groups of participants receiving different interventions. From the intervention grouping variable, we created three dummy variables that compare each experimental group with the control group to examine how each intervention may have affected individual change. For this illustration we use the four *form* scores from day 2 of the study.

Researchers interested in modeling change approach their data with a set of research questions in mind (see Ram & Grimm, 2007). We will approach the sample data with the following research questions: (1) Do participants' squat performances (form scores) improve across the four *blocks* of trials? (2) If yes, how does performance change (e.g., linearly)? (3) Do participants vary in how they change across the four *blocks*? (4) Do any of the three experimental interventions affect particular change components (e.g., the initial scores and the progression of change across the four *blocks*)?

Analysis

We begin our evaluation of these research questions by calculating descriptive statistics and plotting the scores of participants over the four occasions.

Descriptive statistics for the *form* scores over the four occasions are shown in table 7.1. Examining these summary statistics, we see that the mean of the *form* scores increased across the four *blocks*, from 18.78 for *block 1* to 22.20 for *block 4*. Additionally, we see the *form* scores are highly correlated across the four *blocks*, as all correlations are greater than .90, indicating that individuals who performed better at *block 1* were likely to perform better at *block 4*. Finally, we see the standard deviation increased slightly across *blocks*, from 5.71 for *block 1* to 7.05 for *block 4*.

Next, we plot *individual* trajectories for our sample data in figure 7.1. This plot is informative in several ways. First, we can use it for data screening—we can examine whether there are any unusual observations. Second, it helps us understand the trends in the data. For example, we see that most individuals increased their scores over time, but there were a few individuals whose scores increased in *blocks 2* and *3* and then declined in *block 4*. We can see that there is substantial variance in how individuals performed at *block 1* and that individuals appear to change at different rates. Although we do not observe any severe nonlinearity in the trajectories, we will still fit growth models that allow for nonlinear change patterns with respect to time. If we saw strong nonlinear change patterns, we would consider what types of nonlinear change models would be appropriate (e.g., quadratic, exponential, logistic; see Grimm & Ram, 2009; Ram & Grimm, 2007). After this initial look at the data, we can fit a series of growth models to statistically examine within-person change and between-person differences in change.

Latent Growth Curve Modeling

Latent growth curve analysis (McArdle & Epstein, 1987; Meredith & Tisak, 1990) is a method for

■ Table 7.1 ■

Descriptive Statistics for the Four Form Scores From Day 2

Correlations	Block 1	Block 2	Block 3	Block 4
Block 1	1.00			
Block 2	.94	1.00		
Block 3	.94	.96	1.00	
Block 4	.90	.92	.95	1.00
Mean	18.78	20.38	21.70	22.20
Standard deviation	5.71	6.44	6.94	7.05

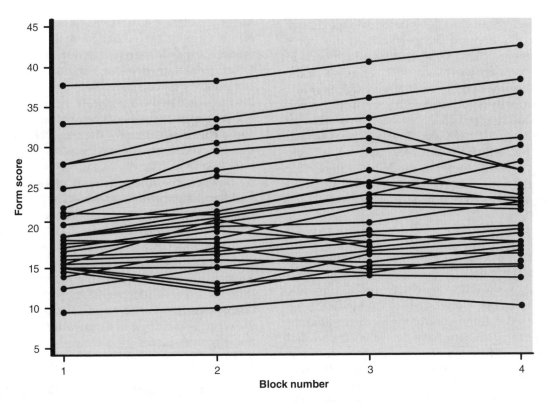

Figure 7.1   Longitudinal plot of observed trajectories of *form* scores of participants.

describing within-person change processes and between-person differences in the within-person change processes. For our sample data, we describe and fit three specific growth curves commonly considered in applied research:

Intercept-Only Growth Curve. The intercept-only growth model is an appropriate starting point in any change study. The model posits that people differ in their level of performance but do not change over time. In most applications, we hope to reject this model, as we expect people to change over time. The model can be written as

$$y_{nt} = i_n + e_{nt},$$ **7.1**

where y_{nt} are the repeated measures of attribute y for individual n at time t (i.e., *form* scores for each participant at each *block*), i_n is the intercept for individual n, and e_{nt} is a time-specific residual score for individual n at time t. The individual intercepts are assumed to be normally distributed and therefore can be described by a mean (μ_i) and variance (σ_i^2). Similarly, time-specific residual scores are assumed to be normally distributed with a mean of 0.0 and a single variance (σ_e^2).

Linear Growth Curve. The linear growth model is probably the most commonly fit growth curve in applied research. The linear growth model posits that people differ in the level (i.e., intercept) of the

attribute at an initial point in time (i.e., *block 1*) and linearly change from that initial level. The linear growth model is similar to fitting a linear regression model to each individual's data. From these regressions, we get an intercept and slope for each individual and can examine the distribution and associations of these *change components*. The linear growth model can be written as

$$y_{nt} = i_n + s_n \cdot \frac{(t - k_1)}{k_2} + e_{nt},$$ **7.2**

where y_{nt} are the repeated measures of attribute y for individual n at time t, i_n is the intercept or predicted score for individual n when $t = k_1$, s_n is the linear slope or the predicted amount of change in y for individual n for a unit change in $(t - k_1) / k_2$, and e_{nt} is a time-specific residual score for individual n at time t. For our sample data, t is the *block* number (1, 2, 3, and 4), k_1 equals 1.0 to center the intercept at the first *block*, and k_2 equals 3.0 to scale the slope as the amount of change from the first to the last *block*. In this format, the intercept term represents the initial status and the slope term represents each individual's rate of change across the four *blocks*. As with the intercept-only model, the intercept and slope are assumed to be normally distributed, and their distributions can be described by means (μ_i and μ_s), variances (σ_i^2 and σ_s^2), and covariance

$(\sigma_{i,s})$. These parameters describe the average change function, the amount of between-person differences in the intercept and slope, and how variations in the intercept are associated with variations in the slope. The time-specific residual scores are assumed to be normally distributed with a mean of 0.0 and a single variance (σ_e^2).

Latent Basis Growth Curve. The latent basis growth model (McArdle & Epstein, 1987; Meredith & Tisak, 1990) is a flexible growth model that allows for modeling nonlinear change patterns. The latent basis growth model can be written as

$$y_{nt} = i_n + s_n \cdot (\alpha_t) + e_{nt}, \qquad 7.3$$

where y_{nt} are repeated measures of attribute y for individual n at time t, α_t are basis coefficients representing how the individual change process unfolds, i_n is the intercept or predicted score for individual n when $\alpha_t = 0$, s_n is the slope or the predicted amount of change in y for a unit change in α_t for individual n, and e_{nt} is a time-specific residual score for individual n at time t. For example, if the individual change process is linear, then α_t equals $(t - k_1) / k_2$. As in the linear model, the distributions of the intercept and slope can be described by means (μ_i and μ_s), variances (σ_i^2 and σ_s^2), and a covariance ($\sigma_{i,s}$). The residual scores have a mean of 0.0 and a single variance (σ_e^2).

Identification constraints must be placed on the basis coefficients to define the slope, s_n, similar to identifying a factor in confirmatory factor analysis. Often, the first basis coefficient, α_1, is set to 0.0 and the last basis coefficient, α_T, is set to 1.0, where T represents the final occasion. These constraints make i_n interpreted as the initial status and the slope interpreted as the total amount of change that occurs during the time of observation. Imposing these identification constraints in our example means that the basis coefficients for the second and third *blocks* are estimated as opposed to being fixed, as they are in a linear growth model. Because these two basis coefficients are estimated, we allow for the individual rate of change to vary across the four *blocks*. For example, we may find that the *form* scores change rapidly across the first and second *blocks* and then do not change from the second through the fourth *blocks*. This pattern of change would indicate that all of the learning took place between the first and second *blocks* and was simply maintained across the remaining *blocks*.

Fitting Latent Growth Curves

Latent growth curves can be fit in the SEM and MLM frameworks (see Ferrer, Hamagami, &

McArdle, 2004; Ghisletta & Lindenberger, 2004; Ram & Grimm, 2007). As an SEM, the linear growth model is fit as a restricted common factor model with a constrained mean structure. The change components, i_n and s_n, are latent factors with factor loadings set equal to 1 and $(t - k_1) / k_2$, respectively. These change components have means, variances, and a covariance. Finally, the residual variance of the observed scores is often forced to be equal over time (see Grimm & Widaman, 2010). In the MLM framework, the linear growth model is fit as a multilevel regression with occasions nested within persons, with $(t - k_1) / k_2$ as an observed variable in the data. For the intercept-only model, s_n is removed from the model. For the latent basis model, the first and last factor loadings for s_n are fixed to 0 and 1, respectively, and the remaining factor loadings are estimated. The Mplus input script for fitting the latent basis growth curve and notes regarding how the script is modified to fit the intercept-only and linear growth curves are contained in the appendix at the end of this chapter.

Results From Fitting Latent Growth Curves

The results from fitting the three growth curves are described in the following paragraphs. Fit statistics and parameter estimates for these growth curves are shown in table 7.2. The fit of the growth models was evaluated using the chi-square misfit statistic (χ^2), comparative fit index (CFI), Tucker-Lewis index (TLI), root mean square error of approximation (RMSEA), and standardized root mean square residual (SRMR). Generally, CFI and TLI values greater than .90 and RMSEA values less than .10 indicate adequate fit, while CFI and TLI values greater than .95 and RMSEA values less than .05 indicate good fit. SRMR is a standardized difference between observed and expected covariance matrices, and values less than .08 indicate good fit.

Intercept-Only Growth Curve. The intercept-only growth curve resulted in $\chi^2(11) = 77.5$, *CFI* = .703, *TLI* = .838, *RMSEA* = .428 (.341-.520), and *SRMR* = .130 and was found to be an inadequate representation of the change process based on the global fit indexes. This finding suggests that *form* scores were not stable but tended to change across the four *blocks*. Even though the intercept-only model did not fit well, it's important to understand what this model is predicting about the change process. Thus, we turn to the parameter estimates. The intercept-only growth model has three estimated parameters, which are the intercept mean (μ_i = 21.03), intercept variance (σ_i^2 = 39.60), and residual variance (σ_e^2 = 5.65). Thus, based on this model, the average person has a predicted score of 21.03 at the

Parameter Estimates and Fit Statistics
for the Intercept-Only, Linear, and Latent Basis Growth Curves

	Intercept only	Linear	Latent	Linear + prediction
PARAMETER ESTIMATES				
Intercept mean (μ_i)	21.03** (1.12)	19.29** (1.02)	19.06** (1.01)	17.36** (1.65)
Slope mean (μ_s)	—	3.54** (0.55)	3.51** (0.53)	2.50** (0.93)
BASIS COEFFICIENTS (A_1-A_4)				
α_1	—	= 0	= 0	= 0
α_2	—	= .333	.456** (.085)	= .333
α_3	—	= .666	.839** (.090)	= .666
α_4	—	= 1	= 1	= 1
Intercept variance (σ_i^2)	39.60** (10.11)	32.99** (8.53)	31.72** (8.28)	22.96** (0.07)
Slope variance (σ_s^2)	—	5.34* (2.49)	4.73* (2.31)	3.51 (2.06)
Intercept–slope correlation (ρ_{is})	—	.44 (.24)	.49* (.24)	.37 (.30)
Residual variance (σ_e^2)	5.65** (0.82)	2.33** (0.41)	2.25** (0.40)	2.33** (0.41)
PREDICTION OF INTERCEPT				
Modeling	—	—	—	6.79** (2.34)
Imagery	—	—	—	−1.53 (2.50)
Combination	—	—	—	1.69 (2.41)
PREDICTION OF SLOPE				
Modeling	—	—	—	1.72 (1.35)
Imagery	—	—	—	−0.53 (1.40)
Combination	—	—	—	2.90* (1.35)
FIT STATISTICS				
χ^2(df)	77.5(11)	11.6(8)	6.8(6)	17.4 (14)
CFI	.703	.984	.997	.985
TLI	.838	.988	.997	.981
RMSEA (C I\	.428 (.341-.520)	.117 (.000-.253)	.063 (.000-.241)	.077 (.000-.178)
SRMR	.130	.040	.024	.031

SE contained within parentheses; = denotes a fixed parameter; * denotes parameter estimate is significantly different from 0 at $p < .05$; ** denotes parameter estimate is significantly different from 0 at $p < .01$.

first occasion and does not change across the four *blocks*. However, there was significant variation in the intercept, suggesting that subjects differed in their intercept scores. A plot of individual *predicted* trajectories based on this model is contained in figure 7.2*a*. As seen in this figure, participants were expected to differ in the *form* scores, and these scores remain perfectly stable across time. Thus, this model is an inadequate representation of our data.

Linear Growth Curve. For the linear growth curve, $\chi^2(8) = 11.6$, $CFI = .984$, $TLI = .988$, $RMSEA = .117$ (.000-.253), and $SRMR = .040$. Thus the linear growth curve was found to be an adequate representation of the change process based on the global fit indexes. The linear growth curve also fit significantly better than the intercept-only model did, with $\Delta\chi^2(3) = 65.9$, $p < .01$. The linear growth model has six estimated parameters and several fixed parameters. The estimated parameters are the intercept mean ($\mu_i = 19.29$), linear slope mean ($\mu_s = 3.54$), intercept variance ($\sigma_i^2 = 32.99$), slope variance ($\sigma_s^2 = 5.34$), intercept–slope correlation ($\rho_{is} = .44$), and residual variance ($\sigma_e^2 = 2.33$). The fixed parameters include the intercept loadings, which were fixed to 1.0, and the slope loadings, which were fixed to change linearly with respect to time for the four occasions (i.e., = 0, .333, .666, 1). Thus, based on this model, the average person has a predicted *form* score of 19.29 at the first occasion, and the *form* score increases 3.54 points from the first to the fourth *block*. Additionally, there was significant variation in both the intercept and slope, indicating that there were individual differences in both the level of performance during the first block (intercept) and the rate of improvement (slope). Thus, some participants have higher (or lower) scores on the first block and higher (or lower) rates of change. Finally, the intercept–slope correlation informs us that participants with higher intercept scores tended to have a faster rate of change; however, this correlation was not statistically significant. A plot of individual predicted trajectories based on the linear growth model is shown in figure 7.2*b*. As seen in this figure, participants differed in their predicted scores for the first *block* and in their rate of change, which was constant across time.

Latent Basis Growth Curve. For the latent basis growth curve, $\chi^2(6) = 6.8$, $CFI = .997$, $TLI = .997$, $RMSEA = .063$ (.000-.241), and $SRMR = .024$. Thus the latent basis growth curve was also found to be an adequate representation of the change process based on the global fit indexes; however, the latent basis growth curve did not fit significantly better than the linear model did, with $\Delta\chi^2(2) = 4.8$, $p = .09$. The latent basis growth model has eight estimated

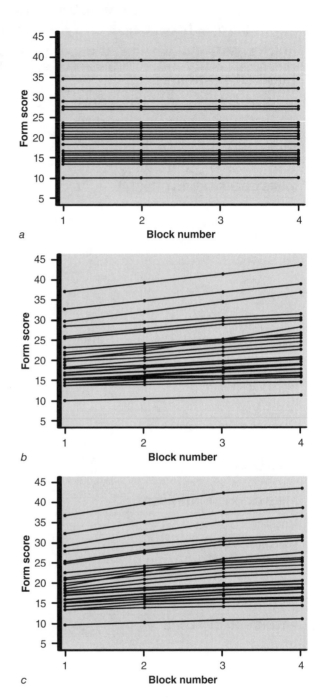

Figure 7.2 Predicted longitudinal trajectories based on *(a)* intercept-only, *(b)* linear, and *(c)* latent basis growth models.

parameters, which are the intercept mean ($\mu_i = 19.06$), slope mean ($\mu_s = 3.51$), intercept variance ($\sigma_i^2 = 31.72$), slope variance ($\sigma_s^2 = 4.73$), intercept–slope correlation ($\sigma_{is} = .49$), residual variance ($\sigma_e^2 = 2.25$), and two estimated basis coefficients ($\alpha_2 = .456$ and $\alpha_3^2 = .839$). The estimated basis coefficients allow for a nonlinear change pattern. For our data, these coefficients indicate that approximately 46% of the total change occurred between the first and second *blocks*. Another 38% (.839 − .456 = .383) of the total change occurred between the second and third *blocks*, which left 16% of the total change between the third and fourth *blocks* (1 − .839 = .161). Thus, from this model, it appears that the rate of change is decreasing (i.e., decelerating). This model predicts that the average person has a *form* score of 19.06 at the first occasion and that the *form* score increases 3.51 points by the fourth *block* but that the rate of change decelerates over time. As with the linear model, there was significant variation in both the intercept and the slope, indicating that participants had sufficiently different intercept and slope scores. The intercept–slope correlation was positive and significantly different from 0, suggesting that participants with higher intercept scores tended to have a faster rate of change. A plot of individual predicted trajectories based on this model is shown in figure 7.2c. As seen in this figure, participants differed in their predicted scores for the first *block* and in their rate of improvement, which decelerated across time.

Model Choice

After fitting this series of growth curves, we are left with the decision of which model provides a reasonable representation of our data. Obviously, the linear and latent basis models fit much better than the intercept-only model. Now, we must decide between the linear and latent basis models. The latent basis model appears to have better global fit indexes, but it does not fit significantly better than the linear model fits based on the chi-square difference test. Thus, we can decide that the linear model is an appropriate model based on statistical fit and parsimony. Now that we have chosen the linear growth model as the best representation of our data, we can answer the first three questions with which we approached our data. First, the mean of the linear slope was significantly different from 0, and thus we can conclude that, on average, squat performance did improve across the four *blocks*. Second, we can conclude that participants changed more or less linearly. Third, the slope variance was significantly different from 0, and we can conclude that participants varied in how they changed across the four *blocks*. Now, let's pursue our fourth question by examining how the experimental manipulation relates to the intercept and slope from the linear growth model.

Examining Predictors of Intercept and Slope

Once the individual change process and between-person differences therein are adequately modeled, we can move to question the determinants of those differences. In our example, we are interested in knowing whether the experimental manipulation affects how individuals change over time, which we can learn by looking at their intercepts and slopes. As in the regression framework, the experimental manipulation variable is treated as a predictor. The individual intercepts and slopes (i.e., change components) are the outcome variables of interest. Three dummy variables (*d_image*, *d_model*, and *d_combo*) were created to compare each experimental condition with the control condition. The resultant (regression) equations can be written as

$$i_n = \beta_{0i} + \beta_{1i} \cdot d\_image + \beta_{2i} \cdot d\_model +$$
$$\beta_{3i} \cdot d\_combo + d_{in}$$
$$s_n = \beta_{0s} + \beta_{1s} \cdot d\_image + \beta_{2s} \cdot d\_model +$$
$$\beta_{3s} \cdot d\_combo + d_{sn}$$

7.4

where i_n and s_n are the two change components (the individual intercepts and slopes from our linear growth model), β_{0i} and β_{0s} are the mean intercept and slope for the control group, β_{1i} and β_{1s} indicate the differences in the mean intercept and slope for the imagery group (compared with the control group), β_{2i} and β_{2s} indicate the differences in the mean intercept and slope for the modeling group (compared with the control group), β_{3i} and β_{3s} indicate the differences in the mean intercept and slope for the combination group (compared with the control group), and d_{in} and d_{sn} are residuals. Please note that even though we're discussing equations 7.2 and 7.4 as distinct components, they represent components of a single model and are estimated simultaneously. Equation 7.4 represents the prediction of latent variables in the SEM framework or the level 2 equation in the MLM framework.

Parameter estimates and fit statistics for the linear growth curve with the three dummy variables predicting the intercept and slope are also contained in table 7.2 (last column). The mean intercept and slope for the control group were estimated to be 17.36 and 2.50, respectively. The modeling group was found to have a greater mean intercept score ($\beta_{2i} = 6.79$, $p < .01$), and the combination group was found to have a greater rate of change ($\beta_{3s} = 2.90$, $p < .05$). Thus, modeling appears to have affected the *form* scores by influencing individuals' intercept scores (first retention *block*). However, the individuals who received the combined modeling and imagery intervention tended to show greater short-term improvement, as their mean slope was significantly greater than that of the controls. Individuals in the imagery group did not, on average, improve differently from the individuals in the control group. Average predicted trends for each experimental group are shown in figure 7.3 on page 72.

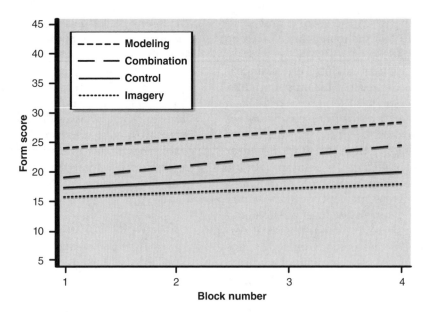

Figure 7.3   Predicted mean trajectories for each experimental group based on the linear model.

Conclusion

Typically, data from intervention studies of this kind are analyzed using group difference methods. For instance, ANOVA is often used to test for differences in group means. Additional within-subject factors (e.g., repeated trials or blocks) may be incorporated to determine when, in time, *group* differences appear. Longitudinal (e.g., multitrial) data also afford the opportunity to examine and model how various treatments affect the pattern or speed of skill acquisition at the *individual* level. For instance, in the present study imagery and modeling interventions affected individual rates of improvement differentially. Latent growth curve modeling is an important analytical tool that can help us describe, examine, and understand within-person change processes. Rather than describing changes in *group-level* averages, these analytical models provide information about average *individual-level* changes (i.e., see discussion of the ecological fallacy in Robinson, 1950).

The latent growth models discussed here are only the beginning, and we have only touched the surface of the many exciting possibilities such analytical tools provide for inquiry into within-person change processes and their determinants (see also McArdle, 2009; Preacher, Wichman, MacCallum, & Briggs, 2008). Extensions have been developed and are available for evaluating multiple phases of development (Cudeck & Klebe, 2002), multiple groups (McArdle & Hamagami, 1996), complex non-linear forms (Browne & Du Toit, 1991), and lead–lag relationships (McArdle & Hamagami, 2001). Excellent introductions to some of these more advanced models can be found in McArdle and Nesselroade (2003), Bollen and Curran (2006), Grimm and Ram (2009), and Ram and Grimm (2007). We encourage researchers to consider when and how latent growth models can further our progress in understanding how, why, and when individuals change over time.

Acknowledgments

Kevin J. Grimm was supported by REECE Program Grant DRL-0815787 from the National Science Foundation. Nilam Ram was funded by the National Institute on Aging RC1-AG035645, R21-AG032379, and R21-AG033109. The content is solely the responsibility of the authors and does not necessarily represent the official views of the funding agencies.

Appendix

TITLE: Latent Basis Model;
DATA: FILE = skalingraw.dat;
VARIABLE:
NAMES =
     id modeling imagery group out1-out8 form1-form8;
     MISSING = .;
     USEVARIABLES = form5-form8;
     IDVARIABLE = id;
ANALYSIS: TYPE = MEANSTRUCTURE;
MODEL:
!Defining Intercept & Slope;
     intercept BY   form5-form8@1;
     slope BY   form5@0
                    form6*.333
                    form7*.666
                    form8@1;
!Variance of Intercept & Slope;
     intercept slope;
!Mean of the Intercept & Slope;
     [intercept slope];
!Variance of Residuals;
     form5-form8 (ve);
!Mean of Residuals;
     [form5-form8@0];
OUTPUT: SAMPSTAT STANDARDIZED;
!To estimate the linear growth curve change the slope definition to:
!   slope BY   form5@0
!   form6@.333
!   form7@.666
!   form8@1;
!To estimate the intercept only growth curve remove
!all terms related to the slope

Rasch Modeling in Sports

Bernd Strauss, PhD, Dirk Büsch, PhD, and Gershon Tenenbaum, PhD

The aim of diagnostic testing is to explain people's response behaviors (i.e., observable, manifest behaviors) in test situations through nonobservable, latent traits or variables such as abilities, strategies, and characteristics. When doing so, it is not only helpful but also necessary to construct formal models describing the relationship between response behavior and latent variables. These models are item response theory (IRT) models (e.g., Hambleton, Swaminathan, & Rogers, 1991; Lord, 1980: see chapter 5 in this book, in contrast to classical test theory (CTT) models (Gulliksen, 1950; Lord & Novick, 1968). The latter assumes axiomatic partition of the observed score X into a true score T and an error score E ($X = T + E$). CTT is a concept that deals with the quality criteria of test scores (reliability, validity), and its major concern is minimizing measurement error and misinterpretation of test scores. However, there is no corresponding measurement theory on how the item responses emerge in a test situation in the absence of a defined origin (i.e., a zero point).

A major limitation of CTT is that item statistics (e.g., difficulty level) are derived from characteristics of persons or samples. It is not a sample-free measurement. In comparison, one of the major advantages of IRT models, the Rasch model in particular, is that all parameters are determined sample free (Rasch, 1960). See also chapter 5 in this book regarding how IRT models can be useful in measurement through instrument development.

The Basic Idea of the Rasch Model

The development of IRT models began in 1927 when Thurstone pointed out that scale values, such as specific sum scores, present all the information about a variable exhaustively if they possess a defined zero point or an origin. This is a feature that is not met by CTT but is taken into consideration by the Rasch model (Rasch, 1960).

The basic idea of the original Rasch model, known as a *probabilistic model*, is as follows: The probability of responding to an item correctly (i.e., the response behavior on the manifest variable) increases as the latent variable increases (e.g., the person's ability such as motor coordination or intelligence increases). In the original Rasch (1960) model, the manifest variable is always coded dichotomously (0 and 1). The latent variable is quantitative. This variable is the parameter of the person (θ). The original model has only one person parameter and so is termed the *unidimensional Rasch model*. The Rasch model assumes item difficulty, which is the parameter of the item (σ). The probabilistic relationship between the manifest variable and the person and item parameters is presented in equations 8.1 and 8.2.

$$p(x_{vi} = 1) = \frac{e^{(\theta_v - \sigma_i)}}{1 + e^{(\theta_v - \sigma_i)}} \qquad \textbf{8.1}$$

or

$$\ln\left(\frac{p(x_{vi} = 1)}{p(x_{vi} = 0)}\right) = \theta_v - \sigma_i, \qquad \textbf{8.2}$$

where e is Euler's constant ($e = 2.71$), and $p(x_{vi} = 1)$ denotes the response probability that a person v will succeed on an item i. Equation 8.1 can also be written in terms of logits, which are often used in the presentation of Rasch-related results. Equation 8.2 shows that the response probabilities (in logits) are equal to the difference between the person's ability θ_v and the item difficulty σ_i. These equations determine the item characteristic curve (ICC), which has an exponential form (see figure 8.1).

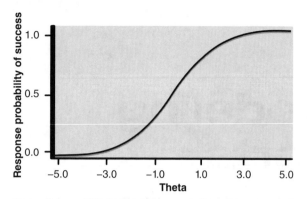

Figure 8.1 ICC of 1 item (θ represents the person parameter).

Reprinted, by permission, from B. Strauss, D. Büsch, and G. Tenenbaum, 2007, New developments on measurement and testing in sport psychology. In *Handbook of sport psychology*, 3rd ed., edited by G. Tenenbaum and R. Eklund (Boston, MA: Wiley), 737-756.

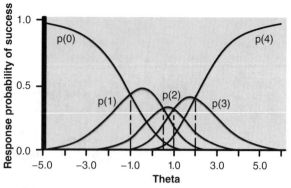

Figure 8.2 CCCs for the response categories.

Reprinted, by permission, from B. Strauss, D. Büsch, and G. Tenenbaum, 2007, New developments on measurement and testing in sport psychology. In *Handbook of sport psychology*, 3rd ed., edited by G. Tenenbaum and R. Eklund (Boston, MA: Wiley), 737-756.

The curve approximates to 0 and 1 but is asymptotic. Person ability is also plotted on the *x*-axis. It corresponds exactly to the value of θ_i when $p(x_{vi} = 1)$ = .5. If item difficulty parameters are greater, the ICCs shift to the right parallel to the ICC plotted in figure 8.1 without bisecting. If the item difficulties are smaller, the ICCs shift to the left parallel to the ICC in figure 8.1. ICCs are ideally parallel and should not intersect, because each item has the same slope parameter of 1.

One major problem in the original Rasch model is that it is restricted to dichotomous manifest variables. Questionnaires, however, often use a response format with more than two categories (e.g., a polytomous format) that are ordered on the assumption that they are ordinally scaled. Therefore, more powerful extensions of the original Rasch model are the *ordinal Rasch models* such as the rating scale model by Andrich (1978) and the partial credit model by Masters (1982) that have been developed to handle items with more than two ordered categories. The equations of the partial credit model are presented in the sidebar.

The basic idea of ordinal Rasch models is that a rater must overcome a step threshold in order to move from one response category to another (Wright & Masters, 1982; Wright & Stone, 1979). If there are five response categories (e.g., a rating from 0 to 4), for example, the rater must cross four thresholds (from category 0 to 1, 1 to 2, 2 to 3, and 3 to 4) in order to select category 4 (the highest category). The step-threshold parameters, which are added to equations 8.1 and 8.2, can be interpreted as the difficulty of making that crossing. All response categories have a *category characteristic curve* (CCC), analogous to the ICC, indicating the probability that a certain category is preferred over the other one. This is depicted in figure 8.2.

The probability for selecting the lowest response category (e.g., 1 = "Disapprove of the statement completely") *decreases* as a function of increasing values for the person parameter. Note that these ordinal Rasch models are also unidimensional probabilistic models. As figure 8.2 shows, the probability of choosing both categories is identical at their point of intersection and then increases as one crosses over into the next category. The distance between two neighboring threshold parameters defines the size of the intervening category.

An Example Using the Ordinal Rasch Model

Tenenbaum, Furst, and Weingarten (1985) used the rating scale model (Andrich, 1978; Wright & Masters, 1982) to evaluate whether the items in the State-Trait Anxiety Inventory (STAI; Spielberger, Gorsuch, & Lushene, 1970) can reliably measure anxiety trait and state in athletes. For this study, 100 young student-athletes responded to the trait scales and 55 high-level athletes responded to the state scales within 30 min before a competition. The Rasch analyses estimates for the trait anxiety scale on both persons and items indicated that the items did not produce equal intervals along the linear continuum of the trait anxiety measure. The number of items was sufficient to differentiate athletes high and low on trait anxiety; 6 of the 20 items elicited unexpected responses and thus resulted in unacceptable fit values ($\delta > |2|$), indicating that uniformity is either selecting a response category or selecting a category that is not in agreement with the person's anxiety level. Several items shared the same locations on the linear continuum, and the efficiency of the entire trait scale was only moderate (69.63%). A similar analysis performed on the state anxiety scale disclosed similar problems: Items failed to be spaced equally along the linear continuum; 15 of the 20 items were located within less of that 1 logit range, thus limiting the discrimination of athletes high and

Important Extended Rasch Models

Partial Credit Model

$$p(x_{vi} = x) = \frac{\exp(\theta_{vx} - \sigma_{ix})}{\sum_{s=0}^{m} \exp(\theta_{vs} - \sigma_{is})}$$

with $\sigma_{ix} = \sum_{s=0}^{x} \tau_{is}$ and $\sigma_{i0} = 0$

x = response category

v = person

i = item

θ_{vx} = person parameter of person v with regard to dimension x

σ_{ix} = difficulty parameter of item i with regard to category x respective cumulated threshold parameter

LLTM

$$p(X_{vi} = 1) = \frac{\exp\left(\theta_v - \sum_{j=1}^{h} q_{ij}\eta_j - c\right)}{1 + \exp\left(\theta_v - \sum_{j=1}^{h} q_{ij}\eta_j - c\right)}$$

j = component

η_j = difficulty of component j

q_{ij} = weight matrix

c = constant

Many-Faceted Model

$$\ln\left[\frac{p_{vijk}}{p_{vijk-1}}\right] = \theta_v - \beta_i - \alpha_j - \tau_k$$

or

$$p(X_{vit} = 1) = \frac{\exp(\theta_v - \sigma_i - \delta_t)}{1 + \exp(\theta_v - \sigma_i - \delta_t)}$$

p_{vijk} = probability of person v with regard to item i through rater j in category k

p_{vijk-1} = probability of person v with regard to item i through rater j in category k − 1

θ_v = person parameter of person v

β_i = difficulty parameter of item i

α_j = rigidity parameter of rater j

τ_k = difficulty parameter of category k

θ_v = trait parameter

σ_i = content parameter

δ_t = situation parameter

MRM

$$p(X_{vi} = 1) = \sum_{g=1}^{G} \pi_g \frac{\exp(\theta_{vxg} - \sigma_{ixg})}{\sum_{s=0}^{m} \exp(\theta_{vsg} - \sigma_{isg})}$$

g = latent class

π_p = class-size parameter

G = a priori fixed number of classes

---

low on state anxiety; 6 items produced misfit values; many items shared similar locations on the linear continuum; and the efficiency of the scale was moderate (72.75%). Hence, this Rasch analysis indicates that the STAI scales need further improvements before they can be suitable for measuring trait and state anxiety in athletes.

Extensions and Generalizations of Rasch Modeling

The development and application of Rasch models make up a very rapidly growing field in psychological research and methodology. Reasons for this include the possibilities of testing the content of models and theories, optimizing diagnostic processes, and gaining insight into the most varied properties of scales and questionnaires as well as motor tests.

Numerous extensions of the dichotomous Rasch models have been developed recently, permitting the study of even more complex research content. The numerous textbooks and articles now published provide an excellent overview of the models and their uses (e.g., von Davier & Carstensen, 2007; Fischer & Molenaar, 1995; Hagenaars & McCutcheon, 2002; Rost & Langeheine, 1997). This interest has been encouraged further in the last decade by the development of powerful and easy-to-use statistical software tools, including RUMM2020 based on the earlier Ascore (Andrich, Sheridan, & Luo, 2004), Winmira 2001 (von Davier, 2001), ConQuest (Wu, Adams, & Wilson, 1999), Facets (Linacre, 2004), and Winsteps (Linacre, 2005). Strauss, Büsch, and Tenenbaum (2007) describe several of these programs and discuss their advantages and disadvantages.

Extensions to the models have been, among others, to increase the number of item parameters (e.g., the additional item discrimination parameter in Birnbaum's 1968 two-parameter model), to modify the underlying probability function (e.g., the assumption of a binominal distribution in the Poisson model for count data from Rasch, 1960), or, in particular, to increase the number of latent traits and item parameters. Nowadays, there are also a great number of *multidimensional* or *item component models*. Generally speaking, these are models in which the response to an item depends on several latent variables or components. These extended Rasch models for dichotomous and polytomous items with ordered categories such as Likert scales can be formulated as multivariate and generalized mixture Rasch models. One major line in this research is to consider the Rasch model as a *log-linear model* (for an overview, see Kelderman, 2007). The edition by von Davier and Carstensen (2007) gives an excellent overview on such extensions of the Rasch model as well as several applications of these extensions.

One early basic model in this framework is Fischer's (1983) *linear-logistic test model* (LLTM). This model decomposes item difficulty into further additive components such as, for example, various elements involved in processing a task. The LLTM equation can be found in the sidebar on page 77. However, not only the item parameter but also the trait (e.g., the person parameter) can vary in the LLTM. This produces multidimensional models in which one person is assigned several person parameters. A special case of the LLTM is Linacre's (1989, 2004) *many-faceted Rasch analysis*. This model is now used widely because it permits detailed psychometric analyses of judgments in a wide range of applied fields.

In a facet design, data is not just organized into a two-dimensional matrix (with the facets persons × items). Rather, the design allows additional facets to be studied, such as the judgments of the raters classifying the responses. This already delivers a three-dimensional data structure (persons × items × raters). In principle, this design can be extended by any arbitrary number of facets including person characteristics, such as gender, age, and so forth, and situations, such as the paired comparisons

typically found in tournaments (Linacre, Wright, & Lunz, 1990). Different model variants are associated with the facet design. The simplest variant has two facets—that is, when persons work on only one task. However, some variants also permit the analysis of interactions between facets, and this is the reason why the many-faceted Rasch model belongs to the set of models permitting an analysis of DIF.

DIF analysis, like the many-faceted model, can be used to test, for example, the invariance of item properties, such as item difficulty, in different groups. It allows for testing the independence of the sample. For example, Asci, Fletcher, and Caglar (2009; see also Fletcher & Hattie, 2004) compared the physical self-concepts (particularly the gender-related ones) of 3,883 adolescents aged 12 to 18 y from New Zealand and Turkey. The item analysis revealed a strong group dependence of item difficulty—that is, there were items favored very strongly by New Zealand versus Turkish youths and vice versa.

As a rule, such DIF analyses form groups a priori on the basis of manifest criteria (e.g., different nationalities). Nonetheless, one very powerful method is to identify these groups a posteriori by forming latent classes with the help of multivariate mixed distribution models (for details, see von Davier & Carstensen, 2007). These models can be used to identify groups of persons as latent classes in which different traits apply.

One mixed distribution extension of the Rasch model that offers the possibility of performing DIF analyses and has been applied several times in sport psychology (e.g., Rost, 1990) is the *mixed Rasch model* (MRM) for dichotomous and ordered categories. The MRM assumes that the same Rasch model does not hold for the whole sample. Instead, it posits Rasch models with unique item parameters for different, unknown subsamples (the latent classes). Hence, the MRM is essentially a combination of the Rasch model and latent class analysis (for the origins of latent class analysis, see Lazarsfeld & Henry, 1968). The MRM assumes that "the Rasch model holds for all persons within a latent class, but it allows for different sets of item parameters between the latent classes" (Rost, 1990, p. 271). The equation of the ordinal MRM is presented in the sidebar on page 77.

If a Rasch model can be fitted to the data for the whole sample (i.e., one latent class), then this is regarded as evidence that the scale is sample free and unbiased, because all persons respond to the items with respect to the same latent trait. If more than one group (i.e., latent class) is necessary, different Rasch models hold in each group; there is evidence for more than one latent trait in the entire sample. Note that these groups are identified according to their response behavior, which is a direct consequence of their latent trait, and not according to manifest criteria such as gender or nationality.

An Example Using the Mixed Rasch Model

The German *Allgemeiner Sportmotorischer* Test (Boes, 2001), a general test of sport fitness and coordination for children, continues to be very popular in Germany, particularly in schools. It consists of 6 items (e.g., 6 min run, ball throwing, and so on) that are assumed to measure both conditioning and coordination. However, only a few studies have investigated its construct validity, and most of these used inappropriate statistical methods.

To test the construct validity in a more robust method, Büsch and colleagues (2009) applied confirmatory analyses as well as the MRM (Rost, 1990) to data derived from 1,567 students who completed all 6 items. Using several goodness-of-fit tests (e.g., bootstrapping statistics, information criteria), they found that the two-class solution provides the best fit. Approximately 61% of the students could be assigned to class 1 and 39% could be assigned to class 2 with a probability of more than 81%. A detailed DIF analysis showed that the Rasch model held in each of the two classes; however, it held with different item parameters. Figure 8.3 depicts the item parameters in each class. Lower scores indicate better performance.

The items could not be separated according to conditioning and coordination. Members of class 1 scored better on *locomotion items* (20 m sprint [20S],

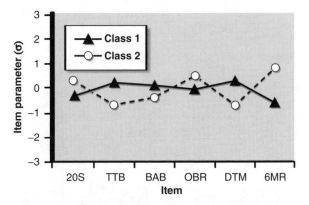

Figure 8.3 Item parameters of the 6 items of the *Allgemeiner Sportmotorischer* Test. 20S = 20 m sprint; TTB = hitting a target with a tennis ball; BAB = bouncing a ball off a wall; OBR = obstacle run; DTM = distance throwing a medicine ball; 6MR = 6 min run.

6 minute run [6MR], and obstacle run [OBR]) and not as well on *object manipulation items* (hitting a target with a tennis ball [TTB], bouncing a ball off a wall [BAB], and distance throwing a medicine ball [DTM]). Hence, locomotion items were easier for members of class 1, while object manipulation items were easier for members of class 2.

Probabilistic Test Models in Sport Psychology and Exercise Sports

Although Rasch models and all their extensions right up to generalized Rasch models are applied in numerous areas in social sciences (for overviews, see Rost & Langeheine, 1997; von Davier & Carstensen, 2007), they are used far less frequently in sport psychology (Strauss, 1999; von Davier & Strauss, 2003). In Duda's (1998) comprehensive textbook on measuring procedures in sport psychology, for example, there is only one article referring to Rasch models or IRT models in general (Tenenbaum & Fogarty, 1998).

In the English-speaking countries, Gershon Tenenbaum and his research team and Weimo Zhu and his colleagues were the first to establish the use of Rasch models in sport psychology and the human movement sciences in the 1980s (e.g., Tenenbaum, 1984, 1999; Tenenbaum & Forgarty, 1998; Tenenbaum, Forgarty, & Jackson, 1999; Tenenbaum, Fogarty, Stewart, et al., 1999; Tenenbaum & Furst, 1985; Tenenbaum, Furst, & Weingarten, 1985; Zhu, 2001; Zhu & Cole, 1996; Zhu & Kurz, 1994). They used the models to perform dimensional analyses of questionnaires and motor scales and to calibrate item parameters. In Germany, it was particularly Klaus Roth, Heinz Mechling, and Klaus Boes who were the first to point out the usefulness and the potentials of Rasch modeling (e.g., Boes & Mechling, 1983; Roth, 1982).

Recent years have revealed a marked increase in the number of studies applying Rasch modeling. Strauss, Büsch, and Tenenbaum (2007) as well as Tenenbaum, Strauss, and Büsch (2007) have provided detailed reviews of studies using probabilistic models and particularly Rasch models in the context of sport. The breadth of issues addressed is now substantial. In addition to classic analyses of the dimensions of questionnaires, such as the Task and Ego Orientation in Sport Questionnaire (TEOSQ; e.g., Tenenbaum & Fogarty, 1998), the STAI (Tenenbaum, Furst, & Weingarten, 1985), the Physical Self-Description Questionnaire (PSDQ; e.g., Fletcher & Hattie, 2004), the Coaching Efficacy Scale (CES; e.g., Myers, Feltz, Chase, Reckase, & Hancock, 2008), the Edinburgh Handedness Inventory (e.g.,

Büsch, Hagemann, & Bender, 2010), the Perfectionism Inventory for Sport (Anshel, Weatherby, Kang, & Watson, 2009), or the German Sport Spectator Identification Scale (SSIS; Strauss, 1995, 1999), Rasch models have also been used to address rehabilitation research (e.g., Avery, Russell, Raina, Walter, & Rosenbaum, 2003), physical disability (Kang, Zhu, Ragan, & Frogley, 2007; Wuang, Lin, & Su, 2009) and judgment situations in sports (e.g., Linacre et al., 1990; Looney, 1996). One major field is the analysis of human movements, such as motor abilities (e.g., Büsch et al., 2009; Cepicka, 2003; Hands & Larkin, 2001; Zhu, 2001) and motor strategies (e.g., Büsch & Strauss, 2005).

Conclusion

The extension of the classic Rasch model into multidimensional and item component models has led to an enormous increase in the range of options for analyzing data in the social and behavioral sciences. These models permit very detailed DIF analyses that help explain response behavior in the sense of IRT. Numerous easy-to-use and powerful computer programs are also available (for an overview, see Strauss et al., 2007). In the Anglo-American world, the field of sport psychology is increasingly using the many-faceted model and its variants and is thereby working with the Facets software of Linacre (2004). European sport psychology, in contrast, shows a recent trend toward Winmira (von Davier, 2001) and the MRM (Rost, 1990).

In 1987 Spray pointed out that Rasch models should not be viewed as an alternative to CTT but as a significant addition to it, and he saw this view as representing the "future of measurement research in physical education" (p. 208). CTT continues to be useful for assessing test properties such as accuracy and validity. However, Rasch models, by being based on a formal modeling of response behavior, provide a detailed insight into the scales and the items, thus making it possible to study the psychological process through which a response comes about. The further development of diagnostics in sport and exercise psychology and the research on the analysis of human movements could benefit greatly from paying more attention to the advantages of Rasch modeling.

Idiosyncratic Measures in Sport

W. Alex Edmonds, PhD, Michael B. Johnson, PhD, Gershon Tenenbaum, PhD, and Akihito Kamata, PhD

Neurobiological examinations in the sport sciences have delineated the role that affective and cognitive states play in an athlete's ability to achieve superior performances (Tenenbaum et al., 2009; see also Hatfield & Kerick, 2007; Tenenbaum & Land, 2009). Furthermore, examinations utilizing idiosyncratic methodologies have indicated the factors related to choking and performing under pressure in addition to the physiological and introspective indexes that influence performance quality (Tenenbaum, Edmonds, & Eccles, 2008; see also Hanin & Stambulova, 2002). Based on these research findings, this chapter elucidates the affective factors related to performance and operationalizes an eight-step idiosyncratic method that reveals the probability of a certain performance level (poor, moderate, or optimal) based on an individual's level of affective intensity (psychological or physiological).

The probabilistic technique presented here updates research that has been of interest for at least a century (see figure 9.1 and Yerkes & Dodson's 1908 inverted-U law) with current statistical techniques that account for the curvilinear relationship between variables (i.e., performance and affect). Additionally, there are salient differences between the method operationalized in this chapter and other methods for determining the relationship between emotional intensity and performance level. These include the multidimensional anxiety theory (Martens, Burton, Vealey, Bump, & Smith, 1990), the catastrophe model (Hardy, 1990, 1996), reversal theory (Kerr, 1997), and the individual zone of optimal functioning model (IZOF; Hanin, 2000).

Hanin (2000) developed the IZOF model, which has served as the conceptual framework that undergirds the analyses of the conceptual and practical association between emotional states and performance quality. Hanin's original conceptualization focused on emotion and mood states, which are considered *feeling* states and can be characterized as pleasant or unpleasant. Kamata, Tenenbaum, and Hanin (2002) expanded the original IZOF methodology to handle the incorporation of multiple, online, and immediately recalled introspective and physiological indexes to determine various performance zones. This methodology includes all the various emotions simultaneously, but not interactively, as well as the *affect* in predicting performance quality (i.e., poor, moderate, and optimal). The consideration of affect as an all-encompassing construct (Watson & Tellegen, 1985) allows for the incorporation of psychological and physiological indexes. More specifically, affect is a global construct and is defined conceptually as episodes of feelings that are influenced, in this case, by responses to performance-related stimuli and can be measured

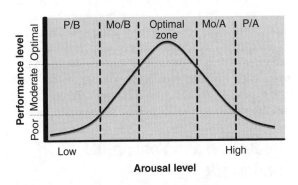

Figure 9.1 The Yerkes and Dodson (1908) curve as it relates to individual affect-related performance zones. P/B and P/A = poor performance below and above the optimal level; Mo/B and Mo/A = moderate performance below and above the optimal level.

by introspective (i.e., self-report) methods or physiological monitoring (e.g., galvanic skin response or electromyography). The term *affect-related performance zone* (APZ) was developed, as it adequately represents the nature (nonlinear nature) of the affect–performance relationship and can account for the idiosyncratic and psychophysiological aspects of behavior.

Conceptually, an APZ is the zone (poor, moderate, or optimal) that encompasses the specific *range* of affective intensity (subjective or objective) and the respective probability (0.0-1.0) of attainment. The concept of applying probability estimates to performance zones was first introduced in crisis theory (Bar-Eli & Tenenbaum, 1989). Crisis theory applies Bayesian inference to derive probabilistic estimates of variables related to a performance-related crisis. In contrast to the probabilistic approach of crisis theory, the APZ method considers the reciprocal relationship (observations in the form of perceived or actual performance versus any perceived or objective affective state) between the intensity or valence of an affective state and the quality of an ensuing performance.

The research methodology for examining APZs is a correlational approach with a predictive design (with affect as the predictor and performance as the criterion) that allows for the inclusion of the individual (a single case) as the unit of analysis and is referred to as an *individual APZ* (IAPZ; for a review, see Johnson, Edmonds, Tenenbaum, & Kamata, 2009). In order to determine an IAPZ, there must be a clear definition of performance that can be rated subjectively or objectively (discrete or continuous data). Because of the idiographic nature of the IAPZ model, the case study approach (see Yin, 2009) paired with the APZ-specific methodology is well suited for APZ investigations. Although the case study approach traditionally has utilized the qualitative method, combining the quantitative aspects of APZ findings with qualitative inquiries would provide a deep and insightful mixed-method approach to determining IAPZs. Examples of data reduction strategies for various types of performance data are offered later in his chapter.

Theoretical and Conceptual Framework

The theoretical underpinning that provides the foundation for the IZOF model (Hanin, 2000) also serves as the conceptual framework for the scientific approach to identifying affect–performance relationships by means of IAPZ analyses. In oversimplified terms, the IZOF model maintains that a relationship exists between a person's emotional state and performance quality. Historically, linking emotions and athletic performance has relied on popular theoretical approaches within the field, such as Yerkes and Dodson's (1908) inverted-U law, Hull's (1943) drive theory, Hardy's (1990) catastrophe model, and Martens and colleagues' (1990) multidimensional anxiety theory; all have focused on the relationship between anxiety and performance, thus creating a negative bias (i.e., giving anxiety a negative stigma). Anxiety was the most frequently investigated emotion because of its known stressful effects on both cognitive functioning and physical (somatic) activity (Martens et al., 1990; Tenenbaum & Bar-Eli, 1995). Hanin's (1978) idiographic approach for defining the zone of optimal functioning originally used anxiety as a correlate with performance, although it has since evolved to encompass a wider range of emotional states.

The IZOF principle implies a distinct relationship between the perceived intensity of functional and dysfunctional emotional states and the quality of a relative performance outcome. An optimal performance state is one in which the best internal conditions (cognitions and emotions) result in a complete involvement in the task and the best possible recruitment of coping resources. However, Hanin posited that a broader range of emotions must be considered to develop a clearer understanding of the link between emotion and performance—one that includes negative and positive emotional states. He indicated that recent developments in the IZOF model provide a solution for this problem. Though the research is equivocal as a consequence of methodological shortcomings, all findings indicate that optimal and functional emotions are related to the task characteristics, interpersonal differences, and environmental conditions under which the task is performed.

A characteristic feature of the IZOF model is that individual differences in optimal emotional levels cannot be predicted from task characteristics or from the performer's level of experience. Rather, IZOFs must be determined either by direct repeated measurement of emotions and the subsequent performances or by retrospective recall of emotional intensities before optimal performances. However, serious concerns arise when emotions are assessed directly during competition. Athletes may perceive self-ratings immediately before or during important competitions as invasive, distracting, or disturbing to their preparation strategies. Despite these measurement difficulties, it is critical to assess emotions experienced during performance in order to determine whether the dynamic emotional states occurring throughout sport events interact with performance. IZOF profiles must therefore be modeled on a systematic observation of performers in real-life situations.

Based on Lacey and Lacey's (1958) contention that interindividual differences exist and that individuals differ widely in the way they experience emotions, the IZOF model indicates that it is unlikely for there to be a single set of optimal levels of emotions resulting in best or poor performance for different athletes in the same sport realm. The determination of IZOFs is context specific and an ideographic approach that emphasizes the within-individual dynamics of perceived emotional experiences in relation to optimal, moderate, and poor performances. For example, one athlete may perform optimally while maintaining pleasant emotions (e.g., happiness) and a relatively low level of physiological arousal in one context, while another may need to feel more unpleasant emotions (e.g., anger) and a higher level of arousal to obtain an optimal performance within another context. Thus, these two athletes have substantially different affective zones.

Researchers utilizing the original IZOF methodological approaches develop profiles from an athlete's retrospective reports of competitive emotional experiences, which include quantitizing the data (i.e., the process of converting qualitative data to numbers for further statistical analysis and illustrations). However, determining an individual's performance zones via this methodology can be improved on, as the IZOF approach does not account for the fact that (a) a single competition may evoke multiple and differing emotional states; (b) an event's outcome may bias the retrospective recall of emotion (Russell, 2003); (c) relatively new and younger athletes may not have access to a requisite number of previous competitions and their associated emotional experiences; (d) self-reported emotions embody solely that aspect of human experience located in conscious awareness, thereby possibly omitting valuable data; and (e) such an approach dichotomizes an emotional intensity into either in the zone or out of the zone.

The probabilistic estimation of the affect–performance relationship for an individual (i.e., the IAPZ methodology) responds to these concerns by (a) explicitly considering the intrapersonal ebbs and flows within many athletic competitions; (b) relying on current, multiple, and online affective states and performance measures rather than historically recalled data of emotions; (c) including athletes who have limited past experiences from which to draw data; (d) permitting data manipulation in a more continuous rather than strictly dichotomous manner; and (e) accounting for the nonlinear relationship between affect and performance.

Originally, IZOFs were developed solely on an athlete's single perception and retrospective report of emotional levels. This created limitations in the model's utility within various research paradigms. More specifically, the empirical assessment of emotions in the IZOF framework was treated as the conscious aspect of perceived emotions and considered apart from bodily changes. However, the organization and processes underlying emotional experiences may be far subtler than their apparent expressions are (Cacioppo, Bernston, Klein, & Poehlman, 1997). That is, language sometimes fails to capture emotional or affective experiences (Ortony & Fainsilber, 1989). As a result, corresponding performance pressures are known to influence levels of activation. Thus the research on affect and performance should attend to psychophysiological states to further account for the interdependence among perceptions, physiology, and performance (Parfitt, Hardy, & Pates, 1995; Raedeke & Stein, 1994). Covert physiological processes (e.g., skin conductance and heart rate) occurring as a result of affective modulation can be measured free from the constraints of the participant's awareness and memory. The probabilistic method that Kamata and colleagues (2002) designed to create IAPZs links affect and performance and builds on the methodology utilized in the classic IZOF model.

The approach to examine IAPZs considers the individual as the unit of analysis and reveals the reciprocal relationship between the *intensity* or *valence* of an affective state and the quality of an ensuing performance. This conceptualization avoids the issue of dichotomizing performances into either in the zone or out of the zone and enables the determination of zones for multiple affect-related performance categories (e.g., optimal, moderately below optimal, moderately above optimal, and poor). This method also assigns probability estimates for each performance zone (poor, moderate, or optimal) given the performer's specific affective state (see the example in figure 9.2 on page 84). The idiosyncratic nature of the affect–performance relationship is supported by previous research (Edmonds at al., 2008; Johnson et al., 2009), including Lacey and Lacey's (1958) principle of system specificity, which posits that individuals maintain idiosyncratic and distinctive patterns of responding. Therefore, in IAPZ research it is appropriate to generalize the technique (i.e., methodology) rather than generalize the findings across samples.

Parameter Estimates

		Estimate	Standard error	Wald	df	Significance	95% confidence interval	
							Lower bound	Upper bound
Threshold	[Ractive = 0]	2.878	0.813	12.537	1	.000	1.285	4.471
	[Ractive = 1.0]	5.312	0.92	33.354	1	.000	3.509	7.115
	[Ractive = 2.0]	7.101	1.062	44.713	1	.000	5.02	9.183
	[Ractive = 3.0]	8.912	1.177	57.307	1	.000	6.605	11.22
Location	activ	0.96	0.16	35.854	1	.000	0.645	1.274

a   Link function: Logit.

Description

By providing appropriate information, this worksheet produces a probability curve plot for model 4, which is an adaption by M. Johnson of Kamata, Tenenbaum, and Hanin (2002). Model 4 assumes following five performance outcome categories: 0 = poor performance (PP/B), 1 = moderate performance (Mo/B), 2 = optimal performance, 3 = moderate performance (Mo/A), and 4 = poor performance (PP/A).

Procedure

1. Enter the estimates from the ordinal regression in SPSS.

Slope	Beta 1	Beta 2	Beta 3	Beta 4
0.96	2.878	5.312	7.101	8.912

2. Enter the scale of emotion intensity.

Lower	Upper
1	9

b   **3.** Look at the *Plot* worksheet.

Figure 9.2   Logistic ordinal regression output from SPSS *(a)* for the athlete's arousal data and *(b)* utilizing the regression coefficients identified from the arousal data.

Eight-Step Idiosyncratic Approach

Affect can be measured from observations made across three main elements: physiological indexes, observable behaviors, and subjective accounts (Deci, 1980). When utilizing data categorized as affect, the probabilistic methodology more closely adheres to the psychometric restrictions imposed by idiosyncratic ordinal data. Previously used emotion–performance methods tend to treat subjectively reported emotion–performance data from a perspective that is more consistent with the manipulation of interval data. The approach delineated in this chapter focuses directly on the individual athlete's within-competition intrapersonal affective experiences. Because of the ordinal nature of much of the data collected in this line of research, the current method does not espouse to be generalizable across individuals or across substantially different domains for a single individual. Psychometric information underlying the steps relating to the idiosyncratic method is provided in the 2002 article by Kamata and colleagues.

Users of the IAPZ methodology must be aware of one additional factor. Performing one of the steps described in this section (the logistical ordinal regression detailed in step 4) necessitates a minimum number of data points in order for the computation to be valid. For example, if the situation requires a greater number of data points than can be collected in a sport of limited duration (e.g., a 60 m sprint in indoor track), then an alternative to the IAPZ methodology should be employed.

The eight-step approach presented here succinctly and purposefully describes the requisite steps for creating an individual performer's IAPZ probability curves and profile charts. These eight steps include (1) collecting data, (2) categorizing performances by outcome level (e.g., poor, moderate, or optimal), (3) converting the data for the calculation of regression coefficients, (4) performing a series of logistic ordinal regressions (LORs) to create the coefficients necessary for calculating IAPZs, (5) creating IAPZ curves, (6) creating IAPZ profile charts, (7) plotting within-competition states onto the IAPZ profile charts, and (8) presenting and implementing the findings.

Step 1: Collecting Data

Previous empirical work establishing IAPZs utilized an affect grid (a 9 × 9 grid) conceptualized along the two primary affective dimensions of arousal (intensity) and pleasure (valence; Russell, Weiss, & Mendelsohn, 1989). This circumplex model of affect, in which affective experience is represented in a two-dimensional space defined by hedonic tone and activation, is one of the foundations upon which this applied work is constructed. Following an explanation of the terms *arousal* and *pleasure*, a performer checks a box within the grid or verbally reports the subjectively perceived arousal and pleasure intensity at a single point in time. Performers can and should be encouraged to provide introspective reports of affect quickly and with minimal thought or disruption to their performances. Additionally, objective physiological measures of affect can be collected via physiological recording devices. Due to the orthogonal nature of arousal and pleasure, the two affective factors should never be combined, as each provides unique insight into the affect–performance relationship.

A performance level must also be recorded and matched with its respective report of affective intensity and valence. There are a variety of ways to operationalize an individual's report of performance. Athletes can subjectively rate their performance on a scale ranging from 1 (worst) to 9 (best) or can use an objective measure of performance.

Affect can also be measured with objective measures such as physiological indexes. These parameters include, but are not limited to, skin conductance, standard heart rate (HR), and, more recently, heart rate variability (HRV). There are many software programs and physiological recording devices that can be utilized to collect these measures (e.g., Biopac MP150, NeXus, J&J, ProComp Infiniti). A vital aspect of collecting physiological data is to ensure that the appropriate performance data point is associated with the relevant physiological data point. For example, when utilizing a Biopac MP150 system, a program written in LabVIEW can be used to trigger a separate channel on the MP150 system that locks a verbal response or performance-related time point to a corresponding epoch in the physiological data. This technique facilitates off-line data reduction and analysis and ensures that the appropriate data points are matched.

HR can be measured with a blood volume pulse (BVP) sensor or an electrocardiogram (ECG). For clinical applications, the BVP sensor usually is sufficient and is more comfortable because it is simply placed on a finger. However, for research data collection, the ECG sensor is recommended for its greater sensitivity. Chest placement or lead II configuration is a common placement of ECG electrodes, but this technique may be problematic. The wrist placement is a strong alternative. The wrist placement of the ECG sensor includes placing pregelled disposable snap electrodes on the interior of the left and right forearms. A ground electrode is placed on the participant's nondominant forearm. Data should be collected at a sampling rate of 1,024 samples per second to provide a high-resolution signal, and the series of interbeat intervals should be corrected for abnormal beats and artifacts (Berntson et al., 1997).

Unlike HR, which is measured in beats per minute, raw HRV data (i.e., the beat-to-beat changes in HR) are measured in milliseconds and must be reduced or summarized before the data are converted for IAPZ analysis. Niskanen, Tarvainen, Ranta-aho, and Karjalainen (2004) provided details regarding the software used for advanced HRV analysis and the analysis of R-R intervals (the intervals between consecutive R peaks). The measures introduced are statistical (e.g., SDNN), geometric (e.g., Poincaré plots), and spectral (e.g., low frequency).

Skin conductivity can be measured with nonpolarized silver–silver chloride (Ag/AgCl) electrodes placed on the medial edge of the nondominant hand. Alternatively, Ag/AgCl sensors can be snapped into two straps that can be placed on the index and middle finger. The hand and electrodes should be prepared using Omniprep with distilled water and ECI electrode gel, respectively. The recording device should be set to detect a range of 0 to 50 μmhos, with a band-pass filter set from 0.05 to 1.0 Hz. The signal should be amplified 500 times.

Step 2: Categorizing Performances by Outcome Level

Performance measures must be defined appropriately and are a critical element of data collection and analysis. Performance indexes can be measured subjectively or objectively. Regardless of how the data are collected, if three performance levels are deemed to be most meaningful for the purposes of analysis, then the performance data must be coded into three levels (poor, moderate, and optimal).

Other performance ranges can be used depending on the domain, the practitioner, and the person from whom data are elicited. Moreover, additional performance levels can be identified provided there are adequate data points to perform the statistical procedures described in step 4. One method that can be used to define performances as optimal, moderate, or poor is to first identify the athlete's average performance. Any performance outcome score that exceeds this value by one-half of a standard deviation can be considered optimal, while any outcome that is at least one-half of a standard deviation below this value can be designated as poor. The remaining performances are considered to be moderate. A second method that can be used is to identify the athlete's top third of performances as optimal, the next third as moderate, and the final third as poor. These are simply two of the many ways to categorize outcome data. One of the strengths of the IAPZ method is that the idiosyncratic nature of an athlete's objective performance level is considered the unit of analysis. Decisions on the terminology used should be based on what is meaningful for the athlete, coach, and practitioner. Furthermore, performances considered optimal for one athlete may be defined as poor for another. And finally, the IAPZ methodology also allows for monitoring intrapersonal changes over time or for identifying intrapersonal differences due to the domains of interest.

Take, for example, the times it takes a race car driver to complete segments of a race on a track. Performance can be assessed by measuring the time in seconds it takes to cross each segment of the race. Each performance must be assessed individually and relative to the driver's own personal optimal, moderate, and poor times throughout all the trials. To determine the performance categories, all performance data can be combined and then ordered for the first segment into ascending order using a frequency tabulator. Next, the performance times can be trichotomized and designated as optimal, moderate, or poor.

Golf putting performance in the laboratory, for example, can also be coded into three levels. First, the nondirectional radial distance (in inches or centimeters) from the hole is recorded. The target (i.e., golf hole) is supplemented with an imposed grid used for assessing accuracy and consistency. The matrix should progress in 1 in. (2.5 cm) increments on both the vertical and horizontal axes and

can be projected onto the putting surface. The next step is to reduce and trichotomize the data. This can be achieved by averaging the score (i.e., nonradial distance from the hole measured in inches or centimeters) and using the standard deviation (SD) as the discriminating factor. A hole in one can equate to optimal performance, any shot within and up to 1 SD from the mean can be coded as moderate performance, and any shot that exceeds 1 SD above the mean can be coded as poor performance. Thus, at the conclusion of step 2 each performance data point is categorized as optimal, moderate, or poor, while each data point continues to be associated with its respective affective intensity or valence state.

Step 3: Converting Data

The trichotomized performance data from step 2 are coded in a manner that identifies each poor and moderate performance as occurring with an affective intensity level either greater than or less than the affective intensity that occurs during optimal performances. This step is done in order to recognize the likelihood that some poor and moderate performances are associated with an affective intensity level above or below that which is associated with an optimal performance, as is suggested by the Yerkes and Dodson law (1908) illustrated in figure 9.1.

The coding described in this step begins with the calculation of the mean affective intensity exclusively for the individual's optimal performances. This is done for each of the performer's affective domains that were measured in step 1. A spreadsheet package is very helpful with this step; it can be used to resort the entire data set by performance, allowing the user to identify every data point relative to its specific performance level. A simple spreadsheet formula can be used to calculate the average affective intensity for the athlete's optimal performances for any affective domain, as can the Compare Means function in SPSS. The outcome measures of the affective dimensions are evaluated and coded as poor performance above or below the optimal zone (PP/A, PP/B), optimal performance (OP), or moderate performance above or below the optimal zone (Mo/A, Mo/B), depending on the performance zone (optimal, moderate, or poor) with which they coincide.

Step 4: Performing a Series of Logistic Ordinal Regressions

Step 4 provides direction on obtaining the regression coefficients necessary to create IAPZ probability curves via a series of logistic ordinal regressions (LOR; for the psychometric underpinnings of this process, see Kamata et al., 2002). The LOR procedure assumes and accounts for the nonlinear relationship between affect and performance. The procedures in this step are performed on each possible raw data point and its respective APZ pair (i.e., the link between performance and affective intensity). Specifically, the combinations of affective and performance categories are analyzed for each condition by regressing the performance zone (criterion variable) on the corresponding affective dimension (predictor variable) when using LOR (i.e., the criterion is regressed on the predictor). This process provides regression coefficients that are then used to create a series of ordinal regression curves (probabilistic curves) to represent the IAPZs for each affective dimension.

Step 5: Creating Individual Affect-Related Performance Zone Curves

Kamata and colleagues (2002) provided a tool for developing the IAPZ curves from the LOR coefficients. The work by Johnson and coworkers (2009) contains information regarding the spreadsheet tool for creating IAPZ curves. Figure 9.2*b* shows a sample of the spreadsheet input area that, once filled in, yields IAPZ probability curves. The input numbers for these fields come directly from the information in figure 9.2*a*. That is, the Estimate in the row designated Location provides the slope input for the spreadsheet (e.g., 0.96 for the archer). The Betas in the spreadsheet come directly from their corresponding Threshold outputs from the SPSS Estimate column. The final input to consider in figure 9.2*b* is the scale of affective intensity. If the

participant is using the affect grid, then the lower limit is 1 and the upper limit is 9. However, if the participant's HR is being used, then another scale is appropriate (e.g., a scale in beats per minute). Operationalizing the affective domain of HR may require the researcher to set a lower limit of 50 and an upper limit of 200 in order to provide an adequate range of HRs for future analyses. Once these data are entered into the first worksheet within this spreadsheet, the second worksheet calculates and displays the resultant IAPZ curves. Figure 9.3 provides these IAPZ curves for the example cited. In this example, five IAPZs for the affective domain of arousal are defined.

The performance level with the highest probability within a specific affective intensity range is the one used to define the IAPZ as poor, moderate, or optimal (Kamata et al., 2002). This is a very powerful addition to the IZOF methodology (Hanin, 2000) and the inverted-U law (Yerkes & Dodson, 1908). For example, figure 9.3 illustrates that at an arousal intensity of 6.5, the athlete has approximately a 42% probability of performing optimally and is within an optimal IAPZ. However, the athlete also has a lesser probability of performing moderately and a small probability of performing poorly. All probability rates at each point add up to 100%.

Step 6: Creating Individual Affect-Related Performance Zone Profile Charts

IAPZ profile charts are constructed to facilitate the analysis of a performer's affective consistency and are created as follows. Consider the archer's

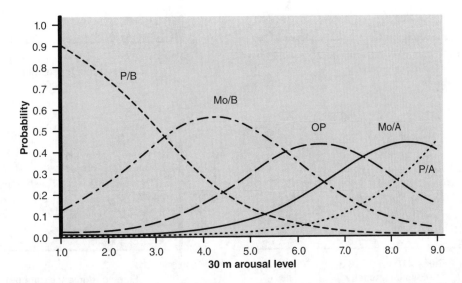

Figure 9.3 Example of an IAPZ and the probability curves produced by an LOR for an archer shooting from a distance of 33 yd (30 m). P/B and P/A = poor performance below and above the optimal level; Mo/B and Mo/A = moderate performance below and above the optimal level; OP = optimal performance.

data described in figure 9.3. The ranges of arousal associated with each IAPZ (i.e., the *ranges of arousal intensity* at which each of the archer's five performance levels are the most likely) are translated onto the *y*-axis of figure 9.4. Each IAPZ now has its unique range on the *y*-axis. For example, the range of arousal associated with an optimal IAPZ for the archer, which can be found on the *x*-axis of figure 9.3, is 5.8 to 7.4. Therefore, this range identifies the lower and upper boundaries for the IAPZ of optimal arousal found on the *y*-axis of figure 9.4. The proce-

dure described here can also be used to create the IAPZ profile charts for other affective dimensions. For example, figure 9.5 shows IAPZs determined for arousal, pleasure, HR (in beats per minute), and skin conductance.

Step 7: Plotting Within-Competition States Onto Profile Charts

At this stage of data analysis, the original, within-competition reports of affective (arousal) intensity

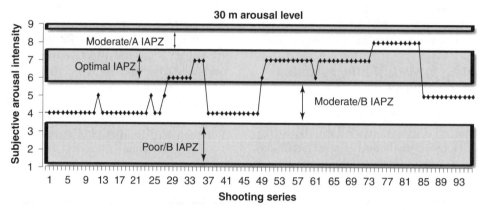

Figure 9.4   IAPZ profile chart.

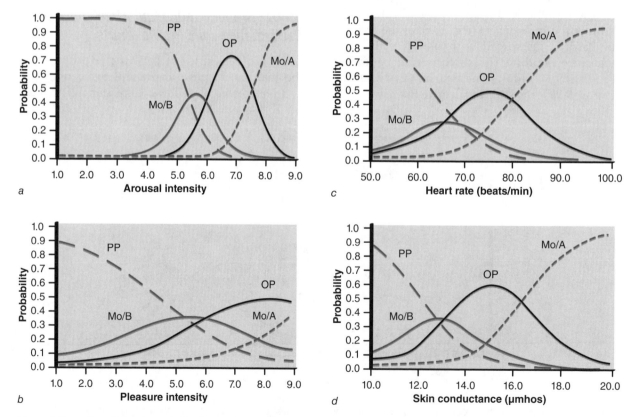

Figure 9.5   Four dimensions of affect presented graphically as four distinct IAPZ curves. PP = poor performance; Mo/B and Mo/A = moderate performance below and above the optimal level; OP = optimal performance.

can be graphed onto the IAPZ profile charts. This methodology emphasizes the notion of momentum states described by Bar-Eli and Tenenbaum (1989). Proponents of momentum states assert that there are dynamic performance and affective components within athletic competition, and the athlete's subjective and idiosyncratic interpretation of this dynamic can greatly influence performance. This is congruent with Russell's (2003) description of core affect fluctuating over the course of an episode. Figure 9.4 identifies, via a line graph, how an archer's arousal fluctuates among five IAPZs during a 33 yd (30 m) shooting competition.

Step 8: Presenting and Implementing the Individual Affect-Related Performance Zone Method in Research and Practice

Research. Researchers have a number of opportunities in the area of idiosyncratic measures in sport. The theoretical foundation of research that takes into account the idiosyncratic differences between individuals has grown in interest. Individuals are known to differ not only in the efficiency of specific mechanisms but also in the frequency with which particular mechanisms are recruited (Lacey & Lacey, 1974). Therefore, it is not recommended to pool data across subjects in order to derive zones, as doing so is often misleading (i.e., distinctive pattern variations among participants can be washed out when combining the data of all the members in each group). When appropriately collected, group data can provide a strong starting point, but individual differences need to be respected if researchers are to understand the underlying mechanisms that sustain the relationship between the biology and the psychology of behavior (Kosslyn et al., 2002). However, from a purely cognitive perspective, it is also important to understand how and why there is variability between individuals within their unique zones. We believe that a sound methodology to investigate such individual differences will be developed in the future.

Examinations should consider outcome and process cues of performance, which can provide more adequate and detailed information relevant to revealing IAPZs. In addition, researchers should not only aim at determining the introspective affective parameters of performers but also examine the neuronal and autonomic changes associated with the development of cognitive and visuomotor skills. Specifically, with more precise information from varied physiological indexes (e.g., HRV and EEG) concerning a performer's idiosyncratic tendencies, we can develop accurate and well-defined techniques to improve arousal regulation and cognitive strategies, particularly in high-level performers attempting to reach levels of expertise.

High-level or expert performers should be the focus for the advancement of future IAPZ research. The substantial practice-related changes in psychophysiology (cognitive and affective) are not necessarily related to the task-related activation, which would control for the general executive processes associated with learning a novel task (i.e., learning effects).

To date, idiosyncratic measures have been tested empirically in archery, tennis, golf, and simulated race car driving (for review, see Johnson et al., 2009). Research in other domains that permit such investigation is warranted, as each sport brings unique challenges that can lead to creative solutions that allow for an ever-improved understanding of the relationship between affective state and performance level. Determining and developing a strong methodological design to determine IAPZs from online objective and introspective measures, in addition to varied levels of performance, can prove to be timely and costly. Nonetheless, researchers should strive to examine IAPZs utilizing multifaceted designs and to account for the inherent limitations (e.g., attrition, practice effects, carryover effects), as this provides the foundation for future endeavors.

Practice. Implementing the IAPZ method is highly congruent with its unit of analysis—that is, the individual athlete's performance. The practical knowledge of the relationship between arousal and athletic performance is highly useful to the individual. The fact that a single athlete's IAPZs cannot be generalized to other athletes is not a weakness but a strength of the process in that it provides the individual with the necessary tools (e.g., increased self-awareness) to improve performance. Additionally, the individual athletes can continue to refine their personal model of affect and performance as they move through a specific career path. This very idea has been addressed hypothetically by Tate, Tenenbaum, and Delpish (2006).

Practitioners who are comfortable with applied work that entails the transtheoretical model (TTM; Prochaska & DiClemente, 2005) or motivational interviewing (MI; Miller & Rollnick, 2002) are acutely aware of the role that self-awareness plays in a client's subjective state. The five stages of the TTM include a focus on raising awareness, which is the initial focus of idiosyncratic measures in sport. MI is a "client-centered, directive method for enhancing intrinsic motivation to change by exploring and resolving ambivalence" (Miller & Rollnick, 2002, p. 25). While avoiding direct coercion, MI enhances the clinician's ability to help the client identify and elaborate on a desire to change behavior (e.g., help the client improve performance and understand how the IAPZ curves can help with this goal) while providing support and alternative views or behavioral options (Miller, 1983). Only after athletes are aware of their inner states and the roles those states play in performance can a practitioner help them to manage their affect in a goal-directed manner. The idiosyncratic measures presented in this chapter provide tools allowing for such discrete feedback. These tools can be used with particular effectiveness if the athlete is a visual learner, as the IAPZ curves carry a large amount of data that can be used in sessions with athletes.

Conclusion

The purpose of the IAPZ methodology presented in this chapter is to: (a) extend and provide further explanations to the original IZOF methodology by applying a probabilistic method to accurately reveal the affect–performance linkage, (b) detail the idiosyncratic nature of IAPZs, and (c) exemplify the utility of the probabilistic approach in an applied setting. The primary purpose of this overview is to aide researchers and practitioners in their ability to establish IAPZs. These will help reveal an individual's probabilistic affect-related performance zones and thereby create interpretable affect-related performance profiles, which later can be applied in the field for establishing and monitoring the effectiveness of idiosyncratic affective regulatory mechanisms. The linkage between affect and performance can be determined for any individual in most contexts. However, when determining affect–performance zones in specific contexts, it should be noted that a valid form of performance must be conceptually identified. From there, accurate and reliable indices of performance must be accessible in order to fully enter it as a criterion variable in the equation.

Explicitly stated throughout, the coping and self-regulation strategies designed to help one stay in his or her "optimal" IAPZs, and thereby enhance performance, have been shown to be idiosyncratic (i.e., unique). The procedures presented in this chapter are intended to be a valid and viable methodology for accomplishing this goal. Therefore, it is important to continue searching and refining techniques that allow practitioners to examine the effects of various strategies utilized by performers to reach optimal performance states. Specifically, the main goals for reaching optimal performance are to (1) determine what the optimal zone is, (2) become more familiar (i.e., increase self-awareness) with that optimal zone, and (3) apply the appropriate self-regulatory strategy associated with achieving that optimal zone, which is in sequence to increasing the probability of performing optimally on a more consistent basis. By demonstrating the dynamic nature of affect and performance within competition, an individual is likely to be better equipped to implement idiosyncratically appropriate activation or relaxation techniques that are specific to the individual and the context.

Dynamic Assessment in Sport

Thomas Schack, PhD

This chapter examines test procedures that go beyond traditional status diagnosis in sport psychology by focusing on activating and assessing an athlete's learning and action potential. It is proposed that dynamic assessment is an appropriate diagnostic strategy for measuring this potential for change and for experimentally identifying the relevant variables. Dynamic assessment is introduced within a framework of current approaches to intelligence testing. This chapter then shows how the various approaches to testing integrate feedback and prompts into their procedures in order to elicit a learning process and estimate learning potential. The development of a dynamic approach to testing motor learning potential in Europe and the United States is sketched. Comparisons with static approaches in various applied fields are used to show some of the advantages of dynamic test procedures. The chapter then focuses on applied fields such as top-level competitive sports, aviation performance domains, and curriculum-oriented procedures for children with motor impairments. Further advantages are confirmed through current trends in different areas of sport psychology. Finally, the potentials and drawbacks of dynamic assessment are discussed along with the consequences of a research perspective that places more emphasis on change.

Dynamic Assessment

The easiest way to study the *developmental potential* of athletes, children, or elderly persons is to train them. It is during such interactions that we can best observe how far novices are capable of responding to an expert's assistance and whether novices possess the "ability to improve under specific training" (Weerdt, 1927, p. 557). Although measuring the potential for change, or plasticity,

is important for judging performance, there has been little systematic research on how to diagnose *learning and action potential* in the training, school, mental coaching, or rehabilitation sport settings. Diagnostic practice focuses far more on assessing various aspects of sport performance and aptitude on the basis of isolated measurements of the *current* level of performance. This practice often neglects the fact that such a diagnosis reveals little about an athlete's *potential* but marks solely the *current state of development*.

Researchers interested in psychodiagnosis have been looking for alternatives and additions to traditional status measurement for several years. Initially, such alternatives emerged independently in different countries, where they became known under names such as *dynamic assessment, diagnosis of the zone of proximal development, testing the limits, response to intervention,* or *learning tests*. These test procedures have been subsumed under the heading of *dynamic assessment* or *dynamic testing* in both Europe (Guthke & Wiedl, 1996) and the United States (Grigorenko & Sternberg, 1998; Sternberg & Grigorenko, 2002; Grigorenko, 2009). Accordingly, *dynamic assessment* is an umbrella term (Elliott, 2003) for approaches that are creating a specific link among *testing, intervention,* and *error analysis* to measure the *learning potential* of subjects in different areas such as intelligence, attention, personality, and motor performance (Guthke & Wiedl, 1996; Grigorenko, 2009; Schack & Guthke, 2003).

Although first developed for aptitude and intelligence testing, dynamic test procedures are now applied in a far broader field. For example, the dynamic approach is increasingly proving its worth as an *experimental diagnosis strategy* that can be applied to questions in the domain of achievement and personality diagnosis. It is worth paying closer attention to parameters related to the motor aspect of human activity, which are related to sport psychology. Therefore, this chapter looks at a series of appropriate approaches to diagnosing intraindividual variability in sports and relates them to the perspective of dynamic assessment. Studying dynamic assessment in sport psychology will supplement those applied fields in which the assessment and dynamic testing approach is well established—namely, educational, clinical, and industrial psychology (see Guthke & Wiedl, 1996; Grigorenko & Sternberg, 1998; Sternberg & Grigorenko, 2002)—and will make basic statements on the domain of *sport psychology* (Schack & Guthke, 2001, 2003).

Dynamic Assessment Concept and Procedures

Conventional test diagnosis has equipped us with a series of diagnostic instruments, attendant routines, rituals, and experiences, but it is based on a few assumptions that still require a more thorough examination. One such assumption is that one-off measurements in standard situations suffice to obtain valid statements on a person's competencies.

Although this assumption has been well established for several decades, the suitability of this testing philosophy needs to be reconsidered. Most of the time, tests are applied in contexts in which development takes on a central role. During learning in preschool and school, vocational training, college, work, and numerous other life situations, the concern is to cope with new tasks. Novices do this by drawing on specific cultural means (learning aids) that the environment places at their disposition. When they solve a task, novices receive specific feedback, and many tasks are solved in some form of expert–novice interaction. The interesting point here is what learning and development potential a person actually possesses.

In a traditional diagnosis it is assumed that more interest should be given to the differences among the test scores of several persons at one point in time than to the learning potential of a single person across two measurement points or to the differences in the learning potentials of several persons. It is assumed that *past learning ability*, which is essential in shaping the *learning history* and is reflected in the current test outcomes, predicts *future learning ability*. It is precisely this assumption that is questioned by the concept of dynamic assessment in sport psychology.

There are several major differences between the static and dynamic testing paradigms. One concerns the object of testing and the necessary measurement points. Static testing focuses on the current mental state and thus on the degree to which a feature is expressed at a specific time of measurement. In contrast, dynamic assessment aims at arriving at statements on the learning potential and associated processes and functions within the framework of a process diagnosis covering several measurements. Whereas status testing focuses solely on more or fewer existing skills and features, dynamic testing targets not only the current level of a characteristic but also the level that is not immediately apparent but potentially present. Hence, dynamic testing strives to make statements not only on whether skills and abilities are present and can be measured at a certain point in time but also on how far such skills are developed and changed.

Further differences between the test paradigms pertain to the test procedure. In conventional testing, tasks and instructions are set in advance, and the tester–testee interaction is designed to be as neutral and asymmetric as possible. Any deviations from this procedure are viewed as interference. In dynamic testing, testees are acquainted with the tasks, and learning aids are provided to help them cope with task demands. In addition, specific feedback is given on the quality of their solutions. The learning aids are tailored to fit the individual testee. They provide specific learning opportunities and permit a greater interaction with the tester. Because learning aids and feedback are not considered as interference but as an essential component of the test procedure, dynamic testing moves away from the conventional test. This strongly recalls the procedures in the development contexts suggested earlier. Also, whereas the traditional status test tends to simulate an *examination*, the learning test combines this examination with a *teaching situation*. The fundamental analyses of the theoretical basis and operationalization of learning and developmental potential have already been performed by Vygotsky (1978) within the concept of a *zone of proximal development*. This concept is sketched next.

Zone of Proximal Development

Keeping in line with his cultural-historical theory of higher cognitive functions, Vygotsky assumed that essential elements of the development process lie in the interaction of socialization partners. To permit a differentiated study of such processes and to consider a *dynamic component* in the process of development, he introduced the concept of the *zone of proximal development*. Because certain learning processes in children (or novices) profit from interaction with adults (or experts), the zone of proximal development is defined as the difference between the level on which the child (or novice) is currently able to solve tasks alone and the level on which the child (or novice) is able to solve tasks when given specific guidance and feedback from experts (see Vygotsky, 1978). Vygotsky (1992) characterized the methodological approach as follows:

> The methods we apply may be called "experimentally genetic." This is because it artificially elicits the genetic process of mental development. At this point, it should be noted that this is also the main task of that dynamic analysis toward which we are striving. (pp. 162-163, translated from German)

Although this methodology provided a fundamental access to the study of higher cognitive functions in humans (see Vygotsky, 1992), Vygotsky (1964) worked out only theoretical ideas on differential diagnosis. Other researchers used this approach to improve diagnosis and transform it into concrete procedures. There is no room here to deal more closely with the theoretical arguments (referring mostly to Vygotsky) that have been used to justify dynamic testing in philosophy (epistemology) or differential, cognitive, learning, and developmental psychology. Nor will we tackle the methodological differences among the individual approaches to dynamic or interactive assessment (see Grigorenko, 2009; Grigorenko & Sternberg, 1998; Guthke & Wiedl, 1996; Haywood & Tzuriel, 1992). However, all approaches share the demand of integrating standardized or nonstandardized feedback and learning incentives into the test process in order to elicit a learning process in the testee. This approach has become particularly well established in intelligence testing, in which it is expected to produce statements on the *true* intellectual potencies of the testee that are more valid than those obtained with status tests.

Dynamic Test Procedures in the Diagnosis of Intelligence

Corresponding diagnostic procedures emerged in the 1960s and 1970s at roughly the same time but for different reasons in Israel, the United States, Russia, and Germany. Throughout the world, the traditional intelligence status test was becoming subject to hefty criticism, particularly when applied to disadvantaged, underachieving children and adolescents. Proposed alternatives included Feuerstein's (1970) Learning Potential Assessment Device (LPAD) and Budoff's (1975) Learning Potential Assessment. However, some of these approaches were criticized because of their low level of standardization and their neglect of psychometric principles (see Büchel

& Scharnhorst, 1993; Embretson, 1990; Glutting & McDermott, 1990; Grigorenko & Sternberg, 1998).

One specific and psychometrically oriented variant of dynamic testing is the *learning test concept* (Guthke, 1972, 1992; Guthke, Beckmann, & Dobat, 1997). Whereas its roots reach far back into European and American psychology, the learning test concept refers predominantly to Vygotsky's approach (see Grigorenko, 2009; Guthke & Wiedl, 1996; Guthke & Beckmann, 2003). Accordingly, the *learning test*, in contrast to the traditional status test, responds to a testee's initial false solutions by simplifying the conditions in the form of specific aids in what can be called a *repeated measurement*. *Long-term learning tests* follow up on an explicit training phase by presenting parallel items in the posttest; *short-term learning tests*, in contrast, provide assistance and feedback tailored to each error in only one session. Such tests record how far the testee can improve performance as a result of the built-in standardized learning incentives or how many learning steps, what kind of assistance, and which additional tasks the testee requires to solve the task. The 1980s saw the development of a new variant of the short-term learning test (see Guthke, 1980; Guthke, Räder, Caruso, & Schmidt, 1991). This was called the *diagnostic program*. It opened up the first paths toward a *psychometrically based diagnosis of the learning process*. One of the aims of diagnostic programs is to construct the item pool on a sound psychological basis while simultaneously ensuring not only a learning gain, as in the traditional learning test, but also better opportunities to analyze the learning process and perform a qualitative analysis of errors. Some diagnostic programs additionally try to link the learning test concept with the idea of *adaptive testing*. In this context, *adaptive* means that the testee's individual errors specify the further item presentation and the assistance given. Hence, adaptive testing should meet the call for an *individualization* of testing without simultaneously impairing the standardization and comparability of the testing procedure (see Beckmann & Guthke, 1999; Guthke, Beckmann, Stein, Rittner, & Vahle, 1995).

Hence, dynamic assessment establishes a specific link among *testing*, *error analysis*, and *intervention*, thereby focusing on both the *learning process* and its *outcome* (see Grigorenko, 2009; Grigorenko & Sternberg, 1998). To summarize, we propose a more comprehensive definition of dynamic assessment: *Dynamic assessment diagnosis* is a term covering approaches to diagnostic testing that aim toward a more valid assessment of the current state of a psychological characteristic or its ability to change through intentionally evoking and assessing the intraindividual variability in the test process.

Comprehensive studies on construct validity (see Beckmann & Guthke, 1999; Guthke & Wiedl, 1996) have shown that the learning test also delivers the diagnostic information provided by a status test with identical items. However, the opposite is not true; the status test does not contain the information contained in the learning test. This property of the learning test not only thoroughly increases the accuracy of predictions but also suggests a different perspective on the area diagnosed in intelligence testing.

Areas Diagnosed in Intelligence Testing

The methodological potentials of dynamic testing provide access to a new perspective on the relevant constructs and areas diagnosed. This can be specified in the following way for the field of intelligence testing.

Drawing on Hebb (1949) and Vernon (1962), three intelligence concepts (see figure 10.1) can be discriminated from a genetic and methodological perspective: (1) *intelligence A*, the innate, mostly genetically determined preconditions for later intellectual performance (that still cannot be ascertained); (2) *intelligence B*, the intellectual ability that can be ascertained at a certain time during development in the sense of an intelligence status that represents a product (a product of learning) of the interaction between given preconditions and environmental or learning conditions; and (3) *intelligence C*, a psychometrically assessed and more or less representative excerpt of the intelligence status

in a *specific* intelligence test. Furthermore, we can postulate an *intelligence D* that might be named *intelligence potency, learning ability, learning potential,* or *intellectual learning ability*. Intelligence D presents the range of the characteristic that intelligence has as an intraindividual variable under the influence of feedback and learning incentives; in other words, it reports how far a person is able to increase momentary intellectual ability in the way that it expresses itself in the test (see figure 10.1).

These conclusions from research on intelligence can also be related to sport psychology and the diagnosis of motor abilities. The next section presents the potentials of applying dynamic assessment to various fields of motor control, motor development, sport psychology, and physical training.

Dynamic Assessment of Motor Learning Potential

Both the importance and the need for dynamic test procedures in obtaining more valid diagnoses in various domains of sport and physical activity have been pointed out repeatedly (e.g., Bös, 1992; Schack, 1997a, 1997b; Stott, Henderson, & Moyes, 1986). However, up to now, there has been neither a systematic processing of the existing approaches nor any formulation of a theoretical basis for dynamic testing in this field.

The most comprehensive approaches to dynamic assessment in sports and physical activity have emerged in the field of motor behavior assessment. Numerous approaches, assessment procedures,

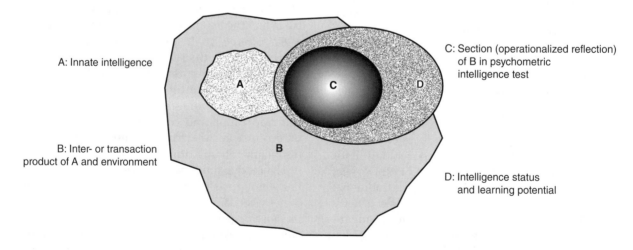

A: Innate intelligence

B: Inter- or transaction product of A and environment

C: Section (operationalized reflection) of B in psychometric intelligence test

D: Intelligence status and learning potential

Figure 10.1 Intelligence A, B, C, and D.[1]

Modified from T. Schack, & J. Guthke, 2003, "Dynamic testing," *International Journal of Sport and Exercise Psychology, 1*(1), 40-60. By permission of Routledge Press.

[1]Note that comparable results were obtained in Eißfeldt's work on dynamic testing in the training of air-traffic controllers for Lufthansa, the German national airline (cited in Guthke & Wiedl, 1996, pp. 233-234).

and specific tests on general motor abilities, motor educability, and fundamental specialized or functional skills have been developed since the 1920s. Various phases of development can be distinguished in which, for example, a more strongly product-oriented approach to movement skill assessment in the 1970s and 1980s gave way to a *process-oriented approach* (see Burton & Miller, 1998). The process-oriented label refers to the process of gathering data at *one* measurement time for the diagnosis of motor skills. An example is the very frequently used Test of Gross Motor Development (TGMD; Ulrich, 1985), an instrument that assesses the movement process while the subject performs different test movement skills. However, the TGMD is still a norm- and criterion-oriented instrument, and, like other process-oriented tests within the framework of motor skill assessment, it does not follow what we consider to be the typical experimental diagnosis strategy for dynamic testing.

However, it is not only *how* we measure a motor behavior at a certain point in time but also *what* we measure that matters. Several researchers have noted conceptual problems with this approach (for example, see Stott et al., 1986). It is therefore worth forging links to the construct domains of the intelligence concept (A, B, C, and D) and specifying these in general terms for the motor domain.

A meta-construct of similar complexity to cognitive intelligence (B) on the motor level is *motor intelligency* or *motor kinesthetic intelligence* (e.g., Gardner, 1985). Motor intelligency is the main category for all the integral psychophysical abilities (factors, dimensions) that form the basis for the ability to define movement problems clearly and solve movement tasks correctly, quickly, and appropriately. In the sense of a working definition, this diagnostically interesting ability can also be viewed as the spatio-temporal interplay of motor operations (functions) under a dominant control level. In particular, this ability makes it possible to cope with the degrees of freedom in the movement system and makes the movement controllable (see Bernstein, 1996; Schack & Bar-Eli, 2007).

Testing the *status* of motor intelligency (baseline performance according to Baltes & Willis, 1982), individual coordination abilities, or movement skills is comparable with testing intelligence C. However, dynamic testing targets the learning and action potential (cognitive or motor intelligence D). The major concept here, and the counterpart to intellectual learning ability, is *motor learning potential* or *motor educability*. Motor learning potential pertains to the ability to learn quickly and effectively or to perfect the necessary sequences of movement for attaining movement goals. Hence, it can be viewed as a *developmental reserve capacity* (Baltes & Willis, 1982) and thus as an integral *higher-order ability* that is actualized as a process under conditions that promote achievement. From this perspective, the movement system is a developing system. This is the reason why future research should pay more attention to the relationships between the dynamic system approach (see Kugler, Kelso, & Turvey, 1982; Turvey, 1977) and dynamic testing. For example, Thelen (1995) has written that "in broad strokes, a developing system is a dynamic system in that patterns of behavior act as collectives—attractor states—of the component parts within particular environmental and task contexts" (p. 84). What is worth examining in this approach is the idea that a person's movement system shifts from one performance level to another. To do so, the system has to overcome its own history in the form of stable patterns and attractor states. This also raises questions about how the *intrinsic dynamics* of the movement system are brought into line with the *task dynamics* and about which change potential the system is able to access for this (see Kelso, 1995). With such an understanding of movement, there is little sense in ascertaining the range of abilities a person has at a given point in time. It is far more appropriate to study the change potential of the movement system through a systematic and experimental modification of the task dynamics and to perform diagnoses in the sense of dynamic testing (see also Corbetta & Vereijken, 1999).

As is shown next, sport science reveals a series of promising approaches to the assessment of motor educability. These approaches range from slightly modified status tests to various approaches to dynamic testing in the diagnosis of performance.

Initial Approaches to Diagnosing Motor Educability in the United States

One of the first major studies to measure motor ability in a standardized way was that of Brace (1927). McCloy (1937) was the first to tackle how to assess motor educability. He modified the Brace Test on the basis of comprehensive studies performed at Iowa State University. This resulted in a battery of 21 scaled tests (the Iowa-Brace Test). Further attempts to measure motor educability came from Johnson (1932), who developed a battery of 10 tests designed to permit a homogeneous sectioning of students into special units. Using empirical research, Metheny (1938) concluded that this battery could be reduced to 4 tests without any loss in information (the Johnson-Metheny Test). Furthermore, Adams

(1954) differentiated the ability to learn gymnastics elements from play elements and compiled a test battery for ball games. This led him to propose a *motor educability score* based on regression analyses.

A major disadvantage of these initial approaches was the insufficient consideration given to the *motor learning processes* during the test procedures (see Bös, 1987). This disadvantage was particularly evident in the design of the tests as *status tests* and in the resulting failure to distinguish between motor action performance C (baseline performance) and learning and motor potential (motor intelligency D, developmental reserve capacity) on either a construct or a diagnosis level. This finding is supported by a series of studies indicating that these initial tests lacked validity.

Brace (1941) examined whether the Brace Test and the Iowa-Brace Test actually assess motor educability. He found only low correlations with other learning tests focusing more strongly on motor learning. Because of this result, Brace developed his learning tests further for a supplementary study (Brace, 1946). But these further developed learning tests were conducted without an explicit training phase and with only one measurement session. Nonetheless, they were designed to enable spontaneous learning processes by presenting a high number of trials (e.g., 30 trials in the Ball Bounce Test). Brace used these learning tests to define learning criteria that he related to various Brace and Iowa-Brace scores as well as to scores on scales developed specially by McCloy (1937). Results showed only low correlations between test scores and learning criteria. Brace concluded that it is doubtful whether the Brace Test and Iowa-Brace Test actually assess motor educability.

In 1942, Gire and Espenschade pointed out that studies on motor educability hardly ever defined learning criteria and did not determine the scores within the educability tests experimentally. They designed a study in which 195 girls learned or relearned skills in basketball, volleyball, and baseball. The skills learned in the different sports were measured across five time points. These measurements were then used to define various learning criteria, such as a total learning score based on the difference between the fifth and the first measurement of the skills. Finally, the learning scores were correlated with scores on the Brace, Iowa-Brace, and Johnson Tests. The correlations were low and nonsignificant. Gross, Griesel, and Stull (1956) reported similar findings for wrestling. They trained 56 college students with no previous experience of wrestling for 8 wk and then applied the Iowa-Brace Test and the Johnson-Metheny Test. Results showed

that the educability test failed to be a good predictor of individual learning success.

The majority of American and European studies (see Schack & Guthke, 2001, 2003) examining the tests of motor educability described thus far in this chapter cast doubt on their validity. In part, these results are due to the lack of differentiation in the construct of motor educability. However, the main problem is a procedure oriented to status testing that excludes motor learning and thus any diagnosis of motor educability.

European Trends in Dynamic Performance Assessment

Europe saw an intensive interest in motor learning ability during the 1960s and 1970s. Particularly in Eastern Europe, this research was linked conceptually to the work of the Bernstein group. Initial attempts to diagnose motor educability were based, to a large extent, on the American tests of McLoy, Metheny, and Brace. However, as in the American studies, these tests proved to have little validity.

As a result, Herzberg (1968) tried to go one step further by developing a *status test with modified conditions*. His test battery comprises a *test of change*, a *self-selected test*, and a *forwards-backwards test*. In the forwards-backwards test, testees run forward through a series of obstacles and then traverse the same obstacles while running backward. In the self-selected test, they choose the obstacles they wish to surmount. In the test of change, the sequence of obstacles is changed for the second trial. This test battery was developed within the framework of aptitude testing for judo. Herzberg and Lehmann (1968) found a significant relationship between scores on this test battery and competitive performance 1.5 y later. However, further studies on other sports produced only low correlations between test scores and later performances (see Thomas, 1977). Therefore, it is important to inquire whether the Herzberg Test diagnoses learning ability. Although the Herzberg Test modifies conditions, it still lacks the learning aids (conditions to promote performance) that characterize the learning tests in the intelligence domain. Hence, the structure of the Herzberg tasks indicates that this test aims more toward diagnosing a combination of coordination skills and adaptability than diagnosing motor educability (see Bös, 1992). Therefore, the tests for diagnosing motor educability presented thus far either try to make statements on a postulated *structure of motor educability* through a status diagnosis (e.g., McCloy, 1937; Metheny, 1938) or try to gain access to motor educability through a *variation of conditions* (e.g., Herzberg, 1968). Both approaches try to derive statements on the learning and action potential of persons by studying their current state of development (with status tests). This is one of the reasons why some authors point to the need for including several measurement time points when diagnosing motor educability (Bös, 1992; Meinel & Schnabel, 1998; Stott et al., 1986).

This conceptualization is the basis of the *dynamic testing*, or *dynamic assessment*, of motor educability. In general, dynamic testing of motor educability can be understood as the goal-directed elicitation and assessment of motor learning processes in order to diagnose the motor learning and action potential or the coordination abilities that the action potential involves. Several interesting approaches can be found; in 1976, Bös, Hörtdörfer, and Mechling referred to the learning test concept found in intelligence testing to propose the development of learning goal control tests. The idea behind their diagnosis strategy was to elicit learning processes in physical education, to diagnose interindividual differences in learning across several measurement time points, and to relate these to the learning goal.

In 1980, Hörtdörfer presented a learning test for diagnosing equilibrium and coordination. The design was a long-term learning test made up of three parts: (1) a pretest (balance test), (2) a training phase to develop equilibrium and coordination (two 40 min sessions), and (3) a posttest (balance test). To standardize and ascertain the effectiveness of the training program, Hörtdörfer compared two programs (training on a stable versus unstable surface). Although the training program was developed with care, the available empirical studies permit no statements on its predictive validity.

In studies unrelated to those being performed in West Germany, Rauchmaul (1984) attempted to diagnose motor educability in terms of the learning test concept in intelligence testing in East Germany. Depending on the class of learning activities addressed, he discriminated between a *general* and a *special motor educability*. This led him to produce three general and four volleyball-specific learning tests. Because the test procedure involved a sequence of pretest, training, and posttest conducted in one session, Rauchmaul (1984) described his approach as a *short-term learning test*. When developing the general learning test, he tried to apply the task construction in the Herzberg Test (obstacle courses) while going beyond the one-shot measurement (and the inappropriate interpretation of a status test as a learning test). He did this by positioning training sections to activate learning processes between the obstacle courses in the pre- and posttests (the time required to complete this test procedure was approximately 45 min for 15 participants). To diagnose volleyball-specific motor educability, Rauchmal developed four short-term tests. These recorded, among other things, the levels of volleyball-specific skills within the pre- and posttest phases. The training phase was oriented toward the further acquisition and development of these skills. Within the process of developing his short-term learning tests, he assessed construct validity with a total of 21 (status) tests of general and specific coordination abilities in a sample of 125 persons. Test outcomes were also related to judgments by trainers. Results (of correlations and factor analyses) indicated that this was a valid test. Unfortunately, data on the predictive validity are still unavailable.

In a recent study, Schack and Guthke (2001) developed a version of dynamic testing that can also tap information on the learning process between pretest and posttest phases. In this long-term learning test for gymnastics (*Langzeit-Lerntest Turnen*, LLTT), the training phase between pretest and posttest has a specific structure. Testees must run through a hierarchy of learning steps that are directed toward learning or improving the exercise to be performed in the posttest. Error-related learning aids are available at each learning stage during this training phase. This means that after the LLTT posttest, diagnostic information is available from the *pretest*, the *posttest*, the *course of learning*, and the *types of error*. The LLTT was given to 87 students before a 6 wk gymnastics course, and its predictive validity was examined by comparing it with other motor educability tests. The criterion variables were a standardized observation and the final grade in gymnastics. Results showed significant correlations ($r = .61$-$.72$) between LLTT and performance after training. However, relationships between other motor educability tests (Herzberg Test and Iowa-Brace Test) and the criterion variables were less pronounced (Schack & Guthke, 2001).

Dynamic Assessment in Top-Level Competitive Sports

Other interesting approaches to dynamic assessment have been developed for *aptitude testing* in top-level sports (see Schack & Guthke, 2003). In competitive sports, there is a particularly strong demand for tests with a high predictive validity for forming suitable training groups, for individualizing training, and for selecting particularly talented athletes. From 1960 to 1990, there was a particularly strong demand for valid aptitude testing in Eastern European countries producing top international athletes despite their small populations. The former East Germany (German Democratic Republic) presents an interesting and unique example for such a trend.

At a set date once a year from 1973 onward, sport-related motor skills and abilities were surveyed in a standardized inspection and selection of all 1st, 3rd, and 7th grade children in the German Democratic Republic. Physical education teachers at the schools carried out tests and measurements. This made comprehensive data on all children in the country available for predictive judgments on performance. Athletes who passed this first stage of selection were subjected to more rigorous selection through provisional training and an integrated test battery assessing condition and coordination skills. The final and decisive third stage of selection applied dynamic test procedures in various sports.

The development of preliminary approaches toward dynamic testing had already commenced at the beginning of the 1960s in East German top-level team sports, gymnastics, and swimming (Schulz, 1964). However, these approaches contained very little standardization, and the training phases were far too extensive. Particularly for aptitude testing, there was a need for fast and standardized procedures. The development of the first dynamic intelligence tests proved beneficial here. Pechtl (1974) drew on the learning test concept (Guthke, 1972) to develop a procedure for detecting talent in gymnastics to be applied in the third and final stage of selection in first graders. This short learning program (SLP) contained sets of exercises in gymnastics. In each set of exercises, students had to work through a linear succession of progressive learning steps of increasing skill complexity. Instructions and specific feedback were given during learning. The SLP consisted of five 90 min training units that could be completed within 1 wk. Progress in learning was ascertained through specific test phases in each training unit. Predictive validity was assessed from 1970 to 1973 within the framework of aptitude testing for admission to gymnastics training centers. In the first step, 7,700 children were selected through screening procedures. The second step was a selection based on status tests of coordination. Finally, in the last step, 237 athletes were selected with the help of dynamic testing (SLP). There were significant relationships between the results obtained with SLP and performance criteria in gymnastics collected 18 mo after testing. Because of this unequivocal confirmation of this procedure's predictive validity, it was applied more frequently after 1973 for aptitude testing in all gymnastics associations.

In Russian top-level sports, a specific approach to dynamic testing was developed by Siris (1974), Balsevic (1980), and others. This approach measured the developmental rate of acceleration in motor properties across four testing sessions (at 6 mo time lags). Jumping and running tests as well as training between measurements were standardized across all athletes. Results were illustrated through a study by Siris (1974) of 25 male track-and-field athletes (aged 13 y at the beginning of the study). The goal was to obtain statements on the validity of the diagnostic strategies applied. Status tests permitted only weak statements on the final ability of athletes. Therefore, it seems worth comparing such statements with ones obtained from dynamic test procedures. The aggregated rates of acceleration achieved during the first 6 mo were compared with competitive performance after 5 y. At this stage, the relationship between the two scores was weak ($r = .461$ for the 100 m sprint and $r = .379$ for the long jump). However, performing the same computation with the rates of acceleration during the first 18 mo increased these correlations to .946 and .876, respectively. Considering the time interval involved, this correlation is remarkable and indicates how advantageous dynamic test procedures can be.

Dynamic Assessment in Aviation Performance Domains

Interesting approaches to dynamic testing of perceptual and motor tasks have been developed in aptitude testing for various national air forces. Since the 1920s, nearly all countries possessing an air force have tried to improve aptitude testing for pilots, bombardiers, or navigators. The reasons for doing so are self-evident: Training is very expensive, and a high number of persons selected to train as pilots (65%-81%) drop out during training because of mental factors (see Chi-cheng & Chung-hsien, 1962). The mental factors considered relevant vary from country to country. Before World War II, France and Italy paid more attention to specific domains such as reaction time, whereas Germany concentrated on complex abilities closely related to real conditions (flight simulation). During World War II, almost all countries increased their emphasis on coordination factors. The U.S. Army set up a special psychological agency, the Aviation Psychology Program, under the leadership of J.C. Flanagan. One of its tasks was to develop corresponding tests. From 1942 onward, more attention was paid to perceptual-motor tests that then became integrated into the aircrew test battery. Dynamic test forms were also developed, such as the phase checks found particularly in flexible gunnery training. Each phase check was based on carefully prepared items that correspond precisely with a step in the real task. Such phase checks were developed for all procedures before, during, and after flight. All task-related items were given dichotomous ratings, and scores were computed on the basis of errors in task performance. Phase checks were used extensively for both tests and training. However, the mean correlation between these dynamic phase checks and a status-oriented, printed multiple-choice test in the final gunnery examination was 0 (Flanagan, 1948).

In Russia, it was assumed initially that at least 90% of real performance could be predicted through status testing of individual components such as will-power or emotional stability. Because these diagnoses proved to be of little use in real life, aircrew selection agencies shifted the emphasis toward dynamic test procedures after 1935. They then tried to gain valid statements on psychological and perceptual-motor skills through a multiple application of tests under changing conditions (Platonow, 1960). Chinese scientists took similar stances after World War II (Chi-cheng & Chung-hsien, 1962). They assumed that pilots require complex abilities to engage in a dynamic interaction between sensorimotor skills and other variables, such as emotional components of self-control. Therefore, they proposed dynamic test procedures for both aircrew and astronaut selection using realistic task simulations.

In more recent studies, Regian and Schneider (1990) examined how performance can be predicted on perceptual-motor tasks such as air-traffic control or naval air intercept control. They started by analyzing the perceptual-motor and cognitive components (such as working memory) involved. Then, they ascertained the rate of learning on these task components with a combination of tests and training in the sense of dynamic assessment. This allowed a better discrimination between the trainee's previous experience and ability than was possible in earlier status tests.

Curriculum-Oriented Procedures for Children With Motor Impairments

In recent years, efforts have been made within educational assessment to link assessment and training more closely together. The concern has been to pay more attention to a dynamic, development-oriented perspective in the teaching process. Here as well, the main arguments emerged from criticism of traditional status-oriented skill assessment. The idea was that the skills or capabilities that children do not yet possess at the first measurement are not only *descriptive* for the current developmental status but also *prescriptive* for future schooling (see Bagnato & Neisworth, 1981).

One approach that is currently receiving attention is curriculum-based assessment (CBA; see Bagnato,

Neisworth, & Capone, 1986; Hamers, Pennings, & Guthke, 1994; Haywood, Tzuriel, & Vaught, 1992). CBA uses the data obtained through assessment as an important source of information and relates the objectives of the curriculum to the instruction. The content of the assessment then depends on the school curriculum. "Essentially, CBA involves a test-teach-test approach wherein children are assessed on objectives to be learned, provided with instruction, and then assessed on achievement of these objectives" (Bagnato et al., 1986, p. 97).

Various CBA instruments have been developed that specifically target motor development (e.g., the Peabody Developmental Motor Scales; see Folio & Fewell, 1983) or that assess motor skills along with other domains, such as cognitive and social curriculum domains (e.g., the Assessment, Evaluation, and Programming System; see Bricker, 1993). Burton and Miller (1998) have discussed an interesting top-down assessment strategy that permits a coordination of assessment and instruction on different levels. They suggest that CBA instruments should pay more attention to functional movement outcomes instead of sometimes focusing too exclusively on assessing isolated skills. One current functionally oriented procedure that can be classified to CBA is Bidabe and Lollar's (1993) Mobility Opportunities Via Education (MOVE) curriculum. This program was developed for children who lack the necessary abilities to sit, stand, or walk by themselves. Its goal is to achieve progress in these skills and in the activities depending on them while measuring this progress formatively. The program consists of six stages: testing, setting goals, task analysis, measuring prompts, reducing prompts, and teaching skills. The Top-Down Motor Milestone Test (TDMMT) was developed for the test phases. The TDMMT is a criterion-referenced test for estimating a total of 74 skills for various levels of functioning in daily life. The goal in the second stage of the MOVE program is to develop functional activities in daily life (e.g., eating or using a toilet) related to the skills evaluated in the first step. The third step selects appropriate components of these functional activities for teaching. The fourth step estimates the aids that are used according to a special support system for sitting, standing, walking, and using arms and hands. The fifth step reduces the prompts systematically according to an aid-reduction plan. The final step teaches skills in accordance with this aid-reduction plan. This teaching of skills is coordinated with the categories to be assessed with the TDMMT.

The MOVE program provides a good example of the value of moving from a more strongly test-oriented perspective to a combination of assessment and instruction or testing and teaching. Its design strongly recalls the learning test presented at the beginning of this chapter and reveals its links with other dynamic testing approaches mentioned earlier. However, CBA instruments such as the MOVE program take more time and are more strongly teaching oriented than test oriented. The same applies to other educational approaches such as ecological task analysis (see Balan & Davis, 1993; Burton & Davis, 1996) as well as to approaches proposed within the framework of a goal-attainment scaling (see Palisano, Haley, & Brown, 1992). The differences between a teaching-oriented and a test-oriented perspective can best be seen by linking them to the different interests of the teacher and the researcher. However, these perspectives are complementary and supplement each other by paying stronger attention to the developmental potential of the student or testee.

Further Areas for Applying Dynamic Assessment in Sport Psychology

Current studies show that dynamic testing can be used not only to ascertain learning potential but also to assess performance deterioration under stress. In particular, various research questions in the context of sport activities could benefit from ascertaining an individual *stress tolerance potential*. Nitsch (1990) has presented interesting approaches for testing concentration. The diagnosis is carried out during increasing bicycle ergometer stress with an adaptive concentration test instrument assisted by computers. Participants must react to auditory stimuli by pressing sensor keys (while stress is being increased in successive stages). The adaptive diagnosis strategy is particularly interesting: A correct response to the stimulus sequence leads to an increase in the number of further stimuli errors (wrong key presses or omissions), which leads to an increase in the time interval between the stimuli. This ensures continuous data collection at the stress threshold for concentration while successively increasing physical stress. The results of this study permit differential statements on reaction time, work tempo, and the number of errors within a *zone of maximal stress exposure*. We consider that this method could be developed further by improving opportunities for purposefully induced learning processes, particularly through error-related interventions. Further current approaches to the previously mentioned diagnosis of learning and action potential that might be of interest for sports have been reported for spatial

orientation ability (Embretson, 1992) and for mental control (Schack, 1999). In the field of neurocognitive sport psychology there are some interesting approaches that measure, for instance, the learning ability after brain injuries. Recent studies (Braun et al., 2007, 2008; Uprichard, Kupshik, Pine, & Fletcher, 2009) have shown that dynamic assessment offers advantages over the traditional standard tests in predicting the developmental potential for people with brain injuries. Additionally, dynamic assessment procedures offer new opportunities for a more precise and development-oriented rehabilitation process.

Conclusion

Hacking (1983) distinguished between two basic modes of inquiry in science: *representing* and *intervening*. We agree with Wittmann and Süß (1999) that research and diagnosis in differential psychology, unlike in experimental psychology, can be characterized as being tied almost exclusively to the representing principle. This statement also applies for broad sectors of research and diagnosis in sport psychology. However, psychodiagnoses, or diagnoses within the framework of research and practice in sport science, will fulfill the demand for more reliable predictors of future behavior and more relevant interventions in the sense of a potential- and intervention-oriented diagnosis only when they pay more attention to the intervening principle. The dynamic testing approaches presented here provide notable ways of doing this.

Further potential application fields for dynamic testing can be found in the context of sport activities. These range from individual functions of action regulation (such as attention, imagery, decisiveness, and so on) to complex competencies (such as game intelligence). Complex diagnosis strategies could be gained from combining the experimental diagnostic strategy of dynamic assessment with models that distinguish among different levels of movement regulation (e.g., Bernstein, 1996; Glencross, Whiting, & Abernethy, 1994, p. 47; Schack, 2004; Schack & Hackfort, 2007; Tenenbaum et al., 2009). These strategies would permit statements on the potential at each respective level (e.g., dynamically driven versus mentally controlled). It would also be interesting to ascertain which system potential first becomes activated through the integration of various levels. Up to now, these possibilities have been exploited only in part. Although this certainly has something to do with the higher costs of dynamic test procedures in terms of time and methods, it may also be linked to the fact that the usefulness of this strategy for improving diagnoses has yet to be discussed and questioned explicitly. This chapter has attempted to take a first step in this direction.

However, there are still unresolved problems, including the lack of a learning process analysis based on psychomotor research and cognitive psychology to ensure, among other things, that the tasks and learning aids presented in the learning test actually follow a hierarchical sequence. Furthermore, a closer understanding of the relationship between movement coordination (motor educability) and learning from the perspective of differential psychology would be helpful (see Adams, 1987; Fleishman, 1972). At the same time, increased interest in such questions should not just benefit diagnosis. For example, dynamic testing could help to focus more attention on the learning potential of persons within the framework of perfecting sport techniques, sport rehabilitation, and health measures as well as within further fields of practical action and research in sport science.

Acknowledgments

Parts of this chapter are based on T. Schack, & J. Guthke, 2003, "Dynamic testing," *International Journal of Sport and Exercise Psychology, 1*(1), 40-60. By permission of Routledge Press.

Verbal Reports of Cognitive Processes

David W. Eccles, PhD

Since the cognitive revolution in mainstream psychology, researchers within psychology, including sport and exercise psychology, have become increasingly interested in studying the cognitions that are thought to underpin human behavior and in the methods for studying such cognitions. Researchers within sport and exercise psychology who are interested in answers to questions such as "To what extent do overweight exercisers experience negative self-evaluations in public exercise settings?" and "What mental strategies do ultraendurance athletes use to help them complete their difficult tasks?" (see Hollander & Acevedo, 2000) have sometimes taken the research approach of simply posing these questions to the target participants, with the expectation that the participants will provide useful information about their thinking (see Ericsson, 2006). However, this is not always the case, and missing from sport and exercise psychology is a consideration of the conditions under which participants are most likely to provide useful information in response to requests for verbal reports of their cognitive processes. Furthermore, there are no accessible guidelines within the field about research designs that create these conditions.

The goal of this chapter is to provide the researcher of sport and exercise psychology with this information. The chapter begins with a discussion of the state of the science in terms of a person's ability to report validly about cognitions and continues with Ericsson and Simon's (1980) proposals of experimental conditions that maximize the validity of verbal reports of cognitions. Following this is an attempt to demonstrate the shortcomings of methods currently used in sport and exercise psychology to elicit verbal reports of cognitions, which is achieved by examining the methods used in recent studies of psychological skill use by sport

performers with regard to the framework proposed by Ericsson and Simon (1980). Guidelines and examples are then provided for designing studies that afford the elicitation and capture of valid verbal reports of cognitive processes.

Validity of Verbal Reports of Cognitive Processes

While concerns over the validity of self-reports of cognitive processes have a long history in both philosophy and psychology, the focus here is on the contemporary debate in mainstream psychology (for a broader historical review, see Ericsson, 2006). In particular, the focus is on the influential reviews of this topic published in *Psychological Review* by Nisbett and Wilson (1977) and Ericsson and Simon (1980).

The 1977 Nisbett and Wilson Review

In the 1960s and 1970s, psychologists, especially those in the emerging discipline of cognitive psychology, questioned the individual's ability to provide valid reports of cognitive processes. However, it was social psychologists Nisbett and Wilson (1977) who provided the strongest critique of these methods in a now widely cited paper. Following a review of the research literature in social psychology, and after undertaking a series of studies on reports on mental processes, these authors found that individuals seldom report accurately about their cognitions. The research these authors cited as providing evidence supporting their propositions included a classic study of problem solving undertaken by Maier (1931). In the study, two cords were hung from a laboratory ceiling. The participant was informed that the problem was to tie the ends of the two cords together. As the participant discovered, the cords were far enough apart that it was impossible to reach the end of one cord while holding onto the end of the other. While there were several possible solutions to the problem, Maier was interested in the relatively unobvious solution of tying an object to the end of one of the cords so that it could be used as a pendulum and then swinging the pendulum so that it would pass near the other cord, whereupon both cord ends could be grasped and tied. If this solution was not discovered within 10 min, Maier provided hints about the solution to the participants. One hint involved an experimenter accidentally brushing one cord while walking about the laboratory so that the cord swung slightly. Despite the 10 min provided for the discovery of the pendulum solution before the hint, all 16 participants in Maier's study made the discovery of this solution an average of 42 s (with a maximum of 150 s) following the hint.

However, when the participants were asked how they discovered the solution, only 1 from the 16 made reference to the hint. The remainder offered a variety of explanations, such as "It was the only thing left" and, more surprisingly, "[I saw] imagery of monkeys swinging through trees. This imagery appeared simultaneously with the solution" (Maier, 1931, p. 189). When specifically asked whether they had seen the hint, 11 participants suggested that they were unaware of it but could understand how it could have been useful in eliciting their discovery of the solution. By contrast, the remaining 4 were adamant that the hint played no role in their discovery of the solution.

Maier, keen to explore the potential for his participants to provide invalid reports about the thinking involved in their solution discoveries, undertook a subsequent study in which participants were provided with the original brushing-the-cord hint or a new hint. The new hint consisted of an experimenter twirling a weight tied to the end of one cord while drawing the participant's attention to it "as a possible help" (1931, p. 188). Thus, it differed from the original hint in that its presentation was intentional rather than accidental and that the participant was informed that it was potentially useful. However, the results indicated that the original hint was more effective than the new hint in eliciting discoveries of the pendulum solution. Maier then undertook a study in which participants received the new hint several minutes before the original hint. The results revealed that the presentation of both hints was required for a discovery of the solution. However, all participants who discovered the solution reported that the new hint helped them. None mentioned the original hint. Thus, the participants not only failed to report the hint that helped them (i.e., the original hint) but also reported a hint that did not (i.e., the new hint).

Nisbett and Wilson (1977) also studied the validity of verbal reports on cognitive processes. One study involved asking shoppers in a store to evaluate clothing goods such as stockings under the guise of a consumer survey. Participants were presented with four items of clothing arranged in a row and asked to choose the item with the highest quality and then describe their reasoning behind their choice. Participants were found to choose the rightmost item of clothing over the leftmost by a factor of almost 4 to 1. While many participants offered reasons for their choice, none reported that their choice was influenced by the position of the item. Furthermore, when asked directly about the influence of position on their decision, nearly all participants denied its influence. Nisbett and Wilson proposed their own theory to explain the position effect, and the interested reader is referred to their work (p. 244).

The proposition by Nisbett and Wilson (1977) that individuals have specific limits on access to the thoughts mediating their decisions and actions is supported throughout the cognitive sciences (e.g., Dennett, 2003; Ericsson & Simon, 1993; Pinker, 1999; Wegner, 2002). As Dennett (2003) proposed,

> for Descartes, the mind was perfectly transparent to itself, with nothing happening out of view, and it has taken more than a century of psychological theorizing and experimentation to erode this ideal of perfect introspectability, which we can now see gets the situation almost backward. Consciousness of the springs of action is the exception, not the rule, and it requires some remarkable circumstances to have evolved at all. (p. 246)

A theoretical question promoted by empirical evidence of invalid reports on cognitive processes is why so much of cognition should be inaccessible to consciousness. Pinker (1999) has argued that inaccessibility "is not a bug, it's a feature" (p. 142) because conscious access to all the processes involved in the mediation of decisions and actions would overload the human's information processing faculties (Newell & Simon, 1972).

Having established that individuals have limited conscious access to their cognitions, a question arises as to the source of the reports about thinking provided by the participants in the studies reviewed and undertaken by Nisbett and Wilson (1977). Despite the evidence that they were often invalid, these reports were reliably provided and often comprehensive. Nisbett and Wilson's answer to this question was that individuals asked to provide such reports under conditions in which the cognitions being sought were not accessible instead accessed *implicit theories* about their thought processes. Implicit theories are defined as an individual's fundamental assumptions about how the world generally works. These theories, it was proposed, can be created via different mechanisms. First, the culture or a subculture in which the individual operates may have explicit social rules stating the relationship between a particular stimulus and a particular response: "I came to a stop because the light started to change" (Nisbett & Wilson, 1977, p. 248). Second, the culture or a subculture may supply implicit theories about these relationships. "Jim gave flowers to Amy [me]; that's why she's [I'm] acting pleased as punch today" (Nisbett & Wilson's brackets, p. 248). Third, individuals may create their own theories based on previous observations of the covariation between stimuli of the general type and responses of the general type: "I'm grouchy today. I'm always grouchy when I don't break 100 in golf" (p. 248). However, there is reason to suspect that actual covariation in the environment may play less of a role in informing an individual's reports than do the individual's theories about covariation. Fourth, in the absence of a culturally supplied rule or implicit theory or a self-generated theory of covariation, people may be able to generate causal hypotheses linking even novel stimuli and novel responses.

Regardless of how these theories are created, when an individual is asked to report on cognitive processes, then the individual will report on the basis of an implicit causal theory that effectively matches the stimulus and response conditions of the given situation. If, based on the individual's previously constructed causal theory, a given stimulus within the situation implies the response provided by the individual, or if a stimulus seems to approximate the types of stimuli that might influence the response, the individual is likely to report that the stimulus influenced the response. In contrast, if, according to the individual's causal theory, the stimulus does not seem to be a plausible cause of the response, then the individual is likely to report that the stimulus did not influence the response. Nisbett and Wilson (1977) also asserted that verbal reports on cognitive processes can sometimes be correct. However, correct reports arise not because the individual is able to obtain access to a memory trace of the cognitive process that mediated the response to a given stimulus but because the individual has incidentally employed a causal theory that is correct.

In summary, the findings of the review undertaken by Nisbett and Wilson (1977) appear damaging to the validity of verbal reports of cognitive processes. To paraphrase Nisbett and Wilson (p. 231), perhaps participants are frequently asked to report "more than they can know."

The 1980 Ericsson and Simon Review

Three years after the work of Nisbett and Wilson, Ericsson and Simon (1980) published a paper suggesting that valid reports on mental processes are obtainable. While the research described previously indicated that much of cognition is not available to consciousness, this same research indicated that *some* information about ongoing cognition is available to consciousness. Within the information processing paradigm, this is the information presented in short-term memory (STM) during ongoing cognition. STM represents the blackboard of consciousness upon which a subset of the information being processed during ongoing cognition is written (Goldman-Rakic, 1996). Thus, Ericsson and Simon (1980) set out to explore and subsequently specify the conditions under which it is possible to verbalize this limited information. The central features of their framework are described here.

First, in line with the research described previously, the only information about mental processes that an individual is thought to be able to access and in turn verbalize is that attended to (hereafter, heeded) in STM during the execution of a task. The cognitive processes operating are not verbalizable themselves. However, with some exceptions, the intermediate and end products of those processes are held in STM during task execution. It is these products that are verbalizable and can allow the experimenter to make inferences about the processes themselves. Ericsson and Simon (1980) termed the process of directly reporting heeded information *level 1 verbalization*. They also proposed that information heeded during a given task that is not in a verbal mode (e.g., visually imaged information) can be verbalized but requires an intermediary process to recode the information into a verbal mode before it can be verbalized; this process is termed *level 2 verbalization*.

Ericsson and Simon (1980) proposed specific experimental conditions that offer the constraints necessary for participants to provide level 1 or 2 verbalization. As the departure from these conditions increases, these constraints change so that, in moderate cases, the participant is not constrained to providing only level 1 and 2 verbalization. By contrast, the participant is afforded opportunities to verbalize information that is not directly heeded during the performance of a task and thus is not a product of any cognitive process mediating performance (e.g., by accessing implicit causal theories). This process is termed *level 3 verbalization*. In more extreme cases, the participant is constrained from level 1 and 2 verbalization and only afforded opportunities to provide level 3 verbalization. These conditions are described as follows.

Concurrent and Retrospective Verbalization

During ongoing activity, information in STM is available only briefly, on the order of single seconds, owing to the finite size of STM (see Newell & Simon, 1972). As new information is heeded, previous information is lost. Thus, unless information heeded in STM during task execution is also encoded in long-term memory (LTM), the principal means of obtaining a direct trace of this information and thus achieving level 1 or 2 verbalization is to instruct participants to report on their mental processes as they are experienced. Ericsson and Simon (1980) termed this method *concurrent reporting*. However, some information remains in STM briefly after the termination of the task. Thus, instructions to report given immediately after the task may provide access to this information. This method was termed *immediate retrospective reporting*.

While concurrent or immediate retrospective reporting methods are preferred, information heeded in STM during task execution may also be indirectly accessible after task execution via LTM. If heeded information was also encoded into LTM during task execution, participants instructed to recall memory traces of this information from LTM should provide level 1 or 2 verbalization. However, a key problem with this method is that similar tasks experienced after the criterion tasks can produce substantial retroactive interference in LTM (e.g., Delaney, Ericsson, & Knowles, 2004). To elaborate, when tasks are similar, the information presented in STM during task execution is likely to be similar across those tasks. If the information presented in similar tasks is encoded into LTM, it is likely to be represented within LTM with a similar rather than differentiated encoding, and this similarity in coding causes interference. Such interference contaminates or makes impossible the recall of information heeded during the criterion task (Delaney et al., 2004). Therefore, verbalization based on recall from LTM of information previously heeded in STM is likely to be valid only for the most recent task within a task type. This method is termed *delayed retrospective reporting*.

Forms of Probing

Ericsson and Simon (1980) also proposed that level 1 and 2 verbalization is most likely to occur when participants are provided with *undirected probes*. To elaborate, when a concurrent report method is used, participants should be asked to simply think aloud thoughts as they are experienced during task execution. Individuals often think aloud naturally when undertaking a task alone. For example, it is sometimes natural to think aloud intermediate products of the cognitive processes involved in arithmetic, such as "Err, 23, carry the 9, ah, 478." However, when an individual is asked to think aloud in the company of others (e.g., an experimenter), the social dynamic often leads the individual to augment verbalization with descriptions and explanations of thoughts that are not part of the actual thoughts being experienced; that is, the social dynamic leads to level 3 verbalization. This effect can be reduced by instructing a participant not to describe or explain thoughts but to think thoughts aloud as they are experienced and to act as if alone in the room and to be unconcerned with how disjointed the thoughts may sound.

These instructions should be adapted slightly when an immediate or a delayed retrospective report method is used. For the immediate retrospective report method, level 1 and 2 verbalization is most likely to occur when participants are instructed to report the thoughts they just experienced during the task, beginning with the first thought they can recall. For the delayed retrospective report method, access to heeded information encoded in LTM is most likely to occur when participants are instructed to report aloud only those thoughts they can definitely recall having experienced during the criterion task without describing or explaining them. Furthermore, for both immediate and delayed retrospective report methods, natural social pressures to report the recall of thoughts when none can be recalled can be reduced by informing participants that saying nothing is perfectly acceptable when no thoughts can be recalled.

However, as Ericsson and Simon (1980) noted, many studies of cognitive processes involve *directed probes* that direct participants to interpret their thoughts and thus to provide level 3 verbalization. To paraphrase Ericsson and Simon (1980, p. 222), how does the researcher lose any data by asking the third versus the first or second of the following questions?

1. Directed probe 1. Q: Did you use any form of self-talk strategy to help you prepare mentally just before your dive? A: Yes.

2. Directed probe 2. Q: Please tell me about any psychological skills you might have used to help you prepare mentally just before your dive.

A: Well, I tried to talk myself into feeling good about the dive.

3. Undirected probe. Q: Please start with the first thought you remember having just before your dive. Immediate retrospective report: The first thought I remember having was, "OK Michelle, this feels good . . . just do it smooth . . . just like in practice."

The last probe not only affords the same information as (if not more information than) the first and second probes but also provides information of sounder validity because the probe avoids constraining the participant to interpret thoughts. As Ericsson and Simon proposed, the interpretation is best left to the experimenter.

When directed probes in the form of questions are accompanied by a specific, fixed set of alternative answers, such as those appearing in most questionnaires, there is greater concern because the participant is provided with a set of fixed constraints on how to respond. There might be no response within the set of response alternatives that approximates any thought process that the participant might be able to recall from the criterion task. Furthermore, there is typically no way to detect the extent to which a response provided by a participant approximates a recalled thought process.

Particular and General Reports

As the only information about cognitive processes that is thought to be verbalizable is that presented to STM during a given task, instructions to verbalize should constrain participants to verbalize only information that is (or was) heeded during the criterion task. However, as Ericsson and Simon (1980) noted, many studies of cognitive processes involve instructions that do not constrain participants to report about thinking experienced during a particular task but afford the participant opportunities to report about thinking in more general terms or constrain the participant to report only about thinking in more general terms. For example, researchers are often concerned with investigating what Ericsson and Simon termed *general strategies*, which are thoughts mediating a participant's performance not during a particular event but during a particular set of events such as a set of trials that make up an experimental session or a set of events that make up a military mission or a sport competition. A typical question asked of participants in an attempt to identify general strategies might be, "How did you solve these problems?"

Ericsson and Simon (1980) proposed that there are several means by which a participant might provide a report of general strategies rather than a report of specific thoughts experienced during an individual task. First, a participant might be aware of the general strategies used and might have used the same strategies during most of the criterion tasks and so can recall and report these strategies directly and without reference to the specific behavior they produced. Second, a participant might recall part of a thought process or an entire process experienced during one or more of the criterion tasks and then attempt to generalize this recalled information into a general procedure, which is then reported. Third, a participant might recall the nature of a specific task and then mentally reattempt or resolve the task and use the thoughts experienced during the mental reattempt to infer the general strategies used during the original attempt. Finally, the participant might draw on information unrelated to any task experienced to generate a verbal report of a general procedure, such as that supplied by the implicit causal theories described by Nisbett and Wilson (1977). There is reason to doubt the validity of the reports obtained by all but the first means, and as the participant would not be constrained to report *only* via the first means, the validity of any resulting reports would be questionable.

Ericsson and Simon (1980) also noted that researchers are often interested in the general characteristics of the thinking involved in a type of task; they termed these characteristics *general states*. Consequently, when studying general states, the instructions given to the participant provide few if any constraints on recalling thoughts experienced during a particular task. Instead, participants are instructed to report how they generally think while performing a type of task. Under these conditions, it is even less clear whether the participant attempts to recall any thoughts experienced during any particular performance of the criterion task. Indeed, Ericsson and Simon (1980) proposed that reports elicited when probes for general states are used bear no relation to level 1 and 2 verbalization because the probes afford the participant maximum opportunities to draw on alternative sources of information (p. 224). It is proposed here that requests for general states maximize the likelihood of the participant drawing on information unrelated to any actual task experienced and in particular on implicit causal theories to provide a report.

In summary, the framework proposed by Ericsson and Simon (1980) suggests that it is possible to obtain valid reports on cognitive processes under specific study conditions, particularly those that constrain the participant to only report or recall information heeded during an actual performance of the task of interest. In the next section, the extent to which current published studies within sport and exercise psychology have involved conditions that constrain participants to report in this way is explored.

Methods Used in Studies of Psychological Skill Use With Regard to the Verbal Report Framework Proposed by Ericsson and Simon (1980)

This section assesses the extent to which studies within sport and exercise psychology interested in examining cognitive processes and strategies have employed verbal report methods providing level 1 or 2 verbalization. A review of the entire discipline is unfeasible, so instead this section focuses on one topic within sport and exercise psychology: the use of psychological skills by sport performers (i.e., athletes and coaches). For the purpose of this chapter, psychological skills refer to the big four proposed by Hardy, Jones, and Gould (1996): goal setting, imagery, relaxation, and self-talk.

The decision to examine studies of psychological skills was made for several reasons. First, while detailed definitions of psychological skills are rare, reviewing the selected research revealed that most researchers consider the skills to have a cognitive basis even if they have some behavioral components. For example, psychological skills have been described as *cognitive skills*, *cognitive strategies*, and *processing strategies* (e.g., Gould, Dieffenbach, & Moffett, 2002, p. 176; Hanton & Jones, 1999, p. 3). Furthermore, Vealey (1994) has stated that a "major premise of PST [psychological skills training] is that athletes . . . may need to learn cognitive skills and strategies to cope with the various demands of sport competition. For example, imagery, relaxation, and goal-setting may be used to cope with competitive stress, facilitate attentional control, and enhance self-confidence" (p. 495). Thus, given that psychological skills essentially involve cognitive processes, reports about psychological skills are essentially reports about cognitive processes. Consider how the following interview question taken from a study of psychological skills directs the participant to report on cognitive processes: "What mental strategies did you use to help you complete this before, during . . . and after [the swim]" (Hollander & Acevedo, 2000, p. 4). Consider also how this is the case for the following questionnaire response items, which are also from studies of psychological skills: "I image alter-

native strategies in case my event/game plan fails" from the Sport Imagery Questionnaire (SIQ; Hall, Mack, Paivio, & Hausenblas, 1998) and "I manage my self-talk effectively during competition" from the Test of Performance Strategies (TOPS; Thomas, Murphy, & Hardy, 1999).

The second reason for focusing on psychological skill use is that the topic is prominent within the research on sport psychology and is influential within applied sport psychology. This is evidenced by the publication of nearly 100 studies of psychological skill use by sport performers in sport psychology journals between 1970 and 2006 (Eccles & Ward, 2006) and more than 100 intervention studies based on psychological skills within and beyond sport psychology journals between 1960 and 2006 (Gardner & Moore, 2006). A third reason is that more than a decade ago Hardy and Jones (1994) called for the development of valid and reliable measures of psychological skills. Hopefully, this chapter constitutes a useful response to this call. A final reason is that the topic is likely to be representative of sport and exercise psychology in terms of self-report methods used.

Literature Search

A literature search was undertaken to identify research studies published in 2008 (the year preceding the preparation of this chapter) concerning psychological skill use by sport performers. Focusing on a single year of published studies might yield unrepresentative results. However, a review of studies of psychological skill use published in every year since 1970 finds 2008 to be representative. The literature search sought peer-reviewed full articles involving one or more empirical studies yielding results providing insight into the use of one or more psychological skills by a sport population. Using the criterion that the results rather than the objectives presented in the articles were related to psychological skills not only enabled the inclusion of studies directly focused on psychological skills but also allowed the inclusion of studies involving an objective to explore topics other than psychological skills that had yielded results relating to these skills. The search was constrained to journals (a) listed on the ISI Web of Science and (b) focused on the publication of studies in sport psychology. These were as follows: *International Journal of Sport Psychology*, *Journal of Applied Sport Psychology*, *Journal of Sport and Exercise Psychology*, *Journal of Sports Sciences*, *Psychology of Sport and Exercise*, *Research Quarterly for Exercise and Sport*, and *The Sport Psychologist*.

The extant studies of psychological skills have made noteworthy contributions to the current understanding of psychological preparation for competition. The objective of this review is not to discredit these contributions but simply to offer guidelines on how to improve the methods used in these studies. Furthermore, it might be proposed that critiquing studies of psychological skill use using a methodological framework that has not been adopted within any of the studies being critiqued is inappropriate and even unfair. Nonetheless, it is proposed that this review can expose important shortcomings of the current methods used within (and beyond) studies of psychological skill use. This will likely promote further studies of psychological skills that are informed by this review and thus offer stricter tests of current hypotheses about the use of these skills by sport performers.

Classification

The literature search identified 16 studies of psychological skill use published in 5 of the 7 journals reviewed (see table 11.1); no relevant studies were published in the *International Journal of Sport Psychology* or the *Journal of Sport and Exercise Psychology*. Each identified study was subsequently examined in terms of the population studied, the method employed, and the psychological skills featured. Studies involving the use of a verbal self-report method were classified according to Ericsson and Simon's (1980) framework. First, each study was inspected to identify whether participants were *undirected*, meaning they were asked to simply report or recall their thoughts and experiences (from here on just *thoughts*), or *directed*, meaning they were asked to report on some specific aspect of their thinking. Second, each study was classified in terms of whether participants were probed by the experimenter to provide reports about their thinking (a) during a particular episode (a *particular report*), (b) during multiple episodes or over an extended time (a *general report*), or (c) during a type of episode (or some broader class of episodes, such as the entire athletic career; see Ericsson, 2006, p. 230) in general (a *report on general states*).

Next, the studies were classified in terms of whether the elicited reports (in the form of raw quotes appearing within the study) provided evidence of (a) a particular report, (b) a general report, or (c) a report on general states. Finally, if a study involved the elicitation of particular or general reports, it was classified in terms of whether the reports were provided (a) during the episode of interest (a *concurrent report*), (b) retrospectively immediately after the episode of interest but before any similar episode was experienced (an *immediate retrospective report*), or (c) retrospectively after the

episode of interest when it was likely other similar episodes had been experienced (a *delayed retrospective report*).

Table 11. on page 110 displays the results of the classification exercise. The first key finding is that of the 16 studies, all involved a self-report method. Only 1 of these also involved an alternative method (study 8 in table 11.1). Second, of the 16 studies, 14 made use of an interview method (the exceptions were studies 7 and 10). The review begins with a discussion of the studies using an interview and follows with a discussion of the studies using a questionnaire.

Results Relating to Interviews

Two studies that were considered to involve an interview actually involved surveys comprising open-ended questions (studies 1 and 4). Inspection of each survey revealed that the surveys essentially functioned as interviews, so, for the purpose of this chapter, the two studies were considered to involve an interview.

Use of Undirected Versus Directed Probes

Of the 14 studies involving an interview, 12 provided evidence of using directed probes only or at least provided constraints within the interview so that participants reported on the topic of interest (the exceptions were studies 9 and 16). Recall that Ericsson and Simon (1980) proposed that level 1 and 2 verbalizations are more likely to occur when an undirected probe is used. For example, in study 1 (Buman, Omli, Giacobbi, & Brewer, 2008), there was interest in identifying how marathon runners cope when they hit the wall. The question used was, "When you hit the wall, what do you do to try to cope with it?" (p. 286). An undirected probe could have been used by first asking the participants if they could recall with definiteness a marathon event in which they felt as if they had hit the wall. If such an event could be recalled with definiteness, then the participants could be asked if they could recall with definiteness any thoughts experienced during this episode. Such a question avoids constraining the participant to report only about coping efforts. The experimenter could then decide whether the elicited reports were consistent with coping efforts, perhaps on the basis of hypotheses derived from coping theory about what kind of reports are consistent with coping.

Of the two remaining studies using an interview method, one provided no description of the interview protocol (study 16). The other (study 9) appeared to use directed probes such as "Was this

■ Table 11.1 ■

Classification of Studies on Use of Psychological Skills Undertaken in 2008 According to the Verbal Report Framework Proposed by Ericsson and Simon (1980)

Study number	Authors and year	Populations	Psychological skills featured	Method	Undirected versus directed	Particular versus general reports versus general states: Type of report probed	Predominant elicited report type	For particular and general reports, concurrent versus immediate retrospective versus delayed retrospective
JOURNAL OF APPLIED SPORT PSYCHOLOGY								
1	Buman, Omli, Giacobbi, & Brewer (2008)	57 marathon runners	Goal setting, imagery, relaxation, self-talk	Internet survey	Directed	General states	General reports and states	General reports: delayed retrospective; delay time not specified
2	Gucciardi, Gordon, & Dimmock (2008)	11 coaches	Goal setting	Interview	Directed	General states	General states	—
3	Jones & Harwood (2008)	5 soccer players	Goal setting, relaxation	Interview	Directed	General states	General states	—
4	Nordin & Cumming (2008)	144 dancers and 124 aesthetic athletes (e.g., artistic gymnasts)	Imagery	Sport Imagery Questionnaire (SIQ), Dance Imagery Questionnaire (DIQ), and survey	Directed	Questionnaires and survey: general states	Questionnaires: assumed general states Survey: general states	—
JOURNAL OF SPORTS SCIENCES								
5	Connaughton, Wadey, Hanton, & Jones (2008)	7 athletes from a variety of sports	Goal setting, imagery, self-talk	Interview	Directed	General states	Particular and general reports and general states	Particular and general reports: delayed retrospective; delay time not specified
6	Mellalieu, Hanton, & Shearer (2008)	2 rugby union players	Imagery, self-talk	Interview	Directed	General states	General states	—
7	Munroe-Chandler, Hall, & Fishburne (2008)	122 soccer players	Imagery	Sport Imagery Questionnaire for Children (SIQ-C)	Directed	General states	Assumed general states	—

8	Fournier, Deremaux, & Bernier (2008)	Experiment 1: 2 skydivers / Experiment 2: 32 skydivers	Imagery	Experiment 1: interview / Experiment 2: verbal self-report method not used	Experiment 1: directed	Experiment 1: general states	Experiment 1: general states	—
9	Nieuwenhuys, Hanin, & Bakker (2008)	1 sailor	Goal setting	Interview	Undirected and directed	Particular report	General reports and general states	General reports: delayed retrospective; delay time not specified
10	Kee & Wang (2008)	182 athletes in various sports	Goal setting, imagery, relaxation, self-talk	Test of Performance Strategies (TOPS) questionnaire	Directed	General states	Assumed general states	—
RESEARCH QUARTERLY FOR EXERCISE AND SPORT								
11	Wadey & Hanton (2008)	15 athletes in various sports	Goal setting, imagery, relaxation, self-talk	Interview	Directed	General states	General states	—
THE SPORT PSYCHOLOGIST								
12	Hanton, Wadey, & Mellalieu (2008)	8 elite performers	Goal setting, imagery, relaxation, self-talk	Interview and Test of Performance Strategies (TOPS) questionnaire	Directed	Interview and questionnaire: general states	Interview and questionnaire: general states	—
13	Hare, Evans, & Callow (2008)	1 athlete from an aquatic sport	Imagery	Interview and Athletic Injury Imagery Questionnaire (AIIQ)	Directed	Interview: general reports / Questionnaire: general states	Interview: general reports / Questionnaire: assumed general states	General reports: delayed retrospective; delay time not specified
14	MacPherson, Collins, & Morriss (2008)	4 javelin throwers	Imagery	Interview	Directed	General reports	General states	—
15	Thelwell, Weston, Greenlees, & Hutchings (2008)	13 coaches in various sports	Goal setting, imagery, relaxation, self-talk	Interview	Directed	General states	General states	—
16	Tremayne & Ballinger (2008)	2 ballroom dancers	Imagery, relaxation	Interview	Unspecified	Unspecified	Particular report and general states	Particular report: delayed retrospective; delay time not specified

. . . situation . . . helpful or harmful for your performance?" as well as undirected probes (or at least less directed probes) such as "What did you think when that happened?" (Nieuwenhuys, Hanin, & Bakker, 2008, p. 66).

Type of Report Probed

Of the 13 studies that involved an interview *and* provided some description of the interview protocol, 12 predominantly involved probes for general states (study 9 was the exception and is discussed later). Ericsson and Simon (1980) proposed that level 1 and 2 verbalizations are more likely if probes are used for verbal reports about particular episodes. For example, in study 5 (Connaughton, Wadey, Hanton, & Jones, 2008), there was interest in identifying "the perceived underlying mechanisms responsible" for maintaining mental toughness (p. 85). While the exact questions posed to the participants were not provided, it can be inferred from the description of the interview guide that participants were asked about how mental toughness is maintained in general (see p. 85). A more preferable design would involve first asking participants to recall situations that were highly stressful and demanding and thus might be hypothesized to require mental toughness. Participants would then be asked to recall any thoughts experienced during these episodes, again with the hypothesis that their reports should contain the thoughts making up the cognitive strategies (i.e., psychological skills) being used to cope during these episodes.

Study 9 differed from the other 12 studies (i.e., those that made use of an interview method and provided some description of the interview protocol) in that the participant was directed to recall a particular episode: "The interview started by asking the participant to remember a very good race that he sailed in the past . . ." (Nieuwenhuys et al., 2008, p. 66). Thus, this was the only study that involved a probe to provide a particular report. Nonetheless, further inspection of the interview protocol revealed the use of other probes directing the participants to describe and explain their thoughts: "Was this (or were these) [situations, thoughts, or feelings] helpful or harmful for your performance?" (Nieuwenhuys et al., 2008, p. 66). This question likely introduced information into the participant's reports that was not part of the actual thoughts being recalled—that is, it likely led to level 3 verbalization. In contrast, Ericsson and Simon (1980) recommended that the participant should report only on thoughts that can be recalled with definiteness and should not attempt to explain, justify, or qualify those thoughts.

Elicited Report Type

Inspection of the raw quotes provided in the 14 studies that involved an interview revealed that the studies on average contained 20.14 quotes (minimum = 1, maximum = 33, and sum = 282). In 13 of these studies, participants predominantly provided reports on general states. This finding is probably owing in part to the predominant use of probes for general states (study 9 was the exception and is discussed later). Of these 13 studies, 9 contained quotes that provided evidence only of reports on general states (the exceptions were studies 1, 5, 13, and 16). Stated alternatively, these studies provided no evidence of a participant having recalled any actual thought from any specific episode. For example, the opening line of the first quote from study 8 (Fournier, Deremaux, & Bernier, 2008) provides evidence of reports on general states: "When I visualize from the ground, I have to learn the order of the formation of the sequence [of skydiving]" (p. 740). Recall that according to Ericsson and Simon (1980), reports on general states have the least validity of the report types within their framework, as these reports bear "no relation" to previously heeded information (p. 224). The remaining four studies (studies 1, 5, 13, and 16), while still predominated by reports on general states ($n = 66$ across the four studies), also contained a smaller number of general reports ($n = 12$) and particular reports ($n = 2$).

Study 5 (Connaughton et al., 2008) contained quotes providing evidence of particular reports, general reports, and reports on general states. Thus study 5 provides an opportunity to contrast these reports. An example of a report on a general state from the study is, "My psychological skills helped maintain my mental toughness. I used self-talk, I used controlled imagery, I set realistic goals, and I stopped negative thoughts and brought in positive ones" (p. 93). No evidence is provided within the quote that the participant recalled having a particular thought or thought process in (a) any specific series of episodes (e.g., a series of attempts to complete a section of river by a kayaker), which would constitute a general report, or (b) any single episode (e.g., a single attempt to complete a section of river by a kayaker), which would constitute a particular report. An example of a general report from the study is, "I just left a team with all my mates. It was difficult, as some of the boys had a go at me. They were saying I was glory hunting . . ." (p. 92). Here, there is evidence that the participant is recalling a specific experience but is doing so by generalizing across multiple episodes, which is evidenced in particular by "they were saying." Finally, an example of a quote from the study that comes closest to providing evidence of a particular report is, "I remember one of my first competitions where I dropped the ball. I started crying my eyes out. . . . I thought my world was going to cave in . . ." (p. 90). Here, the participant provides evidence of recalling a specific episode.

Recall that study 9 differed from the other 12 studies making use of an interview method and providing some description of the interview protocol in that the participant was probed to provide a particular report. However, the quotes presented in this study provided little evidence of particular reports: 4 out of 5 of the quotes contained evidence of general reports and the remaining quote contained evidence of general states. The following quote provides evidence that the participant is recalling thoughts experienced during a specific race but is generalizing about the thoughts experienced across the duration of the race. The experimenter asked, "What was the goal [in the race]?" The participant answered, "I don't know. I didn't make a clear decision about that. Things just happened. During the race I was thinking continuously" (p. 69).

Time of Original Episode

Quotes that provided evidence of particular or general reports (i.e., quotes from studies 1, 5, 9, 13, and 16) were inspected to identify when the episode recalled originally occurred. No study provided information about the length of the delay between the time of the original episode and the time of the report. However, it could be inferred from each quote that the delay was on the order of weeks, months, or years rather than minutes, hours, or days, which would have been preferable. Consequently, it is likely that other episodes similar to the recalled episode occurred during the delay and likely created substantial retroactive interference.

Results Relating to Questionnaires

Of the 16 studies within the review, 5 (studies 4, 7, 10, 12, and 13) employed a questionnaire that measured a performer's use of psychological skills. These questionnaires included the Athletic Injury Imagery Questionnaire-2 (AIIQ-2; Sordoni, Hall, & Forewell, 2002), Dance Imagery Questionnaire (DIQ; Nordin & Cumming, 2006), SIQ (Hall et al., 1998), Sport Imagery Questionnaire for Children (SIQ-C; Hall, Munroe-Chandler, Fishburne, & Hall, 2009), and TOPS (Thomas et al., 1999). One study (study 13) also included a questionnaire (the Vividness of Movement Imagery Questionnaire-2, or VMIQ-2; Roberts, Callow, Hardy, Markland, & Bringer, 2008) measuring an athlete's ability to image actions such

as jumping off a wall that are unlikely to directly represent actions within his or her sport . This questionnaire was not included in the review.

Inspection of the items from each questionnaire revealed that all the questionnaires essentially probed the participants to provide reports on general states. Consider the following items as examples: "I image alternative strategies in case my event/game plan fails" (from the SIQ). "I manage my self-talk effectively during competition" (from the TOPS). In addition, all of the items on the questionnaires were accompanied by a fixed set of alternative responses. Thus, even if participants did draw on an actual memory of a specific episode (despite being probed for a report on general states), they might have found no response within the set of response alternatives approximating any thought process recalled from the episode.

Summary of Methods Used in Studies of Psychological Skill Use With Regard to the Verbal Report Framework

In summary, most of the studies featured in the review provided few constraints on participants to provide level 1 and 2 verbalization. Most of the studies allowed or even constrained participants to provide reports on general states. General states are considered to have the least validity of the report types within the framework proposed by Ericsson and Simon (1980). So, if the participants in these studies were unlikely to be drawing on memories of specific thoughts experienced during a particular episode when providing their reports, what were they drawing on? Recall that Ericsson and Simon (1980) suggested that, in the best case, participants might be aware of the *general* strategies (psychological skills) they used during a particular episode or series of episodes, which they can recall and report directly and without reference to any specific instance within an episode when the strategy was actually applied. However, in the worst case, the participants might draw on information unrelated to any actual episode to generate a verbal report of a general procedure, such as information supplied by implicit causal theories, as described by Nisbett and Wilson (1977). It might be proposed that such theories are readily available within a sport performer's culture. Most modern performers have had some exposure to applied sport psychology and thus psychological skills. One hypothesis, then, is that when sport performers are presented with questions (i.e., directed probes) about mental toughness, psychological skills, or coping under stress, they may simply report what they have heard about and perhaps even think they use (Eccles & Ward, 2006).

Over the last 6 years, feedback has been requested from researchers of sport psychology about concerns over the predominant reliance on interview and questionnaire methods within studies of psychological skills. One researcher responded to the request by noting that studies of psychological skills have yielded consistent findings, one of which is that sport performers who are more skilled report greater use of psychological skills. The researcher proposed that this consistency can be considered good evidence that sport performers make use of psychological skills. The problem with this observation is that reliability is necessary but not sufficient for validity. Sport performers exposed to the same culture might draw on the same or similar implicit theories to provide their reports, which would result in similar (i.e., consistent) reports being elicited from multiple performers. Unfortunately, the reports would also be consistently invalid (Eccles & Ward, 2006).

Enhancing the Validity of Verbal Reports of Cognitive Processes by Using Concurrent and Immediate and Delayed Retrospective Report Methods

In this section, guidelines are proposed first for the use of concurrent and immediate retrospective methods and second for the use of a delayed retrospective report method. Further information on the use of these methods in general is available in Ericsson and Simon (1980, 1993). Information on the use of these methods in sport and exercise settings as well as in other domains involving human movement is available from Eccles via personal communication and published research (e.g., Calmeiro, Tenenbaum, & Eccles, 2010; McRobert, Eccles, Ward, & Williams, in press; McRobert, Williams, Ward, & Eccles, 2009; Ward, Suss, Eccles, Williams, & Harris, in press).

Guidelines for Using Concurrent and Immediate Retrospective Methods

These guidelines are provided through the use of a sample study undertaken by Jackson and Baker (2001). These authors examined psychological elements of the prekick routine of an elite rugby union goal kicker. The routine included the use of psychological skills. The routine was first examined at a

behavioral level by asking the participant to attempt kicks varying in difficulty on an empty rugby field and observing how kick difficulty affected the number of preparatory behaviors included within the routine. Behavioral measures included the number of physical steps taken between the point in time at which the participant placed the ball in the kicking tee and the point in time at which he assumed a kicking stance, along with the duration of this phase. They also included the number of glances from the ball to the goalposts between the point in time at which he assumed a kicking stance and the point in time at which he attempted the kick, along with the duration of this phase. Following this testing, the authors interviewed the participant in the clubhouse of the rugby ground about the psychological skills he incorporated into his prekick routine. Finally, Jackson and Baker also obtained the same behavioral measures from film of the participant's kicks in real games in an attempt to establish the ecological validity of their test condition.

Although Jackson and Baker (2001) provided no examples of the questions asked of the participant during the interview, it can be inferred that, as in most of the studies described in the previous sections, the questions involved probes that were both directed and for reports of general states, such as, "What type of psychological or mental skills and strategies do you use as part of your prekick routine?" The quotes from the participant provided in the paper support this inference: Of the 13 quotes presented, all provided evidence of reports of general states, such as, "I imagine putting all my problems into a black box, and closing the black box and putting them behind me out of the way" (p. 59).

So, with knowledge of the framework proposed by Ericsson and Simon (1980), how might the design of this study be altered to enhance the validity of the participant's verbal reports of his cognitive strategies during his prekick routine? There are various options, and these could be used jointly in an attempt to provide converging evidence of his cognitive strategies. First, during a subset of the kicking trials, the participant could be asked to provide concurrent verbal reports of his thinking. Preliminary training in how to provide such concurrent reports by thinking aloud, including warm-up exercises, should be provided to the participant before testing (Ericsson, 2002, p. 983). Such training typically involves an initial description of what thinking aloud entails and how this way of reporting differs from normal conversation. This is then followed by an exercise that demonstrates the difference between reporting aloud and conversing.

A simplified version of this exercise is described as follows. The participant is asked to think aloud, as if he is alone, as he answers the following question: "What is the fourth letter in the alphabet after the letter *L*?" In normal conversation, there is a social imperative to augment normal thought processes with explanations. Thus, even with the instruction to think aloud as if alone in the room, the presence of the experimenter can lead the participant to interpret or explain his thoughts at the first attempt to answer the question. This might sound something like, "Emm, you want me to find the fourth letter after *L*, well, I'm just going to count forward from *L*, ermm, *M*, that's one, *N, O, P*, the letter is *P*." To demonstrate how thinking aloud differs from this, the experimenter could ask the participant to pose the same question to the experimenter but to choose a different starting letter. Imagine that the participant chooses the starting letter *D*. The experimenter could think aloud as she generates the answer, which might sound something like, "The fourth letter after *D*, ermm, *E, F, G, H*, it's *H*." The experimenter could then invite the participant to try similar problems so that he can gain practice thinking aloud. A few trials are usually required for a participant to be able to reliably think aloud. Once this has been achieved, he could then be invited to think aloud during the criterion task, which in this case is the prekick routine. Other useful considerations for training include having the experimenters position themselves out of sight to reduce the participant's natural tendency to provide explanations during thinking and to ensure that the participant understands that it is not only acceptable but also preferable that he report nothing if he can recall nothing.

A second option for enhancing the validity of the participant's verbal reports of cognitive strategies during the prekick routine is to ask the participant to provide an immediate retrospective report of thinking after each trial within a subset of the kick trials. Ericsson (2006) proposed that participants are unlikely to recall with definiteness all thoughts experienced during a task when the duration of the task lasts longer than 10 s and certainly when the task lasts longer than 30 s. Thus, the duration of the prekick preparation routine meets this requirement. Like the provision of a concurrent report, the provision of an immediate retrospective report requires initial training. The goal of the training is for the participant to be able to simply report those thoughts he can recall with definiteness from the immediate preceding trial and without explaining those thoughts. A third option, which can be contrasted with the interview undertaken by Jackson and Baker (2001), is to ask the participant after the

testing phase to provide a delayed retrospective report of a very recent kick in competition. This report should follow the guidelines described in the next section.

Guidelines for Using a Delayed Retrospective Report

A delayed retrospective report may be used to elicit recalled thoughts from a recent episode (Eccles et al., 2005). The basics of eliciting such a report are as follows. First, a target episode or episodes should be identified. For example, consider that a study objective is to identify thoughts experienced following major errors in sailboat races (Nieuwenhuys et al., 2008), perhaps to identify psychological skills used to cope and refocus after errors are made. The participant should then be directed to identify a very recent (to minimize retroactive interference) sailboat race in which he can recall having made an important error.

Next, there is an attempt to identify a target time within the episode that is short enough (ideally under 10 s but certainly under 30 s; Ericsson, 2006) for the participant to be able to recall thoughts during that time. In the sailboat race example, the participant could be directed to recall when the important error was committed within the race. If the error was committed as the participant rounded the fourth buoy, the target time might begin immediately before the error was committed and end a few seconds after the error was committed. If so, the participant should be asked to report any thoughts that can be recalled immediately before committing the error. The next step involves asking the participant to report the next thought he can recall with definiteness, and the participant is asked to recall successive thoughts in an attempt to trace the thought process across the target time. Once again, the participant should understand that it is not only acceptable but also preferable to report nothing if nothing can be recalled. As with concurrent and immediate retrospective reports, eliciting a delayed retrospective report benefits from initial training.

Concerns Over Using Verbal Report Methods

Over the last 6 years, feedback has been solicited from researchers within sport and exercise psychology on the proposed use of the verbal report methods outlined here for tracing the cognitive processes of sport performers. Two concerns have been expressed by these researchers; these concerns are addressed here. Two other concerns, raised in an excellent review of this chapter, are also addressed here.

Concerns About Automaticity

Some researchers have voiced concerns that sport performers, especially those at the skilled and expert level, might report few if any thoughts (or recall few if any thoughts in retrospective cases) owing to the decreased conscious control of their actions. This leaves the researcher with few data and thus few insights into a performer's thinking. These researchers certainly have a valid point; increases in automaticity are likely to lead to decreases in reportable information. The current alternative, however, is to interview or provide a questionnaire to participants about their thoughts. In these cases, the participant is presented with strong social constraints to respond—but, if the performance during the episode was largely automatic, the participant will be able to draw on few if any memories of actual thoughts to provide a response. As stated earlier, these alternative available means of reporting all involve level 3 verbalization. Thus, it is proposed here that it is better to elicit a few good data points via the verbal report method than many poor data points by the available alternative methods.

Concerns About Reactivity

Another concern is that the performance of the primary task might be affected by concurrent thinking aloud. Reviews of studies that have involved this method for evidence of such reactivity have revealed that, while the method tends to increase the time required to complete the primary task, it seldom affects the structure of the thought processes involved in the task or the actual task performance in terms of accuracy (Ericsson & Simon, 1993; Fox, Ericsson, & Best, 2011). Thus, while the slowing effect might make the method inappropriate for certain situations (e.g., performance during competition), it does not restrict its use in many other situations such as task simulations of the kind used in Jackson and Baker's (2001) study of the rugby goal kicker. Also, checks for reactivity can be made by comparing various behavioral measures of task performance between trials that include a concurrent report and trials that do not. For example, regarding the goal kicker study, reactivity could be explored by comparing kick trials that include a concurrent verbal report and kick trials that do not in terms of behavioral measurements of the kick routine (e.g., number and latencies of steps and glances) and actual kick performance.

Epistemological Issues

A reviewer of the chapter suggested that concerns over the validity of verbal reports are not an issue for many researchers who reject realist notions of cognition, validity, memory, and verbal reports. Researchers influenced by social constructionism, poststructuralism, or discursive psychology assert that thoughts cannot be captured in the sense outlined here. By contrast, they can only be constructed.

These concerns apply to the extent that researchers within sport and exercise psychology adopt these philosophies of science and consequently reject realist notions of cognition. However, the majority of researchers within the field do not adopt these philosophies. They adopt, often implicitly, a more traditional philosophy of science grounded in positivism and empiricism, likely because this philosophy predominates within psychology in general, and most researchers in the field are trained in this philosophy. While researchers within sport and exercise psychology have often turned to qualitative research methods as a means of investigation, which has occasionally exposed them to alternative epistemologies, they have in general used these methods with the belief that more or less valid information will be obtained, consistent with the traditional approach (see Sparkes, 1998).

For example, the research on psychological skills is clearly underpinned by theoretical frameworks from mainstream psychology and from cognitive and experimental psychology in particular—psychologies that are characterized by the traditional approach to science. Furthermore, historically there has been concern within sport and exercise psychology with issues of validity in relation to sport performers' recall of performance episodes (e.g., Brewer, Linder, Van Raalte, & Van Raalte, 1991). There is also evidence of these concerns within the studies featured in the review undertaken here (e.g., Mellalieu, Hanton, & Shearer, 2008, p. 814). Thus, while researchers in sport and exercise psychology remain interested in issues of validity, as it has been construed traditionally, the methods proposed here should be of interest to them.

No One Best Way

A reviewer of the chapter suggested that it might read like a prescription or like the one best way for using self-report methods. This is not the intent for this chapter. Certainly, other useful and meritorious methods exist. Nonetheless, many of these approaches have an established history within sport and exercise psychology, whereas there has been little if any consideration within the field of the methods outlined here and how these methods might inform and enhance the design of studies that involve self-report data.

Conclusion

While it might be tempting to rely solely on participants' reports of their cognitive processes in an attempt to understand, for example, how a participant decides to pass versus keep the ball or to change at the last minute from choosing a healthy option to choosing fast food, the state of the science suggests that these reports may be of limited validity except under specific conditions. This chapter describes these conditions and then demonstrates how an increased understanding of collecting verbal reports within sport and exercise psychology might enhance the quality of studies within the field. Guidelines and examples are provided for designing studies that create these conditions and thus afford the elicitation and capture of valid verbal reports of cognitive processes. It is hoped that the methods described here will afford researchers of sport and exercise psychology new insights into how to enhance the quality of the verbal report data they collect.

Acknowledgments

The author would like to thank Dr. Brett Smith for his insightful and constructive comments on an earlier version of this chapter. The writing of this chapter was made possible in part by generous support to the author from the Financial Industry Regulatory Authority Investor Education Foundation, grant number 2007-06-015.

12

Making Sense of Words and Stories in Qualitative Research

Strategies for Consideration

Brett Smith, PhD, and Andrew C. Sparkes, PhD

Qualitative researchers draw on numerous sources of data to make meaning of the world of sport and exercise. One source is words, which become stories. In this chapter, we explore a number of ways in which researchers might make sense of the stories told to them. These ways can be placed under the umbrella of *analysis*. As Amis (2006) commented, the purpose of analysis is "to make sense of the data that rapidly accumulates" (p. 128). Likewise, for Patton (1990), "analysis involve[s] making sense out of what people have said, looking for patterns, putting together what is said in one place with what is said in another place, and integrating what different people have to say" (p. 347). All this is supported by Coffey and Atkinson (1996) and Gubrium and Holstein (2008), who argue that in terms of making sense of stories, researchers should turn their analytical attention not only to *what* is told in stories but also to *how* stories are told. This is because stories have two sides to them: the *whats* and the *hows*. Thus, in relation to enhancing, enriching, and expanding our sense making, an important goal of analysis is to understand both *what* is said in stories and *how* stories are told.

Therefore, in this chapter we consider four ways in which the stories sport and exercise psychologists elicit and collect as researchers or applied practitioners can be analyzed to incorporate the *whats* and the *hows* of their telling. These are a hierarchical content analysis, a thematic narrative analysis, a performative analysis, and a creative analytical practice (CAP). Exemplars of each approach are pro-

vided to give a flavor of how each form of analysis works to make sense of the stories people tell. First the hierarchical content analysis and the thematic narrative analysis are highlighted. These analyses focus mainly on the *whats* of narrative. Next we consider performative analysis, an approach that focuses on the *hows* of narrative. Expanding our analytical attention further, we then explore CAP, a way of making sense that incorporates an analysis of both *what* people say and *how* they say it.

Before turning to each analysis, it must be recognized that other analyses do exist that can help us make sense of stories we hear. In qualitative work these include discourse analyses, visual analyses, interpretive phenomenological analyses, and grounded theories. Since it is beyond the scope of this chapter to explore all analyses available to sport and exercise psychologists, the ones explored here are intended to be illuminative rather than definitive. In addition, we do not privilege any one analysis outlined here over another. As Coffey and Atkinson (1996) have remarked, there are no formulae for the best or right way to analyze the stories we collect. This, however, should not be seen as a problem. On the contrary, as Coffey and Atkinson noted, one of the strengths of thinking about our data as stories is that doing so opens up possibilities for using a variety of analytical strategies.

With the aforementioned points in mind, we can now turn our attention to the delights and dilemmas of a variety of analyses that sport and exercise psychologists might use to make sense of stories in ways that explore *what* is told and *how* it is told. Our hope in focusing on these ways of making sense is to widen our analytical scope within qualitative inquiry and to expand, enable, and enrich our abilities to make sense of qualitative data within our field.

Analyzing the *Whats*: Content

Content analysis, as Lieblich, Tuval-Mashiach, and Zilber (1998) pointed out, has many variations. For example, depending on the purpose of the study, the narrative materials, practical considerations, and personal preferences, the stories we collect as researchers or applied practitioners may be processed analytically by subjecting them to either *descriptive* and *interpretive* treatment or *measurement* and *statistical* treatment. Furthermore, some variations of content analysis are supported by an *interpretivist paradigm*, while others are guided by a *postpositivist paradigm*. As Lieblich and colleagues (1998) put it, preference for one variation of content analysis over another is related to the researcher's adherence to "criteria of objectivity and quantitative processing, on the one hand, as opposed to hermeneutic and qualitative perspectives on the other" (p. 112). Thus, we need to talk about content analysis in the plural as opposed to the singular. Knowing there are variations in content analysis also means that we need to articulate and recognize the differences among each type of analysis.

At the same time, it needs to be recognized that while there are variations among types of content analysis, points of contact do exist. All content analyses share a concern with the *whats* of storytelling. As part of this concern, the analytical lens of each focuses on an analysis *of* stories (Polkinghorne, 1995; Smith & Sparkes, 2009). Instead of analytically foregrounding the position that analysis *is* the story and thereby producing an actual story, an analysis *of* narratives uses stories as data, and the outcomes of the analysis are paradigmatic categories, classifications, or typologies. In conducting an analysis *of* what is said, the researcher is also called on to think *about* the stories collected rather than *with* them (Frank, 1995). That is, a story in the analytical process is thought of as an object and the researcher seeks to reduce the story to content and then abstractly analyze that content.

With these variations, differences, and points of contact in mind, hierarchical content analysis is one type of content analysis sport and exercise psychologists might use to make sense of the sea of words and stories they swim in.

Hierarchical Content Analysis

A hierarchical content analysis is a popular way of analyzing qualitative data. The analyst using this variation of a content analysis makes sense of the *whats* of talk by subjecting these data to measurement procedures and quantifying its content. For example, by measuring what is said in the data in relation to a specific unit of meaning, the analyst using a hierarchical content analysis seeks to identify first-order or subthemes in the data and then categorize these themes into larger, more inclusive groupings termed *second-order* or *higher-order themes* and *general dimensions*. The researcher also seeks to represent these themes in a matrix or treelike format (e.g., see table 12.1). Furthermore, the procedures used in hierarchical content analysis and the ways these are articulated often (but certainly not always) suggest a (post)positivist-like commitment to reliability, method as a repository of procedural objectivity, techniques for sorting out trustworthy from untrustworthy interpretations of data, and a psychological reality that can be found and known, at least in principle, independently of the researcher. That is, a hierarchical content analysis is positioned within what Sparkes and Smith (2009) termed a *criteriologist* standpoint.

A hierarchical content analysis is the most popular way to make sense of qualitative data within the field of sport and exercise psychology. It appeared initially in the work of Scanlan, Stein, and Ravizza (1989) and has since been employed by numerous researchers in the field, including Eklund (1996); Gould, Eklund, and Jackson (1992a, 1992b); Gould, Tuffey, Udry, and Loehr (1996); Bianco, Malo, and Orlick (1999); Gammage, Hardy, and Hall (2001); and, more recently, Lally (2007); Martinent and Ferrand (2009); and McKay, Niven, Lavallee, and White (2009). A good recent illustration of a hierarchical content analysis within sport and exercise psychology is provided by Bertollo, Saltarelli, and Robazza (2009) in their work on mental preparation strategies and coping responses that elite modern pentathletes display across precompetition, competition, and postcompetition.

Following interviews with six women and eight men, Bertollo and colleagues (2009) subjected the qualitative data to hierarchical content analysis. For them, this "procedure attempts to provide reliability, credibility, and trustworthiness to the qualitative data" (p. 246). As part of this procedure and implied move toward a criteriologist standpoint, each investigator independently identified raw data themes (quotes or paraphrased quotes that captured the major ideas conveyed) characterizing each interviewee's responses within each subsection of the interview (i.e., mental preparation strategies and behaviors the days preceding the event, before competition, during competition, and after competition). The raw data were tagged to obtain a set of concepts representative of the information included in the interview transcripts. Furthermore, the authors independently grouped the raw data themes into meaningful categories that seemed to fit together. This analysis resulted in a grouping of raw data themes within categories of greater generality (subthemes). These themes were subsequently classified into more inclusively meaningful groupings (higher-order themes and general dimensions), with each given a title deemed to represent the themes contained within each category. Bertollo and colleagues also commented that consensus among the investigators was reached at all levels of analysis, and they verified that all themes and categories were represented.

▪ Table 12.1 ▪

Sub-Themes, Higher-Order Themes, and General Dimensions Related to Mental Preparation Strategies and Behaviors Just Before the Event

Sub-themes	Higher-order themes (a/c)	General dimensions
Focusing on technique	Focusing on technique (8/24)	Emotion control
Keeping calm	Reappraisal (10/14)	
Decreasing worry		
Emotional detachment	Emotional detachment (9/12)	
	Attenuation of emotional symptoms (8/15)	
Maintaining relaxation	Attenuation of emotional symptoms (8/15)	
Decreasing tension		
Maintaining tension	Intensification of emotional symptoms (4/8)	
Increasing tension		
Increasing relaxation or tension	Increasing relaxation or tension (3/5)	
Anticipating competition tasks	Anticipation of the competition (11/27)	Mental practice
Rehearsing optimal execution		
Insecurity	Anticipation of difficulties (8/15)	
Strong opponent		
Fatigue		
Self-talk	Self-talk (2/6)	
Consistent warm-up	Warm-up and seclusion (10/10)	Precompetitive routines
Competition focus and seclusion		
Bodily check-up	Bodily check-up (7/10)	
Muscular relaxation	Relaxation for shooting (6/10)	
Breathing		
Behavioral strategies	Behavioral strategies (6/10)	

Adapted from Bertollo et al. 2009.

In relation to mental preparation before competition, for example, the hierarchical content analysis conducted by Bertollo and colleagues (2009) of mental preparation strategies and behaviors athletes adopted before competition yielded 166 raw data themes, which "were classified into 21 sub-themes, and 13 higher-order themes. Similar higher-order themes were grouped into three general dimensions: (1) Emotion control; (2) Mental practice; and (3) Pre-competitive routines" (p. 248). These results are shown in table 12.1.

As demonstrated by Bertollo and colleagues (2009) and many others (e.g., Gould et al., 1996; McKay et al., 2009), for certain purposes a hierarchical content analysis is eminently useful. It holds a number of strengths that make it appealing for sport and exercise psychologists to use in making sense of the stories told to them in interviews, fieldwork, visual materials, and so on. For example, the analyst using a hierarchical content analysis organizes the data into meaningful themes and categories by employing a relatively linear set of prescribed step-by-step procedures. This means that sport and exercise psychologists are provided with a standardized, formulaic, recipe-like way to make sense of stories. For some researchers, therefore, a hierarchical analysis might be an attractive way to make sense of data, as it provides a clear and preset procedure to follow. Furthermore, given that a hierarchical content analysis is often talked about in ways that suggest a commitment to objectivity, to procedures that can sort out trustworthy from untrustworthy interpretations, and to a psychological reality that through methods can be made contact with independently of our knowledge and interests, this type of content analysis may appeal to researchers who commit to postpositivism. Moreover, a hierarchical content analysis focuses on the *whats* of storytelling in such a way that it can assist in developing general knowledge about the themes that make up the content of the stories collected. In a hierarchical content inductive analysis, as with a computer-generated factor analysis, the building process of creating themes and developing general knowledge is iterative.

Despite such strengths, a hierarchical content analysis, like any analysis, has a number of weaknesses. For example, a hierarchical content analysis tends to wash out the contextual nature of storytelling and the messiness of people's experiences. In aggregating lives in higher-order categories, it also washes out the quality of embodiment, thereby disembodying psychological phenomena. Likewise, we gain little sense of the participant's life history and how this history shapes the content of

storytelling. In developing hierarchical themes, the researcher often trades breadth for depth, resolution for scope, and thick description for thin description. Furthermore, there is the risk of deconstructing stories to the extent that what makes a story a story is lost. Additionally, in a hierarchical content analysis the *whats* of storytelling are the central concern. As significant as this contribution is, the equally important *hows* of stories are placed in the background.

Regarding the issue of validity and the problem of sorting out good sense making from not-so-good sense making, a researcher using a hierarchical content analysis often (but not always) adopts a criteriologist position. For example, to sort out trustworthy from untrustworthy interpretations, the researcher often appeals to and advocates specific procedures, as outlined by Lincoln and Guba (1985), including member checks and triangulation. However, there are several serious problems with Lincoln and Guba's positioning. It is beyond the scope of this chapter to detail all the problems and to specify how Lincoln and Guba's work in relation to validity and a criteriologist position is, for some, seriously flawed (see Sparkes & Smith, 2009). It is sufficient to say that Lincoln and Guba's work is philosophically contradictory. On the one hand Lincoln and Guba accept a world of multiple, constructed, and mind-dependent realities (ontological relativism), but on the other hand they espouse epistemological foundationalism in the form of procedures to sort out trustworthy from untrustworthy interpretations of reality. These two positions are *incompatible*. Attempts to square a philosophical circle lead to an untenable situation from which there are only two ways to escape: (1) The existence of foundations, of a reality independent and outside of ourselves that can be known objectively through the appropriate use of procedures, has to be confirmed, and this assumption (the reality) has to be cashed in to do its work of adjudication. (2) There has to be an acceptance that in a relativistic world of multiple mind-dependent realities there is no technical court of last resort to appeal to in order to sort out trustworthy interpretations from untrustworthy ones. Methods alone will not sort out the trustworthy from the untrustworthy. It is worth noting that Lincoln and Guba have significantly changed their position since 1985 and, in light of the criticisms of their work, have stated they would not now use techniques such as member checks in the ways they once proposed for judging the quality of research.

Thematic Narrative Analysis

Another type of content analysis is thematic narrative analysis, or what Lieblich and colleagues (1998) termed *categorical-content analysis* and Polkinghorne (1995) called a *paradigmatic analysis*. On one level, a thematic type of content analysis is very much like a hierarchical content analysis and like many other analytical approaches to making sense of data such as grounded theories and interpretive phenomenological analysis in that it is concerned primarily with content—with *what* is said in interviews, fieldwork, and so forth. Furthermore, like researchers using a hierarchical content analysis, researchers using a thematic analysis carry out an analysis *of* stories. Researchers in the analytical process also often think *about* the stories participants tell.

Despite the common strands, there are key differences between a thematic narrative analysis and a hierarchical content analysis. These differences do not call for hostile arguments over which analysis is superior. On the contrary, following Rorty (1982), they are differences that need to be recognized and lived with. One difference lies in the methodological assumptions that inform each type of analysis. Rather than being supported by (post)positivist assumptions, as is often the case in uses of a hierarchical content analysis, a thematic narrative analysis is often framed by interpretivist assumptions. Instead of adopting a criteriologist position, the researcher adopts a relativist position with regard to validity and judging good sense making from not-so-good sense making. That is, the researcher rejects any claims that we can gain access (via whatever analytical method) to a reality in ways that are independent of our interests, purposes, and languages. This being the case, the reality itself and the analytical method alone cannot provide a reference point for sorting out claims to knowledge or sorting trustworthy from untrustworthy research. Researchers adopting a relativist position when making sense of stories can only appeal to time- and place-contingent lists of characteristics to sort out good and trustworthy sense making from the not-so-good and untrustworthy sense making (see Sparkes & Smith, 2009; J. Smith, 2009). This means that when making sense of stories, researchers "must learn to live with uncertainty, with the absence of final vindications, with the hope of solutions in the form of epistemological guarantees" (Schwandt, 1996, p. 59). It means that when using and interpreting the results from a thematic analysis, we shift from analytical certainty to contingency (Smith, J., 2009).

A second difference relates to what counts as theme and the prevalence of a theme within each data item and across the entire data set. In a thematic analysis, more instances of a theme do not necessarily mean that the theme itself is crucial (Braun &

Clarke, 2006). There is no hard-and-fast answer to the question of what proportion of the data needs to display evidence of the theme for it to be considered a theme. In a thematic analysis, it is not the case that something present in 45% of data items is a theme while something present in only 25% of items is not a theme. Nor is it the case that a theme is something to which many data items—rather than just a sentence or two—give considerable attention. A theme might be given considerable space in some data items and little or no space in others, or it might appear in relatively little of the data set in a thematic analysis.

A third difference is that a thematic narrative analysis frequently seeks to illuminate the social context, however tentatively, rather than wash it out in the analysis. Fourth, there is an absence of clear and step-by-step guidelines around a thematic analysis, and there is no clear agreement about how to go about doing the analysis. Fifth, unlike a hierarchical content analysis, a thematic analysis is not a linear process of simply moving from one phase to the next. Instead, it is a more messy and recursive process, where movement is back and forth throughout the phases as needed. A sixth difference is that scholars who use a thematic narrative analysis often strive to preserve the sequence and wealth of detail contained in long sequences rather than thematically code segments and fracture data, as is customary in many other forms of qualitative analysis, such as a hierarchical content analysis, grounded theories, and interpretive phenomenological analysis.

A seventh difference between a thematic narrative analysis and a hierarchical content analysis flows from a case-centered commitment. The objective in using a hierarchical content analysis is often to generate inductively or deductively (or both) a set of stable concepts that can be used to theorize across cases. By contrast, as Riessman (2008) pointed out, a researcher using a thematic narrative analysis seeks to keep a story intact for interpretive purposes by theorizing from the case. Here, the researcher seeks themes, typologies, or instances of categories not just across but also within the narratives told by one person or by a number of people about a similar issue, such as experiences of flow or motivation to exercise. Thus, as Ezzy (2002) proposed, what often distinguishes a narrative thematic analysis is that it "refers to the whole of a person's account. The parts of the story become significant only as they are placed within the context of the whole narrative" (p. 95).

Accordingly, while both a thematic narrative analysis and a hierarchical content analysis focus on the *whats* of storytelling, they are not one and the same. Examples of researchers in sport and exercise using a thematic narrative analysis include Carless and Douglas (2009) and Jowett and Frost (2007). A thematic narrative analysis is also evident in the work of Smith and Sparkes (2005) in their study of 14 men who experienced a spinal cord injury through playing sport and stories of hope. After transcribing more than 200 h of interview data collected from these former athletes, Smith and Sparkes first assumed the posture of indwelling and immersed themselves in the data in order to understand the participants' points of view from an empathetic position. Next, they read through the transcripts again and identified narrative segments and categories within the data. Simultaneously, they wrote analytical memos that began to make tentative and preliminary connections to various theoretical concepts that they thought might be related to issues emerging from each participant's story. These memos and codes helped frame the questions and themes that were explored in the interviews as part of a recursive process. As the interviews progressed and data was accumulated, Smith and Sparkes searched for connections and themes across the narrative segments in an attempt to identify patterns and meanings as they emerged in a participant's story.

Using this thematic narrative analysis, Smith and Sparkes (2005) identified that for 2 of the 14 men in their sample, the most common kind of hope was what they termed *transcendent hope*. For 1 man, despair was prominent. For the remaining 11 men, concrete hope was most prominent, and this kind of hope operated to shape their lives in ways that instilled a strong belief that through a medical cure they could make a comeback and return to their past body–self relationships and ways of being in the world. The following comments illuminate this concrete hope:

> Interviewer: Did you ever think that you might one day become disabled through rugby?
>
> Eamonn: No, never. I knew there was the possibility that it could happen, and I've heard of it happening to people. But I never thought it would happen to me. You don't, otherwise you'd never play. So becoming disabled was not what I expected, and when it happened I lost everything. It was, *is*, such a huge crisis and because of it I've lost my life. So, everyday I tell myself that I'll walk again. That's what gets me out of bed in the morning. I don't work and don't play sport anymore. So, what do I really have to look forward to? Well, I have hope. It's about every single day hoping that I'll walk again. Which might sound crazy to some people but at least in this miserable existence I have hope . . . I look forward to the day when I can get everything back that I had before the accident. Stand, and walk. So, really,

the main thing that keeps me going is the hope that I'll recover. Hope that medicine will keep progressing and find a cure. Hope that there will be an end to all this. (Smith & Sparkes, 2005, p. 1097)

According to Smith and Sparkes (2005), one potential strength of a thematic narrative analysis, and thus one reason for using it, lies in its capacity to develop general knowledge about the core themes that make up the stories collected with a view to identifying narrative segments and categories not just across but *within* people's stories. Likewise, because the researchers strive to preserve the wealth of detail contained in long sequences and to place themes of interest within the context of the whole story a person tells, over time they can become sensitized to the content world in which development of key events or interested areas of thematic focus (e.g., stress) takes place. The researcher using this kind of analysis may also identify unanticipated phenomena and influences and generate meaningful core ideas about a specific psychological phenomenon grounded in people's stories.

Another potential strength of a thematic narrative analysis is its flexibility. This method has few prescribed or preset steps and recipe-like procedures, and the resulting flexibility allows for a wide range of analytical options. Therefore the potential range of things that can be said about the data is broad. Furthermore, as Phoenix and Howe (in press) demonstrated in their study of sport injury, researchers using thematic narrative analysis can illuminate the context of storytelling and how the context influences what things and to whom things are said. It can also sensitize researchers to evocative slices of human life, provide them with insights into the complexity of what experiences are meaningful for people, and help illuminate how lives are shaped from stories that circulate outside them, in their culture.

Thus a thematic narrative analysis has strengths that are lacking in many other analyses that focus on the *whats* of storytelling, such as a hierarchical analysis. However, thematic narrative analysis also has limitations. For example, by seeking themes in stories, researchers often miss the fine details and functionality of talk. Furthermore, while the flexibility of the method—which allows for a wide range of analytical options—is viewed as a strength by some, for others it is a weakness. In other words, the purposeful lack of a definitive way to go about doing a thematic narrative analysis can be a problem for some. The flexibility makes developing specific guidelines for higher-phase analysis difficult, and this can be troubling for the researcher trying to decide which aspects of the data deserve focus (Braun & Clarke, 2006). Another potential weakness is that a thematic analysis has limited interpretative power beyond mere description *if* it is not used within an existing theoretical framework that anchors the analytical claims being made. Furthermore, as Riessman (2008) pointed out, the role of investigators in constructing the narratives being analyzed tends to remain obscure. Finally, a thematic narrative analysis is not suited to all research questions. There is minimal focus on *how* a story is told. Thus, while the attention of a thematic analysis is directed to the substantive side of what is going on in talk, it's important not to forget the artful side of storytelling—that is, the *hows*.

Analyzing the *Hows*: Performative Narrative Analysis

In qualitative research in sport and exercise psychology, the dominant analytical focus has been on the *whats* of storytelling. However, as noted in the introduction, making sense of words and stories through qualitative analysis is as much about *how* things are said as about *what* things are said. There are various ways to explore the *hows* of talk. These include conversational analysis and various types of discourse analysis (see Locke, 2008; McGannon & Spence, in press). Another possible way to explore the *hows* is through a performative analysis or what is sometimes termed a *dialogical analysis* (Riessman, 2008). As when using content analyses, the researcher using this kind of analysis conducts an analysis *of* stories and often thinks *about* the story an athlete, coach, or exerciser tells. However, a performative analysis focuses on the *hows* of talk. This focus on the *hows* of the story in a performative analysis, as illustrated in sport psychology by Locke (2008) and Smith, Allen Collinson, Phoenix, Brown, and Sparkes (2009), initiates reflection on the manner in which people *do* talk. It initiates reflection on how stories are artfully constructed for particular purposes at particular times and in specific contexts. Thus, the question of "What does the story tell us about X?" becomes "How is X constructed in the telling?"

Adopting this kind of stance, Sparkes and Partington (2002) explored the manner in which flow is constructed in life stories told by white-water canoeists. Instead of asking *what* flow is in a definitive sense, as is traditionally done within sport and exercise psychology, they changed analytical tact to ask *how* flow is achieved and constructed, thereby directing their attention toward the *artful* practices through which athletes *do* flow. Their analysis highlighted *how* experiences of flow are shaped and constrained by the organization and structure of the white-water canoe club as well as by the gendered relationships within the club.

The analysis of the *hows* of people's experiences of flow led Sparkes and Partington (2002) to argue that flow is not simply a natural phenomenon. For them, experiences of flow are not something a person simply has but instead are strongly shaped through the heroic-epic narrative that circulates in society, including within the subculture of the white-water canoe club. This heroic-epic narrative involves pushing yourself to the limits; meeting a challenge; displaying bravery, skill, and courageous risk taking; battling successfully against nature; and competency. Such characteristics of the heroic-epic narrative, Sparkes and Partington argued, led participants to understand flow as an adrenaline buzz. For example, as suggested in the following comments from the captain (Patrick) of the white-water canoe club, flow was experienced by incorporating the theme of competence so that adrenaline becomes the culmination of successfully facing danger via the application of consummate skill.

> It happens all the time, but if I have to pick one, then the one that stands out the most was last winter in a river in Wales. It stands out because it is the hardest piece of white water paddled in Britain. You can be seriously injured or killed on this river, even if you don't make a mistake, let alone if you do. It was big water as well; it was really high. I was with a group of very good paddlers, and we were all paddling extremely well, because we were all so hyped up about the river and concentrating massively. Because we were all paddling well, we started to paddle better. So the better we were all paddling, the better everyone else paddled and you just started to drag your ability up further and further and further. Everyone was really going for it. You just felt extremely focused, just totally, with exactly what you're doing. You know exactly what you're doing and you can respond. I don't think I've ever raised myself up to that level of concentration before or since. I would do it again on something as hard. If I went and did that river again, I would do it again. But just that river and the extreme nature of it meant that I was totally and utterly focused. . . .
>
> You always get a huge adrenaline rush, because it's very dangerous. It can be very, very intense. In the middle of a rapid, the adrenaline is chunking away. And then you get to the bottom and you sort of sit around and you go "Wow! That was pretty wild!" Yeah, you get a real buzz and you feel quite puffed up about it. I think the closest sensation to that is nearly crashing the car and then rescuing it. It's just a massive feeling of "Ha! Cheated death that time!" And you sort of think "Oh shit, some things went wrong, but I was able to get away with it today, yes!" But it's not down to luck, the buzz is a combination of the adrenaline of doing something dangerous, and the satisfaction of being able to do it and get away with it. Adrenaline definitely kicks in, so not only do you get that extra notch of

concentration, but you always get a real strength of paddle. You definitely get an adrenaline impetus to your paddle stroke. When the adrenaline fires up you can make the boat move much more quickly than you would normally. But it's not unusual, when the adrenaline's flowing you can paddle harder. It happens every time I paddle a hard river. (Sparkes & Partington, 2002, pp. 310-311)

Reprinted, by permission, from A. Sparkes and S. Partington, 2002, "Narrative practice and its potential contribution to sport psychology: The example of flow," *The Sport Psychologist* 17: 210-311.

According to Sparkes and Partington (2002), when stories of flow are made sense of through a performative analysis rather than located within the mind or are seen as something cognitive, flow experiences seen as structured in relation to stories that circulate out there in social contexts such as the white-water canoe club. Flow becomes a communicative and relational act. It is a performance that requires narrative skills in terms of, for example, the strategic selection of narrative topics such as bravery and competency.

Why might sport and exercise psychologists use a performative narrative analysis? As suggested by the canoeing example, one good reason for using a performative analysis is that it can change the researcher's angle of vision from the *whats* to the *hows* of telling stories. In doing so, it can expand and potentially enrich our theoretical imagination. For example, as Sparkes and Partington (2003) have argued, emphasis in research on flow within sport psychology has been on identifying in a definitive way just *what* flow actually is. This quest, however, has faced continual difficulties. One difficulty is that researchers have recorded different articulations of the flow experience between groups, sports, and individuals. As a result, researchers who seek to identify definitively what flow is have been left with the problem of inconsistency in identifying what flow really is and thus a lack of a definitive answer to identifying what flow is. This being the case, instead of foregrounding the question of *what* flow is, Sparkes and Partington changed tact to ask *how* flow is constructed. One upshot of this analytical shift is that different articulations of the flow experience between groups, sports, and individuals are no longer a problem. Instead, for Sparkes and Partington, different articulations are a resource for understanding the artful construction of a specific movement-related experience such as flow. With this resource, more complex understandings of flow are developed.

Furthermore, a performative analysis is an attractive way to make sense of stories because it can explicitly illuminate how stories are not simply personal but also social. For example, it can foreground the researcher's analytical lens on interactions (see Smith et al., 2009). Riessman (2008, p. 105) puts it as follows:

Stories don't fall from the sky (or emerge from the innermost "self"); they are composed and received in contexts—interactional, historical, institutional, and discursive—to name a few. Stories are social artifacts, telling us as much about society and culture as they do about a person or group. How do these contexts enter into storytelling? How is a story co-produced in a complex choreography—in spaces between teller and listener, speaker and setting, text and reader, and history and culture? Dialogic/performance analysis attempts to deal with these questions. . . . The investigator becomes an active presence in the text. As a kind of hybrid form, the approach pushes the boundaries of what is and is not included in narrative analysis. It draws on and extends theoretical traditions that emphasise the importance of interaction.

Therefore, according to Riesmann (2008), and as illustrated within sport psychology in the work of Smith and colleagues (2009), a strength of the performative approach is that it analytically shifts the researcher's attention from the *telling*—the events to which language refers—to include both the *doing* and the *telling*. It calls on researchers to interrogate "how talk among speakers is interactively (dialogically) produced and performed as narrative" (Riesmann, 2008, p. 105). For example, it asks questions such as, "Why was the narrative developed that way and told in that order? How does the speaker locate herself in relation to the audience, and vice versa? How does the speaker locate characters in relation to one another and in relation to herself? How does the speaker strategically make preferred identity claims? What other identities are performed or suggested? What was the response of the listener or audience, and how did it influence the development and interpretation of the narrative?" Another good reason for using a performative analysis is that, in contrast to many content analyses, it asks researchers to foreground their analytical lens on the fine details of talk and the contradictions and tensions within the stories told.

Despite such strengths, a performative narrative analysis has a number of weaknesses and risks. For instance, it is difficult to learn. On the one hand, for researchers in sport and exercise psychology who are focused on finding out what X (e.g., flow) really is, its results might be difficult to digest. On the other hand, in light of the weaknesses of content forms of analysis, researchers might turn to a performative analysis as the analytical solution to the limits of a content form of analysis and then disregard the content analysis altogether. However, all analyses have weaknesses, and content analyses do have strengths that, for certain purposes, make them very useful. The *hows* of storytelling are the central concern of a performative analysis, and the equally important *whats* of talk are placed in the background. We should not forget these too. Furthermore, due to the large amount of time it takes to analyze a stretch of narrative using performative analysis compared with other analyses, a performative analysis does not easily permit an overview of all the data generated in a study. Likewise, there is the potential risk that sections of the individual narrative are dissected from and not interpreted within the context of other parts of the individual's life story or history.

Showing the *Whats* and *Hows*: Creative Analytical Practices

Another way a sport and exercise psychologist might make sense of qualitative data is through CAP. *CAP*, as described by Richardson (2000), is an umbrella term for different kinds of research practices, such as ethnodrama, autoethnography, and poetic representations (see Sparkes, 2002), that are both analytical and creative. CAP is very different from the analytical methods highlighted thus far. For example, in CAP the researcher seeks to shift back and forth between *showing* the *whats* and *showing* the *hows*. The researcher moves from the role of *declarative author and persuader* to the role of the *artfully persuasive storyteller* who shifts from telling the readers what the story is about and how it performs actions to trusting the readers and allowing them the freedom to interpret and evaluate the text from their unique vantage points (Barone, 1995).

Moreover, in contrast to content analyses and performative analysis, which conduct an analysis *of* stories, in CAP analysis *is* the story. As Ellis (2004) commented, CAP proposes "a good story is itself analytical and theoretical. When people tell their stories, they employ analytic techniques to interpret their worlds" (pp. 195-196). Or as Smith and Sparkes (2009) put it, researchers show a "story and, in turn, a theory through CAP: Data is recast to produce a story and the story is a theory" (p. 283). As such, rather than generating categories out of stories and adding an abstract layer of analysis to the stories, researchers and readers of CAP respect the integrity of the story *as a story*. This leads to another general difference between CAP and content analyses and performative analyses. While the latter primarily orientates the researcher to think about stories, CAP foregrounds thinking *with* the story. For Frank (1995), "thinking with stories takes the story as already complete; there is no going beyond it. To think with a story is to experience it affecting one's own life and to find in that effect a certain truth of one's life" (p. 23).

Within sport and exercise psychology, a number of researchers have recently begun to use the various kinds of CAP to make sense of the stories they generate. For example, Sparkes and Douglas (2007) used poetic representations to explore the motivations of becoming and being an elite female golfer. Krane (2009) used autoethnography to explore the social constructions of sport, gender, and identity, while Stone (2009) used this genre to examine the relationship between exercise and eating disorders. Using fictional techniques and drawing on data generated from multiple interviews and participant observations with a small group of men who became disabled through playing sport, Smith (2008) crafted a creative ethnographic nonfiction to show what stories people tell within a spinal rehabilitation unit and how these people perform certain stories to shape health behaviors and well-being. To get an idea of what this kind of CAP is like, consider the following abbreviated extract (please read aloud):

"Jon, you OK mate?" asked Mark, one of the forwards on the rugby team Jon played for.

"Yeah, fine," replied Jon, blinking slowly. With a shake of the head, he lifts himself from the mud, spits out a glob of blood and its acrid taste, and tries to push the throbbing sensations that work their way down the left side of his scratched face.

"Go off, we're nearly done anyway," said Mark, patting him gently on the back.

"I'm fine. And anyway, that centre needs taking down a peg or two," Jon said over his shoulder as he jogged back into position.

The ref nods at Jon, to see if he's OK, and blows the whistle to start.

Jon's team has possession and the ball sails smoothly up the line. Players adjust their pace accordingly, dodging and dipping. A long ball is flung out to Jon, who at full speed, stretches, his fingers curling around the ball. It's his. BANG. A shoulder cracks into skull. Darkness. Bodies collide, Jon's feet are lifted off the ground, and he drops down.

"Jon, Jon," shouts Mark a few moments later. "Someone, call an ambulance. Get a fucking ambulance. Don't move Jon. Nobody move him. Where's the ambulance. Get the ambulance."

Seven Months Later

Jon glided through the maze of corridors in the spinal injury unit. The corridors were graying white, the wall paint fading and flaking. In the air, wafts of disinfectant mingle with the smell of shit from morning bowel regimes. The ca-thunk, shhhhhhhh, ca-thunk, shhhhhhhh, ca-thunk, shhhhhhhh sound of Jon and other men repetitively grabbing the metal wheel rails of their wheelchairs and then pushing themselves forward floated down the corridors he passed through. Jon was just getting used to the feeling of his hands touching the cold metal and the repetitive sensations of pushing a wheelchair. But being a body that moved so close to the ground and without being vertical still felt strange. It was not "him." It had been seven months since he was told by a doctor he'd probably never walk again....

Gliding through the final corridor, and thankful of having left the claustrophobic space he slept in and shared daily with two other men paralyzed, he came to the automatic doors that opened to the unit's neat and small garden. The doors opened as he approached with a gentle whssssssshhhhhh sound. Pushing his wheelchair, he moved through them. . . . Alone in the peace and quiet of the small garden, slouched in his wheelchair, Jon pushed his hand into the waistband of his thick cotton jogging pants and lumbered to pull out the pack of Marlboros. . . . A moment later he heard the whir of the garden door opening automatically.

"Pass up us fag," Paul said with a smile on his face as he emerged through the door, and moved next to Jon. . . . With the tips of his fingers, Jon tossed a cigarette, and then the lighter across onto Paul's lap.

"You looking forward to the rugby on TV later?" asked Jon.

"Yeah, can't wait to beat those Welsh. I can't believe you still want to watch though after how you ended up in this," Paul said, patting the cold metal arm of his wheelchair.

"Just one those things. I was unlucky," Jon said, shrugging his shoulders. "When you play rugby there's always the risk of something like this happening. But you don't think about it. And anyway, the risks are so small, and sport's good for your health, isn't it. . . ."

"And disabled sport," Paul asked. "Are you going to join a team? I've seen the guys in the gym here play basketball. Bloody amazing."

"No chance!" snapped Jon. "That's not a proper sport. And disabled sport bores me. No adrenalin rush, no drinking socials after, and these guys that I see play, they're full bravado, all talk. I bet they were crap at sport before they ended up in here. They were the kids at school who got picked last to play football or rugby. And where's the skill in disabled sport? Where's the rush, the stinking kit, the deep heat, and taste of mud? And anyhow, I won't be in this chair forever, so why bother."

"Fair point," replied Paul. "But don't pin all your hopes on walking again soon, and getting out of your chair." Patting his legs that hung lifelessly down, and dropping ash on his back jogging bottoms, he added, "I agree it's sometimes crap being like this, but finding a cure is long way off if you ask me. You've got to make the most of life now."

"Yeah right," said Jon, with a shake of his head. "It's not about now. A cure, a breakthrough is around corner. I read the other day in a newspaper my Dad brought in that there's a doctor in Portugal who uses stem cells to treat spinal injured people. He's had success. People are walking. I'll pass the paper on to you. At some point in the future mate we'll be back to our old lives, and playing rugby. It'll happen soon."

"Maybe," answered Paul. "But, what if we don't. What are you going to do then? Who are we going to be?"

The various kinds of CAP, such as ethnographic creative fictions, have various strengths. Acting as artfully persuasive storytellers, the writers of CAP seek not to prompt a single, closed, and convergent reading of the story by telling readers what theoretically or morally they think the story is and can be about. Instead, writers of CAP produce an open text in which readers are given the freedom to interpret the text from their unique vantage points. This openness has the potential to reposition the reader away from being a relatively passive receiver of knowledge toward being an active participant in the creation of meaning, theory, and different ways of understanding. An open text, as Richardson (2000) suggests, can also enhance our connection with others, thereby making communion more possible. Likewise, for Richardson, CAP can enhance and enrich sense making of the topic in question, since the methods of CAP are themselves "a *method of inquiry,* a way of finding out about yourself and your topic" (p. 923). They are, moreover, Richardson argues, a way of knowing—a method of discovering new aspects of our topic and our relationship to it, and thus they are a key means of making sense of our topic. In breaking with the conventions of traditional writing genres such as realist or scientific tales, CAP also allows us to include the irregularities and messiness of personal experience as well as tales that lack cohesion and plot. When done well, CAP can evoke the emotional texture of human experience and help us hear the heartbeats of others. CAP calls on researchers and readers to think not just *about* stories but also *with* stories.

Furthermore, when compared with a conventional journal article, CAP can be a much more accessible type of research product for athletes, policy makers, and coaches. As such, when compared with traditional academic dissemination practices, CAP methods may be better able to represent and disseminate lived experiences from multiple and contested perspectives to a much wider audience. For example, regarding coaching and sport psychology, Douglas and Carless (2008) argue the following:

> While traditional scientific forms of communication (e.g., statistical analyses) have their place, coaches are often *not* statisticians or scientists. As a result, a reliance on scientific forms of communication may serve to alienate or de-motivate some coaches. In contrast, we suggest that most coaches are active *storytellers*; many routinely cultivate stories in order to, for example, motivate athletes. By drawing on a storied form of communication, we are thereby utilising a method of dissemination that coaches and athletes are probably already familiar with. (p. 36)

Having highlighted the strengths of CAP, it would be remiss of us not to point out some of the potential weaknesses and risks. One potential weakness is that CAP fetishizes form and runs the risk of elevating style, or panache, over content and focus. Likewise, as a part of scholarly research, CAP methods are flawed when they are theoretically vacuous—that is, when they fail to show theory. Furthermore, given that CAP can allow another person's experience to inspire reflection on personal experience, there is also the risk that CAP may not always be a pleasing experience. When a text or performance stirs people emotionally, it can change them, and the direction of change might not be positive. Another risk is that producers of CAP can, in some quarters, be greeted with suspicion, even hostility, and questions are raised as to whether CAP constitutes proper research. Finally, turning to CAP because it is novel will not do. Like all qualitative research, CAP needs to be held to high and difficult standards (Richardson & St. Pierre, 2005; Sparkes & Smith, 2009).

Conclusion

In this chapter, we have described four different ways in which sport and exercise psychologists might make sense of the stories they hear. These methods focus on the respective *hows* and *whats* of storytelling. In offering these analyses for consideration, it is important that we do not fall victim to methodolatry (Chamberlain, 2000; Smith, in press), which is the privileging and reifying of methods over other considerations in qualitative research, such as research questions, epistemology, ontology, and reflexivity (Smith, in press). Furthermore, when considering the use of any analysis, we should avoid privileging one type of analysis (e.g., thematic content) over another (e.g., a hierarchical content analysis or performative analysis). It is much more preferable to open up our analytical possibilities, consider certain purposes using different types of analysis, and, when appropriate, shift our analytical visions. That is, we should consider using a variety of analyses in order to understand our data in different ways.

This need for pluralism is supported by Lieblich and colleagues (1998), who repeatedly returned to the same qualitative data from a variety of angles with "different hearing aids, lenses, which produced a myriad of readings" (p. 167). These different readings revealed similarities as well as contradictions and conflicts, which is part and parcel of qualitative inquiries that seek to understand the multilayered and complex nature of human lives. Likewise, Coffey and Atkinson (1996) suggested that analytical diversity is useful since researchers "can use different analytic strategies in order to explore different facets of our data, explore different kinds of order in them, and construct different versions of the social world" (p. 14). Equally important, the juxtaposition or combination of different analytical techniques does not reduce the complexity of our understandings. Rather, as Coffey and Atkinson remind us, the more we examine our data from different viewpoints, "the more we may reveal—or indeed construct—their complexity" (p. 14). Revealing and constructing the complexity of stories told about sport and exercise are worthy goals. As this chapter has attempted to illustrate, if we wish to enhance, enrich, and expand our sense making, we should consider for certain purposes shifting our analytical visions and using different types of analysis.

Acknowledgments

We would like to thank the editor for inviting us to contribute to this textbook. Thanks also to the reviewer for comments on an early draft of this chapter as well as Amy Latimer, Kathleen Martin Ginis, and Kerry McGannon for their generous feedback when developing this chapter.

Developmentally Informed Measurement in Sport and Exercise Psychology Research

Alan L. Smith, PhD, Travis E. Dorsch, MS, and Eva V. Monsma, PhD

Whether developmental issues are of direct interest or serve as a backdrop in a given sport and exercise psychology investigation, they warrant careful attention in the framing, execution, and interpretation of the work. Though a host of theoretical perspectives on human development exist (see Horn, 2004b; Lerner, 2002), the defining feature of development is change. Importantly, this change must, at a minimum, be systematic and successive to be considered developmental (Lerner, 2002). As Lerner points out, not all change necessarily reflects a developmental process. Ebbs and flows in sport performance are common yet can stem from a variety of circumstances. The variation in opposition from competition to competition may largely explain performance variations; such a pattern of performance variation would not be considered a developmental phenomenon. However, performance variations stemming from learning, accommodation to training regimens, or adaptation to emerging cognitive capacities could be considered developmental. Thus, measurement selection and design that are developmentally informed are likely to yield the most valid and useful knowledge. It behooves sport and exercise psychology researchers to consider carefully how developmental processes may or may not underpin the phenomena that capture their attention.

Recognition of the importance of developmentally informed work in sport and exercise psychology is long standing. It is possible to find research published in the first issue of the *Journal of Sport Psychology* that exhibits sensitivity to developmental concerns. For example, in an examination of children's success predictions as linked to sex typing of motor activities and cross-sex competition, Corbin and Nix (1979) selected participants based on developmental literature on socialization as well as issues surrounding the ability of participants to understand and offer valid responses to questionnaire items. Also appearing in the issue is the widely cited work of Smith, Smoll, and Curtis (1979) showing the effectiveness of training coaches to employ youth-centered behaviors in addressing desirable and undesirable performances of Little League baseball players.

Psychological work on youth sport increased in the 1980s, when important conceptual papers by Gould (1982), Weiss and Bredemeier (1983), and Duda (1987) were published. Gould warned against uncritically applying adult-based theories and psychological processes to youth sport research, reminding us that "the young athlete is not a miniature adult" (p. 211). Weiss and Bredemeier concluded that, based on a content analysis of youth sport psychology research, few researchers considered cognitive-developmental criteria in participant selection. They described selected theories that could be used to frame developmentally sensitive work and offered several guidelines for pursuing developmental sport psychology research. Specifically, they recommended that researchers review theoretical constructs and models available in the developmental psychology literature, evaluate the validity of such constructs in sport settings, formulate testable hypotheses that are developmentally anchored, pursue lines of interrelated studies to capture systematic differences among and change within developmental groups, formulate conceptual working models from these efforts, and test such working models with further investigations. In line with these recommendations, Duda offered a thoughtful treatment of Nicholls' (1984) developmental theory of achievement that stimulated much research activity. In short, throughout the 1980s there was a substantial increase in attention paid to developmental concerns in sport psychology research targeting young people.

As sport and exercise psychology has broadened and matured, so too has appreciation for and understanding of developmental considerations in research. Attention is now paid to the full life span in contemporary treatments of developmental sport and exercise psychology (see Horn, 2004b; Whaley, 2007). Youth-based work has become more programmatic and theoretically driven than it has been in the past (Weiss & Raedeke, 2004). Finally, practical and technical issues surrounding the collection and treatment of developmental data have become accessible to sport and exercise psychology researchers (Brustad, 1998; Schutz & Park, 2004). Nonetheless, our understanding of developmental phenomena operating in sport and exercise contexts is restricted by overreliance on cross-sectional research designs, and we could improve both how we conceptualize our work and how we measure developmentally important constructs. As Whaley (2007) put it, "The knowledge base is there; what we seem to lack is the incentive to follow through" (p. 657).

Therefore, this chapter strives to raise awareness of developmental issues that are salient to measurement in sport and exercise psychology and to offer strategies for addressing these issues. Given the considerable scope of development-related concerns and the constraints inherent in presenting these concerns in a single chapter, we offer a treatment of selected issues that appear to be of particular importance to current research in sport and exercise psychology. Moreover, given the considerable amount of research activity on developmental issues in young people and our background in youth sport research, our discussion predominantly addresses the early years of the life span. We cover cognitive, social, and biological development in distinct subsections. We then reinforce the idea that considering change in multiple domains (e.g., cognitive *and* biological domains) is necessary to achieve the best understanding of development. Within this discussion we also note the importance of context and behavioral assessment in developmental research. Across the sections we describe both global and specific considerations in pursuing developmentally informed measurement. That is, we showcase the importance of carefully framing research questions and selecting measures as well as address selected particulars of constructing and evaluating measurement tools. We reinforce these points with illustrations from extant sport and exercise psychology investigations that have pursued measurement in a developmentally informed way.

Cognitive Abilities and Structures

Cognitive developmental matters have garnered particular attention in discussions of developmental phenomena in sport and exercise psychology (Brustad, 1998; Horn, 2004b). This is a function of the predominant focus on cognitive variables in contemporary sport and exercise psychology theory and research. Investigators seek to understand sport and exercise behavior by tapping constructs such as motivational orientations, perceptions of the self, attitudes, and intentions. Importantly, underlying these constructs are capacities such as the ability to plan, reason in an abstract way, and acquire relevant information. Conducting developmentally informed measurement, therefore, requires careful attention to age-related differences in such capacities and familiarity with developmental theory.

The ability to process information is critical to a host of concerns in sport and exercise settings, such as skill learning, interpreting feedback, accurately deciphering the actions of teammates and opponents, and judging the causes of performance outcomes. Matters pertaining to information processing include speed of accessing information, perceptual sensitivity, and memory, all of which show age-related changes as well as experience-related changes (Thomas, Gallagher, & Thomas, 2001). Changes in the capacity for information processing are particularly rapid across childhood (see Kail, 1991) and must be considered carefully in sport and exercise psychology research on young people. Weiss, Ebbeck, and Wiese-Bjornstal (1993) offered an example of learning how to bat a baseball by viewing a batting demonstration. Younger children (approximately age 7 y or younger) have limited information processing capacities and are expected to capture only selected features of a visual demonstration. At about age 7, children are expected to shift toward attending to a breadth of visual information, including both relevant and irrelevant components (e.g., features of batting as well as what the demonstrator is wearing). Selective attention to relevant components of the demonstration is expected around the age of 12.

The ages in the batting example are based on cognitive developmental milestones but must be considered flexible. There is considerable variability in the expression of cognitive capacities as a function of individual differences such as the amount of experience with a task. The upshot is that in studying psychological phenomena in sport and exercise settings, researchers should consider whether information processing is germane to the targeted phenomena. If so, participant selection must be considered carefully. It may also be necessary to control for individual differences associated with information processing or to include relevant measures of information processing. Alternatively, experimental measures, survey instruments, or other measurement tools should be developed for simplicity and to accommodate those participants least capable at information processing. Careful attention to information processing does not address all possible measurement challenges, as information processing is but one developmental consideration, but it does move researchers toward measurement that is more developmentally sensitive than what is often exhibited in extant research.

Another cognitive developmental consideration relevant to the study of psychological phenomena in sport and exercise is the ability to reason in abstract ways. Piaget's (1952) work has been widely influential in shaping thought on cognitive development. Piaget proposed that schemes, or mental structures underlying behavioral sequences, change over development through intellectual adaptation. More sophisticated schemes evolve as individuals assimilate experiences into their existing cognitive structures and accommodate for novel experiences that foster reconfiguration of those structures. It is through this process that egocentric reasoning characteristic of what Piaget called the preoperational period (on average, from age 2-6 y) gives way to concrete operational reasoning. Abstract thought is evident in the concrete operational stage, although it is bound by what the child can directly perceive. Ultimately, formal operational reasoning emerges around age 12. Hypothetical events can be considered, with the reasoning process drawing from what is tangibly perceived as well as the intangible. Thus, through assimilation and accommodation, cognitive structures become progressively more diverse and interconnected.

Regardless of a scholar's level of agreement with the particulars of Piaget's (1952) perspective, the differences in abstract reasoning across childhood are evident and must be considered when studying psychological phenomena in sport and exercise. In youth-based research, theories incorporating abstract concepts such as goals, friendship, group cohesion, and intention must be applied with particular care. For example, it is not uncommon for researchers to administer to young children a questionnaire designed to assess a concept that is relatively abstract for adults. The researchers may go to the trouble of ensuring that the item wording accommodates the young children's reading skills, avoiding compound questions (i.e., questions possessing more than one element, such as those asking about X *and* Y), and offering a straightforward Likert-type response set. This is a responsible approach in light of children's information processing limitations. The children, of course, are able to select a response option for each question. The questions are similar in nature, the responses accordingly hang together, and the researchers move ahead assuming that the theoretical construct of interest is successfully measured. However, whether the questions fully or best represent the construct as expressed in children is not known. The starting point was an adult-based construct and possibly a measure that was initially developed using adult samples. A better starting strategy is to draw from developmental theory and empirical work deliberately targeting young children.

For example, researchers wishing to study achievement motivation in children must consider that the abstract concepts of ability, effort, task difficulty, and luck come to be distinguished from one another through a developmental process that extends throughout childhood and, for some, into early adolescence. In his widely cited theory of achievement motivation, Nicholls (1978, 1984, 1989; Nicholls & Miller, 1983, 1985) posited that younger children are not good at differentiating such concepts in academic domains until they acquire a mature understanding of ability and the cognitive capacity to differentiate between ability and other concepts of achievement, such as effort, relative to performance outcomes. Specifically, Nicholls suggested that children progress through several stages of development as they come to fully understand these concepts. In the earliest stage, young children cannot conceive of trying hard at something and not doing well or having high ability and not trying hard. Around age 12 y, children attain the capacity to fully disentangle these concepts such that they understand high ability is expressed when one requires little effort to achieve a top performance.

In an effort to test these ideas and extend them to the physical domain, Fry (2000a, 2000b; Fry

& Duda, 1997) conducted structured interviews with boys and girls aged 5 through 13 y after exposing them to scenarios or photos that could be interpreted differently depending on the developmental level of understanding of the target concepts of ability, effort, luck, and task difficulty. Fry adopted a Piagetian structural analysis of interview responses, assuming that the reasoning strategies children use at one stage build on the reasoning used in previous stages in a hierarchy of logic. The results of Fry's work overwhelmingly confirmed Nicholls' developmental hypotheses. In extending Nicholls' original stages, Fry and Duda also proposed a *stage 0* level of understanding, at which children are unable to identify hard work or differentiate effort from ability. Furthermore, Fry's results illuminated substantial variability within age groups in the ability to maturely differentiate tasks of varying difficulties as well as the effort and ability of individuals attempting those tasks. Relative to understanding of ability, effort, and luck, roughly one-third of participants aged 13 y had not yet achieved a fully mature discrimination of these concepts, whereas nearly all participants at this age exhibited a fully mature understanding of task difficulty. This finding reminds us that we must exercise caution with participant selection in youth-based achievement motivation research and that grouping participants by age is not a fail-safe strategy for addressing developmental questions in sport and exercise psychology that involve cognitive variables. Moreover, as Brustad (1998) pointed out, measures that require respondents to engage in complex and hypothetical reasoning must be used cautiously, if at all, with children.

The cognitive structures underlying the development of the capacity to distinguish between effort and ability are linked to other matters of deep interest to researchers in sport and exercise psychology. As an example, perspectives on moral development emphasize the reasoning about right and wrong that underlies moral action and how cognitive and social development are inextricably tied to this reasoning (see Shields & Bredemeier, 1995; Weiss, Smith, & Stuntz, 2008). In pursuing work on moral behavior in sport, therefore, researchers must take care to link cognitive capacities with the selection of participants and measures. Researchers must understand what may or may not be perceived by the target group as constituting a circumstance that involves judgments of right and wrong, because this has implications for the content of measures or for measurement strategy (e.g., open-ended structured interviews, surveys). It is expected that with greater cognitive maturity more complex reasoning

can (though might not) underlie moral behavior in sport. Therefore, attention must be paid not only to what is considered a moral concern by target participants but also to the reasoning underlying these judgments and the motivations offered for behaving a particular way.

The structure of self-descriptions and self-evaluations is also coupled with cognitive development and has been extensively researched by sport and exercise psychologists. How individuals perceive themselves and the abilities they possess evolves through cognitive maturation and life experiences (for developmental treatments relative to the physical domain, see Horn, 2004a; Whaley, 2007). Young children make self-assessments in a constrained set of domains but move toward assessment of global self-worth and discernible domains of competence (e.g., scholastic, athletic, behavioral) as they move into middle childhood. As individuals move through adolescence and adulthood, additional domains of competence become salient to the self (see Harter, 1999, 2003). This progression aligns closely with cognitive development. As the child forms the capacity to consider abstract concepts, differentiate ability from effort, and so forth, the self becomes more complex with regard to the number of competence domains and hierarchical structure. Moreover, the number of sources of competence information used to generate competence judgments increases, the salience of particular sources of competence information changes, and the competence judgments that are formed grow in accuracy (Horn, 2004).

Measuring features of the self is clearly an involved process in light of the close tie of the self system to cognitive development. The assessment strategy or tools used to capture constructs reflecting the self will necessarily differ across various phases of the life span. As showcased elsewhere (see Brustad, 1998), Susan Harter has contributed substantially to measurement of the self system across childhood and beyond. Her measures incorporate increasing and changing components of the self system across time and provide distinct tools for developmental groups spanning young childhood through late adulthood (for a table summarizing this instrumentation, see Horn, 2004a). Moreover, Harter addressed the tendency of children to offer socially desirable evaluations of the self by designing the questions to have what she termed a *structure alternative format* (Harter, 1982). The format has the respondent identify with one of two statements that describe a type of child (e.g., "Some kids often forget what they learn, but other kids can remember things easily"; Harter, 1982, p. 89). In presenting items in this fashion, a message is communicated that half of children view themselves as falling into one category and half of children view themselves as falling into the other, legitimizing either selection (Harter, 1982). After identifying with a type of child, the respondent indicates whether the statement is "Sort of true for me" or "Really true for me," enabling the assignment of an item score on a 4-point scale.

In extending this work to preschoolers through second graders, Harter and Pike (1984) developed a picture-based version of the measure that assesses general competence, containing cognitive and physical competence items, and social acceptance, containing peer and maternal acceptance items. Given the limited attentional capacity of young children and their inability to read and reason in abstract ways, Harter and Pike (1984) developed picture-based items that exhibit skills and specific actions in a concrete behavioral form. As with the measures employed with older respondents, the structure alternative strategy was used with this measure to reduce socially desirable responding. Two pictures are contrasted for selection by the respondent and a subsequent judgment is made with regard to how similar the respondent is to the child in the selected picture. The similarity judgment is made with the assistance of differently sized circles that correspond to appropriate descriptive statements, with higher competence or acceptance judgments corresponding to a score of 4 on a 4-point scale. Items are administered by an examiner who sits across from the child, which helps address the attentional and cognitive limitations of young children. Taken collectively, Harter's measurement work across developmental phases has offered a useful foundation (and template) for assessing psychological constructs that are expected to evolve developmentally.

Social Development

How individuals come to understand, form attitudes about, and behave with others over time constitutes social development (Hartup, 1991). Social development is inextricably linked with cognitive development, as is evident in perspectives such as Piaget's (1952), where social interaction can be an important stimulus for assimilation and accommodation processes. Indeed, social relationships constitute an important context for the development of the self, personality, moral functioning, and other qualities that shape how a person interacts with the environment (Hartup & Laursen, 1999). The upshot for sport and exercise psychology scholars is that social agents and social relationships may require

attention in investigations that include participants of varying developmental maturity or that target particular developmental groups. Also, because conceptions of relationships can vary developmentally, measurement of social constructs must be pursued with care.

As an example, research on the sources of information that individuals use to judge their physical competence suggests that social agents must be carefully considered in examinations of physical self-perceptions. Horn has pursued a line of research (see Horn, 2004a; Horn & Amorose, 1998) exploring the importance that young people place on various information sources such as social comparison, evaluative feedback, goal achievement, and game outcome when judging their competence. This work suggested that as youths move through the later childhood years and toward the early adolescent years, peer comparison information and peer and coach evaluative information increase in importance, whereas parent feedback declines in importance. Adult feedback comes to be considered as one piece of information among several options and is not necessarily taken at face value, reflecting a more mature understanding of others as well as of concepts such as ability. As a person advances through the adolescent years, feedback sources are further differentiated from one another, and internal sources of information become increasingly important (Horn, 2004a). Progressing through the adult years, the person must come to terms with potential decline in physical capabilities, a process that can interconnect goals, self-perceptions, and the tendency to compare personal physical capacities with those possessed by others (see Frey & Ruble, 1990; Semerjian & Stephens, 2007; Whaley, 2007). In short, there is developmental change in the magnitude and form of social influence on physical self-perceptions. Therefore, scholars pursuing work on well-being, physical activity motivation, or other topics in which physical self-perceptions hold a prominent role should consider measuring relevant social constructs.

Researchers should draw from developmental theoretical perspectives and empirical work in selecting the relevant social constructs. Given the work by Horn, a researcher interested in physical activity motivation of middle schoolers, for example, may wish to specifically assess peer constructs to complement the assessment of physical self-perceptions and other motivation-related constructs. There is a rich literature on peer relationships within developmental psychology and an emerging literature within sport and exercise psychology (see Smith & McDonough, 2008; Weiss

& Stuntz, 2004). Much of the work is inspired by Sullivan's (1953) interpersonal theory of psychiatry. This theory suggests that in older children and adolescents it is important to consider both broader acceptance by the peer group and specific friendships. Peer acceptance and friendship are related constructs, and yet they offer distinct contributions to development and can accommodate for one another in circumstances where either construct is experienced at a suboptimal level. For example, poor acceptance by the larger peer group in middle school physical education might be buffered by a high-quality friendship in that setting. Ideally, then, these constructs are distinctly measured and considered simultaneously in data analyses.

Considering the level of social complexity of focal social constructs is important in formulating a measurement plan (see Holt, Black, Tamminen, Fox, & Mandigo, 2008; Rubin, Bukowski, & Parker, 2006). Peer acceptance, for example, can be gleaned from an individual-level measure of perceived acceptance, an assessment of behavioral interactions among peers, interactions over time among actors of particular characteristics (i.e., a relationship level), or group-level sociometric information. Thus, choosing the most appropriate measure or battery of measures to employ in an investigation requires careful attention to relevant theory and the specific research aim. The target sample must be considered in this decision-making process. Ideally, measures of the social (and other) constructs exist that are developed specifically for use with the target sample. If such measures do not exist, either an existing measure for a different target group needs to be modified or a new measure needs to be carefully constructed and evaluated. The latter strategy is preferable for a variety of reasons, though often the former is used because of the intensive time demands involved in producing a new measurement tool. One key reason why the effort may be worthwhile is that social and other constructs often take on a different form or meaning as a function of developmental status. We showcase this next by using the construct of group cohesion.

Group cohesion is a key group variable in sport. It is tightly associated with personal, team, environmental, and leadership factors as well as group and individual outcomes (see Carron, Hausenblas, & Eys, 2005). Carron (1982) defined group cohesion as "a dynamic process which is reflected in the tendency for a group to stick together and remain united in the pursuit of its goals and objectives" (p. 124). With his colleagues, Carron forwarded a conceptual model and associated measure of cohesion called the Group Environment Questionnaire

(GEQ; Carron, Widmeyer, & Brawley, 1985). The GEQ taps four constructs corresponding to group integration and individual attractions to the group crossed with task and social aspects of the group, respectively. The conceptual model and GEQ were generated in an effort to bring order to the cohesion research literature, and in the more than two decades of work since, there has been tremendous benefit to the knowledge base (see Carron et al., 2005; chapter 35 in this book). One troublesome challenge in the study of group cohesion in sport, however, is associated with using the GEQ with athletes other than young adults. The nature and function of interpersonal relationships are known to vary developmentally (see Rubin et al., 2006), and the measure is appropriately generalized only to young adult samples. There is particular interest in understanding group cohesion in adolescent athletes, and yet work employing the GEQ with such samples has shown suboptimal reliability and issues surrounding factor structure (Schutz, Eom, Smoll, & Smith, 1994; Westre & Weiss, 1991). These findings point to the need to pursue deliberate, foundational work on cohesion in adolescents.

Eys, Loughead, Bray, and Carron (2009a, 2009b) pursued such work to enhance the conceptual understanding and measurement of group cohesion in adolescent sport. As a first step, Eys and colleagues (2009b) pursued qualitative work to obtain an understanding of what cohesion means to young athletes. Specifically, team sport athletes ranging from 14 to 17 y were recruited to participate in focus groups. The discussion groups included participants from both sexes and from a variety of sports so that a comprehensive understanding of cohesion could be obtained. Relative to team or physical activity groups, participants were asked how they would define cohesion, characteristics of cohesive and noncohesive groups, and ways cohesion can be developed. Analysis of responses involved deductive categorization into task or social aspects of cohesion followed by inductive categorization of meaning units into similar themes. Themes falling within task cohesion included working together, effective communication, chemistry/bonding, understanding the abilities of others, shared task experiences, unselfishness, effective peer leadership, commitment, status parity, and the coach relationship with team. Themes falling within social cohesion included knowing one another, friendship, getting along, provision of support, lack of conflict, engaging in outside activities, and lack of cliques. Participants reported coach behaviors, practice structure, shared task experiences, development of commitment, and development of task support as means of developing task cohesion in sport and physical activity groups. They reported getting to know each other, engaging in outside activities, and developing friendships as ways to develop social cohesion. Of note relative to the extant literature on adults, the researchers did not find the participants to offer meaning units corresponding with individual attractions to the group. Rather, the group integration aspect of Carron and colleagues' (1985) model characterized the bulk of responses.

Eys and coworkers (2009a) used these reports of cohesion as well as open-ended responses of another 280 adolescents who were current and former team sport athletes and a search of the cohesion literature to generate items for the Youth Sport Environment Questionnaire (YSEQ). Because responses did not suggest dimensions of cohesion beyond those represented in the GEQ, items were generated to tap the four components of cohesion represented in the GEQ. The wording of the items and the instructions was designed to be at a lower grade or reading level than that of the original GEQ, so as to be appropriate for youths. After careful evaluation and trimming of items by the investigators, 120 items were submitted to three sport psychologists with group cohesion expertise and five high school athletes for commentary on conceptual appropriateness and understandability. Following this process, a reduced set of 87 items was retained for subsequent administration to a group of adolescent team sport athletes. Response distribution patterns of items from this administration were examined, resulting in the removal of 30 more items from the YSEQ. Scores on the remaining items were submitted to a set of principal components analyses, with the final analysis yielding 17 items represented by two principal components. The two components reflected social and task aspects of group cohesion, respectively.

In the final phase of the research effort by Eys and colleagues (2009a), the 17-item version of the YSEQ was administered to 352 adolescent team sport athletes. Confirmatory factor analysis specifying the two-factor social and task model showed acceptable fit to the data with the removal of 1 underperforming item. The final YSEQ that emerged from this process is expected to yield group cohesion scores that offer a more valid account of this important group construct in adolescents than would the adult-validated GEQ. Theory informed the initial production of items, and yet the item content came from adolescents themselves. The data suggests that, unlike what has been observed in adults, adolescents do not distinguish between group integration and individual attractions to the

group dimensions of cohesion. Overall, this work provides a nice example of how a social construct can take on different forms across developmental groups. This highlights the importance of considering social development in sport and exercise psychology measurement.

Biological Maturation

The bulk of growth and maturation research focuses on changes occurring up to young adulthood because of the dominant biological activities that occur throughout the first two decades of life—a time that coincides with widespread involvement in sport and other physical activities. According to a review by Eisenmann and Wickel (2009), determinants of physical activity are biologically inherent, as represented by heredity, sex, adiposity, and sexual maturation, and these are especially important for research examining habitual physical activity. Moreover, as noted in a recent review by Dorn, Dahl, Woodward, and Biro (2006), while puberty is often conceived of as a predominantly biological process, it is not simply a matter of physical change. Puberty includes a synchrony of physiological, neurobehavioral, and social changes that affect individual perceptions, cognitions, emotions, and behaviors. Thus, consideration of biological factors is important when designing research investigations in sport and exercise psychology.

Though biological factors are integral to psychological phenomena in sport and exercise, adequate assessments of biological variables are surprisingly absent from most research designs. Many researchers collect information on the age of participants; however, age is simply the marking of time (Wohlwill, 1973) and is not a reliable indicator of developmental stage. This is particularly the case when pubertal processes are under way. Dorn and colleagues (2006) have argued that pubertal assessments are at least as important as specifying the age of participants when conducting adolescent research. Unfortunately, as these authors point out, there is considerable inconsistency in the methods, definitions, and conceptualizations of puberty and its stages. This inconsistency likely has served as a disincentive to include pubertal assessments in sport and exercise psychology investigations.

Considering biological growth and maturation can be especially helpful in shedding light on developmental sport and exercise psychology questions. *Growth* is defined as an increase in size or body mass, whereas *maturation* refers to the timing and tempo of progress toward a mature biological state (Malina, Bouchard, & Bar-Or, 2004). Height, weight, and body mass index (BMI; the ratio of weight in kilograms to height in meters squared) are the most common assessments found in the literature, but researchers can also consider skeletal breadths (e.g., shoulder-to-hip ratio), sitting height, leg length, and the ratio of sitting height to stature when seeking understanding of growth and maturation. Biological maturation is often discussed in terms of status and timing. *Maturity status* refers to the state of maturation at a given point in time. Assessments include skeletal age or a variety of methods for calculating the percentage of mature height at a specific chronological age (see Malina et al., 2004). Children who are the same chronological age can be categorized as prepubertal, pubertal, and postpubertal. In addition, girls can be categorized as pre- and postmenarcheal when age at menarche is ascertained through questionnaire or interview. On average, girls reach their greatest tempo of growth, termed *peak height velocity* (PHV), at 11.5 to 12.0 y, while boys reach PHV at 13.5 to 14.0 y. Velocity is faster for boys. They grow approximately 3.5 in. (9 cm) a year, whereas girls grow about 3.1 in. (8 cm) a year. Growth in stature tapers off at about 14 y in girls and 17 y in boys (Beunen & Malina, 1988). The longer growth time frame for boys accounts for the height difference, which is attributed to growth in the long bones (i.e., leg length), generally seen between adult men and women. Although weight is susceptible to extrinsic factors such as nutrition and physical activity, peak weight velocity follows PHV by 2.5 to 5 mo in boys and 3.5 to 10.5 mo in girls (see Haywood & Getchell, 2009).

An individual's state of biological maturity is relevant for several reasons. Boys advanced in maturation tend to be more successful in sports such as soccer and hockey, whereas girls later in maturation tend to be more successful in gymnastics and figure skating. Thus maturity status can influence sport selection (Malina, 1998). Maturity assessments also can help inform practitioners about training loads appropriate for young athletes and therefore can help to reduce injury risk (Johnson, Doherty, & Freemont, 2009). There is greater risk associated with heavy training loads when an individual has not reached a biologically mature state. Of course, with such physical risks also come potential psychological risks, such as diminished physical self-perceptions, sport motivation, and overall well-being. This is a connection deserving of close research attention. Suggestions that intensive training during the adolescent growth spurt delays achievement of physical maturity, particularly in females (Bass et al., 2000), must be balanced with an understanding of the heritability of menarcheal timing (Towne

et al., 2005). This more comprehensive treatment of maturity can help researchers refine questions pertaining to physical activity outcomes such as the female athlete triad (disordered eating, amenorrhea, and osteoporosis). Clearly, research designs that capture biological maturity, and not just age, enable more robust explanations of various sport and exercise phenomena.

Timing of biological maturation refers to when specific biological events take place. For example, the average age at menarche among Caucasian girls is 12.8 ± 1.0 y (Malina et al., 2004). This age has been used to categorize study participants as early (<11.8 y), average (11.8-13.8 y), and late (>13.8 y) maturers. Because age at menarche is a continuous variable, it can be used as a covariate, as can the number of years since menarche (chronological age – menarcheal age). Other events such as the timing of PHV and how quickly or slowly children pass through sexual maturation (tempo) vary considerably among individuals and can significantly influence sport and exercise experiences among children. For example, two athletes on a team may be the same age and the same height at a given assessment time, but one may have attained 80% of adult stature while the other may have attained 65% of adult stature. Both athletes will attain fully ossified skeletal systems but will do so at different times, and the later-maturing athlete will grow for a longer time frame, surpassing the earlier-maturing athlete in adult stature.

In an effort to account for interindividual size variation when addressing developmental or other questions, researchers frequently use weight and BMI as control variables. For example, in studies examining physical self-perceptions, body image, or disordered eating, BMI may be partialled out in correlation analyses, entered in preliminary steps of hierarchical regression analyses, or used as a covariate in mean difference tests. BMI, though, is only a proxy for fatness, a quality of interest in some investigations. A widely known limitation of BMI is that the distribution of fat and muscle mass is not differentiated in the weight component of the index, meaning that individuals can have a high BMI because of lean muscle, a characteristic common to some athletic populations. Other estimates of body fat are available and found in the extant literature; however, they also should be interpreted with caution. Fat mass is inherently unstable, especially during adolescence, and there is error associated with the assessment techniques (for a review, see Malina et al., 2004). Technological methods that partition body composition into fat mass and fat-free mass (e.g., dual-energy X-ray absorptiometry, or DXA) are available, but they are costly and impractical for large-scale sport and exercise psychology investigations.

Quantifying physique is another way to account for physical characteristics. Assessments include shoulder-to-hip ratio (i.e., the ratio of bicristal to biacromial breadths), the androgyny index, and somatotype, an objective indicator of physique representing relative fatness, muscularity, and linearity. Somatotype is expressed in terms of endomorph, mesomorph, and ectomorph components that can range from 0 to infinity; however, most values are less than 7.0 (Carter & Heath, 1990). While such objective physique indicators should be appealing to researchers, anthropometric assessment training and reliability establishment are time consuming. Compared with using X rays for skeletal maturity assessment, estimating the time before or after PHV from age (Mirwald, Baxter-Jones, Bailey, & Beunen, 2002), which is known as *maturity offset*, is a less intrusive, more robust alternative for assessing maturity status that can be used in psychological investigations. For example, maturity offset has been linked to correlates of disordered eating, such as social physique anxiety, among adolescent athletes (Gay, Monsma, & Torres-McGehee, in press). However, maturity offset also has limitations; equations are valid only for males and females aged 9 to 16 y, and there are validity limitations for homogenous samples of participants short in stature (Malina et al., 2006). Thus, as is the case when selecting cognitive, social, and other biological measures, it is important for researchers to consider carefully their research aims and their target subject population when using this measure.

Change in Multiple Domains

The presentation of the previous sections offers structure to the present chapter but is somewhat artificial in that clearly many of the developmental changes described coincide and interact with one another. For example, the relative timing of physical maturation in light of the social concerns of young people appears to influence the development of the self in girls, whereby early onset of puberty is a disadvantage (Malina, 2002). Physical maturational timing can also link to skill development outcomes, serving as a person cue that shapes performance expectations of important social agents such as teachers and coaches, who may in turn behave in ways that result in the expectations being confirmed (see Horn, Lox, & Labrador, 2010). Most certainly the confluence of developmental experiences faced by participants in sport and physical activity can

influence socialization, motivation, performance, and other outcomes of interest to researchers.

For us to understand developmental experiences, our research designs must systematically consider variables from both biological and psychological paradigms (Burwitz, Moore, & Wilkinson, 1994; Sherar, Cumming, Eisenmann, Baxter-Jones, & Malina, 2010), or what is often termed the *biocultural perspective* (e.g., Malina, 2002). There are useful models that offer insight as to how biological and psychological factors interplay in contextually specific ways. For example, Newell's (1986) model of developmental constraints suggests that movement-related outcomes arise from interactions among structural (physical) and functional (behavioral) characteristics of the individual, environmental influences, and specific task features. Lerner's (1985) contextual theory also calls for including physical characteristics and specifies a matching hypothesis that helps to explain positive and negative valences of behaviors as the quality of match, or mismatch, between the individual (physical and psychological characteristics) and the task demands. These models showcase the importance of the individual interacting with the environment and serve to inform research designs. In a review of adolescent physical activity behavior, Sherar and colleagues (2010) suggested important future research directions, including (1) considering the discordance between subjective self-reported indicators and objective assessments of maturity status and how these measures associate with psychosocial variables; (2) sampling boys and girls from the extreme ends of the developmental continuum to capture what maturational timing means to individuals at varying ages; (3) considering social desirability, as it may be associated with self-reported maturational timing; and (4) assessing how to alter contexts to decrease possible negative outcomes stemming from variation in maturational timing.

Attending to context when pursuing understanding of psychological phenomena is also critical in developmental research (Kagan, 2007). Body-related perceptions, for example, may be especially salient in sport contexts in which aesthetics are subjectively judged, significant others emphasize weight control, and athletes reach their performance prime before adulthood (see Malina, 2002). A person's perceived social acceptance may vary as a function of the specific peer context within which the person interacts with others, be it highly competitive sport, physical education, or the neighborhood setting. Of course, broader community and cultural factors come into play as well, making for many layers of potential influence on developmental outcomes. For this reason, ecological viewpoints that emphasize the interaction of individual and extraindividual influences on human behavior have begun to capture the attention of developmental sport and exercise psychologists (e.g., see García Bengoechea, 2002;Welk, 1999). From a measurement standpoint, it behooves researchers to consider carefully how extraindividual influences might be accommodated and operationalized within sport and exercise psychology investigations.

Developmental researchers should also carefully attend to observable behaviors, an endeavor that has been argued to be underemphasized in contemporary sport and exercise psychology research (Andersen, McCullagh, & Wilson, 2007; Hagger & Chatzisarantis, 2009; Weiss & Raedeke, 2004). Behavioral assessment is critical for the understanding of, for example, sport and exercise motivation, learning of movement skills, and interpersonal relationships in sport. Such consideration goes hand in hand with measurement of internal states and perceptions, which helps capture underlying motives, understandings, and self- and other-directed evaluations that are theoretically and practically important. Assessing observable behaviors and internal states in tandem can allow clearer understanding of psychological phenomena, as often it is the combination of these elements that offers explanatory value. In fact, relying on only one assessment strategy can lead to significant misunderstanding of a phenomenon of interest.

The study of observational learning illustrates this point. Observational learning, also referred to as modeling, is defined as the cognitive, affective, and behavioral changes that result from observing others (Weiss et al., 1993). Coaches and physical education teachers rely heavily on demonstrations to teach new physical skills, and researchers in sport psychology and motor learning have taken interest in the effectiveness of such demonstrations. By adopting a narrow measurement strategy, a researcher or practitioner interested in a young child's learning of a movement skill may rely only on that child's ability to physically reproduce what has been demonstrated. However, the failure of a young child to produce the movement may not necessarily reflect an absence of learning. The child may indeed understand the steps involved in and the purpose of a given movement. This understanding reflects learning at a cognitive level. The inability to physically reproduce the task could be tied to an absence of foundational skills, insufficient physical strength, a context that is not well suited to displaying the behavior (e.g., trying to use adult-sized implements or having

insufficient practice time), or some combination of these (see Bandura, 1986; McCullagh & Weiss, 2001). Thus, sound measurement requires researchers to pay attention to the breadth of components that undergird a phenomenon of interest.

Beyond directing attention to the importance of global measurement strategy in sport and exercise psychology, this example offers a platform for discussing developmentally informed measurement. Previous skill exposure, current strength levels, and the fit of the performance context with a performer's capacities are intertwined with the developmental status of the performer. Had the young child in the example been an adolescent with intensive sport experience, we might generate different hypotheses about why a modeled movement task that is cognitively learned is not physically reproduced. Presumably the adolescent would have an extensive movement skill background and possess the physical qualities needed to produce the modeled task. In this case, a motivational explanation for the absence of successful movement production might be forwarded based on Bandura's (1986) perspective on observational learning. This perspective specifies that attention to and retention of information, behavioral reproduction, *and* motivation are fundamental considerations in the observational learning process. Perhaps the adolescent prefers to display only well-learned behaviors in front of peers or will only halfheartedly attempt to adopt new skills when the current skill set has afforded competitive success. Thus, incorporating measures of motivation-related constructs into the study of observational learning in adolescents may be warranted. This example illustrates the critical importance of considering development (and, of course, theory) when adopting a measurement strategy to understand psychological phenomena within sport and exercise contexts.

Conclusion

Considering developmentally informed measurement from a global standpoint, meaningfully advancing the sport and exercise psychology knowledge base requires careful attention to measurement across cognitive, social, and biological dimensions of human functioning along with other individual (e.g., emotional) and extraindividual (e.g., behavioral context) contributors to human development. Moreover, researchers can benefit from considering the integration of these factors in their work and drawing from developmental theory when designing investigations. Relative to the particulars of conducting developmentally informed work, among other things it is important for researchers to understand the limitations of age as a proxy for developmental status. It is also essential that measures be designed and assessed using participants from the population of interest rather than to presume that modifications of assessments used on other developmental groups suffice to capture target constructs. These recommendations and many of the other points in this chapter are not new; however, as mentioned before, they are often not put into practice. This may reflect the lack of incentive noted by Whaley (2007) that owes in large part to the labor-intensive nature of conducting developmentally informed research. However, as sport and exercise psychology matures, it becomes increasingly necessary for us to go to the trouble of attending to these issues if we are to meaningfully advance the knowledge base.

Cultural Sport Psychology

Special Measurement Considerations

Tatiana V. Ryba, PhD, Robert J. Schinke, EdD, and Natalia B. Stambulova, PhD

The cultural turn in sport and exercise psychology has gained considerable attention as of late. During the writing of this chapter, a special edition of the *International Journal of Sport and Exercise Psychology* (Ryba & Schinke, 2009) pertaining to research methodology of cultural sport psychology was released. Concurrently, in 2009-2010 two edited textbooks were published pertaining to applied practice (see Schinke & Hanrahan, 2009) and to the implications of the cultural turn for the theory and practice of psychological research in the field (see Ryba, Schinke, & Tenenbaum, 2010). This emerging trajectory can be traced back to progressive sport psychology authors—the pioneering feminist sport psychologists in particular—who brought issues of sociocultural difference, identity, power, meaning, reflexivity, and praxis into debates over knowledge production and legitimation (see Gill, 1994; Griffin, 1988, 1992; Harris, 1971, 1972; Oglesby, 1978). We also want to acknowledge the contribution of Rainer Martens (1979, 1987), who called more generally for research relevant within the field and informed by sport and exercise participants within their contexts.

In 1991, Lee and Rotella considered the practices of African American varsity athletes, including what the authors regarded as a tendency to express openly, and perhaps not so subtly, elation after a good performance. Lee and Rotella were interested in the athletes they observed and worked with perhaps because the athletes' overt expressiveness appeared from the authors' vantage to lack in humility and restraint. Such expressiveness, whether it was perceived or real, seemed to serve as a counterpoint to the authors' own socialization.

Though the authors were correct in their suspicions that groups of athletes can be considered in terms of their race and that uniqueness can (and does) in fact exist among groups of athletes in the field, the consideration was and continues to be more challenging than initially proposed.

Andersen (1993) correctly pointed out that there are as many within-culture as across-culture differences that practitioners (and researchers, as we have found) need to consider within their work. The cultural turn is a burgeoning trajectory within sport and health psychology in which space must be made for an open and candid discussion among participants and researchers (please note the ordering of the two parties) regarding how best to achieve understanding and to seek novel solutions to old problems by working collaboratively in a form of an active partnership guided by the participant. The means through which dialogue is negotiated (and when necessary, renegotiated) are meant to forefront the practices and deeper standpoint of the participant, sometimes entirely in the place of the researcher's methodological preferences, training, and personal orientation. The methodological approach and subsequent method are guided by relevant (to the participant) aspects borrowed from the participant's cultural origin, perhaps pertaining to socioeconomic background, socialization, religion, race, gender, and sexuality. Though *culture* as a general term is the point of departure within the immediate chapter, remember that the cultural turn extends well beyond the confines of broad characteristics such as race and nationality (Schinke, Hanrahan, & Catina, 2009).

Cultural and within-cultural norms can be found within pockets of people where shared practices such as euphemisms, gestures, and dress codes become small, though not definitive, parts of how people relate and conversely silence one another. The intent through the cultural turn is to share the richness of the participant's standpoint—a richness that is arguably lost when sport researchers employ a mainstream approach (among the researchers) to present research about the cultural other. Previously, the participant's standpoint when diverging from that of the researcher was inadvertently presented to the reader as strange and exotic (Denzin & Lincoln, 1998; see also Ryba, 2009). Through the cultural turn we might ponder how strange and exotic the practices of researchers journeying into unfamiliar places must have seemed to the participants and the people to whom they recounted their research experiences. Researchers engaging in the cultural turn reconsider how participants are constituted—presenting them not as autonomous and value free but as "saturated with cultural meanings and social norms" (Ryba & Schinke, 2009, p. 264), where people produce such meaning in and through their and our respective cultural practices (see Bruner, 1990; Kral, Burkhardt, & Kidd, 2002).

Inherent in the cultural turn and the tenets that inform it is cultural praxis (Ryba & Wright, 2005). Cultural praxis is an ongoing process in which theory is considered in relation to social practice and in which the manifestations of that intersection are meant to contribute to meaningful social action and human progress among people who are marginalized (see also Bredemeier, 2001). When researchers consider what is achieved through the cultural turn, several unique aspects surface that serve as a potential counterpoint to previous malpractice in and through research. These are identified within the literature by authors such as Linda Smith (1999). On one level, the information gleaned through culture-informed projects offers a richness to the data that correctly situates the participants in their lived reality, where what matters includes not only thoughts, behaviors, and words but also what informs such facets of daily existence. When a more informed approach is used—one in which the researcher meets the participant on level ground and the practices of both people become part of the research—embedded within the work is the encouragement to speak and share openly and more thoroughly on life experiences (Schinke et al., 2008). Arguably, some researchers might respond that to integrate and forefront culture within research is far too challenging and likely messy. However, to proceed with an awareness that culture is a part of how the participant is constituted and then to turn a blind eye to that aspect of the person oversimplifies, silences, and, in some cases, misrepresents the willing participant. In consequence, what is written on paper and then read incorrectly educates the reader, misinforms future research and practice, and constrains potential growth opportunities among researchers, practitioners, and clients. The cultural turn offers many areas for growth. Uncharted in sport and exercise psychology are the in-depth practices of most groups and subgroups. Through a closer consideration of who the participants are in a more holistic sense, in which cultural aspects are a part of how the participants are constituted, the researcher and those touched by the researcher's written words can seek to understand and, through understanding, help affirm the participant on a much deeper level. Hence, the cultural turn promises a potent approach to research and practice that is intuitively appealing and even emancipating.

What follows is an introductory methodological discussion of key tenets pertaining to cultural psychological research. We preface our discussion with a caveat. The present work is meant as a starting point for others fascinated by the topic. As such, this chapter is written as a catalyst and not as a definitive work meant to encapsulate and thus prematurely oversimplify a burgeoning and uncharted trajectory.

Assumptions and Principles of Cultural Sport Psychology

Culture . . . shapes human life and the human mind, . . . gives meaning to action by situating its underlying intentional states in an interpretive system. It does this by imposing the patterns inherent in the culture's symbolic systems—its language and discourse modes, the forms of logical and narrative explication, and the patterns of mutually dependent communal life. (Bruner, 1990, p. 34)

Since the publication of the often cited "Cross-Cultural Analysis in Exercise and Sport Psychology: A Void in the Field" by Duda and Allison (1990), in which the authors challenged scholars of sport and exercise psychology to give serious consideration to the role of race and ethnicity in producing human behavior, there has been an increase in cross-cultural research activity in the field. Much of the work has been devoted to cultural validation of psychological instruments and identification of similarities and variations in psychological constructs across cultures (e.g., Alfermann, Stambulova, & Zemaityte, 2004; Si, Rethorst, & Willimczik, 1995; Stambulova, Stephan, & Järphag, 2007). In that sense, we can talk about scholars turning their gaze to culture while maintaining their epistemological anchors in positivism. Another reading of the shift to culture in sport psychology is linked to the cultural turn, which swept through social sciences in the 1960s and is a permutation of the postmodernist critique of the production of knowledge. The cultural turn gave rise to discourses such as cultural studies and cultural and indigenous psychology that are firmly positioned in social constructionism. While cross-cultural and cultural researchers are interested in understanding the role of culture in psychological processes, they approach the study of culture from different perspectives.

The conceptualization of culture within psychology tends to take either an etic or an emic perspective. According to Ponterotto (2005), the etic view involves universal laws and behaviors that transcend nations and cultures to apply to all humans, while the emic view involves constructs and behaviors that are unique to the individual or group in a particular sociocultural context. Etic studies typically are taken within cross-cultural psychology, where psychological aspects of performance are compared across cultures. Culture is used to indicate some type of belonging to a group and is usually based on a geographical location or linguistic identification. Hence, for cross-cultural researchers culture is a coherent given, "theorized as an independent variable and assumed to influence the psychological functioning of individuals" (O'Dell, de Abreu, & O'Toole, 2004, p. 138).

Emic studies are commonly found within cultural and indigenous psychology, where psychological processes are assumed to be realized through cultural contexts. This is a crucial point to grasp: Mental processes and behaviors such as motivation, emotion, and well-being are not simply influenced but also constituted by sociocultural contexts. Emphasizing this point, Markus and Hamedani (2007) have stated that "just as neuroscientists scan the brain, seeking to produce a neural mapping of the mind, so must psychologists scan the sociocultural environment to generate a sociocultural mapping of the mind" (p. 8). Within this approach, therefore, the main goal is to understand how the varied cultural meanings and practices afford psychological activity or functioning.

Cultural psychology emphasizes the study of meaning from the point of view of cultural members and the understanding of how identity, belonging, and culture are produced in and through everyday practices. Hence, for cultural researchers, there is no separation between subject and context, as they "live together, require each other, and dynamically, dialectically, and jointly make each other up" (Shweder, 1990, p. 1). Given the theorized inter-

dependence of human psyche and sociocultural context, the main assumption of cultural psychology is that the psychological nature of human beings is culturally and historically variable (Shi-xu, 2002; Shweder, 1990, 2003). To substantiate this point, Markus and Hamedani (2007) have contended that results obtained in many cultural psychological studies vary from normative white, middle-class North American understandings. For example, Tsai, Knutson, and Fung (2006) identified that in Taiwanese contexts, feeling good is more likely to be associated with feeling calm and tranquil rather than feeling energized and excited; Uchida, Nora-sakkunkit, and Kitayama (2004) suggested that in Japanese contexts, happiness includes sadness; and Schinke and colleagues (2007) observed that in Canadian indigenous contexts, an elite athlete's sport career is likely to be a communal endeavor.

Methodologically, it is a challenging task to analyze intentional psychological worlds permuted by sociocultural textuality. Cultural researchers are confronted not only by traditional ontological and epistemological questions but also by the necessity to tease out the psychological from the sociocultural. Challenging the Cartesian separation between the psychological and the cultural, the focus is on processes of making each other up to understand the mutually constituting relationship between human psyche and context. As Jaan Valsiner (2004), the editor of *Culture and Psychology* has asserted, a crucial breakthrough in cultural psychology can come from the move from psychology's assumptions of linear causal entities to those of catalytic processes in the causal system involved in specific outcomes. The need for novel, wide-spectrum, and context-linked research designs is evident, akin to a critical rethinking and reformulation of universal psychological concepts as potentialities or tendencies contingent on sociocultural context. We now turn to the notions of culture and meaning, which are central to cultural research.

Culture as Patterns

Raymond Williams, one of the founding fathers of cultural studies, contended that *culture* is one of the most contested words in the English language (see Williams, 1983). The most widespread use of the term involves the works and practices of intellectual and especially artistic activities, such as painting, sculpture, literature, music, theater, and film. Such an understanding of culture as material production is prevalent in the German, Scandinavian, and Slavonic language groups, and this understanding arguably has become normative in cultural anthropology and archeology. Another usage of the word in English, which is distinctly dominant in Italian and French, relates to aesthetic, spiritual, and intellectual learning and gives a sense of a general process of human development. *Culture* can also be used to indicate a particular way of life of a historical period, a people, or a group. According to Williams (1983),

> it is the range and overlap of meanings that is significant. The complex of senses indicates a complex argument about the relations between general human development and a particular way of life, and between both and the works and practices of art and intelligence. (p. 91)

What we have in Williams' account of culture is an insightful identification of the explicit and implicit patterns of historically contingent discursive meanings embodied in social structures, everyday practices, and material artifacts; a naming of the catalytic interdependence between cultural patterns and human actions; and an explication that culture is not a monolithic and fixed set of beliefs and norms that groups possess as "internally homogenous, externally distinctive objects" (Hermans & Kempen, 1998, p. 1113). An important caveat here, offered by Markus and Hamedani (2007), is that while cultural meanings, practices, and artifacts are contested and shifting, they nevertheless create and maintain the social reality (in a given cultural context) within which meaningful actions are produced. Hence, in cultural psychological research, culture is conceptualized as a pattern of constituting processes.

Underscoring the dynamic transaction between the psychological and the sociocultural, Thorpe (2009, 2010) critiqued the extant sport psychology research on extreme sports. The dominant approach taken by sport psychologists appears to be on establishing an associative link between participation in extreme sports and individual dispositions. By equating observed behaviors within extreme sport cultures with individual attributes or traits, such as type T or sensation-seeking personalities, researchers have created a monolithic representation of the behavioral differences between extreme and traditional sport participants. In doing so, many studies reviewed by Thorpe repeatedly reinforced stereotypes of extreme sports and their participants; glossed over complex cultural dynamics and geopolitical differences within the extreme sports; and presented participants as a homogenous group with similar personality types, motives, and experiences.

When Thorpe adopted an ethnographic approach to develop a contextual understanding of snowboarding culture, a complex cultural pattern emerged that elucidated the psychological enterprise of acquiring dispositions, perceptions, and appreciations through a persistent engagement in

snowboarding realities. A particularly revealing lesson of the cultural psychological analysis was given through the reexamination of an incident that involved American snowboarder Lindsey Jacobellis at the 2006 Winter Olympics. The Jacobellis story drew enormous media attention, as the athlete was criticized for performing a needlessly risky aerial maneuver in the last 109 yd (100 m) of her winning race—a maneuver that cost her the Olympic gold. The official verdict was that Jacobellis lost her concentration by celebrating the victory prematurely. Highlighting on the example of Lindsey Jacobellis the catalytic interdependence between the individual and the context, Thorpe arrived at an assessment of the infamous Lindsey leap that is entirely different from the one offered by culture-blind sport psychology (for full details, see Thorpe, 2009).

Meaning

Integral to understanding how cultural narratives and social practices "regulate, express, transform, and permute the human psyche" (Shweder, 1990, p. 1) and in turn are products of human action is the concept of *meaning* (Adams & Markus, 2001; Bruner, 1990; Geertz, 1973). Meaning, as a unit of analysis, illuminates the interdependence and mutual constitution of the psychological and sociocultural. Indeed, meanings for self and identity, well-being, motivation, and other concepts cannot be autonomously produced in the individual's head, just as they cannot be located solely in the works and practices of the external world. Eagleton (1983) explicated the cultural ontology of being when he asserted that "we emerge as subjects from inside a reality which we can never fully objectify, which encompasses both 'subject' and 'object', which is inexhaustible in its meaning, and which constitutes us quite as much as we constitute it" (p. 62). The idea that the world can be read in a multiplicity of ways (i.e., be inexhaustible in its meaning) is significant and marks a crucial break from positivism that assumes that an objective perception of reality is theoretically possible. For cultural psychologists, reality is constructed in the social network of power and knowledge relations and becomes meaningful to us through engagement with worldly phenomena and the interpretation of our experiences. The interpretation, of course, is achieved through symbolic systems of language and discourse that are culturally and historically contingent. Meaning then is not fixed and universal but is discursively produced. Moreover, meaning is negotiated as well as contested along various discourses of class, gender, race, ethnicity, sexuality, and so on (Shi-xu, 2002; Weedon, 1997).

The growing cultural and indigenous research has contested naturalized and taken-for-granted meanings that appear to organize white, middle-class North American psyches as *basic* human needs, drives, or psychological processes that still provide "the unmarked framework of reference for most work in psychology" (Markus & Hamedani, 2007, p. 9). As the power structure between Western and non-Western nations changes, people who traditionally were silenced have acquired the means to articulate the clash between images and realities imposed from the outside (etic perspective) and ontological concepts coming from the inside (emic perspective). The important goal of cultural sport psychology, therefore, is to analyze the complex of meanings for staple sport psychological concepts such as motivation, emotion, cognition, development, self, and identity in various sociocultural contexts (loosely associated with nation, religion, ethnicity, gender, sexuality, class, ability, and so on). It is culture that constitutes psychological worlds and gives meanings to actions; therefore, in the attempt to understand the processes through which psychological functioning is realized in a particular context, the focus is not on groups (e.g., the Americans, the Europeans, the blacks) but on the implicit and explicit patterns of cultural meanings embedded in social practices and cultural artifacts.

Measuring Culture

The key premise of cultural research in psychology is that culture inhabits human psychological worlds, transforming behavior into meaningful acts. Hence cultural psychologists attempt to give accounts of culture in psychological processes. Most cultural researchers in sport psychology advocate the use of qualitative methods and reflexivity in making sense of how sociocultural context and psyche make each other up. Krane and Baird (2005), for example, offered ethnography to extend and enhance our understanding of applied sport psychology. They argued that "it is impossible to comprehend athletes' mental states and behaviors without understanding the social norms and culture that encompass them" (p. 88). In a similar vein, Smith and Sparkes (2010), in their attempts to understand how stories and storytelling organize subjective experiencing of "interrupted body projects" (p. 77), approached sport narratives as cultural artifacts produced in particular sociocultural fields.

While researchers rely on the same building blocks of qualitative research—interview, observation, and document or artifact collection—not all qualitative inquiries fall into the category of cultural

research. Similar methods can be used from different epistemological stances. It is the enhanced sensitivity to epistemological groundings of the project that offers a possibility to reimagine traditional fieldwork in order to derive findings grounded in cultural ontology of a socially constructed reality. The following two examples explore the cultural epistemology of knowing in their depiction of how conventional qualitative methods such as interview, observation, and text or artifact collection can be rearticulated to open a conceptual window of cultural understanding.

Research Example 1: Scandinavian Project on Athletic Talent Development Environment

The Scandinavian Project on Athletic Talent Development Environment (Henriksen, Stambulova, & Roessler, 2010a; 2010b) is a multiple case study of three clubs or teams (one in Denmark, one in Sweden, and one in Norway) with a successful history of producing top-level senior athletes from among its juniors. The project is based on a holistic ecological perspective (Henriksen et al., 2010a; 2010b) that shifted its focus from talented athletes to their context or environment. From such a perspective, an *athletic talent development environment* (ATDE) is defined as "a young athlete's social relationships both inside and outside the world of sport—social relationships that have a sport club or team as their core but also include the larger context in which the club or team is embedded" (Henriksen et al., 2010a, p. 213). Each ATDE is considered as a unique system with elements, structure, activities, organizational culture, and development embedded in the broader sociocultural context. For all the case studies in the project, the first objective was to describe the ATDE and the second was to explain why the particular ATDE was successful in nurturing athletic talents.

In the Scandinavian Project, cultural turn ideas were already incorporated on a conceptual level, being a part of the two working models created by the research group—the ATDE model and the environment success factors (ESF) model (Henriksen et al., 2010a)—that guided the data collection. In the ATDE working model, the athlete's environment is considered holistically—that is, it is considered as consisting of athletic and nonathletic domains, microlevels and macrolevels, and a time frame. The athletic domain covers the part of the environment directly related to sport, whereas the nonathletic domain presents all the other spheres of an athlete's life. Directly surrounding the young athletes is the club environment, with coaches, managers, elite senior and younger athletes, and experts. Other components include school, family, peers, and related teams and clubs (at the microlevel), as well as sport federations, the media, reference groups, and the educational system (at the macrolevel). Some of the components (e.g., school) clearly belong to one level and one domain, whereas others (e.g., the family) may transcend levels or domains. The macroenvironment also involves various cultural contexts, such as national culture, general sport culture, the culture of the specific sport, and youth culture.

The ESF working model outlines a set of factors, such as the preconditions (human, material, financial), the process (practices, camps, competitions, social events), the organizational culture, and the individual and team development and achievements, that all interact to create the ATDE's effectiveness in developing prospective elite athletes and helping them to transition to the senior elite level in their sports. *Organizational culture* is central to the ESF model and consists of three levels: cultural artifacts, espoused values, and basic assumptions (Schein, 1992). *Cultural artifacts* include stories and myths told in the environment, customs and traditions, and physical cultural manifestations such as clothing, buildings, and organization charts. *Espoused values* are the social principles, norms, goals, and standards that the organization shows to the world; they exist in the minds of the members and serve as visible motivations for actions. *Basic assumptions* are underlying reasons for actions. They consist of beliefs and assumptions that are no longer questioned but are taken for granted and that exist at a level below that of the members' consciousness. They are therefore derived by the researchers. Organizational culture is characterized by the integration of the key basic assumptions into a *cultural paradigm* guiding socialization of new members, providing stability, and adapting the organization to a constantly changing environment.

The ESF and ATDE models complement each other in such a way that the ATDE model provides a framework to describe the environment and the ESF model helps to summarize factors influencing its effectiveness. In both working models culture is visible as a patterned process constituting an ATDE.

As of Spring 2011, two case studies—the Danish 49er sailing team and the Swedish track-and-field club IFK Växjö—had been completed and published (Henriksen et al., 2010a; 2010b). The Norwegian case study is in progress. The aspects relevant to the cultural measurement and findings related to organizational cultures of the ATDEs in the two completed cases are presented briefly here based on the two aforementioned publications.

In both the Danish and Swedish cases, the two working models (the ATDE and ESF models) guided the data collection from *multiple perspectives* (in-depth interviews with administrators, coaches, and athletes), from *multiple situations* (observation of training, competitions, meetings, and so on), and from the *analysis of club or team written or website documents*. In the framework of these traditional qualitative methods, the research group focused on meanings the participants attached to their activities and interactions within their environments. Participant observation of the team or club's daily life conducted by the principal researcher was especially important for understanding the organizational cultures of the respective ATDEs. Such observation included about 300 h of living in the Danish ATDE and more than 100 h of living in the Swedish ATDE. This made it possible to study the athletes in diverse contexts, such as at training, in competition, and at various official and unofficial social events. The fieldwork also included a number of informal conversations with parents, athletes, and coaches (some of whom were not really members of the focal environments but provided additional insights into the cultures). Moreover, the observer was closely involved in the activities of the team or club members (e.g., helping to organize equipment, move buoys, measure wind direction, make food for social events, and so on) and got a profound feel of the organizational culture and its basic assumptions not only through talking with and watching the members but also through doing things together with them. Data from all the sources (interviews, observation, and analysis of documents) were treated together, and the two working models were transformed into empirical models capturing the specifics of each environment in terms of its structure (the ATDE empirical model) and the factors contributing to its success in talent development, with organizational culture as a core (the ESF empirical model).

The Danish 49er sailing team and the IFK Växjö track-and-field club appeared different in many ways. For example, the former is really small and consists of a coach and a group of athletes divided into two subgroups: the national team (6 athletes) and the talent group (8 athletes); all are males. The latter is a big club with about 550 athletes and 90 coaches; 50 prospective elite athletes aged 15 to 17 y represent both genders and various track-and-field disciplines. The Danish team does not support parental involvement in the team, while in the Swedish club parents are actively involved as coaches and co-organizers of all the events. The Swedish club has a number of indoor and outdoor training facilities (e.g., several running tracks and a weight training gym) and club offices, whereas the Danish environment is not situated in a specific location: The team travels the world and practices at the sites of the major competitions or where the weather provides good training conditions.

Although each of the two successful ATDEs is unique, some of their characteristics are rather similar. On a descriptive level, the two environments share the following: (a) They contain relationships and interactions of different components in the environment with a central component coordinating these relationships (the Danish Sailing Federation in the 49er sailing environment and the management group in the IFK Växjö track-and-field club); (b) elite athletes play an important role in the development of prospective elite athletes; (c) prospective elite athletes have obligations toward younger athletes, which accustoms them to a position of responsibility; and (d) the environments constantly evolve, adjusting to current tendencies and progress in the sports. The two environments also share a number of factors contributing to their success, the most important of which are (a) strong organizational cultures pervading every aspect of daily life in the environment and (b) basic assumptions revolving around groups of athletes and coaches openly sharing their knowledge in traditionally secretive cultures of both sailing and track and field.

Organizational Culture of the Danish 49er Sailing Team

During initial observations of this team, what stood out immediately were a marked informality, a high degree of interaction among the athletes, a continual drive for perfection in every detail, and verbal artifacts as dominating the environment. As an essential part of living on the beach, many anecdotes are told everyday, mostly by the elite athletes. These stories seldom highlight sport results; rather, they are about experiences of the world, humorous incidents, lessons learned, difficulties faced, and mutual support. Key values expressed by the participants in the environment include working together as a group, helping each other, and having fun while aiming for top-level performance. The athletes often referred to *the Danish model*, which one elite athlete explained as follows: "Every country wants to be the best. At the same time their athletes compete among themselves. We are the only nation that has chosen to solve this dilemma by working together. And I am damned proud of that." The coach highlighted the fact that this approach has characterized the group from the outset: "It is like a tradition that you are willing to pass on your knowledge. What you

are given, you give back to the next generation." Analyses of interviews but mainly experiences of the principal researcher while living within the culture allowed for the structuring of a cultural paradigm of the Danish 49er sailing team. There are six interconnected basic assumptions: (1) The individual athlete must take responsibility for his own excellence, (2) a strong team is a precondition for the elite performance of its members, (3) the elite athletes have priority but also have a duty to help younger athletes, (4) you can always improve, (5) top results are achieved through a focus on performance process and development rather than on results, (6) through open sharing of knowledge and cooperation, everybody improves. Autonomy is considered a key attribute of a prospective winner in sailing, as was demonstrated clearly one afternoon in the yacht club (from observation material):

> While having a cup of coffee, a group of Danish sailors discussed the dismissal of the American coach of a Danish elite boat (not a 49er). The sailors agreed that, with him as a coach, the crew had performed well. But rather than teaching the crew to analyze and make decisions, the coach had told them exactly how to do things. An elite sailor from a different type of boat commented: "That way they will never learn how to handle things for themselves and make their own decisions on the water. Weather conditions change all the time. A coach like that can push them a bit of the way, but he will never be able to take them all the way to the top." The other athletes agreed.

As a fundamental governing principle, openness and cooperation are at the core of the team's cultural paradigm. The coach explained how learning is promoted in the whole group through open sharing of knowledge:

> We always put our cards on the table, even with foreign partners. I have always had the idea that, if we train for a period with one other crew, we will give them something that makes them better. But we will also receive something back and improve. If we then do the same with another crew, then we will learn something from them. So it's all about keeping close relations to the international environment and being open.

Organizational Culture of the IFK Växjö Track-and-Field Club

The principal researcher's first impressions of this club's organizational culture were the family-like interactions, the high level of feedback and discussion among coaches, and the difficulty of understanding which athletes belonged to which groups. Publications and posters explicitly state the club's mission, and a special booklet presents core values of the club to new coaches, parents, athletes, and business sponsors. A member of the board explained the role of the booklet: "Our blue book represents a mindset. . . . We have deliberately compiled a philosophy, rather than a manual." The IFK Växjö club's cultural paradigm was derived by the research group based on the club documents, interviews, and a feel of the principal researcher during his observations. This paradigm is characterized by seven interrelated basic assumptions: (1) Excellence can be reached through cooperation and openness; (2) we are a family, in which everybody contributes; (3) group and team organization is a precondition for the development and continued motivation of athletes and coaches; (4) attitude beats class; (5) an athlete is a whole person; (6) successful development is more important than early results; and (7) the club can always improve. The first and central basic assumption is well illustrated in the story told by an elite coach:

> I was called up by an American coach who asked me about some training issues in heptathlon. I told him it was difficult to describe over the phone, but I could just send him Carolina's last seven years training plans. He was stunned and said: "You are crazy, man. You should make a fortune on those plans." I told him it was just training, not secrets, just a lot of papers with numbers on them. What counts is what you make of it, how you make the athlete train with focus and intensity. He did not understand.

One elite athlete used the metaphor of a forest to present her image of IFK Växjö: "We have many branches and twigs representing different ways one can go. But the roots are intertwined and grow in the same soil." Some prospective elite athletes directly refer to the club as their second home. The club puts in an effort to maintain large groups of athletes, offering friendship, a sense of belonging, and fun. As explained by a coach, "many of these athletes . . . will not become elite. Still, as friends of athletes who may reach elite level, they are important members of the group." Coaches expect the athletes to show focus, discipline, and drive for excellence in training and evaluate the athletes' attitudes more often than their skill level.

Summary

The organizational cultures of the Danish 49er sailing team and the IFK Växjö track-and-field club are characterized by high degrees of coherence among their different levels. Artifacts, espoused values expressed by the participants, and basic assumptions, derived from analysis of actual behaviors, are highly consistent (e.g., what athletes and coaches say they do and what they actually do are the same), allowing the cultures to be an effective stabilizing force in the environment. Owing to a lack of preconditions (e.g., financial resources and professional coaching), in both ATDEs there has been an increased focus on building and maintaining the organizational cultures that underpin the athletic and personal development of their members. Such cultures are constituted in the team or club members' activities and interactions, but these cultures also pervade and constitute every aspect of the environment's life, including how the members relate to the lack of natural advantages and what happens in training and at competitions and meetings.

Communicative validity of these studies was provided through a stakeholder check. In both ATDEs under study, the principal researcher presented related empirical models and cultural paradigms to members of the environments, which led to several new initiatives on their part to improve their practices. The participants commented on the value of feedback from the research group, which helped them to identify blind spots and to optimize their respective environments.

Research Example 2: Working With Coresearchers From Wikwemikong Unceded Indian Reserve

There are arguably many ways to engage in research while working with participants and coresearchers from groups whose cultural orientation is different from yours. In Northern Ontario, Canada, the population comprises residents from a variety of backgrounds, with the largest populations stemming from Anglophone and Francophone Canadians and Canadian Aboriginal peoples (as noted in Smith, 1999, each Aboriginal community is made up of a people). When I (Robert) relocated to Northern Ontario in order to accept a university faculty position, I was already aware that when athletes and coaches come from differing cultures, there is a challenge though also an opportunity to seek a shared understanding through an appreciation of both cultural standpoints. During our earliest work with Canadian Aboriginal athletes, my mainstream colleagues and I asked through semistructured interviews what motivational practices were employed, both personally and through community resources, in order to persist in elite mainstream sport contexts. Most of the athletes were delighted by the topic matter, as they recognized, similar to the experience conveyed by Waneek Horn-Millar (Brant et al., 2002) at the North American Indigenous Games, that when Aboriginal athletes enter into mainstream sport contexts, the expectation is that adaptation is solely the responsibility of the Aboriginal athletes. As such, the questions posed through the project allowed the participants to convey, based on their firsthand experiences, how mainstream sport experiences at the elite level can silence athletes from minority or marginalized groups.

Considering the initial research my colleagues and I did with Canadian Aboriginal athletes more closely, there were a few strengths in the work. One strength was an attempt at consultation with community-appointed coresearchers throughout the project. Consultation was sought in terms of question development and wording, recruitment, refinements throughout the data collection and also with the data analysis, and finally through coauthoring and copresenting. The intent through the research was to add a level of authenticity to the research while also forging a stronger and more trusting relationship with the coresearchers and their community. Though we (the mainstream authors only) believed such endeavors were noteworthy, upon reflection the methods were critically flawed. In fact, I recall that toward the end of the first project, the editor from one sport psychology journal rejected one of our submissions, with both reviewers indicating that our work was research done on another's culture but was not cultural research. Though the criticism at first blush was highly critical, the editor and reviewers were correct in their assessment. The project was mainstream in many respects, and one of the many worthwhile examples of the mainstream orientation within the work was the use of semistructured interviewing (see Schinke, Peltier, et al., 2009). Though researchers often employ various unstructured to structured one-on-one interviewing protocols with participants in their projects, such strategies are inherently culturally informed. For example, consider that in some cultures, meetings with strangers are meant to happen within a group setting or at the very least with the accompaniment of a friend or family member (see Hanrahan, 2004, 2009). Researchers also should consider what the objective of the research is and whether the questions should be posed more generally to a cultural community as opposed to individuals, out of respect for the multiplicity of voices passionate about the subject. Individual interviews are inherently individual, and when the participant originates from a collectivist orientation, such experiences might be regarded as petrifying; participant comfort may be possible only through a group gathering such as a community meeting or a culturally informed group interview such as, in our case, a talking circle (see Blodgett et al., 2008).

Our project team's more recent work is slightly more culturally infused by local Aboriginal knowledge and practices, as are the methods we now use to gather information. In terms of the project focus, it was proposed partway through the team's earliest work that we shift our focus from elite athletes to youth sport participants engaging in physical activity on the reserve. The proposed shift in focus stemmed from poor retention of youths in physical activity within Wikwemikong. Paralleling more general statistical findings (see Canadian Institute for Health Information, 2009), Aboriginal youths on reserve are an at-risk population. Health risks encountered by on-reserve youths include higher rates than the national average of type 1 diabetes, substance misuse, violence, educational dropout, teenage pregnancy, and overall despondence. Arguably, the answers to such challenges are not easily resolved, due to the sociohistorical challenges, which are outlined elsewhere (see Schinke et al., 2009). As a counterstrategy to resolve the challenges posed to Aboriginal youths on reserve, the Wikwemikong community coresearchers proposed an exploration into what the intended youths would like from their community programs. Consequently, the conception of the idea and the potency of the subject matter were determined and led from within Wikwemikong.

Pushing the point of group strategies in data collection further, the project team reconsidered who elicits information from participants. The intent is to build trust in the participants through the research approach, while also creating an environment that is comfortable for the participants. When the team transitioned to group-level data collection strategies, the researchers and coresearchers in collaboration led the discussions. Closer to the present, we revisited our data collection strategies once more and reconceptualized who asks questions and listens to answers, especially when information is being gathered from outside the team's age cohort. For example, because the focus in our more recent project was on how to engage more on-reserve youths in sport and activity, when we met with youth participants in the schools, the talking circles were led by youths, for youths. When meetings were held with elders, those meetings were led by an elder, with discussions entered into in the local Aboriginal dialect. Through the reconceptualizing of who should be the researcher within a given context, beyond the data collection strategies, we learned what many qualitative researchers before us, such as Patton (2002), have known for some time: The researcher is part of and not apart from the instrumentation. If the participants do not feel able to express themselves through appropriate methods and through the most suitable investigator given the context, the method can silence. When researchers engage in a research experience with people from a marginalized culture, silencing extends beyond the immediate history, possibly to a series of silencing experiences in and through research that can be traced back in time (see Smith, 1999). Consequently, the intent through the development of appropriate methods is to empower oppressed communities and, in so doing, develop more sensitive and inclusive research.

Conclusion

The major tenet of cultural psychology is that the psychological nature of human beings is culturally and historically variable. Therefore, we advocate a psychological study of sport participants' behaviors and mental processes within a culturally meaningful context. Our research examples highlighted the use of qualitative methods in gaining in-depth knowledge of particular (sport) cultures, their development and unique sociocultural dynamic, and the values of cultural members embodied in social relationships and everyday practices. In both cases, this groundwork was essential in gaining an insight into the culture meaning systems that guided observed behaviors and representations of cultural members. Living the culture allowed researchers to grasp the elusive constitutive link between cultural worldview and material practices, including the supposedly neutral research methods. In addition, both examples, although to a different extent, emphasized the role of research in articulating sport psychological theories with cultural contextual specificity into praxis.

As our society becomes more diverse due to the increased mobility associated with politicized globalization processes, there is an urgency to undertake the psychology of sociocultural difference in sport and exercise. Indeed, the social context in which sport behavior occurs has changed profoundly. The constituting unity of psyche and context is saturated with the multiplicity of conflicting, hybrid, and migratory cultural meanings that underlie intentional states and afford actions. Yet much of sport psychological research continues to be culture blind, focusing on an autonomous, sterile individual and individual attributes. Although there has been an increase in cross-cultural research in the field, it tends to draw on positivistic methodology to test theories and concepts and make statements about sport behavior in various cultural contexts. Conceptualizing culture as a coherent entity—internally homogenous, externally distinctive—that affects behavior, cognition, and emotion (almost like a trait in and of itself) contributes very little to our understanding of conditions and processes through which culture unleashes psychological functioning. Rather, this approach to the study of culture tends to normalize the constitution of white, middle-class, and Anglo-American psyche, perpetuating the construction of stereotypes about disenfranchised sociocultural groups.

In this chapter, we have outlined cultural sport psychology as a trajectory in the field that is concerned with theoretical, methodological, and practical implications of the cultural, sociopolitical, and historical constitution of human psychological worlds. The goal of cultural sport psychology is to extract meanings for psychological concepts that are embedded in, but also constructed through, the cultural symbolic systems of linguistic, discursive, and material practices. The focus is on understanding the complex processes of cultural construction of the subject; the way cultural resources and social practices enable (or disable) agency, emotion, experience, kinship, and action; and the construction of inclusive and just sport environments. In that sense, cultural research offers conceptual and methodological tools to begin to tackle sociocultural inequality of health and sport and exercise participation and to develop sport psychological theories that are ontologically relevant to a given symbolic system of meanings.

15

Synthesizing Measurement Outcomes Through Meta-Analysis

Betsy Jane Becker, PhD, and Soyeon Ahn, PhD

This chapter looks at measurement issues in sport psychology from a different perspective—the perspective of meta-analysis. *Meta-analysis*, or the analysis of analyses, is a term that Gene Glass (1976) coined to mean the quantitative review of related study results. Meta-analysis enables researchers to evaluate whether results are similar across studies and, if they are not similar, to explore reasons why different results may have occurred. It also provides a means for examining whether results generalize across different settings, treatment implementations, types of participants, and, most critically for this chapter, types of measures.

We begin this chapter with a brief introduction to the process of meta-analysis and its use in sport and exercise psychology, drawing on work by Cooper (1982, 2009). We then describe each of the five stages of meta-analysis. For each one we delineate the roles that measures and measurement issues play throughout the process. We draw on examples from a variety of meta-analyses in sport and exercise science. We finish the chapter with concluding thoughts.

This chapter also describes how meta-analyses can provide information about the constructs and measures important to sport and exercise psychology. We accomplish this by looking at several examples of meta-analyses that focus on specific measures and how those measures behave. A large portion of the literature on meta-analysis concerns validity generalization (Hunter & Schmidt, 2004). Validity generalization studies ask whether par-

ticular predictor–outcome relationships hold across contexts, often focusing on test validity for a specific measure or construct. One such meta-analysis concerns the relationship between scores on Borg's rating of perceived exertion (RPE) scale and a variety of physiological measures (Chen, Fan, & Moe, 2002). Some reviews focus on a single measure to examine a theoretical proposition or hypothesis rather than to study test validity. An example of research in this vein is a review on using the Profile of Mood States (POMS) to capture the iceberg profile (Rowley, Landers, Kyllo, & Etnier, 1995). Similarly, Craft, Magyar, Becker, and Feltz (2003) examined the subscales of the Competitive State Anxiety Index-2 (CSAI-2) as predictors of sport outcomes.

In this chapter we also discuss how measurement concerns, particularly the conceptualization and operationalization of measures, play important roles in meta-analysis even when the focus of the meta-analysis is not on the measures per se. To this end we draw on a number of different meta-analyses concerning exercise (Arent, Landers, & Etnier, 2000; Netz, Wu, Becker, & Tenenbaum, 2005; Wipfli, Rethorst, & Landers, 2008) and on one meta-analysis regarding self-efficacy and sport performance (Moritz, Feltz, Fahrbach, & Mack, 2000).

Many of the other chapters in this book focus on particular constructs—how they are conceptualized, their theoretical bases, and how they are measured. This chapter is not about specific constructs and measures but rather gives an overview of how meta-analysis can be used to inform us about the constructs and measures used in sport research. Also, meta-analysis forces the reviewer to be cognizant of the effects that choosing a single operationalization (or any particular set of operationalizations) of a construct can have on findings and conclusions.

Consequently, this chapter (in spite of its title) adopts a fairly broad view of measurement. We focus not only on the measurement of outcomes, although that is our primary focus. We argue that meta-analysts must also consider the measurement of predictors, especially when a relationship between variables is of interest. Because many meta-analyses in sport and exercise concern group differences, including treatment effects, we also consider the measurement of treatments. In such cases the treatment or grouping variable (such as gender or level of expertise) is the predictor. Proper characterization of (measurement of) treatment features is an important aspect of good research reporting that is critical to meta-analytical practice and to the reviewer's capacity to generalize across studies in sport and exercise psychology.

What Is Meta-Analysis?

Meta-analysis follows the same steps that the more familiar primary research process follows. The key difference is that meta-analysis focuses on and draws data from a series of studies rather than individual participants or cases. Cooper (1982, 2009) laid out five stages or steps in the process of meta-analysis and discussed the details of each one. Cooper's initial set of stages included problem formulation, data collection, data evaluation, data analysis, and presentation of results.

More recently, Cooper split two of the original stages into smaller parts. Data collection now includes searching the literature and gathering information from studies, while data analysis now includes analyzing and integrating the outcomes of studies and interpreting the evidence (2009, p. 12). In essence, to perform a meta-analysis the reviewer collects and processes data in much the same way that data are collected and processed in primary research—by following organized scientific principles, using rigorous methods, and being transparent at each step so that the work can be replicated. We now provide details on each of Cooper's five stages.

Problem Formulation

Before beginning a meta-analysis, the reviewer needs to have a problem in mind. Usually the starting point is a basic question such as, "What are the effects of exercise?" This question may seem very broad, so the reviewer might ask other questions to narrow the focus: "What kind of exercise is of interest? Who is exercising, and how often are they doing it? Is the exercise done in a group or by individuals? How long does each exercise session last?" By answering each of these questions, as well as others discussed in the following paragraphs, the reviewer arrives at a more clearly specified question. This is the task of problem formulation.

In writing these additional questions that might be asked, we have very quickly gotten quite concrete about the variables to be studied. It is useful to think about both the *conceptualization* and the *operationalization* of the variables or constructs of interest. Both must be considered during problem formulation. A simple concrete example makes this idea clear. Netz and colleagues (2005) conducted a meta-analysis on the effects of physical activity on "psychological well being in advanced age" (p. 272). This focus required a definition of advanced age. How old must a person be to be of advanced age? As Netz and colleagues noted, "any definition of old is arbitrary" (p. 274). However, to determine whether a study should be included in the review, it was necessary to set a criterion for identifying studies with older participants. Initially the authors required the samples to have mean ages older than 55 y. However, several studies were located with mean ages of 54 y, and the authors decided that excluding them would be inconsistent with past reviews. So, they operationally defined *advanced age* for a sample as having an average age of 54 y or older. Next we examine how a variety of issues related to measurement appear during problem formulation.

Problem formulation can't be done in a vacuum. Unlike a primary research study, where the researchers are often very happy that no one has done a study like the one they're planning to do, a meta-analysis cannot occur if no one has addressed the question the reviewer is asking. Because meta-analyses are based on series of studies, the reviewer needs to arrive at a question that has been addressed by more than one researcher in one existing study. The question must be narrow enough to be manageable but broad enough to be of general interest and broad enough that a reasonable number of studies have addressed it. To determine if a sufficient amount of evidence exists to address the question, reviewers often do some data collection while formulating the problem to be sure that enough evidence exists in the literature. Netz and colleagues (2005), for example, modified their definition of advanced age after collecting and examining a few studies. Thus the next critical step is data collection.

Data Collection

Data collection includes a variety of activities. Cooper's new breakdown—searching for studies and getting data out of them—captures much of what is done at this stage. The key question being asked here is what information should be included in the review. The meta-analyst asks what articles are eligible for inclusion and what information is needed from each article. The first part of the task usually entails developing search rules for use with databases, selecting the databases and journals to search, and developing initial lists of sources from past reviews and personal article collections. Usually at this point a reviewer will be able to assess whether a meta-analysis is possible and sensible. If no past reviews exist, and few articles are located in initial searches, it may be premature to attempt a meta-analysis. (Though technically a researcher needs only 2 studies to conduct a meta-analysis, it is very unusual to see a meta-analysis done with fewer than 5-10 studies.)

It is much more likely, though, that the meta-analyst will find many articles. This may raise the need to refine the search strategy by adding further limiting rules. One way to limit a search is to search only for studies in a limited time frame or for studies using particular instruments. While the Cochrane and Campbell Collaborations (organizations that promote evidence-based decision making) recommend writing a protocol and setting out the search strategies well before beginning the work of a systematic review, in our experience it is almost always necessary to revise the initial search strategies laid out in the protocol after completing a few preliminary searches.

As the searches proceed and studies are screened, the meta-analyst must then decide what information to gather from the studies included in the review. This task is easier to accomplish if clear definitions of all variables are developed during problem formulation. Decisions will hinge on the specific questions being asked. For example, in the review by Netz and colleagues (2005), one critical variable to be coded was the type of exercise (e.g., walking, stretching, and so on) that was being done by the participants in all groups in the studies. Also, the meta-analyst must record effect sizes or the data needed to compute them.

Again, the questions that drive the meta-analysis determine what is needed, but it often makes sense to code information about the nature of the measures used, even if that is not a focus of the investigation. Information about the independent and dependent variables (both the constructs and the ways in which they are measured) is among the most important information gathered. Finally, at this stage the coders are trained, coding manuals are created that give definitions and descriptions of the information to be abstracted, and checks are made on the reliability of the data that coders have recorded.

Data Evaluation

The next task in a meta-analysis involves assessing the quality of the studies and evidence in the review. The quality of the methods used is evaluated, and studies may be excluded if they do not meet preset quality standards. Later on we will show that a focus on measurement may lead the meta-analyst to examine features of the instruments used in each study. Issues commonly evaluated here concern study design, treatment implementation, and the like. For example, some studies on exercise use strict experimental designs, assigning participants at random to exercise or control conditions (e.g., Jensen & Kenny, 2004), while others allow participants to choose their exercise (e.g., Sridevi & Krishna Rao, 1996) or do not use comparison groups at all (e.g., Bhushan & Sinha, 2001). Meta-analysts might choose to examine only randomized controlled studies, as did Gu and Conn (2008) and Wipfli and colleagues (2008). Other meta-analysts may include studies using a variety of designs and thus at this stage would be careful to code the different design types used in each study. Only if the meta-analyst has coded information about study features such as design used, type of measure, and so on can questions be asked about whether the features have an effect on study outcomes.

Later we discuss a variety of ways that measurement figures at this stage of the review, with a primary focus on examining study features related to measurement issues. We also point out that the task of evaluating study quality and other study features is itself a measurement task.

Data Analysis and Public Presentation

At the data analysis stage, statistical methods for meta-analysis are used to explore the strength of effects and to explore variation in study outcomes. Typically, the meta-analyst desires to make statements about overall effects and to address questions such as, "On average, does exercising have an effect on psychological well-being in the elderly?" or "Does level of self-efficacy relate to level of performance on a sport task?" Often meta-analysts also ask the overall question of whether results appear to vary across studies, although it is not necessary to ask this question before addressing more specific issues concerning subgroups of studies and the like. In any case, it is wise to incorporate any identified between-study variations into the analyses in order to appropriately reflect the uncertainty in the data. (For a discussion of using random versus fixed effects models in meta-analysis, see Hedges and Vevea, 1998.)

Often the most interesting questions in a meta-analysis are the more specific questions, such as whether the effects of exercise differ according to the type of exercise or whether participant characteristics such as age or level of expertise affect the relationship or treatment effect under study. For example, in their examination of Borg's RPE scale, Chen and colleagues (2002) asked whether the RPE scale validity coefficients varied according to the gender and fitness level of the participants as well as the exercise protocol followed in the study. These analyses of potential predictors, often called *moderator analyses*, give the meta-analyst the ability to explain variation in effects—that is, they allow the meta-analyst to understand why study results vary.

This chapter does not cover specific statistical methods for meta-analysis, as to do so would require a book or more, and indeed such books have been written (e.g., Cooper, Hedges, & Valentine, 2009; Hedges & Olkin, 1985). Instead, we discuss the sorts of analyses that can be used to incorporate information about the measures used in studies and to investigate questions about differences related to the measures used in studies in the review.

The final stage of meta-analysis is public presentation of the results. We will not spend much time here, except to say that a key principle is to be explicit in reporting the details of the meta-analysis, so that other reviewers could replicate the meta-analysis if desired. Usually this means being as complete as possible in reporting methods and results, though practical considerations (e.g., page limits and journal restrictions) may limit the amount of detail that can be included. Later in the chapter we focus on aspects of reporting that relate to measurement issues.

Meta-Analysis in Sport and Exercise Psychology

Since its early days in the 1980s, meta-analysis has seen rapid growth in a variety of fields. Searches of Medline and PsycInfo in September 2009 with no restrictions other than entering *meta-analysis* as a keyword produced 22,133 hits and 8,215 hits, respectively. Clearly meta-analysis has become a widely used approach for summarizing the research literature.

To get a clearer sense of the growth of meta-analysis in sport and exercise research, we performed searches of PsycInfo over 5 y intervals beginning in 1976 (the year when Glass coined the term). We searched for *sport or exercise or athlete* with the keyword *meta-analysis*. The results are shown in figure 15.1.

While this plot is based on a rather small and arbitrary selection of search terms, the trend for the increasing use of meta-analysis is clear. The trend line is exponential and fits the observed counts so well that R^2 for this equation is .99! The number of meta-analyses in sport and exercise topics appears to be increasing at an exponential rate. Comparable results for Medline were not available because the term *meta-analysis* was not systematically assigned as a keyword before 1996. However for the last two 5 y intervals, the counts in Medline were 68 and 273 hits—ending well above the count from PsycInfo.

This growth and the good fit of meta-analysis with sport and exercise science may result from the large number of quantitative studies in the field. As early as 1997, Biddle noted that the preponderance of studies in the *Journal of Sport and Exercise Psychology* and *International Journal of Sport Psychology*—more than 90% of studies examined—were quantitative. Weed (2009) also mentioned the positivist nature of much of the research in the field. In any case, meta-analysis has become a popular tool for examining the literature in sport and exercise psychology, and even early on the importance of measurement concerns was evident.

Many meta-analyses in this arena concern exercise and other interventions designed to improve motor performance or physical outcomes. One of the first examples of such a meta-analysis was that of Feltz and Landers (1983). Feltz and Landers examined nearly 150 effect sizes to clarify the role of

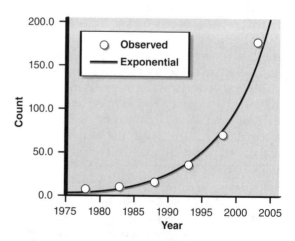

Figure 15.1 Number of hits for *meta-analysis* and *sport or exercise or athlete* per year in PsycInfo.

mental practice in motor performance on a variety of physical tasks. They looked for differences related to the nature of the task (called *task type*) and the level of experience the participants had with that kind of task. Even though the methods they used are not consistent with what we now know about analyzing effect sizes, Feltz and Landers examined variation in the effects of mental practice due to the type of task being measured and found notable and significant differences. Also, participants with more experience showed slightly higher effects for mental practice than novices showed.

A few years later an early tutorial by Thomas and French clearly urged meta-analysts in exercise and sport sciences to consider variables related to measurement issues:

> Characteristics which could influence the findings of the study should be coded. Examples of characteristics which are commonly coded include the internal validity of the study, *how the dependent variable was measured, the scale of measurement*, whether the study was published or unpublished, the age of the subjects and the gender of the subjects. (Thomas & French, 1986, p. 197, emphasis added)

These days, most meta-analysts acknowledge that the characteristics of measures of the outcomes of studies in their syntheses are important (though attention to the treatment variables is less consistent).

Measurement Issues in Meta-Analysis

Let's illustrate how measurement-related issues arise in each of Cooper's five original stages of meta-analysis. For each stage, we outline and illustrate tasks that are particularly related to measurement issues by describing how they have been handled in existing meta-analyses.

Problem Formulation

Meta-analysis begins with a specific description of the research problem. The research problem in a meta-analysis can often be formulated by defining the variables of interest and describing the type of relationship between the variables that is anticipated. As is true in other empirical studies, the variables must be *conceptually* as well as *operationally* defined. This helps the meta-analyst to distinguish research that is relevant (and irrelevant) to the problem of interest. At this stage, the questions are, "What are the constructs or concepts to be examined in the meta-analysis?" and "How are the constructs or concepts defined?"

Predictors

Often meta-analyses aim to examine relationships between a predictor and an outcome or outcomes. An example of such a meta-analysis is that performed by Chen, Fan, and Moe (2002) to examine Borg's RPE scale. This meta-analysis is in fact a validity study aimed at understanding what kinds of outcomes relate most closely to Borg's RPEs. In their review, these authors included only studies that used Borg's RPE scale, although the studies used different variations of the scale (RPE has been measured on 9-, 15-, and 21-point scales as well as on a category-ratio scale; Chen and colleagues called this *scale type*). In this review the construct is nearly identical to the instrument used to measure it.

Table 15.1 on page 158 shows how the questions relevant to problem formulation were answered for two additional meta-analyses. Both of these syntheses considered only one specific measure of one of their constructs. As mentioned earlier, Craft and colleagues (2003) used the CSAI-2 to represent anxiety, and Rowley and colleagues (1995) used the POMS scales to provide profiles of mental health in athletes.

A more common case is one in which a predictor construct is represented by a number of different measures. Moritz and colleagues (2000) examined a variety of measures of self-efficacy as predictors of sport performance. They included both general and task-specific self-efficacy measures and hypothesized that more general measures would show weaker relationships to their sport outcomes. Moritz and coworkers gave a detailed description of the self-efficacy construct based on the work of Bandura and noted that some of the simpler self-efficacy measures were not based on his conception of the construct.

For treatment or intervention meta-analyses, the predictor construct is the treatment itself. For Feltz and Landers (1983) that intervention was mental practice. Their task at this stage was to characterize mental practice. Curiously, however, they did not give a definition or even a description of the treatment, aside from saying that mental instructions were given. Similarly, Netz and colleagues (2005) examined the effects of physical activity, but they also did not define or describe this variable. This unfortunately appears to be extremely common in treatment-oriented meta-analyses on exercise (see also Campbell & Hausenblas, 2009; Gillison, Skevington, Sato, Standage, & Evangelidou, 2009; Wipfli et al., 2008), though an exception is the meta-analysis by Gu and Conn (2008), who referenced definitions of both exercise and physical activity developed by the National Institutes of Health.

Measurement Issues Related to Problem Formulation

Stage	Measurement-related questions	EXAMPLE	
		Rowley et al. (1995)	Craft et al. (2003)
Problem formulation	What constructs were of interest?		
	• Predictors	Mental health in athletes	State anxiety
	• Outcomes	Level of success or expertise of athletes	Athletic performance
	How were constructs and concepts defined?		
	• How were the predictors defined and operationalized?	*Mental health* was defined by the six scales measured by the Profile of Mood States (POMS): tension, depression, anger, vigor, fatigue, and confusion.	*State anxiety* was defined as cognitive anxiety, somatic anxiety, and self-confidence measured by the Competitive State Anxiety Index-2 (CSAI-2).
	• How were outcomes defined and operationalized?	*Elite* • Ranked in the top 10 in the United States • Member of a national team or professional • Best marathon: men: under 2.5 hours; women under 2.75 hours • Best IOK: women: under 35 minutes *Advanced* • Ranked, but not in top 10 • Member of a state team or winner of a state tournament • College athletes • High School: member of a national team or nationally ranked • Black belt in martial arts • Best marathon: under 4 hours • Able to run an ultramarathon (50 miles or more) *Intermediate* • High school athletes • Colored belt in martial arts • Able to run a marathon, triathlon, or 15 miles per week regularly *Novice* • Ranked as novice • Regular participant for less than one year at time of assessment" (pp. 190-191)	*Athletic performance* was defined as objective or subjective ratings by judges or officials, subjective self-ratings by athletes, and subjective ratings by coaches.
	What was the index of relationship between predictors and outcomes?	The *difference in mean POMS scores between groups* defined according to levels of expertise	The *correlation* between state anxiety and sport performance

Failing to clearly define the treatment intervention in a meta-analysis can lead to a lack of clarity at the second stage, where decisions must be made about what studies to include. Conversely, by clearly defining treatments and their characteristics during problem formulation, the meta-analyst may identify variations that can be coded and investigated using moderator variables at the data analysis stage.

Outcomes

It is much more common to find good descriptions of the *outcomes* of interest. The title of the Feltz and Landers meta-analysis on mental practice suggests a focus on motor learning and performance, but how will these two constructs be captured? Many reviews of the effects of exercise focus on immediate physical or physiological outcomes of exercise, such as changes in blood pressure, HR, or respiration. Are long-term physical variables, such as weight loss or changes in body composition, also of interest? Or does the reviewer want to know about psychological outcomes such as changes in anxiety levels, self-image, or self-efficacy? Consideration of such questions about outcome constructs helps the meta-analyst to define a clear problem for meta-analysis.

For instance, in their meta-analysis on the effects of physical activity on psychological well-being among the elderly, Netz and colleagues (2005) asked two key questions: "What is *psychological well-being* among the elderly population?" and "How is *psychological well-being* conceptualized?" The authors drew on the literature to define *psychological well-being* as a multidimensional construct consisting of four general components: emotional well-being, self-perceptions, physical well-being (including perceptions of physical symptoms), and global perceptions. The authors further delineated these four components of psychological well-being into the 11 classes shown in table 15.2. For each of the classes a set of operationalizations was collected.

Others have focused more closely on one aspect of well-being. For example, Long and van Stavel (1995), Schlicht (1994), and Wipfli and colleagues (2008) all focused on anxiety as an outcome. However, their collections of studies differed, in part because of the way anxiety was conceptualized and categorized and in part because of other restrictions put on the study collections. For example, Wipfli and colleagues included only randomized trials of exercise.

Meta-analyses on the same topic might differ in their definitions of target variables. Discrepancies can arise due to differences in the breadth and detail of the definitions of the focal variables. These can eventually lead to differences in review conclusions as well as to differences in the meta-analyst's abil-ity to generalize the conclusions of the review. For instance, Arent and coworkers (2000) looked at the effect of physical exercise on psychological well-being among the elderly, a research topic essentially identical to that of Netz and colleagues. However, Arent and coworkers conceptualized psychological well-being in terms of a change in mood state and suggested a two-factor model (positive affect and negative affect), whereas Netz and colleagues used a definition of psychological well-being that included the four general components and 11 specific classes mentioned earlier. This definition of the construct seems broader and thus more inclusive than that of Arent and coworkers (2000), and thus it may lead to a potentially broader domain of generalization.

When specifying operational definitions of variables, the meta-analyst must make sure that the underlying construct is fully represented by the operational measures to be included. Sometimes the goal is to examine just one particular measure, as in the meta-analysis of Borg's RPE scale (Chen et al., 2002) and the work with the CSAI-2 (Craft et al., 2003) described in table 15.1. In these cases, including studies of only one measure may make sense. However, many research synthesists use multiple operational measures of the variables they are studying. According to Cooper (2009), the rationale for this is similar to the reasoning behind classical measurement theory, in which a test can

▪ Table 15.2 ▪

Netz and Colleagues' (2005) Classification of Psychological Well-Being Measures

Component	Classes of measures
Emotional well-being	Anger
	Anxiety (including stress and tension)
	Confusion
	Depression
	Positive affect
Self-perceptions	Self-worth, self-esteem, and sense of mastery
	Exercise or physical self-efficacy
Physical well-being	Perceived physical symptoms
	Energy
Global perceptions	Overall well-being
	Life satisfaction

reach higher reliability by including a larger number of valid items. Similarly, the underlying constructs in a meta-analysis often can be better represented by a set of interrelated measures.

Indeed, Cook (1991) has argued that including multiple operations, in conjunction with homogenous or consistent research findings, leads to much stronger conclusions. He called differences (in exactly how a construct is measured) that do not relate to study outcomes *heterogeneous irrelevancies*, meaning that these differences are irrelevant to the strength of the findings. In such cases, using multiple operations of the variables increases the meta-analyst's confidence to make inferences from the conclusions, because the review finds the same results across many instantiations of the construct of interest. For instance, Chen and colleagues (2002) found that the scale types used with Borg's RPE scale were unrelated to the strength of the validity coefficients for 5 of 6 physiological outcomes, suggesting that scale type is largely irrelevant to the scale's validity.

How similar the effects have to be is a matter of judgment. In some cases it may be enough to say that effects were always of the same sign, whereas in others a meta-analyst may wish to say effects were similar in magnitude as well. For example, for two of the outcomes in the 2002 review by Chen and colleagues (ventilation and respiration rate), the mean correlations were identical across scale types. For three other outcomes the means differed but not significantly.

Connection Between Predictor and Outcome

Another task during problem formulation is to determine the type of relationship to be explored among the variables. This task is not directly related to the measurement of the variables, but it determines the kinds of research designs that should be included in a meta-analysis. Two types of research problems are examined in most meta-analyses. One focuses on an association between variables and the other considers a causal effect of one variable on another (as in most treatment meta-analyses). Most treatment efficacy meta-analyses (e.g., Netz et al., 2005; Wipfli et al., 2008) use some type of standardized mean difference index. While both of the syntheses described in table 15.1 concerned predictive relationships or associations, they used different indexes of effect size to represent those relationships.

At this stage, the meta-analyst must also consider other potential influences on study effects. Often this involves further consideration of the measurement of the treatment. Among Netz and

colleagues' (2005) moderators were type and intensity of exercise. Also, aspects of exercise duration (number and length of sessions) were considered as potential predictors of the effects of the physical activity. Defining how such potential moderators are operationalized in the literature helps the meta-analyst plan for study screening and for coding so that relevant information can be collected.

Data Collection

The next step in meta-analysis involves searching the literature and gathering information from the collected studies. When searching the literature, the meta-analyst often uses the most comprehensive and exhaustive set of search terms to help locate all relevant studies. Search terms can be generated from the definitions of the key variables and potential moderators identified at the problem formulation stage. For example, search terms used by Netz and colleagues (2005) included (1) terms related to psychological well-being, such as *wellbeing, psychological health, anxiety, depression, body image, self-concept, self-efficacy, life satisfaction, self-perception*, and *happiness*; (2) terms that help define the target population of the elderly, such as *middle age, old age, elderly*, and *older adults*; and (3) terms that are related to physical activity, such as *physical activity, exercise, physical fitness, sport, endurance training*, and *strength training*. Unfortunately, many meta-analyses (including the two described in table 15.3) do not report the keywords used in searching.

In some meta-analyses a very focused approach can be taken during the literature search. That is, if the meta-analyst is willing to focus on only one operationalization of a construct, the name of the specific measure or instrument can be used in the search. Chen and coworkers (2002) used the terms *perceived exertion* and *Borg* to find studies of Borg's RPE scale. Both of the meta-analyses in table 15.3 had this situation for the predictor variable of interest.

After locating potentially relevant studies, the meta-analyst often uses detailed inclusion and exclusion rules to filter out irrelevant studies, retaining only the relevant ones. The process of setting up the inclusion and exclusion rules is closely related to defining the variables and determining the relationships of interest among the variables performed during problem formulation. For example, Arent and colleagues (2000) defined the *older adult* as a person whose age is greater than 65 y. Therefore, their meta-analysis included studies having at least one exercise group with a mean age greater than 65 y. In contrast, Netz and colleagues (2005) limited their studies to those with samples whose mean

■ Table 15.3 ■

Data Collection and Data Evaluation Issues Related to Measurement

Stage	Measurement-related questions	EXAMPLE	
		Rowley et al. (1995)	Craft et al. (2003)
Data collection	What key search terms were used to locate studies?	Not reported, but POMS must have been used as a search term.	Not reported, but CSAI-2 must have been used as a search term.
	Which variables were coded?		
	• Variables related to methods of measurement	Time of mood assessment Presence of a lie scale Presence of demand characteristics Differences in physical training state Confidence in rating of expertise Operational definition of performance (e.g., personal best, ranking, and so on)	Time of CSAI-2 administration (before or during competition) Length of time between inventory administration and competition (15 min or less before competition, 16-30 min before competition, 31-59 min before competition, or 1-4 h before competition)
	• Other variables related to outcomes or predictors	*Activity characteristic:* Aerobic or strength task	*Performance characteristics:* Actual sport Sport type (team versus individual) Type of performance measure (e.g., objective rating by judge or official, subjective rating by coach, and so on) Skill type (open versus closed skills)
	How was reliable and valid data extraction ensured?	Studies were double coded by two authors. Interrater reliability ranged from .8 for variables such as outcome reliability and analysis to 1.0 for variables such as publication year and gender.	Not specified.

(continued)

■ Table 15.3 ■

(continued)

Stage	Measurement-related questions	EXAMPLE	
		Rowley et al. (1995)	Craft et al. (2003)
Data evaluation	Which studies were included or excluded?	Inclusion and exclusion rules were specified as follows: • Studies that assessed mental health with POMS and that had at least two groups of athletes in the same sport at different levels of success were included. • Studies with insufficient data for calculating effect size were excluded. • Studies that duplicate data in another study were excluded.	Inclusion and exclusion rules were specified as follows: Studies that investigated the relationship between state anxiety as measured by the CSAI-2 and athletic performance were included.
	How did the meta-analysts judge the quality of studies?		
	• Did items on measures represent the content of interest?	Confidence in the expertise categorization was coded. The definition of performance was coded as questionable or valid.	Not explicitly specified.
	• Were scores on the measures reliable?	Not explicitly specified.	Not explicitly specified.
	• Was the outcome measure properly aligned to the intervention condition?	The number of threats to internal validity was coded.	Not explicitly specified.
	• To what extent were important classes of outcome measures included?	Many levels of expertise were included.	A diverse selection of sport outcomes was included.
	• Was the time of measurement tested as an influence of the intervention's effect?	Yes, the time of mood assessment was coded as more than 24 h before performance, less than 24 h before performance, or after performance.	Yes, studies were coded for the length of time before competition that the inventory was administered (15 min or less, 16-30 min, 31-59 min, or 1-4 h).

age was greater than 54 y. At this stage the meta-analyst needs to clearly spell out the inclusion and exclusion rules in terms of the operational measures representing the underlying constructs.

Coding Variables

The other task at this stage is to extract information from the studies included in the meta-analysis. This information gathering, which is also known as *coding*, requires several measurement-related activities. First of all, the meta-analyst develops coding sheets containing items that systematically document the nature of the studies and their outcomes. Although the information to be coded is unique to each research review, it can usually be separated into the following categories: article characteristics (e.g., publication year, publication type, and source of funding), design characteristics (e.g., sampling method, whether matching is used, assignment method), setting characteristics (e.g., geographic location; nature of the intervention, if there is one; and context, such as competitive athletics or individual sport), sample characteristics (e.g., gender, ethnicity, and age), measure characteristics (e.g., value and type of reliability and others discussed later), and statistical outcomes (e.g., effect size and sample size). The coding sheet can serve as a valid tool for data collection when the items are stated with clear and easy-to-use response options that capture all the information that should be collected.

Because studies often use diverse measures of the variables of interest, the reviewer must gather detailed information about those measures. Meta-analysts often record extensive measurement characteristics, including measure name, measure type (e.g., standardized versus researcher made), the scale of measurement (e.g., categorical, continuous, dichotomous), score type (e.g., total score, average), number of items, who reports the information (e.g., self-report versus other report), whether reliability information is reported, the value and type of reliability, whether validity information is reported, and so forth. These measurement characteristics have a variety of important uses. They can be used to evaluate the quality of studies at the data evaluation stage, even to the extent of being used to eliminate studies. For example, outcomes based on measures with reliabilities less than .50 (or some other cutoff) may be excluded from analyses. Information on reliability can also be used to correct study findings for potential artifacts related to measurement errors; this is discussed later. Nearly all measure characteristics may be useful in explaining variation in results via moderator analyses at the data analysis stage.

To ensure reliable and valid data extraction, meta-analysts should, using two or more independent coders, double code all included studies. Potential coding errors can be reduced by training coders in advance and by using a well-developed coding manual that clearly describes the definitions of items to be coded and that standardizes coding procedures. One more option for reducing coding errors is to check intercoder reliability. Reliability is often estimated simply by using the percentage of agreement between two coders. For instance, Arent and colleagues (2000) used an agreement rate of .90 to represent acceptable agreement. More complex approaches are also available (Orwin & Vevea, 2009). Finally, the coders must resolve coding discrepancies before the analysis begins.

Data Evaluation

The important tasks during data evaluation are to identify whether studies continue to be eligible for inclusion and to further evaluate the quality of the studies included in the meta-analysis. Many reviewers have reported that study quality is related to study outcomes (e.g., Bérard & Bravo, 1998; Jüni, Altman, & Egger, 2001; Moher et al., 1999), though no clear pattern of the relationship between the quality of a primary study and its outcome has emerged.

In the meta-analysis literature, study quality has been handled in numerous ways. One way is to exclude low-quality studies, and another is to use quality information to correct individual study findings for measurement errors arising from the unreliability of measures (e.g., Hunter & Schmidt, 2004). We discuss this approach later in the section on data analysis. Perhaps the most common approach is to use quality information to try to model differences in study findings. For example, a weighted analogue to ANOVA (Hedges, 1982) can be used to compare effect sizes of low-quality studies and high-quality studies (e.g., Murphy, Nevill, Murtagh, & Holder, 2007) or of studies with different measurement conditions. Table 15.3 lists a variety of measure characteristics available as moderators to Rowley and colleagues (1995) and Craft and coworkers (2003).

Even though no universally accepted tool has been used to assess the quality of primary studies in meta-analysis, many researchers have pointed out that study quality is a multidimensional construct (Valentine & Cooper, 2008). Various scales using diverse quality dimensions exist to assess the quality of studies. One example is the Study Design and Implementation Assessment Device (Study DIAD) created by the What Works Clearinghouse, which evaluates the quality of studies based on both internal and external validity issues. Among the features of study quality examined on the Study DIAD are several measurement-related quality questions. These include the following (Valentine & Cooper, 2008, p. 144):

- Do items on the outcome measure appear to represent the content of interest?
- Were the scores on the outcome measure acceptably reliable?
- Was the outcome measure properly aligned to the intervention condition?
- To what extent were important classes of outcome measures included in the study?
- Was the time of measurement (relative to the end of intervention) tested as an influence on the intervention's effect?

We describe in table 15.3 how Rowley and colleagues (1995) and Craft and coworkers (2003) addressed each of these points. Regardless of what approach is used to handle differences in study quality, it is a good idea to explicitly evaluate the quality of each study and in particular to scrutinize the measures used.

Data Analysis

Three general statistical outcomes can be obtained from a meta-analysis. Two represent overall results: the overall effect size and the variance of effects between studies. The third provides information about the effects of potential predictors on between-study variations in study findings. Many characteristics can be used to model between-study variations, but several measurement-related factors such as type of measure, measure format, and whether the reliability is reported are of particular interest when dealing with multiple measures.

Overall Results

Most reviews report overall average results. Netz and colleagues examined measures of change in their studies of activity in the elderly, estimating an overall effect size of 0.19 *SD* of change in well-being across all treatment and comparison groups and across all outcomes. They next obtained separate overall weighted effect sizes for change in treatment and control groups of 0.24 and 0.09 *SD* of change, respectively. These effects more clearly represent the effect of physical activity on psychological well-being. Moritz and colleagues (2000) reported an average correlation of .38 between self-efficacy and

any sport performance outcome. In contrast, Chen and colleagues (2002) did not report any overall correlation, beginning instead by separating the studies of Borg's RPE scale according to the particular physiological outcome measured. Overall effects for the two other meta-analyses are described in table 15.4. While none of these meta-analyses presented estimates of between-study variance, all tested for variation in effects across studies.

Moderator Effects

As part of problem formulation, most meta-analysts identify variables that they believe relate to study outcomes. Such hypotheses can be examined using analogues to ANOVA and regression that incorporate weights reflecting the precision of the effect sizes in the meta-analysis. (We discuss these analyses here briefly, but for details of such analyses see chapters 14 through 23 in Cooper et al., 2009.) Theoretically interesting variables such as type of treatment regimen or subject characteristics (e.g., male versus female, novice versus expert) are often examined. However, it also makes sense to examine features related to the nature of the measures used. In some cases, the nature of the measures may be of theoretical importance, such as when different measures represent different aspects of a construct, as did Chen and colleagues' six physiological criterion measures. Even if methods variables do not hold theoretical interest, analyzing these variables may help the reviewer to eliminate nuisance variables from consideration as sources of variance in the outcomes.

The ANOVA-like approach involves creating subsets of studies that share some characteristic (e.g., that use the same measures) and comparing the means of the subsets. A weighted average effect is calculated for each subset (see Hedges & Olkin, 1985; Hunter & Schmidt, 2004; Shadish & Haddock, 2009), and a chi-square test of differences provides an analogue to the ANOVA *F*-test. Also, a chi-square test of model fit allows the meta-analyst to assess whether the grouping variable explains all of the between-study variation in effects. Netz and coworkers used type of outcome measure in an ANOVA-like model for explaining between-study variation and computed average effect sizes for each of their 11 subcategories of psychological well-being. Another example is Moritz and colleagues' coding of the concordance of measures of their predictor (self-efficacy) with various sport outcomes. Their analyses showed that self-efficacy

---

[1]Both Chen and colleagues (2002) and Rowley and colleagues (1995) used traditional unweighted ANOVA methods, which are inappropriate because they do not account for the heteroscedasticity that arises because of differences in sample size across studies.

Data Analysis and Public Presentation Issues Related to Measurement

Stage	Measurement-related questions	EXAMPLE	
		Rowley et al. (1995)	Craft et al. (2003)
Data analysis	What was the overall effect of interest?	• The *overall effect size with all dependent effect sizes* was 0.15 (SD = 0.89), indicating that successful athletes possess a mood profile approximately one-sixth of a standard deviation healthier than that of less successful athletes. • The *overall effect size* after eliminating the total mood score and having one set of effect sizes per study was 0.19 (SD = 1.09). • Variance components were not reported.	• Multivariate fixed-effect analyses resulted in a mean overall correlation of .01 (SE = .02) for the cognitive anxiety–performance relationship, −.03 (SE = .02) for somatic anxiety with performance, and .25 (SE = .02) for self-confidence and performance. • The overall multivariate test of homogeneity for the entire matrix was significant, as were univariate homogeneity tests for each subscale. • Overall slope coefficients for the relationship of each subscale to performance (controlling for the other subscales) were computed. • Variance components were not reported.
	Were moderator variables related to measurement issues examined?	Effect sizes were compared across different levels of moderator variables using one-way ANOVA.[1] Effects for studies where expertise level was unclear showed larger effects ($\bar{d}$ = .51) than studies with clear performance measures ($\bar{d}$ = .13) showed.	Exploratory modeling using a multivariate approach was conducted to examine potential moderator variables. Slope coefficients associated with the CSAI-2–performance relationship were computed and compared across levels of moderators using z-tests.
	Did measurement error influence the effect?	Effect sizes were not corrected for measurement errors.	Correlations were not corrected for measurement errors.
	How were multiple outcomes handled?	Overall effect sizes were computed by eliminating total POMS scores and having one effect size reflect the two most extreme success groups per study.	Interdependence among the three subscales of the CSAI-2 was modeled using multivariate meta-analytical techniques.
Public presentation	What key components of methods were presented?		
	• Definitions of variables	Page 190	Pages 45-47
	• Search procedures	Page 189	Page 50
	• Inclusion and exclusion criteria	Page 189	Page 50
	• Coding characteristics and procedures	Pages 189-191	Page 51
	• Computation of effect size	Page 192	Page 51
	• Analysis procedures	Page 192	Pages 51-52

[1]Using the traditional ordinary-least-squares one-way ANOVA is not correct because meta-analytical data violate assumptions of homoscedasticity. The correct analysis should be a weighted ANOVA to compare the means of subsets of studies.

measures that were more targeted to the specific measured physical outcomes showed stronger relationships. Table 15.4 points out that Craft and colleagues tested for differences due to the timing of the administration of the CSAI-2, and Rowley and colleagues found differences according to the confidence raters had in coding the performance variable (expertise).[1]

As mentioned earlier, Chen and colleagues (2002) used a moderator analysis to compare results based on two different aspects of the RPE scale. One aspect was the type of scale. RPE has been measured with scales using 9, 15, and 21 points as well as with a category-ratio scale. As noted earlier, these authors found that scale type was largely irrelevant to the findings. Also, RPE can be measured according to two different protocols, or modes—the estimation and production modes (Chen et al., 2002, p. 877). The estimation mode asks respondents to project what they think their exertion levels would be after completing a particular sort of exercise, and the production mode has respondents exercise at a certain intensity level before reporting their RPE. Although some caution is needed in interpreting the tests of significance from this meta-analysis,1 RPE mode proved to be a significant moderator for several of the physiological outcomes that Chen and colleagues surveyed.

A regression modeling approach can be used when characteristics of measures (or other predictors) are on a quantitative scale. Dummy variables can be included as predictors, and multiple regressions are possible. Again, chi-square tests are available to test the overall significance and fit of regression models, and tests of individual slopes can be obtained. Variables such as number of items in the measure or length of a task in terms of minutes or sessions may be appropriate as regression predictors. Moritz and coworkers (2000) used this approach to look at seven characteristics of the measures and tasks in their meta-analysis of self-efficacy and performance. Their analysis showed that measure concordance and task novelty, as well as the time of assessment of self-efficacy (before or after performance), predicted the strength of the efficacy–performance relationship.

Measurement Error

One further consideration in the analysis phase is whether it is possible to correct for measurement error or unreliability in either the predictors or the outcomes of interest. In the case of treatment or group-difference syntheses, only outcome unreliability can be considered, but for studies of relationships such as those of Chen and coworkers (2002)

and Moritz and coworkers (2000), unreliability exists in both predictor and outcome variables.

An extensive literature exists on the idea of correcting for artifacts such as unreliability, invalidity, and range restriction in meta-analysis. The primary authors in this domain have been Hunter and Schmidt (e.g., 1990, 2004) and their colleagues, whose work originated largely from the domain of employment testing. Hunter and Schmidt have described how to correct for various sources of dispersion in study results, and of primary concern in our chapter are the corrections for measurement error. Although most of the discussions on using these corrections have been limited to correlation coefficients, the correction formulas can be used with other measures of effect size such as standardized mean differences (Hunter & Schmidt, 1990, 2004; Schmidt, Le, & Oh, 2009).

It has long been known that measurement error attenuates correlations (e.g., Forsyth & Feldt, 1969). Thus if different studies use measures that are differentially unreliable, the meta-analyst may see variation in the observed r-values simply because of this fact. Hunter and Schmidt have argued that the typical correction for attenuation should be applied to all effects in a meta-analysis, thereby adjusting the effects for this influence. Measurement error does not relate to the true correlation between the constructs, which is our real interest. Specifically, if r_{XY} is the observed correlation in a study and r_{XX} and r_{YY} are the test reliabilities for the predictor and outcome measures, we can compute the corrected correlation r_{XY}^C as

$$r_{XY}^C = \frac{r_{XY}}{\sqrt{r_{XX}r_{YY}}},$$ **15.1**

which will be larger than the observed correlation in proportion to the degree of unreliability. A similar correction is available for the standardized mean difference d, where we can correct only for unreliability in the outcome Y. Specifically, if $d = (\bar{Y}^T - \bar{Y}^C) / S$, where $\bar{Y}^T$ is the mean of a treatment group on some outcome Y, $\bar{Y}^C$ is the mean of the control group, and S is the pooled within-group standard deviation, then the corrected effect size d^C is

$$d^C = \frac{d}{\sqrt{r_{YY}}}.$$ **15.2**

The biggest problem with using this correction (as well as others advocated by Hunter and Schmidt) outside of the realm of employment testing is that needed information is often not reported in the primary studies themselves. Sometimes reliabilities can be obtained from test manuals, but they may not apply to the scores in the samples in the collected studies. Some people have advocated using artifact distributions (Schmidt et al., 2009, pp. 327-331), but these distributions were developed for employment testing, and it is unclear how appropriate the values of reliabilities used there are for the sport context.

Also, for some other artifacts, no one has suggested how relevant information can be obtained from primary studies (though for a discussion of one approach using external raters, see Ahn, 2008). In particular, construct validities of both predictor and outcome variables, mentioned by Hunter and Schmidt (1990, 2004), are seldom if ever reported in primary studies. The application of corrections for invalidity will be limited in practice unless validities are reported or methods are developed for obtaining unreported values.

Multiple Outcomes

In most meta-analyses, univariate statistical approaches are used due to their ease of application. However, such approaches are problematic when many correlated outcomes are measured, because univariate methods ignore possible dependence in the data and thus can lead to inaccurate conclusions (Becker, 2000; Gleser & Olkin, 2009). Also, univariate analyses are limited when the meta-analyst is interested in an overall picture of interrelationships among sets of variables included in a model, such as in the analysis of the predictive value of the CSAI-2 for sport performance (Craft et al., 2003).

The most common approach to dependence due to multiple measures is to separate the effects from correlated measures into different, hopefully independent subsets. Netz and coworkers (2005) used this approach when they classed the 11 types of well-being outcomes into separate categories. Because some studies used multiple measures within those 11 domains (e.g., by administering several depression or anxiety scales), this approach did not totally remove dependence, but it greatly reduced its influence.

Another approach for combining dependent effect sizes from multiple measures is to use multivariate methods. The most frequently used multivariate approach is a generalized least squares (GLS) method suggested by Raudenbush, Becker, and Kalaian (1988). By using multivariate methods, intercorrelations (dependencies) among several effects can be taken into account. This approach was used by Craft and colleagues (2003) and should lead to a more accurate error rate and ensure that samples with more data do not overinfluence the results (Becker, 2000). However, the application of the GLS method is problematic for very sparse data

sets, in which few studies use the same measures of variables of interest. Also, this approach requires information about the degree of dependence among outcomes, and, as was true for the reliabilities needed to correct for measurement error, that information is not often reported in primary studies, where the focus is on means of the different outcomes and not their interrelationships.

Public Presentation

All procedures in each stage of a meta-analysis should be clearly and completely documented in the report of the research synthesis. The APA created a working group to develop standards for reporting of journal articles as well as a set of meta-analysis reporting standards (MARS) outlining components that should be included in each section of a meta-analysis report (APA Publications and Communications Board Working Group, 2008). Key topics include definitions of the variables, search procedures, inclusion and exclusion criteria, coding characteristics and procedures, computation of effect size, and analysis procedure. In table 15.4 we show where in each of the two featured meta-analyses the authors covered these key points. Regarding measures, the guidelines ask that meta-analysts report on "types of predictor and outcome measures used, [and] their psychometric characteristics" (p. 849). For more information, see the detailed table on page 849 of the APA working group's report. The MARS suggest that two key considerations in every meta-analyst's discussion should be the extent to which results can be generalized across treatment variations and across different outcome variables. The fact that these issues are two of only four listed reflects the critical importance of measurement-related issues to generalization.

Conclusion

In this chapter we explain how a variety of measurement issues can be examined via meta-analysis. We identify measurement concerns at all stages of the review process, and while our chapter focuses on meta-analyses, these issues arise whenever a person does a review of the literature, regardless of whether a quantitative synthesis is performed. Key principles of meta-analysis (and systematic reviewing in general) are replicability and transparency. Readers of meta-analyses that are replicable and transparently reported can better assess whether they agree with the review's evidence base and conclusions. While meta-analysts tend to be quite attuned to providing clear definitions and operationalizations of their outcomes, they tend to pay less attention to delineating the nature of treatments. By beginning with a clear definition of the treatment at the problem formulation stage and carrying it through the other stages, the meta-analyst can provide a richer picture of the treatment construct. This picture should enable later research-ers to refine the treatment via further work or to abandon ineffective aspects of the treatment. Only if we specify and measure all aspects of the studies in our syntheses can we ask whether those aspects matter to our conclusions and the generalizability of our results.

Ethics

Assessment and Measurement in Sport and Exercise Psychology

Jack C. Watson II, PhD, Edward F. Etzel, EdD, and Justine Vosloo, PhD

> ❝ A long habit of not thinking a thing wrong gives it a superficial appearance of being right. ❞
>
> **Thomas Paine**

Polarized views often appear when sport and exercise psychology educators, researchers, and consultants are presented with information related to ethical issues in the field. It seems that either we are fascinated by ethics and discussions of ethical professional practice or we avoid such discussions like the plague. Indeed, considerations of ethics frequently elicit a "paralyzing combination of boredom and fear" among professionals in our field (Hayes & Brown, 2003, p. 251). Given the uncomfortable feelings that are often attached to presentations and readings on ethics, many professionals take part in such discussions only when forced to do so by their institutions, licensure boards, or professional organizations. In professional psychology, continuing education in ethics and legal issues is required regularly. However, such requirements are not a part of the current model of sport and exercise psychology training or certification in the United States.

While many if not most of us like to consider ourselves as ethical professionals, are we really? On occasion, ethical behavior has been compared with driving skills. Most of us believe that we are good drivers and those around us have many driving faults. Such biased self-perceptions can certainly lead to harm. Similarly, it is important that we keep our knowledge about ethics current so that we do not knowingly or unknowingly make mistakes that hurt our professional reputations, profession, or, more importantly, clients and research participants.

Ethics and Ethics Codes

Ethics are philosophy applied to the world of work. Ethics make up a facet of the discipline that attempts to help us describe and make sense of what is right and wrong in an effort to affect our thinking so that we continuously strive to provide quality services and avoid making harmful mistakes. Most professional organizations craft ethical codes. These codes are adopted by members of the organizations and should be modified regularly over time to meet the ever-changing challenges of their work. The people being protected by ethics codes may be students, clients, research participants, supervisees, or others. To develop a better understanding of the different codes of ethics, try visiting the websites of the various sport and exercise psychology organizations listed in the appendix at the end of this chapter.

What do the codes of ethics of major sport and exercise psychology organizations say about issues related to measurement and assessment? Interestingly, the ethics codes for the Association for Applied Sport Psychology (AASP) and the International Society of Sport Psychology (ISSP) do not have sections addressing measurement, assessment, or testing. Furthermore, these codes contain very little related information, although they do contain sections related to research that include some facets that may overlap with measurement and assessment. However, the omission of these topics does seem to suggest the need to address measurement and assessment issues in future code revisions.

The omission of measurement and assessment information from the ethics codes for the major sport and exercise psychology organizations means that students and professionals in this field should turn to the codes of ethics for their governing psychology organization, such as the APA, Australian Psychological Society (APS), British Psychological Society (BPS), Canadian Psychological Association (CPA), and European Federation of Psychologists' Associations (EFPA). The codes of ethics for these organizations often include information related to measurement and assessment. Therefore, much of the information discussed in this chapter is related to the codes from these organizations.

Ethical practice is an essential part of all facets of assessment and measurement. Professionals are charged by their ethics codes to minimize all potentially negative effects of interventions or procedures (e.g., testing and measurement) on others (APA, 1982). Do no harm is the cornerstone to ethical assessment, measurement, research, and practice. It is assumed that professionals are people of good moral character, although as human beings they are vulnerable to "dark forces" (Kagan, 1998, p. 7) that may undermine principled professional behavior. Thus, professional ethical challenges are widespread and ever present. Who has not engaged in unethical behavior or at least confronted an ethically challenging situation in working life? Some of these ethical situations appear clear cut and easy to resolve, while others appear layered with many intricate issues that confound the resolution of the situation. Following a brief overview of ethics, this chapter outlines many of the important ethical considerations that affect measurement and assessment.

Ethics Codes: Their Nature, Purposes, and Application

Ethics codes typically comprise principles and standards. Ethical principles are broad-spectrum statements that summarize and reflect the values of the parent organization or governing body. These general and aspirational statements set the underlying tone for the more specific codes and guide the work-related ethical decision making of professionals. In contrast, ethical standards specify both proscribed and prescribed member behaviors. While not always black and white, these standards serve as a more clear cut and enforceable guide for professional behavior.

Members should apply both the aspirational principles and enforceable standards to shape their thinking and behavior in work settings. Ideally, members self-monitor their own behavior. In an effort to remain ethical, professionals are encouraged to consult with colleagues about ethically challenging situations and to provide constructive feedback about perceived possibly unethical behavior they witness in others.

Assessment and Measurement

A central question to be addressed in this chapter is what are assessment and measurement. Sundberg (1977) defines *assessment* as the processes used "for developing impressions and images, making decisions and checking hypotheses about another person's pattern of characteristics that determines his or her behavior in interaction with the environment" (p. 21). The assessment process involves collecting and assembling a broad range of objective and subjective information about persons or groups to develop impressions about them; identify their needs; predict how they might think, feel, and behave in future situations; and select and apply interventions based on the content and dependability of that information. Professionals may use multiple assessment methods that include observations of behavior, symptom checklists, surveys and questionnaires, structured and unstructured interview materials, and standardized tests (Bennett et al., 2006). Gardner and Moore (2006) emphasize using a triad of psychological assessment strategies in the practice of clinical sport psychology: (1) initial interviews, (2) behavioral observation, and (3) psychological testing. The nature and assumptions underlying assessment approaches are usually grounded in the theoretical orientation of the professional (Andersen, 2002).

In contrast, *measurement* can mean many things to many people. It is one of the most common words in the English language and can be used as both a noun and a verb (Lorge, 1967). For the purposes of this chapter, measurement is viewed as an extension of assessment processes. It can be thought of more narrowly as the process of collecting information about psychological characteristics of interest (e.g., attitudes, behaviors, state experiences) using one or more methods or tools (such as those mentioned earlier) to monitor change, the effect of intervention, or treatments postassessment. For example, an educational sport psychology consultant might administer a measure of team cohesion over the course of a competitive season to see how team members perceive their relationships. Another consultant might conduct a preseason baseline screening assessment of cognitive functioning in hockey players and then reevaluate players who incur a mild traumatic brain injury (i.e., concussion) later in the season.

In this chapter, the terms *measurement* and *assessment* are used interchangeably. Furthermore, these terms are used to describe the decisions and opinions made by professionals regarding clients with whom they work. As such, measurement and assessment techniques include all methods of gathering information about clients, such as (a) psychological, educational, and neurological tests; (b) data gathered during clinical interviewing; (c) information gathered from significant others (e.g., family members, teachers, friends); (d) direct and indirect observation; and (e) interactions with people via teletherapy (e.g., Internet, phone; Fisher, 2009).

Competence and Education

In order to excel in our professional duties and do well for those we serve, teach, study, and otherwise interact with, we must know what to do and how to do it in a capable manner. The ethics codes mentioned earlier identify the necessity of being knowledgeable and capable in our work. For example, the APA ethical standards provide guidance for organization members in this area, including information about (a) competence limitations, (b) keeping up competence, (c) making sound professional and scientific judgments, (d) delegating work responsibilities to others, (e) engaging in activities in emergencies, and (f) impairment (APA, 2002). Competence in professional behaviors is a personal matter that is frequently challenged. It is the responsibility of professionals to know their limitations and how their knowledge and skills change and require constant upgrading. The APA ethics code also emphasizes the importance of making sound work-related decisions based on scientific knowledge and appropriate discipline-specific practice. This portion of the APA code cautions professionals to be careful when delegating work to others, describes how a professional is responsible for others' work, and explains the necessity of avoiding multiple relationships with those to whom work is delegated. The APA standards note that we can occasionally be thrown into situations in which our competence is stretched; in such cases we need to be very careful, seek supervision if available, and end such work as soon as possible.

Measurement Referral Questions and Appropriateness of Instruments

When selecting assessment instruments, the professional must consider the referral questions that prompted this process (Fisher, 2009; Smith, 1976). The instruments selected should reflect these referral questions and utilize assessment strategies that have appropriate validity and reliability. For example, if a professional is interested in measuring state anxiety for research purposes, an appropriate assessment may be the Competitive State Anxiety Index-2 (CSAI-2; Martens, Burton, Vealey, Bump, & Smith, 1990) as opposed to the State-Trait Anxiety Inventory (STAI; Spielberger, Gorsuch, & Luschene, 1970), which measures both trait and state anxiety. When selecting the assessment, the professional should be aware of limitations or biases regarding cultural sensitivity (see the later section on cultural issues); gender considerations (Etzel, Yura, & Perna, 1998); and age, language, or disability factors that may influence the psychometric qualities of the assessment differently from the way they influenced the normative groups used for the development and validation of the instrument (APA, 2002; Fisher, 2009). It is also important to consider the method of delivery. For example, assessments based on paper and pencil may not have been validated for online use (see the later section on technology), and instruments with elevated reading levels may not be appropriate for certain age or developmental groups. Therefore, the professional should always verify the assessment's validity and reliability when a modified assessment method or group is used (Fisher, 2009). Furthermore, the professional should also attempt to conduct in-person assessments when possible, as a great deal of information can be learned about clients from the way in which they present themselves during the assessment process. This information can affect the richness of the assessment data.

It is also important for professionals to be aware of and competent to assess and use appropriate psychometric strategies for establishing validity and reliability of the instruments they use (AERA, APA, & NCME, 1999). All instruments have unique psychometric properties that affect how they should be administered and interpreted. When validity and reliability issues are not taken into consideration, it is possible to choose and utilize instruments to assess factors that they were not designed to assess. Furthermore, practitioners should be well aware of other psychometric properties such as content and criterion validity and standard error of measurement that may affect how results are interpreted and used. The ethical practitioner needs to be aware of psychometric issues in order to choose appropriate instruments with regard to the referral questions, client characteristics, assessment strategies, and environmental factors.

Consent and Assent

As discussed earlier, the ethical principles for sport and exercise psychology emphasize doing no harm to the client and respecting the individual's rights and dignity (AASP, 1996; APA, 2002). The test taker's right to privacy and confidentiality applies here as well, and the professional should take all necessary precautions to maintain the confidentiality and privacy of the client. To protect the test taker, informed consent must be obtained at the start of the relationship (e.g., research, consultation, therapy). Beyond the informed consent process and before formal assessment, the client or participant should be informed of all pertinent information regarding the assessment process. This information includes (a) the nature and purpose of assessment; (b) any applicable fees; (c) potential involvement of third parties such as a coach, athletic trainer, or manager; (d) limits of privacy and confidentiality (as discussed in the next section); and (e) the timeline for the process and potential feedback (Fisher, 2009). This information should be presented in a clear and understandable manner. Furthermore, this information should be agreed to by the test taker, who thereby gives informed consent. Test takers should engage in assessment of their own free will and must be given the option to withdraw participation without consequences (APA standard 3.10). All necessary information about assessment procedures and findings should be provided in a language or level appropriate for the participant. Furthermore, it is unethical to necessitate or coerce individuals to take part in measurement and assessment for research or practice purposes.

Privacy and Confidentiality and Release of Information

Typically, the ethical standards of organizations with ties to sport psychology (APA ethical standard 4.01 and the AASP) suggest that professionals should not reveal information about clients, test takers, or others without their signed approval to release information or legal requirement. These legal situations may include (a) a test taker who indicates possible self-harm or harm to others (i.e., suicide or homicide), (b) a test taker whose results are subpoenaed by the court, or (c) a test taker who is a minor, in which case the parent or guardian may have access to the data (Etzel et al., 1998). If the test taker or, in the case of a minor, the parent or guardian provides explicit written permission, the specific information identified by the client may be released to the identified parties. Unless these circumstances are met, information from the test taker may not be disclosed to anyone (e.g., coaches, management, parents, administration, athletic trainers, and so on).

In situations where the assessment is requested by a third party (e.g., coaches, management, the court), this third party may also request results from the assessment. It is important for the professional to establish a priori who is the "real client" (Ogilvie, 1979) and to have the ability to control access to the results. Etzel and colleagues (1998) suggest that information about the assessment should be shared only with one predetermined person, unless a release of information form has been completed. Therefore, when engaging in assessments, the professional should set clear boundaries and avoid dual relationships, thereby identifying who is being served (APA standard 4.02a). Another complication of these situations is the role of trust. If athletes or test takers suspect the test results will be used without their permission in decisions regarding performance or other aspects of participation, they may be less likely to respond honestly, thus affecting the validity of the results (see the section on demand characteristics).

Raw Data and Data Storage

Raw data such as the test taker's responses to items, including the professional's notes and final reports, should be stored in locked file cabinets inside the professional's office or in password-protected computer files (Fisher, 2009). Other methods to ensure confidentiality may include limiting access to records to only those people who have a need to know this information and have been trained to handle and understand it, deidentifying records using code numbers, and appropriately disposing of identifiable records (Fisher, 2009). A good policy for data maintenance is that data should be kept for a minimum of 7 y after the last service delivery date or 3 y after a minor reaches the age of 18 (whichever is later), as is recommended by the APA record-keeping guidelines (APA, 2002; Fisher, 2009). Raw data and the instruments used for assessment purposes should not be released to third parties unless a release of information form has been completed and the third party is trained competently to use such information.

Results Discussion

Test feedback and results discussion should be provided in the form of a carefully constructed report using clear language that fully explains the assessment results. Labels and jargon should be eliminated to increase readability. Information necessary to the purpose of the test should be included, and the inclusion of unnecessary and unrelated information should be avoided (APA, 2002; Fisher, 2009). Additionally, as recommended by the APA (APA, 2002), interpretations should take into consideration the participant's gender, race, ethnicity, age, national origin, sexual orientation, religion, disability, language, or socioeconomic status. Participants should receive assessment information and feedback related to their performance on the assessment and should be informed of ways in which they could personally use the test results or how this information may be used by a third party (only if written permission was given to release such information). The information released to the participant should be presented in a verbal or written report and presented in such a way that it may not cause harm to the test taker (Etzel et al., 1998). However, information such as numerical scores or specific responses should not be released to individuals not qualified to interpret such information (Fisher, 2009; Tranel, 1995).

Demand Characteristics

In the sport context, several groups of individuals may be interested in the assessment results of athletes. Interested parties may include coaches, managers, teams, students, or administrators. However, the potential of a third party reviewing the test results may increase social desirability and result in invalid and unreliable information. Therefore, undue pressure to complete an instrument or battery should be considered as a contextual factor.

Another potentially undesirable effect of a third party viewing the test taker's results may be assessment anxiety. The APA standards state that if a test taker is observed to be anxious or reports feeling anxious, this feeling should be taken into account and become a limitation in the interpretation of test data (APA, 2002). Assessment anxiety may be exaggerated in situations where a third party may have access to results. These situations may also lead to faking good or faking bad on the part of respondents who are concerned about how the results may be used. This must also be considered when evaluating the results.

Supervision of Subordinates

In some cases, professionals may hire and train subordinates to help with assessment and measurement tasks. These subordinates may administer, score, and even interpret the results of measurement and assessment. Standard 2.05 of the APA ethics code (APA, 2002) states that professionals utilizing employees, supervisees, or research and teaching assistants for such purposes should take reasonable precautions to put subordinates in situations where (a) they do not face possibly harmful multiple relationships with the client that could affect their objectivity, (b) they are competently trained to perform the delegated task on their own or with supervision, or (c) they are supervised for competent service delivery. Therefore, when using subordinates to help with tasks such as administration, scoring, or interpretation, the professional assumes primary responsibility and liability to ensure that the services are being provided competently. The professional needs to ensure that subordinates are well trained with all potential instruments. To do so, the professional must provide appropriate training, experience, and supervision as well as continue to check the subordinates' work to ensure its quality. As with licensed professionals, not all subordinates have the same competencies with regard to all instruments.

Use of Technology

Technological advancements occur on a daily basis. With these changes in technology come opportunities for researchers, teachers, and practitioners to use this new technology to help them perform their duties. However, very little guidance exists in the applicable ethics codes to help practitioners navigate the uncharted waters created by these new and ever changing innovations.

Electronic Scoring Systems

Many of the most popular psychological instruments used today (e.g., Minnesota Multiphasic Personality Inventory-2, or MMPI-2) come with automated computer scoring programs. While computer scoring programs can speed up the process of getting results back to clients, they can also involve several legal and ethical concerns. Because of the ease of scoring and evaluation, individuals who are not competently trained academically or experientially to have access to, use, or score such instruments, without fear of negative consequences, may take it upon themselves to perform these tasks (Etzel et al., 1998).

Professionals who do have sufficient training and competence to administer, score, and interpret specific assessments may feel compelled at times to utilize the computer assessments for their ease and speed of delivery to clients. When computer assessments are used without competent human intervention, the risk of misinformation and harm to clients increases (Etzel et al., 1998). Computers are unable to take into account observational information specific to the client or the client's current situation and mind-set, concerns about testing and the environment, and many other pieces of personal and contextual information. For many of these reasons, section 9.09 of the APA code of ethics clearly states that professionals using scoring services to help with assessment should choose these services "on the basis of evidence of the validity of the program and procedures as on other appropriate considerations" and that the professional "retains responsibility for the appropriate application, interpretation and use of the assessment instruments" even when not personally scoring the instruments (APA, 2002, p. 1072).

Internet-Related Technology

While the Internet provides many unique opportunities for professionals to stay in touch with and even conduct assessments with clients and research participants located at a distance or traveling around the globe for competitions, many ethical issues arise when conducting assessment via distance technology. The most important of these issues are confidentiality, validity of assessment, credentialing, and client identification (Allemen, 2002; Watson, Tenenbaum, Lidor, & Alfermann, 2001).

Confidentiality

Confidentiality is one of the most important tenants of psychology practice because of the personal and private nature of information transmitted between client and professional. Without rules and regulations in place to protect the privacy and private information of clients, professionals in psychology would find it much more difficult to be effective at their jobs. These assumptions of confidentiality are just as important with regard to measurement and assessment as they are to therapy. Therefore, when making the decision to conduct assessment or measurement over the Internet, the professional should be very clear of the nonconfidential nature of information transmitted via this medium (Watson et al., 2001).

Given the potential for information to be intercepted, professionals should take several potential steps to remain ethical and protect assessment information collected via the Internet. First, if assessment information will be distributed and collected via e-mail, professionals should provide the client or participant with a waiver outlining the limitations to confidentiality of information transmitted via e-mail and the Internet. Second, they should take reasonable steps to protect assessment information using easily purchased and affordable encryption software. Third, they should make state-

ments of confidentiality standard in the signature line of all professional communications. Fourth, if information is being sent from a distance using nonelectronic means (e.g., mail or fax), professionals should guarantee that they have a secure reception method where all personnel who may have contact with this information are trained how to handle the information.

Assessment Validity

While it may seem logical to assume that an instrument developed and validated for dissemination using one medium may continue to be valid in another medium, this may not always be the case. Professionals should be careful about converting traditional paper-and-pencil instruments for Internet delivery and assuming that they will continue to be valid (Allen, Sampson, & Herlihy, 1988). When using a modified means of delivery, professionals should ensure that the modified instrument is still valid and reliable. For guidance in modifying instruments, professionals should consult the AERA, APA, and NCME guidelines (AERA, APA, & NCME, 1999).

Credentialing

When providing any psychological service from a distance, professionals need to consider credentialing issues. For instance, a professional providing psychological services to a client currently located in a state, province, or country other than that in which the professional is licensed could be considered to be providing services without a license (Watson et al., 2001). Such issues are not always clear, but credentialing issues need to be considered by ethical professionals.

Client Identification

Working with individuals from a distance, especially via text-based interactions, makes it difficult to confirm the identity of the client or participant. It becomes easy for clients to pretend to be someone else (e.g., a minor pretending to be at the age of consent). Another person can pretend to be the client or can even manipulate the client during the session. When assessing a client or research participant, professionals should take steps to verify the identity of the client (Watson et al., 2001). Practitioners may also want to use code words to ensure that clients are not under duress while completing information. This becomes even more important when the professional does not have control over the environment where the client or participant is completing the assessment or the effects of this environment on the client and responses.

Billing for Services

Measurement and assessment services are often billed to clients at a high hourly rate because of the special training and experiences required for competent service delivery and the cost of the instruments. This may not always be the case in sport and exercise psychology due to the often open access to instruments in the field. An elevated hourly rate may also occur because of the time it takes outside of sessions to score a client's completed assessment, evaluate the results of the assessment, write a report about the assessment results, and report the results to the client. While all of these reasons for charging clients additional fees for assessment or having a different rate for assessment than for other services provided are legitimate, practitioners must take reasonable steps to ensure that they communicate these issues and the fee structure to the clients. To be consistent with APA standard 6.04a, professionals performing an assessment should make every effort to specify compensation and billing arrangements with clients as early in the relationship as possible (APA, 2002).

Cultural Issues

An important factor to consider in assessment and measurement is the background of the person the professional is consulting with, teaching, or studying (AERA, APA, & NCME, 1999). Among many factors, taking into consideration the cultural background of others is critical to effective and ethically sound work. However, it is often challenging for professionals to understand the numerous and typically complex cultural and multicultural factors (similarities and differences) that may affect their work and the psychological functioning of others. Professionals are charged with meeting people where they are. However, it is difficult to understand what obvious and subtle factors may help or hinder their doing so. Indeed, it is quite difficult to even define what culture is beyond standard forms such as socioeconomic status, social class, country of origin, and religious background (Cohen, 2009). Steps should be taken to use assessments that are appropriate for the group being assessed. However, as culture-free tests do not exist, professionals should (a) use instruments that minimize cultural biases, (b) consider the population for which the instrument was created, and (c) weigh the limitations of specific instruments (Etzel et al., 1998). Furthermore, professionals should use caution when forced to use assessments not developed for the specific population under assessment, and any results or recommendations should be clearly described in all resulting reports (Fisher, 2009).

Conclusion

Our professional ethics reflect the values-based moral high ground of the members who belong to the professional organizations in sport and exercise psychology. Without a solid understanding of the ethical principles and standards associated with competent work-related behavior to guide our work-related thinking and behavior, we are at risk to intentionally or unintentionally do harm to those with whom we interact. The topic of ethics as it relates to measurement and assessment is essential to good practice in the work of consultants, faculty members, researchers, and others. Educators and psychologists have been concerned with this topic for numerous years (Jackson & Messick, 1967).

This chapter discusses many important ethical issues and potential challenges within the measurement process. Professionals are encouraged to make themselves familiar with these issues and take steps to avoid the potential ethical pitfalls that often accompany the practice of measurement and assessment. We trust that this chapter provides a useful overview of potential challenges in assessment and measurement and some helpful thoughts on how to respond to those challenges.

Appendix: Codes of Ethics for Related Organizations

American College of Sports Medicine
www.tinyurl.com/acsmethics

American Psychological Association
www.apa.org/ethics/code2002.html

Association for Applied Sport Psychology
www.appliedsportpsych.org/about/ethics/
code

Australian Psychological Society
www.psychology.org.au/Assets/Files/Code_
Ethics_2007.pdf

British Psychological Society
www.tinyurl.com/bpsethics

Canadian Psychological Association
www.tinyurl.com/cpaethicspdf

European Federation of Psychologists' Associations
www.efpa.eu/ethics

International Society of Sport Psychology
www.issponline.org/p_codeofethics.asp

PART II

Cognition, Perception, and Motivation Measurement

The chapters in part II relate to specific issues encountered in sport and exercise psychology. Part II covers measurement issues that relate to cognitive, anticipatory, and mental representation in sport and exercise; self-perception measures such as the physical self, self-perception, self-efficacy, collective efficacy, and effort perception in exercise and sport; and motivation measurements in sport and exercise, a broad concept that is further broken down into achievement motivation processes, intrinsic–extrinsic framework, and exercise-related motivation.

Cognitive Measures Related to Exercise and Physical Activity

Jennifer L. Etnier, PhD

The term *cognition* comes from the Latin word *cognoscere*, which means "to know" or "to recognize." Although this definition may seem straightforward and relatively simple, research designed to advance our understanding of cognition demonstrates that the construct is complex and evolving. To see an example of how this term has evolved, we only have to examine how research foci have changed over time. In the early and middle 1800s, research in cognition focused on understanding general intelligence. In the late 1800s, researchers began to use experimental methods to study cognitive abilities such as reaction time, sensory perception, and memory. In the early 1900s, interest moved back to understanding intelligence, and theories of intelligence were proposed that represented both unidimensional perspectives (e.g., Spearman's *g* factor [Spearman, 1904]) and multidimensional perspectives (e.g., Thorndike's three dimensions of intelligence [Thorndike, 1920]). In the late 1900s, researchers returned to exploring particular cognitive abilities and demonstrated an interest in understanding how these abilities relate to one another. For example, using the results of factor analyses, Carroll (1983) proposed that cognitive abilities should be classified into three hierarchical categories: (1) general ability (similar to Spearman's *g* factor), (2) broad abilities (including fluid intelligence, crystallized intelligence, memory and learning, visual perception, auditory perception, retrieval ability, speed of processing, and cognitive speediness), and (3) narrow abilities (specific abilities housed under each of the broad abilities). A survey of recently published cognitive psychology textbooks (Balota & Marsh, 2004; Lamberts &

Goldstone, 2005; Reisberg, 2006) suggests that the current view of cognition includes the domains of perception, recognition, attention, memory (working, episodic, visual, spatial), language, knowledge and expertise, meta-memory, judgment, decision making, and reasoning. Thus, defining *cognition* as "to know" is only a very broad conceptualization of a complex term that has been operationalized as consisting of the various abilities through which a person comes to know and interact mentally with the environment.

In exercise psychology, cognition is again very broadly defined, and empirical studies have focused on a variety of cognitive abilities in furthering our understanding of how physical activity might affect cognitive performance. As in the parent discipline of psychology, exercise psychology uses behavioral measures and measures of cerebral structure and activation to ascertain the effects of physical activity on cognitive outcomes. Behavioral measures are typified by tasks that require the participant to perform a cognitive activity with performance operationalized in various ways, including number of correct responses, number of errors, failure to respond, and speed of response. There are literally hundreds of behavioral measures of cognition, and each is expected to assess at least one underlying cognitive ability. Measures of cerebral structure usually involve magnetic resonance imaging (MRI) and provide measures of the volume and density of cerebral structures at both the cortical and subcortical levels. Based on the link between cerebral structure and cognitive performance, findings from these studies are used to make inferences regarding the effects of physical activity on cognitive abilities.

Measures of cerebral activation typically are taken concurrently with the performance of a cognitive task, and these measures are used to identify the influence of physical activity on patterns and amounts of activation during task performance. The measures of cerebral activation that have been used in the extant literature include electroencephalographic (EEG) activity, event-related potentials (ERPs), diffusion tensor imaging (DTI), functional MRI (fMRI), magnetoencephalography (MEG), and near-infrared spectroscopy (NIRS).

Theoretical Framework

Several theories have been proposed to explain the relationship between physical activity and cognition. The theories relevant to the effects of acute exercise and to the effects of chronic exercise are distinct and reflect the expectation that the effects of a single bout of exercise on cognitive performance are transitory, while the effects of chronic exercise are more enduring.

Theories Relevant to Acute Exercise

Theories proposed to explain the effects of a single bout of exercise on cognitive activity include the *central fatigue hypothesis* (Douchamps-Riboux, Heinz, & Douchamps, 1989; Hogervorst, Riedel, Jeukendrup, & Jolles, 1996), the *inverted-U law* (Yerkes & Dodson, 1908), and the *transient hypofrontality hypothesis* (Dietrich, 2003). All of these hypotheses have been used to explain the effects of physical activity on cognitive tasks performed during the exercise bout. Additionally, the inverted-U law has been applied to explain the effects on cognitive tasks performed shortly following the exercise bout (when arousal is still elevated).

Central Fatigue Hypothesis

The central fatigue hypothesis suggests that exhaustive exercise challenges the resources of the central nervous system (CNS) in such a way that cognitive performance is dampened (Douchamps-Riboux et al., 1989; Hogervorst et al., 1996). Researchers testing this hypothesis typically have been interested in this effect for practical reasons—because of an interest in cognitive performance by elite athletes performing exhaustive exercise in their sport (e.g., Welsh, Davis, Burke, & Williams, 2002) or by military personnel required to perform cognitively demanding tasks during or after exhaustive activities (e.g., Amos, Hansen, Lau, & Michalski, 2000). Several researchers interested in the effects of exhaustive exercise on cognitive performance have also considered the potential influences of dehydration, heat stress, and

carbohydrate ingestion on this relationship (Cian, Barraud, Melin, & Raphel, 2001; Cian et al., 2000; Gopinathan, Pichan, & Sharma, 1988; Tomporowski, Beasman, Ganio, & Cureton, 2007; Welsh et al., 2002). Contrary to the central fatigue hypothesis, the work of Brisswalter, Collardeau, and Rene (2002) found that results from this line of research generally suggest that exhaustive exercise improves cognitive performance and that providing fluids or carbohydrate can augment this effect.

Inverted-U Law

The inverted-U law (Yerkes & Dodson, 1908) was proposed to explain the relationship between increased arousal and performance (generally speaking). As applied to cognitive outcomes, this hypothesis predicts that cognitive performance improves with increasing arousal up to a moderate level of arousal, at which point performance plateaus and then declines. Given the close relationship between exercise and arousal, the inverted-U law has been proposed to explain cognitive performance during an exercise bout and shortly after the termination of the exercise bout (before arousal has returned to resting levels). Several researchers have designed empirical studies to test this hypothesis; some demonstrated a positive linear relationship between exercise-induced arousal and cognitive performance (Aks, 1998; Allard, Brawley, Deakin, & Elliott, 1989; Tenenbaum, Yuval, Elbaz, Bar-Eli, & Weinberg, 1993) and others supported an inverted-U relationship (Arent & Landers, 2003; Brisswalter, Durand, Delignieres, & Legros, 1995; Chmura, Nazar, & Kaciuba-Uscilko, 1994; Reilly & Smith, 1986). Importantly, the relationship may vary as a function of the particular cognitive outcome assessed. Recently, Chang and Etnier (2009) demonstrated that the relationship between exercise intensity during a resistance exercise bout and cognitive performance immediately following the exercise session is task specific. In particular, they observed linear relationships for tasks involving information processing or simple attention and curvilinear relationships for tasks involving executive function and more complex attention. Thus, the inverted-U law remains viable as a descriptor of the relationship between exercise-induced arousal and performance on particular types of cognitive tasks.

Transient Hypofrontality Hypothesis

The transient hypofrontality hypothesis (Dietrich, 2003) suggests that during exercise the fixed resources available in the brain are made available to those areas of the brain that are responsible for performing the physical activity. Hence, this hypothesis predicts that demands placed on the prefrontal cortex during exercise impede the performance of cognitive functions reliant on the prefrontal cortex. The hypothesis further predicts that these decrements in cognitive performance are observed only during exercise and that the decrements abate relatively quickly following the termination of activity. Evidence supporting the negative effects of exercise on the performance of frontally dependent cognitive tasks was presented by Dietrich and Sparling (2004), who demonstrated that performance on two measures expected to be reliant on frontal lobe functioning (the Wisconsin Card Sorting Test, or WCST, and the Paced Auditory Serial Addition Task) was hindered during a bout of moderately intense exercise (70%-80% of maximum HR), while measures of general intelligence and vocabulary were not affected by the exercise. Additional research is necessary to assess the viability of this hypothesis as an explanation for the effects of acute exercise on cognitive performance.

Theories Relevant to Chronic Exercise

Theories that have been proposed to explain the benefits of chronic physical activity on cognitive performance include the cardiovascular fitness hypothesis (North, McCullagh, & Tran, 1990) and the cognitive reserve hypothesis (Stern, 2002). These hypotheses focus on the physiological changes that result from regular long-term exercise training. In studies testing these hypotheses, researchers typically assess cognitive performance on a day when the participant has not exercised so that the results are not influenced by any effects of acute exercise.

Cardiovascular Fitness Hypothesis

The cardiovascular fitness hypothesis originally was proposed as an explanation for the beneficial effects of chronic physical activity on depression (North, McCullagh, & Tran, 1990). As applied to cognitive performance, this hypothesis suggests that the positive effects of physical activity on cognitive performance are a result of gains in cardiorespiratory fitness that occur in response to the physical activity program (Etnier, 2008; Etnier, Nowell, Landers, & Sibley, 2006). Numerous studies have been conducted to assess the role of aerobic fitness in this relationship (Aleman et al., 2000; Barnes, Yaffe, Satariano, & Tager, 2003; Blumenthal et al., 1991; Chodzko-Zajko & Moore, 1994; Chodzko-Zajko, Schuler, Solomon, Heinl, & Ellis, 1992; Dustman, Emmerson, & Shearer, 1994; Dustman et al., 1990; Emery, Schein, Hauck, & MacIntyre, 1998; Izquierdo-Porrera & Waldstein, 2002; Offenbach, Chodzko-Zajko, & Ringel, 1990; van Boxtel et al.,

1997); however, recent meta-analytic evidence fails to support cardiorespiratory fitness as a mediator of the relationship. This finding suggests that gains in aerobic fitness are not the critical predictor of cognitive performance gains (Angevaren, Aufdemkampe, Verhaar, Aleman, & Vanhees, 2008; Colcombe & Kramer, 2003; Etnier et al., 2006).

Cognitive Reserve Hypothesis

The cognitive reserve hypothesis has been applied to the literature on physical activity and cognitive performance as a way to explain the observation that physical activity appears to be more beneficial for older adults than it is for younger adults. According to the cognitive reserve hypothesis, individuals who have a greater cognitive reserve maintain their cognitive function better in the face of advancing age and are at less risk of dementia (Fratiglioni, Paillard-Borg, & Winblad, 2004; Scarmeas & Stern, 2003; Stern, 2002; Whalley, Deary, Appleton, & Starr, 2004). Cognitive reserves are thought to be enhanced by a variety of lifestyle factors, including formal education, occupational complexity, and physical activity (Whalley et al., 2004). Thus, it is predicted that physical activity enhances cognitive reserves and that this benefit is more important for older adults, whose cognitive reserves are challenged by advancing age, and less important for younger adults, whose cognitive reserves are intact. The underlying variables that contribute to a person's cognitive reserves are thought to include brain and cerebrospinal volume, brain metabolic activity, microvascular cerebral pathology, and extent of damage due to oxidative stress (Stern et al., 2005; Whalley et al., 2004). The cognitive reserve hypothesis is supported by evidence that physical activity is more beneficial to older adults than it is to younger adults (Etnier & Landers, 1997; Hillman et al., 2006), that physical activity is beneficial to people with chronic illnesses expected to negatively affect cognitive performance (Etnier & Berry, 2001; Etnier et al., 2009; Heyn, Abreu, & Ottenbacher, 2004), and that physical activity and aerobic fitness are especially beneficial for people at genetic risk for Alzheimer's disease (Deeny et al., 2008; Etnier et al., 2007; Rovio et al., 2005; Schuit, Feskens, Launer, & Kromhout, 2001). However, future study is necessary to test empirically the role of the proposed cognitive reserves as mechanisms that can explain the benefits of physical activity for cognitive performance.

Physiological Mechanisms

Recent nonhuman animal studies and neuroimaging studies with humans have pointed toward physiological mechanisms in addition to the afore-mentioned hypotheses that might explain the benefits of physical activity for cognitive performance. For example, research using rodent models has impli-cated brain-derived neurotrophic factor (BDNF) as a potential mechanism of the effects (Cotman & Berchtold, 2002; Cotman & Engesser-Cesar, 2002; Gomez-Pinilla, 2008; Gomez-Pinilla, Ying, Roy, Molteni, & Edgerton, 2002; Neeper, Gomez-Pinilla, Choi, & Cotman, 1996; Vaynman & Gomez-Pinilla, 2005, 2006; Vaynman, Ying, & Gomez-Pinilla, 2003, 2004). Research with humans has been mixed, with one study failing to support BDNF as a mediator of the relationship (Ferris, Williams, & Shen, 2007) and another implicating BDNF as a mediator of short-term learning (Winter et al., 2007). Future research is needed to clarify the potential role of BDNF in the relationship between both acute and chronic exercise and cognitive performance.

Other nonhuman animal studies have demon-strated that chronic physical activity results in both angiogenesis and neurogenesis in areas of the brain predicted to be important for cognitive performance (Black, Isaacs, Anderson, Alcantara, & Greenough, 1990; van Praag, Christie, Sejnowski, & Gage, 1999; van Praag, Kempermann, & Gage, 1999; van Praag, Shubert, Zhao, & Gage, 2005). Recent studies have shown that changes in cerebral structure as a func-tion of participating in physical activity can also be observed in humans. Neuroimaging techniques (MRI) have shown that regular physical activity protects against age-related declines in cerebral tissue (Colcombe et al., 2003; Colcombe et al., 2006).

Additionally, researchers have recently become interested in the potential role of oxidative stress as a mediator of the relationship between advancing age and cognitive decline and between physical activity and cognitive performance (Asha Devi, 2009). The free radical theory of aging (Harman, 1956, 1969, 1972, 1994) has been touted as one of the most viable theories to explain age-related cognitive decline and clinical cognitive impairment (Berr, 2000; Butterfield, Howard, Yatin, Allen, & Carney, 1997; Joseph et al., 1998; Liu & Ames, 2005; Meydani, 1999). According to this theory, as the human body ages, the production of free radicals increases or the quantity or quality of antioxidants decreases (or both). As a result, the body experiences an increase in oxidative stress. The brain is thought to be par-ticularly vulnerable to oxidative insults, so this theory posits that the damage caused by increased oxidative stress plays a role in age-related cognitive decline and in the risk of Alzheimer's disease (Berr, 2000; Clausen, Doctrow, & Baudry, 2008; Hasnis & Reznick, 2003). Studies with nonhuman animals

have shown that moderate chronic physical activity decreases oxidative stress (Aksu, Topcu, Camsari, & Acikgoz, 2008; Harris, Mitchell, Sood, Webb, & Venema, 2008; Leeuwenburgh et al., 1997; Powers et al., 1994, 1993; Radak et al., 2000, 2001; Venditti, Masullo, & Di Meo, 1999). Although research with humans is more limited, there is evidence that chronic exercise improves antioxidant defenses in younger men and women (Evelo, Palmen, Artur, & Janssen, 1992; Sato, Nanri, Ohta, Kasai, & Ikeda, 2003) and in older men (Fatouros et al., 2004). Thus, evidence supports the notion that physical activity reduces oxidative stress. Future research is needed to test the role of oxidative stress as a mediator of the relationship between physical activity and cognitive performance.

Limitations and Sources of Confusion

There are two primary limitations in the extant literature on physical activity and cognition. The first is the limited ability to compare findings across studies due to the variety of measurement tools (and dimensions) that have been used as outcomes in this literature. The second limitation is that most studies have focused on laboratory measures of cognitive performance and have not made comparisons with published norms, provided appropriate compari-sons to real-world functioning, or incorporated measures of applied cognition.

Synthesizing the findings from the research on physical activity and cognition is made difficult by the variety of assessments being used on cognitive performance. As previously described, cognition has been measured with behavioral measures as well as measures of cerebral structure and activa-tion. Comparisons across these studies is made chal-lenging by the simple fact that these measures are so different. Further difficulty arises from the variety of measures used within each of these broad categories of outcomes. This concern is particularly relevant for the behavioral measures, but it also affects our ability to synthesize findings from studies assessing cerebral structure and activation.

As just mentioned, the issue of a large variety of measurement tools is most relevant to studies using behavioral outcomes. In their reference on neuropsychological assessment, Lezak, Howeison, and Loring (2004) identified approximately 450 dif-ferent tests of cognitive performance. Although all of these measures have not been used in the exercise psychology literature, the number of tasks used in the extant literature is still large. Meta-analytic reviews of the literature on physical activity and cognition highlight this diversity. In a review of 134 studies, Etnier and colleagues (1997) identified 106 cognitive tests; in a review of 37 studies testing the relationship between aerobic fitness and cognitive performance, Etnier and colleagues (2006) identified 29 tests; in a review of 18 randomized controlled trials with older adults, Colcombe and Kramer (2003) identified 58 cognitive measures; and in a review of 11 randomized controlled trials with cognitively intact older adults, Angevaren and coworkers (2008) identified 27 cognitive outcomes. To further our understanding of how physical activity affects particular domains of cognition, meta-analytic reviewers typically have identified each of the numerous cognitive tests as belonging to a smaller number of broad cognitive dimensions. However, this approach is challenging because there is no gold standard for categorizing these tests. For example, Lezak and colleagues (2004) categorized tests of cognition as falling into the dimensions of orientation and attention, perception, memory, verbal functions and language skills, construction, concept formation and reasoning, and executive function or of representing broad neuropsychological assessment batteries. In contrast, Carroll (1983) described broad cognitive abilities of fluid intelligence, crystallized intelligence, memory and learning, visual perception, auditory perception, retrieval ability, speed of processing, and cognitive speediness.

As a result of the different methods available for categorizing the individual tests, meta-analyses on physical activity and cognition are varied even in terms of the broader cognitive categories that are identified. An examination of four meta-analyses in this area provides a clear example of how this is problematic. Etnier and coworkers (1997) used subjective judgments to categorize cognitive tests into the dimensions of memory, mathematical ability, verbal ability, reasoning, creativity, academic achievement, mental age, intelligence quotient, dual-task paradigms, reaction time, and perception. Colcombe and Kramer (2003) also used a subjective system to categorize the tests in their meta-analysis, but they used only four categories (speeded tasks, spatial tasks, controlled tasks, and executive function tasks). Additionally, Colcombe and Kramer allowed cognitive tests to be categorized as belonging to more than one of these categories. In another meta-analytic review, Etnier and colleagues (2006) used Carroll's factor analysis work in combination with Lezak and colleagues' (2004) cognitive domains to code the cognitive tests included. Similarly, Angevaren and coworkers (2008) used Lezak and colleagues' (2004) cognitive domains in

combination with categories used in another meta-analytic review (Kessels, Aleman, Verhagen, & van Luijtelaar, 2000) for their categorization system. Clearly, there is great variety in the individual cognitive tests used and in the methods used to identify the cognitive domains of these tests. Thus, comparisons across studies (and even meta-analytic reviews) are challenging.

Although there has been substantial variability in the manner in which cognition has been assessed, the cognitive measures that have been used in the exercise psychology literature have been dominated by measures that Lezak and colleagues would consider to be measures of orientation and attention (e.g., reaction time, Stroop Color Test, or word tests), memory (e.g., Auditory Verbal Learning Test or California Verbal Learning Test), and executive function (e.g., Trail Making Test, or TMT, or Stroop Interference Test). Thus, there is a growing body of literature that provides findings relative to each of these commonly used tasks.

Variability is also evident in studies assessing cerebral activation. At the most basic level, the methods used to measure cerebral activation are numerous and include EEG, ERPs, DTI, fMRI, MEG, and NIRS. Each measure provides its own unique type of data, which, of course, makes comparisons across studies difficult. Furthermore, there are differences in the behavioral tasks that participants are asked to perform while cerebral activity is measured. For example, Prakash and coworkers (2007) reported on relationships between aerobic fitness and fMRI data obtained during performance of a Paced Visual Serial Addition Test (a test of attention and concentration), whereas studies using ERPs have often used an oddball paradigm (Hillman, Buck, Themanson, Pontifex, & Castelli, 2009; Hillman, Pontifex, et al., 2009; Hillman, Snook, & Jerome, 2003; Kamijo et al., 2009; Kamijo, Nishihira, Higashiura, & Kuroiwa, 2007; Stroth et al., 2009; Themanson & Hillman, 2006). Given the relatively few studies that have examined the relationship between physical activity or aerobic fitness and cerebral activation and the variety in the methods of measurement, it is currently difficult to draw general conclusions regarding this relationship.

An additional challenge with the cognitive measures is that the focus has been on laboratory-based cognitive tests rather than on applied cognition, and there is a general failure to translate findings from laboratory-based measures into implications for real-world functioning. Applied cognition is a field that focuses on the ability to "understand cognition in the uncontrolled world of interesting people" (Durso, 2007, p. xix). Although researchers have tested the effects of acute exercise on the performance of sport-specific cognitive tasks (McMorris & Graydon, 1997; McMorris et al., 1999) and have assessed the relationship between physical activity and perceived ability to perform instrumental activities of daily living (Langhammer, Stanghelle, & Lindmark, 2009; Mercer, Freburger, Chang, & Purser, 2009), there is no research to date that has tested the effects of exercise on behavioral measures of applied cognition in real-world settings. One example of applied cognition that might be assessed relative to exercise is the ability of older adults to perform cognitively during home functioning (e.g., balancing a check book, following a recipe, taking medications as prescribed; Rogers, Pak, & Fisk, 2007). Clearly, this is a direction for future research aimed to have more immediate practical application.

Very few studies on physical activity and cognition provide information necessary to make inferences from laboratory-based tests to real-world cognitive performance. Although journals that follow APA guidelines typically require the inclusion of effect sizes in published articles, most of the empirical studies on physical activity and cognition do not translate their findings into an effect on real-world functioning, and this is considered a critical shortcoming of the sport and exercise psychology literature in general (Anderson, McCullagh, & Wilson, 2007). That is, authors may report that a moderate effect size was observed in their study, but they do not typically explain what this might mean in terms of performing real-world activities such as driving a car, shopping for groceries, or using a computer. Furthermore, although normative data are available for many of the commonly used cognitive measures, such as the Stroop Test (Steinberg, Bieliauskas, Smith, Ivnik, & Malec, 2005; Troyer, Leach, & Strauss, 2006; Van der Elst, Van Boxtel, Van Breukelen, & Jolles, 2006), in the extant literature on physical activity and cognitive performance, comparison to this normative data is typically lacking.

One exception to this limitation involves studies using clinical outcomes as a measure of cognitive performance. There are several studies in which prospective designs have been used to test the potentially protective effects of physical activity participation on the subsequent experience of clinical cognitive impairment (Abbott et al., 2004; Broe et al., 1998; Larson et al., 2006; Lindsay et al., 2002; Podewils et al., 2005; Rovio et al., 2005; Verghese et al., 2003; Wilson et al., 2002). The results from these studies are usually presented as hazard ratios, which allow for a comparison of relative risk of clinical impairment, and thus make the real-world implications evident.

A second notable exception is the line of research looking at physical activity training as a means of improving cognitive performance for automobile driving. For example, the Useful Field of View Test (UFOV) is a computerized test designed to assess visual processing speed, attention, and higher-order cognitive abilities. Although this is a laboratory-based measure, performance on the UFOV has been linked to driving performance in older adults (Anstey, Wood, Lord, & Walker, 2005). Researchers have demonstrated that physical activity is predictive of better performance on the UFOV, and inferences have been made relative to driving performance (Roth, Goode, Clay, & Ball, 2003). Similarly, researchers have tested the effects of physical activity on attention and have drawn conclusions relative to driving (Marmeleira, Godinho, & Fernandes, 2009).

Primary Measurement Tools

Of relevance to this line of research is further discussion of the measurement tools used to assess the relationship between physical activity and cognitive performance. For ease of presentation, the behavioral measures of cognition are categorized and described according to Lezak and colleagues' (2004) dimensions of cognitive function.

Attention and Orientation

The cognitive tasks used in the exercise psychology literature are frequently measures of attention and orientation. This is particularly true for studies on acute exercise, which are dominated by measures such as reaction time (Brisswalter, Arcelin, Audiffren, & Delignieres, 1997; Brisswalter et al., 1995; Collardeau, Brisswalter, & Audiffren, 2001; Davranche, Burle, Audiffren, & Hasbroucq, 2005; Hogervorst, Riedel, Kovacs, Brouns, & Jolles, 1999; Kashihara & Nakahara, 2005; Lemmink & Visscher, 2005; Pesce, Cereatti, Casella, Baldari, & Capranica, 2007; Scott, McNaughton, & Polman, 2006) and the Stroop Test (Aks, 1998; Ferris et al., 2007; Hogervorst et al., 1996, 1999; Kubesch et al., 2003; Lichtman & Poser, 1983; McMorris & Graydon, 1997; Welsh et al., 2002).

Reaction time tasks are implemented in a variety of ways, but the basic goal is to identify the time it takes for a participant to respond to a stimulus. The stimulus may be administered to any sensing system but is typically an auditory or a visual stimulus. The response may also be provided in a variety of ways but most often is a verbal response or a motor response (which is typically made on a computer keyboard or by pushing a response key). Reaction time tasks may be simple (with only one possible stimulus and one preprogrammed response), choice or complex (with multiple possible stimuli, each one associated with a particular response), or discriminant (with one stimulus requiring a response and another stimulus requiring not making a response). The number of trials used represents a balance between a desire for reliable measures and a desire to limit fatigue and loss of interest. Some studies distinguish motor movements from cognitive processes by dividing reaction time into its subcomponents (premotor time, motor time, movement time) using electromyographic (EMG) techniques (Chang, Etnier, & Barella, 2009; Clarkson, 1978; Etnier, Sibley, Pomery, & Kao, 2003; MacRae et al., 1996).

The Stroop Test is also a frequently used measure of attention and orientation. The two conditions of the Stroop Test that are considered measures of attention and orientation are the Word Test and the Color Test. The Stroop Word Test requires participants to identify the color name that is presented (e.g., the word *blue*). The Stroop Color Test requires participants to identify the color of ink of a symbol or string of symbols (e.g., *XXX* written in blue ink). There is great variety in the method of stimuli administration (e.g., presented one at a time on a computer screen or presented as a list on a piece of paper), in the response method (e.g., verbally, pressing a push button, striking a key on a computer keyboard), and in the performance measures (e.g., average time to response or total number correct in a given time). There is also variety in whether the performance on one of the two tests or the average performance on the two tests together is used as the measure of cognitive performance.

Memory

Measures of memory have also been popular in the exercise psychology literature and have been used in both acute exercise studies (Coles & Tomporowski, 2008; Emery, Honn, Frid, Lebowitz, & Diaz, 2001; Hogervorst et al., 1999; Krebs, Eickelberg, Krobath, & Baruch, 1989; Netz, Tomer, Axelrad, Argov, & Inbar, 2007; Schramke & Bauer, 1997) and chronic exercise studies (Blumenthal et al., 1989; Emery & Gatz, 1990; Fabre, Chamari, Mucci, Masse-Biron, & Prefaut, 2002; Hassmen, Ceci, & Backman, 1992; Hoffman et al., 2008; Lautenschlager et al., 2008). Various forms of word lists (Auditory Verbal Learning Test or California Verbal Learning Test) require a participant to recall 15 to 16 words that have been presented verbally. Typically, the participant is asked to recall the list immediately following the list presentation (immediate recall) and then again following a 30 min delay (delayed recall). The Digit Span Test is another common memory task. In this task, participants are read a series of single digits (from 2-8) and are asked to repeat those digits either forward (in order) or backward (in reverse order). Once a participant is unable to repeat back the digits at a given difficulty level on two occasions, the task is terminated. At this time, human studies on the effects of physical activity on memory have not assessed the various forms of memory (e.g., working, episodic, visual, spatial) within a given study, and thus our understanding of the potential specificity of the effects is limited.

Executive Function

Measures of executive function have become increasingly popular in the exercise psychology literature. This is likely in response to evidence suggesting that the frontal lobe is most affected by physical activity (Kramer, Humphrey, Larish, Logan, & Strayer, 1994) and to the Colcombe and Kramer (2003) meta-analysis, which showed larger effects on executive function tasks ($g = 0.68$) than on controlled ($g = 0.46$), spatial ($g = 0.43$), and speeded ($g = 0.27$) tasks. Executive function is a higher-order cognitive ability thought to reflect planning, scheduling, inhibition, and working memory (Etnier & Chang, 2009). In the exercise psychology literature, commonly used measures of executive function are the Stroop Test, the TMT, and the Flanker Test.

For executive function assessment, the relevant Stroop Test is the Stroop Interference Test. In this test, cognitive interference is increased by asking participants to identify the color of ink in which a color name is written and to disregard the color name itself (e.g., give the response "blue" when the word *red* is written in blue ink). As previously mentioned, the Stroop Test can be administered in a variety of ways. Additionally, the score used to reflect executive function may be the time required for test completion, the difference between time to completion for the Interference Test and time to completion for either the Color Test or the Word Test, or the difference between time to completion for the Interference Test and the average time to completion for the Color and Word Tests.

The TMT is another frequently used measure of executive function. This task also consists of two tests. Test A (TMT A) requires participants to connect the dots by drawing a line to connect the numbers 1 through 13 in consecutive order as quickly as possible. TMT A measures attention and orientation. Test B (TMT B) measures executive function by asking participants to alternate between consecutive numbers and consecutive letters (e.g., draw a line from *1* to *A* to *2* to *B*) as they connect the dots as quickly as possible. The difference in performance between TMT A and TMT B (i.e., TMT B – TMT A) is used as the measure of executive function.

The Flanker Test is a measure of executive function that is common in studies that also incorporate measures of cerebral activation (Hillman, Buck, et al., 2009; Hillman, Pontifex et al., 2009; Hillman et al., 2003; Kamijo et al., 2009; Kamijo et al., 2007; Stroth et al., 2009; Themanson & Hillman, 2006; Themanson, Pontifex, & Hillman, 2008). The stimulus in this test consists of five symbols, the center one of which is typically an arrow pointing to the left or right. Participants are instructed to respond as quickly as possible by pressing a key corresponding to the direction in which the center arrow points (left or right). The two symbols on either side of the center stimulus are squares (neutral condition), arrows pointing in the same direction as the center stimulus (congruent condition), or arrows pointing in the opposite direction of the center stimulus (incongruent condition). Performance in the incongruent condition is used as the measure of executive function.

Broad Neuropsychological Assessment Batteries

Many prospective studies use a single general measure of cognition such as the Mini-Mental Status Exam (MMSE; Barnes et al., 2003; Dik, Deeg, Visser, & Jonker, 2003; Lytle, Vander Bilt, Pandav, Dodge, & Ganguli, 2004; van Gelder et al., 2004; Yaffe, Barnes, Nevitt, Lui, & Covinsky, 2001). The MMSE (Folstein, Folstein, & McHugh, 1975) assesses orientation, attention, arithmetic, memory, language, and motor skills and has a maximum possible score of 30. A score of 20 to 26 indicates potential cognitive impairment, and a score of less than 20 suggests severe cognitive impairment. The MMSE is best used as an assessment of changes in clinical cognitive impairment and so only demonstrates appropriate sensitivity when used with large samples from a population expected to experience cognitive impairment.

Cerebral Structure and Activation

Measures of cerebral structure and activation have also been used in the exercise psychology literature to identify the effects of physical activity on brain morphology and on neural activity purported to underlie cognitive task performance. The most commonly used measure of cerebral structure is MRI. MRI is a relatively noninvasive technique that provides cross-sectional images of the brain. These images are then analyzed using voxel-based morphometry to distinguish gray matter, white matter, and cerebrospinal fluid. MRI typically has been used to identify differences in cerebral structure that are associated with chronic participation in physical activity or with differences in levels of aerobic fitness (Burns et al., 2008; Carlson et al., 2009; Colcombe et al., 2003; Colcombe et al., 2006; Dubbert, Penman, Evenson, Reeves, & Mosley, 2009; Gordon et al., 2008; Rovio et al., 2008).

ERPs are the most frequently used measure of cerebral activation in the literature on physical activity and cognition. ERPs are collected via EEG, and measurements are taken relative to a time-locked stimulus. ERPs have exceptional temporal resolution but poor spatial resolution (Irani, Platek, Bunce, Ruocco, & Chute, 2007). When ERPs are assessed in the exercise psychology literature, P300 is the component typically considered. P300 is a positive-going waveform that is observed approximately 300 ms after stimulus presentation. It is associated with the attentional processes that are necessary when a new, relevant stimulus is detected. P300 amplitude (the difference between baseline EEG activity before stimulus presentation and the largest positive activity between 250 and 500 ms following stimulus presentation) is thought to indicate the allocation of attentional resources (Polich, 2007). P300 latency (the time from stimulus presentation to the time at which the P300 amplitude is identified) is used as a measure of classification speed and is thought to relate to the time needed to identify a relevant stimulus (Polich, 2007). Thus, these measures are used to enhance our understanding of how physical activity affects underlying neurological indexes of cognitive performance.

Other measures of cerebral activation such as DTI, fMRI, MEG, and NIRS have been used much less frequently in the extant literature. DTI is an MRI method that measures neural tract directional activation and allows for inferences regarding white matter connectivity. Marks and colleagues (2007) used DTI to ascertain the relationship between aerobic fitness and white matter integrity. Similarly, fMRI provides a noninvasive means of examining cerebral activation. fMRI is used to measure blood oxygenation and blood flow, and these measures are then used to infer neural activity. In terms of measuring cognitive activation, fMRI has excellent spatial resolution but limited temporal resolution (Irani et al., 2007). Prakash and coworkers (2007) used fMRI to examine cerebral activation relative to aerobic fitness in patients with multiple sclerosis.

MEG is a noninvasive technique that is similar to EEG in that it is used to detect electrical potentials generated by neural activity. MEG has excellent temporal resolution and good spatial resolution. Deeny and colleagues (2008) used MEG to demonstrate that physical activity is associated with greater temporal lobe activation during a working memory task performed by people at genetic risk for Alzheimer's disease. NIRS is another technique that is beginning to receive attention in the neuropsychology literature. NIRS allows for the measurement of hemodynamic responses from which inferences about neural activity are made. NIRS provides good spatial and temporal resolution (Irani et al., 2007). It has been used in the general exercise psychology literature to advance our understanding of cerebral blood flow during exercise, but inferences to cognitive function have not yet been made (Ekkekakis, 2009).

Example Studies

The 2003 study by Barnes and colleagues provides an excellent example of a study testing the relationship between aerobic fitness and cognitive performance by using a general measure of cognition as well as individual cognitive tests targeting particular cognitive domains. These authors were interested in testing the protective effects of aerobic fitness against cognitive decline experienced over a 6 y time frame. Community-dwelling older adults (>55 y) involved in an ongoing longitudinal study were invited to participate. Volunteers performed a maximal aerobic fitness test on a treadmill and completed the modified MMSE at baseline and 6 y subsequently. In year 6, participants completed additional cognitive tests that included measures of memory (California Verbal Learning Test), executive function (Stroop Interference Test, TMT B, Digit Symbol Substitution Test), and verbal function and language skills (verbal fluency). Of the 998 who completed the baseline measures, 902 were identified as being cognitively healthy at baseline, and 349 agreed to complete the additional cognitive tests in year 6. Results indicated that the baseline measure of aerobic fitness was predictive of better maintenance of MMSE performance from baseline to year 6 and was predictive of better performance on all of the additional cognitive tests. The authors thus concluded that in cognitively normal older adults, aerobic fitness is protective against age-related cognitive decline when operationalized as either general cognitive performance or performance of specific cognitive abilities.

Research conducted by Colcombe and coworkers (2006) provides a good example of a study in which measures of cerebral structure were used as an outcome. These authors randomly assigned sedentary older adults ($n = 59$; 60-79 y) to an aerobic training group or a stretching control group for 6 mo. Participants were scanned with MRI 1 wk before and 1 wk following the intervention, and voxel-based morphometry methods were used to ascertain changes in gray and white matter as a function of time by treatment group. Results indicated that participants in the aerobic training group experienced significantly greater increases in gray matter in the frontal regions of the brain and significantly greater increases in white matter in areas of the brain thought to be important to the experience of age-related cognitive decline. Given the changes in cerebral structure observed relative to participation in aerobic exercise, the authors concluded that aerobic training is causally linked to cerebral structure and inferred that aerobic training is likely to be protective against age-related cognitive decline.

Other scientists have used measures of cerebral activation and behavioral measures of cognition concurrently to further our understanding of the effects of exercise on cognitive performance. Kamijo and colleagues (2007) tested the interactive effects of task difficulty and exercise intensity on performance of the modified Eriksen Flanker Test. The Flanker Test was modified so that participants were asked to respond to an *F* with their left thumb and to an *X* with their right thumb. In the incongruent condition, the target stimulus (e.g., *F*) was flanked by the other possible target stimulus (e.g., *X*). In the neutral condition, the flankers were irrelevant letters (e.g., *L*). EMG activity from the right and left flexor pollicis brevis muscles was recorded so that reaction time could be operationalized as the time from stimulus presentation to the first observable indication of muscle activation to initiate the motor response. On the first day, participants performed 30 practice trials and 300 actual trials while EEG activity was recorded. The trials consisted of equal numbers of neutral (easy) and incongruent (difficult) trials. Participants also performed a maximal aerobic exercise test so that exercise intensities corresponding to low, moderate, and high were identified for each individual. On 3 subsequent days, participants exercised at the assigned intensity level for 20 min and then performed the Flanker Test within 3 min of the termination of the exercise bout. Results indicated that exercise of any intensity resulted in a reaction time that was quicker than that observed at baseline. Additionally, light and moderate exercise resulted in amplitudes for P300 that were larger than those observed at baseline. After exercise, P300 latency was shorter in the incongruent condition but not in the neutral condition. Because behavioral measures and measures of cerebral activation were used concurrently, the authors were able to interpret their results as being indicative of differential effects of acute exercise on cognitive parameters. In particular, the authors concluded that acute exercise might benefit the stimulus evaluation processes more than it benefits the response processes.

Recommendations for Researchers and Practitioners

The assessment of cognitive function is not a trivial undertaking. In particular, the effects of physical activity (whether acute or chronic) on cognitive performance appear to be task dependent, making task selection critical for the observation of effects. Furthermore, the selection of the particular cognitive instruments for a study should be made with consideration of the study design, relevant theory, underlying mechanisms, and study population. For example, Etnier and Chang (2009) discussed the fact that interest in executive function blossomed in response to the Colcombe and Kramer (2003) meta-analysis but pointed out that those findings were derived from studies testing the effects of chronic physical activity interventions on cognitive performance by older adults. Thus, the findings of the Colcombe and Kramer meta-analysis should not be used to justify a focus on executive function in other populations (e.g., children). That being said, researchers are encouraged to consult meta-analytic reviews to identify expected effect sizes for the cognitive measures to be used with their particular sample so that appropriate sample sizes are recruited.

A second comment with respect to the selection of cognitive tasks is that our ability to synthesize the literature is hampered by the huge variety in tasks used and the different methodologies used to administer these tasks. It would be a benefit if researchers could come to some agreement on the appropriate measures to use to assess the various dimensions of cognitive performance. Clearly this is not an easy undertaking, especially given the particular nuances and subtle differences among tasks within a given dimension. For example, both the TMT and Stroop Test measure executive function, but the TMT has been described as measuring inhibition, cognitive flexibility, and maintenance of a response set (Arbuthnott & Frank, 2000; Kortte, Horner, & Windhan, 2002), while the Stroop Test has been purported to assess inhibition, selective attention, and shifting ability (Miyake et al., 2000).

A further consideration is using cognitive tasks that have normative data available and that have clear implications for real-world functioning or are measures of applied cognition. Clearly, this is an important point to emphasize as we strive to further our appreciation for the potential public health benefits of physical activity. Similarly, when using measures of cerebral structure and activation, we should strive to pair the use of these techniques with behavioral measures of cognition so that the link between mechanisms and performance is clear.

The following recommendations for practitioners are presented relative to the age groups of children, older adults, and all other ages. With respect to older adults, research consistently shows that as people age, cognitive performance declines (Salthouse, 2003; Schaie, 1994), the rate of cognitive decline increases (Bors & Forin, 1995; Brayne et al., 1999; Schonknecht, Pantel, Kruse, & Schroder, 2005), and the risk of Alzheimer's disease increases (Jorm & Jolley, 1998; Lindsay et al., 2002; Rubin et al., 1998). The evidence regarding the beneficial effects of physical activity for cognitive performance by older adults consistently supports a small to moderate effect (Angevaren et al., 2008; Colcombe & Kramer, 2003). Furthermore, the evidence suggests that participating in physical activity is most beneficial to cognitive performance for people at genetic risk for Alzheimer's disease (Deeny et al., 2008; Etnier et al., 2007; Rovio et al., 2005; Schuit et al., 2001) and for people who have chronic illnesses that negatively affect their cognitive functioning (Etnier & Berry, 2001; Etnier et al., 2009; Heyn et al., 2004). Given these promising findings and the importance of cognitive functioning for the quality of life of older adults, it is appropriate for professionals working with older adults to implement physical activity programs to benefit cognitive performance.

Research with children is not as well developed, but the extant literature also supports the efficacy of physical activity as a means of positively affecting cognitive performance. In a meta-analytic review of the literature, Sibley and Etnier (2003) reported a small positive effect of physical activity on the cognitive performance of children. A recent empirical study in which physical activity was manipulated in a randomized controlled trial also demonstrated a beneficial effect of physical activity on cognitive performance by children (Davis et al., 2007). Although the evidence is much more limited, the extant literature does support the use of physical activity as a means of improving cognitive performance by children, and practitioners are encouraged to consider cognitive benefits as an additional advantage of participating in physical activity.

In people of other ages, the effects of chronic physical activity appear to be more minimal (Etnier et al., 1997); however, physical activity performed during young or middle adulthood may serve to increase cognitive reserves and be protective of cognitive performance in later life (Dik et al., 2003). In addition, in young adults acute bouts of physical activity have been shown to be beneficial to particular types of cognitive tasks (Chang et al., 2009; Coles & Tomporowski, 2008; Hogervorst et al., 1996;

McMorris & Graydon, 1997; McMorris et al., 1999; McMorris, Swain, Lauder, Smith, & Kelly, 2006) and to benefit underlying neuropsychological indexes of cognitive performance (Kamijo et al., 2004; Kamijo et al., 2007; Magnie et al., 2000). Thus, physical activity by young adults can improve cognitive performance in the short term and may provide an important foundation for preserving cognitive abilities in the face of age-related decline.

■ Table 17.1 ■

Measures of Cognitive Performance Commonly Used in Studies Testing the Effects of Physical Activity

Variable or concept	Measure or tool	Dimension or characteristic	Source	Website
Attention and orientation	Reaction time	Computer administered		www.pstnet.com www.lafayetteinstrument.com
Attention and orientation	Stroop Color and Word Tests	Paper version	Stroop (1935)	www.parinc.com www.mhs.com www.stoeltingco.com
Memory	California Verbal Learning Test	Paper version and computer administered	Delis, Kramer, Kaplan, & Ober (1987)	www.pearsonassess.com/pai/
Memory	Auditory Verbal Learning Test	Paper version	Rey (1941)	www.parinc.com
Memory	Digit Span Test	Paper version	Wechsler (1997)	www.pearsonassess.com/pai/
General cognition	Mini-Mental Status Exam (MMSE)	Paper version	Folstein, Folstein, & McHugh (1975)	www.parinc.com
Executive function	Stroop Interference Test	Paper version	Stroop (1935)	www.parinc.com www.mhs.com www.stoeltingco.com
Executive function	Trail Making Test (TMT)	Online version	Partington (1949)	www.parinc.com
Executive function	Trail Making Test (TMT)	Paper version	Partington (1949)	www.mhs.com www.stoeltingco.com www.parinc.com
Executive function	Flanker Test	Computer administered	Eriksen & Schultz (1979)	www.pstnet.com

Anticipation and Decision Making

Skills, Methods, and Measures

Andrew Mark Williams, PhD, and Bruce Abernethy, PhD

Anticipating the intentions of opponents and formulating an appropriate response based on the current context as well as overriding strategic and tactical considerations are key components of performance in many sports, particularly team ball sports and racket sports. In many sports, performers are confronted with extreme temporal pressure. For example, in tennis the time it takes for the ball to travel from one player to another is often shorter than the combined total of the receiver's reaction time and movement time, implying that the receiver must commence a response before the ball leaves the opponent's racket (Abernethy & Russell, 1983; Williams, Davids, & Williams, 1999). An increasing body of empirical evidence highlights the superior anticipation and decision-making skills of experts compared with novices (for recent reviews, see Williams & Ward, 2007; Hodges, Huys, & Starkes, 2007) as well as the notion that these skills are increasingly important as athletes progress to higher levels of performance (Williams & Reilly, 2000).

As a result of increased awareness of the importance of anticipation and decision making in expert performance, scientists have attempted to develop methods that capture these skills under controlled conditions in both laboratory and field settings (Ericsson & Williams, 2007). Moreover, process-tracing measures such as eye movement recording, think-aloud protocols, and brain imaging have been employed in order to identify the mechanisms underpinning effective performance (Williams & Ericsson, 2005) as well as the acquisition of these mechanisms through prolonged engagement in the performance domain (Baker, Côté, & Abernethy,

2003a, 2003b; Berry, Abernethy, & Côté, 2008). The ability to effectively measure these skills helps to identify the strengths and weaknesses of athletes, to monitor improvements in these skills over time, and to develop training programs that facilitate the acquisition of these skills.

This chapter examines recent research in order to provide an understanding of the skills that contribute to superior anticipation and decision making in sport. We highlight the methods that may be used to assess these skills in the laboratory and, where appropriate, in the field and illustrate some of the measures that may be used to examine the mechanisms governing successful performance.

Anticipation in Sport: Capturing Performance

In recent decades, scientists have been successful in identifying a number of component skills that reliably contribute to superior anticipation in sport. These components are frequently referred to as *perceptual-cognitive skills*, illustrating the importance of perceptual and cognitive processes in anticipation. These skills are assumed to be closely interrelated during expert performance, with the relative importance of each varying as a function of the task and situation (Williams, 2009; Williams & Ward, 2007). As a result of extensive engagement in sport, elite athletes develop complex, task-specific encoding skills and associated retrieval structures in long-term memory (LTM; Ericsson & Kintsch, 1995). These retrieval structures allow athletes to index and store information at encoding, such that features or collections of features can permit superior representation of current scenarios and facilitate both recognition and anticipation of events (Ericsson, Patel, & Kintsch, 2000). These complex information structures in the LTM are accessible through cues held in the short-term memory (STM). The proposal is that long-term working memory (LTWM) helps performers develop an encoding for a situation that in turn facilitates monitoring, formulation of planning actions, and continual evaluation of the present situation and planned actions. This section briefly reviews these perceptual-cognitive skills and the manner in which they may be assessed.

Advance Cue Utilization

Skilled athletes are able to anticipate the intentions of others by picking up information from postural orientation ahead of key events such as foot-to-ball or ball-to-racket contact. For example, in soccer skilled goalkeepers are able to anticipate the intentions of an opponent during a penalty kick by processing information from the opponent's run up and bodily movements just before the foot-to-ball contact (Williams & Burwitz, 1993; Savelsbergh, Williams, van der Kamp, & Ward, 2002), whereas in tennis skilled players are able to make use of advance visual cues when trying to anticipate what type of serve an opponent will deliver (Williams, Ward, Knowles, & Smeeton, 2002).The skilled performer's ability to process advance visual cues has been demonstrated in a range of sports as well as in different situations within each sport, such as the penalty kick and outfield play in soccer (Williams & Davids, 1998) or facing spin and swing bowlers in cricket (McRobert, Williams, Ward, & Eccles, 2009; Müller, Abernethy, & Farrow, 2006). Several methods have been developed to measure the time course of information pickup (i.e., the *when*) and to identify the location of the specific postural cues (i.e., the *where*) that performers use to make anticipation judgments. The most popular of these methods have been the temporal and spatial occlusion approaches, although others such as the response time paradigm and biomechanical profiling methods have gathered support recently. We review each method in turn.

Temporal Occlusion

The ability of performers to utilize advance postural cues can be evaluated using temporal occlusion approaches that limit the time course of information available to the viewer. Sport-specific action is captured on video by placing a camera in the position normally occupied by the performer so as to replicate, as closely as possible, the view that is available, for example, to the goalkeeper in field hockey or to the batter in baseball. A number of athletes are then filmed completing the typical actions of an opponent, such as a penalty flick in field hockey or a pitch in baseball, respectively. These clips are then edited to present varying extents of advance and ball flight information. For example, video sequences may be occluded 120 ms before, 80 ms before, at, and 120 ms after foot-to-ball contact by the penalty taker or ball release by the pitcher. Participants then indicate either verbally or using pen and paper where the ball will be placed by the opponent. In order to make the task as realistic as possible, images may be projected onto a large screen to replicate the participant's perspective during actual competition and participants may be required to move physically as if to intercept or strike the ball (e.g., see Abernethy & Russell, 1987; Williams & Davids, 1998). An illustration of the conditions employed in a temporal occlusion paradigm is highlighted in figure 18.1.

Skilled athletes are more accurate on these judgment tasks than their less skilled counterparts are, frequently obtaining scores above chance at even the earliest occlusion conditions. These findings highlight the early time course of information extraction in sport and illustrate the ability of elite athletes to pick up advance (e.g., before foot-to-ball contact or before ball release) information from the postural orientation of opponents. Athletes with less skill are generally less sensitive (or less attuned) to this early information, and the expert advantage on this type of task has been shown to relate to the specific pickup of early information from the opponent's movement pattern rather than to any generic capacity for faster processing of all types of visual information (Farrow, Abernethy, & Jackson, 2005). The types of prediction errors made by players of different skill levels may also be informative. For example, soccer players tend to predict at levels above chance the correct side that the ball will be placed before foot-to-ball contact, whereas errors in judging the height of the kick only reduce significantly after the soccer players view the first portion of ball flight (Williams & Burwitz, 1993).

Although the temporal occlusion approach has been used extensively across a number of sports, it is not without its limitations. Most notably, the experimenter must acquire some preconceived notion of the key time window for information extraction in order to decide on the specific temporal occlusion conditions. While there have been attempts to determine the most appropriate time windows based on an analysis of the kinematics of the movement (e.g., Abernethy & Zawi, 2007), the process remains largely intuitive, which may result

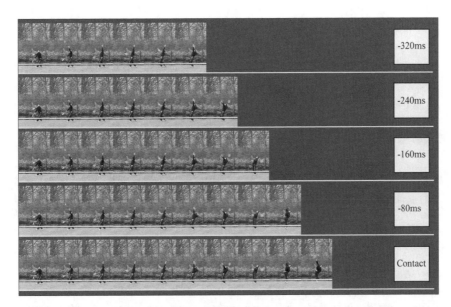

Figure 18.1 The temporal occlusion approach in tennis. Varying the time of display occlusion at different points during the time course from the commencement of action to a critical event such as racket-to-ball contact permits determination of when information pickup occurs and the extent to which pickup is influenced by the skill and experience of the receiving player (or viewer).

in the selection of less-than-optimal time windows. Another concern relates to the absence of realistic constraints on the time available for response, as personified by the customary use of pen and paper, although technological advances allowing in situ testing reduce this limitation. When athletes are asked to perform without the normal temporal pressures that exist during competition, they may be inclined to use a different-than-usual strategy to solve the problem. Finally, when used in isolation, the temporal occlusion approach only indicates the time frames in which critical information is picked up—it does not permit direct identification of the specific sources of information used for making anticipation judgments.

A field-based alternative to the film occlusion technique involves the use of liquid crystal occlusion glasses (see Farrow & Abernethy, 2003; Farrow et al., 2005; Müller & Abernethy, 2006; Starkes, Edwards, Dissanayake, & Dunn, 1995). These glasses may be triggered by a range of electronic devices, including infrared beams, pressure-sensitive pads, and optoelectronic motion analysis systems, to occlude at varying times relative to a key event (see Oudejans & Coolen, 2003). The main difficulty when using field-based methods of this nature is that there are problems in test reliability, particularly in comparisons of performance between players or groups. The repeatability of the stimuli may be improved by using trained individuals to act out the action sequences in a consistent manner. There may also be concerns over participant safety, particularly in situations where a physical response is required.

The advantage of these glasses is that they enable performance to be captured in situ with participants having complete access to relevant cues and some opportunity to respond physically to the action. The ability to incorporate interceptive responses into the paradigm used to examine anticipation may be important given that it is thought that only with such a response requirement is the use of the specialized, dorsal, vision-for-action pathway invoked (Milner & Goodale, 1995; van der Kamp, Rivas, van Doom, & Savelsbergh, 2008). An example of using the liquid crystal glasses to gather data on the tennis court is provided in figure 18.2 on page 194.

Spatial Occlusion

The spatial or event occlusion technique may be used to identify the specific information cues that players use to anticipate an opponent's intentions. This approach is similar to the temporal occlusion technique, but while the time of occlusion usually remains constant, different areas of the display may be occluded for the entire duration of the clip. For example, the hips or nonkicking leg of a penalty kicker may be occluded. If performance declines when a particular area of the display is occluded, the assumption is that this area provides an important source of information for the performer (e.g., see Abernethy & Russell, 1987; Williams & Davids, 1998; Müller et al., 2006). A repeated measures design is employed, with participants being shown the same set of clips, occasionally under different temporal occlusion conditions, in an effort to identify the *what* and *when* of information extraction. It

Figure 18.2 Liquid crystal goggles can be used to manipulate temporal occlusion in the natural setting. In this example the experimenter manually controls when the goggles change from transparent to opaque. The player's task is to complete a successful return stroke. Whether the player moves in the correct direction to intercept the ball following occlusion can be used as a measure of successful information pickup.

Illustration courtesy of Damian Farrow.

is customary to include a control condition involving the occlusion of an irrelevant display area. The experimenter may use the same presentation and response modes employed in the temporal occlusion approach. Another variation of the traditional occlusion approach is to present only a key source of information, such as the hand or arm, while removing all other information sources. This is opposed to the more traditional method of occluding a single source while presenting the remaining information (e.g., see Müller et al., 2006). This newer approach indicates what information can be used in isolation, whereas the older approach indicates what information is essential and unique and cannot be replaced by information pickup from alternative sources.

A difficulty with the spatial occlusion approach is that the editing work involved is extensive and time consuming (Williams et al., 1999). Although recent advancements in digital technology have greatly simplified the process, the time required to produce the edited sequences remains somewhat prohibitive. Another difficulty relates to the need to present the same stimuli on repeated trials; there is a risk of participants becoming familiar with the particular clip or action sequence. The potential for order effects needs to be carefully monitored and controlled. Unlike the temporal occlusion approach, for which occlusion goggles make possible in situ analogues of the original laboratory-based method, the spatial occlusion approach currently lacks a simple in situ equivalent to the laboratory-based testing.

Response Time Paradigm

The same film footage and response methods employed with the temporal occlusion approach may be used with the response time paradigm. In this approach, the viewing duration is controlled by the participant rather than by the tester. In other words, participants initiate a response as soon as they feel that they can make an accurate decision based on the duration of film viewed. Response time and response accuracy are taken as dependent measures. A variety of methods can be used to measure response characteristics, including pressure-sensitive floor-mounted pads, pressure switches, infrared beams, and optoelectronic motion analysis systems (for a more detailed review, see Williams & Ericsson, 2005).

This type of paradigm has been used successfully to assess anticipation and decision making during various offensive (Helsen & Starkes, 1999; Vaeyens et al., 2007a,b) and defensive (Williams & Davids, 1998; Williams, Davids, Burwitz, & Williams, 1994) scenarios in soccer and during the penalty flick in field hockey (Williams, Ward, & Chapman, 2003). Skilled players typically respond more quickly than less skilled players respond while maintaining a high level of accuracy. A limitation with this approach is that it is difficult to isolate the key moment when information is extracted from the display; a player may be reasonably confident of making the correct decision earlier in the sequence but may wait a few moments longer to be certain that the intended response is correct. Subtle trade-offs between speed and accuracy can therefore make analysis and interpretation of findings difficult. Moreover, in actual competition, participants rarely have to respond quickly and accurately; rather, they are required to respond accurately within the time available. Therefore, to some degree the response time paradigm places unrealistic constraints on performance. Like the temporal occlusion approach, the response time paradigm provides no direct indication as to the specific information cues performers extract from the display to guide anticipation.

A field-based version of this paradigm exists (Howarth, Walsh, Abernethy, & Snyder, 1984; James, Caudrelier, & Murray, 2006). Various incidents from a particular sport are filmed during actual competition and then coded after the event. In the case of tennis, for instance, an anticipatory movement is defined as the first displacement of the receiver's body in the direction necessary to intercept the oncoming stroke. Viewing time is regarded as the time necessary to make a perceptual assessment of the environment and to make a judgment; it is estimated to be in the region of 200 ms. Howarth and coworkers (1984) used this approach in squash to report that highly skilled players make their initial anticipatory movements significantly earlier than their less skilled counterparts make them, with the highly skilled players typically initiating a response 100 ms before the opponent strikes the ball. This chronometric approach is limited both by the veracity of the assumption that the perceptual and decision-making processes necessarily occur in a strict serial manner and by the accuracy with which individual differences in measures of visual simple reaction time provide an adequate estimation of processing latencies for different individuals and skill groupings.

Biomechanical Analysis and Profiling

The analysis and profiling of movement skill have been undertaken in clinical and applied biomechanics for many years. The main focus in this type of work has been to identify clinical abnormalities in gait patterns (see Troje, 2002). Only recently have scientists started using these techniques to identify how the specific nature of the information available to the performer may differ across subtle variations of the same skill in sport. A motion analysis system may be employed to capture detailed two- or three-dimensional kinematic information for different skills such as the forehand crosscourt and down-the-line shots in tennis. Identifying the biomechanical differences between these shots provides a principled basis for identifying subtle

differences in the perceptual cues that may be visible to performers (see Cañal-Bruland & Williams, 2010; Huys, Smeeton, Hodges, Beek, & Williams, 2008; Huys, Cañal-Bruland, Hagemann, & Williams, 2009; Shim, Carlton, & Kwon, 2006; Williams, Huys, Cañal-Bruland, & Hagemann, 2009).

These biomechanical data may be analyzed at varying levels. The simplest level of analysis involves using angle–angle plots or extracting simple quantitative measures such as joint range of motion, angular displacement, and angular and liner velocity profiles. Cross-correlations can be used to examine aspects of intralimb coordination (see Horn, Williams, & Scott, 2002). A more sophisticated approach is to use assumption-free data reduction techniques such as principal component analysis to identify component modes that differentiate subtle variations in shot direction. Principal component analysis reduces high-dimensional data sets into a smaller number of structures or components (see Daffertshofer, Lamoth, Meijer, & Beek, 2004). The technique can tease apart the structural components (or invariance) of the task and identify the factors that discriminate potentially subtle variations of the same shot (e.g., down-the-line and crosscourt shots in tennis).

An added advantage of collecting biomechanical data is that researchers can use these data to create computer simulations of the skill in question or to create point-light displays or stick figure images. Computer simulations can be viewed from any angle or perspective, and aspects of the display such as a particular limb may be highlighted, removed, or distorted. Such manipulations may be useful for testing and training purposes. Several researchers have used point-light displays to examine the importance of relative motion information when anticipating the actions of an opponent (e.g., Abernethy, Gill, Parks, & Packer, 2001; Ward, Williams, & Bennett, 2002). The argument is that performers determine an opponent's intentions based on their perception of the relative motions between specific bodily features rather than the extraction of information from more superficial features or an isolated area or cue. The method of presenting images in point-light form can be combined with temporal and spatial occlusion techniques such that images are temporally occluded at predetermined time points or individual or collective markers are removed for all or part of a trial in an effort to identify the minimal essential information guiding skilled perception (e.g., Abernethy & Zawi, 2007; Abernethy, Zawi, & Jackson, 2008). Some examples of point-light presentations are provided in figure 18.3 on page 196.

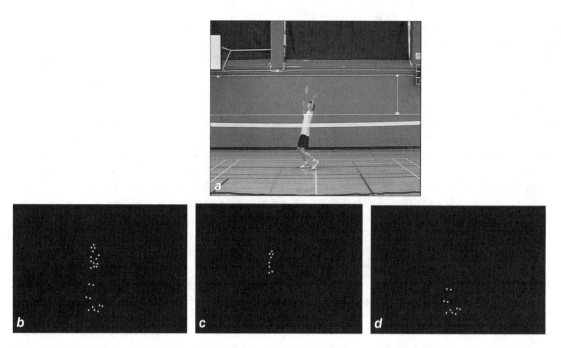

Figure 18.3 Presenting normal video displays (*a*) in point-light format (*b*) reduces the available display information to purely kinematic information. Selectively presenting only some points, such as those of the (*c*) racket and playing arm or (*d*) the lower body, permits determination of the information content of specific elements within the opposing player's movement pattern.

Identifying Sequences of Play

Several researchers have argued that the ability to identify a familiar sequence of play early in its development is an important component of anticipation skill, particularly in team ball sports such as soccer, rugby, and American football (Abernethy, Wann, & Parks, 1998; Williams & Davids, 1995). Typically this skill has been examined using the recall and recognition paradigms, although neither paradigm provides a direct measure of pattern recognition per se (North, Williams, Hodges, Ward, & Ericsson, 2009; North, Williams, Ward, & Ericsson, 2010).

Recognition Paradigm

In the recognition paradigm, players are presented with filmed sequences of play taken directly from actual matches. These sequences are either structured (e.g., footage involving a typical offensive move) or unstructured (e.g., footage of players warming up before a match). The level of structure presented by each sequence may be determined via an independent panel of expert coaches. These sequences typically last between 3 and 10 s. In a subsequent recognition phase, players are presented with a similar sample of clips, some of which are repeats of clips presented in the earlier viewing phase and some of which are novel. Players are required to indicate either verbally or on paper which sequences are new and which are repeats. The

accuracy with which players are able to recognize previously viewed clips is taken as the dependent measure.

Recognition accuracy is known across a host of cognitive tasks to be proportional to the level at which the information to be remembered is processed on initial encoding. When compared with their less skilled counterparts, skilled players are more accurate in recognizing structured sequences only. The proposal is that experts are able to combine low- and high-level cognitive processes. Performers are thought to extract motion information and temporal relationships between features (e.g., teammates, opponents, the ball) before matching this stimulus representation with internal semantic concepts or templates stored in memory (Dittrich, 1999). In contrast, novices are unable to pick up important relational information and have fewer semantic concepts or templates that they can access. This constrains them to employ more distinctive surface features when making such judgments. This approach has been used successfully in soccer (Ward & Williams, 2003; Williams & Davids, 1995) and field hockey (Smeeton, Ward, & Williams, 2004).

A novel variation to the film-based approach is presenting action sequences as point-light displays. Players are presented as points of light against a black background that includes the pitch markings and position of the ball, as is illustrated in figure 18.4. Such sequences may be used to examine the rela-

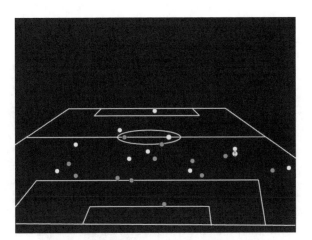

Figure 18.4 A typical pattern of play in soccer with the positions of players represented as points of light against a black background. These images are presented as dynamic sequences, and subjects have to make familiarity-based judgments as to whether or not they have already seen these clips in an initial viewing phase. These images may also be manipulated by removing points of light or by distorting the pattern of play by moving certain players into different positions.

tive importance of isolated display features and the relational information on players, the ball, and pitch markings. Skilled players maintain their superiority over novices under point-light conditions, implying that the crucial information is conveyed by the relative motions between players and the higher-order strategic information conveyed (Williams & North, 2009; Williams, Hodges, North, & Barton, 2006). Moreover, this information emerges at relatively discrete moments as the pattern of play unfolds and is not continuously available throughout each action sequence (North & Williams, 2009).

Recall Paradigm

An alternative approach to assess the ability to identify information is the recall paradigm. Participants are presented with structured and unstructured film sequences of play lasting 3 to 10 s and are required to recall the positions of some or all of the players at the end of each sequence. The positions of players are entered onto a blank representation of the field of play using pen and paper or using a computer keyboard or mouse. The radial, vertical, and horizontal error scores are computed by comparing each player's actual position with that recalled by participants. A skill effect is usually observed on the structured sequences only. Compared with less skilled players, skilled players demonstrate a superior knowledge of related sequences of play that enables them to more accurately recall the positions of players. This skill effect has been demonstrated in soccer (Ward & Williams, 2003;

Williams & Davids, 1995; Williams, Davids, Burwitz, & Williams, 1993), rugby (Nakagawa, 1982), American football (Garland & Barry, 1991), field hockey (Starkes, 1987), volleyball (Borgeaud & Abernethy, 1987), and snooker (Abernethy, Neal, & Koning, 1994). The expert advantage in recall has been reported to hold not only in the specific sport but also across sports with related offensive and defensive structures (Abernethy, Baker, & Côté, 2005; Smeeton et al., 2004).

A more recent development has been a focus on identifying the information that players use when making familiarity-based judgments. For example, verbal reports, eye movement data, and spatial occlusion techniques have been used to identify the essential information used to make such judgments (North et al., 2009, 2010; Williams & North, 2009). Moreover, the extent to which anticipation and recognition skills are correlated has been examined in relation to performance as well as the underlying processes employed when making each type of judgment (Cañal-Bruland & Williams, 2010; North et al., 2009, 2010).

Knowledge of Event Probabilities

Skilled players develop accurate expectations of what their opponents will do in advance of the actual event. It is thought that experts are able to assign accurate probabilities to each event that may occur so that they are able to allocate attention only to the most important sources of information, facilitating the anticipation process. Anticipation is presumed to be optimal if probabilistic expectations match the available sensory evidence. The human brain is presumed to employ some form of Bayesian strategy based on the statistical distribution of likely event probabilities and the level of uncertainty in the sensory feedback evolving from the emerging display (Kording & Wolpert, 2004).

The role of event probabilities in sport typically has been examined using laboratory-based choice reaction time paradigms (Alain & Proteau, 1980; Dillon, Crassini, & Abernethy, 1989). However, recently there have been attempts to develop more representative paradigms using sport-specific stimuli (e.g., Crognier & Féry, 2005; Ward & Williams, 2003). Ward and Williams presented skilled and less skilled players with filmed action sequences from soccer matches. At the end of each 10 s action sequence, the filmed footage was paused and the player in possession of the ball was highlighted. Participants were required to highlight the potential offensive passing options of the player in possession of the ball and to rank these in order of their likelihood of occurrence. The ratings were then compared with those of a panel of expert coaches. The skilled participants were more accurate than the less skilled participants were in highlighting and ranking players most likely to receive a pass from the player with the ball.

Although it seems evident that this skill should contribute significantly to anticipation, there have been relatively few systematic attempts to develop innovative methods to evaluate the contribution of this perceptual-cognitive skill to sport performance. A difficulty is the need to accurately measure the specific probabilities associated with each action open to an opponent. While in the past the opinions of expert coaches have been used as criterion measures for assessing the judgments of elite athletes, recent developments in using real-time player and event tracking should enable the collection of extensive databases that can be used to test and potentially train athletes on this particular component of performance (Carling, Reilly, & Williams, 2008).

Decision Making in Sport: Capturing Performance

In comparison to the number of published reports focusing on anticipation in sport, relatively few researchers have focused on decision making. While anticipation involves the ability to predict the future (i.e., what will happen next), decision making involves selecting the best response based on the information available as well as overriding strategic and tactical considerations. Although progress has been made in developing valid and reliable measures of decision making (typically involving film simulations and response measures similar to those used to measure anticipation), there have been very few attempts to identify the mechanisms underpinning skilled performance (for examples of this type of early work, see Starkes & Deakin, 1984; McMorris & Graydon, 1996).

A few published reports have mapped out the visual search behaviors employed by athletes when choosing an appropriate response. Helsen and Starkes (1999) examined the search behaviors employed by expert and nonexpert soccer players attempting to decide whether to shoot, pass, or dribble the ball in a number of open and set play situations. The decision-making scenarios were simulated by actors on the actual field of play and then captured on film to provide controlled and repeatable stimuli. An eye movement registration technique was employed to analyze the visual behaviors adopted by the soccer players. Skill-based differences were reported for decision time and accuracy. Systematic differences in visual behav-

ior were also observed, with the skilled players employing fewer fixations of longer durations and focusing for a longer time on areas of free space that could be exploited or exposed. Vaeyens and colleagues (2007a) reported similar results in tests of elite players, subelite players, regional players, and nonplayers using 2v1, 3v1, 3v2, 4v3, and 5v3 offensive simulations in soccer. The differences in visual search behaviors between groups were most pronounced when participants were grouped according to a within-task criterion (i.e., actual performance on the decision-making test) rather than their level of attainment within the sport (Vayeans et al., 2007b). Figure 18.5 highlights the typical experimental setup used in a film-based simulation test (data published in Roca et al., 2011).

An alternative approach involves collecting verbal report protocols from athletes either during performance (McPherson & Kernodle, 2003) or immediately after the event (McAllister et al., 2009, 2010). McRobert and colleagues (2009) collected verbal reports from skilled and less skilled cricket batters immediately after the batters viewed film simulations of spin and pace bowlers. Verbal reports were coded based on a structure adapted from Ericsson and Simon (1993). Cognitions were conceptualized as statements representing current actions or recalled statements about current events and evaluations. Planning statements were divided into predictions and deep planning. Predictions reflected statements about what would occur next, while deep planning concerned searching possible alternatives beyond the next move by strategically developing potential action outcomes. Compared with the less skilled batters, the skilled batters made more statements that were coded as predictions and deep planning. In contrast, less skilled batters made more statements that were coded as cognitions. The retrospective verbal reports of thinking indicated that skilled batters engage in systematic deep planning of potential outcomes that resulted in superior decision making. Such studies reflect initial attempts to improve understanding of how elite athletes engage perceptual-cognitive processes when making decisions. However, a significant amount of work still needs to be done to provide a better understanding of the factors that influence decision making in sport.

Anticipation and Decision Making: Identifying Causal Mechanisms Using Process Measures of Performance

The discussion in the preceding sections has focused mainly on capturing and measuring anticipation

Figure 18.5 A typical experimental setup used to measure decision-making skill and to record visual search data in sport. Life-size images are presented and athletes are encouraged to move in response to the images. Verbal reports and eye movements may be recorded simultaneously to identify the processes used in successfully completing the task.

and decision making. It is also important for scientists and, perhaps to a lesser extent, practitioners to identify the strategies and processes that are employed by performers attempting to anticipate and make appropriate decisions. The measures commonly used to make inferences about the underlying processes include the collection of eye movement data and verbal reports. Modern brain imaging techniques offer future promise as a means of merging behavioral measurement of skill components with neurophysiological and neuroanatomical correlates.

Eye Movement Recording

Eye movement recording may be used to evaluate the visual search behaviors employed by participants in anticipation and decision making (for a review of this literature, see Williams, Janelle, & Davids, 2004). The head-mounted corneal reflection system is the favored approach in sport settings. This system works by detecting the position of the pupil and the reflection of a light source off the surface of the cornea in a video image of the eye. The relative positions of these two signals are used to compute point of gaze with respect to the optics. Recent advances involve tetherless eye-tracking systems that can be used when total freedom of movement is required and video with overlaid cursor is the desired output. Newer systems are easy for an active participant to wear. The eye-tracking optics are now lightweight and unobtrusive, and the recording devices are small enough to be worn on a belt. The eye and scene image are typically interleaved and saved on video tape. The taped data are analyzed to ascertain several measures of search behavior, most notably fixation duration, frequency of fixations, fixation areas, and search order (for a more detailed review of this technology, see Williams et al., 1999). A recent extension enables the eye movement data to be analyzed concurrently with the athlete's physical actions in a vision-in-action paradigm (Vickers, 2007).

While the processing of eye movement data collected from moving scenes can be time consuming, the biggest limitation remains the fact that gaze behavior offers only a proxy measure of attention allocation or information pickup. While the line of gaze and the allocation of attention may often coincide, they can also dissociate (such as when attention is allocated to the visual periphery), so concurrent behavioral measures of information pickup are needed to constantly complement and confirm gaze behavior as measured through eye movement recording.

Verbal Reports

Verbal reports can provide a valid method for identifying the processing strategies underlying performance (e.g., Ericsson & Simon, 1993; Nisbett & Wilson, 1977). Ericsson and Simon (1993) described the conditions under which participants are able to report accurately on their mediating thought processes either concurrently during task performance using think-aloud protocols or retrospectively immediately after completing the task. The key factor is to ensure that individuals are instructed properly to give verbal expression to their thoughts rather than to explain their solution for the task to the experimenter or to provide a summary of the general strategy adopted. For example, rather than being instructed to report the number of players considered when attempting to anticipate an opponent's intentions in field hockey, participants should be instructed to report the thought process that comes to mind as they react to a presented representative situation. Participants normally require 15 min of instruction and warm-up to give such reports, but in some dynamic situations the participant needs longer durations of experience with non-domain-specific tasks to become sufficiently familiar with this procedure. Additional effort is required to undertake a detailed task analysis of each situation before data collection and to transcribe, collate, and analyze verbal protocols. McRobert and colleagues (2009, 2010) have provided examples of how this type of approach may be used to explore perceptual-cognitive expertise in cricket. Verbal reports in the sport domain are more likely to provide insight into the processes of strategic, conscious decision making (of the type that accompanies a change in playing tactics, for example) than they are to provide insight into the processes of visuomotor control that typically are either automated or controlled below the level of consciousness. Requiring verbal reports on movement control processes, such as those involved in interceptive actions (e.g., hitting a tennis ball), can produce data of questionable validity (Bahill & LaRitz, 1984).

Brain Imaging

Historically, attempts to describe and explain perceptual-cognitive expertise have been based almost exclusively on behavioral data, and speculations about underlying cognitive processes have been made in the absence of parallel data on brain activity. In the past two decades, in particular, the advances in both the quality and the availability of brain imaging techniques have made it increasingly feasible to measure brain activity in tasks requiring anticipation and decision making (for a review, see Yarrow, Brown, & Krakeaur, 2009). In fMRI, changes in blood flow are mapped as a measure of neural activity within the brain. Contrasts in the blood oxygen level dependence between tasks requiring anticipation, for example, and control tasks providing comparable visual stimulation without the anticipatory requirements offer a new window into the neural basis of skilled performance.

The few researchers that have used fMRI to examine the component skills of sport expertise suggest that there are differences in brain activation between highly skilled and less skilled performers that mirror some of the differences evident in task performance. Wright, Bishop, Jackson, and Abernethy (2010) examined brain activation in expert and novice badminton players attempting to anticipate the direction of an opponent's stroke (within a temporal occlusion paradigm). Activation was evident for both skill groups in the mirror neuron network known to be involved in both the perception and the production of movement. It was most pronounced for the early occlusion conditions, which required the greatest dependence on pickup of information from the kinematics of the opponent's movements. The level of activation, importantly, was greater for the more skilled players (see also Wagg, Williams, Vogt, & Higuchi, 2009).

The main advantages of fMRI for examining underlying control processes include its low invasiveness (compared with other imaging procedures), its high spatial resolution, and its increasingly wide availability. The principal difficulties of fMRI include the substantial movement constraints that limit responses to simple finger-press responses, the cost of magnetic time, the need for specialized image processing, and the challenge of finding appropriate control conditions to help subtract out brain activity that is unrelated to the task of interest. Nevertheless, it is probable that a rise in fMRI studies in the near future will provide valuable information to improve our understanding of the processes underlying skilled anticipation and decision making in sport.

Recommendations for Researchers and Practitioners

A difficulty for practitioners and scientists is deciding which perceptual-cognitive method and measure to administer to their athletes. A key issue is that in most sports the different perceptual-cognitive skills interact dynamically during performance (Williams, 2009), which makes measurement and evaluation (and potentially the development of suitable perceptual-cognitive training programs) difficult. It is likely that the relative importance of each of these perceptual-cognitive skills varies from one sport to another. In a racket sport such as tennis, players may be more reliant on advance cue usage and situational probabilities than on pattern recognition, whereas in a team sport such as soccer or rugby the latter skill may be more important.

The importance of each skill within a sport may also vary from one situation to the next. In a team sport such as field hockey, a player positioned on the edge of her defensive third may rely more on pattern recognition or situational probabilities when the opponent with the ball is in the center circle and may rely more on postural cues when the opponent with the ball is positioned nearer to the defender's goal. Other factors that may influence the relative importance of the different perceptual-cognitive skills include the specific context, such as the score in the match; the time remaining; and the associated cost–benefit assessment (the cost of anticipating incorrectly versus the benefits of making the correct judgment). Also, individual athletes likely vary significantly in their ability to make use of these skills. For example, when anxious, some athletes reduce their search rate and narrow their focus of attention. This reaction potentially reduces their capacity to use peripheral vision and influences the relative importance of different sources of information (Williams & Elliott, 1999). Similar changes in visual search during fatigue may influence the manner in which players make anticipation judgments (Vickers & Williams, 2007).

A potential solution to problems with task selection is to adopt a multitask approach using a battery of the tests outlined in this section. Then, the relative importance of each test to anticipation or decision making in the sport can be determined statistically using multivariate statistical analysis techniques (see Starkes, 1987; Ward & Williams, 2003). The amount of variance between each skill group accounted for by the different perceptual-cognitive tests can be identified and their relative importance ranked. This approach provides a parsimonious method for deciding which tests should be administered to players in each sport. A similar approach may be used to examine how the importance of each skill varies across different types of situations within a sport (Williams, Ward, Smeeton, & Ward, 2008).

A number of other practical considerations should be taken into account by professionals interested in undertaking routine testing in this area. Which skill levels and ages should be employed when creating the test film? How many different actors should be employed? How frequently should this type of testing take place? Can the results of such tests be used to identify talent? Answering such questions is not easy, particularly given that several factors can influence the answers. Ideally, the skill levels and ages of the performers used to create the test footage should not differ greatly from those of the sample group to be tested. As many actors as possible should be used to create the test footage, but certainly more than one actor should be employed so as to eliminate the potential effect of idiosyncrasies in technique. Testing should be performed at least annually so as to monitor the longitudinal development of skills. It is unclear whether such tests may be used for talent identification, mainly because there have been no longitudinal studies in this area. Although evidence suggests that perceptual-cognitive skills develop at an early age (e.g., Abernethy, 1988; Tenenbaum, Sar-El, & Bar-Eli, 2000; Ward & Williams, 2003), as of yet there are no data to suggest that a player who scores well on these tests at an early age (10-12 y) will continue to perform above average at an older age (15-16 y). The predictive value of these tests has yet to be established (Williams, 2000; Weissensteiner, Abernethy, Farrow, & Müller, 2008).

Several process measures are available to help researchers identify the mechanisms underlying anticipation and decision making in sport. Although each of the measures reviewed in this chapter has certain strengths and weaknesses, all potentially contribute to our understanding of perceptual-cognitive expertise in sport. These techniques should be viewed as complementary, and a combination of approaches may be needed to identify the important processes that mediate exceptional performance. Some of these measures, such as eye movement recording and film occlusion, focus more on identifying the underlying perceptual strategies (i.e., what information is extracted from the display), whereas others, such as verbal report protocols, provide a better measure of how performers use the information extracted from the display to determine an appropriate course of action (i.e., what to do next). To this end, there would appear to be considerable benefit in combining think-aloud protocols with a measure of information extraction in order to achieve a more complete overview of the anticipation and decision-making processes (e.g., McRobert et al., 2009, 2010).

A practitioner or young scientist should seek suitable guidance from an experienced researcher before deciding on which particular methods or measures to employ. Professionals using these methods and measures need to have a firm understanding of the strengths and weaknesses of the different approaches and a clear picture of the specific questions that need to be answered. They also need to have an idea of how any information gathered will feed into the testing and training process. Scientists and practitioners need to work together to promote understanding and ensure that valid, reliable, and objective methods may be used for the routine testing of anticipation and decision making in elite athletes.

Measuring Mental Representations

Thomas Schack, PhD

To help provide an understanding of measurement methods addressing mental representation in motor action, this chapter begins by establishing a model that places mental representation in a functional relationship to motor action. Mental representations are characterized by well-integrated networks of basic action concepts (BACs). Each BAC corresponds to functionally meaningful body postures and movement elements. Next, this chapter considers relevant issues in research methodology and presents a method for the experimental assessment of mental representation structures. Because rating and sorting methods do not allow a *psychometric* analysis of the representational structure, a methodical procedure called *structural dimensional analysis of mental representation* (SDA-M) is applied. The SDA-M contains four steps: (1) A special split procedure involving a multiple sorting task is used to create a distance scaling among the BACs of a suitably predetermined set. (2) A hierarchical cluster analysis is used to transform the set of BACs into a hierarchical structure. (3) A factor analysis is used to reveal the dimensions in this structured set of BACs. (4) The cluster solutions are tested for invariance within and between individuals and groups. A practical implication of the measurement of mental representations with SDA-M arises from the fact that the measured representation structures can be analyzed not only on a *group level* but also on an *individual level*. Empirical studies using this method in sport, dance, and rehabilitation are used to demonstrate the procedure of the SDA-M method and to discuss the opportunities this method opens for research and practical work.

Mental Representations

Mental representations play a central role in the control and organization of actions. Regardless of whether a surgeon is selecting the appropriate instrument for an operation or a basketball player is deciding to pass a ball to a teammate, the performer must use a mental representation to sort through an exceptionally large amount of information. Frequently in sport, the action-relevant information is available only under extreme time pressure. Hence, mental representations must be rapidly available and provide clear criteria for selecting the appropriate motor response required for skilled performance.

The relationship between mental representations and motor performance not only is an issue for basic research (e.g., Jeannerod, 2004; Koch, Keller, & Prinz, 2004) but also has implications for practical work with athletes (see Ericsson & Starkes, 2003). A long-standing discussion here is addressing the functional status of mental representations within the organization of actions. The approach assumes that *effect representations* functionally mediate between the perception of events and the execution of actions (e.g., Ericsson, 2003; Hommel, Müsseler, Aschersleben, & Prinz, 2001). This functional linkage is supported by empirical findings on bimanual coordination (Mechsner, Kerzel, Knoblich, & Prinz, 2001; Weigelt, Rieger, Mechsner, & Prinz, 2007), serial learning (Koch & Hoffmann, 2000), neurophysiological research (Decety & Grèzes, 1999; Jeannerod, 2004), and sport events (e.g., Ericsson, 2003; Schack & Mechsner, 2006). Ericsson (2003) took this approach in expertise research to show that mental representations mediate expert performance. Abernethy, Farrow, and Berry (2003) argued that expert performance is not necessarily mediated by mental representations, leaving this area open for further research.

Cognitive Representation and Performance: Perspectives and Methods

Research in the last 40 years has revealed the close relationship between knowledge representation and performance. Also, the research has introduced a wide range of methods to measure mental representations. For example, the chess studies of De Groot (1965), Chase and Simon (1973), and Chi (1978) have shown that experts are better than novices are at storing task-relevant information in *short-term memory* (STM). To learn about the cognitive mechanism of expert performance, these authors used different methods. De Groot used *think-aloud protocols*, in which subjects were instructed to verbalize their thoughts during the task, while Chase and Simon used a 5 s *recall task* to learn about the chunking of meaningful game constellations. As mentioned, these chess studies revealed that experts are better than novices are at storing task-relevant information in STM. However, this superiority is limited to meaningful game constellations. It is no longer evident when players must reproduce meaningless constellations of chess pieces. Chase and Simon's recall paradigm was later generalized to studies on knowledge in sport (e.g., Allard, Graham, & Paarsalu, 1980; Allard & Burnett, 1985; Starkes, 1987). Such work made major contributions to our knowledge about coding and chunking processes in STM, and it demonstrated that *capacity* for task-related information storage increases as a function of performance in various expert domains. However, it is quite speculative to make direct statements as to how far mental representations in long-term memory (LTM) mediate the formation of such chunks (see Ericsson, 2003, pp. 375-376) and whether chunk formation has any major influence on the performance of experts in real-world situations.

A further group of studies addressed the storage of knowledge components in *LTM*. Compared with the studies focused on information storage capacity in working or STM, these studies were more concerned with how knowledge is structured and networked. The major issue in this domain is whether we can confirm that improved performance is accompanied by a higher degree of order formation in the sense of knowledge structuring and hierarchies (Anderson, 1982; Chi & Rees, 1983; Schack & Ritter, 2009). Many methods have been used to study the structures of mental representations in LTM (for an overview, see Hodges, Huys, & Starkes, 2007; McPherson & Kernodle, 2003). One of the first studies in sports was that of French and Thomas (1987). These authors assessed various components of basketball performance (e.g., control of the basketball and cognitive decisions, dribbling and shooting skills) along with declarative knowledge in children aged 8 to 12 y. Declarative knowledge was measured via a *paper-and-pencil test*. Results confirmed relationships between knowledge and the decision component of performance, suggesting that knowledge plays an appreciable role in skilled sport performance. Additionally, specific *sorting techniques* and *interview methods* have been used to confirm expertise-dependent differences in the classification and representation of context-specific problem states in springboard divers, judokas, triathletes, and weightlifters (Huber, 1997; Russell, 1990). Research on springboard diving has revealed that the nodes of the representation structures in experts possess far more features than those of novices possess. This result replicates findings in the problem-solving domain (Chi & Glaser, 1980). Likewise, expert springboard divers revealed a greater number of connections between nodes, just as experts in problem solving revealed (see Huber, 1997). Studies using *categorization tasks* have shown that experts classify problems according to underlying functional principles, whereas novices operate more strongly with superficial features (e.g., Allard & Burnett, 1985; Russell & Salmela, 1992). Furthermore, *questionnaire methods* and *interviews* have revealed the structure and organization of movement knowledge in, for example, tennis (McPherson & Thomas, 1989; McPherson & Kernodle, 2003), volleyball (McPherson & Vickers, 2004), and basketball (French & Thomas, 1987).

Research perspectives focusing more strongly on the functional links between mental representation and performance require new methods to delineate this relationship. Although experimental methods have been used to analyze STM storage (e.g., Starkes, 1987), visual search (e.g., Allard & Starkes, 1980), and perceptual processes (e.g., Borgeaud & Abernethy, 1987), most previous studies of knowledge components in LTM have used *interviews, questionnaires, paper-and-pencil tests, sorting* and *categorization tasks,* and specific forms of *protocol analysis.* However, using such methods leads to problems with objectivity and reliability (see Thomas & Thomas, 1994). It is also worth distinguishing knowledge that is functionally relevant for the control and organization of actions from knowledge that merely accompanies actions or justifies actions in retrospective. We cannot assume that the knowledge that high performers report is identical to the knowledge required for actual performance. Hence, the existing repertoire of methods would benefit from approaches that determine *experimentally* the representation structures in LTM. The goal of this chapter is to provide a theoretical foundation for the link between mental representations and action and to present an *experimental approach* to determine mental representations in motor action.

Mental Representations: A Theoretical Framework

Mental representations about the *task*, the *environment*, and the anticipated steps of *action* are key cognitive elements of motor actions. The term *mental* in this regard aims to elicit the potential and partial consciousness of cognitive representations in memory and is related to the level of action organization where the representations are located (Schack & Hackfort, 2007). In various fields such as bimanual coordination (Weigelt et al., 2007), manual action (Rosenbaum, Cohen, Jax, Van Der Wel, & Weiss, 2007), complex sport movements (e.g., Schack & Mechsner, 2006), robotics (Schack & Ritter, 2009), and decision making (Tenenbaum et al., 2009), it has been shown that central costs and interference in actions depend greatly on how these movements are represented on a mental level. Mental representations in motor action might involve different formats such as propositions, relational structures of many kinds, and concepts. Some studies (see Schack, 2004a, 2004b; Schack & Mechsner, 2006; Schack & Ritter, 2009; Tenenbaum et al., 2009) have provided evidence for BACs in analogy to the well-established notion of basic concepts in object representation (Rosch, 1978). BACs are cognitive compilations of movement elements and body postures that share functions in the attainment of action goals. They are mental tools to transform the movement system into a *controllable system*.

In descriptions of mental representations, the *representation units* and the *structural composition* of these cognitive representations in LTM are of main interest. BACs generally are not represented in isolation. Furthermore, they are part of a hierarchical representation system. The *structure* of a knowledge representation is understood as the internal grouping or clustering of conceptual units (BACs) in individual subdomains. This approach views the relationships among conceptual units as being fea-

ture based. These relationships can be characterized according to the type (feature classes), number, and weighting (relevance) of the features of a conceptual representation system. This assignment of features is called *dimensioning*. Dimensioning is characterized in object concepts through the shared features of objects (e.g., color, size, purpose) or in BACs through the shared properties of movements (e.g., temporal control, amplitude, purpose). Hence, it is not just the *structural design* of a concept system but also the *dimensioning* (feature binding and feature weighting) that is of interest. The relationship between these two aspects of a mental representation is also of interest (Lander, 1991; Schack, 2010b). Methodical approaches for measuring mental representation must consider and analyze the structure and feature dimensions of representation. This is why the method is termed *structural dimensional analysis of mental representation* (SDA-M).

Another important demand for such a method is to measure the *similarity (invariance)* between different representation structures (see Olson & Biolsi, 1991; Schack, 2004a). Expertise in cognitive operations and in the motor domain is accompanied by order formation in memory. Order formation reduces the cognitive effort needed to activate relevant information. This is where individual differences in the type and efficiency of problem solving also appear. In general, cognitive structures improve when more classifications (concepts) related to problem solving are formed. Such mental structures in action knowledge can be assessed, judged, and compared using the help of specific methods.

Measurement of Mental Representations

The integration of representation units into structures of representation has been studied with a wide range of methods (e.g., Hodges et al., 2007). In principle, however, two methodological approaches are used to study representation structures in complex actions: methods that derive them from *response behaviors* and methods that derive them from *reaction times*. Whereas the first approach is used for studying order formation in LTM, the second approach is used to ascertain chunk structures in working memory (Schack, 2004a). Because this chapter addresses the measurement of mental representation in LTM, it focuses on the former method.

The first step in measuring mental representations is to use a specific procedure to obtain data on the proximity of the representation units in the LTM. Various scaling procedures can be used to obtain such proximity data (see Olson & Biolsi,

1991). These include the popular sorting method (Champagne & Klopfer, 1981; Kluwe, 1988), the paired and triple comparison (Friendly, 1977), and the structure set test (Tergan, 1989). The first and last procedures are not considered further because of their limited psychometric capabilities. They do not deliver the metric data necessary for a structural measurement of action knowledge. Moreover, the sorting and triple comparison methods provide only one individual incidence matrix with binary data (0, 1) that is difficult to analyze to obtain knowledge structures. These and other problems with the existing procedures led us to develop our own method (splitting procedure to obtain proximity data). In line with the assumptions on the structure and dimensioning (feature assignment) of action knowledge formulated here, this method was conceived as a structure dimensional analysis of mental representations. The SDA-M is a procedure that presents the structure–dimensional relationships of a conceptually ordered representation *psychometrically* based on metrical data input (operationalized by the splitting procedure) for both single cases and groups (Lander, 1991; Schack, 2010b).

The SDA-M method (figure 19.1) uses the following four steps to assess the structure–dimensional relationships of BACs in a mental representation structure:

1. A distance scaling between the selected representation units (BACs) relevant for a problem-solving domain or a particular motor action

2. A structure analysis of the applied representation by means of a hierarchical cluster analysis

3. A dimension analysis of the established representation structure by means of factor analysis and a special cluster-oriented rotation procedure; the factor analysis delivers the features (factors) and their weights (factor loadings) according to which the cluster formation (structuring) proceeds in each single case

4. An intra- and interindividual invariance analysis of the established cluster solutions (Lander & Lange, 1992; Schack, 2004a, 2004b)

Step 1: Analyzing the Proximity of Basic Action Concepts in Long-Term Memory

The SDA-M of a representation system initially seeks information on the distances between selected representation units (BACs) that are relevant for a problem-solving domain. It is assumed that the structure of movement representations can be explicated only to a limited degree, and thus a splitting technique is used for this purpose. This

technique is based on the selection and presentation of a group of concepts (BACs) that are a valid component of the larger set of concepts from which they come and are absolutely necessary for a certain problem-solving or working domain. This group of concepts is obtained through work analysis, survey, or experiment.

Each concept is offered as an anchor (i.e., reference object, at the top of the list) to which the remaining $N - 1$ concepts are either classified or declassified according to an individually chosen similarity criterion. This procedure continues with the emerging (positive or negative) partial quantities by retaining the reference concept (anchor) until an individual discontinuance criterion is reached. By this procedure N decision trees are established, as each concept occupies an anchor (reference) position (at the top of the list). Subsequently, the algebraic branch sums (Σ) are determined on the partial quantities per decision tree and are submitted to a Z-transformation for standardization and finally combined into a Z-matrix. This matrix forms the starting point of all further analyses. If the Z-values are distributed normally, N(0, 1), then the classification probabilities of the concepts of the reference concept (which are found in the last joint of the decision tree) can be established.

Step 2: Measuring the Hierarchical Structure of Representation

The Z-matrix is transferred into a euclidean distance matrix for a structure analysis that forms the basis for a hierarchical cluster analysis (in accordance with the average linkage method). As a result, an individual cluster solution on the N concepts is formed as a dendrogram. Each cluster solution is established when determining an incidental euclidean distance (d_{krit}). All junctures, which lie underneath the incidental value, form the apical pole of an underlying concept cluster. The incidental distance is defined as

$$d_{krit} = \sqrt{2N} \cdot \sqrt{1 - r_{krit}} \left(\alpha, FG \,/\, H_0 : r = 1 \right), \quad \textbf{19.1}$$

where r_{krit} denotes the incidental value of the correlation of two line vectors of the Z-matrix, provided that H_0 is valid. The value for r_{krit} results from the t-distribution for α (to be determined), with $FG = N - 2$ degrees of freedom.

Step 3: Analyzing the Feature Dimensions of Representations

The Z-matrix is transformed into a correlation matrix that then forms the data basis for an

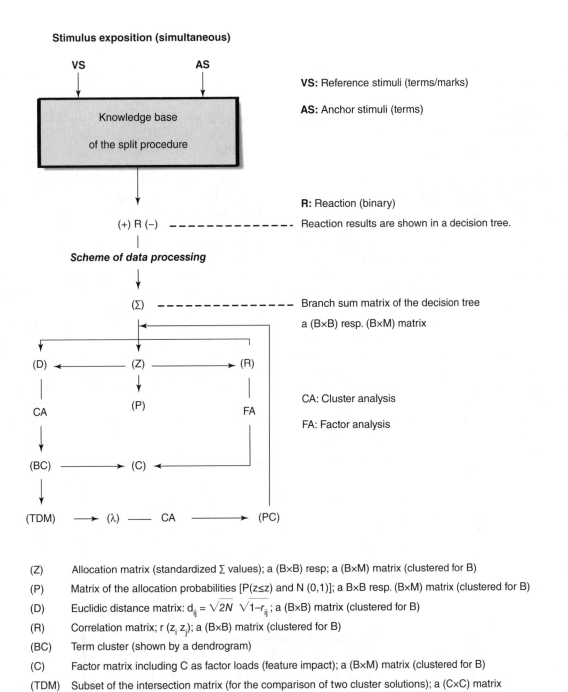

Stimulus exposition (simultaneous)

VS: Reference stimuli (terms/marks)

AS: Anchor stimuli (terms)

R: Reaction (binary)

Reaction results are shown in a decision tree.

Branch sum matrix of the decision tree

a (B×B) resp. (B×M) matrix

CA: Cluster analysis

FA: Factor analysis

(Z) Allocation matrix (standardized Σ values); a (B×B) resp; a (B×M) matrix (clustered for B)

(P) Matrix of the allocation probabilities [P(z≤z) and N (0,1)]; a B×B resp. (B×M) matrix (clustered for B)

(D) Euclidic distance matrix: $d_{ij} = \sqrt{2N} \ \sqrt{1-r_{ij}}$; a (B×B) matrix (clustered for B)

(R) Correlation matrix; r $(z_i\ z_j)$; a (B×B) matrix (clustered for B)

(BC) Term cluster (shown by a dendrogram)

(C) Factor matrix including C as factor loads (feature impact); a (B×M) matrix (clustered for B)

(TDM) Subset of the intersection matrix (for the comparison of two cluster solutions); a (C×C) matrix

(λ) Invariance matrix of two cluster solutions; a (P×P) matrix

(PC) Pearson-related group cluster (shown by a dendrogram)

Figure 19.1 The SDA-M procedure. Various computer programs are available to perform this method (www.promentcenter.de/portal).

(orthogonal) factor analysis with a subsequent cluster-oriented rotation procedure. The result is a factor matrix classified according to the concept cluster, the elements of which are factor charges (*c*), the property values. A cluster within an individual (or group-specific) cluster solution stands out in that its elements (concepts) are in one factor at least equally and highly charged. The incidental value for

the factor charges results from the basic equation of the factor analysis and is defined by

$$c_{krit} = \sqrt{\frac{1}{m} r_{krit} \left(\alpha, FG\ /\ H_0 : r = 0 \right)}, \qquad \textbf{19.2}$$

where *m*, the number of factors that are to be extracted, is estimated in advance. Here r_{krit} stands for the incidental value of the correlation of two part vectors of the Z-matrix, assuming the validity of H_0. The value for r_{krit} again results from the t-distribution for a defined α with $FG = N - 2$ degrees of freedom. This factor matrix, classified according to the clusters, forms the final solution of the individual SDA-M as a concept quantity selected according to certain criteria.

Step 4: Measuring the Intra- and Interindividual Differences of Representations

In case the cluster solution is of relevance, the determined individual cluster solutions are to be examined pair wise for their (structural) invariance. The following values are necessary for determining the invariance measure λ (see figure 19.2).

Accordingly, the number of made-up clusters of the pair-wise cluster solutions (r, s) must be compared with each other. The number of elements (concepts) within the made-up clusters (partial quantities n_j, n_k) and the average quantities (n_{ik}) of the made-up clusters are used for the structural invariance measure of two cluster solutions determined by

$$\lambda_{ik} = \sqrt{k_{ik} \times \mathrm{GAM}(p_{ik})}.0 \leq \lambda_{in} \leq 1$$

19.3

in which $k_{ik} = \dfrac{Min(r,s)}{Max(r,s)}$, with $k_0 = 2/3$ as limiting

value, and $P_{ik} = \dfrac{n_{ik}}{\sqrt{n_i \times n_k}}, 0 \leq p_{ik} \leq 1,$

with $p_0 = .7$ as limiting value.

$GAM(p_{ik})$ comprises the weighted arithmetic means of all relative average quantities (p_{ik}). The differential threshold is definitely determined by using the top two interval criteria with $\lambda_0 = .683$ (i.e., all λ values equal to or larger than λ_0). The corresponding cluster solutions are homogenously structured pair wise excepting a few deviations. As a result of an invariance analysis, an invariance matrix (λ) is established, the complementary value of which the database for a subsequent hierarchical cluster analysis is formed against. The personal clusters obtained here represent personal groups (subgroups) with homogenous cluster solutions of the applied concept quantities. In order to determine subgroup-specific cluster solutions, the Z-matrix for the subgroups is made up by additionally sum-

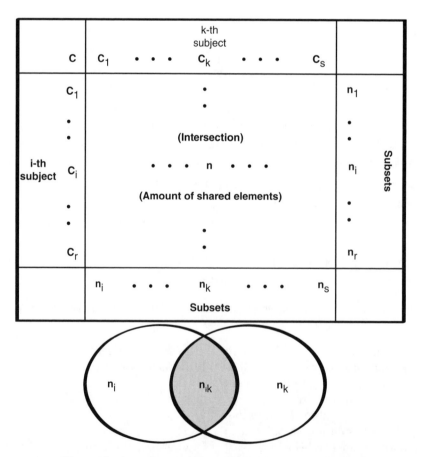

Figure 19.2 Part–average quantities matrix of two cluster solutions. The matrix is a subset intersection matrix (SIM).

ming the Z-matrices of the persons belonging to the subgroup with a subsequent restandardization of the Z-summary values. Therefore, the following equation is valid:

$$\sum_j z_{ij} = 0 \text{ and } \sum_j z^2{}_{ij} = N \qquad \textbf{19.4}$$

with $i = 1, 2, \ldots, N$ as index of rows.

The SDA-M establishes group-specific cluster and factor solutions similarly to individual cases. If groups already exist (e.g., experts versus novices), the individual cluster solutions are established and group-specific cluster solutions are determined by the invariance measure. If the group-specific cluster solutions are found to be of invariance pair wise, this can be regarded as a sufficient differential criterion.

Special computer programs have been developed to help researchers and practitioners complete the SDA-M analyses within a reasonable time frame (10-15 min; the programs are available from the author on request at www.promentcenter.de/portal). Using these and other methods (Schack, 2004a), it is possible to determine mental representations economically and to compare persons or groups on the structure of their knowledge. At the same time, these methods can be used to deliver important diagnostic information for deriving intervention procedures to improve performance (Braun et al., 2007; Schack & Heinen, 2000). The following section presents an SDA-M example from the field of performance sport.

Measuring Mental Representations in Sport

To illustrate how the SDA-M methods work, we examined a movement technique from tennis—the tennis serve (Schack & Mechsner, 2006). In a preparatory step, we characterized the task-adequate functional organization of the tennis serve and compiled a plausible and workable set of BACs in collaboration with nonplayers, athletes of different levels of expertise, and coaches. Then we used reaction time experiments to test whether the concepts were really basic in character. Photographs of tennis submovements along with linguistic markers of varying generality were presented to experts. The BAC level was then defined, in analogy to classical methods (Rosch, 1978), as the shortest time taken to decide whether the photo–word combination was adequate.

A tennis serve consists of three phases, each of which fulfils distinct functional and biomechanical demands. First is the preactivation phase, when the body and ball are brought into position and tension

energy is provided to prepare the strike. The following BACs were identified for the preactivation phase: (1) ball throw, (2) forward movement of the pelvis, (3) bending the knees, and (4) bending the elbow. Second is the strike phase, when energy is conveyed to the ball. The following BACs were identified for the strike phase: (5) frontal upper-body rotation, (6) racket acceleration, (7) whole-body stretch motion, and (8) hitting point. Third is the swing phase, when the body is prevented from falling and the racket movement is decelerated after the strike. The following BACs were identified for the swing phase: (9) wrist flap, (10) forward bending of the body, and (11) racket follow-through. To determine subjective distances between BACs, we had participants perform the following split procedure as the *first step* in the SDA-M: On a computer screen, a selected BAC was displayed continuously as a standard unit in red writing. In addition, the rest of the BACs were presented in yellow writing as a randomly ordered list. The participant had to judge whether each yellow BAC was functionally close to the standard red BAC. This produced two subsets that were then submitted to the same procedure repeatedly until the referee decided to perform no further splits. Because the anchor role of standard was assigned to each BAC in succession, we ended up with 11 decision trees whose nodes contained the resulting subsets and whose borders took either a negative or a positive sign depending on whether the element was judged as belonging to or not belonging to the standard. To obtain a measure of the distance between the successively judged elements and the standard (with interval scaling), we computed algebraic sums over the subsets located on one branch of the decision tree. These sums were then Z-transformed.

In the *second step* of the SDA-M, we determined the individual partitioning by means of a hierarchical cluster analysis. The *third step* of the SDA-M was a dimensioning of the cluster solutions through a factor analysis linked to a specific cluster-oriented rotation process. This resulted in a factor matrix classified by clusters. Finally, the *fourth step* of the SDA-M was to perform a within- and between-group comparison of the cluster solutions using an invariance measure λ to indicate whether differences were significant. An alpha level of $p = .05$ was used in all analyses. This means that there was a significant difference between clusters when $\lambda < \lambda_{crit} = .68$.

Figure 19.3 on page 210 presents dendrograms for the subjective distances of BACs based on the hierarchical cluster analysis of the means of two groups (experts and low-level players). In experts the cognitive structure came close to the functional structure of the tennis serve. The three functional phases (preactivation, strike, and swing) produced clearly separated treelike structured clusters in the dendrograms. In experts, the BACs seemed to be grouped in memory according to generic terms that conform to the solution of special movement problems. An invariance analysis (step 4 of SDA-M) confirmed this interpretation. There was no significant difference between the cognitive BAC framework in experts and the biomechanical demand structure of the movement ($\lambda = .70$; $\lambda_{crit} = .68$). Results looked rather different for the low-level group (see figure 19.3): The clustering of the BACs did not mirror the functionally and biomechanically demanded phases so well. The BACs were less clearly grouped, with no close neighborhoods, and the partial clusters usually failed to attain significance. The difference between the cognitive BAC framework and the functionally demanded structure of the movement was even significant in low-level players ($\lambda = .53$; $\lambda_{crit} = .68$) and nonplayers ($\lambda = .31$; $\lambda_{crit} = .68$; for more details, see Schack & Mechsner, 2006).

The *individual* clusters of BACs (not shown here) revealed that, in experts, the three functionally and biomechanically demanded movement phases of the tennis serve were virtually always represented distinctly in the form of significantly separated partial trees. The individual clusters were rather similar between individuals, with an invariance analysis revealing no significant differences. Significantly distinct subclusters could be seen in individual low-level players, though they were not as functionally well structured as those in experts. Although the

functionally and biomechanically required phases could be discerned regularly, they were not matched so well and consistently. There were rather arbitrary associations based on surface or unfathomable criteria that often varied from person to person. Interindividual differences were significant. In nonplayers, significantly distinct subclusters were rare and arbitrary. The structures of the clustering trees, which varied greatly between persons, revealed no clear grouping principles.

The determinants of the revealed memory structure were evaluated with a factor analysis (step 3 of SDA-M). Table 19.1 reports the results for the expert group. Two factors, both with bipolar loadings, explained 74.3% of the variance. One factor had a bipolar loading on the preactivation cluster (corresponding to phase 1) and the strike cluster (corresponding to phase 2). Its dimension was movement direction—that is, vertical versus frontal. The other factor had a bipolar loading on the strike cluster (phase 2) and the final swing cluster (phase 3). Its dimension was ball-oriented versus follow-through swing movement. Within the context of a skilled tennis serve, these factors seem highly plausible.

In sum, our investigation of mental representations in the tennis serve revealed that applying SDA-M to appropriately determined BACs produces hierarchical clustering structures whose characteristics can be related systematically to performance on different levels of expertise. These results reflect differences in the grouping of BACs in LTM and its determinants. Movement-related mental representations seem to be much better structured and

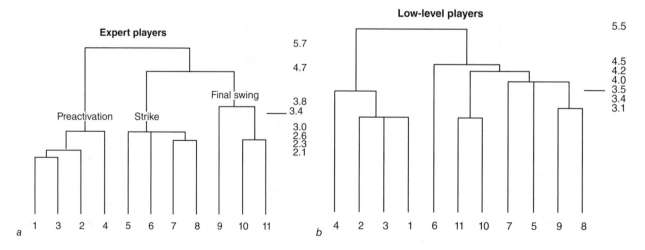

Figure 19.3 Dendrograms for two expertise groups based on the hierarchical cluster analysis of BACs in the tennis serve. The lower the value of a link between two items (see the scale of euclidean distances on the right), the lower the distance between the BACs in LTM. The value for d_{crit} is displayed as a bar splitting the scale of euclidean distances; it separates the relevant structural links from the less relevant ones (above d_{crit}) for a given α probability. For every group, $n = 11$; $p = .05$; $d_{crit} = 3.46$.

From *Neuroscience Letters*, Vol. 391, T. Schack and F. Mechsner, "Representation of motor skills in human long-term memory," pgs., 77-81, Copyright 2006, with permission of Elsevier.

▪ Table 19.1 ▪

Factor Analysis Solution
for the Expert Group (n = 11; c_{krit} = .207)

Cluster	BAC		1	2	h^2
1	1	Throwing ball	**.86**	.02	.75
1	2	Moving pelvis forward	**.83**	.06	.70
1	3	Bending knees	**.93**	−.02	.86
1	4	Bending elbow	**.80**	−.05	.65
2	5	Turning upper body	**−.60**	**.62**	.76
2	6	Accelerating racket	**−.56**	**.68**	.78
2	7	Stretching whole body	**−.52**	**.70**	.77
2	8	Hitting ball	**−.58**	**.74**	.79
3	10	Bending body forward	−.48	**−.65**	.68
3	11	Slowing down	−.45	**−.68**	.69
Σc^2			4.65	2.77	7.43
%			46.5	27.7	74.3

For the numbering of BACs, see text. h^2 is the communality, a standard value in factory analysis. Bold numbers are factor loadings that are above c_{krit} = .207.

From *Neuroscience Letters*, Vol. 391, T. Schack and F. Mechsner, "Representation of motor skills in human long-term memory," pgs., 77-81, Copyright 2006, with permission of Elsevier.

adapted to functional and biomechanical demands in experts compared with novices.

Measuring Mental Representations in Sport: Insight From Empirical Studies

Several studies in sport (Schack, 2004a, 2004b; Schack & Bar-Eli, 2007; Schack & Hackfort, 2007; Weigelt, Ahlemeyer, Lex, & Schack, in press), dance (Bläsing, Tenenbaum, & Schack, 2009; Bläsing, 2010; Geburzi, Engel, & Schack, 2004; Schack, 2010a), movement rehabilitation after stroke (Braun et al., 2007), music (Schack, 2010b), and cognitive robotics (Schack & Ritter, 2009) have used the SDA-M-approach to measure the structure and dimension of mental representation in motor action. Most of the studies in sport are conducted to investigate the nature and role of mental representation in skilled athletic performance and to derive new technolo-

gies in mental training and technical preparation (Schack & Hackfort, 2007; Schack & Bar-Eli, 2007; Schack, 2010a). The results of investigations in various sports such as golf, soccer, tennis, windsurfing, volleyball, gymnastics, and judo (Schack, 2003, 2004a; Schack & Mechsner, 2006; Schack & Bar-Eli, 2007; Schack & Hackfort, 2007) have shown that the mental representation structures relate to performance. These representation structures are the outcome of an increasing and effort-reducing order formation in LTM. In high-level experts, these representational frameworks are organized in a distinctive hierarchical treelike structure that is remarkably similar among individuals and well matched to the functional and biomechanical demands of the task. In comparison, action representations in low-level players and nonplayers are organized less hierarchically and more variably among individuals. The SDA-M has been used to do more than compare the representation structures of different expertise groups at a given point of time. With the help of the individual representation measure of the SDA-M method, it has become possible to observe how individual and group-dependent mental representation structures develop and change in the learning process (Heinen, Schwaiger, & Schack, 2002).

A practical implication of the measurement of mental representations in skilled performance arises from the fact that these representation structures can be analyzed not only on a *group level* but also on an *individual level*. On the one hand, this provides the opportunity to gain knowledge about an athlete's specific movement problems, and on the other hand, it gives coaches a tool to provide performance-related instructions and to optimize mental training and technical training—a tool that goes beyond traditional methods such as nonstandardized questionnaires or observation methods from biomechanics (i.e., measurement of movement kinematics).

This makes the SDA-M important for developing new forms of mental training (Schack, 2004a, 2004b; Schack & Hackfort, 2007). The main disadvantage of traditional procedures is that they try to optimize performance through repeated movement imaging without taking an athlete's mental technique representation into account (i.e., they are representation blind). However, if the movement's cognitive reference structure has structural gaps or errors, these tend to be stabilized rather than overcome by repeated practice. The SDA-M method aims at measuring the mental representation of the movement before the athlete engages in mental training and then integrating these results into that training. This *mental training based on mental representations* (MTMR) has been applied successfully for several years in professional sports such as golf, volleyball (Schack, 2004a, 2004b), gymnastics, windsurfing, and soccer (Schack & Bar-Eli, 2007; Schack & Hackfort, 2007).

An example of using SDA-M in mental training can be seen in the way professional volleyball players address the ball on a spike. This movement requires at least 12 substeps (BACs) that are stored in memory. Because the primary focus is on the memory structure of the movement, in preparation for a mental training program, Schack (2004a) studied this structure in members of a German women's national volleyball youth team. To examine the findings in detail, we can compare findings from quick spikers with good movement performance (figure 19.4) with findings from quick spikers with specific movement problems. In quick spikers with good movement performance, four different clusters can be identified in the mental representation of the spike: (1) run-up (substeps 1-3), (2) takeoff (substeps 4-5), (3) hit preparation (substeps 6-8), and (4) hit (substeps 10-12). These substructures are spatially distinct and are ordered in chronological sequence. Figure 19.4 presents the results of a hierarchical cluster analysis for the group of quick spikers from the Germany youth national team. As shown in figures 19.4 and 19.5, it is possible to use *pictures* and *words* for the splitting procedure and for the presentation of the results from the cluster analysis.

Mental movement representation is structured exactly the same as the movement is organized. Furthermore, the categories determined by the clusters (run-up, takeoff, hit preparation, hit) are spatially distinct and ordered in a temporal sequence. Therefore, the specific BAC structures are used to solve specific subproblems in the movement. For several years, player B (see figure 19.5) had difficulties in optimally executing the spike. The current analysis

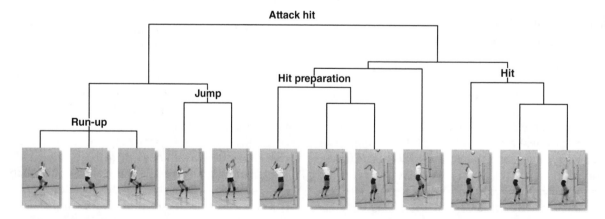

Figure 19.4 Results of the hierarchical cluster analysis of the SDA-M for experts in volleyball (quick spikers) reveal a hierarchical representation structure containing four clusters. The mental movement representation is structured in exactly the same way that the movement is organized. The categories determined by the clusters (run-up, takeoff, hit preparation, hit) are spatially distinct and ordered in a temporal sequence.

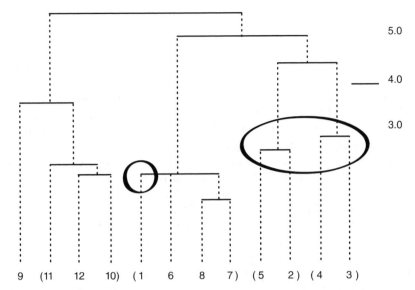

Figure 19.5 Individual representation structure of a German national team player (player B) displaying specific movement problems in the quick spike shown as a result of cluster analysis (α = 5%; d_{krit} = 3.98). The highlighted positions are explained in the text.

Adapted, by permission, from T. Schack, 2004, "The cognitive architecture of complex movement," *International Journal of Sport and Exercise Psychology* 2(4): 403-438. By permission of Routledge Press.

reveals the cause: BACs 1 through 3 and 4 through 5, which are important for the sequence of impulses during run-up and takeoff, point to a less precise memory structure. For player B, run-up and takeoff are broken down into two inefficient memory sections: (1) substeps 5 and 2 and (2) substeps 4 and 3.

Subsequently, an individualized applied mental training program was used to tackle the athlete's memory structure and develop movement imagery for an ideal takeoff and a proper spike. Additionally, player B went through a series of run-up and takeoff drills designed to train the optimal motion sequence. The focus was on making player B aware of the altered movement so she could develop a new feeling for it. Additionally, the mental training program aimed to generate this optimal perception of the movement in the complementary mental training. This process paid off with appreciable improvement in player B's spike, and player B is now a member of the German women's national volleyball team. The advantage of using mental training and memory analysis in combination is derived from the fact that individual memory structures are integrated into mental training, providing sufficient consideration of the individual dispositions of athletes.

Mental representations are also important components of dancing. In different areas of dance (e.g., ballet; Latin American dances; classical dance; solo, pair, or group dance), mental representation makes it possible to select and combine effective sources of information. Interesting findings about the mental representations in dance extracted with the SDA-M method were presented in a recent study by Bläsing and colleagues (2009), who demonstrated differences in the mental representations for two complex ballet skills among novices, advanced dancers, and expert dancers (see also Bläsing, 2009). A noticeable detail of their study was that advanced dancers showed initial clustering but were more variable in their structures than the experts were, while the novices did not show any reliable representations of the two ballet skills. From this observation, it can be inferred that becoming an expert in a particular sport may also rely on the development of individual mental skill representations and that the measurement of mental representation is an important tool to support the learning process.

Investigators and practitioners may also apply the results of such experimental diagnoses in the *consulting process* so that athletes or patients in rehabilitation receive feedback on their memory structure (Braun et al., 2007; Braun et al., 2008; Schack & Hackfort, 2007). This diagnosis is important when deciding whether an athlete or patient possesses a good disposition for specific kinds of mental or psychological training. Braun and coworkers (2007) asked explicitly in the title of their paper, "Is it possible to use the SDA-M to investigate representations of motor actions in stroke patients?" In their study, each control patient participated in the SDA-M once and each patient with stroke participated in the SDA-M 3 times within 1 wk. In the SDA-M, the subject was presented with 10 BACs involved in drinking from a cup and asked to state whether each BAC was functionally close to each of the other 9 BACs. All subjects were able to perform the assessment. Healthy controls all had a similar set of representation structures measured via cluster analysis. Four patients with stroke had treelike diagrams (results of cluster analysis) that were close to those of the control group. The remaining eight patients with stroke had treelike diagrams that differed greatly from those of the control group and from other diagrams within their own group, with much less clustering of actions. Patients with more severe stroke appeared to have more disordered treelike diagrams. The authors concluded that "the Structural Dimension Analysis of Motor Memory (SDA-M) is a feasible method for investigating the mental representation of internal motor action plans in stroke patients, giving similar data in stable healthy people and revealing abnormal patterns in patients after stroke" (Braun et al., 2007, p. 822). Because Braun and colleagues (2007) used the SDA-M method 3 times a week in every stroke patient, they learned that the measured representation structures in patients are stable over time. With the help of the invariance measure, these authors found statistically stable representation structures for every subject. They interpreted these results as clear evidence for the reliability of the SDA-M method. Because the results demonstrated plausible differences with healthy controls, the authors concluded that the SDA-M is a valid measure of mental representation in motor actions.

Recommendations for Researchers and Practitioners

Coaches and athletes often hold a different learning background or preference. Therefore, it is important to get a closer insight into the development and change of the cognitive systems of athletes. In this light, methods such as SDA-M come into play and may help practitioners to increase their understanding of the mental representations of athletes. Measuring the cognitive representations of complex skills provides an effective tool to gain further knowledge about an athlete's individual skill representation. Most importantly, such skill diagnostics can inform coaches (and athletes) about specific movement problems that are reflected in the athlete's LTM structures. This provides coaches with the opportunity to improve performance-related instructions and with an additional diagnostic tool to optimize technical training routines. SDA-M goes beyond the traditional assessments in biomechanics, such as measuring kinematic parameters of human motion, by revealing the cognitive representation structures of complex skills in the LTM. The present findings, particularly the use of SDA-M as a diagnostic tool to measure individual skill representations, should have further implications for practical work in coaching, technical preparation, and mental training (Schack & Bar-Eli, 2007; Schack & Hackfort, 2007).

A very important *preparatory step* in measuring mental representation is to characterize the movement task and the structure of the movement technique (for more information, see Schack & Bar-Eli, 2007). In this context it is important to define a plausible and workable set of key points (BACs) of the selected movement in collaboration with nonplayers, athletes at different levels of expertise, and coaches.[1] Using these special programs, practitioners and scientists can carry out such experiments and the resulting data analysis within a reasonable time frame (10-20 min). The programs can present the results immediately after the session at the computer, and they allow using cluster analysis as an important tool in the mental coaching process. This is interesting, because athletes and coaches can see and discuss the mental representation of the athlete as well as can study the representation of another athlete (for instance, a top athlete) or the coach. With SDA-M, it is possible to determine mental representation in an economical way and to compare persons or groups in terms of the structure of their knowledge. At the same time, SDA-M provides an experimental diagnosis that delivers important information for deriving intervention procedures to improve performance (Braun et al., 2007; Schack & Heinen, 2000).

---

[1] Additionally, practitioners can find information about BACs of different movement techniques at www.promentcenter.de/portal.

Physical Self-Concept

Herbert W. Marsh, PhD, and Jacqueline H.S. Cheng, PhD

The new emphasis in psychology is on positive psychology—on how healthy, normal, and exceptional individuals can get the most from life (e.g., Marsh & Craven, 2006; Seligman & Csikszentmihalyi, 2000; Vallerand et al., 2003). Consistent with this emphasis, a positive self-concept is valued as a desirable outcome in sport, exercise, and health psychology as well as in many other disciplines (e.g., developmental, mental health, social, personality, and educational psychology). Methodologists are concerned with particular measurement and methodological issues inherent in the study of self-concept. Researchers with a major focus on other constructs also are often interested in how constructs in their research are related to self-concept. Professionals, practitioners, and policy makers in many areas of social services and welfare seek to improve the self-perspectives of their clients. Hence, self-concept is valued widely as a desirable outcome.

The study of self-concept has a long (and often controversial) history, and it is one of the most established areas of research in the social sciences. Despite a long chapter in William James' 1890 textbook on the self, advances in theory, research, and measurement of self-concept have been slow, particularly during the heyday of behaviorism in the 1950s. Before the 1980s, reviewers typically emphasized the lack of theoretical basis in most studies, the poor quality of measurement instruments used to assess self-concept, the methodological shortcomings, and a general lack of consistent findings (e.g., Shavelson, Hubner, & Stanton, 1976; Wells & Marwell, 1976; Wylie, 1979). However, there has been a substantial improvement in the quality of self-concept research in the last quarter of a century, partly due to the development of better measurement instruments, theoretical models, and research designs.

This chapter provides an overview of the conceptual and measurement aspects of self-concept, focusing in particular on physical self-concept (PSC). We begin with the theoretical and historical underpinnings of the self-concept construct. We then discuss how these differences in conceptual frameworks have led to differences in the development of PSC instruments.

Construct Definition of Physical Self-Concept

One cornerstone for the resurgence of self-concept research in the last 25 years was the classic review article by Shavelson and colleagues (1976). They reviewed existing research and self-concept instruments and provided a theoretical definition for and model of self-concept. This seminal work has had a profound influence on subsequent research (see Marsh & Hattie, 1996), providing a theoretical definition of self-concept and a blueprint for the later development of multidimensional self-concept instruments. Shavelson and colleagues stressed that self-concept is important both as an outcome and as a mediating variable that helps to explain other outcomes. However, they noted critical deficiencies in self-concept research, including inadequate definitions of the self-concept construct, a dearth of appropriate measurement instruments, and a lack of rigorous tests of counterinterpretations. They concluded, "it appears that self-concept research has addressed itself to substantive problems before problems of definition, measurement, and interpretation have been resolved" (p. 470).

In their review, Shavelson and coworkers (1976) identified 17 different conceptual definitions of self-concept. Integrating features from many definitions, they defined *self-concept* as a person's self-perceptions that are formed through experience with and interpretations of the environment. Self-concept is especially influenced by evaluations by significant others, reinforcements, and attributions for personal behavior. Shavelson and colleagues emphasized that self-concept is not an entity within the person but is a hypothetical construct that is potentially useful in explaining and predicting how a person acts. These self-perceptions influence the way a person acts, and these acts in turn influence the person's self-perceptions. Consistent with this perspective, Shavelson and coworkers noted that self-concept is important as both an outcome and a mediating variable that helps to explain other outcomes. Thus, for example, PSC may be an important outcome that is influenced by an experimental intervention. Alternatively, PSC may mediate the influence of an exercise intervention that is designed to enhance health-related physical activity and fitness (e.g., Marsh & Peart, 1988). In this second example, the intervention effect on physical outcomes is due partly to the effect of the intervention on PSC, which in turn influences physical fitness. In this sense, the effect of the intervention on physical fitness is facilitated by the effect of the intervention on PSC even though the enhancement of PSC may not be the main aim of the study.

Even in studies where self-concept is not the major focus, evaluating self-concept is useful because of its importance as a mediating variable that facilitates the attainment of other desired outcomes. In sport and exercise psychology, self-concept frequently is posited as a mediating variable that facilitates the attainment of desired outcomes such as physical skills, health-related physical fitness, physical activity, exercise adherence in nonelite settings (Fox & Corbin, 1989; Marsh, 1997, 2002; Sonstroem, 1978), and improved performance in elite sports (Marsh & Perry, 2005). Thus, for example, if an intervention unintentionally undermines self-concept, then it is unlikely to have lasting effects on its intended outcomes. In contrast, if an intervention enhances self-concept as well as its desired outcome (e.g., performance or fitness), then the effects are more likely to last. The rationale behind these findings is that individuals who perceive themselves to be more effective, confident, and able accomplish more than individuals with less positive self-perceptions accomplish (i.e., "I believe, therefore I am").

Historically, self-concept researchers have argued either that self-concept is unidimensional or that the multiple dimensions of self-concept are so highly correlated that they cannot be distinguished (see review by Marsh & Hattie, 1996). Byrne (1984) noted, "many consider this inability to attain discriminant validity among the dimensions of SC [self-concept] to be one of the major complexities facing SC researchers today" (pp. 449-450). Shavelson and colleagues (1976) posited a hierarchical, multidimensional model of self-concept (figure 20.1)

in which the *general self* appears at the apex and is divided into *academic* and *nonacademic* self-concepts at the next level. Academic self-concept is divided further into self-concepts in particular subject areas (e.g., mathematics, English, and so on). Nonacademic self-concept is divided into three areas: (1) *social self-concept*, which is divided into relationships with peers and with significant others; (2) *emotional self-concept*; and (3) *PSC*, which is divided into physical ability and physical appearance.

At the time when Shavelson and colleagues (1976) first developed their model, there was only modest support for the hypothesized domains, and no one instrument considered in their review was able to differentiate among even the broad academic, social, and physical domains. In this respect, this model provided a theoretical background for the development of new theory, measurement, and research. However, the model also provided a blueprint for the next generation of self-concept instruments (see Marsh & Hattie, 1996). Particularly relevant to the present chapter is the set of Self-Description Questionnaires (SDQs) developed by Marsh and colleagues in the mid-1980s (for an overview of this research, see Marsh, 2007). Starting with Shavelson and colleagues' model and using stronger statistical procedures than had been used previously, Marsh and colleagues developed instruments that successfully assessed self-concept factors posited by Shavelson and coworkers. Subsequent research in a variety of different disciplines provided strong support for this multidimensional perspective of self-concept (e.g., Marsh & Craven, 2006).

Dimensions and Sources of Confusion: Self-Esteem Versus Self-Concept and Self-Efficacy

As self-concept research has a long history that incorporates studies from many disciplines, the literature is fraught with potential sources of confusion (e.g., Shavelson et al., 1976; Marsh, 2007). In the social sciences, particularly in the motivation and self-belief areas, researchers tend to focus on favorite constructs without seriously testing how (or if) they differ from other constructs. This leads to jingle-jangle fallacies (Marsh, 1994) in which two scales with similar names might measure different constructs while two scales with apparently different names might measure similar constructs. This section attempts to clarify some of the prevalent areas of confusion.

The difference between self-esteem and self-concept has been a source of confusion and controversy.

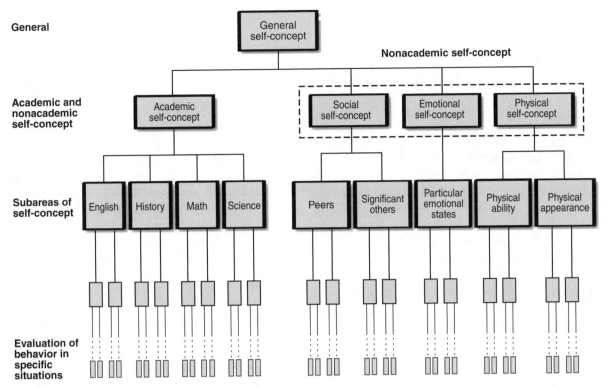

Figure 20.1 A hierarchical and multidimensional model of PSC.

Reprinted, by permission, from R.J. Shavelson, J.J. Huber, and G.C. Stanton, 1976, "Self-Concept: Validation of construct interpretations," *Review of Educational Research* 46: 401-477.

Particularly since the development of Shavelson and colleagues' (1976) model, researchers (e.g., Blascovich, & Tomaka, 1991; Hattie, 1992) have viewed general self-esteem as a global and relatively stable construct that appears at the apex of the hierarchy, thus reflecting the broad views that people hold about themselves (see figure 20.1). Marsh (2007) argued that self-esteem items such as those on the widely used Rosenberg Self-Esteem Scale (1965) are specifically constructed so that they do not refer to any specific domain. Historically, some theoretical models distinguished between self-esteem as the evaluative component of self-concept and self-concept as the description. Shavelson and colleagues (1976) addressed this issue, arguing that self-concept has both a descriptive and an evaluative aspect such that individuals may describe themselves ("I am happy") as well as evaluate themselves ("I do well in sports"). Evaluations can be made against an absolute ideal such as the 5 min mile (about a 3 min kilometer) or a personal internal standard such as a personal best. Following Shavelson and colleagues, it is generally accepted that self-concept is both descriptive and evaluative (e.g., Byrne, 1996; Marsh, 2007), so evaluation versus description is not a useful distinction between self-esteem and self-concept.

As emphasized by Bong and Skaalvik (2003) and others, academic self-efficacy and academic self-concept constructs have much in common: an emphasis on perceived competence; a multidimensional and hierarchical structure; content specificity; and the prediction of future performance, emotion, and motivation. Historically, it was argued that self-concept is a global measure, whereas self-efficacy is domain specific. However, in modern approaches to self-concept, it is reasonable to measure self-concept facets that are as domain specific as typical self-efficacy measures are, while some researchers focus on global measures of self-efficacy. Hence, this distinction does not seem very useful.

Bandura (2006) and others have suggested that self-efficacy describes people's beliefs about what they can do, whereas self-concept also includes a personal evaluation of the behavior. Consistent with this distinction, Marsh and colleagues (Marsh, Walker, & Debus, 1991; Marsh, 2007) found that when compared with self-concept responses, pure measures of self-efficacy are affected much less by frame-of-reference effects and social comparisons. For example, being in a physical education class with very physically skilled classmates should not have much effect on physical self-efficacy measures but should have a negative effect on PSC. Making a similar point, Bong and Skaalvik (2003) argued that "assessing one's capability in academic self-concept relies heavily on social comparison information"

(p. 9), whereas "self-efficacy items solicit goal referenced evaluations and do not directly ask students to compare their abilities to those of others" (p. 9) and "self-efficacy items provide respondents with a specific description of the required referent against which to judge their competence" (p. 9). However, much of the power of self-beliefs to motivate and predict future behavior depends on the evaluation placed on a pure performance expectation. Whereas the self-efficacy belief that I can run 100 m in 12 s might be descriptive in nature, the self-evaluation of this outcome—whether this is a great or terrible performance—has important implications. Nevertheless, even this distinction between self-concept and self-efficacy depends on how the constructs are measured.

Tools to Measure the Physical Self

Reflecting the general historical trends in self-concept research, self-concept instruments used in early sport and exercise research focused on global self-esteem (Marsh, 1997, 2002). However, following the research of Shavelson and colleagues (1976), a number of multidimensional self-concept instruments containing one or more PSC scales were developed. Thus, in a 1974 review, Wylie concluded that at the time most self-concept instruments focused on global self-concept or self-esteem rather than specific domains such as PSC. Although several of the instruments reviewed by Shavelson and colleagues (1976) contained items relating to physical skills and elements of physical appearance, none provided a clearly interpretable measure of PSC. From a practical perspective, these older instruments appear to be of little value for sport and exercise psychologists. The major exception, perhaps, is the Physical Estimation and Attraction Scale (PEAS; Sonstroem, 1978, 1997), along with the theoretical model on which it is based. This instrument was designed to measure two global components: *estimation* (competency) and *attraction*. While the PEAS may not be the instrument of choice today, it has a historical significance in that its research incorporated many of the features of the construct validity approach advocated in this chapter, it was heuristic, and it provided an important basis for subsequent research.

In a subsequent 1989 review, Wylie identified several multidimensional self-concept instruments measuring one or more components of PSC that can be differentiated from other specific domains of self-concept and general self-concept. Included in the list were the three SDQ instruments already discussed. Wylie also evaluated Harter's (1985) Self-Perception Profile for Children, which contains two PSC scales (*athletic competence* and *physical appearance*). Other multidimensional instruments containing physical scales that were not reviewed by Wylie include the Self-Rating Scale (Fleming & Courtney, 1984), which measures *physical ability* and *physical appearance*; the Song and Hattie Test (Hattie, 1992), which measures *physical appearance*; and the Multidimensional Self-Concept Scale (Bracken, 1996), which has a physical scale that includes *physical competence*, *physical appearance*, *physical fitness*, and *health*. The Tennessee Self-Concept Scale (Fitts, 1965) is a multidimensional self-concept instrument that also purports to measure PSC. In their review and empirical evaluation of this instrument, Marsh and Richards (1988) found distinguishable physical components reflecting *health*, *neat appearance*, *physical attractiveness*, and *physical fitness* that were incorporated into a single PSC score. This detailed breakdown of the Tennessee physical scale was supported by relationships with the SDQ physical ability and physical appearance scales in an MTMM study comparing responses to the two instruments. Because each of the clusters based on responses to the Tennessee instrument is represented by only a few items, it is not appropriate to use the instrument to measure these distinct components of PSC. Marsh and Richards argued that PSC measures that combine and confound a wide range of differentiable physical components—such as those based on the Tennessee Self-Concept Scale—should be interpreted cautiously (see similar comments by Fox & Corbin, 1989).

In summary, although multidimensional self-concept instruments based on Shavelson and colleagues' (1976) model provided good support for the construct validity of the physical ability and appearance scales (e.g., Marsh, 2002; Marsh & Peart, 1988), they left unanswered the question of whether PSC is more differentiated than can be explained in terms of one (physical ability) or two (ability, appearance) physical scales. Subsequent PSC instruments were developed specifically to address the issue of the multidimensionality of PSC.

Physical Self-Perception Profile

The Physical Self-Perception Profile (PSPP; Fox, 1990; Fox & Corbin, 1989) is a 30-item inventory that consists of four specific scales and one general physical self-worth factor. The PSPP was developed to document the physical self-perceptions of college students. It was designed to reflect the advances made by Harter (1985) and Shavelson and colleagues (1976) in identifying the physical self as an important construct to measure in its own right and to reflect the hierarchical, multidimensional nature of the physical self. A qualitative approach was used to reveal dimensions of physical self-esteem salient to the population sampled (Fox & Corbin, 1989). The PSPP consists of five 6-item scales of sport (perceived sport competence), body (perceived bodily attractiveness), strength (perceived physical strength and muscular development), condition (perceived level of physical conditioning and exercise), and physical self-worth. Fox (1990) recommended that the 10-item Rosenberg Self-Esteem Scale (Rosenberg, 1965) be used alongside the PSPP to provide a global measure. Fox (1990) reported factor analyses indicating that each item loads most highly on the factor that it is designed to measure and that individual scale reliabilities are in the .80s.

The PSPP research demonstrates (a) good reliability (coefficient alpha of .80-.95; Fox, 1990; Page, Ashford, Fox, & Biddle, 1993; Sonstroem, Speliotis, & Fava, 1992); (b) good test–retest stability over the short term (rs of .74-.89; Fox, 1990); (c) a well-defined, replicable factor structure as shown by CFA (Fox & Corbin, 1989; Sonstroem, Harlow, & Josephs, 1994); (d) convergent and discriminant validity in studies showing PSPP relationships with external criteria such as exercise behaviors, mental adjustment variables, and health complaints (Fox & Corbin, 1989; Sonstroem & Potts, 1996); and (e) applicability for an older adult population (Sonstroem et al., 1994). However, correlations among the PSPP scales are consistently so high (.65-.89 when disattenuated for measurement error; Marsh, Richards, Johnson, Roche, & Tremayne, 1994) that they detract from the instrument's ability to differentiate among the different PSC factors it purports to measure.

Subsequently, a version of the PSPP for children and adolescents was developed and validated—the Children and Youth Physical Self-Perception Profile (CY-PSPP; Eklund, Whitehead, & Welk, 1997; Whitehead, 1995). Like the PSPP, the CY-PSPP is a 30-item inventory consisting of the same five 6-item scales. The CY-PSPP is a substantially revised version of the PSPP that is most appropriately thought of as a different instrument. The CY-PSPP body, strength, and conditioning subscales are based on minor adaptations of the PSPP to make them more suitable for children. However, the global self-worth (self-esteem) and sport scales are completely different. The PSPP did not have a self-esteem scale of its own but included 6 items adapted from the Rosenberg Self-Esteem Scale. On the CY-PSPP, global self-esteem and sport scales from the PSPP were dropped and replaced with corresponding scales from Harter's (1985) Self-Perception Profile for Children. Correlations among factors remained high (e.g., physical self-worth with attractive body adequacy = .8). Eklund and colleagues (1997) suggested that these results are consistent with the developmental patterns among children, as differentiation in self-concept is less defined at younger ages (Harter, 1985). CFAs have supported the instrument's factor structure, with both the CFI (comparative fit index) and NNFI (non-normed fit index) indexes exceeding the .90 criterion for good model fit (Eklund et al., 1997). Moderate correlations (r = .39-.45) with external criteria such as physical activity and physical fitness have demonstrated its convergent and discriminant validity (Welk & Eklund, 2005). The CY-PSPP has been validated with adolescents (Jones, Polman, & Peters, 2009; Welk, Corbin, & Lewis, 1995; Whitehead, 1995) and younger children (Welk, Corbin, Dowell, & Harris, 1997) and has been validated and translated into other languages (Åsci, Eklund, Whitehead, Kirazci, & Koca, 2005; Raustorp, Ståhle, Gudasic, Kinnunen, & Mattsson, 2005; Raustorp, Mattsson, Svensson, & Ståhle, 2006).

Both the PSPP and CY-PSPP use a nonstandard response format based on Harter (1985), in which each item consists of a matched pair of statements, one negative and one positive (e.g., "Some people feel that they are not very good when it comes to sports" *but* "Others feel that they are really good at just about every sport"). Each item consists of two contrasting descriptions, and respondents are asked which description is most like them and whether the description they select is "Sort of true of me" or "Really true of me." Responses are scored on a scale of 1 to 4, with 1 representing a "Really true of me" response to the negative statement and 4 representing a "Really true of me" response to the positive statement. Whereas this response format is designed to reduce the influence of social desirability, Wylie's (1989) review of Harter's original instruments provided little or no support for this suggestion, and Marsh and colleagues (1994) suggested that there were substantial method effects associated with the nonstandard response scale. This format has also been shown to be confusing, particularly for children (Eiser, Eiser, & Haversmans, 1995), and even for adults (Marsh, Bar-Eli, Zach, & Richards, 2006; Marsh et al., 1994), unless special care is taken to explain the response scale. Using the suggestion of Marsh and colleagues (1994) that confusion over the structured alternative response scale could be overcome by more detailed instructions at the outset, researchers implementing the CY-PSPP used large illustrations for a sample item (Whitehead,

1995). Wichstrom (1995) found that responses for this format were psychometrically stronger when based on typical Likert responses rather than the structured alternative format, but Welk and colleagues (1997) suggested that the nonstandard response scale on the CY-PSPP worked better than Likert responses worked.

In summary, the PSPP and the CY-PSPP are established instruments that have been translated into several languages and have been used with a range of populations. However, the format and the high correlations among factors in both instruments may limit their usefulness in some settings. The CY-PSPP is a substantially revised version of the PSPP specifically developed for children. Although the CY-PSPP should be used instead of the PSPP for child and adolescent samples, it might even be stronger than the original PSPP is for adult samples.

Subsequent to the completion of this chapter, Lindwall and colleagues (2011) published a revised version of the PSPP (PSPP-R). They reviewed critiques of the PSPP response scale such as those noted here (e.g., Marsh, Bar-Eli, Zach, & Richards, 2006; Marsh et al., 1994) and acknowledged that "the idiosyncratic alternative response format has been difficult to understand for some participants" (pp. 310-311). In recognition of these problems, the idiosyncratic response scale that has been such a salient feature of the PSPP was dropped altogether and replaced with a 4-point Likert response using only positively worded items. Lindwall and colleagues (2011) demonstrated the appropriateness of the revised PSPP-R based on a large sample (N = 1,831) of participants from four countries (Sweden, Great Britain, Portugal, and Turkey). However, they did not indicate whether the PSPP-R supersedes the PSPP or is merely an alternative to it. There also wasn't any discussion of the implications for other instruments using similar idiosyncratic response scales (e.g., PSPP- related instruments such as CY-PSPP or Harter's instruments more generally).

Physical Self-Inventory

The Physical Self-Inventory (PSI) is a French adaptation of the PSPP that was originally developed for use with Francophone adults (Ninot, Delignières, & Fortes, 2000). In two preliminary studies, Ninot and colleagues used the nonstandard response scale from the PSPP. However, consistent with previous research (Marsh et al., 1994), they reported that this response scale was problematic. In a third study, the authors used a 6-point Likert response scale; factor analysis results were reasonable, but reliability coefficients were not completely satisfactory.

Next the authors replaced the PSPP global physical items with items from the SDQ physical scale and the PSPP global self-esteem items with items from Coopersmith (1967). The final PSI consists of 25 items measuring six PSC factors (four specific and two global, as with the PSPP) and has satisfactory psychometric properties that have been confirmed in subsequent French studies of adults (Masse, Jung, & Pfister, 2001; Stephan, Bilard, Ninot, & Delignières, 2003; Stephan & Maïano, 2007).

Maïano and coworkers (2008) subsequently constructed a short form of the PSI for use with adolescents. They found that not all items from the adult PSI worked with adolescents, but they were able to construct 18-item (PSI-SF, 3 items per scale) and 12-item (PSI-VSF, 2 items per scale) versions that had good psychometric properties. In particular, the measurement and hierarchical structures were consistent with proposals by Fox and Corbin (1989) and were fully invariant across gender. Maïano and coworkers also noted that PSI-SF responses showed very high test–retest stability. Comparison of the PSI-SF and PSI-VSF demonstrated that the measurement model, mean structure, structural parameters, and criterion-related validity were equivalent across samples and versions. Nevertheless, the authors noted a serious limitation that all versions of the PSI share with the PSPP: Very high correlations among the six PSC factors (correlations among latent factors) that, according to the authors, bring "into question the real independence of some of the models' sub-dimensions, and by extension their discriminant validity, a finding that has already been observed by Marsh (2002; Marsh et al., 2006) on analyses of the PSPP" (Maïano et al. 2008, p. 844). However, Maïano and colleagues also noted that because they used a traditional Likert response scale, the high correlations apparently were not due to the structured alternative format used in the PSPP. In summary, particularly the short and very short forms of the PSI have made a potentially important contribution to applied research. However, further research is needed to evaluate more fully the robustness of support for construct validity and application in non-French-speaking settings.

Richards Physical Self-Concept Scale

The Richards Physical Self-Concept Scale (RPSCS; Marsh et al., 1994; Richards, 1988) is a 35-item instrument designed to measure six specific components of PSC (body build, appearance, health, physical competence, strength, action) and one general physical satisfaction factor. Each item is a simple declarative statement, and subjects respond on an 8-point true–false scale. Extensive research in

Australia (e.g., Marsh et al., 1994; Richards, 1988) has indicated that RPSCS responses have good psychometric properties. The factor structure is very robust, generalizing well over ages from 8 to 80 y and over gender.

RPSCS research has demonstrated (a) good reliability (coefficient alpha of .79-.93; Marsh et al., 1994; Richards & Marsh, 2005); (b) good test–retest stability over the short term (coefficient alpha of .77-.90 over 3 wk; Richards, 1988); (c) a well-defined, replicable factor structure as shown by CFA (Marsh et al., 1994; Richards, 2004); (d) a factor structure that is invariant across gender, as shown by multiple-group CFA (Richards, 2004), and across a wide age range; (e) convergent and discriminant validity as shown by MTMM studies of responses to three PSC instruments (Marsh et al., 1994; Richards & Marsh, 2005); and (f) applicability for participants aged 8 to 60 y and for both genders (Marsh et al., 1994; Richards, 1988, 2004; Richards & Marsh, 2005). In summary, the RPSCS is regarded as a valid, reliable, and structurally sound instrument that has been tested across both genders and a wide population of ages. The applicability across such a wide range of ages is a particular strength.

Physical Self-Description Questionnaire

Extending Fleishman's (1964) classic research on the structure of physical fitness, the Physical Self-Description Questionnaire (PSDQ) scales reflect some of the original SDQ scales and parallel physical fitness components identified in a CFA of physical fitness measures (Marsh, 1993). The PSDQ consists of nine specific components of PSC (strength, body fat, activity, endurance and fitness, sport competence, coordination, health, appearance, and flexibility), a global physical scale, and a global self-esteem scale. Each of the 70 PSDQ items is a simple declarative statement, and individuals respond on a 6-point true–false scale. The PSDQ is designed for adolescents but is also appropriate for older participants.

PSDQ research has demonstrated (a) good reliability (median coefficient alpha of .92) across the 11 scales (Marsh, 1996b; Marsh et al., 1994); (b) good test–retest stability over the short term (median r = .83 over 3 mo) and longer term (median r = .69 over 14 mo; Marsh, 1996b); (c) a well-defined, replicable factor structure as shown by CFA (Marsh, 1996b; Marsh et al., 1994); (d) a factor structure that is invariant over gender as shown by multiple-group CFA (Marsh et al., 1994); (e) convergent and discriminant validity as shown by MTMM studies of responses to three PSC instruments (see Marsh et al., 1994); (f) convergent and discriminant validity as

shown by PSDQ relationships with external criteria (e.g., measures of body composition, physical activity, endurance, strength, and flexibility; see Marsh, 1996a, 1997); and (g) applicability for participants aged 12 to 18 y (or older) and for elite athletes and nonathletes (Marsh, Hey, Roche, & Perry, 1997; Marsh, Perry, Horsely, & Roche, 1995). In summary, the PSDQ is a psychometrically strong instrument.

Marsh, Martin, and Jackson (2010) recently presented a new short form of the PSDQ (PSDQ-S). This short form balances brevity and psychometric quality in relation to established guidelines for evaluating short forms (e.g., Marsh, Ellis, Parada, Richards, & Heubeck, 2005; Smith, McCarthy, & Anderson, 2000) with the construct validity approach that is the basis of PSDQ research. Based on the PSDQ normative archive, 40 of 70 items were selected and evaluated in a new cross-validation sample (N = 708 Australian adolescents). To test the generalizability of results, the authors considered four additional samples: Australian adolescent elite athletes (n = 349), Spanish adolescents (n = 986), Israeli university students (N = 395), and Australian senior citizens (n = 760). Reliabilities for the 40 PSDQ-S items were consistently high in the cross-validation sample (.81-.94; median = .89) and senior sample (.81-.94; median = .91) and reliabilities in the cross-validation sample were higher than they were in comparable groups completing the 70-item PSDQ. The PSDQ-S factor structure in the cross-validation sample was well defined and highly similar to that based on the archive sample as well as to those based on the other four groups. Study 1, using a missing-by-design variation of multigroup invariance tests, showed that invariant factor structures were invariant based on 40 PSDQ-S items and 70 PSDQ items. Study 2 demonstrated factorial invariance of responses over 1 y (test–retest correlations of .57-.90; median = .77) and good support for convergent and discriminant validity in relation to time. Study 3 showed good and nearly identical support for convergent and discriminant validity of PSDQ and PSDQ-S responses in relation to responses on the PSPP and PSC instruments. The four studies reported by Marsh and coworkers demonstrated new, evolving strategies for the construction and evaluation of short forms that support the PSDQ-S. The authors concluded that the strong support for the psychometric properties and construct validity of the widely used PSDQ instrument generalizes very well to the PSDQ-S.

Elite Athlete Self-Description Questionnaire

The PSC instruments discussed thus far may be suitable for elite athletes (e.g., Marsh et al., 1995).

There may, however, be other components to PSC that are particularly relevant for elite athletes, and thus the Elite Athlete Self-Description Questionnaire (EASDQ; Marsh, Hey, Roche, et al., 1997; Marsh, Hey, Johnson, & Perry, 1997) was developed to address these other components. For the EASDQ, it was hypothesized that overall performance by elite athletes is a function of skill level, body suitability, aerobic and anaerobic fitness, and mental competence. Thus Marsh and colleagues developed the EASDQ to measure these six factors. For each scale, they developed a pool of items that sport psychologists at the Australian Institute of Sport evaluated for their suitability for elite athletes. Pilot studies were conducted to select the best items to represent each factor. A compromise between brevity and psychometric soundness was achieved, with acceptable levels of reliability (e.g., all scales having reliability estimates of at least .8) based on short scales (4-6 items per scale).

EASDQ research demonstrates (a) adequate reliability (median coefficient alpha of .85) across the six scales (Marsh, Hey, Johnson, et. al., 1997); (b) a well-defined, replicable factor structure as shown by CFA (Marsh, Hey, Johnson, et. al., 1997; Marsh, Hey, Roche, et al., 1997); (c) applicability for elite athletes aged 12 y or older (Marsh, Hey, Roche, et al., 1997); and (d) predictive validity as shown by its ability to predict swimming performances in world championships after controlling for previous personal best performances (Marsh & Perry, 2005). In summary, the EASDQ is a reliable and valid instrument for elite athletes of all ages. More research is needed, however, to relate EASDQ responses to external validity criteria such as those used in PSDQ research and to criteria that are more specific to elite athletes (e.g., actual performance in competition).

Examples From the Literature

Now that the main instruments for measuring physical self-concept have been introduced, the next section presents some examples from the research literature where these measures have been used.

Comparison of the Measures

Marsh, Bar-Eli, and colleagues (2006) compared the results for three major multidimensional PSC instruments: the PSDQ, PSPP, and RPSCS. In a sample of 395 Israeli university students (60% women) aged 18 to 54 y, a total of 23 components of PSC were measured by the three instruments, and an initial CFA provided support for all 23 factors. Using MTMM analysis, Marsh, Bar-Eli, and colleagues (2006) showed support for convergent and dis-

criminant validity. In this application, the multiple traits were the 23 PSC components, whereas the multiple methods were the three different PSC instruments. Convergent validity was demonstrated in that matching (the same or similar) components from the three instruments were substantially correlated. For example, each of the three PSC instruments had a physical strength scale, and the correlations among these three scales were substantial (.74-.94). In contrast to convergent validity, discriminant validity is demonstrated when measures that are supposed to measure different constructs are not highly correlated. Across the 23 PSC components, the average correlation among the closely matching scales was $r = .81$ (in support of convergent validity), whereas the mean correlation among nonmatching components was only $r = .31$ (in support of discriminant validity).

The results based on the sample of Israeli university students provided a strong replication of Marsh and colleagues' (1994) results based on the sample of Australian high school students. A comparison of the results from both studies provided reasonably similar outcomes for reliability estimates and for convergent validities. The Israeli study results, like those of the Australian study, suggested that all three instruments performed well and, coupled with previous research, supported the generalizability of these conclusions over age and nationality. As in the previous research, however, responses to the PSDQ and the RPSCS were psychometrically stronger than those based on the PSPP. In particular, there was clear evidence of method halo effects in PSPP responses that resulted in substantially inflated correlations among PSPP factors in relation to responses on the other two instruments (for similar results based on PSDQ-S responses, see Marsh et al., 2010).

Reciprocal Effects of Self-Concept and Performance

Do changes in self-concept lead to changes in subsequent performance? This is one of the most vexing questions in self-concept research. It has been the focus of considerable research due to the important theoretical and practical implications. Calsyn and Kenny (1977) contrasted self-enhancement and skill development models of this relationship. The self-enhancement model posits self-concept as a primary determinant of performance and supports self-concept enhancement interventions explicit or implicit in many programs. In contrast, the skill development model implies that self-concept emerges as a consequence of academic achievement so that the best way to enhance self-concept is to develop stronger skills. Using more advanced statistical tools, empirical results, and self-concept theory, Marsh (1990; Marsh

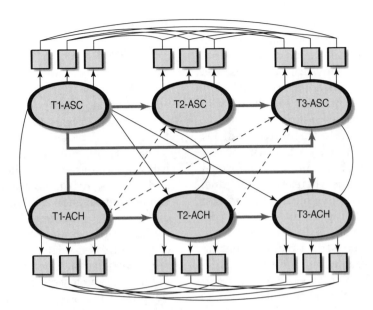

Figure 20.2   Prototype causal ordering model for testing self-enhancement, skill development, and the reciprocal effects model (REM). In this full-forward, multiwave, multivariable model, multiple indicators of self-concept (ASC) and performance-achievement (ACH) are collected in three successive waves (T1, T2, and T3). Each latent construct (oval) has paths leading to all latent constructs in subsequent waves. Within each wave, self-concept and performance are assumed to be correlated. Curved lines at the top and bottom of the figure reflect a correlated uniqueness between responses to the same measured variable (box) collected on different occasions. Paths connecting the same variable on multiple occasions reflect stability (solid gray paths). Dashed lines reflect effects of previous performance achievement on subsequent self-concept, whereas solid black lines reflect the effects of previous self-concept on subsequent performance.

& Craven, 2006) argued that a more realistic compromise between the self-enhancement model and the skill-development model is a *reciprocal effects model* (REM), in which previous self-concept affects subsequent performance *and* previous performance affects subsequent self-concept (figure 20.2).

A considerable body of support for the REM, based primarily on educational research, and even a comprehensive meta-analysis (Valentine, DuBois, & Cooper, 2004) currently exist. There are also a number of applications of the REM in sport and exercise settings. Using a longitudinal design, Marsh, Chanal, Sarrazin, and Bois (2006) evaluated predictions about the effects of T1 gymnastics self-concept and T1 gymnastics performance skills collected at the start of a gymnastics training program on T2 gymnastics self-concept and T2 gymnastics performance skills collected at the end of the 10 wk program. Consistent with the REM predictions, gymnastics self-concept and gymnastics performance were reciprocally related. Similarly, Marsh, Papaioannou, and Theodorakis (2006) found that both the effect of T1 PSC on T2 exercise behavior and the effect of T1 exercise behavior on T2 PSC paths were significant. In subsequent analyses, PSC effects were significant even after controlling for key constructs from the theory of planned behavior (behavioral intentions, perceived behavioral control,

exercise attitudes). This finding suggests that self-concept should be used to supplement the theory of planned behavior. Marsh, Gerlach, Trautwein, Lüdtke, and Brettschneider (2007) demonstrated support for the REM in a 4 y longitudinal study in the physical domain for young German boys and girls (*N* = 1,135; mean age = 9.67 y). After controlling for previous physical performance (skill-based tests and teacher assessments in year 3, primary school), PSC had a positive effect on subsequent physical performance in both grade 4 (primary school) and, following the t1ransition to secondary school, grade 6. Marsh and Perry (2005) tested REM predictions on a large sample of swimmers competing at the Pan Pacific Swimming Championships in Australia and the World Short Course Championships in Greece. Scores on an EASDQ specially adapted for swimmers significantly predicted championship performance beyond what could be explained by previous personal best times, which is consistent with the REM. These results were replicated across different events swum by each swimmer.

Experimental Manipulations: Competitive and Cooperative Interventions

Marsh and Peart (1988) contrasted two different physical education programs that manipulated the type of performance feedback given to high school girls. Participants were randomly assigned to one of two experimental groups or to a control group. They completed a physical fitness test and a multidimensional self-concept instrument before and immediately after undergoing a 6 wk intervention consisting of 14 classes lasting 35 min each. The social comparison and competitive feedback condition emphasized the relative performances of different students and focused on who performed best on a particular exercise, whereas the individual improvement and cooperative feedback condition emphasized individual progress in relation to previous personal performances. In the cooperative group, participants exercised in pairs so that no one person could succeed without the cooperation of another, whereas in the competitive group participants completed exercises individually.

Both the cooperative and competitive conditions significantly enhanced physical fitness relative to pretest scores and to the control group; there were no differences between these two experimental groups in terms of short-term gains in fitness. The cooperative group also had significantly enhanced PSC, but the competitive group experienced a significant decline in PSC. Apparently, the competitive intervention forced participants to compare their own physical accomplishments with those of the participants who were best on each individual exercise to a much greater degree than what they had done before the intervention or what was done in the control group. Even though girls in the competitive condition had substantial gains in actual fitness levels, these gains did not translate into increased PSC. Critical features in this study were frame-of-reference effects and social comparison processes. Students in the competitive group knew their fitness had improved but were forced to compare their performances with the best performing student on each exercise. Thus, the frame of reference that they used to evaluate their performances changed even more than that of their fitness levels. The net effect of the competitive intervention on PSC was negative. In highly competitive environments, there are often many losers and few winners, and this is likely to lead to lower levels of self-concept. This study shows why it is important to measure self-concept even if the focus of the study is on skill development—unintended negative effects associated with the competitive intervention can undermine any long-term gains associated with it. More generally, as shown in the REM, performance and self-concept are reciprocally related; thus, the best way to enhance and maintain development in either one is to enhance both.

Recommendations for Researchers and Practitioners

Measures in sport and exercise psychology before the 1990s were typically weak. In a monumental effort to catalog sport and exercise measures used over the past 25 years, Ostrow (1990) developed the *Directory of Psychological Tests in the Sport and Exercise Sciences.* He included all instruments from the published sport and exercise literature with reliability and validity information. In addition to providing valuable information about individual measures, the directory also provides a barometer for evaluating the quality of measurement in our field. Indeed, one of the expressed intents of the directory is to force researchers, test authors, reviewers, journal editors, publishers, and test consumers to embrace a higher standard of measurement quality. Of the 175 instruments summarized in the directory, however, only 33% have items based on a conceptual or theoretical framework, less than 25% report factor analyses, and less than 10% show evidence of extensive reference support. Apparently, measurement practice in the 25 years before 1990 did not measure up to the high ideals espoused by leading researchers.

Measurement in sport and exercise psychology has progressed substantially in the time since Ostrow's 1990 directory, as demonstrated by reviews in the second edition of the directory (published in 1996) and by much subsequent research. This progress is the result of more carefully developed instruments; better articulation of the links among instrument design, theory, and practice; and improved application of methodological and statistical techniques. This improvement may also reflect the higher standards being placed on researchers and test constructors. No longer can sport psychology researchers simply pull together an ad hoc set of items that are more or less related to the construct of interest and claim, with any credibility, that they have developed a new instrument. The emphasis on psychometrically strong instruments is particularly evident in the development of PSC research.

Self-concept plays a salient role in the mentality of athletes. The development of sound definitions and reliable instruments not only serves the purpose of meeting statistical criteria but also is important for applying these constructs in practice. For example, in nonelite settings, people may have a low PSC, thinking that they are unable to carry out physical exercises, which may lead to more serious consequences such as obesity. If instruments are not developed carefully to measure the appropriate construct, practitioners will have a tougher job of diagnosing the problem.

▪ **Table 20.1** ▪

Measures Assessing Physical Self-Concept

Variable or concept	Measure	Dimension	Source
Self-perceptions of physical fitness as a component of global self-esteem and interest in vigorous physical activity	Physical Estimation and Attraction Scale (PEAS)	Physical estimation and attraction	Sonstroem (1978, 1997)
Multidimensional perspectives of the physical self	Children and Youth Physical Self-Perception Profile (CY-PSPP)	Perceived sport competence, perceived bodily attractiveness, perceived physical strength and muscular development, perceived level of physical conditioning and exercise, and physical self-worth	Eklund, Whitehead, & Welk (1997); Welk & Eklund (2005); Whitehead (1995)
Multidimensional perspectives of the physical self	Physical Self-Perception Profile (PSPP)	Perceived sport competence, perceived bodily attractiveness, perceived physical strength and muscular development, perceived level of physical conditioning and exercise, and physical self-worth	Fox & Corbin (1989)
Self-perceptions of physical well-being	Richards Physical Self-Concept Scale (RPSCS)	Body build, appearance, health, physical competence, strength, action, and satisfaction	Richards (1988); Marsh, Richards, Johnson, Roche, and Tremayne (1994)
Multidimensional, hierarchical PSC	Physical Self-Description Questionnaire (PSDQ)	Strength, body fat, activity, endurance and fitness, sport competence, coordination, health, appearance, flexibility, global PSC, and global esteem	Marsh et al. (1994); Marsh (1997, 2002)
	Physical Self-Description Questionnaire short form (PSDQ-S)		Marsh, Martin, & Jackson (2010)
	Physical Self-Inventory (PSI)		Maïano et al. (2008); Ninot, Delignières, & Fortes (2000)
Self-concept in elite athletes	Elite Athlete Self-Description Questionnaire (EASDQ)	Skill level, body suitability, aerobic fitness, anaerobic fitness, mental competence, and performance	Marsh, Hey, Johnson, & Perry (1997)

The direction of causality posited in the REM has important practical implications for mentors (e.g., coaches, trainers, sport psychologists, managers, and perhaps parents). If the direction of causality was from self-concept to performance (the self-enhancement model), then mentors might be justified in putting more effort into enhancing self-concepts rather than fostering skills and performance outcomes. On the other hand, if the direction of causality was from performance to self-concept (the skill development model), then mentors would need to focus primarily on improving skills and performance as the best way to improve self-concept. In contrast to both of these overly simplistic models, the REM implies that self-concept and performance are reciprocally related and mutually reinforcing. Studies carried out by Marsh, Chanal, and colleagues (2006, 2007) and Marsh and Perry (2005) have supported the REM in nonelite and elite settings across a wide range of ages. Improved self-concept leads to better performance *and* improved performance leads to better self-concept. Hence, according to the REM, mentors should strive to improve self-concept and skill simultaneously.

Exercise and Self-Perception Constructs

Catherine Sabiston, PhD, James R. Whitehead, EdD, and Robert C. Eklund, PhD

The self has been described as a psychological tool that fosters conscious thought about a person's roles, identities, and descriptions (Leary & Tangney, 2003). Historical evidence suggests that the self is an active agent in human development and is shaped through interaction with others (Harter, 1999). Within the context of exercise, the self has been studied from multiple interrelated perspectives that would be impossible to review in a chapter and perhaps even in a book. This chapter focuses on the main self-perceptions studied in exercise and physical activity contexts, including physical self-concept and self-perceptions, exercise identity and physical activity self-definition, exercise self-schemata, and possible selves (Fox, 1997; Kendzierski, 1990; Kendzierski, Furr, & Schiavoni, 1998). Sport-related literature on these or other self-constructs is not considered in this chapter.

Self-Esteem and Self-Concept

Self-esteem is the evaluative feeling that people have about themselves. This self-ascribed worth has been described as being either true and stable (intrapsychic feelings of personal worth and autonomy) or contingent on outcomes and achievement (based on inter- or intrapersonal standards; Deci & Ryan, 1995). Self-esteem has also been explored from explicit (i.e., controlled and conscious) and implicit (i.e., unaware, automatic, and intuitive) perspectives. In this regard, explicit self-esteem involves conscious and reflective self-appraisals, whereas implicit self-esteem involves a predisposition to evaluate oneself in a spontaneous and unconscious way (Greenwald & Banaji, 1995). *Self-concept* is defined broadly as an individual's self-description. Much like self-esteem, self-concept can also be explored for implicit and explicit roots (Wylie,

1974). Self-concept and self-esteem are often used interchangeably, yet self-concept is the cognitive component of the self and self-esteem is an affective and evaluative component of the self. Self-concept becomes increasingly complex and differentiated during childhood and adolescence and so is conceptualized as a multidimensional construct (Harter, 1999; Marsh, 1994b; Shavelson, Hubner, & Stanton, 1976). The physical self is one domain that is often studied among exercise psychology researchers. *Physical self-concept* refers to an individual's physical self-description, which includes both physical abilities and physical appearance (Fox, 1997).

Theories of Self-Concept and Self-Esteem

According to William James (1892), there are two fundamental aspects of the self: the self as a subject (I-self) and the self as an object (me-self). The me-self came to be called self-concept and was viewed by James as having multidimensional constituents (material self, social self, and spiritual self) ordered hierarchically. James' theoretical framework has garnered much attention as being the first to identify the self as a multidimensional construct—a view that is now widely endorsed (Harter, 1999; Marsh, 1994b; Shavelson et al., 1976).

In the multidimensional and hierarchical models of self-concept, global self-worth (i.e., self-esteem) comprises a number of developmentally specific domains such as academic, emotional, social, and, of importance here, physical domains (Marsh, 1989, 1994b; Shavelson et al., 1976). These models illustrate how each domain is structured and help to explain the associations between specific self-perceptions and behavioral outcomes such as exercise.

The exercise and self-esteem model (EXSEM; Sonstroem & Morgan, 1989) explicitly links self-esteem, physical self-perceptions, and exercise self-efficacy (which is tied to exercise behavior). The original model proposed that exercise enhances perceptions of exercise self-efficacy, which in turn improves perceptions of physical competence. Perceptions of competence are linked to physical acceptance (defined as the personal regard and liking that people hold for themselves), and both of these factors lead to higher self-esteem. Sonstroem and colleagues (Sonstroem, 1997; Sonstroem, Harlow, & Josephs, 1994) later expanded the model to include additional self-perceptions based on Fox and Corbin's (1989) model of the physical self. In the expanded model, exercise is postulated to improve physical self-efficacy. In turn, physical self-efficacy affects physical self-perceptions relating to sport competence, conditioning competence, body attractiveness, and strength competence. These self-perceptions are subsequently affected by assessments of physical self-worth, which in turn has a causal effect on global self-esteem.

Drawing from James' (1892) original work, Harter (1990) proposed that self-esteem is a function of an individual's perceived competence in the various self-domains in relation to the perceived importance of each competence. The act of ascribing low importance to self-domains with low levels of perceived competence is termed *discounting* and is a self-enhancement strategy. The inability to discount perceptions of importance in areas of low competence leads to discrepancies between importance and competence that may negatively influence self-esteem. Successful discounting leads to higher levels of self-esteem (Harter, 1990). Fox (1997) has presented evidence on the discounting hypothesis in the physical domain. For example, females tend to report low mean scores on perceptions of sport and strength competence as well as low ratings of importance, indicating a congruence. In contrast, individuals are often incongruent on the appearance or body physical self-perceptions, such that they tend to report it is important to be physically attractive or thin and yet also report low scores on these competencies. Marsh and Sonstroem (1995) have presented evidence challenging the discounting hypothesis.

Measures Assessing Physical Self-Concept and Self-Esteem

There are two main measurement tools used to capture the domains of physical self-concept and self-worth. The first tool, the 30-item Physical Self-Perception Profile (PSPP; Fox, 1990; Fox & Corbin, 1989), was developed using a two-stage process. First, following a review of previous research, open-ended responses from college-aged students were used to identify the salient contributors to physical self-esteem. Subsequent factor analysis of data from three independent samples identified, consistent with theoretical tenets, four physical self-perception subdomains (condition competence, sport competence, body attractiveness, strength competence) and one global domain construct of physical self-worth.

A structured alternative response format was employed for PSPP items. Specifically, respondents are presented with a pair of contrasting statements (e.g., "Some people feel that they are physically stronger than most people of their sex" but "Others feel that they lack physical strength compared with most others of their sex") and are asked to choose which of the statements is most like them. The respondents are then asked to indicate if the statement is "Really true of me" or "Sort of true of me." As a consequence, responses vary along a 4-point scale. Fox and Corbin (1989) reported internal consistency and test–retest coefficients in the original work with college students. Many EFAs and CFAs (e.g., Marsh, Richards, Johnson, Roche, & Tremayne, 1994; Page, Ashford, Fox, & Biddle, 1993; Sonstroem et al., 1994) have confirmed the four-factor structure of the PSPP with males and females, and there is some evidence of age and gender factorial invariance among high school students (Hagger, Biddle, & Wang, 2005).

The PSPP was adapted for use with children and youth in the Children and Youth Physical Self-Perception Profile (CY-PSPP; Whitehead, 1995). In addition to modifying many of the items of the original PSPP to make them appropriate for younger populations, the CY-PSPP retained Harter's (1985) measure of appearance competence and global self-esteem tool. Evidence of the content and structure of physical self-worth has been reported with younger populations of boys and girls (Eklund, Whitehead, & Welk, 1997; Welk & Eklund, 2005; Whitehead, 1995).

The Physical Self-Description Questionnaire (PSDQ; Marsh et al., 1994) is a 70-item questionnaire that measures nine physical self-perceptions (health, strength, body fat, physical activity, endurance and fitness, sport competence, coordination, health, appearance, and flexibility), global physical self-concept, and self-esteem. The PSDQ was developed and theoretically grounded in previous work with more general self-concept scales and was also informed by the results of factor analysis of data from physical fitness tests. Each item is a statement (e.g., "I am a physically strong person") in which individuals respond on a 6-point Likert-type scale ranging from 1 = "False" to 6 = "True." Evidence of internal consistency, support for the factor structure, and invariance across males and females were originally presented (Marsh et al., 1994). Strong associations between field measures and each of the PSDQ subscales demonstrated construct validity (Marsh, 1997).

Examples in the Literature

Research targeting physical self-concept and self-worth has focused predominantly on cross-cultural psychometrics, testing the multidimensional and hierarchical nature of the self, and linking physical self-perceptions to affect and behavior. The PSPP, CY-PSPP, and PSDQ have been translated into many languages and used in cross-cultural research worldwide (e.g., Asci, Eklund, Whitehead, Kirazci, & Koca, 2005; Marsh, Marco, & Asci, 2002; Moreno & Cervello, 2005).

The postulated multidimensional and hierarchical structure of the physical self has appeared quite robust in analyses of cross-sectional data (e.g., Crocker, Eklund, & Kowalski, 2000; Dishman et al., 2006; Fox & Corbin, 1989). However, tests of the hierarchical structure of the physical self with longitudinal data using the PSDQ (Marsh & Yeung, 1998) and PSPP (Kowalski, Crocker, Kowalski, Chad, & Humbert, 2003) have suggested that earlier conclusions based on cross-sectional analyses were provisional at best. Empirical evidence supporting the multidimensional nature of the physical self continues to be robust, but the hierarchical structure of the physical self has been drawn into question. For example, Marsh and Yeung found limited support for the influence of global self-concept factors on specific self-concept factors and for the influence of physical self-perceptions on global self-concept factors over a 1 y time frame when using the PSDQ. They concluded that physical self-perceptions are most likely to influence respective physical self-perceptions over time, a phenomenon they called *horizontal effects*. Using a similar procedure with the PSPP, Kowalski and colleagues found little evidence of a hierarchical structure across a 1 y time frame and reported that the horizontal effects model was most parsimonious. These studies suggest that the evidence on a hierarchical model of the physical self is inconclusive.

Researchers have also examined the relationships involving physical self-concept (or self-worth), self-perceptions, and a range of health behaviors and affective outcomes among predominantly adolescent female samples. Moderate relationships between perceptions of sport competence and physical conditioning and physical activity behavior have been observed consistently (Crocker et al., 2000; Crocker, Sabiston, Kowalski, McDonough, &

Kowalski, 2006; Dunton, Jamner, & Cooper, 2003). Changes in physical conditioning self-perceptions (assessed using the PSPP) and in physical activity appear to covary over time among adolescent girls (Crocker et al., 2003). Also, the physical self-perceptions and physical self-worth of adolescent girls have been shown to decrease over time (3 y), and these changes have been linked to change in physical activity (Crocker et al., 2003). Interestingly, in cross-lagged analyses, the link between conditioning self-perceptions and physical activity across time was stronger than the link between physical activity and conditioning self-perceptions across time. This finding provides evidence of a potential bidirectional, although nonequivalent, causal association between self-perceptions and physical activity (Crocker et al., 2006). Finally, Dishman and colleagues (2006) found cross-sectional evidence that physical activity and sport participation are indirectly associated with depression, with several PSDQ-assessed physical self-perceptions acting as mediators of this relationship. Thus, positive changes in self-perceptions resulting from physical activity may help attenuate depressive symptoms among older adolescent girls (Dishman et al., 2006). This conclusion requires longitudinal assessment.

Exercise Identity

Identities are integral components of self-concept, making it difficult to operationally differentiate the two constructs in practice (Brettschneider & Heim, 1997; Stryker, 1987; Stryker & Burke, 2000). The concept of identity takes on multiple meanings depending on the context or field in which it is studied. In the physical domain, the term *identity* tends to be used to refer to unique and distinctive self-descriptions situated in the context of a particular role, such as the role of an exerciser (Anderson & Cychosz, 1995; Brettschneider & Heim, 1997; Cardinal & Cardinal, 1997; Hardcastle & Taylor, 2005; Strachan, Woodgate, Brawley, & Tse, 2005; Whaley & Ebbeck, 2002). Identity is a result of (a) a person's interactions with others, (b) self- and other evaluations, and (c) a clearly delineated self-definition that is meaningful to the individual and to which the individual is committed (Anderson & Cychosz, 1995; Brettschneider & Heim, 1997; Waterman, 1985). As such, identity has important personal and social aspects. The exerciser identity helps give meaning and salience to past behavior and directs future behavior (Anderson & Cychosz, 1995; Anderson, Cychosz, & Franke, 1998) and hence offers potential utility for understanding exercise adherence and maintenance.

Identity Theory

With the exception of two studies (Strachan & Brawley, 2008; Strachan et al., 2005), much of the work describing exercise identity and related antecedents and outcomes has been atheoretical. Identity theory (Stryker, 1987; Stryker & Burke, 2000) emphasizes both the social structural sources of identity and the relationships among multiple identities as well as internal cognitive processes. The social element of identity theory includes a person's commitment to relationships, such that the social ties depend on a certain identity and role. For example, an individual who does not cycle is less likely to have a social network of cyclist friends than the person who does cycle. Commitment shapes identity salience, which is described as the probability that an identity will be invoked across a variety of situations (Stryker & Burke, 2000). For example, a strong identity salience for cycling means that the individual describes herself as a cyclist even when among a group of runners or swimmers. Therefore, identities are stable. Based on identity theory, it is proposed that identity salience (e.g., "I'm a cyclist") leads to behavioral choices (e.g., cycling) that match the expectations attached to that identity. In this way, identity salience may direct role behavior (Burke, 2006; Stryker, 1987; Stryker & Burke, 2000). Generally, identity theory provides a framework to understand behavioral regulation such that behavior (e.g., going to the gym) is either congruent with a person's identity (e.g., an exerciser) or not congruent with a person's identity (e.g., a couch potato). Identity congruent behavior is thought to lead to positive affective states and increased confidence for the behavior (Stryker & Burke, 2000). Alternatively, incongruence is thought to lead to negative emotions, and this affective state is thought to motivate changes (e.g., to engage in the congruent behavior, diminish commitment to the social network, or decrease salience) to reduce the mismatch (Burke, 2006).

Measures Assessing Exercise Identity

Findings from the study of *athletic* identity, as assessed by the Athletic Identity Measurement Scale (AIMS; Brewer, Van Raalte, & Linder, 1993), likely have been a part of the impetus for work on *exercise* identity. Nonetheless, this chapter is focused on exercise and physical activity, and hence the AIMS is not dealt with substantively here (see chapter 25).

Similarities to AIMS can be found in the 9-item Exercise Identity Scale (EIS) of Anderson and Cychosz (1994). The EIS was designed to assess the extent to which exercise behavior is descriptive of a person's self-concept with items such as, "I consider myself an exerciser" and "Exercising is something I think about often." A Likert-type response format is used for EIS measurement (from 1 = "Strongly disagree" to 7 = "Strongly agree"), and items are summed to create a total exercise identity score ranging from 9 to 63. Across diverse samples, a unidimensional factor structure has been demonstrated consistently, and reasonable indexes of internal consistency have been reported (Anderson & Cychosz, 1994; Anderson et al., 1998; Anderson, Cychosz, & Franke, 2001; Storer, Cychosz, & Anderson, 1997). In addition to using the EIS, some researchers have assessed exercise-related identities using scales developed for specific research questions. These assessments include the Physical Activity Identity Scale (PAIS; Miller, Ogletree, & Welshimer, 2002) and a modified version of the AIMS used to assess runner identity (Brewer et al., 1993; Strachan et al., 2005).

Examples in the Literature

EIS research has predominantly involved adult samples. In these samples, exercise identity has been associated with multiple indicators of exercise behavior, including number of exercise sessions per week, minutes of exercise per session, intensity levels, and levels of perceived exertion (Anderson & Cychosz, 1994, 1995; Anderson et al., 2001; Strachan & Brawley, 2008) as well as injury tolerance (Lantz, Rhea, & Mesnier, 2004). Exercise identity has also been observed to be positively related to physiological indicators such as muscular endurance and maximum oxygen uptake and negatively associated with percent body fat (Anderson et al., 1998). In addition, associations in expected directions have been observed with measures of positive and negative affect, intentions to exercise, self-regulatory efficacy (Strachan & Brawley, 2008), and health attitudes such as eating (Lantz et al., 2004). Cardinal and Cardinal (1997) found that a 14 wk intervention enhanced exercise identity (and behavior) among female college students attending an exercise class compared with female students not attending an exercise class over the same time frame. There is also cross-sectional evidence indicating that exercise identity tends to decrease with age (Anderson et al., 1998, 2001). Overall, research examining longitudinal patterns in exercise identity and covarying exercise-related constructs is needed to advance this area of study.

Research using others measures of exercise and physical activity identity generally corroborates EIS findings. Exercise identity is associated with exercise behavior, adherence, and self-efficacy (Miller, Ogletree, & Welshimer, 2002; Strachan et al., 2005).

Physical Activity Self-Definitions

According to Kendzierski and Morganstein (2009), *physical activity self-definitions* "are aspects of the self-concept related to physical activities in which people voluntarily engage for exercise, sport, or recreation" (p. 485). They are hierarchically organized and vary in specificity (e.g., an exerciser versus a runner).

Theoretical Perspectives

Drawing from self-perception (Bem, 1972) and identity (Stryker & Burke, 2000) theories and exercise motivation literature, Kendzierski and colleagues (Kendzierski et al., 1998; Kendzierski & Morganstein, 2009) developed and tested a model examining the correlates of physical activity self-definitions. This model describes why people have or do not have a physical activity self-definition, and it may therefore provide researchers with a foundation for designing interventions to promote positive self-definitions as well as exercise adherence (Kendzierski & Morganstein, 2009). The most recent work supports a model in which perceived commitment and perceived ability specific to the activity are the most proximal correlates of self-definition. Perceived wanting and trying to do the activity are antecedents of commitment, whereas trying to do the activity is an antecedent to perceptions of ability. Enjoyment of the activity is described as being a correlate of perceived wanting to do the activity. The model can be used at a more general level (e.g., exerciser) or a more specific level (e.g., runner) to describe self-definitions (Kendzierski et al., 1998; Kendzierski & Morganstein, 2009). The researchers also proposed that there are both social and nonsocial triggers for self-reflection, although the mechanisms associated with the social context are not yet understood. "It is also possible that members of the social world surrounding the individual at the time may affect the self-definitional process, either by affecting the variables in the model or by affecting the weight those variables have in self-definitional inferences" (Kendzierski & Morganstein, 2009, p. 500).

Measures Assessing Physical Activity Self-Definition

Measures of specific physical activity self-definitions have been developed and used to assess weightlifting, basketball, exercise, jogging, and cycling self-definitions (Kendzierski et al., 1998; Kendzierski & Morganstein, 2009). In these studies, self-definition has been assessed with a total of 4 to 6 items, such as, "How important to you is being a *runner*" and "To what extent do you consider yourself a *weightlifter*" (for a list of the questions, see the appendix in Kendzierski et al., 1998). The items are assessed on 7-point Likert-type scales with the anchors appropriately reflecting the topic of the question. For example, the response anchors for "How important to you is being a *runner*" are 1 = "Not at all important" to 7 = "Extremely important," while the response anchors for "To what extent do you consider yourself a *weightlifter*" are 1 = "Not at all" to 7 = "To a great extent." A specific physical activity self-definition is calculated by summing the items in the scale. Evidence of reliability and validity has been reported (Kendzierski et al., 1998; Kendzierski & Morganstein, 2009).

Examples in the Literature

The study of physical activity self-definition, along with its antecedents and outcomes, remains an understudied area. Nevertheless, initial studies on physical activity self-definitions have been conducted with adult samples and have shown that behavioral criteria (e.g., past experiences, current performance) are more important to self-definitions than affective criteria (e.g., enjoyment) and achievement goal criteria (e.g., setting goals) (Kendzierski et al., 1998). With youth samples, physical activity self-definition was positively associated with measures of aerobic fitness and future physical activity self-definition (Robbins, Pis, Pender, & Kazanis, 2004). In this study, adolescent boys reported higher physical activity self-definitions compared with girls (Robbins et al., 2004). This latter finding may highlight the need to consider gender differences in future research on physical activity self-definitions.

Exerciser Self-Schemata

Self-schemata are underlying belief systems about the self that are a result of experience and reflected appraisal (Nurius, 1991). These cognitive structures act as guides for the processing and retrieval of stored information about the self and others (Kendzierski, 1988, 1990). For example, an individual's experiences associated with exercise, such as thoughts, feelings, and motor and autonomic responses to exercise, constitute the exercise self-schema stored in the long-term memory (Kendzierski, 1988, 1990). There are three types of individuals based on the importance and descriptiveness of their exercise-related self-schema: exerciser schematics, nonexerciser schematics, and aschematics

(Kendzierski, 1990; Marcus, 1977). Also, some individuals are not classified by either the importance or the descriptiveness of their self-schema. *Exerciser schematics* are individuals who consider the attribute of exercising to be extremely descriptive and important to their sense of self. *Nonexerciser schematics* do not describe themselves in terms of exercise attributes but consider exercising to be important. *Aschematics* are individuals who do not consider exercise attributes to be extremely descriptive of or extremely important to their self-image (Kendzierski, 1990; Marcus, 1977). The presence of a self-schema for a behavior is important to future participation in that activity (Cross & Markus, 1994).

Schema Theory

Schema theorists posit that individuals are active agents in processing information that is formulated through experience in a specific activity or with a certain concept (Marcus, 1977). Information can come from feedback from others, objects and equipment, and physiological effects (increased heartbeat during an aerobics class). Self-schemata guide the perception and selection of incoming information, influence the organization of information in memory, and direct how the information is used (Fiske & Taylor, 1984). Self-schemata may increase processing time and enhance the quality of information, are readily available in memory, and are resistant to information that is inconsistent with a schema (Marcus, 1977). As they relate to exercise behavior, schemata act as an impetus to initiate an exercise program and enhance motivation to continue to exercise (Kendzierski, 1988). Whereas schemata originate in social cognition, the behavioral outcomes of schemata are often explored within established frameworks of motivation and behavior, such as the theory of planned behavior and social cognitive theory (Estabrooks & Courneya, 1997; Kendzierski, 1990, 1994; Yin & Boyd, 2000).

Measures Assessing Self-Schemata

Based on theoretical propositions (Marcus, 1977), the Exerciser Self-Schema Scale (Kendzierski, 1988) was developed to assess whether individuals are exerciser schematics, nonexerciser schematics, or aschematics. The first set of questions assesses the extent to which individuals perceive themselves to be someone who "exercises regularly," "keeps in shape," and "is physically active." Responses to these questions are recorded on a Likert-type scale ranging from 1 = "Does not describe me" to

11 = "Describes me"). The second set of questions comprises filler questions, such as "friendly" or "spontaneous," which are included to avoid biases. The last set of questions assesses the importance individuals attribute to "the image you have of yourself, regardless of whether or not the trait describes you" on a Likert-type scale ranging from 1 = "Not at all important" to 11 = "Very important." Since self-schemata involve self-descriptiveness and importance to self-image, assessments of self-schemata need to include both the importance and the descriptiveness dimensions.

Individuals who score 8 or more on the 11-point Likert-type scales for 2 of the 3 descriptive *and* importance questions are considered to be exerciser schematics. Individuals who report at least 2 of the 3 descriptive questions at the low end of the scale (i.e., a score of 1-4 on the 11-point Likert-type scale) *and* at least 2 of the 3 importance questions as extremely important to self-image (i.e., a score of 8-11 on the 11-point Likert-type scale) are classified as nonexerciser schematics. Individuals are classified as aschematics if their scores for at least 2 of the 3 descriptive questions fall in the midrange of the 11-point scale (i.e., a score of 5-7) *and* at least 2 of the 3 exercise descriptors are reported as dimensions that are not extremely important (i.e., a score of 1-7 on the 11-point Likert-type scale) to their self-image.

Examples in the Literature

Research exploring the relationship between exerciser self-schema and behavior has consistently revealed a positive direct association among predominantly college-aged and adult samples. In her original work, Kendzierski (1988) found that exerciser schematics participate in more activities, exercise more frequently, demonstrate greater past experiences with exercise, report higher levels of future intention and commitment to exercise, and have more plans in place to face barriers when compared with nonexerciser schematics and aschematics. Primarily cross-sectional research has confirmed many of these findings. Exerciser schematics report greater caloric expenditure, higher frequency of exercise, higher self-efficacy, and more positive exercise-related attitudes when compared with the nonexerciser schematics and aschematics (Yin & Boyd, 2000). Exerciser schematics make less stable attributions for a personal exercise lapse than aschematics make (Kendzierski & Sheffield, 2000; Kendzierski, Sheffield, & Morganstein, 2002). Also, exerciser schematics are more likely to have exercise intentions and greater future expectancies to exercise compared with other schematics (Estabrooks & Courneya, 1997; Sheeran

& Orbell, 2000; Yin & Boyd, 2000). There is some evidence that exerciser self-schemata also mediate the intention-to-behavior relationship (Banting, Dimmock, & Lay, 2009).

When compared with the other schematic groups, exerciser schematics also tend to judge exercise-related stimuli as being self-descriptive and have different reaction times to these descriptive words or stimuli (Kendzierski, 1990). In one study, exerciser schematics demonstrated attentional bias for exercise-related words (i.e., had a delayed response latency) when compared with aschematics, who themselves showed attentional bias for sedentary lifestyle stimuli (Berry, 2006). Taken together, the works of Kendzierski (1990) and Berry (2006) suggest that health promotion messages may be less effective for aschematics and nonexerciser schematics. Banting and colleagues (2009) also used an association test as an implicit measure of exercise self-schemata and the Exerciser Self-Schema Scale as an explicit measure of exercise self-schemata. They found a small significant correlation between explicit and implicit exerciser self-schemata, and both self-schemata were significant correlates of exercise behavior among regular exercisers. These researchers did not classify individuals according to self-schemata based on the Exerciser Self-Schema Scale responses. Finally, in a review of the literature, Long and Flood (1993) suggested that exerciser self-schemata are likely coping resources to help manage work-related stress.

Whereas the literature demonstrates consistent differences among exerciser self-schematics and associations with various exercise-related cognitions, affects, and behaviors, one of the limitations of this work has been the avoidance or exclusion of the individuals who do not meet any exerciser self-schema criteria. This is usually a substantial percentage (18%-45%) of individuals (Berry, 2006; Estabrooks & Courneya, 1997; Kendzierski, 1988, 1990; Yin & Boyd, 2000). There is some evidence for combining these individuals into a reclassified group of *no exerciser self-schematics*, in which the aschematics and nonexerciser schematics are collapsed and grouped with the individuals not otherwise classified (Kendzierski et al., 2002). Nonetheless, future work is needed to help us assess and understand the individuals who do not have an exerciser schema.

Possible Selves

Conceptually, *possible selves* are self-schemata subcomponents (Marcus & Nurius, 1987). Possible selves are future-oriented self-perceptions that include both positive or hoped-for selves (e.g., the attractive fit self, the esteemed self) and negative or feared selves (e.g., the self as a failure, the unhealthy self). Possible selves are mental representations that may include plans and behavioral control strategies for achieving goals (Aloise-Young, Hennigan, & Leong, 2001; Whaley & Redding, 2001). In a way, they act as blueprints for goal achievement (Whaley & Redding, 2001) and are critical motivational resources.

Theoretical Considerations for Possible Selves

Possible selves are incentives for future behavior in the way that they represent the self to be approached or avoided (Oyserman & Markus, 1990). Markus and Nurius (1986) proposed that the desired or hoped-for self and the feared possible self organize, provide meaning, and direct cognition and behavior toward (in the case of the hoped-for self) or away from (in the case of the feared self) the pursuit of the end state.

Within the larger frameworks of motivation that are frequently used in the exercise domain, possible selves lead to feelings of self-efficacy (Bandura, 1997), effectance and competence (Eccles & Wigfield, 2002; Harter, 1978), and control (Carver & Scheier, 1982). They also lead to various health behaviors such as physical activity.

Measures Assessing Possible Selves

There are three ways to assess possible selves. Closed-ended possible selves measures involve having individuals report on the number of positive and negative possible selves that they endorse from a provided list (Markus & Nurius, 1986). Closed-ended measures specific to domains (primarily academic and social, with no evidence of physical) have also been used (see Oyserman & Fryberg, 2006) to yield summed scores for positive and negative possible selves. To assess possible selves more qualitatively (i.e., an Open-Ended Possible Selves Questionnaire), individuals are provided with a page with lines to write down their hoped-for selves and another page to write down their feared possible selves (Cross & Markus, 1991). The instructions on the scale provide a short description of possible selves. This measure can be administered to children, adolescents, and older adults either in paper-and-pencil format or in a verbal interview setting. In work with adult women, Whaley (2003) employed a combination of open-ended and closed-ended (exercise-specific) measures to gather extensive information on possible selves.

Scoring of the open-ended possible selves measure involves counting the number of hoped-for and feared possible selves to get total scores. The types of hoped-for and feared possible selves can also be coded. Cross and Markus (1991) suggested the following content domains for coding: personal, physical, educational, lifestyle, family, relationships, occupational, material, and leisure. Whaley (2003) amended these categories for the physical domain to include body image (weight and attractiveness), physical (activity level, condition), health (medical concerns), independence and dependence (requiring care), personal projects (leisure and material), retirement, education and occupation, and family and relationships.

Drawing from other areas in psychology dealing with the assessment of behavior change, it is also an option to assess the *number* of possible selves that relate to engagement and adherence or dropout and avoidance of physical activity. A *possible selves balance* refers to having both feared (e.g., dropout or avoidance) and hoped-for (e.g., regular engagement and adherence) possible selves for the same domain (Dunkel, Kelts, & Coon, 2006). This balanced approach seems to provide the greatest motivation for behavior change (Oyserman & Markus, 1990). To date, few researchers have employed this perspective in the physical activity context.

Examples in the Literature

The area of exercise-related possible selves has yet to be extensively researched. Nonetheless, Whaley (2003) compared reports of possible selves from exercising and inactive women. The results showed that the inactive women had more hoped-for and feared selves for body image. Exercise-related possible selves distinguished among exercise levels, as did self-regulatory variables of the possible self (outcome expectancy, self-efficacy, and importance).

There is also evidence that manipulating possible selves can change exercise behavior (Ouellette, Hessling, Gibbons, Reis-Bergan, & Gerrard, 2005). In one study, college-aged students read a scenario about future-oriented selves in exercise and had their actual behavior measured before and after the manipulation. The results revealed that individuals who were concerned with their future self were influenced by the possible selves manipulation and increased their exercise behavior over the 4 wk of the study. The study also focused on prototypes, which are current self-descriptors rather than future-oriented images (Ouellette et al., 2005). These findings suggest it is possible to design interventions focused on possible selves.

Dimensions and Sources of Confusion

Given the multitude of constructs pertaining to the self, it is no wonder that there are debates and areas of confusion. Perhaps much of the ambiguity can be found in the lack of definitional consensus on the various self-related constructs. This lack of consensus has resulted in undifferentiated and interchangeable use of construct labels. Somewhat related, these many constructs are organized into various theories that often seem to overlap conceptually.

1. *Are jingle-jangle fallacies confusing or obscuring our understanding of the self?* Jingle-jangle terminology is used when scales with similar names reflect different constructs or when scales with different names measure the same construct (Marsh, 1994a). As alluded to throughout this chapter, it is at times difficult to differentiate self-concept and self-esteem, identity and self-definition, and self-schemata and possible selves. Many of these are used interchangeably and remain indistinguishable in research reports.

2. *Can these varied approaches to the self be subsumed into a broader, more integrated theory?* A primary source of confusion may be rooted in issues arising from the ongoing debate about what the term *theory* means in psychology. Bannister and Fransella (1971) were quite direct in making that point several decades ago:

> The term theory should be reserved for extensive and elaborated systems of ideas cast in terms of an integrated language. Users should not have to borrow, in every intellectual emergency, from elsewhere and conclude by assembling a ragbag of concepts which cannot be cross-related. (p. 11)

So, can constructs such as physical self-concept, physical self-worth, exercise identity, and exerciser schemata be more fruitfully understood from the perspective of an umbrella, or broader integrated, theory? To answer that question and to provide some direction to efforts at reducing the confusion in this theoretical area, we must first decide which umbrella would best cover the conceptual area. Arguably, the answer is not too difficult to come by, since all these perspectives can be applied to an understanding of physical activity and exercise behavior. Thus, as the various authors (several cited in this chapter) frequently suggest, the primary concern is with *motivation* to do or not do those behaviors.

Self-determination theory (SDT, described in detail in chapter 26) may be a logical choice as an umbrella theory of human motivation (Deci & Ryan, 1985, 2008; Ryan & Deci, 2000). For example, many contemporary measures of self-esteem and self-worth (e.g., Fox & Corbin, 1989; Harter, 1985; Marsh et al., 1994) tap competence perceptions, a key construct of SDT. Also, the physical activity self-definition (PASD) model has ability perceptions at its core. Furthermore, the positive or negative affective states posited as consequences of congruence or incongruence of personal identity with personal behavior are suggestive of integrated or introjected regulations, respectively, which are also key constructs of SDT. Moreover, the similarities between concepts such as *true* and *contingent* self-esteem seem easier to link to wider theory and to apply to various behaviors when put into the SDT motivational perspective (Deci & Ryan, 2008; Ryan & Brown, 2003). Finally, Kendzierski and Morganstein (2009), in their discussion of the PASD model, mentioned possible effects of the competitive orientations of individuals, how the "social world" may affect self-definitional processes, and whether "social recognition" plays a role (p. 500). All are suggestive of controlled orientations as discussed within SDT. A controlled orientation is associated with contingent self-esteem. Thus, the conceptual linking of self-esteem theory to SDT is evident, and there may be heuristic advantages to subsuming the constructs into the wider motivation theory rubric. Of course, the question of whether conceptual confusion would be reduced and clarity and theoretical application would be enhanced by subsuming the self-based theories under a wider umbrella of a meta-theory such as SDT will have to be answered by empirical research rather than the general applications of logic attempted here.

Recommendations for Researchers and Practitioners

There are many constructs related to the self and exercise, and researchers should identify the construct and theoretical framework that best fits with their research questions. With this in mind, we focus the recommendations made here on issues related to developing and testing instruments (e.g., reliability, validity, social desirability), expanding research to underrepresented populations (e.g., age, ethnicity, gender), exploring untapped constructs of the self (e.g., self-compassion), and using different methods of data collection (e.g., qualitative methodologies). Furthermore, we suspect that advancement of research might be facilitated by subsuming many of the constructs discussed in this chapter under a broader motivation theory such as SDT.

Existing measures of the self should not be modified and then expected to function appropriately in unique contexts or with different samples. Appropriate tests of reliability and validity must be conducted in preliminary work before authors can be confident in modified versions of scales. While tests of social desirability have been used very little in the reviewed literature, researchers are encouraged to account for social desirability in self-esteem and self-concept research (e.g., Sonstroem & Potts, 1996). Furthermore, newly developed measures should emanate from theory and pilot work and be tested thoroughly before being applied in the field. Whereas estimates of reliability are easy to access once data are collected, tests of validity often require careful planning and the inclusion of additional measures in the data collection process. Researchers are encouraged to conduct more formal tests of validity. According to Messick (1995), validity assessments are essential to "help disentangle some of the complexities inherent in appraising the appropriateness, meaningfulness, and usefulness of score inferences" (p. 744). Researchers in exercise psychology should be particularly interested in demonstrating the multiple aspects of construct validity in order to make meaningful interpretations of test scores (Messick, 1995). These aspects include content validity (content representativeness and relevance), substantive validity (theoretical rationales for test scores), structural validity (a match between the scoring structure and the intended construct structure), generalizability (similarity of score properties and interpretations across populations, environments, and tasks), external validity (convergent and discriminant evidence and criterion relevance), and consequential validity (an appraisal of the value of score interpretations for practical use and actual or potential consequences of test use). We endorse the view of Marsh (1994a), who suggested that validity research should critically evaluate psychological measures that may confuse research because of jingle-jangle fallacies in which scales with similar names measure different constructs and scales with different names measure similar constructs.

Underrepresented populations should be studied to inform research of the effects of sociocultural factors such as age, ethnicity, culture, socioeconomic position, and gender (among others) on constructs related to the self. Many of the constructs reviewed here have been studied in predominantly North American (i.e., Westernized) female Caucasians of moderate to high socioeconomic status (if reported). It is important not only to test the psychometrics of the scales independently for a range of subsamples and to determine if the measures are being interpreted similarly among the subgroups but also to build research capacity in understanding the possible sociocultural differences in mechanisms linking the self and exercise.

There are also additional self-related constructs in the study of exercise behavior that may merit consideration. For example, there is emerging research on understanding self-compassion in the context of health and exercise. Self-compassion is defined as having three dimensions (Neff, 2003): self-kindness (understanding and being kind to the self rather than being critical and imposing harsh criticisms), common humanity (being immersed in a larger human experience rather than seeing personal experiences as separate and isolating; acknowledging personal limitations), and mindfulness (maintaining a balanced state of awareness of feelings). Self-compassion is conceptualized as an alternative to self-esteem, and both constructs are usually positively related to one another and to psychological well-being (Neff, 2003, 2004). In the context of exercise and the physical self, Magnus, Kowalski, and McHugh (2009) found that self-compassion is uniquely associated with indicators of exercise and well-being, such as introjected motivation (e.g., being motivated to exercise out of guilt or to avoid shame), ego goal orientation, social physique anxiety, and obligatory exercise, above and beyond the associations between these constructs and self-esteem. Therefore, self-compassion may be an important target both in theory and in practice within the exercise domain.

Finally, qualitative research may be useful for informing future instruments or modifications to instruments for unique populations, identifying factors that may be related to the self, and developing a better understanding of the main constructs of self as they relate to exercise (Bond & Batey, 2005; Hardcastle & Taylor, 2005; Sabiston, McDonough, & Crocker, 2007; Whaley & Ebbeck, 2002). Working with a group of older adult women, Whaley and Ebbeck found that an exercise identity is not part of a comprehensive schema for exercise. Many of the women reported exercise as being important to their sense of self but not descriptive of them. For many women, avoiding the label of *old* was a primary motivator to exercise—not an identity of exercise. This research showed the importance of changing the language and using appropriate descriptors for older adult populations. Focusing on a population of middle-aged and older inactive adults, Hardcastle and Taylor found that women with a primary care referral to a community physical activity program developed an exercise identity

by prioritizing and promoting exercise and staying committed to the program. Participants scheduled and planned for their exercise and in turn experienced achievement, feelings of autonomy, and a sense of belonging within the network of exercisers. This research highlighted the processes by which exercise identity is developed in inactive women. In others studies, survivors of breast cancer discussed changes to their physical self-perceptions and the development of physical activity identities when taking part in dragon boat programs (McDonough, Sabiston, & Crocker, 2008; Sabiston et al., 2007). Taken together, interviews and focus groups are rich data-gathering tools that help delve into lingering questions and concerns about the self and relationships to exercise behavior across genders, cultures, and ages.

Practitioners are encouraged to understand their clients' perspectives and attitudes toward the self. First, the individual's contingent versus true self-esteem and implicit versus explicit self-esteem can be factored into many decisions regarding program, treatment, and follow-up. Second, practical strategies aimed at helping individuals discount domains of the physical self in which they do not feel competent may foster positive affective and behavioral outcomes both from Harter's (1990) perspective and from identity theory tenets (Stryker & Burke, 2000). Alternatively, practitioners can help individuals change their perceptions of competence or develop such perceptions (Harter, 1999). Third, possible selves scenarios can be used as intervention tools to increase short-term physical activity levels (Ouellette et al., 2005). This line of intervention work needs to be expanded and explored with multiple affective and behavioral outcomes. Finally, practitioners may target various elements outlined in the PASD model (Kendzierski & Morganstein, 2009) to help foster physical activity self-definitions. For example, helping individuals realize their desires for physical activity and learn ways to prioritize and plan for physical activity can enhance self-definitions. Furthermore, enhancing importance and competence perceptions, thus supporting congruence, helps with the development of physical activity self-definitions.

Taken together, there are many perspectives related to the self that can inform the development and implementation of exercise and mental health programs. Practitioners are encouraged to draw from the perspectives outlined in this chapter as well as to consider the broader motivational theoretical tenets that may be foundational to the understanding of the various constructs of the self and the associated links to exercise and well-being.

■ **Table 21.1** ■

Measures Assessing the Self in the Physical Domain

Variable or concept	Measure	Dimension or characteristic	Source and web site (if applicable)
Physical self-worth	Physical Self-Perception Profile (PSPP)	Self-perceptions of conditioning, strength, sport, and body; global physical self-worth	Fox (1990); Fox & Corbin (1989)
Physical self-worth	Children and Youth Physical Self-Perception Profile (CY-PSPP)	Self-perceptions of conditioning, strength, and sport; appearance self-perceptions and global physical self-worth are assessed by Harter's (1985) scales	Whitehead (1995)
Physical self-concept	Physical Self-Description Questionnaire (PSDQ)	Self-perceptions of health, strength, physical activity, endurance and fitness, sport competence, coordination, appearance, flexibility, and body fat; global physical self-concept; global self-esteem	Marsh, Richards, Johnson, Roche, & Tremayne (1994) www.self.ox.ac.uk/Instruments/packages.htm
Exercise identity	Exercise Identity Scale (EIS)	Exercise identity (unidimensional)	Anderson & Cychosz (1994)
Physical activity identity	Physical Activity Identity Scale (PAIS)	Physical activity identity (unidimensional)	Miller, Ogletree, & Welshimer (2002)
Runner identity	Modified Athletic Identity Measurement Scale (AIMS)	Runner identity (unidimensional)	Brewer et al. (1993); Strachan et al. (2005)
Exercise self-definition	Physical activity self-definition (PASD) items	Self-definitions measured either globally (exerciser) or specific to the type of activity (e.g., runner, weightlifter, cyclist)	Kendzierski et al. (1998); Kendzierski & Morganstein (2009)
Exercise schema	Exerciser Self-Schema Scale	Self-description and importance of being an exerciser	Kendzierski (1988)
Possible selves	Open-Ended Possible Selves Questionnaire	Hoped-for and feared possible selves	Cross & Markus (1991); Dunkel et al. (2006)
Possible selves	Closed-ended possible selves measure	Positive and negative possible selves	Markus & Nurius (1986)

Exercise-Related Self-Efficacy

Edward McAuley, PhD, Siobhan M. White, PhD,
Emily L. Mailey, MS, and Thomas R. Wójcicki, BS

More than a decade ago, McAuley and Mihalko (1998) critically reviewed the extant literature on the measurement of exercise-related self-efficacy. They made the case that physical activity is both an important health behavior implicated in physical and psychological health and a notoriously difficult behavior for people to adopt and maintain over the long term. Little has changed in this regard. Physical activity is still associated with disease reductions (Laaksonen et al., 2005; Lee, 2003; Sesso, Paffenbarger, & Lee, 2000) and psychological health (Brown et al., 2003; Fox, 1999), and participation remains abysmally poor (Haskell & Lee, 2007). This chapter updates the McAuley and Mihalko (1998) review by using more stringent inclusion criteria to review 488 articles in which self-efficacy was used as a correlate of physical activity behavior. We begin with a brief overview of social cognitive theory (SCT) and the role of self-efficacy within this theoretical framework. Next, we classify the efficacy measures that are most consistently used in the literature into the three dimensions of (1) barriers self-efficacy, (2) task-specific self-efficacy, and (3) adherence self-efficacy. We discuss the psychometric properties of these measures and give an overview of how each class of efficacy measures has been demonstrated to relate to physical activity and associated outcomes. We conclude with recommendations for both the research and the practice communities.

Self-Efficacy and Social Cognitive Theory

SCT (Bandura, 1986, 1997, 2004) has provided a theoretical foundation that has served as the impetus for a considerable body of literature documenting the correlates and determinants of health behavior change. The core set of determinants underlying SCT (i.e., self-efficacy, outcome expectations, goals, facilitators, and impediments) and the manner in which they are theorized to influence behavior have been well articulated by Bandura (2004). The active agent in SCT is self-efficacy. Self-efficacy expectations are beliefs that individuals hold regarding their capabilities to carry out a course of action (Bandura, 1977). They may be considered a situation-specific form of self-confidence. The situation-specific nature of self-efficacy is nontrivial, as it is a characteristic that distinguishes efficacy cognitions from more stable, dispositional qualities such as self-confidence and subjects them to external and internal influences, making them ideal targets for manipulation (McAuley, Talbot, & Martinez, 1999) and interventions (McAuley, Courneya, Rudolph, & Lox, 1994). The primary sources of efficacy information include past performance accomplishments or mastery experiences, social persuasion, social modeling, and interpretations of physiological and emotional states (Bandura, 1997). Efficacy expectations influence the activities individuals choose to pursue, the degree of effort they expend in pursuit of their goals, and the levels of persistence they demonstrate in the face of setbacks, failures, and difficulties. It is difficult to argue that choice, effort, and persistence are unrelated to adopting and maintaining an exercise regimen. Thus, self-efficacy appears to be a very natural correlate of this complex health behavior. Indeed, it has been one of the most consistently reported correlates of exercise behavior and its outcomes (McAuley & Blissmer, 2000).

It is important to differentiate self-efficacy expectations from another core construct of SCT, outcome expectations. Outcome expectations are beliefs about the expected outcomes an individual associates with engaging in a specific health behavior (Bandura, 1997). Often these outcomes are seen in the context of perceived costs and benefits. Importantly, outcome expectations are theorized to lie along three dimensions: physical, social, and self-evaluative (Bandura, 1997). These dimensions closely reflect outcomes typically associated with physical activity. To distinguish between efficacy expectations and outcome expectations, it may be illustrative to consider the example of physical activity and weight loss. An outcome expectation regarding this behavior (physical activity) and its outcome (weight loss) might be, "If I exercise for 150 min/wk for the next several months, I will effectively manage my weight." The attendant efficacy expectation might be, "I am confident that I can exercise for 150 min/wk for the next several months even when the weather is bad or I have competing commitments."

A much ignored but important construct within the SCT model involves the goals that individuals set for themselves relative to physical activity and health outcomes and the strategies and plans they devise to achieve these goals. Additionally, physical and social barriers to behavior change and the presence or absence of support systems and facilitators for such change are also theorized to influence behavior in the SCT model. Importantly, self-efficacy is considered the primary factor for influencing behavior change by operating directly on behavior and indirectly through outcome expectations, goals, and facilitators and impediments (Bandura, 2004). Knowing how to change physical activity is not sufficient because unless people believe they have the capabilities to bring about change, they most likely will not be moved to action. Thus, individuals with higher levels of self-efficacy have more positive expectations about what the behavior of interest will bring about, set higher goals for themselves, and are more likely to take the view that they are capable of overcoming difficulties and barriers with effort and coping skills.

As noted earlier, self-efficacy has been demonstrated to influence a wide array of health behaviors (Bandura, 1997; McAuley & Blissmer, 2000). However, it is equally important to consider that behavioral outcomes associated with physical activity take the form of elements other than actual physical activity. For example, there is a considerable literature detailing the effects of physical activity on psychological well-being in the form of anxiety (Taylor, 2000), depression (Craft & Landers, 1998), affect (Biddle, 2000), and quality of life (Rejeski &

Mihalko, 2001; McAuley & Morris, 2007). In all such associations, evidence suggests that self-efficacy is one of a number of potential mediators of the effects of physical activity on these psychological outcomes. In addition, there is a growing literature to suggest that physical activity plays an important role in the attenuation of functional limitations (Keysor, 2003) and the enhancement of functional performance in older adults (Stewart, 2003). For example, self-efficacy mediated the influence of an exercise intervention on stair-climbing in older adults with osteoarthritis of the knee (Rejeski, Ettinger, Martin, & Morgan, 1998). Li and colleagues (2002) provided further evidence for the relationship between self-efficacy and physical function performance in a randomized controlled exercise trial. Moreover, Seeman and colleagues (Seeman & Chen, 2002; Seeman, Unger, McAvay, & Mendes de Leon, 1999) reported that self-efficacy expectations are related to disability and functional declines and that self-efficacy influences disability independent of physical abilities. These important physical activity outcomes represent vital areas in which self-efficacy measures can be validated systematically.

In the following sections, we provide an overview of the exercise-specific measures that have been used the most frequently in the literature. It is beyond the scope of this chapter to systematically review each measure. Therefore, we first classify these measures into three broad categories and then we discuss the properties of and support for such categories.

Primary Self-Efficacy Measures

The measures of self-efficacy related to physical activity or exercise that we selected for our review were identified through literature searches conducted in 2009 using the PubMed, Google Scholar, PsycInfo, Web of Science, and Scirus search engines. A combination of the following terms was used: *physical activity*, *exercise*, and *self-efficacy*. Our initial search identified 488 articles in which a self-efficacy measure could be identified. Given the volume of articles and the fact that numerous measures were developed specifically for use in individual studies, we refined our search by including only the measures meeting the following three criteria:

1. The measure was specific to physical activity or exercise.

2. The original measure development paper was cited in the literature a minimum of 10 times.

3. The scale was published in English.

Three broad categories effectively capture the content of the scales retained for discussion: *barriers self-efficacy*, *adherence self-efficacy*, and *task-specific self-efficacy*. The retained measures are shown in table 22.1. In the following sections, we briefly describe the three categories, detail their overall internal consistency, and discuss their use and relationship with exercise behavior and outcomes (e.g., affect, function).

Barriers Self-Efficacy

Measures of barriers self-efficacy assess a person's confidence to engage in regular exercise in the face of common barriers to exercise. There has been a consistently reported positive relationship between barriers self-efficacy and exercise participation (McAuley & Blissmer, 2000). For example, cross-sectional studies of individuals at various stages of the exercise process (e.g., contemplation, preparation, maintenance) have demonstrated that participants in the action and maintenance stages report greater self-efficacy to overcome barriers than participants in the earlier stages report (Resnick & Nigg, 2003). Individuals who strongly believe they are capable of overcoming common barriers are more likely to engage in regular exercise.

Of the measures included for review, 19 were barriers self-efficacy scales (see table 22.1). The format is quite similar on most of these scales. A preceding stem such as "I believe I can exercise regularly . . . " is followed by individual items identifying specific barriers, such as "when the weather is bad." Some scales quantify regular exercise (e.g., 3 times per week for 20 min), whereas others refer to exercise more generally (e.g., stick to your exercise program).

Although a variety of approaches to developing barriers efficacy scales have been adopted, one useful approach is to ask participants to identify the factors that have led them to drop out of exercise programs in the past. The most frequent responses are used to formulate scale items. Importantly, the most common barriers (e.g., not enough time, too tired, bad weather, feeling stressed, program is not enjoyable, no one to exercise with) were identified consistently by almost all adult samples, and many of these appear in the identified barriers self-efficacy scales (Blanchard, Rodgers, Courneya, Daub, & Knapik, 2002; McAuley, 1992; Rogers et al., 2006).

Several of the barrier scales include relatively few items, which may be problematic, as it is likely that different barriers are more salient to some individuals than they are to others. For example, for someone who enjoys exercising alone, not having an exercise partner would not be a major barrier to exercise

participation. Thus, barriers efficacy scales should be long enough to incorporate an array of barriers. Given the variable importance placed on different items by different individuals, the items do not need to be in any particular order, as the hierarchy of challenges will differ for each individual. We have one further recommendation, however. Participants should be given the option of indicating whether the barrier is not applicable. Forcing participants to rate a non-relevant barrier may artificially inflate or deflate efficacy values.

Task-Specific Self-Efficacy

The second category of self-efficacy measures is task-specific self-efficacy, which reflects the confidence that individuals have in their ability to perform essential components of a specified task (McAuley & Mihalko, 1998). Although self-efficacy is considered a situation-specific construct, in order to execute a behavior of interest it is often necessary to complete subcomponents of that behavior (Bandura, 1986). For example, in an intervention designed to increase daily step counts, measuring the participants' efficacy for exercise may be too broad or vague of an assessment to portray the participants' confidence in successfully performing the outcome of interest (walking). It may be more appropriate to use a task-specific measure of efficacy (e.g., self-efficacy for walking at various increments of duration over time) rather than a general measure of exercise self-efficacy to determine the participants' confidence in their ability to perform the task at hand (Bandura, 1986). Thus, task-specific self-efficacy measures explicitly assess a person's belief in an ability to accomplish a specific exercise-related task (walking, strength training, cycling), often at specified levels (e.g., 1 mi or 1.6 km, 10 repetitions, 30 min).

Although the potential benefits of using a task-specific measure are evident, few task-specific scales have been developed for exercise, and even fewer have been consistently used and validated throughout the literature. We identified five task-specific measures (table 22.1).

Although these measures focused on different tasks (walking or jogging, cycling, performing tai chi, stair-climbing), they were all structured in the hierarchical manner recommended by Bandura (2006). For example, rather than simply asking participants to evaluate their capabilities of walking continuously at a moderate pace for 40 min, a walking scale might include 8 increasingly difficult items that start with walking continuously for 5 min and increase in 5 min increments until the end goal of walking continuously for 40 min is reached. Similarly, a stair-climbing scale might range from 2 flights to 10 flights of stairs. In general, task-specific scales may be more appropriate for evaluating self-efficacy for a particular behavior and may represent a more accurate reflection of what people believe they can accomplish successfully. Conversely, a more general measure may attenuate the strength of a person's perception for a specific exercise-related activity and its associations with related constructs.

Adherence Self-Efficacy

The final category of self-efficacy measures is adherence self-efficacy in the context of physical activity and exercise. These measures assess people's beliefs in their ability to adhere to a specified regimen of physical activity or exercise. Self-efficacy has been associated consistently with adherence to exercise regimens (McAuley & Blissmer, 2000), although many of the self-efficacy measures used in the literature do not specifically measure adherence self-efficacy. As the ultimate goal of most physical activity and exercise programs is short-term adherence and long-term maintenance, assessing individuals' beliefs with respect to their capabilities in these areas is important. Additionally, given that attrition from exercise programs is greater in the beginning stages, such assessment might be useful in developing strategies to enhance adherence self-efficacy. It may also be critical for terminal programs and interventions, as there is evidence that individuals who have higher levels of adherence self-efficacy are more likely to maintain physical activity postintervention (McAuley, 1993).

Adherence self-efficacy measures assess individuals' beliefs in their capabilities to continue an exercise program at specified temporal increments. These scales can take a number of forms but typically specify the frequency and duration (e.g., accumulated or per session) that the activity will be performed. Thus, a sample item might state, "I am able to continue to exercise 3 times per week at a moderate intensity for 40+ min without quitting for the next month." Alternatively, the format might be more general, with items such as, "I am able to accumulate 30 min of physical activity on 5 or more days of the week for the next 6 mo." Such an approach reflects assessment of self-efficacy that is in line with public health recommendations for physical activity (U.S. Department of Health and Human Services, 2008). Like task-specific self-efficacy measures, adherence self-efficacy measures should be designed hierarchically, with the frequency and duration remaining unchanged

but with progressive increments in the time frame in which the activity is to be performed (e.g., next 1 month, 2 month, 3 month, and so on). We identified two scales (see table 22.1, p. 298) designed to measure adherence self-efficacy.

Scale Construction

Bandura (1977, 2006) has been forthright in explicating how efficacy scales should be constructed. The recommended approach is to assess each item on a 100-point percentage scale comprising 10-point increments ranging from 0%, or "Not at all confident," to 100%, or "Completely confident." These item scores are aggregated and divided by the total number of items to arrive at a single efficacy score ranging from 0 to 100. In essence, this approach assesses what Bandura terms *strength of self-efficacy* (Bandura, 1977). Earlier derivations of this approach had the respondents first check whether they believed they could execute each item. If they checked "Yes," they completed the confidence ratings. This aspect of measurement was referred to as the *level* of self-efficacy, whereas the confidence ratings were reflective of the *strength* of self-efficacy. However, most contemporary measures of self-efficacy rely solely on the latter aspect of measurement.

There has been concern that respondents do not understand the 100% confidence rating scales, which has prompted researchers to construct simple Likert-type scales ranging from 1 to 5 (e.g., Dwyer, Allison, & Makin, 1998) or from 1 to 10 (e.g., Blanchard et al., 2002). These approaches do not appear to have any significant effect on how self-efficacy is associated with hypothesized outcomes, although to our knowledge no psychometric tests have been conducted to directly compare the methods. One final issue for consideration reflects the wording of self-efficacy measures. As defined, self-efficacy reflects people's confidence in their beliefs that they can successfully execute a course of behavior (Bandura, 1977). Thus, items should be worded accordingly, with stems such as, "I believe that I am capable of. . . ." Items that use statements such as "I think . . ." or "I am . . ." or that assess the perceived ease or difficulty of an activity do not accurately capture the self-efficacy construct (Bandura, 1997).

Psychometric Properties

Traditionally, the internal consistency of a self-efficacy measure has been the primary indicator of the scale's reliability. The majority of exercise self-efficacy scales have excellent internal consistency. In particular, well-constructed measures of adherence self-efficacy and task-specific self-efficacy report coefficient alphas of ≥.90 (e.g., McAuley, 1993), in large part because they follow very similar formats. The barriers self-efficacy scales also show good internal consistencies, although the range (coefficient alpha of .54-.97) is more variable due to differing lengths and compositions of this type of scale.

Construct validity is, of course, an ongoing process. For the scales reviewed here, we have inferred support for construct validity as evidence that the self-efficacy measure is associated with physical activity behavior and other theoretically appropriate variables such as affective responses, functional performance, and well-being.

Evidence for Support: Examples From the Literature

SCT proposes that self-efficacy plays a role in human health at two different levels (Bandura, 1992, 1997). The first level is the basic biological level. Evidence has shown that individuals with higher levels of self-efficacy tend to have higher levels of health status and functioning, whereas the opposite is true for individuals with lower levels of self-efficacy (Bandura, 2000). The second level is concerned with health habits and progression of biological aging (Bandura, 2000). People's beliefs in their efficacy to regulate their own motivation and behavior influence their decisions to participate in healthy habits such as physical activity. Thus, self-efficacy acts as a determinant that regulates motivation (e.g., adopting an exercise program), affect (e.g., depression, mood responses to acute or long-term physical activity), health status and functioning (e.g., quality of life, activities of daily living), and behavior (e.g., exercise adherence and maintenance). Thus, exercise self-efficacy is expected to be associated with these outcomes (Bandura, 2000). Additionally, because the relationship between physical activity and self-efficacy is reciprocal, self-efficacy should influence physical activity participation just as physical activity participation should influence self-efficacy (McAuley & Blissmer, 2000). In the following sections, we briefly discuss the relationships between the three categories of self-efficacy measures and the exercise-related outcomes.

Barriers Self-Efficacy

It is beyond the scope of this chapter to provide a comprehensive review of all the support for the barriers self-efficacy construct. Therefore, we have elected to focus on several examples that testify to the relationship between this construct and exercise-related outcomes. Numerous cross-sectional

studies have supported the relationship between barriers self-efficacy and exercise behavior. For example, individuals with higher barriers efficacy report engaging in more physical activity, and this relationship appears to be consistent across various intensities (e.g., moderate, vigorous), modes (e.g., walking, jogging, resistance training), and measurement approaches (e.g., accelerometer, self-report) of physical activity (Allison, Dwyer, & Makin, 1999; Motl, Snook, McAuley, & Gliottoni, 2006; Oliver & Cronan, 2005). McAuley, Jerome, Elavsky, Marquez, & Ramsey (2003) provided longitudinal evidence that higher barriers self-efficacy at the end of a 6 month exercise intervention is associated with greater physical activity levels at 6 and 18 month postintervention. Importantly, this relationship held when controlling for previous exercise behavior. Given that individuals leaving structured or organized programs to become active on their own face an additional set of barriers, targeting strategies for overcoming these barriers should be considered an important aspect of exercise trials.

Unsurprisingly, the majority of support for the construct validity of barriers self-efficacy measures comes from studies of exercise behavior. However, other studies have demonstrated significant associations between barriers self-efficacy and exercise-related outcomes. For example, in a recent study of survivors of breast cancer (Rogers, McAuley, Courneya, & Verhulst, 2008), women with higher self-efficacy to overcome exercise barriers also reported greater physical activity enjoyment and lower levels of fatigue. In a study of women who were obese and initiating a physical activity program, Annesi (2007) found that changes in barriers self-efficacy significantly predicted weight loss. In all likelihood, task-specific or adherence self-efficacy measures may be more appropriate to examine such relationships, given that we might expect a dose–response relationship between exercise and outcomes such as affect and physiological status. However, it is not unremarkable that barriers self-efficacy is also related to such outcomes, as these scales often share common variance with other exercise efficacy measures.

Task-Specific Self-Efficacy

Bandura (1986) noted the primacy of task-specific measures over more general measures of efficacy, given the malleable nature of these cognitions. Self-efficacy is specific to domains of functioning. Thus, Maddux (1995) argued that the assessment of task efficacy can be useful when examining the potential performance of exercise-related activities that require specific skills or have specific demands.

Task-specific efficacy scales have proved quite useful in examining theoretical associations between self-efficacy and outcomes associated with exercise. One particularly useful area to establish the validity of these efficacy measures has been the examination of the relationship between self-efficacy and affect (Bozoian, Rejeski, & McAuley, 1994; Jerome et al., 2002; Treasure et al., 1998). SCT (Bandura, 1986) suggests that a more positive sense of self-efficacy is associated with improved affective states. To test this experimentally, McAuley and colleagues (Jerome et al., 2002; Marquez, Jerome, McAuley, Snook, & Canaklisova, 2002; McAuley et al., 1999) manipulated exercise-related self-efficacy in a series of studies by providing false feedback based on physiological testing. Participants randomized into a high-efficacy condition reported more positive well-being and reduced levels of psychological distress and fatigue during a single bout of activity than their low-efficacious counterparts reported (McAuley et al., 1999). In a subsequent follow-up study, Marquez and colleagues (2002) reported similar associations relative to state anxiety. In addition, Jerome and coworkers (2002) replicated, in large part, the findings of McAuley and colleagues in a sample of white and Latina women.

Task-specific self-efficacy has also been shown to be associated with health, as evidenced by its relationship to quality of life, physical functioning, and cognitive functioning (White, Wójcicki, & McAuley, 2009; McAuley, Morris, Doerksen, et al., 2007; Elavsky et al., 2005). Typical correlations in this area are in the moderate range. Exercise self-efficacy is viewed as a mediator in the relationship between changes in physical activity and changes in health variables. The positive relationship between exercise and health status and functioning has been exhibited in older adults (McAuley, Morris, Doerksen, et al., 2007) and in populations with chronic disease (Motl, Snook, McAuley, Scott, & Gliottoni, 2007; Rogers et al., 2006). For example, Rogers and colleagues (2006) examined the task-specific exercise beliefs regarding walking briskly, running or jogging, climbing stairs, and exercising to specifically increase heart rate and breathing in a sample of patients with breast cancer currently undergoing treatment. In general, strength of self-efficacy for these activities was low to moderate, and participants reported being more confident in their ability to walk and climb stairs than to jog or run.

Finally, changes in task-specific self-efficacy have been shown to be related to changes in specific behaviors. McAuley, Courneya, and Lettunich (1991) conducted a study examining the effects of acute and long-term exercise participation on self-efficacy for successful completion of incremental units of sit-ups, cycling, and walking or jogging in older adults. Self-efficacy was assessed before and immediately after an acute bout of activity (e.g., a graded exercise test) both before and after a 20 wk intervention. This approach allowed the researchers to examine the effects of two sources of mastery experiences on self-efficacy: the acute bout and the cumulative 20 wk intervention. The data demonstrated significant main effects for time for each of the task-specific measures, suggesting that the mastery experiences gained as a result of active participation in the intervention influenced future task-specific efficacy beliefs. Importantly, this work highlighted gender differences, with females reporting significantly less efficacy than males reported before and after the preintervention acute bout. However, the 20 wk exposure to organized activity resulted in the women becoming as efficacious as the men before and after the postintervention acute bout.

Taken in total, these findings suggest that task-specific measures of self-efficacy are significantly associated with changes in the behavior of interest. In addition, these measures are significantly associated with psychological outcomes of exercise participation.

Adherence Self-Efficacy

There is considerable evidence to support the construct validity of the measures developed to assess adherence and maintenance of physical activity. Adherence self-efficacy has been shown to be reciprocally related to physical activity participation (Marquez & McAuley, 2006; Morris, McAuley, & Motl, 2008) and to adherence to an exercise intervention: Individuals who have higher levels of adherence self-efficacy exhibit higher levels of physical activity and greater session attendance (McAuley, Motl, et al., 2007; Morris et al., 2008), and individuals with higher levels of adherence exhibit higher levels of adherence self-efficacy (McAuley, Jerome, Marquez, Elavsky, & Blissmer, 2003). However, this is not to suggest that the relationship between exercise participation and self-efficacy is always positive. A study by McAuley and colleagues (McAuley, Morris, Motl, et al., 2007) found that during a 6 month exercise intervention, adherence self-efficacy actually decreased. Although this finding may seem counterintuitive, it is important to consider that when individuals leave a highly structured exercise program to embark on their own exercise regimen, an initial attenuation of efficacy expectations may be expected. Given that adherence self-efficacy is associated with postintervention exercise behavior independent of other factors such as fitness and program adherence (McAuley, 1993), it appears prudent to structure interventions (e.g., taper the level of supervision) to facilitate a strong sense of adherence self-efficacy for long-term maintenance of physical activity.

Adherence self-efficacy has also been shown to be related to an array of physical activity outcomes. In a number of cases, this has been done by incorporating the self-efficacy construct into models of function, quality of life, and self-esteem. For example, the exercise and self-esteem model (EXSEM; Sonstroem, Harlow, & Josephs, 1994) posits that the effects that physical activity factors have on subdomains of self-esteem work largely through self-efficacy. However, there is some dispute as to whether self-efficacy acts in a parallel fashion to influence self-esteem (Elavsky & McAuley, 2007; McAuley, Elavsky, Motl, et al., 2005). Nevertheless, it appears that self-efficacy is implicated in the formation of esteem. Adherence self-efficacy has also been shown to be both directly and indirectly related to global quality of life through its relationship to physical health status, mental health status, and functional limitations in older adults as well as in individuals with multiple sclerosis (Elavsky et al., 2005; McAuley, Konopack, Morris, et al., 2006; Motl, McAuley, & Snook, 2007; Motl & Snook, 2008; White et al., 2009). Additionally, adherence self-efficacy has been shown to be directly related to positive well-being (McAuley, Elavsky, Jerome, Konopack, & Marquez, 2005), functional performance (Konopack et al., 2008), and functional limitations (Motl & McAuley, 2009a, 2009b) and indirectly related to fatigue (Motl & McAuley, 2009b).

Thus, there is consistent and relatively strong evidence to suggest that the measures of exercise efficacy identified here demonstrate adequate psychometric properties. That is, these self-efficacy measures are associated with elements of physical activity behavior, such as adherence, and outcomes associated with physical activity participation, such as well-being, functional performance and limitation, and quality of life.

Further Issues

As the central active agent in SCT (Bandura, 1986), self-efficacy has received considerable attention as a consistent correlate of physical activity and the outcomes associated with physical activity. However, some issues regarding the measurement of exercise-related self-efficacy need to be considered. These include the proliferation of self-efficacy measures, the use of single-item scales, and the confusion of other self-related constructs with self-efficacy.

McAuley and Mihalko (1998) posed the question of "why are there so many self-efficacy measures?" In spite of employing considerably stricter inclusion criteria than McAuley and Mihalko employed in their review, we still identified 26 measures in our review. In particular we found a considerable number of scales assessing barriers self-efficacy (see table 22.1). Given that the items that make up most barriers to self-efficacy scales demonstrate considerable overlap across scales and, in all probability, could be applied across populations, we see little need for the development of more scales to assess this construct in the general population. There may, however, be a need to expand existing measures to accommodate special populations (see our subsequent recommendations).

Measures of task-related self-efficacy are an exception to this rule as different tasks require different measures, although some measures will retain predictive qualities across tasks. As self-efficacy is a situation-specific construct, having a single generic or global scale to assess any element of self-efficacy is erroneous. Indeed, some researchers (Chen, Gully, & Eden, 2001; Schwarzer & Jerusalem, 1995; Sherer et al., 1982) have attempted to develop general self-efficacy measures, but such measures have shown little consistency in their relationships with health and behavioral outcomes. Additionally, the nature of the scale used is driven by the outcome in question. That is, if the primary outcome is increasing the number of steps taken within a day across a set number of days, item content should reflect the target behavior (e.g., 10,000 steps per day) and gradations of this goal (e.g., 2,000, 4,000, 6,000, and 8,000 steps). Additionally, researchers must be circumspect in how they expect to see change in efficacy across time. For example, an older individual who attends a walking program 3 days a week at the local mall may demonstrate significant improvements in self-efficacy for walking increasingly longer durations but may show little, if any, change in barriers self-efficacy. The importance of carefully considering the nature of exercise studies or interventions and employing appropriate measures of self-efficacy cannot be overstated.

Although excluded from this review, there are numerous single-item scales assessing exercise self-efficacy (e.g., Clark, Patrick, Grembowski, & Durham, 1995; Demark-Wahnefried, Peterson, McBride, Lipkus, & Clipp, 2000; Grembowski et al., 1993). These are formulated as statements such as, "How confident would you be to stick to a regular exercise program?" Using single-item scales is a practice that we strongly recommend against. For example, using only a few items to assess barriers self-efficacy restricts the possible range of exercise barriers that might prevent exercise participation. Similarly, using a single item to assess task or adherence self-efficacy is imprudent, as such practice fails to take into consideration the hierarchical measurement structure recommended by Bandura (1977, 2006).

The exercise and health psychology literature is burgeoning with applications of self-related constructs to understand and explain health behaviors (Bandura, 1997, 2004). This has led to researchers confusing constructs such as self-esteem, self-confidence, and perceived behavioral control with self-efficacy. For example, global self-esteem and self-confidence are broader constructs spanning an array of domains, whereas self-efficacy is concerned with a person's confidence to be successful in specific contexts (Bandura, 1986, 1997). As such, these constructs are relatively stable in contrast to self-efficacy, which can wax and wane with successes and failures. Even assessing esteem at the domain level (e.g., physical self-worth) is still not isomorphic with assessing self-efficacy, although there is certainly variability at this level. This is a practice that may have been occurring inadvertently with use of the Physical Self-Efficacy Scale (PSES; Ryckman, Robbins, Thornton, & Cantrell, 1982). This scale has been used heavily in the literature as a measure of self-efficacy, although the item content, particularly of the perceived physical ability (PPA) scale, appears to more closely reflect the self-evaluative component of self-esteem (Feltz, 1994). To address this issue, Hu, McAuley, and Elavsky (2005) conducted a multi-trait, multi-method analysis of four data sets. They concluded that the PPA converges with measures of physical self-esteem rather than measures of self-efficacy, thus calling into question the veracity of using this measure to assess physical self-efficacy.

Perceived behavioral control (PBC; Ajzen, 1985) is another construct that is often used as a proxy for self-efficacy. Conceptually, however, the two constructs differ in that PBC (Ajzen & Madden, 1986) is defined as the individual's perception of how easy or difficult it will be to execute a behavior. As noted previously, self-efficacy reflects people's beliefs in their capabilities to carry out a given behavior effectively and successfully. Thus, a person may perceive a task to be difficult (thereby demonstrating low perceived behavioral control) but have moderate to high efficacy for carrying out that task. Armitage and Connor (1999) have provided empirical data to support the conclusion that, at best, these two constructs are weakly to moderately correlated with each other and that each construct makes a unique contribution in predicting behavior (Armitage & Conner, 2001).

Recommendations for Researchers and Practitioners

There are four important areas of recommendations to consider. First, at this juncture, the development of new measures of exercise self-efficacy is not prudent. There are already a number of well-validated measures of barriers self-efficacy, many with significant overlap in item content. Having said this, there are some situations in which the development of new measures may be warranted. For example, there is increasing interest in applying social cognitive models and in particular the self-efficacy construct to special populations who may be facing unique barriers to exercise (e.g., individuals with multiple sclerosis, survivors of stroke, and so on). Although many of the common exercise barriers likely are relevant to these populations, the addition of items reflecting special circumstances may prove useful in accurately predicting behavior. Such an approach reflects the situation-specific nature of self-efficacy. In addition, there are certainly instances in which developing new measures for task-specific physical activity behaviors may be appropriate. We recommend that developers adhere to the guidelines for self-efficacy measurement outlined by Bandura (2006). That is, task-specific measures should be hierarchical to reflect gradations of challenge, and the response scale should include multiple options (e.g., a 100-point scale for each item ranging from 0 to 100 in 10-point increments) to bolster sensitivity and reliability. Employing single-item measures of exercise self-efficacy is not recommended.

Although self-efficacy is considered the primary active agent in SCT (Bandura, 1986, 1997), it is proposed to have both direct and indirect influence on behavior. The indirect pathways may operate through a number of social cognitive constructs, including outcome expectations, goals, and facilitators and impediments to behavioral performance (Bandura, 2004). Rarely, however, have researchers tested the full social cognitive model, and examining the extent to which the different types of self-efficacy influence behavior through the theoretical pathways proposed is needed. Exceptions to this include Rovniak, Anderson, Winett, and Stephens (2002) and Anderson, Wojcik, Winett, and Williams (2006). An additional concern with applying the full social cognitive model is the lack of reliable and valid measures that accurately reflect model constructs other than self-efficacy. To this end, Wójcicki, White, and McAuley (2009) recently developed a multidimensional outcome expectations scale that assesses physical, self-evaluative, and social outcome expectations, as proposed by Bandura (1997). Determining whether exercise-related self-efficacy influences physical activity in different ways through the different outcome expectations is warranted.

Finally, researchers should continue to explore the meditational role that self-efficacy plays in explaining the effects of physical activity and exercise participation on health-related outcomes such as functional limitations and disability, quality of life, affect, and fatigue. McAuley, Konopack, Motl, and colleagues (2006) have argued that these outcomes reflect more distal effects of exercise and physical activity participation and that self-efficacy is a more proximal outcome. Thus, the pathway from physical activity to, for example, global quality of life encompasses self-efficacy and health status as mediators of this relationship. Initial evidence for such a position has been encouraging (McAuley et al., 2008; McAuley, Morris, Doerksen, et al., 2007), although replication and extension of these findings are necessary. The importance of this recommendation lies in the fact that self-efficacy is a modifiable construct. As such, the exercise or physical activity experience can be tailored to provide experiences that enhance self-efficacy and, in turn, outcomes such as quality of life.

The judicious use of reliable and valid self-efficacy measures has considerable application for exercise and health care practitioners. For example, assessing the self-efficacy of participants and patients entering a program is essentially an assessment of psychological readiness to face up to the challenges and barriers that are no small difficulties for individuals who may be sedentary or facing a long and possibly painful rehabilitation. Having this initial gauge of what participants think they are capable of allows the practitioner to structure the planned exercise programs and regimens effectively. This assessment also serves another purpose in that it provides the individual with a baseline level of efficacy to monitor while progressing through the program. We might caution, however, that our experience in conducting randomized controlled trials suggests that efficacy expectations are often overestimated on entry into a program (McAuley et al., 2011). Whether this is a reflection of being buoyed by optimism or simply wanting to please exercise leaders is not known. Thus, we recommend that self-efficacy be reevaluated after a few weeks to determine more accurately what individuals believe

they are capable of and that program requirements are adjusted accordingly.

Additionally, practitioners can use estimations of self-efficacy to design strategies for overcoming specific barriers that may be prevalent in participant responses. Such strategies may include providing alternative solutions to overcoming barriers or creating exercise environments that minimize the perception of the barrier. Further strategies include using the primary sources of efficacy information to enhance the efficacy-building approach to the exercise experience. As noted earlier, these sources include focusing on the provision and identification of mastery experiences, targeting appropriate modeling, building elements of social persuasion within the exercise content, and teaching participants to interpret the physiological and psychological responses to the exercise experience. Periodic measurement of self-efficacy can be tied back to individual progress and serve as a source of information for establishing future exercise goals or making adjustments to current goals and plans. Self-efficacy measures can also be a useful method for monitoring the effectiveness and success of the overall exercise program and informing practitioners on how effective their programs are at increasing self-efficacy and potentially leading to long-term behavior change.

As noted, these recommendations are not limited to individuals who work in exercise-related settings with predominantly healthy individuals. We strongly believe that the suggestions offered here have considerable utility for rehabilitation specialists (e.g., cardiac rehabilitation staff members, physical and occupational therapists), who deal on a daily basis with a client population facing considerable challenges in the quest to return to good health. Indeed, self-efficacy may play a particularly potent role in behavior change in such populations, as efficacy expectations are better predictors of behavior in more challenging situations. Regardless of the domain in which they are utilized, validated exercise self-efficacy measures can be very useful resources for helping practitioners to better understand and meet the needs of their clients by developing strategies to improve and monitor confidence levels over time.

Acknowledgments

This chapter was prepared with the support of grants 5R57 AG025667, 2R01 AG020118, and 1F31 AG034025 from the National Institute on Aging and a Shahid and Ann Carlson Khan Professorship in Applied Health Sciences.

Measures Assessing Self-Efficacy Related to Physical Activity and Exercise

Measure	Dimensions and subscales	Source[*]	Internal consistency
BARRIERS SELF-EFFICACY			
Self-Efficacy for Physical Activity	One: Common barriers	Armstrong, Sallis, Hovell, & Hofstetter (1993)	NR
Self-Efficacy to Regulate Exercise	One: Common barriers	Bandura (2006)	NR
Exercise Barriers Self-Efficacy	One: Common barriers for cardiac rehabilitation patients	Blanchard, Rodgers, Courneya, Daub, & Knapik (2002)	.86
Scheduling Self-Efficacy Scale	One: Common barriers	DuCharme & Brawley (1995)	.89-.90
Physical Activity Self-Efficacy Scale	Two: External barriers and internal barriers	Dwyer, Allison, & Makin (1998)	.83-.89
Physical Activity Self-Efficacy	One: Barriers to aerobic exercise	Edmundson et al. (1996)	.67
Self-Efficacy for Exercise Questionnaire	One: Common barriers	Garcia & King (1991)	.90
Cardiac Exercise Self-Efficacy Instrument	One: Barriers to cardiac exercise	Hickey, Owen, & Froman (1992)	.90
5-Item Self-Efficacy Questionnaire	One: Common barriers	Marcus, Selby, Niaura, & Rossi (1992)	.82
Barriers Self-Efficacy Scale	One: Common barriers	McAuley (1992)	.88
8-Item Questionnaire for Adolescent Girls	One: Common barriers	Motl et al. (2000)	NR
Self-Efficacy for Exercise Scale	Two: Self-efficacy (barriers) and response efficacy (outcomes)	Plotnikoff & Higginbotham (2002)	.80-.91
Self-Efficacy for Exercise Scale	One: Common barriers	Resnick & Jenkins (2000)	.92
Barriers Self-Efficacy Scale	One: Barriers for cancer patients	Rogers et al. (2006)	.96

Scale	Subscales	Source	Reliability
Self-Efficacy for Exercise Behavior	Two: Resisting relapse and making time for exercise	Sallis, Pinski, Grossman, Patterson, & Nader (1988)	.83
Self-Efficacy: Confidence in Ability to be Physically Active	Three: Support seeking, barriers, and positive alternatives	Saunders et al. (1997)	.54-.71
Exercise Self-Efficacy Scale (modified for Korean adults)	Three: Situational/interpersonal, competing demands, and Internal feelings	Shin, Jang, & Pender (2001)	.94
Tai Chi Exercise Self-Efficacy	One: Barriers to Tai Chi	Taylor-Piliae & Froelicher (2004)	.95-.97
Child Physical Activity Self-Efficacy	One: Common barriers for children	Trost et al. (2003)	.85
ADHERENCE SELF-EFFICACY			
Self-Efficacy for Exercise Scale (modified)	One: Continued exercise participation	Duncan & McAuley (1993)	NR
Exercise Self-Efficacy Scale	One: Continued exercise participation	McAuley (1993)	NR
TASK-SPECIFIC SELF-EFFICACY			
Physical Activity Efficacy for Cardiac Patients	Six: Lifting, jogging, walking, climbing, sex, push-ups	Ewart & Taylor (1985)	NR
Self-Efficacy for Walking/Jogging; Bicycling; Sit-Ups	Three: Sit-ups, Bicycling, Walking/jogging	McAuley, Courneya, & Lettunich (1991)	.80
Task Self-Efficacy Scale	One: Aerobic activity	Rogers et al. (2006)	.89
Self-Efficacy for Running Duration	One: Running duration	Rudolph & McAuley (1996)	.95
Tai Chi Exercise Self-Efficacy	One: Tai Chi duration	Taylor-Piliae & Froelicher (2004)	.95-.97

NR = not reported in original source.

*Please refer to reference list in the chapter for full citations.

Self-Efficacy and Collective Efficacy

Lori Dithurbide, PhD, and Deborah L. Feltz, PhD

The self-efficacy construct is a well-studied cognitive variable related to achievement strivings in sport (Feltz, Short, & Sullivan, 2008). Since the first publication on the self-efficacy construct (and its collective efficacy extension) in 1977 (Bandura), there have been more than 300 research articles published on self- and collective efficacy related to sport and motor performance. This research supports the important place that efficacy beliefs have in influencing sport performance (Moritz, Feltz, Fahrback, & Mack, 2000). Given the powerful predictive value of these beliefs to sport performance, the importance of how these beliefs are measured and used to study cognition in sport cannot be underestimated. In this chapter, we define the terms *self-efficacy* and *collective efficacy*, provide the theoretical framework within which they fit, describe the main tools for their measurement, and provide recommendations for researchers.

Definitions

Researchers have used different terms to describe the cognitive process by which people make judgments about their capabilities to accomplish a particular goal in sport or physical activity (Feltz & Chase, 1998). We have used the terms *self-confidence* and *self-efficacy* interchangeably to describe a person's perceived capability to accomplish a certain level of performance (Feltz, Short, et al., 2008). Others have employed *sport confidence* (Vealey, 1986) to measure the belief that a person has, more broadly, to perform successfully in a sport context. Because the collective extension of self-efficacy—collective efficacy—has its own set of definitions, we discuss the two efficacies separately in this chapter.

Self-Efficacy

Bandura (1997) defined *self-efficacy* as the "beliefs in one's capabilities to organize and execute the courses of action required to produce given attainments" (p. 3). Efficacy beliefs are not about the levels of ability that individuals or teams possess; rather, they are what people believe they can do with their abilities at any given circumstance (Bandura, 1997). These beliefs vary along three dimensions: level, strength, and generality (Bandura). Level, or magnitude, of self-efficacy refers to an athlete's achievement of a task at different levels of difficulty. Strength refers to the athlete's certainty in achieving each level of performance. Generality, although rarely studied in the sport arena (e.g., Samuels & Gibb, 2002), refers to the transferability of an athlete's efficacy beliefs across different tasks or even different sports.

Sport confidence is the degree of certainty individuals possess about their ability to be successful in sport (Vealey, 1986). Sport confidence is conceptualized as having both trait and state components, but it is still based on athletes' beliefs about what they can do to be successful, and thus it is still considered within the efficacy belief family (Feltz, Short, et al., 2008). However, review of the sport confidence concept and measurement is beyond the scope of this chapter.

Collective Efficacy

In a number of sports, athletes compete as members of teams, rather than as individuals, who work together toward a collective goal. An individual's perception of the team's capacity to accomplish a certain goal may have an underlying effect on the team's performance as a whole. Zaccaro, Blair, Peterson, and Zananis (1995) have stated that whereas self-efficacy expresses beliefs about how well individuals can organize their psychological and physical abilities to accomplish a task, collective efficacy reflects a group member's beliefs of how well the group as a whole can assemble and coordinate its collective resources. For example, a group of all-stars who are playing on the same team but are playing only for their own purposes may quickly diminish any sense of collective efficacy. The definition of collective efficacy cited most often is that of Bandura (1997), who defined *collective efficacy* as "a group's shared belief in its conjoint capability to organize and execute the courses of action required to produce given levels of attainment" (p. 477). This definition is a group-level attribute regarding the team's ability rather than the sum of the group members' personal efficacies. The level of collective efficacy has an effect on what a team chooses to do, how much effort the team instills into a task, and how persistent the team is (Bandura, 1997).

Coaching Efficacy

One of the most important factors contributing to an athlete's or team's sense of efficacy is the coach, as a coach can significantly affect an athlete's or team's motivation and performance. Feltz, Chase, Moritz, and Sullivan (1999) defined *coaching efficacy* as the extent to which coaches believe they have the ability to affect the learning and performance of their athletes and teams. However, as with sport confidence, a review of coaching efficacy and its measurement is beyond the scope of this chapter and is not addressed further.

Theoretical and Conceptual Framework

Efficacy beliefs are the core of social cognitive theory (SCT). In SCT, human behavior is defined as a triadic, dynamic, and reciprocal interaction of personal factors, behavior, and the environment (Bandura, 1986). According to this theory, an individual's behavior is uniquely determined by each of these three factors (Bandura, 1986). SCT hypothesizes that individuals take a proactive approach to their own behavioral outcomes and can help make things happen by the actions they choose to perform. Additionally, individuals possess self-beliefs that allow them to control their thoughts, feelings, and actions, and this in turn controls how they behave (Bandura, 1986).

Efficacy beliefs should not be confused with outcome expectations or beliefs. Whereas efficacy beliefs are the beliefs that a person has about being able to perform certain behaviors successfully, outcome expectations are the beliefs that certain behaviors will lead to certain outcomes (Bandura, 1977). In other words, outcome beliefs concern a person's environment and efficacy beliefs concern a person's competencies.

Efficacy judgments are the result of a complex process of self- or team appraisal and persuasion that is dependent on varying sources of efficacy information (Bandura, 1990). These varying sources include past performance accomplishments or mastery experiences, vicarious experiences, verbal persuasion, physiological states, and imaginal states (Bandura, 1977, 1997; Maddux, 1995).

■ *Mastery Experiences.* Of all the sources, mastery experiences are the most influential because they present the most realistic evidence of whether individuals or teams can succeed. If people have succeeded in the past, they are more likely to believe they can succeed in the future (Bandura, 1977, 1986, 1997). Whereas success can build a sense of efficacy, failure can undermine it.

■ *Vicarious Experiences.* The efficacy beliefs of individual athletes or teams can be influenced by observing other individuals or teams perform, evaluating their performance, and then using the cognitive information gained to make judgments regarding their own efforts (Maddux, 1995). These vicarious experiences occur through modeled achievements. So, in turn, modeling serves as an effective tool for promoting a sense of efficacy. When athletes observe others who are successful, especially others who share similar personal characteristics, abilities, and competencies, their efficacy beliefs will increase (Bandura, 1997).

■ *Verbal Persuasion.* Persuasive methods, whether pep talks from parents, coaches, or peers; evaluative feedback from a manager; or an individual's self-talk, can also influence efficacy beliefs. These methods can also include information from spectators and the media (George & Feltz, 1995). Verbal persuasion is probably used the most widely due to its ease and its availability (Bandura, 1977; 1986); however, verbal sources are theorized to be less influential than those based on an individual's own performance (Bandura, 1997).

■ *Emotional and Physiological States.* Physiological and affective states also affect efficacy beliefs. Physiological information, such as increased HR, increased sweating, and tensed muscles, can be perceived as both positive and negative. When individuals become aware of unpleasant physiological arousal, they are more likely to doubt themselves and to decrease their sense of efficacy

(Bandura, 1986, 1997). More specifically, in activities demanding strength and stamina, individuals tend to read their fatigue, windedness, aches, and pains as indicators of physical inefficacy (Bandura, 1997).

This bodes the same for emotional states and reactions. Emotional states, or moods, provide an additional source of efficacy, as they often accompany changes in quality of functioning (Bandura, 1977, 1997). Individuals are also more likely to have an increased sense of efficacy about their performance when their affect is positive (e.g., happiness, exhilaration, calmness) than when it is negative (e.g., sadness, anxiety, depression; Maddux, 1995).

■ *Imaginal States.* Although Bandura (1997) refers to imaginal experiences as a form of self-modeling, Maddux (1995) argues that imaginal experiences can be considered as a separate source of efficacy information. Athletes who continuously imagine themselves failing are likely to have lower efficacy beliefs that can in turn lead to poor performance. On the other hand, athletes who imagine themselves winning against an opponent may experience a rise in efficacy judgments. This has been shown in past research examining imagery and efficacy beliefs in an endurance task (Feltz & Riessinger, 1990).

These sources of efficacy beliefs rarely operate independently. For example, people not only experience their own performances and efforts but also observe the performances and efforts of others. How information sources are specifically weighted and judged regarding tasks, situations, and abilities is still unknown. However, the outcomes of these judgments determine how motivated people are, which activities they choose, how much effort they put into reaching their goals, and how they persevere when facing obstacles (Bandura, 1997).

The relationship between efficacy sources and performance outcomes is not a simple direct relationship. For example, mastery experiences influence efficacy beliefs, which in turn influence a performance that becomes another mastery experience. Consequently, the relationship between mastery attempts and efficacy beliefs can be considered temporally recursive. Bandura (1977, 1986, 1997) has stated that efficacy beliefs are a determinant of behavior only when individuals have enough reason to act on their perception of efficacy and when individuals possess the right skills and abilities to perform. People who have the right skills and abilities to perform at their potential but have no incentive to do so could have efficacy beliefs that exceed their actual performance. In contrast, people who have a high level of efficacy beliefs to perform

at a certain level may not possess the right skills and abilities to do so. These discrepancies between efficacy beliefs and performance also occur when tasks or situations are novel and unknown, such as when a person is first learning a new activity.

Sources of Collective Efficacy Information

Collective efficacy is rooted in self-efficacy, which means that team members consider the individual beliefs of their teammates when judging their collective capabilities (Bandura, 1997). Most collective efficacy sources of information are very similar to self-efficacy sources but occur at the group level. Mastery experiences are based on the team's performances, vicarious experiences involve the social comparison of another similar team, persuasive methods are directed to the group as a whole, and physiological and affective states reflect the state of the entire team. Furthermore, because self-efficacy and collective efficacy are so closely related, levels of collective efficacy can theoretically be influenced indirectly by the sources informing the self-efficacy of each team member (Feltz, Short, et al., 2008).

However, groups possess different structures and processes than individuals possess, and this holds true in the sport arena. Zaccaro and colleagues (1995) hypothesized that group size is related to collective efficacy. They stated that in general smaller teams have an increased likelihood to coordinate their behaviors when compared with larger teams. On the other hand, larger teams may have an extended pool of resources when compared with smaller teams. Some researchers argue that the more resources a team possesses, the greater likelihood the team has of succeeding.

Zaccaro and colleagues (1995) also suggested that the leadership process may influence a team's collective efficacy beliefs. Leaders may influence collective efficacy beliefs through modeling, encouragement, persuasion, feedback, and enhancement of team functioning (Chow & Feltz, 2008). Leaders who positively encourage their team, provide constructive feedback, and model confidence are more likely to have a team with an increased sense of collective efficacy.

A variable related to leadership is the motivational climate that a coach sets for the team (Feltz, Short, et al., 2008). Athlete perceptions of the motivational climate (mastery or performance) set by the coach represent the goal structures the athletes believe are being emphasized by the coach (Magyar, Feltz, & Simpson, 2004). In a mastery climate, positive reinforcement is provided to athletes on the basis of hard work, improvement, and good team-work. In a performance climate, coaches emphasize punishment for mistakes and poor performance and promote competition among team members. Magyar, Feltz, and Simpson investigated perceived motivational climate at the team level as a source of collective efficacy beliefs in rowing teams. They found that the more that teams perceived their coach to be emphasizing a mastery climate focused on learning, improving, and working together, the greater their collective beliefs in the team's ability to row successfully.

Group cohesion has been argued to be a source of collective efficacy in addition to collective efficacy being a mediator in the cohesion–performance relationship (Heuzé, Raimbault, & Fontayne, 2006; Zaccaro et al., 1995). It is hypothesized that the more cohesive a team is, the greater the sense of collective efficacy a team has. On the other hand, being successful is hypothesized to reinforce collective efficacy beliefs, and these beliefs affect the cohesiveness of the team (Chow & Feltz, 2008). Past research has shown that group cohesion positively influences collective efficacy beliefs in interdependent teams; however, this has not been examined in teams lacking interdependence (Kozub & McDonnell, 2000; Paskevich, Brawley, Dorsch, & Widmeyer, 1999).

An additional correlate unique to collective efficacy may be the length of time a team has been together (Feltz, Short, et al., 2008). Newly formed teams do not serendipitously form a sense of collective efficacy, whether negative or positive. Collective efficacy beliefs need time to develop; teams need to have shared experiences in order to form collective efficacy beliefs.

Dimensions and Sources of Confusion in Self-Efficacy and Collective Efficacy

The concept of self-efficacy is widely used in multiple research arenas, including sport. However, the nature of efficacy beliefs is highly dependent on the specific research question being examined (Feltz, Short, et al., 2008). Multiple forms of efficacy beliefs have been applied to the sport arena. The following sections present some of the commonly used types of efficacy beliefs applied to sport.

Task Self-Efficacy

Maddux (1995) has defined *task self-efficacy* as a person's perceived capability to perform a simple motor act. However, in the sport psychology field,

where tasks can be complex, task self-efficacy may be used to study an individual's beliefs regarding particular tasks (such as hitting a slice backhand in tennis) that vary in degrees of difficulty depending on the individual's sport or expertise (Feltz, Short, et al., 2008). Task-based beliefs may also be applied to teams.

Self-Regulatory Efficacy

Self-regulatory efficacy involves a person's beliefs in personal or team capabilities to exercise influence over barriers and impediments, thought processes, emotional states, and patterns of behavior (Bandura, 1997). Self-regulatory efficacy may be examined in sport by studying, for example, an individual's beliefs in following an off-season training regimen or an individual's beliefs in being able to manage a competitive, training, and educational schedule in collegiate sport.

Ameliorative and Coping Efficacy

Ameliorative efficacy is referred to by Bandura (1997) as the perceived ability to manage perceived threats. Ameliorative efficacy is also often referred to as *coping efficacy*. This type of efficacy can be examined in sport by studying athletes' beliefs in controlling negative thoughts and feelings toward their performance and how these beliefs affect subsequent performance.

Preparatory Efficacy

Preparatory efficacy involves the beliefs about a task or competition that a person holds during the preparation phase (Feltz & Wood, 2009). It does *not* involve the beliefs that people have in their ability to prepare. Bandura (1997) suggests that in the preparatory phase of competition, some self-doubt may be necessary to motivate the person to put forth the effort in practicing the task in question Thus, ultimately, greater preparatory effort should lead to stronger competitive performance because of greater effort in practice. However, too much self-doubt can become unnecessary stress and impede practice (Feltz & Wood, 2009).

Competitive Efficacy

Feltz and Chase (1998) define competitive efficacy as the beliefs people have in their ability to compete successfully against opponents. This type of efficacy can be studied in sport by examining an athlete's beliefs regarding the ability to beat various opponents or teams in various aspects of competition. As with all efficacy measures, competitive efficacy is not a single-item assessment but assesses multiple aspects of competition.

Related Constructs for Measuring Self-Efficacy

Although there are many types of efficacy, even just in sport-related research, there are other similar yet distinct constructs that are also used in sport research. Table 23.1 (Feltz, Short, et al., 2008) compares self-efficacy and other related constructs in sport research. Some of these other constructs, such as sport confidence, are also goal striving (Vealey, 1986), while some, such as self-esteem, are related to the self but do not necessarily measure a person's abilities in goal-striving contexts. For an in-depth discussion of how these constructs are similar to and different from self-efficacy beliefs, see Feltz, Short, and colleagues (2008).

Collective Efficacy

Because the construct of collective efficacy stems from self-efficacy, dimensions and sources of confusion in self-efficacy can also be related to the group form of efficacy. In addition, collective efficacy has its own intricacies. These are discussed in the following paragraphs.

When examining the sport performances of athletes or teams, the first inclination is to assess their physical capabilities. The majority of sport-specific collective efficacy measures used in previous research (see the Collective Efficacy Examples section on page 261) have focused solely on the physical requirements of the sport. However, the ability to perform successfully does not rely solely on physical capabilities. A team's effort, persistence, and teamwork may contribute to overall success. Bandura (1997) has argued that efficacy beliefs include different types of abilities, such as thought, emotional, motivational, and behavioral management. Short, Sullivan, and Feltz (2005) constructed a generalized collective efficacy measure (the Collective Efficacy Questionnaire for Sports, or CEQS) that assesses five dimensions of collective efficacy, including preparation, effort, persistence, unity, and ability.

Team potency is defined by Shea and Guzzo (1987) as a "collective belief of a group that it can be effective" (p. 335). Team potency has also been described as a general group attribute, whereas collective efficacy is more situation specific. Stajkovic, Lee, and Nyberg (2009) pointed out that in the past, authors often used collective efficacy and group potency interchangeably (Shea & Guzzo, 1987), hardly acknowledged team potency (Bandura, 1997), or explicitly differentiated between the two (Gully, Incalcaterra, Joshi, & Beaubien, 2002). Like collective efficacy, group potency has been found to have a positive relationship with group performance. For a more detailed comparison of the two constructs, see the meta-analytical review by Stajkovic and colleagues (2009).

Zaccaro and colleagues (1995) defined *collective efficacy* as "a sense of collective competence shared among members when allocating, coordinating, and integrating their resources as successful, concerted response to specific situational demands" (p. 309). Zaccaro and colleagues emphasized the coordination, interaction, and integration components of collective efficacy, whereas Bandura (1997) emphasized the *perceptions* of a team's capabilities to perform a task to account for the coordination and interaction within teams. Researchers such as Heuze and colleagues (2006) and Paskevich and colleagues (1999) have interpreted this definition to mean that athletes should rate their team's collective efficacy beliefs and not their own individual beliefs in their team's abilities (Myers & Feltz, 2007). This particular method suggests that the individual athlete acts as an informant of the team's collective efficacy beliefs (Moritz & Watson, 1998). Myers and Feltz recommended, however, that researchers aggregate the individual responses of team members to collective efficacy items that are preceded by the stem that asks an individual to assess the team's confidence in its capabilities because individuals are better able to assess their own beliefs, when compared with the group's beliefs, about the group's abilities. They argued that a group is an inanimate social system that cannot have beliefs.

Collective efficacy is a group-level construct that most of the time is derived from individual perceptions. These individual perceptions are often aggregated to represent a group-level assessment. This results in a multilevel method of analysis. Perceptions at the individual level are aggregated to a higher-level construct where the mean of the individual responses is used to represent the collective interpretation (Rousseau, 1985). This process may occur when perceptual consensus has been demonstrated within the individual responses (James, 1982). However, Moritz and Watson (1998) noted that by focusing solely on the aggregated means, the researcher dismisses the within-team variability and the lack of independence; the independence of responses is assumed in statistical processes. Raudenbush and Bryk (2002) added that analyzing data at only the group level may result in loss of power, inefficient estimation of fixed effects when using unequal group sizes, and difficulty in interpreting the amount of variance explained by group-level predictors.

Comparisons of Self-Efficacy and Related Constructs in Sport

Construct	Description	Goal-striving context	Sample item in sport
Self-efficacy	Belief in being able to organize and execute a course of action to reach a specific goal	Yes	How "confident" are you that you can kick a soccer goal in a penalty kick against this goaltender?
Sport confidence (Vealey, 1986)	Degree of certainty about the ability to be successful in sport	Yes	Compared with the most confident athlete you know, how confident are you that you can perform under pressure?
Self-confidence from Competitive State Anxiety Index-2 (CSAI-2; Martens, Vealey, & Burton, 1990)	Belief in being able to perform successfully in competition	Yes	In this competition, I'm confident I can meet the challenge.
Perceived competence and perceived ability	Belief in personal ability in a certain domain or across a set of behaviors that develops as a result of cumulative interactions with the environment	Yes	How likely do you feel that you are better than others your age at sports?
Outcome expectancy	Belief that a certain behavior will lead to a certain outcome	Yes	How confident are you that the goals you score will lead to approval from your coach?
Self-concept	Self-description profile, whether global or domain specific, formed through evaluative experiences and interactions with the social environment	No	I am athletic.
Self-esteem	Global or domain-specific judgment of self-worth and feelings of self-satisfaction	No	On the whole, I am satisfied with myself as an athlete.
Level of aspiration	Estimation of a given level of task-specific performance before attempting the task	Yes	How many targets will you hit in the next trial?
Locus of control	Global or specific expectancy that outcomes are within personal control or determined by external forces	Yes	Winning this event is under my control.
Sport confidence from Carolina Sport Confidence Inventory (CSCI) (Manzo, Silva, & Mink, 2001)	Dispositional belief that incorporates perceived optimism and competence in sport	Yes	I feel that if something can go right for me during sports, it will. (optimism) In the company of my peers, I feel that I am always one of the best when it comes to joining sport activities. (competence)

Reprinted, by permission, from D.L. Feltz, S.E. Short, and P.J. Sullivan, 2008, *Self-efficacy in sport: Research and strategies for working with athletes, teams, and coaches* (Champaign, IL: Human Kinetics), 25-26

Guidelines for Constructing Self-Efficacy and Collective Efficacy Scales

Although years of sport research have indicated a robust positive relationship between efficacy and performance across sports and physical task domains (Moritz et al., 2000), the methods and measurement of self-efficacy beliefs have not been consistent. Because most general measures of efficacy beliefs do not specify the activities performed or the conditions under which those activities must be performed, Bandura (2006) recommends using efficacy belief measures that are specific to particular domains of functioning. Most measures that have been used in sport are domain specific and constructed by the authors specifically for their study. Unfortunately some researchers have used other established measures of similar constructs (e.g., self-esteem, global self-confidence) to describe and assess self-efficacy beliefs in athletes. Consequently, this section outlines the recommendations of Feltz, Short, and colleagues (2008) for constructing self-efficacy measures that are based on Bandura's (2006) guidelines. In addition, this section briefly describes the different approaches used in past research and highlights the unique approaches used in the measurement of collective efficacy.

Feltz, Short, and colleagues (2008) summarized Bandura's (1997, 2006) most pertinent efficacy measurement guidelines specific to sport-related research. The first guideline, and likely the most important of the guidelines, involves the *domain specification*, which refers to the specificity of the situation in which efficacy beliefs are being assessed. Generally there are three levels of domain specification (Bandura, 1997). Measures that assess beliefs regarding a particular performance under a certain set of conditions are the most specific. An example is assessing a hockey player's self-efficacy beliefs in taking a penalty shot against a certain goaltender in sudden-death overtime during a tie game. A less specific measure might assess self-efficacy beliefs in taking penalty shots at various points and under various conditions during the game. These measures assess beliefs in performance for a certain activity (ice hockey) under certain conditions (penalty shot situations) that have common properties (the mechanics and mental focus are common in penalty shots, regardless of the goaltender). Lastly, the third level of domain specification is the most general measure. This measure does not specify the activity or the condition under which the activity is performed. A sample item might be "How confident

are you that you can be mentally ready to perform successfully in your sport?"

Task-linked efficacy scales are more predictive of specific behavior because individuals are likely to vary in their efficacy beliefs across the different task demands in their respective sport. For example, a basketball player may have a high level of self-efficacy in her ability to shoot free throws but may have a low level of self-efficacy in her ability to slam-dunk the ball. In their meta-analysis of self-efficacy and performance in sport, Moritz and colleagues (2000) found that even when using a validated general sport confidence measure (e.g., Vealey's 1986 Sport Confidence Inventory or Martens, Vealey, and Burton's 1990 Competitive State Anxiety Index-2) with the stem "In your sport," sport- and task-specific efficacy measures were more predictive of performance behavior than the generalized sport confidence measures were. Consequently, Feltz, Short, and coworkers (2008) recommended that scales be tailored to the level of specificity that matches the performance specificity of interest.

Second, in constructing efficacy measures, researchers and practitioners should develop items through a conceptual and contextual analysis (Feltz, Short, et al., 2008). These analyses may include interviews or consultations with experts in the field to help produce a list of subskills necessary to perform the task in question and other situational demands regarding this particular task. An example of this is Feltz and Lirgg's (1998) benchmark collective efficacy study conducted with ice hockey teams. The authors consulted with collegiate ice hockey coaches to determine what areas within the sport were deemed the most important for measuring players' self- and collective efficacy beliefs.

Bandura (2006) also recommended that all items be piloted and that items displaying ceiling or floor effects be discarded. Ceiling effects seem to be more of a problem among athletes (Feltz, Short, et al., 2008). Thus, another solution to the ceiling effect is to increase the difficulty of the task in the particular item to increase the challenge while still remaining realistic. In addition to including enough gradations of challenges, measures should include multiple items in order to incorporate all sport or task components (Feltz, Short, et al., 2008).

Another recommendation based on Bandura's guidelines and put forth by Feltz, Short, and colleagues (2008) concerns *content relevance*. Earlier in this chapter, we differentiated between efficacy expectations ("I can") and outcome expectations ("I will"). Items in an efficacy measure should be written in terms of "can do" to properly assess efficacy beliefs. Another issue related to this recommendation is using the term *efficacy scales* to describe scales that may not be measuring efficacy. An example of this is the Physical Self-Efficacy Scale (PSES; Ryckman, Robbins, Thornton, & Cantrell, 1982). Feltz and Chase (1998) argued that this scale resembles more of a self-concept measure than a self-efficacy measure. In fact, Hu, McAuley, and Elavsky (2005) provided empirical support for this argument. Items from the PSES are worded as "I have" and "I am," whereas efficacy scales should be worded as "I can."

The next step in constructing an efficacy scale is to determine the proper *response scale*. Typically, athletes are asked whether, and to what degree, they believe they *can* accomplish the task in question. If they believe they can (the level of efficacy), then they rate their degree of certainty (the strength of efficacy). Athletes can rate their degree of certainty along a continuum, or rating scale, ranging from 0 to 10 (or 0 to 100 in increments of 10); a rating of 0 indicates that the athlete does *not* believe he can perform the task. To obtain a measurement of efficacy strength, the scores across items athletes believe they can accomplish are summed, and then this sum is divided by the number of performance items (Bandura, Adams, & Beyer, 1977). The level of efficacy is simply the number of items to which the participant answered anything but 0. Most researchers examining efficacy beliefs in sport have relied solely on strength measurements or on both level and strength scores (Feltz, Short, et al., 2008; see Feltz & Lirgg, 2001).

There has been debate over the number of response categories, or width, of the rating scale. Bandura (2006) argued that the 11-point scale (0-10) is more sensitive and reliable than scales using fewer categories. On the other hand, Myers and Feltz (2007) noted that fewer response categories may be more practical and may increase measurement stability and accuracy, especially when used in SEM. In pre- and postintervention studies, where participants become familiar with the response categories, the 11-point scale may be more sensitive to changes that occur during the intervention.

Like any measurement scale, efficacy scales should have face validity—that is, they should measure what they are hypothesized to measure. For example, if a researcher wishes to study the running efficacy and performance of sprinters, the efficacy scale should not focus on running endurance. Efficacy measures should also have construct validity. For nonhierarchical scales, factor analysis should be used to measure the homogeneity of the items; if these results indicate multiple dimensions, the data should be analyzed accordingly.

Lastly, the items of efficacy scales should be written in a way that is suitable to the reading abilities of the participants and should include the appropriate sport-related terms (Bandura, 2006). Pilot testing should be conducted with participants who are similar to the study participants to ensure that there are no ambiguities or problem items.

Types of Scales

There are two types of scales that have been constructed in sport psychology research: hierarchical and nonhierarchical scales. The choice of which scale to use depends on the focus of the research question. For instance, a researcher interested in the self-regulatory efficacy of athletes to maintain a particular training regimen could assess the level and strength of maintaining the regimen over different lengths of time (a hierarchical scale). Or, the researcher could assess the athletes' beliefs toward overcoming different types of challenges or impediments to adhering to the regimen (a nonhierarchical scale).

Hierarchical Scales

Most commonly used in earlier efficacy research, hierarchical scales list tasks in a hierarchical fashion according to difficulty, usually beginning with the easiest task. For example, a hierarchical scale might range from making a putt 1 out of 10 times to making the putt 10 out of 10 times. Hierarchical scales can also be used in endurance tasks, where time is increased in each item. Because the items in hierarchical scales are the same except for the degree of difficulty, factor analysis and internal reliability need not be computed (Feltz, Short, et al., 2008).

Nonhierarchical Scales

As mentioned earlier, nonhierarchical scales, which may not have items ranging in difficulty for a single task, should be analyzed conceptually and contextually and pilot tested to ensure the adequacy and applicability of the measures. These items must be challenging but realistic in order to avoid floor or ceiling effects. It is also important to report the internal reliabilities of these scales because past internal reliabilities cannot be assumed to remain the same with all samples (Feltz, Short, et al., 2008).

When employing nonhierarchical scales, a researcher can sum the strength of each item and divide the sum by the number of items to get an average strength score, or the researcher can use a microanalytical approach.[1] In this approach,

---

[1]Cervone (1985) suggested that a microanalytical approach is unnecessary with hierarchical scales.

advocated by Bandura (1986, 1997) as the strongest test of the relationship between efficacy belief and behavior, the researcher analyzes the congruence between efficacy belief and performance evaluation at the level of each item by computing a percentage of items in which belief matches performance. As Bandura (1977) noted, calculating the percentage match provides a more precise index of predictive accuracy than an aggregate correlation between efficacy and performance provides.

Measurement of Efficacy Beliefs Over Time

Measuring the contributions of efficacy beliefs over time requires special conditions and analyses. First, as Bandura and colleagues (Bandura, 1997; Bandura & Locke, 2003) have stated, a dynamic environment should be used to test the efficacy–performance relationship over time. The dynamic environment is preferred over the static environment because performance tends to stabilize when the environment stabilizes; in a stable environment, therefore, there is no reason to reevaluate efficacy beliefs. Second, a previous performance evaluation includes the previous efficacy beliefs in addition to other sociocognitive factors (Bandura, 1997; Bandura & Locke, 2003). In other words, when efficacy beliefs are assessed before the first performance attempt, the subsequent performance score represents a conglomerate index that includes those efficacy beliefs as well as other factors (Bandura, 1997). Unless this first efficacy assessment is partialled out of the variance in the first performance attempt, the predictive strength of the first performance on the second performance will be inflated (i.e., residualized performance; for self-efficacy examples, see Feltz, Chow, & Hepler, 2008; for collective efficacy examples, see Myers, Payment, & Feltz, 2004).

Guidelines Specific to Collective Efficacy

Collective efficacy can be measured in different ways depending on how the construct is defined (Feltz, Short, et al., 2008). First, the researcher can aggregate the team members' responses regarding their own individual capabilities of performing within their team. Second, the researcher can aggregate the team members' perceptions of the team's capabilities as a whole. These responses are still individual perceptions, but they are perceptions of the team's ability. Examples of both methods are provided by Feltz and Lirgg (1998), who asked ice hockey players to rate their individual abilities and their team's abilities in multiple aspects of performance. Research examining collective efficacy in sport has mostly used the second method, which

Bandura (1997) contended encompasses the coordinative and interactive influences that operate within the group. Bandura also contended that the team's interdependence determines the predictive strength of the method used. When additive teams, such as those in golf, gymnastics, and swimming, are assessed, the first method may have enough power to predict team performance. However, when highly interdependent teams, such as those in basketball, ice hockey, or volleyball, are assessed, the second method is a better predictor of performance (Feltz & Lirgg, 1998).

Third, some sport psychology researchers (e.g., Heuze et al., 2006; Paskevich et al., 1999) have used Zaccaro and colleagues' (1995) definition of collective efficacy, which emphasizes the coordination, interaction, and integration components of collective efficacy, to argue that individual teammates should rate *their team's beliefs* in its capabilities (i.e., the individual should act as an informant of the team) rather than rate *their own beliefs in their team's* capabilities (Myers & Feltz, 2007). Even though there is a discrepancy between definitions, subsequent research has shown no differences between the two, and both have been deemed adequate (Short et al., 2002).

A fourth method of measuring collective efficacy stems from the argument that teams should respond to measures as a group, providing one single answer for the team as a whole (Prussia & Kinicki, 1996). This particular approach has been used in sport psychology research (Bray, 2004; Moritz, 1998) and eliminates the need for agreement analyses and avoids potential aggregation issues. On the other hand, as Bandura (1997) noted, team members rarely are of one mind in their beliefs, and group decision making is subject to persuasion and conformity pressures. Lastly, this group discussion method may be highly impractical when conducting longitudinal field studies with real teams (Myers, Feltz, & Short, 2004). In the two studies using this method, one used groups of three participants in a controlled laboratory environment (Bray, 2004), and the other used only dyads (Moritz, 1998). These small teams and controlled environments may have minimized the impracticality of the method.

Regarding the level of analysis to use when analyzing collective efficacy, there is a concern in using only aggregated data because doing so dismisses the within-team variability and the lack of independence, that is, the assumption of independence in observations may be. In addition, analyzing data at the group level ignores potential effects that make interpreting the results problematic (Raudenbush & Bryk, 2002). Consequently, multilevel modeling

(MLM), or hierarchical linear modeling (HLM), is the optimal method for analyzing collective efficacy data (Myers & Feltz, 2007). MLM can also be used when performance measures or other independent or dependent variables are measured at the group level (e.g., Dithurbide, Sullivan, & Chow, 2009; Myers, Feltz, & Short, 2004; Myers, Payment, & Feltz, 2004). Although MLM software programs do not require that a certain consensus value be reached in order to proceed with multilevel analyses, reporting consensus is recommended for descriptive purposes and for explaining variance around an average team-level effect as a group-level variable within MLMs (Myers & Feltz, 2007).

Collective efficacy is a relatively new construct when compared with self-efficacy; however, several sport-specific collective efficacy measures have been used in sport psychological research. Measures of collective efficacy have been constructed for adventure racing teams (Edmonds, Tenenbaum, Kamata, & Johnson, 2009), basketball (Bray & Widmeyer, 2000; Heuze et al., 2006), bowling (Moritz, 1998), football (Myers, Feltz, & Short, 2004), ice hockey (Feltz & Lirgg, 1998), rowing (Magyar et al., 2004), rugby (Greenlees, Nunn, Graydon, & Maynard, 1999; Kozub & McDonnell, 2000), and volleyball (Paskevich et al., 1999).

In addition to these sport-specific measures, Short and colleagues (2005) developed the CEQS to measure collective efficacy beliefs across sports. A common measure is desirable in order to examine these beliefs across sports and compare these beliefs between sports. The CEQS represents collective efficacy as a multidimensional construct based on Bandura's (1997) argument that efficacy beliefs include beliefs not only concerning the physical task but also concerning the capability to manage thoughts, emotions, actions, and motivation. The CEQS is also conceptualized as a state measure in which beliefs are assessed on current capabilities.

For the CEQS, a five-factor structure was supported. The five subscales each contain 4 items, for a total of 20 items. The five subscales include ability or physical skill (e.g., playing more skillfully than the opponent), effort (e.g., playing to the team's capabilities), persistence (e.g., persisting in the face of failure), preparation (e.g., mentally preparing for competition), and unity (e.g., being united). Validity for the CEQS was shown in the initial paper (Short et al., 2005). Short and colleagues also stated that if the correlations between all five factors of the CEQS and the total score of the measure are statistically significant, the total score of the five subscales can be used to measure collective efficacy beliefs. However,

subsequent CFAs should be conducted to support the one-factor structure.

Examples From the Literature

In this section, we provide some examples of efficacy belief scales that have been used in research in sport psychology. These include hierarchical and non-hierarchical self-efficacy scales used in laboratory and field settings, as well as collective efficacy scales used with sport teams.

Self-Efficacy Examples

Examples of hierarchical self-efficacy scales are most common in earlier studies examining efficacy beliefs in leg endurance tasks. One of these is the study by Feltz and Riessinger (1990) that examined the effectiveness of in vivo emotive imagery and performance feedback on self-efficacy in a leg endurance task. Respondents were asked how confident they were that they could hold their leg up for a certain length of time. They were first asked to indicate whether they believed they could hold their leg up for the given length of time, and they were then asked to indicate their certainty (i.e., strength) on an 11-point Likert scale. Time increased in 30 s increments, beginning at 30 s and progressing to 5 min. The results of the study indicated that participants who used imagery had a significant increase in self-efficacy beliefs and had the longest endurance times.

Studies using true sport tasks and participants, as opposed to physical tasks in a laboratory, also use nonhierarchical scales. An example of a nonhierarchical self-efficacy scale is a study by Treasure, Monson, and Lox (1996), who examined self-efficacy, performance, and precompetitive affect in wrestling. The authors asked participants to rate their confidence for the following moves against an opponent: escape, get reversal, get back points, pin opponent, not get taken down, get takedown by throw, get takedown single leg, ride opponent, get takedown double leg, and not be pinned. Participants rated their certainty on an 11-point Likert scale. Results of this study indicated that self-efficacy beliefs were positively related to positive affect and negatively related to negative affect. Self-efficacy was also a predictor of wrestling performance, and self-efficacy was the only variable that differentiated between winners and losers.

Because most sport psychological studies have used hierarchical scales and thus have eliminated the need for congruence analysis, the microanalytical approach has not been common in the sport psychology literature. In fact, we are unaware of any published sport psychology studies that have used this approach. However, we provide a hypothetical example of such an approach using selected items from Chow and Feltz's (2008) study with track athletes on relay teams (see table 23.2).

Lastly, an example of the temporal approach is provided by Feltz and colleagues (2008) in their reanalysis of Feltz's (1982) original diving study data set. This reanalysis was conducted in order to compare the predictive validity of self-efficacy on performance in three different statistical models. These path analysis models included the use of raw past performance, residual past performance, and both residual past performance and residual self-efficacy. As mentioned earlier, Bandura (1997) has argued that residualizing past performance removes the previous contribution of self-efficacy that is embedded in past performance scores. Results of the reanalysis by Feltz and coworkers indicated that self-efficacy beliefs were a stronger predictor of diving performance in the residualized past performance model compared with the raw, unadjusted past performance model.

Collective Efficacy Examples

As mentioned earlier, several sport-specific measures have been developed to assess collective efficacy beliefs in sport. One of the first sport-specific collective efficacy measures was constructed to measure collective efficacy beliefs in ice hockey teams. Feltz and Lirgg developed this measure in 1998 and used it again years later in 2004 (Myers et al., 2004). They developed this measure in consultation with expert ice hockey coaches and used it to examine the relationships among team efficacy, player efficacy, and team performance in men's collegiate ice hockey. The authors conducted a meta-analysis (due

to the small number of participating teams) of the regression equations generated from each team's player efficacies and team efficacies across games. Results indicated that team efficacy was a better predictor of team performance than aggregated values of player efficacy were. Results also revealed that team efficacy significantly increased after a team win and significantly decreased after a team loss.

Using the same measure for female collegiate ice hockey teams, Myers and colleagues (2004) examined the reciprocal relationship between collective efficacy and team performance. Data collection was performed in instances where teams played the same opponent over 2 consecutive days. Results indicated that the level of collective efficacy moderately and positively influenced the team's performance for that same day when the previous day's performance was accounted for. The previous day's performance also had a small and positive effect on the next day's collective efficacy scores.

Edmonds, Tenenbaum, Kamata, and Johnson (2009) designed a collective efficacy measure to assess the relationship between collective efficacy and performance in adventure team racing. Teams ranged from 2 to 4 members, and each member assessed the team's confidence in its ability with respect to the performance areas of adventure racing—marathon and trekking, canoeing, mountain biking, climbing, and orienteering—at three different race checkpoints. The team was used as the unit of analysis, and results indicated a consistent and moderate relationship between collective efficacy and subsequent performance at each stage of the race.

Using a sport that is considered unitary additive according to Steiner's (1972) task typology,

■ Table 23.2 ■

Illustration of Congruence Scores on a Nonhierarchical Scale

Performance items	Efficacy scale (level)	Performance	
Track relay race items		Scale	Match
1. Accelerate off the start	Yes	Yes	x
2. Do not drop the baton	Yes	Yes	x
3. Use good running form	Yes	No	
4. Have a clean exchange	Yes	No	
5. Have a fast exchange	No	No	x
Score	4	2	3

Congruence = 3 / 5 × 100 = 60%.

Magyar and colleagues (2004) examined individual and boat-level determinants of collective efficacy among adolescent rowers. Each boat represented a team. The authors constructed self-efficacy and collective efficacy questionnaires, each with 22 items that represented four different sections of the race: warm-up, start, middle, and final sprint. The authors also included items related to coordination, communication, and motivation. The questionnaires had good internal reliabilities, but factor analyses were not performed to test for multidimensionality in the instruments. Using MLM, Magyar and colleagues found that task self-efficacy significantly predicted individual perceptions of collective efficacy, while perceptions of a mastery climate significantly predicted average collective efficacy scores at the boat level.

Lastly, Paskevich and coworkers (1999) developed a collective efficacy measure specific to volleyball to examine the relationship between group cohesion and collective efficacy. Items in the measure were determined through past collective efficacy research and through conceptual analysis with expert coaches and athletes. The task-related dimensions of cohesion were strongly correlated with collective efficacy beliefs in that athletes who perceived their team as having a high degree of cohesion also tended to perceive their team as having a higher level of collective efficacy.

Recommendations for Researchers and Practitioners

In this chapter, we have described the theoretical framework on which self-efficacy and collective efficacy measures are based, the various types of efficacy beliefs, the types of measures used, the scale structures used, and the guidelines for constructing these measures. As noted by Feltz, Short, and colleagues (2008), self-efficacy judgments appear to be most useful in explaining sport behavior and performance when measures have been constructed within the tenets of the theory (i.e., when proper incentives and requisite skills are present). Although we have made recommendations throughout the chapter, we make the following explicit recommendations here to help researchers to continue the advancement of self-efficacy and collective efficacy research. As most efficacy measures have been used for research purposes, practitioners should be careful when using such measures in applied or diagnostic work. We do not recommend that efficacy measures following Bandura's (2006) guidelines be used for diagnosing efficacy in athletes or teams.

First, we recommend that researchers examine the multidimensional aspects of sport performance. Bandura (1997) stated that a common mistake in self-efficacy sport research is the assessment of efficacy judgments on physical skills only. He contended that people judge their efficacy across the full range of task demands within a given domain (Feltz, Short, et al., 2008). Therefore, we recommend that self-efficacy also be measured through the evaluation of beliefs in strategy, decision making, and self-regulation, as there is more to success than physical skill.

Second, we recommend that researchers pay careful attention to the gradations of self-efficacy items before analysis in order to determine any ceiling or floor effects. As mentioned previously, hierarchical efficacy scales should include enough gradations so that the highest level is difficult and yet still realistic. When using nonhierarchical scales, researchers should conduct conceptual and contextual analyses to determine appropriate challenges in the performance task.

Third, just as the smallest of margins in time or distance separate Olympic medal winners from nonwinners, it may be the smallest of margins in self-efficacy beliefs that contribute to these performance accomplishments (Feltz, Short, et al., 2008). Therefore, we recommend that efficacy measures for elite athletes be constructed in such a way as to capture these fine differences. One possible way of doing so is to include more difficult efficacy items; however, these items should be pilot tested before data collection.

Fourth and last, as mentioned earlier, there is debate regarding the width of scales used in efficacy measures. We believe that the choice between a narrow (4- or 5-point) and a broader (11-point) scale should depend on the research question. However, if the intention is to measure change in efficacy beliefs, then an 11-point scale should be used in order to capture any change, be it small or large.

We have a few recommendations specific to collective efficacy. First, it has become more common, and is often required, for collective efficacy data to be analyzed at multiple levels. Because data are collected at the individual level, and these individuals are nested within teams, potentially within leagues, and so on, there is a lack of independence of the data. This lack of independence violates one of the main assumptions of inferential statistics. Therefore, along with Myers and Feltz (2007), who provided an in-depth critique of MLM in the assessment of collective efficacy in sport, we suggest that for most cases MLM is the optimal choice in analyzing collective efficacy data.

Our second recommendation concerns the choice of stem used in collective efficacy measures. Myers and Feltz (2007) noted that individuals are better able to assess their own beliefs regarding the team's abilities than to assess the group's beliefs about the team's abilities. Consequently, we support previous recommendations (Feltz, Short, et al., 2008; Myers & Feltz, 2007) to use "Rate your confidence in your team's capabilities" as the stem. In addition, this stem corresponds with Bandura's (1997) definition of collective efficacy beliefs.

Effort Perception

Selen Razon, MS, Jasmin Hutchinson, PhD, and Gershon Tenenbaum, PhD

Over the past 50 years, there has been growing clinical and practical interest in the conceptualization and measurement of what we have come to know as perceived exertion. The term *perceived exertion* is used in the first part of this chapter because of its widespread use in the literature. *Perceived effort* is used in the latter part of this chapter, as it is believed to be a better term to describe an array of related perceptions, of which exertion is only one. In this chapter, we review the historical and conceptual frameworks of perceived exertion and then present the measurement tools used to operationalize perceived exertion or effort and related symptoms. We begin with a detailed background of how this field of study started and then expanded. Next we review the design and validation processes of a number of perceived exertion scales. Then we introduce theoretical frameworks and important concepts, most of which originated from the disciplines of psychophysics, physiology, and psychology. In the second part of this chapter, we discuss challenges in perceived exertion measurement. We introduce the main measurement tools currently in use and describe the application of these to research and practice. We also present a multidimensional approach to the measurement of perceived effort.

Historical Perspective on Perceived Exertion

In the first part of this chapter we describe how the concept of effort perception was defined and conceptualized. As such, the psychophysiological (i.e., multidisciplinary) view of the term is discussed, and the need for a multidimensional measurement of effort is emphasized. From a biophysical standpoint, we first give an overview of a number of early attempts to quantify effort sensations including the earlier assessments of stimulus and terminal thresholds. A number of flaws (i.e., inconsistencies

associated with these initial biophysical measures) are discussed. Following, we introduce Borg's framework and the ways in which Borg's measures and scales attempted to circumvent the flaws associated with the early measures of efforts in biophysics. To move toward more inclusive approaches to effort measurement, we then present the central governor model (Saint-Clair & Lambert, 2005), which helped shift the definition of fatigue to include effort sensations (i.e., more than the physical manifestations only). We then discuss calibration methods to measure effort and help curb the subjectivity associated with the psychological components of effort. Following, models of psychobiological responses to exercise are brought up and the gate control theory of pain (Melzack & Wall, 1965) is introduced. Following the psychophysical and psychobiological frameworks, psychological models of effort perceptions including Tenenbaum's effort-related model (2001) are introduced as accompanied by a number of psychological constructs that are worthy of consideration in the conceptualization of effort (i.e., coping strategies, self-efficacy, and affect).

In the second part of this chapter we shift our attention to the measurement of perceived exertion. We discuss the difficulties inherent in measuring the rate of perceived exertion (RPE) by examining factors such as social influence, trait characteristics, and attention focus. Next, we review the reliability and validity of established RPE scales and newer scales designed for special populations. We conclude by offering evidence to support a proposed multidimensional approach to the measurement of RPE and providing detailed recommendations for researchers and practitioners in this area.

Background and Development

A psychophysiological term, *perceived exertion* has been given much attention since the early 1960s. Borg (1961a) was the first to define and measure perceived exertion, discussing it in his original studies on how individuals adjust to physical effort and exercise. Later, Borg (1962) defined *perceived exertion* as perceived fatigue, distinguishing between perceived force and perceived fatigue or exertion. Accordingly, Borg argued that perceived force is associated with short-term exercise, whereas perceived fatigue or exertion is largely associated with aerobic exercise that is of long duration. Experiences of effort, breathlessness, tiredness, muscle pain, and heat underpinned early conceptualizations of the term (Borg, 1998). In fact, drawing from a Gestalt view, Borg held *perceived exertion* as a rather psychological term incorporating all the sensations inherent in physical effort. We do not concur with this framework but instead draw on two major resources—Borg's original publications and Noble and Robertson's (1996) book on perceived exertion—to provide a review of the ways in which these views were presented to the field. Our view is that effort perceptions comprise differentiated perceptions, including exertion, fatigue, mood states, motivation, and additional sensations, that result in unique patterns of perception during the effort experience. Adequate measures of effort perception need to account for these distinct effort-related inputs that shape the perceptual exercise experience.

When dealing with perceived exertion, it is important to acknowledge that scientific interest in human sensations originally emanated from both psychology and physiology. Indeed, a subdiscipline of psychology, psychophysics, provided the initial methodological and validation foundations underlying the majority of current conceptual frameworks and scales (Noble & Robertson, 1996).

Effort Sensations in Psychophysics

As specified by Marks (1974), psychophysics is the field that links perceived sensations with given stimuli, addressing both as measurable quantities. Consistent with Marks' specification, classical psychophysicists such as Weber and Fechner attempted to answer questions of whether individuals can in fact identify the presence of or changes in a given sensory stimulus. Thus, scales equipped with 0 and final end points were developed. On these scales, the 0 points were termed the *stimulus threshold*, while the end points were termed the *terminal threshold*. It was, for instance, on the basis of these scales that the classical psychophysicists were able to determine the lowest and highest sound frequencies audible by the human ear. Additional thresholds of interest, including the *just noticeable difference* (jnd) and the *difference threshold* (DL), also received considerable attention from the classical psychophysicists. The

DL is the amount of change in the sensory stimulus required for the occurrence of a jnd in the human system (for review, see Noble & Robertson, 1996). According to Noble and Robertson, as early as 1834, Weber stipulated that the change in a perceptual stimulus produces a constant ratio of the original stimulus. Weber's law is expressed as $K = \Delta S \, / \, S$, where ΔS is the incremental change in a stimulus (S) required for the change to be detected and K is a constant. Later, in 1860, Fechner failed to prove Weber's law and its implied prediction of a linear relationship. To circumvent this problem, Fechner proposed that the ratio is not constant but grows with the logarithm of the perceptual stimulus. That is, as the stimulus increases, the response (R) increases logarithmically, so that $S = K\log R$. This method does not directly measure the perceptual response but instead measures the subject's understanding of perceptual response through *observation* of the change in the perceptual stimulus (the method was indirect). At that time, no direct approaches to measurement of human perceptions were deemed conceivable or even valuable.

In reference to modern psychophysics and its direct methodology, it is important to mention that Stevens (1957) introduced the concept of ratio methods into psychophysics. The relevance of ratio methods to the study of human perception lies in direct ratio assessments of perceptual sensations. As such, ratio scales are equipped with a point of absolute zero as well as with equal intervals that allow respondents to report their perceptions on a ratio scale. Addressing the same question that Fechner examined many years earlier, Stevens used direct scaling methods to propose that the magnitude of a subjective sensation increases proportionally to a power of the stimulus intensity. This became known as *Stevens' power law* and is expressed as *sensation* $= aI^b$, where I is the intensity, or power, of the perceptual sensation; a is the constant value relative to the specific sensory dimension; and b is the exponent of the power function (usually with a value of 1.7 for muscle force). Stevens (1974, 1989) relied on several studies measuring psychophysical functions for isometric force, in which the exponent ranged between 1.5 and 1.8. Others studying physical force and perception of muscle force reported a power of 1.6 (Borg, 1973a; Stevens & Mack, 1959). These inconsistent findings were the result of subjects making effort judgments rather than force judgments (Jones, 1986).

Borg Era

In the early 1960s, Gunnar Borg introduced a scale currently known as *Borg's rating of perceived exertion*

(RPE) scale (Borg, 1961b). Initially, the scale ranged from 0 to 20 points (a 21-point scale). As indicated by Noble and Robertson (1996), the scale was constructed with the explicit intent to provide perceptual data that were linearly related to HR and power output. However, the 21-point scale was not linearly associated with HR (Borg, 1961b). To address this deficiency, Borg designed a 15-point scale ranging from 6 to 20 (Borg, 1971). An additional aim embedded in Borg's original conceptualization was to use RPE responses to predict HRs. Thus, the 15-point scale was designed to parallel the HR range of a normal healthy male (60-200 beats/min). HR was predicted by multiplying an individual's RPE score by 10: $RPE \times 10 = HR$ (Borg, 1971). Even though the HR equation did not hold true, a number of studies confirmed the linear relationship between RPE and HR for the 15-point scale (Noble & Robertson, 1996). In their careful review, Noble and Robertson (1996) attributed Borg's accomplishment of linearity to a number of reasons. Among them were the reduction of categories from 21 to 15, the appropriate selection of verbal anchors (Gamberale, 1985), and the choice of well-defined and interindividually consistent (in terms of their meaning) terms (Borg, 1962).

In his early work, Borg defined his scale as a *rating scale* (Borg, 1961b), while later he defined it as a *category scale* (Borg, 1973a). Borg (1978) then asserted that his scale meets the criteria of an interval scale. Despite Borg's assertions, Gamberale (1985) reported that Borg's scale fails to meet the equal interval criterion, thus qualifying the scale as a rating scale. Borg's assertion of equal intervals was also proven false by Tenenbaum, Falk, and Bar-Or (2002) in their analysis comparing HR and RPE ratings. Nevertheless, Noble and Robertson (1996) stated that sufficient evidence exists to characterize the scale as a category scale.

Borg's initial attempt to develop a ratio scale was prompted by theoretical considerations (Borg, 1973b). Borg felt that a category scale lacked satisfactory metrical features. According to Noble and Roberson (1996), Borg sought to develop a scale that satisfied the psychophysical requirements of ratio scaling but was capable of generating interindividual comparisons. To achieve this, Borg combined Stevens' ratio scaling methods with those of category scaling, thus "using verbal expressions and numbers in a congruent way for determinations of direct levels on a ratio scale" (Borg, 2004, p. 1). The result was the CR10 scale (Borg, 1982), which has a primary numerical range of 0 to 10, with the first verbal anchor at 0.5. The upper anchor of "Extremely strong, maximal" is at 10, although there is no fixed upper end point. This gives the option to select a maximum intensity greater than 10 by using free magnitude estimation (see Borg, 1998). Occasionally, a more finely graded scale is needed, so Borg constructed the CR100 scale as a modification of the CR10 scale (see Borg, 2007). The CR10 scale satisfied the requirement for ratio properties and led to a strong correlation of .88 with HR. As noted by Noble and Robertson (1996), the scale also accounted for sensations of curvilinear physiological responses, including lactate production and pulmonary ventilation. Even so, the failure to meet the equal distance criterion between categories and the use of a number of unclear terms complicated the effective use of the scale. As concluded by Noble and Robertson (1996), the 15-point scale remains the scale of choice, especially when a direct relationship between power output and physiological variables is sought. Borg (1973b) also suggested using the 15-graded scale in most cases, due to its universality and ease of administration.

Modern Psychophysics

Psychophysical methods are purported to be "consistent, reproducible, quick, inexpensive, and convenient in assessing strain" (King & Finet, 2004, p. 412). They are built on the assumption that individuals can detect and integrate stimuli arising from biomechanical and physiological loads in order to provide a subjective evaluation of physical stresses. Psychophysical methods measure perception, which cannot otherwise be directly obtained, and also allow for quantitative task analysis and guidelines (Nussbaum & Lang, 2005). Thus, psychophysical methods provide an integrative measure in that they synthesize the many signals elicited from the working muscles, joints, and CNS (Borg, 2007). However, there is debate as to whether individuals make force judgments on the basis of afferent information arising from muscular, articular, and cutaneous receptors or judge some central variable related to the efferent motor command (Van Doren, 1996). Indeed, it has been suggested that RPE is not purely the result of afferent sensory feedback but instead is set at the beginning of the exercise bout as part of a feed-forward control mechanism.

Central Governor Model

Noakes, St. Clair-Gibson, and Lambert (2005) proposed the central governor model (CGM), which suggests that exercise is regulated by a complex system that integrates afferent sensory feedback with anticipatory feed-forward control in a process termed *teleoanticipation*. The integration of this information generates a conscious perception of effort (i.e., RPE), which regulates the extent of skeletal muscle activation during exercise in order to ensure that a potentially catastrophic failure of homeostasis does not occur (Noakes et al., 2005). The feed-forward component of central motor command subconsciously determines exercise intensity (pace) at the onset of exercise by recruiting the appropriate number of motor units in the active muscles. This pace is based on preexercise expectations of task duration and intensity as well as on other potential influences such as past experiences and the relative importance of the exercise bout. Feedback from organs that monitor the internal and external environment then modify the pace by altering the number of motor units recruited in the exercising limbs. Symptoms of fatigue progress in severity during exercise in order to ensure that the activity terminates within a predetermined and safe duration. Thus, the perception of exertion results from the interpretation of afferent sensations against an expected outcome. The CGM shifts the definition of *fatigue* from a physical event (i.e., a decline in the ability to produce power) to a sensation or emotion separate from an overt physical manifestation.

Support for the CGM comes from studies demonstrating that RPE rises as a linear function of the duration of exercise that remains (e.g., Noakes, 2004). As Tucker (2009) pointed out,

> if exercise was ultimately limited by the depletion of energy substrates, with no anticipatory component, then it would be expected that the RPE would increase rapidly only at the end of exercise when the muscle glycogen stores were approaching critically low levels. (p. 393)

This is not the case. In addition, Swart, Lamberts, Lambert, and colleagues (2009) observed that "regardless of its intensity or duration, the exercise bout always terminates at approximately the same (sub)maximal RPE levels, and before there is evidence for any failure of whole body or local homeostasis" (p. 782). The CGM also accounts for the underperformance of tasks for which athletes are provided with misleading feedback regarding exercise duration (e.g., Baden, McLean, Tucker, Noakes, & St. Clair Gibson, 2005), the effect of placebos (which must be mediated by a central process) on fatigue during prolonged (Clark, Hopkins, Hawley, & Burke, 2000) and short-term exercise (Beedie, Coleman, & Foad, 2007), and the characteristically observed end spurt that occurs when power output or running speed increases significantly during the final stages of self-paced trials (e.g., Marino, Lambert, & Noakes, 2004).

The CGM is not without its detractors; indeed, it has been the subject of much debate in the exercise physiology literature. Marcora (2008) suggested that the CGM is overly complex and argued that the conscious brain makes the decision of when to terminate exercise. Presenting a model based on motivational intensity theory, Marcora suggested that

> task disengagement (i.e., exhaustion) occurs when (a) the effort required by the constant-power test is equal to the maximum effort the subject is willing to exert to succeed in the exercise task or (b) when the subject believes to have exerted a true maximal effort and continuation of exercise is perceived as impossible. Within the limit set by B, an increase in A (the so-called potential motivation) will improve exercise tolerance. (p. 930).

Other counterarguments include the fact that physiological catastrophes can and do occur in athletes, which means that humans can override the central governor (Esteve-Lanao, Lucia, deKoning, & Foster, 2008). Also, numerous studies have demonstrated that exercise performance can be limited not only by motor unit recruitment but also by loss of contractile performance of the skeletal muscle itself (see Weir, Beck, Cramer, & Housh, 2006).

Calibration Methods

Psychophysical measures are inherently subjective and therefore are suspected to lack validity, which exists in direct measures such as force measurement and EMG. Psychophysical measures, however, can improve in precision with task-specific experience (see Marshall, Armstrong, & Ebersole, 2004). Recent efforts have been made to calibrate perceived sensations. For example, Spielholz (2006) measured participants' maximal voluntary contractions (MVCs) on two handgrip tasks and then asked the participants to perform the task at two RPE levels using Borg's CR10 scale. In other words, the participants were asked to "grip to a 2 on the scale" and then "grip to a 5" (a grip-to-scale procedure). Participants then performed another contraction, during which they were guided verbally by a researcher to 20% and then 50% MVC. At that point they were asked to stop and rate the exertion on the Borg CR10 scale (a guided-grip procedure). These data were used separately to define relationships between scale ratings and actual force application. In this way, the use of regression allowed the researchers to produce equations to calibrate the perceptual values and arrive at measures believed to be more valid and representative of the real physical load. In Spielholz's study, both procedures significantly reduced rating error on a subsequent power grip task. When not calibrated and adjusted to objective measures, *magnitude production techniques* (i.e., "squeeze to 40% of your maximal squeeze capacity") have been shown to yield inaccurate force estimates with low rates of repeatability (Lowe, 1995). For example, King and Finet (2004) provided evidence that using psychophysical methods of grip force measurement distorted the real force used in a handgrip task. Nussbaum and Lang (2005) found some relationships, but also inconsistencies, relating load acceptability, RPE, and relative joint demands posed by a static load.

Models of Psychobiological Responses to Exercise

The sensory link between subjective symptoms and physiological processes related to exercise was first described by Kinsman and Weiser (1976). Kinsman and Weiser's original four-level model was revised first by Pandolf (1982) and then by Noble and Robertson (1996) into a model with four levels of psychobiological responses. The first level of the model, or the *physiological substrata*, consists of several physiological mediators of the subjective symptoms of fatigue and exertion intolerance during exercise. At the second, or *subordinate*, level is the *perceptual-cognitive reference filter*. This filter encompasses a broad range of psychological and cognitive processes. These processes are not directly related to the underlying physiological substrata, and yet they systematically account for individual differences in perceptual responses during physical exercise (see Noble & Robertson, 1996). Also at the subordinate level are *discrete symptoms*. These encompass a range of exercise sensations such as sweating, panting, heart pounding, heavy and shaky legs, tiredness, drive, vigor, and determination. At the third, or *ordinate*, level, discrete symptoms are clustered into differentiated subcategories that represent mode-specific (i.e., *respiratory-metabolic* and *peripheral*) fatigue during exercise. The last, or *superordinate*, level is associated with *undifferentiated fatigue* and physical exhaustion. At this stage, the exerciser cannot identify specific sensations such as muscle aches and breathing but instead experiences extreme general fatigue and exhaustion (Tenenbaum, 2001). A major difference between the original Kinsman and Weiser (1976) model and the later adaptation by Noble and Robertson (1996) is the location of cognitive and psychological factors within the model. In the original model, these factors (task aversion and motivation) are located at the ordinate level of subjective report, just before the formation of undifferentiated fatigue. However, Noble and Robertson believed that these factors influence exertional sensations at all levels of subjective report. Their revised model reordered this sequence of sensory processing during exercise and combined the symptom clusters of task aversion and motivation into a single conceptual classification, the perceptual-cognitive reference filter, which is located at the subordinate level. This is an important distinction, because it accounts for the role of the filter in "modulating sensory signals as they travel from their physiological or neuromotor origins to conscious expression of both differentiated and undifferentiated exertional perceptions" (Noble & Robertson, 1996, p. 100). As just described, the perceptual-cognitive reference filter encompasses a wide range of psychological and cognitive processes, so it is also broader in scope compared with the factors in Kinsman and Weiser's model.

Gate Control Theory of Pain

Naturally occurring neuromuscular pain, especially in the limbs or chest, is frequently experienced during high-intensity or prolonged exercise (Robertson, 2004). The International Association for the Study of Pain (IASP) defines *pain* as "an unpleasant sensation and emotional experience associated with actual or potential tissue damage, or described in terms of such damage" (Merskey & Bogduk, 1994, p. 211). RPE and pain are two independent yet related constructs that develop more or less simultaneously during exercise. Both have strong underlying physiological and psychological dimensions. Thus, we can look to established psychophysical theories of pain to help us understand the experience of perceived exertion.

The first comprehensive theory of pain to account for the influence of psychological and cognitive factors in the perception of pain—gate control theory (GCT; Melzack & Wall, 1965)—proposed that signals from the brain stimulate neural gating circuits in the dorsal horns of the spinal cord. Neural circuits in return increase or decrease the flow of incoming nerve impulses to the CNS. The extent to which the neural gating circuits influence sensory transmission is thought to depend on the activity of A-beta fibers (large diameter), A-delta fibers, and C-fibers (small diameter) as well as on descending impulses from the brain. Accordingly, the theory holds that when the level of neural impulses flowing through the gate exceeds a given threshold, it activates those areas responsible for pain experience and pain response (Melzack & Wall, 1965). As a theory that does not conceptualize pain as merely an afferent sensory sensation (Melzack, 1973), GCT accounts for the possibility of controlling pain volitionally through the mediation of three psychological dimensions.

Tenenbaum and colleagues (1999) conceptualized perceived effort as being closely related to GCT and its three dimensions, which are as follows:

1. The *sensory-discriminative dimension*, which is associated with the location, quality, and intensity of the painful sensation

2. The *cognitive-evaluative dimension*, which is associated with the cognitive appraisal (e.g., the meaning) of the painful stimuli

3. The *motivational-affective dimension*, which is associated with the emotional reaction to the painful stimuli and the motivation to avoid any possible harm associated with these stimuli (Hutchinson & Tenenbaum, 2006; Melzack & Casey, 1968)

As such, the sensory-discriminative dimension involves the physiological aspect of the exertion experience, the cognitive-evaluative dimension involves the subjective interpretation of physiological inputs associated with perceived effort and exertion, and the motivational-affective dimension involves an extensive range of motivations and emotions associated with the discomfort state. The motivational-affective dimension of the exertion experience also accounts for task-related mental toughness, determination, and concentration in the face of exertion (Tenenbaum et al., 1999).

Psychological Models of Effort Symptoms and Perceptions

Most of the physiological processes related to perceptual signs of effort occur at an unconscious level. These include HR, oxygen consumption, blood pressure, and lactate accumulation. However, as the exercise intensity, task duration, and power output increase, more conscious attention is allocated to variables such as pulmonary ventilation and regional pain (Noble & Robertson, 1996). Perceived effort is also a psychological process determined by the interaction of several other mechanisms. Tenenbaum's (2001) effort-related model describes the psychological processes that guide the perception of effort and exertion in physical activity settings. Tenenbaum's model, which stems from the social cognitive theoretical perspective, postulates three categories of mediating factors external to perceived effort. The first category consists of the *physical load and duration* of the work, including the nature and extent of the activity. The second category includes the *environmental conditions*, such as the temperature, humidity, and specifics of the activity context. The third category comprises the *task characteristics*; that is, the unique requirements of the specific task (e.g.,

cycling, walking). The model also incorporates a set of internal factors mediating perceived effort. These include task familiarity, coping strategies, and self-regulations as well as social cognitive components representing motivational factors such as determination, commitment, perceived competence, self-efficacy, perceived and sustained effort, and readiness to invest effort.

Similarly to the physiological models of exertion that conceptualize the perceptual-cognitive reference filter, Tenenbaum's (2001) model conceptualizes psychological (i.e., cognitive) factors as important mediators of perceived effort and exertion. One important nuance, however, lies in the recognition of the limits associated with these factors at increased levels of exercise intensity. As hypothesized in models preceding Tenenbaum's, psychological factors are most influential when the physical task is of a submaximal nature and imposes low to moderate physiological demands (Rejeski, 1981). Beyond submaximal levels, however, "there is a point in the physical stress of exercise at which sensory cues, due to their strength, dominate perception. Under these conditions, it is unreasonable to expect mediation through psychological factors" (Rejeski, 1985, p. 372).

Related Constructs

Coping Strategies. An important determinant of perceived effort, coping strategies (e.g., self-regulation) involve an individual's attentional styles and strategies. The conceptualization of attentional strategies was initiated by Morgan and Pollock (1977). In a pioneering study, these authors examined the specific attention allocation of runners during marathon races. Two broad attentional strategies relative to exertional experiences emerged and were termed *association* and *dissociation* (Morgan & Pollock, 1977). In the domain of physical activity, the term *dissociation* does not have its common clinical connotation of psychopathology; rather, it refers to a division between cognitive processes and perception of somatic awareness that is under the individual's control. Associative and dissociative attentional strategies are internally and externally oriented, respectively. Associative strategies lead performers to shift their focus inward and toward physiological or bodily symptoms of exertion. Dissociative strategies, on the other hand, redirect the focus of attention outward and away from the bodily symptoms of exertion (Scott, Scott, Bedic, & Dowd, 1999). Dissociation of sensory input was shown to reduce the sensations of distress, often resulting in the enhancement of exertion tolerance (Morgan, Hortsman, Cymerman, & Stokes, 1993). The two strategies represent distinct cognitive approaches that indicate the extent to which exercisers allocate their attention to physiological feedback relative to perceived effort and exertion (Tenenbaum, 2005). Across low exercise intensities, attention can easily be switched back and forth between associative and dissociative styles. However, once the intensity becomes high enough, the focus of attention naturally shifts from dissociation to association, compromising the distracting capabilities of the dissociative focus (Hutchinson & Tenenbaum, 2007; Tenenbaum et al., 2004).

Self-Efficacy. Self-efficacy is the "belief in one's capabilities to organize and execute the courses of action required to produce given attainments" (Bandura, 1997, p. 3). In Tenenbaum's (2001) model, when people have adequate motivation to perform, their self-efficacy beliefs help determine exertion tolerance (Litt, 1988). Exercisers with high self-efficacy beliefs have been found to report less perceived exertion than others with low self-efficacy beliefs report (McAuley & Courneya, 1992). Recently, significant improvement of exertion tolerance to a handgrip protocol was observed among participants with increased self-efficacy beliefs (Hutchinson, Sherman, Martinovic, & Tenenbaum, 2008). In addition, self-efficacy cognitions have been found to correlate negatively with RPE in several studies (Hall, Ekkekakis, & Petruzzello, 2005; Pender, Bar-Or, Wilk, & Mitchell, 2002).

Affect. Engaging in exercise produces demands on the system that can result in considerable variations in affect. Affect refers broadly to the experience of feeling or emotion. As defined by Ekkekakis, Hall, and Petruzzello (2005), affect is the "experiential component of all valenced (i.e., 'good' or 'bad') responses, including emotions and moods" (p. 77). Ekkekakis (2003) developed a dual-mode model of exercise-induced affective responses that suggests that affective responses to exercise are determined by complex and multidimensional mechanisms. In the dual-mode model, particular emphasis is placed on the interaction of interoceptive cues such as respiratory and muscular signals and cognitive mediators such as physical self-efficacy and social physique anxiety. The equilibrium between these two groups of determinants is predicted to depend on exercise intensity; cognitive factors prevail at low exercise intensities, while interoceptive cues take over at high exercise intensities (Ekkekakis, 2003). When exercise intensities allow the preservation of a physiologically homeostatic state, homogenous pleasure responses result. Across high exercise intensities, the maintenance of physiological homeostasis is challenged, and, as

the physiological system approaches exhaustion, homogeneous displeasure results. Also stipulated by the model is that across intensities nearing the transition between aerobic and anaerobic metabolism, a divergence in affective response patterns may be observed. Specifically, around these limits, some people experience pleasure, while others experience displeasure. According to the model, response patterns exhibit this variability because the level of intermediate intensity involves a trade-off between the benefits (e.g., adaptational advantages resulting from performing more physical work) and the costs (e.g., increased risk for injury, cardiovascular complications, and immune problems) of exercise. The model and its assumptions were supported in a recent series of hypothesis-testing studies (Ekkekakis 2003, 2005; Ekkekakis & Lind, 2005). Main practical implications emanating from the model include the proposition that cognitive interventions will demonstrate limited effectiveness in helping beginner exercisers cope with exercise-related displeasure. As a result, practitioners are advised to teach exercisers skills for self-monitoring and self-regulating exercise intensity as an adjunct to cognitive coping techniques.

Measurement of Perceived Effort

The measurement of perceived effort is inherently difficult because the object of inquiry is internal to the participant and not directly observable to others. Thus, as with any self-report instrument, the measure is based on the assumption that people are able to evaluate and articulate their perceptions of effort accurately. A further compound to this problem is that participants are involved in physical activity when perceptions of effort occur, making recording them a challenging task. This problem is particularly salient during research based outside of the laboratory.

Outside of a laboratory setting, the social context in which perceptions occur requires consideration. An issue frequently encountered in RPE measurement is social influence. Self-presentation theory suggests that individuals try to present themselves in a socially desirable manner (Baumeister, 1982). In the case of perceived effort, this results in under-reporting of RPE in an attempt to appear physically strong or competent. Hardy, Hall, and Prestholdt (1986) found that males reported lower RPE when performing a cycling task in the presence of a coactor. This effect manifested particularly at moderate (50% maximal oxygen uptake, or $\dot{V}O_2$max) exercise intensities as opposed to hard (75%) or light (25%) intensities. Even in a tightly controlled laboratory environment, experimenter gender can influence RPE. Males have been shown to report significantly lower RPE in the presence of female experimenters compared with male experimenters. However, the reverse does not appear to be true, and females do not moderate their RPE in the presence of a male experimenter (Boutcher, Fleischer-Curtian, & Gines, 1988). It has been suggested that this effect is limited to the nonelite athlete or recreational exerciser. Sylva, Byrd, and Magnum (1990) found that RPEs of male and female track athletes were unaffected by the presence of a coactor (of either gender). Other situational factors shown to influence RPEs include expected duration (Baden et al., 2005), performance feedback (Nethery, 2002), verbal encouragement (Andreacci, Robertson, Goss, Randall, & Tessmer, 2004), state anxiety (Focht & Koltyn, 1999), and task-specific self-efficacy (Hutchinson et al., 2008).

An individual's disposition, or stable psychological characteristics, can also influence perceived effort. Morgan (1994) reported that extraversion is negatively related to RPE, a finding that Hall and coworkers (2005) confirmed at exercise intensities below and at the ventilatory threshold but not above the ventilatory threshold (i.e., high intensities). Evidence also suggests that effort perception varies with the age (Bar-Or, 1977) and sex-role typology (Hochstetler, Rejeski, & Best, 1985) of subjects.

Perhaps the most difficult issue facing researchers in this field relates to attentional focus. The process of assessing effort perceptions alters the performer's focus of attention. An associative attentional focus is required in order to appraise effort accurately, but associative cognitive strategies have been shown to increase RPE (e.g., Stanley, Pargman, & Tenenbaum, 2007). Thus, the very act of measurement can distort the measure. In this case, an individual's internal perception of effort might differ from the reported RPE (Rejeski, 1985). Such concerns are heightened when RPE is measured frequently (Corbett, Vance, Lomax, & Barwood, 2009) and when study designs seek a comparison between different attentional distractions. In addition, when the independent variable of interest is a factor hypothesized to influence perceived effort via attentional disruption (e.g., music), then the measurement of effort during the exercise bout may compromise the internal validity of the research. An alternative method of measurement that might circumvent this issue is obtaining retrospective measures of RPE. However, such measures may be unreliable and invalid. It is questionable whether individuals can recall with accuracy how hard they felt to be working during a previous exercise bout and even more so at various stages of a previous exercise bout. It is also thought that retrospective RPE measures are heavily influenced by cognitive appraisal (Hall et al., 2005) and retrospective recall bias.

Although the measurement of perceived effort presents unique challenges, the information that can be gathered from this measurement is invaluable. It is clear that perception of effort cannot be described in terms of physiological input alone. Perhaps a panel of experts on workload measurement phrased it best when they concluded the following: "If a person tells you that he is loaded and effortful, he is loaded and effortful, whatever the behavioral and performance measures may show" (Moray, 1979, p. 105). To this end, much effort has been directed toward developing tools and methods for measuring this complex phenomenon as consistently and accurately as possible (see table 24.1, p. 277).

Borg's Scales

Borg's 15-point scale (Borg, 1971) and CR10 scale (Borg, 1982) have been used in a multitude of experimental situations. In clinical diagnostics for perceived exertion, these scales have been used for symptom evaluation, pain, and so on (Borg, 2007). In the field of ergonomics, they have been used to evaluate perceived difficulty, effort, and other aspects of mental and physical workload (e.g., Finsen, Søgaard, Jensen, Borg, & Christensen, 2001). They have also been used in cardiac, pulmonary, and musculoskeletal rehabilitation settings and in sport and exercise settings, both as descriptive and as prescriptive measures. Both the ACSM (1998) and British Association of Sport and Exercise Sciences (BASES, 1997) endorse RPE scales as valid tools in the monitoring of intensity in exercise training programs. An exhaustive review of the many applications of Borg's RPE scales is outside the scope of this chapter (see Borg, 1998; Noble & Robertson, 1996).

Borg's scale has been shown to be an accurate and reliable instrument to measure exercise intensity in a number of investigations (e.g., Dunbar et al., 1992; Eston, Davies, & Williams, 1987; Eston & Williams, 1988) and across many modes of exercise (e.g., Marriott & Lamb, 1996; Ueda & Kurokawa, 1991, 1995; Walker, Lamb, & Marriott, 1996). The most relevant evidence of the validity of the RPE scale is criterion related. Criterion-related validity describes the empirical relationship between RPE and physiological measures that reflect exercise intensity more directly, such as HR, blood lactate concentration, and oxygen uptake (Chen, Fan, & Moe, 2002). These physiological variables, however, are confounded by potential psychological variables, which may undermine the relationship between RPE and physiological indicators of exercise intensity (Chen et al., 2002). See chapter 8 in Noble and Robertson (1996) for a review of psychological mediators of RPE.

Borg's 15-point RPE scale and CR10 scale have been studied to determine their reliability and validity. Research has concluded that both scales provide a valid assessment of perceived exertion. Test–retest reliability coefficients ranging from .71 to .91 indicate that the scales are also a reliable measure of perceived exertion (see Noble & Robertson, 1996). However, recent research has questioned the validity of Borg's scales. Chen and colleagues (2002) undertook a meta-analysis to determine the strength of the relationship between RPE scores and six physiological measures of physical exertion: HR, blood lactate concentration, percent maximal oxygen uptake (%$\dot{V}O_2$max), oxygen uptake ($\dot{V}O_2$), ventilation, and respiration rate. The weighted mean validity coefficients were .62 for HR, .57 for blood lactate, .64 for %$\dot{V}O_2$max, .63 for $\dot{V}O_2$, .61 for ventilation, and .72 for respiration rate. These findings suggested that although Borg's RPE scale is a valid measure of exercise intensity, its validity may not be as high as previously thought ($r = .80$- $.90$). The results of this meta-analysis also suggested that respiration rate is probably the best indicator of physical exertion. In addition, respiration rate is the only criterion measure that yields a higher mean validity coefficient when using *estimation mode* as opposed to *production mode*. Given that breaths can be counted easily by an observer and by the person doing the exercise, respiration rate may be the most reliable and valid measure of physical exertion in both research and clinical settings (Chen et al., 2002).

Since "correlation coefficients do not actually assess the level of agreement between repeated measures; instead, they quantify the degree of association (Lamb, Eston, & Corns, 1999) it is not yet known whether the RPE scale yields repeatable values when applied in a typical test–retest investigation" (p. 336). Lamb and colleagues proposed that the 95% limits of agreement technique is a more appropriate statistical approach. Using this method of analysis, they reported a test–retest variability of up to 3 RPE units (in either direction) across two identical multistage (incremental) treadmill running protocols. The 95% limits of agreement were found to widen as exercise intensity increased, while intraclass correlations decreased as exercise intensity increased. The authors concluded that these findings "cast doubt on the test–retest reliability of the established 6-20 Borg RPE scale for estimating exercise effort during progressive exercise" (p. 339).

Tools for Special Populations

Pediatric RPE Scales. Growing clinical and experimental interest in measuring children's perceptions of physical exertion has resulted in the development of several pediatric RPE scales. RPE scales specific to children and adolescents were developed because some children lack the cognitive ability or vocabulary to understand the descriptors of exercise intensity associated with adult scales (Eston, Parfitt, Campbell, & Lamb, 2000; Groslambert & Mahon, 2006).

Williams, Eston, and Furlong (1994) first attempted to tackle the problem of children's comprehension of exercise effort with the Children's Effort Rating Table (CERT). Initial investigations using the CERT provided evidence for its utility with children (Eston, Lamb, Bain, Williams, & Williams, 1994; Lamb, 1995). However, subsequent work utilizing the CERT demonstrated diminished scale sensitivity over the upper HR range during dynamic exercise as well as significant individual variability in correlations between perceived and objective measures of exercise intensity (Lamb & Eston, 1997). Attempts to improve the CERT resulted in the development of the Cart and Load Effort Rating (CALER) scale (Eston et al., 2000) and the Pictorial Children's Effort Rating Table (PCERT; Yelling, Lamb, & Swaine, 2002). The CALER scale is an abridged version of the CERT, with identical numbers and wording, that portrays a figure of a child pulling a cart loaded progressively with bricks. The PCERT uses all of the original numerical and verbal descriptors of the CERT, along with adjacently placed pictures of a child becoming increasingly fatigued while climbing stairs. The CALER scale has been shown to be an effective tool for regulating exercise intensity in children (Eston et al., 2000; Parfitt, Shepherd, & Eston, 2007), and it shows concurrent validity relative to HR ($r = .88$) and oxygen consumption ($r = .92$) within a perceptual estimation paradigm (Barkley & Roemmich, 2008). The validity of the PCERT has been established for submaximal exercise using a perceptual estimation paradigm ($r = .89$-$.90$) by Roemmich and colleagues (2006). In addition, the PCERT has been shown to correlate more highly with physiological measures ($r = .62$-$.88$) and to demonstrate greater reliability (intraclass correlation coefficients = .77-.97) than either Borg's CR10 scale (Marinov, Mandadjieva, & Kostianev, 2008) or Borg's 6-20 RPE scale (Leung, Chung, & Leung, 2002) demonstrates.

The Children's OMNI Scale of Perceived Exertion is a pediatric RPE scale with several activity-specific derivatives, including cycling (OMNI-Bike; Robertson et al., 2000), resistance training (OMNI-RES;

Robertson et al., 2003), stepping exercise (OMNI-Step; Roberson et al., 2005a), and walking and running (OMNI-Walk/Run; Utter, Robertson, Nieman, & Kang, 2002). The OMNI-Bike scale demonstrated concurrent and construct validity when using a simple estimation-of-effort paradigm during aerobic cycle ergometer exercise (Robertson et al., 2000) and when using a perceptual estimation paradigm (Barkley & Roemmich, 2008). The OMNI-Bike scale also showed validity for producing a prescribed exercise intensity in children (Robertson et al., 2002) and for identifying response-normalized undifferentiated and differentiated RPEs corresponding to the ventilatory break point in young children (Robertson et al., 2001). Similar findings supported the validity of the OMNI-Walk/Run scale (Roemmich et al., 2006; Utter et al., 2002), OMNI-RES scale (Robertson et al., 2005b), and OMNI-Step scale (Robertson et al., 2005a) as well as different language versions of the OMNI scales (Suminski, Robertson, Goss, & Olvera, 2008).

Aside from the OMNI-RES scale, the OMNI scales share a common verbal anchor, "tired." Eston and Parfitt (2006) suggested that using the word *tired* might be ascribing a negative connotation to the feelings experienced during physical activity. "From a purely semantic and literal perspective, feeling 'tired' is a general condition of fatigue, weariness, or sleepiness, rather than effort. It is not an indication of exertion" (Eston & Parfitt, 2006, p.289). The terminology of the CERT, which uses the verbal descriptors "easy" and "hard," seems to describe the concept more accurately. Interestingly, the OMNI-RES scale uses the "easy" to "hard" verbal anchor range, although no rationale was offered for this change in scale terminology.

Adult versions of the OMNI scale have been developed and also show good concurrent and construct validity (Irving et al., 2006; Lagally & Robertson, 2006; Robertson et al., 2004; Utter et al., 2004). The adult OMNI scale has been shown to be effective not only in establishing the target intensity at the onset of exercise but also in maintaining the intensity throughout a 20 min exercise session (Kang, Hoffman, Walker, Chaloupka, & Utter, 2003). In the aforementioned validity studies, construct validity was established by correlating RPE derived from the various adult OMNI scales with RPE from Borg's (6-20) RPE scale. This led Faulkner and Eston (2008) to express concern about the scientific merit of the adult OMNI scales. They observed that since various validity studies confirm that Borg's scale is a sound tool for monitoring, prescribing, and regulating exercise intensities, it appears that Borg's RPE scale does not need to be replaced. Furthermore,

there is no strong rationale for propagating pictorial scales for normal, literate adults (Faulkner & Eston, 2008).

Braille RPE Scale. Noting that blindness or vision impairment presents a barrier to physical activity and that the advent and proliferation of modern gyms may provide people who are blind with a greater opportunity to become more physically active, Buckley, Eston, and Sim (2000) sought to examine the reliability and validity of a braille version of Borg's standard 6-20 RPE scale. Buckley and colleagues used a production mode protocol, in which participants were asked to produce different exercise intensities for a given RPE on a cycle ergometer. In the study, 10 healthy participants who were blind performed an initial graded exercise test to determine maximal HR (HR_{max}) and $\dot{V}O_2max$. This was followed by three trials of three exercise bouts at RPEs of 9, 11, and 13. Bouts were performed in random order and trials were performed on separate days within the same week. ANOVA showed no significant differences in either %HR_{max} or %$\dot{V}O_2max$ among trials at each of the three RPE levels, but there was a significant difference in both %HR_{max} and %$\dot{V}O_2max$ among the three RPE levels. Thus, the participants in this study were able to successfully use the braille RPE scale while performing cycle ergometry, and they were able to use RPE to differentiate between intensity levels. Buckley and colleagues (2000) concluded that, like the RPE scale used by people who can see, a braille RPE scale can be used by people who are blind during cycle ergometry.

Multidimensional Approach

Single-item measures of RPE, as outlined previously, have been well validated and represent reliable measures of perceptual intensity that have proved robust in their usefulness (Noble & Noble, 1998). However, a number of researchers have questioned the efficacy of a single-item measure of RPE (e.g., Hardy & Rejeski, 1989; Hutchinson & Tenenbaum, 2006; McAuley & Courneya, 1992; Parfitt, Markland, & Holmes, 1994; Tenenbaum, 2005), arguing that a one-dimensional scale is insufficient to capture the whole range of perceptual sensations that people experience when exercising or being physically active.

Differentiated Rating of Perceived Exertion

Single-item measures of RPE, such as Borg's scale, represent an individual's integration of various sensations that have different subjective weightings. Borg (1998) has conceptualized perceived exertion within a Gestalt framework: a configuration of sensations such as strain, aches, and fatigue that stem from the peripheral muscles, pulmonary system, somatosensory receptors, cardiovascular system, and other sensory organs and cues. Within this Gestalt conceptualization of RPE, motivation and emotions are psychological variables that are an integral part of the experience of exertion. However, it has been proposed that differentiated exertion signals provide a more precise definition of the physiological and psychological processes that shape the perceptual context during exercise (Noble & Robertson, 1996).

Differentiated RPEs have been used to examine in greater detail the central and local factors contributing to an individual's RPE (Demura & Nagasawa, 2003; Marsh & Martin, 1998). In these studies, RPE scores were assigned to central (cardiopulmonary) and peripheral (muscle and joint) sources either alone or in conjunction with an overall RPE (RPE-O) score (Marsh & Martin, 1998). The intensities of the various differentiated perceptual signals usually differ from that of the undifferentiated signal at a given point in time during submaximal exercise (Noble & Robertson, 1996). Peripheral RPE is generally higher than central RPE is (Garcin, Vautier, Vandewalle, Wolff, & Monod, 1998), particularly at the anaerobic threshold (Green, Crews, Bosak, & Peveler, 2003; Mahon, Gay, & Stolen, 1998). Peripheral signals also dominate RPE in cycling (Pandolf, 1982; Robertson & Noble, 1997), typically resulting in greater leg RPE responses (versus central RPE or RPE-O) during this mode.

Psychological Factors

Certain types of effort symptoms are not specifically related to physiological processes. These nonspecific psychological factors represent distinct inputs in the perceptual report (Noble & Robertson, 1996). In addition to addressing physical components, measures of exercise-related effort must take into account the different psychological components that reflect signals of motivation and affect (Hardy & Rejeski, 1989; Parfitt, Markland, & Holmes, 1994).

Tenenbaum and colleagues (1999) developed a questionnaire to elicit the feelings and thoughts of people engaged in running activities. The authors asked 10 runners to express their feelings and thoughts during a demanding 5.5 mi (9 km) run they had just completed. These responses constituted the first version of the Running Discomfort Scale (RDS). These items were then given to 171 runners in different distance races during the competitive season. The ratings of the 171 runners were analyzed using EFA techniques and Rasch probability analyses as well as traditional reliability and validity procedures. The final version of the questionnaire consisted of 32 items divided into eight correlated subscales: proprioceptive symptoms, leg symptoms, respiratory difficulties, dryness and heat, head or stomach symptoms, mental toughness, disorientation, and task completion thoughts. These eight categories were subsequently collapsed into three global dimensions: the *sensory-discriminative*, *motivational-affective*, and *cognitive-evaluative* dimensions (for details, see Tenenbaum et al., 1999). These dimensions of effort were drawn from the three-factor conceptualization proposed by Melzack and Wall's (1965, 1996) GCT of pain.

While the RDS is innovative in applying GCT to the field of effort perception, it is limited in that it is specific only to running activities. To address this, Hutchinson and Tenenbaum (2006) used two different tasks (a stationary cycling task and an isometric strength task) to examine differentiated physiological and psychological factors in perceived effort. The isometric task involved a handgrip contraction at 25% maximum grip strength sustained to fatigue using a calibrated handgrip dynamometer. The cycling task involved pedaling on a stationary cycle ergometer at 50%, 70%, and 90% of previously established $\dot{V}O_2$max to volitional exhaustion. The same three dimensions of perceived effort (sensory-discriminative, motivational-affective, and cognitive-evaluative sensations) were measured, via self-report, at regular intervals for the duration of the cycling and handgrip tasks. Results indicated that the three dimensions were perceived distinctly and operated differently during the two physically demanding tasks. Throughout both tasks, motivational-affective sensations were consistently rated higher than sensory-discriminative sensations and cognitive-evaluative sensations were rated. Cognitive-evaluative sensations were, in turn, rated more highly than sensory-discriminative sensations were rated. Over the time course of the two tasks, both sensory-discriminative and cognitive-evaluative sensations increased monotonically (by an average of 72% and 60% for the handgrip and cycling tasks, respectively). In contrast, motivational-affective responses remained more stable over time, showing a slight increase (by 27%) from the outset in the handgrip task and remaining unchanged during the cycling task.

Recommendations for Researchers and Practitioners

The general aim of RPE is to quantify an individual's subjective perception of exertion as a means of determining or regulating exercise intensity

(Borg, 1998). However, for researchers who examine RPE as the main variable of interest, a single-item measure (such as Borg's scale) represents an oversimplification of the psychophysiological construct. Within RPE are many distinct variables that should be measured in parallel. We recommend that researchers use differentiated measures incorporating sensory-discriminative, motivational-affective, and cognitive-evaluative dimensions (see figure 24.1). The exact variables of interest within each dimension will vary according to the research question or specific practical application of the scale. For example, a specific peripheral input such as backache might be of interest to an ergonomic investigation in an occupational setting; on the other hand, a motivational-affective variable such as state arousal might be important for research examining the effects of different arousal states on perceived effort.

Established principles of administration must be followed carefully to ensure the validity and reliability of the measure. We echo the conclusions of Noble and Robertson (1996) that preparation of participants, through the presentation of comprehensive instructions, is critical to the correct use of rating scales. Instructions should include an explanation of the concept (or concepts) under examination, anchoring of the perceptual range via relevant examples and expressions, an explanation of how the numbers and expressions on the scale are to be used (e.g., as a category of sensations ordered according to intensity), a description of how differentiated ratings are to be used, and a description of how differentiated ratings are distinguished from undifferentiated ratings. Participants should also be advised that there are no correct answers and should be encouraged to provide ratings without judgment. Finally, the participant should be given the opportunity to ask questions and to practice making perceptual estimates (see Maresh & Noble, 1984; Noble & Robertson, 1996). Other instructions must be specific to the task (e.g., explaining how to express ratings if the participant is wearing a breathing apparatus), to the participants (e.g., using different verbal descriptors for children), to the exact research question at hand, or to the practical rationale for incorporating perceptual effort ratings.

A more comprehensive model should replace the traditional (Gestalt) concept of perceived exertion in the study and measurement of effort perception. Adequate measures of effort perception need to account for the distinct inputs that shape the perceptual milieu during sustained physical activity. More research is needed to establish a comprehensive concept of perceived effort and to develop an associated multidimensional measure of perceived effort. We reiterate Noble and Noble's (1998) call

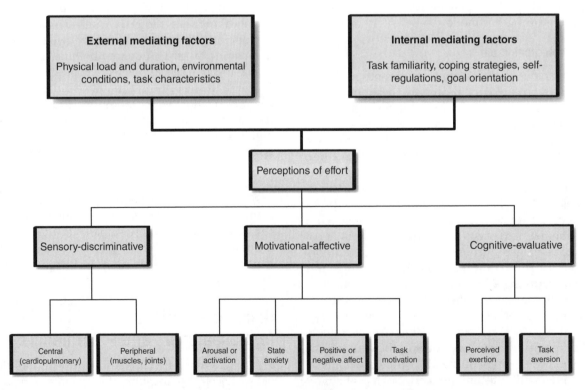

Figure 24.1 A conceptual framework for differentiated perceptions of effort.

for greater eclecticism in the measurement of effort perceptions. They recommended that the research question, and not instrument availability, should be the primary determinant of measurement choice: "Emphasis should be placed on understanding perception, not on studying the results of the Borg scale. Until that is done, the study of perceptual response during physical activity will reflect only what the Borg scale measures" (p. 356).

Progress toward a comprehensive concept of perceived effort is offered in figure 24.1. The multidimensional nature of perceived effort is central to the model. Consistent with the empirical evidence presented earlier, the model suggests three global dimensions of perceived effort: the *sensory-discriminative, motivational-affective,* and *cognitive-evaluative* dimensions. Within these global dimensions are specific sensations that can be measured during physical activity. The two boxes at the top of the model represent the influence of internal and external mediating factors on perceived effort. These factors can influence specific effort sensations differently. For example, listening to music (a coping strategy) can facilitate an increase in arousal and task motivation but a decrease in central and peripheral sensory discriminative sensations (Karageorghis & Terry, 1997). Physical load, an external mediating factor, can also mediate this relationship, such that the effects of music are less salient at high exercise intensities.

■ Table 24.1 ■

Tools for Measuring Perception of Effort and Exertion

Variable	Tool	Dimension or characteristic	Source
Perceived exertion	Rating of perceived exertion (RPE) scale	RPE	Borg (1971)
Perceived exertion	CR10 scale	RPE	Borg (1982)
Perceived exertion	CR100 scale	RPE	Borg (1998)
Effort rating	Children's Effort Rating Table (CERT)	Pictorial	Williams, Eston, & Furlong (1994)
Effort rating	Cart and Load Effort Rating (CALER) Scale	Pictorial	Eston, Parfitt, Campbell, & Lamb (2000)
Effort rating	Pictorial Children's Effort Rating Table (PCERT)	RPE, pictorial	Yelling, Lamb, & Swaine (2002)
Running discomfort	Running Discomfort Scale (RDS)	Sensory-discriminative, motivational-affective, and cognitive-evaluative dimensions	Tenenbaum et al. (1999)
Perceived exertion	OMNI scales	RPE, pictorial, multiple derivations	Robertson et al. (2000)
Perceived exertion	Braille RPE scale	RPE	Buckley, Eston, & Sim (2000)

Intrinsic and Extrinsic Motivation in Sport and Exercise

Robert J. Vallerand, PhD, Eric G. Donahue, BSc, and Marc-André K. Lafrenière, BS

In 1998, Vallerand and Fortier conducted a critical review of existing instruments assessing intrinsic and extrinsic motivation toward sport. These authors concluded that the necessary methodological tools were now in place and that "the future would appear to be rather promising in the intrinsic and extrinsic motivation research area" (p. 98). The next decade proved Vallerand and Fortier right, as research on intrinsic and extrinsic motivation in sport and exercise has exploded (see Hagger & Chatzisarantis, 2007). The research conducted since the Vallerand and Fortier review has provided valuable information on existing motivation instruments. Furthermore, new scales have been published. This chapter reviews and critiques existing measures of intrinsic and extrinsic motivation in sport and exercise by focusing mostly on research that has been published since the Vallerand and Fortier (1998) review. First, we discuss definitional aspects of intrinsic and extrinsic motivation. In so doing, we also briefly present theories that are useful to our research review. Second, we present and evaluate the different motivation measures in terms of their validity and reliability. Finally, in the last section, we draw implications for researchers and practitioners.

Defining Intrinsic and Extrinsic Motivation

The construct of motivation can be defined as "the hypothetical construct used to describe the internal and/or external forces that produce the initiation, direction, intensity, and persistence of behavior" (Vallerand & Thill, 1993, p. 18, translated from

French). This definition fits well with the constructs and theories of intrinsic and extrinsic motivation, in which factors both inside and outside the individual are hypothesized to affect intrinsic and extrinsic motivation. As we shall see, definitions and theories are intertwined in no small measure in this area.

Nature of Intrinsic and Extrinsic Motivation

Intrinsic motivation generally involves the impetus to perform an activity for itself and the pleasure and satisfaction derived from participation (Deci & Ryan, 1985, 2000). Basketball players who play because they enjoy the feeling of gracefully jumping, running, and shooting the ball are representative of individuals who are intrinsically motivated. Contrary to intrinsic motivation, extrinsic motivation involves engaging in an activity as a means to an end and not for its own sake. Thus, extrinsically motivated individuals do not participate in an activity for the inherent pleasure they may experience while performing it; rather, they participate in order to receive something positive or to avoid something negative that is separate from the activity (Deci & Ryan, 2000; Kruglanski, 1978). Athletes who play in order to obtain trophies and medals represent individuals who are extrinsically motivated.

Given these definitions, it is possible to distinguish between intrinsic and extrinsic motivation on at least two counts. First, these two forms of motivation differ fundamentally from a teleological (or purposive) perspective (Bolles, 1967). Whereas for intrinsic motivation the purpose of participation lies within the process itself, the purpose of extrinsic motivation focuses on benefits that are separate from the activity. The rewards being sought are located in different loci. When intrinsically motivated, people seek to experience affective rewards (pleasure, enjoyment, feelings of competence) during task engagement. Conversely, when extrinsically motivated, people seek awards that are usually experienced after the activity (e.g., having lost some weight). Second, intrinsic and extrinsic motivation can be distinguished from a phenomenological perspective. Being intrinsically motivated feels different from being extrinsically motivated. Being intrinsically motivated leads individuals to experience pleasant emotions, such as enjoyment, and to feel free and relaxed. When intrinsically motivated, individuals experience little pressure or tension, and they focus more easily on the task. Conversely, when extrinsically motivated, individuals tend to feel tense and pressured. Social approval, for instance, depends on others and is therefore to a large extent outside of personal control. This can help us to understand the pressure that can be experienced when extrinsically motivated. However, as we will see, there are different types of extrinsic motivation, some of which are self-determined and thus minimize the experience of tension and pressure.

Multidimensional View of Intrinsic and Extrinsic Motivation

Historically, intrinsic motivation has been defined as unidimensional (e.g., Csikszentmihalyi & Nakamura, 1989; Lepper & Hoddell, 1989). That is, intrinsic motivation has been assumed to represent a general form of motivation that leads people to engage in activities out of enjoyment. However, can it be assumed that certain tasks, situations, and individuals are more conducive to certain types of enjoyment? Indeed, certain theorists such as White (1959), Harter (1981), and Deci (1975) have proposed that intrinsic motivation might be differentiated into more specific motives (a multidimensional perspective). Vallerand and colleagues (Vallerand, 1997; Vallerand, Blais, Brière, & Pelletier, 1989; Vallerand et al., 1992, 1993) expanded this view and posited the existence of three types of intrinsic motivation: intrinsic motivation to know, intrinsic motivation toward accomplishment, and intrinsic motivation to experience stimulation.

Intrinsic motivation toward accomplishment focuses on engaging in a given activity for the pleasure and satisfaction that people experience while *attempting* to surpass themselves or to accomplish or create something. The focus is on the process of accomplishing something and not on the end result.

For instance, swimmers who swim for the intense pleasure they experience while trying to improve their time display this type of intrinsic motivation. On the other hand, *intrinsic motivation to experience stimulation* takes place when people engage in an activity in order to experience pleasant sensations associated mainly with the senses (e.g., sensory and aesthetic pleasure). People who engage in hang gliding because they enjoy the pleasant sensations they experience while their bodies soar through the air display this type of intrinsic motivation. Finally, *intrinsic motivation to know* refers to engaging in an activity for the pleasure and the satisfaction that people experience while learning, exploring, or trying to understand something new. For instance, people who exercise because they enjoy discovering different exercises to keep in shape display intrinsic motivation to know.

Research in different contexts, such as education (Fairchild, Horst, Finney, & Barron, 2005; Hein, Müür, & Koka, 2004; Vallerand et al., 1989, 1992), work (Blais, Brière, Lachance, Riddle, & Vallerand, 1993), leisure (Pelletier, Vallerand, Green-Demers, Blais, &, Brière, 1996), and sport (Brière, Vallerand, Blais, & Pelletier, 1995; Pelletier et al., 1995), supports the existence of the three types of intrinsic motivation. Furthermore, Hein and colleagues (2004) showed that the intrinsic motivation to accomplish and to experience stimulation toward physical activity predicted intentions to engage in exercise during free time. Finally, Carbonneau and Vallerand (2011) showed in five studies that each type of intrinsic motivation is linked to distinct determinants and outcomes.

Originally it was believed that extrinsic motivation pertains only to behaviors prompted by external sources of control (e.g., coaches, fitness instructors) and performed largely in the absence of self-determination. Based on self-determination theory (SDT; Deci & Ryan, 1985, 2000; Ryan & Connell, 1989), extrinsic motivation has also been considered from a multidimensional perspective, including some types of motivation self-determined in nature. That is, although not engaged in out of pleasure (i.e., out of intrinsic motivation), some behaviors may still be emitted by choice.

Four types of extrinsic motivation that vary in terms of the underlying level of self-determination have been proposed. *External regulation* refers to behavior regulated through external means such as rewards and constraints. For instance, a hockey player might say, "I'm going to tonight's practice because if I don't, the coach will be mad at me." In this case, the player goes to practice in order to avoid punishment and is therefore externally regulated.

With *introjected regulation*, the individual begins to internalize the reasons for action. However, such internalization is not truly self-determined because it is limited to past external contingencies. For instance, exercisers who train because they feel guilty and anxious when they don't train display introjected regulation toward exercise. It is only with the third type of extrinsic motivation, *identified regulation*, that behavior is emitted out of choice and is thus self-determined. With this type of motivation, the behavior (e.g., participating in sport or physical activity) is performed freely even if the activity is not pleasant. For instance, a basketball player might say, "I want to improve my jumping ability. It is important for me. Thus, although I don't like weight training, I've decided to start doing it for my own good." In this case, the athlete has chosen freely (without any external or internal prodding either from the coach or from unpleasant emotions) to engage in weight training although this activity is not intrinsically motivating. The fourth and final type of extrinsic motivation, *integrated regulation*, also entails engaging in an activity out of choice. However, the choice is not simply limited at the activity level but is now a coherent part of the organization of the self. That is, the person's choices are now made as a function of the fit between the activity and other aspects of the self. Thus, the integrated exerciser may choose to do weight training early in the morning so as to prevent conflict with work and family activities during the rest of the day.

Deci and Ryan (1985) have also proposed a third construct: *amotivation*. This concept is similar to that of learned helplessness (Abramson, Seligman, & Teasdale, 1978) and refers to the relative absence of motivation, intrinsic or extrinsic (Vallerand, 1997). When amotivated, individuals do not perceive contingencies between their actions and the outcomes of their actions and can no longer find good reasons to continue participation in the activity. Thus, the amotivation construct may prove helpful in predicting a lack of persistence in sport and exercise.

SDT posits that the various types of motivation can be ordered along a self-determination continuum. From lower to higher levels of self-determination, they are as follows: amotivation, external regulation, introjection, identification, integrated regulation, and intrinsic motivation. Research supports the validity of the self-determination continuum in a variety of contexts, including sport (e.g., Chatzisarantis, Hagger, Biddle, Smith, & Wang, 2003; Li & Harmer, 1996). For instance, through the use of SEM and the Sport Motivation Scale (SMS; Pelletier et al., 1995), Li and Harmer (1996) confirmed the placement of the various motivation constructs on the self-determination continuum. This placement has led to predictions regarding the pattern of relationships among the various types of motivation, called the *simplex pattern*. Such a pattern implies that the correlations between adjacent constructs on the self-determination continuum (e.g., intrinsic motivation and identified regulation) are positive and higher than those between constructs farther apart (e.g., amotivation and intrinsic motivation). While some authors have used statistical techniques such as SEM to test the presence of the simplex pattern (Li & Harmer, 1996), most researchers have simply looked at the relative strength of the correlations among the various motivation subscales.

Other research has revealed that consequences are decreasingly positive as motivations move on the continuum from intrinsic motivation to amotivation (for reviews, see Vallerand, 1997, 2001, 2007). Whereas the positive effects of intrinsic motivation and integrated and identified regulation are clear (Vallerand, 2007; Wilson, Mack, & Grattan, 2008), the role of external regulation and especially introjected regulation in outcomes is less clear, as at times they have predicted negative outcomes (e.g., Pelletier, Fortier, Vallerand, & Brière, 2001) and at other times have been unrelated to outcomes (Koestner, 2008). Introjected regulation has even been found to predict some positive outcomes (e.g., Chantal, Guay, Dobreva-Martina, & Vallerand, 1996). Future research is needed on this issue. Finally, the strong negative effects of amotivation have been clearly confirmed.

Intrinsic and Extrinsic Motivation at Different Levels of Generality

The hierarchical model of intrinsic and extrinsic motivation (HMIEM; Vallerand, 1997, 2001, 2007) makes a number of propositions with respect to human motivation. One of these propositions is that intrinsic and extrinsic motivation exist at different levels of generality in a hierarchical fashion. More specifically, Vallerand proposed that motivation is represented at three levels of generality: the global, the contextual, and the situational levels. At the global level, motivation refers to a general motivational orientation to interact with the environment in an intrinsic or extrinsic way. It is akin to a personality dimension. The Global Motivation Scale (see Pelletier & Dion, 2007) assesses motivation at this level. Because this level has not been examined or applied in the sport context so far, we do not discuss it further. The contextual level is of particular interest for our present discussion. The term *context* refers to distinct spheres of activities, such as education, work, interpersonal relationships, and sport and exercise (see Vallerand, 1997). In such life contexts, individuals develop motivational orientations that, although still somewhat responsive to the environment, are moderately stable (Vallerand, 1997). This can be likened to a domain-specific motivational disposition. Scales used to assess motivation at the contextual level include the SMS (Brière et al., 1995; Pelletier et al., 1995) and the Behavioral Regulation in Exercise Questionnaire (BREQ; Mullan, Markland, & Ingledew, 1997).

The situational level represents the third and last level of generality proposed by Vallerand (1997). This level involves the motivation that an individual experiences while currently engaged in an activity. This level captures the here and now, or the state aspect, of motivation. The Situational Motivation Scale (SIMS; Guay, Vallerand, & Blanchard, 2000) is an example of a scale used to assess intrinsic and extrinsic motivation and amotivation at the situational level.

The levels of generality have important implications for intrinsic and extrinsic motivation measures. A first implication pertains to scale construction. Scales at the situational and contextual levels should not be formulated in the same fashion. For instance, while the SIMS (Guay et al., 2000) asks respondents to indicate why they are *currently* engaging in the activity, the SMS (Pelletier et al., 1995) asks respondents to indicate why they *generally* participate in their sport. Furthermore, items for each type of scale should reflect the appropriate level of generality. A valid scale should display items that are clearly in line with the desired level of generality. A second implication is that scales at the situational and contextual levels should not be expected to have similar psychometric properties or to behave in the same fashion. For instance, contextual measures should display a relatively high level of temporal stability (as exemplified by high test–retest correlations), while situational measures should not. Contextual measures reflect a relatively enduring broad motivational orientation in a circumscribed context such as sport, whereas situational measures assess motivation that may fluctuate to a large extent as a function of situational factors. Therefore, a criterion of moderately high test–retest temporal stability is appropriate for contextual measures but not for situational measures.

Finally, a third implication of the different levels of generality is that the level may help clarify the assessment of a scale's construct validity. Construct validity is analyzed by testing relationships between the scale being assessed and various other

instruments as predicted by theory. For instance, in light of SDT (Deci & Ryan, 1991, 2000), perceptions of competence should be positively related to intrinsic motivation. However, in order to properly test this relationship, a researcher must assess both constructs at the same level of generality. Failing to do so may lead the researcher to conclude wrongly that there is an absence of relationship when the null result actually stems from an improper selection of instruments.

In sum, recent conceptual contributions have led to the conclusion that the constructs of intrinsic and extrinsic motivation and amotivation should be assessed at different levels of generality and in a multidimensional fashion.

Evaluation of Measures of Intrinsic and Extrinsic Motivation in Sport and Exercise

In this section, a critical review of the different measures used to assess intrinsic and extrinsic motivation in sport and exercise research is conducted. Certain criteria have guided the selection of the measures presented in this section. First, we have selected measures that are fully developed instruments that have gone through extensive validation steps. Second, we have chosen scales that have been used in research, published or unpublished, during the past 10 years. Scales that have not been used during that time frame are considered to be obsolete and are not reviewed. Finally, in light of recent theoretical development and because of space limitation, we have focused on motivation scales that assess intrinsic and extrinsic motivation independently of determinants and outcomes, while focusing on the perceived reasons of behavior. Our earlier discussion on the definitions of intrinsic and extrinsic motivation makes it possible to classify the different measures. The measures can vary in terms of the level of generality (situational versus contextual level) and the area (sport versus exercise). This classification appears in table 25.1. Table 25.2 (see p. 291) provides additional information on the concept of, dimensions of, publication source of, and where to obtain the scale. As can be seen, seven measures are reviewed. For each one, we present (a) a description of the instrument, (b) the conceptual and theoretical rationale underlying its scale development, (c) the available evidence concerning its psychometric properties (e.g., factorial validity, reliability, and construct validity), and (d) a broad assessment of the strengths and weaknesses associated with each measure.

■ **Table 25.1** ■

Types of Measures of Intrinsic and Extrinsic Motivation in Sport and Exercise Research

Type	Sport	Exercise
Contextual measures	Sport Motivation Scale (SMS; Pelletier et al., 1995) Sport Motivation Scale-6 (SMS-6; Mallet, Kawabata, Newcombe, et al., 2007) Behavioral Regulation in Sport Questionnaire (BRSQ; Lonsdale, Hodge, & Rose, 2008) Pictorial Motivation Scale (PMS; Reid, Vallerand, Poulin, Crocker, & Farrell, 2009)	Behavioral Regulation in Exercise Questionnaire (BREQ; Mullan, Markland, & Ingledew, 1997) Exercise Motivation Scale (EMS; Li, 1999)
Situational measures	Situational Motivation Scale (SIMS; Guay, Vallerand, & Blanchard, 2000)	—

Measures Used in Sport

In this section, we review the SMS (Brière et al., 1995; Pelletier et al., 1995), the Sport Motivation Scale-6 (SMS-6; Mallett, Kawabata, Newcombe, Otero-Rorero, & Jackson, 2007), the Behavioral Regulation in Sport Questionnaire (BRSQ; Lonsdale, Hodge, & Rose, 2008), the Pictorial Motivation Scale (PMS; Reid, Vallerand, Poulin, Crocker, & Farrell, 2009), and the SIMS (Guay et al., 2000).

Sport Motivation Scale

The SMS was developed (Brière et al., 1995; Pelletier et al., 1995) in order to assess contextual intrinsic and extrinsic motivation from a multidimensional perspective, as well as amotivation. The SMS has been the most often used motivation measure in sport, being employed with a variety of athletes (recreational to elite), age groups (adolescent to senior), and cultures (e.g., Canada, United States, United Kingdom, Bulgaria, Australia, Spain, and New Zealand). In fact, the SMS has been translated and validated in several languages (see Pelletier & Sarrazin, 2007). The SMS is based on SDT (Deci & Ryan, 1985) and is made up of seven subscales assessing amotivation; external, introjected, and identified regulation; and intrinsic motivation to know, to experience stimulation, and to accomplish. In line with SDT, motivation is assessed as the perceived reasons for participation, or the *why* of behavior. At the beginning of the scale, participants are asked, "In general, why do you practice your sport?" The items represent the perceived reasons for engaging in the activity, thus reflecting the different types of motivation.

The original scale was developed in French as *L'Échelle de Motivation dans les Sports* (Brière, Valle-rand, Blais, & Pelletier, 1995) and was validated in three steps. The first step involved generating a pool of items explaining various reasons for sport participation through interviews with French Canadian athletes (aged 17-20 y). These reasons were then used to formulate items for the seven subscales of the French SMS. In the second step, a committee of experts evaluated the content validity of the items and eliminated those that were thought to be inadequate. Another sample of athletes from various sports completed the scale. Results from an exploratory factor analysis (EFA) provided support for a seven-factor structure with 4 items per subscale; this second step thus resulted in a 28-item scale. In the third and final step, two additional studies were conducted to further validate the scale. These studies included approximately 500 individuals, most of whom were involved in recreational sports. Results from confirmatory factor analyses (CFA) and correlational analyses confirmed the seven-factor structure, the subscale internal consistency (ranging from .65-.96), and moderate to high indexes of temporal stability (ranging from .54-.82) over 1 month. Furthermore, inspection of correlations among the seven SMS subscales provided support for the simplex pattern proposed by SDT. Results of correlations also showed that (in line with SDT) the most self-determined forms of motivation (intrinsic motivation and identified regulation) were related more strongly to determinants such as autonomy support from coaches and feelings of competence than to other forms of motivation (external and introjected regulation) and amotivation. Similar results were obtained with motivational outcomes such as positive affect, concentration, and intentions to pursue engagement in sport. In sum, adequate construct validity was obtained for the French form of the SMS.

The translation of the French SMS into English involved back-translation and committee procedures as suggested by Vallerand (1989). Pelletier and colleagues (1995) conducted two studies involving college athletes from various sports in order to assess the psychometric properties of the English form of the SMS. Results from CFA with a sample of 593 Canadian university athletes revealed adequate fit indices or the hypothesized seven-factor model (see the Adjusted Goodness of Fit Index and the Normed Fit Index both > .90 and the Root Mean Square Residual < .08), and correlations with determinants and outcomes supported the simplex model. Moreover, internal consistency above .70 was obtained on all of the subscales except the identified subscale (.63). Test–retest correlations were acceptable and very similar to those obtained with the French SMS, as was the scale construct validity.

Since 1995, the SMS has been used extensively in sport psychology research. The seven-factor structure has been supported repeatedly (e.g., Doganis, 2000; Gillet, Vallerand, & Rosnet, 2009; Li & Harmer, 1996; Shaw, Ostrow, & Beckstead, 2005; Standage, Duda, & Ntoumanis, 2003). In addition, Hu and Bentler (1999) obtained support for a five-factor model by combining the three types of intrinsic motivation into one factor. Similar results were obtained by Gillet and colleagues (2009) with the French SMS. However, some studies have not supported the seven-factor model (Hodge, Allen, & Smellie, 2008; Mallett, Kawabata, & Newcombe, 2007; Mallett, Kawabata, Newcombe, & Otero-Rorero, 2007; Martens & Webber, 2002). Why is there such a discrepancy between these two sets of studies? One possibility lies in the populations from which the different samples were taken. Specifically, the SMS was validated using adolescent and young adult athletes and not older athletes. Because of this specific focus, some of the items may reflect a participation rather than an elite orientation, which is more in line with the younger population. For instance, an identified regulation item reads, "Because sport is one of the best ways to maintain good relationships with my friends." Such an item seems more relevant for a younger population. An older, high-level athlete may disagree with this item but still display a high level of identified regulation for a sport (but not for relationship reasons). Future research using the SMS with different age groups and proficiency levels is needed to clarify this issue.

Whereas the internal consistency of the SMS has systematically shown adequate values, some values below .70 have been found. This is especially the case for the identified regulation subscale (Brière et al., 1995; Kingston, Horrocks, & Hanton, 2006; Li & Harmer, 1996; Pelletier et al., 1995), although some lower values (below .70) have been obtained with the introjected (McNeill & Wang, 2005; Perreault & Vallerand, 2007; Riemer, Fink, & Fitzgerald, 2002; Standage, Duda, & Ntoumanis, 2003) and external regulation (Standage, Duda, & Ntoumanis, 2003) and amotivation subscales (Standage, Duda, & Ntoumanis, 2003). However, very few instances of values below .60 have been obtained. It should be noted that a Cronbach alpha of .60 with only 4 items is acceptable because, as noted by Cronbach (1951), the coefficient alpha underestimates the internal consistency of scales with a low number of items. This is because the coefficient alpha includes the number of items in the formula. For instance, given the same average interitem correlation, a 3-item scale coefficient alpha value of .56 is equivalent to an alpha value of .81 on an 8-item scale!

In line with the original work of Ryan and Connell (1989) and the initial SMS validation procedures (Brière et al., 1995; Pelletier et al., 1995), construct validity has been assessed by other authors in two fashions: (1) with the simplex pattern of correlations among the subscales and (2) with correlations between motivational factors and their determinants and consequences. We do not have space to review all studies. However, overall, there is overwhelming support for the construct validity of the SMS both in French and English. For instance, in addition to finding support for the simplex pattern, Pelletier and Sarrazin (2007) concluded in their review of the evidence that the SMS has been used with success to predict a great variety of specific outcomes and consequences (such as burnout, exercise dependence among endurance athletes, fear of failing, adaptive coping skills, perceptions of constraints, flow, vitality and well-being, sporting behavior orientations, aggression, and performance) in a manner that is consistent with SDT. These findings provide strong support for the construct validity of the SMS.

In sum, the SMS has some positive features. First, it is a multidimensional instrument that assesses different types of intrinsic and extrinsic motivation as well as amotivation. Second, the scale focuses on the why of behavior and thus items are not confounded with determinants and consequences. Finally, it has some excellent psychometric properties. Nevertheless, some limitations should be underscored. First, although internal consistency levels have been acceptable overall, some subscales, especially the identified regulation subscale, have yielded relatively low coefficient alphas at times. Second, the SMS does not assess integrated regulation. Third, the seven-factor structure has not always been supported by CFAs. According to Pelletier, Vallerand, and Sarrazin (2007), this may be explained by a host of factors, including differences in sample sizes, variations in the way the instrument is administrated, or some other characteristics specific to the context of the study. However, as already indicated, it is also possible that the SMS is better suited for a younger, nonelite athlete population. Clearly, future research on this issue is in order.

Sport Motivation Scale-6

Mallett, Kawabata, Newcombe, and Otero-Rorero (2007) developed another version of the SMS, the SMS-6. This scale has the same underlying rationale that the original SMS scale but was designed to improve the original version of the SMS by including an integrated regulation subscale and attempting to solve some of the inconsistencies with the factor structure and some of the relatively low internal consistency values (below .70). The SMS-6 comprises 24 items, 4 for each of the six subscales, which include amotivation; external, introjected, identified, and integrated regulation; and general intrinsic motivation. Mallett, Kawabata, Newcombe, and Otero-Rorero (2007) developed 5 items for the integrated regulation subscale as well as 7 other items (4 of which were kept in the final scale) to replace some items in the original SMS. Two samples were used to validate the SMS-6. Sample 1 was composed of 501 first-year university students participating in competitive sport at least twice per week and 113 elite athletes representing Australia at the international level (for a total of 614 participants). Sample 1 was used to derive a factor structure that included the SMS items as well as the reformulated and integrated regulation items. Sample 2 was composed of 557 university students who were engaged in a variety of sports or physical activities twice per week. The second sample was used to confirm the structure of the SMS-6. Participants also completed the Dispositional Flow Scale (DFS).

Results of a CFA with the SMS-6 (with sample 2) provided support for the factor structure as well as for the internal consistency values (all above .70). Concerning the construct validity of the SMS-6, Mallett, Kawabata, Newcombe, and Otero-Rorero (2007) reported a rather weak simplex pattern of correlations among the subscales. More specifically, external regulation correlated highly with intrinsic motivation ($r = .54$), while the correlation between identified regulation and intrinsic motivation was very high ($r = .91$) and was higher than the one between integrated regulation and intrinsic motivation ($r = .75$). The construct validity of the SMS-6

was not fully supported, as some of the correlations involving the SMS and flow were not as expected by SDT. For instance, the distinctions among integrated regulation, identified regulation, and intrinsic motivation were not always clear. Furthermore, external regulation revealed some positive and sometimes strong correlations with flow, contrary to hypotheses derived from SDT.

In sum, the SMS-6 contains some nice features. First, it contains an integrated regulation subscale. Furthermore, the addition of 4 new items may make the SMS more acceptable for older and more experienced athletes. Second, Mallett, Kawabata, Newcombe, and Otero-Rorero (2007) presented results supporting the validity of a variation of the SMS-6, the SMS-8. The SMS-8 contains the same items that the SMS-6 contains but assesses the three types of intrinsic motivation rather than general intrinsic motivation. The SMS-6 also shows some limitations. First, Mallett, Kawabata, Newcombe, and Otero-Rorero (2007) proposed 7 new items to replace those that were presumably problematic in the original SMS. However, only 4 of these items made it to the final version. Thus, it appears that the SMS-6 retained much of the original SMS. Second, even some of the new items appear problematic and may not assess the desired construct (see Pelletier et al., 2007). For instance, a new amotivation item ("I don't seem to be enjoying my sport as much as I previously did") seems to reflect a decrease in intrinsic motivation rather than amotivation. Finally, results from Mallett, Kawabata, Newcombe, and Otero-Rorero (2007) demonstrated that the integrated regulation subscale may lack discriminant validity, leading to results with flow highly similar to identified regulation and intrinsic motivation.

Behavioral Regulation in Sport Questionnaire

Lonsdale and colleagues (2008) developed the BRSQ to create an alternative measure of elite sport motivation as conceptualized by SDT. However, in contrast to Mallett, Kawabata, Newcombe, and Otero-Rorero (2007), these authors used a complete new pool of items developed by SDT experts and competitive athletes. There are two versions of the BRSQ. The BRSQ-8 contains 32 items assessing integrated, identified, introjected, and external regulation; amotivation; and the three forms of intrinsic motivation (knowledge, experience stimulation, and accomplishment) identified by Vallerand (1997). The BRSQ-6 contains the same items but assesses general intrinsic motivation rather than all three types of intrinsic motivation, for a total of 24 items.

Lonsdale and colleagues (2008) conducted a series of three studies to validate the scale. In the first study, the factorial validity and the internal consistency were assessed with 382 New Zealand elite athletes. Results from a CFA on the 32 items supported the factor structure of the BRSQ. Specifically, fit indexes were acceptable and all items loaded significantly on the appropriate factors (they ranged from .58-.91). Finally, internal consistency of the eight subscales, measured with the Cronbach alpha, showed high values ranging from .71 to 91. Additionally, 1 wk test–retest reliability was tested with 34 competitive adult athletes. Coefficient alphas for all subscales supported the temporal reliability (values ranged from .73-.90).

In a second study with 343 athletes from New Zealand, the results of a CFA on the BRSQ-8 supported once more the factor structure as well as the subscale internal consistency. Lonsdale and colleagues (2008) also showed that the factor structure of the BRSQ-6 model fit the data very well and that subscale coefficient alphas all exceeded .78. Moreover, the construct validity of the BRSQ-6 was assessed by testing for a simplex pattern of correlations among the six subscales. While some relationships were in line with predictions (e.g., amotivation was negatively related to intrinsic motivation), there was a lack of discrimination between some subscales. More specifically, there was no difference between external and introjected regulation scores in terms of their relationships with amotivation. A similar pattern was evident with the identified and integrated regulation subscales, which both had similar high correlations with intrinsic motivation. These results with the simplex pattern were replicated in a third study conducted with nonelite athletes. In this third study, Lonsdale and colleagues also assessed the relationships between the BRSQ-6 and indexes of burnout (Lemyre, Treasure, & Roberts, 2006; Raedeke & Smith, 2001) and flow (Jackson & Eklund, 2002). Overall, results supported hypotheses in line with SDT. Specifically, amotivation and external and introjected regulation showed negative correlations with flow and positive correlations with burnout. The opposite pattern of correlations was found for the self-determined subscales (intrinsic motivation and identified and integrated regulation). However, there was a lack of discrimination between integrated regulation and general intrinsic motivation. Results of another study on burnout (Lonsdale, Hodge, & Rose, 2009) replicated these findings. Thus, overall, the support for the construct validity of the BRSQ-6 appears to be mixed.

It should be underscored that the BRSQ has some nice features. First, the scale is designed in such a way that the researcher can decide to use a multidimensional (BRSQ-8) or unitary (BRSQ-6) conceptualization of intrinsic motivation. Second, the scale is rather short, with 4 items per subscale. Finally, it assesses integrated regulation. At the same time, the BRSQ also displays some limitations. First, additional research is needed on the construct validity of the scale. Whereas there is support distinguishing the self-determined subscales (intrinsic motivation and identified and integrated regulation) from the non-self-determined subscales (external and introjected regulation), the finer discrimination within each type of category appears to be lacking. Such evidence is crucial, and future research is needed in order to show that this scale does indeed assess the SDT constructs rather than two broad sets of subscales tapping self-determined versus non-self-determined motivation. Second, this scale is designed specifically for older participants in competitive sport; it remains to be seen if the BRSQ can be used with younger participants, for whom the integrated regulation subscale may not have full meaning. Finally, research is needed to test the temporal stability of the scale over a time framed longer than 1 week.

Pictorial Motivation Scale

The PMS was designed to measure intrinsic and extrinsic motivation for sport and exercise in people with an intellectual disability. It assesses participants' reasons for engaging in sport and exercise. The scale's main characteristics are drawings depicting each of the 20 items. There are 5 items (pictures) for each of four subscales: intrinsic motivation, self-determined extrinsic motivation (a mixture of integrated and identified regulation), non-self-determined extrinsic motivation (a mixture of introjected and external regulation), and amotivation. These pictures are used to help participants with cognitive difficulties and to help represent the motivational concept depicted in each item.

The original scale was developed in French (Reid, Poulin, & Vallerand, 1994). Results of a study with 62 participants supported the internal consistency, temporal stability, and construct validity, as exemplified by the presence of a simplex pattern among the four subscales. However, the amotivation subscale had poor reliability ($\alpha = .52$). The French version (Reid et al., 2009) was translated into English according to the back-translation and committee procedures outlined in Vallerand (1989). Then, 6 new items were generated for the less reliable amotivation subscale. Participants in the Special Olympics ($n = 160$) completed the English version. Results of the CFA confirmed the four-factor structure of the PMS. Furthermore, the internal consistency (Cronbach alphas) ranged from .60 to .71. Finally, the construct validity was assessed by testing for a simplex pattern of correlations among the four subscales. The intercorrelations among latent variables from the CFA provided support for the simplex pattern.

Results from a study conducted with the English version of the PMS involving 80 high school students with mild intellectual disability provided support for the internal consistency, temporal stability (over 3 wk), and construct validity of the PMS with respect to the simplex pattern of correlations among the PMS subscales as well as correlations between the PMS subscales and motivational antecedents (skill and perceived competence) and outcomes (perceived effort) as rated by the physical education teacher. Finally, the internal consistency of each subscale was tested without the pictorial dimension with a subset of 47 high school students with mild intellectual disability. Results indicated poor internal consistency (.91 for intrinsic motivation, .27 for self-determined extrinsic motivation, .20 for non-self-determined extrinsic motivation, and .60 for amotivation). This finding suggests that the scale is not reliable without the drawings.

The preliminary findings with the English version of the PMS are encouraging. Furthermore, this scale is the only one geared for individuals with intellectually disability. The use of drawings to depict the various items makes this scale unique in the field. Nevertheless, the PMS shows some limitations. First, the scale does not differentiate among all forms of intrinsic (knowledge, stimulation, and accomplishment) or extrinsic (integrated, identified, introjected, and external regulation) motivation. Second, construct validity was tested with only a limited number of variables. Third, it is not known if the scale is usable with children who have severe forms of intellectual disabilities. Clearly additional research is needed on the reliability and validity of the PMS.

Situational Motivation Scale

The SIMS is one of the few scales to assess intrinsic and extrinsic motivation and amotivation at the situational level (Guay et al., 2000). The SIMS is a multidimensional tool that measures four types of motivation: intrinsic motivation, identified regulation, external regulation, and amotivation. The SIMS is made up of 16 items (4 items per subscale) and asks this question: "Why are you currently engaged in this activity?" The items represent potential reasons for task engagement. The scale is worded in such a way that it can be used in most situations (sport and nonsport).

Five studies were reported in the original article. In study 1, the original scale was developed by a committee of experts and completed by 195 French Canadian college students. Results of an EFA revealed a four-factor structure with the final 16 items loading on their respective factor. In study 2, a CFA confirmed the factor structure as well as its invariance across gender. Across the five studies, the internal consistency values of the subscales were acceptable, ranging from .62 to .95 (see Guay et al., 2000). Moreover, across all studies, support was obtained for the construct validity of the SIMS through results from correlations in line with the simplex pattern among the subscales as well as between the SIMS subscales and motivational determinants and consequences. Perhaps of greater interest for the present discussion were the results of study 4, which showed that some subscales (intrinsic motivation and identified regulation) were sensitive enough to detect changes in motivation that took place during two games of a basketball tournament.

Other researchers have also obtained support for the psychometric properties of the SIMS. First, all studies reported acceptable internal consistency values for each subscale (Blanchard, Mask, Vallerand, de la Sablonnière, & Provencher, 2007; Conroy, Coatsworth, & Kaye, 2007; Law & Ste-Marie, 2005; Ntoumanis & Blaymires, 2003; Standage, Treasure, Duda, & Prusak, 2003). The coefficient alpha values of all but the amotivation subscale (α = .58) in the Conroy and colleagues study were above .60. Second, support for the factorial validity of the SIMS was obtained through CFAs with one qualification. Whereas the CFA results with the 16 items yielded acceptable fit indexes, removal of 1 item (Jaakkola, Liukkonen, Laakso, & Ommundsen, 2008) and even 2 items (Gillet, Berjot, & Paty, 2009; Standage, Treasure, et al., 2003) yielded better fit indexes. Moreover, Standage, Treasure, and colleagues (2003) conducted multisample CFAs and showed that the pattern of factor loadings was largely invariant across four different samples.

Construct validity of the SIMS was also assessed in several studies (Blanchard et al., 2007; Conroy et al., 2007; Law & Ste-Marie, 2005; Ntoumanis & Blaymires, 2003; Standage, Treasure, et al., 2003). In addition to supporting the simplex pattern among the SIMS subscales and between the SIMS subscales and need satisfaction (study 2 of Blanchard and colleagues, 2007), results also supported the postulate from the HMIEM (Vallerand, 1997) for the top-down effect, in which contextual sport motivation was found to predict situational sport motivation (studies 1 and 2 of Blanchard et al., 2007; Jaakkola et al.,

2008; Ntoumanis & Blaymires, 2003). Specifically, the more self-determined the motivation was found to be in a specific context (in this case, sport), the more self-determined the motivation was found to be in a given situation. Furthermore, Blanchard and colleagues (2007, studies 1 and 2) found support for another postulate from the HMIEM that suggests that over time, situational motivation in the realm of sport (basketball) has recursive effects on contextual motivation. The more that situational motivation is self-determined, the more that contextual motivation becomes self-determined over time. Finally, Jaakkola and coworkers (2008) demonstrated that, as predicted by the HMIEM, situational self-determined motivation was better than contextual motivation in predicting the situational intensity (as assessed by HR) displayed by students in a physical education class. Overall, these findings provide strong support for the reliability and factorial and construct validity of the SIMS.

The SIMS has several positive features, one of them being that it is the only scale to assess intrinsic and extrinsic motivation and amotivation at the situational level. Furthermore, it does so using only 16 items. Nevertheless, it also has some weaknesses. First, the SIMS does not assess the different types of intrinsic motivation and integrated and introjected regulation, because it was designed to be short. Second, while the factor structure has been supported, it is not clear if some items should be replaced (Gillet, Berjot, et al., 2009; Jaakkola et al., 2008; Standage, Treasure, et al., 2003). Third, research so far has not assessed the validity of the scale with high-performance athletes. Thus, additional research is needed to further test the psychometric properties of the SIMS in sport.

Motivation Scales for Exercise

In this section, we review scales used to assess intrinsic and extrinsic motivation in exercise settings. Specifically, we review the BREQ (Mullan et al., 1997) and the Exercise Motivation Scale (EMS; Li, 1999).

Behavioral Regulation in Exercise Questionnaire

Mullan and colleagues (1997) developed the BREQ to measure the different forms of motivation for exercise. The BREQ assesses external, introjected, identified, and intrinsic regulations. In line with other scales (e.g., Pelletier et al., 1995), the scale starts with a stem containing the question "Why do you engage in exercise?" Participants indicate the extent to which each item represents a reason why they exercise on a 5-point Likert scale ranging from 0 = "Not true for me" to 4 = "Very true for me." In

the first validation study (study 1 of Mullan et al., 1997), items derived from the Academic Motivation Scale (AMS; Vallerand et al., 1992) and the Self-Regulation Questionnaire (SRQ; Ryan & Connell, 1989) were adapted to reflect reasons for exercise. This preliminary version of the BREQ (with 30 items) was administered to 298 exercisers. Results from a CFA provided support for the four-factor structure of the BREQ with 15 items. Results also revealed that the BREQ has satisfactory internal consistency (with coefficient alphas ranging from 0.76-.90). The second validation study (study 2 of Mullan et al., 1997) involved 310 exercise participants and confirmed the four-factor structure of the BREQ through a CFA. In addition, a multisample analysis established factorial invariance across gender. The internal consistency of the subscales was also replicated. Furthermore, in line with SDT, subscale intercorrelations revealed a simplex pattern, thereby providing some elements of support for the construct validity of the BREQ. Surprisingly, Mullan and colleagues (1997) did not report test–retest correlations for the BREQ.

Research by other authors has also provided support for the psychometric properties of the BREQ. For instance, Wilson, Rodgers, and Frazer (2002, study 1) demonstrated through CFA that the proposed four-factor structure is acceptable. In addition, following Li and Harmer's (1996) procedures, Wilson and colleagues (2002, study 1) found support for the simplex model for the BREQ using SEM. Other research has supported the construct validity of the BREQ by demonstrating a simplex pattern between the BREQ subscales and motivational antecedents such as need satisfaction of autonomy, competence, and relatedness (Edmunds, Ntoumanis, & Dudas, 2006; Wilson et al., 2002). Similar findings have been obtained between the BREQ subscales and outcomes such as increased intention to exercise (Hagger, Charzisarantis, Barkoukis, Wang, & Baranowski, 2005; Thogersen-Ntoumani & Ntoumanis, 2006), higher objective intensity of exercise (Standage, Sebire, & Loney, 2008), and more intense exercise participation (Edmunds et al., 2006). Moreover, the BREQ has shown that more autonomously regulated individuals do exercise more (Landry & Solomon, 2004). One consistent finding in such research is that identified regulation to exercise is typically more positively associated with exercise participation than intrinsic motivation is (i.e., Edmunds et al., 2006; Landry & Solomon, 2004; Standage et al., 2008; Thogersen-Ntoumani & Ntoumanis, 2006). These results are in line with a hypothesis posited by Vallerand (1997; see also Burton, Lydon, D'Alessandro, & Koestner, 2006;

Koestner, Losier, Vallerand, & Carducci, 1996; Vallerand & Fortier, 1998) that when the task is not purely interesting (as is often the case for exercise), the most important predictor of outcomes is not intrinsic motivation but involves the highest forms of autonomous extrinsic motivation (identified and integrated regulation).

The BREQ has led to some variations since its development. For instance, Markland and Tobin (2004) added an amotivation subscale to the BREQ, whereas Wilson, Rodgers, Loitz, and Scime (2004) added an integrated regulation subscale to the original BREQ (that did not contain the amotivation subscale). These modified versions of the BREQ have all displayed appropriate levels of validity and reliability. However, no test of the entire BREQ revised with all subscales (amotivation; external, introjected, internal, and integrated regulation; and intrinsic motivation) has been conducted.

The BREQ contains some nice features. First, it assesses both intrinsic and extrinsic motivation (the latter in a multidimensional fashion). It has few items and can readily be used in most exercise settings. Furthermore, the psychometric properties of the scale are highly supportive of its reliability and validity. Nevertheless, some limitations should be kept in mind when using the BREQ. First, as mentioned previously, several versions of the BREQ have been developed over the years. Future research is needed to assess the reliability (including test-retest correlations) and validity of the complete version of the BREQ. Second, contrary to other scales, the BREQ does not assess the three types of intrinsic motivation. This distinction might prove useful, as some authors (Hein et al., 2004) have shown that some types of intrinsic motivation are better than others at predicting a person's intentions to engage in exercise during free time. Future research on this issue is needed.

Exercise Motivation Scale

Li (1999) developed and validated the EMS to assess amotivation; external, introjected, identified, and integrated regulation; and the three types of intrinsic motivation for exercise. As in the BREQ, motivation is operationalized as the perceived reasons for exercising. The EMS asks, "Why are you currently participating in this activity?" Participants indicate their degree of agreement with each item using a 6-point Likert scale ranging from 1 = "Strongly disagree" to 6 = "Strongly agree." In the first validation study (study 1 of Li, 1999), 101 college students were recruited from physical activity classes and interviewed about the reasons why they and their friends participate in exercise activi-

ties. Then, a panel of experts evaluated the content of the responses and classified the responses. This procedure created a total of 32 items. In the second validation study (study 2 of Li, 1999), these 32 items were administered to 371 college students also recruited from physical activity classes. Results of a CFA demonstrated poor fit of the model. Removal of 1 amotivation item improved the fit indexes, but it did not improve them up to acceptable values. Results also revealed that the EMS had satisfactory internal consistency (with coefficient alphas ranging from .75-.90). Finally, in the third validation study (study 3 of Li, 1999), the eight-factor EMS was administered to 598 college students involved in one of a variety of physical activity classes. Results of a CFA once again provided poor fit for the model although all factors were well defined. Finally, results demonstrated that the temporal stability of the scale was acceptable (with test-retest correlations ranging from .78-.88) over 1 wk.

In study 3, Li (1999) looked at the construct validity of the EMS in four ways. First, following Li and Harmer's (1996) procedures, Li found general support for the simplex model among the EMS subscales through SEM. However, the integrated regulation was correlated more strongly with introjected regulation than it was with identified regulation. Second, support was obtained through correlations between the EMS subscales and need satisfaction of competence, autonomy, and relatedness. Third, correlations between the EMS subscales and motivational consequences such as exercise interest and effort were in line with predictions from SDT. However, there was a lack of finer discrimination among the self-determined subscales as well as among the non-self-determined subscales pertaining to their correlations with both determinants and outcomes. Finally, the EMS was found to distinguish between frequent exercisers and nonfrequent exercisers, with autonomous regulated individuals exercising more.

To the best of our knowledge, only one other study has examined the psychometric properties of the EMS (Winninger, 2007). In study 1, the EMS was administered to 143 undergraduate students. Results revealed that the EMS shows satisfactory internal consistency (with coefficient alphas ranging from .75-.90). However, the results from the pattern of correlations were not fully supported, as several departures were obtained. Of interest is that all EMS subscales were unrelated to social desirability, with the exception of introjected regulation, which was weakly but significantly and positively related. Finally, results from study 2 showed that the more self-determined forms of motivation were positively associated with exercise identity as measured by the Exercise Identity Scale (EIS; Anderson & Cychosz, 1994).

In sum, the EMS offers some positive features, including the fact that it is the only validated scale assessing exercise motivation that covers the entire self-determination continuum, including the three different forms of intrinsic motivation and integrated regulation. However, the EMS has not been used extensively and has some limitations. First, additional research is needed to further examine the factorial validity of the EMS, as it appears to be problematic. One explanation may have to do with the question posed to the respondents. The EMS asks, "Why are you *currently* participating in this activity?" This is a question that is typically used at the situational level. And yet, the items reflect motivation at the contextual level. Changing the question to a more contextual one ("In general, why do you exercise?") might improve the scale factorial validity. Second, research (Li, 1999; Winninger, 2007) revealed that while there is some support for the construct validity of the EMS, such support is not complete. Third, the EMS has been validated only with college and undergraduate students. We have no information on the psychometric properties of the scale with the general population. Finally, the temporal stability of the scale was assessed only over a 1 wk time frame. Future research is needed in order to address all of these issues.

Recommendations for Researchers and Practitioners

From the review of existing measures of intrinsic and extrinsic motivation presented in this chapter, we can make a number of conclusions. In this section we formulate conclusions that lead to suggestions for future research that may appeal to motivation researchers. In addition, throughout the chapter, we have highlighted areas where improvement is needed; researchers may find in these suggestions food for thought pertaining to research ideas.

A first conclusion it that most scales display relatively high levels of validity and reliability. This is reassuring for researchers who rely on proper methodological tools to conduct their research and move the field forward. However, not all scales are created equal, and we recommend that researchers make an informed choice regarding which scale to use in their research based on the information that we report and the conclusions that we draw.

A second conclusion is that all seven scales assess the motivation of only one type of sport participant—namely, athletes or exercisers (depending on the scale). In their review, Vallerand and Fortier (1998) underscored the importance of developing scales to assess the motivation of other sport participants, especially that of coaches. More than 10 years later, we not only reiterate the necessity of doing so but also add that scales are needed to assess the motivation of referees, fans, and fitness instructors. This represents an important future research agenda for motivation researchers.

A third conclusion is that there has been a clear move toward a multidimensional assessment of motivation since the Vallerand and Fortier (1998) paper. In fact, all the scales reviewed here are multidimensional. This is an important change, as historically intrinsic and extrinsic motivation were viewed as unidimensional constructs. However, as theory has evolved, so have assessment tools. It should be underscored, however, that amotivation is not assessed in a multidimensional fashion. Researchers may want to determine empirically if the multidimensional amotivation taxonomy developed for the environment by Pelletier, Dion, Tuson, and Green-Demers (1999) might be useful for the sport and exercise domain.

A fourth conclusion is that research so far has not assessed the level of social desirability displayed by the various motivation scales (see the EMS for an exception). Because self-report instruments may be subject to some social desirability, and all the motivation scales reviewed here use self-report, such research appears to be important. It also appears important to develop and validate alternative assessment procedures. Doing so would allow researchers to assess whether the findings obtained with self-reports can be replicated. A possible alternative procedure is interviews. A nice example is the work of Mallett and Hanrahan (2004), who, through interviews with high-level athletes, found support for SDT and the HMIEM. Similar procedures could be used to assess intrinsic and extrinsic motivation with exercisers. A second assessment alternative deals with implicit motivational processes. Recent research has shown that nonconscious factors (e.g., subliminal priming) may affect intrinsic and extrinsic motivation (e.g., Levesque & Pelletier, 2003; Ratelle, Baldwin, & Vallerand, 2005), including motivation on a sport-related task (Radel, Sarrazin, & Pelletier, 2009). If intrinsic and extrinsic motivation are affected without the person being aware of such effects, participants may not be able to report motivational changes. The alternatives to self-report measures might include implicit measures such as the Implicit Association Test (IAT; Greenwald, McGhee, & Schwartz, 1998). The IAT rests on methodological procedures used with lexicon tasks in cognitive psychology and deals with comparisons of reaction times following the presentation of stimulus words on a computer screen. Levesque and Brown (2007) developed an implicit intrinsic and extrinsic motivation measure toward a task and have shown that it is basically unrelated to explicit (self-report) measures of motivation. Thus it may predict different outcomes. The challenge will be to devise an IAT measure that can be used in field settings and administered rather quickly. Future research on these issues appears particularly exciting for the realm of sport and exercise.

In this chapter, we have examined seven scales used regularly in contemporary research. Practitioners may ask themselves, "Which one should I use?" The answer to this question depends on the goal of the assessment. For instance, practitioners interested in understanding the predominant types of motivation that athletes have in general toward their sport should use a contextual measure of motivation. These practitioners can select one of the sport motivation questionnaires (SMS, SMS-6, or BRSQ). On the other hand, practitioners who want to identify the intrinsic and extrinsic motivations that athletes experience in specific situations should use a situational measure—the SIMS. Thus, consideration should be given to assessing motivation at the appropriate level of generality. Other considerations include ensuring that all pertinent constructs (the different types of intrinsic and extrinsic motivation) are assessed by the selected scale and making sure that the scale is appropriate for the subject population (age, level of cognitive complexity).

Another issue pertains to the best way to assess the effects of interventions. Research (e.g., Conway & Ross, 1984) has revealed that when people are involved in an intervention, they typically expect to change. Self reports may thus be biased. Practitioners may thus want to use a triangulation method, in which various measures completed by different people are used. Reports from fitness instructors, spouses, or fitness buddies of the participants, in addition to reports from the participants themselves, can be used to see if there is a coherent pattern of results (see Reiss & Havercamp, 1998).

Measurement represents a crucial aspect of scientific inquiry. In part because of the quality of the motivation measures, the field of intrinsic and extrinsic motivation in sport and exercise has exploded over the past decade. No one can predict what the field will be like in ten years from now. However, by remaining strongly anchored in methodological rigor and sound theory, our instruments should allow us to continue moving forward on the quest for scientific knowledge.

■ Table 25.2 ■

Measures Assessing Intrinsic and Extrinsic Motivation

Concept	Measure	Dimension	Source	Website
Intrinsic and extrinsic motivation in sport	Sport Motivation Scale (SMS)	7 subscales: amotivation; external, introjected, and identified regulations; and intrinsic motivation to know, to experience stimulation, and to accomplish	Pelletier et al. (1995); Briere et al. (1995)	www.er.uqam.ca/ nobel/r26710/LRCS/ echelles_en.htm
Intrinsic and extrinsic motivation in sport	Sport Motivation Scale-6 (SMS-6)	6 subscales: amotivation; external, introjected, identified, and integrated regulations; and general intrinsic motivation	Mallett et al. (2007)	None

(continued)

Concept	Measure	Dimension	Source	Website
Intrinsic and extrinsic motivation in sport	Behavioral Regulation in Sport Questionnaire (BRSQ)	8 subscales: amotivation; external, introjected, identified, and integrated regulations; intrinsic motivation to know, to experience stimulation, and to accomplish	Lonsdale et al. (2008)	None
Intrinsic and extrinsic motivation in sport	Pictorial Motivation Scale (PMS)	4 subscales: intrinsic motivation, self-determined extrinsic motivation (a mixture of integrated and identified regulation), non-self-determined extrinsic motivation (a mixture of introjected and external regulation), and amotivation	Reid et al. (2009)	www.er.uqam.ca/nobel/r26710/LRCS/echelles_en.htm
Intrinsic and extrinsic motivation in sport	Situational Motivation Scale (SIMS)	4 subscales: intrinsic motivation, identified regulation, external regulation, and amotivation	Guay et al. (2000)	www.er.uqam.ca/nobel/r26710/LRCS/echelles_en.htm
Intrinsic and extrinsic motivation in exercise	Revised Behavioral Regulation in Exercise Questionnaire (BREQ)	5 subscales: amotivation and external, introjected, identified, and intrinsic regulations	Mullan, Markland, & Ingledew (1997)	www.bangor.ac.uk/~pes004/exercise_motivation/breq/breq.htm
Intrinsic and extrinsic motivation in exercise	Exercise Motivation Scale (EMS)	6 subscales: amotivation and external, introjected, identified, integrated, and intrinsic regulations	Li (1999)	None

Exercise Motivation

Philip M. Wilson, PhD

It is difficult to envision a concept in exercise psychology that has drawn more attention than motivation. Such popularity is not surprising considering the many people who initiate exercise programs and then fail to adhere to exercise over the long term and the widespread belief that motivational theory provides a platform to understand this paradox (Deci & Ryan, 2002). The past 30 years have generated a substantial amount of research concerning exercise motivation. The topic of measurement has served as a focal point integrating research themes across numerous theories. Lack of attention to measurement issues can stifle progress in any field (Crocker & Algina, 1986), so it is partially reassuring that scholars interested in the psychology of exercise have focused their research efforts in this direction. It is equally perplexing, however, to gauge the amount of progress that has been made in measuring exercise motivation given (a) the breadth of this research agenda, (b) the proliferation of exercise motivation instruments, and (c) the diverse range of theories addressing motivation issues frequently utilized in exercise psychology.

This chapter focuses on instruments designed to measure exercise motivation. It begins by outlining issues of domain clarity based on the conceptualization of motivation within psychological theory that is the foundation for instrument development. The next section reviews published data concerning select instruments designed to assess both intrinsic and extrinsic motives for exercise in line with relevant theory. The chapter concludes with directions for advancing research and practice in exercise psychology. The intent is to illustrate issues and challenges in the field that affect future exercise motivation research.

Key Concepts and Theoretical Frameworks

Defining *motivation* is a key challenge given the breadth and scope of different theories and frameworks examining this psychological construct. Providing a universal definition of motivation that transcends diverse theories and frameworks is a pivotal challenge, particularly when such definitional clarity is integral to the measurement process (Messick, 1995). Classic approaches to the definition of motivation in the general psychology literature suggest that this concept is characterized by the energization and direction of human behavior (Deci & Ryan, 2008). The conceptual origins of these classic definitions can be traced to early research by psychologists grappling with issues such as physiological and psychological needs as the driving forces of human behavior in conjunction with intentional and nonintentional acts as goal-directed actions (Deci, 1992). Contemporary approaches to human motivation in psychology built on this early work and led to the evolution of three concepts, amotivation, extrinsic motivation, and intrinsic motivation, which Vallerand (1997) contended are integral for a "complete analysis of motivation" (p. 278). These concepts distinguish among major sources, or types, of motivation with reference to their intrinsic or extrinsic orientation and also differentiate the extent to which a person is motivated or not motivated (known as *amotivation*) toward a target behavior. The following section provides a conceptual overview of the defining features that distinguish amotivation from intrinsic or extrinsic motivation. The section culminates with a synopsis of two major approaches to human motivation that are prevalent in psychology and that elucidate the nature and function of these concepts: self-determination theory (SDT; Deci & Ryan, 2002) and the hierarchical model of intrinsic and extrinsic motivation (HMIEM; Vallerand, 1997). Measurement issues inherent to the study of exercise motivation using social cognitive theories are addressed in chapter 25.

Intrinsic Motivation

Intrinsic motivation refers to "doing an activity for its own sake" (Ryan & Deci, 2007, p. 2). As a concept, intrinsic motivation has enjoyed one of the longest traditions in motivational psychology. The original concept was developed in reaction to dominant views in psychology contending that behavior is motivated by environmental reinforcements or the desire to ameliorate deficiencies in physiological needs (see Deci, 1992). Contemporary views suggest that intrinsic motivation is a natural endowment of all human beings that occurs when people find an activity to be inherently satisfying and interesting and thus do not require environmental prompts to participate (Deci & Ryan, 2008). Examination of the available literature suggests that the content domain characterizing intrinsic motivation is defined by feelings of enjoyment, fun, interest, and inherent satisfaction derived solely from participating in the target activity (Deci & Ryan, 2002). In other words, the participant perceives the behavior itself as autotelic or self-rewarding (Deci & Ryan, 2002).

Vallerand (1997) has advanced a more differentiated view of intrinsic motivation within the HMIEM in which feelings of knowledge, stimulation, and accomplishment characterize distinct intrinsic motives. This tridimensional conceptualization of intrinsic motivation goes beyond the unitary phenomenon often depicted in the literature. *Intrinsic motivation to know* is defined by a person's innate curiosity to experience pleasure while exploring and comprehending novel tasks or experiences. *Intrinsic motivation toward accomplishment* pertains to the personal satisfaction associated with trying to accomplish a given task rather than the rewards associated with the end product of those strivings. Finally, *intrinsic motivation to experience stimulation* concerns the pleasure a person receives from sensory activation.

Extrinsic Motivation

Extrinsic motivation refers to activities undertaken as a means to an end. The impetus motivating participation is external to and distinct from the behavior itself (Deci & Ryan, 2002). In other words, extrinsic motivation concerns participation because

the activity "leads to some separable consequence" (Deci & Ryan, 2008, p.15). Initial research in this area used a "binary approach" (Vallerand, 1997, p. 282) in which both intrinsic and extrinsic motives were considered unitary and often pitted against one another or combined in an additive manner to index overall motivation. Subsequent research and theorizing by Deci and Ryan (2002) promoted a differentiated view of extrinsic motivation that accounted for the degree to which the target behavior is internalized and integrated with an individual's sense of self. Organismic integration theory (OIT) is the subfacet of SDT concerned with the nature of extrinsic motivation (Deci & Ryan, 2002). In contrast to early conceptualizations of extrinsic motivation, OIT includes four extrinsic motives that are also embraced within the HMIEM. These extrinsic motives vary across a continuum in the degree to which the instrumental reasons motivating the target behavior are internalized by the person and integrated with the sense of self. The content domain characterizing the different extrinsic motives outlined within OIT includes the following:

1. *External Regulation:* Motivation toward the target behavior that occurs via external means. In other words, the origin of motivation resides outside the individual and within the social environment. Examples include rewards, punishments, threats, and deadlines.

2. *Introjected Regulation:* Motivation toward the target behavior that occurs by self-imposed contingencies such as the desire to avoid negative emotions (e.g., guilt or shame) or to support contingent self-worth. Introjected regulation focuses on self-imposed contingencies, as opposed to external regulation, in which the motivating source resides with an external agent or environmental prompt.

3. *Identified Regulation:* Motivation toward the target behavior that occurs via the personal value or purpose an individual ascribes to the behavior itself, usually because the behavior promotes outcomes that the person deems important. Identified regulation is an autonomous form of extrinsic motivation. Reasons compelling action have been internalized within the self to a greater extent when compared with controlling extrinsic motives such as introjected and external regulations.

4. *Integrated Regulation:* Motivation toward the target behavior is prompted by the instrumental value of the activity itself that is congruent with other value structures that make up the individual's psyche. Integrated regulation concerns the extent to which participating in the target activity (e.g., exercise) is symbolic of the person's identity. The

motives regulating this behavior align harmoniously with reasons that motivate other activities (e.g., eating).

Amotivation

Amotivation has received considerably less research attention in the exercise psychology literature when compared with intrinsic or extrinsic motivation (Vallerand, 1997). The defining characteristic of amotivation concerns the lack of intention to act. In essence, this means that a person is "literally without motivation for an activity" (Ryan & Deci, 2007, p. 10). Amotivation can stem from the target behavior lacking instrumental value to the person, feelings of perceived incompetence with respect to the target behavior, or failure to recognize the range of outcomes contingent on participation (Deci & Ryan, 2002; Vallerand, 1997). The key characteristics defining the content domain of amotivation include futility with respect to the target behavior and lack of intention to act. These characteristics rarely motivate behavior and at best compel the individual to act by merely going "through the motions" (Deci & Ryan, 2002, p. 17).

Theory and Measurement

Measurement experts contend that domain clarity, or establishing the boundary conditions that define key concepts (Crocker & Algina, 1986), is an integral step in the development (and refinement) of instruments designed to measure latent concepts such as motivation. Issues of domain clarity within exercise motivation research typically adhere to the conceptual principles outlined within the framework or theory guiding the investigation. Given the importance of domain clarity to advancing progress in measurement, the following section provides an overview of the key features defining motivation in accordance with SDT (Deci & Ryan, 2002) and the HMIEM (Vallerand, 1997). Comprehensive reviews of SDT and the HMIEM in psychology (Deci & Ryan, 2002; Vallerand, 1997) and in applications to exercise (Ryan & Deci, 2007; Vallerand, 2007) have been provided in the literature.

Self-Determination Theory and Motivation

SDT is a macrolevel approach to studying human motivation that was initially developed to assimilate research concerning intrinsic and extrinsic sources of human motivation (Vallerand, 1997). The current iteration of SDT comprises four minitheories, each designed to account for a distinct yet related aspect of human development and function (Deci

& Ryan, 2002). Cognitive evaluation theory (CET) focuses on intrinsic motivation and delineates the environmental factors that can forestall (or support) this natural propensity in humans. OIT provides a differentiated account of extrinsic motivation and presents a range of behavioral regulations that vary in quantity (amotivational versus motivational) and quality (less to more self-determined). Causality orientations theory (COT) is concerned with individual differences that lead a person to approach broad domains of life with a global autonomous, controlled, or impersonal orientation toward functioning. Finally, basic needs theory (BNT) accounts for the energizing nature of fulfilling psychological needs for competence, autonomy, and relatedness in terms of their effects on integration, growth, and well-being. The conceptual thread permeating each minitheory in SDT is the "organismic-dialectical meta-theory" (Deci & Ryan, 2000, p. 228), which in plain language suggests that humans are naturally endowed toward growth and development. These natural tendencies are optimized when social environments provide opportunities to fulfill basic psychological needs in an authentic and ongoing manner (Deci & Ryan, 2002).

The development of SDT as a framework to understand human motivation provided the foundation for several key postulates that collectively guide instrument development based on this theory (Deci & Ryan, 2002). The following is a synopsis of the postulates embedded within SDT: (a) Motivation is complex and is best represented as a continuum that differentiates sources of extrinsic motivation based on their degree of internalization and integration with the self (Deci & Ryan, 2002). (b) The central distinction of motives within the SDT approach concerns those that are autonomous (identified, integrated, and intrinsic regulations) versus those that are controlled (external and introjected regulations). These differ from amotivation in both quantity and quality (Deci & Ryan, 2008). (c) Motives in SDT can be distinguished from goals (or aspirations) in that motives concern the regulatory processes driving goal-directed behavior (*why*; Deci & Ryan, 2000), while goals define the outcomes anticipated to accrue from participating in the behavior (*what*; Deci & Ryan, 2000).

A key corollary derived from this theorizing concerns the "quasi-simplex pattern" (Deci & Ryan, 2002, p. 18) of relationships that is hypothesized to occur in research using the motivational continuum postulated within SDT. Deci and Ryan (2002) argued that the continuum represents the extent to which reasons motivating behavior have been internalized and integrated with the self. Therefore, adjacent points on the continuum (e.g., external and introjected regulations) should be more positively correlated than distal points on the continuum (e.g., external and intrinsic regulations).

Motivation and the Hierarchical Model of Intrinsic and Extrinsic Motivation

The pioneering work that culminated in the SDT framework served in part as the impetus for the development of the HMIEM by Vallerand (1997) and colleagues. Since the inception of the HMIEM, a considerable amount of research has tested and largely supported the five postulates that make up the model across various life domains. The postulates collectively articulate the nature, function, and determinants of amotivation, extrinsic motivation, and intrinsic motivation (for a review, see Vallerand, 1997). In brief, the HMIEM presents a four-stage causal sequence of motivational processes that exist at three distinct levels of generality (global, contextual, and situational). The model can be depicted as follows: Social factors → mediators (psychological needs) → types of motivation → consequences (Vallerand, 1997). Vallerand introduced the HMIEM as a unifying framework predicated on integrating existing literature concerned with motivation and generating novel hypotheses to advance study in this area. The research base informing and testing the HMIEM has advanced instrument development to assess exercise motivation in numerous ways. These include but are not limited to (a) clarifying item wording to differentiate motivation at the global level from instruments measuring motivation at either the contextual or the situational level and (b) offering a clear nomological network (Cronbach & Meehl, 1955) that anchors a program of construct validation research to an underlying conceptual framework.

Exercise Motivation Instruments

This section presents a review of four instruments (see table 26.1) used to measure intrinsic and extrinsic motivation toward exercise behavior. A series of inclusion criteria facilitated the identification and selection of instruments for review in this section of the chapter. Instruments were included if they (a) were initially developed on the basis of SDT or the HMIEM, (b) assessed both extrinsic and intrinsic motives for exercise or assessed amotivation, (c) included exercise as the focal reference point for item content, and (d) were used primarily as an index of exercise motivation rather than motivation for sport or rehabilitation.

The Motivation for Physical Activity Measure-Revised (MPAM-R; Ryan, Frederick, Lepes, Rubio, & Sheldon, 1997) is included in this section given the pioneering role of research using this instrument in the development of subsequent instruments concerned with the assessment of exercise motivation in line with the SDT framework (Frederick-Recascino, 2002). The information presented includes a brief description of the instrument, the source used to generate items embedded within the instrument, and the evidence for the reliability and construct validity of scores derived from the instrument available in the exercise psychology literature.

Motivation for Physical Activity Measure-Revised

The MPAM-R (Ryan et al., 1997) is an extension of the Motivation for Physical Activity Measure (MPAM; Frederick & Ryan, 1993). The MPAM is a 23-item instrument developed to assess interest, enjoyment, competence, and body-related reasons motivating involvement in physical activity (Frederick & Ryan, 1993). Ryan and colleagues (1997) developed the MPAM-R to address two content validity issues inherent with the MPAM. The first issue concerned differentiating items within the MPAM's body-related subscale to assess distinct extrinsic motives based on appearance (e.g., "Because I want to define my muscles") versus health (e.g., "Because I want to improve my cardiorespiratory fitness"). The second issue concerned the content represented by the pool of MPAM items, which omitted social interactions as a plausible extrinsic motive. The MPAM-R (Ryan et al., 1997) is a 30-item instrument designed to represent five physical activity motives with these subscales: competence, enjoyment, appearance, health and fitness, and social.

The nature of the stem for the MPAM or MPAM-R was unclear, but subsequent research has used the following stem with the MPAM-R in exercisers: "Why do you exercise?" (Wilson, Rodgers, & Fraser, 2002). The MPAM and MPAM-R use a (5-point and 7-point, respectively) Likert response format. The two instruments use the same verbal anchors at the extremes, with 1 = "Not at all true for me" and 5 (MPAM) or 7 (MPAM-R) = "Very true for me."

Source of Items. Frederick and Ryan (1993) developed the original MPAM items based on available literature, pilot testing, and the need for an instrument to assess motives that could apply broadly across both sport contexts and exercise contexts. Subsequent development of the MPAM-R (Ryan et al., 1997) involved the addition of 7 new items. Of the new items, 5 were written to represent social motives (e.g., "Because I want to meet new

■ **Table 26.1** ■

Instruments Used to Measure Exercise Motivation Developed Within Self-Determination Theory and the Hierarchical Model of Intrinsic and Extrinsic Motivation

Variable or concept	Instrument	Dimension	Source	Website
Fitness, appearance, competence and challenge, enjoyment, social motives	Motivation for Physical Activity Measure-Revised (MPAM-R)	Extrinsic and intrinsic motivation	Ryan, Frederick-Recascino, Lepes, Rubio, & Sheldon (1997)	www.psych.rochester.edu/SDT/measures/mpam_description.php
Stress management, revitalization, enjoyment, challenge, social recognition, affiliation, competition, health pressures, ill-health avoidance, positive health, weight management, appearance, strength and endurance, and nimbleness	Exercise Motivation Inventory-2 (EMI-2)	Extrinsic and intrinsic motivation	Markland & Ingeldew (1997)	http://pages.bangor.ac.uk/~pes004/exercise_motivation/emi/emi-2.htm
External, introjected, identified, and intrinsic regulation	Behavioral Regulation in Exercise Questionnaire (BREQ)	Extrinsic and intrinsic motivation	Mullan, Markland, & Ingledew (1997)	http://pages.bangor.ac.uk/~pes004/exercise_motivation/breq/breq.htm
Amotivation and external, introjected, identified, and intrinsic regulation	Behavioral Regulation in Exercise Questionnaire-2 (BREQ-2)	Amotivation and extrinsic and intrinsic motivation	Markland & Tobin (2004)	http://pages.bangor.ac.uk/~pes004/exercise_motivation/breq/breq.htm
Amotivation; external, introjected, identified, and integrated regulations; and intrinsic motivation to know, to experience sensations, to learn, and to accomplish	Exercise Motivation Scale (EMS)	Amotivation and extrinsic and intrinsic motivation	Li (1999)	None

people") and 2 were added to the fitness and health subscale ("Because I want to maintain my physical strength to live a healthy life" and "Because I want to maintain my physical health and well-being"). Three items from the original MPAM body-related subscale define the full complement of MPAM-R items measuring health and fitness (see Ryan et al., 1997). The etiology of the items added to the MPAM-R is not clear, although Ryan and colleagues (1997) noted that the MPAM-R "was developed on the basis of pilot testing of items" (p. 345).

Summary. A limited number of studies have used the MPAM-R, and thus appraising the instrument's utility is challenging and likely premature. The

available evidence suggests that MPAM-R scores are minimally affected by measurement error. Internal consistency reliability estimates (Cronbach alphas) range considerably for scores across MPAM-R subscales (Frederick-Recascino & Schuster-Smith, 2003; Moreno, Galindo, & Pardo, 2008; Ryan et al., 1997; Sit, Kerr, & Wong, 2008; Wilson et al., 2002), with .70 being the lowest reported value for the health and fitness subscale. In the literature, there are concerns regarding the integrity of the MPAM-R measurement model. Two studies reported analyses pertaining to the structural validity of the MPAM-R measurement model, and neither study provided convincing support for the instrument's scores in samples of adult exercisers from North America (Ryan et al., 1997; Wilson et al., 2002). Notwithstanding this caveat, there is evidence to support the nomological validity of MPAM-R scores in terms of relationships with psychological need fulfillment (Wilson et al., 2002) and behavior in the form of adherence patterns (Ryan et al., 1997) and physical activity status (Sit et al., 2008). Studies of young North American adults (Ryan et al., 1997) and middle-aged Chinese women (Sit et al., 2008) indicated that appearance motives do not seem to correlate with exercise behavior, whereas the other four MPAM-R subscales were associated with higher adherence or more active group classification. A study of Spanish adults engaged in aquatic exercise (Moreno et al., 2008) revealed that more self-determined exercise motives were positively associated with all MPAM-R subscales expect appearance. In summary, the MPAM-R may be useful for measuring a broad range of motives that conceptually represent either intrinsic or extrinsic reasons for physical activity behavior.

Exercise Motivation Inventory-2

The Exercise Motivation Inventory-2 (EMI-2; Markland & Ingledew, 1997) was developed as an extension of the Exercise Motivation Inventory (EMI; Markland & Hardy, 1993). The EMI-2 contains 51 items defining 14 constructs measuring "a broad range of males' and females' exercise motives" (Markland & Ingledew, 1997, p. 374). The EMI-2 assesses the following exercise motives: weight management, ill-health avoidance, revitalization, appearance, social recognition, stress management, positive health, strength and endurance, enjoyment, affiliation, health pressures, competition, nimbleness, and challenge.

Four additional items have been created for use with the EMI-2 to assess muscular development (Loze & Collins, 1998). A stem—"Personally, I exercise (or might exercise) . . ."—focuses participants on their current or potential reasons for exercise. The EMI-2 items are followed by a 6-point Likert scale with verbal anchors located at 0 = "Not at all true for me" and 5 = "Very true for me."

Source of Items. Markland and Hardy (1993) developed the original pool of EMI items from two sources. These are (1) open-ended responses provided by a sample of regular exercisers (*N* = 76) asked to state the three main reasons they choose to exercise (*n* = 45 items) and (2) items embedded within the Personal Incentives for Exercise Questionnaire (Duda & Tappe, 1989) or evident in the exercise motivation literature (*n* = 31 items). The final set of 44 EMI items were

derived from an iterative process of item elimination using exploratory factor analyses (EFA). An additional 25 items were included with the original EMI items to form the initial EMI-2 item pool. Markland and Ingledew (1997) used a hypothesis-testing approach to confirmatory factor analyses (CFA) to identify and discard 18 original EMI items to arrive at the final 51-item version of the EMI-2. The items proposed by Loze and Collins (1998) to assess muscular development emerged from a synthesis of expert opinions concerning why people engage in resistance training and a subsequent EFA.

Summary. The availability of the EMI-2 in seven different languages suggests that the instrument holds broad appeal as a method of assessing exercise motivation reflecting the archetypal intrinsic and extrinsic distinction. Estimates of internal consistency (Markland & Ingledew, 1997; Ingledew & Sullivan, 2002; Ingledew, Markland, & Medley, 1998) and temporal stability (Ortís et al., 2007) are evident, yet select studies indicate no sample-specific reliability data (Ortís et al., 2007). Cronbach alpha values reported in the literature vary considerably across EMI-2 subscales (ranging from .56-.95), yet it seems that health pressures (α= .69; Ingledew et al., 1998; Markland & Ingledew, 1997) and revitalization (α = .56; Ingledew & Sullivan, 2002) are the only subscales displaying consistently lower reliability estimates. Evidence of structural validity for responses to the EMI-2 is difficult to appraise. The different solutions reported in the literature based on factor analysis tests make it difficult to interpret the evidence informing the measurement model underpinning the EMI-2. Studies have reported the results of measurement model analyses for EMI-2 scores based on single-factor measurement models in adolescents (Ingledew & Sullivan, 2002), grouping conceptually related EMI-2 subscales together before evaluating structural validity (Markland & Ingledew, 1997), and not using the full complement of EMI-2 items (Dacey, Baltzell, & Ziachkowsky, 2008). A series of investigations has linked more intrinsic EMI-2 motives with later stages of change pertaining to exercise adoption defined by sustained exercise behavior (Dacey et al., 2008; Ingeldew et al., 1998; Ortís et al., 2007) and higher indexes of well-being (Maltby & Day, 2001). Overall, the EMI-2 appears useful if the primary interest is to measure a broad array of exercise motives that reflect either intrinsic or extrinsic reasons for behavior.

Behavioral Regulation in Exercise Questionnaire

The Behavioral Regulation in Exercise Questionnaire (BREQ; Mullan, Markland, & Ingledew, 1997) was developed to assess the motivational continuum outlined within OIT (Deci & Ryan, 2002). The BREQ includes subscales to assess the following concepts: external regulation, introjected regulation, identified regulation, and intrinsic regulation.

Markland and Tobin (2004) created the BREQ-2, which includes 4 items measuring amotivation. The stem preceding the BREQ and BREQ-2 items is "Why do you engage in exercise?" The response options are provided on a 5-point Likert scale with verbal anchors affixed at 0 = "Not true for me," 2 = "Sometimes true for me," and 4 = "Very true for me." One study reports the development of 4 additional items to assess integrated regulation when using either the BREQ or the BREQ-2 (Wilson, Rodgers, Loitz, & Scime, 2006).

Source of Items. Mullan and colleagues (1997) developed the BREQ and BREQ-2 items by modifying the wording of existing items from the Academic Motivation Scale (AMS) and Self-Regulation Questionnaire (SRQ). The BREQ initially contained 30 items modified from the AMS and SRQ to "reflect reasons for exercise" (Mullan et al., 1997, p. 747). The integrated regulation items developed by Wilson and colleagues (2006) were modified from existing instruments that assess this extrinsic motive (Pelletier, Dion, Slovinec-D'Angelo, & Reid, 2004).

Summary. Most of the research addressing exercise motivation using SDT as a framework has included the BREQ or BREQ-2. This suggests that these instruments have been pivotal in advancing this line of inquiry. Evidence for construct validity is available in five different languages for both instruments and generally supports the conceptualization of exercise motivation along a continuum of self-determination advanced within SDT (Deci & Ryan, 2002). Intrinsic regulation scores display the least error variance (Cronbach alpha values range from .74-.98), while amotivation and introjected regulation scores occasionally demonstrate lower reliability estimates (Edmunds, Ntouamnis, & Duda, 2008). Select investigations have reported internal consistency reliability estimates for combinations of BREQ and BREQ-2 subscales that conceptually represent autonomous and controlled motives (Sebire, Standage, & Vansteenkiste, 2008; Standage, Sebire, & Loney, 2008), although it is not entirely clear if these reliability estimates used raw or weighted BREQ and BREQ-2 scores. Investigations supporting the structural validity of the BREQ (Mullan et al., 1997) and BREQ-2 (Markland & Tobin, 2004) have been reported using CFA techniques. Research has demonstrated positive links between more self-determined motives assessed by the BREQ and BREQ-2 and frequent physical activity behavior

(Wilson, Rodgers, Fraser, & Murray, 2004), overall well-being (Edmunds, Ntouamnis, & Duda, 2007), greater psychological need satisfaction (Wilson & Rogers, 2008), and stronger endorsement of intrinsic relative to extrinsic goals for exercise (Sebire et al., 2008). Select investigations have supported variations in the scoring protocol applied to BREQ responses by creating either a single score called the *Relative Autonomy Index* (RAI; Mullan & Markland, 1997) or two global scores posited to represent autonomous and controlled exercise motives (Sebire et al., 2008). Comparable scoring protocols haven been forthcoming in the broader SDT literature and remain consistent with the meta-theoretical roots of SDT; however, the extent to which such approaches can be applied to the BREQ-2 or studies that include an assessment of integrated regulation remains unclear at present. Overall, the evidence informing the interpretation of BREQ and BREQ-2 scores is impressive both in depth and scope. The literature has shown systematic efforts to test multiple aspects of construct validity advanced by Messick (1995). In brief, it seems reasonable to suggest that the BREQ and BREQ-2 are the instruments of choice for research assessing the regulation of exercise behavior in line with OIT.

Exercise Motivation Scale

The Exercise Motivation Scale (EMS; Li, 1999) assesses the quantity and quality of exercise motivation in line with the HMIEM (Vallerand, 1997). The EMS comprises 31 items assessing three types of intrinsic motivation (to learn, to experience sensations, and to accomplish), four types of extrinsic motivation (external, introjected, identified, and integrated regulations), and amotivation toward exercise. The EMS stem focuses respondents on their current physical activity: "Why are you currently participating in this activity?" EMS items are followed by a 6-point Likert response scale with verbal anchors fixed to each option, with 1 = "Strongly disagree" and 6 = "Strongly agree."

Source of Items. Li (1999) developed the EMS items in three phases to produce an initial pool of 32 items balanced equally across 8 HMIEM constructs (4 items per construct). The original EMS items were generated from existing literature concerned with "descriptive reasons why people exercise" (Li, 1999, p. 100) and from focus group data using college students enrolled in physical activity classes who indicated why they (or their friends) engaged in exercise. Li (1999) used a Delphi method across at least two iterations of expert review ($N_{reviewers}$ = 5-6) to produce the initial 32-item EMS. It is not clear to what extent the item content of the original 32 EMS items reflected experiences noted in the focus group data or other sources utilized by Li (1999).

Summary. Research concerning the EMS remains scant in the exercise psychology literature. Only Wininger's (2007) study reported subscale-specific internal consistency reliability estimates for EMS scores (Cronbach alphas ranged from .68-.92). Three investigations reported no reliability data (Lutz, Lochbaum, & Turnbow, 2003; Lutz, Karoly, & Okun, 2008; Stevenson & Lochbaum, 2008). Li (1999) reported a range of internal consistency and temporal stability estimates of reliability without providing specific values for each EMS subscale. Research examining structural validity issues with reference to EMS scores has been insufficient aside from Li's (1999) investigation, which did not provide convincing evidence supporting the hypothesized EMS measurement model in samples of young active college students. Additional studies have linked more internalized motives assessed by the EMS with postexercise affect (Lutz et al., 2003), exercise identity (Wininger, 2007), and exercise behavior indexed by either stage of change for exercise (Wininger, 2007) or frequency of strenuous exercise participation (Lutz et al., 2008). Overall, construct validity evidence for EMS scores has been forthcoming, but more research is needed before definitive conclusions regarding the EMS's merit for assessing motivation in line with the HMIEM can be made.

Recommendations for Researchers and Practitioners

Exercise motivation research focused on measurement issues has produced a rich and diverse literature aiding theory development at the expense of creating an array of instruments assessing the focal constructs, which can be daunting. Progress in terms of instrument development to assess exercise motivation is evident, but sustained attention to construct validation remains a fundamental issue for advancing this area of research. Few systematic reviews of the literature appraising the construct validity evidence have been conducted that could serve as a guide to inform the selection and use of exercise motivation instruments (Vallerand & Fortier, 1997; Wilson, Mack, & Grattan, 2008). The final section of this chapter offers recommendations addressing the unresolved issues that pervade research and practice concerning the measurement of exercise motivation.

Messick (1995) argued that instrument development via construct validation is an ongoing challenge for research that requires the constellation of evidence from multiple sources to clarify test score interpretations. The following areas seem ripe for additional research to advance the measurement of exercise motivation based on the existing literature:

■ Measurement experts have long extolled the importance of examining issues germane to reliability and validity within the sample under study (Crocker & Algina, 1986; Messick, 1995). It seems reasonable to echo this sentiment by encouraging scholars to report both sources of evidence in investigations using exercise motivation instruments. It is also recommended that researchers clearly articulate that reliability and validity appraisals concern scores (not instruments) to avoid the misleading claims that an instrument is reliable and valid (Messick, 1995).

■ Instrument selection within a study is best guided by joint consideration of the research question and the available data supporting the interpretation of an instrument's scores. It seems reasonable to suggest that a range of instruments measuring exercise motivation already exists, such that developing new instruments may be unnecessary or may at least warrant considerable justification. The EMI-2 and MPAM-R appear suitable for questions concerning broad intrinsic or extrinsic motives for exercise. On the contrary, for research questions concerned with testing the motivational continuum proposed within SDT and embedded within the HMIEM, the BREQ and BREQ-2 and EMS are more suitable. An index of integrated regulation could accompany the BREQ and BREQ-2 in future research to advance our understanding of this concept in exercise contexts with respect to instrument development and theoretical issues.

■ Attention to the different scoring protocols used with exercise motivation instruments is a useful line of inquiry. Three scoring protocols concerning the BREQ have been published and can be summarized as follows: (1) four subscale scores representing each BREQ concept, (2) two composite scores representing autonomous (identified and intrinsic regulation) and controlled (introjected and external regulation) motives for exercise, and (3) one composite RAI score derived by combining weighted BREQ subscales with the formula Σ[intrinsic(2) + identified(1) + introjected(−1) + external(−2)].

A fourth scoring protocol to accommodate the assessment of integrated regulation and amotivation in conjunction with concepts embedded within the BREQ and EMS is available (see Vallerand, Pelletier, & Koestner, 2008). Comparative research examining the merits (and costs) of each scoring protocol and research on the potential scoring configurations that could be applied to data collected with the MPAM-R and EMI-2 await further inquiry.

■ Item content relevance and representation influence the range of plausible interpretations (or construct validity) derived from scores assessing exercise motivation. Loevinger (1957) noted some time ago that the items used to measure a concept (such as exercise motivation) should "sample all possible contents that might comprise the putative trait" (p. 659). Even a cursory examination of the literature suggests that the research on developing and evaluating instruments designed to assess exercise motives has paid limited attention to issues of relevance and representation beyond testing the strength and direction of factor loadings as evidence of item content relevance. Mullan and colleagues (1997) were among the first to recognize the importance of this measurement issue in exercise motivation instruments. In the initial article detailing the development of the BREQ, these authors noted that 4 BREQ items originally designed to assess introjected regulation were discarded, leaving the 3 BREQ items assessing this construct subject to underrepresentation problems (Messick, 1995). Future studies would do well to address both item content relevance and representation issues using empirical procedures to avoid construct underrepresentation that stifles progress in the measurement of exercise motivation.

The following issues are gathered into a synopsis of recommendations pertaining to the use of instruments designed to measure exercise motivation in practical contexts where research may not be the primary agenda. These recommendations may serve as a guide for the health professionals who invest in the arduous process of optimizing motivation with the intent of changing or sustaining exercise behavior.

■ The instruments measuring exercise motivation that are reviewed in this chapter were developed for research purposes as opposed to clinical use in applied settings. Insufficient research has examined the use of criterion-referenced (binary) scoring approaches with instruments designed to assess exercise motivation. It remains uncertain if instruments (such as the MPAM-R or BREQ-2) could be used with a binary scoring protocol to aid clinical judgments regarding participant motivation toward exercise behavior. Messick (1995) cautioned against dichotomizing participant responses around a criterion score, given that such an approach could yield negative consequences (e.g., aversive emotional reactions to labels or diagnoses given based on scores). Health professionals should use exercise motivation instruments for their intended purpose and should avoid the temptation of classifying individuals as motivated or unmotivated based on deviation around a solitary, and at this point arbitrary, criterion score.

■ Exercise motivation instruments typically lack test manuals to guide clinical or practical use, and little attention has been given to creating normative values for specific instruments across target populations. Nonetheless, the instruments reviewed in this chapter have a solid theoretical foundation, appear in published studies that could help with the interpretation of scores, and represent superior choices compared with ad hoc instruments that rarely provide useful information for practical use. It is recommended that health professionals consult with instrument developers to determine if the test they select is viable for the target population of interest and suitable for clinical (or practical) use alongside other sources of information that can illuminate key concepts integral to motivating exercise participation. One useful approach to garnering additional information aligned with SDT is motivational interviewing, which is showing promise in exercise contexts as a mechanism to facilitate behavioral change (Markland & Vansteenkiste, 2007). Combining motivational interviewing techniques with available instrumentation (such as the BREQ-2) could provide a rich source of information about exercise motivation that can inform the health professional as well as offer insight into usability issues pertaining to an instrument that aids the ongoing process of construct validation.

Acknowledgments

Dr. Wilson's research program is supported by the Social Sciences and Humanities Research Council of Canada, the Canada Foundation for Innovation, and the Ontario Innovation Trust. I would like to thank Dr. Catherine M. Sabiston (McGill University, Canada) for her insightful and helpful remarks provided on an initial draft of this chapter.

Achievement Motivation Processes

David E. Conroy, PhD, and Amanda L. Hyde, MS

The pursuit of competence is fundamental to physical activity, regardless of whether that activity occurs in organized competitive sport or in less structured leisure-time pursuits. People naturally strive to feel effective in their physical activities, but such competence can be pursued in a variety of ways with different consequences. Achievement motivation theories attempt to explain the processes that energize and orient these competence strivings. This chapter reviews the psychometric properties of measures used to assess the most common and relevant achievement motivation processes for people engaged in sport and exercise activities.

The psychometric enterprise does not exist in a vacuum, so some context is required for this review. We begin—and ultimately end—with the premise that in an ideal world, theory, research design, and statistical models are integrated seamlessly (Collins, 2006). Research that integrates these components effectively is elegant and yields strong, robust conclusions. To the extent that two or more components depart from each other, the rigor and yield of the research may be compromised. Thus, for this review and evaluation of the psychometric properties of achievement motivation measures, it is necessary to contextualize the measures in contemporary theorizing and methods used to study achievement motivation. In addition to providing the context needed to evaluate achievement motivation measures, this background on theory and methods also informs the critique and recommendations offered to close the chapter.

History of Achievement Motivation Theories

Several excellent reviews of major achievement motivation theories are available (e.g., Elliot &

Dweck, 2005; Eccles & Wigfield, 2002; Thrash & Hurst, 2008). The earliest studies of achievement motivation focused on the level of aspiration (e.g., Hoppe, 1930), and studies have since broadened their focus to include motives, attributions, self-efficacy, goals, and implicit theories (among other constructs). This chapter focuses on achievement motives and goals. We selected *achievement motives* because of their historical prominence in the achievement motivation literature, their relevance to theorizing about the self and emotions, and their function as robust antecedents of achievement goals. *Achievement goals* were selected because of their current prominence in the literature and their significant role in self-regulation during achievement pursuits.

In a seminal work on achievement motives, McClelland (1951) conceived of individual differences in approach–avoidance tendencies based on anticipatory affective states associated with specific incentives (i.e., end states). With respect to achievement motivation, these motives are referred to as the *need for achievement* (or hope for success) and the *fear of failure* (or motive to avoid failure; McClelland, Atkinson, Clark, & Lowell, 1953). The need for achievement (nAch) is based on anticipatory pride for succeeding, while the fear of failure (FF) is based on anticipatory shame and humiliation for failing. These emotions are important elements of motives because they connect motivation to powerful self-evaluative processes that are shaped in early childhood (Elliot, Conroy, Barron, & Murayama, 2010).

One of the most confounding issues in this work was psychometric in nature. McClelland and colleagues (1953) used a data-driven approach to develop a coding system for assessing the achievement motive from open-ended responses to the well-known Thematic Apperception Test (TAT).

Other researchers attempted to develop self-report measures of the achievement motives, and correlations between scores from the projective TAT and self-reports were often disappointingly small (Spangler, 1992). Debate flourished as scholars sought to determine which method had superior psychometric status. Ultimately, these methods were determined to be tapping into separate motivational systems. The distinction between these systems is discussed in the section on achievement motives.

The next burst of achievement motivation research focused on the developmental roots of achievement motivation. Dweck and colleagues (Diener & Dweck, 1978, 1980; Dweck, 1975) characterized mastery and helpless responses to failure in young children. Mastery responses were characterized by persistence, low effort attributions, selecting challenging tasks, increased competence expectancies, and improved performance on subsequent trials. Helpless responses were characterized by unpleasant affect, low ability attributions, selection of easy tasks, decreased competence expectancies, and reduced performance. Dweck proposed that these responses reflected differences in children's goals (Dweck, 1986; Dweck & Elliott, 1983; Elliott & Dweck, 1988). Children were more likely to exhibit mastery responses when they viewed tasks as opportunities to learn and develop their competence (learning goals), and they were more likely to exhibit helpless responses when these tasks were opportunities to demonstrate their standing relative to their peers (performance goals).

Nicholls (1976, 1978, 1984a) arrived at a similar framework through a developmental analysis. He argued that children possess an undifferentiated concept of ability in early childhood, which leads them to equate competence with learning and effort. By the end of middle childhood, children are able to differentiate the concepts of effort and ability, and this differentiation forms the basis for different achievement goals (Nicholls, 1984a). Children who focus on effort and learning are pursuing competence in an undifferentiated sense and are held to be task involved. Others who focus on outperforming their peers with as little effort as possible are pursuing competence in a differentiated sense and are held to be ego involved.

By the end of the 20th century, the goal-based approach for explaining achievement strivings had become extremely popular in many branches of psychology, including sport and exercise psychology (for a review, see Roberts, Treasure, & Conroy, 2007). A robust literature developed with parallel models of goals using different terminology (e.g., *learning*, *task*, and *mastery goals* and *performance*, *ego*,

and *competitive goals*). In a thoughtful analysis of the broad achievement motivation literature, Elliot (1997) attempted to integrate the classic, motive-based approach with the contemporary, goal-based approach. In his view, these approaches were complementary rather than mutually exclusive. The motive-based approach was well suited to describing approach and avoidance behavior as well as stable patterns of behavior. It was less adept at capturing intraindividual variability in achievement behavior. In contrast, the goal-based approach was well suited to explaining why achievement behavior varied over time but was less adept at accounting for approach–avoidance variability. This analysis led to two important and related developments: (1) an expanded achievement goal framework that more specifically described how people orient their achievement strivings and (2) a hierarchical model of achievement motivation that emphasized the interdependence of constructs in an achievement motivation system (Elliot, 1997, 1999; Elliot & Church, 1997; Elliot & McGregor, 2001).

2 × 2 Achievement Goal Framework

One of the most prominent features of the hierarchical model of achievement motivation is its reconceptualization of the structure of achievement goals. By crossing the definition of competence with the valence of the competence-based outcome, Elliot (1997, 1999) produced a more detailed achievement goal framework. Elliot (1999) focused on two definitions of competence (mastery and performance) and two valences for the competence-based incentives (competence and incompetence). *Mastery* definitions of competence involved task- and self-referenced competence. In other words, did the athlete perform the task as it should be performed (task-referenced standard) or did the athlete perform the task better than in previous attempts (self-referenced standard)? These two standards typically have been combined into a single mastery definition of competence; however, they could easily be differentiated in future work (Elliot & Conroy, 2005). *Performance* definitions of competence involved normatively referenced competence (i.e., did the athlete perform better than other athletes performed?). Likewise, competence-based goal incentives could have two valences: People could orient themselves toward competence (leading to *approach* goals) or away from incompetence (leading to *avoidance* goals).

Combining the definitions of competence with the valence of strivings yielded the four achievement goals shown in figure 27.1. Mastery-approach (MAp) goals are exemplified by athletes whose purpose at

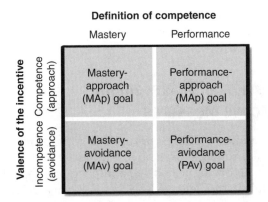

Figure 27.1 The 2 × 2 achievement goal framework proposed by Elliot (1999).

Based on Elliot 1999.

a particular moment is to improve their skill level. Mastery-avoidance (MAv) goals are exemplified by athletes whose purpose is to minimize deterioration in their ability. Performance-approach (PAp) goals are exemplified by athletes whose focus is on outperforming competitors. Performance-avoidance (PAv) goals are exemplified by athletes whose focus is on not being outperformed by competitors.

This 2 × 2 framework is a useful expansion of the dichotomous model of achievement goals. It accounts for previously equivocal findings (e.g., performance goals having mixed effects on intrinsic motivation; Rawsthorne & Elliot, 1999) and integrates the best of the classic and contemporary approaches to achievement motivation. Time will tell whether the 2 × 2 framework is the best taxon-

omy for describing the achievement goals that play such an important role in regulating achievement-related thoughts, feelings, and behaviors. There may be other dimensions that should be added. Existing dimensions may benefit from further specification. For example, it is possible that task- and self-referenced standards that have been combined in the mastery-based definition of competence could be differentiated. The keys to justifying any further complexity when describing achievement goals are (1) to ensure that the goals remain fully and unambiguously grounded in the concept of competence and (2) to demonstrate sufficient increases in predictive value gained from the additional complexity to the goal framework.

Hierarchical Model of Achievement Motivation

Historically, the antecedents and consequences of achievement goals have not always been distinguished clearly, and this critique is as true in the sport and exercise psychology literature as it is in the social, educational, or industrial-organizational psychology literatures. As the research base on goals has grown and greater attention has been invested in identifying causal relations, it has become necessary to clarify both the antecedents and the consequences of achievement goals. Elliot (1999) proposed the hierarchical model of achievement motivation shown in figure 27.2 as a conceptual tool for organizing findings and surfacing tacit assumptions. In its simplest form, the hierarchical model

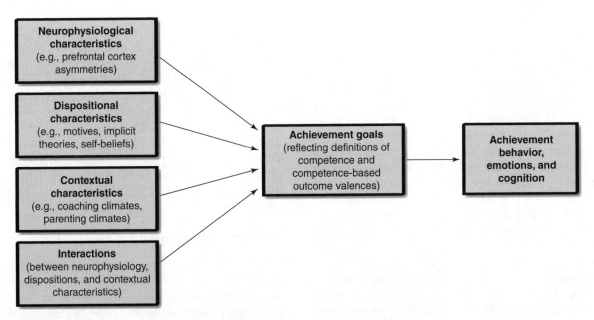

Figure 27.2 The hierarchical model of achievement motivation proposed by Elliot (1999).

Based on Elliot 1999.

of achievement motivation proposes that goals are the most proximal predictor of achievement outcomes and goals can be predicted by neurophysiological characteristics of the person, dispositional characteristics of the person, characteristics of the achievement context, and interactions among those variables. In essence, goals serve as "concrete . . . midlevel motivational surrogates" for higher-order achievement motives (among other antecedents; Elliot & Church, 1997, p. 219). Evaluations of this model in sport psychology have been favorable, and the model offers a promising platform for future research because of its conceptual clarity, integrative nature, and effectiveness in accounting for available observations.

The remainder of this chapter focuses on reviewing the psychometric properties of measures for achievement motives and goals in the hierarchical model of achievement motivation. Whereas achievement motive measures have not been reviewed recently in the sport and exercise psychology literature, Duda and Whitehead (1998) published an extensive review of achievement goal measures. This chapter attempts to build on their conclusions in light of empirical and theoretical developments in the intervening decade.

The unified theory of construct validity (Messick, 1995) provides the basis for evaluating the psychometric properties of measures in this chapter. This theory integrates common sources of evidence for interpreting the meaning of scores into a unified framework. Note that this evidence speaks to the validity of how score meaning is interpreted—validity is a property of score interpretations rather than a property of measures. Readers should be careful to evaluate the performance of the motive or goal measures they use in their own data before interpreting the scores.

Although Messick (1995) identified six distinguishable aspects of score validity, our review focuses primarily on empirical evidence for structural and external validity. *Structural validity* refers to the model presumed to underlie responses to a measure. When items are aggregated to create a scale score, is the scoring model consistent with the latent structure of responses? *External validity* refers to evidence of convergent and discriminant associations with theoretically related and unrelated constructs, respectively. It includes what has often been referred to as *criterion validity*, or evidence that scores predict critical criteria for a particular construct. In our discussion of the structural and external validity evidence, we comment on aspects of *content validity* (content relevance and representativeness), *substantive validity* (the

theoretical basis for a measure), and *generalizability* (different populations that have been studied with the measure).

Review of Achievement Motive Measures

In addition to the approach–avoidance motives noted earlier, two separable motivational systems can be distinguished—one implicit and the other explicit (McClelland, Koestner, & Weinberger, 1989; Spangler, 1992). The implicit motivational system is held to be the more primitive system because it is based on affective arousal, whereas the explicit motivational system is based on an "elaborate system of explicit goals, desires, and commitments" (McClelland et al., 1953, p. 700). Bargh (1997) proposed that implicit processes ground individuals in the here and now and are therefore ideally suited to organizing habitual behaviors that occur without conscious reflection. Explicit processes, on the other hand, capitalize on the cognitive ability to shift perspective and reflect on the past or anticipate the future when self-regulating. These systems differ in their developmental antecedents (for a review, see Elliot et al., 2010) as well as in their consequences for affect, behavior, and cognition.

Very little sport psychology research has focused on implicit achievement motives. In other areas, implicit motives have been assessed using the Picture Story Exercise (Schultheiss & Pang, 2007; see also Conroy, Elliot, & Thrash, 2009), coding systems for running text (Winter, 1994), a modified Implicit Association Test (IAT; Brunstein & Schmitt, 2004), and the Multi-Motive Grid (Schmalt, 1999, 2005; Sokolowski, Schmalt, Langens, & Puca, 2000). Schultheiss (2007) proposed that the implicit motive system is grounded in nondeclarative memory, is not consciously accessible, and regulates spontaneous or automatic behavior over time. In contrast, the explicit motivational system has its roots in declarative memory, is consciously accessible via introspection, and is thought to regulate declarative outcomes that derive from semantic or episodic memories (e.g., enjoyment). These motives are typically assessed with self-report methods.

Need for Achievement

Very few sport and exercise studies have included nAch measures; however, there are several measures of explicit nAch. Jackson (1994) developed the Personality Research Form (PRF), which includes an achievement scale, based on Murray's (1938) taxonomy of human needs. This scale has 16 true–

false items and provides a single score representing nAch. Questions have been raised about the dimensionality of scores from this measure (Jackson, Ahmed, & Heapy, 1976; Jackson, Paunonen, Fraboni, & Goffin, 1996).

The Work and Family Orientation Questionnaire (WOFO) is another commonly used measure in achievement motivation research (Helmreich & Spence, 1978). As described by Spence and Helmreich (1983), the "items are relatively free of references to specific situational contexts, and individuals' responses to the items are assumed to reflect dispositional tendencies that may influence behavior in a variety of settings" (p. 41). The WOFO provides scores for mastery (8 items), work (6 items), competitiveness (5 items), and personal unconcern with achievement (4 items). Participants rate each item on a scale ranging from A = "Strongly agree" to E = "Strongly disagree." The work and mastery scores are conceptually similar to the nAch construct and are often strongly correlated, so they are usually combined into a single nAch score representing favorable attitudes toward effort, a preference for difficult and challenging tasks, and a need to meet internal standards of excellence. Competitiveness scores, which focus on interpersonal competition for status, have been found to moderate some work and mastery effects; however, the item content on this scale is inconsistent with an intrinsic achievement motive and so it is not suitable as a measure of nAch. The personal unconcern is never used to indicate nAch. Spence and Helmreich (1983) reviewed findings linking WOFO scores with outcomes in a variety of achievement domains.

One of the most surprising observations of the achievement motivation literature is how few studies there are of nAch in sport and exercise contexts. Given the role of nAch in the hierarchical model of achievement motivation and its demonstrated links with important consequences in other domains, research on the consequences of nAch in sport and exercise is sorely needed.

Fear of Failure

Several paper-and-pencil measures have been used to measure explicit FF. Measures that have been used to assess FF in sport include those published by Alpert and Haber (1960, Debilitating Anxiety Scale); Hermans (1990); Passer (1983); and Smith, Smoll, Cumming, and Grossbard (2006, Sport Anxiety Scale-2, or SAS-2) and Smith, Smoll, and Schutz (1990, Sport Anxiety Scale, or SAS). One problem that has emerged in studies using these measures is that many contain an undesirable amount of irrelevant content. For example, although FF is related

to performance anxiety, the two concepts are not isomorphic, and performance anxiety measures include variance that is irrelevant to FF. Interpreting scores from these measures as indicators of FF reduces the construct validity of scores. Such problems with content validity may help to explain the historical difficulty of obtaining strong convergent validity between these measures and discriminant validity from measures of distinct constructs (Gelbort & Winer, 1985; Jackaway & Teevan, 1976; MacDonald & Hyde, 1980; Mulig, Haggerty, Carballosa, Cinnick, & Madden, 1985). In the interest of preserving content validity and optimizing the construct validity of FF scores, we recommend using measures specifically designed to assess FF with as little content-irrelevant variance as possible.

The most popular measure of explicit FF in the sport literature has been the Performance Failure Appraisal Inventory (PFAI; Conroy, 2001; Conroy, Willow, & Metzler, 2002). To establish preliminary evidence of content validity, the PFAI was developed based on descriptions by elite performers of the aversive consequences of failing (Conroy, Poczwardowski, & Henschen, 2001). A 25-item long form and a 5-item short form exist. The long form provides scores for five lower-order beliefs in aversive consequences of failing that predispose an individual to fearing failure. These consequences include experiencing shame and embarrassment, devaluing a self-estimate, having an uncertain future, losing the interest of important others, and upsetting important others. Relationships among these lower-order beliefs can be represented by a single higher-order factor representing the FF (Conroy et al., 2002; Conroy, Metzler, & Hofer, 2003). The short form includes 1 item from each of the 5 lower-order belief scales to index FF.

Structural Validity

The factor structures of responses to the long and short forms of the PFAI have been investigated vigorously. Work from our laboratory has provided evidence supporting the factor structure in youth and college-aged samples (Conroy, 2001; Conroy et al., 2002; Conroy, Metzler, et al., 2003; Conroy & Coatsworth, 2004; Conroy, Coatsworth, & Fifer, 2005). Model coefficients have demonstrated invariance across groups (Conroy, Metzler, et al., 2003). This factor structure also demonstrates strict invariance over durations of up to 2 mo (a very high standard for longitudinal factorial invariance; Conroy, Metzler, et al., 2003; Conroy & Coatsworth, 2004). Responses to the long and short forms of the PFAI have consistently demonstrated internal consistency coefficients greater than .70. Collectively, this evidence suggests that the PFAI score model has strong structural validity.

External Validity

General FF scores from the long and short forms of the PFAI have been associated with greater avoidance motivational temperaments, perfectionistic concerns, dispositional performance anxiety (worry, concentration disruption, somatic anxiety), problem behaviors, and self-criticism while failing (Conroy, 2003; Conroy et al., 2002; Conroy, Coatsworth, & Kaye, 2007; Kaye, Conroy, & Fifer, 2008). FF has been associated with less dispositional optimism, state hope before an achievement task, self-esteem, sport competence (for youths), physical self-concept, academic competence, and peer competence (Conroy et al., 2002). People with high FF also report feeling less pleasant and less dominant while viewing failure-themed stimuli (Duley, Conroy, Morris, Wiley, & Janelle, 2005).

With respect to discriminant validity, FF scores from the PFAI have shown evidence of null associations with fear of success and approach-valenced achievement goals (Conroy et al., 2002; Conroy & Elliot, 2004). In a young adult sample, FF was unassociated with perceptions of competence in an activity; however, a negative association between FF and perceived competence has emerged in youth sport samples (Conroy et al., 2005; Conroy, Coatsworth, et al., 2007). Changes in FF and perceived competence appear to occur independently over time, suggesting that these measures capture different processes despite their baseline correlation (Conroy et al., 2005). FF scores have also been unassociated with intrinsic and extrinsic motivation in youth sport (Conroy et al., 2005; Conroy, Coatsworth, et al., 2007).

The five lower-order FF-related beliefs show similar patterns of bivariate relationships with most external measures (Conroy, 2004; Conroy et al., 2002; Conroy & Elliot, 2004; Conroy, Kaye, & Fifer, 2007). This finding is to be expected given the higher-order factor structure of responses. Nevertheless, some unique and interesting patterns have also been identified. For example, fears of experiencing shame and embarrassment seem to be the beliefs most closely linked to avoidance goal adoption (Conroy, 2004). These lower-order belief scores may be useful for cognitively oriented researchers; however, the higher-order FF score should be more than adequate for most other research applications. Researchers who opt to focus on the lower-order belief scores should consider the consequences of the expected collinearity among scores when drawing conclu-

sions (e.g., unreliable beta weights in regression equations).

Predictive Validity

FF scores have been linked to attentional biases, avoidance-based self-regulation, and interpersonal problems. Individuals who score high in FF allocate more natural selective attention to failure-themed stimuli when compared with peers who do not score high in FF (Duley et al., 2005). FF also increases the likelihood of adopting avoidance-valenced achievement goals over time and plays a role in regulating affective arousal and dominance during competence pursuits (Conroy & Elliot, 2004; Schantz & Conroy, 2009). Finally, self-reports and peer reports indicate that people who have high FF experience greater interpersonal distress and specific problems involving excessive aggression and appeasement (Conroy, Elliot, & Pincus, 2009; Wright, Pincus, Conroy, & Elliot, 2009).

A brief note about appropriate applications for this measure is in order. The PFAI has been evaluated for use as a research or evaluation tool. The level of evidence available suggests that it may also be valuable for assessment purposes in clinical or educational consultations. There is no basis for using scores from this measure for any sort of personnel selection.

Review of Achievement Goal Measures

Achievement goal measures have proliferated in the literature. The most commonly used measures in sport and exercise studies have been the Task and Ego Orientation in Sport Questionnaire (TEOSQ; Duda & Nicholls, 1992) and the Perceptions of Success Questionnaire (POSQ; Roberts, Treasure, & Balague, 1998). Both of these measures are based on the dichotomous model of achievement goals and provide scores for task and ego goal orientations. Goal orientations are theorized to be orthogonal dispositional tendencies that generalize across situations and time (Duda & Nicholls, 1992; Nicholls, 1984b, 1989; Roberts et al., 1998). Evidence attesting to the validity of scores from these two measures was reviewed by Duda and Whitehead (1998). We seek to update conclusions from that review with evidence that has accrued in the decade since that chapter first appeared. Additionally, we review the psychometric properties of a newer measure based on the 2 × 2 goal framework and methods used to assess states of achievement goal involvement during activities.

Task and Ego Orientation in Sport Questionnaire

The TEOSQ was developed to assess achievement goals in sport (Duda & Nicholls, 1992). The measure was based on Nicholl's (1984b, 1989) theories of goal orientation and a dispositional goal perspectives assessment used for classroom settings, the Motivational Orientation Scale (Nicholls, 1989). The two goal orientation domains sampled by the TEOSQ are task and ego orientations. People high in task orientation incorporate criteria for success that include personal improvement, learning, and mastery of tasks. People high in ego orientation base success on the demonstration of ability and competence compared with normative references (i.e., compared with others).

Duda and Whitehead (1998) reviewed the creation process and revisions by which the TEOSQ was finalized as a measure comprising a 6-item ego subscale and a 7-item task subscale. In an effort to assess an overall tendency for goal orientation involvement, each item begins with this stem: "I feel successful in sport when. . . ." Several studies have adapted the stem to assess more domain-specific goal orientations. Examples include "I feel most successful in physical education when . . ." (Barkoukis, Ntoumanis, & Nikitaras, 2007) and "I feel most successful in hockey when . . ." (Bergin & Habusta, 2004). This modification to increase contextual specificity is desirable because of the potential for goals to vary across contexts (and time).

One group of researchers has suggested that the task orientation items on the TEOSQ do not fully represent the content universe of task orientations (Harwood, Hardy, & Swain, 2000). The argument is that the task goal items focus on learning and task mastery and fail to sample task goal orientations that are self-referenced. The same group also suggested that responses to the TEOSQ are inconsistent across situational contexts and therefore may not be measuring dispositional traits (Harwood & Hardy, 2001). Though some potential issues in content validity have been discussed, the field appears to have confidence in the validity of TEOSQ scores, as is evident by the widespread use of the measure.

Structural Validity

Duda and Whitehead (1998) reported that the task and ego scales of the TEOSQ are supported with acceptable factorial validity and internal consistency for two orthogonal scales across youth, adolescent, and adult athlete populations. When the TEOSQ is applied to nonelite populations (e.g., physical education students, recreational sport participants),

the task orientation dimension may split into two factors (Duda & Whitehead). Since that review, several studies on the original and translated versions of the TEOSQ (e.g., Barkoukis, Tsorbatzoudis, & Grouios, 2008; Flores, Salguero, & Marquez, 2007; Li, Harmer, Duncan, Duncan, Acock, & Yamamoto, 1998; Mohsen, 2007; Wang & Liu, 2007) have reported results supporting the structural validity of the scores as comprising two orthogonal factors. It should be noted that one study found the item "I do my very best" to load onto both the ego and the task scales (Hodge, Allen, & Smellie, 2008). In studies of nonelite samples, a two-factor structure was supported (Barkoukis et al., 2007; Barkoukis et al., 2008; Wang & Liu, 2007). Acceptable internal consistency has been reported consistently for both the original and the translated TEOSQ (e.g., Balaguer, Duda, Atienza, & Mayo, 2002; Bortoli, Bertollo, & Robazza, 2009; Kuan & Roy, 2007; Xiang & Lee, 1998).

External Validity

Duda and Whitehead (1998) reported that the task and ego orientation scales of the TEOSQ positively correlated with corresponding goal orientations in classrooms. Since that review, a study comparing goal orientations with the 2 × 2 achievement goal assessment revealed that *task orientation* scores were positively related to mastery goals and negatively related to performance goals, whereas *ego orientation* scores were positively correlated with both mastery and performance goals (Barkoukis et al., 2007). *Task orientation* scores have been positively correlated with incremental self-theories of ability (Wang & Liu, 2007). *Ego orientation* scores have been positively associated with perfectionism (Brannan & Petrie, 2008; De Bruin, Bakker, & Oudejans, 2009; Hall, Kerr, Kozub, & Finnie, 2007). Incremental theories of ability have been positively associated with both task and ego goal orientation scores, although relationships were stronger for task than ego orientation scores (Wang & Liu, 2007).

With respect to the consequences of TEOSQ scores, Duda and Whitehead (1998) reported a pattern of relationships with a range of relevant constructs, including motivation, perceptions of success, enjoyment, sporting behavior, motives, learning strategies, and coping strategies. *Task orientation* scores demonstrated positive relationships with theoretical consequences such as task enjoyment and commitment (Allen, 2003; Stuntz & Weiss, 2009; Hodge et al., 2008), interest in sport (Newton, Watson, Kim, & Beacham, 2006), pleasant psychobiosocial states (Bortoli et al., 2009), positive emotions in physical education class (Mouratidis, Vansteenkiste, Lens, & Auweeele, 2009), concern for opponent and graciousness (Lavoi & Stellino, 2008), self-determined reasons for discipline (Papaioannou, 1998), motivation by enhancing self-esteem (Ryska, 2003), attributing success to effort (Van Yperen & Duda, 1999), perceived improvement of individual physical aspects of the game and perceived improvement of team technical and tactical aspects of the game (Balaguer et al., 2002), and overall satisfaction with coach and competitive results (Balaguer, Duda, & Crespo, 1999). *Ego orientation* scores demonstrated positive relationships with cognitive and somatic symptoms of anxiety (Ntoumanis & Biddle, 1998a), competitiveness (Ryska, 2003), motivation by social status and recognition (Allen, 2003; Ryska, 2003), and public self-consciousness and social anxiety (Hatzigeorgiadis, 2002). Task orientation has been reported to positively relate to perceptions of mastery climate, whereas ego orientation has been reported to positively relate to perceptions of performance climate (Bortoli et al., 2009; Kouli & Papaioannou, 2009; Magyar & Feltz, 2003; Magyar, Feltz, & Simpson, 2004; Ntoumanis & Biddle, 1998a, 1998b; Williams, 1998).

Elliot (1999) proposed that perceived competence specifically affects the approach–avoidance dimension of goals rather than the definition of competence; therefore, differences in relationships between perceived competence and task or ego orientation scores are not expected. There are mixed results concerning how the task and ego orientation scales of the TEOSQ relate to perceived competence. Some studies suggest that task and ego orientations both relate to greater perceived competence (Hodge et al., 2008; Mouratidis et al., 2009; Wang & Liu, 2007); however, others report a positive relationship between perceived competence and task orientation alone (Allen, 2003; Stuntz & Weiss, 2009). In a separate study, ego orientation scores related to perceived ability, whereas task orientation did not (Hall et al., 2007). The pattern of relationships between TEOSQ scores and perceived competence has not been replicated.

Perceptions of Success Questionnaire

Similar to the TEOSQ, the POSQ was created to assess the goal orientations theorized by Nicholls (1984b, 1989; Roberts et al., 1998). Originally referred to as *mastery* and *performance* goal orientations, the scales have since been relabeled to coincide with Nicholls' theories of task and ego orientations. Each scale includes 6 items. The major emphasis in the creation of the POSQ was to specify achievement goal assessment to sport contexts. Items such as "I outperform my opponents" and "I win" illustrate the sport-specific content of the POSQ. Both the

TEOSQ and the POSQ item stems orient respondents to general rather than specific response sets.

There have been concerns that some TEOSQ and POSQ items tap into consequences of goals rather than specific goal involvement (Harwood et al., 2000). For example, items such as "I reach a goal" and "I overcome difficulties" may speak to consequences of a task goal as opposed to a task goal directly (for a response, see Treasure et al., 2001). Harwood and colleagues (2000) favored the POSQ over the TEOSQ because items on the former are more "conceptually attuned to measuring a self-referent conception of achievement" (p. 248) consistent with mastery goals, but both measures are mainstays in the literature.

Structural Validity

Duda and Whitehead (1998) concluded that the POSQ demonstrated acceptable test–retest reliability and internal consistency in samples of student and athlete populations of various ages. Few recent studies have evaluated the factorial structure fit of the POSQ; however, there is support for the hypothesized two-factor structure based on responses to English and translated versions of the POSQ (Barić & Horga, 2006; Duda & Whitehead, 1998; Fonseca, 2001). Results have not been unequivocal, and one study found that deleting selected task orientation items (e.g., "I work hard," "I show clear personal improvement") and ego orientation items (e.g., "I accomplish something others can't do") improved model fit (Kavussanu & Ntoumanis, 2003). Further evaluation of the latent structure of POSQ responses appears to be warranted. The original and translated versions of the POSQ have exhibited acceptable internal consistency for the task and ego orientation scales (Abrahamsen, Roberts, & Pensgaard, 2008; Harwood, Cumming, & Hall, 2003; Lemyre, Hall, & Roberts, 2008; Wang, Chatzisarantis, Spray, & Biddle, 2002).

External Validity

Duda and Whitehead (1998) reported that the POSQ goal orientations correlated positively with corresponding TEOSQ scales. Since that review, *task orientation* scores have exhibited a positive correlation with incremental self-theories of ability and a negative correlation with entity self-theories of ability (Wang et al., 2002). Relationships between the task orientation scale and aspects of perfectionism are mixed (Appleton, Hall, & Hill, 2009; Lemyre et al., 2008). The POSQ *ego orientation* scores positively correlate with entity self-theories of ability (Wang et al., 2002) and aspects of perfectionism (Appleton et al., 2009; Lemyre et al., 2008). Ego orientation also shows a small positive association with incremental self-theory of ability (Wang et al., 2002).

With respect to the theoretical consequences of goals, Duda and Whitehead (1998) reported that POSQ task orientation scores show positive relationships with satisfaction from mastery experiences and intrinsic motivation. They also reported that the POSQ ego orientation scale shows expected positive relationships to satisfaction from demonstrations of normatively referenced ability and state anxiety. Since that review, the POSQ *task orientation* scale has exhibited positive relationships with intrinsic motivation, prosocial behavior, high moral functioning, adaptive coping styles, life satisfaction, and self concept (Kavussanu & Boardley, 2009; Kavussanu & Ntoumanis, 2003; Kristiansen, Roberts, & Abrahamsen, 2008; Poulsen, Ziviani, & Cuskelly, 2006; Sage & Kavussanu, 2007; Standage & Treasure, 2002; Wang et al., 2002). The POSQ *ego orientation* scores have been positively associated with external motivation, antisocial behavior, hypercompetitive attitudes, and performance anxiety (Dru, 2003; Grossbard, Cumming, Standage, Smith, & Smoll, 2007; Kavussanu & Boardley, 2009; Sage & Kavussanu, 2007; Standage & Treasure, 2002; Wang et al., 2002).

Recent research shows that perceived competence is related to both ego and task orientation, although in most cases, sex differences may exist (Abrahamsen, Roberts, & Pensgaard, 2008; Abrahamsen, Roberts, Pensgaard, & Ronglan, 2008; Poulsen et al., 2006; Wang et al., 2002). In one study, neither task nor ego orientation scores were related to perceived ability (Lemyre et al., 2008). The lack of relationship between perceived competence and either ego or task orientation is consistent with the hypothesis that perceived competence should affect only the approach–avoidance dimension of goal adoption (Elliot, 1999).

Associations between goal orientation and environmental factors are not expected due to the presumed stability of goal orientations; however, studies have shown relationships between the goal orientation scales on the POSQ and perceived mastery and performance climates (Abrahamsen, Roberts, & Pensgaard, 2008; Abrahamsen, Roberts, Pensgaard, & Ronglan, 2008; Lemyre et al., 2008). Of course, the reported associations may be a result of the effects that goal orientations have on the perception of the environment rather than the effects that aspects of the environment have on goal orientations.

2 × 2 Achievement Goal Questionnaire for Sport

The 2 × 2 Achievement Goal Questionnaire for Sport (AGQ-S) was developed to assess approach–avoid-ance goals within the 2 × 2 framework that was becoming popular in the educational and social psychology literatures (Conroy, Elliot, & Hofer, 2003). This measure was based closely on the original Achievement Goal Questionnaire (AGQ; Elliot & McGregor, 2001). A French translation also appears in the literature (Schiano-Lomoriello, Cury, & Da Fonseca, 2005). The AGQ-S was designed to assess MAp, MAv, PAp, and PAv goals based on the model proposed by Elliot (1999). The major modifications made to the original AGQ involved increasing the emphasis on normative definitions of competence in the performance goal items and phrasing the items to be more relevant to athletic versus academic performance.

Structural Validity

The factor structure of AGQ-S responses has been investigated in several studies. In the initial study of this measure, Conroy, Elliot, and Hofer (2003) found that the a priori model with four correlated factors outperformed a variety of plausible alternative models and exhibited acceptable fit in a college-aged sample of recreational athletes. Nien and Duda (2008) found broad support for the invariance of this solution in female and male competitive athletes, although two problems were noted. First, one item on the MAp scale related to multiple factors. The authors removed this item from the model. Second, one item on the MAv scale had a stronger item factor regression coefficient for women than for men. Both coefficients for that MAv item were positive and statistically significant, so the difference was just in magnitude, with squared multiple correlations of .79 (women) and .59 (men). Responses to the four individual factors in this model have demonstrated longitudinal factorial invariance over 6 wk in a sample of youth swimmers (Conroy, Kaye, & Coatsworth, 2006). In general, responses to the MAv, Pap, and PAv scales have exhibited adequate internal consistency; however, the MAp scale tends to have lower and occasionally unacceptable internal consistency. One explanation for these undesirable properties may involve the ceiling effect frequently observed in the high mean MAp scores. The reduced variability in this situation may have a number of adverse effects, including biasing the overall internal consistency estimates. Overall, the evidence supports the structural validity of responses to the 2 × 2 AGQ-S.

External Validity

The 2 × 2 goals assessed by the AGQ-S have been linked to a variety of antecedents. The hierarchical model attempts to distinguish between antecedents and consequences of goals. Most research designs used in achievement goal research do not permit valid tests of causal sequences, so conceptual arguments have been used to group correlates of each goal in the review that follows.

MAp goals have been linked with conceptual antecedents such as greater perfectionistic strivings, incremental theories of ability, perceived mastery climates within a team, and perceived learning and enjoyment climates from parents (Kaye et al., 2008; Morris & Kavussanu, 2008; Nien & Duda, 2008; Stoeber, Stoll, Pescheck, & Otto, 2008; Stoeber, Stoll, Salkmi, & Tiikkaja, 2009; Warburton & Spray, 2009). One study also found MAp goals to be negatively associated with perfectionistic concerns (Kaye et al., 2008), but that finding has not been replicated. With respect to their consequences, MAp goals have been linked with behavioral regulations such as more intrinsic motivation and identified behavioral regulations and less external behavioral regulations and amotivation (Conroy et al., 2006; Nien & Duda, 2008). People who adopt MAp goals are more likely to make challenge appraisals and less likely to make threat appraisals (Adie, Duda, & Ntoumanis, 2008). MAp goals have been linked with more positive and less negative affect (Adie et al., 2008). Athletes with MAp goals are also more likely to use mental training strategies, experience less daily distress, use less alcohol and get inebriated less frequently, and rate their practice quality more positively (Conroy, Cassidy, & Elliot, 2008).

MAv goals have been linked with conceptual antecedents such as greater FF, greater perfectionistic concerns, greater incremental theories of ability, greater perceptions that coaches were creating a motivational climate that emphasized MAv goals, and greater perceptions that parents created a learning and enjoyment climate (Conroy, Elliot, & Hofer, 2003; Conroy et al., 2006; Kaye et al., 2008; Stoeber et al., 2008; Stoeber, Stoll, et al., 2009; Warburton & Spray, 2009). With respect to their consequences, MAv goals have been linked to reduced intrinsic motivation and greater external behavioral regulation and amotivation (Conroy et al., 2006). MAv goals have also been linked positively with daily distress, threat appraisals, and negative affect (Adie et al., 2008; Conroy et al., 2008).

PAp goals have been linked with conceptual antecedents such as greater FF, greater perfectionistic strivings, greater perfectionistic concerns, greater entity theories of ability, and greater performance climates within a team (Conroy, Elliot, & Hofer, 2003; Conroy et al., 2006; Kaye et al., 2008; Morris & Kavussanu, 2008; Nien & Duda, 2008; Stoeber et al., 2008; Stoeber, Stoll, et al., 2009; Warburton & Spray,

2009). With respect to their consequences, PAp goals have been linked with greater extrinsic motivation (i.e., external regulations) and amotivation (Conroy et al., 2006; Nien & Duda, 2008). PAp goals have been associated with greater threat appraisals and negative affect (Adie et al., 2008). These goals have also been linked with superior athletic performance (Bois, Sarrazin, Southon, & Boiché, 2009; Stoeber, Uphill, & Hotham, 2009).

PAv goals have been linked with conceptual antecedents such as greater FF, perfectionistic concerns, perceptions that coaches were creating a motivational climate that emphasized PAv goals, and perceptions that parents created a climate conducive to worry (Conroy, Elliot, & Hofer, 2003; Conroy et al., 2006; Kaye et al., 2008; Morris & Kavussanu, 2008; Nien & Duda, 2008; Stoeber et al., 2008; Stoeber, Stoll, et al., 2009; Warburton & Spray, 2009). With respect to their consequences, PAv goals have been linked with reduced intrinsic motivation, greater external behavioral regulations, and greater amotivation (Conroy et al., 2006; Nien & Duda, 2008). PAv goals have been associated with fewer challenge appraisals, more threat appraisals, less positive affect, and more negative affect (Adie et al., 2008). These goals have also been linked with relatively inferior athletic performance (Stoeber, Uphill, et al., 2009).

Some inconsistent findings were not included in the review just presented. First, perceptions of competence have inconsistent relationships with the 2×2 achievement goals. Warburton and Spray (2009) found that perceptions of competence positively predict all four achievement goals, whereas others have found that competence perceptions are associated only with approach-valenced achievement goals (Morris & Kavussanu, 2008; Nien & Duda, 2008). Second, Adie and colleagues (2008) conceived of self-esteem as a consequence of goals and reported a positive relationship with MAp goals and negative relationships with the remaining goals. From our perspective, stable and broad entities such as self-esteem are better conceived of as antecedents of goals in a particular context.

Other Measures

Our review has included three popular measures of achievement goals in sport and exercise contexts, but this review is far from comprehensive. A number of other noteworthy measures have been developed in the past decade. Some of these tap into dichotomous achievement goals; an example is the Achievement Goal Scale for Youth Sports (Cumming, Smith, Smoll, Standage, & Grossbard,

2008). Others are like the AGQ-S, being derivatives of the original AGQ (Elliot & McGregor, 2001), and assess goals in the 2 × 2 framework. These include the Achievement Goal Questionnaire-Physical Education (Guan, McBride, & Xiang, 2007; Guan, Xiang, McBride, and Bruene, 2006), the 2 × 2 Achievement Goals in Physical Education Questionnaire (Wang, Biddle, & Elliot, 2007), and the AGQ for strenuous physical activity (Lochbaum, Stevenson, & Hilario, 2009). These measures do not have a comparable body of evidence supporting the meaning of their scores as of this writing; however, the initial evidence for these scores is promising.

States of Achievement Goal Involvement

In contrast to the voluminous research on achievement goal orientations, the research on states of achievement goal involvement is less prolific. These states of goal involvement are theoretically powerful because they focus on intraindividual changes in goal levels. Goals have shown lower reliability than motives have shown (e.g., Conroy, Elliot, & Hofer, 2003; Conroy, Metzler, et al., 2003), and elements of both stability and instability are present in longitudinal goal assessments (Fryer & Elliot, 2007). This dynamic quality introduces unique assessment challenges for researchers. Three general strategies have emerged for assessing these states: (1) using existing scales with modified instructions, (2) using video-assisted recall, and (3) using single items in a repeated measures fashion.

Using Existing Scales With Modified Instructions

The most obvious measure for assessing states of goal involvement involves adapting existing multi-item scales such as the ones described earlier to meet the needs for temporal and contextual specificity. Simply modifying the instructions or item stems on a measure may be sufficient to capture the goals that a participant adopted at a particular moment in time. It is critical when assessing states of goal involvement that participants rate their goals for a specific activity at a particular point in time. Such contextual and temporal specificity distinguishes states of involvement from more global achievement goal orientations. The AGQ-S lends itself well to this approach. In fact, the AGQ-S *should* be administered in reference to a specific upcoming activity, although the timescale for the activity and outcomes may vary, for example, from hole-by-hole outcomes during a round of golf (Schantz & Conroy, 2009) to pre- to midseason outcomes in track and field (Conroy et al., 2008). This modification approach

has been applied with other measures (e.g., Simons, Dewitte, & Lens, 2003).

Hall and Kerr (1997) used this approach in their study of achievement goals and state anxiety in junior fencers. Fencers completed a standard TEOSQ 1 wk before a tournament competition and a TEOSQ with modified instructions 30 min before the competition. The standard and modified instruments used the following item stems, respectively: "I feel most successful in fencing when . . ." and "I will feel most successful in this tournament if. . . ." Internal consistency estimates for both the standard and modified TEOSQ responses were comparable and above traditional cutoff criteria. Correlation coefficients for the goal assessments 1 wk and 30 min before competition were both statistically significant: r_{task} = .57, r_{ego} = .66 ($ps < .01$). Williams (1998) used a similar approach in a study of female softball players. As in the study of Hall and Kerr (1997), the results demonstrated both consistency and variability in states of goal involvement. These findings indicate that goal orientations positively predict states of involvement but are not strong enough predictors to serve as proxies for states that are assessed immediately before a performance.

Some limitations to this approach should be noted. First, full-length scales can burden and fatigue participants unnecessarily, so this approach is not ideal for longitudinal research with intensive goal assessments conducted over a short time frame. In cross-sectional research, however, the temporal and contextual specificity of these ratings is likely to produce less biased estimates of relationships between achievement goals and their consequences. Second, given that states of involvement can shift over time, care must also be taken to align the temporal focus of the outcome measures with the goals assessment.

Single-Item Measures

A second approach to assessing states of goal involvement is to shorten existing multi-item scales into single-item scales and ask participants to rate their goals for a specific activity occurring shortly thereafter (e.g., Harwood & Swain, 1998; Swain & Harwood, 1996). This approach has the benefit of minimizing the demands made on participants during an event and lends itself well to intensive sampling of goal states during an activity.

Schantz and Conroy (2009) demonstrated this approach by conducting repeated assessments of collegiate golfers during a round of golf. The assessments consisted of single items for each of the 2 × 2 achievement goals. Before every hole in a practice round, golfers rated a single item for each of the goals with instructions to rate their goals for that hole. Immediately after completing the hole, they recorded their score and rated their affect along the dimensions of valence, arousal, and dominance. By adopting a multilevel modeling (MLM) approach, Schantz and Conroy (2009) were able to decompose goal variance into components that varied within golfers (i.e., hole-to-hole fluctuations around the golfer's average level of each goal) and between golfers (i.e., the average level of a goal over the entire round). Each of these parameters could then be linked to the intraindividual variability in that outcome over time (e.g., affective fluctuation) and the average level of an outcome variable (e.g., mood). This MLM approach also provided an opportunity to control third variables that may have threatened the validity of conclusions (e.g., individual differences in ability or hole-to-hole fluctuations in performance). Best of all, the intensive sampling of goals, affect, and performance over a round of golf made it possible to evaluate temporal sequences that would be impossible to test in research that did not treat time as a meaningful dimension. This approach revealed that dominant and unpleasant moods over the entire round reduced the strength of prehole MAv and PAp goals, respectively, but had no effect on prehole MAp and PAv goals. Complex affect regulation processes also were revealed in this study. For example, golfers with high FF who adopted stronger-than-usual MAp goals at the beginning of a hole increased their arousal level over the course of the hole, whereas golfers with low FF who adopted stronger-than-usual MAp goals at the beginning of a hole decreased their arousal level over the course of the hole. These findings (and others described in the paper) illustrate the powerful insights that can be gained from using single items for intensive sampling of motivational processes.

One trade-off with this approach is that single items may not be representative of the domain being assessed. They also have unknown reliability. Contemporary theorizing about goals has shifted toward very specific, competence-based aims devoid of surplus meaning. We believe that a single, well-written item can be sufficient for assessing well-defined, concrete goals (e.g., "my aim is to outperform my playing partners on this hole"). Of course, this issue is an empirical question that has preliminary support and awaits further examination. The unknown reliability of single items in cross-sectional research is an unmistakable concern (Nunnally, 1994); however, in longitudinal studies with repeated measurements, reliability for such items can be estimated so this criticism is moot.

Moreover, Wanous, Reichers, and Hudy (1997) have demonstrated that single items can provide valid and reliable assessments of psychological constructs and therefore may be justified in research contexts that do not permit the use of full-length scales. One consideration when using this approach is that analyses of intensive within-person data require statistical techniques that have been uncommon in contemporary achievement motivation research in sport and exercise psychology.

Stimulated Recall

The final approach used to assess states of achievement goal involvement is stimulated, or video-assisted, recall. Lyle (2003) reviewed this method and highlighted its utility for conducting research in naturalistic research settings. It minimizes intrusion into the performer's experience and provides a high-frequency sampling of goal involvement states. This innovative technique involves recording a participant's performance and then replaying it for the participant to watch. While watching, the participant describes a recalled experience at that point in time (e.g., state of goal involvement). These ratings can be made with single- or multi-item measures.

One innovative application of this method was demonstrated by Gernigon, d'Arripe-Longueville, Delignières, and Ninot (2004) with two judo competitors. These competitors were videotaped in a 5 min practice combat session. Afterward, the competitors watched the video recording while using the mouse paradigm to record their state of involvement for a particular goal (Vallacher, Nowak, Froehlich, & Rockloff, 2002). A single item describing an achievement goal was shown at the top of the screen, and participants used the mouse to move the cursor left or right along a horizontal axis to indicate the strength of the state of involvement corresponding to the goal item shown on screen. This process was repeated for each goal under consideration. The computer sampled and recorded cursor movements 5 times per second. The authors then linked changes in cursor movement (goal involvement) with events that occurred on the video and for the other participant. Smith and Harwood (2001) used stimulated recall to assess goal involvement during a tennis match. While watching a video recording of his match, a tennis player rated his goal involvement at the end of each point using a single item. Both of these studies revealed substantial intraindividual variability in goal involvement during relatively brief time frames.

The stimulated recall technique has its limitations. It is vulnerable to retrospective biases associated with the time delay between the activity and the rating. Knowledge of future events in the behavioral sequence may also contaminate retrospective accounts of goal involvement. These limitations aside, this innovative technique is capable of providing unique and valuable measures of achievement goal involvement.

Recommendations for Researchers and Practitioners

From our review of the literature, we see several opportunities for increasing the clarity of future findings in achievement motivation. Following our description of recommendations for researchers, we also offer recommendations for practitioners who use achievement motivation theories in their work.

From a conceptual perspective, the 2 × 2 achievement goal framework has sharpened our understanding of achievement goals. By grounding goals explicitly in competence, it is possible to distinguish goals from indirectly related surplus meaning. All of the scales described in this chapter have problems with at least some content-irrelevant variance (e.g., effort and worry, neither of which refers to a definition of competence but is clearly a consequence of certain achievement goals). Increased precision will be valuable for clarifying the processes associated with goal-related variability (see Elliot & Murayama, 2008). If the 2 × 2 achievement goal framework is expanded someday, it will be important to ensure that any new goals are clearly grounded in the concept of competence.

On a related note, differentiating approach goals from avoidance goals has increased the predictive validity for goals in relation to important achievement-related criteria. It may not be necessary to assess all goals in every study. For example, performance-based definitions of competence may not be particularly relevant for studies of achievement goals in rehabilitation contexts. Nevertheless, it would be valuable to contextualize conclusions based on which goals were and were not assessed in a particular study.

The hierarchical model of achievement motivation also provides a valuable framework for researchers to differentiate goals from their antecedents and consequences. Even if a particular research design does not permit a clear temporal sequencing of measures that minimizes the threat of state effects and captures motivational processes as they unfold over time, researchers can benefit from the conceptual exercise of identifying antecedents and consequences of goals. Strong theoretically driven arguments about causal sequences should outweigh

atheoretical arguments driven by sample-specific findings when evaluating competing statistical models.

The bandwidths of motives and goals differ, and this difference should be reflected in assessments. Achievement motives are deeply rooted in self-evaluative tendencies that are unlikely to change dramatically from one achievement context to another. Competence valuation for two activities may differ, but that is insufficient justification for context-specific assessments of broad-based, dispositional motives. Context-specific assessments may inflate shared variance between motives and potential outcomes; however, such an increase in predictive power should be viewed cautiously because it may be an artifact of shared method variance if both measures require respondents to focus on their experience in a particular context. Absent a compelling theoretical rationale, motives are best assessed without regard to a specific achievement context.

Goals, on the other hand, require both contextual and temporal specificity. Achievement goal questionnaires should inform respondents which activity and which time frame to consider when rating each item. States of involvement assessed with here-and-now instructions may be appropriate for some research questions. Other research questions may require respondents to consider their goals for a longer duration (e.g., this season). Either way, the key is for researchers to consider the temporal resolution of their outcomes and match that to their goals assessment.

Achievement motivation research has relied strongly on cross-sectional studies that do not control for initial levels of outcomes or attempt to manipulate goals. These research designs have many limitations, and there is great value to be gained from introducing more sophisticated research designs. Temporally separating assessments of motivation and outcomes is a valuable, albeit insufficient, design feature. Longitudinal—not just prospective—assessments of goals and outcomes (e.g., Schantz and Conroy, 2009) and experimental manipulation of states of goal involvement (e.g., Cury, Elliot, Sarrazin, Da Fonseca, & Rufo, 2002) will help to shed further light on motivational processes and strengthen the basis for causal inferences.

Finally, from a data analysis perspective, some positive associations are expected between goals in the 2 × 2 framework. Collinearity of predictor variables complicates multiple regression analyses by creating the potential unstable regression weights (i.e., bouncing betas). Researchers should carefully evaluate the collinearity in goal scores and use appropriate caution when analyzing their data. Multiple regression remains a valuable tool even with a degree of collinearity between predictor variables; however, interpretations of regression weights should be supplemented by careful consideration of structure coefficients before drawing conclusions from such analyses (see Courville & Thompson, 2001).

Practitioners can also take some guidance from this review. First, more immediate effects will be realized from interventions targeting goals rather than motives. Goals are dynamic cognitive entities that respond to situational cues (as well as dispositional qualities), whereas motives are stable dispositions deeply rooted in self-evaluative processes. Motives can change over time in the right environment; however, such changes require a longer time frame than changes in goals require. It is also worth noting that changes in motives are more likely to endure.

In addition to changing quickly, goals—relative to motives—are proximal predictors of many important achievement-related outcomes. In the sport and exercise domains, these outcomes include performance and many aspects of subjective experiences. Selecting which goal to promote may not be as straightforward as previously thought. No single goal has desirable effects on every achievement outcome. Practitioners should carefully consider the consequence profile of the goals in light of their objectives before implementing any achievement goal interventions.

Finally, evidence supporting the hierarchical model of achievement motivation leads us to encourage practitioners to think broadly about achievement motivation and not limit their focus to achievement goals. Motives predispose people to adopting particular achievement goals and can facilitate or hinder progress toward desired achievement outcomes. The available evidence suggests that achievement motives are one of the most robust dispositional antecedents of achievement goals, so practitioners are encouraged to include them in any assessments of achievement motivation.

Motivation in general, and achievement motivation in particular, is a process of initiating and orienting behaviors to attain specific incentives. Processes are characterized by change over time (*Merriam-Webster Online Dictionary*, 2009). Unless our designs and measures are sensitive to temporal dynamics and intraindividual variability, they risk an undesirable disconnection from a fundamental premise of these theories. Cattell (1952) conceived of a three-dimensional cube—a data box—defined by persons × variables × occasions. To date, the vast majority of achievement motivation research in sport and exercise has been located on the persons × variables plane of this data box, and the temporal dimension (i.e., occasions) has been largely neglected. We propose that it is time to extend ourselves beyond such plane research designs and become edgier by incorporating the temporal dimension of motivation so we can exploit the richness of the data box. Of course, this approach challenges existing methods for designing studies, assessing motivation, and analyzing data, but critical reflection can be valuable. Analytical tools are emerging in related bodies of literature that can be adapted to overcome many of the methodological limitations of the past (e.g., see the recent special issue edited by Ram and Gerstorf, 2009). We eagerly await the advances in understanding that will derive from greater convergence of theories, data, and methods in achievement motivation research. Indeed, we anticipate that the next generation of advances in achievement motivation will come from reinvigorating the role of process in our research.

Acknowledgments

This publication was made possible by grant number RC1 AG035645 from the National Institute of Aging at the National Institutes of Health. Its contents are solely the responsibility of the authors and do not necessarily represent the official views of NIA.

Measures Assessing Achievement Motivation Processes

Variable or construct	Measure or tool	Dimension or characteristic	Source	Website
Explicit need for achievement	Personality Research Form (PRF)	Achievement sub-scale, 16 true–false items	Jackson (1994)	www.sigmaassess-mentsystems.com/assessments/prf.asp
Explicit need for achievement	Work and Family Orientation Questionnaire (WOFO)	Work and mastery scales, 14 items with 5-point response scale	Helmreich & Spence (1978); Spence & Helmreich (1983)	None
Explicit fear of failure	Performance Failure Appraisal Inventory (PFAI)	Fear of failure (higher-order factor) and five related (lower-order) beliefs about aversive consequences of failure, 25-item long form and 5-item short form with 5-point response scale	Conroy (2001); Conroy, Willow, & Metzler (2002)	None
Task and ego goal orientations	Task and Ego Orientation in Sport Questionnaire (TEOSQ)	Task and ego orientation scales, 13 items with 5-point response scale	Duda & Nicholls (1992)	None
Task and ego goal orientations	Perceptions of Success Questionnaire (POSQ)	Task and ego orientation scales, 12 items with 5-point response scale	Roberts, Treasure, & Balague (1998)	None
2 × 2 achievement goals in sport	Achievement Goal Questionnaire for Sport (AGQ-S)	Mastery-approach, mastery-avoidance, performance-approach, and performance-avoidance scales, 12 items with 7-point response scale	Conroy, Elliot, & Hofer (2003)	None

PART III

Emotion, Affect, and Coping Measurement

Similiar to part II, the chapters in part III relate to specific issues encountered in sport and exercise psychology. In part III, issues of interest are affect, mood, emotions, flow, burnout, and the psychological skills and coping strategies used for self-regulation and adaptation. A Bayesian approach to measuring psychological crisis is also included in part III.

Affect, Mood, and Emotion

Panteleimon Ekkekakis, PhD

The study of emotions, moods, and affect (collectively referred to here as *affective phenomena*) presents a considerable challenge for researchers. This is an area characterized by a bewildering multiplicity of constructs, several alternative theories for each construct, and multiple measures based on each theory. The history of research and theorizing on affective phenomena is long, and the associated literature is vast. On certain key topics, such as the interface between cognition and emotion, the first substantive debates date to antiquity. Furthermore, the issues are often complex and, in many cases, have been the subject of intense controversy. Consequently, there is an overwhelming amount of information that a researcher needs to master before being ready to make a meaningful contribution. This means that while on the one hand, the dedicated and patient scholar will discover a fascinating wealth of ideas within this field, on the other hand, the impatient researcher with an ephemeral interest is likely to feel bemused, fall easy victim to uninformed advice, and, perhaps more importantly, reproduce more misinformation into an already confusing literature. Simply put, this is not an area that a researcher can enter after reading just one or even a few papers on the subject. Therefore, given the space constraints of this chapter, those who are now embarking on a study in this field should view this chapter as a very brief introduction and not a sole resource. Researchers are strongly encouraged to consult the cited references and to conduct their own in-depth study of the original material before selecting a construct or a measure.

Choosing a Measure: A Three-Step Process

The process of choosing a measure ideally includes three steps (Ekkekakis, 2008). The first step involves deciding which construct to target among the three main constructs that constitute the affective domain, namely *emotion*, *mood*, and *core affect*. The differences in these constructs are summarized in the following section.

The second step involves choosing among different theoretical models that have been proposed for conceptualizing the chosen construct. Measures do not evolve in a theoretical vacuum; when researchers choose a measure, they presumably also accept the theoretical infrastructure upon which the measure was built. Thus, the researchers must have a good knowledge of the underlying theory and must be able to explain the reasons for choosing one theory over another.

The third step consists of considering the psychometric information—namely, whether a measure meets or surpasses conventional criteria for evaluating reliability and validity. Was the Cronbach alpha value greater than .70? Was the goodness-of-fit index greater than .90 or .95? Are the coefficients for convergent and discriminant validity satisfactory? This is certainly important information that requires considerable experience and expertise in psychometrics to evaluate properly. However, this step should be considered only as the *last* step in this multistep process and not as the sole step. Its meaningfulness is questionable if the previous two steps are missing.

Understanding the Differences Between Affect, Emotion, and Mood

In the early 1990s, Batson, Shaw, and Oleson (1992) noted that, in general psychology, "most often, the terms *affect*, *mood*, and *emotion* are used interchangeably, without any attempt at conceptual differentiation" (p. 295). Today, progress is being made in drawing some lines of demarcation (Alpert & Rosen, 1990; Batson et al., 1992; Beedie, Terry, & Lane, 2005; Russell, 2003; Russell & Feldman Barrett, 1999). Thanks to considerable convergence among the stated views, a workable classification scheme has started to emerge.

Core Affect. This term is defined as a "neurophysiological state consciously accessible as a simple primitive non-reflective feeling most evident in mood and emotion but always available to consciousness" (Russell & Feldman Barrett, 2009, p. 104). Examples of core affect include pleasure and displeasure, tension and relaxation, energy and tiredness. A person experiences core affect constantly, although the nature and intensity of affect vary over time. Core affect can be a component of emotions and moods (defined next), but it can also occur in pure, or isolate, form. For example, according to Russell (2003), *"pride* can be thought of as feeling good about oneself. The 'feeling good' is core affect and the 'about oneself' is an additional (cognitive) component" (p. 148). As explained next, this qualifies *pride* as an *emotion.*

Emotion. Russell and Feldman Barrett (1999) defined a "prototypical emotional episode" (what is commonly called an occurrence of an *emotion*) as a "complex set of interrelated sub-events concerned with a specific object" (p. 806), such as a person, an event, or a thing, whether past, present, future, real, or imagined. The co-occurring components that compose a prototypical emotional episode include (a) core affect, (b) overt behavior congruent with the emotion (e.g., a smile or a facial expression of fear), (c) attention directed toward the eliciting stimulus, (d) cognitive appraisal of the meaning and possible implications of the stimulus, (e) attribution of the genesis of the episode to the stimulus, (f) the experience of the particular emotion, and (g) neural (peripheral and central) and endocrine changes consistent with the particular emotion.

Because emotional episodes are elicited *by* something, are reactions *to* something, and are generally *about* something, the cognitive appraisal involved in the transaction between person and object is considered a defining element. Some examples of emotions—which comprise all the elements listed here, including cognitive appraisal—are anger, fear, jealousy, pride, and love.

Mood. One distinguishing feature of moods is that they typically last longer than emotions. Other authors have emphasized that a more meaningful differentiating feature of moods might be that they are diffuse and global as opposed to specific. According to Frijda (2009), *mood* is "the appropriate designation for affective states that are about

nothing specific or about everything—about the world in general" (p. 258). For example, when a person is in an anxious mood, the object might be something as general as the whole future or as distant as life in 20 years; when a person is in a depressive mood, the object might be the totality of self; and when a person is in an irritable mood, the object could be anything and anyone. In such cases, moods essentially have a cause. However, unlike emotions, which follow their eliciting stimuli closely or even instantaneously, a mood is usually temporally remote (Morris, 1992) from its cause (e.g., a person can wake up in a bad mood in the morning as a result of a confrontation the previous evening). Consequently, the cause of a mood may not always be easy to identify.

An important consideration when choosing a measure is whether the goal is to assess a specific, narrowly defined state (or a set of distinct states) or broad dimensions that are theorized to underlie a global domain of content (such as *mood* or *core affect*). Despite the fundamental importance of this consideration, it is not one that is addressed explicitly in most published reports. However, this issue has direct relevance to the ability of a researcher to make generalizations. If what was assessed is a narrowly defined state (or even an assortment of distinct states), then the researcher is not justified in drawing inferences about the global domain in which the specific state belongs. This is because the domain presumably includes more content than is reflected in a measure of a narrowly defined state.

Let's consider an example. The Profile of Mood States (POMS; McNair, Lorr, & Droppleman, 1971) remains one of the most frequently used measures of mood in exercise psychology. This questionnaire taps six distinct mood states: tension, depression, anger, vigor, fatigue, and confusion. There is no claim, either explicit or implicit, in the theoretical basis of the POMS that these six distinct states collectively capture the entire content domain of mood. Another frequently used measure is the Positive and Negative Affect Schedule (PANAS; Watson, Clark, & Tellegen, 1988). In contrast to the POMS, the PANAS was developed not to assess distinct mood states but rather to assess "the two primary dimensions of mood" (p. 1069)—namely, positive affect and negative affect. Both dimensions are theorized to be bipolar and orthogonal to each other. They are primary dimensions because together they are believed to account for the majority of the variance (differences and similarities) among distinct mood states. Positive affect is a dimension that "reflects the extent to which a person feels enthusiastic, active, and alert." Its high pole has been described as "a state of high energy, full concentration, and pleasurable engagement," whereas its low pole has been described as a state "characterized by sadness and lethargy." In contrast, negative affect has been described as a "general dimension of subjective distress and unpleasurable engagement." Its high pole "subsumes a variety of aversive mood states, including anger, contempt, disgust, guilt, fear, and nervousness," whereas its low pole is characterized by "calmness and serenity" (Watson et al., 1988, p. 1063).

If a researcher intends to draw inferences about the effects of an exercise intervention on the global domain of mood, then the POMS, a measure of just six distinct mood states, is not the most appropriate option. It is easy to think of other mood states not captured by the POMS, some of which might be influenced by an exercise intervention (e.g., cheerfulness). Thus, if a researcher did use the POMS and the exercise intervention resulted in no significant changes, it would be erroneous for the researcher to conclude that exercise had no effect on the broad domain of *mood*. This is because it is possible that exercise might have influenced components of mood other than the six being tapped by this measure.

On the other hand, there are situations in which a researcher may wish to examine the effect of manipulating an exerciser's specific cognitive appraisal. Cognitive theories predict that such a manipulation induces a change in specific states. For example, a decrease in efficacy is expected to lead to anxiety (Bandura, 1988), while an attribution of success to internal causes should evoke a sense of pride (Weiner, 1985). In such cases, a measure of broad dimensions of mood, such as the PANAS, is not the most appropriate option. If the manipulation targets a specific pattern of appraisal theorized to elicit a specific response, then the most appropriate option is a measure that specifically targets the response predicted by theory (e.g., anxiety or pride).

As these examples illustrate, the distinction between the distinct-states approach and the dimensional approach is clearly of fundamental importance. Therefore, this consideration should be addressed explicitly in justifying the selection of a measure. According to the distinct-states approach, each state is a distinct entity. For example, the emotion of anxiety is associated with a unique pattern of antecedent appraisal (facing a perceived threat); a unique experiential quality; characteristic attention-related biases; a possibly distinct signature of visceral and somatic symptoms; tense facial, postural, and vocal expressions; and a repertoire of coping responses. For researchers specifically interested

in anxiety, focusing on this one emotion and its unique characteristics is the only way to understand it deeply and fully.

Although the distinct-states approach highlights the unique features of different states, it has been proposed that such states are not entirely independent of one another but are interrelated systematically. These systematic relationships can be modeled by a small number of underlying dimensions. Hence, this conceptual approach has been labeled *dimensional*.

Although numerous dimensional models were proposed during the 20th century, the most widely accepted contemporary dimensional models are two dimensional. First is the circumplex model proposed by Russell (1980). This model is based on the idea that two orthogonal and bipolar dimensions—affective valence and perceived activation—define the affective space. The various affective states are combinations of these two basic constituents in different degrees. As a result, affective states are arranged along the perimeter of the circle defined by the two dimensions. States that are close together (e.g., happy and glad) represent similar mixtures of valence and activation. States that are positioned diametrically from each other (e.g., happy and sad) differ maximally in terms of one or the other dimension (e.g., valence). States that are separated by a 90° angle are statistically independent of each other.

Second is the two-dimensional solution that Zevon and Tellegen (1982) and Watson and Tellegen (1985) arrived at via factor analyses of inter- and intraindividual data from self-reports. In agreement with Russell's analyses, these authors identified one dimension reflecting affective valence (ranging from items such as happy and pleased to unhappy and sad) and a second dimension reflecting perceived activation, although they decided to label this dimension as *strong engagement to disengagement* (ranging from items such as aroused and astonished to quiescent and still). However, because most of the items that were subjected to factor analysis did not reflect pure valence and activation but instead reflected mixtures of these two dimensions, following a varimax rotation, the axes passed through the areas with the highest concentration of items. Thus, one axis extended from high-activation pleasant affect (e.g., elated, enthusiastic, excited) to low-activation unpleasant affect (e.g., drowsy, dull, sluggish). This dimension was initially labeled *positive affect* and later renamed *positive activation* (PA). The other axis extended from high-activation unpleasant affect (e.g., distressed, jittery, nervous) to low-activation pleasant affect (e.g., calm, placid, relaxed). This dimension was initially labeled *negative affect* and later renamed *negative activation* (NA). It should be clear from this description that Russell's (1980) circumplex model and the PA/NA dimensional model are 45° rotational variants of one another rather than fundamentally different conceptualizations.

One highly controversial aspect of the PA/NA model that has been the cause of much confusion in the literature was the decision to name the dimensions using descriptors that connote unipolarity (i.e., *positive affect*, *negative affect*) when the dimensions were identified in the original analyses as bipolar. Zevon and Tellegen (1982) tried to explain this decision by stating that the dimensions "are best characterized as *descriptively bipolar* but *affectively unipolar*" (p. 112). This enigmatic statement was based on the argument that only high-arousal states can be conceived of as genuinely affective, whereas low-arousal states (e.g., calmness or fatigue) are nonaffective. Thus, the dimensions were defined (and named) solely by their high-arousal poles. This debatable position generated considerable confusion. For example, *calm* is not a marker of what most people call *positive affect* but is a marker of low negative affect. Furthermore, *happy* is not a marker of positive affect, and *sad* is not a marker of negative affect. Instead, these states are markers of the two opposite poles of a different bipolar dimension named *pleasantness-unpleasantness*. This led to additional confusion, since the dimensions of PA and NA were theorized to be orthogonal to each other (i.e., statistically unrelated), whereas pleasantness and unpleasantness were theorized to be bipolar opposites. Many researchers who did not notice the difference used the PA/NA model as a basis for arguing that people can feel both happy and sad at the same time (see the review by Larsen and Diener, 1992). The PA/NA model clearly does not make such a prediction.

A third variant of a two-dimensional structure was proposed by Thayer (1989). His model again postulates two bipolar dimensions. One, named *energetic arousal* (EA), extends from energy to tiredness. The other, named *tense arousal* (TA), extends from tension to calmness. It is easy to detect the compatibility of this model with the PA/NA model. Indeed, Thayer (1989) and Watson and Tellegen (1985) have made it clear that EA overlaps with PA and TA overlaps with NA. Empirical evidence for the compatibility of these models within a two-dimensional framework was provided by Yik, Russell, and Feldman Barrett (1999). After correcting for as many sources of random and systematic error (which tend to distort the relationships between constructs) as possible, these researchers found

that, for unipolar constructs (e.g., Thayer's energy scale or Watson and Tellegen's PA), valence and activation explained between 53% and 90% of the variance, with a mean of 72%. For bipolar dimensions (e.g., Thayer's EA), valence and activation explained between 73% and 97% of the variance, with a mean of 85%.

Hierarchical Structure of the Affective Domain: An Integrative Framework

After decades of referring to dimensional models as models of *emotions*, it is now becoming widely recognized that the true heuristic value of dimensional models is limited to the study of *core affect*. According to Russell and Feldman Barrett (1999), "we now believe that this dimensional structure (i.e., the circumplex) represents, and is limited to, the core affect involved" (p. 807). Along the same lines, Russell (2003) acknowledged more recently that "by themselves, pleasure and arousal do not fully account for most emotional episodes," and the circumplex "does not provide a sufficiently rich account of prototypical emotional episodes" because it "fails to explain adequately how fear, jealousy, anger, and shame are different." He concluded that "the dimensional perspective must be integrated with the categorical perspective" (p. 150). The critical insight that led to this development was the distinction between *core affect* and *emotions* (what Russell called *prototypical emotional episodes*). This underscores the importance of what was considered here as the crucial first step—namely, recognizing the differences among the various affective phenomena.

Recognizing both the strengths and the limitations of dimensional models early on, Watson and Tellegen (1985) proposed that the affective domain could be described as having a hierarchical structure. Broad dimensions can capture the differences and similarities between states on a macroscopic scale. Beyond this, however, the distinct-states approach is also required for a microscopic analysis of the uniqueness of the different states. Explaining this position, Watson and Clark (1997) wrote the following:

> We want to emphasize that these two basic approaches—dimensions and discrete affects—are not incompatible or mutually exclusive; rather, they essentially reflect different levels of a single, integrated hierarchical structure. . . . That is, each of the higher order dimensions can be decomposed into several correlated yet ultimately distinct affective states, much like a general factor of

personality (e.g., neuroticism) can be subdivided into several narrower components or "facets" (e.g., anxiety, vulnerability). In this hierarchical model, the lower level reflects the unique descriptive/explanatory power of the individual discrete affects (i.e., specificity), whereas the general dimensions reflect their shared, overlapping qualities (i.e., nonspecificity). (p. 269)

What are the practical implications of these integrative, hierarchical models for the exercise psychology researcher? Perhaps the most important point is that both the distinct states and the dimensional approach have their place, so this issue is not an either-or question. Which approach is most suitable for a given study depends on the specific aim of the study. If a study involves an experimental manipulation that is likely to induce a pattern of cognitive appraisal underlying a specific emotion, then the focus of the investigation should be on that particular emotion (and use a distinct-states perspective). For example, if a study places sedentary women or women highly anxious about their physical appearance in front of mirrors while they exercise (i.e., the study involves a manipulation of a very specific self-evaluative appraisal), then the appropriate target is the distinct emotion of anxiety (i.e., the specific emotional state that is theorized to emerge from that particular appraisal) rather than general affect. If, on the other hand, the purpose of a study is to examine the effects of a more general manipulation (e.g., different levels of intensity or duration) or a manipulation for which the effects cannot be predicted on the basis of current theory (e.g., hydration or glucose supplementation), then it makes more sense to broaden the investigative scope by assessing the global domain of core affect. This can be done effectively and efficiently by using a two-dimensional model (Ekkekakis & Petruzzello, 2002).

Review of Specific Measures

In the last 20 years, more than 20 different measures of affective constructs have been used in studies of acute exercise (i.e., to examine the effects of single bouts of exercise). An even larger number of measures has been utilized in studies of chronic exercise (i.e., to examine the effects of exercise training programs lasting for several weeks or months). Those in the latter category include measures designed for clinical and healthy populations; questionnaires and clinician-administered interview protocols; measures of distinct states and broad dimensions; and measures of affect, mood, emotions, and broader constructs such as perceived quality of life or satisfaction with life. Furthermore, not all studies have employed self-reports to operationalize affective constructs. A small but growing number of studies have employed psychophysiological measures (e.g., prefrontal hemispheric asymmetry assessed by EEG or acoustic startle responses assessed by EMG) to draw inferences about affective responses. Given the space constraints of this chapter, only a very selective review can be presented here. Before researchers decide to adopt any of the measures cited here, they are strongly encouraged to conduct a thorough and in-depth review of the theoretical basis, the developmental history, and the relevant conceptual and psychometric critiques that have appeared in the literature. There are measures developed in recent years that have been used or discussed in no more than a handful of published articles. However, there are also measures developed decades ago that have been used in thousands of studies and have been the subject of several critical reviews. Thus, researchers who intend to use such measures should be prepared to invest considerable time and effort in familiarizing themselves with the issues and contemplating the pros and cons of different theoretical perspectives and measures before making a decision.

Single-Item Dimensional Measures of Affect

Single-item measures take only a few seconds to administer, shortening the interruptions of any ongoing tasks and minimizing respondent fatigue. Thus, researchers find single-item measures to be convenient in studies in which the need to track a rapidly changing affective state makes repeated measurements necessary. On the other hand, because scores on single-item measures depend entirely on only one response, and this response could be erroneous (e.g., due to carelessness or confusion), single-item measures generally tend to be less reliable than multi-item measures of the same constructs. Nevertheless, when appropriate care is taken to control the sources of random measurement error, single-item measures can be very informative, as evidenced by the wealth of information that single-item measures of perceived exertion have contributed to the exercise science literature.

Self-Assessment Manikin

The Self-Assessment Manikin (SAM; Bradley & Lang, 1994; Lang, 1980) assesses three dimensions of affect using pictures of a cartoon character as opposed to a numerical scale with verbal anchors. First, the valence scale depicts a character with facial expressions ranging from pleasure (smiling face) to displeasure (frowning face). Second, the arousal scale depicts a character with facial expressions ranging from sleepiness (eyes closed) to high arousal (shaking and heart pounding). Third, the dominance scale depicts a figure ranging from small size (indicating submissiveness) to large size (indicating dominance). The SAM has been used in only a few exercise studies (e.g., Ekkekakis, Hall, Van Landuyt, & Petruzzello, 2000; Smith, O'Connor, Crabbe, & Dishman, 2002). A bout of exercise has been found to increase arousal, but the changes in valence depend on exercise intensity. Higher intensities are typically associated with declines in pleasure.

Affect Grid

The Affect Grid (AG; Russell, Weiss, & Mendelsohn, 1989) was developed on the basis of Russell's (1980) circumplex model of affect. Accordingly, it provides two scores, one for pleasure and one for arousal. The format of the AG is a 9×9 grid, with the horizontal dimension representing affective valence (ranging from unpleasantness to pleasantness) and the vertical dimension representing perceived activation (ranging from sleepiness to high arousal). Respondents place a single X in 1 of the 81 cells of the grid, and this response is scored along both the valence and the arousal dimensions. The AG has been used in several studies in sport psychology but in surprisingly few studies in exercise psychology (e.g., Ekkekakis et al., 2000). Given the potential problems associated with the somewhat unfamiliar formats of the SAM (i.e., cartoons) and the AG (i.e., a grid), more researchers have opted to assess affective valence and arousal using simple rating scales.

Feeling Scale and Felt Arousal Scale

The Feeling Scale (FS; Hardy & Rejeski, 1989) is an 11-point bipolar scale of pleasure and displeasure that ranges from –5 to +5. Anchors are provided at 0 = "Neutral" and at all odd integers, ranging from –5 = "Very bad" to +5 = "Very good." The Felt Arousal Scale (FAS) of the Telic State Measure (Svebak & Murgatroyd, 1985) was originally developed as a measure of the construct of felt arousal in the context of reversal theory. It is a 6-point single-item scale ranging from 1 to 6, with anchors only at 1 = "Low arousal" and 6 = "High arousal." The FS and FAS have been adapted for children with the addition of a series of stylized drawings of faces ranging from very happy to very sad and from very sleepy to very alert (Hulley et al., 2008).

Multi-Item Measures of Distinct Mood States

Multi-item measures take longer to administer than single-item measures. This makes them less conve-

nient for repeated administrations within a short time frame, as they can increase respondent fatigue and reactivity to testing (e.g., irritation or noncompliance with instructions). They may also distract from ongoing tasks. On the other hand, multi-item measures are generally less susceptible to sources of random measurement error than single-item measures. Because of these characteristics, multi-item measures are typically used to investigate the effects of chronic exercise interventions (with days, weeks, or months between administrations) or in studies of acute exercise in which researchers are interested only in pre-to-post changes rather than closely tracking the trajectory of change over time. When researchers use multi-item measures of distinct mood states, they should explain the reasons why they opted to focus on these particular states and should avoid making unwarranted generalizations to the global domain of *mood*.

Multiple Affect Adjective Checklist

The Multiple Affect Adjective Checklist (MAACL; Zuckerman & Lubin, 1965) was one of the first self-report measures designed to assess transient states as opposed to stable traits and to be geared toward the general population as opposed to clinical groups. The first version of the MAACL combined scales for anxiety, depression, and hostility (Zuckerman, Lubin, Vogel, & Valerius, 1964). When factor analysis became more readily available, the 132-item pool was analyzed and a new structure emerged (Zuckerman, Lubin, & Rinck, 1983). Specifically, anxiety-present, depression-present, and hostility-present items formed three separate factors, while the positively worded items formed two factors, one named *positive affect* and the other *sensation seeking*. However, given the strong intercorrelations among factors within each category, Zuckerman and colleagues (1983) proceeded to merge anxiety, depression, and hostility into a dysphoria (DYS) factor and to merge positive affect (PA) and sensation seeking (SS) into a combined PASS factor. The hierarchical structure (five first-order factors and two second-order factors) formed the basis for the revised edition of the MAACL (MAACL-R; Lubin et al., 1986; Zuckerman & Lubin, 1985), which comprised 66 scored and 66 filler items. The MAACL was used in several earlier studies in exercise psychology (e.g., Goldfarb, Hatfield, Sforzo, & Flynn, 1987; Hardy & Rejeski, 1989). However, its popularity has declined in recent years.

Profile of Mood States

The POMS (McNair et al., 1971) remains one of the most popular self-report measures, not only in exercise psychology but also in psychology in general. The now-famous initials appeared for the first time in 1964, although they did not originally stand for *Profile of Mood States* but rather for *Psychiatric Outpatient Mood Scale* (McNair & Lorr, 1964). The original goal of the POMS was to "construct and develop a useful method for identifying and assessing mood states in psychiatric outpatient populations" (p. 620). The developers of the POMS initially identified six mood states that they considered of interest in this population (tension, anxiety, anger, depression, vigor, and fatigue). These were somewhat different from those assessed by the present-day version of the POMS, which emerged from subsequent factor analyses. It is important for current and prospective users of the POMS to understand that the item pool was composed of items drawn from various adjective lists, a dictionary, and a thesaurus with the purpose of matching them to the six hypothesized mood states. In other words, the item pool of the POMS was never intended to reflect the global content domain of mood. It was meant only to reflect certain states that were deemed of interest specifically for the study of psychiatric outpatients. A series of factor analyses based on data gathered from neurotic psychiatric outpatients led to a merger of the tension and anxiety items into one group and the emergence of a confusion factor. If any users of the POMS in exercise psychology were wondering about the inclusion of a confusion scale in a measure of mood, it can be explained by the fact that this particular state, although arguably not a mood *per se*, was of interest to the developers of the POMS because confusion is a common side effect of psychotropic drugs. The unabated popularity of the POMS in exercise psychology, despite the facts that it was developed for research within a very different context and that it has been rendered obsolete by conceptual developments in the study of affective phenomena, is a fascinating case study for epistemologists and historians of science. It is perhaps unsurprising that the only argument that is presented by researchers who continue to use this instrument is that it has been used in numerous previous investigations.

Multi-Item Dimensional Measures of Affect

Unlike measures that represent conglomerations of several distinct states, dimensional measures were developed with the explicit goal of capturing a global domain of content. This is accomplished by measuring dimensions that are theorized to underlie and define this global domain. In selecting a dimensional measure, researchers should articulate their reasons for endorsing the theoretical framework

upon which their measure of choice was built (i.e., why they believe that the targeted domain of content should be defined by one set of underlying dimensions as opposed to another).

Positive and Negative Affect Schedule

The PANAS (Watson et al., 1988) was developed as the operationalization of the orthogonal dimensions of positive affect (now called *positive activation*) and negative affect (now called *negative activation*) that emerged from the analyses of Zevon and Tellegen (1982) and Watson and Tellegen (1985). Since its publication, the PANAS has become one of the most widely used measures of affect. It consists of 20 items, 10 for the PA scale (e.g., interested, excited) and 10 for the NA scale (e.g., distressed, upset). Each item is accompanied by a 5-point scale ranging from "Very slightly or not at all" to "Extremely." There are two important limitations of the PANAS that should concern researchers. First, the items of the PANAS appear to represent a mixture of emotions, moods, and affects. For example, the items proud, guilty, and ashamed are commonly considered to be emotions; the items irritable, upset, and hostile could be considered moods; and the items distressed, nervous, and jittery probably fall under the category of core affects (Russell, 2003, 2005). It is debatable whether some of the other items (e.g., interested, strong, inspired, determined, attentive) even belong in any of these categories at all. The fact that the PANAS was described as a measure of *mood* and yet was named a measure of (positive and negative) *affect* implies that Watson did not recognize a difference between the constructs described by these two terms. Second, several authors have criticized the PANAS for an obvious inconsistency between the conceptual model that formed its basis (i.e., Watson & Tellegen, 1985; Zevon & Tellegen, 1982) and its eventual content and structure. Specifically, the PA and NA dimensions that emerged from the analyses of Zevon and Tellegen (1982) and Watson and Tellegen (1985) were clearly bipolar. Yet, as described earlier, Zevon and Tellegen (1982) argued that although the dimensions were "descriptively bipolar," they should be viewed as "affectively unipolar" because states of low activation represent "the absence of affect" (p. 112). Accordingly, the items for the PA and NA scales were selected to represent only the high-activation poles of the PA and NA dimensions. As a result, the scales of the PANAS "include no terms assessing fatigue and serenity" (Watson & Clark, 1997, p. 276). The PANAS has been used extensively in exercise psychology research (e.g., Bixby, Spalding, & Hatfield, 2001; Bodin &

Martinsen, 2004; Miller, Bartholomew, & Springer, 2005). However, given that low-activation pleasant states (e.g., serenity) and low-activation unpleasant states (e.g., fatigue) are of exceptional interest in the context of exercise investigations, the exclusion of such states from the PANAS constitutes a critical limitation.

Activation Deactivation Adjective Check List

In its present form, the Activation Deactivation Adjective Checklist (AD ACL; Thayer, 1989) taps two bipolar dimensions. One is termed *Energetic Arousal* (EA) and extends from high-activation pleasant affect (labeled *Energy*, with 5 items such as energetic, vigorous, and lively) to low-activation unpleasant affect (labeled *Tiredness*, with 5 items such as sleepy, tired, and drowsy). The other is termed *Tense Arousal* (TA) and extends from high-activation unpleasant affect (labeled *Tension*, with 5 items such as jittery, clutched-up, and tense) to low-activation pleasant affect (labeled *Calmness*, with 5 items such as placid, calm, and at rest). Each of the 20 items is accompanied by a 4-point response scale, with *vv* = "Definitely feel," *v* = "Feel slightly," *?* = "Cannot decide," and *no* = "Definitely do not feel." The AD ACL can be scored either in terms of the two bipolar dimensions (EA, TA) or in terms of four unipolar scales (Energy, Tiredness, Tension, Calmness). Since the PA and NA scales of the PANAS tap only the high-activation poles of the respective dimensions, Nemanick and Munz (1994) have suggested that the AD ACL is a more complete operationalization of the theoretical space defined by PA and NA. Ekkekakis, Hall, and Petruzzello (2005) examined whether the 20 items of the AD ACL conform to a circumplex before and after a walk. Using stochastic process modeling (the only confirmatory technique that is currently available to test for circumplex structure), they showed that the fit to a circumplex was satisfactory at both time points. However, some problems have also been noted. For example, in exercise studies with healthy and active college samples, there have been problems associated with floor effects. Specifically, the item *fearful* (of the Tension pole of the TA scale) exhibits very low mean and variance (Ekkekakis, Hall, & Petruzzello, 1999; Ekkekakis et al., 2005; Jerome et al., 2002). Furthermore, in some cases, the meaning of the item *intense* has been seen as ambiguous. These problems manifest themselves as reduced indexes of internal consistency of the respective scales.

A measure with a structure similar to that of the AD ACL was recently developed. The state version of the Four-Dimension Mood Scale (4DMS; Gregg & Shepherd, 2009) measures Positive Energy, Tiredness, Negative Arousal, and Relaxation. Unlike the Tiredness scale of the AD ACL, which comprises items that refer mainly to sleepiness and wakefulness (sleepy, drowsy, wide awake, wakeful), the Tiredness scale of the 4DMS comprises items that refer more directly to tiredness and fatigue (exhausted, fatigued, tired, weary, worn out). Because of this difference, Gregg and Shepherd (2009) speculated that "the 4DMS could be more sensitive to the effects of physical exercise" (p. 153).

Multi-Item Measures of Specific Emotions

Both the exercise stimulus and the exercise context are highly variable. Likewise, exercise participants are characterized by tremendous variation in their physiological and psychological constitutions (e.g., temperament or personality traits). The interaction of these factors may result in extremely diverse patterns of cognitive appraisals during acute and chronic exercise. Consequently, a similarly diverse array of appraisal-dependent emotions may occur and thus constitute relevant objects of scientific study within exercise psychology. However, an examination of the literature shows that the one emotion that has received the most attention is *anxiety*. Of the numerous measures of anxiety that are available in the literature, the State-Trait Anxiety Inventory (STAI; Spielberger, Gorsuch, & Lushene, 1970; Spielberger, 1983) is the one used most frequently, and it is the focus of this section.

The STAI was based on Spielberger's highly influential theory of state and trait anxiety (Spielberger, 1972). According to the theory, *state anxiety* is defined as a "transitory psychobiological emotional state or condition that is characterized by subjective, consciously experienced thoughts and feelings relating to tension, apprehension, nervousness, and worry that vary in intensity and fluctuate over time" (Spielberger & Reheiser, 2004, p. 70). *Trait anxiety*, on the other hand, is defined as "relatively stable individual differences in anxiety proneness as a personality trait" or "differences in the strength of the disposition to respond to situations perceived as threatening with elevations in state anxiety" (pp. 70-71). Accordingly, the STAI includes two scales, each consisting of 20 items. One is for state anxiety (with items such as "I am worried" and "I feel frightened") and the other is for trait anxiety (with items such as "I worry too much over something that really doesn't matter" and "I lack self-confidence"). The state anxiety items are accompanied by a 4-point scale of intensity ranging from "Not at all" to "Very much so." The trait anxiety items are accompanied by a 4-point scale of frequency ranging from "Almost never" to "Almost always." The state anxiety scale has been used in exercise psychology to investigate the anxiolytic effects of single bouts of activity (e.g., Bodin & Martinsen, 2004), whereas the trait anxiety scale has been used as a measure of the effects of exercise training studies lasting for weeks or months (e.g., DiLorenzo et al., 1999). The original version of the STAI (Form X; Spielberger et al., 1970) was published in 1970. A revised version (Form Y; Spielberger, 1983) was published in 1983 with the goal of reducing content overlap with depression and replacing certain items with ambiguous meanings.

Despite its unquestionable popularity across many areas of clinical and applied psychology, the STAI has also been the target of considerable criticism. Outside of exercise psychology, the STAI has been criticized for its factor structure (with both the state and the trait scales having been shown to be multidimensional despite the fact that scoring instructions treat them as unidimensional) and its unacceptably high content overlap with depression (which persisted even after the 1983 revision). Within exercise psychology, the criticism has been focused mainly on the state anxiety scale. As first shown by Rejeski, Hardy, and Shaw (1991) and later elaborated on by Ekkekakis and colleagues (1999), during exercise, scores on items indicative of perceived physiological activation (e.g., calm, relaxed) tend to increase (i.e., participants feel less calm and less relaxed, which are scored as increased state anxiety), whereas scores on items indicative of cognitive components of anxiety (e.g., worried) tend to decrease. This divergent pattern of responses suggests that during exercise the different items of the scale become indexes of different constructs rather than a unitary construct of state anxiety. Weakened item intercorrelations lead to declines in the internal consistency of the scale (e.g., $\alpha = .33$ in Rejeski et al., 1991).

Although this is a serious problem, perhaps the most critical problem associated with the STAI in exercise psychology is that the measure has been misused and misinterpreted as a proxy measure of mood and negative affect. The origins of this problem can be traced back to the early days of research on the feel-better effect of exercise, in the early 1970s. At that time, the STAI was one of only a handful of self-report measures that could be used with nonclinical samples and that contained a scale for the assessment of transient states. Thus, it was chosen out of necessity by research pioneers who were eager to operationalize and document exercise-induced feel-better effects. Since both the state and the trait scales demonstrated decreased

scores with acute and chronic exercise interventions, respectively, the STAI quickly became the measure of choice for an increasing number of investigators. In the process, the fact that the STAI was a measure of a very specifically demarcated emotion was forgotten. This led to the STAI being used in numerous exercise studies in which the participants were not anxious and anxiety was not experimentally elevated. In such cases, findings that exercise further reduced already low STAI baseline scores by one or two units were interpreted as evidence of the feel-better phenomenon or exercise-induced anxiolysis. After four decades of research with the STAI in exercise psychology, it seems prudent to return to Spielberger's definition of anxiety and to recall that the STAI is a measure of the very specifically demarcated emotion of anxiety.

Multi-Item Measures of Specific Moods

Similar to the narrow focus of exercise psychology research on the emotion of anxiety, research on specific moods has concentrated primarily on depression. This is perhaps unsurprising given the prevalence and societal effects of depression. The phenomenon of selecting measures on the basis of their extensive use in other areas of psychological research is also quite common in this case. For example, certain measures such as the Beck Depression Inventory (BDI; Beck, Steer, & Garbin, 1988) and the Hamilton Rating Scale for Depression (HRSD; Hamilton, 1960) have ascended to the status of gold standard and thus represent default choices in randomized clinical trials investigating the effects of exercise (Blumenthal et al., 1999, 2007; Dunn, Trivedi, Kampert, Clark, & Chambliss, 2005). However, when judged more critically, even these venerable measures show considerable weaknesses. Critical reviewers, for example, have pointed out that the BDI suffers from controversial factorial validity, susceptibility of scores to momentary changes in environmental conditions, and relatively poor discriminant validity against anxiety (Richter, Werner, Heerlein, Kraus, & Sauer, 1998). Similarly, the HRSD has been criticized for an unclear and unreliable factor structure, poor interrater and retest reliability, and questionable content validity for some items (Bagby, Ryder, Schuller, & Marshall, 2004).

Exercise-Specific Measures of Affect

A new trend appeared in exercise psychology in the 1990s. Following the development of several sport-specific self-report measures in sport psychology, researchers proposed that exercise is characterized by unique stimulus properties and it therefore elicits unique affective responses that are not captured by domain-general measures of affect. This proposal resulted in the development of the Exercise-Induced Feeling Inventory (EFI; Gauvin & Rejeski, 1993), the Subjective Exercise Experiences Scale (SEES; McAuley & Courneya, 1994), and the Physical Activity Affect Scale (PAAS; Lox, Jackson, Tuholski, Wasley, & Treasure, 2000), which was formed by merging scales from the EFI and the SEES. A shortened version of the EFI (Annesi, 2006) and a version intended for use with chronic exercise (Rejeski, Reboussin, Dunn, King, & Sallis, 1999) have also been developed. Given space constraints, a thorough review of these measures is not possible here, and interested readers are referred to other published sources (Ekkekakis & Petruzzello, 2000, 2001a, 2001b). The main problems with these measures were (a) the absence of a guiding theoretical framework (a consequence of the argument that the affective changes associated with exercise are unique), and (b) the derivation of the item pools on the basis of the experiences of a very select group (young, healthy, and active college students).

Problem (a) resulted in structures that are inconsistent with contemporary models of affect. Problem (b) likely resulted in domain underrepresentation, meaning that the domain of content reflected in these measures probably leaves out variants of affect that may be experienced by other segments of the population, such as people who are older, physically inactive, or facing a chronic disease or disability.

Recommendations for Researchers and Practitioners

To reiterate a statement made in the introduction, the study of affect, mood, and emotion is not an area of singular constructs, singular theories, or singular measurement options. To the contrary, it is an area characterized by a very long history, a vast literature, an astounding diversity of theoretical views, and considerable confusion and controversy. As a result, the measurement of affective constructs is an enormously challenging undertaking, requiring an extraordinarily high level of preparation and critical thinking on the part of the researcher. Having to study, critically analyze, and distill a century of research on affective phenomena before being truly ready to choose a measure (and articulately defend this decision) can certainly seem daunting. The alternative, such as choosing a measure that is popular, is much simpler and more tempting by comparison.

When authors attempt to justify the selection of a measure, their arguments tend to focus solely on numeric psychometric indexes. If the Cronbach alpha and, more recently, fit indexes from a CFA are above a certain threshold, then the measure is characterized as psychometrically strong. In actuality, the evaluation should begin at a much earlier stage. Of the different constructs that fall under the umbrella of affective phenomena, which was the target of this particular investigation and why? Of the various theoretical models that have been proposed to describe this particular construct, which one was selected and why? Is this theoretical model satisfactory when examined against the background of theoretical advances in the respective field? Finally, does the chosen measure offer a faithful and comprehensive representation of the intended domain of content? Then, and only then, should the researcher start considering whether the fit indexes or internal consistency coefficients are high enough. Getting numbers from a computer printout is easy but, by itself, meaningless. The challenge lies in carrying out the intensive and critical work of evaluating the underlying theory and the correspondence between the measure and the theoretical postulates it is supposed to represent.

For example, the fact that the factor structure of the PANAS (Watson et al., 1988) was found to be replicable in a sample of youth sport participants (Crocker, 1997), with a goodness-of-fit index of .95, does not constitute adequate evidence of the appropriateness and applicability of the measure in youth samples. As noted earlier, the PANAS does not include items or scales that assess either pleasant (e.g., calmness, serenity) or unpleasant (e.g., tiredness, fatigue) low-activation states (Watson & Clark, 1997). A researcher contemplating the use of the PANAS in the context of exercise should first evaluate this fundamental aspect of the theoretical basis of the PANAS and decide whether it seems appropriate (using the current state of theoretical development in the field as a criterion) and whether it serves the purpose of the specific study being planned. The value of the goodness-of-fit index should be a secondary concern.

Thus, the single most important recommendation that can be made here is to follow the three-step approach for selecting a measure that was outlined in the introduction:

1. Decide whether the construct of interest is an affect, a mood, or an emotion.
2. Select the most appropriate conceptual model of the construct of interest for the purpose of the particular study.

3. Choose the most psychometrically sound instrument that was developed on the basis of the conceptual model.

The rationale for each of these decisions should always be explained in published reports. "This measure was used because it has been used extensively before" should never be considered an acceptable justification for a measurement decision by authors, reviewers, or journal editors.

The main message of this chapter is that the measurement of affective phenomena is a considerable intellectual challenge given the size and complexity of the associated literature. The purpose of this chapter is not to arrive at a recommendation for or against the use of a specific measure. The issues involved do not lend themselves to such simplistic black-and-white differentiations. For practitioners as well as researchers, the choice of a measure depends on what they want to measure. A professional might be interested in a specific emotion (e.g., self-presentational anxiety in a gymnasium or fear for one's life in a cardiac rehabilitation clinic) or in general affective responses (e.g., when tailoring the intensity or duration of an exercise regimen to a client's preferences or abilities). Choosing the most appropriate measure in each situation must be based on a critical evaluation of the relevant literature, perhaps with the aid of an expert.

The value of monitoring the short-term and long-term affective changes of clients and patients as they engage in exercise is now more clear than ever. Affective constructs are recognized as important both when treated as effects and when treated as causes. For example, exercise has been shown to reduce feelings of fatigue (Puetz, O'Connor, & Dishman, 2006) and to enhance feelings of energy and vigor, both acutely (Reed & Ones, 2006) and chronically (Reed & Buck, 2009). Reducing fatigue and enhancing energy are among the effects most valued by present-day people, who seek to achieve these changes via numerous other means, both legal and illegal.

Similarly, affective responses to exercise are important when considered as a causal factor that influences behavioral decisions. For example, after decades of speculating that people are more likely to continue their exercise participation if they experience pleasure during exercise (and are more likely to drop out if they experience displeasure), the first reliable empirical evidence is beginning to accumulate (e.g., Kwan & Bryan, 2010; Williams et al., 2008). Importantly, in the latest edition of the *Guidelines for Exercise Testing and Prescription*, the ACSM (2010) recommended the use of "measures of affective valence such as the Feeling Scale" as "adjunct measures of exercise intensity" (p. 157). This is a remarkable development; it establishes the measurement of affect as a regular part of the daily practice of exercise professionals worldwide. In doing so, it builds a bridge across the dualistic chasm that has long divided exercise science.

■ **Table 28.1** ■

Self-Reporting Measures Assessing Affect, Mood, and Emotion

Construct	Measure	Dimension	Source	Website
Core affect	Self-Assessment Manikin (SAM)	Valence (pleasant to unpleasant), arousal (excited to calm), dominance (feeling of being controlled versus being in control)	Lang (1980); Bradley & Lang (1994)	None
Core affect	Affect Grid (AG)	Pleasure and arousal	Russell, Weiss, & Mendelsohn (1989)	www2.bc.edu/~russeljm/publications/JPSP1989.pdf
Affective valence (pleasure and displeasure)	Feeling Scale (FS)	Affective valence (pleasure and displeasure)	Hardy & Rejeski (1989)	None
Felt arousal	Felt Arousal Scale (FAS)	Felt arousal	Svebak & Murgatroyd (1985)	None

(continued)

Construct	Measure	Dimension	Source	Website
Multiple distinct affective states	Revised Multiple Affect Adjective Checklist (MAACL-R)	Anxiety (A), depression (D), hostility (H), positive affect (PA), and sensation seeking (SS) *or* dysphoria (DYS; A + D + H) and PASS (PA + SS)	Zuckerman & Lubin (1985)	www.edits.net/component/content/article/53/24-maaclr.html
Multiple distinct mood states	Profile of Mood States (POMS)	Tension and anxiety, anger and hostility, fatigue and inertia, depression and dejection, vigor and activity, confusion and bewilderment	McNair, Lorr, & Droppleman (1971)	www.mhs.com/product.aspx?gr=cli&prod=poms
Mood dimensions	Positive and Negative Affect Schedule (PANAS)	Positive affect and negative affect	Watson, Clark, & Tellegen (1988)	http://works.bepress.com/david_watson/211
Mood dimensions	Activation Deactivation Adjective Checklist (AD ACL)	Energy, tiredness, tension, and calmness *or* energetic arousal and tense arousal	Thayer (1989)	www.csulb.edu/~thayer/thayer/adaclnew.htm
Mood dimensions	Four-Dimension Mood Scale (4DMS), state version	Positive energy, tiredness, negative arousal, and relaxation	Gregg & Shepherd (2009)	None
Anxiety	State-Trait Anxiety Inventory (STAI)	State anxiety and trait anxiety	Spielberger (1983)	www.mindgarden.com/products/staisad.htm
Depression	Beck Depression Inventory (BDI)	Cognitive-affective symptoms and somatic symptoms *of* depression (total score)	Beck, Steer, & Brown (1996)	www.pearsonassessments.com/HAIWEB/Cultures/en-us/Productdetail.htm?Pid=015-8018-370
Depression	Hamilton Rating Scale for Depression (HRSD)	Depression	Hamilton (1960)	www.assessmentpsychology.com/HAM-D.pdf
Exercise-induced feelings	Exercise-Induced Feeling Inventory (EFI)	Revitalization, tranquility, positive engagement, and physical exhaustion	Gauvin & Rejeski (1993)	None
Subjective exercise experiences	Subjective Exercise Experiences Scale (SEES)	Positive well-being, psychological distress, and fatigue	McAuley & Courneya (1994)	www.epl.illinois.edu/meas_see.html
Physical activity affect	Physical Activity Affect Scale (PAAS)	Positive affect, negative affect, tranquility, and fatigue	Lox, Jackson, Tuholski, Wasley, & Treasure (2000)	None

Emotional Reactivity

Christopher M. Janelle, PhD, and Kelly M. Naugle, PhD

The constant vacillation of emotion that accompanies the ebb and flow of athletic competition is universally compelling and fundamental to sport experience. Desirable emotional consequences are often realized through attaining a long sought-after goal such as a national championship, a world record, or a personal best. Athletes are also motivated to avoid the aversive consequences that come with failure, losing, and social ineptitude. Such undesirable emotional experiences can be as intensely devastating as the positive experiences are elating. In addition to the emotional consequences of sport participation, emotions affect the quality of sport performance and social functioning in the sport context. This chapter discusses the measurement of precompetitive and competitive emotional experiences and how these experiences affect sport performance through specific cognitive, physiological, and behavioral mechanisms. We begin by defining the often misunderstood concepts of affect, mood, and emotion. Two specific emotions, fear and anxiety, are then elucidated, followed by a discussion of arousal and stress and their roles in considerations of emotional experience. We then summarize the state of contemporary theory in the study of emotion. A discussion of specific measures and assessment tools used in the study of emotion follows, with an emphasis on anxiety. Throughout this discussion, we highlight empirical works from the extant mainstream sport psychology literature as examples of how the measures of interest can be implemented. Finally, we provide recommendations for both researchers and practitioners.

Definitions and Dimensions of the Variable Construct

From Darwin to James to Selye to modern conceptualizations of emotions and related constructs, scientists have operationalized and defined terms with increasing specification, yielding a set of generally accepted contemporary guidelines for what to call affect-related concepts and how to study them. Still, terms such as *stress, anxiety, arousal, emotion, mood,* and *affect* are used interchangeably, even in the scientific literature. This section provides a context for how such terms are conceptualized based on their use in sport psychology as well as in the broader affective sciences.

Affect

When used clinically, the term *affective disorder* refers to a specific class of mental health problems that are characterized by consistent alterations in mood that influence thoughts, emotions, and behaviors (e.g., depressive disorders, bipolar disorders, anxiety and related disorders; APA, 2000). More generally, however, *affect* is a broadly inclusive term that is descriptive of mental states that involve judgment of feeling states (Coan & Allen, 2007). Moods, emotions, anxiety, depression, and fear can all be considered to be some form of affect, strictly speaking. People can feel good or bad or can like or dislike certain things that can then provide lower or higher thresholds for experiencing other moods, emotions, and feeling states. Affective conditions also vary widely in the time course of their experience, as is specified later.

Mood

While not as broad as affect, *moods* are conceptualized as enduring feeling states that are experienced less intensely and fulfill different functions than those that emotions fill (Ekman & Davidson, 1994). A widely held view is that moods are a summary of a person's affective state rather than a specific isolated instance of affect (Watson & Clark, 1994). Put another way, moods provide the affective backdrop of life onto which other more specific and short-lived affective experiences are overlaid (Ekman & Davidson, 1994).

Emotion

Merriam-Webster defines *emotion* as "a psychic and physical reaction (as anger or fear) subjectively experienced as strong feeling and physiologically involving changes that prepare the body for immediate vigorous action" (Webster, 2005). Evolved from the Latin root *motum*, meaning "to move," emotions, like moods, are affective states. However, they differ from moods both in their time course and in the potential intensity of their experience. Emotions are typically brief and are elicited in response to a particular stimulus or object. While opinions differ (see Ekman & Davidson, 1994; Gray & Watson, 2007), emotions can be considered to be ever present yet constantly fluctuating in intensity as a function of environmental stimuli. A common function of emotion is to motivate attention to the critical internal and external cues that affect the likelihood of attaining a desired goal. Such goals are specific manifestations of our general approach and avoidance motivational orientations, and the emotions experienced function to mobilize behavioral responses that are consistent with desirable affective states. Emotions therefore serve as action dispositions (Lang, 2000) and are critical to human development, survival, health, and performance excellence.

Fear and Anxiety

Anxiety is the primary emotion addressed in this chapter, as it has received the most empirical attention in the sport psychology literature. The construct of anxiety is often confused with fear. *Fear* is a reflexive emotional response to a known threat (Lang, McTeague, & Cuthbert, 2006). It is usually adaptive except when the fear response is exaggerated relative to the provoking stimulus (as is the case with phobias). *Anxiety*, on the other hand, is considered to be fear of the unknown; it is an emotion characterized by uncertainty and a high degree of negative thoughts, worries, and concerns in anticipation of future danger (APA, 2000). Anxiety is an emotional response that is acquired through the learning process, through either direct or vicarious exposure to anxiety-producing conditions. A person can also fear emotional experience (or anxiety) itself (Koerner & Dugas, 2006).

Dimensions and Sources of Confusion

Sources of confusion in the study of emotion have long stemmed from the lack of efforts to define related terms consistently and then operationalize them uniformly, both across and within subdomains of the parent discipline of psychology. Beyond the definitional distinctions just provided, much of this confusion cannot be rectified within the context of this chapter. However, further differentiation from other related terms recurrent in the dominant theoretical frameworks may be helpful. Much debate has centered on the need to consider multiple dimensions of anxiety, which has led to the development of state- and trait-specific foci as well as to the dividing of anxiety into cognitive and somatic components. Interestingly, such divisions have led to further confusion of terms, primarily with regard to the difference between somatic anxiety and arousal.

Somatic anxiety is the perception of (physiological) arousal (Morris, Davis, & Hutchings, 1981). Increases in arousal and activation are represented by heightened physiological preparation for action, which is induced by greater sympathetic nervous system activity. While *arousal* and *activation* are often used interchangeably, Woodman and Hardy (2001) distinguished between the two concepts based on the degree of predictability of the antecedent event. They defined *activation* as a state of heightened cognitive and physiological activity in preparation for a planned response and *arousal* as a response to the onset of novel input. In mainstream affective science, arousal typically refers to the intensity of the emotional experience. The term *arousal* occasionally is used synonymously with attention, (somatic) anxiety, and even motivation, and some researchers contend that arousal can be self-reported (e.g., Lang, Bradley, & Cuthbert, 2008). Others contend that reporting the physiological symptoms of the intensity of emotional experience is actually an index of somatic anxiety. For the sake of clarity, *we consider physiological measures of emotional intensity as measures of arousal* within this chapter.

Another term that has endured while also perpetuating confusion is *stress*. The classic definition popularized by Selye (1955) half a century ago generally holds today. Specifically, stress arises when there is a real or perceived lack of resources available to deal with current demands. Such demands can take on various forms: life stressors, heat, sport-specific stressors, job pressures, personal struggles, coping with illness or injury, overtraining, and so on. While the study of stress is important and the term is used consistently in the empirical literature, researchers generally favor terms that focus on more specific affective states and dispositions (as described earlier). Perhaps motivated by this realization, Lazarus (2000) insightfully wrote the following:

Many scholars who tend to the garden of stress seem blissfully unaware of the research and the thought of those who work in the emotion garden, and vice-versa. This is illogical and counterproductive. Stress is important in its own right, but emotion encompasses all of the important phenomena of stress. (p. 231)

Confusion has also surrounded how emotions are classified for study from *discrete* versus *dimensional* perspectives. In the former case, emotions can be considered categorically, and each of the distinct qualitative aspects of each emotion can be considered. From such a perspective, separate and distinct descriptions (and labels) of anger, anxiety, fear, sadness, jealousy, and so on arise. Discrete emotion theorists (e.g., Ekman, 1984; Lazarus, 2000) contend that understanding such subtle differences among emotional labels is important for understanding the antecedents and functional consequences of the emotion. While not disregarding the subtle qualitative differences among emotions, the theorists who favor a dimensional approach (e.g., Konorski, 1967; Lang, Cuthbert, & Bradley, 1998; Schneirla, 1959) argue that the functional significance of the emotional experience can be gathered through understanding two (or three) dimensions of the emotion—namely, the intensity by which the emotion is experienced and the emotional valence (whether it is pleasant or unpleasant). Discrete emotions, it is argued from this perspective, can be meaningfully classified and studied using such dimensional discriminators. Integrated approaches have also been advanced by well-respected theorists. Of these, perhaps the most notable are the circumplex notions of Russell (1980) and Tellegen (1985), which certainly remain viable today. Consideration of an emotional experience according to its discrete characteristics is widely accepted to be reliant on both automatic and cognitively demanding appraisal processes that are discussed in chapters 14 and 15 and are therefore not discussed further here. Interested researchers are also referred to work by Crocker, Vallerand, and colleagues (e.g., Crocker, Kowalski, Hoar, & McDonough, 2004; Vallerand & Blanchard, 2000).

We now turn to a brief overview of the massive theoretical literature that has evolved over the years. This includes treatment of sport-specific theories as well as theories borrowed from the parent discipline and applied to the study of emotional experience in sport.

Theoretical and Conceptual Frameworks

Current directions in affective science are marked with an explosion of knowledge that is a direct consequence of the consistent interplay between theoretical and methodological advancement. Indeed, some of the dearest theories in all of psychology have evolved from the study of emotion. Prominent affective scientists (e.g., Charles Spielberger, Richard Lazarus, Peter Lang) have more than occasionally dabbled in sport psychology, and their theories have been enriched because of it. Other, more performance-specific theories have been developed and must be robust to the deductive process of theory disproval. While they are not discussed in detail here, the inverted-U hypothesis (Yerkes & Dodson, 1908), drive theory (Hull, 1943), and other theories of arousal, stress, and attention (Hancock & Warm, 1989) have been widely implemented by sport psychologists and have clearly influenced the advancement of emotion and related theories (for recent discussion of the inverted-U hypothesis, see Arent & Landers, 2003). These early notions are reflected in present-day theoretical induction. The remainder of this section focuses on prominent theories that have helped advance the *sport science* of emotion, giving particular consideration to those that have shaped the current knowledge base in mainstream sport psychology.

Anxiety Theories

Relative to other emotions, anxiety has received the lion's share of attention from sport psychology researchers, who are concerned with precompetitive, competitive, and postcompetitive (postevent) emotional states as well as how dispositional anxiety levels interact with such states to affect performance. Popular theoretical approaches adapted by sport psychologists include Spielberger's anxiety theory as well as multidimensional anxiety theory, which highlighted the importance of considering cognitive and somatic aspects of anxiety.

Spielberger's Anxiety Theory

Perhaps the most influential theory that remains a dominant framework for research design in sport psychology is Spielberger's anxiety theory. Forwarded in 1979, this theory described the difference between state anxiety and trait anxiety. The theory and the psychometric tool that emerged from studies of the theory (the State-Trait Anxiety Inventory, or STAI; Spielberger, 1983) have been prevalent in sport and exercise psychology since their publication. The psychometric properties of the STAI are described in detail in the next section.

Multidimensional Anxiety Theory

While not incompatible with Spielberger's theory, multidimensional anxiety theory is a popular theoretical notion that was first forwarded by Martens and colleagues (Martens, Vealey, & Burton, 1990). These authors contended that anxiety should not be considered a unidimensional concept. They suggested that researchers should consider both the somatic (perceptions of physiological arousal) and the cognitive (degree of negative thoughts, worries, and concerns) aspects of anxiety, given that they are distinct constructs that follow unique temporal patterns across the competitive experience. Although the theoretical relationships between cognitive and somatic components of anxiety as related to performance have been generally disregarded, the principles differentiating the constructs remain. More importantly, the self-report tool used to assess cognitive and somatic anxiety, the Competitive State Anxiety Index-2 (CSAI-2), is perhaps (along with its revisions) the most widely used self-report anxiety tool in all of sport psychology research.

Catastrophe Models

Another contemporary notion of anxiety that has remained a prominent framework for sport psychology researchers (Hardy, 1990) is the cusp catastrophe model. The original catastrophe model, and its later iterations, holds distinct advantages over many previous models, given its multidimensional nature and its consideration of the interaction between anxiety and physiological arousal in performance. While anxiety was the focus of earlier models (such as multidimensional anxiety theory and Hanin's zone of optimal functioning), consideration of the physiological mechanisms that are spurred by and then interact with anxiety provides an attractive advancement of the model. In short, the model predicts that at low levels of cognitive anxiety, performance varies as a function of physiological arousal in an inverted-U manner. At high levels of anxiety, however, the likelihood of a performance catastrophe is enhanced, with increases in physiological arousal benefiting performance to an optimal level, after which performance dramatically decreases. While mathematically complex, the central tenets of the model can be examined in a straightforward manner, and they have been studied over the past 20 years. The model holds important measurement implications given that testing it relies on assessing the interacting cognitive and physiological response systems through which emotional reactivity manifests. The model is also attractive from a practical standpoint, as it explains the conditions that lead to drastic and immediate performance failures. As is described later, another significant contribution that emerged from work on the catastrophe model has been the

implementation of the time-to-event paradigm to elicit emotional states.

Interactions of Emotional Experience

While the conceptual approaches described above have been used to account for how anxiety impacts sport performance, sport psychology research has also been conducted within frameworks that consider other emotions. Two popular approaches are briefly summarized in this section.

Reversal Theory

Reversal theory (Apter, 1983) is a psychological theory of motivation, emotion, and personality. It was first adapted to sport by Kerr (1985, 1990). Reversal theory proposes that emotions are produced from the interaction of an individual's arousal level with the current metamotivational state. While the original theory proposed four pairs of metamotivational states, the telic–paratelic motivational pairing has provided the most valuable theoretical contribution to sport psychology research. In a telic motivational state, an athlete prefers low levels of *felt arousal* and consequently interprets high arousal as unpleasant anxiety and low arousal as relaxation. Alternatively, in a paratelic motivational state, the athlete prefers high levels of *felt arousal* and interprets high arousal as pleasant excitement and low arousal as boredom. Reversal theory predicts that performance is best when a highly aroused athlete is in a paratelic state, interpreting high levels of felt arousal as excitement rather than anxiety. Reversal theory also proposes that emotional states can be quickly reversed (from anxiety to excitement) by changing the motivational state. While research on reversal theory has repeatedly demonstrated the importance of felt arousal in sport performance (Cox & Kerr, 1989; Males & Kerr, 1996), few empirical tests of the theory's predictions have been made.

Individual Zone of Optimal Functioning

In contemporary sport psychology, perhaps the most multifaceted and intuitively attractive theoretical notion is the IZOF concept advanced by Hanin (1997, 2000; IZOF is the evolution of the earlier zones of optimal functioning model of state anxiety). The theory is attractive from both a scientific and an applied perspective, primarily due to its emphasis on the need to understand individual differences in susceptibility to emotional reactivity to determine how emotional states influence performance. The basic premise is that the optimal performance state occurs under different emotional conditions for different people. In other words, while one athlete might perform best when extremely angry, this same emotional response might be devastating for another athlete who performs well when calm, cool, and collected. Hanin's original notions were criticized heavily, mainly due to the fact that the initial theory was a theory of individual differences without any explanation for why certain individuals perform better or worse than other individuals perform under different emotional states (Gould & Tuffey, 1996). More recently, however, researchers have begun to examine the dispositional characteristics that might underlie the tendency to experience particular emotional states as either beneficial or detrimental to performance. These notions in the context of the IZOF model are converging with other notions in the broader affective sciences. For the past two decades, a voluminous database has emerged detailing how individuals who are high in trait anxiety exhibit robust attentional biases to certain environmental cues and that such cues are interpreted as more threatening even when they are benign (Bar-Haim, Lamy, Pergamin, Bakermans-Kranenburg, & van Ijzendoorn, 2007). Such notions were also theorized in the early work of Spielberger but now have been advanced from a more mechanistic standpoint.

Mechanisms Affecting Sport Performance as a Consequence of Emotional Reactivity

Anxiety and other emotions are undeniably related to performance variability in sport. Strictly speaking, however, emotions do not change performance. Rather, it is *what* emotions affect that changes performance. Emotion-induced attentional alterations are the primary and most proximal psychological mechanisms that impact behavioral change and performance. Conceptual accounts of these attentional mechanisms are briefly overviewed next. The manner by which emotions impact performance remains a rich area for scientific inquiry, with continued debate surrounding *how* emotions affect performance

Processing Efficiency and Attentional Control Theory

The idea that individuals who are higher in trait anxiety respond differently under emotion-eliciting state-specific conditions is also reflected in the theoretical notions of Eysenck and colleagues. Eysenck and Calvo's (1992) original processing efficiency theory (PET) has served as a fruitful conceptual framework for sport psychologists interested in the attentional shifts that underlie performance alterations. PET is an inherently attentional theory.

The basic notion is that when individuals are anxious, the efficiency of their executive attentional processes is compromised. Under such conditions, performance effectiveness can be maintained but only in situations where the individual deems it worthwhile (is sufficiently motivated) to bring additional attentional resources to the fore. Such resources must be available, however, and when anxiety reaches a level where no further resources are available, performance suffers. Like the catastrophe model and IZOF, PET and its contemporary evolution, attentional control theory (ACT; Eysenck, Derakshan, Santos, & Calvo, 2007), are intuitively appealing because they provide clear explanations for why anxiety is not necessarily detrimental to performance and for how performance alterations likely arise as a function of the interaction between individual dispositional characteristics and the environment. They are also appealing from a scientific standpoint, as they highlight the likely psychological (and physiological) mechanisms that drive performance changes under increasing levels of anxiety.

Conscious Processing Theories

PET and ACT, as well as other theories of anxiety, generally agree that it is attentional mechanisms that are altered as a function of increasing anxiety levels. Attentional alterations can manifest in numerous ways. The final conceptual ideas can be grouped broadly as having a common focus on *conscious processing*. Proponents of conscious processing postulate that as anxiety increases, performers tend to focus attention inward, thereby disrupting the usual coordination patterns that proceed in a relatively autonomous fashion. As a result, the fluid automaticity that typifies high-level performance is compromised, leading to performance errors that can be considered to result from paralysis by analysis. Initial work in this area was advanced by Baumeister (1984), with a seminal paper (Baumeister & Showers, 1986) reviewing evidence that people become more conscious of thinking about performing when under stress. Beilock and Carr (2001) provided confirmatory evidence to this effect, and Masters (1992) made important advances to understanding how the learning process affects the likelihood of susceptibility to conscious processing under stress. In particular, Masters and colleagues (e.g., Maxwell, Masters, & Poolton, 2006; Poolton, Maxwell, Masters, & Raab, 2006) have shown that implicit learners, relative to explicit learners, are stress resistant due to an inability to reinvest in the explicit rules that dominate early stages of learning.

Upon reviewing these theories, it should be immediately evident that academic sport psychologists take theory seriously. Even in the applied sport psychology literature, the vast majority of empirical papers have theoretical roots and help advance theoretical induction. We contend that emotion lies at the heart of the translation from motivated intention to action, and it is inherently intertwined with other important concepts in sport psychology as well as psychology. Emotion, therefore, cannot be isolated from its motivational roots and its attentional and motor consequences. Such centrality is evident in the multiple measurement tools available to sport psychologists.

Overview of Emotion Measures

This section summarizes the wide range of experimental designs, measurement tools, and methodological approaches used to *elicit* and then *assess* affective experience, with an emphasis on assessment. Following a cursory description of the methods for emotion elicitation, emotional assessment measures are reviewed, and examples from the empirical literature of how the assessments have been implemented are provided. While our aim is to be as thorough as possible, comprehensive coverage is beyond what can be portrayed here. As such, we have chosen to center our discussion on measures that have been used primarily within the scope of the theoretical foundations discussed earlier.

Emotion Elicitation

Emotions must first be elicited before their effects can be assessed. Emotional responses are elicited in numerous ways, both generally and sport specifically. Popular laboratory-based manipulations of emotion include designs that feature (1) social threat and self-presentation concerns through the real or implied presence of evaluative others (e.g., Mullen, Hardy, & Tattersall, 2005); (2) ego threat and induction of threats to appraisals of success and failure, often through false feedback (e.g., Murray & Janelle, 2007; Wilson, Vine, & Wood, 2009); (3) reinforcement and punishment via withdrawal of rewards and imposition of penalties (e.g., Janelle, Singer, & Williams, 1999); (4) incentive motivation with provision of intrinsic and extrinsic rewards such as praise, prize money, trophies, and so on (e.g., Murray & Janelle, 2007); and (5) physical threat, such as manipulating height (e.g., Pijpers, Oudejans, Holsheimer, & Bakker, 2003).

Researchers can also take advantage of actual sport competitions and the numerous sources of stress that are present in such situations to elicit emotional variation. Field-based designs are highly desirable due to their inherently greater ecological validity compared with most laboratory environments. Careful attention must be paid, however, to controlling the numerous threats to internal validity that are likely to occur under such conditions. Examples of real-world factors that elicit emotional responses include (but are certainly not limited to) (1) financial gain and loss, (2) public scrutiny, (3) threats to self-esteem, (4) identity threats, and (5) threat of injury.

Researchers have been creative in merging the advantages offered by the laboratory and ecological environments through pretest and posttest or multiple time series designs. An example of such an approach was popularized by Hardy (1996) and colleagues in their studies of the cusp catastrophe model. A time-to-event protocol was implemented in which emotional responses were recorded over the time frame preceding the competition. Such an approach allowed the researchers to gather multiple data points that provided snapshots of the time course of emotional response in the days and hours leading up to an important competition.

Emotion Assessment

While the degree to which emotional states are elicited is typically assessed through self-report measures, researchers can rely on additional modalities to assess emotional reactivity more comprehensively. In particular, a more thorough assessment of emotion can be achieved by triangulating (1) self-report indexes of subjective emotional experience with (2) physiological and (3) behavioral indexes of the critical attentional and motor components of emotion that affect performance proficiency. Given the three dominant response systems that have traditionally been used to index emotional reactivity, we turn our attention to summarizing how each of these response systems is measured.

Self-Report

Most sport psychologists assess the dispositional and state components of emotion using standardized self-report scales. Even though athletes experience a broad array of emotions in sport settings, sport psychology researchers have typically focused on anxiety. Self-report measures of anxiety are therefore the focus of this section, with brief mention of other emotion assessment instruments.

Trait Measures   The two most prominent measures of competitive trait anxiety in sport psychology research are the Sport Competition Anxiety Test

(SCAT; Martens, 1977) and the Sport Anxiety Scale (SAS; Smith, Smoll, & Schultz, 1990). While a general measure of trait anxiety, the trait scale of the STAI (Spielberger, 1983) has also been used to assess trait anxiety in athletes and research participants in sport-related studies (e.g., Murray & Janelle, 2003; Pijpers, et al., 2003). Due to space constraints, our discussion focuses on the more commonly used sport-specific scales.

The SCAT consists of 2 cognitive items and 8 somatic items, which are summed to provide a unidimensional measure of competitive trait anxiety. The SCAT asks responders to indicate how they "usually feel when competing in sports and games." The original validation process of the SCAT showed high internal consistency and test–retest reliability. The SCAT has been used less frequently since the development of the SAS. In contrast to the SCAT, the SAS is a multidimensional measure of sport competition trait anxiety. It consists of three subscales that measure somatic anxiety, worry, and concentration disruption. Participants rate on a 4-point Likert scale the degree to which they generally experience anxiety-related symptoms before or during competition. Prompted by several studies showing major shortcomings in the factorial validity of the SAS (Dunn, Dunn, Wilson, & Syrotuik, 2000; Prapavessis, Maddison, & Fletcher, 2005), Smith and colleagues recently developed a new version of the SAS (SAS-2; Smith, Smoll, Cumming, & Grossbard, 2006) that has improved psychometric properties and replicated the three-component structure of the original instrument. Furthermore, while the original SAS was developed with college-aged and adult samples, the SAS-2 was designed to be used with all age groups (e.g., Smith, Smoll, & Cumming, 2007). Researchers often use these trait measures to classify participants as high or low in competitive trait anxiety to test predictions of anxiety-related theories (e.g., PET) that are based on dispositional differences in anxiety (e.g., Smith, Bellamy, Collins, Newell, 2001; Wilson, Smith, Chattington, Ford, & Marple-Horvat, 2006). While each instrument exhibits certain limitations, the SCAT and the two versions of the SAS have provided sport psychologists with valuable information regarding competitive trait anxiety in athletes.

State Measures During the last two decades, the CSAI-2 (Martens, Burton, Vealey, et al., 1990) has been the instrument of choice to measure sport-specific state anxiety. Based on the conceptualization of anxiety as a multidimensional construct, the CSAI-2 consists of three largely independent subscales measuring cognitive anxiety, somatic anxiety, and self-confidence. Each subscale has 9 items that are rated on a 4-point Likert scale. Athletes are asked to indicate "how you feel right now" for each item. The original version of the CSAI-2 was extended by Jones and Swain (1992) to include a directional scale assessing the facilitative and debilitative characteristics of the intensity of anxiety. Using this modified version of the CSAI-2, researchers have repeatedly demonstrated the importance of assessing athletes' interpretations of anxiety symptoms in understanding the relationship between anxiety and performance (e.g., Jones & Hanton, 2001; Mellalieu, Hanton, & Jones, 2003).

In the past decade, several studies examining the psychometric properties of the CSAI-2 revealed weaknesses in the theoretical factor structure (Lane, Sewell, Terry, Bartram, & Nesti, 1999; Tsorbatzoudis, Varkoukis, Kaissidis-Rodafinos, & Grouios, 1998). Thus, Cox, Martens, and Russell (2003) developed a revised version of the CSAI-2 (CSAI-2R) with theoretically and empirically guided modifications and stronger psychometric properties. The CSAI-2R has been validated on samples of high school and college athletes, providing support for its use in diverse athletic populations. Sport psychology researchers may wish to consider using the CSAI-2R in place of the CSAI-2.

Numerous studies have used the CSAI-2 and the CSAI-2R to investigate the relationships among the subcomponents of precompetitive anxiety and sport performance (for a review, see Craft, Magyar, Becker, & Feltz, 2003). In a seminal study, Burton (1988) used the CSAI-2 to provide the initial evidence for the theoretical underpinnings of the multidimensional anxiety theory, showing that performance of elite swimmers had an inverted-U relationship with somatic anxiety, a negative relationship with cognitive anxiety, and a positive linear relationship with self-confidence. Research has continued to use the CSAI-2 to test the multidimensional anxiety theory (Edwards & Hardy, 1996) as well as the inverted-U hypothesis (Arent & Landers, 2003), the conscious processing hypothesis (Gucciardi & Dimmock, 2008; Mullen & Hardy, 2000), and the effect of anxiety on performance within the framework of the IZOF model (Davis & Cox, 2002; Robazza, Pellizzari, Bertollo, & Hanin, 2008; Woodman, Albinson, & Hardy, 1997).

Several brief self-report measures are available for researchers who need a less intrusive and more expedient alternative to measure competitive state anxiety. These include versions of the Mental Readiness Form-Likert (MRF-L; Krane, 1994) and the anxiety thermometer (Houtman & Bakker, 1989). Similar to the CSAI-2, the MRF-L consists of three subscales measuring cognitive anxiety, somatic anxiety, and self-confidence. Krane (1994) demonstrated that the MRF-L subscales correlate highly with the subscales of the CSAI-2 (cognitive, $r = .76$; somatic, $r = .69$; and self-confidence, $r = .68$). Several studies have used the MRF-L to test the predictions of PET (Smith et al., 2001; Wilson et al., 2006). In a test of the cusp catastrophe model, Cohen, Pargman, & Tenenbaum (2003) used the MRF-L to monitor dart throwers' fluctuations in anxiety through the course of an entire experimental session. The researchers required participants to complete the MRF-L before every throwing trial, using a strategy not possible with longer self-report instruments. Alternatively, the anxiety thermometer, developed by Houtman and Bakker (1989), requires participants to place a cross on a 4 in. (10 cm) continuous scale ranging from 0 to 10 to indicate their level of anxiety at a particular moment. The anxiety thermometer does not distinguish between cognitive and somatic anxiety; therefore, researches wishing to assess both types of anxiety must use a separate thermometer for each type (e.g., Pijpers et al., 2003). Anxiety thermometer scores have shown a moderate correlation with somatic ($r = .62$) and cognitive ($r = .59$) anxiety scores on the CSAI-2.

Other Emotions Much of the sport psychology research on emotion focuses solely on anxiety, which represents only a small portion of the affective spectrum. To assess a broader range of affective states in sport, researchers have used non-sport-specific scales such as the Positive and Negative Affect Schedule (PANAS) and the Differential Emotions Scale (DES-IV) as well as sport-specific scales such as the Sport Emotion Questionnaire (SEQ). For example, the PANAS (Watson, Clark, & Tellegen, 1988), which was designed to assess positive and negative affective responses for daily living, has demonstrated factorial validity in sport (Crocker, 1997) and has been used successfully in sport contexts (e.g., Hadd & Crocker, 2007; Russell & Cox, 2000). Sport psychologists have also used the DES-IV (Izard, 1991) to measure basic emotions as conceptualized by the differential emotion theory (e.g., Cerin, 2003; Cerin & Barnett, 2006). The DES-IV consists of 12 subscales measuring the emotions of interest, enjoyment, surprise, sadness, anger, disgust, contempt, fear, guilt, shame, shyness, and self-hostility. Cerin and Barnett (2006) used the DES-IV to investigate the temporal patterns of basic emotional responses to competition. Athletes reported that they experienced fear, interest, and enjoyment more frequently than all other emotions and intensely 1 hr before competition. Immediately after competition, the athletes reported experiencing positive emotions, such as enjoyment, and emotions contingent on negative outcome, such as guilt, anger, self-hostility, and sadness.

Generalized measures of emotion are not designed to assess competitive experiences specifically, and thus they may not adequately capture the emotional spectrum that exists in this specialized context. With the idea that the measurement of emotion should consider contextual factors, Jones, Lane, Bray, Uphill, and Catlin (2005) recently developed the SEQ, a sport-specific measure of precompetitive emotion. These authors provided evidence that SEQ scores validly assess the emotions of anger, anxiety, dejection, excitement, and happiness as they are experienced by athletes in precompetition settings. While researchers should continue to test the psychometric properties of this relatively new instrument, the SEQ seems to provide a valid and internally reliable alternative to non-sport-specific measures of emotion.

Proponents of the ideographic (individual-oriented) approach to the study of competition-related affects often use lists of idiosyncratic descriptors to allow the athlete to identify pleasant or unpleasant emotions exerting facilitating or debilitating effects on performance (Robazza, Bortoli, Nocini, Moser, & Arslan, 2000; Robazza, Bortoli, & Hanin, 2006). For example, using the IZOF model, Robazza and colleagues (2006) developed a list of emotional symptom descriptors (70 pleasant and unpleasant emotional items) to investigate the link between emotion and performance across the working range of emotional intensity in elite cross-country skiers. The researchers found large interindividual variability in the content of emotions and in the shape of the curves representing the intensity effect contingencies.

Physiological Measures

Currently, sport psychology researchers most frequently assess arousal via the paper-and-pencil measures just described. While these subjective measures provide valid and reliable measures of *perceptions of arousal*, often athletes are not cognizant of the moment-to-moment changes in the physiological manifestation of arousal itself and are therefore incapable of reporting such physiological changes. These challenges can be overcome objectively through the use of psychophysiological measures. In sport psychology research, changes in physiological arousal are often determined by HR, electrodermal, EMG, and EEG activity. These techniques allow researchers to assess covert physiological processes resulting from affective modulation and to do so free from the constraints of participant awareness.

The details of the arrangement of the environment, subjects, and tasks used in psychophysiological studies are beyond the scope of this chapter. For a comprehensive treatment of how to establish and set up the psychophysiology laboratory as well as a detailed description of how to acquire and reduce psychophysiological data, interested readers are referred to excellent chapters in resource manuals such as the *Handbook of Psychophysiology* (Cacioppo et al., 2007), the *Handbook of Affective Sciences* (Davidson et al., 2007), and the *Handbook of Emotion Elicitation and Assessment* (Coan & Allen, 2007). In this section we describe the limited (but expanding) work in sport that has been done to study emotional responses with psychophysiological measures.

Heart Rate Likely because it is the least invasive and easiest of the physiological measures to administer, HR is the most commonly used physiological measure of arousal in sport psychology research. HR has been used in numerous sport psychology studies to indicate participants' physiological responses to anxiety (e.g., Janelle, et al., 1999; Woodman & Davis, 2008). HR is controlled by both the sympathetic and the parasympathetic divisions of the autonomic nervous system (Berntson, Quigley, & Lozano, 2007). Increased arousal is generally associated with elevated HR, as is evidenced by an increase in the average beats per minute (Zaichkowsky & Baltzell, 2001). HR can be derived from two different methods. ECG is used to measure the electrical potentials associated with contractions of the heart muscle. HR is determined by counting the number of large spikes, called *R waves*, per unit of time. Alternatively, HR can be derived from pulse wave recordings produced by a plethysmographic optical sensor placed at the fingertip or earlobe (Cohen, Kessler, & Gordon, 1995). Because they require no electrode hookup, pulse wave recording devices can be used easily in a wide variety of settings.

Sport psychology researchers typically measure HR in conjunction with self-report measures of anxiety. For example, Cottyn, Clercq, Pannier, Crombez, and Lenoir (2006) used both self-report (CSAI-2, retrospective report of nervousness) and physiological measures (HR) to examine the effects of competitive anxiety during balance beam performance. HR was elevated at rest during the competitive sessions compared with the training sessions, whereas the self-report measures of anxiety did not differ between the training and competitive sessions. Thus, a discrepancy existed between participants' actual physiological arousal (HR) and perceived physiological arousal (somatic subscale of CSAI-2). This finding supports the use of both physiological

and subjective measures when studying precompetitive anxiety. Poor performance on the balance beam routine was not linked to HR or CSAI-2 scores but was associated with increased self-reported nervousness at the end of the routine. Interpreting the results in light of catastrophe theory, Cottyn and colleagues concluded that increased physiological arousal did not lead to poorer performance in the competitive setting relative to the training setting because cognitive anxiety remained stable between the two conditions.

HRV provides a promising objective measure of physiological arousal. HRV represents the beat-to-beat changes in the heart rhythm (the interbeat interval). This noninvasive measure of neurocardiac function reflects the activity of both the sympathetic and the parasympathetic divisions of the autonomic nervous system as well as the interaction between the two division inputs into the heart (Aubert, Seps, & Beckers, 2003). Several power frequency bands of HRV have been defined (high = 0.15-0.4 Hz; low = 0.04-0.15; very low = 0.003-0.04 Hz), each associated with different autonomic nervous system activity (Berntson et al., 2007). HR generally becomes less variable as arousal increases, as is evidenced by a shift from equal relative power across frequency bands to higher relative power in the lower-frequency bands. Research has demonstrated support for utilizing HRV as a measure of precompetitive arousal (Murray & Raedeke, 2008) and attentional changes due to increased anxiety (Mullen et al., 2005). When using HRV as an indicator of precompetitive arousal, researchers need to be aware of the other factors influencing HRV, such as age (Ramaekers, Ector, Aubert, Rubens, & Van de Werf, 1998), physical activity (Buchheit et al., 2004), and respiration rate (Grossman, 1992).

Electrodermal Response Although it has been seldom used in sport psychology research, electrodermal activity (EDA) has been widely used to study psychological processes (attention, emotion, information processing) in psychophysiological research. EDA reflects activity of the eccrine sweat glands and thus is a relatively direct representation of sympathetic activation of the autonomic nervous system (Dawson, Schell, & Filion, 2007). The most common measurements in sport psychology research taken from EDA are skin conductance level (SCL) and skin conductance response (SCR) amplitude. These measures are expressed as units of microsiemens (μS). SCL reflects the tonic level of the electrical conductivity of the skin and can vary depending on the emotional state of the individual (Dawson et al., 2007). SCR amplitude is the phasic increase in conductance observed shortly following a novel, significant, or aversive stimulus or event. A stimulus-elicited SCR must achieve a minimum change in conductance (usually 0.01-0.05 μS) and must be observed within a certain latency window (commonly 1 and 4 s) following stimulus onset. The amplitude of SCR has been shown to vary as a function of emotional arousal, with emotionally arousing stimuli producing greater skin conductance reactivity than low-arousing or neutral stimuli (Lang, Greenwald, Bradley, & Hamm, 1993). While SCR and SCL are relatively inexpensive and risk free to record, EDA is a slow-moving response system and is not useful in research investigating rapidly occurring processes. Additionally, SCR can be elicited by a multitude of processes, including activation, attention, and significance or affective intensity of a stimulus. Thus, in using EDA as a physiological response measure, researchers must ensure that they are varying only one EDA-influencing process at a time.

Perkins, Wilson, and Kerr (2001) used HR and SCL as an index of physiological arousal to examine the relationship between felt arousal and physiological arousal, emotional state, and performance on a strength task. Manipulation of telic versus paratelic motivational state via guided imagery increased felt and physiological arousal as indexed by HR and SCL. While handgrip strength significantly differed among the motivational conditions (paratelic > telic > neutral), the physiological variables had no association with these changes in strength performance. In another study integrating physiological measures of arousal (HR, SCR) and perceived affective states (AG), Edmonds, Tenenbaum, Mann, Johnson, and Kamata (2008) determined athletes' individual affect-related performance zones on a simulated racing task and then applied a biofeedback intervention to determine the effect on performance. Participants receiving biofeedback training were taught to regulate and maintain their predetermined optimal level of HR and SCR for driving performance. These individuals improved driving performance on the racing task following the biofeedback intervention. Furthermore, driving performance could be determined by the participant's level of physiological arousal. Several other studies employing biofeedback training to augment performance have successfully used physiological measures of HR and SCR, as well as EMG, as biofeedback indices (e.g., Blumenstein, Bar-Haim, & Tenenbaum, 1995).

Electromyography   Surface EMG is a noninvasive tool used to investigate emotional processes. It continuously records muscle activity while minimally interfering with the behavior under study.

Psychological research has demonstrated that emotional reactions are accompanied by patterns of EMG activity in the facial musculature (Cacioppo, Martzke, Petty, & Tassinary, 1988; Gehricke & Shapiro, 2001; Halberstadt, Winkielman, Niedenthal, & Dalle, 2009), particularly in the brow muscle region (corrugator supercilii) and the cheek muscle region (zygomatic major). Elevated EMG activity during preparatory times and effortful engaging tasks has been used as an indicator of subjective effort expended on tasks, task difficulty, and stress. In sport psychology research, EMG has been used as an index of muscle tension. Increases in muscle tension are generally associated with heightened arousal (Zaichkowsky & Baltzell, 2001). Although seldom used in sport psychology research, EMG can be used as an indirect measure of muscle tension during an isometric contraction. Pijpers and colleagues (2003) demonstrated this on a handgrip dynamometer. The median frequency of the power spectrum of the EMG signal was significantly higher in a high-anxiety condition relative to a low-anxiety condition. As previously mentioned, EMG has also been used as biofeedback to train athletes to reach the optimal level of arousal for successful performance (e.g., Blumenstein et al., 1995).

Electroencephalography   EEG has been robustly employed as a measurement tool in sport psychology since the systematic work of Hatfield, Ray, and Landers at Penn State University in the early 1980s. The vast majority of EEG work completed in sport has been motivated by the desire to evaluate the brain processes that underlie differences in attention and information processing among expert and nonexpert performers. There have also been occasional forays into the emotional domain using EEG methods. Work in this area has typically involved a consideration of how the emotionally charged brain differs from the efficient expert brain in action. Researchers who study emotion in sport through EEG and related measures attempt to ascertain how the bioelectrical signature of expertise is disrupted by emotional input (for a recent review, see Janelle & Hatfield, 2008). Over the years, several indices have been developed to gain a better understanding of the neuroelectrical signals produced in the brain by the fluctuation in electrical potentials over time. The primary measures that have been used include examining the EEG spectrum as well as event-related cortical potentials that are known to index the mental chronometry of brain processes.

Once the raw EEG signal is acquired and cleaned, the spectral characteristics of the EEG record can be extracted and grouped into bands that are categorized based on the frequency of the cortical activity that is being recorded at a given cortical location. These bands are traditionally grouped into the following categories: delta (1-4 Hz), theta (4-7 Hz), alpha (8-12 Hz), beta (13-36 Hz), and gamma (36-44 Hz). While other frequency bands have been investigated, the dominant frequencies that have been of interest in the sport psychology literature are the alpha and beta bands. Generally, greater levels of alpha (higher alpha power) represent synchronization among neuronal firing patterns in a given cortical region (which may have subcortical generators that are reflected at the surface). This synchronization is associated with greater disengagement of the cortical structures relative to the given task or event. As engagement increases, alpha power decreases, which indicates greater desynchronization of the neural structures in the region and more task-specific neurological processing (Hatfield & Hillman, 2001). While views remain debatable and findings are not homogeneous, there are commonalities that can be extracted from the literature to provide an index of how EEG spectral activity can reflect emotional activity.

Relative asymmetry in cortical activation levels between the two cerebral hemispheres has been of great interest in affective science. An extensive body of literature has robustly demonstrated that greater resting left frontal cortical activity is associated with pleasant affect and approach-related behaviors, while greater resting right frontal activation is associated with avoidance-motivated behaviors and unpleasant affect (Davidson, 1995, 2004). Saarela (1999) postulated that a stress manipulation induced through time pressure would lead to greater relative right hemisphere activation and result in detrimental performance relative to a performance in which target shooters were given the typical preparatory time course to execute a regulation round of shots. Their findings supported this hypothesis. The reversal in hemispheric activation was related to decreased performance. Findings were attributed to the stress induction, which led to variability in the motor pathways involved in shooting. A similar effect was noted by Kerick, Iso-Ahola, and Hatfield (2000), who found that induction of positive affect facilitated shot performance, although the positive affect induction did not result in the postulated shift in hemispheric asymmetry (a nonsignificant trend in the predicted direction was found).

While such findings are compelling, it is important to emphasize that a philosophy of more relaxation is better has not been borne out in the spectral studies that have been conducted to date. Specifically, Landers and colleagues (1994) found

that archers exhibiting the highest levels of temporal EEG power performed comparatively poorer than when lower alpha activity was recorded in the temporal region—a region that is thought to be a highly associative area of the brain. Similarly, Hillman, Apparies, and coworkers (2000) found that marksmen chose to abort shots that were characterized by comparatively higher alpha activity (across brain regions). As such, there appears to be an inverted-U relationship between preparatory spectral activation levels and the quality of psychomotor sport performance (Janelle & Hatfield, 2008).

Recently, Kerick, Hatfield, and Allendar (2007) recently reported an increase in cortical activity (i.e., alpha suppression) in a study of U.S. Marines executing a shooting task under cognitive load (i.e., discrimination of enemy and friendly targets during shooting). This increase was observed relative to a nonstressed condition (i.e., shooting at enemy-only targets). The heightened activity under the condition of cognitive load was associated with a decline in performance accuracy and decision making. In sum, though the extant database is limited, findings are beginning to emerge that reliably indicate alterations in spectral EEG activity that reflect less efficiency in cortical dynamics under stress. These alterations detrimentally affect the automaticity associated with expert performance.

Event-Related Potentials Once cleaned and filtered, ERPs can also be used to glimpse into the underlying mental processes that index the time course of specific temporal processes, both in preparation for an event as well as in response to discrete sensory input. ERPs can therefore be thought of as time-locked representations of cortical responses to specific stimuli. The most prevalent component of the ERP investigated in sport is the P300 (P3) component, which is a positive deflection in the ongoing EEG signal that occurs 200 to 800 ms after the onset of an obligatory stimulus. The P3 component is thought to reflect the resources devoted to discriminating and processing an attended stimulus. Accordingly, greater P3 amplitude means that more attention is being allocated to processing an obligatory stimulus. Murray and Janelle (2007) evaluated the effect of anxiety in the context of a dual-task protocol in which P3 amplitude to a secondary stimulus was recorded while participants performed simulated auto racing. They found that, as predicted, the P3 amplitude was smaller under higher-anxiety conditions. This finding suggests that more attention was devoted to the racing task under higher-anxiety conditions, leaving less available processing space for detection of the obligatory stimulus.

Pupil Diameter A final physiological index that has been applied recently to understanding the effect of emotion on performance is the extent of pupil dilation that occurs under heightened anxiety. Pupil diameter has been shown to increase with greater mental effort devoted to task performance (Steinhaur, Siegle, Condray, & Pless, 2004). Believing that anxiety can affect mental effort, Wilson and colleagues (2006) tested the central tenets of PET using a simulated rally driving task. Among findings from other indexes of inefficiency, they found that the pupil dilated as anxiety increased. Though the technique is promising, using pupil diameter as an index of emotional response must be implemented with careful control of conditions due to the pupil's susceptibility to variation from other factors (ambient luminance most prominently). In any case, such efforts should be encouraged, as they provide converging physiological evidence of the effect of anxiety on performance.

Behavioral Measures

Few studies have examined emotional reactivity at the subjective, physiological, and behavioral level. In particular, the overt behavioral manifestations of emotion are largely ignored, aside from rather gross measures of performance changes or outcome measures. While providing an indirect measure of how sport performance is affected by anxiety, outcome measures typically do not assess the direct influence of emotion on the parameters that affect actual movement execution. Here, we briefly describe the few studies that have investigated the effects of anxiety on basic movement parameters and movement fluency. Additionally, while gaze behavior may be considered a physiological measure, it can be argued that eye movements are behavioral indexes. Gaze indexes of emotional reactivity are therefore reviewed in this section.

Movement Efficiency and Effectiveness Pijpers and colleagues (Nieuwenhuys, Pijpers, Oudejans, & Bakker, 2008; Pijpers et al., 2003) examined the effects of anxiety on movement efficiency. Anxiety was manipulated by requiring novice climbers to traverse a route on a climbing wall at high (high-anxiety condition) and low (low-anxiety condition) heights. Subjective measures were used to assess both trait (STAI) and state (anxiety thermometer) anxiety levels immediately before and after the completion of each climbing route. Concomitant physiological changes (HR) were measured during climbing, and indirect measures of muscle tension (EMG) were assessed following each climb. In the first experiment, the high-anxiety condition was associated with increased self-reported anxiety, HR,

and muscle tension when compared with the low-anxiety condition. In the second experiment, Pijpers and colleagues extended the results by showing that participants exhibited more rigid and jerky movements while climbing in the high-anxiety condition.

Studies testing the predictions of PET have included measures of specific movement parameters to index performance efficiency (Williams, Vickers, & Rodrigues, 2002; Wilson et al., 2006). For example, Wilson and colleagues (2006) investigated the effects of anxiety on performance effectiveness and efficiency in a simulated rally driving task. Performance effectiveness was measured as the time taken to complete the course, while efficiency was indexed by variability of wheel and accelerator movements. Participants raced individually under low-threat and high-threat conditions. Compared with low trait anxious participants, high trait anxious individuals demonstrated more variable wheel and accelerator movements, particularly in the high-threat condition. Thus, processing efficiency was impaired in high trait anxious individuals. While not described here, emotional changes also optimize or compromise performance through their critical role in modulating the movement parameters (speed, force, limb trajectory, and so on) that underlie overt physical performance (e.g., Coombes, Cauraugh, & Janelle, 2007; Coombes, Gamble, Cauraugh, & Janelle, 2008; Naugle et al., 2010, 2011).

Gaze Behavior Beginning a decade ago, sport psychologists have been at the forefront of a movement to more directly examine the mechanisms of visual attention reallocation that are theorized to occur with increases in arousal and anxiety (for a review, see Janelle, 2002). Early studies were spawned by interest in how Easterbrook's (1959) notions of attentional narrowing manifest in the search patterns used to gather information from the environment. While numerous sources of performance-based evidence (primarily using dual-task designs) had documented how peripheral and primary task performance vary under different emotional states, little was known concerning how visual gaze itself altered under these conditions. Early studies involved primarily sport activities in which saccadic eye movements were recorded, while more recent efforts have also been concerned with other measures such as the quiet eye period. Given the disparate attentional demands that are required for high-level performance in different sport tasks, widely varied dependent measures have been used to capture the attentional alterations that are experienced in different sports. The methods and measures used in these protocols are described next.

Anxiety and Saccadic Eye Movements. Common dependent measures acquired by eye tracking and used to assess the allocation of attention to environmental cues during the performance of dynamic tasks include the *frequency* and *duration* of fixations made to various areas of interest in a given display. Of great interest to researchers is the combination of these variables to ascertain the rate by which the display is searched (the *search rate*). Each of these measures provides an indication of attention allocation to specific areas. Although it is not possible to infer directly that what is gazed upon is actually attended to, strong evidence supports the contention that attention is closely coupled to saccadic eye movements (Zelinsky, Rao, Hayhoe, & Ballard, 1997).

In their seminal work in this area, Janelle et al., (1999) investigated how search patters alter as a function of increasing anxiety using a time-to-event paradigm and an auto racing simulation. Participants were required to navigate the racecourse while also identifying the intermittent presence of relevant and irrelevant light cues in their peripheral visual field. Eye movements were tracked for the duration of the session, as were performance of the racing task and light detection latency and errors. At high-anxiety levels, performance on both tasks decreased and errors increased. Performance findings were accompanied by search characteristics in which visual gaze became increasingly erratic. More fixations were directed to peripheral locations, decreasing the rate by which peripheral cues were identified, increasing the rate by which the onset of cues was missed, and decreasing the amount of time the eyes fixated on the roadway. These findings have been largely replicated and extended (considering trait and state anxiety interactions) in recent years with similar racing simulations (e.g., Murray & Janelle, 2003; Wilson et al., 2006). A primary finding is that search rate increases under higher anxiety (for a logical exception in a single-task design involving rock climbing, see Niewenhuys et al., 2008). Similar findings, particularly the increase in search rate with greater anxiety levels, have been noted in other sport tasks, including table tennis (Williams, Vickers, et al., 2002), gymnastics (Moran, Byrne, & McGlade, 2002), and billiards (Williams, Singer, & Frehlich, 2002). Importantly, Williams and Elliot (1999) demonstrated that expertise can moderate the typical increase in peripheral narrowing and search rate among karate players exposed to anxiety-inducing circumstances, with experts being more capable of maintaining optimal search strategies under stress.

Anxiety and the Quiet Eye Period. Vickers (1996) defined the *quiet eye period* as the temporal duration between the last fixation to a target and the onset of movement time (the initiation of the motor response). The duration of the quiet eye period is thought to reflect the organization of neural networks involved with orientation and control of visual attention (e.g., Posner & Gilbert, 1999). Since Vickers' initial work in this area more than a decade ago, the quiet eye period has received extensive attention from researchers interested in calibrating the optimal attentional state before the onset of obligatory sport behaviors. The extant corpus of data has robustly demonstrated that longer quiet eye periods are representative of greater sport expertise and better performance, particularly in self-paced tasks (for a meta-analysis, see Mann, Williams, Ward, & Janelle, 2007). The quiet eye period has been associated with other psychophysiological indexes of the expert performance state, such as the hemispheric asymmetry in EEG spectral activity (Janelle et al., 2000). Though initially attributed to the control of visual attention, the quiet eye period has also been theorized to reflect compensatory behaviors (such as emotion regulation, see Janelle & Hatfield, 2008). Given the important role of the quiet eye period in orienting and controlling attention, researchers began to consider it as a potential locus of anxiety's effect on visual attention and ensuing performance. These efforts have proven fruitful in elucidating the effect of anxiety on performance in several sport contexts.

Rodrigues, Vickers, and Williams (2002) examined how manipulating temporal pressure in a table tennis task influenced gaze behavior characteristics. Participants were required to return a serve under successively abbreviated time allotments. As the duration of the precued time frame shortened, the quiet eye period became significantly shorter and performance deteriorated. Collectively, experts in a wide range of sports (see Mann et al., 2007) have been found to exhibit a longer quiet eye period than comparative nonexperts. Longer quiet eye periods are also associated with better performance (Behan & Wilson, 2008; Williams, Singer, et al., 2002). Exposure to emotionally evocative situations, however, reduces the quiet eye period, which has robustly been show to be detrimental to performance in a wide range of sport tasks. In such cases, maintenance of an extended quiet eye period may help preserve performance quality under emotionally evocative conditions (Vickers & Williams, 2007).

Recommendations for Researchers and Practitioners

Understanding the effect of emotion on performance requires consideration of the mechanisms that are altered by emotion. It can be argued that emotion does not directly affect performance. Rather, emotion causes modulation of more proximal predictors of performance—namely, attention and motor coordination. Sport psychologists fulfill a unique role in delineating the effect of emotion on psychomotor function. A central consideration is how performers translate thought into action. Consideration of how emotion affects this translation is therefore of paramount importance. Sport, the performing arts, military maneuvers, and other domains that require movement to realize performance goals hold in common a reliance on physical execution to index aptitude. This is not the case in many other domains of expertise, in which knowing the appropriate response is inherently followed by the appropriate response. How to perform the action not only is common knowledge but also has no bearing on proficiency (e.g., a chess expert knows the right move and moves the piece accordingly).

In sport, the emotional mechanisms that alter motor actions have at least a twofold potential effect on performance outcome: First, they affect the attentional capabilities of the performer, both in planning the response and in executing the movement once planned. Second, emotions alter the set point from which muscles must respond, thereby requiring that movements be planned to accommodate different levels of muscle tension and coordination. Contemporary theoretical notions such as the ACT, IZOF, cusp catastrophe model, and reinvestment and conscious processing provide solid but insufficient frameworks for addressing such mechanisms.

While sport psychologists have made great strides and in many ways set the bar for experimental rigor, greater attention should be paid to increasing the mechanistic bases by which the performance effects of emotion can be explained as theoretical induction proceeds in the field. Interestingly, it has become more commonplace for other fields of inquiry, particularly neuroscience, to look to sport settings and sport participants to evaluate questions of interest (e.g., Milton, Small, & Solodkin, 2004; Yarrow, Brown, & Krakauer, 2009). Recognizing the increasing potential to investigate sport performance issues through a neuroscientific perspective, Janelle and Hatfield (2008) recently forwarded a model of stress-induced cortical dynamics to guide future empirical work. The adoption of advancing affective neuroscientific methods could permit greater insight into currently unanswered questions that have long intrigued sport psychologists. Many of these questions concern the means by which the brain circuits that regulate emotion and

movement interact to affect the quality of resultant motor actions.

Beyond adopting more rigorous neuroscientific approaches to delineating the brain-based mechanisms that drive the performance changes known to occur under heightened emotional states, the field of behavioral genetics has embarked on efforts to define the links among functional measures of individual differences (such as self-reported trait anxiety), variability in behaviorally relevant brain circuitry, the molecular pathways that underlie brain function, and the functional genetic polymorphisms that underlie variability in the molecular signaling pathways (Hariri, 2009). While such models are currently being applied to determine the extent to which anxiety and affective disorders can be predicted from genetic markers, such techniques could be used to enhance the ability to pair promising athletes with sports that fit their genetic profile and to tailor training programs accordingly. There are clear ethical issues that surround such application. It is our contention that sport psychologists should play a prominent gatekeeping role in conducting the research that is at the fore of such technologies so that they are not misapplied in the name of science (or national pride). Indeed, such work could theoretically uncover illness-resistant or neuroprotective characteristics of elite athletes, for example, that could be used to inform genetic therapies to benefit both athletes and nonathletes. Interventions to bolster such adaptive attributes could be optimized in combined gene therapy and behavioral interventions for individuals who have movement or emotional issues.

The accurate and reliable assessment of emotion in sport-specific settings also has important implications for practitioners. Optimal levels of emotion, particularly anxiety, are fundamental to athletic performance. Thus, psychological skills training often incorporates techniques designed to induce the optimal level of anxiety or arousal needed for peak performance. Valid and reliable measures of emotion are therefore critical for several components of the psychological skills training process. First, in the assessment of an athlete's mental skills, a practitioner can supplement information gathered from a semistructured interview with objective self-report instruments. For example, trait measures of sport competitive anxiety, such as the SAS-2, may inform the practitioner that an athlete tends to experience generally elevated anxiety and concentration disruption. Therefore, the practitioner might include precompetitive anxiety regulation strategies as part of the psychological skills training program. Second, state-specific self-report measures of emotion may be used to explore the relationship between emotional state and performance in athletes. Practitioners who assess an athlete's level of cognitive and somatic anxiety, as well as discrete emotional responses across a continuum of (poor, moderate, and optimal) sport performances, can use this information to guide and individualize emotion regulation interventions.

When used with the proper training and equipment, physiological and behavioral assessments of emotion can also be used in the applied setting. Physiological measures of emotion can be used in biofeedback interventions to train athletes to reach and maintain a specific level of arousal. Biofeedback devices provide an athlete with auditory or visual feedback to obviate otherwise hidden physiological responses. Using measures of skin conductance, HR, EEG, and EMG for biofeedback can help train athletes to become aware of autonomic nervous system responses and to regulate these responses with appropriately tailored emotion regulation techniques. The Wingate five-step approach, developed by Blumenstein, Bar-Eli, and Tenenbaum (1997), provides a guide in the application of biofeedback interventions to enhance performance. Several studies have used the Wingate five-step approach as a tool for improving sport performance (Bar-Eli & Blumenstein, 2004; Bar-Eli, Dreshman, Blumenstein, & Weinstein, 2001; Blumenstein & Bar-Eli, 2004). While such studies are promising, there is a clear need for further empirical validation for using biofeedback to improve sport performance.

Sport psychologists fulfill a unique role in psychological science, as they are concerned with optimizing actions that must be executed under dynamic states of emotional flux. Emotions directly affect a person's ability to attend to the right things at the right times, to program the appropriate responses, and then to execute the chosen actions. Given that emotions are ubiquitous, athletes must become attuned to emotional effects on attention and motor function so they can compensate for affective alterations and perform appropriately. In addition to athletes, there are other individuals (firefighters, soldiers, surgeons, performing artists, and astronauts, just to name a few) who must execute skilled movement under pressure; these individuals can also look to sport psychology research to help understand and overcome such challenges. Being able to measure emotion allows researchers to delineate the cognitive, physiological, and behavioral mechanisms that are altered under emotionally intense conditions. The knowledge generated through these empirical efforts can be used to enhance the quality of information delivery to practitioners and consumers of sport psychology.

Acknowledgments

We would like to thank Dr. Peter Crocker for his helpful comments on an earlier version of this chapter.

■ Table 29.1 ■

Measures Assessing Emotional Reactivity

Variable or concept	Measure	Dimension	Source
Trait competitive anxiety	Sport Anxiety Scale-2 (SAS-2)	Somatic anxiety, worry, and concentration disruption	Smith, Smoll, Cumming, & Grossbard (2006)
Trait competitive anxiety	Sport Competition Anxiety Test (SCAT)	Unidimensional measure of competitive trait anxiety	Martens, Vealey, & Burton (1990)
Sport-specific state anxiety	Competitive State Anxiety Index-2 (CSAI-2)	Cognitive anxiety, somatic anxiety, and self-confidence	Martens, Vealey, & Burton (1990)
Sport-specific state anxiety	Revised Competitive State Anxiety Index-2 (CSAI-2R)	Cognitive anxiety, somatic anxiety, and self-confidence	Cox, Martens, & Russell (2003)
Brief measure of state anxiety	Mental Readiness Form-Likert (MRF-L)	Cognitive anxiety, somatic anxiety, and self-confidence	Krane (1994)

(continued)

Table 29.1

(continued)

Variable or concept	Measure	Dimension	Source
Brief measure of state anxiety	Anxiety thermometer	Unidimensional measure of state anxiety	Houtman & Bakker (1989)
Daily affect	Positive and Negative Affect Schedule (PANAS)	Positive and negative affective responses for daily living	Watson, Clark, & Tellegen (1988)
Competitive state emotion	Differential Emotions Scale (DES-IV)	Interest, enjoyment, surprise, sadness, anger, disgust, contempt, fear, guilt, shame, shyness, and self-hostility	Izard (1991)
Precompetitive state emotion	Sport Emotion Questionnaire (SEQ)	Anger, anxiety, dejection, excitement, and happiness	Jones, Lane, Bray, Uphill, & Catlin (2005)
Physiological arousal	HR		Berntson, Quigley, & Lozano (2007)
Physiological arousal	SCR		Dawson, Schell, & Filion (2007)
Physiological arousal	EMG	Anxiety manifested as muscle tension	Pijpers, Oudejans, Holsheimer, & Bakker (2003)
Physiological index of hemispheric asymmetry	EEG (spectral)	Greater left frontal cortical activity indicates greater resting positive affect	Saarela (1999)
Physiological signal extracted from the ongoing raw EEG	EEG (ERPs)	Attention devoted to discrimination of an obligatory stimulus (P3 component)	Murray & Janelle (2007)
Physiological arousal	Pupil diameter	Extent of pupil dilation	Wilson, Smith, Chattington, Ford, & Marple-Horvat (2006)
Behavioral index	Movement efficiency	Efficiency of motor function	Wilson, Smith, Chattington, Ford, & Marple-Horvat (2006)
Behavioral index	Gaze behavior (search rate)	Number and duration of fixations	Janelle, Singer, & Williams (1999)
Behavioral index	Gaze behavior (quiet eye)	Duration of final fixation to the target area until the initiation of the motor response (movement time)	Rodrigues, Vickers, & Williams (2002)

Flow

Susan A. Jackson, PhD, and Robert C. Eklund, PhD

Flow represents those moments when everything comes together to create a special state of absorption and enjoyment in an activity (Csikszentmihalyi, 1975, 1990). Flow occurs when a person is totally involved in the task at hand. When in flow, the performer feels strong and positive, not worried about the self or failure. *Flow* can be defined as an experience that stands out as being better than average in some way, in which the individual is totally absorbed in the activity being performed and the experience is very rewarding in and of itself. Csikszentmihalyi (1975) developed the flow concept after investigating human experience during times when everything seemed to come together during the performance of a person's chosen activity. Included in the early studies were a range of activities, such as surgery, dancing, chess, and rock climbing. Despite the diversity in settings, there was considerable consistency of responses regarding what was felt during moments that stood out as being special in some way.

Csikszentmihalyi (1990) considered flow to be an optimal experience, and he used the terms *flow* and *optimal experience* interchangeably. We consider the study of optimal experience to be just as important as focusing on problems or negative experiences. The tremendous resurgence of the positive psychology approach, initiated by the efforts of the 2000 APA president, Martin Seligman (Seligman & Csikszentmihalyi, 2000), demonstrates considerable support for the significance of understanding positive human experiences. Flow is considered a central positive subjective experience in positive psychology.

Theoretical Framework

Since his initial investigations, Csikszentmihalyi (e.g., 1990, 1997, 2003) has continued to examine the flow construct. The experience of flow has been examined relative to a host of engagements rang-

ing from daily living (Csikszentmihalyi, 1997) to research endeavor leading to major scientific discoveries (Csikszentmihalyi, 1996). The remarkable consistency observed in Csikszentmihalyi's (1975) initial investigation of lived optimal experiences has continued to be encountered across the broadening array of engagements examined. Flow appears to be regarded universally as a special psychological state that is intimately associated with enjoyment. Flow can occur at different levels of complexity but, by definition, is intrinsically rewarding regardless of whether it involves a simple game of throw and catch or a complicated and dangerous gymnastics routine. Csikszentmihalyi (1975) referred to the different levels of flow experience as *microflow* and *macroflow*. Microflow experiences were postulated to fit the patterns of everyday life, whereas the *macroflow* label was reserved for experiences associated with higher levels of complexity and demand on the participant.

There are several defining characteristics of flow, and it is the simultaneous experience of these positive aspects that creates the memorable experience that is flow. These defining characteristics are described in greater detail in the next section and include *total focus, involvement,* and *absorption* in the task at hand, to the exclusion of all other thoughts and emotions. This involvement in the activity is so complete that nothing else seems to matter, and we continue in it "even at great cost, for the sheer sake of doing it" (Csikszentmihalyi, 1990, p. 4). This immersion for the sake of doing links flow with intrinsic motivation, and the initial name that Csiksentmihalyi gave for flow (*autotelic experience*) translates as doing something for its own sake. Hence the links with intrinsic motivation are strong.

A central element in the conceptualization of the flow experience is the need for the challenges of an activity to be balanced with the skills of the participant. This balance is depicted in the flow model shown in figure 30.1 on page 350. The balance is essential

Challenge axis

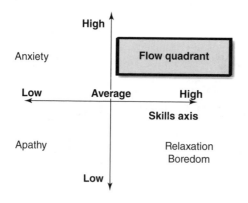

Figure 30.1   The flow state.

Adapted, by permission, from S.A. Jackson and M. Csikszentmihalyi, 1999, *Flow in sports: The keys to optimal experiences and performances* (Champaign, IL: Human Kinetics), 37. Previously adapted from M. Csikszentmihalyi and I. Csikszentmihalyi, 1988, *Optimal experience: Psychological studies of flow in consciousness* (Cambridge: Cambridge University Press).

to the concept of flow as conceptualized by Csikszentmihalyi (1990). It relates to the person's *perception* of the level of challenge and the degree of skill—and the balance between them. When the perceived challenge of the activity is in balance with the perceived skill, the performer is set up for an experience of flow. This means that it is not the objective challenges or skills that determine the quality of the experience but rather what we think of the level of challenge and of the level of skill we *believe* we have to meet the challenge.

Grounding flow in positive psychology. The millennial issue of *American Psychologist* was devoted to the exploration and advancement of positive psychology. Seligman and Csikszentmihalyi (2000) outlined three areas central to the science of positive psychology: positive *subjective experience*, positive *individual traits*, and positive *institutions*.

The aim of positive psychology was characterized as "to catalyze a change in psychology from a preoccupation only with repairing the worst things in life to also building the best qualities in life" (Seligman, 2002, p. 3). Flow, identified as a key construct in the positive subjective experience, has found a home in positive psychology because it epitomizes the goal of positive psychology to understand and promote the "best qualities in life."

Flow Dimensions

Csikszentmihalyi (1990) conceptualized the flow construct in terms of nine dimensions. These dimensions are as follows: challenge–skill balance, action–awareness merging, clear goals, unambiguous feedback, concentration on task, sense of con-

trol, loss of self-consciousness, time transformation, and autotelic experience. Together, they represent the optimal psychological state of flow; by themselves, they signify conceptual elements of the flow experience.

Challenge–Skill Balance. This dimension is critical to the operational definition of flow. Challenges can be thought of as opportunities for actions or goals. Skills are the capacities the individual has to produce desired outcomes. Critical to the challenge–skill balance is the idea that the *perception* of challenge and the *perception* of skill drive the equation. This perception makes our belief in what we are able to do more important than our objective skill levels. Moreover, challenges can be defined in a personal way, separate from any structures of an activity. It is the perception of the defined challenge that is critical to the occurrence of flow.

During the experience of flow, a dynamic balance exists. Maintaining optimal challenge in the demand–skill balance equation appears to be important. In sport, developing athletes constantly challenge themselves with higher skill demands. The structure of sports and levels of competition provide continual opportunities for challenge. For many people, physical activity (be it competitive or recreational) provides one of the most concrete opportunities for setting and striving for personal challenges.

Action–Awareness Merging. When people are asked to describe what it feels like to be in flow, the merging of action and awareness is often central to their descriptions. This dimension involves a feeling of being at one with the activity being performed. It is through total absorption in the activity (see the later description on the total concentration dimension of flow) that the perception of oneness results, bringing harmony and peace to an active engagement with a task. Athletes often describe a sense of effortlessness and spontaneity associated with this flow dimension.

Clear Goals. Individuals describe the flow state as involving a clear sense of knowing what they need to do. During flow, this clarity of purpose occurs on a moment-by-moment basis, keeping the performer fully connected to the task and responsive to appropriate cues. Sport provides an excellent setting for the experience of flow because actions are inherently bound by clear goals and rules. Goal setting is a process that can also move a performer toward flow. The structure of preset intention allows more attention to be focused on immediate tasks. Personal goals can also be set and continually monitored against this backdrop of built-in goals for action. Goals are a necessary part of achieving something worthwhile in any endeavor. The focus that goals provide to action also means that they are an integral component of the flow experience.

Unambiguous Feedback. Hand in hand with having clear goals is the processing of information on how performance is progressing relative to clear goals. Paying attention to feedback is an important step in determining whether the performance is on track toward the goals that have been set. During flow, feedback information is perceived as unambiguous and effortlessly processed in producing performance consistent with the performer's desires.

Feedback can come from many sources. For athletes, one of the most important sources of feedback is kinesthetic awareness, or knowing the spatial location of the body. This awareness is the internal information that an athlete needs in order to optimize movement. Feedback can also come from several external sources, ranging from the environment in which the performance is occurring to the information provided by competitors or spectators. It is not necessary for feedback to be positive for flow to occur or continue. The nature of clear and immediate feedback means that adjustments can be made to keep a performer in flow or enable the performer to achieve the state of flow. When receiving feedback associated with a flow state, the performer does not need to stop and reflect on how things are going. Moment by moment, information is seamlessly integrated into performance.

Total Concentration on the Task at Hand. Being totally connected to the task at hand epitomizes the flow state and is one of its most frequently mentioned characteristics. When in flow, the performer is totally focused in the present on the specific task being performed. There are no extraneous thoughts, and the distractibility that often accompanies involvement in any task is wonderfully absent. This connectedness relies on a present-centered focus. The past and the future are not roads to flow; flow resides in being able to be *in* the present moment.

Sense of Control. Another frequently mentioned flow characteristic is a feeling of being in control. Some athletes describe it as a sense of infallibility. This empowering feeling frees the performer from the all-too-frequent fear of failure that creeps into performance. Failure thoughts are nowhere to be found during flow, enabling the individual to approach the challenges at hand in a positive frame of mind.

Control, like the challenge–skill relationship, is a delicately balanced component of flow. Although the perception of control is inherent to the experience, absolute situational control would be inimical to flow. The performer must experience challenge in order to experience flow, and challenge does not exist under conditions of absolute control. Hence, the experience of total control most likely moves an individual away from the experience of flow and into relaxation or boredom. The possibility of keeping things under control keeps flow alive. Like flow itself, the sense of control usually lasts only a short time. This relates back to remaining at the cutting edge of the challenge–skill balance. If the feeling of being in control continues indefinitely, then the scales tip in favor of skill over challenge, and flow is lost.

Loss of Self-Consciousness. Most people live their lives surrounded by evaluations of how they are doing. Emanating from many sources, one of the most insistent sources is the self. In situations of importance, it is difficult for us to stop constantly evaluating how we are doing in the eyes of others. However, cessation of this evaluation is necessary for flow. When an individual is no longer concerned with what others think, this individual has lost self-consciousness.

Athletes often find it difficult to lose self-consciousness. The very public nature of their sport activity affords many opportunities for evaluation. Criticism—both from others and from on the self—turns attention away from the task and onto the self. The ego, that part of self that questions, critiques, and prompts self-doubt, needs to be quieted for flow. We can think of flow as unself-conscious action. It is liberating to be free of the voice within our head that questions whether we are living up to the standards that we perceive we should meet.

Transformation of Time. Deep moments of flow seem to transform the perception of time. For some, the experience is that time stops. For others, time seems to slow. For still others, time seems to pass more quickly than expected. These sensations come about through the intense involvement of a flow experience. Because nothing else is entering our awareness during flow, we may be surprised to find that significant time has passed while in this state. The intensity of focus may also contribute to the perception that time is slowing and the feeling of having all the time in the world to execute a move that is, in reality, very much time limited. Thus, there seems to be a close link between depth of concentration and time transformation.

Autotelic Experience. Csikszentmihalyi (1990) coined the term *autotelic experience* to describe the intrinsically rewarding nature of flow. As described by Csikszentmihalyi, the word is derived from two Greek words that describe doing something for its own sake: *auto*, which means "self," and *telos*, which means "goal." Flow is such an enjoyable experience that the performer is motivated to return to this state. Once experienced, flow becomes much sought after. Csikszentmihalyi described this dimension as the end result of the other eight flow dimensions. For many people, flow is the defining motivation to keep pushing toward higher limits. It is generally upon reflection that the autotelic aspect of flow is realized and provides high motivation toward further involvement.

Together, these nine dimensions of flow provide an optimal experience. Considerable consistency of the flow experience has been found across many domains (see Csikszentmihalyi, 1990, 1997; Csikszentmihalyi & Csikszentmihalyi, 1988). The dimensions of flow provide a conceptually coherent framework for understanding optimal experience.

Sources of Confusion in the Flow Construct

At least two widely employed constructs are often confused with the construct of flow: *peak experience* and *peak performance*. First, flow—often termed *optimal experience* by Csikszentmihalyi—is not the same concept as *peak experience*. The latter term was coined by Maslow in the 1960s to describe "moments of highest happiness and fulfillment" (Maslow, 1968, p. 69). These relatively rare experiences are highly valued by the individual as particularly memorable because of their intensity, meaning, and richness (Privette, 1983). Another concept distinguishable from flow is *peak performance*. Privette (1983) defined this term as "behavior that transcends or goes beyond predictable functioning to use a person's potentials more fully than could be reasonably expected" (p. 58). The three experiences—flow, peak experience, and peak performance—have phenomenological commonality (Garfield & Bennett, 1984; Jackson, 2000; Privette, 1983; Ravizza, 1984) and can be experienced simultaneously. Nonetheless, each can occur independently of the others. Specifically, peak performance requires exceptional performance—anything less is by definition not peak performance regardless of phenomenological quality. Likewise, neither flow nor peak experience inherently involves exceptional performance. Moreover, an experience of flow does not have to be uniquely memorable. The phenomenological commonalities are interesting, but the conceptual distinctiveness of the constructs is also important to respect.

Another source of confusion, or uncertainty, regarding flow can be found in the question of whether all nine dimensions need to be experienced

simultaneously for flow to occur. Further research is required to tease out the relative contributions of the nine dimensions to flow and the relationships among these dimensions within different contexts and individuals. Jackson, Kimiecik, Ford, and Marsh (1998) and Jackson, Thomas, Marsh, and Smethurst (2001) took a statistical viewpoint to examine the relative contributions of the flow dimensions to other related psychological constructs. In CFAs of the Long Flow Scales (e.g., Jackson & Eklund, 2002; Jackson & Marsh, 1996; Kowal & Fortier, 1999; Vlachopoulos et al., 2000; see next section for a description of the instruments), two flow dimensions—loss of self-consciousness and time transformation—have consistently received lower factor loadings on a higher-order flow construct. An interesting future research direction would be to investigate how these two dimensions are experienced in different settings and across different levels of performers. An exploratory study of the dimensions of flow using IRT analysis (Tenenbaum, Fogarty, & Jackson, 1999) suggested that the loss of self-consciousness and the time transformation dimensions might be experienced only in deeper levels of flow. Continued investigation of the relative endorsement of the flow dimensions may help to advance understanding of how the process of flow operates.

Measurement Tools

Jackson and colleagues (Jackson & Eklund, 2002; Jackson, Eklund, & Martin, 2010; Jackson, Martin, & Eklund, 2008; Martin & Jackson, 2008) developed a suite of scales—the Long, Short, and Core Flow Scales—to provide a range of instrumentation to suit an array of research and applied purposes. One general characteristic of their approach is to assess flow at two levels: (1) the *dispositional level*, or the frequency of flow experience across time in particular domains (e.g., sport, work, or school), and (2) the *state level*, or the extent of flow experienced in a particular event or activity (e.g., a race, a work project, or a test).

The dispositional and state flow scales are parallel forms, with differences in wording reflecting whether the disposition to experience flow or a specific flow experience is being assessed. By administering the two versions of the scales, it is possible to assess flow at both a dispositional level and a state level. That is, general tendency to experience flow as well as particular incidence (or nonincidence) of flow during a specific event can be assessed.

The Long, Short, and Core Flow Scales all include a dispositional and a state version. Brief descriptions of these three main flow instruments follow.

1. Long Flow Scales: These 36-item scales assess Csikszentmihalyi's nine dimensions of flow. The Long Flow Scales (i.e., dispositional and state) are particularly useful when a detailed picture of flow experience is important for research or applied purposes. They provide a multidimensional approach that is grounded in Csikszentmihalyi's conceptualization of flow. These scales are the instruments of choice for targeted interventions and for times when a detailed understanding of the flow dimensions is important.

2. Short Flow Scales: These 9-item (dispositional and state) scales are abbreviated versions of the Long Flow Scales in which 1 item is used to represent each of the nine flow dimensions. The Short Flow Scales provide a brief assessment that is useful when research or practical constraints prevent the use of a longer scale.

3. Core Flow Scales: These 10-item (dispositional and state) scales assess the global phenomenology of flow. The Core Flow Scales provide an assessment of the central subjective experience that complements the dimensional assessments afforded by the Long and Short Flow Scales.

All versions of the scales have been validated through CFA, and the scales have demonstrated good psychometric properties. In the subsequent sections the various scales are described in more detail, beginning with the Long Flow Scales.

Long Flow Scales

The Long Flow Scales are the original scales developed by Jackson and colleagues (e.g., Jackson & Marsh, 1996; Jackson & Eklund, 2002). Comprising 36 items, the Long Flow Scales provide a multidimensional assessment of flow from a dimensional flow perspective.

Flow State Scale-2

Using both qualitative and quantitative methods, Jackson and Marsh (1996) developed a self-report scale called the *Flow State Scale* (FSS) to open up the possibilities for quantitative investigation of the flow state in sport settings. Several years later, Jackson and Eklund (2002) revised the FSS into the Flow State Scale-2 (FSS-2).

The FSS-2, like its predecessor, is a 36-item self-report questionnaire designed to measure the state of flow during participation within a specific activity. It is designed to be given immediately or soon after activity completion. The questionnaire has nine subscales, each with 4 items, to assess the nine flow dimensions. Respondents indicate the extent to which they agree with each statement on a 5-point Likert scale ranging from 1 = "Strongly disagree" to 5 = "Strongly agree." The following are sample items from the FSS-2:

> "My attention was focused entirely on what I was doing."
>
> "I had a strong sense of what I wanted to do."
>
> "I was aware of how well I was performing."

Dispositional Flow Scale-2

A dispositional version of the flow scale was developed to measure the frequency with which a performer typically experiences flow in sport or physical activity (Jackson et al., 1998). The Dispositional Flow Scale (DFS) was based on preliminary validation of the FSS developed by Jackson and Marsh (1996). Jackson and Eklund (2002) developed the DFS-2, a revision of the DFS.

The DFS-2 is essentially a parallel version of the FSS-2. Like the FSS, it is a 36-item self-report questionnaire. However, items are reworded to assess to what degree an individual *generally* experiences the flow state while participating in physical activity. It is therefore designed to be answered away from an immediate involvement in activity. The questionnaire has nine subscales, each with 4 items, corresponding to the nine flow dimensions. Respondents indicate the frequency of each statement on a 5-point Likert scale ranging from 1 = "Never" to 5 = "Always." The following are sample items from the DFS-2:

> "I have a feeling of total control."
>
> "I am not worried about what others may be thinking of me."
>
> "I love the feeling of the performance, and want to capture it again."

Across two large psychometric studies (Jackson & Eklund, 2002; Jackson, Martin, & Eklund, 2008), the FSS-2 and DFS-2 have demonstrated good reliability. FSS-2 coefficient alphas ranged between .76 and .92, and DFS-2 coefficient alphas ranged from .78 to .90.

The DFS-2 and FSS-2 have been translated into several languages, including Greek (Stavrou & Zervas, 2004), French (Fournier et al., 2007), Japanese (Kawabata, Mallett, & Jackson, 2007), Finnish (Pekka

Hämäläinen & Veli-Pekka Räty, personal communication, 2008), Spanish (Martínez-Zaragoza, Benavides, Solanes, Pastor, & Martin del Rio, personal communication, 2008), Hungarian (Bimbo, personal communication, 2009), and Hindi (Singh, personal communication, 2009). More translations are underway.

Short Flow Scales

Although there are psychometric advantages to long, multidimensional instruments, practical considerations often dictate the need for shorter versions. During a sport event, athletes and coaches may be willing to complete a 10-item scale but may balk at answering a scale four times that length. In large-scale projects involving many measures, short forms may be preferable to keep a questionnaire package to a reasonable size for participants or to use when a particular construct is not the central focus and can be reasonably estimated with a short measure. For reasons such as these, Jackson and colleagues (Jackson et al., 2008; Martin & Jackson, 2008) developed two short instruments to assess flow: the Short Flow Scales and the Core Flow Scales.

The Short Flow Scales are abbreviated versions of their predecessors, the FSS-2 and DFS-2. Both the Short Flow State Scale and the Short Dispositional Flow Scale contain 9 items—1 item for each of the nine flow dimensions. The rating scales of the abbreviated instruments are the same as those used in their parent scales. They provide succinct measures of the higher-order dimensional flow model described in CFA research with the 36-item scales. Initial psychometric support for the Short Flow Scales is promising. Because they are new scales, further research is needed to examine their utility. Both the dispositional and state forms have demonstrated good reliability (Jackson, Martin, & Eklund, 2008; Martin & Jackson, 2008). The dispositional form has demonstrated strong CFA results across research with participants from sport, work, school, and music (Jackson, Martin, & Eklund, 2008; Martin & Jackson, 2008). The CFA values for the state form are somewhat weaker, although fewer analyses have been undertaken to date with this version of short flow (Jackson & Martin, 2008). Interestingly, in the research that has been conducted with the short state scale, better values have been obtained with sport-specific versus pooled samples. From this finding, Jackson and Martin concluded that the more situation-sensitive state measures may operate better from a psychometric standpoint when used in specific (compared with generalized) contexts.

Core Flow Scales

While the Short Flow Scales were designed as abbreviated versions of the 36-item Long Flow Scales, the Core Flow Scales were designed to provide a different approach to assessing flow with a succinct measure. The Core Flow Scales contain 10 items describing what it feels like to be in flow during a target activity. The items of the Core Flow Scales were derived from qualitative research in which elite athletes described the experience of being in flow (Jackson, 1992, 1995, 1996). Expressions used by athletes to describe what it is like to be in flow were adapted into short statements. These are rated on scales similar to those used in the other flow instruments. Model fit and reliability for these scales have been strong in the initial research (Martin & Jackson, 2008).

Examples From the Literature

Research has been conducted with the Long Flow Scales in a range of activities in settings such as sport (e.g., Jackson et al., 1998), exercise (e.g., Karageorghis, Vlachopoulos, & Terry, 2000), yoga (Penman, Cohen, Stephens, & Jackson, 2006), music performance (Wrigley, 2005), and web-based instructional activity (Chan & Repman, 1999). Researchers from diverse areas such as gifted education, work addiction, yoga, and business have applied the flow scales to their research setting. Moreover, there is considerable interest in examining flow in relationship to other psychological constructs across diverse settings. Relationships with concepts such as hope, cohesion, personality type, intrinsic motivation, burnout, self-efficacy, self-esteem, and anxiety have all captured the interest of flow researchers. To address the considerable interest in examining flow across a range of settings and in relationship to a diverse set of psychological constructs, the recent introduction of two brief measures of flow provides researchers with several options for including flow as a focal, ancillary, or outcome measure.

In their early research into flow, Jackson and Roberts (1992) demonstrated associations between flow and task-orientated motivation. Kowal and Fortier (1999) subsequently observed similar associations in a study of masters swimmers. They found that swimmers who were motivated in a self-determined way (e.g., were swimming for pleasure, satisfaction, or benefit) were more likely to experience flow. They also found that the situational determinants of perceived *competence*, *autonomy*, and *relatedness* were positively and significantly related to flow experiences. Jackson et al., (1998) also conducted research on flow with masters athletes participating in four sports (swimming, triathlon, cycling, and track and field) at the World Masters Games. They found dispositional flow to be positively associated with perceived ability and intrinsic motivation and negatively associated with anxiety.

In studying U.S. Division I college athletes, Wiggins and Freeman (2000) observed higher flow scores (i.e., global, unambiguous feedback, concentration, loss of self-consciousness) among athletes perceiving their anxiety as facilitative compared with athletes perceiving anxiety as debilitative. Using Long Flow Scales (state and dispositional), Jackson and colleagues (2001) found that the four dimensions of challenge–skill balance, concentration on the task at hand, sense of control, and clear goals were the most strongly associated with psychological skill proficiency and self-concept in a study of 236 competitive orienteers, surf lifesavers, and road cyclists. Moreover, athletes with greater psychological skill proficiency and more positive self-perceptions were more likely to experience flow.

Karageorghis and colleagues (2000) investigated relationships between subjective feelings of enjoyment and flow in exercise. In their sample of 1,231 aerobic dance exercise participants, they found a positive and significant association between levels of flow and postexercise feelings of revitalization, tranquility, and positive engagement. This suggests that the experience of flow might play a role in encouraging adherence to physical activity regimens through the experience of positive postexercise feelings.

A group of Italian researchers investigated the flow experience across a variety of sport settings, and an edited book (Muzio, 2004) summarizes the findings from an array of research into aspects of flow. Included are reports on differences among fencers, skiers, swimmers, cyclists, and track-and-field athletes on an Italian version of the FSS (Jackson & Marsh, 1996). The fencers differed the most from the other groups, which the researchers explained in terms of the high importance assigned to immediate feedback cues in fencing bouts. There was close similarity among the swimming, cycling, and track-and-field groups.

Vea and Pensgaard (2004) examined the relationship between perfectionism and flow in young elite Norwegian athletes. Perfectionism has been shown to have some negative repercussions, and the authors were interested in understanding the performance and well-being implications of perfectionism. Flow was selected as an indicator of potential to perform at optimal levels and as an indicator of subjective well-being. As expected, most of the perfectionism dimensions correlated negatively with flow dimensions, although there were a couple of unexpected positive associations.

Recommendations for Researchers and Practitioners

The triad of flow scales developed by Jackson and colleagues (Jackson & Eklund, 2002; Jackson et al., 2008; Martin & Jackson, 2008) provides researchers with a variety of options for assessing flow. The 36-item Long Flow Scales have been shown to be robust instruments that provide a detailed assessment of the dimensional flow model. These scales are the best choice when a detailed description of flow characteristics according to the dimensional flow model of Csikszentmihalyi (1990) is desired. The Long Flow Scales are also ideally suited to intervention-based research, providing assessment of modifiable flow characteristics in the nine dimensions of flow.

The Short Flow Scales provide a useful tool for a brief assessment of flow from the nine-dimensional conceptualization. Grounded in a solid psychometric base, the 9-item flow scales are useful when an aggregate measure of the nine flow dimensions is desired. The equally short Core Flow Scales provide a valid and reliable assessment of the central, or core, subjective experience of being in flow. The two brief flow scales offer different but complementary ways of assessing flow and should open up more possibilities for including flow as a focal construct across a range of settings.

The original Long Flow Scales were designed to assess flow in physical activity settings. A qualitative database of athletes' descriptions of being in flow was used when developing the original items for the scales and again when developing items for Core Flow Scales. While there is a specific focus on movement in a small number of items, there is no reference to activity structure or to competitiveness, which are aspects that might have tied the scales to a sport environment. Since the development of the flow scales, interest in using the scales has come not only from researchers studying optimal experiences in physical activity settings but also from researchers working in many other settings. In the more recent Short and Core Flow Scales, items were developed with a diverse audience in mind, and these scales have been applied successfully to school, work, and extracurricular activity. Because the Long Flow Scales were developed with a physical activity context in mind, Jackson et al., (2009) recently created adapted versions of the DFS-2 and

FSS-2 in which items with a focus on movement or performance were reworded to facilitate their use across a broad range of settings.

The dispositional versions of the three flow scales assess the general tendency to experience flow characteristics within a particular setting nominated by the respondent (or the investigator). The respondent is directed to think about the frequency with which the flow items are experienced in the nominated activity. There are several reasons for the format of these instructions. First is to provide a context for participant responses and to ground participant thinking in a particular setting. Second, the DFS-2 was designed in parallel with the FSS-2, in which respondents report flow experience within a single event. The contextualizing of the DFS-2 enables researchers to compare responses to the same activity across the FSS-2 and DFS-2 and thus examine relationships between state and dispositional factors in experience. Third, most investigations using the DFS-2 will likely focus on activities in which the respondents are personally invested, where they are likely to encounter challenge and for which they have developed some skills (i.e., activities conducive to flow experiences).

While the DFS-2 is meant to be grounded in a particular activity (or type of activity), it should be answered at a time separate from immediate involvement in this activity. As a dispositional measure, the DFS-2 is designed to elicit typical responses, or how the person feels in general about participating in a chosen activity. There are no set time frames in which the respondent is asked to recall experience. Nonetheless, it is possible to assign a time frame by adding to the instructions preceding the scale. For example, the following instructions could be added: "Think about your experience in (name of activity) over the past year, and answer the questions about how you have generally felt while participating." The appropriate time frame to specify for respondents answering the DFS-2 may depend on the research question or the particular characteristics of the sample (e.g., age, amount of time spent in the activity, frequency of participation).

The State Flow Scales were designed as postevent assessments of flow. Instructions (e.g., "During the event") are worded to focus the respondent on the recently completed activity. Respondents are asked to indicate their extent of agreement with each of the flow descriptors in relation to the activity just completed. The FSS-2 should be administered as soon as possible after the completion of the activity in order to promote clear recall. It is recommended that responses to the FSS-2 be collected within 1 h of a completed activity, with the aim of gathering the data as close to the finish of an activity as possible while minimizing intrusion on the participants. Collecting responses close to the conclusion of an activity is more likely to yield a more accurate assessment of the state flow experience.

Another possible use of the FSS-2 is to collect data on particular experiences of significance to the participants. Respondents can be asked to think about a particular experience (e.g., a peak experience) and answer the questions in relation to this event. There is research support for strength of memory in relation to personally significant life events (e.g., Wagenaar, 1986). It can be argued that a high-level flow experience, such as one tied into a peak performance or peak experience, remains a strong memory for the recipient. Qualitative research conducted by Jackson (1996) and Eklund (1994) supports this assertion, with such events being remembered as highlights of an athlete's career. Initial research conducted by Jackson and Marsh (1996) to develop the flow scale used the recalled optimal experiences of respondents. While the recommended usage of the FSS-2 is to ground participant responses in a particular event that has just occurred, there may be users of this scale who are particularly interested in understanding experiences, such as best-ever experiences, that reside further in the past.

Most people would agree that being in flow is a great experience, but how do we know when people are experiencing flow, and what is it like when they are in this state? To what extent are a group of athletes, students, employees, or performers absorbed in and enjoying what they are doing? The flow scales can answer questions such as these. They have been used in a wide range of performance settings, including sport, music, and art. In addition, the scales have been used to assess flow experience in school, work, and leisure-time activities and hobbies. With the suite of Long, Short, and Core Flow Scales, there is a range of instrumentation to suit a diversity of applied purposes.

Practitioners interested in a detailed picture of how their students, clients, or participants are experiencing flow should use the Long Flow Scales, as should practitioners conducting interventions in which changes in subjective experience are a valued outcome. When time or situational constraints are operating, the Short or Core Flow Scales can provide a brief assessment of flow. Choosing between these two instruments comes down to whether there is more interest in assessing flow from a dimensional perspective (Short Flow Scales) or from a more holistic, experiential perspective (Core Flow Scales).

From a practitioner perspective, the flow scales can provide useful information in areas such as tracking client progress, evaluating the effect of interventions, and understanding how individuals experience their involvement in activities. It is important to remember, however, that the flow scales were not designed to be used as diagnostic instruments per se.

■ Table 30.1 ■

Measures Assessing Flow

Flow concept	Measure	Dimension	Source	Website
Multidimensional flow experience	Dispositional Flow Scale-2 (Long DFS-2) and Flow State Scale-2 (Long FSS-2)	Challenge–skill balance, action–awareness merging, clear goals, unambiguous feedback, concentration on task at hand, sense of control, loss of self-consciousness, time transformation, and autotelic experience	Jackson & Marsh (1996); Jackson & Eklund (2002); Jackson, Martin, & Eklund (2008)	www.mindgarden .com
Flow as a global construct	Short Flow Scales (Short DFS and Short FSS)	Unidimensional flow construct	Jackson, Martin, & Eklund (2008); Martin & Jackson (2008)	www.mindgarden .com
Flow as a phenomenological experience	Core Flow Scales (dispositional and state)	Unidimensional flow construct	Jackson, Martin, & Eklund (2008); Martin & Jackson (2008)	www.mindgarden .com

Burnout

Robert C. Eklund, PhD, Alan L. Smith, PhD,
Thomas D. Raedeke, PhD, and Scott Cresswell, PhD

Research on athlete burnout has grown noticeably in recent years (Eklund & Cresswell, 2007; Goodger, Gorely, Lavallee, & Harwood, 2007; Gould & Whitley, 2009; Raedeke & Smith, 2009). This growth can be attributed to several converging developments. As noted by Raedeke and Smith, athlete burnout has been a growing concern among constituents of the sport community, including administrators, scientists, coaches, athletes, parents, and even fans. This concern has led some sport organizations to fund research programs to gain a better understanding of burnout in hopes of ameliorating the problem (Eklund & Cresswell, 2007). Beyond the growing concern and funding increases supporting athlete burnout research, the emergence of measurement tools such as the Athlete Burnout Questionnaire (ABQ; Raedeke, 1997; Raedeke & Smith, 2001, 2009), the Eades Athletic Burnout Inventory (EABI; Eades, 1990), and the Maslach Burnout Inventory-General Survey (MBI-GS; Maslach, Jackson, & Leiter, 1996) has facilitated research efforts. Although qualitative investigations have been revealing and informative (e.g., Cresswell & Eklund, 2006c, 2007a, 2007b; Goodger, Wolfenden, & Lavallee, 2007; Gould, Tuffey, Udry, & Loehr, 1996; Gustafsson, Kenttä, Hassmén, Lundqvist, & Durand-Bush, 2007), the availability of psychometrically sound quantitative measures has greatly facilitated efforts to study athlete burnout. In this chapter, we present important considerations in the measurement of athlete burnout by (a) providing conceptual grounding for understanding this issue as a psychosocial syndrome, (b) identifying sources of confusion about the athlete burnout construct, (c) describing three prominent measurement tools used in sport psychology research to study athlete burnout and highlighting sample studies in the extant literature, (d) providing recommendations for researchers conducting athlete burnout research,

and (e) providing brief recommendations for practitioners seeking to prevent or treat athletes struggling with this aversive experiential state.

Conceptualizing Athlete Burnout as a Syndrome

Burnout emerged as a psychosocial construct in the mid-1970s in Freudenberger's (1974, 1975) and Maslach's (1976) efforts to describe disturbing patterns of mental and physical deterioration and workplace ineffectiveness observed among alternative health care staff members and human services workers. Freudenberger is credited with naming the phenomenon *burnout*. He characterized it as exhaustion due to excessive demands on energy, strength, or resources. The development of a measurement instrument, the Maslach Burnout Inventory (MBI; Maslach & Jackson, 1981, 1986), effectively formalized burnout as a syndrome involving sustained feelings of emotional exhaustion, depersonalization (negative attitudes and feelings toward patients or clients), and perceived inadequate personal accomplishment (a sense of low accomplishment and professional inadequacy).

It did not take long for the term *burnout* to take root in sport settings (Eklund & Cresswell, 2007; Raedeke & Smith, 2009). The notion that negative, amotivated, and exhausted states sometimes described by athletes might be a sport-related manifestation of burnout quickly gained currency among sport scientists and practitioners (e.g., Cohn, 1990; Feigley, 1984; Gould, 1993; Henschen, 1990; Rowland, 1986; Schmidt & Stein, 1991; Smith, 1986; Yukelson, 1990). Nonetheless, scepticism about the relevance and applicability of Maslach and Jackson's (1981, 1986) conceptualization of the burnout syndrome to the experiences of sport participants was salient (e.g., Feigley, 1984; Garden, 1987). As Smith (1986) noted in his influential paper on sport burnout, it is logical to question "the extent to which the nature, causes and consequences are unique and to what extent they are shared by those who experience burnout in other domains of activity" (p. 44). The challenges faced by athletes are substantially different from those faced by human services professionals, and hence there is merit to such scepticism. Too often, however, the arguments have focused on burnout antecedents (as we just did in focusing on "the challenges") instead of the experiential syndrome itself.

It is reasonable to expect that antecedents of burnout vary across settings. This variation, however, does not inherently mean that the experiential consequences of exposure to chronic stress must also differ. In fact, research across a variety of occupational settings characterized by chronic exposure to psychosocial stress indicates that a common burnout syndrome exists (Schaufeli & Enzmann, 1998). Likewise, interview data from athletes indicate that exposure to demanding competitive sport environments results in the same negative experiential syndrome (Cresswell & Eklund, 2006c, 2007a, 2007b; Goodger, Wolfenden, et al., 2007; Gould, Tuffey, et al., 1996; Gustafsson, Hassmén, Kenttä, & Johansson, 2008; Gustafsson, Kenttä, Hassmén, Lundqvist, et al., 2007).

At this point, further consideration of the nature of a syndrome is required to fully grasp what Maslach and Jackson (1981, 1986) accomplished and did not accomplish in conceptualizing burnout in this manner. In broad terms, a syndrome is a constellation of signs and symptoms that present defining features for a condition of epidemiological significance. Identifying the defining manifestations (or symptoms) of the chronic maladaptive state, however, does not amount to understanding the syndrome's nature or underlying causes. Nonetheless, it does help frame scientific inquiry that can offer greater understanding of puzzling and problematic health conditions. Refinements to characterizations of syndromes can occur as evidence emerges on what is core or spurious to the underlying nature. Once the underlying nature and causes of a syndrome have been identified, the syndrome itself largely ceases to be of interest. At that point, the primary research focus is on more fundamental etiological and interventional issues.

Conceptualizing burnout as a syndrome was not an outgrowth of extant psychosocial theory. Rather, it was grounded in grassroots observation of people's experiences in the workplace (Maslach, Schaufeli, & Leiter, 2001). Chronic exposure to work-place-related interpersonal stressors was posited to be the etiological basis of this persistent aversive experiential state. The burnout syndrome has been examined extensively in workplace settings and has been associated with negative consequences such as decreased performance, low motivation, impaired health, personal dysfunction, insomnia, increased use of alcohol and drugs, and marital and family problems (Maslach & Goldberg, 1998; Maslach, Jackson, & Leiter, 1996).

Paralleling the organizational psychology literature, the most widely employed conceptualization of the athlete burnout syndrome has been forwarded by Raedeke (1997; Raedeke & Smith, 2001, 2009; Raedeke, Lunney, & Venables, 2002). In this conceptualization, the burnout syndrome among athletes is characterized by an enduring experience of (a) emotional and physical exhaustion, (b) sport devaluation, and (c) reduced sense of accomplishment.

This sport-specific conceptualization of the syndrome is fundamentally grounded in Maslach and Jackson's (1981, 1986) seminal work, albeit with minor modification. The general notion of a sense of reduced personal accomplishment being symptomatic of athlete burnout was mapped over without problem from Maslach and Jackson's (1981, 1986) syndrome, but other syndrome facets were subject to some alteration. Specifically, Raedeke (1997; Raedeke & Smith, 2001) broadened Maslach and Jackson's (1981, 1986) emotional exhaustion construct to include the chronic experience of physical exhaustion. This decision has intuitive appeal given the central place of physicality in sport, and it is consistent with the broader exhaustion construct assessed in the MGI-GS, which was introduced in the third edition of the MBI manual (Maslach et al., 1996). The depersonalization construct was also modified. It held limited relevance to athlete burnout, given that athletes were not involved in human services. Raedeke replaced it with sport devaluation (i.e., diminished and cynical assessment of the benefits of sport involvement) to better capture the experiential manifestation of burnout among athletes. This decision paralleled depersonalization being reconceptualized in the general burnout literature as a manifestation of the broader issue of cynicism in the workplace (e.g., Maslach et al., 1996; Maslach et al., 2001).

Sources of Confusion About Athlete Burnout

Most of the recent research has been grounded in Raedeke's (1997; Raedeke & Smith, 2001, 2009) psychosocial syndrome conceptualization of athlete burnout. However, other conceptualizations (e.g., Coakley, 1992; Silva, 1990) can be found in the extant sport science literature. This variation in conceptualization can complicate meaningful communication about the construct (Eklund & Cresswell, 2007). Difficulties on this account are exacerbated by widespread, idiomatic use of the term *burnout* in sport (Raedeke et al., 2002). The "everybody knows what it is" problem (Marsh, 1998, p. xvi) is clearly a salient source of confusion surrounding the athlete burnout construct. Most sport-specific usages and conceptualizations are interrelated in important ways, but important differences also exist.

Coakley (1992), for example, viewed burnout as an unwarranted termination of youth sport involvement after intense investment and substantial competitive accomplishment. He postulated that the social organization and constraints of intense sport involvement disempower young athletes by limiting their autonomy and restricting their opportunities for identity development beyond the athletic role. In his view, athletes burn out (i.e., drop out) of sport in order to exercise personal autonomy and explore new self-dimensions rather than remain in aversive circumstances. Eklund and Cresswell (2007) noted that this shooting star conceptualization of athlete burnout (i.e., talented, young athletes who suddenly leave sport before fully reaching their potential) does seem to underlie, at least in part, the interest in funding some research programs on athlete burnout (e.g., Gould, Tuffey, et al., 1996). Nonetheless, Coakley's conceptualization contrasts noticeably with other frameworks (e.g., Raedeke, 1997; Silva, 1990; Smith, 1986) in which dropout is viewed as a potential, but not requisite, *consequence* of burnout. Indeed, athletes experiencing the burnout syndrome do not always withdraw from sport (Eklund & Gould, 2008; Raedeke, 1997; Smith, 1986). It would be unfortunate if these athletes were ignored by practice or research focusing solely on the shooting stars.

Other researchers reference burnout in conceptualizing overtraining or underrecovery (e.g., Gould & Dieffenbach, 2002; Kellman, 2002a, 2002b; Kentta, Hassmen, & Raglin, 2001; Silva, 1990). Silva's views are commonly invoked on this account. Silva (1990) posited that burnout is the most extreme of three maladaptive phases in a regressive training stress syndrome. Specifically, the progression toward burnout is initiated when the athlete experiences a training-induced performance plateau. Progression into the second phase occurs when continued exposure to training stress results in "detectable psychophysiological malfunctions, and is char-

acterized by easily observable changes in mental orientation and physical performance" (p. 10). In the ultimate and burnout phase of the training stress syndrome, "[t]he organism's ability to deal with the psychophysiological imposition of stress is depleted, and the response system is exhausted" (p. 11). The experiential symptoms of this phase are not inconsistent with those characterized in psychosocial syndrome accounts of burnout (e.g., Maslach, 1982; Raedeke, 1997; Raedeke & Smith, 2001). But nontrivial differences are also evident. For example, Silva argued that burnout is an end state preceded by performance plateaus and detectable performance malfunction. In contrast, the syndrome perspective views burnout not as the end state but as an aversive experiential state that is progressively associated with dysfunction both on and off the playing field (e.g., Cresswell & Eklund, 2004, 2006c, 2007a; Gould, Tuffey, et al., 1996; Maslach, 1982; Maslach et al., 1996; Maslach et al., 2001).

Also, in Silva's (1990) account, excessive and chronic exposure to training stimuli is requisite for progression into burnout. This contrasts starkly with the psychosocial syndrome conceptualization, in which training stimuli are among the potential antecedents but are not necessarily the primary antecedents of athlete burnout. A plethora of evidence from outside of sport indicates that training stress is not at all requisite to the attainment of maladaptive levels of the burnout syndrome (e.g., Maslach, 1982; Maslach et al., 2001). Within sport, interview data also suggest that excessive training is not the only pathway to burnout (Cresswell & Eklund, 2006c, 2007a, 2007b; Gould, Tuffey, et al., 1996; Gould et al., 1997; Gustafsson, Kenttä, Hassmén, Lundqvist, & Durand-Bush, 2007). As noted by Raglin and Wilson (2000), some researchers have indiscriminately used the term *burnout* to describe overtrained states among athletes. Raglin's (1993) observation that burnout and overtraining should be regarded as separate conditions requiring distinct interventions remains salient in light of the extant literature.

Finally, the question often arises as to whether burnout and depression are distinct experiential states (Maslach et al., 2001). Freudenberger (1975) clearly believed that there are important differences and argued that burnout is accompanied by anger and frustration whereas depression is accompanied by guilt. The crucial conceptual distinction that is highlighted the most frequently relates to experiential generality. Specifically, a depression diagnosis requires pervasive symptomatology that influences "nearly all activities" (DSM-IV, 1994, p. 320; Leiter & Durup, 1994). Burnout, on the other hand, tends to be situation specific, at least in early stages (Maslach, Jackson, & Leiter, 1997). Moreover, burnout measures have demonstrated discriminant validity when evaluated against measures of depression in both workplace (e.g., Firth, McIntee, McKeown, & Britton, 1986; Glass, McKnight, & Valdimarsdottir, 1993; Leiter & Durup, 1994; Schaufeli, Enzmann, & Girault, 1993) and sport (Cresswell & Eklund, 2006b) samples. The fact remains, however, that despite a long history of conceptual distinctness, there are striking similarities in burnout and depression symptomologies (Glass & McKnight, 1996). Nonetheless, and despite experiential commonalities, important empirically supported conceptual differences exist between burnout and depression constructs.

Overall, several sources of confusion about athlete burnout have been evident in the extant literature. It is in more recent efforts, particularly those of researchers directing their attention to the measurement of athlete burnout, that these points of conceptual confusion have been articulated clearly. Increased awareness of these conceptual distinctions has afforded more coherent and less ambiguous use of term *burnout* in recent literature. In the following section we describe three measurement tools that have been employed in the study of athlete burnout.

Burnout Measurement Tools for Athletes

We limit our discussion here to measurement of the athlete burnout syndrome and do not address measures employed to operationalize burnout-related constructs such as dropout (e.g., Coakley, 1992), failure adaptation (e.g., Tenenbaum, Jones, Kistantas, Sacks, & Berwick, 2003a), underrecovery (e.g., Kellman, 2002a), overtraining (e.g., Silva, 1990), training distress (e.g., Main & Grove, 2009), or depression (e.g., Cresswell & Eklund, 2006b). Kellman's Recovery-Stress Questionnaire for Athletes (RESTQ-Sport), for example, is a widely employed multidimensional instrument that can provide burnout-relevant information. Nonetheless, the RESTQ-Sport was not developed to measure athlete burnout per se, and hence its discussion lies beyond the purview of this chapter. To address the measurement of athlete burnout specifically, we focus our discussion on (a) the MBI (Maslach & Jackson, 1981, 1986; Maslach et al., 1996), (b) the EABI (Eades, 1990), and (c) the ABQ (Raedeke, 1997; Raedeke & Smith, 2001, 2009). A brief overview of these measures is provided in table 31.1, and greater details are offered in the following chapter subsections.

■ **Table 31.1** ■

Measures Assessing Athlete Burnout

Variable or concept	Measure	Subscale	Source	Website
Burnout	Maslach Burnout Inventory-General Survey (MBI-GS)	Professional efficacy (6 items), cynicism (5 items), and exhaustion (5 items)	Maslach, Jackson, & Leiter (1996)	www.mindgarden.com/products/mbi.htm
Athlete burnout	Eades Athletic Burnout Inventory (EABI)	Emotional and physical exhaustion (9 items), psychological withdrawal (7 items), devaluation by coach and teammates (6 items), negative self-concept of athletic ability (8 items), congruent athlete and coach expectations (3 items), and personal and athletic accomplishment (3 items)	Eades (1990)	
Athlete burnout	Athlete Burnout Questionnaire (ABQ)	Reduced sense of accomplishment (5 items), sport devaluation (5 items), and emotional and physical exhaustion (5 items)	Raedeke & Smith (2009)	http://wvuecommerce.wvu.edu/index.cfm?do=product.product&id=738191991%5F91w&product_id=2159

Maslach Burnout Inventories

Maslach and Jackson (1981) produced the first burnout syndrome measure, the MBI. Its incarnations (Maslach & Jackson, 1986; Maslach et al., 1996; Maslach et al., 2001) have come to be regarded as the gold standard for measuring workplace burnout. They also have been employed, in modified or unmodified forms, in a variety of sport-related investigations. Published reports of these efforts, however, have not involved athletes but rather coaches (e.g., Dale & Weinberg, 1989; Kelley, Eklund, & Ritter-Taylor, 1999; Raedeke, 2004; Raedeke, Granzyk, & Warren, 2000), athletic directors (e.g., Martin, Kelley, & Eklund, 1999), and athletic trainers (e.g., Giaccobi, 2009; Hendrix, Acevedo, & Hebert, 2000). Successful use of the MBI in these instances is likely related to the fact that the populations being studied occupied roles paralleling those for which the MBI was developed (i.e., human services personnel, educators). Modification of these MBI versions for use with athletes has been less successful, almost certainly because the athletic role does not parallel the direct service roles for which the educator and human services versions of the MBI were developed (Eklund & Cresswell, 2007). In fact, similar problems were encountered in modifying the original MBI versions for use outside of human services employment roles (Maslach et al., 2001; Schutte, Toppinen, Kalimo, & Schaufeli, 2000). The development of the general survey version (MBI-GS) occurred as a consequence (Schutte et al., 2000). With only minor word substitutions, the MBI-GS, unlike the MBI educator and human services versions, has shown utility for assessing burnout in athletes (Cresswell & Eklund, 2006b).

The MBI-GS contains 16 items that measure burnout on three subscales paralleling the original versions of the MBI: professional efficacy (6 items, such as, "I have accomplished many worthwhile things in this job"), cynicism (5 items, such as, "I have become less enthusiastic about my work"), and exhaustion (5 items, such as, "I feel emotionally drained from my work"). Items are measured on a 7-point response format with anchors of "Never" to "Every day." Scores on the MBI-GS have been reported to exhibit acceptable reliability as well as factorial validity across a range of workplace (Schutte et al., 2000) and athlete (Cresswell & Eklund, 2006b) samples.

Eades Athletic Burnout Inventory

For her master's degree, Eades (1990) tackled the task of creating an inventory to measure athlete burnout. The resulting unpublished instrument, the EABI, was greeted with considerable initial enthusiasm by researchers interested in athlete burnout. As a consequence, it has been employed as a key measure in some published research (e.g., Gould, Udry, Tuffey, & Loehr, 1996; Gustafsson, Kenttä, Hassmén, & Lundqvist, 2007; Vealey, Armstrong, Comar, & Greenleaf, 1998).

Eades (1990) identified potential items by eclectically drawing from the extant burnout literature, the MBI, and anecdotes from athletes deemed to have experienced burnout. Participants respond to items on a 7-point Likert-type scale with anchors of "Never" to "Every day." EFA suggested subscales of emotional and physical exhaustion (9 items), psychological withdrawal (7 items), devaluation by coach and teammates (6 items), negative self-concept of athletic ability (8 items), congruent athlete and coach expectations (3 items), and personal and athletic accomplishment (3 items).

Despite the initial enthusiasm, the EABI has been found to have both conceptual and psychometric shortcomings. The atheoretical and idiosyncratic nature of the EABI renders data interpretation difficult because the subscales represent a mix of burnout syndrome facets and antecedents (Raedeke & Smith, 2001). Moreover, CFA procedures revealed the factor structure to be tenuous even after removal of 5 problematic items (Vealey et al., 1998) or the two 3-item subscales (Gustafsson, Kenttä, Hassmén, & Lundqvist, 2007). Unsatisfactory internal consistency reliability is typical for the two 3-item subscales (e.g., Gould, Udry, et al., 1996; Gustafsson, Kenttä, Hassmén, & Lundqvist, 2007; Vealey et al., 1998). Overall, though development of the EABI can be credited with catalyzing athlete burnout research, there seems to be little reason to employ this instrument in future research given its conceptual and psychometric weaknesses.

Athlete Burnout Questionnaire

Stimulated by EABI inadequacies and an interest in studying athlete burnout, Raedeke (1997; Raedeke & Smith, 2001, 2009) developed the ABQ. The ABQ is a 15-item instrument designed to quantify Raedeke's (1997) conceptualization of the athlete burnout syndrome. The stem for each item is, "How often do you feel this way?" Athletes respond to each item on a 5-point Likert scale with 1 = "Almost never," 2 = "Rarely," 3 = "Sometimes," 4 = "Frequently," and 5 = "Almost always."[1] Items are designed to measure the key burnout symptoms of (a) reduced sense of

---

[1]"Most of the time" was used by Raedeke and Smith (2001) in their initial version of the ABQ, and it has subsequently been used elsewhere (e.g., Cresswell & Eklund, 2006c).

accomplishment (e.g., "It seems that no matter what I do, I don't perform as well as I should"), (b) sport devaluation (e.g., "I have negative feelings toward sport"), and (c) emotional and physical exhaustion (e.g., "I am exhausted by the mental and physical demands of my sport"). Raedeke and Smith (2001) presented construct validation evidence for ABQ responses and reported acceptable internal consistency reliability (with subscale coefficient alphas ranging from .71-.87) and test–retest reliability (with intraclass correlations ranging from .86-.92). In addition, the proposed factor structure of the items has been supported through CFA (for a review, see Raedeke & Smith, 2009).

Lonsdale, Hodge, and Rose (2006) have presented evidence on the psychometric equivalence of Internet and traditional paper-and-pencil collection of ABQ data. Raedeke and Smith (2001, 2009) advocate a minor word substitution strategy (e.g., replacing *sport* with *swimming*) to make the instrument more specific for a particular sample, as is the long-standing practice with the MBI. Other researchers have also found this tactic to be useful. For example, Cresswell and Eklund (2005b) changed *sport* to *rugby* in their study of burnout among amateur New Zealand rugby union players.

Subsequent to the initial three-study validation evidence presented by Raedeke and Smith (2001), Cresswell and Eklund (2006b) reported additional compelling ABQ validity evidence from MTMM analyses of data obtained from elite amateur New Zealand rugby players. These MTMM analyses were conducted with data obtained from two measures of athlete burnout (the ABQ and a version of the MBI-GS modified for athletes) as well as a general measure of depression and anxiety (the Depression Anxiety Stress Scale; Lovibond & Lovibond, 1995). Overall, the ABQ and MBI-GS scores displayed acceptable convergent validity, with matching subscales highly correlated, and satisfactory internal discriminant validity, with lower correlations between nonmatching subscales. In the MBI-GS, 2 of the items from the cynicism subscale exhibited psychometric difficulties in the New Zealand rugby player data. Importantly, scores on both scales indicated adequate discrimination between depression and burnout constructs. The psychometric results, construct validity analysis, and practical considerations (e.g., development for use in sport settings) of the ABQ support its use to assess athlete burnout.

Sample Studies Using the ABQ From the Literature

In assessing the construct validity of responses to athlete burnout measures, it is important to conduct theory-grounded efforts that offer what is referred to as *between-network* (Marsh, 1998), or *nomological* (Rowe & Mahar, 2006), evidence. With the introduction of measurement tools for assessing athlete burnout in the literature, theory-grounded studies have been conducted that address the link between athlete burnout and various individual difference, stress-related, and motivation-related constructs (e.g., Black & Smith, 2007; Cresswell & Eklund, 2004, 2005a, 2005b, 2005c, 2006a; Hill, Hall, Appleton, & Kozub, 2008; Lemyre, Treasure, & Roberts, 2006; Lemyre, Hall, & Roberts, 2008; Lonsdale, Hodge, & Rose, 2009; Perreault, Gaudreau, Lapoint, & Lacroix, 2007; Raedeke & Smith, 2004). Given recent reviews of the athlete burnout literature (e.g., Eklund & Cresswell, 2007; Goodger, Gorely, et al., 2007; Gould & Whitley, 2009; Raedeke & Smith, 2009), only a couple of the most recently published studies are reviewed here (i.e., Hill et al., 2008; Lonsdale et al., 2009).

Lonsdale and colleagues (2009) examined the potential mediating effects of self-determined motivation in the relationship between psychological need satisfaction in sport (i.e., autonomy, competence, relatedness) and athlete burnout symptoms. Cross-sectional data were obtained from elite Canadian athletes (121 females, 80 males; mean age = 22.9 y), with the ABQ used to tap athlete burnout perceptions. Overall, less self-determined motives showed positive associations and more self-determined motives showed negative correlations with burnout. These findings replicated the results of several of other studies (e.g., Cresswell & Eklund, 2005a, 2005b, 2005c; Lemyre et al., 2006; Raedeke, 1997). Moreover, the mediation analyses suggested that the extent of self-determined motivation (as indicated by the use of a self-determination index) fully mediated the relationships between satisfaction of competence and autonomy needs and the burnout symptom of emotional and physical exhaustion as well as the relationship between autonomy and sport devaluation. Motivation partially mediated the relationships of competence and autonomy with the burnout symptoms of sport devaluation and decreased sense of accomplishment, respectively. These findings highlight the importance of psychological need satisfaction in efforts to prevent, or perhaps ameliorate, burnout among athletes. Moreover, the findings are in line with theoretical conceptions of the link between burnout and motivation, offering between-network support for the construct validity of ABQ responses.

Perfectionism, a personality characteristic reflecting a compulsive need to pursue excessively high standards accompanied by overly critical self-evaluation, has long been an individual difference factor of interest to burnout researchers and practitioners (e.g., Feigley, 1984; Gould, Udry, et al., 1996). In recent years, several studies have examined this construct relative to athlete burnout (e.g., Appleton, Hall, & Hill, 2009; Chen, Kee, Chen, & Tsai, 2008; Chen, Kee, & Tsai, 2009; Hill et al., 2008; Lemyre et al., 2008). Among these is a youth sport investigation by Hill and colleagues that examined unconditional self-acceptance as a possible mediator of the relationship between perfectionism (self-oriented and socially prescribed dimensions) and athlete burnout as measured by the ABQ in elite junior soccer players. As expected, both perfectionism dimensions were inversely related to unconditional self-acceptance among athletes. Unconditional self-acceptance partially mediated relationships between the two dimensions of perfectionism and athlete burnout. Interestingly, though expected direct effects were observed (i.e., self-oriented perfectionism inversely and socially prescribed perfectionism positively related to burnout), a positive self-oriented perfectionism indirect effect (i.e., mediated through unconditional self-acceptance) was also observed. Hill and colleagues concluded that a contingent sense of self-worth is central to both socially prescribed and self-oriented perfectionism and may underpin maladaptive achievement striving and increased vulnerability to athlete burnout. Clearly this contention awaits experimental confirmation, but the possibility is intriguing nonetheless.

Consistent with extant literature offering support for the construct validity of athlete responses to the ABQ, the two investigations just described offer between-network evidence of the efficacy of ABQ scores in reflecting the experiential syndrome of burnout. Specifically, these investigations showed that individual difference and motivation-related constructs link with burnout in theoretically expected ways. Although the construct validation of athlete burnout responses to the ABQ is an ongoing process, the evidence to date suggests that the ABQ has been a helpful tool in pushing forward the athlete burnout knowledge base.

Recommendations for Researchers and Practitioners

Although recent years have been marked by increased interest in athlete burnout, the scientific study of athlete burnout remains in its infancy (Eklund & Cresswell, 2007; Raedeke & Smith, 2009). As such, many avenues of potential research in the area exist, including those directly related to measurement issues. Clearly, there is a need for research

to delineate burnout syndrome scores, whether obtained on the ABQ or the MBI-GS, into normative categories of reference (i.e., high, medium, low). Epidemiological study of the construct across sports, athlete subgroups, and competitive levels could facilitate the provision of such normative information (Eklund & Cresswell, 2007). Identification of more specific criterion-referenced cutoff points relative to particular burnout-related conditions is also warranted (Raedeke & Smith, 2009).

Extant data on athlete burnout have largely been acquired with the ABQ from English-speaking populations, including athletes in the United States (e.g., Raedeke, 1997), Canada (e.g., Lonsdale et al., 2009), New Zealand (e.g., Cresswell & Eklund, 2004, 2006b; Lonsdale et al., 2006), and the United Kingdom (Appleton et al., 2009). Evaluation of cross-cultural psychometric equivalence of responses to the ABQ English version is warranted but not yet examined. More challenging from a psychometric perspective is the yet unsatisfied need to establish equivalency across translated versions of the ABQ, including Chinese (Chen et al., 2009), French (Perreault et al., 2007), German (Ziemainz, Abu-Omar, Raedeke, & Krause, 2004), Norwegian (Lemyre et al., 2008), Spanish (De Franciso, Arce, Andrade, Arce, & Raedeke, 2009) and Swedish (Gustafsson, Kenttä, Hassmén, Lundqvist, & Durand-Bush, 2007) versions.

Aside from research to address psychometric issues, there are many practical and theoretical issues worthy of investigation. The pursuit of longitudinal monitoring of burnout in athlete populations offers considerable potential for understanding syndrome developmental patterns under a variety of conditions. Both idiographic and nomothetic longitudinal studies would enrich knowledge about this syndrome. Certainly, the examination of process models relative to syndrome facets has been a matter of interest among burnout researchers beyond sport (e.g., Golembiewski, Munzenrider, & Carter, 1983; Maslach et al., 2001; Plana, Fabregat, & Gassió, 2003; Van Dierendonck, Schaufeli, & Buunk, 2001). This also merits further consideration and investigation among athletes. Research on intervention strategies to prevent or ameliorate burnout among athletes is also needed (Eklund & Cresswell, 2007). Research on workplace interventions has shown promise (Maslach, 2003) and may prove useful in shaping intervention directions in sport settings. Certainly, however, the sport setting differs in important ways from the settings investigated in the workplace literature. Therefore, investigations of interventions suitable for and specific to sport are required (Eklund & Cresswell, 2007; Feigley, 1984; Garden, 1987). Such work will meaningfully benefit not only theoretical understanding of athlete burnout but also the prevention and treatment of the athlete burnout syndrome.

Research in general workplaces and in the health and human services indicates that high burnout levels are associated with a variety of undesirable outcomes. These outcomes include decreased performance, low motivation, impaired health, personal dysfunction, insomnia, increased use of alcohol and drugs, and marital and family problems (Maslach & Goldberg, 1998; Maslach et al., 1996). Interview data obtained from professional rugby players provide preliminary evidence of similar difficulties for athletes (Cresswell & Eklund, 2006c, 2007a, 2007b). Interpretation of the extent to which ABQ measurement can provide indications of clinically meaningful levels of burnout on this account, however, is tenuous at this point (Eklund & Cresswell, 2007; Raedeke & Smith, 2009). It seems unreasonable to believe that athletes experiencing symptoms in the range of "Rarely" to "Sometimes" experience meaningful difficulties from burnout. Athletes experiencing symptoms more frequently than that may be at risk for the various burnout-related maladaptive behaviors, but large-scale epidemiological studies providing a reliable normative base on these accounts have yet to be conducted. Moreover, research linking specific threshold values to elevated risk of the emergence of maladaptive behaviors has yet to be conducted. Suggestive findings are evident in the literature, but the empirical basis for supporting conclusions that an athlete might be at risk for the emergence of negative burnout-associated consequences is not yet available—regardless of the level of an observed ABQ score. Even the MBI, with its well-established norms, does not provide this sort of interpretive guidance. The MBI manual suggests the following:

> The coding itself is intended primarily as feedback for individual respondents. It enables each respondent to compare him or herself to the overall norm, and to obtain a rough assessment of the degree of his or her experience with the various aspects of burnout. However, neither the coding, nor the original numerical scores should be used for diagnosis purposes; there is insufficient research on the pattern(s) of scores as indicators of individual dysfunction or the need for intervention. (Maslach et al., 1996, p. 9)

Given that the ABQ should not be used for diagnostic purposes at this point of development,

clinical judgment and ethical practice in interpreting longitudinal monitoring data probably afford the soundest path forward for practitioners. At present, it does not appear that burnout is a substantial problem for most athletes. A relatively small proportion of athletes surveyed to date have reported relatively high scores on burnout dimensions. However, interpreting the magnitude of ABQ scores should be done with caution given the lack of normative data or clinically derived cutoff points indicating high burnout. Also, research to date may underestimate the number of athletes with high burnout scores, as studies have sampled active participants who have volunteered to participate in the research. It is plausible that some athletes experiencing burnout are not represented in such studies. Nonetheless, even if only a small proportion of athletes experience burnout, this issue is of practical significance due to the high cost of burnout in terms of individual experience. Moreover, even a small proportion can represent a large number of athletes in light of the extent of participation in serious competitive sport around the world.

The recent growth in athlete burnout research can, in part, be attributed to the emerging availability of measures to assess the burnout syndrome. Getting to this point has required researchers to carefully consider core signs and symptoms that present defining features of the syndrome as well as the causal sequencing of burnout-related constructs relative to the syndrome conceptualization—in short, to address various sources of extant conceptual confusion about athlete burnout. These endeavors are far from complete, but the availability of tools such as the ABQ and MBI-GS has contributed to progress in scientific understanding of this issue. Of course, assessment of measurement efficacy and adequacy is always an incomplete and ongoing process. Measures of athlete burnout also require continued assessment and, where appropriate, refinement to remain useful in advancing science in this area. Presently, the ABQ and the MBI-GS have shown promise as athlete burnout measurement tools. The ABQ in particular has exhibited considerable practical utility on this account over the past decade. Much research on the athlete burnout construct remains to be conducted, but the availability of promising instruments to extend the present knowledge base is encouraging.

Bayesian Approach of Measuring Competitive Crisis

Michael Bar-Eli, PhD, and Gershon Tenenbaum, PhD

In the first decades of the 18th century, many problems concerning the *forward probability* term were solved. The problems referred to determining the probability of certain events, given specified conditions; for example, what is the probability of drawing a black ball, given a specific number of white and black balls in an urn? A completely converse problem is the following: What can be said about the number of white and black balls in an urn, given that one or more balls have already been drawn from that urn? Such questions refer to *inverse probability*, for which the Reverend Thomas Bayes (1702-1761) was the first to provide a solution.

According to Bellhouse (2004), it was Bayes' friend Richard Price (1723-1791), a minister himself, who revised that paper and communicated it to the Royal Society about 2 years after Bayes' death. Price, who was deeply engaged in theological work, described his own motivation to work on Bayes' essay as resulting from his belief that it provided a proof of the existence of God (Price, 1767). Over the years, Bayes' theorem was shown to rest on a valid theoretical interpretation of probability and has gained importance mainly in diagnostic contexts. For example, when a patient is observed to have a particular symptom (e.g., tests positive for HIV), Bayes' theorem can be applied to compute the probability that given that observation, a proposed diagnosis is correct (e.g., the patient really has an HIV infection).

Such applications rest on using Bayes' theorem to relate the conditional and marginal probabilities of two random events, often to compute posterior probabilities given observations. However, the Bayesian approach has also played a central role in the debate concerning the foundations of statistics by being part of the *frequentist* and Bayesian interpretations debate about how to assign probabilities in applications. Whereas the frequentists (see Reichenbach, 1949; Venn, 1876/1962; Von Mises, 1928/1957) assign probabilities to random events according to their occurrence frequencies or to subsets of populations as proportions of the whole, the proponents of the Bayesian approach describe probabilities in terms of subjective degrees of belief in propositions regarding uncertainty (e.g., De Finetti, 1980; Ramsey, 1931/1980/1990).

Since the 1950s, Bayesian statistics have acquired immense importance and have penetrated many areas, including those where the application of such methods originally appeared to be quite impossible. For example, on February 18, 2009, a computerized search in Google for *applications of Bayesian statistics* resulted in about 534,000 items! Bayesian statistics have been applied in different and remote areas such as actuarial science, auditing, bioinformatics, biological monitoring, biostatistics, ecology, econometrics, educational measurement, engineering, epidemiology, geophysics, hydrology, image retrieval, information processing, law, medicine, meteorology, neurology, pharmacology, quality assurance, schizophrenia diagnosis, spatial data analysis, and terrain navigation (for a recent review, see Upadhyay, Singh, & Dey, 2007).

In essence, Bayesian inference involves collecting evidence that should be consistent or inconsistent with a given hypothesis. As evidence accumulates, the degree of belief in a hypothesis ought to change; with sufficient evidence, it becomes pronounced. Thus, this method can be used to discriminate among conflicting hypotheses; in principle, hypotheses with relatively high support should be accepted as true, and those with relatively low support should be rejected as false. The degree of belief (subjective probability) in any hypothesis before evidence has been observed is later calculated. This process is repeated time and again when additional evidence is obtained.

A logical consequence of this inference process is that the Bayesian approach has become deeply embedded within decision theory. The basic tenets of decision theory are that opinions should be expressed in terms of subjective (i.e., personal) probabilities and that optimal revisions of such opinions, in light of new relevant information, should be conducted using Bayes' theorem, particularly for situations in which it leads to decision making and action. Because of the concern with judgment and decision making, the output of a Bayesian analysis is often a distribution of probabilities over a set of hypothesized states of the world rather than a single prediction. These probabilities can be used, in combination with information about payoffs associated with different states of the world and decision possibilities, to implement any of a number of decision rules. In addition, Bayes' theorem can be used as a normative model that specifies some internally consistent relationships among probabilistic opinions and serves to prescribe how people should think (Rappaport & Wallsten, 1972).

Bayesian Notions in Psychology: An Approach to Judgment and Decision Making

The first person to introduce Bayesian notions to psychology was Ward Edwards (1927-2005) in the early 1960s (e.g., Edwards, 1962a; Edwards, Lindman, & Savage, 1963). He also introduced the concept of subjective expected utility, which rested heavily on the idea of subjective probability (Edwards, 1962b). During the 1960s, Edwards and colleagues conducted several studies to determine how well the Bayesian model describes changes in human behavior as new information is received. This work revealed the phenomenon of conservatism (Edwards, 1968; Phillips & Edwards, 1966; Phillips, Hays, & Edwards, 1966)—that is, the insufficient readiness of people to change their minds in the face of new evidence presented to them. In response to this consistent finding, Edwards (1962a; Edwards, Phillips, Hays, & Goodman, 1968) enthusiastically proposed a system in which a computer could use Bayes' theorem to put together the

pieces of information, with experts providing the likelihood inputs. This system was later dubbed *probabilistic information processing* (PIP). The central principle of such a system can be described as follows: The psychologist lets people (e.g., experts) estimate the probability $P(D|H)$ that a particular datum (D) will be observed when a specific hypothesis (H) is given. Later, the computer integrates all $P(D|H)$ estimations across data and hypotheses using Bayes' theorem. After all relevant data have been processed, the final output (i.e., the revised opinion) is presented in the form of a posterior probability $P(H|D)$ for each hypothesis (H) under consideration, taking into account each and every datum (D) available.

Toward the end of the 1960s, several hundred studies were aimed at investigating how people use information to arrive at a judgment or a decision; much of this work was done within a paradigm based on probability theory, particularly Bayes' theorem. In a seminal article, to which an entire issue of *Organizational Behavior and Human Performance* was devoted, Slovic and Lichtenstein (1971) reviewed this research. They indicated that PIP systems also attempted to cope with another serious limitation of human judgment and decision making—namely, misaggregation (Gettys & Manley, 1968; Hammond, Kelly, Schneider, & Vancini, 1967; Kaplan & Newman, 1966; Schum, Goldstein, Howell, & Southard, 1967). More specifically, it seemed that due to cognitive overload, people confronted with judgment and decision-making tasks often had substantial difficulties in aggregating (i.e., weighing and combining) information. Therefore, many of the decision aids proposed at that time—including the PIP system—reflected the old Roman concept of *divide et impera* ("divide and rule"), according to which larger concentrations of power are divided into less powerful chunks that are more easy to conquer and control. Slovic, Fischhoff, and Lichtenstein (1977) called this strategy *decomposition*, which implies that a decision aid (e.g., PIP system) breaks down an entire problem into smaller, structurally related elements. The decision maker is then requested to provide subjective estimations regarding only smaller—if possible, the smallest—components, which are much simpler to handle compared with the original, global problem. Later on, these estimations are combined with the help of the computer.

The main role of the human participant in a PIP system is to estimate the diagnostic effect of each and every separate datum. The machine (computer), which combines these estimations via Bayes' theorem, relieves the decision maker from the task of integrating the various pieces of information, thereby contributing substantially to coping with the major difficulty of information aggregation. Moreover, PIP systems have been used not only for diagnostic purposes but also for parameter estimation in cases where objective values could not be calculated and only human probabilistic parameter judgments were available.

Theory of Psychological Performance Crisis

Bar-Eli (1984) contended that during the past several decades, the inverted-U hypothesis (Yerkes & Dodson, 1908) has dominated the motor behavior literature in accounting for the relationship between arousal and performance. He indicated that this hypothesis, the Yerkes-Dodson law, was used in many domains of general psychology, such as organizational behavior, motivation, and stress and anxiety. In addition, this law enjoyed wide acceptance among researchers and practitioners in sport and exercise psychology, mainly because of its great deal of appeal for athletes, coaches, and applied sport psychologists. Bar-Eli noticed that despite the fact that it had received fairly consistent empirical support, it had also received a considerable amount of criticism. Thus it seemed that the relationship between arousal and performance was somewhat more complex than the simple inverted-U form.

Most of the alternatives suggested to the inverted-U hypothesis (see Gould, Greenleaf, & Krane, 2002) attempted to clarify either the true arousal–performance relationship or the way to determine the optimal level of arousal required for maximal performance in advance of competition. In contrast, the theory of psychological performance crisis, initially suggested by Bar-Eli (1984) and later developed further by Bar-Eli and Tenenbaum (1989a), was proposed with reference to the inverted-U hypothesis but with a focused attempt to conceptualize the organization (or disorganization) of an athlete's behavior *during* competition. In this context, the Bayesian method was applied, which is unique in the sport and exercise setting.

Summarized in short, the crisis model assumes that athletes in competition frequently experience psychological stress that can elevate their arousal levels and negatively affect their performance. Under extreme levels of arousal, the athlete may enter a psychological performance crisis, a state in which the ability to cope adequately with competitive requirements substantially deteriorates. According to Bar-Eli and Tenenbaum (1989a), a crisis develops when an athlete (conceived of as

a system) is no longer characterized by stability (phase A) but is progressively under- or overcharged and thus is characterized by lability (phase B). In the case of extreme lability, failure of coping may lead to crisis (phase C). If events C (crisis) and C' (no crisis) are defined as mutually exclusive and exhaustive, then $P(C) + P(C') = 1$. In phase A, $P(C) << P(C')$; in phase B, $P(C) < P(C')$ or $P(C) \approx P(C')$ or $P(C) > P(C')$; and in phase C, $P(C) >> P(C')$. The probabilities of all phases sum to 1.

Bayes' Theorem: A Measurement Tool for Developing the Individual Performance Psychological Crisis

The Bayesian method was used to establish a formal diagnostic framework for the development of an athlete's psychological performance crisis in competition (for details, see Bar-Eli & Tenenbaum, 1989a). The probabilistic measure of diagnostic value used for this purpose consists of Bayes' theorem.

Bayesian Principles

The crucial elements of the Bayesian model are conditional probabilities—that is, probabilities with an *if, then* character ("If so and so is true, then the probability of this event must be such and such"). Thus, Bayes' theorem states that given several mutually exclusive and exhaustive hypotheses, H_i (where i is the number of hypotheses), and a datum, D (a new item of information),

$$P(H_i \mid D) = \frac{P(D \mid H_i)P(H_i)}{\Sigma P(D \mid H_i)P(H_i)} . \qquad \textbf{32.1}$$

This formula has three basic elements:

1. Prior probability. $P(H_i)$ is the prior probability of hypothesis H_i. It represents the probability of H_i conditional on all information available before the receipt of datum D.

2. Posterior probability. $P(H_i \mid D)$ is the posterior probability that H_i is true, taking into account the new datum D *as well as* all previous data.

3. Effect of new datum. $P(D \mid H_i)$ is the conditional probability that the datum D will be observed if hypothesis H_i is true.

For a set of mutually exclusive and exhaustive hypotheses, H_i, the values of $P(D \mid H_i)$ represent the effect of the datum D on *each* of the hypotheses. Suppose, for example, that a soccer coach decides to try out a new test for admitting players to the team. In such a case, two exclusive and exhaustive hypotheses may be defined: H_1, the player succeeds in the team, and H_2, the player does not succeed in the team. Before the introduction of the new test (D), the proportion $P(H_1)/P(H_2)$ reflects the chances of each player to succeed or not succeed based on all previous tests that have been conducted (therefore, the term *prior probability*). After the introduction of the new test (D), the chances of each player succeeding or failing are reflected by the proportion $P(H_1|D)/P(H_2|D)$, which takes into account the results of the new test *as well as* the old ones (therefore, the term *posterior probability*). According to the model, however, it is crucial to also know the probability of a particular score in the test (D), given the fact that the player succeeded or failed in the team, $P(D|H_1)/P(D|H_2)$. That is, if the player succeeded or failed in the team, what score did that player (probably) get? This proportion reflects the effect of the new test on both hypotheses.

Equation 32.1 is appropriate for discrete hypotheses, but it can be rewritten, using integrals, to handle a continuous set of hypotheses and continuously varying data (with the denominator in equation 32.1 serving as a normalizing constant). It is, however, often convenient to form the ratio of equation 32.1 taken with respect to two hypotheses, H_i and H_j:

$$\frac{P(H_i|D)}{P(H_j|D)} = \frac{P(D|H_i)P(H_j)}{P(D|H_j)P(H_j)} \qquad \textbf{32.2}$$

For this ratio form, new symbols are introduced:

$$\Omega_1 = LR \cdot \Omega_0, \qquad \textbf{32.3}$$

where Ω_1 represents the posterior odds, *LR* is the likelihood ratio, and Ω_0 represents the prior odds.

Bayes' theorem can be used sequentially to measure the effects of several data. The posterior probability computed for the first datum is considered as the prior probability when processing the effect of the second datum, and so on. Thus the terms *prior* and *posterior* are relative, depending on where a person is in the process of gathering information. The order in which data are processed makes no difference to their effects on posterior opinion; the final posterior odds (given *n* items of data) are

$$\Omega_n = II\ LR_k \cdot \Omega_o. \qquad \textbf{32.4}$$

According to equation 32.4, the data affect the final odds multiplicatively, and the degree to which the prior odds are revised upon receipt of any new datum is dependent on that datum's likelihood ratio (LR). Thus, the LR is an index of data diagnosticity (or importance, analogous to the weights employed in regression models, see Rapoport & Wallsten, 1972; Slovic & Lichtenstein, 1971). This may become

clearer when we think about hypotheses such as sick (H_1) and healthy (H_2) and a particular symptom (D) diagnosed by a medical doctor. Similarly, we could think about events (hypotheses) such as "It will rain tomorrow" or "It will not rain tomorrow" (given that the weather forecast has been such and such), "A defendant is guilty" or "A defendant is not guilty" (given that a particular piece of evidence has been presented to the court), or "The team will win" or "The team will not win" (given that the star player is in such-and-such shape).

The crisis model (summarized briefly earlier in the chapter) was used to diagnose the development of an athlete's psychological performance crisis in competition. The probabilistic measure of diagnostic value used for this purpose was based on the Bayesian approach. H_i and H_j in equation 32.2 were replaced by the two following mutually exclusive and exhaustive hypotheses:

1. C—the athlete is in a psychological performance crisis during the competition.

2. C'—the athlete is not in a psychological performance crisis during the competition.

Equation 32.2 then took the form of

$$\frac{P(C|D)}{P(C'|D)} = \frac{P(D|C)P(C)}{P(D|C')P(C')}. \qquad \textbf{32.5}$$

As noted, when a total problem is fractionated, or decomposed, into a series of structurally related parts and then experts are asked to assess these fractions, processes such as judgment and decision making are substantially improved (e.g., Armstrong, Denniston, & Gordon, 1975; Gettys, Michel, Steiger, Kelly, & Peterson, 1973). In the case of only two hypotheses, H_i and H_j, people estimate $P(D|H_i)$ and $P(D|H_j)$ values, which are integrated across data and across hypotheses by means of Bayes' theorem (see equation 32.2). After all the relevant data have been processed, the resulting output is a ratio of posterior probabilities, $P(H_i|D)/P(H_j|D)$. In this way, a probabilistic diagnosis may be facilitated, as was just demonstrated (Edwards, 1962a; Slovic & Lichtenstein, 1971).

A diagnosis of crisis development requires that diagnostic factors be identified. Through these factors, the problem of diagnosing an athlete's psychological performance crisis in competition was fractionated (decomposed). Each factor included several components (i.e., Bayesian data) that could be assessed separately by experts with regard to their probability of occurrence when a crisis, $P(D|C)$, or a noncrisis $P(D|C')$, occurs. Later on, the ratio of $P(C|D)/P(C'|D)$ could be computed by Bayes' rule (equation 32.3).

At this point, the Bayesian model, as presented in equation 32.5, could be used as follows. Upon exposure to information about the existence of a particular datum (i.e., a component of one of the diagnostic factors), the ratio of probabilities concerning the occurrence of the two events, C and C′, is revised, all previous data being taken into account. For this purpose, however, the technical hurdle of computerizing such a diagnosis process should be overcome. Furthermore, posterior probabilities should be associated preferably with practical measures aimed at coping with players' psychoregulative problems at each phase of crisis development during competition (Bar-Eli & Tenenbaum, 1989a).

Crisis-Related Factors

The principal logic of the Bayesian method initially applied in Bar-Eli's (1984) dissertation and further developed in a series of investigations conducted mainly from 1984 to 1996 (for review, see Bar-Eli, 1997) followed a certain logic. In order to identify crisis-related factors, the athlete's state in competition was systematically decomposed into its various facets. First was what happens to the athlete before the beginning of the contest. This issue had been dealt with intensively in applied contexts, especially in the former Eastern Bloc (the *prestart state*; e.g., Smirnow, 1974); thus, the first factor to be investigated was the athlete's prestart susceptibility to crisis. Since it was maintained from an action theoretical perspective that time in itself has a substantial strain-related meaning (e.g., Nitsch, 1976), the factor of *time phases* was investigated next to address some of the athlete's crisis-related experiences during the contest. These were derived from the concept of strain.

Another factor in the athlete's subjective reality in competition is related to performance on court. Based on action theory (e.g., Nitsch, 1982), the concept of *game standings* was developed and was later labeled *perceived team performance*. However, this factor was suggested to take into account other facets of an athlete's behavior on court beyond performance. Based on theories that emphasized the connection between anxiety and misdirection of attention (e.g., Wine, 1980, 1982) as well as different theoretical notions and empirical findings related to the interplay among aggression, behavioral violations, and crisis (e.g., Gabler, 1976; Nitsch, 1976), it was reasoned that both impaired motor performance and increased frequency and intensity of behavioral violations indicate an athlete's crisis in contest. Accordingly, the factor labeled *performance quality and behavioral violations* was investigated next.

More than three decades ago, teammates, coaches, spectators, and referees were identified as being central components of the athlete's subjectively perceived social environment on court (e.g., Gabler, 1976; Geron, 1975). These factors had been discussed briefly in the original version of crisis theory (Bar-Eli, 1984); however, they were intensively investigated only at the beginning of the 1990s. The design of research conducted on the various social factors—teammates, coaches, spectators, and referees—was similar and reflected the major principles of the Bayesian approach described earlier in this chapter.

Before we introduce the individual psychological crisis in competition, we should briefly demonstrate how Bayesian LRs are derived and then used for further analysis. Assuming that an individual's psychological crisis in team sport depends on teammates' expected or unexpected negative or positive responses to successful, unsuccessful, or independent actions of the player, a *measurement scheme* can be established in the form presented in figure 32.1. The form consists of factor A, the teammates' positive or negative responses to the player's actions; factor B, the expected or unexpected nature of the responses; and factor C, the successful, unsuccessful, or independent nature of the player's actions.

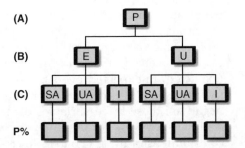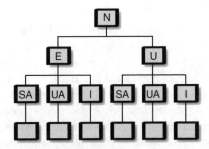

Figure 32.1   A template for assigning LR values (in percent, P%) in events. These LRs comprise three factors: (1) teammates' positive (P) and negative (N) responses; (2) expectations, either expected (E) or unexpected (U); and (3) player's successful actions (SA) or unsuccessful actions (UA) and things independent of the player's actions (I).

Experts are asked to indicate the percent of probability that the player is in a psychological crisis within each cell of interaction among the three factors. Once a sample of experts completes this mission, these LR values can be subjected to any linear or nonlinear statistical procedure such as ANOVA, multivariate ANOVA (MANOVA), regression, and other univariate and multivariate procedures.

Prestart Susceptibility to Psychological Crisis

Prestart susceptibility to psychological performance crisis in competition was investigated by Bar-Eli, Tenenbaum, and Elbaz (1989). The athlete's ability to cope with stress and competitive motivation were considered to be two factors that substantially affect motor performance. The Bayesian approach was used to assess the diagnostic relevance of these two constructs on prestart vulnerability to crisis. German basketball experts and Israeli team handball experts responded to a questionnaire on psychological performance crisis in competition. In this questionnaire, they were requested to estimate the components of the Bayesian LR for each level of coping ability and competitive motivation. Similar results were obtained in both samples; it was revealed that a very high coping ability and a balanced level of motivation were strongly associated with very low competitive crisis vulnerability. In contrast, a very low coping ability and a too high or too low situational motivation might be indicative of psychological crisis. Thus, the advantage gained through possessing an appropriate personality seems to be amplified by having a compatible situational motivation (e.g., by appropriate expectations related to the upcoming competition). It should be noted, however, that while these conclusions are valid for team sports such as basketball and team handball, they have not yet been investigated in other (e.g., individual) sport disciplines.

Time Phases

It was argued that a competition (e.g., in basketball or team handball) can be structured temporally into six psychologically meaningful phases: a beginning phase, a main phase, and an end phase within each half (basketball and team handball are played in two halves). These phases have a considerable crisis-related diagnostic relevance. Based primarily on a previous work of Nitsch (1976), it was maintained that the strain processes that characterize each particular phase in competition are determined by two dimensions: *time phases* and *halves*. Bar-Eli and

Tenenbaum (1988b, 1988c) and Bar-Eli, Tenenbaum, and Elbaz (1990b) examined this concept using the Bayesian method with German and Israeli participants as top experts in basketball and team handball, respectively. It was revealed that the experts in each sport discipline could unanimously determine the time limits among the phases, and that the phases themselves have a considerable diagnostic relevance with regard to a psychological performance crisis during competition. The player is highly vulnerable to crisis in the end phase of the second half, whereas in the other five phases, particularly in the first through the fourth phases, vulnerability to crisis is low. Vulnerability to crisis is the lowest during the beginning phases (in both halves). During the main phases it remains relatively low. At the end phase of the second half (the last phase of the game), crisis vulnerability increases dramatically.

It was concluded that the suggested two-dimensional (time phases and halves) analysis of perceived action, which was investigated empirically in two sport disciplines and two different cultural settings, indicated that the end phase of the second half was the most vulnerable to crisis. More generally, the time phases and halves were considered as very meaningful for the athlete's psychological state in competition. However, in both disciplines (basketball and team handball), the game's structure with regard to an actor's time dimension is quite similar (at least according to the old regulation in basketball; see Nitsch, 1976). Future research should investigate not only whether these findings are valid with regard to the new regulation in basketball (according to which a game is divided into four quarters) but also whether these findings hold in sport disciplines in which the action's time structure is even more different (e.g., boxing, fencing, gymnastics, sailing, swimming, or track and field).

Perceived Team Performance: Game Standings

Bar-Eli and Tenenbaum (1989c) and Bar-Eli, Tenenbaum, and Elbaz (1991) investigated the notion of *game standings*, later labeled *perceived team performance*. Perceived team performance in competition can be conceived of in terms of event expectancy (expected, unexpected event), direction of lead (which team is ahead), and momentum (positive, negative); these three variables determine game standings. In these studies, the perceived relative contributions of these variables to crisis and noncrisis were investigated. German basketball and Israeli team handball experts responded to a Bayesian questionnaire in which they were requested to assess the occurrence probability of all possible game standings under crisis and noncrisis conditions. It was found that under the crisis condition, negative momentum, unexpected event, and lead by opposing team were evaluated as more probable, whereas positive momentum, expected event, and leading the opposing team were estimated to be more likely to occur under the noncrisis condition. Moreover, the athlete's psychological state (crisis versus noncrisis) was judged to be more strongly related to momentum than to event expectancy and direction of lead.

The overall pattern of results obtained from German basketball and Israeli team handball experts was quite similar. The only notable inconsistency regarded prolonged tie score (e.g., a game standing in which maximal uncertainty exists—that is, the chances of each team to win or lose the game objectively approach 50%). In principle, the state of prolonged tie score (either expected or unexpected by the athlete) can be conceived of as a third level of momentum or direction of lead. Bar-Eli and colleagues (1991) found that the effect of prolonged tie score was perceived as being quite similar to that of negative momentum, with both being strongly associated with crisis. Prolonged tie score was more strongly associated with crisis (versus noncrisis) also within the context of direction of lead. Thus, the interpretation of this game standing as an uncertain state and possible source of stress (e.g., McGrath, 1976) was supported in the contexts of momentum and direction of lead.

In contrast to these findings, Bar-Eli and Tenenbaum (1989c) revealed that prolonged tie score was more strongly associated with noncrisis. This finding was somewhat surprising, because prolonged tie score was viewed as an uncertainty arousing stressor, which would indicate a substantially higher crisis vulnerability. Bar-Eli and Tenenbaum (1989c) reasoned that it is possible that when the player subjectively expects a prolonged tie score, this player takes into account (within the framework of game-related plans) a unique self-exertion perspective that is reflected in a readiness for an extreme effort intended to control arousal level in order to cope with the tough demands of competition. Such an approach, which would be much less effective with an unexpected prolonged tie score, might account for the low crisis vulnerability discussed here. This explanation is in line with previous empirical work conducted by Gabler (1976), who revealed that athletes (e.g., basketball players) do indeed exert themselves much more during a prolonged tie score versus game standings in which one of the teams is clearly in the lead. At any rate, the psychological processes underlying prolonged tie score deserve further investigation to clarify these intriguing questions.

Performance Quality and Behavioral Violations

Based on cognitive-attentional anxiety theory (Wine, 1980, 1982; Bar-Eli, 1984), it was assumed that impaired task-relevant motor performance and increased task-irrelevant responses indicate the development of an athlete's psychological performance crisis. Accordingly, in a series of investigations (Bar-Eli, Taoz, Levy-Kolker, & Tenenbaum, 1992; Bar-Eli & Tenenbaum, 1988a; Bar-Eli, Tenenbaum, & Elbaz, 1990a), it was hypothesized that task-related behavior and rule- and norm-related behavior (e.g., fairness and sanctions by officials) are highly relevant to an athlete's crisis vulnerability during competition.

Bar-Eli and Tenenbaum (1988a) and Bar-Eli and colleagues (1990a) initially revealed that athletes from basketball and team handball unanimously differentiated between rule violations that are considered minor and rule violations that are normatively considered major. In their studies, the term *sanctions* was operationally defined by calling or ignoring the violation by the officials. Subsequently, these authors used the Bayesian theorem to investigate the relevance of task-related behavior (e.g., performance quality) and rule- and norm-related behavior (e.g., fairness and officials' responses) to crisis vulnerability in competition using German basketball and Israeli team handball experts. These experts assessed the probability of such behaviors in crisis and noncrisis states. It was revealed that vulnerability to crisis was associated with unexpected poor performance and with unexpected violations such as unfair and called behaviors. Expected behaviors were associated with a noncrisis state.

In both basketball and team handball, the structure of the game with regard to players' actions is quite similar (e.g., Bar-Eli & Tenenbaum, 1988b, 1988c; Bar-Eli et al., 1990b). It was therefore recommended that research apply the crisis concept to sport disciplines in which an athlete's structure of action is substantially different. Accordingly, Bar-Eli and colleagues (1992) investigated the probabilities in which behavioral modes such as performance quality, level of fairness, and the response of officials were estimated as diagnostic to the development of a tennis player's psychological performance crisis in competition. However, the definitions used in the rule- and norm-related domain were revised to conform to the tennis domain.

In basketball and team handball, *violations* referred to modes of behavior that are against the rules of the competition and occur unexpectedly. These unexpected rule violations were further divided into minor (fair) and major (unfair) violations and into violations called or uncalled by the officials. For tennis, the last dimension (officials' response) was found to be highly relevant, but the first dimension (fairness) had to be adapted substantially. More specifically, preliminary consultations with tennis experts revealed that they unanimously differentiated the fairness dimension as follows: (a) expected rule- and norm-conforming behavior, (b) unexpected and unfair behavior not against the rules, and (c) unexpected and unfair behavior against the rules.

Thus, whereas the first category in tennis remained similar to that in basketball and team handball, *unexpected minor violations* were defined by the tennis experts as unfair but not against the rules (instead of against the rules but fair) and *unexpected major violations* were defined as unfair and against the rules (instead of against the rules and unfair). Based on these perceptions, then, the concepts of fairness and officials' response were revised and adapted to tennis.

Israeli tennis experts indicated that vulnerability to crisis was associated with unexpected poor performance, unexpected and major violations, and unexpected behavior evoking official response. Expected behaviors were associated with a state of noncrisis (Bar-Eli et al., 1992). These findings further emphasized the significance of investigating the crisis concept in other (e.g., individual) sport disciplines and taking into account the unique characteristics of each specific sport.

Social Factors

The environment in which an athlete executes tasks in competition includes several factors, which can generally be defined as *social factors*. Leading (European) sport psychologists (e.g., Gabler, 1976; Geron, 1975) indicated more than three decades ago that social factors such as teammates, coaches, spectators, and referees substantially affect athletes' competitive performances. Athletes' perceptions of social factors as related to the crisis concept were not intensively investigated until the beginning of the 1990s (Bar-Eli, Levy-Kolker, Pie, & Tenenbaum, 1995; Bar-Eli, Tenenbaum, & Levy-Kolker, 1992a, 1992b, 1993), although these factors were discussed briefly in the original version of crisis theory (Bar-Eli, 1984). Generally speaking, it seems that the athlete's perceptions of social factors are highly relevant to crisis development.

Teammates and Coaches

The athlete's perceived behavior of teammates (Bar-Eli et al., 1992b) and coaches (Bar-Eli et al., 1993) in competition was analyzed in terms of their response (positive, negative, or lack of response), which expectedly or unexpectedly followed the athlete's successful or unsuccessful action or occurs independently of the athlete's action. To investigate crisis-related behavior of teammates, Bar-Eli and colleagues (1992b) studied elite male basketball, team-handball, soccer, and water polo players and elite female gymnasts. In a crisis state, a negative response, an unsuccessful action, and unexpected events were estimated as being more probable. In turn, a positive response, a successful action, and expected events were assessed as being more likely under a noncrisis state. It was also revealed that the athlete's psychological state (crisis, noncrisis) was estimated as being associated with all other variables but particularly with teammates' response and athlete's action.

To investigate crisis-related behavior in coaches, Bar-Eli and colleagues (1993) used elite ballplayers (e.g., from basketball, team-handball, soccer, and water polo) as participants. They found that under crisis, a negative response, an unsuccessful action, and unexpected events are more probable, whereas during noncrisis, the reverse is true. They also found that the athlete's psychological state relates mainly to the variable of coach's response.

Spectators

Bar-Eli and colleagues (1992a) analyzed the behavior of spectators during competition in terms of *spectators' response* (positive, negative, or lack of response) in reaction to a player's successful or unsuccessful action or independently of a player's action in a home or away game. To investigate spectators' crisis-related behavior, Bar-Eli and colleagues (1992a) used elite ballplayers as participants. They revealed that in the crisis state, a negative response, an unsuccessful action, and a home game were estimated as being more probable, whereas in a noncrisis state, the reverse was true. It was also found that the athlete's psychological state was more strongly related to spectator response than to game location or athlete's action.

Referees

Bar-Eli and colleagues (1995) analyzed the perceived behavior of referees in competition in terms of response in favor of, response against, no response in favor of, and no response against the athlete during a home or away game and during expected or unexpected events. Work with elite ballplayers revealed that psychological performance crisis was highly associated with (a) a referee's response against a player, including no response in the player's favor; (b) an away game; and (c) unexpected events. Under noncrisis conditions, (a) no response against a player and a response in the player's favor, (b) a home game, and (c) an expected event was rated as being more probable.

Social Factors and Crisis: The Riddle of Home Advantage (or Disadvantage)

In general, the results of these four studies on social factors were quite consistent with each other; however, an interesting exception was observed when the findings concerning the location of the game were closely examined. More specifically, in the context of referees' behavior, the results related to game location indicated that the crisis state was more probable in an away game than in a home game. This finding was in line with the well-documented phenomenon of home advantage (e.g., Courneya & Carron, 1992; Nevill & Holder, 1999; Pollard, 2006). As indicated by the interactional effects, a home game was strongly associated not only with noncrisis but also with positive effects, such as an expected absence of a referee's response against the player. In contrast, an away game was strongly related not only to crisis but also to negative effects, such as an unexpected response against the player. These findings seem to imply that referees are biased in favor of the home team or at least that athletes expect referees to be biased in their favor when competing at home, which means that home athletes actually expect referees to respond differently toward the home team versus visiting teams.

Despite the suggested home advantage in relation to referees' behaviors, home games were found to be psychologically problematic for the athlete in the context of spectators' behavior; they were associated with a higher likelihood of crisis, negative spectator responses, and unsuccessful action by the player. In contrast, away games were related to a higher likelihood of noncrisis, positive spectator response, and successful actions. These findings can be interpreted on the basis of previous investigations by Baumeister and colleagues (Baumeister, 1984; Baumeister & Showers, 1986; Baumeister & Steinhilber, 1984) on the *choking under pressure* phenomenon (for a recent review, see Beilock and Gray, 2007), which indicated the existence of a home disadvantage. It is therefore possible that home games do provide circumstances that increase the importance of performing well, resulting in heightened self-awareness, enhanced evaluative attention to the performance process, and self-presentational concerns. These alterations may interfere with optimal task performance, resulting in choking under pressure (Beilock & Gray, 2007). These variables may interact with perceived negative spectator response to an athlete's unsuccessful action, which may significantly increase crisis probability in competition. Thus, it can be concluded that in principle, the athlete's psychological states in a competition are affected by location (home versus away). However, in the context of crisis, it is highly important to maximize the specific conditions under which home advantage or disadvantage exists.

Synthesis

Bar-Eli (1997) used a mapping sentence to formally define and summarize the content of variables (i.e., Bayesian data) discussed thus far. The concept of a mapping sentence was formulated in the 1950s by Guttman (e.g., 1954, 1959). A mapping sentence is made up of facets, which are sets of attributes that belong together in some sense and that represent underlying semantic and conceptual components of a content universe. If *n* facets describe the components of a content universe, then any variable from that universe would be denoted by one element for each of these *n* facets. Such a combination of elements is called a *structuple*; it summarizes the conceptual components of the variable (Guttman & Greenbaum, 1998).

The summarizing mapping sentence used by Bar-Eli (1997) synthesized the factors and variables suggested here to be conceived of as Bayesian data. For clarity, the mapping sentence was transferred into a tabulated form and is presented in table 32.1.

Application

Although it is impossible to predict which events an athlete will experience (i.e., which specific combination of probabilities should be calculated for diagnostic purposes at each moment of a particular competition), it is certainly possible to conduct computer simulations. For instance, if a specific athlete experiences some events while competing in an entire contest, profiles can be produced to represent all possible combinations among the different variables. A probabilistic value can be produced for each profile, and this value can be classified into one of the three phases of crisis development (A, B, C) probabilistically defined by the experts (Bar-Eli, 1984; Bar-Eli & Tenenbaum, 1989a). To illustrate LR profiles across experts and athletes, we will use the three factors used in figure 32.1—namely, (1) teammates' responses, either (2) expected or unexpected, to (3) player's actions. The method and the profiles are illustrated in figure 32.2 on page 378.

■ Table 32.1 ■

Psychological Crisis in Competition: Factors and Associated Bayesian Components

CRISIS-RELATED FACTORS

Prestart susceptibility to crisis		Time phases		Perceived team performance and game standings		
Ability to cope with stress	Very high	1	Beginning	Own team leading	Maintained or extended	Expected or unexpected
	Average		Main		Decreasing	Expected or unexpected
	Very low		End			
Competitive motivation	Too high	2	Beginning	Tie	Maintained	Expected or unexpected
	Balanced		Main			
	Too low		End			
				Opponent leading	Maintained or extended	Expected or unexpected
					Decreasing	Expected or unexpected

Performance quality and violations related to task

Task-related behavior and performance quality	Unexpectedly good		
	Expected		
	Unexpectedly poor		
Rule- and home-related behavior and performance quality	Unexpected behavioral violations	Minor (fair)	Called
			Uncalled
		Major (unfair)	Called
			Uncalled
Behavior and behavioral violations	Expected behavioral violations	Minor (fair)	Called
			Uncalled
		Major (unfair)	Called
			Uncalled

SOCIAL FACTORS

Teammates and coach

Response type	Expectation	Outcome
Positive response	Expected	Successful / Unsuccessful / Independent
	Unexpected	Successful / Unsuccessful / Independent
Negative response	Expected	Successful / Unsuccessful / Independent
	Unexpected	Successful / Unsuccessful / Independent
Lack of response	Expected	Successful / Unsuccessful / Independent
	Unexpected	Successful / Unsuccessful / Independent

Spectators

Response type	Location	Outcome
Positive response	Home	Successful / Unsuccessful / Independent
	Away	Successful / Unsuccessful / Independent
Negative response	Home	Successful / Unsuccessful / Independent
	Away	Successful / Unsuccessful / Independent
Lack of response	Home	Successful / Unsuccessful / Independent
	Away	Successful / Unsuccessful / Independent

Referees

Response type	Location	Expectation
Response in favor	Home	Expected or unexpected
	Away	Expected or unexpected
Response against	Home	Expected or unexpected
	Away	Expected or unexpected
No response in favor	Home	Expected or unexpected
	Away	Expected or unexpected
No response against	Home	Expected or unexpected
	Away	Expected or unexpected

[1] Logically, a prolonged tie score cannot decrease. Accordingly, the relevant data were collapsed in the ANOVAs when necessary (Bar-Eli & Tenenbaum, 1989b; Bar-Eli et al., 1991).

[2] Basically, the facet of minor (fair) and major (unfair) relates only to unexpected behavioral violations. It does not relate to expected behavior. Accordingly, the relevant data were collapsed in the ANOVAs when necessary (Bar-Eli et al., 1990b; Bar-Eli, Taoz et al. 1992).

A	P	P	P	P	P	P
B	E	E	E	U	U	U
C	SA	UA	I	SA	UA	I
P%	5	12	7	6	14	6
.	.	.	.	.	.	.
.	.	.	.	.	.	.
.	.	.	.	.	.	.
.	.	.	.	.	.	.
ΣP% / N	7.8	11.7	6.5	10.6	15.6	5.4

N	N	N	N	N	N
E	E	E	U	U	U
SA	UA	I	SA	UA	I
22	67	72	74	83	54
.	.	.	.	.	.
.	.	.	.	.	.
.	.	.	.	.	.
.	.	.	.	.	.
23.7	61.3	74.5	76.1	86.3	52.5

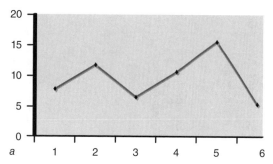
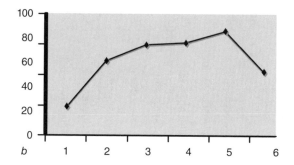

Figure 32.2 Mean LRs (P%) of experts assigned to events that may lead to individual psychological crisis in competition. LR estimates are based on teammates' responses (A; positive or negative), player's expectations (B; expected or unexpected), and player's actions (C; successful, unsuccessful, or independent).

Such profiles are useful for scientific purposes by helping us to understand psychological performance crisis in competition, its antecedents, and its development. From a practical point of view, however, the profiles can be applied to reduce the probability of crisis. The athlete can use such profiles to mentally prepare more efficiently for upcoming events (i.e., particular combinations of variables) that are likely to occur during competition and are especially problematic for the athlete (if not coped with). To improve mental preparation, athletes and coaches may use the naive techniques of psychoregulation (stabilization versus modification, mobilization versus relaxation, prevention versus compensation) that were intensively investigated in the German Sport University almost three decades ago (e.g., Nitsch & Allmer, 1979; Nitsch & Hackfort, 1979) or any of the well-known methods of mental preparation in sport (for reviews, see Hackfort, Duda, & Lidor, 2005; Williams, 2005).

Observational Studies

The Bayesian model presented here to measure psychological performance crisis in competition operates primarily on the verbal level. In principle, human behavior in sport and exercise settings can be measured on three levels (see Bar-Eli, 2002b): verbal (e.g., expressions of subjective experience, such as anxiety, inconvenience, or joy), motor (e.g., particular movements or facial expressions and observed behaviors during contests or practice), and physiological (e.g., increased pulse or breathing frequency or hormonal activity). According to Vealey and Garner-Holman's (1998) review of measurement issues in applied sport psychology, most of the methods used by practitioners in this area are verbal. Such methods are viewed as being introspective (i.e., subjective), and the domain of sport and exercise psychology has often been criticized for relying too heavily on the use of such techniques (e.g., Schutz, 1994). Thus, in order to validate conceptual constructs and theories, researchers in sport and exercise psychology must also conduct measurements on the other two levels of human behavior (i.e., the motor and physiological levels).

In line with this recommendation, Bar-Eli (1997) suggested an alternative approach to the regular practice of observing basketball players during competition. This approach was examined in two field studies (Bar-Eli & Tenenbaum, 1989d; Bar-Eli, Sachs, Tenenbaum, Pie, & Falk, 1996). In the first study, Bar-Eli and Tenenbaum (1989d) systematically observed behavioral rule violations (grouped within time phases) and used them as crisis indicators in basketball competitions. In the second study, Bar-Eli and colleagues (1996) further extended the observational scope of the crisis research by observing a single player's behavior throughout a series of basketball games. Taken together, these behavioral observations, which were related to different combinations of Bayesian variables described in this chapter, strongly supported the predictions derived from crisis theory.

Bar-Eli and Tractinsky (2000) applied crisis theory in a somewhat different yet complementary setting; they attempted to explore psychological performance crises under time pressure toward the end of basketball games. In the study's first stage, experts' judgments indicated that the final phase of the game comprises twice as many highly critical possessions than low-criticality possessions. In addition, the number of highly critical possessions increases dramatically toward the end of the phase. In the study's second stage, results indicated that, in accordance with crisis theory, highly critical possessions were characterized by a lower quality of decision making when compared with low-criticality possessions.

More recently, Bar-Eli, Tenenbaum, and Geister (2006) investigated the consequences of a player's dismissal from a game (i.e., group-size effects) in professional soccer and analyzed these consequences in terms of crisis theory. Using data from 743 games played in 41 German 1. Bundesliga seasons, the authors documented the effects of a player's dismissal on team performance in professional soccer. The aim was to determine whether the punishment meted out for unacceptable player behavior resulted in reduced team performance. It was evident from the data that a player's dismissal does indeed weaken a sanctioned team in terms of the goals made and the final score following the punishment. The chances of a sanctioned team scoring or winning were substantially reduced following the sanction, with most of the cards being issued in the later stages of matches. In addition, the statistics pertaining to outcome results as a function of game standing, game location, and time phases all strongly supported the view that, conceptually, teams can be considered similarly to the way individuals are considered when it comes to the link between psychological crisis and performance on court.

Recommendations for Researchers and Practitioners

The entire concept of applying the Bayesian approach to measuring competitive crisis should be validated in future research. One possible direction is to investigate further whether the present probabilistic estimates do reflect actual competitive states. In all the Bayesian studies summarized in this chapter, a substantial main effect was revealed. This effect demonstrated that overall the state of noncrisis was evaluated as being much more probable than the state of crisis. Indeed, as our naive daily experience reveals, most athletes are in noncrisis most of the time when they perform on court. From a somewhat different perspective, Bar-Eli (2002a) conducted three studies with elite athletes from Israeli professional sport teams (basketball, team-handball, soccer, and water polo) to explore their perception of the psychological performance crisis in competition. It was revealed that across all three studies a well-defined crisis construct existed in the cognition of elite athletes that enables a clear differentiation between the crisis concept and the alternatives of noncrisis and optimal functioning. Bar-Eli (2002a) concluded that the crisis concept derived from theoretical considerations (Bar-Eli, 1984; Bar-Eli & Tenenbaum, 1989a) and presented to the participants for judgment in the Bayesian studies reviewed in this chapter does indeed reflect real perceptions of athletes on court. This finding contributes another dimension of validation to the entire approach.

In future research, then, the relationships between subjective and observational dimensions need further clarification. Such investigations should be continued and should include additional factors (e.g., other social psychological variables) as well as additional sport disciplines. The Bayesian approach can also be applied to additional problem areas in which psychophysiological measures still remain limited (e.g., mainly for technical reasons; for review, see Collins, 2002), allowing for exploration of the underlying mechanisms of psychological crisis. However, as indicated by Bar-Eli and Tenenbaum (1989b), the question of whether probabilistic aggregation helps coaches to diagnose athletes' behaviors during actual competitions depends not only on the ability of the scientist (e.g., sport psychologist) to provide the coach with appropriate computerized diagnostic tools but also on the readiness of the coach to accept such a consultation. For this to happen, continuous and mutual collaboration between coaches and psychologists is required to secure psychological noncrisis as much as possible.

Psychological Skills

Robert Weinberg, PhD, and Samuel Forlenza, MS

The mental or psychological skills of athletes have always been of interest to practitioners and researchers alike. Often when being interviewed after winning (or losing) an important competition, an athlete or coach describes the mental part of the game as being critical to the outcome. We hear things such as "I just felt confident out there, " "I just started to relax and play my game," or "I was able to stay focused for the entire match." Announcers or other media also get into the act with statements such as "He's really getting into the head of his opponent" or "She has a history of losing her cool and just throwing in the towel." Coaches have known the frustration of working with athletes who excel in practice but fail to live up to these standards during games. Then there are athletes who are said to have a lot of potential but never seem able to reach it (which, when reading between the lines, means the athlete is physically skilled but does not have equivalent mental skills). Conversely, there is the gamer, who does not excel in practice but always seems to perform well (above expectations) during actual competitions. Finally, when athletes are asked about how important the mental side of the game is, they usually say it is very important, putting it as high as 95%. Especially when athletes have reached high levels of performance and have perfected the technical aspects of the sport (e.g., professional and Olympic athletes), the difference between good and great performance and winning and losing is often due to mental skills (Orlick & Partington, 1988).

There is little doubt from a practical point of view that mental skills are critical to the success of athletes. Thus, a question that has interested researchers is the notion of the ability of athletes to learn these mental skills. For example, can players learn and practice mental skills in the same way they practice shooting free throws, putting, or hitting a curve ball? If there are such things as mental skills, can these skills be measured and quantified? The short answer to these questions is *yes*. An ever-increasing literature base has demonstrated that psychological interventions can positively influence thoughts and feelings that in turn can influence performance (Fournier, Calmels, Durand-Bush, & Salmela, 2005; Greenspan & Feltz, 1989; Meyers, Whelan, & Murphy, 1996; Weinberg & Comar, 1994). The process of athletes learning these different self-regulatory skills (e.g., imagery, relaxation, goal setting, self-talk) has become known as *psychological skills training* (PST). Weinberg and Gould (2007) defined PST as "systematic and consistent practice of mental or psychological skills for the purpose of enhancing performance, increasing enjoyment, or achieving greater sport and physical activity self-satisfaction" (p. 250). The history, theoretical foundations, and current issues of PST are discussed next.

History and Theoretical Foundations

As was the case in many areas of sport psychology, Coleman Griffith was the first (or most certainly one of the first) to address psychological skills in sport and suggest that athletes differ in these mental skills. This idea was captured by Griffith (as cited in Martens, 1987, p. 74) in the following excerpt:

> We know that some men see better than others . . . some men have a better type of attention than others . . . some men have a better imagination than others . . . if we realize that we are what we are in all of these psychological skills mostly because of the ways in which we have been trained, we shall discover that there is a great deal we can do about some of them. . . . The coach's psychological as well as physical skills.

Therefore, even in the 1920s and 1930s, Griffith was putting forth the idea that there are psychological skills (to complement physical skills) that can be learned and trained. Unfortunately, there was a gap of about 30 years between Griffith's original ideas and the revisiting of the notion of psychological skills relating to performance.

Keeping in line with mainstream psychology, the first concerted effort to investigate the relationship between psychology and athletic performance was couched in personality trait theory. Personality traits were seen as stable over time and dispositional in nature. For example, early personality traits such as anxiety (Spielberger, 1966), achievement motivation (Atkinson, 1974), and confidence (Bandura, 1977) were hypothesized to influence performance. Tutko, Lyon, and Ogilvie (1969) devised the Athletic Motivation Inventory (AMI) specifically to sport performance. The AMI was designed to measure traits such as aggressiveness, determination, drive, and leadership. The claim by the authors that this test could predict athletic performance was met with a great deal of criticism because most other trait measures were not able to predict athletic performance accurately and reliably. Despite the controversy that ensued, the AMI represents an initial attempt to link psychological traits with athletic performance.

Although trait theory dominated the personality landscape for many years, a change occurred in the 1970s and 1980s that emphasized a social learning perspective. The social learning approach argued that the social environment could influence personality traits, which were seen more like dispositions that could be altered and changed. In essence, social cognitive theory (SCT) focused on individual differences that resulted from different environmental learning opportunities. Therefore, it was hypothesized that individuals could learn self-regulation skills such as reducing anxiety, increasing confidence, and enhancing motivation. In fact, many of the training methods used to develop psychological skills in sport were drawn from social learning and SCT approaches, such as the use of Meichenbaum's (1985) stress inoculation training in different self-talk and thought-stopping procedures to reduce cognitive anxiety. The mainstream psychology focus on cognitions in the 1970s fit well with sport psychology, in which coaches were attempting to teach athletes different mental skills.

As the notion of self-regulation and the learning of psychological skills developed, it seemed reasonable to expect that psychological skills might differ among athletes of different physical skills or success. In particular, differences among more successful versus less successful and expert versus novice athletes were investigated from a psychological perspective. One of the initial studies in this area was conducted by Mahoney and Avener (1977), who investigated differences among gymnasts who qualified or did not qualify for the 1976 Olympic team. Results revealed that gymnasts making the team reported being more confident, used more self-

talk in both training and competition, and thought (as well as dreamed) more about gymnastics. Thus, even though both groups were highly skilled and could be considered elite, psychological differences still emerged.

After this initial study, numerous studies investigating individual differences in athletes varying in ability or success were conducted in the 1970s and 1980s, and this area is still generating new research (Auweele, Cuyper, Van Mele, & Rzewnicki, 1993; Gould, Weiss, & Weinberg, 1981; Highlen & Bennett, 1979; Williams & Ericsson, 2008; Vealey, 2002). For example, it has been found that compared with nonexperts, experts exhibit better skills in decision making, anticipation, and attention. Similarly, successful versus less successful athletes exhibit higher levels of confidence, coping ability, concentration, and goal setting. Studies with Olympic athletes (e.g., Gould, Guinan, Greenleaf, Medberry, & Peterson, 1999) found that those who performed up to or exceeded their potential (i.e., who were not supposed to medal but did) had several things in common, including detailed mental plans, daily training goals, consistent use of imagery, high levels of confidence, and facilitating interpretations of anxiety. In summary, individual differences in psychological preparation and skills were found among athletes varying in expertise, ability, and level of achievement.

In addition to research investigating psychological qualities of elite and successful athletes, a parallel line of research emerged focusing on factors common to successful performances. This focus was on peak performance (Krane & Williams, 2006), peak experience (Ravizza, 1984), or flow (Jackson & Csikszentmihalyi, 1999). Consistent across these different but related approaches was the similarity of athletes' experiences when performing at high levels. For example, the commonalities in cognitions and feeling states among these approaches include focused attention, relaxation, confidence, self-motivation, sense of control, and optimal arousal. It is not that these thoughts and feelings cause performance excellence—rather, they appear to be related to high levels of performance. In any case, whether the focus was on the successful athletes or on the successful performances, the individual difference approach revealed a number of psychological qualities related to success.

Besides these primarily quantitative approaches to psychological skills (with the notable exception of research on flow and peak experience), there has been a growing number of qualitative investigations focusing on mental skills relating to high levels of athletic performance. Orlick and Partington (1988) conducted one of the first classic studies in this area, interviewing Olympic athletes in an attempt to determine common elements of success. Results revealed a number of commonalities, including imagery training, simulation training, setting of daily goals, and thorough mental preparation. Since this study, interviews have been used regularly to assess the mental skills of athletes, providing a rich understanding of how mental skills are learned and developed as well as a better understanding regarding why athletes feel and think certain ways. These thoughts and feelings eventually are translated into performance. This research has helped in the development of questionnaires and other inventories to assess these skills objectively.

The most recent approach influencing the development and assessment of psychological skills began with the work of Seligman and Csikszentimalyi (2000). These authors focused on positive psychology and the psychology of excellence. For more than half a century, starting back when soldiers were returning from World War II with a variety of mental and physical disorders, psychology had been focused on healing people and remediating illness. The onus was on getting people back to where they could reenter society as contributing members. Seligman and Csikszentimalyi attempted to reorient this research toward the study of excellence, focusing on mental skills and dispositions that allow people to reach their potential, such as hope, optimism, hardiness, and resiliency. Sport psychologists embraced this because the focus in sport was on improvement and reaching full potential by developing mental skills in addition to physical skills. This focus can be seen in the recent research on mental toughness (discussed later), which to date has used predominantly a qualitative approach, although there has been some attempt to quantify this concept. Mental toughness is seen as a positive attribute (or made up of several positive attributes), and therefore the focus is on the psychology of excellence incorporating different mental skills under the rubric of mental toughness. Next a few of the issues and limitations surrounding the assessment of psychological skills are addressed, before specific inventories attempting to assess psychological skills are described.

Issues and Limitations in the Measurement and Assessment of Psychological Skills

There is no doubt that PST has become a critical part of the sport psychology consultant's orientations.

Of course, within this general orientation, there is diversity in techniques for assessing the current strengths and weaknesses in the psychological skills of a specific athlete. Some consultants prefer interview strategies, some prefer objective inventory assessments, others prefer a combination of these, and still others prefer to use an approach known as *performance profiling* (Butler & Hardy, 1992). In performance profiling, athletes are asked to compare their mental skills with those of an elite performer in their sport by rating themselves in relation to this top performer. This comparison is translated into a pictorial performance profile that the athlete can see visually, which makes the athlete's psychological strengths and weaknesses more apparent. A first difficult question is whether there is a best way to assess psychological skills. To date, the best way has remained a preference of the applied sport psychology consultant, but the strengths and weaknesses of the different approaches should be discussed.

A second area of concern is the question of what skills make up a mental training program. There certainly have been some studies investigating the influence of different package approaches to the study of PST. These packages typically involve teaching or employing several mental skills (e.g., goal setting, imagery, relaxation, self-talk, attentional control). But exactly what skills should a PST program address? Vealey (2007) proposed a model developed from research over the past 25 to 30 years that emphasizes the development of mental skills to achieve performance success as well as personal well-being. This model emphasizes that multiple types of mental skills are important for success and well-being in coaches and athletes, including foundation, performance, personal development, and team skills. Foundation skills (e.g., self-awareness, self-confidence, productive thinking, achievement drive) are intrapersonal resources that are the basic mental skills necessary to achieve success. Performance skills (e.g., energy management, attentional focus, perceptual-cognitive skill) are mental abilities critical to the execution of skills during sport performance. Personal development skills (identity achievement, interpersonal competence) are mental skills that represent significant maturational markers of personal development that allow for high-level psychological functioning through clarity of self-concept, feelings of well-being, and a sense of relatedness to others. Team skills (e.g., leadership, communication, team confidence) are collective qualities of the team that are instrumental to an effective team climate and overall team success. So, should PST focus only on performance skills from this model, or are foundation skills also important?

Along these lines, Morris and Thomas (1995) argued in their model of performance enhancement that the psychological skills of the individual (e.g., self-awareness, motivation, confidence) should be separated from the strategies and techniques used to influence these skills (imagery, relaxation training). More discussion and research on what makes up a PST program and which psychological skills should be included would be an important contribution to this literature.

A third area of concern is that in measuring psychological skills, there is often confusion (either within a scale or across scales) and lack of consistency in what is actually being measured. For example, there is sometimes confusion between asking a trait-oriented question (i.e., how you generally feel) and asking a state-oriented question (i.e., how you feel at a specific moment in time). States and traits are conceptually different and should be viewed differently by coaches, and yet the scales measuring psychological skills often confuse them. For example, in the Psychological Skills Inventory for Sports (PSIS), one item states, "I experience tunnel vision during competitive performance" (state), while another item states, "I am as self-confident as I can be" (trait). In addition, some questions on scales measuring psychological skills focus on the ability of athletes to monitor their current emotions and cognitions (i.e., to know how they are feeling), while others focus on their skill in using an intervention to influence a change in psychological state (i.e., to use imagery to gain confidence). Furthermore, some scales assess simply how often athletes use a technique, assuming that if a technique is used more often, it is effective. For example, the Test of Performance Strategies (TOPS) includes items such as "I practice using relaxation techniques at workouts" and "I visualize my competition going exactly the way I want." Athletes are asked how often they perform these activities but not if they view the activities as effective. Researchers developing new scales and practitioners currently using these scales should be aware of these distinctions in developing questions and interpreting results.

Finally, Murphy and Tammen (1998) argued in their evaluation of the psychological skill literature that athletic performance can be viewed as a three-step process: (1) awareness of psychological states, (2) self-monitoring, and (3) self-regulation. Thus, a PST program may consist of aspects above and beyond the classical skills normally thought to make up a PST program. With these caveats in mind, the next section focuses on the tools typically used in the literature to measure psychological skills.

Psychological Skill Assessment and Measurement

Several sport-specific inventories have been developed to measure different psychological skills. Most of the initial scales assessed only one specific psychological skill or trait; more recently multidimensional inventories assessing a variety of skills have been developed. Some of the more popular inventories are discussed here, along with their psychometric properties. Some popular inventories have lacked the psychometric rigor seen in the development of other scales and thus do not receive as much attention in this review.

Psychological Skills Inventory for Sports

In its time, the PSIS was probably the most popular instrument used to measure psychological skills related to sport performance. It was also probably the first to focus on a multidimensional view of psychological skills. (The AMI focused on 11 different personality traits that were suggested to be related to outstanding athletic performance, but the scale was also mired in controversy and lacked psychometric data attesting to its reliability and validity.) Mahoney, Gabriel, and Perkins (1987) developed the PSIS to assess psychological skills related to elite athletic performance. The development was based on Mahoney and colleagues' (Mahoney, 1979; Mahoney & Avener, 1977; Shelton & Mahoney, 1978) previous work with Olympic and collegiate athletes. The original PSIS had 51 true–false items (a more updated version, the PSIS-R5, uses a 5-point Likert scale while reducing the number of items to 45) and was developed to differentiate among the psychological skills of elite, preelite, and collegiate athletes. Factor analysis revealed six different subscales, including mental preparation, concentration, confidence, team emphasis, and anxiety control. Results demonstrated the ability of the PSIS to discriminate among athletes of different abilities as well as between males and females and between individual and team athletes.

A number of studies subsequently investigated different psychometric properties of the PSIS-R5 (for a review, see Murphy & Tammen, 1998). However, at best, the results have been inconsistent and equivocal regarding different aspects of reliability and validity. For example, one of the underlying premises of the PSIS was that it could differentiate athletes of different ability levels, with the elite athletes having the best psychological skills. However, Mahoney (1989) found that nonelite athletes scored higher than elite athletes scored on five of the six subscales—a finding that contradicts the conceptual basis for the creation of the PSIS. Other studies have found low internal consistencies for several subscales and test–retest reliabilities below .6 on some subscales. In addition, the studies found factor structures different from the original scale as well as a low goodness-of-fit index between the data on new samples and the proposed six-factor solution. Therefore, although the PSIS-R5 provided a needed start in the assessment of psychological skills from a multidimensional perspective, it cannot be recommended for either research or applied perspectives.

Athletic Coping Skills Inventory-28

The Athletic Coping Skills Inventory-28 (ACSI-28) is a popular multidimensional psychological skills assessment that emanated from the original Athletic Coping Skills Inventory (ACSI) used to help predict coping with injury in sport (Smith, Smoll, & Ptacek, 1990). The original 42-item ACSI was revised and shortened to the 28-item ACSI-28 (Smith, Schutz, Smoll, & Ptacek , 1995). The ACSI-28 provides a trait-like measure of psychological skills predicted to improve performance. The original eight-factor solution was reduced to seven factors via CFA and a reasonable goodness-of-fit index (.91). Results revealed seven factors, including coping with adversity, concentration, coachability, confidence, freedom from worry, goal setting and mental preparation, and achievement motivation. The seven subscales can be summed to yield a general measure of psychological coping skills (personal coping resources). However, it is suggested that the ACSI-28 measures a multifaceted construct and that each subscale can be used as a specific measure. Items are scored on a 4-point scale ranging from "Almost never" to "Almost always." Each subscale has 4 items.

A good deal of psychometric analysis has been done on the ACSI-28 to assess its reliability and validity. Specifically, 1 wk test–retest reliability on a sample of almost 1,000 high-level athletes ranged from .47 (coachability) to .87 (peaking under pressure), and five of the scales had coefficients above .70. Internal consistency statistics (Cronbach alpha) ranged from .62 (concentration) to .78 (peaking under pressure), indicating adequate reliability. Construct validity was established by demonstrating meaningful relationships between the ACSI-28 and scales (or subscales) such as the worry subscale from the Sport Anxiety Scale (SAS; Smith, Smoll, & Schutz, 1990), the problem-focused coping sub-

scale from the Ways of Coping Checklist (Vitalino, Russo, Carr, Miuro, & Becker, 1985), and general self-esteem (Smoll, Smith, Barnett, & Everett, 1993). Finally, construct validity was established by relating the ACSI-28 to different measures of performance. For example, overachievers in high school athletics had higher scores on all seven subscales, three of which were significant.

From an applied perspective, Smith and Christensen (1995) studied professional baseball players and found that psychological and physical skills accounted for approximately the same amount of variance in batting average, although psychological skills (34%) accounted for a much larger percentage of explained variance in pitching (earned run average) when compared with physical skills (3%). Although the ACSI-28 is an indirect measure of performance, the study also found that it helped predict which players remained active in professional baseball over a 3 y time frame. In fact the ACSI-28 was better than an assessment of physical skill level at predicting athletic success for pitchers. It is these types of findings that highlight the potential practical use of the ACSI-28 in helping to predict athletic performance and related behavior.

Although there is a lot to recommend the ACSI-28 as a measure of psychological skills, there have been some criticisms of the instrument. First, CFA needs to be conducted on an independent sample (different from the original sample used to confirm the factor structure). Second, the construct validity should involve measures of psychological skills that are not self-report because all self-report measures have the same type of limitations, including cognitive distortions, memory limitations, and social desirability. Third, Crocker, Kowalski, and Graham (1998) have argued that the CSAI-28 was not derived conceptually from theory and so may be a measure of coping skills as opposed to psychological skills. Items may have been put together without specific regard to research findings and current theory. In summary, despite these limitations, the ACSI-28 appears to be an important step in the right direction for measuring psychological skills.

Test of Performance Strategies

The TOPS was developed to provide a test of psychological skills used both in competition and in practice and was based on "the psychological processes thought to underlie successful athletic performance as delineated by contemporary theory" (Thomas, Murphy, & Hardy, 1999, p. 699). EFA of the 64 items yielded eight competition factors and eight practice factors, including goal setting, negative thinking, emotional control, self-talk, imagery, attentional control, activation, relaxation, and automaticity (factors were similar across practice and competition except for attentional control during practice and negative thinking during competition). In a sample of 472 Australian athletes, coefficient alpha values ranged from .66 to .78 for the practice factors and from .74 to .80 for the competition strategies. Furthermore, correlational analysis indicated moderately strong correlations among many of the strategies, suggesting that athletes who tend to use one or more of the competition or practice strategies also tend to use many of the other strategies. Results also indicated differences between elite male and female athletes and their nonelite counterparts in the usage of these practice and competition psychological skills. In addition, international-level athletes used a wider range of psychological strategies than college, regional, and recreational performers used.

The use of the TOPS in relation to the interpretation of anxiety as facilitative or debilitative was explored by Fletcher and Hanton (2001). Results revealed that swimmers who scored lower on relaxation and higher on self-talk exhibited more facilitative interpretations of anxiety symptoms as well as higher levels of self-confidence. Furthermore, the TOPS has successfully linked psychological skills in both practice and competition to perceptions of success (Frey, Laguna, & Ravizza, 2003) and self-efficacy (Lowther, Lane, & Lane, 2002).

The TOPS has offered some additional insight into the development of mental skills by highlighting specific practice and competition psychological strategies. However, further psychometric analysis on the stability of the eight subscales for competition and practice (16 subscales in all) needs to be conducted. In addition, the criterion validity of the scale in helping to predict performance outcomes still needs further refinement and data collection. But the scale does measure a number of different important psychological skills in both practice and competition and thus offers a promising assessment tool for psychological skills. This was demonstrated in a recent study using Olympic athletes from the 2000 Sydney Olympic Games (Taylor, Gould, & Rolo, 2008), in which the TOPS was able to discriminate between medalists and nonmedalists in both competition and practice performance strategies. In addition, gender and age differences were found in some mental skills, leading the authors to conclude that the TOPS created an internally stable instrument with moderate predictive ability relative to the quality of sport performance in elite athletes. Finally, because so much time is spent in practice and the TOPS is the only instrument that specifically focuses on psychological skills in practice, it offers great potential to help train mental skills in practice settings (which then can be transferred to competition).

Ottawa Mental Skills Assessment Tool-3

The Ottawa Mental Skills Assessment Tool-3 (OMSAT-3) is an extension of the original OMSAT developed by Salmela (1992). The initial version contained 14 mental skills grouped into five categories, including foundation skills, psychosomatic skills, cognitive skills, competition skills, and team dynamics. The inventory contained 114 items, and while the subscales had acceptable internal consistency, a shorter version was recommended, especially since there was some overlap among items and a number of items appeared unclear. The revision shortened the scale to 85 items and 12 subscales (still a lot of items) using the same five categories. However, this model displayed an inadequate goodness of fit. A further revision reduced the items to 48 (4 per subscale), and CFA supported the factorial structure of 12 subscales of goal setting, self-confidence, concentration, relaxation, fear control, imagery, refocusing, mental practice, activation, focusing, commitment, and competition planning. In addition to these first-order factors, a second CFA found that these 12 subscales fit into three broader factors, including foundation skills, psychosomatic skills, and cognitive skills. Regarding reliability, internal consistency scores ranged from .68 to .88 with a mean of .78 on the 12 subscales. Intraclass reliability scores ranged from .78 to .96 with a mean of .86. Finally, MANOVA revealed that the five subscales of the OMSAT-3 differentiated between elite and competitive athletes, underscoring its construct validity as well as corroborating other research indicating psychological skill differences between elite and lesser skilled athletes.

In terms of future research, determining predictive validity of the OMSAT-3 through a longitudinal design assessing its relationship with variables such as performance in training and competition, psychological well-being, and dropout rates would be a great addition. Furthermore, the OMSAT-3 should be correlated to other psychological assessments such as self-efficacy, self-esteem, anxiety, attentional control, and imagery to provide additional validity to the scale.

Durand-Bush, Salmela, and Green-Demers (2001) offered some suggestions for using the OMSAT-3 in applied settings. For example, the OMSAT-3 could be used at the outset of a season to gain a better understanding of the strengths and weaknesses of athletes. It only takes 15 min to complete, and scores are easily complied and graphed to provide a mental skills profile. The OMSAT-3 can be especially helpful when working with large groups of athletes, because when working with large groups it is often difficult to meet each athlete individually. The OMSAT-3 can be completed by all athletes, and team tendencies as well as individual profiles can be calculated. These team scores can be displayed visually and discussed in a team session to target areas of intervention. Finally, the OMSAT-3 can be given at different times throughout the season to monitor the progress of the development of mental skills. Thus, overall, the OMSAT-3 can be a useful tool for practitioners who are attempting to get an assessment of the mental skills of their athletes from which specific training programs can be developed.

Mental Toughness

In recent years, the construct of mental toughness has started to receive more attention, starting with the groundbreaking research of Jones, Hanton, and Connaughton (2002). In this initial research, 12 different aspects of mental toughness were identified via a qualitative approach. A number of investigations were conducted subsequently using qualitative approaches, and although findings differed somewhat based on the specific sport, there was a good deal of consistency across studies (for a review, see Connaughton, Wadey, Hanton, & Jones, 2008). Specifically, the four pillars of mental toughness were concentration, confidence, motivation, and coping with pressure. Thus, there seems to be no doubt that mental toughness is a multidimensional concept and that it contains some of the basic (although maybe slightly different) psychological skills assessed by the instruments reviewed. The first quantitative scale, the Mental Toughness Questionnaire (MTQ), was developed by Clough, Earle, and Sewell (2002). The authors created a 48-item version and an 18-item version (to increase its accessibility to athletes and teams, but it has no subscales). They found four reliable factors: control (.73), commitment (.71), challenge (.71), and confidence (.80). Construct validity was established through the scale's relationship with other constructs, including optimism ($r = .48$), self-image ($r = .42$), life satisfaction ($r = .56$), and self-efficacy ($r = .57$). Although other psychometrics were discussed, more research is necessary to test more fully the reliability and validity of the questionnaire.

The most recent attempt to assess mental toughness came from Gucciardi, Gordon, and Dimmock (2008), who specifically targeted Australian football. The development of this qualitative approach (Australian Football Mental Toughness Inventory [AfMTI]) was couched in personal construct psychology in an attempt to understand mental toughness from a holistic perspective. Three overarching categories were found inductively: characteristics (e.g., self-belief, concentration, handling pressure, self-motivation), situations (playing environment, injury and rehabilitation, preparation), and behaviors (consistent performances, playing well no matter the position, superior decision making). One important contribution to the literature was that mental toughness was considered important not only for situations with negative effects (e.g., injuries) but also for some situations with positive effects (e.g., good form). Thus, although mental toughness is somewhat situation (sport) specific, there appears to be a good deal of consistency among sports regarding certain aspects of mental toughness. Future research and practice should focus on what activities, drills, and strategies can be used to build mental toughness.

Individual Assessments of Psychological Skills

The scales just reviewed were multidimensional and thus included a variety of psychological skills in their assessment, although they tended to ask only a few questions on each of the different psychological skills. Typically, PST includes skills such as imagery, relaxation (coping with pressure), self-talk, and goal setting. These are reviewed briefly here.

Imagery

As noted, imagery is usually a key component of PST programs (e.g., Daw & Burton, 1994). The Movement Imagery Questionnaire (MIQ) was developed by Hall, Pongrac, and Buckholz (1985) at approximately the same time the Vividness of Movement Imagery Questionnaire (VMIQ; Isaac, Marks, & Russell, 1986) was developed. The VMIQ has been shown to have test–retest reliability of .76 over 3 wk as well as convergent validity (e.g., correlation of .81 between VMIQ and Vividness of Visual Imagery Questionnaire, or VVIQ). Recently, the VMIQ was revised, and the reliability and validity of this scale have been updated (Roberts, Callow, Hardy, Markland, and Bringer, 2008).

Although it was reported that the MIQ had a test–retest reliability of .83 and Cronbach alphas of .87 (visual) and .91 (kinesthetic), there were some limitations to the measure, such as some participants refusing to perform certain movements and taking too long to complete the entire inventory. Therefore, Hall and Martin (1997) revised the MIQ so that there were only 8 items (4 kinesthetic and

4 visual), all of which were easier to perform. Results showed that the MIQ-R kinesthetic and visual subscales correlated (.77) with the corresponding MIQ kinesthetic and visual subscales, indicating a successful revision. In addition, a more recent test of the MIQ-R correlating EEG measurements to the different imagery subscales supported the reliability and concurrent validity of the MIQ-R.

Since the VMIQ, MIQ, and MIQ-R can all be employed to measure movement imagery ability, some recommendations for when to use the different scales are appropriate. When working one on one or in small groups, the MIQ-R seems most appropriate because it is easily administered and assesses both kinesthetic and visual imagery. When working with teams or other large groups (especially when space is limited), the VMIQ could be used since it requires no actual physical movement, unlike the MIQ and MIQ-R, which require movement. Furthermore, the MIQ and MIQ-R are best employed when the group or team is physically able to perform the movements required. Finally, under optimal conditions, the VMIQ could be used in conjunction with the MIQ since research has found that they do measure two different aspects of imagery (Hall & Martin, 1997).

Although not technically a measure of imagery ability, the Sport Imagery Questionnaire (SIQ) has received a lot of attention and is a measure of the cognitive and motivational functions of imagery (Hall, Mack, Paivio, & Hausenblas, 1998). It measures the frequency of use of different types of imagery, which has been closely correlated with imagery effectiveness. Athletes use different aspects of imagery because they are perceived to be effective in helping performance. The SIQ consists of 30 items and five subscales (measuring different motivational and cognitive functions of imagery) with coefficient alphas above .70 for each subscale.

Self-Talk

Self-talk has been a staple of PST programs, although quantitative measures of self-talk have been developed only recently. One of the first studies on the content of self-talk used a qualitative approach and found that self-talk was multidimensional (Hardy, Gammage, & Hall, 2001). Using these initial findings, Hardy, Hall, and Hardy (2005) developed the Self-Talk Use Questionnaire (STUQ), which contained four sections: when, content, functions, and how. A follow-up study (Hardy & Hall, 2005) found the internal consistency of the items to be high (.94). Test–retest reliability was marginal (.66), and results from the proportion of agreement indicated that all 24 items had agreement values greater than

85%, demonstrating item stability. However, like the SIQ, the STUQ focused mostly on the frequency of use and the types of self-talk, finding differences among male and female athletes, athletes of different skill levels, and athletes playing individual versus team sports.

The Functions of Self-Talk Questionnaire (FSTQ; Theodorakis, Hatzigeorgiadis, & Chroni, 2008) was developed to assess the ways in which self-talk functions. Principal component analysis for the 45-item questionnaire yielded five factors, including effort and motivation, cognitive and emotional control, confidence and belief, automaticity, and attention and concentration. An additional CFA reduced the items to 30 but kept the same factor structure. Coefficient alpha values ranged from .79 to .86. The FSTQ is again a measure of the ways that athletes use self-talk rather than an assessment of their self-talk skills. The major function of self-talk in novel tasks appears to be attention and concentration (Hatzigeorgiadis, Zourbanos, & Theodorakis, 2007). Finally, another Self-Talk Questionnaire (S-TQ) was developed (Zervas, Stavrou, & Psychountaki, 2007) that assessed the cognitive (learning and performing skills, developing strategies) and motivational (focus, encouragement, confidence) functions of self-talk. The scale was developed in three phases using both EFA and CFA, with results supporting a two-factor solution with internal consistencies of .83 for motivational and .92 for cognitive factors. In addition, convergent validity was established through correlations with the Ways of Coping Checklist and the Competitive Worries Inventories. Thus it appears that there are now reliable scales for measuring the functions and content of self-talk, although the skill of self-talk has yet to be adequately assessed. For example, much of self-talk is negative and undermines performance. Although athletes might use some aspects of self-talk productively, their ability to reduce or eliminate negative self-talk is usually viewed as critical to performance excellence. Thus, the refinement of the existing scales or the development of a new scale for measuring self-talk ability would add to the extant literature in this area.

Concentration

Proper attentional focus has long been viewed as a critical factor in performance excellence. Researchers and practitioners have attempted to assess attentional capacity and selectivity in numerous ways. Attentional capacity or mental workload measures have been very popular in cognitive and applied psychology. The more popular ones have been the NASA Task Load Index (NASA-TLX); Hart

& Staveland, 1988) and the Subjective Workload Assessment Technique (SWAT; Reid & Nygren, 1988). Unfortunately, these have not been used in sport and exercise settings. Measures of selectivity include ocular assessments such as using selective occlusion of either specific time frames (temporal occlusion) or specific regions (spatial occlusion) of the visual display. In addition, physiological measures that have been used to measure attentional selectivity include cardiac acceleration and deceleration, ERPs, eye movements, and regional cerebral blood flow. Measures of attentional capacity include pupil diameter, MEG, and cardiac variability.

The subjective assessment of attentional selectivity has been dominated by the Test of Attentional and Interpersonal Style (TAIS) developed by Nideffer (1976). The TAIS and its sport-specific versions (e.g., Van Schoyck & Grasha, 1981) have been used extensively in examining the attentional styles of athletes. The TAIS contains 144 items and has 17 different subscales, 6 of which measure attentional style: broad external, external overload, broad internal, internal overload, narrow focus, and reduced focus. Thus there are three effective attentional styles and three ineffective attentional styles. In Nideffer's original conceptualization, attention varied on only the two dimensions of width (broad to narrow) and direction (internal to external). There has been ongoing debate regarding the psychometric properties of the TAIS and its practical utility. While Nideffer (1976, 1987, 1990, 2007) has argued about the psychometrics and practical use of the TAIS, other researchers have raised serious concerns about the psychometric properties, especially the assumption of subscale independence (e.g., Dewey, Brawley, & Allard, 1989; Ford & Summers, 1992). In summary, there appears to be some support for the use of the TAIS as a diagnostic tool for helping athletes to identify attentional problems that may be affecting performance (Bond & Sargent, 1995). However, "there is little strong empirical support for its use as a research instrument to examine the relationship between attentional abilities and sport performance" (Abernethy, Summers, & Ford, 1998, p. 194). Finally, the TAIS is not a sport-specific measure of attention, and research has clearly indicated that prediction of performance, behavior, affect, and cognitions is better when using a sport-specific measure. Development of such a sport-specific attentional inventory appears to be a worthy goal.

Goal Setting

Most PST interventions include a goal-setting component in which the athlete sets different types of goals using goal-setting principles. There are no established scales for the assessment of goal-setting skill. Rather, the focus has been on goal orientations. That is, assessments are focused on whether athletes are more oriented toward the goal of winning (the outcome of the competition) or the goal of performing the task well regardless of outcome. For example, Gill and Deeter (1988) developed the Sport Orientation Questionnaire (SOQ) to measure individual differences in approaches to sport competition. Factor analysis yielded subscales measuring competitiveness (desire to strive for success), win orientation (focus on outcome of competition), and goal orientation (focus on reaching personal goals).

Duda and Nicholls (1992) developed the Task and Ego Orientation Questionnaire (TEOSQ), which has been used extensively and has additional psychometric analyses regarding its validity and reliability. In the initial study, factor analysis reduced the factors to 13, including task orientation (focus on personal improvement) and ego orientation (focus on outcome and winning). These factors have been confirmed across numerous subsequent studies. To summarize the many studies using the TEOSQ, test–retest reliabilities are typically .70 and higher, while Cronbach alpha values are .79 and .81 for task and ego orientation, respectively (Duda & Whitehead, 1998). Predictive validity has been confirmed by many studies relating task and ego orientations to things such as motives for participation in sport, beliefs about the causes of success, enjoyment and satisfaction, anxiety, social loafing, and learning and competition strategies. The Perceptions of Success Questionnaire (POSQ) also focuses on task and ego orientations and has received a great deal of psychometric support in numerous studies (for a review, see Duda & Whitehead, 1998).

As noted earlier, the focus of goal-setting inventories to date has been on assessing goal orientations. Two points regarding this development are warranted. First, the two goal orientations that have received the most attention by far have been task and ego. However, there are other goal orientations (e.g., social) emanating from the original work of Maehr and Nicholls (1980) as well as other goal orientations appearing in the literature, such as cooperative goals and individualistic goals (being creative and original in performance). These orientations should be more closely investigated. Second, the degree to which these goal orientations are more trait-like or state-like has been an issue of concern. The focus has been on trait-like goal orientations, but single-item measures of situation-specific task and ego involvement have been employed (e.g., Swain & Harwood, 1996). However, in attempting to assess goal states in sport, simply changing the stem of the same items used in the dispositional goal orientation measures (e.g., TEOSQ, POSQ) to focus on a specific moment in time appears problematic (Duda & Whitehead, 1998).

Recommendations for Researchers and Practitioners

This chapter has attempted to review the ever-increasing literature on the assessment of psychological skills. There have been a growing number of multidimensional scales assessing different psychological skills as well as individual scales measuring specific psychological skills (e.g., imagery, self-talk, attention). As noted, many of these inventories have limitations in terms of their psychometric properties, and thus caution should be used when employing these assessments. For example, a common mistake is attempting to use a questionnaire developed and normed on one population (e.g., college male athletes) with another group (e.g., female high school

athletes). Similarly, if a test has not demonstrated predictive validity, then it should not be used to predict behavior or performance. This underscores the need for individuals to be knowledgeable when using these psychological inventories. In addition, due to the many scale limitations, there is a need for increased development of existing scales as well as for new scales to measure emerging constructs. Finally, the difference between using the scales for research and using them for applied purposes should be emphasized. For example, the TAIS has been used successfully in some applied settings, but there is great concern for its use as a research tool. As the use of sport psychology in applied settings continues to grow, the need for reliable and valid scales to measure psychological skills will also grow. This makes it all the more important that the field has developed and continues to develop measures of psychological skills that can be used both to enhance our knowledge in research settings and to increase our effectiveness in assessing and teaching psychological skills in applied settings.

■ Table 33.1 ■
Measures Assessing Psychological Skills

Variable or concept	Measure	Dimension or subscale	Source	Website
Personality traits	Athletic Motivation Inventory (AMI)	Drive, aggression, determination, guilt proneness, leadership, self-confidence, emotional control, mental toughness, conscientiousness, coachability, trust	Tutko, Lyon, & Ogilvie (1969)	None
Psychological skills	Psychological Skills Inventory for Sports (PSIS)	Anxiety, concentration, confidence, mental preparation, team emphasis, motivation	Mahoney, Gabriel, & Perkins (1987)	None
Coping strategies	Athletic Coping Skills Inventory-28 (ACSI-28)	Peaking under pressure, goal setting and mental preparation, freedom from worry, coachability, coping with adversity, concentration, and confidence and achievement orientation	Smith, Schutz, Smoll, & Ptacek (1995)	None
Psychological skills in practice and competition	Test of Performance Strategies (TOPS)	Competition strategies (self-talk, emotional control, automaticity, goal setting, imagery, activation, negative thinking, relaxation) and practice strategies (goal setting, emotional control, automaticity, relaxation, self-talk, imagery, attentional control, activation)	Thomas, Murphy, & Hardy (1999)	www.topsfirst.com

Variable or concept	Measure	Dimension or subscale	Source	Website
Psychological skills	Ottawa Mental Skills Assessment Tool-3 (OMSAT-3)	Foundation skills (goal setting, self-confidence, commitment), psycho-somatic skills (stress reactions, fear control, relaxation, activation), cognitive skills (imagery, mental practice, focusing, refocusing, competition planning)	Durand-Bush, Salmela, & Green-Demers (2001)	www.mindeval.com/shop/product/omsat_3/
Mental toughness	Mental Toughness Questionnaire (MTQ)	Control, commitment, challenge, confidence	Clough, Earle, & Sewell (2002)	None
Mental toughness	Australian Football Mental Toughness Inventory (AfMTI)	Thriving through challenge, sport awareness, tough attitude, desire for success	Gucciardi, Gordon, & Dimmock (2008)	None
Imagery ability	Movement Imagery Questionnaire (MIQ)	Kinesthetic, visual	Hall, Pongrac, & Buckholz (1985)	None
Imagery ability	Movement Imagery Questionnaire-Revised (MIQ-R)	Kinesthetic, visual	Hall & Martin (1997)	http://ses-gcremades.barry.edu/PerformanceEnhancement/Self-report/MIQ-R.doc
Imagery ability	Vividness of Movement Imagery Questionnaire (VMIQ)	Kinesthetic, visual	Isaac, Marks, & Russell (1986)	www.coaching-wales.com/1373.file.dld
Frequency of imagery	Sport Imagery Questionnaire (SIQ)	Motivational general—mastery, motivational general—arousal, motivational specific, cognitive general, cognitive specific	Hall, Mack, Paivio, & Hausenblas (1998)	None
Self-talk use	Self-Talk Use Questionnaire (STUQ)	When, content, functions (practice, competition), how	Hardy, Hall, & Hardy (2005)	None
Functions of self-talk	Functions of Self-Talk Questionnaire (FSTQ)	Effort and motivation, cognitive and emotional control, confidence and belief, automaticity, attention and concentration	Theodorakis, Hatzigeorgiadis, & Chroni (2008)	None
Frequency of self-talk	Self-Talk Questionnaire (S-TQ)	Motivational, cognitive	Zervas, Stavrou, & Psychountaki (2007)	None
Concentration	Test of Attentional and Interpersonal Style (TAIS)	Attentional style (broad external focus, overloaded by external stimuli, broad internal focus, overloaded by internal stimuli, narrow focus, reduced focus)	Nideffer (1976)	www.enhanced-performance.com
Goal orientations	Sport Orientation Questionnaire (SOQ)	Competitiveness, win orientation, goal orientation	Gill & Deeter (1988)	None

(continued)

Variable or concept	Measure	Dimension or subscale	Source	Website
Goal orientations	Task and Ego Orientation Questionnaire (TEOSQ)	Task orientation, ego orientation	Duda (1989)	www.brianmac. co.uk/teosq.htm
Goal orientations	Perceptions of Success Questionnaire (POSQ)	Task orientation, ego orientation	Roberts, Treasure, & Balague (1998)	None

Coping in Sport and Exercise

Ronnie Lidor, PhD, Peter R.E. Crocker, PhD, and Amber D. Mosewich, MSc

The ability of athletes in both individual and team sports to self-regulate their behaviors, feelings, and thoughts before and during their sport activity is crucial in determining proficiency. Take, for example, the kicker performing a 36 ft (11 m) penalty kick in soccer (football)—a kick that may decide the outcome of a championship game. The kicker must evaluate the situational and physical demands of the task as well as the potential social consequences. The kicker must then manage these external and internal demands through behavioral and cognitive strategies in order to execute the most successful kick. Or consider, for example, a gymnast making the final preparations for a floor routine. This performance will determine whether the gymnast advances to the next round of the international competition. The gymnast has to organize thoughts, focus solely on relevant cues while blocking out any internal and external distractions, and be in the right mood. In both examples, the ability of the athlete to cope effectively with the specific demands of the sport activity and the challenging situation influences the outcome of the performance.

Self-regulation is critical in sport and exercise, as participants must manage and adapt to ever-changing physical, cognitive, emotional, and social demands. Effective self-regulation can produce performance success, positive physical and mental well-being, and positive social functioning. Coping is a critical process in managing stress (Hoar, Kowalski, Gaudreau, & Crocker, 2006; Lazarus, 1999; Nicholls & Polman, 2007) and involves coordinating many self-regulating systems composed of cognitive, emotional, physiological, and motor behavior processes (Skinner & Zimmer-Gembeck, 2007).

In this chapter we examine a number of measurement issues associated with instruments and questionnaires given to athletes to assess their coping skills. We also look at preperformance strategies that athletes can use to prepare themselves for coping with the physical, cognitive, and emotional demands of their sport activity. The purpose of this chapter is threefold. First is to discuss a number of measurement issues related to instruments and questionnaires dealing with the coping process in sport and exercise settings from both quantitative and qualitative perspectives. Second is to highlight a number of measurement issues associated with the use of preperformance coping strategies. While there are many different coping strategies available to athletes, in this chapter we focus on only one type of coping strategy—preperformance—that can be used in one type of sport activity—self-paced events. Third is to offer researchers a number of recommendations on how to strengthen the validation process of instruments and questionnaires used to assess coping in sport and how to increase the number of variables measured in studies on preperformance coping strategies as well as to provide practitioners with a number of recommendations for selecting coping instruments, questionnaires, and preperformance coping strategies.

Coping Concept and Definition

The coping process has long been recognized as vital to managing stress and emotion in sport and exercise (Crocker, Alderman, & Smith, 1988; Smith, 1980). The measurement of coping, however, continues to be a challenge because of conceptual and measurement issues. Understanding the strengths and weaknesses of coping measurement approaches requires the elucidation of several issues, including defining coping, identifying macro- and micro-analytical dimensions of coping, distinguishing between trait-like and state-like coping, and recognizing the role of context and stressors in the coping process. These issues have been discussed in detail in previous studies (see Crocker, Kowalski, & Graham, 1998; Crocker, Mosewich, Kowalski, & Besenski, 2010; Hoar et al., 2006; Lazarus, 1990), and so here we provide only a concise overview before reviewing specific quantitative and qualitative measurement techniques.

Theorists have conceptualized coping as a conscious process involving cognitive and behavioral efforts to manage external or internal demands that are taxing the resources of the person involved (Aldwin, 2007; Endler & Parker, 1990; Lazarus, 1991, 2000). Coping mediates the relationship between the appraisal of stressors and the subsequent emotions and performance. Within sport and exercise settings there are countless ways to manage stressful demands (Gould, Eklund, & Jackson, 1993; Kowalski, Mack, Crocker, Niefer, & Fleming, 2006). To identify the basic types of coping, researchers have employed several approaches, many of them guided by previous work in social and clinical psychology. Two primary approaches involve identifying either conceptually distinct coping *functions* or conceptually distinct coping *strategies*. Macroanalytical approaches have identified three broad functional categories (see Hoar et al., 2006; Lazarus, 1991): (1) problem-focused (e.g., task-oriented, active) coping, which involves active efforts to change the situation; (2) emotion-focused (e.g., motion-oriented, accommodation) coping, which involves actions to regulate emotion processes; and (3) avoidance (e.g., disengagement, withdrawal) coping, which involves actively removing the self from the stressful transaction. Other functional dimensions that have been proposed in the sport and exercise literature are distraction-oriented coping (Gaudreau & Blondin, 2004) and approach–avoidance coping (Anshel, 2001).

Microanalytical approaches involve identifying specific categories of coping strategies. These strategies in sport and exercise can include, but are not limited to, increasing effort, problem solving, planning, seeking social support, imagery, relaxation, logical analysis, acceptance, positive reappraisal, mental disengagement, behavioral disengagement, wishful thinking, help seeking, humor, confrontation, venting, arousal control, turning to religion, suppression of competing activities, dietary restrictions, appearance management, and self-blame (see Gaudreau & Blondin, 2004; Gould et al., 1993; Sabiston, Sedgwick, Crocker, Kowalski, & Stevens, 2007). Coping researchers have emphasized that specific coping strategies can vary widely depending on the context and the specific stressor demands (Carver, Scheier, & Weintraub, 1989).

Definitions of coping suggest that it is a dynamic process that can change as a stress transaction unfolds (temporal characteristic) or as stressors change (situational characteristic). Since a key element in a stressful transaction is the person, a critical question in sport and exercise is whether a person has a preferred way of coping (Anshel & Anderson, 2002; Crocker et al., 1998). Assumptions about temporal and situational stability influence a number of measurement factors, such as research design and analysis, wording of instructions, and wording of coping items (see Crocker et al., 1998; Crocker et al., 2010). Empirical evidence indicates weak to moderate evidence of stability of coping in sport studies (Anshel & Anderson, 2002; Crocker & Isaak, 1997; Gaudreau, Lapierre, & Blondin, 2001). However, two recent longitudinal research studies using latent growth analysis indicated that coping in soccer players (Louvet, Gaudreau, Menaut, Genty, & Deneuve, 2007) and referees (Louvet, Gaudreau, Menaut, Genty, & Deneuve, 2009) displayed both trait-like (stable) and state-like (unstable) properties, differing for distinct subgroups. Sport participants (and exercisers) may have preferred ways of coping, but situational demands (and associated appraisals for well-being and coping options) are likely to affect actual coping responses (Hoar et al., 2006).

The valid measurement of coping requires the researcher to evaluate the external and internal demands faced by the participant. These demands are embedded in a sociocultural context that affects not only the appraisal of the stressor but also the expectations and constraints on potential coping options (Aldwin, 2007; Lazarus, 1999; Yoo, 2001). The coping options vary depending on the general domain (e.g., sport competition, work, or social relationships), the situation within a domain, and the different time points in a situation (Gaudreau et al., 2001; Holtzman & DeLongis, 2007). Specific sport and exercise stressors require specific coping strategies for successful adaptation and self-regulation. For example, managing organizational stressors (Hanton & Fletcher, 2005) during the Olympic Games is markedly different from coping with a debilitating knee injury (Udry, 1997). From a measurement perspective, coping assessment must accurately capture how the participant attempts to manage these specific demands. Psychologists in various fields have increasingly recognized the need for context-specific coping measurement protocols (see Endler, Parker, & Summerfeldt, 1998; Holtzman & DeLongis, 2007; Sabiston et al., 2007).

Instruments and Questionnaires Assessing Coping Skills

Researchers have used a variety of quantitative and qualitative methods to investigate how participants in sport and exercise contexts try to manage stressful demands. This section will first review the numerous quantitative instruments commonly used in the field. Most of these instruments recognize the multidimensional nature of coping, focusing on either measuring macroanalytical or microanalytical dimensions of coping. This section will then consider qualitative inquiry approaches.

Quantitative Instruments

The most prevalent method for assessing coping in sport and exercise over the last two decades has involved coping questionnaires. These questionnaires have been developed through both inductive (empirical) and deductive (theory-driven) approaches (Hoar et al., 2006). Sport and exercise coping instruments have been heavily influenced by the Lazarus transactional stress and coping model (e.g., Lazarus & Folkman, 1984) as well as by previous instrument development in clinical and social psychology (Hoar et al., 2006; Nicholls & Polman, 2007). This review covers the most commonly used coping instruments in sport and exercise in the last decade. These instruments include sport modifications of the COPE, the Athletic Coping Skills Inventory-28 (ACSI-28), the Coping Function Questionnaire (CFQ), the Coping Inventory for Competitive Sport (CICS), and questionnaires based on approach–avoidance perspectives. The psychometric information on the instruments and questionnaires reviewed in this section is presented in table 34.1 on page 396.

Modified COPE (MCOPE)

A popular validated measure of dispositional and situational coping in psychology is the COPE (Carver et al., 1989). The COPE was developed on both empirical and theoretical grounds and consists of 13 conceptually distinct scales that assess coping strategies. Crocker and colleagues (Crocker & Graham, 1995; Crocker & Isaak, 1997) modified the COPE for use in sport settings (and named it the *MCOPE*) due to concerns over psychometric weaknesses in sport modifications of the Ways of Coping Checklist (see Crocker, 1992).

The MCOPE consists of 12 distinct coping scales of 4 items each. The MCOPE uses 9 scales from the COPE (active coping, planning, seeking social support for instrumental reasons, seeking social support

for emotional reasons, denial, humor, suppression of competing activities, behavioral disengagement, and venting of emotions) and 3 additional scales from sport modifications of the Ways of Coping Checklist (self-blame, wishful thinking, and increasing effort). Items were reworded to reflect sport competition and are scored on a 5-point scale ranging from 1 = "Used not at all/very little" to 5 = "Used very much." As in the work of Carver and colleagues (1989), scale scores are not combined into problem- or emotion-focused or total score aggregates. The MCOPE consists of both situational and dispositional versions and has been translated into French (Gaudreau et al., 2001).

The MCOPE is a frequently used coping measure in sport settings (Hoar et al., 2006; Nicholls & Polman, 2007) and has shown adequate reliability and validity. Crocker and Graham (1995) examined scale reliability in 235 competitive athletes reporting performance stress. All scales had adequate internal consistency, with the exception of denial. Eklund, Grove, and Heard (1998) evaluated various measurement models using a sample of 621 athletes reporting on coping with performance slumps. The model that fit the best comprised 10 factors that combined the two social support scales as well as the planning and active coping scales. Scale reliabilities were acceptable, but the model fit indexes were modest. Construct validity was established by indirect means through various studies that have found conceptually meaningful relationships with positive and negative affects (Crocker & Graham, 1995), performance goal discrepancy (Gaudreau, Blondin, & Lapierre, 2002), and achievement goal motivation (Ntoumanis, Biddle, & Haddock, 1999).

The MCOPE has several limitations. First, the factorial validity of the MCOPE needs to be established in both situational and dispositional formats across multiple sport stressors. Second, gender and temporal invariance are unclear. Third, the MCOPE or modifications of the COPE have not been validated in exercise settings. Last, although the MCOPE modified items to make them more sport relevant, this instrument was not developed specifically for sport or exercise. It does not assess all relevant coping strategies that are associated with adaptive and maladaptive functioning in sport and exercise settings.

Athletic Coping Skills Inventory-28

The ACSI-28 was developed by Smith, Schultz, Smoll, and Ptacek (1995) to assess psychological coping skills that are thought to be important to performance in the sport domain. It is based on a theoretical model that takes into account life stress,

■ Table 34.1 ■

Psychometric Information on Coping Instruments and Questionnaires

Measure	Source	Sample	Reliability	Validity
MCOPE (situational)	Crocker & Graham (1995)	377 adolescent and adult competitive athletes (169 women, 208 men)	For all scales, reliability is above α = .60, except for the denial scale (α = .42)	*Construct validity* For problem-focused scales related to positive affect, *r* = .26-.46 (*p* < .01) For emotion-focused scales (except humor) related to negative affect, *r* = .22-.46 (*p* < .01)
MCOPE (dispositional)	Eklund, Grove, & Heard (1998)	621 adolescent and adult athletes	For all scales, reliability is above α =.67	*Factorial validity* Indexes of fit (2 samples reported, each with a calibration and cross-validation component):
12-factor model				MCOPE-12: CFI = .88, .88, .89, .87 NNFI = .86, .86, .87, .86
10-factor model				MCOPE-10: CFI = .88, .87, .88, .86 NNFI = .86, .86, .87, .86
Athletic Coping Skills Inventory-28 (ACSI-28)	Smith, Schultz, Smoll, & Ptacek (1995)	Male and female athletes in high school and college (sample sizes vary across studies)	*Subscale 1 wk test–retest reliabilities* (94 college athletes) *r* =.63-.87, except for coachability (*r* = .47) *Subscale internal consistency* (594 male and 433 female high school athletes) All scales reliabilities above α =.66	*Factor validity* All factor loadings were significant for subscales (.46-.77) (579 male and female high school athletes; 135 NCAA Division I football players): *Indexes of fit* CFI =.91 (.90 males, .90 females) RMSEA = .044 (.043 males, .051 females) *Construct validity* (295-771 high school athletes): Significant relationships (*p* < .05) between ASCI-28 subscales and the following: Self-control, *r* = .13-.42 Self-efficacy, *r* = .17-.47

			Internal consistency reliabilities for composite coping scales	
Coping Function Questionnaire (CFQ)	Kowalski & Crocker (2001)	683 high school students (344 boys, 339 girls)	**Internal consistency reliabilities for composite coping scales** Problem-focused coping = .84 (boys) and .83 (girls) Emotion-focused coping = .80 (boys) and .84 (girls) Avoidance = .91 (boys) and .92 (girls)	*Factor validity* All factor loadings were greater than .40 for both genders *Fit indexes:* TLI = .898 (boys), .882 (girls); CFI = .912 (boys), .898 (girls); robust CFI = .920 (boys), .909 (girls); RMSEA = .074 (boys), .083 (girls) *Convergent validity* Problem-focused function scale significantly related to COPE active coping (*r* = .61) and planning (*r* = .38) Avoidance function scale related to avoidance (*r* = .38) and resignation (*r* = .25) on the Life Situations Inventory emotion-focused function scale significantly related to COPE acceptance (*r* = .31), restraint coping (*r* = .26), and seeking social support (*r* = .25)
Coping Inventory for Competitive Sport (CICS)	Gaudreau & Blondin (2002)	306 French Canadian athletes (aged 14-28 y)	*Internal consistency reliabilities* Thought control: α = .72 Mental imagery: α = .74 Relaxation: α = .80 Effort expenditure: α = .79 Logical analysis: α = .67 Seeking social support: α = .70 Social withdrawal: α = .71 Mental distraction: α = .76 Disengagement and resignation: α = .68 Venting of unpleasant emotion: α = .87	*Indexes of fit* CFI = .931, TLI = .921, RMSEA = .036 *Construct validity* Many meaningful significant correlations between CICS task-focused subscales and problem-focused scales on the MCOPE and ways of coping questionnaire (WOCQ) Many meaningful significant correlations between CICS emotion-focused subscales and emotion-focused scales on the MCOPE and WOCQ Subscales of the CICS correlated in the expected direction with perceived relevance of the competition, sense of control, perceived goal attainment, positive affect, negative affect, cognitive state anxiety, and somatic state anxiety

There are some instruments, such as sport modifications of the Ways of Coping Checklist (Madden, Kirkby, & McDonald, 1989), that are now used only rarely and are covered in previous measurement reviews (see Crocker & Graham, 1995).

social support, and psychological coping skills (Smith et al., 1995). The ACSI-28 is made up of seven psychological skills factors, each serving as a subscale: (1) coping with adversity, (2) peaking under pressure, (3) goal setting and mental preparation, (4) concentration, (5) freedom from worry, (6) confidence and achievement motivation, and (7) coachability. These subscales can be summed to generate a composite measure of psychological coping skills, called *personal coping resources*. Alternatively, each subscale can be used as a specific measure.

The items of the ACSI-28 consist of statements about the experiences of other athletes (see Smith et al., 1995). Athletes are asked to rate how often they have had the same experiences on a 4-point Likert scale, with 0 = "Almost never," 1 = "Sometimes," 2 = "Often," and 3 = "Almost always." The subscale scores can range from 0 to 12 and the personal coping resources score (the composite score) can range from 0 to 84. The higher the score, the higher the level of psychological skill.

Extensive reliability and validity evidence has been established for the ACSI-28. The composite score test–retest and internal consistency reliability was high in a sample of high school and college athletes (Smith et al., 1995). All subscales have demonstrated acceptable test–retest and internal consistency reliability. Convergent and divergent validity of the measure was also supported in the Smith and colleagues (1995) study. The ACSI-28 composite was related to cognitive-behavioral coping skills, the problem-focused coping scale on the Ways of Coping Checklist, the Sport Anxiety Scale (SAS), global self-esteem, and self-efficacy.

There is support for the construct validity of the ACSI-28. Overachievers in high school athletics (defined as athletes whose performance ratings exceeded their physical talent ratings as judged by the coach) had higher scores on the ACSI-28 than underachievers or normal achievers had (Smith et al., 1995). However, there was no relationship between performance ratings and the ACSI-28. Additional support for construct validity was found in a study by Smith and Christensen (1995). Psychological and physical skills accounted for approximately equal amounts of variance in batting average, and psychological skills accounted for most of the explained variance in the earned run average of pitchers at the end of the season. However, physical skills were unrelated to the ACSI-28.

After translating the ACSI-28 into Greek, Goudas, Theodorakis, and Karamousalidis (1998) demonstrated adequate internal consistency values for all scales, with the exception of the coping with adversity subscale. This study provided further support

for the factor structure of the ACSI-28 via CFA and also provided discriminant validity evidence for this version of the ACSI-28.

A major strength of the ACSI-28 is that it was designed specifically for sport and employs sport-related questions that reflect the multifaceted nature of psychological skills in the sport domain (Crocker et al., 1998). It has demonstrated strong factor validity and acceptable construct validity. However, little research has examined age and gender invariance or validity across sport situations and in exercise settings. There are inherent limitations with this measure. The ACSI-28 showed higher correlations with the Self-Control Schedule (SCS), which is a measure of cognitive-behavioral skills, than with the Ways of Coping Checklist, which measures coping preferences as opposed to skills (Smith et al., 1995). This suggests that the ACSI-28 is more a measure of psychological skills than a measure of coping skills. The ACSI-28 has also been criticized for being too general to capture the complexities of the coping process, such that it may be assessing general psychological skills and not coping ability (Crocker et al., 1998). However, psychological skills are an important element of coping (see Hoar et al., 2006), and they form an essential component of coping skills training for athletes (Crocker et al., 1988). Lastly, the ACSI-28 instructions assume that psychological skills are relatively stable, and therefore it is not sensitive to dynamic changes in coping across situations and time.

Approach–Avoidance Measures of Sport Coping

Anshel and colleagues (e.g., Anshel, Williams, & Williams, 2000) have used measures of approach–avoidance coping in sport. Approach coping involves taking direct action, either cognitively or behaviorally, to deal with the effects of a stressor (Roth & Cohen, 1986). Avoidance coping involves efforts to reduce or eliminate cues that are perceived to generate threat or harm (Krohne, 1993). Both approach and avoidance coping can be subcategorized as cognitive or behavioral (Anshel, 2001). Several measures designed to assess approach and avoidance coping styles specifically in sport have arisen out of this research. These instruments include the Coping Style Inventory (CSI; Kaissidis-Rodafinos & Anshel, 2000) and the Coping Style in Sport Survey (CSSS; Anshel et al., 2000).

It is difficult to critically evaluate the measurement qualities of the various approach–avoidance scales developed by Anshel and colleagues. Unfortunately, these measures were developed for use in just one study and do not provide specific details on the items and nature of the measure. While the development of a measure that is made specifically for one study has its merits, including being context specific and applicable to the sample in question, a major limitation is the inability to build psychometric validation over the course of a number of studies. None of the approach–avoidance instruments appears to have been systematically evaluated for factor or construct validity. Nevertheless, Anshel and colleagues' work suggests that the approach–avoidance framework may be beneficial in sport settings, but more research is required to develop psychometrically strong instruments.

Coping Function Questionnaire

The CFQ is a sport-specific instrument developed to assess the functions of coping (Kowalski & Crocker, 2001). Conceptually driven, the CFQ assesses three higher-order dimensions of coping and consists of 18 items in three scales: problem-focused coping (6 items), emotion-focused coping (7 items), and avoidance coping (5 items). Responses for each item are scored on a 5-point scale ranging from "Not at all" to "Very much." This instrument has been used to study adolescent athlete perceptions of control over coping (Kowalski, Crocker, Hoar, & Niefer, 2005), differences in coping and perceived coping effectiveness in adult athletes across performance status (current elite, past elite), competitive experience (Hanton, Neil, Mellalieu, & Fletcher, 2008), and the relationship between trait anger and coping in adolescent tennis players (Bolgar, Janelle, & Giacobbi, 2008).

The CFQ was developed through a multistep process involving item development, athlete and expert analysis of items, analysis of item response format (frequency, duration, and use), item analysis, factor validity, and convergent and divergent validity. Kowalski and Crocker (2001) evaluated the CFQ in a sample of 683 high school athletes. The athletes were asked to describe their most stressful athletic situation in the last 12 mo and then indicate how they managed the situation based on the CFQ. The scales demonstrated good psychometric properties. CFA found strong factorial validity and evidence for gender invariance. The three CFQ scales were relatively independent, with interscale correlations of $r < .23$ for both boys and girls. Convergent validity was established through intercorrelation with specific coping strategies scales from previously validated instruments.

Researchers using the CFQ must consider both its strengths and its weaknesses. Some of the strengths are that it assesses three dimensions of coping functions, it is sport specific, it has demonstrated strong psychometric properties, and it has shown acceptable construct validity in adolescent athletes. However, the CFQ has several limitations. First, it requires athletes to make inferences about the actual function of their coping efforts. Second, it does not assess actual coping strategies. Third, it was developed and validated with adolescent athletes; this may limit its use with older athletes and the generalizability of specific findings. Fourth, Kowalski and Crocker (2001) did not report the specific stressors associated with each athlete's coping, and they did not analyze stressor invariance. Although Kowalski and colleagues (2005) reported additional construct validity evidence, the CFQ could benefit from additional work to improve its scale properties and applicability to older athletes (Hoar et al., 2006).

Coping Inventory for Competitive Sport

The CICS is a 39-item, 10-scale instrument designed to assess coping across competitive sport situations as well as temporal phases within a competition (Gaudreau & Blondin, 2002). The 10 scales can be merged into three distinct higher-order coping dimensions: task-oriented coping, distraction-oriented coping, and disengagement-oriented coping. Task-oriented coping includes the scales of thought control, mental imagery, relaxation, effort expenditure, logical analysis, and seeking social support. Distraction-oriented coping consists of the scales of mental distraction and distancing. Disengagement coping includes the scales of venting of unpleasant emotions and disengagement or resignation. While recalling a stressful competition, athletes are asked to rate the extent to which each item represents their actions or thoughts on a 5-point scale ranging from 1 = "Does not correspond at all" to 5 = "Corresponds very strongly." The CICS has become a popular sport coping instrument for examining a number of measurement and conceptual questions. Studies using either the original French version or the English translation have examined questions related to coping, such as coping stability over time (Gaudreau & Blondin, 2004; Louvet et al., 2007); coping and sport motivation (Gaudreau & Antl, 2008); relationships among self-determination, goal attainment, and coping (Amiot, Gaudreau, & Blanchard, 2004); and personality and coping (Nicholls, Polman, Levy, & Backhouse, 2008).

The CICS was developed on strong conceptual and empirical foundations. Gaudreau and Blondin (2002) argued that coping is a dynamic, contextually dependent process that can be organized at the strategy level as well as at a higher-order functional dimension level. Recognizing the need for a sport-specific measure that captures the unique contextual demands of sport competition, Gaudreau and

Blondin identified more than 100 specific coping strategy items by analyzing the sport coping literature and associated literatures related to psychological skills, burnout, peak performance, facilitative anxiety, and flow states. Through a multistep process involving athlete and expert evaluation and a four-step sequential CFA, the 39-item, 10-scale instrument was finalized.

The CICS has demonstrated acceptable reliability and validity across multiple studies. Employing CFA procedures, Gaudreau and Blondin (2002) reported acceptable model fit for the 10-factor model with a sample of 316 Canadian athletes from various sports. In a subsequent validation with 200 Canadian athletes, Gaudreau and Blondin (2004) demonstrated acceptable model fit for the 10-factor model and modest support for the higher-order three-dimensional model. A multigroup analysis found factorial invariance across individual and team sport subsamples. Some research, however, indicated problems with a number of the items and scales. A study on New York City Marathon participants encountered measurement problems with 7 items and the imagery scale (Gaudreau, El Ali, & Marivain, 2005) and revealed a less-than-desirable fit for the three-factor higher-order coping dimensions model.

Construct validity for the 10-scale and three-dimension models was acceptable. Gaudreau and Blondin (2002) found that the 10-factor coping strategy scale was correlated in expected strength and direction with select scales from the MCOPE and with a French version of the Ways of Coping Checklist. The 10-factor coping strategy scale was correlated in conceptually meaningful ways with perception of control, perceived goal attainment, and positive and negative affect. Recent work has demonstrated construct validity for the three higher-order coping dimensions (Gaudreau & Antl, 2008). For example, task-oriented coping was positively related to self-determination motivation and goal attainment; disengagement-oriented coping was negatively related to goal attainment but positively related to nondetermined motivation; and distraction coping was positively related to nondetermined motivation and evaluative concerns perfectionism.

Thus, the CICS has a number of strengths from a measurement perspective. There are, however, several potential limitations that require careful research examination. First, much of the validation evidence is from the French version. Second, there is a lack of evidence of competition stressor invariance. Third, the higher-order dimensions assume that specific coping strategies can be nested under only one higher-order functional dimension. How-

ever, Lazarus (1991) noted that specific strategies can serve different functions across stressors or at different time points in a stress transaction. Lastly, because of its focus on competitive sport, the CICS may have limited utility in other physical activity contexts. Nevertheless, despite these potential limitations, the CICS may be the most promising instrument for quantitative studies in sport coping.

Qualitative Methods

There has been an increased reliance on qualitative methods for examining stress and coping in sport and exercise. The rise in qualitative methods is due to several interrelated reasons. First, qualitative methods focus on the individual's experience and provide a rich data source. Second, qualitative methods are an appropriate method given that coping is dynamic, personal, and contextual. Third, existing quantitative instruments have various limitations in sport and exercise settings. Fourth, there may be too many antecedent, mediating, and outcome variables to consider using traditional quantitative systems research (Lazarus, 1999). Thus, it is not surprising that qualitative methods have been used to study a wide variety of research questions, including coping with performance-related stressors (e.g., Gould et al., 1993; Nicholls & Polman, 2008; Thelwell, Weston, & Greenlees, 2007), gender differences with interpersonal stress in adolescent athletes (Hoar, Crocker, Holt, & Tamminen, 2010), athletic injury (Thing, 2006; Udry, 1997), coping effectiveness profiles (Holt, Berg, & Tamminen, 2007), sport retirement (Lally, 2007), social physique anxiety (Kowalski et al., 2006; Sabiston et al., 2007), and muscularity issues (Kyrejto, Mosewich, Kowalski, Mack, & Crocker, 2008).

A detailed review and systematic evaluation of qualitative methods in the sport and exercise psychology coping research are beyond the scope of this chapter. There are a number of different qualitative methods (e.g., case studies, phenomenological methods, narratives), data collection techniques (e.g., interviews, diaries, open-ended questions, think-aloud techniques, and focus groups), time frames (e.g., cross-sectional and longitudinal), and analytical procedures (see Crocker et al., 2010). There are several other key procedural issues that affect the quality of research studies, including triangulation, member checks, gaining entry and building rapport, and bracketing (see Creswell, 2007; Smith & Sparkes, 2009).

Qualitative methods offer a number of advantages in the study of coping. First, effective data collection and deductive content analysis can help identify both common and unique coping strategies across contexts. For example, Sabiston and colleagues (2007) reported that adolescent females use various coping strategies to manage social physique anxiety (e.g., avoidance and seeking social support). Several of the strategies for managing social physique anxiety were important and unique (e.g., dietary restriction, appearance management, seeking sexual attention). Second, qualitative methods can capture the coping process over time (given appropriate data collection methods). Interviewers are able to probe why participants chose specific strategies to manage particular stressful transactions. This may help clarify the relationship between the actual coping responses and the stressors, appraisal of stressors, and coping options. Third, qualitative analysis may allow the generation of individual or group profiles. For example, Holt and colleagues (2007) employed idiographic chronological analysis to create three group profiles for 10 volleyball players according to whether they reported effective, partially effective, or ineffective coping over a series of competitions.

Qualitative methods also have several potential limitations for the assessment of coping. First, many qualitative studies use only a single assessment. Requiring participants to recall complex and dynamic processes may result in errors of omission or commission. Second, if sufficient rapport and trust are not established, participants may not reveal sensitive or socially undesirable information. Third, researcher bias is a prominent issue, because researchers are an active part of the qualitative research method (interviewing, content analysis, theme generation, and data interpretation). Although these biases can be somewhat minimized or acknowledged, they cannot be eliminated. Fourth, it is not always possible to establish causal relationships among key variables. Lastly, generalization of findings across persons, contexts, and time is very difficult. Despite these limitations, strong qualitative methods are well suited to studying the unfolding nature of stress and coping and can make a significant contribution to the field.

Preperformance Coping Strategies: The Case of Self-Paced Tasks

As indicated previously, athletes can use various coping strategies to cope with the physical, cognitive, emotional, and social demands of their sport activities. Among these strategies are attention focusing, imagery, self-talk, and relaxation. These strategies, if taught appropriately, can help performers ready themselves for the sport act—to anticipate *what* needs to be done during the act, *when* and *how* to perform the act, and *how* to overcome unexpected situations.

One of the measurement issues that researchers studying coping strategies in sport must deal with is how to measure the effectiveness of a selected strategy in sport achievement. In other words, what are the variables that can be measured during the strategy sessions in order to assess the contribution of the learned strategy to the participant's proficiency? To demonstrate what variables are measured in studies on coping strategies and to illustrate a number of measurement issues associated with these variables, we will examine four types of strategies that are used before one type of sport activity—self-paced events. Self-paced events are tasks taking place in a relatively stable and predictable setting in which there is adequate time to prepare for task execution (Lidor, 2007). Examples of self-paced events or sports include archery, bowling, free throws in basketball, drives in golf, and weightlifting. For these self-paced events, the athlete can activate a preperformance coping strategy to facilitate learning, performance, and achievement. Limiting our examination to self-paced events enables us to focus solely on specific measurement issues related to using coping strategies in one category of sport skills. Our assumption is that proficiency is achieved when the selected coping strategies match the unique characteristics of the performed tasks.

Four types of preperformance coping strategies are discussed in this section: biofeedback, preperformance routines, learning strategies, and attentional instructions. There were two reasons for selecting these four strategies. First, these strategies have been found to be the most effective in helping individuals ready themselves for the execution of self-paced motor tasks (see Lidor, 2007). Second, these strategies have been used frequently by athletes preparing themselves for a self-paced event (Blumenstein, 2002; Cohn, 1990). We assess the usefulness of these strategies by looking at two categories of variables typically measured in preperformance coping strategy studies—outcome-related variables and process-related variables. *Outcome-related variables* are those measured to determine achievement. These variables were collected in all the reviewed studies (*n* = 19) in this section. These variables are associated with the final results of the performed task. Speed and accuracy of performance are among the two frequently used outcome-related variables in studies on preperformance coping strategies.

Process-related variables are those measured during the strategy session or at the end of the session; however, they are not related to the outcome of the task. This category comprises two types of variables: (1) biological, physiological, and physical variables and (2) subjective self-report variables. A few of the biological, physiological, and physical variables measured by advanced technology include the electrical activity of the brain (EEG), HR, and muscle tension. These variables can also be observed by examining video recordings of overt behaviors of the participants, such as the physical routines they demonstrate before they perform. These variables assist researchers in determining profiles of various performers, such as novice versus expert performers, or levels of performance (e.g., performing at personal best). The subjective self-report variables are those that are made verbally or reported in writing by the participants during a study. These variables reflect participant feelings, perceptions, and thoughts on the learned strategy or the learning process. Short interviews and questionnaires are typically used to collect the information on self-report variables. Including both types of variables in strategy studies seems to be essential in assessing the contribution of a selected strategy to achievement. Table 34.2 summarizes the variables measured in the studies reviewed in this section.

Preperformance Coping Strategies Incorporating Biofeedback

The effectiveness of preperformance coping strategies incorporating biofeedback, including breathing techniques, imagery, and progressive relaxation, has been examined in a series of laboratory studies (see Blumenstein, 2002). Preperformance coping strategies incorporating biofeedback are used in sport for teaching athletes to deal with anxiety and stress and to reduce pain and fatigue. These strategies help athletes increase self-regulation and effectively manage psychophysiological arousal. They were found to facilitate performance in a number of self-paced events, among them archery (Salazar et al., 1990), golf (Crews & Landers, 1993), and gymnastics (Zaichkowsky, 1983).

An example of a preperformance coping strategy incorporating biofeedback is the five-step approach (5-SA; see Blumenstein, Bar-Eli, & Tenenbaum, 1997). This technique utilizes testing and various simulative materials to enable athletes to transfer the psychoregulative skills performed in sterile laboratory settings to real practice and competition settings. The 5-SA is composed of five stages: (1) introduction (learning various self-regulation techniques, such as imagery, attention focusing, and self-talk), (2) identification (identifying and strengthening the most efficient biofeedback response

modality), (3) simulation (biofeedback training with simulated competitive stress), (4) transformation (bringing mental preparation from the laboratory to the field), and (5) realization (achieving optimal regulation in competition).

In a typical study on using a biofeedback preperformance coping strategy, such as the 5-SA, in sport (see Blumenstein, 2002), a performer was taught a selected strategy (breathing control) while connected to biofeedback equipment. Different modalities were used to provide online feedback on physical state while the performer practiced the preperformance coping strategy. Among the modalities were measurements of muscle tension by EMG (muscle feedback), peripheral skin temperature as an index of peripheral blood flow (thermal feedback), EDA or sweat gland activity (electrodermal feedback), electrical activity of the brain (EEG feedback), and heart activity monitored by ECG (HR feedback and blood pressure feedback; Blumenstein, 2002). Among these modalities, the measurements of EMG, EDA, and HR were the most commonly used by researchers. In addition to the process-related variables, outcome-related variables were also measured. For example, in one study on golf (Crews & Landers, 1993), putting performance was enhanced by the use of relaxation and imagery incorporating biofeedback training.

Studies on preperformance coping strategies incorporating biofeedback in sport demonstrate a combined use of process-related variables (biological and physiological variables) and outcome-related variables. Subjective self-report variables are lacking in these studies.

Preperformance Routines

A preperformance routine is a systematic sequence of motor, emotional, and cognitive behaviors performed immediately before the execution of self-paced tasks (see Lidor, 2007, 2009). The benefits of a well-established preperformance routine in sport include (a) developing a plan of action before the performance begins (Cohn, 1990), (b) improving the process of focusing attention by preventing negative thoughts and reflections and blocking out external distractions (Moran, 1996), and (c) providing the performer with a feeling of being in control of what is going on (Lidor & Mayan, 2005).

Two types of studies have been conducted to examine the usefulness of preperformance routines in sport settings: observational and experimental (for a review, see Lidor, 2007). In observational studies, researchers observe the athlete's overt patterns of behaviors in natural settings, such as when the

Summary of the Measured Variables in the Reviewed Studies on Preperformance Coping Strategies

Preperformance coping strategies	Study (in alphabetical order)	Tasks	Outcome-related variables	Process-related variables: biological, physiological, and physical variables	Process-related variables: self-report variables
Preperformance coping strategies incorporating biofeedback	Crews & Landers (1993)	Strokes in golf	Putting performance	EEG	—
	Salazar et al. (1990)	Archery	Archery performance	EEG, HR	—
	Zaichkowsky (1983)	Gymnastics	Gymnastics performance	EMG, EDA, temperature	—
Preperformance routines	Boutcher & Crews (1987)	Golf putting	Putting performance	Time between addressing and striking the ball and variability of putting	—
	Cohn, Rotella, & Lloyd (1990)	Shots and putts in golf	Shooting and putting performance	—	+
	Hall & Erffmeyer (1983)	Basketball free throws	Accuracy of shooting	—	—
	Jackson (2003)	Kicking in rugby	Kicking performance	Routine time and consistency and rhythmicity of routine	—
	Lidor & Mayan (2005)	Serving in volleyball	Serving success	Physical behaviors (study 1)	+
	Lobmeyer & Wasserman (1986)	Basketball free throws	Accuracy of shooting	—	—
	Wrisberg & Anshel (1989)	Basketball free throws	Accuracy of shooting	—	—

(continued)

▪ **Table 34.2** ▪
(continued)

Preperformance coping strategies	Study (in alphabetical order)	Tasks	Outcome-related variables	Process-related variables: biological, physiological, and physical variables	Process-related variables: self-report variables	
Learning strategies	Kim, Singer, & Radlo (1996)	Brain scramble, golf putting, card sorting, star training with mirror, ball rolling to a target	Accuracy and speed	—	—	
	Lidor (2004)	Basketball free throws	Accuracy of shooting	—	+	
	Singer, Flora, & Abourezk (1989)	Novel complex motor task	Accuracy and speed	—	—	
Attentional instructions	Radlo, Steinberg, Singer, Barba, & Melnikov (2002)	Dart throwing	Accuracy	EEG, HR	—	
	Totsika & Wulf (2003)	Pedal task	Speed	—	—	
	Vance, Wulf, Töllner, McNevin, & Mercer (2004)	Biceps curls with a bar	Angular velocity, range of motion	EMG	—	
	Wulf, Hoss, & Prinz (1998)	Ski-simulator task and stabilometer task	Balance performance	—	—	
	Wulf, Shea, & Park (2001)	Balance task	Balance performance	—	+	
	Zachry, Wulf, Mercer, & Bezodis (2005)	Basketball free throws	Accuracy of shooting	EMG	—	

Muscle tension not measured; self-report variables collected by interviews or questionnaires.

athlete is preparing for self-paced tasks to be carried out in actual competitions or games. In this type of study, the researcher can authentically describe behaviors exhibited by athletes before they perform self-paced tasks in actual competitions or games. For example, researchers have observed physical patterns of behaviors demonstrated by skilled athletes before the initiation of tasks such as serves in volleyball (Lidor & Mayan, 2005), kicking in rugby (Jackson, 2003), and shots and putts in golf (Cohn, Rotella, & Lloyd, 1990).

In most observational studies on preperformance routines, two major process-related variables are measured. First is the type of physical behaviors demonstrated by the performers while they are performing the routine. In basketball, for example, this might include holding the ball, dribbling the ball a number of times, looking at the front area of the rim, and aiming at the target when performing the free throw. Second is the consistency of performers in using similar patterns of behavior each time they prepare themselves for the self-paced act. In one observational study on serving in volleyball (Lidor & Mayan, 2005, study 1), two additional process-related variables were measured: the time interval players used to ready themselves for the act (e.g., a 12 s time interval for preparation before serving) and the servers' perceptions of what they were doing during the time they were preparing themselves for the serving act (e.g., what environmental cue did they focus on while preparing themselves for the act). Outcome-related variables, such as the accuracy of performance, were measured in all the observational studies on preperformance routines.

In the experimental studies of preperformance routines, researchers manipulate conditions or treatments that have the potential to enhance behavior (Lidor, 2007). Two types of manipulations have been performed. The first involves manipulations of the regular routines that the performer already uses. For example, performers were asked to alter their regular routine or to alter the amount of time used to execute their routine. The second involves manipulations of different preparatory treatment routines presented to the participants, such as a physical-oriented routine versus a cognitive-oriented routine (Lidor & Mayan, 2005, study 2) or visuomotor behavioral rehearsal (VMBR) versus visualization (Hall & Erffmeyer, 1983).

Two major findings emerged from a series of experimental studies on preperformance routines (e.g., Hall & Erffmeyer, 1983; Lidor & Mayan, 2005, study 2; Lobmeyer & Wasserman, 1986). First, athletes who consistently used their own established preparatory routines achieved better than athletes who used altered routines. Second, participants who were taught how to use preperformance techniques such as VMBR, visualization, and attention focusing achieved better than those who were not taught to implement these techniques.

In these experimental studies, the researchers assessed the contribution of the routine to achievement by measuring outcome-related variables. For example, in a number of studies on using preperformance routines before shooting free throws in basketball (e.g., Lobmeyer & Wasserman, 1986; Wrisberg & Anshel, 1989), the accuracy of the shots was measured. The researchers in these studies concluded that the routine was the main contributor to success, since those who learned the routine behaviors outperformed those who were not taught how to develop a routine. However, in a number of studies, process-related variables were measured as well. For example, in one study on golf (Cohn et al., 1990), posttreatment interviews were conducted in which the participants were asked if the intervention had helped their performance. Although immediate improvement in performance did not occur, the golfers felt that the intervention had helped them to achieve. In a study examining both male and female golfers (Boutcher & Crews, 1987), the time between addressing and striking the ball and the variability of the putting task were measured. The male and female golfers who were taught how to use a cognitive-behavioral routine increased the time between addressing and striking the ball and decreased the variability of the putting task. However, only the female golfers who were taught a routine improved their putting performances. It is assumed that the participants' input on their feelings and thoughts concerning the learned routine or other variables related to the learning process enables researchers to increase their understanding of the actual contribution of preperformance routines to performance.

Learning Strategies

A learning strategy encompasses the behaviors and thoughts that an individual activates deliberately or subconsciously to improve a skill or to accomplish a goal (Lidor & Singer, 2005). A series of laboratory (e.g., Kim, Singer, & Radlo, 1996) and field (e.g., Lidor, 2004) inquiries showed that participants—youths and adults—who were taught how to implement the principles of a task-pertinent learning strategy were able to perform self-paced tasks, such as throwing darts, shooting free throws in basketball, and serving in table tennis, more accurately than participants who were not told how to use strategy instructions. Learning strategies seem to provide performers with effective tools for organizing, controlling, and directing thoughts before, during, and after the execution of self-paced events (Lidor & Singer). In essence, these strategies teach performers how to learn and perform, how to remember, how to think, and how to discern which thought processes to inhibit.

An example of a learning strategy that can prepare individuals for the execution of self-paced events in sport is the five-step strategy (F-SS; see Lidor and Singer, 2005). This strategy is composed of five steps, each of which has been subjected to a fair amount of scientific inquiry: (1) readying (establishing a ritual that involves optimal positioning of the body, confidence, expectations, and emotion), (2) imagining (creating a vivid picture of a personal best performance), (3) focusing attention (concentrating intensely on the one external cue that is most relevant to the act or environment), (4) executing (performing with a calm mind), and (5) evaluating (using self-feedback information on the quality of the performed act).

The contribution of learning strategies such as the F-SS to achievement in self-paced tasks has been assessed mainly by measuring outcome-related variables (for a review on laboratory and field studies on learning strategies, see Lidor and Singer, 2005). For example, in one strategy study (Singer, Flora, & Abourezk, 1989), two performance variables were measured: accuracy and speed. It was argued by the researchers that the participants who were asked to use the strategy principles (i.e., the F-SS) were able to cope better with the task's demands. No process-related variables were measured during the strategy training.

Process-related variables have been measured in only a small number of studies. For example, in one study (Lidor, 2004), participants were taught three different learning strategies (the F-SS, an awareness strategy, and a nonawareness strategy) while shooting free throws in basketball. After being presented with the strategies, the participants were given one strategy questionnaire that examined whether they understood the strategy instructions. At the end of the study, an additional questionnaire was distributed, in which the participants were asked to report if they had used the principles of the learned strategies while performing the shooting task. If they reported that they had used these principles, they were asked to report if they used them throughout their entire performance or only in a small portion of their performance. These two questionnaires—the understanding questionnaire and the strategy-check questionnaire—provided additional relevant information as to how the participants implemented the strategy instructions.

As mentioned, the contribution of coping learning strategies to performance achievement has been assessed mainly by the measurement of outcome-related variables (e.g., accuracy and speed). However, in order to provide a complete answer to the question of whether the participants use the strategy instructions throughout the study, researchers should also collect process-related variables, particularly those of subjective self-report.

Attentional Instructions

The ability to focus before and during the execution of a self-paced event is crucial in determining proficiency. During the performance of a self-paced task, attention should be narrowed and directed to a target (e.g., the front area of the rim when shooting free throws in basketball) or a zone (e.g., the opponent's zone of serving in tennis). Since self-paced events are performed in stable and predictable settings, performers can be provided with instructions on how to focus their attention effectively.

A series of laboratory studies conducted by Wulf and colleagues (e.g., Totsika & Wulf, 2003; Wulf, Shea, & Park, 2001) on attentional instructions revealed that external focus of attention has an advantage over internal focus in the performance of self-paced tasks. Participants who were taught to focus attention away from their body and onto a specific external cue that was part of the performance setting achieved better than those who were directed to focus on their body and feel their own movements. The researchers proposed that focusing on the movements and attempting to think about the body's movements may interfere with automatic motor control processes that normally dictate the movements. However, focusing on external cues enables the motor system to use the automatic processes.

In a typical laboratory study examining the effectiveness of attentional instructions (Wulf, Hoss, & Prinz, 1998), one group of participants was taught to focus on internal cues (e.g., parts of the body) and a second group was taught to focus on external cues (e.g., an object in the performance setting). After being exposed to the attentional instructions, the participants performed self-paced laboratory tasks such as a ski-simulator task and a balancing task. Outcome-related variables, such as accuracy of performance and time on task, were the main variables measured in the studies on attentional instructions, as in the laboratory and field studies on learning strategies. (For an extensive review of studies on internal and external attentional instructions, see Wulf, 2007.)

A small number of attentional studies measured not only outcome-related variables but also process-related variables. For example, in the study by Wulf and colleagues (2001), participants were interviewed to determine whether they had indeed used their preferred attentional focus during the retention phase of the study or whether they had focused on something else. In other studies (e.g., Radlo, Steinberg, Singer, Barba, & Melnikov, 2002; Vance, Wulf, Töllner, McNevin, & Mercer, 2004; Zachry, Wulf, Mercer, & Bezodis, 2005), process-related biological and physiological variables such as EEG activity, EMG activity, and HR were also measured.

Recommendations for Researchers and Practitioners

Using the measurement issues discussed in this chapter, we can make the following four recommendations for researchers conducting studies on coping in sport and exercise:

1. Since different sports and modes of exercise vary greatly, the validation process of the instruments and questionnaires assessing coping skills should take into account the different situational demands of the sport activity. A basketball player and an archer must cope with two different sets of competitive situational factors. Therefore, coping instruments and questionnaires should be validated across different sports and physical activities as well as across the skill levels of performers.

2. Since coping is a dynamic process, instruments and questionnaires assessing coping skills should be given to athletes on a number of occasions during the training program. Data collected at the beginning of the training program may differ from those collected at the end of the program, when athletes have most likely improved their physical and psychological skills. Therefore, the same instrument or questionnaire should be given at different times during the program, and its validation process should take into account the time frame in which it was administered.

3. Researchers should adopt a more balanced approach when selecting measurement variables in studies on preperformance coping strategies. Outcome-related variables have always been measured. However, there is a need to use more process-related variables, particularly self-reports made by the participants throughout the study. Spe-cific questionnaires and guidelines for interviews should be developed. Information on the feelings and thoughts of the participants engaged in learning a coping strategy is essential for increasing our understanding of the strengths and weaknesses of a given strategy.

4. The outcome-related and process-related variables should be measured not only under sterile conditions, as described in the reviewed studies, but also under more challenging learning situations, such as those including physical exertion and distractions (auditory and visual). Measuring these variables under more challenging conditions will enable researchers to assess the use of the strategy under authentic real-world situations, such as those the participant may face during practices, competitions, and games.

In addition to the recommendations for researchers, we have two practical recommendations for practitioners (applied sport psychology consultants, coaches, and instructors) attempting to assess the psychological skills of their athletes or to teach their athletes a preperformance coping strategy. The two recommendations are as follows:

1. As indicated previously, coping in sport and exercise is a dynamic process, and therefore questionnaires assessing the coping skills of athletes should be given a few times throughout the training program. The coping skills of the athlete may vary over time, and so information on any changes should be collected at different times across the annual program. It is recommended that coping skills be assessed at early phases (e.g., the preparation phase) and late phases (e.g., the beginning of the competition phase) of the training program. In addition, it is important that only qualified individuals administer and interpret coping questionnaires.

2. Practitioners should use the information obtained via the coping questionnaires to select the most appropriate preperformance coping strategy for their athlete. Various preperformance coping strategies are available for athletes preparing themselves for the execution of self-paced events. However, not all the strategies may fit the specific needs of the athlete. Therefore, the information collected from the coping questionnaire should be used to make a careful selection of the appropriate strategy. For example, if the athlete needs to work on focusing and attention skills, attentional instructions should be used. If the athlete experiences difficulty in preparing physically for the task, then a more conceptualized strategy such as the F-SS should be used.

PART IV

Social and Behavioral Measurement

The chapters in part IV relate to specific issues encountered in sport and exercise psychology. Part IV consists of measurement issues related to team processes. These include team cohesion, leadership, communication, pro- and antisocial behaviors, and behavioral measurements that quantify physical activity.

Cohesion

Albert V. Carron, PhD, Mark A. Eys, PhD, and Luc J. Martin, MA

Cohesion has long been acknowledged as the most important small-group variable (Golembiewski, 1962; Lott & Lott, 1965). As a result, it has been the focus of considerable discussion, research activity, and theorizing in a wide cross section of domains, including sociology, psychology (e.g., social psychology), business and industry (e.g., organizational psychology), the military, education, and the sport and exercise sciences. A logical extension of the discussion, research activity, and theorizing is an attempt to develop operational measures to assess cohesion. As Sir Humphrey Davy (quoted in Hager, 1995) observed,

> nothing tends so much to the advancement of knowledge as the application of a new instrument. The native intellectual powers of men in different times are not so much the causes of the different success of their labours, as the particular nature of the means and artificial resources in their possession. (p. 86)

In short, measurement protocols are at the heart of science; they are fundamental to the advancement of knowledge. In this chapter, we introduce cohesion (its definition and conceptualization) and then outline its measurement protocols. Also, moving from the realm of theory to practice, we provide examples from the literature using the various measures of cohesion. To conclude the chapter, we provide recommendations for both researchers and practitioners.

Definitions of Cohesion

The term *cohesion* is derived from the Latin word *cohaesus*, which means to cleave or stick together. As Dion (2000) pointed out,

> in physics and chemistry, cohesion refers to the force(s) binding molecules of a substance together. In psychology and the social sciences, a similar metaphor applies, with the term *cohesion* or *cohesiveness* describing the process(es) keeping a small group or larger social entity (e.g., military unit, business organization, ethnic group, or society) together and united to varying degrees. (p. 7)

The concept of sticking together forms the basis for most definitions of cohesion in social psychology. For example, in an early classic definition, Festinger, Schachter, and Back (1950) proposed that cohesion is the "sum of the forces acting on members to remain in the group" (p. 164). In another classic definition, Gross and Martin (1952) suggested that cohesion is the resistance of the group to disruptive forces. Others have defined cohesion in terms of member commitment to a group task (Goodman, Ravlin, & Schminke, 1987), interpersonal attraction to other group members (Dimock, 1941), interpersonal attraction to the group as a whole, and interpersonal attraction to the group task (Bovard, 1951; Schachter, 1951).

In sport psychology, the definition that provided a conceptual foundation for recent work on cohesion was advanced by Carron (1982) and modified slightly by Carron, Brawley, and Widmeyer (1998). Namely, cohesion is "a dynamic process which is reflected in the tendency for a group to stick together and remain united in the pursuit of its instrumental objectives and/or for the satisfaction of member affective needs" (Carron et al., 1998, p. 213). Carron and colleagues (1998) pointed out that this definition is intended to highlight four properties of cohesion: (1) *multidimensionality* (numerous factors cause groups to remain united), (2) *vivacity* (the degree of unity can change over time), (3) *instrumentality* (groups stick together for a purpose or to achieve an objective), and (4) *affectivity* (sticking together has social ramifications). This definition and an understanding of the nature of cohesion formed the basis for the conceptualization of the construct.

Conceptual Framework for Cohesion

Social cognitive theorists proceed under the assumption that humans are rational beings who consistently evaluate, form judgments about, organize, and interact in and with their environment (e.g., Bandura, 1986). Carron and colleagues (1998) advanced five assumptions associated with the belief that cohesion, a *group* construct, can be assessed through perceptions of *individual* group members. Briefly, these assumptions are as follows:

1. A group has clearly observable properties (e.g., the relative youth and fitness of a professional sport team are evident).

2. Group members experience the social situation of their group, are socialized into the group, and develop a set of beliefs about the group (e.g., members in sport teams develop a status hierarchy).

3. The beliefs that group members have about the group are a product of selective processing and integration of information (e.g., team members are aware of chronic social tensions or intrateam competition and from these develop beliefs about the team's unity).

4. Perceptions about the group held by a group member are a reasonable estimate of various aspects of unity characteristics of the group.

5. The social cognitions that members have about their group and its cohesion can be measured through a paper-and-pencil questionnaire.

Carron and colleagues proposed that each team member develops and holds perceptions about the team that are related to the group as a totality and to the manner in which the group satisfies the member's personal needs and objectives. In turn, the strengths of these perceptions, singly or in combination, account for why groups stick together. These perceptions include the following:

■ *Group Integration.* This reflects the individual's perceptions about the closeness, similarity, and bonding within the group as a whole as well as the degree of unification of the group.

■ *Individual Attractions to the Group.* These reflect the individual's perceptions of the personal factors that attract and retain the individual in the group as well as the individual's personal feelings about the group.

Carron and colleagues also suggested that there are two fundamental foci to a group member's perceptions about group integration and individual attractions to the group:

1. A *task* focus reflects the individual's perceptions of personal involvement with the group from an instrumental perspective.

2. A *social* focus reflects the individual's perceptions of personal involvement with the group from a social perspective.

Combining the types and foci of perception results in four manifestations of cohesion. These are outlined in table 35.1.

Sources of Confusion

More than 20 years ago, Peter Mudrack (1989a) concluded an article on the nature, definition, and measurement of cohesion with the observation that "the history of research into group cohesion has been dominated by confusion, inconsistency, and almost inexcusable sloppiness with regard to defining the construct" (Mudrack, 1989a, p. 45). In another article published in the same year, Mudrack (1989b) also suggested that the Carron (1982) definition for cohesion described earlier might be appropriate for "a reconceptualization of group cohesion" (p. 781). However, even though the

■ **Table 35.1** ■

Dimensions of Group Cohesion

Type of perception	Focus of perception	Definition
Group integration	Task	A member's perceptions of the similarity, closeness, and bonding within the group as a whole around its task
	Social	A member's perceptions of the similarity, closeness, and bonding within the group as a whole around social relationships
Individual attractions to the group	Task	A member's perceptions of personal involvement with the group from a task perspective
	Social	A member's perceptions of personal involvement with the group from a social perspective

nominal definition and the operational definitions emanating from that definition (discussed later) have been in use in sport and exercise psychology for a considerable time, it would be presumptuous to suggest that the result has been unanimity and the elimination of confusion. Therefore, it is useful to discuss some of the points of contention and sources of confusion that bear indirectly or directly on the measures discussed in this chapter.

One long-standing source of discussion pertains to the *locus of measurement*. With few exceptions (e.g., Stogdill, 1964), social scientists have examined the cohesion perceptions of *individual* group members, amalgamated their responses, and then used that amalgamated value to draw conclusions about *group* cohesion. Theorists argue that a group construct should be measured at the group and not the individual level (the former method simply involves having group members provide one summary value). However, the examination of cohesion from the individual perspective emanates from expediency—there are no valid indexes that can be used to directly test the group as a whole.

Another issue that deserves emphasis is that athletes most likely stick with their teams for a *number of reasons* beyond the four included in table 35.1. For example, a factor that may cause athletes who hold little regard for their teams to stay as a member is the social stigma associated with quitting. Nonetheless, Carron, Brawley, and Widmeyer (2002) proposed that a sizeable proportion of the variability in cohesion among sport teams is associated with the four constructs.

Another important issue (and source of confusion) is the tendency for researchers to treat (i.e., statistically analyze) cohesion as if it is a stable enduring *trait*. While cohesion certainly does not change moment to moment—as mood does, for example—it does change over time. It changes in both its degree and its various salient manifestations (e.g., task cohesion, social cohesion) throughout the process of group formation, group development, group maintenance, and group dissolution.

Another source of confusion is the implicit belief of researchers that the most important elements in the measurement of a construct are the items. The items in any questionnaire are simply a means of tapping into an underlying construct. Some researchers attempting to use existing sport cohesion questionnaires in other contexts (e.g., business) or cultures have placed inordinate importance on the utility of individual items. We believe that the conceptual model (discussed earlier) is sound; therefore, it can be used as the basis for any new measures of cohesion developed in other countries

or for other contexts. At the same time, however, some (or all) of the individual items may not be pertinent. Carron, Brawley, and Widmeyer (2002) suggested the following:

> Researchers interested in the measurement of cohesion in other cultures or contexts should (a) directly use any of the original GEQ [Group Environment Questionnaire] items that appear to represent cohesion in the group(s) under focus; (b) revise the wording on any item that appears to be useful but that contains language, terminology, or a situational reference not characteristic of the group(s) under focus; (c) delete those items that, through pilot testing, appear to be inappropriate; and (d) add new items that are more culturally meaningful or better represent the situation for any of the four scales in the conceptual model. The context-specific measure of cohesiveness can then be examined for its psychometric properties. (pp. 40-41)

Finally, there is also confusion about the *multidimensional nature* of cohesion. The dimensions are related to one another only marginally. Thus, to accept the proposition that cohesion is a multidimensional construct does not involve acceptance of the premise that all four dimensions must always be present or must be present in equal amounts in similar types of groups. One intramural basketball team might have exceptionally high individual attractions to the group and task cohesion but little individual attractions to the group and social cohesion, while a second team might have high group integration and social cohesion and little or no group integration and task cohesion.

Questionnaires for Assessing Cohesion

Thus far the discussion in this chapter has focused predominantly on the work of Carron, Brawley, and Widmeyer (e.g., 1998, 2002; Carron, Widmeyer, and Brawley, 1985). Their conceptualization of cohesion highlighting task and social foci in conjunction with personal and group perceptions underlies what has become the most accepted measure of cohesion in the field of sport and exercise psychology: the Group Environment Questionnaire (GEQ; Carron, Widmeyer, & Brawley, 1985). However, it is worth emphasizing that many attempts to measure a group's cohesion were made before the development of the GEQ and, more recently, researchers have created cohesion instruments for specific populations based initially on the structure and items of the GEQ. The present section provides (a) a brief summary of early attempts to measure cohesion; (b) specific details about the GEQ; and (c) a description of recent developments in measuring cohesion within another culture (Francophone population;

Heuzé & Fontayne, 2002), another context (physical activity groups for older adults; Estabrooks & Carron, 2000), and another age group (youths; Eys, Loughead, Bray, & Carron, 2009).

Early Cohesion Measures

The measurement and examination of cohesion within sport psychology were derived from previous research within social psychology. A useful summary of past sport-oriented operational definitions of cohesion within the social psychological literature was provided by Carron and colleagues (1998). In that summary, they outlined the origins of their own conceptual model. For example, various early operational definitions of cohesion emphasized social aspects (e.g., Fiedler, 1954; Lenk, 1969; McGrath, 1962) and task aspects (e.g., Stogdill, 1964) of the group. Furthermore, perceptions of individuals' attractions to the group (e.g., Klein & Christiansen, 1969), interpersonal relationships (McGrath, 1962), and group integration (Stogdill, 1964) were considered in a number of the early measures. Interestingly, compared with recent measures that approach cohesion assessment through paper-and-pencil surveys of participant perceptions, these previous studies utilized a variety of approaches to understand the dynamics of the group. For example, Stogdill had independent raters evaluate the degree of integration football teams displayed on a play-by-play basis. Implicit in this approach was the assumption that cohesion is a very transitory group property (i.e., it can change from moment to moment). Lenk utilized a combination of participant observations and sociometry to assess the social interrelationships within a successful, yet confrontational, rowing group. In all, these earlier studies and assessment tools provided a basis from which subsequent conceptualizations and operational definitions of cohesion arose within sport psychology.

One measure that prompted greater interest in cohesion within sport psychology was the Sport Cohesiveness Questionnaire (SCQ) developed by Martens, Landers, and Loy (1972). The SCQ, based on Festinger and colleagues' (1950) definition of cohesion (Yukelson, Weinberg, & Jackson, 1984), required participants to rate their response to 7 items that measure manifestations of cohesion:

1. The interpersonal attractions among group members

2. The power and influence of group members

3. The individual's sense of belonging to the group

4. The value of group membership perceived by the individual

5. The amount of enjoyment the individual derives from group membership

6. The individual's perception of the amount of teamwork present in the group

7. The degree of closeness the individual perceives within the group

While the SCQ spurred further research in cohesion within sport teams and approached the construct from a multidimensional perspective, sport psychology researchers expressed concerns about the measure. First, Gill (1977) noted that evidence of reliability and certain forms of validity were lacking for the SCQ. Second, it was not clear whether it was better to consider the items independently or combined into subcategories. Carron (1980) suggested that the items could be categorized into three distinct groups, including those measuring individual-to-individual relationships (e.g., friendship), those measuring individual-to-group relationships (e.g., sense of belonging), and those measuring the group as a unit (e.g., teamwork). Finally, Carron and colleagues (1998) pointed out that the items do not allow for the separate examination of task and social aspects of group involvement—a distinction that has "a good deal of support, if not consensus, from cohesion researchers" (Dion, 2000, p. 21).

The Multidimensional Sport Cohesion Instrument (MSCI) developed by Yukelson and colleagues (1984) provides another example of an inventory designed to assess cohesion. Yukelson and colleagues initiated the development of their questionnaire based on the well-founded argument that past measures did not strictly approach cohesion from a multidimensional perspective. Their view, similar to that of Carron (1982) and Dion (2000), was that the consideration of both task and social aspects is imperative toward understanding a group's cohesion.

Yukelson and colleagues (1984) drew together an initial pool of potential items (41 items total) for their questionnaire from (a) other cohesion questionnaires, (b) operational definitions of cohesion proposed by other researchers, (c) literature reviews of complementary research areas (e.g., industrial and organizational psychology), and (d) interviews with sport coaches and social scientists. Through a series of factor analyses on data obtained from the responses of 282 intercollegiate basketball players, the questionnaire was reduced to 22 items distributed within four proposed dimensions. These dimensions were quality of teamwork (e.g., how well the team works together), unity of purpose (e.g., degree to which group members are committed to the goals of the team), valued roles (e.g., degree to which group member contributions are acknowledged within the team), and attractions to the group (e.g., a group member's satisfaction and identification with the team). In a discussion of their findings and the resultant questionnaire, Yukelson and colleagues reiterated that task and social aspects of group involvement are important considerations in the measurement of cohesion. Their proposed dimensions included three task-oriented dimensions (quality of teamwork, unity of purpose, and valued roles) and one dimension containing both task and social items (attractions to the group).

The MSCI and the communication of its development (Yukelson et al., 1984) advanced the measurement of cohesion within sport teams due to its focus on task versus social orientations. However, Carron and colleagues (1998) noted two limitations with respect to this measure. First, since the development of the MSCI in 1984, further evidence on its reliability and validity has been limited or nonexistent. Also, given that the MSCI was developed solely on the responses of intercollegiate basketball players, the generalizability of the questionnaire is restricted. Second, Yukelson and colleagues utilized a data-driven approach in determining the structure and content of their cohesion questionnaire. As a result, a number of the items and one dimension (valued roles) included in the questionnaire likely represent antecedents or consequences of cohesion rather than cohesion itself.

Group Environment Questionnaire

Taking into account the contributions and limitations from previous cohesion research, Carron and colleagues (1985) developed the GEQ. Over the past 25 years, this instrument has come to be the accepted measure of cohesion within sport groups. In fact, in a summary of the extant literature in a variety of fields, Dion (2000) noted that the GEQ is a valuable contemporary assessment tool for group cohesion. The GEQ was based on the assumptions and conceptual model for cohesion outlined in the introduction to this chapter. Again, this conceptual model proposes that cohesion is represented by task-oriented and social-oriented cognitions related to the group as a whole and the degree to which individual needs and objectives are satisfied. As a result, the GEQ assesses an individual's perceptions of the group's *integration* with respect to task (group integration—task; GI-T) and social concerns (group integration—social; GI-S) as well as the individual's *attractions* to the group's task (i.e., individual attractions to the group—task; ATG-T) and social pursuits (i.e., individual attractions to the group—social; ATG-S).

The development of the GEQ proceeded through a number of phases (Carron et al., 1985). The first phase involved individual interviews ($n = 234$), the distribution of open-ended questionnaires ($n = 123$), and a literature search to determine the meaning of cohesion from an athlete's perspective. The information gathered from this first phase was subsequently used to construct potential items for the questionnaire in the second phase. During this second phase, an initial pool of items was created and vetted by both the researchers and an external panel of experts in the field of group dynamics. In later phases of questionnaire development, athletes from a variety of sport teams were asked to respond to 53-item ($n = 212$) and 24-item ($n = 247$) versions of the questionnaire. Their responses were utilized to analyze intrascale equivalence (i.e., degree to which each item correlated with its proposed dimension), interscale equivalence (i.e., degree to which each item correlated with its proposed dimension in contrast to other dimensions), scale reliability (Cronbach alpha; Cronbach, 1951), and the initial principal components.

The resultant questionnaire (Carron et al., 1985; Carron, Brawley, & Widmeyer, 2002) comprised 18 items reflecting the four dimensions of cohesion. The scale referred to as *individual attractions to the group—social* contains 5 items, such as "I do not enjoy being a part of the social activities of this team." The scale named *individual attractions to the group—task* contains 4 items, such as "I do not like the style of play on this team." The *group integration—social* scale contains 4 items, such as "Members of our team do not stick together outside of practice." Finally, the *group integration—task* scale contains 5 items, such as "Our team members have conflicting aspirations for the team's performance." Participants are asked to respond to each item on a 9-point Likert-type scale with anchors at 1 = "Strongly disagree" and 9 = "Strongly agree." In the original study, the intercorrelations among the four dimensions ranged from .30 to .41, and the Cronbach alpha values were .75 (ATG-T), .70 (GI-T), .64 (ATG-S), and .76 (GI-S).

The GEQ has been employed in a number of studies examining cohesion. Overall, strong support has been demonstrated for the instrument's content, concurrent, predictive, and factorial validity (for a summary, see Carron et al., 1998). However, there have been instances in which the four-factor structure of the GEQ was not supported (e.g., Schutz, Eom, Smoll, & Smith, 1994; Sullivan, Short, & Cramer, 2002). In these cases, the participant groups under examination (e.g., youths; Schutz et al., 1994) were dissimilar to those utilized in the development of the GEQ (i.e., young adults aged 18-30 y who were recreational and competitive athletes from heterogeneous sport teams). In fact, Carron, Brawley, and Widmeyer (2002) cautioned that researchers must consider the relevance of the GEQ and its items to the population under examination. Furthermore, these authors suggested that researchers operating in other contexts or cultures should consider revising, adding, or deleting items as needed to better fit their purposes.

In general, researchers assessing cohesion with a modified GEQ in contexts beyond sport, such as activity and exercise groups (Carron & Spink, 1993; Courneya & McAuley, 1995) and university dormitories (Carron & Ramsey, 1994), have been successful in their attempts to make the measure context specific. However, while also basing their underlying definition of cohesion on the work of Carron and colleagues (Carron, 1982; Carron et al., 1998), other researchers have undertaken more comprehensive research projects to develop GEQ-related measures of the construct. These instruments, designed to assess cohesion in (a) Francophone sport teams, (b) physical activity groups for older adults, and (c) youth sport groups, are summarized in subsequent sections. An overview of the various cohesion instruments is provided in table 35.2.

Questionnaire sur l'Ambiance du Groupe

Noting both the need for a French cohesion questionnaire and Dion's (2000) suggestion to test the boundaries of the GEQ, Heuzé and Fontayne (2002) embarked on examining the validity and utility of the GEQ and its underlying conceptual model with French sport teams. Their initial projects involved a direct translation and transcultural validation of the original GEQ items through procedures set forth by Vallerand (1989; Vallerand & Halliwell, 1983). The results from this process did not provide support for the factorial validity of the translated questionnaire. Consequently, Heuzé and Fontayne made a number of adjustments to their instrument, including adding relevant items, deleting inappropriate items, and making slight modifications to retained items. In the latter case, Heuzé and Fontayne noted that there are cultural nuances pertaining to how individuals reference their groups that were lost in translation. Specifically, they explained that cohesion questions with references toward "Our group" or "We" were better asked as "My group" or "My team" within the French culture.

The preliminary revised version of Heuzé and Fontayne's questionnaire (*Questionnaire sur l'Ambiance du Groupe*; QAG) contained 31 items and was given to 286 athletes from a heterogeneous

sample of sport teams for further testing. The responses of the athletes allowed the researchers to develop a more concise instrument (18 items) that was determined to be a good fit to the conceptual model of cohesion proposed by Carron and colleagues (1985). Subsequent testing with a separate sample of 237 athletes provided evidence of the predictive validity of the measure through the analysis of cohesion perceptions based on sport type and athletes' tenure on their teams. These results compared favorably with those obtained with the original GEQ (Brawley, Carron, & Widmeyer, 1987). Buton, Fontayne, Heuzé, Bosselut, and Raimbault (2007) recently created a short version of the QAG (i.e., QAG-a) for the purpose of efficiently and frequently assessing athletes' perceptions of group cohesion in a longitudinal manner. This questionnaire uses a visual analog approach to measurement in which ratings are made on a 4 in. (10 cm) line as opposed to a Likert-type structure with defined incremental points. It contains 8 items designed to assess the four dimensions of cohesion. The authors' intention was to examine the dynamic nature of cohesion proposed within previous research and to highlight an important measurement consideration.

Youth Sport Environment Questionnaire

Eys and colleagues (2009) provided a strong rationale for a more comprehensive approach to the development of a cohesion questionnaire for youth sport groups (aged 13-17 y); this led to the Youth Sport Environment Questionnaire (YSEQ). Eys and colleagues argued that there are issues with respect to the conceptualization and operationalization of cohesion that require a closer examination of cohesion with younger age groups. From a *conceptual* standpoint, the authors highlighted Rubin, Bukowski, and Parker's (2006) suggestion that development plays a critical role in how an athlete perceives the group. Furthermore, evidence that conceptual models developed with adults may not apply to younger populations was provided (i.e., Sport Anxiety Scale; Smith, Smoll, & Barnett, 1995). From an *operationalization* standpoint, Eys and colleagues presented previous research suggesting the need for age-appropriate measures (Cumming, Smith, Smoll, Standage, & Grossbard, 2008) as well as potential pitfalls associated with using the original GEQ with younger participants. These pitfalls included the GEQ's advanced level of readability (as derived from the Flesch-Kincaid assessment of readability; Kincaid, Fishburne, Rogers, & Chissom, 1975) and use of negatively phrased items (Eys, Carron, Bray, & Brawley, 2007).

■ Table 35.2 ■

Recent Measures Assessing Cohesion

Variable or concept	Measure	Dimension or characteristic	Source
Cohesion (general)	Sport Cohesiveness Questionnaire (SCQ)	Multidimensional, 7 items	Martens, Landers, & Loy (1972)
Cohesion (intercollegiate basketball)	Multidimensional Sport Cohesion Instrument (MSCI)	4 dimensions (quality of teamwork, unity of purpose, valued roles, and attractions to the group), 22 items	Yukelson, Weinberg, & Jackson (1984)
Cohesion (general)	Group Environment Questionnaire (GEQ)	4 dimensions (ATG-T, ATG-S, GI-T, and GI-S), 18 items	Carron, Widmeyer, & Brawley (1985); Carron, Brawley, & Widmeyer (2002)
Cohesion (French language)	Questionnaire sur l'Ambiance du Groupe (QAG)	4 dimensions (ATG-T, ATG-S, GI-T, and GI-S), 18 items	Heuzé & Fontayne (2002)
Cohesion (exercise group)	Physical Activity Group Environment Questionnaire (PAGEQ)	4 dimensions (ATG-T, ATG-S, GI-T, and GI-S), 21 items	Estabrooks & Carron (2000)
Cohesion (youth sport)	Youth Sport Environment Questionnaire (YSEQ)	2 dimensions (task and social cohesion), 18 items	Eys et al. (2009)

ATG-T = attractions to the group—task; ATG-S = attractions to the group—social; GI-T = group integration—task; GI-S = group integration—social.

The series of projects undertaken by Eys and colleagues (2009) to develop a youth-oriented questionnaire included (a) the use of focus groups, open-ended questionnaires, and literature reviews to understand how adolescents perceive the concept of cohesion; (b) the development of potential items based on the subsequent results; (c) content analyses by group dynamics experts to create an 87-item preliminary version of the questionnaire; (d) principal component analyses to help trim items and determine the underlying factor structure (which reduced the questionnaire to 17 items); and (e) a CFA with a separate sample to test the proposed questionnaire (which further reduced the questionnaire to 16 items).

Three points should be conveyed with respect to the resultant YSEQ. First, the questionnaire contains 18 items in total—16 items derived from the previous analyses plus 2 negatively phrased and spurious items (i.e., items not to be analyzed). These 2 items were included to aid in the detection of invalidating response sets. Second, the primary 16 items are divided into *only* task (8 items, such as "I like the way we work together as a team," with $\alpha = .89$) and social (8 items, such as "We hang out with one another whenever possible," with $\alpha = .94$) dimensions. Eys and colleagues did not find support for the four-dimension model proposed by Carron and coworkers (1985); they provide a more detailed discussion of the implications of this finding in their article. Finally, a readability assessment of the YSEQ suggested that the measure is age appropriate for its intended population (participants aged 13-17 y).

Physical Activity Group Environment Questionnaire

A second example of a research project examining cohesion in a targeted context is the work of Estabrooks and Carron (2000). Their Physical Activity Group Environment Questionnaire (PAGEQ) was developed specifically to assess older adults' perceptions of cohesion in exercise groups. While researchers previously examining cohesion in an exercise context were able to make slight adjustments to the original GEQ for their purposes, Estabrooks and Carron (2000) presented three issues with the original questionnaire that arose through their research with older adults (e.g., Estabrooks & Carron, 1997). First, the psychometric properties of the original questionnaire were problematic at times (e.g., lower scale reliability). Second, older adults communicated concerns with respect to the negative items contained in the original questionnaire. Specifically, participants had difficulty answering questions phrased negatively and were uncomfortable considering their

groups in a negative fashion. Finally, participants also questioned the relevancy of certain items with respect to their physical activity groups.

As a result, Estabrooks and Carron (2000) undertook a series of projects to develop a psychometrically sound measure of cohesion for older adults. These projects followed a trajectory similar to the one used by Carron and colleagues (1985) for the original questionnaire. Using the conceptual model of cohesion proposed by Carron and colleagues (1985) as a base, Estabrooks and Carron (2000) conducted focus groups with older adults and performed a literature search to develop an initial pool of 55 items. A content analysis by group dynamics experts reduced this pool to 35 items. Subsequent analyses (e.g., principal component analyses) resulted in a final 21-item questionnaire, which was then utilized with two separate samples to provide support for its concurrent (i.e., in relation to responses on the original GEQ) and predictive validity (e.g., in relation to adherence and perceptions of self-efficacy). In sum, the PAGEQ is similar in structure to the GEQ in that it contains items designed to assess four dimensions: ATG-T (e.g., "I like the amount of physical activity I get in this program"), GI-T (e.g., "Our group is united in its beliefs about the benefits of the physical activities offered in this program"), ATG-S (e.g., "This physical activity group is an important social unit for me"), and GI-S (e.g., "Members of our physical activity group often socialize during exercise time"). Responses are made on a Likert-type scale ranging from 1 = "Strongly disagree" to 9 = "Strongly agree." These four dimensions were moderately intercorrelated ($.28 \leq r \leq .69$) and demonstrated strong internal reliability ($.78 \leq \alpha \leq 94$; Estabrooks & Carron, 2000). In contrast to the original GEQ, however, the new cohesion inventory contains more items (21 versus 18), all of which are phrased in a positive manner.

Estabrooks and Carron (2000) concluded that the results of their studies provided support for the utility of the PAGEQ. Interestingly, after comparing younger and older adult responses on the PAGEQ, they suggested that their questionnaire might also be a useful tool for examining cohesion in physical activity groups of younger adults. Contrasting the PAGEQ with modified versions of the original GEQ might provide direction to future researchers interested in the cohesion of physical activity and exercise groups.

Overview of Questionnaire Use

In order to effectively summarize the use of cohesion measures in research, the following discussion is divided into two sections: sport and exercise. The measures highlighted are the GEQ (Carron et al., 1985), the QAG (Heuzé & Fontayne, 2002), and the PAGEQ (Estabrooks & Carron, 2000). The research carried out with questionnaires introduced in the section on early cohesion measures is not discussed, as research has not been carried out with these questionnaires for a quarter of a century. Also, the YSEQ (Eys et al., 2009) has only just been developed, so there is no body of research associated with it at this point.

Sport

Questionnaires are developed for a purpose: namely, to answer questions about the relationship between the construct of interest (cohesion in this case) and other constructs. An overview of research findings is presented in the sections that follow.

Group Environment Questionnaire

For the past 25 years, the GEQ has been the instrument of choice to examine cohesion in sport teams. In order to summarize the resulting large body of research, it is useful to categorize the studies on the basis of whether they focused on situational factors, personal factors, leadership factors, or team factors (Carron, Hausenblas, & Eys, 2005).

Situational Factors. The GEQ has been used to measure the correlation of cohesion to many different situational factors, such as the organization's *orientation* (Spink & Carron, 1994), *level of competition* (Granito & Rainey, 1988), and *group size* (Widmeyer, Brawley, & Carron, 1990, study 1 and 2). For example, Widmeyer and colleagues (1990, study 1) assessed cohesion levels in groups of varying sizes (n = 3, 6, and 9) in a 3-on-3 basketball league. The GEQ was administered at pre- and postseason, and results indicated that task cohesion was greater at both pre- and postseason for the 3-person groups. Social cohesion was also greatest for the 3-person groups at postseason. No difference was found for social cohesion during the preseason, perhaps because participants were too busy competing and did not have time to immediately establish social relationships.

Personal Factors. Researchers have been interested in the relationship between team cohesion and a myriad of personal factors, including *anxiety* (Eys, Hardy, Carron, & Beauchamp, 2003), *stress* (Henderson, Bourgeois, LeUnes, & Meyers, 1998), *depression* (Terry et al., 2000), and *social loafing* (Hoigaard, Tofteland, & Ommundsen, 2006; Hoigaard, Safvenbom, & Tonnessen, 2006). To examine social loafing, Hoigaard and colleagues (2006) administered the

GEQ to 118 junior soccer players in Norway in an attempt to determine the relationship between task and social cohesion and social loafing. The results indicated that both task and social cohesion were negatively correlated with perceived social loafing. Analyses also indicated that a combination of low task cohesion and low team norms seemed to underlie perceptions of social loafing.

Leadership Factors. Leadership style is another important correlate of group cohesion. Westre and Weiss (1991), for example, found that athletes had higher levels of task cohesion when their coaches demonstrated greater amounts of instruction, training behavior, positive feedback, and social support and used a more democratic style of decision making.

Team Factors. A long-standing issue in the cohesion literature has been whether cohesion plays a role in team success. Some studies reported that lower cohesion was associated with higher performance (i.e., success; Landers & Luschen, 1974; Lenk, 1969), others reported that the two were unrelated (Melnick & Chemers, 1974), and still others reported that cohesion is positively associated with performance (Carron & Chelladurai, 1981; Landers, Wilkinson, Hatfield, & Barber, 1982).

In 2002, Carron, Colman, Wheeler, and Stevens conducted a meta-analysis to resolve this issue. A total of 46 studies containing 164 effect sizes were available. The overall relationship between cohesion (a composite of all four dimensions) and team success was positive and moderate to large (effect size = .655, p < .03). Social cohesion (a composite of individual ATG-S and GI-S) exhibited a slightly stronger relationship with performance (effect size = .702) than task cohesion (a composite of individual ATG-T and GI-T) exhibited (effect size = .607); however, the difference was not significant (p > .05).

Questionnaire sur l'Ambiance du Groupe

In 2006, Heuzé, Sarrazin, Masiero, Raimbault, and Thomas used the QAG to investigate the relationship among perceived motivational climate (task- or ego-oriented), cohesion (ATG-T, ATG-S, GI-T, GI-S), and collective efficacy in elite female basketball and handball teams (n = 124 athletes). Results revealed that a task-involved climate positively predicted changes in athletes' perceptions of task cohesion, whereas an ego-involved climate negatively predicted changes in athletes' perceptions of social cohesion. Ego-involving climates were negatively related to both task and social cohesion.

That same year, Heuzé, Raimbault, and Fontayne (2006) examined the relationships among cohesion, collective efficacy, and performance in professional basketball teams. The sample comprised 154 French- and English-speaking professional athletes. Due to the different languages, both the QAG (for French athletes) and the GEQ (for English athletes) were used. Heuze and colleagues reported that three dimensions of cohesion (i.e., ATG-T, GI-T, and GI-S) had positive relationships with collective efficacy. It was also found that individual performance contributed to perceptions of collective efficacy, which then contributed to perceptions of cohesion (GI-T).

Exercise

As stated above, questionnaires are a tool used to answer questions about the relationship between the construct of interest (cohesion in this case) and other constructs. In the sections that follow, an overview of research findings associated with cohesion in physical activity groups is provided.

Group Environment Questionnaire

As pointed out earlier, the GEQ was developed for sport teams; however, some researchers did adapt the items for use in exercise groups (Annesi, 1999; Carron, Widmeyer, & Brawley, 1988; Courneya & McAuley, 1995; Estabrooks & Carron, 1999; Spink & Carron, 1993; Spink & Carron, 1994). In one of those studies, Spink and Carron (1993) used the adapted GEQ with female exercise participants (mean age = 20 y) to examine the effects of a team-building intervention on both the level of cohesion present and the adherence patterns. The team-building group had fewer dropouts, had members show up late less often, and had increased levels of cohesion (i.e., ATG-T) compared with the control group.

In another study, Estabrooks and Carron (1999) used the modified version of the GEQ to examine the relationship between class cohesion and exercise adherence in older adult exercisers. Results demonstrated that ATG-S, GI-S, and GI-T were all significantly related to exercise class attendance.

A third example of the use of the modified GEQ was a study undertaken by Annesi (1999), who investigated the effects of instructor-based warm-up and cool-down sessions on cohesion, exercise adherence, and dropout in a group of healthy adult exercisers. Annesi found that the warm-up and cool-down sessions resulted in a significant increase in ATG-T as well as higher attendance and lower dropout rates.

Physical Activity Group Environment Questionnaire

Burke and colleagues (2005) sought to determine whether perceptions of cohesion in exercise classes

display sufficient intragroup consensus and intergroup variance to allow these classes to be considered real groups. The analyses were undertaken with data from 1,700 participants of 130 exercise classes. Participants were administered either the GEQ or the PAGEQ. Results indicated that the consensus surrounding class cohesion and the differences in cohesion between classes were sufficient to satisfy the statistical criteria necessary to conclude that an exercise class is a real group. Another interesting finding was that the intragroup consensus values (represented by the index of agreement) for the PAGEQ were significantly higher than those for the modified GEQ. A major reason behind the creation of the PAGEQ (Estabrooks & Carron, 2000) was that elderly exercisers did not like the negatively worded items in the modified GEQ. Perhaps this is a common theme in exercise groups, and the PAGEQ originally created for an older adult population can be used with younger participants.

In another study, Watson, Martin Ginis, and Spink (2004) used the PAGEQ to examine the effectiveness of a team-building intervention aimed at improving group cohesion (i.e., GI-T and GI-S) and attendance in 12 elderly exercisers. Attendance was monitored throughout the intervention, while cohesion was measured at baseline and 12 wk. Positive trends were evident for both attendance and cohesion (i.e., GI-T and GI-S) throughout the intervention.

Finally, Burke and colleagues (2005) utilized the PAGEQ in order to examine the relationship between group goal setting and group performance in 6,356 exercisers. In this setup, cohesion was considered as a moderator variable. Results indicated that goal setting had a significant relationship with performance, although cohesion was not found to moderate this relationship.

Recommendations for Researchers and Practitioners

Alfred Binet, who lived from 1857 to 1911, is best known for his contributions to the measurement of human intelligence. Although there have been revisions to his original test (e.g., the Stanford, the Herring, and the Kuhlmann), it is safe to say that his work has stood the test of time—a claim that cannot be advanced for most other scales, questionnaires, or instruments developed in the social sciences in the 19th and 20th centuries. Thus, it may be surprising to learn what Binet (as cited in Gould, 1996, p. 181) had this to say about his test: "The scale, properly speaking, does not permit the measure of the intelligence, because intellectual qualities are not superposable, and therefore cannot be measured as linear surfaces are measured."

We think that most social scientists who develop paper-and-pencil questionnaires to assess a theoretical construct also have (or should have) similar reservations about their contributions. Developing an instrument to describe, explain, and predict as complex an activity as human behavior—whether individual or group behavior—is an ambitious undertaking fraught with limitations. At the same time, however, we think that Sir Humphrey Davy was correct in the sentiment we quoted earlier—that there is nothing that contributes to the advancement of knowledge more than a new instrument.

If this is the case, if new questionnaires are fundamental to the advancement of knowledge, and if cohesion is the most important small group variable (Golembiewski, 1962; Lott & Lott, 1965), then new cohesion measures should be developed for a variety of target populations. One is children. Groups—sport teams and activity groups—are important for the social and skill development as well as for the health and welfare of children. Yet maintaining children's involvement in sport is an increasing societal concern. Of course, the problem of withdrawal from sport is more complex than simply a child's lack of perceptions of cohesion. However, since cohesion has been shown to be strongly linked to adherence in adult populations (Burke, Carron, Eys, Ntoumanis, & Estabrooks, 2006), it is a good place to start, and we can't start if we have no questionnaires for assessment.

A second group comprises the sport and physical activity groups in other cultures. In the test manual for the GEQ, Carron, Brawley, and Widmeyer (2002) noted that "an important issue that must be addressed is whether the GEQ has validity . . . [for] teams in other cultures" (p. 39). The issue is complex, but it is sufficient to say that no researchers other than Heuzé and Fontayne (2002) have undertaken the laborious process of testing, modifying, and then publishing a cohesion questionnaire for widespread use in another culture.

Researchers also should begin to incorporate the more recently developed cohesion inventories — the QAG, PAGEQ, and YSEQ—into their research. Cohesion is a fundamental group property. Thus, even if a researcher's principal question is not directly concerned with cohesion, it is not inconceivable that it might have a moderator or mediator role. Including a cohesion measure into the test protocol could provide greater insights into group or individual behavior.

Approximately 15 years ago, Carron (1993) pointed out the following:

> Theory development, research, and intervention are not (and cannot be approached as) independent activities. They are compatible, complementary, and interdependent. Each is essential to the growth and development of the others. Theory development is of little value if it occurs in a vacuum; ultimately evaluations through research and application are required. And, finally, research is of minimal value if it occurs in a vacuum; ultimately theory development and application are required. (p. 210)

Therefore, practitioners, whether applied sport psychologists, coaches, or teachers, should use the cohesion inventories described in this chapter to assess the status of their groups. Has a team-building intervention been introduced? If so, the practitioner can examine its efficacy by measuring the cohesion of the team. Has the group experienced setbacks that have led concerned observers to question its unity? If so, the practitioner can assess that unity through a cohesion measure and compare the results obtained against the 9-point response scale or against the published norms.

Practitioners are sometimes loath to take the ivory tower approach and use psychometrically sound questionnaires, preferring instead to use anecdotal testimony or personal observation. This attitude may be unique to the social sciences. In the medical sciences, the physical sciences, and the natural sciences, practitioners eagerly await and readily adopt improvements in measurement. To move applied sport psychology further along the continuum from art to science, a greater reliance on psychometrically sound measures is essential.

Sequential Analysis of Team Communications and Effects on Team Performance

Allan Jeong, PhD

This chapter proposes a set of tools and methods for evaluating, modeling, and predicting team performance based on the sequential analysis of team communication patterns. The method of sequential analysis is described along with specific software tools and techniques that facilitate the analysis of dialogue moves and move sequences observed in communications exchanged between team members. The dialogic theory and its assumptions are presented to establish a theoretical framework for determining how to sequentially analyze, model, and interpret observed patterns in team communication processes. Step-by-step instructions are presented to illustrate how (a) to assess the effect of latent variables (e.g., message function, response latency, communication style) and exogenous variables (e.g., gender, discourse rules, context) on when and how certain dialogue moves elicit subsequent moves, and (b) to assess how and to what extent the resulting communication patterns correlate with improvements in group decision making, group problem solving, and team performance.

Introduction to Team Communications

Team performance depends not only on the skills and contributions of individual team members but also on the ways in which team members engage in communication processes that facilitate team decision making and problem solving. In other words, how team members communicate with one another

can shape and determine team performance (Fiore, Salas, Cuevas, & Bowers, 2003; Salas & Cannon-Bowers, 2000) as well as team motivation, concentration, strategy, skill acquisition, attitudes, feelings, and behavior (Yukelson, 1993). However, precise models of team communication processes and the ways in which specific processes affect team performance have not yet been examined adequately (Guerlain, Shin, Guo, Adams, & Calland, 2002). The current state of research on team communications can be attributed to the lack of tools and methods to support the detailed analysis and modeling of team communication processes (Domagoj, Tenenbaum, Eccles, Jeong, & Johnson, 2009).

Some of the tools and methods that can be used to analyze and model team communications and team performance were recently developed to model processes observed in computer-mediated communication (CMC) and computer-supported collaborative learning (CSCL). The tools were developed with the purpose of attaining a deeper understanding of CMC and its effects on group interaction, group performance, and learning (Garrison, 2000; Koschmann, 1999; Mendl & Renkl, 1992). One of these approaches is sequential analysis (Bakeman & Gottman, 1997), a method used to measure and study the sequential nature of messages and responses exchanged within groups to determine how particular processes, and the variables affecting the processes, either help groups achieve or inhibit groups from achieving desired outcomes (Jeong, 2003a; Koschmann, 1999; Soller, 2004). This process-oriented approach enables researchers to develop computational models (represented quantitatively and visually) to explain and predict patterns in group interaction based on specific characteristics of the message and the conditions surrounding the exchange of messages.

A precursor to sequential analysis was *content analysis,* an analytical method commonly used to study verbal exchanges in interpersonal communications. In content analysis, messages (or dialogue moves) are classified into categories, and the message frequencies observed in each category are computed to determine what communication patterns exist (Rourke, Anderson, Garrison, & Archer, 2001). This approach generates results that are descriptive rather than prescriptive, reporting, for example, the frequencies of arguments, challenges, and explanations observed in team deliberations and decision making. Message frequencies, however, provide little information to explain or predict how participants respond to given types of messages (e.g., argument → challenge versus argument → simple agreement), how response patterns are influenced by latent variables (e.g., message function, content, communication style, response latency) and exogenous variables (e.g., gender, personality traits, discussion protocols, type of task), and how particular response patterns help to improve group performance to achieve desired outcomes.

In contrast, sequential analysis enables researchers to determine the *transitional probabilities* between dialogue moves across different categories. In other words, sequential analysis determines how likely one dialogue move of a given category (e.g., claim) will elicit specific types of responses (e.g., challenge, question) based on what is said in conjunction with when, how, who, and why messages are presented (Jeong, 2004, 2006, 2007). Sequential analysis also determines whether the elicited responses help produce sequences of dialogue moves that support critical discourse (e.g., claim → challenge → explain), group decision making, problem solving, and learning. Sequential analysis has been used in studies on interpersonal communication conducted over the last 30 years, including studies on the conversational patterns of married couples, children at play, and mother–infant play (Bakeman & Gottman, 1997, pp. 184-193; Gottman, 1979) and studies on human–computer interaction (Olson, Herbsleb, & Rueter, 1994). More recently, the techniques and tools used to conduct sequential analysis have been refined (Jeong, 2009) and implemented to analyze (as well as visualize) discourse patterns in CMC in response to previous claims that sequential analysis may be the missing factor in research on the effects of computer-mediated environments and computer-based instruction (England, 1985; King & Roblyer, 1984).

To help advance research on team communications and team performance, this chapter describes software tools and a seven-step procedure for sequentially analyzing communication processes based on recent refinements to the original methods developed by Bakeman and Gottman (1997). The procedural descriptions that follow are illustrated with findings from previous studies on group discourse in CMC and computer-supported argumentation (Jeong, 2003a, 2003b, 2004, 2006; Jeong & Juong, 2007) in order to provide a more comprehensive demonstration of the tools and methods. Nevertheless, the described procedures can be readily applied to analyzing team communications in team sports, as was illustrated in a recent study comparing the communication patterns between winning and losing teams in doubles tennis (Domagoj et al., 2009). The discussion begins with a proposed set of theoretical assumptions to establish the foundation underlying the use of sequential analysis and the research designs for investigating the effects of latent and exogenous variables on group interaction patterns in team communications.

Seven-Step Procedure for Sequentially Analyzing Team Communications

The dialogic theory (Bakhtin, 1981) is a theoretical framework that can be used to conceptualize and operationalize team communication measures in group tasks or group learning (Koschmann, 1999). In this theory, language is viewed as part of a social context in which all possible meanings of a word interact, possibly *conflict,* and affect future meanings. As a result, meaning does not reside in any one utterance (or message). Instead, meaning emerges from examining the relationships between multiple utterances (e.g., a message and replies to the message). Through the process of examining the interrelationships and conflicts that emerge from a social exchange, meaning is renegotiated and reconstructed through extended social interaction. Conflicts that emerge from the interactions are what drive further inquiry, reflection and articulation of individual viewpoints and underlying assumptions.

The two main assumptions are that (1) conflict is produced not by only ideas presented in one message, such as an argument or claim, but also by the juxtaposition of opposing ideas presented in a message and responses to the message and (2) conflicts produced in exchanges trigger subsequent responses that can serve to verify (e.g., argument → challenge → evidence) and justify (e.g., argument → challenge

→ explain) stated arguments and claims. These assumptions imply that we should focus on analyzing the frequency of specific message–response pairs (e.g., argument → challenge, challenge → explain) and not the frequency of messages alone (e.g., arguments, challenges, explanations). Support for this theory can be drawn from extensive research on collaborative learning that shows that conflict and the consideration of both sides of an issue are needed to drive inquiry, reflection, articulation of individual viewpoints, and underlying assumptions and ultimately to achieve deeper understanding (Johnson & Johnson, 1992; Wiley & Voss, 1999). The need to explain, justify, or understand is felt and acted on only when conflicts or errors are brought to attention (Baker, 1999). This process plays a key role not only in increasing understanding but also in improving decision making (Lemus, Seibold, Flanagin, & Metzger, 2004).

Step 1: Choose a Metric for Measuring and Comparing Group Interaction Patterns

A number of possible metrics can be used to analyze and identify patterns in message–response sequences. The two metrics that are perhaps the most meaningful are (1) transitional probabilities, which are probabilities that determine, for example, what percentage of the observed responses to arguments are challenges versus supporting evidence versus explanations, and (2) mean response scores, which are the mean number of specific responses elicited per message category, such as the mean number of challenges, supporting evidence, or explanations elicited per stated argument.

Transitional probabilities are computed by tallying the frequency of a particular response posted in reply to a particular message type. The results are reported in a frequency matrix (table 36.1). The observed frequencies are converted into relative frequencies or *transitional probabilities* for each response type for each message category (table 36.2 on page 426). To determine whether the transitional probabilities of each response to each message category are significantly higher or lower than expected and to determine whether a pattern exists in the way in which participants respond to messages in a particular category, z-scores are computed and reported in a Z-matrix (table 36.3 on page 426). As opposed to using the chi-square test for independence, this z-score statistic, which was proposed by Bakeman and Gottman (1997, pp. 108-111), takes into account not only the observed total number of responses to a particular message category but also the marginal totals of each response type observed across all message types.

The transitional probabilities can be conveyed visually in the form of a state diagram (figure 36.1 on page 426) that provides a Gestalt view of team communication processes and a visual means to identify response patterns and predict event sequences that are most likely to occur. For example, the diagram can be used to determine or predict how often arguments will elicit challenges versus counterarguments and how often challenges will elicit explanations versus counterchallenges to determine overall how likely the observed patterns of interaction will lead to constructive dialogue (e.g., argument → challenge → explanation) versus nonproductive dialogue (e.g., argument → opposing argument).

▪ Table 36.1 ▪

Frequency Matrix Produced With the Discussion Analysis Tool

	Arg	But	Evid	Expl	Replies	No replies	Givens	% targets	% givens
Arg	3	**101**	**73**	*16*	193	35	112	.25	.30
But	3	*82*	88	91	264	24	149	.35	.40
Evid	0	64	50	48	162	22	35	.21	.09
Expl	0	51	*22*	**71**	144	55	74	.19	.20
Total responses observed	14	307	233	229	763	136	370		

For example, 101 challenges (But) were posted in response to arguments (Arg). This frequency (in bold) was higher than the expected frequency based on its z-score value of 3.96 at p < .01. Values significantly lower than expected are in bold and italic. Evid = evidence, EXPL = explanations.

From Jeong, 2009.

■ Table 36.2 ■
Transitional Probability Matrix

	Arg	But	Evid	Expl	Replies	No replies	Givens	Reply rate
Arg	.02	**.52**	**.38**	*.08*	193	35	112	.69
But	.01	*.31*	.33	.34	264	24	149	.84
Evid	.00	.40	.31	.30	162	22	35	.37
Expl	.00	.35	*.15*	**.49**	144	55	74	.26
Total responses observed	14	307	233	229	763	136	370	.52

For example, 52% of all responses to arguments (Arg) were challenges (But). Values in bold identify probabilities significantly higher than expected. Values in bold and italic identify probabilities significantly lower than expected. Evid = evidence, Expl = explanations.

■ Table 36.3 ■
z-Score Matrix

	Arg	But	Evid	Expl
Arg	−0.34	**3.96**	**2.54**	*−7.62*
But	−1.05	*−3.76*	1.22	1.95
Evid	−1.96	−0.21	0.10	−0.12
Expl	−1.82	−1.31	*−4.41*	**5.61**

Z-scores < −2.32 (in bold and italic) reveal probabilities that were significantly lower than expected. Z-scores ≥ 2.32 (in bold) reveal probabilities that were significantly higher than expected. Arg = argument, But = challenge, Evid = evidence, Expl = explanation.

The second metric, mean response scores, determines the number of times a given type of message elicits a particular type of response. This metric *describes* the overall level of performance by measuring, for example, the mean number of challenges elicited per argument and the mean number of explanations elicited per challenge. This is similar to measuring the percentage of arguments left unchallenged and the percentage of challenges left unresolved. As a result, this particular metric can be used to determine at what level participants are critically analyzing arguments (e.g., argument → challenge → explain) or are engaging in processes that block critical discourse (e.g., argument → counterargument, argument → no response). When mean response scores are used, statistical methods such as *t*-tests and ANOVA can be used to test for differences in response patterns among experimental conditions, and effect sizes can be computed to determine to what extent the observed differences are meaningful.

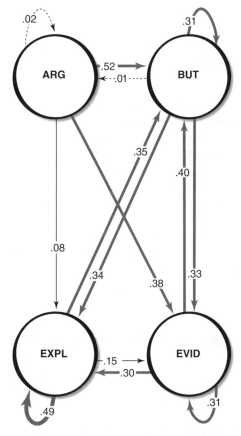

Figure 36.1 Transitional state diagram. ARG = argument, BUT = challenge, EVID = supporting evidence, and EXPL = explanation.

Reprinted by permission from A. Jeong 2009.

Transitional probabilities can be used to explain observed differences in mean response scores. For example, one group might exhibit a tendency to respond to arguments with more challenges and less supporting evidence, whereas another group might exhibit a tendency to respond to arguments with more supporting evidence but fewer challenges. If a significant difference is found in the mean number of challenges elicited per argument between groups, the differences in interaction patterns might suggest that the second group posts fewer challenges in response to arguments because its members allocate more time and resources to developing evidence to support arguments, which leaves less time and resources to challenge arguments. Thus, transitional probabilities and mean response scores can be used simultaneously, with one metric used as the main dependent variable and the other used for post hoc analysis. However, transitional probabilities are best used as the main dependent variable when conducting an exploratory study, whereas mean response scores are best for conducting experimental studies.

Step 2: Specify A Priori Tests for Specific Message–Response Pairs

When using transitional probabilities or mean response scores, the specific message–response pairs to be examined in a study should be defined a priori because the total number of possible event pairs grows exponentially with the addition of each message category to the coding scheme. For example, a coding scheme consisting of four categories (e.g., argument, challenge, explain, evidence) produces a 4 × 4 matrix resulting in 16 possible event pairs (e.g., argument → challenge, challenge → argument, challenge → explain, explain → challenge, and so on). Testing all 16 event pairs for differences in mean response scores involves too large a number of contrasts to adequately control for type I error (finding significant differences when the differences are actually the result of random chance alone). Power can be increased by testing only a select number of event pairs, particularly those that are believed to support group performance (e.g., argument → challenge, challenge → explain).

To identify the most important sequences to examine in a study, the researcher should review existing literature for specific models for achieving specific tasks. The specific message–response sequences that were examined in the previous studies (discussed earlier) were selected on the dialogic theory's assumptions that deeper and more critical inquiry revolves around exchanges in which opposing or conflicting viewpoints are juxtaposed. The other alternative is to closely examine social exchanges while groups perform a particular task (Mandl & Renkl, 1992) and to identify the subordinate skills and skill sequences needed to complete the task by using techniques for analyzing intellectual skills (Dick, Carey, & Carey, 2005, pp. 38-56).

Step 3: Collect Discussions and Messages Parsed and Classified by Dialogue Moves

The next step is to parse transcripts of the team communications into discrete units of analysis. Each unit must be classified by function (or dialogue move) based on an established coding scheme using the same procedures for conducting quantitative content analysis (Rourke, Anderson, Garrison, & Archer, 2001). However, the process of parsing and coding is fraught with a number of methodological challenges in which the reliability, validity, and feasibility of parsing and coding messages pose significant problems. Messages often address multiple topics or functions, making the process of parsing each message into discrete segments extremely difficult to achieve with high interrater reliability. As a result, researchers have debated the merits of parsing and categorizing messages by sentence, paragraph, message, unit of meaning, and dialogue move. The problem with interrater reliability is then compounded when mapping the links between units presented within a message and units presented within responses to the message (Gunawardena, Lowe, & Anderson, 1997; Newman, Johnson, Cochrane, & Webb, 1996).

One approach to this problem (at least in CMC research) is to instruct participants to classify, label, and post messages that address one and only one function (e.g., argument, evidence, challenge, explanation) at a time. Table 36.4 on page 428 provides instructions for structuring online group debates. In this approach, each message is associated with one and only one dialogue move. As a result, the challenges associated with parsing messages into discrete units of analysis are minimized if not eliminated. Another advantage of this approach is that larger data sets can be attained more easily to generate a sufficient number of event pairs to test transitional probabilities and mean response scores.

Message labeling has been implemented in a number of computer-supported collaborative argumentation (CSCA) systems to scaffold argumentation and problem solving (Carr & Anderson, 2001; Cho & Jonassen, 2002; McAlister, 2003; Sloffer, Dueber, & Duffy, 1999; Veerman, Andriessen, & Kanselaar, 1999) and to enable participants to see the overall structure and organization of their arguments (see figure 36.2 on page 428). However, message labeling in itself can affect group interactions and the validity of the findings. At this time, the effects of message labeling have not yet been fully investigated, and initial findings are still inconclusive (Beers, Boshuizen, & Kirschner, 2004; Jeong, 2004; Strijbos, Martens, Jochems, & Kirschner, 2004).

■ Table 36.4 ■

Example Instructions
on How to Label Messages During Online Debates

Symbol	Description of symbol
+	Identifies a message posted by a student assigned to the team *supporting* the given claim or statement.
–	Identifies a message posted by a student assigned to the team *opposing* the given claim or statement.
Arg#	Identifies a message that presents *one and only one* argument or reason for using or not using chats (instead of threaded discussion forums). Number each posted argument by counting the number of arguments already presented by your team. Subarguments need not be numbered.
Expl	Identifies a reply or message that provides additional support, explanation, clarification, or elaboration of an argument or challenge.
But	Identifies a reply or message that questions or challenges the merits, logic, relevancy, validity, accuracy, or plausibility of a presented argument (Arg) or challenge (But).
Evid	Identifies a reply or message that provides proof or evidence to establish the validity of an argument or challenge.

SUPPORT statement because...	Instructor	Sat Oct 2, 2004 11:18 am
. +ARG#1 MediaIsButAMereVehicle	Student	Mon Oct 4, 2004 8:47 pm
. . -EVID MediaIsButAMereVehicle	Student	Tue Oct 5, 2004 7:09 pm
. . . +BUT RelativityTheoryOldToo	Student	Tue Oct 5, 2004 9:43 pm
. . . . -BUT RelativityTheoryOldToo	Student	Sat Oct 9, 2004 10:12 am
. . -BUT Whataboutemotions?	Student	Tue Oct 5, 2004 9:53 pm
. . +EVID DistEdEffectiveAsF2F	Student	Tue Oct 5, 2004 10:40 pm
. . -BUT Mediaamerevehicle	Student	Wed Oct 6, 2004 8:19 pm
. . +EVID MooreConcurs	Student	Wed Oct 6, 2004 10:07 pm
. . . +EXPLMediaSelectionComesAfterInstructionalStrategy	Student	Sun Oct 10, 2004 12:35 am
. . . -BUT WellChosenEffective	Student	Sun Oct 10, 2004 4:31 pm
. . . . +BUT SupportingResearch	Student	Sun Oct 10, 2004 5:37 pm
. . -BUT Mediaismorethenamerevehicle	Student	Fri Oct 8, 2004 5:30 pm
. . . +BUT SupportingEvidence?	Student	Sat Oct 9, 2004 8:51 am
. . . -BUT LearningNotSimplyAPassiveResponseToDeliveryMethod	Student	Mon Oct 11, 2004 9:54 am
. +ARG2 Standards for teaching	Student	Wed Oct 6, 2004 1:48 pm
. . +BUT Clarification?	Student	Sun Oct 10, 2004 5:39 pm
. +ARG3 MediaUnrelatedtoLearningObjectives	Student	Wed Oct 6, 2004 3:12 pm
. . -BUT MediaUnrelatedtoLearningObjectives	Student	Wed Oct 6, 2004 8:26 pm
. . . +BUT MediaSelection	Student	Thu Oct 7, 2004 9:20 am
. . . . -BUT MediaSelection	Student	Sun Oct 10, 2004 11:21 am
. . +EVID MethodNotMedia	Student	Wed Oct 6, 2004 11:04 pm
. . -BUT MediaUnrelatedtoLearningObjectives	Student	Sat Oct 9, 2004 10:59 am
. . . +EXPL Media'sContribution?	Student	Sat Oct 9, 2004 9:10 pm
. . . . -BUT Media'sContribution?	Student	Sun Oct 10, 2004 3:42 pm

Figure 36.2 Example of an online debate with labeled messages in a blackboard forum.

Nevertheless, message labeling provides a practical, although not perfect, solution to a problem that has prevented previous researchers from conducting a thorough and sequential analysis of CMC. These methods could be used when hosting online discussions among team members in team sports. How this particular approach can be applied to facilitate the process of coding team communications in face-to-face contexts is an issue that warrants further research.

Step 4: Organize Dialogue Move Sequences Into Conversational Threads

Although conversations often appear to unfold linearly (to be ordered by chronology), conversations can be, and often are, multithreaded in their semantic structure. Particularly in large groups, participants make responses *not* to the most recent comment but to comments presented earlier in the conversational thread. For example, in figure 36.2 the sixth message down the list (–But What about emotions?) was posted at 9:53 p.m. in direct response to the second message (+Arg#1) posted 2 days earlier and *not* in response to the fourth message (+But) posted only 10 min earlier at 9:43 p.m.

The multithreaded nature of conversations observed in face-to-face contexts can be organized visually into a hierarchical structure using a common spreadsheet (as illustrated in figure 36.2). Each dialogue move listed in the hierarchical structure is tagged with the assigned code (e.g., +But). Following each code is a complete transcript of the dialogue move or some title that conveys the main idea presented in the dialogue move. Finally, each coded dialogue move is assigned a *thread level*—a whole number representing its relative location within the conversational thread. The thread level for each dialogue move is determined by simply counting the number of indentations to the right relative to the first message in each conversational thread. For example, a thread level of 2 is assigned to message +Arg#1 in figure 36.2, a level of 3 is assigned for –Evid, a level of 4 is assigned for +But, a level of 5 is assigned for –But, and a level of 3 is assigned for –But. Thus, the data set is reduced to codes and thread levels so that the dialogue moves can be sequentially analyzed to identify emerging patterns in team communications.

Step 5: Prepare Data for Analysis According to Questions Under Examination

The Discussion Analysis Tool (DAT; Jeong, 2009), which is a software program, can be used to automatically harvest the codes and compute the thread level for each dialogue move recorded in a spreadsheet such as the one illustrated in figure 36.2. All codes are pulled into column A in a DAT spreadsheet (see figure 36.3), and the thread level for each coded dialogue move is recorded in column B. Once all the data are extracted into DAT, the codes must be checked for interrater reliability against the Cohen kappa coefficient (Rourke et al., 2001, p. 6). At this time, DAT is the only tool available for processing data from a hierarchically organized spreadsheet (such as the one in figure 36.2) to produce the data needed to sequentially analyze both linear and multithreaded conversations.

Once all the codes and thread levels have been entered into DAT, the codes in column A can be modified, expanded, and collapsed to examine group interaction patterns from different perspectives depending on the variables that are being examined. For example, the codes in column A of figure 36.3

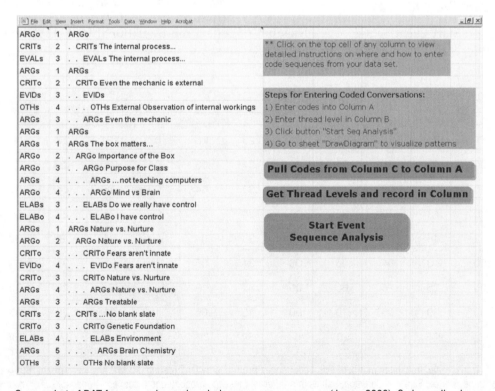

Figure 36.3 Screen shot of DAT for processing and analyzing message sequences (Jeong, 2006). Codes ending in *s* are dialogue moves presented in a conversational style. Codes ending in *o* are dialogue moves presented in a purely expository style.

have been expanded to identify dialogue moves presented in a conversational style (e.g., arguments presented with greetings, emotions, acknowledgments, addresses to other members by name, and so on), which are coded as Args, versus dialogue moves presented in a purely expository style, which are coded as Argo.

By appending additional tags (such as s and o) to the codes, different variables can be taken into consideration to examine their effects on team communication patterns and vice versa. This procedure has been used in research on team communications in online discussions to analyze the effects of either using or not using qualifiers when stating claims (Jeong, 2005) as well as the effects of response time (Jeong, 2004), gender (Jeong & Davidson-Shivers, 2006), and intellectual openness (Jeong, 2007). These studies all examine how characteristics of a dialogue move (based on why, how, when, and who performs the dialogue move) affect the way other team members respond to a move to produce particular communication patterns. Appending tags to identify dialogue moves produced by high- versus low-performing teams produces state diagrams to reveal potential differences in communication patterns—differences that can potentially explain and predict team performance.

Step 6: Compute Transitional Probabilities, Z-Scores, and State Diagrams

By clicking on Start Event Sequence Analysis in DAT (see figure 36.3), the conversational exchanges recorded in the data are translated into a transitional probability matrix (figure 36.4). Comparing the transitional probabilities in the upper-left quadrant of the probability matrix, for example, reveals how often dialogue moves presented in an expository style elicit responses also presented in an expository style. In contrast, the lower-right quadrant reveals how often dialogue moves presented in a conversational style elicit responses also presented in a conversational style. Each quadrant can be converted into a state diagram to compare, identify differences in, and model interaction patterns in conversational threads that consist of dialogue moves presented in an expository versus conversational style (figure 36.5).

One alternative to using DAT is the General Sequential Querier (GSEQ) developed by Bakeman and Quera (1995). GSEQ performs a wide range of statistical functions to analyze event sequences, timed-event sequences, interval sequences, and cross-classified events. What separates DAT from GSEQ is that DAT (a) analyses multithreaded conversations and events, (b) makes more transparent within Excel the formulas and functions used to compute probabilities and z-scores, (c) provides an interface with Excel and tools to support data preparation and analysis, (d) identifies the location of each event pair tallied in frequency matrices, and (e) generates transitional state diagrams using arrows or edges with varying densities that directly reflect the transitional probabilities among the nodes or events.

	Arg	But	Evid	Expl	Arg	But	Evid	Expl	Replies	No replies	Givens	Reply rate
Arg	.01	.35	.20	.10	.00	.20	.06	.07	231	27	143	.81
But	.00	.43	.11	.05	.00	.34	.03	.04	130	133	239	.44
Evid	.00	.38	.09	.18	.00	.31	.04	.00	45	44	81	.46
Expl	.00	.48	.10	.00	.00	.34	.00	.07	29	27	50	.46
Arg	.02	.46	.07	.06	.00	.35	.04	.00	54	8	32	.75
But	.00	.43	.04	.06	.00	.31	.05	.11	94	91	174	.48
Evid	.00	.25	.25	.00	.00	.37	.12	.00	8	22	30	.27
Expl	.00	.20	.05	.10	.00	.45	.05	.15	20	20	37	.46
$n =$	3	238	79	50	0	174	30	37	611	372	786	.68

Figure 36.4 Transitional probability matrix of event sequences produced by DAT (Jeong, 2006). Arg = argument, But = challenge, Evid = supporting evidence, Expl = explanation. Values in bold are a message presented in a conversational style. For example, the 32 arguments presented with conversational style elicited 21 total responses, and 90% of the responses were challenges.

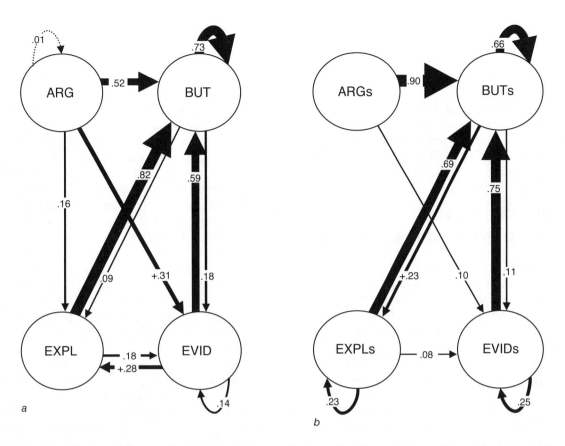

Figure 36.5 Transitional state diagrams illustrating the response patterns produced from messages with or without conversational language (Jeong, 2006).

Reprinted, by permission, from A. Jeong, 2006, "The effects of conversational styles of communication on group interaction patterns and argumentation in online discussions," *Instructional Science* 34(5): 367-397.

Step 7: Interpret the Transitional Probabilities for Interaction Patterns

A visual inspection of the transitional state diagrams in figure 36.5 reveals potential differences in communication patterns produced by dialogue moves that are presented in expository versus conversational style during argumentative discussions. The diagrams show that arguments presented in a conversational style are far more likely to elicit challenges. Also, challenges presented in a conversational style are far more likely to elicit explanations.

A number of statistical tests can be used to determine whether the noted communication patterns are significantly different. One option is to use the chi-square test to determine, for example, if the transitional probabilities of all responses to Argo versus Args are significantly different. In the study by Jeong (2006), DAT was used to output numerical data that counted the number of challenges elicited by *each* argument, the number of explanations elicited by *each* challenge, and so on. These data were then analyzed using a common

statistical software program to test for differences in mean response scores (e.g., the average number of challenges elicited per Argo versus Args) using independent *t*-tests. These *t*-tests revealed that (a) the average number of challenges elicited by arguments presented in a conversational style was significantly higher than the number of challenges elicited by arguments presented in an expository style and (b) the average number explanations elicited by arguments presented in a conversational style was significantly higher than the number of explanations elicited by challenges presented in an expository style.

Arriving at a meaningful interpretation of interaction patterns revealed from sequential analysis is often a difficult process due to the large number of statistical tests that can be performed across the many possible message–response pairs that arise from the complex nature of group interaction. Type I errors can be avoided by minimizing the number of possible tests and comparisons and focusing the analysis on only those message–response sequences that exemplify the processes believed to improve group performance and specified in the a priori hypotheses. The final word of caution is that when a particular pattern of interaction is revealed in a z-score matrix (where the transitional probability of an event sequence is significantly higher or lower than the expected frequency), the researcher should verify that the finding is supported by sufficient cell frequencies in the frequency matrix for the given message–response pair and the finding is not biased by coding errors in the message labels.

Recommendations for Researchers and Practitioners

More detailed discussions of the method and its limitations can be found in the cited references. The limitations noted there provide recommendations and ideas for future research. Nevertheless, here are some recommendations. Researchers should (a) examine multiple discussion groups to prevent the idiosyncrasies of any one particular group from exerting too large an influence on the results, (b) examine the interrelationships among multiple variables and their relative effect using multiple regression, (c) expand the analysis to measure the frequency of three-event sequences to determine whether some event pairs are more effective than others in eliciting desired responses, (d) identify sequences that distinguish experts from novices using multidimensional scaling (Soller, 2004), and (e) test and validate process models across different types of team tasks that take other categories of dialogue moves into consideration to help identify unique patterns of communication that can lead to better team performance.

Despite the noted limitations, the methods and tools described in this chapter provide a road map on how to model and study team communications, the effects of different variables on team communications, and the relationship between team communications and team performance. The tools and methods presented here enable researchers to embark on a microlevel approach to measuring, visualizing, and formalizing models of team communications at a level not seen before in the effort to identify new directions for research and development of methods that improve team performance. From the practitioner's perspective, the research findings resulting from the proposed tools and methods can support an evidence-based approach to designing training and interventions that can improve team communication skills and processes. The developments in CMC research and technologies in themselves might also serve as useful tools to help teams develop more effective communication.

Sequential analysis can be used to model not just patterns in the dialogue exchanged among athletes on the same or opposing teams but also patterns in the communications between trainer and athlete as well as patterns in the overt interactions between athlete and training technologies. Finally, sequential analysis can also be used to model the sequences of cognitive and emotional responses and behaviors observed in training and competition (Calmeiro, 2006). The hope is that these methods and software tools will enable more researchers to apply sequential analysis to the study of human behavior and performance.

37

Models and Measurement of Leadership in Sport

Packianathan Chelladurai, PhD

Leadership, defined as "the behavioral process of influencing individuals and groups toward set goals" (Barrow, 1977, p. 232), has been considered a significant factor in the successes of governments, political movements, business and industrial enterprises, educational institutions, and individuals and teams in sports. The importance of leadership is highlighted by the extensive media coverage of leaders, their behaviors, and their decisions. In addition, the exorbitant rewards that organizations are willing to provide to leaders are another indication of the importance attached to leadership.

This emphasis on leadership is very much pronounced in the context of sport, particularly when it comes to coaches. Since every sport is characterized by competitions, and every competition is a zero-sum game, victories in such contests are critical. While victories are a function of the talented athletes in the team and their performance in specific contests, the coaches of those winning teams are also credited with the successes. The coaches decide on the training regimen, on the strategies and tactics employed in a specific contest, and on the combination of players to be deployed.

In this chapter, the major streams of research on coaching leadership in sport are outlined. The first section describes the multidimensional model of leadership (Chelladurai, 1978; 1993), the mediational model of leadership (Smith, Smoll, & Hunt, 1977; Smoll & Smith, 1989), the model of coaching effectiveness (Horn, 2002), the autonomy-supportive leadership model (Amorose & Horn, 2000, 2001; Amorose & Anderson-Butcher, 2007; Hollembeak & Amorose, 2005; Mageau & Vallerand, 2003; Vallerand, 2007), and the normative model of decision

styles in coaching (Chelladurai & Haggerty, 1978). The next section outlines various scales, such as the Leadership Scale for Sports (LSS; Chelladurai & Saleh) and the Coaching Behavior Assessment System (CBAS; Smith, Smoll, & Hunt, 1977), that have been used to test the propositions of the leadership models. Finally, the concluding section offers recommendations for future research. Interested readers may also refer to earlier reviews of research on leadership in sport (Chelladurai, 1993, 2007; Chelladurai & Riemer, 1998; Horn, 2002).

Theoretical Frameworks of Leadership in Sport

This section briefly describes the models of leadership advanced in the context of sport: the multidimensional model of leadership (Chelladurai, 1978, 1993), the mediational model of leadership (Smith et al., 1977; Smoll & Smith, 1989), coaching effectiveness model (Horn, 2002), and the model of autonomy-supportive leadership (Amorose & Horn, 2000, 2001; Mageau & Vallerand, 2003). In addition, Chelladurai and Haggerty's (1978) normative model of decision styles is described.

Multidimensional Model of Leadership

Chelladurai's (1978, 1993) multidimensional model incorporates three states of leader behaviors: *required behaviors* (behaviors largely influenced by *situational characteristics*), *preferred behaviors* (members' preferences mostly as a function of their *individual characteristics*), and *actual behaviors* (behaviors influenced by *leader characteristics* as well as *required* and *preferred behaviors*). The major proposition of the multidimensional model is that congruence among the three states of leader behavior results in member satisfaction and group performance. In the model, the leader may also engage in transformational leadership in an attempt to (a) change one or more of the situational characteristics that constrain the group in its activities and (b) change member characteristics in terms of their self-esteem and aspirations.

Mediational Model of Leadership

The mediational model of leadership (Smith et al., 1977; Smoll & Smith, 1989) consists of the central elements of (a) coach's behaviors, (b) players' perceptions and recollections of those behaviors, and (c) players' evaluative reactions. These central elements are influenced by situational factors, coach characteristics, and player characteristics.

The situational factors influencing these central elements are the nature of the sport, practice sessions versus games, previous team successes and failures, current status in competitions, level of competition (e.g., recreational versus competitive), and interpersonal attraction within the team. The coach characteristics that influence coach behaviors and perceptions of player attitudes are coaching goals and motives, behavioral intentions, instrumentalities, perceived coaching norms and role conception, inferred player motives, self-monitoring, and sex. Finally, the player characteristics that affect player perception and recall and player evaluative reactions include age, sex, perceived coaching norms, valence of coach behaviors, sport-specific achievement motives, competitive trait anxiety, general self-esteem, and athletic self-esteem.

Model of Coaching Effectiveness

In Horn's (2002) coaching effectiveness model, the identifiable antecedents of sociocultural context, organizational climate, and personal characteristics of the coach influence a coach's behaviors as mediated by that coach's expectancies, values, beliefs, and goals. Furthermore, a coach's behaviors affect athletes' performance and behavior directly as well as indirectly through the athlete's perception, interpretation, and evaluation of the coach's behaviors. Perceived leader behavior influences the athlete's self-perceptions, beliefs, and attitudes, which, in turn, influence the athlete's level and type of motivation. The unique feature of Horn's (2002) model is that she adapted the mediational processes of Smoll and Smith's (1989) model and articulated them as sequential outcomes of leader behaviors that influence athlete performance and behavior.

Autonomy-Supportive Leadership

Using Deci and Ryan's (1985; Ryan & Deci, 2000, 2002) self-determination theory (SDT), Amorose and associates (Amorose & Horn, 2000, 2001) and Vallerand and associates (Mageau & Vallerand, 2003; Vallerand, 2007) recently advanced the model of autonomy-supportive leadership. In Mageau and Vallerand's (2003) view, an autonomy-supportive coach (a) provides choices within specific rules and boundaries, (b) explains the tasks and boundaries, (c) recognizes members' feelings and perspectives, (d) allows individuals to take initiative, (e) provides noncontrolling feedback, (f) avoids criticisms and rewards to control behavior, and (g) reduces ego involvement in members.

Thus, these authors clearly defined *autonomy-supportive style* and articulated the kinds of coach behaviors considered to be autonomy supportive. What is missing is a scale to measure these behaviors. However, it is only a matter of time before these authors or other researchers develop a scale to measure the components of autonomy-supportive coaching.

Amorose and Anderson-Butcher (2007) assessed the perceptions of high school and college athletes by administering the 6-item short version of the Sport Climate Questionnaire (SCQ). They found that the more the athletes felt competent and autonomous and had a sense of relatedness, the more their reasons for participating were self-determined. What is more germane to the present context is that perceptions of coaches as autonomy supportive positively related to each of the three needs and had an indirect effect on the motivational orientation of athletes.

Decision Styles in Coaching

A significant component of leadership is making decisions in every aspect of coaching, such as selecting players, selecting strategies and tactics to be employed during the season and in specific games, developing the training regimen, and choosing competitions. Chelladurai and associates (Chelladurai & Arnott, 1985; Chelladurai & Haggerty, 1978; Chelladurai, Haggerty, & Baxter, 1989; Chelladurai, & Quek, 1995) focused on the degree of involvement of group members in making these decisions. In their normative model of decision styles in coaching, Chelladurai and Haggerty (1978) identified seven attributes that affect the problem (the decision making) in coaching. They are as follows:

1. Time pressure (whether there is enough time for member participation)

2. Decision quality (whether the problem requires an optimal solution)

3. Information location (whether the coach or athletes have the relevant information)

4. Problem complexity (if the problem involves several factors requiring thorough analysis)

5. Group acceptance (if the acceptance of the decision is necessary for implementing the solution)

6. Coach power (if the coach's power base would enlist group acceptance)

7. Group integration (if the team is integrated)

Given a configuration of these attributes, a coach may adopt one of the following decision styles: making an autocratic decision, consulting with a few members or with the whole group before making a decision, letting the group make the decision, or delegating the decision making to one or more members of the group. The studies based on this model (Chelladurai & Arnott, 1985; Chelladurai et al., 1989; Chelladurai and Quek, 1995) employed various scenarios to describe the presence or absence of selected problem attributes and assessed the preferences of athletes for decision style under each scenario. The results showed that overall the respondents preferred their coaches to make the decisions alone, that their preferences for group decision making was minimal, and that the delegate style was almost totally unacceptable in the coaching context.

Sources of Confusion

One source of confusion relative to the multidimensional model of leadership is the concept of required behavior. While several studies have been carried out based on the multidimensional model, they have been confined to assessing the congruence of preferred and actual behaviors. Typically, researchers have administered the perceived and preferred versions of Chelladurai and Saleh's (1980) LSS, assessed the degree of congruence between these two states of leader behavior, and related it to some outcome measure such as member satisfaction or group performance. This focus on just two states of leader behavior while ignoring the third state of required behavior could be attributed to the fact that the actual behaviors and preferred behavior are easily measured. Only Chelladurai (1978) operationalized the construct of required behavior by averaging the preferences of all athletes in one context (Canadian intercollegiate basketball teams). In his view, the influence of individual differences on preferred leadership cancels out when the overall

mean of the subjects is computed. But his argument may not hold when the organizational contexts of various teams in one sport may be vastly different from each other, and so using a single estimate of required behavior for all teams may not be appropriate. Thus, there is the necessity to identify and catalog the behaviors required in a given context (e.g., professional, elite, and participant sports). The problem of assessing required behavior is magnified by the multitude of situational characteristics that determine required behavior. These include the task of the group (e.g., closed versus open sports, independent versus interdependent tasks), the organizational goals (e.g., pursuit of excellence versus pursuit of pleasure), the norms of a particular setting (e.g., cultural differences), and the nature of the group (e.g., youth versus adult teams). At any rate, future research that includes required behavior must ensure that the teams and athletes are under the influence of the same set of situational characteristics. If different situational characteristics are in play, it is necessary to estimate different sets of required behavior.

Another source of confusion pointed out by Chelladurai (2007) is the misconception that the multidimensional model applies only to adult sports and the mediational model applies only to youth sports. He noted that the problem lies in "confounding of (a) the conceptual frameworks (i.e., the two models in question), (b) the measurement systems (i.e., the LSS and the CBAS), and (c) the populations in which the frameworks were developed and tested" (p. 124). He went on to suggest that the models themselves do not restrict their application to any specific population and do not proscribe the use of other measures to test their propositions.

Measures of Leadership

The leadership scales discussed in this chapter are listed in table 37.1 on page 436. The following sections describe each of these scales in turn.

Leadership Scale for Sports

Chelladurai and Saleh's (1980) LSS was developed specifically to test the constructs of the multidimensional model of leadership. The 40 items in the scale measure five dimensions of leader behavior: training and instruction (13 items), democratic behavior (9 items), autocratic behavior (5 items), social support (8 items), and positive feedback (5 items). The dimensions of democratic and autocratic behaviors assess the coach's style of decision making (i.e., the extent to which athletes are

▪ Table 37.1 ▪

Measures Assessing Leadership

Variable	Scale	Source	Website
Training and instruction, democratic behavior, autocratic behavior, social support, and positive feedback	Leadership Scale for Sports (LSS)	Chelladurai & Saleh (1980)	None
Training and instruction, democratic behavior, autocratic behavior, social support, positive feedback, and situational consideration	Revised Leadership Scale for Sports (RLSS)	Zhang, Jensen, & Mann (1997)	None
Reinforcement, nonreinforcement, and mistake contingent Encouragement, mistake-contingent technical instruction, punishment, punitive technical instruction, keeping control, general technical instruction, general encouragement, organization, and general communication	Coaching Behavior Assessment System (CBAS) observational measures	Smith, Smoll, & Hunt (1977).	None
Reinforcement, nonreinforcement, mistake-contingent encouragement, mistake-contingent technical instruction, punishment, punitive technical instruction, keeping control, general technical instruction, general encouragement, organization, and general communication	CBAS-Perceived Behavior Scale (CBAS-PBS)	Cumming, Smith, & Smoll (2006)	None
Praise and reinforcement, nonreinforcement, reinforcement combined with technical instruction, mistake-contingent encouragement, ignoring mistakes, corrective instruction, punishment, and corrective instruction combined with punishment	Coaching Feedback Questionnaire (CFQ)	Amorose & Horn (2000)	None
Negative activation and supportiveness and emotional composure	Coaching Behavior Questionnaire (CBQ)	Williams, Jerome, Kenow, Rogers, Sartain, & Darland (2003)	None
Support for athletes' needs	Sport Climate Questionnaire (SCQ)	Amorose & Anderson-Butcher (2007)	www.psych.rochester.edu/SDT/measures/passport.php
Preferences among autocratic, consultative, and group decision making	Cases for decision styles	Chelladurai & Quek (1995)	None

allowed to participate in decision making), while the dimensions of training and instruction and positive feedback relate to the task. The fifth dimension of social support assesses whether the coach creates a friendly and positive group climate. The response format asks respondents to rate the frequency of the behavior exhibited by the coach on a scale with five categories: "Always," "Often—75% of the time," "Occasionally—50% of the time," "Seldom—25% of the time," and "Never." Three versions of the LSS measure (a) athletes' preferences for specific leader behaviors, (b) athletes' perceptions of their coaches' leader behaviors, and (c) coaches' perceptions of their own behavior. The internal consistency estimates from selected studies were adequate for four of the dimensions. However, the estimates for autocratic behavior were low (<.70).

The subscale structure of the LSS has been verified by several scholars (e.g., Iordanoglou, 1990; Isberg & Chelladurai, 1990; Kim, Lee, & Lee, 1990; Lacoste & Laurencelle, 1989; Serpa, Lacoste, Pataco, & Santos, 1988). These efforts relied on the analysis of item-to-total correlations, a less rigorous technique. In contrast, Chelladurai and Riemer (1998) verified the construct validity of the scale through the more rigorous method of CFA of the preferred and perceived versions of the LSS (n = 317 and 217 university football players, respectively). The results showed that the measurement model fit the data adequately (with χ^2/df < 2 and RMSEA = .06 and .062, respectively, for the preference and perception versions). Similarly, Trail (2004) reported that there was a reasonable fit (RMSEA = .058; χ^2/df = 1.65) between high school basketball players' perceptions and the measurement model, indicating adequate construct validity for the LSS.

Revised Leadership Scale for Sports

In an attempt to revise the LSS into the RLSS, Zhang, Jensen, and Mann (1997) proposed two new dimensions of leader behavior: group maintenance behavior, which involves "clarifying the relationships among the team members, structuring and coordinating the athletes' activities, and improving the coach–athlete relationship and team cohesion" (p.109), and situational consideration behavior, which involves "considering the situation factors such as the time, individual, environment, team, and game; setting up individual goals and clarifying ways to reach the goals; differentiating coaching methods at different stages; and assigning an athlete to the right position" (pp. 109-110).

However, the proposed group maintenance behavior was not supported by the data. The intercorrelations among the rest of the subscales were all less than .30. As in previous studies, the internal consistency estimates for autocratic behavior were only .59 for the preference version, .48 for the perception version, and .35 for the coaches' self-report version. In contrast, these values were higher than .80 in all other dimensions. It is noteworthy that the dimension of autocratic behavior emerged from factor analyses of three different data sets of the RLSS but yet the internal consistency estimates remained low. In a later study, Jambor and Zhang (1997) reported coefficient alpha values of .84 for training and instruction, .66 for democratic behavior, .70 for autocratic behavior, .52 for social support, .78 for feedback, and .69 for situational consideration.

Coaching Behavior Assessment System

Along with proposing their mediational model of leadership, Smith, Smoll, and Curtis (1978) also developed measures of (a) leader behavior, (b) athletes' perceptions and recollections of leader behavior, (c) athletes' affective reactions to the sport experience, and (d) coaches' perceptions of their own behavior. The CBAS is an observational scheme in which 12 categories of leader behaviors are observed and recorded. These 12 categories are further classified as either reactive (i.e., responses to immediately preceding player or team behaviors) or spontaneous (i.e., initiated by the coach and not as a response to an immediately preceding event; Smith et al., 1977). Reactive behaviors include responses to desirable performances, reactions to mistakes, and responses to misbehaviors, while spontaneous behaviors are either game related or game irrelevant.

The measure of the actual behavior is the frequency with which a coach exhibits each one of the 12 categories of leader behaviors as observed and recorded by one or more trained observers. The agreement among raters in coding ranged from 87.5% to 100% (Smith et al., 1977; Smith, Zane, Smoll, & Coppel, 1983). Interrater reliability has also been high, with the correlations ranging from .50 to .99 in different studies (Smith et al., 1977; Smith et al., 1983). Other authors have also provided evidence of a high degree of agreement between raters (e.g., Chaumeton & Duda, 1988; Horn, 1985).

To measure players' perceptions of the coach's behavior, players are provided with a verbal description and example of each of the 12 behavioral dimensions and then asked to indicate how frequently the coach engages in each of those behaviors. Responses are made on a 7-point scale ranging from 1 = "Almost never" to 7 = "Almost always." This scale is called the *CBAS-Perceived Behavior*

Scale (CBAS-PBS; Cumming, Smith, & Smoll, 2006). Similarly, coaches are asked to indicate on 7-point scales (ranging from 1 = "Almost never" to 7 = "Almost always") the extent to which they engage in each of the behaviors. As both the CBAS-PBS and the coaches' self-reports are single-item scales, reliability cannot be established. Evaluative reactions of players have been gathered with a varying number of items, ranging from 6 (Smith et al., 1983) to 8 (Barnett, Smoll, & Smith, 1992; Smoll, Smith, Barnett, & Everett, 1993) to 10 (Smoll, Smith, Curtis, & Hunt, 1978; Smith & Smoll, 1990) and finally to 11 items (Smith et al., 1978). These items were scored on a 7-point Likert-type scale.

Correspondence Between Dimensions of the Leadership Scale for Sports and the Coaching Behavior Assessment System

Chelladurai (1993) noted the correspondence between certain LSS dimensions and CBAS dimensions. Later, Cumming and colleagues (2006) administered the LSS and CBAS to 645 high school athletes from 63 high schools and found that several of Chelladurai's (1993) hypotheses regarding relationships among behavioral categories of the two models were supported. More specifically, the training and instruction dimension of the LSS was significantly correlated with the mistake-contingent technical instruction, keeping control, general technical instruction, organization, and reinforcement and instruction dimensions of the CBAS. The positive feedback dimension of the LSS was significantly correlated with the reinforcement and general encouragement CBAS dimensions and negatively and significantly correlated with the nonreinforcement dimension of the CBAS. Cumming and colleagues (2006) also found that the LSS and CBAS dimensions explained similar and substantial amounts of variance in athletes' liking for their coach and evaluations of their coach's knowledge and teaching ability.

Coaching Feedback Questionnaire

Amorose and Horn (2000) developed the Coaching Feedback Questionnaire (CFQ) to measure athletes' perceptions of the types of feedback provided by their coaches. The 16-item CFQ measures eight categories of feedback, including (a) praise and reinforcement, nonreinforcement, reinforcement combined with technical instruction (as responses to players' performance successes) and (b) mistake-contingent encouragement, ignoring mistakes, corrective instruction, punishment, and corrective instruction combined with punishment (as

responses to players' errors). Amorose and Horn noted that these categories correspond to those of the CBAS—specifically, the reactive behaviors as outlined by Smith and colleagues (1977). The response format involves a 5-point scale ranging from "Very typical" to "Not at all typical" to indicate the extent of the behavior in question. Amorose and Horn extracted three meaningful factors from these 16 items—positive and informational feedback, punishment-oriented feedback, and nonreinforcement and ignoring mistakes. The coefficient alpha values were .72, .83, and .78, respectively. In Smith, Fry, Ethington, and Li's (2005) study involving female high school basketball players, three factors emerged from the CFQ items—positive feedback (4 items), punishment (6 items), and ignoring mistakes (2 items). Furthermore, these three factors were significant in explaining 38% of the variance in perceived task climate and positive feedback. Punishment explained 27% of the variance in perceived ego-involving climate.

In the study in which they administered both the LSS (perceived version) and the CFQ to university athletes, Amorose and Horn (2000) found that individuals high on intrinsic motivation perceived their coaches to be high on training and instruction and democratic behaviors and low in autocratic behavior (LSS dimensions). In addition, intrinsically motivated athletes perceived their coaches to be high on positive and informationally based feedback and low on punishment and ignoring behaviors (CFQ dimensions). However, the relationships between LSS dimensions and CFQ dimensions were not investigated.

Coaching Behavior Questionnaire

Kenow and Williams (1992) developed the 28-item Coaching Behavior Questionnaire (CBQ). The questionnaire included 7 filler items and a 4-point Likert response scale ranging from 1 = "Strongly disagree" to 4 = "Strongly agree." These items were intended to measure athlete's perceptions of (a) the coach's ability to communicate, (b) the confidence displayed by the coach, (c) the coach's composure and emotional control, and (d) the effects of the coach's arousal level on athletes. In this initial study, the authors found higher trait anxiety and state cognitive anxiety and lower self-esteem among athletes with more negative evaluations of their coach's behavior (i.e., the composite of the 21 CBQ items). In a later study, Kenow and Williams (1993) derived five factors from the substantive items: (1) cognitive and attentional effects of coach behavior, (2) supportiveness, (3) emotional control and composure, (4) communication, and (5) somatic effects of coach behavior. They found significant correlations between state somatic anxiety and coaches' emotional control and composure and between cognitive anxiety and perceived somatic effects of coaches' behavior.

Williams and colleagues (2003) carried out an EFA with a random half of the responses to the CBQ and a CFA with the other half of responses to verify the two-factor and three-factor models that were found to be tenable in the previous EFA. In the CFA, the two-factor model emerged as the best (compared with single-factor and three-factor models). There were 7 items in the first factor, which was named *negative activation*, and 8 items in the second factor, which was named *supportiveness and emotional composure*. The internal consistency estimates (Cronbach alpha values) were .82 and .83, respectively. Williams and colleagues (2003) could have carried out a CFA with the a priori factor structure proposed by Kenow and Williams (1992) or the five-factor structure derived by Kenow and Williams (1993) instead of conducting an EFA to derive new factors.

Measures of Decision Style

The method used in the research studies based on Chelladurai and Haggerty's (1978) normative model of decision styles was to present a set of cases representing all possible configurations in the presence or absence (yes or no, high or low) of the selected problem attributes. Following each case, a set of decision styles was presented for the respondents to indicate the one style they would choose or prefer in that particular case. In Chelladurai and Quek's (1995) study, the test–retest correlations (i.e., reliability scores) in 21 of the cases were significant and ranged from .39 to .82 for a mean of .55. The correlations in nine other cases ranged from .20 to .37 for a mean of .30. The test–retest correlations in two cases were rather low ($r = .05$ and .03). However, the test–retest correlation of the total participation score (i.e., the mean of the scores on all 32 cases) of .83 ($p < .001$) was sufficiently high. To investigate the internal consistency of the 32 cases, the authors focused on each of the five attributes at a time and divided the cases into two subsets (16 cases in each subset) based on the high–low rating of the attribute in question. The internal consistency was estimated by computing the Cronbach alpha and the Spearman-Brown equal-length split-half reliability coefficient for each subset of cases. This was repeated for all five attributes. Cronbach alpha values ranged from .69 to .83 for a mean of .77, and Spearman-Brown coefficients ranged from .68 to .88 for a mean of .79.

Measurement of Autonomy-Supportive Behavior

In their earlier studies of autonomy-supportive behavior of coaches, Amorose and Horn (2000, 2001) used the LSS to infer that higher levels of training and instruction, democratic behavior, and positive feedback and low levels of autocratic behavior reflected autonomy-supportive leadership. Recently, Amorose and Anderson-Butcher (2007) used the short version of the SCQ to examine this subject. Sample items included the following: "I feel that my coach provides me choices and options," "My coach conveys confidence in my ability to do well at athletics," and "I feel understood by my coach." The response format was a 7-point scale ranging from "Strongly disagree" to "Strongly agree," with higher scores indicating a more autonomy-supportive coaching style. The website from which the scale was extracted does not report any psychometric properties of the SCQ.[1] However, Amorose and Anderson-Butcher (2007) reported that the alpha values for all their scales ranged from .70 to .96, and so, although the specific value for the SCQ is not known, it must have been at least .70 or higher. However, Amorose and Anderson-Butcher acknowledged that "the items do not reflect the specific autonomy-supportive behaviors exhibited by the coach, but rather the general perception on the part of the athlete that the coach demonstrates an interpersonal style that is supportive of the athletes' needs" (p. 660). Future research may address the issue of whether the existing scales on leadership do or do not measure the construct of autonomy-supportive behaviors. If not, attempts should be made to develop a new scale to measure the specific coach behaviors that reflect autonomy support.

Confusion in Purposes of Sport Participation

It is not uncommon for a field to have several theories on a particular topic, each emphasizing specific constructs and the interrelationships among them (consider, for example, the extant motivational theories). It is also common for such theories to identify divergent pathways to a terminal outcome. It is seldom, however, that any two theories on a topic advocate opposing (not simply diverging) perspectives,

[1]The University of Rochester hosts a website at www.psych.rochester.edu/SDT/measures/passport.php dedicated to self-determination theory. In it, the SCQ is described in detail. The website does not show the psychometric properties of the scale or the authors of the scale.

which seems to be the case with the emphasis on autonomy-supportive leadership advanced by Amorose and associates (Amorose & Horn, 2000, 2001; Amorose & Anderson-Butcher, 2007) and Mageau and Vallerand (2003) versus the results of Chelladurai and associates (Chelladurai & Arnott, 1985; Chelladurai, Haggerty, & Baxter, 1989) on decision styles. Autonomy-supportive leadership is oriented toward cultivating the sense of autonomy and competence in the individual, which, in turn, fosters intrinsic motivation and well-being in the individual. In contrast, the decision styles research shows that the autocratic style of decision making is acceptable to, and indeed preferred by, athletes—a notion that appears to be antithetical to the notion of autonomy. Furthermore, Chelladurai (2007) has advanced a different leadership style (including demanding, commanding, and controlling) for pursuit of excellence in sport that is not consistent with the central thrust of autonomy-supportive leadership.

These contrasting approaches can be reconciled if we consider the outcomes (or goals) that are sought in each of the paradigms. The autonomy-supportive leadership is oriented toward individual motivation and well-being. The issue of performance is rarely mentioned in that context. But Chelladurai's (2007) leadership in the pursuit of excellence focuses largely on performance and progressive attainment of excellence. Similarly, the studies on decision styles involve competitive basketball teams in which performance is emphasized. Competitive teams in interdependent sports (such as basketball) may not be so conducive for participative or autonomy-supportive leadership because of the conflict of interests inherent in such tasks. For instance, the 12 players on a basketball team vie with each other for a position in the starting lineup or for a chance to play in competition. Given this intrateam competition, it may not be a good idea to ask the players who should be among the starting 5 players. Thus, the differences in the approaches to the study of leadership may be viewed as a function of the goals of participation (pursuit of pleasure or skill versus pursuit of excellence) and the type of sport (individual versus team sports). Future research should clarify the purpose of the venture and the nature of the task at hand and advance a leadership style appropriate to each contingency.

Recommendations for Researchers and Practitioners

A persistent issue with the LSS has been the low internal consistency estimates for the dimension of autocratic behavior. In Chelladurai and Riemer's

(1998) view, the items in the subscale do not reflect autocratic behavior in the traditional sense of being the opposite of democratic behavior. They suggest that the dimension be renamed as aloof behavior, authoritarian behavior, or inflexible behavior. But renaming the dimension does not solve the problem of low internal consistency. One option is to drop the dimension altogether, but this step may not be prudent because autocratic behavior with the same items emerged as a distinct factor in four different data sets. Therefore, it might be wise to retain the dimension and strengthen it by adding more homogeneous items, as was done by Price and Weiss (2000), who then found that the added items lifted the internal consistency to .71. It must be noted, however, that this increase in coefficient alpha could be a result of the larger number of items rather than the result of the substance of those items.

An alternative and more meaningful strategy is to split the dimension into (a) aloof behavior and (b) authoritarian behavior. This would require the generation of more items reflecting these two new dimensions. In the process of revising this subscale, researchers might also consider revising the entire scale. Chelladurai and Saleh (1980) employed EFA of 99 items gathered from existing scales. They accepted a five-factor solution and selected items to represent a factor based on their high loading on one factor (.40 or more) and low loadings on any other factor (.30 or less). As a result, disparate numbers of items (from 5-13 items) were selected to represent the emergent five dimensions. In a future revision of the LSS, the dimensions of the scale should be defined a priori and the items should be specified to represent each dimension. It might also be prudent to select fewer and equal numbers of items to represent each dimension. Then, the resultant measurement model should be subjected to CFA.

Also, the method used in the research studies based on Chelladurai and Haggerty's (1978) normative model of decision styles was to present a set of cases representing all possible configurations of the presence or absence (yes or no, high or low) of the selected problem attributes. Following each case, a set of decision styles was presented for the respondents to indicate the one style they would choose or prefer in that particular case. This line of research on decision styles has not been rigorous enough to place much confidence in the results. For instance, the attributes defining the problem situation and the various decision styles were transported from the mainstream management literature. While such a process is not entirely invalid, it does not take into account the unique exigencies of sport participation. Therefore, this line of research should be extended by interviewing past and present coaches to elicit their views and experiences of decision making in the coaching context. Such in-depth interviews can yield insights into the attributes of problems specific to coaching and the decision styles appropriate for such problems.

A second issue with the past research on decision styles is that these studies employed at the most five attributes to define a problem attribute, and then they crossed the presence or absence of the attributes to derive the number of scenarios. Even this restriction resulted in 32 cases (as in Chelladurai et al., 1989; Chelladurai & Quek, 1995), which might be tedious for the respondents. Future research should gather the problem attributes most relevant to the coaching context and employ all of them in investigating the perceptions of, or preferences for, specific decision styles appropriate to the coaching context. In addition, such research may resort to conjoint analysis, which could reduce the need to present a large number of cases to the respondents. Presenting fewer cases would allow the decision situation to be presented in greater detail.

The various models of sport leadership described in this chapter incorporate some common elements. For instance, the situational factors in Smoll and Smith's (1989) mediational model of leadership,

the sociocultural context and organizational climate of Horn's (2002) model of coaching effectiveness, and the coaching context in Mageau and Vallerand's (2003) motivational model of coach–athlete relationships are subsumed under the situational characteristics in Chelladurai's (1978, 1993) multidimensional model of leadership. Similarly, the coach's individual difference variables of Smith and Smoll, the coach's personal characteristics of Horn, and the coach's personal orientation of Mageau and Vallerand are encompassed by leader characteristics in Chelladurai's model. Finally, player individual difference variables in Smith and Smoll's model and athletes' personal characteristics in Horn's model are reflected in Chelladurai's member characteristics.

However, Chelladurai's (1978, 1993) model focused only on member satisfaction and group performance, while Horn (2002), Mageau and Vallerand (2003), and Amorose and Horn (2000) focused on athletes' motivation, which is a function of athletes' perceptions of competence, autonomy, and relatedness. However, this differential emphasis on varied outcomes is easily accommodated by including athlete motivation and personal growth as outcome variables along with performance and satisfaction, as is shown in figure 37.1. This figure

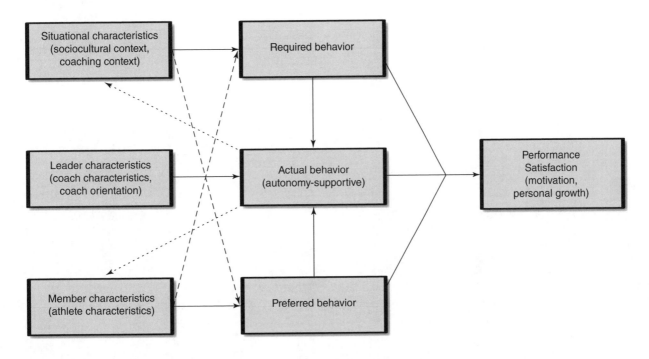

- – – – – – – ▸ Partial influence of situation on preferred behavior and of member (group) characteristics on required behavior

⋯⋯⋯⋯⋯▸ Leader behaviors transform situational or member characteristics

Figure 37.1 Incorporation of major leadership constructs.

also shows (in parentheses) how critical constructs of other models of leadership are subsumed under the multidimensional model.

The challenge lies in revising existing scales or developing new ones to measure the outcome variables, particularly individual motivation and personal growth. Similarly, the measurement of autonomy-supportive leadership needs serious consideration. The challenges in this regard have been discussed earlier. New scales should be developed or existing scales should be revised to include autonomy-supportive leadership as a separate dimension. Furthermore, it is necessary to identify and measure the elements of transformational leadership pertinent to the coaching context.

Moral Behavior

Maria Kavussanu, PhD, and Ian D. Boardley, PhD

In 2008, in a softball game at Central Washington University, an incident occurred that captured the attention of many Americans. Western Oregon's Sara Tucholsky tore one of her knee ligaments while trying to reach first base, and since she was unable to move and her teammates were not allowed to touch her, she could not achieve her goal of hitting her first-ever home run. Instead of taking advantage of this injury, Mallory Holtman and Liz Wallace—two players from the opposing team—carried her to touch second and then third base and finally home plate thereby helping her achieve her goal. This incident was described as an unbelievable act of sportspersonship and was a shining example of a social act that had positive consequences for its recipient. Unbelievable acts with *negative* consequences for others also occur in sport. Some examples are rugby player Tom Williams faking an injury to his mouth by biting on a fake blood capsule in an English Premiership rugby game and boxer Mike Tyson biting off part of Evander Holyfield's ear in response to repeated head butting during a boxing match. Although these are extreme acts, other behaviors with positive or negative consequences for others are more common in sport. In this chapter, we review measures and research dealing with such behaviors.

Definitions of the Construct

Within the sport literature, the terms *prosocial behavior* and *antisocial behavior* have been used to refer to acts such as those described above (see Kavussanu, 2008). Prosocial behavior is voluntary behavior intended to help or benefit another individual or group of individuals (Eisenberg & Fabes, 1998). Examples in sport are lending equipment to an opponent; helping another player off the floor; and encouraging, supporting, or congratulating a teammate. In contrast, antisocial behavior is voluntary behavior intended to harm or disadvantage another individual or group of individuals (Kavussanu, 2006; Sage, Kavussanu, & Duda, 2006). Sport examples are trying to injure an opponent, teasing or verbally abusing another player, breaking the rules, and cheating.

Prosocial and antisocial behaviors typically have positive and negative consequences, respectively, for others. Thus, helping an injured player should alleviate the player's distress, and hitting a player should cause pain. However, if the player does not feel any pain (e.g., due to distraction or taking analgesic medication), the behavior will not have such negative consequences. Similarly, encouraging a teammate may not benefit the athlete who does not need such encouragement, verbally abusing a player may not cause psychological harm to the individual who is able to ignore this behavior, and cheating may not have a negative consequence for others if the cheat is caught and the situation is rectified. Thus, prosocial and antisocial behaviors have the *potential* to affect others. In our view, these behaviors are morally relevant because one of the criteria used to classify behaviors within the moral domain is the perception of their consequences for the recipient (Turiel, 1983). In this chapter, we use the term *moral behavior* to refer to a broad range of *intentional* acts that could result in positive or negative consequences for others. Although such behaviors are typically discussed in moral development reviews (e.g., Carlo, 2006; Eisenberg, 2000; Tisak, Tisak, & Goldstein, 2006), the term *moral behavior* is used with a different meaning by different authors.

Several researchers have used the same or different terms to describe behavioral constructs that are similar to prosocial and antisocial behaviors as defined above. For example, the same terms have been used by Hassandra and colleagues (Hassandra, Goudas, Hatzigeorgiadis, & Theodorakis, 2007), who referred to these behaviors collectively as *fair play*, defined as respect for rules, teammates, opponents, and officials and their decisions. In this line of research, which stems from the work of Lee, Vallerand, and colleagues (Lee, Whitehead, & Ntoumanis, 2007; Lee, Whitehead, Ntoumanis, & Hatzigeorgiadis, 2008; Vallerand, Briere, Blanchard, & Provencher, 1997), *prosocial behavior* has been defined as respect for teammates and conventions, whereas the term *antisocial behavior* has been used to refer to cheating and gamesmanship acts (Hassandra et al., 2007). Conventions are positive social behaviors, cheating is an attempt to break the rules of the game while escaping detection and punishment, and gamesmanship is the use of legal but morally dubious tactics to settle the opponents (Hassandra et al., 2007; Lee et al., 2007).

Two other behavioral constructs that appear similar to prosocial and antisocial behaviors as defined here (Eisenberg & Fabes, 1998; Sage et al., 2006) are *good* and *bad* or *poor* sport behaviors. These terms were introduced by Shields, Bredemeier, LaVoi, and Power (2005) in a large-scale study of predominantly team-sport athletes and were subsequently applied to ice hockey by LaVoi and Babkes Stellino (2008). However, *good behaviors* were defined only by LaVoi and Babkes Stellino (2008) as positive acts that players do on and off the ice during games and practices. Obviously, such behaviors are not restricted to ice hockey players. *Poor sport behaviors* were described as negative things that hockey players do on and off the ice during games and practices (LaVoi & Babkes Stellino, 2008) and as ethically problematic behaviors reflecting cheating, aggression, and disrespect (Shields et al., 2005). Poor sport behaviors have also been referred to as (poor) *sportspersonship* and described as sport behaviors that carry moral connotations because of their connection to issues of respect and fairness (Shields, LaVoi, Bredemeier, & Power, 2007).

Finally, the most widely investigated class of antisocial behavior is *aggressive* behavior, which has been defined as overt behavior (verbal or physical) that is purposeful (nonaccidental), is chosen with the intent of causing injury, and has the capacity to cause psychological or physical injury to another (Husman & Silva, 1984; Stephens, 1998). The distinction has also been made between instrumental aggression, which is behavior directed at the target as a means to an end (e.g., injuring a player to get a competitive advantage), and hostile aggression, which is behavior toward another who has angered or provoked the individual and is an end in itself (Husman & Silva, 1984). Aggression has long been viewed as a moral issue and discussed in reviews of moral behavior (e.g., Shields & Bredemeier, 1995).

Theoretical and Conceptual Framework

Moral behavior in sport has been studied using a variety of theoretical frameworks. Several studies have used Rest's (1984) model to study different components of morality, one of which is behavior. However, as the present chapter focuses only on behavior, this model is not reviewed here. The framework that has been used in most aggression studies is Bandura's (1977) social learning theory, which has evolved into the social cognitive theory (SCT) of moral thought and action (Bandura, 1991). The latter theory is briefly reviewed next.

In the SCT of moral thought and action, Bandura (1991) proposed that through the course of socialization, children develop moral standards from a variety of influences, including approving and disapproving reactions to their behavior by significant others and observation of the behavior of siblings, peers, parents, and other adults. These moral standards regulate conduct through evaluative self-reactions. For example, individuals feel pride when behaving in ways that match their moral standards and guilt when their actions violate these standards. These evaluative self-reactions regulate conduct anticipatorily: People do things that they expect will give them self-satisfaction and refrain from behaving in ways that bring self-disapproval (Bandura, 1991).

Bandura (1991) also suggested that individuals use multidimensional rules or standards in determining whether behavior is reprehensible such as the consequences of the action, whether it causes personal injury or property damage, the perceived personal motivators for the conduct, and whether the conduct is directed at other people. Individuals must integrate the morally relevant information in the situations that confront them to judge the morality of conduct. Bandura (1991) also highlighted the importance of the consequences of the action for others in the social labeling of behavior and viewed those consequences as more important than the motives of the actor in determining whether behavior is reprehensible.

Finally, Bandura (1999) proposed that morality has two aspects: *proactive* and *inhibitive*. Proactive morality is manifested in the power to behave humanely, whereas inhibitive morality is expressed in the power to refrain from behaving inhumanely. In this view of morality, "people do good things as well as refrain from doing bad things" (Bandura, 1999, p. 194). In sport research, the terms *prosocial* and *antisocial behavior* have been used to refer to proactive and inhibitive morality, respectively (e.g.,

Sage et al., 2006). High levels of morality are evident when a person engages in prosocial behaviors and refrains from engaging in antisocial acts.

Dimensions and Sources of Confusion

Several researchers have emphasized the importance of moral action in the study of morality. For example, Rest (1984) argued that moral development theorists should ultimately try to understand behavior, Blasi (1980) pointed out that few would disagree that morality ultimately lies in action, and Shields and Bredemeier (1995) have recognized that action is the cornerstone of morality. Despite the widely accepted view that researchers interested in morality should study (and therefore measure) behavior, in a comprehensive review of moral assessment in sport psychology, Bredemeier and Shields (1998) stated that there are no generally accepted instruments measuring moral behavior in sport. This was attributed to a number of reasons, including the need for a philosophically defensible definition of moral behavior, the need for the participant to perceive the situation as one that involves moral choice, the importance of assessing the actor's intent, and the utilization of an ethically sound assessment technique. In 1998, no instrument satisfied completely all these criteria (Bredemeier & Shields, 1998); this is probably still the case today.

It is also rare to find a clearly stated definition of moral behavior in the sport psychology literature. In some cases, Blasi's (1987) definition—behavior that is intentional and a response to some sense of obligation, with the latter being a response to an ideal—has been cited (e.g., Kavussanu & Roberts, 2001; Shields & Bredemeier, 1995). Despite the lack of clear definitions of the construct, references to moral behavior in empirical studies and reviews of the relevant sport literature are abundant (e.g., Shields & Bredemeier, 1995, 2007; Stephens, Bredemeier, & Shields, 1997; Weiss, Smith, & Stuntz, 2008). In some instances, researchers have devoted entire sections to moral action, discussing research on poor sporting behavior, temptation to play unfairly, prosocial behavior, and most notably aggression.

This state of affairs reflects a clear paradox: The lack of adequate measurement technology that assesses moral behavior implies that researchers have not been able to measure, and therefore study, this construct (at least from a certain perspective). In this case, one should be unable to review research on moral action in sport because such research should not exist! Using the term *moral behavior* without clearly defining it or with defining it but

then discussing research pertaining to other relevant constructs in sections labeled *moral action* can be confusing. Thus, to maintain conceptual clarity, researchers who use this term should explain what they mean by it and ensure that the variables they discuss, and measure, conform to this meaning.

Perhaps this paradox can be resolved. It seems to us that the term *moral behavior* has been used with two different meanings. Specifically, when some researchers define moral behavior, they refer to the conditions in which an act is right, or *ethical*; when these conditions are met, the act can be called *moral*. For example, Rest (1984) explicitly stated that without knowing what produced the behavior we cannot call it *moral*. Similarly, Shields and Bredemeier (1995) have repeatedly emphasized the importance of assessing a person's motives in the study of moral behavior and referred to Blasi's (1987) definition to indicate when a behavior can be considered moral. When Bredemeier and Shields (1998) concluded that there are no generally accepted instruments measuring moral behavior, they seemed to us to be referring to the measurement of *ethical* behavior. However, when researchers discuss a range of behaviors in sections called *moral action*, they seem to refer to acts that are encompassed within the moral domain—that is, intentional acts that have consequences for others' rights and welfare (Turiel, 1983). This could explain why a broad range of behaviors with unknown motives are discussed as *moral action*.

A second source of confusion concerns the use of terms that reflect proactive morality to refer to behaviors that represent inhibitive morality. For instance, in the Horrocks Prosocial Play Behavior Inventory (HPPBI) developed in 1979 and used in a few sport studies (e.g., Gibbons, Ebbeck, & Weiss, 1995; Gibbons & Ebbeck, 1997), only 1 of the 10 behaviors measured was prosocial (i.e., sharing equipment). The remaining items referred to *antisocial* acts such as teasing others and arguing with teammates. Similarly, Shields and colleagues (2007) used the term *sportspersonship* to refer to sport behaviors that carry moral connotations because of their link to issues of respect and fairness, but the examples of cheating, arguing, and trash-talking they provided could be more accurately classified as *unsportsperson-like* acts. The term *poor sportspersonship*, which was used to refer to cheating, is slightly awkward because a negative term (*poor*) is used to describe a positive or desirable construct (*sportspersonship*).

Finally, there is overlap in the definitions and items used to measure moral behavior. With respect to the definition of two main constructs reviewed in this chapter—antisocial and aggressive behavior—

the overlap is substantial. Both entail the intended infliction of harm on another person. The main difference is that the term *antisocial* refers to a broader class of acts, some of which can be classified as *aggressive*. Other antisocial acts, as defined by Sage and colleagues (2006), are cheating and breaking the rules of the game. With regard to the item overlap, the same items are used in different behavior measures. For example, helping a player off the floor appears in measures of prosocial behavior, good behavior, and fair play as well as in measures of sportspersonship orientations (e.g., Vallerand et al., 1997). Thus, there has been an unnecessary proliferation in the labels used for essentially the same construct.

Main Tools for Measuring the Variables

In this section, we review the main tools for measuring moral behavior. Due to space restrictions, we focus on measures that have been developed and used in the past two decades. Readers interested in older measurement tools are advised to consult other authoritative sources (e.g., Bredemeier & Shields, 1998; Stephens, 1998). In cases where behavior was measured as part of a range of moral constructs (e.g., Kavussanu & Roberts, 2001; Stuart & Ebbeck, 1995), we describe only the part of the measure that is relevant to behavior itself. First, we discuss paper-and-pencil tools, followed by teacher and coach ratings, fouls and penalties, and observational measures. We use the term *moral behavior* when referring collectively to a broad range of behaviors that could be classified within the moral domain, but we use the specific term employed by each researcher (e.g., *aggression, prosocial behavior, antisocial behavior*, and so on) when discussing each measure.

Paper-and-Pencil Tools

One approach to measuring moral behavior in sport is presenting participants with moral dilemmas (i.e., scenarios) describing hypothetical behaviors likely to occur during a game and asking them to indicate whether they engaged in the described behaviors during a specified time frame. Using this approach, Kavussanu and Roberts (2001) presented basketball players with four moral dilemmas: (1) pushing another player when the referee is not looking, (2) faking an injury, (3) risking injuring an opposing player, and (4) injuring an opposing player. An example of a dilemma is "Imagine yourself during the last minute of a critical basketball game. A player

from the opposite team is going for a fast break, and you are the sole defender. Because of your position, the only way to stop the player from making the basket may result in an injury. You have to decide whether to risk injuring the player to prevent the basket." Participants were asked to indicate on a scale ranging from 1 = "Never" to 5 = "Very often" how often they engaged in each behavior during the last five games, and responses were averaged across the four scenarios. The reliability of the scale was acceptable (α = .70); however, the described acts were highly specific and the time frame of five games was relatively short. Thus, players may not have engaged in these acts during that time frame but might have displayed other behaviors during other games. Finally, this instrument assessed only inhibitive morality.

In an attempt to address these issues, Sage and Kavussanu (2007) developed a soccer-specific instrument that consists of 6 items measuring prosocial behavior (e.g., helping an opponent off the floor, returning the ball to an opponent for a free kick) and 13 items measuring antisocial behavior (e.g., pushing an opponent from behind, diving to fool the referee). Participants were asked to indicate how often they engaged in each behavior during the season on a scale ranging from 1 = "Never" to 5 = "Very often." Sage and Kavussanu (2007) assessed factorial validity using both EFA and CFA in one sample; factor loadings were acceptable to strong (.40-.77), and the two-factor model had an acceptable fit to the data. The internal consistency was excellent for the antisocial behavior subscale (α = .92) but below traditionally acceptable levels for the prosocial behavior subscale (α = .64). In addition, some of the items were relevant only to soccer. Finally, the instrument measured behaviors directed mainly toward opponents.

We addressed these issues by developing the Prosocial and Antisocial Behavior in Sport Scale (PABSS; Kavussanu & Boardley, 2009). Through extensive discussions with seven players involved in football, rugby, basketball, hockey, and netball, we identified behaviors common to these sports, developed items referring to these behaviors, established item content validity, and finally administered a long version of the scale to a large sample of team-sport athletes (N = 1,213) recruited from 103 teams. EFA and CFA on three subsamples revealed four factors reflecting prosocial behavior toward teammates (e.g., encouraged a teammate) and opponents (e.g., helped an injured opponent) and antisocial behavior toward teammates (e.g., verbally abused a teammate) and opponents (e.g., physically intimidated an opponent). Participants rated the frequency with which they engaged in each behavior over a set time frame (e.g., the previous season) on a scale ranging from 1 = "Never" to 5 = "Very often." The scale has shown good concurrent and discriminant validity, acceptable-to-very-good internal consistency (α range = .73-.86), and measurement invariance across five team sports and the two sexes.

Hassandra and colleagues (2005) developed the Fair Play in Physical Education Questionnaire (FPPEQ) by adapting two questionnaires measuring moral attitudes (Lee et al., 2007) and sportsperson-ship orientations (Vallerand et al., 1997) to the physical education context. The questionnaire consists of two subscales measuring prosocial fair play: respect for teammates (e.g., verbally supporting and helping teammates) and respect for conventions (e.g., shaking hands with the opponent after the game). Two subscales also measure antisocial fair play: cheating (e.g., "I cheat if it helps my team win") and gamesmanship (e.g., faking injury and trash-talking). The questionnaire consists of 16 items (4 in each subscale) scored on a scale ranging from 1 = "Never" to 5 = "Always." In this instrument, some of the items (e.g., shaking hands with the opponent after the game) may better reflect what Turiel (1983) has termed *social convention*—that is, agreed uniformities in social behavior that are determined by the social system in which they are formed.

Shields, LaVoi, Bredemeier, and Power (2007) developed a questionnaire to measure poor sport behavior (or sportspersonship) using athletes from a range of team sports. Their scale consists of 7 items (e.g., cheated to help the team win, tried to hurt an opponent to help the team win). Participants were asked to indicate whether they had engaged in these behaviors; if the answer was affirmative, they were asked whether they had done so "Once or twice," "A few times," or "Often" during the current season. Responses were given a score from 1 = "No" to 4 = "Often." The items were developed to have face validity; however, it is unclear how they were selected and whether they represent a broad range of poor sport behaviors. Principle component analysis showed that the scale was unidimensional, and internal consistency was very good (α = .80).

Poor *and* good sport behaviors have been measured with an instrument designed specifically for ice hockey (LaVoi & Babkes Stellino, 2008). The scale contained two poor behavior subscales—play and talk tough (e.g., trash talk to opponents) and complain and whine (e.g., complain about ice time)—and two good behavior subscales—concern and respect for opponents (e.g., help opponent up

off ice) and graciousness (e.g., thank the coach). Respondents were asked to indicate how much they thought the behaviors were like them on a scale ranging from 1 = "Very much like me" to 5 = "Not at all like me." EFA was used in one sample to select items and determine the dimensions of the final scale. The internal consistency of the four subscales ranged from marginally acceptable to very good (α = .67-.84).

This scale differs somewhat from the other instruments reviewed in this section. Specifically, although play and talk tough and concern and respect for opponents can have consequences for others, such consequences are not very obvious for complain and whine and graciousness. In addition, the authors referred to good and poor *behaviors*, but the way these variables were measured seems more appropriate for a measure of personal *characteristics* rather than behavior: Participants were asked to indicate their opinion of whether the behaviors characterized them (i.e., to indicate the extent of agreement that the behaviors were like them) rather than the frequency with which they engaged in these behaviors. Thus, this instrument measured a disposition to act in a certain way, particularly because no time frame (e.g., a game, a season) was specified for the players' acts. In all likelihood, high ratings on this scale should correspond to high ratings on a behavior frequency scale, but we are not aware of any data that verify this.

Some researchers have adapted nonsport instruments to the sport context. For example, Rutten and colleagues (2008) adapted two questionnaires measuring prosocial and antisocial behavior in nonsport contexts and named their scale the *Sports Behavior Inventory* (SBI). The scale measures antisocial behavior (e.g., "I shout abuse to others during matches") and prosocial behavior (no example provided) on the field and includes two other subscales that measure prosocial and antisocial behavior off the field. Respondents indicate the frequency of behavior on a scale ranging from 1 = "Never" to 4 = "Always." Principal component analysis supported the hypothesized four-factor structure, and internal consistency was very good for antisocial on-field behavior (α = .80) but only marginally acceptable for prosocial on-field behavior (α = .66). Antisocial behaviors were negatively related (r range = −.21 to −.44) while prosocial behaviors were positively related (r range = .21-.29) with moral reasoning, athlete fair play attitudes, and sociomoral team atmosphere, thus providing evidence for the concurrent validity of the scales.

The studies reviewed in this section clearly suggest that in the past two decades, researchers' interest in measuring moral behavior in sport has increased dramatically, as indicated by the multiple attempts to develop instruments to measure various aspects of this construct. However, a few points are in order. First, although in most cases measures were constructed because no adequate instruments were available at the time of data collection, typically the researchers' main interest was in the research question rather than the development of the measure (e.g., Kavussanu & Roberts, 2001; Sage & Kavussanu, 2007; Shields et al., 2007). Perhaps because scale development in this domain has largely been a means to an end, many of these tools have not been given a formal name. Second, there is variation in the items used in the available scales, with some referring strictly to behavior (i.e., faking an injury) and others including the motive of the act (i.e., cheating *to help the team win*). If a researcher is interested in measuring behavior when specific motives are present, the latter items are appropriate. However, if the interest is in measuring behavior per se, scales that do not refer to motives are preferable. Third, there is considerable variability in the scale development procedures employed in different studies, ranging from simple construction of items that appear to have face validity to a systematic procedure that adheres to established guidelines for scale development. Obviously, scales that have been developed using more rigorous procedures are preferable. Fourth, it is important to remember that self-report measures involve some risk of socially desirable responding, even though this may be minimal (e.g., Kavussanu & Roberts, 2001), and such instruments measure *reported* rather than *actual* behavior.

Coach and Teacher Ratings

One of the earliest attempts to assess aggressive behavior in sport using coach ratings was by Bredemeier and Shields (1984). These authors asked coaches to rate their players' aggressiveness on a scale ranging from 1 = "Extremely low aggression level" to 5 = "Extremely high aggression level" and to rank players in each team from the least aggressive to the most aggressive. A very strong correlation ($r = -.89$) between ratings and rankings evidenced agreement across the two methods.

Horrocks (1979) developed the HPPBI to enable teachers to assess the behavior of upper-elementary students. It consists of items measuring 10 behaviors (e.g., arguing with teammates, showing off, teasing others, sharing equipment) on which children are rated. The response scale ranges from 1 = "Not at all like the child" to 4 = "Very much like the child." The 10 behaviors were selected from an initial list

of 25 on the basis of being the easiest for teachers to observe. Correlations of HPPBI scores with moral reasoning ($r = .55$) and sportspersonship ($r = .63$) supported the concurrent validity of the scale, while internal reliability ranged from .96 to .98 in two samples (Horrocks, 1979). However, as only 1 of these 10 behaviors (i.e., sharing equipment) could be classified as prosocial, the name of this questionnaire does not reflect its content.

Gibbons and colleagues (1995) asked teachers to rate physical education students on the 10 HPPBI behaviors. An example of an item from the scale is "The child accepts defeat without complaining." Teachers rated children on a scale ranging from 1 = "Not at all like the child" to 4 = "Very much like the child" in one study (Gibbons & Ebbeck, 1997), and the scale showed excellent levels of internal consistency (α range = .90-.92). Finally, Stuart and Ebbeck (1995) presented coaches with 5 items (e.g., injuring another player to prevent a basket, pushing an opposing player when the referee is not looking, teasing a teammate), and asked them to indicate how often athletes engage in these behaviors throughout the season. The coaches' ratings were averaged to produce a single score for the behavior of each athlete.

Coach and teacher ratings are easy to use and avoid socially desirable responding. However, coaches and teachers are likely to have preexisting opinions that may affect the objectivity of their scoring. Thus, although they represent a good alternative to self-reports of athletes, coach and teacher ratings can be influenced by various factors such as level of personal interaction and similarity of values between coaches and players (Bredemeier & Shields, 1998). Employing multiple observers has been recommended (Bredemeier & Shields, 1998) but has not been used to date in research examining moral behavior in sport.

Fouls and Penalties

A few researchers have used fouls and penalties as a measure of aggression. For example, in a study of basketball players, Bredemeier and Shields (1984) computed the average number of fouls committed per minute per game per season for each player and used this statistic as an indicator of athletic aggression. Player fouls had a moderately strong positive relationship with coach rankings ($r = .46$) and ratings ($r = .37$) of aggression. The most recent example of this method is by Gee and Leith (2007), who utilized the penalty records from the first 200 games of the 2003-2004 Canadian National Hockey League (NHL) season. In their measure of aggression, they included 14 behaviors (e.g., fighting, spearing, high-sticking, elbowing) reported by athletes to be committed with the intent of harming an opponent at least 80% of the time. A total of 2,185 penalties were issued in the 200 games; of these, 1,266 were 1 of the 16 aggressive behaviors of interest.

Although the use of penalties or fouls seems to be an objective way of measuring aggressive behavior in sport, this method has weaknesses: Not all penalties or fouls are given for aggressive behavior; some aggressive acts are not identified and therefore are not penalized by officials (Kirker, Tenenbaum, & Mattson, 2000); and officials may be biased toward some teams as a result of crowd loyalties, the score, or previous aggressive acts (Stephens, 1998). For these reasons, researchers have recently started to use naturalistic observation to measure behavior.

Observational Methods

Observational methods, in which the frequency of behavior from videotaped matches is recorded, have increased in popularity in recent years. Although most studies using this method have measured aggression, prosocial and antisocial behaviors have also been examined. Kavussanu, Stamp, Slade, and Ring (2009) recorded 24 soccer games and coded the frequency of 7 prosocial behaviors (e.g., helping an opponent off the floor, congratulating an opposing player, returning the ball to opponents) and 11 antisocial behaviors (e.g., late tackle, shirt pulling, elbowing). Operational definitions for each behavior were given to observers before recording behavior frequency. To account for imbalance in match length between male and female teams, behavior frequency was recorded as number of behaviors per hour per team.

Aggression in ice hockey and basketball was examined in an observational study by Kirker and colleagues (2000). The recorded behaviors (e.g., push, kick, punch) were selected by four experts (i.e., officials and players). Ten behaviors were sport-specific and 12 were common to both sports, with each being classified as physical or nonphysical and assertive or aggressive. They were also classified according to typical severity, which was rated on a scale anchored by 1 = "Least severe" and 5 = "Most severe"; only behaviors given a severity score of 2 or more were considered aggressive. Coding of a behavior and its severity occurred only after two observers came to agreement.

Sheldon and Aimar (2001) also coded aggressive behaviors from videotaped ice hockey games. Examples of coded behaviors were checking or cross-checking, using the stick to impede or harm an opponent, elbowing or punching, and tripping.

Jones, Bray, and Olivier (2005) videotaped a random selection of 21 professional rugby league games and recorded aggressive behaviors that were identified in a focus group of seven players with considerable experience playing rugby league. Examples of behaviors coded are high tackle, head butt, late tackle, and gouge or bite. The total number of behavior frequencies was used in all analyses.

Coulomb and colleagues developed two observation grids to examine instrumental and hostile aggression: one for handball (Rascle, Coulomb, & Pfister, 1998) and one for soccer (Coulomb & Pfister, 1998). In handball, actions were coded in general categories such as repelling, retaining, hitting, and cheating for instrumental aggression and insulting; threatening; making obscene gestures; and shoving against opponents, referees, teammates, and others for hostile aggression. In soccer, behaviors were illegal tackling or tripping, holding, and striking for instrumental aggression and actions against the opponents, referees, and teammates for hostile aggression. CFA showed a good fit of the hypothesized two-factor model for both grids (Coulomb-Cabagno & Rascle, 2006). Factor loadings were moderate to high (.53-.99) for most behaviors, and test–retest reliability was excellent (.93 for soccer and .92 for handball). Behavior frequency was calculated as number of behaviors per 15 min in order to allow for comparisons between the two sports and between the two sexes, who played over varying time frames.

The studies examining observed behavior in sport provide more reliable and objective information than other methods about the behaviors that actually occur in the sport context. Unfortunately, this type of research is very time consuming; thus, it is difficult to recruit a large number of participants or to observe them for an extended period of time. Also, verbal behaviors are not easily captured and for this reason they are often not recorded. Importantly, the success of this method relies heavily on training the observers to ensure objective observation and high levels of interrater reliability. However, the strengths of this methodology outweigh its weaknesses, and we recommend using this approach whenever it is possible.

Examples From the Literature

The instruments reviewed in the previous section have been used to measure moral behavior in sport with varying frequency. In this section, we provide examples from the literature using each of the measures reviewed in the previous section. We begin with studies using paper-and-pencil tools and continue with studies on coach and teacher ratings, fouls and penalties, and observed behaviors. We use the term *antisocial behavior* when referring to variables that reflect inhibitive morality when describing studies in which researchers used a term not discussed in this chapter or simply referred to as behavior (e.g., Stuart & Ebbeck, 1995).

Paper-and-Pencil Tools

Several studies have examined antisocial behavior using the instrument developed by Kavussanu and Roberts (2001). In some cases, the scenarios were adapted slightly to fit a different sport. In these studies, researchers have been typically interested in team influences on behavior, and two of the variables investigated are the motivational climate and moral atmosphere of the team. For example, Miller, Roberts, and Ommundsen (2005) found that Norwegian youth soccer players who perceived a performance motivational climate in their team (i.e., an emphasis on normative success) were more likely to report engaging in antisocial acts, such as faking an injury and risking injuring an opposing player. However, no significant relationship between this type of motivational climate and antisocial behavior was revealed among American college basketball players (Kavussanu, Roberts, & Ntoumanis, 2002). In both studies, perceptions of a moral atmosphere (created by the coach and teammates) that sanctioned antisocial behavior corresponded to a greater reported frequency of such behavior.

The soccer-specific instrument developed by Sage and Kavussanu (2007) to measure prosocial and antisocial behavior has been used in two studies, both of which employed adolescent soccer players. The first study established a link between achievement and social goals and the two types of behavior. Specifically, players who pursued task and social affiliation goals while playing soccer were more likely to display prosocial behaviors such as helping an opponent off the floor, whereas players who pursued ego and social status goals were more likely to engage in antisocial acts such as faking an injury (Sage & Kavussanu, 2007). In the second study, the main interest was in the temporal stability of the behaviors, and both types of acts displayed relative stability across a soccer season (Sage & Kavussanu, 2008).

The more generic measure of prosocial and antisocial behavior—the PABSS developed by Kavussanu and Boardley (2009)—has been used in two studies to date. In the first study (Boardley & Kavussanu, 2009), perceptions of a team environment that emphasized learning and skill mastery (i.e., mastery climate) positively predicted proso-

cial behavior and negatively predicted antisocial behavior toward teammates in hockey and netball. Prosocial and antisocial behavior toward opponents were predicted by moral disengagement, which refers to a set of psychological mechanisms that people use to justify their antisocial conduct and minimize negative emotional reactions (e.g., guilt, shame) when engaging in such conduct (see Bandura, 1991). Moral disengagement was also a strong positive predictor of antisocial behavior toward opponents and teammates in a second study of male soccer players (Boardley & Kavussanu, 2010).

The FPPEQ has been used in a study reporting a 10 wk intervention intended to promote fair play during games (Hassandra et al., 2007). Four classes formed the experimental group, and another four classes acted as the control group. In the experimental group, strategies derived from social learning (Bandura, 1977) and structural developmental (Kohlberg, 1984) theories were used to promote fair-play behaviors. Both groups completed the FPPEQ 1 wk before the first lesson and 1 wk after the last lesson. The experimental group also completed the measure 2 mo after the postmeasures. The experimental group significantly increased their fair-play behaviors from pre- to posttest and maintained this increase at the 2 mo follow-up, whereas the control group showed no change.

Poor sport behaviors have been investigated in relation to a variety of personal and social influences, which were assessed via players' perceptions in a large sample of young athletes drawn from six team sports (Shields et al., 2007). Players who thought that it was okay to engage in poor sport behaviors, and perceived that their coach and the spectators had engaged in similar acts, were more likely to report higher frequency of such behaviors. In addition, players' perceptions that their teammates would engage in poor sport behaviors to help the team win were associated with poor behavior frequency. Finally, players' perceptions that their parents or coach would be disappointed if they (for parent perceptions) or a team member (for coach perceptions) engaged in poor sport behaviors corresponded to a lower reported frequency of these behaviors.

Poor (or bad) and good behaviors have been examined in relation to parental influences, which were measured via perceptions of male youth ice hockey players (LaVoi & Babkes Stellino, 2008). Players, whose parents encouraged learning and enjoyment and were involved with the child's sport participation, were more likely to report good behaviors (i.e., concern for opponent and graciousness) and less likely to report poor behaviors (i.e., play and talk tough and whine and complain) when playing ice hockey. Interestingly, parents' expectations that their children perform at a high level were positively associated with bad behaviors, which were also more likely in players who perceived that their parents emphasized concerns about failure and mistakes. Thus, parents seem to play an important role in their children's good and bad sport behaviors.

Prosocial and antisocial behaviors were measured using the SBI and investigated in relation to team characteristics, such as relational support from the coach and fair-play attitudes of both athletes and coaches, in a sample of adolescent soccer players (Rutten et al., 2008). Fair-play attitudes of athletes and coaches (i.e., respect for the opponent and the rules of the game) negatively predicted antisocial behavior. In addition, players who reported fair-play attitudes and experienced relational support by their coach (i.e., acceptance, emotional support, respect for autonomy, quality of communication, and convergence of goals) were more likely to engage in prosocial behaviors while playing soccer.

Coach and Teacher Ratings

Researchers have used coach and teacher ratings in several studies. In some cases, the interest was in variables associated with behaviors. For example, Bredemeier and Shields (1984) examined moral reasoning (i.e., the criteria that players use to resolve moral conflicts) in relation to coach ratings of aggressive on-court behavior of American intercollegiate basketball players. Players characterized by less mature moral reasoning were more likely to be rated by their coaches as displaying aggressive behavior on court.

An adapted version of the HPPBI (Horrocks, 1979) was used in intervention studies aimed at enhancing the moral development of young people. For example, Gibbons and colleagues (1995) administered the Fair Play for Kids intervention over a 27 wk time frame in elementary students. At the posttest, children in the intervention group were rated by their teachers as being more prosocial than children in the control group. In another study, Gibbons and Ebbeck (1997) examined the effectiveness of two fair-play interventions based on teaching strategies derived from the social learning (Bandura, 1977) and structural developmental (e.g., Haan, 1991) theories on the moral development of physical education students. Both intervention groups scored higher on prosocial behavior than the control group at mid- and postintervention.

Coach ratings of antisocial behaviors were used in a study by Stuart and Ebbeck (1995) that investigated the relationship between coach-rated antisocial behavior and perceptions of youth basketball players that such behaviors were approved by four significant others: mother, father, coach, and teammates. Players in grades 7 and 8 (but not 4 and 5), who perceived that significant others approved of the antisocial behaviours, were more likely to be rated by their coaches as engaging in these behaviors. Overall, these studies indicate that coach and teacher ratings can be used effectively to measure behavior in sport morality research.

Fouls and Penalties

Several studies have utilized penalties as a measure of aggression. An example of this approach is a study of ice hockey players (McGuire, Courneya, Widmeyer, & Carron, 1992) in which penalties received for aggressive acts were used as an indicator of aggression. Data were collected from the official game reports and penalty records of the NHL during one season. Results showed that home teams won 58.3% of matches. There was a significant interaction between game location and performance, such that home teams incurred more penalties in games they won, whereas visiting teams incurred more penalties in games they lost. In a more recent study of professional ice hockey players (Gee & Leith, 2007), the penalties given for aggressive acts in the first 200 matches of the NHL season were identified and used as a measure of aggression. Players of North American origin committed significantly more aggressive acts than European-born athletes. The authors suggested that early learning experiences may have long-term implications for aggressive behavior in ice hockey.

Observed Behaviors

A few studies have examined moral behavior using naturalistic observation. For example, the soccer observation grid developed by Kavussanu and colleagues (2009) was used to measure prosocial and antisocial behavior of soccer teams (players ages ranged from 15 to 47 years). A 90 min soccer game was videotaped for each team. The researchers investigated sex differences in behaviors and whether potential differences were explained by personal and social variables. Males engaged in more antisocial acts than females, but the two sexes did not differ in the frequency of prosocial behavior. Females also reported higher empathy, lower perceived performance climate in their team, and less soccer experience than their male counterparts.

These variables accounted for the sex differences in antisocial behavior.

Kirker and colleagues (2000) filmed two ice hockey and two basketball games and coded aggressive acts, as well as antecedent and consequent events to each aggressive act, in five teams competing in a men's top division in Australian state competition. Results showed that aggressive behaviors occurred in clusters. In addition, the most severe aggressive acts were preceded by less severe acts and were followed by other aggressive acts, most commonly verbal acts. Other events preceding severe aggressive acts were forceful play and anger toward the target of aggression in ice hockey and missed shots and a close score differential in basketball. In both sports, examples of events that followed the aggressive acts were verbal abuse between players and teammate support.

The observation grids developed for soccer and handball by Coulomb and Pfister (1998) and Rascle and colleagues (1998) were used to record hostile and instrumental aggression and to examine sex and competition-level differences in a large-scale study of 90 handball and 90 soccer games (Coulomb-Cabagno & Rascle, 2006). In both sports, male players displayed significantly more instrumental and hostile aggressive behaviors than female players. Moreover, in soccer, instrumental aggression increased and hostile aggression decreased with an increase in competitive level. However, a different pattern emerged in handball, in which players competing at the national level displayed more instrumental and hostile behaviors than those competing at the lower competition levels.

Recommendations for Researchers and Practitioners

As the studies reviewed in this chapter demonstrate, substantial progress has been made over the past two decades in the measurement of moral behavior in sport. Although different terms have been used by different researchers to label constructs, a careful examination of the content of the various instruments reveals substantial overlap not only in the behaviors measured but also in the definitions used. We recommend that researchers do not introduce new terms into the study of moral behavior in sport in order to avoid further confusion (unless, of course, a clearly distinct new construct is proposed). Instead, researchers are encouraged to explore different *dimensions* of prosocial and antisocial behaviors. For example, we have distinguished between prosocial behaviors directed at teammates and prosocial behaviors directed at

opponents (Kavussanu & Boardley, 2009). Those are also qualitatively different in that the prosocial opponent behaviors are also helping acts. A similar dimension of prosocial helping behavior could also exist for teammates and is worth exploring.

To date, very few studies have examined prosocial sport behavior, and in these investigations alpha coefficients have ranged from unacceptable to good (e.g., Kavussanu & Boardley, 2009; Sage & Kavussanu, 2007; Rutten et al., 2008). A measure of prosocial behavior that has *very good* levels of internal consistency is still needed. Future research should revise the present instruments to include more items describing other prosocial behaviors to increase their internal consistency. Moreover, with the exception of one study investigating behaviors in tennis, some of which were aggressive (Hanegby & Tenenbaum, 2001), moral behavior has not been examined in individual sports (to our knowledge). Some of the items included in current measures of prosocial behavior (e.g., encouraged or supported a teammate) and antisocial behavior (e.g., verbally abused an opponent) could be adapted and used in individual sports. It would be interesting to obtain data on the frequency of these behaviors in individual sports.

Typically, researchers examine behavior *during* competition, which might explain why they have had considerable difficulty in identifying a large number of prosocial behaviors. Such behaviors are less likely to occur during competition, as there is a clear conflict in the interests of the two parties involved in the competition. Prosocial behaviors may be more frequent in the training context, which also constitutes a significant part of the athletic experience. Thus, researchers need to examine behaviors that occur in other contexts that are part of the athletic experience. Some of the items used in current scales should be applicable to the training context or a measure specific to that context may need to be developed.

Only a few researchers have used CFA to perform a stringent examination of the factor structure of their scale. When using an instrument for which limited information on its psychometric properties is reported, researchers should examine the factor structure of the instrument using CFA. Similarly, when developing a new scale, researchers should evaluate its factor structure and ensure that it is unidimensional before aggregating responses to form a single score (see Cortina, 1993). Finally, current measures of moral behavior need to be validated more extensively. For example, researchers could examine whether participants change their responses to the scale as a result of an experimental intervention aimed to promote prosocial behavior.

With regard to the research questions asked, most studies have examined *antecedents* of moral behavior. However, moral behavior may also have consequences, such as team cohesion, positive interpersonal relationships, and satisfaction with being a member of the team, and these should be examined. In addition, the effect of emotion on moral behavior in sport needs to be investigated. For example, anticipation of pleasant (e.g., pride) and aversive (e.g., guilt) emotions may have important implications for moral behavior (see Bandura, 1991). Finally, researchers are encouraged to implement interventions to examine whether we can change athlete behavior. At present, such interventions have been conducted in the physical education context but not the sport context. In sum, although research has improved the measurement of moral behavior in sport, much remains to be done.

For practitioners who wish to promote moral behavior in sport, we recommend videotaping games and reviewing these games with athletes to identify prosocial and antisocial behaviors and the events that precede and follow these behaviors (see Kirker et al., 2000). Although a temporal relationship is a necessary but not sufficient condition for a causal relationship between two events, identifying the conditions that surround prosocial and antiso-cial acts may help practitioners better understand the immediate causes and consequences of these behaviors. One of these important consequences is performance, and we need to understand its relationship with prosocial and antisocial behavior.

Practitioners may also wish to know which theoretical perspectives should guide their interventions. Research that has investigated the effectiveness of fair-play interventions can offer guidance in this area (Gibbons & Ebbeck, 1997; Hassandra et al., 2007). The findings of these studies suggest that approaches based on social learning theory or structural developmental theory or both theories (Gibbons & Ebbeck, 1997; Hassandra et al., 2007) may be effective in promoting prosocial behavior and deterring antisocial conduct. Although these studies were conducted in educational settings, they provide useful ideas for practitioners designing interventions aimed at influencing moral conduct in sport. However, the most critical issue is educating coaches about the important role that they play in affecting moral behavior in sport through their interaction with their athletes.

Acknowledgments

The authors thank Brenda J. Light Bredemeier and Gershon Tenenbaum for their insightful comments on earlier drafts of this chapter.

▪ **Table 38.1** ▪

Measures Assessing Moral Behavior

Variable or concept	Tool	Dimension or characteristic; scale	Source
Moral behavior (antisocial)		4 scenarios followed by 1 question each; 5-point scale	Kavussanu & Roberts (2001)
Prosocial and antisocial behavior		Prosocial (6) and antisocial (13) behavior; 5-point scale	Sage & Kavussanu (2007)
Prosocial and antisocial behavior	Prosocial and Antisocial Behavior in Sport Scale (PABSS)	Prosocial opponent (3) and teammate (4) behavior, antisocial opponent (8) and teammate (5) behavior; 5-point scale	Kavussanu & Boardley (2009)
Fair play	Fair Play in Physical Education Questionnaire (FPPEQ)	Respect for teammates (4), convention (4), cheating (4), gamesmanship (4); 5-point scale	Hassandra, Hatzigeorgiadis, & Goudas (2005)
Poor sportsperson-ship		Poor sport behavior (7); 4-point scale	Shields, LaVoi, Bredemeier, & Power (2007)

(continued)

Variable or concept	Tool	Dimension or characteristic; scale	Source
Poor and good sport behavior		Play and talk tough (10), complain and whine (5), concern and respect for opponents (4), graciousness (3); 5-point scale	LaVoi & Babkes Stellino (2008)
Prosocial and anti-social behavior	Sport Behavior Inventory (SBI)	Prosocial (5) and antisocial (8) behavior; 4-point scale	Rutten et al. (2008)
Aggression		Coach ratings and rankings (1); 5-point scale; highest to lowest on team	Bredemeier & Shields (1984)
Prosocial behavior	Horrocks Prosocial Play Behavior Inventory (HPPBI)	Prosocial behavior (10); 4-point scale	Horrocks (1979)
Moral behavior (antisocial)		Moral behavior (5); 5-point scale	Stuart & Ebbeck (1995)
Aggression		Player fouls; fouls per minute per season per game	Bredemeier & Shields (1984)
Aggression		Aggressive and nonaggressive penalties	Gee & Leith (2007)
Prosocial and anti-social behavior		Prosocial and antisocial behavior	Kavussanu, Stamp, Slade, & Ring (2009)
Aggression		Instrumental and noninstrumental aggression	Kirker, Tenenbaum, & Mattson (2000)
Aggression		Aggressive behavior	Sheldon & Aimar (2001)
Aggression		Aggressive behavior	Jones, Bray, & Olivier (2005)
Aggression		Instrumental and hostile aggression	Rascle, Coulomb, & Pfister (1998)
Aggression		Instrumental and hostile aggression	Coulomb & Pfister (1998)

Numbers in parentheses next to subscale names indicate the number of items in that subscale.

Behavioral Measurement in Exercise Psychology

Claudio R. Nigg, PhD, Patricia J. Jordan, PhD, and Angela Atkins, MPH

> " It is impossible to change things that cannot be measured. "
>
> **Claudio R. Nigg**

The Department of Health and Human Services recently, and for the first time, published national physical activity guidelines. The United States Department of Health and Human Services' (DHHS) 2008 Physical Activity Guidelines for Americans (DHHS, 2008) affirm that regular physical activity reduces the risk of many adverse health outcomes. The guidelines state that all adults should avoid inactivity; that some physical activity is better than none; and that adults who participate in any amount of physical activity gain some benefit to their health. In fact, the guidelines emphasize that for most positive health outcomes, additional benefits accrue as the amount of physical activity increases in higher intensity, frequency, and/or duration. We acknowledge the differences between physical activity, exercise, and sport and provide the definitions in the "Conceptual Issues" section.

The accurate measurement of regular physical activity is essential to study of the relationship between exercise and health (Esliger & Tremblay, 2007). The majority of measurement tools generate data that are accurate at a temporal level, such as energy expenditure over time, pedometer step counts over a certain time period, or minutes of moderate to vigorous physical activity per day or per week; but none of these provide a definitive view of overall health. It is fundamental to exercise psychology that the behavioral variables/constructs upon which we rely provide accurate, valid, reliable and accessible data that help us better understand and monitor the relationship of physical activity with health.

The five types of behavioral measures most common among researchers and practitioners are: (1) intensity, (2) duration, (3) frequency, (4) mode, and (5) adherence.

The first three of these dimensions are interdependent with the mode or type of activity, and understanding their impact on health can only be effective if the normal fluctuations in adherence are considered.

Concept Definitions

The American Heart Association (2007) applies the FIT formula for optimizing physical fitness: **F** for frequency; **I** for intensity; and **T** for time (or duration). Two additional salient concepts are presented here: mode and adherence.

Frequency. The number of times an activity is performed in a day or a week is its frequency. Personal exercise prescriptions vary; typically a minimum of 3 alternating days a week (more if possible) is sufficient to improve overall health (Heyward, 2006). In 2007, the American College of Sports Medicine improved their physical activity recommendations by acknowledging that longer, less frequent sessions of aerobic exercise provide no clear advantage over shorter, more frequent sessions of activity.

Intensity. Intensity refers to the amount of effort the individual expends at the activity. It may be assessed through perceived exertion scales or physiological indicators, such as heart rate or self-report questionnaires addressing involvement in activity at different intensity levels. Scaled measures for intensity are not unique and may include ordinal categories (e.g., mild, moderate, vigorous) or may be continuous (e.g., heartbeats per minute). Physical activity performed at an intensity that increases the heart rate into a target heart rate zone (THRZ) of 55% to 90% of an individual's maximum heart rate (MHR) or 40% to 85% of their maximal amount of oxygen uptake ($\dot{V}O_2$max) provides optimal cardiovascular health benefits. [The updated formula of: [208 − (.7 x age)] is also used to calculate MHR.] In order to maintain or improve aerobic fitness, an individual's THRZ must be calculated by multiplying the MHR by a percentage between 55% and 90% to find out the necessary total number of beats per minute (National Association for Sport & Physical Education, 2005). Intuitively, in order to achieve desired outcomes when performing strength exercises, individuals should increase intensity but decrease intensity for endurance exercises (Tipton, 2006). Intensity of exercise must also consider the fitness goals, age, capabilities, and current fitness level of the individual (Heyward, 2006).

Time (Duration). The length of an activity session is equivalent to its time or duration. Current recommendations suggest that health can be improved with an accumulation of 30 minutes or more of moderate physical activity on most, preferably all days of the week. The accumulated fitness time can be achieved all at once or in multiple bouts of shorter duration throughout the day (e.g., 10 minute sessions 3 times a day) (Heyward, 2006). Duration can be determined through direct observation, using objective activity monitors, or self-reports, and data usually take the form of minutes/hours.

Mode. Mode describes the type of activity being measured. Mode can be summarized in categories such as leisure time, occupational, and transport; or by physiologically determined categories such as aerobic or anaerobic (Smith & Biddle, 2008). More descriptive classifications may reference the major physiological benefits incurred, including cardiovascular (e.g., walking, cycling, and step aerobics), strengthening (e.g., stair climbing and free weights), or flexibility (e.g., yoga and pilates) activities. As a result, measurement of mode is inherently nominal and descriptive.

Adherence. According to Buckworth and Dishman (2002) exercise adherence refers to conforming faithfully to a standard of behavior that has been set as part of a negotiated agreement. This has been measured as exercise class attendance (Marcus & Stanton, 1993; McAuley & Jacobson, 1991; Weber & Wertheim, 1989); weekly distance or time goals (Cauley et al., 1987; King et al., 1991; Wood, Ste-

fanick, Williams, & Haskell, 1991); and responses to questionnaires, such as retrospective self-report instruments of physical activity (Svendsen, Hassager, & Christiansen, 1994), or stage of exercise behavior (Cardinal & Sachs, 1996; Marcus et al., 1992; Nigg, 2001). Exercise diaries or self-reporting are increasingly popular, and encourage individuals to track their adherence online or in places that can be monitored, updated, and referenced (Woods et al., 2005).

In order to minimize negative influences that can result from the lack of consistent of exercise, the American College of Sports Medicine recommends frequent modification and increasing motivational strategies within exercise programs in an effort to increase long-term adherence.

Conceptual Issues

In order to properly select a measure or to evaluate if a proper measure has been applied, several conceptual issues need to be understood. These issues help clarify the context of the behavior that impacts the measurement.

Capturing Physical Activity and Exercise

The measurement of physical activity is difficult because of the high level of variability between individuals in the energy expenditure of various modes of activity, as well as the types of physical activities performed (Kriska & Caspersen, 1997). Further, differences in environmental conditions (e.g. temperature, humidity, wind, etc.) affect the level of energy expenditure (Montoye, Kemper, Saris, & Washburn, 1996). In addition, physical fitness and health status often affect the levels and types of physical activity performed. Type of physical activity may affect different aspects of physical fitness. For example, energy expenditure through aerobic activity impacts most aerobic capacity and body composition, while resistance (weight) training will impact on muscle and bone mass (Kriska & Caspersen, 1997).

Measuring What We Can't See

All physical activities require energy expenditure. Metabolic equivalents (METs) are the most common representation for rate of oxygen consumption, and are expressed as multiples of the resting metabolic rate, which is assigned a value of one MET. The Compendium of Physical Activities standardizes the measurement of energy expenditure by assigning MET levels to more than 600 activities, (Ainsworth et al., 2000). In the laboratory, energy expenditure can be measured by direct or indirect calorimetry or physical fitness can be measured (e.g., maximal oxygen uptake) as a criterion reflecting habitual physical activity. Field methods may include doubly labeled water (DLH_2O), physical activity diaries and self-report questionnaires, motion accelerometers and heart rate monitoring (HRM). There is no perfect method for measurement of energy expenditure or physical activity; therefore, it is impossible to determine the actual validity of any one method (Montoye et al., 1996). All methods of assessment have error associated with them and the advantages and disadvantages of using one or more of these approaches to measurement depend on the research question and the population being studied (Kriska, 1997; Montoye, 1996). Further, the units of measurement between the various methods are different, making it difficult to correlate alternate methods as a measure of validity.

Semantics in Labeling, or Real Operational Differences

One of the most important components of measurement is the definition. The semantic expressions used to qualify and quantify human movement can lead to confusion, particularly where context is uncertain. The definition of a concept or variable should contain a semantic definition and an operational definition. The semantic definition uses plain language to capture the basic meaning of the concept; while the operational definition provides the rules for measuring the concept, including how relevant information can actually be quantified. Practically speaking, semantic definitions are used to translate abstract concepts into something that can be measured; whereas operational definitions of these concepts describe how the data that are collected actually represent the concept being measured.

Physical Activity versus Exercise

Physical activity has been defined by Caspersen (1989) as any bodily movement produced by skeletal muscles that result in energy expenditure. There are several components of energy expenditure, including basal metabolic rate (60-70% total energy expenditure [TEE]), thermic effect of food (7-10%TEE), and physical activity (Kriska & Caspersen, 1997). The level of energy expenditure during physical activity is the most variable component of TEE and is related to the force generated by the total muscle mass, which is producing the movements, and by the duration and frequency of these muscle contractions (Caspersen, 1989). Essentially, physical activity

is the act of moving and includes physical activities done as part of daily living, occupation, leisure, exercise, and sports (Montoye et al., 1996). Exercise is therefore a subcategory of physical activity that is structured, repetitive, and planned; and results in the improvement or maintenance of one or more physical fitness facets (Montoye et al., 1996).

Physical Fitness versus Physical Function

Physical fitness is a health attribute that is the result of regular physical activity, and consists of four components: aerobic or cardiorespiratory fitness, muscular strength and endurance, flexibility, and body composition (Bouchard, Shephard, & Stephens, 1994).

Physical function (or functional ability) is the ability to carry out activities of daily living (Huang, Macera, Blair, Brill, Kohl, & Kronenfeld, 1998). It is different from physical fitness in that it involves the assessment of applied physical function (e.g., the ability to complete a specific task) rather than the physiological derived attributes measured in fitness assessment.

The interrelationship between physical activity, physical fitness, and physical function provides a holistic view of health as a product of these components. For example, a lack of physical activity will result in lower physical fitness and may result in a decrement in the ability to carry on activities of daily life. The reverse is also true. The interrelationship between physical activity, fitness, and function are shown in figure 39.1.

Duration versus Adherence

There are unique challenges associated with the measurement of physical activity, including whether to emphasize amount of time over amount of effort or actual health benefit. Essentially all of these things are important, but balancing motivation and maintenance can sometimes prove difficult. Two critical factors in any exercise program are duration and adherence. While they are often seen as interchangeable, they are in fact two very

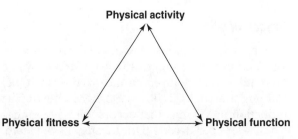

Figure 39.1 Inter-relations of physical activity, fitness, and function

different components. *Adherence* is the term used to describe how well an individual sticks to a prescribed exercise regimen. *Duration* refers to the time an individual has actually spent exercising during one bout or session.

Typical adherence rates range from 50-80% for most research studies (Martin, Bowen, Dunbar, & Perri, 2000); in part because there is little consistency in how adherence is defined and measured. For example, adherence comprises frequency, duration and intensity, and can be measured at specified time points or using self-report or objective instruments. Many factors influence any one individual's adherence to a regular exercise program, including demographics (e.g., age, gender), environment (e.g., nearby facilities, transportation options), social/cultural considerations (e.g., family role, customs), and behavior (e.g., smoking). In general physical activity interventions should focus on factors that are potentially modifiable, while acknowledging how moderator variables influence the system.

Tools for Measuring Physical Activity

A myriad of tools exist for the assessment and measurement of physical activity. Each tool has its advantages and disadvantages that must be appropriately balanced and recognized. The assessment tools below have been divided into three reference categories: Criterion measures, or possible "gold standard" assessments; objective measures, or unbiased, fact-based assessments; and subjective measures, or those derived from personal experience.

Criterion Measures

Criterion measures are thought to represent the most accurate measure of whatever aspect of physical activity is being assessed (Mahar & Rowe, 2002). There is no single criterion measure of physical activity; therefore, researchers must choose among several possible measures and evaluate the evidence of its validity.

Oxygen Uptake

Maximal oxygen uptake ($\dot{V}O_2$max) decreases with age, and evidence suggests that this trend can be favorably altered with endurance exercise (aerobic) training (Kasch, 1972; 1976; 1993; Ready, 1996). The reduction in $\dot{V}O_2$max that occurs with age ranges from 0-34% per decade (Drinkwater, 1975; Heath, 1981; Kasch, 1976; Kasch, 1993; Ogawa, 1992; Rogers, 1990). After age 25-30, sedentary adults generally experience a 9%-13% reduction in $\dot{V}O_2$max per decade, but the $\dot{V}O_2$max of active individuals' declines at a lesser rate and remains higher than age-matched sedentary individuals (Hagberg, 1989; Pollock, 1997; Trappe, 1996).

Age is not a deterrent to aerobic endurance or resistance training (Fiatarone, 1990; Fiatarone, 1994; Hagberg, 1989; Ready, 1996; Rogers, 1993). In fact, the relative increase in maximal oxygen uptake resulting from regular participation in aerobic exercise training in the elderly is similar to that reported in middle-aged and younger adults (Hagberg, 1989; Hartley, 1969; Kohrt, 1991; Meredith, 1989; Mitchell, 1992; Pollock, 1976; Sidney, 1977; Sidney, 1978; Wallace, 1995). Furthermore, there appears to be no gender differences in the responses to endurance exercise training (Hagberg, 1989; Kohrt, 1991; Ogawa, 1992). While $\dot{V}O_2$max is a good marker of physiologic change consequent to endurance exercise training, there is a genetic component (Bouchard et al., 1999). Nonetheless, the cross sectional and longitudinal data show that active individuals have consistently higher $\dot{V}O_2$max levels compared with sedentary individuals.

Doubly Labeled Water

Doubly labeled water (DLH$_2$O) is one method for estimating energy expenditure that can be used in field and laboratory studies (Westerterp, 1988; Schoeller, 1996). The method uses the principles of indirect calorimetry (i.e., CO_2 production) to measure total energy expenditure through the turnover rates of two stable isotopes of water — H$_2$18O and either 2H$_2$O or 3H$_2$O (Ritz & Coward, 1995). The method involves ingestion of a quantity of labeled water with a known concentration of hydrogen ions that equilibrates with total body water (Montoye, 1996; Ritz, 1995). The labeled hydrogen leaves the body as water (e.g., sweat, urine, breath/water vapor) and carbon dioxide (Montoye et al., 1996). Labeling total body water can also provide an estimate of body composition and measurement of water outflow rates (Ritz & Coward, 1995). This method requires special laboratory equipment and techniques, and only some laboratories are able to accurately measure energy expenditure in this way (Roberts, Dietz, Sharp, Dallal, & Hill, 1995). Given that radioisotopes are in short supply and the measurement equipment is expensive, this method remains impractical for use in large studies (Montoye et al., 1996). Further, this method provides limited information pertaining to public health guidelines since they are phrased in terms of frequency, intensity, duration and mode which cannot easily be extracted from this technique.

Direct Observation

Direct observation offers several advantages for studying physical activity. Direct observation provides detailed objective information about levels of activity (mild, moderate, strenuous), as well as the context in which the activity is taking place (e.g., leisure, occupational, etc.). Essentially direct observation requires a trained observer to unobtrusively watch a particular individual or group of individuals and record various aspects of the physical activity taking place (McKenzie et al., 1991, 2000, 2004). Advantages to direct observation include its accuracy, assessment of a natural setting, ability to simultaneously observe multiple dimensions of the activity taking place, and its use as a validation measure for other instruments. Although direct observation techniques require relatively few resources, several disadvantages also need to be considered. For example, direct observation is time-consuming, and some forms require approximately one observer for each participant. This also makes it relatively expensive compared with other assessment methods. Direct observation can also lead to participant reactivity, whereby individuals under observation alter their normal routines in response to being watched.

Blood Pressure

Primary risk factors for the development of hypertension include increasing age, overweight, sodium intake, alcohol consumption, family history of hypertension, and physical inactivity (Horan & Lenfant, 1990). Physical inactivity is related to both hypertension and overweight. Lifestyle modification including physical activity has been recommended for primary prevention of hypertension and as adjunctive therapy (National Heart, Lung, and Blood Institute, 1997).

Longitudinal studies of exercise training in normotensive individuals have resulted in reductions in blood pressure particularly in older and heavier subjects (Pollock, 1973; Tipton, 1984; Tipton, 1991). Cross sectional studies have noted lower resting blood pressures in normotensive athletes of young and middle age, and in physically active hypertensive subjects (Tipton, 1984; Tipton, 1991). The results of numerous studies of middle aged and older subjects with hypertension have led to the conclusion that exercise training is associated with a 525 mmHg decline in systolic and a 315 mmHg decline in diastolic blood pressure measures (Tipton, 1991). Even normotensive individuals experience a decline in resting systolic and diastolic blood pressure with exercise training (Gilders, 1989). Resting blood pressure is a good biologic marker of the effects of regular training and acts as a good criterion variable for validation of the physical activity instruments.

Objective Measures

If the data being collected is not cognitively or perceptually processed by the participant then it is classified as objective. In other words, the data exists irrespective of what the participant believes and perceives about them. It needs to be noted that criterion measures are usually the best available objective measures.

Pedometers

Pedometers have become increasingly popular among people of all ages as a convenient means of objectively tracking number of steps taken. According to Tudor-Locke (2002), pedometers contain a spring suspended, lever arm that moves up and down. This motion opens and closes the horizontal arm as a response to the vertical accelerations of the waist that occur while walking and running (Tudor-Locke, 2002). Carron, Hausenblas, and Estabrooks (2003) explain that optimal recording accuracy is obtained when the device is clipped onto a belt or worn around the ankle. Pedometers are lightweight and do not interfere with lifestyle or activity; but, pedometers do not incorporate temporal measurement; therefore intensity and duration cannot be determined. Further, pedometers accurately record walking, running, and biking, but are not sensitive to isometric activities and do not evaluate movement of the upper body (Carron et al., 2003). New pedometer technologies often include a time feature in order to measure velocity because the original style pedometers only count steps and do not take into account duration of exercise (Tudor-Locke, 2002).

Behavior modification and motivation levels are often influenced by immediate feedback (Carron et al., 2003), which is why pedometers are commonly used in physical activity interventions Welk (2002). This intervention effect of pedometers needs to be taken into account when using it as an assessment tool.

Accelerometers

Portable accelerometers have been used in a variety of field settings to estimate energy expenditure and/or physical activity (Montoye et al., 1996). These devices measure acceleration and deceleration by use of a piezoelectric bender (Montoye et al., 1996). The Caltrac (Hemokinetics, Madison, WI) is a commonly used device and it is made to fit firmly at the waist on a belt or clothing. The device can estimate caloric expenditure, but it is more often used to give motion counts as an index of physical activity. The device measures acceleration on the horizontal plane and therefore does not measure motion on other planes, or when the hip does not move, such as during upper body motion or cycling (Montoye et al., 1996). This device is unlikely to be useful in measuring physical activity performed by older adults, because so many activities they perform are without horizontal displacement of the hip, such as household tasks and other physical activities (e.g., arm exercise).

The Caltrac has been validated in a variety of subjects engaging in a variety of activities. Several studies have reported that the estimation of energy expenditure by the Caltrac was greatly affected by exercise mode and intensity and that it does not accurately reflect variation in the level of physical activity (Fehling, 1999; Pambianco, 1990; Richardson, 1995). Work using the Caltrac in older adults has shown that the Caltrac provides inaccurate estimates of energy expenditure in this population. The Caltrac significantly underestimates daily energy compared with DLH$_2$O (Starling, Matthews, Ades, & Poehlman, 1999) and, when compared with oxygen uptake during exercise, the Caltrac overestimated treadmill walking and underestimated stepping exercise (Fehling, Smith, Warner, & Dalsky, 1999).

Triaxial accelerometers (such as the Actical: Bio-Lynx, Montreal, Canada) measure vertical, horizontal and lateral acceleration and raw data can be analyzed to provide an objective measure of the intensity, duration and frequency of physical activity throughout the day. The detected accelerations are filtered, converted to a numerical value and summed over a specified time interval or epoch. The recorded counts for each epoch can be used to represent the activity intensity. In order to accurately quantify PA intensity and duration, short (2-5 sec.) epoch durations are necessary (Baquet, Stratton, Van Praagh, & Berthoin, 2007; Nilsson, Ekelund, Yngve & Sjostrom, 2002). These monitors store data over long periods, allowing analysis of patterns of physical activity in free-living participants over the course of several days to weeks. The small size of the device is unobtrusive and allows monitoring of participants without interfering with normal movement. Studies have concluded that accelerometers can be effectively used in free-living individuals to measure levels of physical activity (e.g., Freedson, Pober & Janz, 2005). In addition, relatively short periods of monitoring (4-7 days) have been found to be reliable (Trost, Pate, Freedson, Sallis & Taylor, 2000).

Heart Rate Monitors

Heart rate (HR) is a physiologic variable that is easy to apply in the field using portable HRM, which can be used to estimate energy expenditure or oxygen uptake (Astrand, 1970; Montoye, 1996). Physiologically, the relationship between heart rate and oxygen uptake can be understood by the Fick equation, whereby oxygen uptake is equal to the product of the cardiac output (HR x stroke volume) and the arteriovenous oxygen difference (Astrand & Rodahl, 1970). Stroke volume and arteriovenous oxygen difference do not change much during exercise, so HR becomes the main determinant of the oxygen uptake throughout a broad range of exercise intensity and can be used as a surrogate measure of oxygen uptake (Rowell, 1986).

The efficacy of heart rate monitoring for estimating total daily energy expenditure (TDEE) has been studied in various populations. Heart rate monitoring has been compared with other methods of measuring energy expenditure, including indirect calorimetry, oxygen uptake, and DLH$_2$O. Several studies have found a strong positive relationship between HRM and wholebody calorimetry and oxygen uptake (Ceesay, 1989 Davidson, 1997; Dauncey, 1979; McCrory, 1997; Rutgers, 1997; Spurr, 1988), although it has been known to overestimate TDEE for the individual (Kalkwarf, Haas, Belko, Roach, & Roe, 1989). HRM has also compared favorably with DLH$_2$O in the evaluation of TDEE, despite variability in the estimations, and depending upon which heart rate oxygen uptake calibration method is used (Kashiwazaki, 1999; Li, 1993; Livingstone, 1990; Morio, 1997; Rothenberg, 1998; Sawaya; 1996). It should be noted that there is considerable day to day variability in heart rate (Rutgers, 1977; Li, 1993), so most experts recommend at least four days of HRM data for reliable measurement of mean heart rate (Montoye et al., 1996). Heart rate monitoring is an inexpensive and noninvasive method of evaluating an individual's free living energy expenditure (Montoye et al., 1996).

Body Composition

Within the 2008 Physical Activity Guidelines for Americans (DHHS, 2008) body composition is defined as a health related component of physical fitness that applies to body weight and the relative amounts of muscle, fat, bone, and other vital tissues of the body. Most often, the components are limited to fat and lean body mass (or fat-free mass).

The recommended body composition varies considerably for men and women and by age, but the minimum percent of body fat considered safe for good health is 8% for males and 16% for females (Heyward, 2006). The average adult body fat is about 13% for men and 28% for women. Heyward (2006) recommends body fat percentages for young females between 15% and 25% and young males between 10% and 25%. Body composition has been directly linked overall health status. The term obese refers to body composition consisting of too much fat; for men over this is 22%, young males over 31%, women over 35% and young females over 36% (Heyward, 2006). Currently, one of the main contributors to preventable causes of death is obesity (Daniel, Sizer, & Latman, 2005). According to Welk and Blair (2000) obesity has been linked to a variety of serious diseases and metabolic disorders including type 2 diabetes, hypertension, dyslipidemia, coronary heart disease, gall bladder disease, respiratory diseases, various cancers and osteoarthritis.

With aging, there is a substantial decline in fat free mass primarily due to the loss of bone mineral and muscle mass (Heyward & Wagner, 2004). These changes in body composition have important effects on physical function and overall health status of older adults. Sharkey and Gaskill (2007) state that with each decade above 25 years old, the body loses about 4% of its metabolically active cells which usually leads to weight gain that is a result of decrease of muscle and increase in percentage of body fat. The loss of muscle mass is associated with an age-related decrease in strength, which may result in a loss of functional independence and quality of life. For example, Jette and Branch (1981) found that 45% of women aged 65-74 and 65% of women aged 75-84 were unable to lift 4.5 kg. A high percentage of these women reported they were unable to perform some aspects of normal household tasks.

Regular exercise results in positive changes in body composition in people of all ages, even if they have been previously sedentary. Endurance exercise training reduces the percentage of body fat in older men, with a preferential loss from central fat depots (Schwartz, 1991). Resistance training increases the strength and muscle mass in older adults (Fiatarone, 1990; Fiatarone, 1994; Frontera , 1988). It is therefore possible to use changes in body composition to validate self-reported increases in exercise behavior. In fact, percentage of body fat has been used to validate The Godin Leisure-Time Exercise Questionnaire, (Godin, & Shepard, 1985). The Lipid Research Clinic Questionnaire (Ainsworth, 1993; Jacobs, 1993), The Minnesota Leisure Time Physical Activity Questionnaire (Richardson, Leon, Jacobs, Ainsworth, & Serfass, 1994), and The Paffenbarger Physical Activity Questionnaire (Jacobs, Ainsworth, Hartman, & Leon, 1993).

Subjective Measures

These measures require some cognitive or perceptual processing by the participant to produce the data. This usually takes the form of the participant thinking about and recording their physical activity information.

Diaries and Logs

Diary methods involve having an individual regularly record or log physical activity, and may include information such as duration, intensity, mode, emotional state, environment, etc. (Woods et al., 2005). The diary or log technique requires very little expense, and information can be gathered from many individuals at once. There are several shortcomings to this particular method, which make it less desirable as a form of measurement, and more useful as a motivational tool. First and foremost, the quality of the logged data is reliant solely on the cooperation and precision of the participant's reporting. Secondly, coding diary entries is not only time-consuming but tedious, and often requires more than one analyst to maximize inter-rater reliability. Finally, this method is only appropriate for persons who are not limited by any physical or cognitive challenges that could prevent them from writing.

Interviews and Questionnaires

Physical activity questionnaires are wholly subjective measures of physical activity—most commonly used method in population studies. Questionnaires are an ideal application since they are cost effective, can be adapted to a variety of settings and populations, and they have validity and reliability compared with laboratory and field methods, as well as health outcomes (Kriska & Caspersen, 1997). Physical activity questionnaires can be used to rank individuals or subgroups of individuals in a population and then compared with standardized physiological measures (e.g., body composition, aerobic capacity) and disease outcomes (Kriska & Caspersen, 1997). Physical activity questionnaires differ on several attributes: complexity, time frame, type of activity, and scoring. The choice of questionnaire for any particular application must take each of these factors into consideration with regard to the study hypotheses, population of interest (e.g., gender, age, and ethnicity), time, financial resources, and a myriad of other factors (Kriska & Caspersen, 1997).

It is important to keep in mind that older adults may not engage in the same physical activity intensity as young adults; therefore, any instruments that are used need to reflect and detect very specific changes for a broad range of physical activities. For example, there are several physical activity questionnaires that have been developed for and validated in older adults (Caspersen, 1991; Di Pietro, 1993; Stewart, 1997; Voorips, 1991; Washburn, 1993). The Modified Baeke Questionnaire (Caspersen, 1991; Voorips, 1991), and the Zutphen Questionnaire were both designed for European older adults; whereas the Yale Physical Activity Survey (YPAS) (Di Pietro et al., 1993) and the Community Healthy Activities Model Program for Seniors CHAMPS (Stewart et al., 1997) questionnaires have been carefully validated and are used more commonly with American older adults.

Challenges of self-report questionnaires include bias, such as recall or reporting bias, whereby answers rely on the respondent's memory or honesty; social desirability or response bias, in which respondents answer what they think the research wants to know, or in a way that makes them appear more favorable. The potential for missing data is high where self-report methods are concerned, since respondents may systematically, intentionally or unintentionally not provide answers. Table 39.1 presents a summary of the various measurement approaches.

Recommendations for Researchers and Practitioners

There is no one instrument or measure of physical activity that satisfactorily incorporates intensity, duration, frequency, mode, and adherence. As a result, consideration for physical activity researchers and practitioners must realize that the instrument and measure selection should be based on the research question at hand. In other words, the program or project should drive the instrument and measure selection. For example, if a program promotes activity on elementary school playgrounds and the purpose is to investigate frequency of children's activity when in the playground area; then observation might be the instrument of choice. In this instance, one can observe frequency reliably and with validity while there are self-report challenges with children in grade 3 and lower, maturational issues with some of the physiological indicators, and feasibility issues of other approaches. Whenever possible, triangulation of physical activity measures is recommended (Treuth, 2002). This is the inclusion

of three or more different physical activity instruments (preferably including 3 different types of measures), which essentially provides multiple lines of evidence and a more complete picture of physical activity. For example, when assessing walking on older adults, self-report could be complemented by a pedometer and/or HRM as a balance between subjective and objective indicators.

Whatever the decision, we emphasize developing well documented standardized scripts and protocols, with detailed rules of how data is collected, quality controlled, cleaned, and processed. This ensures the reproducibility of your measurement approach.

As practitioners in this field, we recommend that you encourage individuals to meet published guidelines in a safe manner. Inactive individuals should start slowly and build up gradually to these guidelines. All kinds of activity should be promoted to allow the individual to find what they like and make the physical activity experience enjoyable for the participant.

Attention to measurement is paramount, especially in the planning stages of program development. Using resources to develop and implement a physical activity program (be it strength training for employees of a company, aerobics for high school students, or a flexibility program for older adults, etc.) and neglecting appropriate measurement means there is no way of knowing if a program was worthwhile. The same recommendation that applies to the researchers applies with the practitioner. Target the measure to what the program is trying to change or promote.

Challenges that practitioners face are the length, resources, and practicality of some published instruments. Our recommendation to this is threefold:

1. A brief, valid instrument is better than no assessment at all.

2. Ask an expert at your local university (phone or email if you don't have direct access). Most likely there is a feasible and specific solution for the purposes of the program.

3. Hire a research or evaluation person/unit that can do the measurement for you. This has the added advantage of decreasing a perceived conflict of interest (i.e., if *you* measure whether your own program is effective, some bias (perceived or real) may be assumed. Using an external evaluator reduces this perception).

Measures Assessing Behavioral Physical Activity

Variable	Measure	Pros	Cons	Sources	Websites
Intensity	Indirect calorimetry	• Validates other measures • Provides accurate measure of short-term energy expenditure • Avoids biases and inaccuracy • Provides quantitative data	• Confined to unnatural laboratory setting • Highly invasive • Requires a lot of equipment	Carron, Hausenblas, & Estabrooks (2003); Smith & Biddle (2008)	None
Intensity	Doubly labeled water	• Little interference with everyday life—noninvasive • No time constrains • Avoids biases and inaccuracy • Provides quantitative data • High validity for all ages • Valuable for small, controlled studies	• High cost of equipment and required analysis • Not a specific measure of physical activity because it measures all forms of energy expenditure • Does not provide data on type, frequency, intensity, or duration of activity	Carron, Hausenblas, & Estabrooks (2003); Kang (2008)	None
Frequency, intensity, and mode	Direct observation	• Valid and reliable for controlled studies • Captures whole-body movement • Convenient for large groups • Provides quantitative and qualitative information • Provides valuable and detailed information • Little interference with activity	• Observation done by a trained individual • May produce biased results (on trainer's or participant's behalf) • Time intensive • Provides measurement for time frame observed • Accuracy decreases over time	Carron, Hausenblas, & Estabrooks (2003); Sharpe & Koperwas (2003); Smith & Biddle (2008); Welk (2002)	www.noldus.com/human-behavior-research www.skware.com/softwaredata/BestCD.pdf www.drjamessallis.sdsu.edu/Documents/sofitprotocol.pdf www.drjamessallis.sdsu.edu/Documents/SOPLAYprotocol.pdf
Frequency and intensity	Pedometer	• Inexpensive and easy to use • Used in a variety of settings • Captures low intensity • Provides incentive and motivation • No additional equipment required to record or interpret results • Reliable and valid instrument • Provides quantitative data	• May not account for time • Accuracy can be affected by alteration in gait or placement of device • Cannot measure upper-body activity • Intensity cannot be measured	Carron, Hausenblas, & Estabrooks (2003); Jago et al. (2006); Reiser & Schlenk (2009); Schmidt et al. (2007); Smith & Biddle (2008); Tudor-Locke (2002); Welk (2002)	www.thepedometercompany.com www.accusplit.com www.sportline.com

(continued)

▪ **Table 39.1** ▪

(continued)

Variable	Measure	Pros	Cons	Sources	Websites
Duration, frequency, and intensity	Acceler-ometer	• Records movement in several planes simultaneously • Objective measure • Measures complex activities • Avoids biases and inaccuracy • Provides quantitative data	• Expensive • High sensitivity may record background vibrations • Unit of measurement is not standardized • No direct translation to energy expenditure	Carron, Hausenblas, & Esta-brooks (2003); Reiser & Schlenk (2009); Smith & Biddle (2008); Welk (2002)	www.theactigraph.com www.biotrainerusa.com www.bio-lynx.com/actical.html
Adherence, duration, frequency, and intensity	Heart rate monitor	• Accurately measures physical exertion • Valid in laboratory and field settings • Indicator of true physiological stress on the body • Monitors target HR during exercise • Avoids biases and inaccuracy • Provide quantitative data • Easy and quick data collection and analysis	• Limited accuracy during low levels of activity • Results can be affected by medications, pathology, or stress levels • Provides only indirect informa-tion about energy expenditure • Highly individualized • Strap can be inconvenient and uncomfortable • Other electronic devices can interfere with data	Carron, Hausenblas, & Esta-brooks (2003); Reiser & Schlenk (2009); Smith & Biddle (2008); Welk (2002)	www.polarusa.com www.consumersearch.com/heart-rate-monitors www.sportline.com
Adherence, duration, frequency, intensity, and mode	Diary or log	• Increases accountability and awareness • Inexpensive • Able to reference long term • Does not require an observer • Can be completed by large group simultaneously • Captures quantitative and qualitative information	• Subjective • Memory limitations • Reliability and validity can be affected with recall • Time consuming • May not be consistently updated	Carron, Hausenblas, & Esta-brooks (2003); Reiser & Schlenk (2009); Smith & Biddle (2008); Welk (2002)	www.cdc.gov/healthyweight/pdf/Physical_Activity_Diary_CDC.pdf www.shapeup.org/support/maintain/logform1.php
Adherence, duration, frequency, intensity, and mode	Interview or ques-tionnaire	• Easy administration • Inexpensive and immediate • Ability to assess large sample • Captures quantitative and qualitative information • Facilitates understanding of concepts and questions	• Subjective • Memory limitations • Terms used can be misunder-stood • Reliability and validity can be affected with recall	Carron, Hausenblas, & Esta-brooks (2003); Di Pietro et al. (1993); Smith & Biddle (2008); Stewart, Sepsis, King, McLellan, & Ritter (1997); Welk (2002)	www.ipaq.ki.se/ipaq.htm

REFERENCES

Chapter 1

Abell, N., Springer, D.W., & Kamata, A. (2009). *Developing and validating rapid assessment instruments.* New York: Oxford University Press.

DeVellis, R.F. (2003). *Scale development: Theory and applications.* (2nd ed.). Thousand Oaks, CA: Sage.

Embretson, S.E., & Reise, S.P. (2000). *Item response theory for psychologists.* Mahwah, NJ: Erlbaum.

Mehrens, W.A., & Lehmann, I.J. (1991). *Measurement and evaluation in education and psychology.* (4th ed.). Orlando, FL: Harcourt Brace.

Osterlind, S.J. (2006). *Modern measurement: Theory, principles, and applications of mental appraisal.* Upper Saddle River, NJ: Pearson.

Wilson, M. (2005). *Constructing measures: An item response modeling approach.* Mahwah, NJ: Erlbaum.

Chapter 2

Asci, F.H., Fletcher, R.B., & Caglar, E. (2009). A differential item functioning analysis of the PSDQ with Turkish and New Zealand/Australian adolescents. *Psychology of Sport and Exercise, 10,* 12-18.

American Educational Research Association, American Psychological Association, & National Council on Measurement in Education. (1985). *Standards for educational and psychological testing.* Washington, DC: Author.

American Educational Research Association, American Psychological Association, & National Council on Measurement in Education. (1999). *Standards for educational and psychological testing.* Washington, DC: Author.

American Psychological Association. (1954). Technical recommendations for psychological tests and diagnostic techniques. *Psychological Bulletin, 51*(Suppl. 2), part 2.

American Psychological Association. (1966). *Standards for educational and psychological tests and manuals.* Washington, DC: Author.

American Psychological Association. (1974). *Standards for educational and psychological tests and manuals (revised).* Washington, DC: Author.

Andersen, M.B., McCullagh, P., & Wilson, G.J. (2007). But what do the numbers really tell us? Arbitrary metrics and effect size reporting in sport psychology research. *Journal of Sport and Exercise Psychology, 29,* 664-672.

Baker, F.B. (1985). *The basics of item response theory.* Portsmouth, NH: Heinemann.

Barclay-Goddard, R., Epstein, J.D., & Mayo, N.E. (2009). Response shift: A brief overview and proposed research priorities. *Quality of Life Research, 18,* 335-346.

Barrett, L.F., & Barrett, D.J. (2001). An introduction to computerized experience sampling in psychology. *Social Science Computer Review, 19*(2), 175-185.

Baumgartner, T.A. (1989). Norm-referenced measurement: Reliability. In M.J. Safrit & T.M. Wood (Eds.), *Measurement concepts in physical education and exercise science* (pp. 45-72). Champaign, IL: Human Kinetics.

Baumgartner, T.A. (2006). Reliability and error of measurement. In T. Wood and W. Zhu (Eds.), *Measurement theory and practice in kinesiology* (pp. 27-52). Champaign, IL: Human Kinetics.

Bennett, R.E. (2008). *Technology for large-scale assessment* (ETS Report No. RM-08-10). Princeton, NJ: Educational Testing Service.

Berk, R.A. (Ed.). (1980). *Criterion-referenced measurement: The state of the art.* Baltimore: Johns Hopkins University Press.

Berk, R.A. (Ed.). (1982). *Handbook of methods for detecting test bias.* Baltimore: Johns Hopkins University Press.

Berk, R.A. (Ed.). (1984). *A guide to criterion-referenced test construction.* Baltimore: Johns Hopkins University Press.

Biddle, S.J.H., Markland, D., Gilbourne, D., Chatzisarantis, N.L.D., & Sparkes, A.C. (2001). Research methods in sport and exercise psychology: Quantitative and qualitative issues. *Journal of Sports Sciences, 19,* 777-809.

Bingham, W.V. (1937). *Aptitudes and aptitude testing.* New York: Harper Brothers.

Bollen, K.A. (1989). *Structural equations with latent variables.* New York: Wiley.

Brennan, R.L. (1983). *Elements of generalizability theory.* Iowa City, IA: American College Testing Program.

Brennan, R.L. (2001). *Generalizability theory* (2nd ed.). New York: Springer.

Byrne, B.M. (1998). *Structural equation modeling with LISREL, PRELIS, and SIMPLIS: Basic concepts, applications, and programming.* Mahwah, NJ: Erlbaum.

Byrne, B.M. (2010). *Structural equation modeling with AMOS: Basic concepts, applications, and programming* (2nd ed.). New York: Routledge.

Cattell, R.B. (1978). *The scientific use of factor analysis in behavioral and life sciences.* New York: Plenum Press.

Child, D. (1990). *The essentials of factor analysis* (2nd ed.). London: Cassel Educational Limited.

Cohen, A. (2006). Item bias and differential item functioning. In T. Wood and W. Zhu (Eds.), *Measurement theory and practice in kinesiology* (pp. 113-126). Champaign, IL: Human Kinetics.

Colcombe, S.J., Kramer, A.F., Erickson, K.I., Scalf, P., McAuley, E., Cohen, N.J., Webb, A., Jerome, G.J., Marqueq, D.X., & Elavsky, S. (2004). Cardiovascular fitness, cortical plasticity, and aging. *Proceedings of the National Academy of Sciences, 101*(9), 3316-3321.

Cronbach, L.J. (1949). *Essentials of psychological testing.* New York: Harper & Row.

Cronbach, L.J., Gleser, G.C., Nanda, H., & Rajaratnam, N. (1972). *The dependability of behavioral measurements: Theory of generalizability for scores and profiles.* New York: Wiley.

Cronbach, L.J., & Meehl, P.E. (1955). Construct validity in psychological tests. *Psychological Bulletin, 55,* 281-302.

Culver, D.M., Gilbert, W.D., & Trudel, P. (2003). A decade of qualitative research in sport psychology journals: 1990-1999. *The Sport Psychologist, 17,* 1-15.

Dishman, R.K. (1991). The *failure of sport psychology* in the exercise and *sport* sciences. *American Academy of Physical Education Papers, 24,* 39-47.

Dorans, N.J., & Holland, P.W. (1993). DIF detection and description: Mantel-Haenszel and standardization. In P.W. Holland & H. Wainer (Eds.), *Differential item functioning* (pp. 35-66). Hillsdale, NJ: Erlbaum.

Drasgow, F., & Olson-Buchanan, J.B. (1999). *Innovations in computerized assessment.* Mahwah, NJ: Erlbaum.

Duda, J.L. (Ed.). (1998). *Advances in sport and exercise psychology measurement.* Morgantown, WV: Fitness Information Technology.

Duncan, T.E., Duncan, S.C., Strycker, L.A., Li, F., & Alpert, A. (1999). *An introduction to latent variable growth curve modeling: Concepts, issues, and applications.* Mahwah, NJ: Erlbaum.

Embretson, S.E., & Hershberger, S.L. (Eds.). (1999). *The new rules of measurement: What every psychologist and educator should know.* Mahwah, NJ: Erlbaum.

Embretson, S.E., & Reise, S.P. (2000). *Item response theory for psychologists.* Mahwah, NJ: Erlbaum.

Etnier, J.L., Salazar, W., Landers, D.M., Petruzzello, S.J., Han, M., & Nowell, P. (1997). The influence of physical fitness and exercise upon cognitive functioning: A meta-analysis. *Journal of Sport and Exercise Psychology, 19,* 249-277.

Fletcher, R. (1999). Incorporating recent advances in measurement in sport and exercise psychology. *Journal of Sport and Exercise Psychology, 21,* 24-38.

Frederiksen, N., Mislevy, R.J., & Bejar, I.I. (Eds.). (1993). *Test theory for a new generation of tests.* Mahwah, NJ: Erlbaum.

Gershon, R.C., & Bergstrom, B.A. (2006). Computerized adaptive testing. In T. Wood and W. Zhu (Eds.), *Measurement theory and practice in kinesiology* (pp. 127-143). Champaign, IL: Human Kinetics.

Gill, D.L. (1997). Measurement, statistics, and research design issues in sport and exercise psychology. *Measurement in Physical Education and Exercise Science, 1*(1), 39-53.

Gill, D.L. (2000). *Psychological dynamics of sport and exercise* (2nd ed.). Champaign, IL: Human Kinetics.

Gorsuch, R.L. (1983). *Factor analysis* (2nd ed.). Hillside, NJ: Erlbaum.

Hambleton, R.K., & Swaminathan, H. (1985). *Item response theory: Principles and applications.* Boston: Kluwer-Nijhoff.

Hambleton, R.K, Merenda, P.F., & Spielberger, C.D. (2004). *Adapting educational and psychological tests for cross-cultural assessment.* Mahwah, NJ: Erlbaum.

Hayduk, L.A. (1987). *Structural equation modeling with LISREL: Essentials and advances.* Baltimore: Johns Hopkins University Press.

Hillman, C.H., Pontifex, M.B., Raine, L.B., Castelli, D.M., Hall, E.E., & Kramer, A.F. (2009). The effect of acute treadmill walking on cognitive control and academic achievement in preadolescent children. *Neuroscience, 159*(3), 1044-1054.

Holland, P.W., & Thayer, D.T. (1988). Differential item functioning and the Mantel-Haenszel procedures. In H. Wainer & H. Brain (Eds.), *Test validity* (pp. 129-145). Hillsdale, NJ: Erlbaum.

Jackson, S.A., Martin, A.J., & Eklund, R.C. (2008). Long and short measures of flow: The construct validity of the FSS-2, DFS-2, and new brief counterparts. *Journal of Sport and Exercise Psychology, 30,* 561-587.

Jöreskog, K.G., & Sörbom, D. (1984). *LISREL VI* [Computer software]. Chicago, IL: Scientific Software International.

Kane, M.T. (1992). An argument-based approach to validity. *Psychological Bulletin, 112*(3), 527-535.

Klein, S. (2008). Characteristics of hand and machine-assigned scores to college students' answers to open-ended tasks. In D. Nolan & T. Speed (Eds.), *Probability and statistics: Essays in honor of David A. Freedman* (pp. 76-89). Beachwood, OH: Institute of Mathematical Statistics.

Kolen, M.J. & Brennan, R.L. (2004). *Test equating, scaling, and linking: Methods and practices* (2nd ed.). New York: Springer.

Landers, D.M. (1983). Whatever happened to theory testing in sport psychology? *Journal of Sport Psychology, 5,* 135-151.

Lenders, D.M., Boutcher, S.H., & Wang, M.Q. (1986). The history and status of the *Journal of Sport Psychology:* 1979-1985. *Journal of Sport Psychology, 8,* 149-163.

Leighton, J.P., & Gierl, M.J. (Eds.). (2007). *Cognitive diagnostic assessment for education: Theory and practices.* New York: Cambridge University Press.

Lindquist, E.F. (1953). *Design and analysis of experiments in psychology and education.* Boston: Houghton Mifflin.

Llewellyn, D., Hodrien, A., & Llewellyn, V. (2008). Neuroimaging in psychology: The portrayal of key radiological techniques in contemporary texts. *Psychology Learning and Teaching, 7*(1), 46-51.

Loehlin, J.C. (1987). *Latent variable models: An introduction to factor, path, and structural analysis.* Hillsdale, NJ: Erlbaum.

Looney, M.A. (1989). Criterion-referenced measurement: Reliability. In M.J. Safrit & T.M. Wood (Eds.), *Measurement concepts in physical education and exercise science* (pp. 137-152). Champaign, IL: Human Kinetics.

Looney, M.A., Spray, J.A., & Castelli, D. (1996). The task difficulty of free throw shooting for males and females. *Research Quarterly for Exercise and Sport, 67*(3), 265-271.

Long, J.S. (*1983*). *Confirmatory factor analysis.* Beverly Hills, CA: Sage.

Lonsdale, C., Hodge, K., & Rose, E. (2008). The Behavioral Regulation in Sport Questionnaire (BRSQ): Instrument development and initial validity evidence. *Journal of Sport and Exercise Psychology, 30,* 323-355.

Lord, F.M. (1980). *Application of item response theory to practical testing problems.* Hillsdale, NJ: Erlbaum.

Lord, F.M., & Novick, M.R. (1968). *Statistical theories of mental test scores.* Reading, MA: Addison-Wesley.

Mantel, N., & Haenszel, W. (1959). Statistical aspects of the analysis of data from retrospective studies of disease. *Journal of the National Cancer Institute, 22,* 719-748.

Marsh, H.W. (1998). Foreward. In J.L. Duda (Ed.), *Advances in sport and exercise psychology measurement* (pp. xv-xix). Morgantown, WV: Fitness Information Technology.

Martens, R. (1977). *Sport competition anxiety test.* Champaign, IL: Human Kinetics.

McAuley, E., & Duncan, T.E. (1990). Cognitive appraisal and affective reactions following physical achievement outcomes. *Journal of Sport and Exercise Psychology, 12,* 415-426.

McCullagh, P. (1995). Sport psychology: A historical perspective. *The Sport Psychologist, 9*(4), 363-365.

McDonald, R.P. (1985). *Factor analysis and related models*. Hillsdale, NJ: Erlbaum.

Meier, S.T. (1994). *The chronic crisis in psychological measurement and assessment: A historical survey*. New York: Academic Press.

Messick, S. (1989). Validity. In R.L. Linn (Ed.), *Educational measurement* (3rd ed., pp. 13-103). New York: Macmillan.

Messick, S. (1996a). Standards-based score interpretation: Establishing valid grounds for valid inferences. *Proceedings of the Joint Conference on Standard Setting for Large Scale Assessments*. Washington, DC: U.S. Government Printing Office.

Messick, S. (1996b). Validity of performance assessment. In G. Philips (Ed.), *Technical issues in large-scale performance assessment* (pp. 1-18). Washington, DC: National Center for Educational Statistics.

Michell, J. (1999). *Measurement in psychology: Critical history of a methodological concept*. New York: Cambridge University Press.

Morgan, W.P. (1978). The mind of the marathoner. *Psychology Today, April*, 38-49.

Morgan, W.P. (1994). Sport psychology in exercise science and sports medicine. In *American College of Sports Medicine—40th anniversary lecture* (pp. 81-92). Indianapolis: American College of Sports Medicine.

Morgan, W.P., & Pollock, M.L. (1977). Psychologic characterization of the elite distance runner. *Annals of the New York Academy of Sciences, 301*, 382-403.

Morrow, J., Jr., Jackson, A., Disch, J., & Mood, D. (2005). *Measurement and evaluation in human performance* (3rd ed.). Champaign, IL: Human Kinetics.

Mulaik, S.A. (1972). *The foundations of factor analysis*. New York: McGraw-Hill.

Muthén, L.K., & Muthén, B.O. (2007). *Mplus user's guide* (5th ed.). Los Angeles: Muthén & Muthén.

Myers, N.D., Feltz, D.L., & Wolfe, E.W. (2008). A confirmatory study of rating scale category effectiveness for the Coaching Efficacy Scale. *Research Quarterly for Exercise and Sport, 79*, 300-311.

Myers, N.D., Wolfe, E., & Feltz, D.L. (2005). An evaluation of the psychometric properties of the Coaching Efficacy Scale for American coaches. *Measurement in Physical Education and Exercise Science, 9*, 135-160.

Myers, N.D., Wolfe, E.W., Feltz, D.L., & Penfield, R.D. (2006). Identifying differential item functioning of rating scale items with the Rasch model: An introduction and an application. *Measurement in Physical Education and Exercise Science, 10*, 210-240.

Myers, N.D., Wolfe, E.W., Maier, K.S., Feltz, D.L., & Reckase, M.D. (2006). Extending validity evidence for multidimensional measures of coaching competency. *Research Quarterly for Exercise and Sport, 77*, 451-463.

National Association for Sport and Physical Education Assessment Task Force. (2008). *PE metrics: Assessing the national standards, Standard 1*. Reston, VA: Author.

Nichols, P.D., Chipman, S.F., & Brennan, R.L. (Eds.). (1995). *Cognitively diagnostic assessment*. Hillsdale, NJ: Erlbaum.

O'Craven, K.M., & Kanwisher, N. (2000). Mental imagery of faces and places activates corresponding stimulus-specific brain regions. *Journal of Cognitive Neuroscience, 12*(6), 1013-1023.

Ostrow, A.C. (Ed.). (1990). *Directory of psychological tests in the sport and exercise sciences*. Morgantown, WV: Fitness Information Technology.

Ostrow, A.C. (Ed.). (1996, 2002). *Directory of psychological tests in the sport and exercise sciences*. Morgantown, WV: Fitness Information Technology.

Parshall, C.G., Spray, J.A., Kalohn, J.C., & Davey, T. (2002). *Practical considerations in computer-based testing*. New York: Springer.

Patterson, P. (1997). Measurement approaches to sport psychology questions. In T.M. Wood (Ed.), *Exploring the kaleidoscope: Proceedings of the 8th Measurement and Evaluation Symposium* (pp. 60-67). Corvallis, OR: Oregon State University.

Quellmalz, E.S., & Pellegrino, J.W. (2009). Technology and testing. *Science, 323*(5910), 75-79.

Roberts, R., Callow, N., Hardy, L., Markland, D., & Bringer, J. (2008). Movement imagery ability: Development and assessment of a revised version of the Vividness of Movement Imagery Questionnaire. *Journal of Sport and Exercise Psychology, 30*, 200-221.

Roussos, L., & Stout, W. (1996). A multidimensionality-based DIF analysis paradigm. *Applied Psychological Measurement, 20*(4), 355-71.

Rowe, D.A., & Mahar, M.T. (2006). Validity. In T. Wood & W. Zhu (Eds.), *Measurement theory and practice in kinesiology* (pp. 9-26). Champaign, IL: Human Kinetics.

Sands, W.A., Waters, B.K., & McBride, J.R. (Eds.). (1997). *Computerized adaptive testing: From inquiry to operation*. Washington, DC: American Psychological Association.

Safrit, M.J. (1989). Criterion-referenced measurement: Validity. In M.J. Safrit & T.M. Wood (Eds.), *Measurement concepts in physical education and exercise science* (pp. 119-135). Champaign, IL: Human Kinetics.

Safrit, M.J., Atwater, A.E., Baumgartner, T.A., & West, C. (Eds.). (1976). *Reliability theory*. Washington, DC: American Alliance for Health, Physical Education, Recreation and Dance.

Safrit, M.J., & Wood, T.M. (Eds.). (1989). *Measurement concepts in physical education and exercise science*. Champaign, IL: Human Kinetics.

Safrit, M.J., & Wood, T.M. (1995). *Introduction to measurement in physical education and exercise science* (3rd ed.). St. Louis: Times Mirror/Mosby.

Schutz, R.W. (1989). Research methodology: New procedures for comparative physical education and sport. In F.H. Fu, M.L. Ng, & M. Speak (Eds.), *Comparative physical education and sport* (Vol. 6, pp. 53-66). Hong Kong: Physical Education Unit, The Chinese University of Hong Kong.

Schutz, R.W. (1994). Methodological issues and measurement problems in sport psychology. In S. Serpa, J. Alves, & V. Pataco (Eds.), *International perspectives on sport and exercise psychology*. Morgantown, WV: Fitness Information Technology.

Schutz, R.W., & Gessaroli, M.E. (1993). Use, misuse, and disuse of psychometrics in sport psychology research. In R.N. Singer, M. Murphey, & L.K. Tennant (Eds.), *Handbook of research on sport psychology* (pp. 901-917). Don Mills, ON: Maxwell Macmillan Canada.

Schutz, R.W., & Park, I. (2004). Some methodological considerations in developmental sport and exercise psychology. In M.R. Weiss (Ed.), *Developmental sport and exercise psychology: A lifespan perspective* (pp. 73-99). Morgantown, WV: Fitness Information Technology.

Shealy, R., & Stout, W. (1993). A model-based standardization approach that separates true bias/DIF from group ability differences and detects test bias/DTF as well as item bias/DIF. *Psychometrika, 58*, 159-194.

Shermis, M.D., & Burstein, J.C. (2003). *Automated essays scoring: A cross-disciplinary perspective*. Mahwah, NJ: Erlbaum.

Shinkareva, S.V., Mason, R.A., Malave, V.L., Wang, W., Mitchell, T.M., & Just, M.D. (2008). Using fMRI brain activation to identify cognitive states associated with perception of tools and dwellings. *PLoS ONE, 3*(1), e1394.

Silva III, J.M., & Weinberg, R.S. (Eds.). (1984). *Psychological foundations of sport*. Champaign, IL: Human Kinetics.

Singer, R.N. (1989). Applied sport psychology in the United States. *Journal of Applied Sport Psychology, 1*(1), 61-80.

Smith, D., & Bar-Eli, M. (Eds.). (2007). *Essential readings in sport and exercise psychology*. Champaign, IL: Human Kinetics.

Spearman, C. (1904). General intelligence objectively determined and measured. *American Journal of Psychology, 15*(2), 201-293.

Spray, J.A. (1987). Recent developments in measurement and possible applications to the measurement of psychomotor behavior. *Research Quarterly for Exercise and Sport, 58*, 203-209.

Spray, J.A. (1989). New approaches to solving measurement problems. In M.J. Safrit & T.M. Wood (Eds.), *Measurement concepts in physical education and exercise science* (pp. 229-248). Champaign, IL: Human Kinetics.

Stevens, S.S. (1951). Mathematics, measurement and psychophysics. In S.S. Stevens (Ed.), *Handbook of experimental psychology* (pp. 1-41). New York: Wiley.

Tatsuoka, K.K. (2009). *Cognitive assessment: An introduction to the rule space method*. New York: Routledge Academic.

Tenenbaum, G. (1986). Critical reflections of measurements in sport psychology. In L.-E. Unestahl (Ed.), *Contemporary sport psychology: Proceedings from the VI World Congress in Sport Psychology* (pp. 57-64). Orebro, Sweden: VEJE.

Tenenbaum, G., & Bar-Eli, M. (1995). Contemporary issues in exercise and sport psychology research. In S.J.H. Biddle (Ed.), *European perspectives on exercise and sport psychology* (pp. 292-323). Champaign, IL: Human Kinetics.

Thomas, J., Nelson, J., & Silverman, S. (2005). *Research methods in physical activity* (5th ed.). Champaign, IL: Human Kinetics.

Thompson, B. (Ed.). (2003). *Score reliability: Contemporary thinking on reliability issues*. Thousand Oaks, CA: Sage.

Thorndike, R.M., & Lohman, D.F. (1990). *A century of ability testing*. Chicago: Riverside.

Thurstone, L.L. (1947). *Multiple-factor analysis: A development and expansion of the vectors of the mind*. Chicago: University of Chicago Press.

Tryon, W.W. (Ed.). (1991). *Activity measurement in psychology and medicine*. New York: Plenum.

Tucker, B. (2009). *Beyond the bubble: Technology and the future of student assessment*. Washington, DC: Education Sector.

van de Vijver, F.J.R., & Tanzer, N.K. (2004). Bias and equivalence in cross-cultural assessment: An overview. *European Review of Applied Psychology, 54*(2), 119-135.

von Eye, A., & Clogg, C.C. (Eds.). (1994). *Latent variables analysis: Applications for developmental research*. Thousand Oaks, CA: Sage.

Wainer, H., Dorans, N.J., Flaugher, R., Green, B.F., Mislevy, R.J., Steinberg, L., & Thissen, D. (1990). *Computerized adaptive testing: A primer*. Hillsdale, NJ: Erlbaum.

Weinberg, R.S., & Gould, D. (1995, 1999). *Foundations of sport and exercise psychology*. Champaign, IL: Human Kinetics.

Weiss, D.J. (Ed.). (1983). *New horizons in testing: Latent trait testing theory and computerized adaptive testing*. New York: Academic Press.

Weiss, M.R. (2008). "Riding the wave": Transforming sport and exercise psychology within an interdisciplinary vision. *Quest, 60*, 63-83.

Weiss, M.R., & Gill, D.L. (2005). What goes around comes around: Re-emerging themes in sport and exercise psychology. *Research Quarterly for Exercise and Sport, 76*(Suppl.), S71-S87.

Wiggins, D.K. (1984). The history of sport psychology in North America. In J.M. Silva III & R.S. Weinberg (Eds.), *Psychological foundations of sport* (pp. 9-22). Champaign, IL: Human Kinetics.

Williams, A.M., Davids, K., Burwitz, L., & Williams, J.G. (1994). Visual search strategies in experienced and inexperienced soccer players. *Research Quarterly for Exercise and Sport, 65*, 127-135.

Williams, J.M., & Straub, W.F. (2006). Sport psychology: Past, present, future. In J.M. Williams (Ed.), *Applied sport psychology: Personal growth to peak performance* (pp. 1-14). New York: McGraw-Hill.

Wood, T.M. (1987). Putting item response theory into perspective. *Research Quarterly for Exercise and Sport, 58*, 216-220.

Wood, T.M. (1989). The changing nature of norm-referenced validity. In M.J. Safrit & T.M. Wood (Eds.), *Measurement concepts in physical education and exercise science* (pp. 23-44). Champaign, IL: Human Kinetics.

Wood, T., & Zhu, W. (Eds.). (2006). *Measurement theory and practice in kinesiology*. Champaign, IL: Human Kinetics.

Wright, B.D., & Masters, G.N. (1982). *Rating scale analysis: Rasch measurement*. Chicago: MESA Press.

Wright, B.D., & Stone, M.H. (1979). *Best test design*. Chicago: MESA Press.

Zhu, W. (1998a). Comments on "Development of a Cadence Curl-Up Test for College Students" (Sparling, Millard-Stafford, & Snow, 1997): Concerns about validity and practicality. *Research Quarterly for Exercise and Sport, 69*(3), 308-310.

Zhu, W. (1998b). Test equating: What, why, how? *Research Quarterly for Exercise and Sport, 69*, 11-23.

Zhu, W. (2001). An empirical investigation of Rasch equating of motor function tasks. *Adapted Physical Activity Quarterly, 18*(1), 72-89.

Zhu, W. (2006a). Constructing tests using item response theory. In T. Wood and W. Zhu (Eds.), *Measurement theory and practice in kinesiology* (pp. 53-76). Champaign, IL: Human Kinetics.

Zhu, W. (2006b). Scaling, equating and linking to make measures interpretable. In T. Wood & W. Zhu (Eds.), *Measurement theory and practice in kinesiology* (pp. 93-111). Champaign, IL: Human Kinetics.

Zhu, W., & Kurz, K.A. (1996). Graphical DIF analysis for assessing biased motor items/tasks. *Research Quarterly for Exercise and Sport, 67*(Suppl. 1), A-63-A-64.

Zhu, W., Plowman, S.A., & Park, Y. (2010). A primary test centered equating method for cut-off score setting. *Research Quarterly for Exercise and Sport*.

Zhu, W., Timm, G., & Ainsworth, B.A. (2001). Rasch calibration and optimal categorization of an instrument measuring women's exercise perseverance and barriers. *Research Quarterly for Exercise and Sport, 72*(2), 104-116.

Zumbo, B.D. (1999). *A handbook on the theory and methods of differential item functioning (DIF): Logistic regression modeling as a unitary framework for binary and Likert-type (ordinal) item scores*. Ottawa, ON: Directorate of Human Resources Research and Evaluation, Department of National Defense.

Chapter 3

Abell, N., Springer, D.W., & Kamata, A. (2009). *Developing and validating rapid assessment instruments.* New York: Oxford University Press.

Cook, T.D., & Campbell, D.T. (1979). *Quasi-experimentation: Design and analysis issues for field settings.* Chicago: Rand McNally.

Cronbach, L.J. (1951). Coefficient alpha and the internal structure of tests. *Psychometrika, 16,* 297-334.

Mattens, R. (1977). *Sport Competition Anxiety Test.* Champaign, IL: Human Kinetics.

McAuley, E., Duncan, T., & Tammen, V. (1989). Psychometric properties of the intrinsic motivation inventory in a competitive sport setting: A confirmatory factor analysis. *Research Quarterly for Exercise and Sport, 60,* 48-58.

Netemeyer, R.G., Bearden, W.O., & Sharma, S. (2003). *Scaling procedures: Issues and applications.* Thousand Oaks, CA: Sage.

Nunnally, J.C. (1978). *Psychometric theory* (2nd ed.). New York: McGraw-Hill.

Nunnally, J.C., & Bernstein, I.H. (1994). *Psychometric theory* (3rd ed.). New York: McGraw-Hill, 264-265.

Zimmerman, D.W., & Zumbo, B.D. (1993). Coefficient alpha as an estimate of test reliability under violation of two assumptions. *Educational and Psychological Measurement, 53,* 33-50.

Chapter 4

Abell, N., Springer, D.W., & Kamata, A. (2009). *Developing and validating rapid assessment instruments.* New York: Oxford University Press.

Althauser, R.P., Heberlein, T.A., & Scott, R.A. (1971). A causal assessment of validity: The augmented multitraitmultimethod matrix. In H.M. Blalock, Jr. (Ed.), *Causal models in the social sciences* (pp. 374-399). Chicago: Aldine.

American Educational Research Association, American Psychological Association, & National Council on Measurement in Education. (1999). *Standards for educational and psychological testing.* Washington, DC: American Psychological Association.

Bagozzi, R.P. (1978). The construct validity of the affective, behavioral, and cognitive components of attitude by analysis of covariance structures. *Multivariate Behavioral Research, 13,* 9-31.

Bagozzi, R.P. (1981). An examination of the validity of tow models of attitude. *Multivariate Behavioral Research, 16,* 323-359.

Campbell, D.T., & Fiske, D.W. (1959). Convergent and discriminant validity by the mutitrait- multimethod matrix. *Psychological Bulletin, 56,* 81-105.

Carless, S.A., & De Paola, C. (2000). The measurement of cohesion in work teams. *Small Group Research, 31,* 71-88.

Eys, M., Loughead, T., Bray, S.R., & Carron, A.V. (2009). Development of a cohesion questionnaire for youth: The youth sport environment questionnaire. *Journal of Sport and Exercise Psychology, 31*(3), 390-408.

Grant, D.A., & Berg, E.A. (1993). *Wisconsin Card Sorting Test (WCST).* San Antonio: Psychological Corporation.

Hagger, M.S., & Chatzisarantis, N.L.D. (2009). Assumptions in research in sports and exercise psychology. *Journal of Sport and Exercise Psychology, 10,* 511-519.

Kline, T. (2005). *Psychological testing: A practical approach to design and evaluation.* Thousand Oaks: Sage.

Marsh, H.W. (1989). Confirmatory factor analyses of multitrait-multimethod data: Many problems and few solutions. *Applied Psychological Measurement, 13,* 335-361.

Netemeyer, R.G., Bearden, W.O., & Sharma, S. (2003). *Scaling procedures: Issues and applications.* Thousand Oaks, CA: Sage.

Sanchez-Burks, J., Lee, F., Choi, I., Nisbett, R., Zhao, S., & Koo, J. (2003). Conversing across cultures: East-West communication styles in work and nonwork contexts. *Journal of Personality and Social Psychology, 85*(2), 363-372.

Widaman, K.F. (1985). Hierarchically nested covariance structure models for multitrait- multimethod data. *Applied Psychological Measurement, 9,* 1-26.

Chapter 5

Ackerman, T.A. (1992). A didactic explanation of item bias, item impact, and item validity from a multidimensional perspective. *Journal of Educational Measurement, 29,* 67-91.

Adams, R.J., Wilson, M.R., & Wang, W. (1997). The multidimensional random coefficients multinomial logit model. *Applied Psychological Measurement, 1,* 1-23.

Baur, T., & Lukes, D. (2009). An evaluation of IRT models through Monte Carlo simulation. *Journal of Undergraduate Research, 12,* 1-7.

Bock, D.R. (1972). Estimating item parameters and latent ability when responses are scored in two or more nominal categories. *Psychometrika, 37,* 29-51.

Brown, T.A. (2006). *Confirmatory factor analysis for applied research.* New York: Guilford Press.

Embretson, S.E., & Reise, S.P. (2000). *Item response theory for psychologists.* Mahwah, NJ: Erlbaum.

Fletcher, R., & Hattie, J. (2005). Gender differences in physical self-concept: A multidimensional differential item functioning analysis. *Educational and Psychological Measurement, 65,* 657-667.

Hambleton, R.K., & Jones, R.W. (1993). Comparison of classical test theory and item response theory and their applications to test development. *NCME Instructional Module,* 253-262.

Hambleton, R.K., & Swaminathan, H. (1990). *Item response theory.* New York: Wiley.

Hattie, J., Krakowski, K., Rogers, H.J., & Swaminathan, H. (1996). An assessment of Stout's index of essential unidimensionality. *Applied Psychological Measurement, 20,* 1-14.

Kamata, A., & Bauer, D.J. (2008). A note on the relationship between factor analytic and item response theory models. *Structural Equation Modeling, 16,* 136-153.

Kline, R.B. (2005). *Principles and practices of structural equation modeling* (2nd ed.). New York: Guilford Press.

Linacre, J.M. (1994). Sample size and item calibration stability. *Rasch Measurement Transactions, 7,* 328.

Marsh, H.W., & Hau, K.T. (1999). Confirmatory factor analysis: Strategies for small sample size. In R.H. Hoyle (Ed.), *Statistical strategies for small sample research* (pp. 251-284). Thousand Oaks, CA: Sage.

Martens, R., Vealey, R.S., & Burton, D. (1990). *Competitive anxiety in sport.* Champaign, IL: Human Kinetics.

McDonald, R.P. (1979). The structural analysis of multivariate data: A sketch of general theory. *Multivariate Behavioral Research, 14,* 21-38.

McKinley, R.L., & Mills, C.N. (1985). A comparison of several goodness-of-fit statistics. *Applied Psychological Measurement, 9,* 49-57.

Muthen, B., & Lehman, J. (1985). Multiple group IRT modeling: Applications to items bias analysis. *Journal of Educational Statistics, 10*, 133-142.

Muthen, L.K., & Muthen, B.O. (2002). How to use a Monte Carlo study to decide on sample size and determine power. *Structural Equation Modeling, 9*, 599-620.

Nunnally, J.C., & Bernstein, I. (1994). *Psychometric theory* (4th ed.). New York: McGraw-Hill.

Ostini, R., & Nering, M.L. (2006). *Polytomous item response theory models.* Thousand Oaks, CA: Sage.

Petscher, Y., & Kim, Y.S. (2011). Efficiency of predicting risk in word reading using fewer, easier letters. *Assessment for Effective Intervention.*

Rasch, G. (1960). *Probabilistic models for some intelligence and attainment tests.* Copenhagen: Danish Institute for Educational Research.

Rupp, A.A., & Zumbo, B.D. (2003). Which model is best? Robustness properties to justify model choice among unidimensional IRT models under item parameter drift. *The Alberta Journal of Educational Research, 49*, 264-276.

Rupp, A.A., & Zumbo, B.D. (2004). A note on how to quantify and report whether item parameter invariance holds: When Pearson correlations are not enough. *Educational and Psychological Measurements, 64*, 588-599.

Rupp, A.A., & Zumbo, B.D. (2006). Understanding parameters invariance in unidimensional IRT models. *Journal of Educational and Psychological Measurement, 66*, 63-84.

Safrit, M.J., Cohen, A.S., & Costa, M.G. (1989). Item response theory and the measurement of motor behavior. *Research Quarterly for Exercise and Sport, 60*, 325-335.

Samejima, F. (1969). *Estimation of latent ability a response pattern of graded scores* (Psychometric Monograph No. 17). Iowa City, IA: Psychometric Society.

Stout, W. (1990). A new item response theory modeling approach with applications to unidimensional assessment and ability estimation. *Psychometrika, 55*, 293-296.

Tenenbaum, G., Fogarty, G., & Jackson, S. (1999). The flow experience: A Rasch analysis of Jackson's Flow State Scale. *Journal of Outcome Measurement, 3*, 278-294.

Thissen, D. (2003). Psychometric engineering as art: Variations on a theme. In H. Yanai, A. Okada, K. Shigemasu, Y. Kano, & J.J. Meulman (Eds.), *New developments in psychometrics: Proceedings of the International Meeting of the Psychometric Society IMPS 2001* (pp. 3-18). Tokyo: Springer-Verlag.

Van der Linden, W.J., & Hambleton, R.K. (1997). *Handbook of Modern Item Response Theory.* New York: Springer-Verlag.

Wainer, H. (Ed.). (2000). *Computer adaptive testing: A primer* (2nd ed.). Mahwah, NJ: Erlbaum.

Chapter 6

Ahmavaara, Y. (1954). The mathematical theory of factorial invariance under selection. *Psychometrika, 19*, 27-38.

Baker, F. (2001). *The basics of item response theory.* College Park, MD: University of Maryland, ERIC Clearinghouse on Assessment and Evaluation.

Bentler, P., & Bonett, D.G. (1980). Significance tests and goodness of fit in the analysis of covariance structures. *Psychological Bulletin, 88*(3), 588-606.

Bentler, P., Lee, S., & Weng, J. (1987). Multiple population covariance structure analysis under arbitrary distribution theory. *Communication in Statistics-Theory, 16*, 1951-1964.

Bollen, K.A. (1989). *Structural equations with latent variables.* New York: Wiley.

Bollen, K.A., & Long, J.S. (1993). *Testing structural equation models.* Newbury Park, CA: Sage.

Bontempo, D.E., & Hofer, S.M. (2007). Assessing factorial invariance in cross-sectional and longitudinal studies. In A.D. Ong & M.H.M. van Dulmen (Eds.), *Oxford handbook of methods in positive psychology* (p. 153-175). New York: Oxford University Press.

Burt, C.L. (1948). The factorial study of temperamental traits. *British Journal of Psychology, I*, 178-203.

Byrne, B.M., & Stewart, S.M. (2006). The macs approach to testing for multigroup invariance of a second-order factor structure: A walk through the process. *Structural Equation Modeling, 13*, 287-321.

Cattell, R.B. (1944). 'Parallel proportional profiles' and other principles for determining the choice of factors by rotation. *Psychometrika, 9*, 267-283.

Cattell, R.B. (1978). *The scientific use of factor analysis in behavioral and life sciences.* New York: Plenum Press.

Chan, W., Ho, R.M., Leung, K., Chan, D.K.-S., & Yung, Y.-F. (1999). An alternative method for evaluating congruence coefficients with procrustes rotation: A bootstrap procedure. *Psychological Methods, 4*, 378-402.

Cheung, G., & Rensvold, R. (1998). Cross-cultural comparisons using non-invariant measurement items. *Applied Behavioral Science Review, 6*, 93-110.

Cheung, G., & Rensvold, R. (1999). Testing factorial invariance across groups: A reconceptualization and proposed new method. *Journal of Management, 25*, 1-27.

Cronbach, L.J., & Meehl, P.E. (1955). Construct validity in psychological tests. *Psychological Bulletin, 52*, 281-302.

Drasgow, F. (1982). Biased test items and differential validity. *Psychological Bulletin, 92*, 526-531.

Embretson, S.E., & Reise, S.P. (2000). *Item response theory for psychologists.* Mahwah, NJ: Erlbaum.

Hambleton, R.K., Swaminathan, H., & Rogers, H.J. (1991). *Fundamentals of item response theory.* Newbury Park, CA: Sage.

Horn, J., McArdle, J.J., & Mason, R. (1983). When invariance is not invariant: A practical scientist's view of the ethereal concept of factorial invariance. *The Southern Psychologist, 1*, 179-188.

Horn, J., Wanberg, K.W., & Appel, M. (1973). On the internal structure of the MMPI. *Multivariate Behavioral Research, 8*, 131-172.

Horn, J.L., & McArdle, J.J. (1992). A practical and theoretical guide to measurement invariance in aging research. *Experimental Aging Research, 18*, 117-144.

Hu, L., & Bentler, P.M. (1993). Evaluating model fit. In R.H. Hoyle (Ed.), *Structural equation modeling: Concepts, issues, and applications* (pp. 16-99). Newbury Park, CA: Sage.

James, L.R., Mulaik, S.A., & Brett, J.M. (1983). *Causal analysis: Assumptions, models, and data.* Beverly Hills, CA: Sage.

Joreskog, K.G. (1971). Simultaneous factor analysis in several populations. *Psychometrika, 36*, 409-426.

Kamata, A., & Bauer, D. (2008). A note on the relation between factor analytic and item response theory models. *Structural Equation Modeling, 15*, 136-153.

Loehlin, J.C. (1998). *Latent variable models: An introduction to factor, path, and structural analysis* (4th ed.). Mahwah, NJ: Erlbaum.

Lord, F.M., & Novick, M.R. (1968). *Statistical theories of mental test scores.* Reading, MA: Addison-Wesley.

Lorenzo-Seva, U., & Berge, J.M.F. ten. (2006). Tuckers congruence coefficient as a meaningful index of factor similarity. *Methodology, 2*, 57-64.

MacCallum, R. (1986). Specification searches in covariance modeling. *Psychological Bulletin, 100*(1), 107-120.

McArdle, J. (1980). Causal modeling applied to psychonomic systems simulation. *Behavior Research Methods and Instrumentation, 12*(2), 193-209.

McArdle, J.J., & McDonald, R.P. (1984). Some algebraic properties of the reticular action model for moment structures. *British Journal of Mathematical and Statistical Psychology, 27*, 234-251.

McDonald, R.P. (1985). *Factor analysis and related methods.* Hillsdale, NJ: Erlbaum.

Meredith, W. (1964a). Notes on factorial invariance. *Psychometrika, 29*, 177-185.

Meredith, W. (1964b). Rotation to achieve factorial invariance. *Psychometrika, 29*, 186-206.

Meredith, W. (1993). Measurement invariance, factor analysis and factor invariance. *Psychometrika, 58*, 525-543.

Millsap, R.E., & Everson, H. (1993). Methodology review: Statistical approaches for assessing measurement bias. *Applied Psychological Measurement, 17*, 297-334.

Millsap, R.E., & Meredith, W. (2007). Factorial invariance: Historical perspectives and new problems. In R. Cudeck & R.C. MacCallum (Eds.), *Factor analysis at 100: Historical developments and future directions* (pp. 131-152). Mahwah, NJ: Erlbaum.

Mulaik, S.A. (1972). *The foundations of factor analysis.* New York: McGraw-Hill.

Muthén, B. (1981). Factor analysis of dichotomous variables: American attitudes toward abortion. In D. Jackson & E.F. Borgotta (Eds.), *Factor analysis and measurement in sociological research* (pp. 201-213). London: Sage.

Muthén, B. (1984). A general structural equation model with dichotomous, ordered categorical and continuous latent variables indicators. *Psychometrika, 49*, 115-132.

Muthén, B., & Christoffersson, A. (1981). Simultaneous factor analysis of dichotomous variables in several groups. *Psychometrika, 46*, 407-419.

Muthén, L., & Muthén, B. (1998-2007). *Mplus user's guide* (5th ed.). Los Angeles: Muthén and Muthén.

Nesselroade, J.R., Baltes, P.B., & Labouvie, E.W. (1971). Evaluating factor invariance in oblique space: Baseline data generated from random numbers. *Multivariate Behavioral Research, 6*(2) 233-241.

Nesselroade, J.R., & Estabrook, R. (2008). Factor invariance, measurement, and studying development over the lifespan. In C.K. Hertzog & H. Bosworth (Eds.), *Aging and cognition: Research methodologies and empirical advances* (pp. 39-52). Washington, DC: American Psychological Association.

Nesselroade, J.R., Gerstorf, D., Hardy, S.A., & Ram, N. (2007). Idiographic filters for psychological constructs. *Measurement: Interdisciplinary research and perspectives, 5*, 217-235.

Raykov, T., & Marcoulides, G.A. (2008). *An introduction to applied multivariate analysis.* New York: Taylor & Francis.

Rensvold, R., & Cheung, G. (2001). Testing for metric invariance using structural equation models: Solving the standardization problem. *Research in Management, 1*, 25-50.

Rupp, A.A., & Zumbo, B. (2006). Understanding parameter invariance in unidimensional IRT models. *Educational and Psychological Measurement, 66*, 63-84.

Satorra, A. (1993). Asymptotic robust inferences in multi-sample analysis of augmented-moment structures. In C.M. Cuadras & C.R. Rao (Eds.), *Multivariate analysis: Future directions* (pp. 211-229). Barcelona: Elsevier.

Satorra, A., & Saris, W. (1985). Power of the likelihood ratio test in covariance structure analysis. *Psychometrika, 50*(1), 83-90.

Schmitt, N., & Kuljanin, G. (2008). Measurement invariance: Review of practice and implications. *Human Resource Management Review, 18*(4), 210-222.

Sorbom, D. (1989). Model modification. *Psychometrika, 54*, 371-384.

Tabachnick, B.G., & Fidell, L.S. (1996). *Using multivariate statistics* (3rd ed.). New York: Harper Collins.

Thomson, G.H. (1939). *The factorial analysis of human ability.* London: University of London Press.

Thurstone, L.L. (1947). *Multiple factor analysis.* Chicago: University of Chicago Press.

Tucker, L.R. (1951). *A method for synthesis of factor analysis studies* (Personnel Research Section Report No. 984). Washington, DC: Department of the Army.

Vandenberg, R.J., & Lance, C.E. (2000). A review and synthesis of the measurement invariance literature: Suggestions, practices, and recommendations for organizational research. *Organizational Research Methods, 3*(1), 4-69.

Widaman, K.F., & Reise, S.P. (1997). Exploring the measurement invariance of psychological instruments: Applications in the substance use domain. In K.J. Bryant, M. Windle, & S.G. West (Eds.), *The science of prevention: Methodological advances from alcohol and substance abuse research* (pp. 281-324). Washington, DC, US: American Psychological Association.

Chapter 7

Bollen, K.A., & Curran, P.J. (2006). *Latent curve models: A structural equation perspective.* Hoboken, NJ: Wiley.

Browne, M., & Du Toit, S.H.C. (1991). Models for learning data. In L. Collins & J.L. Horn (Eds.), *Best methods for the analysis of change* (pp. 47-68). Washington, DC: American Psychological Association.

Cudeck, R., & Klebe, K.J. (2002). Multiphase mixed-effects models for repeated measures data. *Psychological Methods, 7*, 41-63.

Ferrer, E., Hamagami, F., & McArdle, J.J. (2004). Modeling latent growth curves with incomplete data using different types of structural equation modeling and multilevel software. *Structural Equation Modeling: A Multidisciplinary Journal, 11*, 452-483.

Ghisletta, P., & Lindenberger, U. (2004). Static and dynamic longitudinal structural analyses of cognitive changes in old age. *Gerontology, 50*, 12-16.

Grimm, K.J., & Ram, N. (2009). Nonlinear growth models in Mplus and SAS. *Structural Equation Modeling: A Multidisciplinary Journal, 16*, 676-701.

Grimm, K.J., & Widaman, K.F. (2010). Residual structures in latent growth curve modeling. *Structural Equation Modeling: A Multidisciplinary Journal, 17*, 424-442.

McArdle, J.J. (2009). Latent variable modeling of differences and changes with longitudinal data. *Annual Review of Psychology, 60*, 577-605.

McArdle, J.J., & Epstein, D. (1987). Latent growth curves within developmental structural equation models. *Child Development, 58*, 110-133.

McArdle, J.J., & Hamagami, F. (1996). Multilevel models from a multiple group structural equation perspective. In G. Marcoulides & R. Schumacker (Eds.), *Advanced structural equation modeling techniques* (pp. 89-124). Hillsdale, NJ: Erlbaum.

McArdle, J.J., & Hamagami, F. (2001). Latent difference score structural models for linear dynamic analysis with incomplete longitudinal data. In L. Collins & A. Sayer (Eds.), *New methods for the analysis of change* (pp. 137-175). Washington, DC: American Psychological Association.

McArdle, J.J., & Nesselroade J.R. (2003). Growth curve analysis in contemporary psychological research. In J.A. Schinka & W.F. Velicer (Eds), *Handbook of psychology: Research methods in psychology* (Vol. 2, pp. 447-480). New York: Wiley.

Meredith, W., & Tisak, J. (1990). Latent curve analysis. *Psychometrika, 55,* 107-122.

Preacher, K.J., Wichman, A.L., MacCallum, R.C., & Briggs, N.E. (2008). *Latent growth curve modeling.* Thousand Oaks, CA: Sage.

Ram, N., Riggs, S.M., Skaling, S., Landers, D.M., & McCullagh, P. (2007). A comparison of modeling and imagery in the acquisition and retention of motor skills. *Journal of Sports Sciences, 25,* 587-597.

Ram, N., & Grimm, K.J. (2007). Using simple and complex growth models to articulate developmental change: Matching method to theory. *International Journal of Behavioral Development, 31,* 303-316.

Robinson, W.S. (1950). Ecological correlations and the behavior of individuals. *American Sociological Review, 15,* 351-357.

Chapter 8

Andrich, D. (1978). A rating formulation for ordered response categories. *Psychometrika, 43,* 561-573.

Andrich, D., Sheridan, B., & Luo, G. (2004). *RUMM2020. Rasch unidimensional measurement models (Version 4.0 for Windows).* Perth, Australia: RUMM Laboratory.

Anshel, M.H., Weatherby, N.L., Kang, M., & Watson, T. (2009). Rasch calibration of a unidimensional perfectionism inventory for sport. *Psychology of Sport and Exercise, 10,* 210-216.

Asci, F.H., Fletcher, R.B., & Caglar, E. (2009). A differential item functioning analysis of the PSDQ with Turkish and New Zealand/Australian adolescents. *Psychology of Sport and Exercise, 10,* 12-18.

Avery, L.M., Russell, D.J., Raina, P.S., Walter, S.D., & Rosenbaum, P.L. (2003). Rasch analysis of the gross motor function measure: Validating the assumptions of the Rasch model to create an interval-level measure. *Archives of Physical Medicine and Rehabilitation, 84,* 697-705.

Birnbaum, A. (1968). Some latent trait models and their use in inferring an examinee's ability. In F.M. Lord & M.R. Novick (Eds.), *Statistical theories of mental test scores* (pp. 395-479). Reading, MA: Addison-Wesley.

Boes, K. (2001). *Handbuch motorischer tests* [Handbook of motor tests]. Goettingen, Germany: Hogrefe.

Boes, K., & Mechling, H. (1983). *Dimensionen sportmotorischer Leistungen* [Dimensions of motor performance in sports]. Schorndorf, Germany: Hofmann.

Büsch, D., Hagemann, N., & Bender, N. (2010). The dimensionality of the Edinburgh Handedness Inventory: An analysis with models of the item response theory. *Laterality: Asymmetries of Body, Brain and Cognition.*

Büsch, D., & Strauss, B. (2005). Qualitative differences in performing coordination tasks. *Measurement in Physical Education and Exercise Science, 9,* 161-180.

Büsch, D., Strauss, B., Seidel, I., Pabst, J., Tietjens, M., Müller, L., Wirszing, D., & Kretschmer, J. (2009). *Die Konstruktvalidität des Allgemeinen Sportmotorischen Tests für Kinder* [Construct validity of the German general motor fitness and coordination test for children]. *Sportwissenschaft, 39*(2), 95-103.

Cepicka, L. (2003). The Rasch model in the motor ability testing. *Journal of Human Kinetics, 10,* 99-106.

Duda, J.L. (Ed.). (1998). *Advances in sport and exercise psychology measurement.* Morgantown, WV: Fitness Information Technology.

Fischer, G.H. (1983). Logistic latent trait models with linear constraints. *Psychometrika, 48,* 3-26.

Fischer, G.H., & Molenaar, I.W. (Eds.). (1995). *Rasch models: Foundations, recent developments, and applications.* New York: Springer.

Fletcher, R.B., & Hattie, J.A. (2004). An examination of the psychometric properties of the physical self-description questionnaire using a polytomous item response model. *Psychology of Sport and Exercise, 5,* 423-446.

Gulliksen, H. (1950). *Theory of mental tests.* New York: Wiley.

Hagenaars, J.A., & McCutcheon, A.L. (Eds.). (2002). *Applied latent class analysis.* Cambridge, MA: Cambridge University Press.

Hambleton, R.K., Swaminathan, H., & Rogers, H.J. (1991). *Fundamentals of item response theory.* Newbury Park, CA: Sage.

Hands, B., & Larkin, D. (2001). Using the Rasch measurement model to investigate the construct of motor ability in young children. *Journal of Applied Measurement, 2*(2), 101-120.

Kang, M., Zhu, W., Ragan, B.G., & Frogley, M. (2007). Exercise barrier severity and perseverance of active youth with physical disabilities. *Rehabilitation Psychology, 52,* 170-176.

Kelderman, H. (2007). Loglinear multivariate and mixture Rasch models. In M. von Davier & C. Carstensen (Eds.), *Multivariate and mixture distribution Rasch models* (pp. 77-98). New York: Springer.

Lazarsfeld, P.F., & Henry, N.W. (1968). *Latent structure analysis.* Boston: Houghton Mifflin.

Linacre, J.M. (1989). *Many-faceted Rasch measurement.* Chicago: MESA Press.

Linacre, J.M. (2004). *FACETS Rasch measurement computer program.* Chicago: Winsteps.com.

Linacre, J.M. (2005). *WINSTEPS Rasch measurement computer program.* Chicago: Winsteps.com.

Linacre, J.M., Wright, B.D., & Lunz, M.E. (1990). *A facets model for judgmental scoring.* Chicago: University of Chicago.

Looney, M.A. (1996). Figure skating fairness. *Rasch Measurement Transactions, 10*(2), 500.

Lord, F.M. (1980). *Applications of item response theory to practical testing problems.* Hillsdale, NJ: Erlbaum.

Lord, F.M., & Novick, M.R (1968). *Statistical theories of mental test scores.* Reading, MA: Addison-Wesley.

Masters, G.N. (1982). A Rasch model for partial credit scoring. *Psychometrika, 47,* 149-172.

Myers, N.D., Feltz, D.L., Chase, M.A., Reckase, M.D., & Hancock, G.R. (2008). The Coaching Efficacy Scale II—High School Teams. *Educational and Psychological Measurement, 68,* 1059-1076.

Rasch, G. (1960). *Probabilistic models for some intelligence and attainment tests.* Copenhagen: Nielsen & Lydiche.

Rost, J. (1990). Rasch-models in latent classes. An integration of two approaches to item analysis. *Applied Psychological Measurement, 14,* 271-282.

Rost, J., & Carstensen, C. (2002). Multidimensional Rasch measurement via item component models and faceted designs. *Applied Psychological Measurement, 26*, 42-56.

Rost, J., & Langeheine, R. (Eds.). (1997). *Applications of latent trait and latent class models in the social sciences.* Münster, Germany: Waxmann.

Roth, K. (1982). *Strukturanalyse koordinativer Fähigkeiten* [Structural analysis of coordination abilities]. Bad Homburg, Germany: Limpert.

Spielberger, C., Gorsuch, R., & Lushene, R. (1970). *STAI manual for the State-Trait Anxiety Inventory.* Palo Alto, CA: Consulting Psychologist Press.

Spray, J.A. (1987). Recent developments in measurement and possible applications to the measurement of psychomotor behavior. *Research Quarterly for Exercise and Sport, 58,* 203-209.

Strauss, B. (1995). *Die Messung der Identifikation mit einer Sportmannschaft: Eine deutsche Adaption der "Team Identification Scale" von Wann und Branscombe* [Measuring identification with a sports team: A German adaptation of the TIS]. *Psychologie und Sport, 2,* 132-145.

Strauss, B. (1999). IRT models in sport psychology. *International Journal of Sport Psychology, 30,* 17-40.

Strauss, B., Büsch, D., & Tenenbaum, G. (2007). New developments on measurement and testing in sport psychology. In G. Tenenbaum & Eklund, R. (Eds.), *Handbook of sport psychology* (3rd ed., pp. 737-756). Boston, MA: Wiley.

Tenenbaum, G. (1984). A note on the measurement and relationships of physiological and psychological components of anxiety. *International Journal of Sport Psychology, 15,* 88-97.

Tenenbaum, G. (1999). The implementation of Thurstone's and Guttman's measurement ideas in Rasch analysis. *International Journal of Sport Psychology, 30,* 3-16.

Tenenbaum, G., & Fogarty, G. (1998). Application of the Rasch analysis to sport and exercise psychology measurement. In J.L. Duda (Ed.), *Advances in sport and exercise psychology measurement* (pp. 410-421). Morgantown, WV: Fitness Information Technology.

Tenenbaum, G., Fogarty, J., & Jackson, S. (1999). Stages of the flow experience: A Rasch analysis of Jackson's Flow State Scale. *Journal of Outcome Measurement, 3,* 278-294.

Tenenbaum, G., Fogarty, G.J., Stewart, E., Calcagnini, N., Kirker, B., Thorne, G., & Christensen, S. (1999). Perceived discomfort in aerobic-type tasks: Scale development and theoretical considerations. *Journal of Sport Sciences, 17,* 183-196.

Tenenbaum, G., & Furst, D. (1985). Similarities between retrospective and actual anxiety states. *The Journal of Psychology, 119,* 185-191.

Tenenbaum, G., Furst, D., & Weingarten, G. (1985). A statistical re-evaluation of the STAI Anxiety Questionnaire. *Journal of Clinical Psychology, 41,* 239-244.

Tenenbaum, G., Strauss, B., & Büsch, D. (2007). Applications of generalized Rasch models in the sport, exercise and the motor domains. In M. von Davier & C. Carstensen (Eds.), *Multivariate and mixture distribution Rasch models* (pp. 347-356). New York: Springer.

Thurstone, L.L. (1927). The unit of measurement in educational scales. *Journal of Educational Psychology, 18,* 505-524.

von Davier, M. (2001). Winmira 2001 (Version 1.45) [Computer Software]. St. Paul: Assessment Systems Corporation.

von Davier, M., & Carstensen, C. (Eds.). (2007). *Multivariate and mixture distribution Rasch models.* New York: Springer.

von Davier, M., & Strauss, B. (2003). New developments in testing probabilistic models. *International Journal of Sport and Exercise Psychology, 1,* 61-82.

Wright, B.D., & Masters, G. (1982). *Rating scale analysis.* Chicago: MESA Press.

Wright, B.D., & Stone, M.N. (1979). *Best test design.* Chicago: MESA Press.

Wu, M.L., Adams, R.J., & Wilson, M.R. (1999). *ConQuest.* Melbourne, Australia: ACER.

Wuang, Y.-P., Lin, Y.-H., & Su, C.-Y. (2009). Rasch analysis of the Bruininks-Oseretsky Test of Motor Proficiency—Second Edition in intellectual disabilities. *Research in Developmental Disabilities, 30*(6), 1132-1144.

Zhu, W. (2001). An empirical investigation of Rasch equating of motor function tasks. *Adapted Physical Activity Quarterly, 18,* 72-89.

Zhu, W., & Cole, E.L. (1996). Many-faceted Rasch calibration of a gross motor instrument. *Research Quarterly for Exercise and Sport, 67,* 24-34.

Zhu, W., & Kurz, K.A. (1994). Rasch partial credit analysis of gross motor competence. *Perceptual and Motor Skills, 79,* 947-961.

Chapter 9

Annesi, J.J. (1998). Applications of the Individual Zones of Optimal Functioning model for the multi-model treatment of precompetitive anxiety. *The Sport Psychologist, 12,* 300-316.

Bar-Eli, M., & Tenenbaum, G. (1989). A theory of individual psychological crisis in competitive sport. *Applied Psychology: An International Review, 38,* 107-120.

Bernston, G.G., Bigger, J.T., Eckberg, D.L., Grossman, P., Kaufmann, P.G., Malik, M., Nagaraja, H.N., Porges, S.W., Saul, J.P., Stone, P.H., & Van Der Molen, M.W. (1997). Heart rate variability: Origins, methods, and interpretive caveats. *Psychophysiology, 34,* 623-648.

Cacioppo, J.T., Bernston, G.G., Klein, D.J., & Poehlman, K.M. (1997). The psychophysiology of emotion across the lifespan. *Annual Review of Gerontology and Geriatrics, 17,* 27-74.

Cohen, A.B., Tenenbaum, G., & English, R.W. (2006). Emotions and golf performance: An IZOF-based applied sport psychology case study. *Behavioral Modification, 30,* 259-280.

Deci, E.L. (1980). *The psychology of self-determination.* Lexington, MA: Free Press.

Edmonds, W.A., Mann, D.T.Y., Tenenbaum, G., & Janelle, C. (2006). Analysis of affect-related performance zones: An idiographic approach using physiological and introspective data. *The Sport Psychologist, 20*(1), 40-57.

Edmonds, W.A., Tenenbaum, G., Mann, D.T.Y., Johnson, M., & Kamata, A. (2008). The effect of biofeedback training on affective regulation and simulated race car performance: A multiple case study analysis. *Journal of Sport Sciences, 26,* 1-13.

Ericsson, K.A. (1998). The scientific study of expert levels of performance: General implications for optimal learning and creativity. *High Ability Studies, 9,* 75-100.

Golden, A.S., Tenenbaum, G., & Kamata, A. (2004). Affect-related performance zones: An idiographic method for linking affect to performance. *International Journal of Sport and Exercise Psychology, 2,* 24-42.

Gould, D., & Udry, E. (1994). Psychological skills for enhancing performance: Arousal regulation strategies. *Medicine and Science in Sports and Exercise, 26,* 478-485.

Hanin, Y.L. (1978). A study of anxiety in sports. In W.F. Straub (Ed.), *Sport psychology: An analysis of athlete behavior* (pp. 236-249). Ithaca, NY: Mouvement.

Hanin, Y.L. (2000). *Emotions in sport.* Champaign, IL: Human Kinetics.

Hanin, Y.L., & Stambulova, N.B. (2002). Metaphoric description of performance states: An application of the IZOF model. *The Sport Psychologist, 18,* 396-415.

Hardy, L. (1990). A catastrophe model of anxiety and performance. In J.G. Jones & L. Hardy (Eds.), *Stress and performance in sport* (pp. 81-106). Chichester, UK: Wiley.

Hardy, L. (1996). Testing the prediction of the cusp catastrophe model of anxiety and performance. *The Sport Psychologist, 10,* 140-156.

Hardy, L., Jones, G., & Gould, D. (1996). *Understanding psychological preparation for sport: Theory and practice of elite performers.* Chichester, UK: Wiley.

Hatfield, B.D., & Kerick, S.E. (2007). The psychology of superior sport performance: A cognitive and affective neuroscience perspective. In G. Tenenbaum & R.C. Eklund (Eds.), *Handbook of sport psychology* (3rd ed.) (pp. 84-112). Chichester, UK: Wiley.

Hull, C.L. (1943). *Principles of behavior.* New York: Appleton.

Jackson, S.A., & Marsh, H.W. (1996). Development and validation of a scale to measure optimal experience: The flow state scale. *Journal of Sport and Exercise Psychology, 18,* 17-35. Johnson, M.B., Edmonds, W.A., Moraes, L.C., Filho, E.S.M., & Tenenbaum, G. (2007). Linking affect and performance of an international level archer: Incorporating an idiosyncratic probabilistic method. *Psychology of Sport and Exercise, 8,* 317-335.

Johnson, M.B., Edmonds, W.A., Tenenbaum, G., & Kamata, A. (2009). Determining individual affect-related performance zones (IAPZs): A tutorial. *Journal of Clinical Sports Psychology, 3,* 34-57.

Johnson, M.B., Tenenbaum, G., Edmonds, W.A., & Kamata, A. (2007). Individual affect-related performance zones (IAPZs) during tennis competition: A dynamic conceptualization and application. *Journal of Clinical Sport Psychology, 1,* 130-146.

Jokela, M., & Hanin, Y.L. (1999). Does the individual zone of optimal functioning model discriminate between successful and less successful athletes? A meta analysis. *Journal of Sports Sciences, 17,* 873-887.

Kamata, A., Tenenbaum, G., & Hanin, Y.L. (2002). Individual zone of optimal functioning (IZOF): A probabilistic estimation. *Journal of Sport and Exercise Psychology, 24,* 189-208.

Kerr, J.H. (1997). *Motivation and emotion in sport: Reversal theory.* New York: Psychology Press.

Kosslyn, S.M., Cacioppo, J.T., Davidson, R.J., Hugdahl, K., Lovallo, W.R., Spiegal, D., & Rose, R. (2002). Bridging psychology and biology: The analysis of individuals in groups. *American Psychologist, 57,* 341-351.

Lacey, B.C., & Lacey, J.I. (1974). Studies of heart rate and other bodily processes in sensorimotor behavior. In P.A. Orbist, A.H. Black, J. Brener, & L.V. DiCara (Eds.), *Cardiovascular physiology* (pp. 538-564). Chicago: Aldine.

Lacey, J.I., & Lacey, B.C. (1958). Verification and extension of the principle of autonomic response-stereotype. *American Journal of Psychology, 71,* 50-73.

Lang, P.J. (2000). Emotion and motivation: Attention, perception, and action. *Journal of Sport and Exercise Psychology, 20,* 122-140.

Lazarus, R.L. (2000). Cognitive–motivational–relational theory of emotion. In Y.L. Hanin (Ed.), *Emotions in sport* (pp. 39-63). Champaign, IL: Human Kinetics.

Martens, R., Burton, D., Vealey, R.S., Bump, L.A., & Smith, D.E. (1990). Development and validation of the Competitive State Anxiety Inventory-2. In R.S. Martens, R.S. Vealey, & D. Burton (Eds.), *Competitive anxiety in sport, Part III* (pp. 117-190). Champaign, IL: Human Kinetics.

Miller, W.R. (1983). Motivational interviewing with problem drinkers. *Behavioural Psychotherapy, 11,* 147-172.

Miller, W.R., & Rollnick, S. (2002). *Motivational interviewing: Preparing people for change* (2nd ed.). New York: Guilford Press.

Niskanen, J., Tarvainen, M.P., Ranta-aho, P.O., & Karjalainen, P.A. (2004). Software for advanced HRV analysis. *Computer Methods and Programs in Biomedicine, 76,* 7-81.

Ortony, A., & Fainsilber, L. (1989). The role of metaphors in descriptions of emotions. In Y. Wilks (Ed.), *Theoretical issues in natural language processing* (pp. 178-182). Hillsdale, NJ: Erlbaum.

Parfitt, G., Hardy, L., & Pates, J. (1995). Somatic anxiety and physiological arousal:

Their effects upon a high anaerobic, low memory demand task. *International Journal of Sport Psychology, 26,* 196-213.

Pons, D., Balaguer, I., & Garcia-Merita, M.L. (2001). Is the breadth of individual ranges of optimal anxiety (IZOF) equal for all athletes? A graphical method for establishing IZOF. *Spanish Journal of Psychology, 4,* 3-10.

Prochaska, J.O., & DiClemente, C.C. (2005). The transtheoretical approach. In J.C. Norcross & M.R. Goldfried (Eds.), *Handbook of psychotherapy integration* (2nd ed., pp. 147-171). New York: Oxford University Press.

Raedeke, T., & Stein, G. (1994). Felt arousal, thoughts/feelings, and ski performance. *The Sport Psychologist, 8,* 360-375.

Robazza, C., & Bortoli, L. (2003). Intensity, idiosyncratic content and functional impact of performance-related emotions in athletes. *Journal of Sport Sciences, 21,* 171-189.

Russell, J.A. (1991). Culture and the categorization of emotion. *Psychological Bulletin, 110,* 426-450.

Russell, J.A. (2003). Core affect and the psychological construction of emotions. *Psychological Review, 110,* 145-172.

Russell, J.A., & Mehrabian A. (1977). Evidence for a three-factor theory of emotions. *Journal of Research in Personality, 11,* 273-294.

Russell, J.A., & Pratt, G. (1980). A description of the affective quality attributed to environments. *Journal of Personality and Social Psychology, 38,* 259-288.

Russell, J.A., Weiss, A., & Mendelsohn, G.A. (1989). Affect grid: A single-item scale of pleasure and arousal. *Journal of Personality and Social Psychology, 57,* 493-502.

Smith, R., Smoll, F., & Wiechman, S. (1998). Measurement of trait anxiety in sport. In J. Duda (Ed.), *Advances in sport and exercise psychology measurement* (pp. 105-127). Morgantown, WV: Fitness Information Technology.

Tate, R.L., Tenenbaum, G., & Delpish, A. (2006). Hierarchical linear modeling of individual athlete performance-affect relationships. *Journal of Quantitative Analysis in Sports, 2,* 1-27.

Tenenbaum, G., & Bar-Eli, M. (1995). Contemporary issues and future directions in

exercise and sport psychology. In S.J.H. Biddle (Ed.), *Exercise and sport psychology: A European perspective* (pp. 292-323). Champaign, IL: Human Kinetics.

Tenenbaum, G., Edmonds, W.A., & Eccles, D. (2008). Emotions, coping strategies, and performance: A conceptual framework for defining affect-related performance zones. *Military Psychology, 20*(S.1), S11-S37.

Tenenbaum, G., Hatfield, B., Eklund, R.C., Land, W, Camielo, L., Razon S., & Schack T. (2009). Conceptual framework for studying emotions-cognitions-performance linkage under conditions which vary in perceived pressure. In M. Raab, J.G. Johnson, & H. Heekeren (Eds.), *Progress in brain research: Mind and motion—the bidirectional link between thought and action* (pp. 159-178). Cambridge, MA: Elsevier.

Tenenbaum, G., & Land, W.M. (2009). Mental representations as an underlying mechanism for human performance. In M. Raab, J.G. Johnson, & H. Heekeren (Eds.), *Progress in brain research: Mind and motion—the bidirectional link between thought and action* (pp. 251-266). Cambridge, MA: Elsevier.

Watson, D., & Clark, L.A. (1992). Affects separable and inseparable: On the hierarchical arrangement of the negative affects. *Journal of Personality and Social Psychology, 62,* 489-505.

Watson, D., & Tellegen, A. (1985). Toward a consensual structure of mood. *Psychological Bulletin, 98,* 219-235.

Yerkes, R.M., & Dodson, J.D. (1908). The relation of strength of stimulus to rapidity of habit formation. *Journal of Comparative Neurology and Psychology, 18,* 459-482.

Yin, R.K. (2009). *Case study research: Design and methods* (4th ed.). Thousand Oaks, CA: Sage.

Chapter 10

Adams, A.R. (1954). *A test construction of sport type motor educability test for college men.* Unpublished doctoral dissertation, Louisiana State University, Baton Rouge, LA.

Adams, J.A. (1987). Historical review and appraisal of research on the learning, retention, and transfer of human motor skills. *Psychological Bulletin, 1,* 41-74.

Bagnato, S.J., & Neisworth, J.T. (1981). *Linking developmental and curricula: Prescriptions for early intervention.* Rockville, MD: Aspe.

Bagnato, S.J., Neisworth, J.T., & Capone, A. (1986). Curriculum-based assessment for the young exceptional child: Rationale and review. *Topics in early childhood special education, 6,* 97-110.

Balan, C.M., & Davis, W.E. (1993). Ecological task analysis: An approach to teaching physical education. *Journal of Physical Education, Recreation, and Dance, 64,* 54-61.

Baltes, P.B., & Willis, S.L. (1982). Plasticity and enhancement of intellectual functioning in old age. In F.I.M. Craik & E.E. Trehub (Eds.), *Aging and cognitive processes* (pp. 353-389). New York: Plenum Press.

Balsevic, V.K. (1980). Metodologiceskie principy issledovanij po probleme otbora i sportivnoj orientacii [Methodological principles of studies on the problem of selection and sport orientation]. *Teorija i Praktika fiziceskoi Kultura, 1,* 31-39.

Beckmann, J.F., & Guthke, J. (1999). *Psychodiagnostik des schluß-folgernden Denkens* [Psychodiagnosis of inferential thinking]. Göttingen, Germany: Hogrefe.

Bernstein, N.A. (1996). On dexterity and its development. In M. Latash & T. Turvey (Eds.), *Dexterity and its development* (pp. 3-236). Hillsdale, NJ: Erlbaum.

Bidabe, L., & Lollar, J.M. (1993). *MOVE-Mobilitätstraining für Kinder und Erwachsene* [MOVE mobility training for children and adults]. Dortmund, Germany: Borgmann.

Bös, K. (1987). *Handbuch sportmotorischer Tests* [Handbook of motor tests in sports]. Göttingen, Germany: Hogrefe.

Bös, K. (1992). Diagnostik motorischer Fähigkeiten und Fertigkeiten [Diagnosing motor abilities and skills]. In R.S. Jäger & F. Petermann (Eds.), *Psychologische diagnostik* (pp. 602-618). Weinheim, Germany: Psychologie-Verlags-Union.

Bös, K., Hörtdörfer, B., & Mechling, H. (1976). Leistungs- oder Lernleistungsmessung? Zur Theorie einer pädagogischen Diagnostik im Sport [Measuring performance or learning performance? On the theory of educational diagnosis in sports]. In ADL (Ed.), *Sport, Lehren und Lernen.* Schorndorf, Germany: Hofmann.

Brace, D.K. (1927). *Measuring motor ability.* New York: Barnes.

Brace, D.K. (1941). Studies in the rate of motor learning gross body motor skills. *Research Quarterly, 12,* 181-185.

Brace, D.K. (1946). Studies in motor learning of gross bodily motor skills. *Research Quarterly, 17,* 242-253.

Braun, S.M., Beurskens, A.J.H.M., Schack, T., Marcellis, R.G., Oti, K.C., Schols, J.M., & Wade, D.T. (2007). Is it possible to use the SDA-M to investigate representations of motor actions in stroke patients? *Clinical Rehabilitation, 21,* 822-832.

Braun, S.M., Kleynen, M., Schols, J.M., Schack, T., Beurskens, A.J., & Wade, D.T. (2008). Using mental practice in stroke rehabilitation: A framework. *Clinical Rehabilitation, 7,* 579-591.

Bricker, D. (Ed.). (1993). *Assessment, evaluation and programming system for infants and children. Vol. 1: AEPS measurement for birth to three years.* Baltimore: Brookes.

Budoff, M. (1975). Measuring learning potential: An alternative to the traditional intelligence test. In G.R. Gredler (Ed.), *Proceedings of the First Annual Conference in School Psychology* (pp. 74-88). Philadelphia: Temple University Press.

Büchel, F.P., & Scharnhorst, U. (1993). The Learning Potential Assessment Divide (LPAD): Discussion of theoretical and methodical problems. In J.H.M. Hamers, K. Sijtsma, & A.J.J.M. Ruijssenaars (Eds.), *Learning potential assessment. Theoretical, methodical and practical issues* (pp. 83-111). Amsterdam: Swets & Zeitlinger.

Burton, A.W., & Davis, W.E. (1996). Ecological task analysis: Theoretical and empirical foundations. *Human Movement Science, 15,* 285-314.

Burton, A.W., & Miller, D.E. (1998). *Movement skill assessment.* Champaign, IL: Human Kinetics.

Chi-cheng, C., & Chung-hsien, L. (1962). Problems concerning the prediction of successful aircraft pilots. *Acta Psychologica Sinica, 3,* 248-261.

Corbetta, D., & Vereijken, B. (1999). Understanding development and learning of motor coordination in sport: The contribution of dynamic systems theory. *International Journal of Sport Psychology, 30,* 507-530.

Elliott, J.G. (2003). Dynamic assessment in educational settings: Realising potential. *Educational Review, 55,* 15-32.

Embretson, S.E. (1990). Diagnostic testing by measuring learning processes : Psychometric considerations for dynamic testing. In N. Frederiksen, R. Glaser, L. Lesgold, & M.G. Shafto (Eds.), *Diagnostic monitoring of skill and knowledge acquisition.* Hillsdale, NJ: Erlbaum.

Embretson, S.E. (1992). Measuring and validating cognitive modifiability as an ability: A study in the spatial domain. *Journal of Educational Measurement, 29,* 25-50.

Feuerstein, R. (1970). A dynamic approach to the causation, prevention and alleviation of retarded performance. In

H.C. Haywood (Ed.), *Social-cultural aspects of mental retardation* (pp. 341-377). New York: Appleton-Century-Crofts.

Flanagan, J.C. (Ed.). (1948). *The aviation psychology program in the army air forces: Report No. 1*. Washington, DC: Army Air Forces Aviation Psychology Program Research Reports, U.S. Government Printing Office.

Fleishman, E.A. (1972). On the relation between abilities, learning, and human performance. *American Psychologist, 27,* 1017-1032.

Folio, M.R., & Fewell, R.R. (1983). *Peabody developmental motor scales and activity cards.* Austin, TX: PRO-ED.

Gardner, H. (1985). *Frames of mind: The theory of multiple intelligences.* London: Paladin Books.

Gilbert, D. (1980). Sports in the GDR: The miracle machine. New York: McCann.

Gire, E., & Espenschade, A. (1942). The relationship between measures of motor educability and the learning of specific skills. *Research Quarterly, 13,* 43-52.

Glencross, D.J., Whiting, H.T.A., & Abernethy, B. (1994). Motor control, motor learning and the acquisition of skill: Historical trends and future directions. *International Journal of Sport Psychology, 25,* 32-52.

Glutting, J., & McDermott, P.A. (1990). Principles and problems in learning potential. In C.R. Reynolds & R.W. Kamphaus (Eds.), *Handbook of psychological and educational assessment of children* (pp. 296-347). New York: Guilford Press.

Grigorenko, E.L. (2009). Dynamic Assessment and Response to Intervention—Two sides of one coin. *Journal of Learning Disabilities, 42*(2), 111-132.

Grigorenko, E.L., & Sternberg, R. (1998). Dynamic testing. *Psychological Bulletin, 124*(1), 75-111.

Gross, E.A., Griesel, D.C., & Stull, A. (1956). Relationship between two motor educability tests, a strength test, and a wrestling ability after eight week instruction. *Research Quarterly, 27,* 395-401.

Guthke, J. (1972). *Zur Diagnostik der intellektuellen Lernfähigkeit* [Diagnosing intellectual educability]. Berlin: Verlag der Wissenschaften.

Guthke, J. (1980). *Ist Intelligenz meßbar* [Can intelligence be measured]? Berlin: Verlag der Wissenschaften.

Guthke, J. (1992). Learning tests: The concept, main research findings, problems and trends. *Learning and Individual Differences, 4,* 137-151.

Guthke, J., & Beckmann, J.F. (2003). Dynamic assessment with diagnostic problems. In R.J. Sternberg, J. Lautrey, & T.I. Lubart (Eds.), *Models of intelligence: International perspectives* (pp. 227-242). Washington, DC: American Psychological Association.

Guthke, J., Beckman, J.F., & Dobat, J. (1997). Dynamic testing: Problems, uses, trends and evidence of validity. *Educational and Child Psychology, 14*(4), 17-32.

Guthke, J., Beckmann, J.F., Stein, H., Rittner, S., & Vahle, H. (1995). *Adaptive computergestützte Intelligenz-Lerntestbatterie (ACIL)* [Adaptive computer-assisted battery of intelligence learning tests]. Mödling, Germany: Dr. Schuhfried.

Guthke, J., Räder, E., Caruso, M., & Schmidt, K.D. (1991). Entwicklung eines adaptiven computergestützten Lerntests auf der Basis der strukturellen Informationstheorie [Development of an adaptive computer-assisted learning test based on structural information theory]. *Diagnostica, 37,* 1-29.

Guthke, J., & Wiedl, K.H. (1996). *Dynamisches Testen* [Dynamic testing]. Göttingen, Germany: Hogrefe.

Hacking, I. (1983). *Representing and intervening: Introductory topics in the philosophy of natural science.* Cambridge, UK: Cambridge University Press.

Hamers, J.H.M., Pennings, A., & Guthke, J. (1994). Training-based assessment of school achievement. *Learning and Instruction, 4,* 347-360.

Haywood, H.C., & Tzuriel, D. (Eds.). (1992). *Interactive assessment.* New York: Springer.

Haywood, H.C., Tzuriel, D., & Vaught, S. (1992). Psychoeducational assessment from a transactional perspective. In H.C. Haywood & D. Tzuriel (Eds.), *Interactive assessment* (pp. 38-63). New York: Springer.

Hebb, D.O. (1949). *The organization of behavior.* New York: Wiley.

Herzberg, P. (1968). Zum Problem der motorischen Lernfähigkeit und zu den Möglichkeiten des Diagnostizierens mit motorischen Tests [The problem of motor educability and the possibiliteis of diagnosing it with motor tests]. *Theorie und Praxis der Körperkultur, 17*(9), 799-804.

Herzberg, P., & Lehmann, G. (1968). *Motorische Lernfähigkeit-technische Leistung-Wettkampfleistung* [Motor educability, technical performance, and competitive performance]. Unpublished manuscript, University of Leipzig, Germany.

Hörtdörfer, B. (1980). Zur Diagnostik im Sport - Möglichkeiten und Probleme mit motorischen Lerntests [Diagnoses in sport: Potentials and problems of motor learning tests]. In R. Dieckmann (Ed.), *Sportpraxis und Sportwissenschaft* (pp. 150-164). Schorndorf, Germany: Hofmann.

Johnson, G.B. (1932). Physical skill tests for sectioning classes into homogeneous units. *Research Quarterly, 3,* 128-134.

Kelso, J.A.S. (1995). *Dynamic patterns: The self-organization of brain and behavior.* Cambridge, MA: Bradford Books, MIT Press.

Kugler, P.N., Kelso, J.A.S., & Turvey, M.T. (1982). On the control and coordination of naturally developing systems. In J.A.S. Kelso & J.E. Clark (Eds.), *The development of movement control and coordination* (pp. 5-78). New York: Wiley.

Laszlo, J.I., & Bairstow, P.J. (1985). *Perceptual-motor behaviour: Developmental assessment and therapy.* London: Holt, Reinhart & Winston.

McCloy, C.H. (1937). An analytical study of a stunt type tests as a measure of motor educability. *Research Quarterly, 8,* 46-55.

Meinel, K., & Schnabel, G. (1998). *Bewegungslehre—Sportmotorik* [Movement theory: Motorics in sport]. Berlin: Sport Verlag.

Metheny, E. (1938). Studies of the Johnson Test of Motor Educability. *Research Quarterly, 9,* 105-114.

Nitsch, J. (1990). *Untersuchungen mittels Adaptivem Konzentrationstestgerät (AKG) zum Verlauf der Konzentrationsleistung unter Belastung* [Studies on the course of concentration under stress with the AKG test instrument]. Unpublished manuscript, Deutsche Sporthochschule, Köln, Germany.

Palisano, R.J., Haley, S.M., & Brown, D.A. (1992). Goal attainment scaling as a measure of change in infants with motor delays. *Physical Therapy, 72,* 432-437.

Pechtl, V. (1974). *Die Diagnostik koordinativer Fähigkeiten mittels eines Kurzlernprogramms-Ein Beitrag zur inhaltlichen Gestaltung des Auswahlprozesses für die Trainingszentren Gerätturnen* [Diagnosing coordinative skills with a short-term learning program: A contribution to the design of selection procedures for gymnastic training centers]. Unpublished doctoral dissertation, University of Leipzig, Germany.

Platonow, K.K. (1960). Psichologija letnowo truda. [Psychology of aviation]. *Psichologisheskaja nauka w SSSR, II,* 362-387.

Rauchmaul, H. (1984*). Zur Struktur der motorischen Lernfähigkeit* [The structure of motor educability]. Unpublished doctoral dissertation, University of Leipzig, Germany.

Regian, J.W., & Schneider, W. (1990). Assessment procedures for predicting and optimizing skill acquisition after extensive practice. In N. Frederiksen, R. Glaser, A. Lesgold, & M.G. Shafto (Eds.), *Diagnostic monitoring of skill and knowledge acquisition* (pp. 297-323). Hillsdale, NJ: Erlbaum.

Rubinstein, S.L. (1946). Osnovy obshchei psikholgii [Foundation of general psychology]. Moscow: Uchpedgic.

Schack, T. (1997a). Zum Ansatz der Kulturhistorischen Schule [The approach of the culture-historical school]. In H. Ilg (Ed.), *Gesundheitsförderung-Konzepte, Erfahrungen, Ergebnisse aus sportpsychologischer und sportpädagogischer Sicht* (pp. 340-351). Köln, Germany: BPS.

Schack, T. (1997b). *Ängstliche Schüler im Sport—Interventionsverfahren zur Entwicklung der Handlungskontrolle* [Anxious students in sport: Intervention procedures for developing action control]. Schorndorf, Germany: Hofmann.

Schack, T. (1999). Zur Entwicklung mentaler Funktionskomponenten—Dynamisches Testen mittels Prä-Posttest-Analyse [The development of mental function components: Dynamic testing with the pre-posttest analysis]. In E. Witruk & H.-J. Lander (Eds.), *Informationsverarbeitungsanalysen—kognitionspsychologische und meßmethodische Beiträge* (pp. 161-177). Leipzig, Germany: Universitätsverlag.

Schack, T. (2004). The cognitive architecture of complex movement. *International Journal of Sport and Exercise Psychology, 2*(4), 403-438.

Schack, T., & Bar-Eli, M. (2007). Psychological factors of technical preparation. In B. Blumenstein, R. Lidor, & G. Tenenbaum (Eds.), *Psychology of sport training. Perspectives on sport and exercise psychology* (Vol. 2, 62-103). Oxford, United Kingdom: Meyer & Meyer Sport.

Schack, T., & Guthke, J. (2001). Dynamisches Testen im Sport—Zugänge zur Diagnostik des individuellen Lernpotentials [Dynamic testing in sport: Ways of diagnosing individual learning potential]. *Psychologie und Sport, 2*, 1-11.

Schack, T., & Guthke, J. (2003). Dynamic testing. *International Journal of Sport and Exercise Psychology, 1*(1), 40-60.

Schack, T., & Hackfort, D. (2007). Action-theory approach to applied sport psychology. In G. Tenenbaum & R.C. Ecklund (Eds.), *Handbook of sport psychology* (3rd ed., pp. 332-351). New Jersey: Wiley.

Schulz, H. (1964). Untersuchungen zum Erkennen sportlichen Talents [Studies on recognizing sports talent]. *Wiss. Zeitschrift DHfK, 6*, 169-173.

Siris, P. (1974). Das Wachstumstempo der motorischen Eigenschaften—Ein Faktor der potentiellen Möglichkeiten von Sportlern [The developmental rate of acceleration in motor properties: One factor in the potential of athletes]. *Leistungssport, 4*, 339-342.

Sternberg, R.J., & Grigorenko, E.L. (2002). *Dynamic testing.* New York: Cambridge University Press.

Stott, D.H., Henderson, S.E., & Moyes, F.A. (1986). The Henderson Revision of the Test of Motor Impairment: A comprehensive approach to assessment. *Adapted Physical Activity Quarterly, 3*, 204-216.

Tenenbaum, G., Hatfield, B., Eklund, R.C., Land, W.M., Calmeiro, L., Razon, S., & Schack, T. (2009). A conceptual framework for studying Emotions-Cognitions-Performance linkage under conditions that vary in perceived pressure. *Progress in Brain Research, 174*, 159-178.

Thelen, E. (1995). Motor development: A new synthesis. *American Psychologist, 50*, 79-95.

Thomas, A. (1977). Zur Anwendung psychomotorischer und sportmotorischer Testverfahren bei bewegungs- und zielzentrierten Sportarten [Applying psychomotor and sportmotor test procedures in motion- and goal-centered types of sport]. In A. Thomas, D. Simons, & R. Brackhance (Eds.), *Handlungspsychologische Analyse sportlicher Übungsprozesse* (pp. 179-192). Schorndorf, Germany: Hofmann.

Turvey, M.T. (1977). Preliminaries to a theory of action with reference to vision. In R. Shaw & J. Bransford (Eds.), *Perceiving, action and knowing: Towards an ecological psychology* (pp. 211-265). Hillsdale, NJ: Erlbaum.

Ulrich, D.A. (1985). *Test of gross motor development.* Austin, TX: Pro-Ed.

Uprichard, S., Kupshik, G., Pine., K., & Fletcher, B.(2009). Dynamic assessment of learning ability improves outcome prediction following acquired brain injury. *Brain Injury, 23*(4), 278-290.Vernon, P. (1962). *The structure of human abilities.* London: Methuen.

Vygotsky, L.S. (1964). *Denken und Sprechen* [Thinking and talking]. Berlin: Akademie-Verlag.

Vygotsky, L.S. (1978). *Mind in society—the development of higher psychological processes.* Cambridge, MA: Harvard University Press.

Vygotsky, L.S. (1992). *Geschichte der höheren psychischen Funktionen* [History of higher mental functions]. Münster, Germany: Lit.

Weerdt, E.H. de. (1927). A study of the improvability of fifth grade school children in certain mental functions. *Journal of Educational Psychology, 18*, 547-557.

Wittmann, W., & Süß, H.M. (1999). Investigating the paths between working memory, intelligence, knowledge and complex problem solving performances via Brunswik symmetry. In P.L. Ackerman, P.C. Kyllonen, & R.D. Roberts (Eds.), *Learning and individual differences: Process, trait and content determinants* (pp. 77-104). Washington, DC: American Psychological Association.

Chapter 11

Brewer, B.W., Linder, D.E., Van Raalte, J.L., & Van Raalte, N.S. (1991). Peak performance and the perils of retrospective introspection. *Journal of Sport and Exercise Psychology, 13*, 227-238.

Buman, M.P., Omli, J.W., Giacobbi, P.R., & Brewer, B.W. (2008). Experiences and coping responses of "hitting the wall" for recreational marathon runners. *Journal of Applied Sport Psychology, 20*, 282-300.

Calmeiro, L., Tenenbaum, G., & Eccles, D.W. (2010). Event-sequence analysis of appraisals and coping during trapshooting performance. *Journal of Applied Sport Psychology, 22*, 392-407.

Connaughton, D., Wadey, R., Hanton, S., & Jones, G. (2008). The development and maintenance of mental toughness: Perceptions of elite performers. *Journal of Sports Sciences, 26*, 83-95.

Delaney, P.F., Ericsson, K.A., & Knowles, M.E. (2004). Immediate and sustained effects of planning in a problem-solving task. *Journal of Experimental Psychology: Learning, Memory, and Cognition, 30*, 1219-1234.

Dennett, D.C. (2003). *Freedom evolves.* New York: Penguin.

Eccles, D.W., & Ward, P. (2006). Is self-talk all talk and imagery imagined? Prospects and limits of research on the role of psychological skills in expert sports performance. *Proceedings of the Association for the Advancement of Applied Sports*

Psychology Annual Conference (p. 50). Madison, WI: Association for the Advancement of Applied Sports Psychology.

Eccles, D.W., Ward, P., Ericsson, K.A., Harris, K.R., Sacks, D.N., Williams, A.M., & Hassler, L.B. (2005). Using a delayed retrospective report method to increase the reliability of verbal reports of past events. *Proceedings of the Association for the Advancement of Applied Sports Psychology Annual Conference* (pp. 15-16). Madison, WI: Association for the Advancement of Applied Sports Psychology.

Ericsson, K.A. (2002). Towards a procedure for eliciting verbal expression of non-verbal experience without reactivity: Interpreting the verbal overshadowing effect within the theoretical framework for protocol analysis. *Applied Cognitive Psychology, 16*, 981-987.

Ericsson, K.A. (2006). Protocol analysis and expert thought: Concurrent verbalizations of thinking during experts' performance on representative tasks. In K.A. Ericsson, N. Charness, P.J. Feltovich, & R.R. Hoffman (Eds.), *The Cambridge handbook of expertise and expert performance* (pp. 223-241). Cambridge, UK: Cambridge University Press.

Ericsson, K.A., & Simon, H.A. (1980). Verbal reports as data. *Psychological Review, 87*(3), 215-251.

Ericsson, K.A., & Simon, H.A. (1993). *Protocol analysis: Verbal reports as data* (Rev. ed.). Cambridge, MA: MIT Press.

Fournier, J.F., Deremaux, S., & Bernier, M. (2008). Content, characteristics and function of mental images. *Psychology of Sport and Exercise, 9*, 734-748.

Fox, M.C., Ericsson, K.A., & Best, R. (2011). Do procedures for verbal reporting of thinking have to be reactive? A meta-analysis and recommendations for best reporting methods. *Psychological Bulletin, 137*, 316–344.

Gardner, F.L., & Moore, Z.E. (2006). *Clinical sport psychology.* Champaign, IL: Human Kinetics.

Goldman-Rakic, P.S. (1996). Regional and cellular fractionation of working memory. *Proceedings of the National Academy of Sciences USA, 93*, 13473-13480.

Gould, D., Diffenbach, K., & Moffett, A. (2002). Psychological characteristics and their development in Olympic championships. *Journal of Applied Sport Psychology, 14*, 172-204.

Gucciardi, D.F., Gordon, S., & Dimmock, J.A. (2008). Towards an understanding of mental toughness in Australian Football. *Journal of Applied Sport Psychology, 20*, 261-281.

Hall, C.R., Mack, D.E., Paivio, A., & Hausenblas, H.A. (1998). Imagery use by athletes: Development of the Sport Imagery Questionnaire. *International Journal of Sport Psychology, 29*, 73-89.

Hall, C.R., Munroe-Chandler, K.J., Fishburne, G.J., & Hall, N.D. (2009). The Sport Imagery Question for Children (SIQ-C). *Measurement in Physical Education and Exercise Science, 13*, 93-107.

Hanton, S., & Jones, G. (1999). The acquisition and development of cognitive skills and strategies: I. Making the butterflies fly in formation. *The Sport Psychologist, 13*, 1-21.

Hanton, S., Wadey, R., & Mellalieu, S.D. (2008). Advanced psychological strategies and anxiety responses in sport. *The Sport Psychologist, 22*, 472-490.

Hardy, L., & Jones, G. (1994). Current issues and future directions for performance-related research in sport psychology. *Journal of Sports Sciences, 12*, 61-92.

Hardy, L., Jones, G., & Gould, D. (1996). *Understanding psychological preparation for sport.* New York: Wiley.

Hare, R., Evans, L., & Callow, N. (2008). Imagery use during rehabilitation from injury: A case study of an elite athlete. *The Sport Psychologist, 22*, 405-422.

Hollander, D.B., & Acevedo, E.O. (2000). Successful English Channel swimming: The peak experience. *The Sport Psychologist, 14*, 1-16.

Jackson, R.C., & Baker, J.S. (2001). Routines, rituals, and rugby: Case study of a world class goal kicker. *The Sport Psychologist, 15*, 48-65.

Jones, M.I., & Harwood, C. (2008). Psychological momentum within competitive soccer: Players' perspectives. *Journal of Applied Sport Psychology, 20*, 57-72.

Kee, Y.H., & Wang, C.K.J. (2008). Relationships between mindfulness, flow dispositions and mental skills adoption: A cluster analytic approach. *Psychology of Sport and Exercise, 9*, 393-411.

MacPherson, A., Collins, D., & Morriss, C. (2008). Is what you think what you get? Optimizing mental focus for technical performance. *The Sport Psychologist, 22*, 288-303.

Maier, N.R.F. (1931). Reasoning in humans: II. The solution of a problem and its appearance in consciousness. *Journal of Comparative Psychology, 12*, 181-194.

McRobert, A., Eccles, D.W., Ward, P., & Williams, A.M. (in press). The effect on perceptual-cognitive processes of manipulating context-specific information during a simulated anticipation task. *British Journal of Psychology.*

McRobert, A., Williams, A.M., Ward, P., & Eccles, D.W. (2009). Tracing the process of expertise in a simulated anticipation task. *Ergonomics, 52*, 474-483.

Mellalieu, S.D., Hanton, S., & Shearer, D.A. (2008). Hearts in the fire, heads in the fridge: A qualitative investigation into the temporal patterning of the precompetitive psychological response in elite performers. *Journal of Sports Sciences, 26*, 811-824.

Munroe-Chandler, K., Hall, C., & Fishburne, G. (2008). Playing with confidence: The relationship between imagery use and self-confidence and self-efficacy in youth soccer players. *Journal of Sports Sciences, 26*, 1539-1546.

Newell, A., & Simon, H.A. (1972). *Human problem solving.* Englewood Cliffs, NJ: Prentice Hall.

Nieuwenhuys, A., Hanin, Y.L., & Bakker, F.C. (2008). Performance-related experiences and coping during races: A case of an elite sailor. *Psychology of Sport and Exercise, 9*, 61-76.

Nisbett, R.E., & Wilson, T.C. (1977). Telling more than we can know: Verbal reports on mental processes. *Psychological Review, 84*, 231-259.

Nordin, S.M., & Cumming, J. (2006). Measuring the content of dancers' images: Development of the Dance Imagery Questionnaire (DIQ). *Journal of Dance Medicine and Science, 3&4*, 85-98.

Nordin, S.M., & Cumming, J. (2008). Exploring common ground: Comparing the imagery of dancers and aesthetic sport performers. *Journal of Applied Sport Psychology, 20*, 375-391.

Pinker, S. (1999). *How the mind works.* New York: Norton.

Roberts, R., Callow, N., Hardy, L., Markland, D., & Bringer, J. (2008). Movement imagery ability: Development and assessment of a revised version of the Vividness of Movement Imagery Questionnaire. *Journal of Sport and Exercise Psychology, 30*, 200-221.

Sordoni, C., Hall, C., & Forewell, L. (2002). The use of imagery in athletic injury rehabilitation and its relationship to self-efficacy. *Physiotherapy Canada, Summer*, 177-185.

Sparkes, A.C. (1998). Validity in qualitative inquiry and the problem of criteria: Implications for sport psychology. *The Sport Psychologist, 12*, 363-386.

Thelwell, R.C., Weston, N.J.V., Greenlees, I.A., & Hutchings, N.V. (2008). A qualitative exploration of psychological-skills use in coaches. *The Sport Psychologist, 22,* 38-53.

Thomas, P.R., Murphy, S.M., & Hardy, L. (1999). Test of performance strategies: Development and preliminary validation of a comprehensive measure of athletes' psychological skills. *Journal of Sports Sciences, 17,* 697-711.

Tremayne, P., & Ballinger, D.A. (2008). Performance enhancement for ballroom dancers: Psychological perspectives. *The Sport Psychologist, 22,* 90-108.

Vealey, R.S. (1994). Current status and prominent issues in sport psychology interventions. *Medicine and Science in Sport and Exercise, 26,* 495-502.

Wadey, R., & Hanton, S. (2008). Basic psychological skills usage and competitive anxiety responses: Perceived underlying mechanisms. *Research Quarterly for Exercise and Sport, 79,* 363-373.

Ward, P., Suss, J., Eccles, D.W., Williams, A.M., & Harris, K.R. (in press). Skill-based differences in option generation in a complex task: A verbal protocol analysis. *Cognitive Processing.*

Wegner, D. (2002). *The illusion of conscious will.* Cambridge, MA: MIT Press.

Chapter 12

Amis, J. (2006). Interviewing for case study research. In D. Andrews, D.

Mason, & M. Silk (Eds.), *Qualitative methods in sport studies* (pp. 65-103). Oxford: Berg.

Barone, T. (1995). Persuasive writings, vigilant readings, and reconstructed characters: The paradox of trust in educational storysharing. *Qualitative Studies in Education, 8,* 63-74.

Bertollo, M., Saltarelli, B., & Robazza, C. (2009). Mental preparation strategies of elite modern pentathletes. *Psychology of Sport and Exercise, 10,* 244-254.

Bianco, T., Malo, S., & Orlick, T. (1999). Sport injury and illness: Elite skiers

describe their experiences. *Research Quarterly for Exercise and Sport, 70,* 157-169.

Braun, V., & Clarke, V. (2006). Using thematic analysis. *Qualitative Research*

in Psychology, 3, 77-101.

Carless, D., & Douglas, K. (2009). "We haven't got a seat on the bus for you" or "All the seats are mine": Narratives and career transition in professional golf. *Qualitative Research in Sport and Exercise, 1,* 53-68.

Chamberlain, K. (2000). Methodolatry and qualitative health research. *Journal of Health Psychology, 5,* 285-296.

Coffey, A., & Atkinson, P. (1996). *Making sense of qualitative data.* London: Sage.

Douglas, K., & Carless, D. (2008). Using stories in coach education. *International Journal of Sports Science and Coaching, 3,* 33-49.

Eklund, R.C. (1996). Preparing to compete: A season-long investigation with collegiate wrestlers. *The Sport Psychologist, 10,* 111-131.

Ellis, C. (2004). *The ethnographic I.* Oxford: AltaMira Press.

Ezzy, D. (2002). *Qualitative analysis.* London: Routledge.

Frank, A. (1995). *The wounded storyteller.* Chicago: University of Chicago Press.

Gammage, K., Hardy, J., & Hall, C. (2001). A description of self-talk in exercise. *Psychology of Sport and Exercise, 2,* 233-247.

Gould, D., Eklund, R.C., & Jackson, S.A. (1992a). 1988 U.S. Olympic wrestling excellence: I. Mental preparation, precompetitive cognition, and affect. *The Sport Psychologist, 6,* 358-382.

Gould, D., Eklund, R.C., & Jackson, S.A. (1992b). 1989 U.S. Olympic wrestling excellence: II. Thoughts and affect occurring during competition. *The Sport Psychologist, 6,* 383-402.

Gould, D., Tuffey, S., Udry, E., & Loehr, J. (1996). Burnout in competitive junior tennis players: II. A qualitative analysis. *The Sport Psychologist, 10,* 341-366.

Gubrium, J., & Holstein, J. (2008). *Analysing narrative reality.* London: Sage.

Jowett, S., & Frost, T. (2007). Race/ethnicity in the all male coach-athlete relationship: Black footballers' narratives. *International Journal of Sport and Exercise Psychology, 3,* 255-269.

Krane, V. (2009). A sport odyssey. *Qualitative Research in Sport and Exercise, 1,* 221-238.

Lally, P. (2007). Identity and athletic retirement: A prospective study. *Psychology of Sport and Exercise, 8,* 85-99.

Lieblich, A., Tuval-Mashlach, R., & Zilber, T. (1998). *Narrative research.* London: Sage.

Lincoln, Y., & Guba, E. (1985). *Naturalistic inquiry.* Thousand Oaks, CA: Sage.

Locke, A. (2008). Managing agency for athletic performance: A discursive approach to the zone. *Qualitative Research in Psychology, 5,* 103-126.

Martinent, G., & Ferrand, C. (2009). A naturalistic study of the directional interpretation process of discrete emotions during high-stakes table tennis matches. *Journal of Sport and Exercise Psychology, 31,* 318-336.

McGannon, K., & Spence, J. (in press). Speaking of the self and understanding physical activity participation: What discursive psychology can tell us about an old problem. *Qualitative Research in Sport and Exercise.*

McKay, J., Niven, A., Lavallee, D., & White, A. (2009). Sources of strain among elite UK track athletes. *The Sport Psychologist, 22,* 143-163.

Patton, M. (1990). *Qualitative evaluation and research methods* (2nd ed.). Newbury Park, CA: Sage.

Phoenix, C., & Howe, A. (in press). Working the when, where, and who of social context: The case of a traumatic injury narrative. *Qualitative Research in Psychology.*

Polkinghorne, D. (1995). Narrative configuration in qualitative analysis. In J. Hatch & R. Wisniewski (Eds.), *Life history and narrative* (pp. 5-24). London: Falmer Press.

Richardson, L. (2000). Writing: A method of inquiry. In N.K. Denzin & Y.S. Lincoln (Eds.), *Handbook of qualitative research* (2nd ed., pp. 923-948). London: Sage.

Richardson, L., & St. Pierre, E. (2005). Writing: A method of inquiry. In N. Denzin & Y. Lincoln (Eds.), *Handbook of qualitative research* (3rd ed., pp. 959-978). London: Sage.

Riessman, C. (2008). *Narrative methods for the human sciences.* London: Sage.

Rorty, R. (1982). *Consequences of pragmatism (Essays 1972-1980).* Minneapolis: University of Minnesota Press.

Scanlan, T.K., Stein, G.L., & Ravizza, K. (1989). An in-depth study of former elite figure skaters: II. Sources of enjoyment. *Journal of Sport and Exercise Psychology, 11,* 65-83.

Schwandt, T. (1996). Farewell to criteriology. *Qualitative Inquiry, 2,* 58-72.

Smith, B. (2009). *Rehabilitation, sport, and spinal cord injury: An ethnographic creative non-fiction.* Paper presented at the 12th

International Society of Sport Psychology (ISSP) Conference, Morocco.

Smith, B. (2008). Imagining being disabled through playing sport: The body and alterity as limits

to imagining others lives. *Sport, Ethics and Philosophy, 2*(2), 142-157

Smith, B. (2010). Narrative inquiry: Ongoing conversations and questions for sport psychology

research. *International Review of Sport Psychology, 3*(1), 87-107.

Smith, B., Allen Collinson, J., Phoenix, C., Brown, D., & Sparkes, A. (2009). Dialogue, monologue, and boundary crossing within research encounters: A performative narrative analysis. *International Journal of Sport and Exercise Psychology, 7*, 342-358.

Smith, B., & Sparkes, A. (2005). Men, sport, spinal cord injury, and narratives of hope. *Social Science and Medicine, 61*, 1095-1105.

Smith, B., & Sparkes, A. (2009). Narrative analysis and sport and exercise psychology: Understanding stories in diverse ways. *Psychology of Sport and Exercise, 10*, 279-288.

Smith, J. (2009). Judging research quality: From certainty to contingency. *Qualitative Research in Sport and Exercise, 1*, 91-100.

Sparkes, A. (2002). *Telling tales in sport and physical activity: A qualitative journey.* Champaign, IL: Human Kinetics.

Sparkes, A., & Douglas, K. (2007). Making the case for poetic representations: An example in action. *The Sport Psychologist, 21*, 170-189.

Sparkes, A., & Partington, S. (2002). Narrative practice and its potential contribution to sport psychology: The example of flow. *The Sport Psychologist, 17*, 292-317.

Sparkes, A., & Smith, B. (2009). Judging the quality of qualitative inquiry: Criteriology and relativism in action. *Psychology of Sport and Exercise, 10*, 491-497.

Stone, B. (2009). Running man. *Qualitative Research in Sport and Exercise, 1*, 67-71.

Chapter 13

Andersen, M.B., McCullagh, P., & Wilson, G.J. (2007). But what do the numbers really tell us?: Arbitrary metrics and effect size reporting in sport psychology research. *Journal of Sport and Exercise Psychology, 29*, 664-672.

Bandura, A. (1986). *Social foundations of thought and action: A social cognitive theory.* Englewood Cliffs, NJ: Prentice Hall.

Bass, S., Bradney, M., Pearce, G., Hendrich, E., Inge, K., Stuckey, S., Lo, S.K., & Seeman, E. (2000). Short stature and delayed puberty in gymnasts: Influence of selection bias on leg length and the duration of training on trunk length. *The Journal of Pediatrics, 136*, 149-155.

Beunen, G., & Malina, R.M. (1988). Growth and physical performance relative to the timing of the adolescent spurt. *Exercise and Sport Sciences Reviews, 16*, 503-540.

Brustad, R.J. (1998). Developmental considerations in sport and exercise psychology measurement. In J.L. Duda (Ed.), *Advances in sport and exercise psychology measurement* (pp. 461-470). Morgantown, WV: Fitness Information Technology.

Burwitz, L., Moore, P.M., & Wilkinson, D.M. (1994). Future directions for performance-related sports science research: An interdisciplinary approach. *Journal of Sports Sciences, 12*, 93-109.

Carron, A.V. (1982). Cohesiveness in sport groups: Interpretations and considerations. *Journal of Sport Psychology, 4*, 123-138.

Carron, A.V., Hausenblas, H.A., & Eys, M.A. (2005). *Group dynamics in sport* (3rd ed.). Morgantown, WV: Fitness Information Technology.

Carron, A.V., Widmeyer, W.N., & Brawley, L.R. (1985). The development of an instrument to assess cohesion in sport teams: The Group Environment Questionnaire. *Journal of Sport Psychology, 7*, 244-266.

Carter, J.E.L., & Heath, B.H. (1990). *Somatotyping: Development and applications.* New York: Cambridge University Press.

Corbin, C.B., & Nix, C. (1979). Sex-typing of physical activities and success predictions of children before and after cross-sex competition. *Journal of Sport Psychology, 1*, 43-52.

Dorn, L.D., Dahl, R.E., Woodward, H.R., & Biro, F. (2006). Defining the boundaries of early adolescence: A user's guide to assessing pubertal status and pubertal timing in research with adolescents. *Applied Developmental Science, 10*, 30-56.

Duda, J.L. (1987). Toward a developmental theory of children's motivation in sport. *Journal of Sport Psychology, 9*, 130-145.

Eisenmann, J.C., & Wickel, E.E. (2009). The biological basis of physical activity in children: Revisited. *Pediatric Exercise Science, 21*, 257-272.

Eys, M.A., Loughead, T.M., Bray, S.R., & Carron, A.V. (2009a). Development of a cohesion questionnaire for youth: The Youth Sport Environment Questionnaire. *Journal of Sport and Exercise Psychology, 31*, 390-408.

Eys, M.A., Loughead, T.M., Bray, S.R., & Carron, A.V. (2009b). Perceptions of cohesion by youth sport participants. *The Sport Psychologist, 23*, 330-345.

Frey, K.S., & Ruble, D.N. (1990). Strategies for comparative evaluation: Maintaining a sense of competence across the life span. In R. Sternberg & J. Kolligian (Eds.), *Competence considered* (pp. 167-189). New Haven, CT: Yale University Press.

Fry, M.D. (2000a). A developmental analysis of children's and adolescents' understanding of luck and ability in the physical domain. *Journal of Sport and Exercise Psychology, 22*, 145-166.

Fry, M.D. (2000b). A developmental examination of children's understanding of task difficulty in the physical domain. *Journal of Applied Sport Psychology, 12*, 180-202.

Fry, M.D., & Duda, J.L. (1997). A developmental examination of children's understanding of effort and ability in the physical and academic domains. *Research Quarterly for Exercise and Sport, 68*, 331-344.

García Bengoechea, E. (2002). Integrating knowledge and expanding horizons in developmental sport psychology: A bioecological perspective. *Quest, 54*, 1-20.

Gay, J., Monsma, E.V., & Torres-McGehee, T.M. (in press). Developmental and contextual risks of social physique anxiety among female athletes. *Research Quarterly for Exercise and Sport.*

Gould, D. (1982). Sport psychology in the 1980s: Status, direction, and challenge in youth sports research. *Journal of Sport Psychology, 4*, 203-218.

Hagger, M.S., & Chatzisarantis, N.L.D. (2009). Assumptions in research in sport and exercise psychology. *Psychology of Sport and Exercise, 10*, 511-519.

Harter, S. (1982). The perceived competence scale for children. *Child Development, 53*, 87-97.

Harter, S. (1999). *The construction of the self: A developmental perspective.* New York: Guilford Press.

Harter, S. (2003). The development of self-representations during childhood and adolescence. In M.R. Leary & J.P. Tangney (Eds.), *Handbook of self and identity* (pp. 610-642). New York: Guilford Press.

Harter, S., & Pike, R. (1984). The pictorial scale of perceived competence and social acceptance for young children. *Child Development, 55*, 1969-1982.

Hartup, W.W. (1991). Social development and social psychology: Perspectives on interpersonal relationships. In J.H. Cantor, C.C. Spiker, & L. Lipsitt (Eds.), *Child behavior and development: Training for diversity* (pp. 1-33). Norwood, NJ: Ablex.

Hartup, W.W., & Laursen, B. (1999). Relationships as developmental contexts: Retrospective themes and contemporary issues. In W.A. Collins & B. Laursen (Eds.), *Relationships as developmental contexts: The Minnesota symposia on child psychology* (Vol. 30, pp. 13-35). Mahwah, NJ: Erlbaum.

Haywood, K.M., & Getchell, N. (2009). *Life span motor development* (5th ed.). Champaign, IL: Human Kinetics.

Holt, N.L., Black, D.E., Tamminen, K.A., Fox, K.R., & Mandigo, J.L. (2008). Levels of social complexity and dimensions of peer experiences in youth sport. *Journal of Sport and Exercise Psychology, 30*, 411-431.

Horn, T.S. (2004a). Developmental perspectives on self-perceptions in children and adolescents. In M.R. Weiss (Ed.), *Developmental sport and exercise psychology: A lifespan perspective* (pp. 101-143). Morgantown, WV: Fitness Information Technology.

Horn, T.S. (2004b). Lifespan development in sport and exercise psychology: Theoretical perspectives. In M.R. Weiss (Ed.), *Developmental sport and exercise psychology: A lifespan perspective* (pp. 27-71). Morgantown, WV: Fitness Information Technology.

Horn, T.S., & Amorose, A.J. (1998). Sources of competence information. In J.L. Duda (Ed.), *Advances in sport and exercise psychology measurement* (pp. 49–63). Morgantown, WV: Fitness Information Technology.

Horn, T.S., Lox, C.L., & Labrador, F. (2010). The self-fulfilling prophecy theory: When coaches' expectations become reality. In J.M. Williams (Ed.), *Applied sport psychology: Personal growth to peak performance* (6th ed., pp. 81-105). New York: McGraw-Hill.

Johnson, A., Doherty, P.J., & Freemont, A. (2009). Investigation of growth, development, and factors associated with injury in elite schoolboy footballers: Prospective study. *British Medical Journal, 338*, b490.

Kagan, J. (2007). The limitations of concepts in developmental psychology. In G.W. Ladd (Ed.), *Appraising the human developmental sciences: Essays in honor of Merrill-Palmer Quarterly* (pp. 30-37). Detroit: Wayne State University Press.

Kail, R. (1991). Developmental change in speed of processing during childhood and adolescence. *Psychological Bulletin, 109*, 490-501.

Lerner, R.M. (1985). Adolescent maturational changes and psychosocial development: A dynamic interactional perspective. *Journal of Youth and Adolescence, 14*, 355-372.

Lerner, R.M. (2002). *Concepts and theories of human development* (3rd ed.). Mahwah, NJ: Erlbaum.

Malina, R.M., (1998). Growth and maturation of young athletes—is training for sport a factor? In K.M. Chan & L.J. Micheli (Eds.), *Sports and children* (pp. 133-161). Hong Kong: Williams & Wilkins Asia-Pacific.

Malina, R.M. (2002). The young athlete: Biological growth and maturation in a biocultural context. In F.L. Smoll & R.E. Smith (Eds.), *Children and youth in sport: A biopsychosocial perspective* (2nd ed., pp. 261-292). Dubuque, IA: Kendall/Hunt.

Malina, R.M., Bouchard, C., & Bar-Or, O. (2004). *Growth, maturation, and physical activity* (2nd ed.). Champaign, IL: Human Kinetics.

Malina, R.M., Claessens, A.L., Van Aken, K., Thomis, M., Lefevre, J., Philippaerts, R., & Beunen, G.P. (2006). Maturity offset in gymnasts: Application of a prediction equation. *Medicine and Science in Sports and Exercise, 38*, 1342-1347.

McCullagh, P., & Weiss, M.R. (2001). Modeling: Considerations for motor skill performance and psychological responses. In R.N. Singer, H.A. Hausenblas, & C.M. Janelle (Eds.), *Handbook of research in sport psychology* (2nd ed., pp. 205-238). New York: Wiley.

Mirwald, R.L., Baxter-Jones, A.D.G., Bailey, D.A., & Beunen, G.P. (2002). An assessment of maturity from anthropometric measurements. *Medicine and Science in Sports and Exercise, 34*, 689-694.

Newell, C. (1986). Constraints on the development of coordination. In M.G. Wade & H.T.A. Whiting (Eds.), *Motor development in children: Aspects of coordination and control* (pp. 341-361). Amsterdam: Nijhoff.

Nicholls, J.G. (1978). The development of the concepts of effort and ability, perception of academic attainment, and the understanding that difficult tasks require more ability. *Child Development, 49*, 800-814.

Nicholls, J.G. (1984). Achievement motivation: Conceptions of ability, subjective experience, task choice, and performance. *Psychological Review, 91*, 328-346.

Nicholls, J.G. (1989). *The competitive ethos and democratic education.* Cambridge, MA: Harvard University Press.

Nicholls, J.G., & Miller, A.T. (1983). The differentiation of the concepts of difficulty and ability. *Child Development, 54*, 951-959.

Nicholls, J.G., & Miller, A.T. (1985). Differentiation of the concepts of luck and skill. *Developmental Psychology, 21*, 76-82.

Piaget, J. (1952). *The origins of intelligence in children.* New York: International University Press.

Rubin, K.H., Bukowski, W.M., & Parker, J.G. (2006). Peer interactions, relationships, and groups. In N. Eisenberg (Ed.), *Handbook of child psychology: Vol. 3. Social, emotional, and personality development* (6th ed., pp. 571-645). Hoboken, NJ: Wiley.

Schutz, R.W., Eom, H.J., Smoll, F.L., & Smith, R.E. (1994). Examination of the factorial validity of the Group Environment Questionnaire. *Research Quarterly for Exercise and Sport, 65*, 226-236.

Schutz, R.W., & Park, I. (2004). Some methodological considerations in developmental sport and exercise psychology. In M.R. Weiss (Ed.), *Developmental sport and exercise psychology: A lifespan perspective* (pp. 73-99). Morgantown, WV: Fitness Information Technology.

Semerjian, T., & Stephens, D. (2007). Comparison style, physical self-perceptions, and fitness among older women. *Journal of Aging and Physical Activity, 15*, 219-235.

Sherar, L.B., Cumming, S.P., Eisenmann, J.C., Baxter-Jones, A.D.G., & Malina, R.M. (2010). Adolescent biological maturity and physical activity: Biology meets behavior. *Pediatric Exercise Science, 22*, 332-349.

Shields, D.L.L., & Bredemeier, B.J.L. (1995). *Character development and physical activity.* Champaign, IL: Human Kinetics.

Smith, A.L., & McDonough, M.H. (2008). Peers. In A.L. Smith & S.J.H. Biddle (Eds.), *Youth physical activity and sedentary behavior: Challenges and solutions* (pp. 295-320). Champaign, IL: Human Kinetics.

Smith, R.E., Smoll, F.L., & Curtis, B. (1979). Coach effectiveness training: A cognitive-behavioral approach to enhancing relationship skills in youth sport coaches. *Journal of Sport Psychology, 1*, 59-75.

Sullivan, H.S. (1953). *The interpersonal theory of psychiatry.* New York: Norton.

Thomas, K.T., Gallagher, J.D., & Thomas, J.R. (2001). Motor development and skill acquisition during childhood and adolescence. In R.N. Singer, H.A. Hausenblas, & C.M. Janelle (Eds.), *Handbook of sport psychology* (2nd ed., pp. 20-52). New York: Wiley.

Towne, B., Czerwinski, S.A., Demerath, E.W., Blangero, J., Roche, A.F., & Siervogel, R.M. (2005). Heritability of age at menarche in girls from the Fels longitudinal study. *American Journal of Physical Anthropology, 128,* 210-219.

Weiss, M.R., & Bredemeier, B.J. (1983). Developmental sport psychology: A theoretical perspective for studying children in sport. *Journal of Sport Psychology, 5,* 216-230.

Weiss, M.R., Ebbeck, V., & Wiese-Bjornstal, D.M. (1993). Developmental and psychological factors related to children's observational learning of physical skills. *Pediatric Exercise Science, 5,* 301-317.

Weiss, M.R., & Raedeke, T.D. (2004). Developmental sport and exercise psychology: Research status on youth and directions toward a lifespan perspective. In M.R. Weiss (Ed.), *Developmental sport and exercise psychology: A lifespan perspective* (pp. 1-26). Morgantown, WV: Fitness Information Technology.

Weiss, M.R., Smith, A.L., & Stuntz, C.P. (2008). Moral development in sport and physical activity. In T.S. Horn (Ed.), *Advances in sport psychology* (3rd ed., pp. 187-210). Champaign, IL: Human Kinetics.

Weiss, M.R., & Stuntz, C.P. (2004). A little friendly competition: Peer relationships and psychosocial development in youth sport and physical activity contexts. In M.R. Weiss (Ed.), *Developmental sport and exercise psychology: A lifespan perspective* (pp. 165-196). Morgantown, WV: Fitness Information Technology.

Welk, G.J. (1999). The youth physical activity promotion model: A conceptual bridge between theory and practice. *Quest, 51,* 5-23.

Westre, K.R., & Weiss, M.R. (1991). The relationship between perceived coaching behaviors and group cohesion in high school football teams. *The Sport Psychologist, 5,* 41-54.

Whaley, D.E. (2007). A life span developmental approach to studying sport and exercise behavior. In G. Tenenbaum & R.C. Eklund (Eds.), *Handbook of sport psychology* (3rd ed., pp. 645-661). Hoboken, NJ: Wiley.

Wohlwill, J.F. (1973). *The study of behavioral development.* New York: Academic Press.

Chapter 14

Adams, G., & Markus, H.R. (2001). Culture as patterns: An alternative approach to the problem of reification. *Culture and Psychology, 7,* 283-296.

Alfermann, D., Stambulova, N., & Zemaityte, A. (2004). Reactions to sports career termination: A cross-national comparison of German, Lithuanian, and Russian athletes. *Psychology of Sport and Exercise, 5*(1), 61-75.

Andersen, M. (1993). Questionable sensitivity: A comment on Lee and Rotella. *The Sport Psychologist, 7,* 1-3.

Blodgett, A.T., Schinke, R.J., Fisher, L.A., George, C.W., Peltier, D., & Ritchie, P. (2008). From practice to praxis: Community-based strategies for aboriginal youth sport. *Journal of Sport and Social Issues, 32,* 393-414.

Brant, R., Forsyth, J., Horn-Miller, W., Loutitt, J., Sinclair, C., & Smith, M. (2002). North American Indigenous Games sport research panel. In R. Brant & J. Forsyth (Eds.), *2002 North American Indigenous Games conference proceedings* (pp. 67-70). Winnipeg, MB: University of Manitoba Press.

Bredemeier, B. (2001). Feminist praxis in sport psychology research. *The Sport Psychologist, 15,* 412-418.

Bruner, J.S. (1990). *Acts of meaning.* Cambridge, MA: Harvard University Press.

Denzin, N.K., & Lincoln, Y.S. (1998). Entering the field of qualitative research. In N.K. Denzin & Y.S. Lincoln (Eds.), *Strategies of qualitative inquiry* (pp. 1-34). London: Sage.

Duda, J.L., & Allison, M.T. (1990). Cross-cultural analysis in exercise and sport psychology: A void in the field. *Journal of Sport and Exercise Psychology, 12,* 114-131.

Eagleton, T. (1983). *Literary theory: An introduction.* Minneapolis: University of Minnesota Press.

Geertz, C. (1973). *The interpretations of cultures.* New York: Basic Books.

Gill, D.L. (1994). A feminist perspective on sport psychology practice. *The Sport Psychologist, 8,* 411-426.

Griffin, P. (1988). How to identify homophobia in women's athletic programs. In M.J. Adrian (Ed.), *National Coaching Institute applied research papers* (pp. 33-36). Reston, VA: American Alliance for Health, Physical Education, Recreation and Dance.

Griffin, P. (1992). Changing the game: Homophobia, sexism, and lesbians in sport. *Quest, 44,* 251-265.

Hanrahan, S.J. (2004). Sport psychology and indigenous performing artists. *The Sport Psychologist, 18,* 60-74.

Hanrahan, S.J. (2009). Working with Australian aboriginal athletes. In R.J. Schinke & S.J. Hanrahan (Eds.), *Cultural sport psychology* (pp. 191-198). Champaign, IL: Human Kinetics.

Harris, D.V. (Ed.). (1971). *DGWS research reports: Women in sports.* Washington, DC: American Alliance for Health, Physical Education, Recreation and Dance.

Harris, D.V. (Ed.). (1972). *Women and sport: A national research conference.* University Park, PA: Pennsylvania State University Press.

Canadian Institute for Health Information. (2009). *Mentally healthy communities: Aboriginal perspectives.* Ottawa, ON: Canadian Institute for Health Information.

Henriksen, K., Stambulova, N., & Roessler, K.K. (2010a). Holistic approach to athletic talent development environment: A successful sailing milieu. *Psychology of Sport and Exercise, 11,* 212-222.

Henriksen, K., Stambulova, N., & Roessler, K.K. (2010b). Successful talent development in athletics: Considering the role of environment. *Scand J Med Sci Sports, 20,* 122–132.

Hermans, H.J.M., & Kempen, H.J.G. (1998). Moving cultures: The perilous problems of cultural dichotomies in a globalizing society. *American Psychologist, 53,* 1111-1120.

Kral, M.J., Burkhardt, D.J., & Kidd, S. (2002). The new research agenda for a cultural psychology. *Canadian Psychology* [Online serial]. http://findarticles.com/p/articles/mi_qa3711/is_200208/ai_n9145557.

Krane, V., & Baird, S. (2005). Using ethnography in applied sport psychology. *Journal of Applied Sport Psychology, 17,* 87-107.

Lee, C.C., & Rotella, R.J. (1991). Special concerns and considerations for sport psychology consulting with black student athletes. *The Sport Psychologist, 5,* 365-369.

Markus, H.R., & Hamedani, M.G. (2007). Sociocultural psychology: The dynamic interdependence among self systems and social systems. In S. Kitayama & D. Cohen (Eds.), *Handbook of cultural psychology* (pp. 3-39). New York: Guilford Press.

Martens, R. (1979). About smocks and jocks. *Journal of Sport Psychology, 1*, 94-99.

Martens, R. (1987). Science, knowledge, and sport psychology. *The Sport Psychologist, 1*, 29-55.

O'Dell, L., de Abreu, G., & O'Toole, S. (2004). The turn to culture. *The Psychologist, 17*(3), 138-141.

Oglesby, C. (1978). *Women and sport: From myth to reality.* Philadelphia: Lea & Febiger.

Patton, M.Q. (2002). *Qualitative research and evaluation methods* (3rd ed.). Thousand Oaks, CA: Sage.

Ponterotto, J.G. (2005). Qualitative research in counseling psychology: A primer on research paradigms and philosophy of science. *Journal of Counseling Psychology, 52*(2), 126-136.

Ryba, T.V. (2009). Understanding your role in cultural sport psychology. In R.J. Schinke & S. Hanrahan (Eds.), *Cultural sport psychology: From theory to practice* (pp. 35-44). Champaign, IL: Human Kinetics.

Ryba, T.V., & Schinke, R.J. (2009). (Eds.). Decolonizing methodologies: Approaches to sport and exercise psychology from the margins (Special Issue). *International Journal of Sport and Exercise Psychology, 7*(3).

Ryba, T.V., & Schinke, R.J. (2009). Methodology as a ritualized Eurocentrism. *International Journal of Sport and Exercise Psychology, 7*, 263-274.

Ryba, T.V., Schinke, R.J., & Tenenbaum, G. (Eds.). (2010). *The cultural turn in sport psychology.* Morgantown, WV: Fitness Information Technology.

Ryba, T.V., & Wright, H.K. (2005). From mental game to cultural praxis: A cultural studies model's implications for the future of sport psychology. *Quest, 57*, 192-212.

Schein, E. (1992). *Organizational culture and leadership.* San Francisco: Jossey-Bass.

Schinke, R.J., Hanrahan, S.J., & Catina, P. (2009). Introduction to cultural sport psychology. In R.J. Schinke, & S. Hanrahan (Eds.), *Cultural sport psychology* (pp. 3-12). Champaign, IL: Human Kinetics.

Schinke, R.J., Hanrahan, S.J., Eys, M.A., Blodgett, A., Peltier, D., Ritchie, S., Pheasant, C., & Enosse, L. (2008). The development of cross-cultural relations with a Canadian aboriginal community through sport research. *Quest, 6*, 357-369.

Schinke, R.J., & Hanrahan, S. (Eds.). (2009). *Cultural sport psychology: From theory to practice.* Champaign, IL: Human Kinetics.

Schinke, R.J., Ryba, T.V., Danielson, R., Michel, G., Peltier, D., Enosse, L., Pheasant, C., & Peltier, M. (2007). Canadian aboriginal elite athletes: The experiences of being coached in mainstream culture. *International Journal of Sport and Exercise Psychology, 5*, 125-143.

Schinke, R.J., Blodgett, A., Ritchie, C., Pickard, P., Michel, G., Peltier, D., Pheasant, C., Wabano, M.J., Wassangeso-George, C., & Enosse, L. (2009). Entering the community of Canadian indigenous athletes. In R.J. Schinke & S.J. Hanrahan (Eds.), *Cultural sport psychology* (pp. 91-102). Champaign, IL: Human Kinetics.

Schinke, R.J., Peltier, D., Hanrahan, S., Eys, M.A., Recollet-Saikkonene, D., Yungblut, H.E., Ritchie, S., Pickard, P., & Michel, G. (2009). The progressive integration of Canadian indigenous culture within a sport psychology bicultural research team. *International Journal of Sport and Exercise Psychology, 7*, 309-322.

Shi-xu. (2002). The discourse of cultural psychology. *Culture and Psychology, 8*, 65-78.

Shweder, R.A. (1990). Cultural psychology—what is it? In J.W. Stigler, R.A. Shweder, & G. Herdt (Eds.), *Cultural psychology: Essays on comparative human development* (pp. 1-43). Cambridge: Cambridge University Press.

Shweder, R.A. (2003). *Why do men barbecue? Recipes for cultural psychology.* Cambridge, MA: Harvard University Press.

Si, G., Rethorst, S., & Willimczik, K. (1995). Causal attribution perception in sports achievement. *Journal of Cross-Cultural Psychology, 26*, 537-553.

Smith, B., & Sparkes, A.C. (2010). The narrative turn in sport and exercise psychology. In T.V. Ryba, R.J. Schinke, & G. Tenenbaum (Eds.), *The cultural turn in sport psychology.* Morgantown, WV: Fitness Information Technology.

Smith, L.T. (1999). *Decolonizing methodologies: Research and indigenous peoples.* Dunedin, New Zealand: University of Otago Press.

Stambulova, N., Stephan, Y., & Järphag, U. (2007). Athletic retirement: A cross-national comparison of elite French and Swedish athletes. *Psychology of Sport and Exercise, 8*, 101-118.

Thorpe, H. (2009). Understanding "alternative" sport experiences: A contextual approach for sport psychology. *International Journal of Sport and Exercise Psychology, 7*, 359-379.

Thorpe, H. (2010). Psychology of extreme sports. In T.V. Ryba, R.J. Schinke, & G. Tenenbaum (Eds.), *The cultural turn in sport psychology* (pp. 361-384). Morgantown, WV: Fitness Information Technology.

Tsai, J., Knutson, B., & Fung, H.H. (2006). Cultural variation in affect valuation. *Journal of Personality and Social Psychology, 90*, 288-307.

Uchida, Y., Norasakkunkit, V., & Kitayama, S. (2004). Cultural construction of happiness. *Journal of Happiness Studies, 5*, 223-239.

Valsiner, J. (2004). Three years later: Culture in psychology—between social positioning and producing new knowledge. *Culture and Psychology, 10*(5), 5-27.

Weedon, C. (1997). *Feminist practice and poststructuralist theory* (2nd ed.). Cambridge, MA: Blackwell.

Williams, R. (1983). *Keywords.* New York: Oxford University Press.

Chapter 15

Ahn, S. (2008). *Application of model-driven meta-analysis and latent variable framework in synthesizing studies using diverse measures.* Unpublished doctoral dissertation, Michigan State University, East LansinAmerican Psychological Association Publications and Communications Board Working Group on Journal Article Reporting Standards. (2008). Reporting standards for research in psychology: Why do we need them? What might they be? *American Psychologist, 63*(9), 839-851.

Arent, S.M., Landers, D.M., & Etnier, J.L. (2000). The effects of exercise on mood in older adults: A meta-analytic review. *Journal of Aging and Physical Activity, 8*(4), 407-430.

Becker, B.J. (2000). Multivariate meta-analysis. In H.E.A. Tinsley & S.D. Brown (Eds.), *Handbook of applied multivariate statistics and mathematical modeling* (pp. 499-525). San Diego: Academic Press.

Bérard, A., & Bravo, G. (1998). Combining studies using effect sizes and quality scores: Application to bone loss in postmenopausal woman. *Journal of Clinical Epidemiology, 51*(10), 801-807.

Biddle, S.J.H. (1997). Current trends in sport and exercise psychology research, *The Psychologist: Bulletin of the British Psychological Society, 10,* 63-69.

Bhushan, S., & Sinha, P. (2001). Yoganidra and management of anxiety and hostility. *Journal of Indian Psychology, 19*(1-2), 44-49.

Campbell, A., & Hausenblas, H.A. (2009). Effects of exercise interventions on body image: A meta-analysis. *Journal of Health Psychology, 14,* 780-793.

Chen, M.J., Fan, X., & Moe, S. (2002). Criterion-related validity of the Borg ratings of perceived exertion scale in healthy individuals: A meta-analysis *Journal of Sports Sciences, 20,* 873-899.

Cook, T.D. (1991). Meta-analysis: Its potential for causal description and causal explanation within program evaluation. In G. Albrecht & H. Otto (Eds.), *Social prevention and the social sciences: Theoretical controversies, research problems, and evaluation strategies* (pp. 245-285). New York: Walter de Gruyter.

Cooper, H.M. (1982). Scientific guidelines for conducting research reviews. *Review of Educational Research, 52*(2), 291-302.

Cooper, H.M. (2009). *Research synthesis and meta-analysis: A step by step approach* (4th ed.). Thousand Oaks, CA: Sage.

Cooper, H.M., Hedges, L.V., & Valentine, J.C. (Eds.). (2009). *The handbook of research synthesis and meta-analysis.* New York: Russell Sage Foundation.

Craft, L.L., Magyar, T.M., Becker, B.J., & Feltz, D.L. (2003). The relationship between the Competitive State Anxiety Index-2 and athletic performance: A meta-analysis. *Journal of Sport and Exercise Psychology, 25*(1), 44-65.

Feltz, D.L., & Landers, D.M. (1983). The effects of mental practice on motor skill learning and performance: A meta-analysis. *Journal of Sport Psychology, 5*(1), 25-57.

Forsyth, R.A., & Feldt, L.S. (1969). An investigation of empirical sampling distributions of correlation coefficients corrected for attenuation. *Educational and Psychological Measurement, 29,* 61-71.

Gillison, F.B., Skevington, S.M., Sato, A., Standage, M., & Evangelidou, S. (2009). The effects of exercise interventions on quality of life in clinical and healthy populations; a meta-analysis. *Social Science and Medicine, 68*(9), 1700-1710.

Glass, G.V. (1976). Primary, secondary, and meta-analysis of research. *Educational Researcher, 5,* 3-8.

Gleser, L.J., & Olkin, I. (2009). Stochastically dependent effect sizes. In H.M. Cooper, L.V. Hedges, & J.C. Valentine (Eds.), *The handbook of research synthesis and meta-analysis* (pp. 357-376). New York: Russell Sage Foundation.

Gu, M.O., & Conn, V.S. (2008). Meta-analysis of the effects of exercise interventions on functional status in older adults. *Research in Nursing and Health, 31,* 594-603.

Hedges, L.V. (1982). Fitting categorical models to effect sizes from a series of experiments. *Journal of Educational Statistics, 7*(2), 119-137.

Hedges, L.V., & Olkin, I. (1985). *Statistical methods for meta-analysis.* New York: Academic Press.

Hedges, L.V., & Vevea, J.L. (1998). Fixed- and random-effects models in meta-analysis. *Psychological Methods, 3*(4), 486-504.

Hunter, J.E., & Schmidt, F.L. (1990). *Methods of meta-analysis: Correcting error and bias in research findings.* Newbury Park, CA: Sage.

Hunter, J.E., & Schmidt, F.L. (2004). *Methods of meta-analysis: Correcting error and bias in research findings.* Newbury Park, CA: Sage.

Jensen, P.S., & Kenny, D.T. (2004). The effects of yoga on the attention and behavior of boys with attention-deficit / hyperactivity disorder (ADHD). *Journal of Attention Disorders, 7,* 205-216.

Jüni, P., Altman, D.G., & Egger, M. (2001). Assessing the quality of controlled clinical trials. *British Medical Journal, 323,* 42-46.

Long, B.C., & van Stavel, R. (1995). Effects of exercise training on anxiety: A meta-analysis. *Journal of Applied Sport Psychology, 7*(2), 167-189.

Mann, D.T.Y., Williams, A.M., Ward, P., & Janelle, C.M. (2007). Perceptual-cognitive expertise in sport: A meta-analysis. *Journal of Sport and Exercise Psychology, 29,* 457-478.

Moher, D., Cook, D.J., Eastwood, S., Olkin, I., Rennie, D., & Stroup, D.F. (1999). Improving the quality of reports of meta-analyses of randomised controlled trials: The QUOROM statement. *The Lancet, 354*(9193), 1896-1900.

Moritz, S.E., Feltz, D.L., Fahrbach, K.R., & Mack, D.E. (2000). The relation of self-efficacy measures to sport performance: A meta-analytic review. *Research Quarterly for Exercise and Sport, 71*(3), 280-294.

Murphy, M.H., Nevill, A.M., Murtagh, E.M., & Holder, R.L. (2007). The effect of walking on fitness, fatness and resting blood pressure: A meta-analysis of randomised, controlled trials. *Preventive Medicine, 44*(5), 377-385.

Netz, Y., Wu, M.-J., Becker, B.J., & Tenenbaum, G. (2005). Physical activity and psychological well-being in advanced age: A meta-analysis of intervention studies. *Psychology and Aging, 20*(2), 272-284.

Orwin, R.G., & Vevea, J.L. (2009). Evaluating coding decisions. In H.M. Cooper, L.V. Hedges, & J.C. Valentine (Eds.), *The handbook of research synthesis and meta-analysis* (pp. 177-203). New York: Russell Sage Foundation.

Raudenbush, S.W., Becker, B.J., & Kalaian, H. (1988). Modeling multivariate effect sizes. *Psychological Bulletin, 103*(1), 111-120.

Rowley, A.J., Landers, D.M., Kyllo, L.B., & Etnier, J.L. (1995). Does the iceberg profile discriminate between successful and less successful athletes? A meta-analysis. *Journal of Sport and Exercise Psychology, 17*(2), 185-199.

Schlicht, W. (1994). Does physical exercise reduce anxious emotions? A meta-analysis. *Anxiety, Stress and Coping: An International Journal, 6*(4), 275-288.

Schmidt, F.L., Le, H., & Oh, I.-S. (2009). Correcting for the distorting effects of study artifacts in meta-analysis. In H.M. Cooper, L.V. Hedges, & J.C. Valentine (Eds.). *The handbook of research synthesis and meta-analysis* (pp. 317-334). New York: Russell Sage Foundation.

Shadish, W.R., & Haddock, C.K. (2009). Combining estimates of effect size. In H.M. Cooper, L.V. Hedges, & J.C. Valentine (Eds.). *The handbook of research synthesis and meta-analysis* (pp. 257-277). New York: Russell Sage Foundation.

Sridevi, K., & Krishna Rao, P.V. (1996). Yoga practice and menstrual distress. *Journal of the Indian Academy of Applied Psychology, 22,* 47-54.

Thomas, J.R., Jr., & French, K.E. (1986). The use of meta-analysis in exercise and sport: A tutorial. *Research Quarterly for Exercise and Sport, 57*(3), 196-204.

Valentine, J.C., & Cooper, H. (2008). A systematic and transparent approach for assessing the methodological quality of intervention effectiveness research: The Study Design and Implementation Assessment Device (Study DIAD). *Psychological Methods, 13*(2), 330-349.

Weed, M. (2009). Research quality in sport and exercise psychology: Introduction to the collection. *Psychology of Sport and Exercise, 10*(5), 489-490.

Wipfli, B.M., Rethorst, C.D., & Landers, D.M. (2008). The anxiolytic effects of exercise: A

meta-analysis of randomized trials and dose-response analysis. *Journal of Sport and Exercise Psychology, 30*(4), 392-410.

Chapter 16

Allen, V.B., Sampson, J.P., & Herlihy, B. (1988). Details of the new 1988 AACD Ethical Standards. *Journal of Counseling and Development, 67*, 157-158.

Allemen, J.R. (2002). Online counseling: The Internet and mental health treatment. *Psychotherapy: Theory, Research and Practice, 39*, 199-209.

American Educational Research Association, American Psychological Association, & National Council on Measurement in Education. (1999). *Standards for educational and psychological testing.* Washington, DC: American Educational Research Association.

American Psychological Association. (1982). *Ethical principles in the conduct of research with human participants.* Washington, DC: American Psychological Association.

American Psychological Association. (2002). Ethical principles of psychologists and code of conduct. www.apa.org/ethics/code2002.html#3_09.

Andersen, M. (2002). *Comprehensive interventions.* In J. Van Raalte & B. Brewer (Eds.), *Exploring sport and exercise psychology* (2nd ed., pp.13-24). Washington, DC: American Psychological Association.

Association for Applied Sport Psychology. (1996). AASP code of ethical principles and standards. http://appliedsportpsych.org/about/ethics.

Bennett, B.E., Bricklin, P.M., Harris, E., Knapp, S., Vandecreek, L., & Younggren, J.N. (2006). *Assessing and managing risk in psychological practice: An individualized approach.* Washington, DC: American Psychological Association.

Cohen, A. (2009). Many forms of culture. *American Psychologist, 64*(3), 194-204.

Etzel, E., Yura, M., & Perna, F. (1998). Ethics and testing in applied sport psychology. In J. Duda (Ed.), *Advances in measurement in sport and exercise psychology* (pp. 423-432). Morgantown, WV: Fitness Information Technology.

Fisher, C. (2009). *Decoding the ethics code: A practical guide for psychologists.* Thousand Oaks, CA: Sage.

Gardner, F., & Moore, Z. (2006). *Clinical sport psychology.* Champaign, IL: Human Kinetics.

Hayes, K.F., & Brown, C.H. (2003). *You're on! Consulting for peak performance.* Washington, DC: American Psychological Association.

Jackson, D., & Messick, S. (Eds.). (1967). *Problems in human assessment.* New York: McGraw-Hill.

Kagan, J. (1998). *Three seductive questions.* Cambridge, MA: Harvard University Press.

Lorge, I. (1967). The fundamental nature of measurement. In D. Jackson & S. Messick (Eds.), *Problems in human assessment* (pp. 43-56). New York: McGraw-Hill.

Martens, R., Burton, D., Vealey, R.S., Bump, L.A., & Smith, D.E. (1990). Development and validation of the Competitive State Anxiety Inventory-2. In R. Martens, R.S. Vealey, & D. Burton (Eds.), *Competitive anxiety in sport* (pp. 117-190). Champaign, IL: Human Kinetics.

Ogilvie, B. (1979). The sport psychologist and his professional credibility. In P. Klavora & J.V. Daniel (Eds.), *Coach, athlete and the sport psychologist* (pp. 44-55). Champaign, IL: Human Kinetics.

Smith, W. (1976). Ethical, social, and professional issues in patients' access to psychological test reports. *Bulletin of the Menninger Clinic, 42*, 150-155.

Spielberger, C.D., Gorsuch, R.L., & Luschene, R.L. (1970). *Manual for the State-Trait Anxiety Inventory.* Palo Alto, CA: Consulting Psychologists.

Sundberg, N. (1977). *The assessment of persons.* New York: Prentice Hall.

Tranel, D. (1995). The release of psychological data to nonexperts: Ethical and legal considerations. In D. Bersoff (Ed.), *Ethical conflicts in psychology* (pp. 275-280). Washington, DC: American Psychological Association.

Watson, J.C., II, Tenenbaum, G., Lidor, R., & Alfermann, D. (2001). Ethical uses of the Internet in sport psychology: A position stand. *International Journal of Sport Psychology, 32*, 207-222.

Chapter 17

Abbott, R.D., White, L.R., Ross, G.W., Masaki, K.H., Curb, J.D., & Petrovitch, H. (2004). Walking and dementia in physically capable elderly men. *Journal of the American Medical Association, 292*(12), 1447-1453.

Aks, D.J. (1998). Influence of exercise on visual search: Implications for mediating cognitive mechanisms. *Perceptual and Motor Skills, 87*, 771-783.

Aksu, I., Topcu, A., Camsari, U.M., & Acikgoz, O. (2008). Effect of acute and chronic exercise on oxidant-antioxidant equilibrium in rat hippocampus, prefrontal cortex and striatum. *Neuroscience Letters, 452*(3), 281-285.

Aleman, A., de Haan, E.H., Verhaar, H.H., Samson, M.M., de Vries, W.R., & Koppeschaar, H.P. (2000). Relationship between physical and cognitive function in healthy older men: A role for aerobic power? *Journal of the American Geriatrics Society, 48*(1), 104-105.

Allard, F., Brawley, L.R., Deakin, J., & Elliott, D. (1989). The effect of exercise on visual attention performance. *Human Performance, 2*(2), 131-145.

Amos, D., Hansen, R., Lau, W.M., & Michalski, J.T. (2000). Physiological and cognitive performance of soldiers conducting routine patrol and reconnaissance operations in the tropics. *Military Medicine, 165*(12), 961-966.

Anderson, M.B., McCullagh, P., & Wilson, G.J. (2007). But what do the numbers really tell us? Arbitrary metrics and effect size reporting in sport psychology research. *Journal of Sport and Exercise Psychology, 29*(5), 664-672.

Angevaren, M., Aufdemkampe, G., Verhaar, H.J., Aleman, A., & Vanhees, L. (2008). Physical activity and enhanced fitness to improve cognitive function in older people without known cognitive impairment. *Cochrane Database of Systematic Reviews* [Online], *3*, CD005381. www2.cochrane.org/reviews/en/ab005381.html.

Anstey, K.J., Wood, J., Lord, S., & Walker, J.G. (2005). Cognitive, sensory and physical factors enabling driving safety in older adults. *Clinical Psychology Review, 25*(1), 45-65.

Arbuthnott, K., & Frank, J. (2000). Trail Making Test, part B as a measure of executive control: Validation using a set-switching paradigm. *Journal of Clinical and Experimental Neuropsychology, 22*(4), 518-528.

Arent, S.M., & Landers, D.M. (2003). Arousal, anxiety, and performance: A reexamination of the inverted-U hypothesis. *Research Quarterly for Exercise and Sport, 74*(4), 436-444.

Asha Devi, S. (2009). Aging brain: Prevention of oxidative stress by vitamin E and exercise. *The Scientific World Journal, 9,* 366-372.

Balota, D.A., & Marsh, E.J. (Eds.). (2004). *Cognitive psychology: Key readings.* New York: Psychology Press.

Barnes, D.E., Yaffe, K., Satariano, W.A., & Tager, I.B. (2003). A longitudinal study of cardiorespiratory fitness and cognitive function in healthy older adults. *Journal of the American Geriatrics Society, 51*(4), 459-465.

Berr, C. (2000). Cognitive impairment and oxidative stress in the elderly: Results of epidemiological studies. *Biofactors, 13*(1-4), 205-209.

Black, J.E., Isaacs, K.R., Anderson, B.J., Alcantara, A.A., & Greenough, W.T. (1990). Learning causes synaptogenesis, whereas motor activity causes angiogenesis, in cerebellar cortex of adult rats. *Proceedings of the National Academy of Sciences of the United States of America, 87*(14), 5568-5572.

Blumenthal, J.A., Emery, C.F., Madden, D.J., George, L.K., Coleman, R.E., Riddle, M.W., McKee, D.C., Reasoner, J., & Williams, R.S. (1989). Cardiovascular and behavioral effects of aerobic exercise training in healthy older men and women. *Journal of Gerontology, 44*(5), M147-M157.

Blumenthal, J.A., Emery, C.F., Madden, D.J., Schniebolk, S., Walsh-Riddle, M., George, L.K., McKee, D.C., Higginbotham, M.B., Cobb, F.R., & Coleman, R.E. (1991). Long-term effects of exercise on psychological functioning in older men and women. *Journal of Gerontology, 46*(6), P352-P361.

Bors, D.A., & Forin, B. (1995). Age, speed of information processing, recall, and fluid intelligence. *Intelligence, 20,* 229-248.

Brayne, C., Spiegelhalter, D.J., Dufouil, C., Chi, L.Y., Dening, T.R., Paykel, E.S., O'Connor, D.W., Ahmed, A., McGee, M.A., & Huppert, F.A. (1999). Estimating the true extent of cognitive decline in the old. *Journal of the American Geriatrics Society, 47*(11), 1283-1288.

Brisswalter, J., Arcelin, R., Audiffren, M., & Delignieres, D. (1997). Influence of physical exercise on simple reaction time: Effect of physical fitness. *Perceptual and Motor Skills, 85*(3, Pt. 1), 1019-1027.

Brisswalter, J., Collardeau, M., & Rene, A. (2002). Effects of acute physical exercise characteristics on cognitive performance. *Sports Medicine (Auckland, N.Z), 32*(9), 555-566.

Brisswalter, J., Durand, M., Delignieres, D., & Legros, P. (1995). Optimal and nonoptimal demand in a dual-task of pedaling and simple reaction time: Effects on energy expenditure and cognitive performance. *Journal of Human Movement Studies, 29,* 15-34.

Broe, G.A., Creasey, H., Jorm, A.F., Bennett, H.P., Casey, B., Waite, L.M., Grayson, D.A., & Cullen, J. (1998). Health habits and risk of cognitive impairment and dementia in old age: A prospective study on the effects of exercise, smoking and alcohol consumption. *Australian and New Zealand Journal of Public Health, 22*(5), 621-623.

Burns, J.M., Cronk, B.B., Anderson, H.S., Donnelly, J.E., Thomas, G.P., Harsha, A., Brooks, W.M., & Swerdlow, R.H. (2008). Cardiorespiratory fitness and brain atrophy in early Alzheimer disease. *Neurology, 71*(3), 210-216.

Butterfield, D.A., Howard, B.J., Yatin, S., Allen, K.L., & Carney, J.M. (1997). Free radical oxidation of brain proteins in accelerated senescence and its modulation by N-tert-butyl-alpha-phenylnitrone. *Proceedings of the National Academy of Sciences of the United States of America, 94*(2), 674-678.

Carlson, M.C., Erickson, K.I., Kramer, A.F., Voss, M.W., Bolea, N., Mielke, M., McGill, S., Rebok, G.W., Seeman, T., & Fried, L.P. (2009). Evidence for neurocognitive plasticity in at-risk older adults: The Experience Corps Program. *The Journals of Gerontology. Series A, Biological Sciences and Medical Sciences, 64*(12): 1275-1282.

Carroll, J.B. (1983). *Human cognitive abilities: A survey of factor-analytic studies.* New York: Cambridge University Press.

Chang, Y.K., & Etnier, J.L. (2009). Exploring the dose-response relationship between resistance exercise intensity and cognitive function. *Journal of Sport and Exercise Psychology, 31*(5), 640-656.

Chang, Y.K., Etnier, J.L., & Barella, L.A. (2009). Exploring the relationship between exercise-induced arousal and cognition using fractionated response time. *Research Quarterly for Exercise and Sport, 80*(1), 78-86.

Chmura, J., Nazar, K., & Kaciuba-Uscilko, H. (1994). Choice reaction time during graded exercise in relation to blood lactate and plasma catecholamine thresholds. *International Journal of Sports Medicine, 15*(4), 172-176.

Chodzko-Zajko, W.J., & Moore, K.A. (1994). Physical fitness and cognitive functioning in aging. *Exercise and Sport Sciences Reviews, 22,* 195-220.

Chodzko-Zajko, W.J., Schuler, P., Solomon, J., Heinl, B., & Ellis, N.R. (1992). The influence of physical fitness on automatic and effortful memory changes in aging. *International Journal of Aging and Human Development, 35*(4), 265-285.

Cian, C., Barraud, P.A., Melin, B., & Raphel, C. (2001). Effects of fluid ingestion on cognitive function after heat stress or exercise-induced dehydration. *International Journal of Psychophysiology: Official Journal of the International Organization of Psychophysiology, 42*(3), 243-251.

Cian, C., Koulmann, N., Barraud, P.A., Raphel, C., Jimenez, C., & Melin, B. (2000). Influence of variations in body hydration on cognitive function: Effect of hyperhydration, heat stress, and exercise-induced dehydration. *Journal of Psychophysiology, 14,* 29-36.

Clarkson, P.M. (1978). The effect of age and activity level on simple and choice fractionated response time. *European Journal of Applied Physiology and Occupational Physiology, 40*(1), 17-25.

Clausen, A., Doctrow, S., & Baudry, M. (2008). Prevention of cognitive deficits and brain oxidative stress with superoxide dismutase/catalase mimetics in aged mice. *Neurobiology of Aging, 31*(3), 425-433.

Colcombe, S., & Kramer, A.F. (2003). Fitness effects on the cognitive function of older adults: A meta-analytic study. *Psychological Science, 14*(2), 125-130.

Colcombe, S.J., Erickson, K.I., Raz, N., Webb, A.G., Cohen, N.J., McAuley, E., & Kramer, A.F. (2003). Aerobic fitness reduces brain tissue loss in aging humans. *The Journals of Gerontology. Series A, Biological Sciences and Medical Sciences, 58*(2), 176-1Colcombe, S.J., Erickson, K.I., Scalf, P.E., Kim, J.S., Prakash, R., McAuley, E., Elavsky, S., Marquez, D.X., Hu, L., & Kramer, A.F. (2006). Aerobic exercise training increases brain volume in aging humans. *The Journals of Gerontology. Series A, Biological Sciences and Medical Sciences, 61*(11), 1166-1170.

Coles, K., & Tomporowski, P.D. (2008). Effects of acute exercise on executive processing, short-term and long-term memory. *Journal of Sports Sciences, 26*(3), 333-344.

Collardeau, M., Brisswalter, J., & Audiffren, M. (2001). Effects of a prolonged run on simple reaction time of well trained runners. *Perceptual and Motor Skills, 93*(3), 679-689.

Cotman, C.W., & Berchtold, N.C. (2002). Exercise: A behavioral intervention to enhance brain health and plasticity. *Trends in Neurosciences, 25*(6), 295-301.

Cotman, C.W., & Engesser-Cesar, C. (2002). Exercise enhances and protects brain function. *Exercise and Sport Sciences Reviews, 30*(2), 75-79.

Davis, C.L., Tomporowski, P.D., Boyle, C.A., Waller, J.L., Miller, P.H., Naglieri, J.A., & Gregoski, M. (2007). Effects of aerobic exercise on overweight children's cognitive functioning: A randomized controlled trial. *Research Quarterly for Exercise and Sport, 78*(5), 510-519.

Davranche, K., Burle, B., Audiffren, M., & Hasbroucq, T. (2005). Information processing during physical exercise: A chronometric and electromyographic study. *Experimental Brain Research, 165*(4), 532-540.

Deeny, S.P., Poeppel, D., Zimmerman, J.B., Roth, S.M., Brandauer, J., Witkowski, S., Hearn, J.W., Ludlow, A.T., Contreras-Vidal, J.L., Brandt, J., & Hatfield, B.D. (2008). Exercise, APOE, and working memory: MEG and behavioral evidence for benefit of exercise in epsilon4 carriers. *Biological Psychology, 78*(2), 179-187.

Delis, D.C., Kramer, J.H., Kaplan, E., & Ober, B.A. (1987). *The California Verbal Learning Test.* San Antonio: Psychological Corporation.

Dietrich, A. (2003). Functional neuroanatomy of altered states of consciousness: The transient hypofrontality hypothesis. *Consciousness and Cognition, 12*(2), 231-256.

Dietrich, A., & Sparling, P.B. (2004). Endurance exercise selectively impairs prefrontal-dependent cognition. *Brain and Cognition, 55*(3), 516-524.

Dik, M., Deeg, D.J., Visser, M., & Jonker, C. (2003). Early life physical activity and cognition at old age. *Journal of Clinical and Experimental Neuropsychology, 25*(5), 643-653.

Douchamps-Riboux, F., Heinz, J.-K., & Douchamps, J. (1989). Arousal as a tridimensional variable: An exploratory study of behavioural changes in rowers following a marathon race. *International Journal of Sport Psychology, 20,* 31-41.

Dubbert, P.M., Penman, A.D., Evenson, K.R., Reeves, R.R., & Mosley, T.H., Jr. (2009). Physical activity and subclinical MRI cerebral infarcts: The ARIC Study. *Journal of the Neurological Sciences, 284*(1-2), 135-139.

Durso, F.T. (Ed.). (2007). *Handbook of applied cognition* (2nd ed.). Chichester, UK: Wiley.

Dustman, R.E., Emmerson, R., & Shearer, D. (1994). Physical activity, age, and cognitive-neuropsychological function. *Journal of Aging and Physical Activity, 2,* 143-181.

Dustman, R.E., Emmerson, R.Y., Ruhling, R.O., Shearer, D.E., Steinhaus, L.A., Johnson, S.C., Bonekat, H.W., & Shigeoka, J.W. (1990). Age and fitness effects on EEG, ERPs, visual sensitivity, and cognition. *Neurobiology and Aging, 11*(3), 193-200.

Ekkekakis, P. (2009). Illuminating the black box: Investigating prefrontal cortical hemodynamics during exercise with near-infrared spectroscopy. *Journal of Sport and Exercise Psychology, 31*(4), 505-553.

Emery, C.F., & Gatz, M. (1990). Psychological and cognitive effects of an exercise program for community-residing older adults. *The Gerontologist, 30*(2), 184-188.

Emery, C.F., Honn, V.J., Frid, D.J., Lebowitz, K.R., & Diaz, P.T. (2001). Acute effects of exercise on cognition in patients with chronic obstructive pulmonary disease. *American Journal of Respiratory and Critical Care Medicine, 164*(9), 1624-1627.

Emery, C.F., Schein, R.L., Hauck, E.R., & MacIntyre, N.R. (1998). Psychological and cognitive outcomes of a randomized trial of exercise among patients with chronic obstructive pulmonary disease. *Health Psychology, 17*(3), 232-240.

Era, P., Jokela, J., & Heikkinen, E. (1986). Reaction and movement times in men of different ages: A population study. *Perceptual and Motor Skills, 63*(1), 111-130.

Eriksen, C.W., & Schultz, D.W. (1979). Information processing in visual search: A continuous flow conception and experimental results. *Perception and Psychophysics, 25,* 249-263.

Etnier, J.L. (2008). Interrelationships of exercise, mediator variables, and cognition. In W.W. Spirduso, L.W. Poon, & W. Chodzko-Zajko (Eds.), *Exercise and its mediating effects on cognition* (Vol. 2, pp. 13-32). Champaign, IL: Human Kinetics.

Etnier, J.L., & Berry, M. (2001). Fluid intelligence in an older COPD sample after short- or long-term exercise. *Medicine and Science in Sports and Exercise, 33*(10), 1620-1628.

Etnier, J.L., Caselli, R.J., Reiman, E.M., Alexander, G.E., Sibley, B.A., Tessier, D., & McLemore, E.C. (2007). Cognitive performance in older women relative to ApoE-epsilon4 genotype and aerobic fitness. *Medicine and Science in Sports and Exercise, 39*(1), 199-207.

Etnier, J.L., & Chang, Y.K. (2009). The effect of physical activity on executive function: A brief commentary on definitions, measurement issues, and the current state of the literature. *Journal of Sport and Exercise Psychology, 31,* 469-483.

Etnier, J.L., Karper, W.B., Gapin, J.I., Barella, L.A., Chang, Y.K., & Murphy, K.J. (2009). Exercise, fibromyalgia, and fibrofog: A pilot study. *Journal of Physical Activity and Health, 6*(2), 239-246.

Etnier, J.L., & Landers, D.M. (1997). The influence of age and fitness on performance and learning. *Journal of Aging and Physical Activity, 5,* 175-189.

Etnier, J.L., Nowell, P.M., Landers, D.M., & Sibley, B.A. (2006). A meta-regression to examine the relationship between aerobic fitness and cognitive performance. *Brain Research Reviews, 52*(1), 119-130.

Etnier, J.L., Salazar, W., Landers, D.M., Petruzzello, S.J., Han, M., & Nowell, P. (1997). The influence of physical fitness and exercise upon cognitive functioning: A meta-analysis. *Journal of Sport and Exercise Psychology, 19,* 249-277.

Etnier, J.L., Sibley, B.A., Pomery, J., & Kao, J.C. (2003). Components of reaction time as a function of age, physical activity, and aerobic fitness. *Journal of Aging and Physical Activity, 11,* 319-332.

Evelo, C.T., Palmen, N.G., Artur, Y., & Janssen, G.M. (1992). Changes in blood glutathione concentrations, and in erythrocyte glutathione reductase and glutathione S-transferase activity after running training and after participation in contests. *European Journal of Applied Physiology and Occupational Physiology, 64*(4), 354-358.

Fabre, C., Chamari, K., Mucci, P., Masse-Biron, J., & Prefaut, C. (2002). Improvement of cognitive function by mental and/or individualized aerobic training in healthy elderly subjects. *International Journal of Sports Medicine, 23*(6), 415-421.

Fatouros, I.G., Jamurtas, A.Z., Villiotou, V., Pouliopoulou, S., Fotinakis, P., Taxildaris, K., & Deliconstantinos, G. (2004). Oxidative stress responses in older men during endurance training and detraining. *Medicine and Science in Sports and Exercise, 36*(12), 2065-2072.

Ferris, L.T., Williams, J.S., & Shen, C.L. (2007). The effect of acute exercise on serum brain-derived neurotrophic factor levels and cognitive function. *Medicine and Science in Sports and Exercise, 39*(4), 728-734.

Folstein, M.F., Folstein, S.E., & McHugh, P.R. (1975). "Mini-mental state." A practical method for grading the cognitive state of patients for the clinician. *Journal of Psychiatric Research, 12*(3), 189-198.

Fratiglioni, L., Paillard-Borg, S., & Winblad, B. (2004). An active and socially integrated lifestyle in late life might protect against dementia. *Lancet Neurology, 3*(6), 343-353.

Gomez-Pinilla, F. (2008). The influences of diet and exercise on mental health through hormesis. *Ageing Research Reviews, 7*(1), 49-62.

Gomez-Pinilla, F., Ying, Z., Roy, R.R., Molteni, R., & Edgerton, V.R. (2002). Voluntary exercise induces a BDNF-mediated mechanism that promotes neuroplasticity. *Journal of Neurophysiology, 88*(5), 2187-2195.

Gopinathan, P.M., Pichan, G., & Sharma, V.M. (1988). Role of dehydration in heat stress-induced variations in mental performance. *Archives of Environmental Health, 43*(1), 15-17.

Gordon, B.A., Rykhlevskaia, E.I., Brumback, C.R., Lee, Y., Elavsky, S., Konopack, J.F., McAuley, E., Kramer, A.F., Colcombe, S., Gratton, G., & Fabiani, M. (2008). Neuroanatomical correlates of aging, cardiopulmonary fitness level, and education. *Psychophysiology, 45*(5), 825-838.

Harman, D. (1956). Aging: A theory based on free radical and radiation chemistry. *Journal of Gerontology, 11*, 298-300.

Harman, D. (1969). Prolongation of life: Role of free radical reactions in aging. *Journal of the American Geriatrics Society, 17*(8), 721-735.

Harman, D. (1972). The biologic clock: The mitochondria? *Journal of the American Geriatrics Society, 20*(4), 145-147.

Harman, D. (1994). Free-radical theory of aging. Increasing the functional life span. *Annals of the New York Academy of Sciences, 717*, 1-15.

Harris, M.B., Mitchell, B.M., Sood, S.G., Webb, R.C., & Venema, R.C. (2008). Increased nitric oxide synthase activity and Hsp90 association in skeletal muscle following chronic exercise. *European Journal of Applied Physiology, 104*(5), 795-802.

Hasnis, E., & Reznick, A.Z. (2003). Antioxidants and healthy aging. *The Israel Medical Association Journal, 5*(5), 368-370.

Hassmen, P., Ceci, R., & Backman, L. (1992). Exercise for older women: A training method and its influences on physical and cognitive performance. *European Journal of Applied Physiology and Occupational Physiology, 64*(5), 460-466.

Heyn, P., Abreu, B.C., & Ottenbacher, K.J. (2004). The effects of exercise training on elderly persons with cognitive impairment and dementia: A meta-analysis. *Archives of Physical Medicine and Rehabilitation, 85*(10), 1694-1704.

Hillman, C.H., Buck, S.M., Themanson, J.R., Pontifex, M.B., & Castelli, D.M. (2009). Aerobic fitness and cognitive development: Event-related brain potential and task performance indices of executive control in preadolescent children. *Developmental Psychology, 45*(1), 114-129.

Hillman, C.H., Motl, R.W., Pontifex, M.B., Posthuma, D., Stubbe, J.H., Boomsma, D.I., & de Geus, E.J. (2006). Physical activity and cognitive function in a cross-section of younger and older community-dwelling individuals. *Health Psychology, 25*(6), 678-687.

Hillman, C.H., Pontifex, M.B., Raine, L.B., Castelli, D.M., Hall, E.E., & Kramer, A.F. (2009b). The effect of acute treadmill walking on cognitive control and academic achievement in preadolescent children. *Neuroscience, 159*(3), 1044-1054.

Hillman, C.H., Snook, E.M., & Jerome, G.J. (2003). Acute cardiovascular exercise and executive control function. *International Journal of Psychophysiology, 48*(3), 307-314.

Hoffman, B.M., Blumenthal, J.A., Babyak, M.A., Smith, P.J., Rogers, S.D., Doraiswamy, P.M., & Sherwood, A. (2008). Exercise fails to improve neurocognition in depressed middle-aged and older adults. *Medicine and Science in Sports and Exercise, 40*(7), 1344-1352.

Hogervorst, E., Riedel, W., Jeukendrup, A., & Jolles, J. (1996). Cognitive performance after strenuous physical exercise. *Perceptual and Motor Skills, 83*(2), 479-488.

Hogervorst, E., Riedel, W.J., Kovacs, E., Brouns, F., & Jolles, J. (1999). Caffeine improves cognitive performance after strenuous physical exercise. *International Journal of Sports Medicine, 20*(6), 354-361.

Irani, F., Platek, S.M., Bunce, S., Ruocco, A.C., & Chute, D. (2007). Functional near infrared spectroscopy (fNIRS): An emerging neuroimaging technology with important applications for the study of brain disorders. *The Clinical Neuropsychologist, 21*(1), 9-37.

Izquierdo-Porrera, A.M., & Waldstein, S.R. (2002). Cardiovascular risk factors and cognitive function in African Americans. *Journal of Gerontology, 57*(4), P377-P380.

Jorm, A.F., & Jolley, D. (1998). The incidence of dementia: A meta-analysis. *Neurology, 51*(3), 728-733.

Joseph, J.A., Shukitt-Hale, B., Denisova, N.A., Prior, R.L., Cao, G., Martin, A., Taglialatela, G., & Bickford, P.C. (1998). Long-term dietary strawberry, spinach, or vitamin E supplementation retards the onset of age-related neuronal signal-transduction and cognitive behavioral deficits. *Journal of Neuroscience, 18*(19), 8047-8055.

Kamijo, K., Hayashi, Y., Sakai, T., Yahiro, T., Tanaka, K., & Nishihira, Y. (2009). Acute effects of aerobic exercise on cognitive function in older adults. *The Journals of Gerontology: Series B, Psychological Sciences and Social Sciences, 64*(3), 356-363.

Kamijo, K., Nishihira, Y., Hatta, A., Kaneda, T., Wasaka, T., Kida, T., & Kuroiwa, K. (2004). Differential influences of exercise intensity on information processing in the central nervous system. *European Journal of Applied Physiology, 92*(3), 305-311.

Kamijo, K., Nishihira, Y., Higashiura, T., & Kuroiwa, K. (2007). The interactive effect of exercise intensity and task difficulty on human cognitive processing. *International Journal of Psychophysiology, 65*(2), 114-121.

Kashihara, K., & Nakahara, Y. (2005). Short-term effect of physical exercise at lactate threshold on choice reaction time. *Perceptual and Motor Skills, 100*(2), 275-291.

Kessels, R.P., Aleman, A., Verhagen, W.I., & van Luijtelaar, E.L. (2000). Cognitive functioning after whiplash injury: A meta-analysis. *Journal of the International Neuropsychological Society, 6*(3), 271-278.

Kortte, K.B., Horner, M.D., & Windhan, W.K. (2002). The Trail Making Test, part B: Cognitive flexibility or ability to maintain set? *Applied Neuropsychology, 9*(2), 106-109.

Kramer, A.F., Humphrey, D.G., Larish, J.F., Logan, G.D., & Strayer, D.L. (1994). Aging and inhibition: Beyond a unitary view of inhibitory processing in attention. *Psychology and Aging, 9*(4), 491-512.

Krebs, P., Eickelberg, W., Krobath, H., & Baruch, I. (1989). Effects of physical exercise on peripheral vision and learning in children with spina bifida manifesta. *Perceptual and Motor Skills, 68*(1), 167-174.

Kubesch, S., Bretschneider, V., Freudenmann, R., Weidenhammer, N., Lehmann, M., Spitzer, M., & Gron, G. (2003). Aerobic endurance exercise improves executive functions in depressed patients. *The Journal of Clinical Psychiatry, 64*(9), 1005-1012.

Lamberts, K., & Goldstone, R.L. (Eds.). (2005). *The handbook of cognition.* London: Sage.

Langhammer, B., Stanghelle, J.K., & Lindmark, B. (2009). An evaluation of two different exercise regimes during the first year following stroke: A randomised controlled trial. *Physiotherapy Theory and Practice, 25*(2), 55-68.

Larson, E.B., Wang, L., Bowen, J.D., McCormick, W.C., Teri, L., Crane, P., & Kukull, W. (2006). Exercise is associated with reduced risk for incident dementia among persons 65 years of age and older. *Annals of Internal Medicine, 144*(2), 73-81.

Lautenschlager, N.T., Cox, K.L., Flicker, L., Foster, J.K., van Bockxmeer, F.M., Xiao, J., Greenop, K.R., & Almeida, O.P. (2008). Effect of physical activity on cognitive function in older adults at risk for Alzheimer disease: A randomized trial. *Journal of the American Medical Association, 300*(9), 1027-1037.

Leeuwenburgh, C., Hollander, J., Leichtweis, S., Griffiths, M., Gore, M., & Ji, L.L. (1997). Adaptations of glutathione antioxidant system to endurance training are tissue and muscle fiber specific. *The American Journal of Physiology, 272*(1, Pt. 2), R363-R369.

Lemmink, K.A., & Visscher, C. (2005). Effect of intermittent exercise on multiple-choice reaction times of soccer players. *Perceptual and Motor Skills, 100*(1), 85-95.

Lezak, M.D., Howieson, D.B., & Loring, D.W. (2004). *Neuropsychological assessment* (4th ed.). New York: Oxford University Press.

Lichtman, S., & Poser, E.G. (1983). The effects of exercise on mood and cognitive functioning. *Journal of Psychosomatic Research, 27*(1), 43-52.

Lindsay, J., Laurin, D., Verreault, R., Hebert, R., Helliwell, B., Hill, G.B., & McDowell, I. (2002). Risk factors for Alzheimer's disease: A prospective analysis from the Canadian Study of Health and Aging. *American Journal of Epidemiology, 156*(5), 445-453.

Liu, J., & Ames, B.N. (2005). Reducing mitochondrial decay with mitochondrial nutrients to delay and treat cognitive dysfunction, Alzheimer's disease, and Parkinson's disease. *Nutritional Neuroscience, 8*(2), 67-89.

Lytle, M.E., Vander Bilt, J., Pandav, R.S., Dodge, H.H., & Ganguli, M. (2004). Exercise level and cognitive decline: The MoVIES project. *Alzheimer Disease and Associated Disorders, 18*(2), 57-64.

MacRae, P.G., Morris, C., Lee, C.Y., Crum, K., Giessman, D., Greene, J.S., & Ugolini, J.A. (1996). Fractionated reaction time in women as a function of age and physical activity level. *Journal of Aging and Physical Activity, 4,* 14-26.

Magnie, M.N., Bermon, S., Martin, F., Madany-Lounis, M., Suisse, G., Muhammad, W., & Dolisi, C. (2000). P300, N400, aerobic fitness, and maximal aerobic exercise. *Psychophysiology, 37*(3), 369-377.

Marks, B.L., Madden, D.J., Bucur, B., Provenzale, J.M., White, L.E., Cabeza, R., & Huettel, S.A. (2007). Role of aerobic fitness and aging on cerebral white matter integrity. *Annals of the New York Academy of Sciences, 1097,* 171-174.

Marmeleira, J.F., Godinho, M.B., & Fernandes, O.M. (2009). The effects of an exercise program on several abilities associated with driving performance in older adults. *Accident; Analysis and Prevention, 41*(1), 90-97.

McMorris, T., & Graydon, J. (1997). The effect of exercise on cognitive performance in soccer-specific tests. *Journal of Sports Sciences, 15*(5), 459-468.

McMorris, T., Myers, S., MacGillivary, W.W., Sexsmith, J.R., Fallowfield, J., Graydon, J., & Forster, D. (1999). Exercise, plasma catecholamine concentrations and decision-making performance of soccer players on a soccer-specific test. *Journal of Sports Sciences, 17*(8), 667-676.

McMorris, T., Swain, J., Lauder, M., Smith, N., & Kelly, J. (2006). Warm-up prior to undertaking a dynamic psychomotor task: Does it aid performance? *The Journal of Sports Medicine and Physical Fitness, 46*(2), 328-334.

Mercer, V.S., Freburger, J.K., Chang, S.H., & Purser, J.L. (2009). Step Test scores are related to measures of activity and participation in the first 6 months after stroke. *Physical Therapy, 89*(10), 1061-1071.

Meydani, M. (1999). Dietary antioxidants modulation of aging and immune-endothelial cell interaction. *Mechanisms of Ageing and Development, 111*(2-3), 123-132.

Miyake, A., Friedman, N.P., Emerson, M.J., Witzki, A.H., Howerter, A., & Wager, T.D. (2000). The unity and diversity of executive functions and their contributions to complex "frontal lobe" tasks: A latent variable analysis. *Cognitive Psychology, 41,* 49-100.

Neeper, S.A., Gomez-Pinilla, F., Choi, J., & Cotman, C.W. (1996). Physical activity increases mRNA for brain-derived neurotrophic factor and nerve growth factor in rat brain. *Brain Research, 726*(1-2), 49-56.

Netz, Y., Tomer, R., Axelrad, S., Argov, E., & Inbar, O. (2007). The effect of a single aerobic training session on cognitive flexibility in late middle-aged adults. *International Journal of Sports Medicine, 28*(1), 82-87.

North, T.C., McCullagh, P., & Tran, Z.V. (1990). Effect of exercise on depression. *Exercise and Sport Sciences Reviews, 18,* 379-415.

Offenbach, S.I., Chodzko-Zajko, W.J., & Ringel, R.L. (1990). Relationship between physiological status, cognition, and age in adult men. *Bulletin of the Psychonomic Society, 28,* 112-114.

Partington, J. (1949). Detailed instructions for administering Partington's pathways test. *Psychological Service Center Journal, 1,* 46-48.

Pesce, C., Cereatti, L., Casella, R., Baldari, C., & Capranica, L. (2007). Preservation of visual attention in older expert orienteers at rest and under physical effort. *Journal of Sport and Exercise Psychology, 29*(1), 78-99.

Podewils, L.J., Guallar, E., Kuller, L.H., Fried, L.P., Lopez, O.L., Carlson, M., & Lyketsos, C.G. (2005). Physical activity, APOE genotype, and dementia risk: Findings from the Cardiovascular Health Cognition Study. *American Journal of Epidemiology, 161*(7), 639-651.

Polich, J. (2007). Updating P300: An integrative theory of P3a and P3b. *Clinical Neurophysiology, 118*(10), 2128-2148.

Powers, S.K., Criswell, D., Lawler, J., Ji, L.L., Martin, D., Herb, R.A., & Dudley, G. (1994). Influence of exercise and fiber type on antioxidant enzyme activity in rat skeletal muscle. *The American Journal of Physiology, 266*(2, Pt. 2), R375-R380.

Powers, S.K., Criswell, D., Lawler, J., Martin, D., Lieu, F.K., Ji, L.L., & Herb, R.A. (1993). Rigorous exercise training increases superoxide dismutase activity in ventricular myocardium. *The American Journal of Physiology, 265*(6, Pt. 2), H2094-H2098.

Prakash, R.S., Snook, E.M., Erickson, K.I., Colcombe, S.J., Voss, M.W., Motl, R.W., & Kramer, A.F. (2007). Cardiorespiratory fitness: A predictor of cortical plasticity in multiple sclerosis. *NeuroImage, 34*(3), 1238-1244.

Radak, Z., Kaneko, T., Tahara, S., Nakamoto, H., Pucsok, J., Sasvari, M., Nyakas, C., & Goto, S. (2001). Regular exercise improves cognitive function and decreases oxidative damage in rat brain. *Neurochemistry International, 38*(1), 17-23.

Radak, Z., Sasvari, M., Nyakas, C., Taylor, A.W., Ohno, H., Nakamoto, H., & Goto, S. (2000). Regular training modulates the accumulation of reactive carbonyl derivatives in mitochondrial and cytosolic fractions of rat skeletal muscle. *Archives of Biochemistry and Biophysics, 383*(1), 114-118.

Reilly, T., & Smith, D. (1986). Effect of work intensity on performance in a psychomotor task during exercise. *Ergonomics, 29*(4), 601-606.

Reisberg, D. (2006). *Cognition: Exploring the science of the mind.* New York: Norton.

Rey, A. (1941). Psychological examination of traumatic encephalopathy. *Archieves de Psychologic, 28,* 286-340.

Rogers, W.A., Pak, R., & Fisk, A.D. (2007). Applied cognitive psychology in the context of everyday living. In F.T. Durso (Ed.), *Handbook of applied cognition* (2nd ed.) (pp. 3-28). Chichester, UK: Wiley.

Roth, D.L., Goode, K.T., Clay, O.J., & Ball, K.K. (2003). Association of physical activity and visual attention in older adults. *Journal of Aging and Health, 15*(3), 534-547.

Rovio, S., Kareholt, I., Helkala, E.L., Viitanen, M., Winblad, B., Tuomilehto, J., Soininen, H., Nissinen, A., & Kivipelto, M. (2005). Leisure-time physical activity at midlife and the risk of dementia and Alzheimer's disease. *Lancet Neurology, 4*(11), 705-711.

Rovio, S., Spulber, G., Nieminen, L.J., Niskanen, E., Winblad, B., Tuomilehto, J., Nissinen, A., Soininen, H., & Kivipelto, M. (2008). The effect of midlife physical activity on structural brain changes in the elderly. *Neurobiology of Aging, 31*(11), 1927-1936.

Rubin, E.H., Storandt, M., Miller, J.P., Kinscherf, D.A., Grant, E.A., Morris, J.C., & Berg, L. (1998). A prospective study of cognitive function and onset of dementia in cognitively healthy elders. *Archives of Neurology, 55*(3), 395-401.

Salthouse, T.A. (2003). Memory aging from 18 to 80. *Alzheimer Disease and Associated Disorders, 17*(3), 162-167.

Sato, Y., Nanri, H., Ohta, M., Kasai, H., & Ikeda, M. (2003). Increase of human MTH1 and decrease of 8-hydroxydeoxyguanosine in leukocyte DNA by acute and chronic exercise in healthy male subjects. *Biochemical and Biophysical Research Communications, 305*(2), 333-338.

Scarmeas, N., & Stern, Y. (2003). Cognitive reserve and lifestyle. *Journal of Clinical and Experimental Neuropsychology, 25*(5), 625-633.

Schaie, K.W. (1994). The course of adult intellectual development. *The American Psychologist, 49*(4), 304-313.

Schonknecht, P., Pantel, J., Kruse, A., & Schroder, J. (2005). Prevalence and natural course of aging-associated cognitive decline in a population-based sample of young-old subjects. *American Journal of Psychiatry, 162*(11), 2071-2077.

Schramke, C.J., & Bauer, R.M. (1997). State-dependent learning in older and younger adults. *Psychology and Aging, 12*(2), 255-262.

Schuit, A.J., Feskens, E.J., Launer, L.J., & Kromhout, D. (2001). Physical activity and cognitive decline, the role of the apoli-poprotein e4 allele. *Medicine and Science in Sports and Exercise, 33*(5), 772-777.

Scott, J.P., McNaughton, L.R., & Polman, R.C. (2006). Effects of sleep deprivation and exercise on cognitive, motor performance and mood. *Physiology and Behavior, 87*(2), 396-408.

Sibley, B.A., & Etnier, J.L. (2003). The relationship between physical activity and cognition in children: A meta-analysis. *Pediatric Exercise Science, 15*(3), 243-256.

Spearman, C. (1904). "General Intelligence," objectively determined and measured. *The American Journal of Psychology, 15*(2), 201-292.

Steinberg, B.A., Bieliauskas, L.A., Smith, G.E., Ivnik, R.J., & Malec, J.F. (2005). Mayo's Older Americans Normative Studies: Age- and IQ-adjusted norms for the Auditory Verbal Learning Test and the Visual Spatial Learning Test. *The Clinical Neuropsychologist, 19*(3-4), 464-523.

Stern, Y. (2002). What is cognitive reserve? Theory and research application of the reserve concept. *Journal of the International Neuropsychology Society, 8,* 448-460.

Stern, Y., Habeck, C., Moeller, J., Scarmeas, N., Anderson, K.E., Hilton, H.J., Flynn, J., Sackeim, H., & van Heertum, R. (2005). Brain networks associated with cognitive reserve in healthy young and old adults. *Cerebral Cortex, 15*(4), 394-402.

Stroop, J.R. (1935). Studies of interference in serial verbal reactions. *Journal of Experimental Psychology, 18,* 643-662.

Stroth, S., Kubesch, S., Dieterle, K., Ruchsow, M., Heim, R., & Kiefer, M. (2009). Physical fitness, but not acute exercise modulates event-related potential indices for executive control in healthy adolescents. *Brain Research, 1269,* 114-124.

Tenenbaum, G., Yuval, R., Elbaz, G., Bar-Eli, M., & Weinberg, R. (1993). The relationship between cognitive characteristics and decision making. *Canadian Journal of Applied Physiology, 18*(1), 48-62.

Themanson, J.R., & Hillman, C.H. (2006). Cardiorespiratory fitness and acute aerobic exercise effects on neuroelectric and behavioral measures of action monitoring. *Neuroscience, 141*(2), 757-767.

Themanson, J.R., Pontifex, M.B., & Hillman, C.H. (2008). Fitness and action monitoring: Evidence for improved cognitive flexibility in young adults. *Neuroscience, 157*(2), 319-328.

Thorndike, E.L. (1920). Intelligence and its uses. *Harper's Monthly Magazine, 140,* 227-235.

Tomporowski, P.D., Beasman, K., Ganio, M.S., & Cureton, K. (2007). Effects of dehydration and fluid ingestion on cognition. *International Journal of Sports Medicine, 28*(10), 891-896.

Troyer, A.K., Leach, L., & Strauss, E. (2006). Aging and response inhibition: Normative data for the Victoria Stroop Test. *Neuropsychology, Development, and Cognition. Section B, Aging, Neuropsychology and Cognition, 13*(1), 20-35.

van Boxtel, M.P., Paas, F.G., Houx, P.J., Adam, J.J., Teeken, J.C., & Jolles, J. (1997). Aerobic capacity and cognitive performance in a cross-sectional aging study. *Medicine and Science in Sports and Exercise, 29*(10), 1357-1365.

Van der Elst, W., Van Boxtel, M.P., Van Breukelen, G.J., & Jolles, J. (2006). The Stroop color-word test: Influence of age, sex, and education; and normative data for a large sample across the adult age range. *Assessment, 13*(1), 62-79.

van Gelder, B.M., Tijhuis, M.A., Kalmijn, S., Giampaoli, S., Nissinen, A., & Kromhout, D. (2004). Physical activity in relation to cognitive decline in elderly men: The FINE Study. *Neurology, 63*(12), 2316-2321.

van Praag, H., Christie, B.R., Sejnowski, T.J., & Gage, F.H. (1999). Running enhances neurogenesis, learning, and long-term potentiation in mice. *Proceedings of the National Academy of Sciences of the United States of America, 96*(23), 13427-13431.

van Praag, H., Kempermann, G., & Gage, F.H. (1999). Running increases cell proliferation and neurogenesis in the adult mouse dentate gyrus. *Nature Neuroscience, 2*(3), 266-270.

van Praag, H., Shubert, T., Zhao, C., & Gage, F.H. (2005). Exercise enhances learning and hippocampal neurogenesis in aged mice. *The Journal of Neuroscience, 25*(38), 8680-8685.

Vaynman, S., & Gomez-Pinilla, F. (2005). License to run: Exercise impacts functional plasticity in the intact and injured central nervous system by using neurotrophins. *Neurorehabilitation Neural Repair, 19*(4), 283-295.

Vaynman, S., & Gomez-Pinilla, F. (2006). Revenge of the "sit": How lifestyle impacts neuronal and cognitive health through molecular systems that interface energy metabolism with neuronal plasticity. *Journal of Neuroscience Research, 84*(4), 699-715.

Vaynman, S., Ying, Z., & Gomez-Pinilla, F. (2003). Interplay between brain-derived neurotrophic factor and signal transduction modulators in the regulation of the effects of exercise on synaptic-plasticity. *Neuroscience, 122*(3), 647-657.

Vaynman, S., Ying, Z., & Gomez-Pinilla, F. (2004). Hippocampal BDNF mediates the efficacy of exercise on synaptic plasticity and cognition. *The European Journal of Neuroscience, 20*(10), 2580-2590.

Venditti, P., Masullo, P., & Di Meo, S. (1999). Effect of training on H(2)O(2) release by mitochondria from rat skeletal muscle. *Archives of Biochemistry and Biophysics, 372*(2), 315-320.

Verghese, J., Lipton, R.B., Katz, M.J., Hall, C.B., Derby, C.A., Kuslansky, G., Ambrose, A.F., Sliwinski, M., & Buschke, H. (2003). Leisure activities and the risk of dementia in the elderly. *The New England Journal of Medicine, 348*(25), 2508-2516.

Wechsler, D. (1997). *Wechsler Memory Scale* (3rd ed.). San Antonio: The Psychological Corporation.

Welsh, R.S., Davis, J.M., Burke, J.R., & Williams, H.G. (2002). Carbohydrates and physical/mental performance during intermittent exercise to fatigue. *Medicine and Science in Sports and Exercise, 34*(4), 723-731.

Whalley, L.J., Deary, I.J., Appleton, C.L., & Starr, J.M. (2004). Cognitive reserve and the neurobiology of cognitive aging. *Ageing Research Reviews, 3*(4), 369-382.

Wilson, R.S., Mendes De Leon, C.F., Barnes, L.L., Schneider, J.A., Bienias, J.L., Evans, D.A., & Bennett, D.A. (2002). Participation in cognitively stimulating activities and risk of incident Alzheimer disease. *Journal of the American Medical Association, 287*(6), 742-748.

Winter, B., Breitenstein, C., Mooren, F.C., Voelker, K., Fobker, M., Lechtermann, A., Krueger, K., Fromme, A., Korsukewitz, C., Floel, A., & Knecht, S. (2007). High impact running improves learning. *Neurobiology of Learning and Memory, 87*(4), 597-609.

Yaffe, K., Barnes, D., Nevitt, M., Lui, L.Y., & Covinsky, K. (2001). A prospective study of physical activity and cognitive decline in elderly women: Women who walk. *Archives of Internal Medicine, 161*(14), 1703-1708.

Yerkes, R.M., & Dodson, J.D. (1908). The relation of strength of stimulus to rapidity of habit-formation. *Journal of Comparative Neurology and Psychology, 18*, 459-482.

Chapter 18

Abernethy, B. (1988). The effects of age and expertise upon perceptual skill development in a racquet sport. *Research Quarterly for Exercise and Sport, 59*(3), 210-221.

Abernethy, B., Baker, J., & Côté, J. (2005). Transfer of pattern recall skills may contribute to the development of sport expertise. *Applied Cognitive Psychology, 19*, 705-718.

Abernethy, B., Gill, D.P., Parks, S.L., & Packer, S.T. (2001). Expertise and the perception of kinematic and situational probability information. *Perception, 30*, 233-252.

Abernethy, B., Neal, R.J., & Koning, P. (1994). Visual-perceptual and cognitive differences between expert, intermediate, and novice snooker players. *Applied Cognitive Psychology, 8*, 185-211.

Abernethy, B., & Russell, D.G. (1983). Skill in tennis: Considerations for talent identification and skill development. *Australian Journal of Sport Sciences, 3*(1), 3-12.

Abernethy, B., & Russell, D.G. (1987). Expert-novice differences in an applied selective attention task. *Journal of Sport Psychology, 9*, 326-345.

Abernethy, B., Wann, J.P., & Parks, S. (1998). Training perceptual-motor skills for sport. In B.C. Elliott (Ed.), *Training in sport: Applying sport science* (pp.1-68). Chichester, UK: Wiley.

Abernethy, B., & Zawi, K. (2007). Pick-up of essential kinematics underpins expert perception and action. *Journal of Motor Behavior, 39*, 353-367.

Abernethy, B., Zawi, K., & Jackson, R. (2008). Expertise and attunement to kinematic constraints. *Perception, 37*, 931-948.

Alain, C., & Proteau, L. (1980). Decision making in sport. In C.H. Nadeau, W.R. Halliwell, K.M. Newell, & G.C. Roberts (Eds.), *Psychology of motor behavior and sport* (pp. 465-477). Champaign, IL: Human Kinetics.

Bahill, A.T., & LaRitz, T. (1984). Why can't batters keep their eyes on the ball? *American Scientist, 72*, 249-253.

Baker, J., Côté., J., & Abernethy, B. (2003a). Sport-specific practice and the development of expert decision making in team ball sports. *Journal of Applied Sport Psychology, 15*, 12-25.

Baker, J., Côté., J., & Abernethy, B. (2003b). Learning from the experts: Practice activities of expert decision makers in sport. *Research Quarterly for Exercise and Sport, 74*(3), 342-347.

Berry, J., Abernethy, B., & Côté., J. (2008). The contribution of structured activity and deliberate play to the development of expert perceptual and decision-making skill. *Journal of Sport and Exercise Psychology, 30*(6), 685-708.

Borgeaud, P., & Abernethy, B. (1987). Skilled perception in volleyball defence. *Journal of Sport Psychology, 9*, 400-406.

Cañal-Bruland, R., & Williams, A.M. (2010). Recognizing and predicting movement effects identifying critical movement features. *Experimental Psychology, 57*(4), 320-326.

Carling, C., Reilly, T.P., & Williams, A.M. (2008). *Performance assessment in field sports*. London: Routledge.

Crognier, L., & Féry, Y. (2005). Effect of tactical initiative on predicting passing shots in tennis. *Applied Cognitive Psychology, 19*, 1-13.

Daffertshofer, A., Lamoth, C.J.C., Meijer, O.G., & Beek, P.J. (2004). PCA in studying coordination and variability: A tutorial. *Journal of Clinical Biomechanics, 19*(4), 415-428.

Dillon, J.M., Crassini, B., & Abernethy, B. (1989). Stimulus uncertainty and response time in a simulated racquet-sport task. *Journal of Human Movement Studies, 17*, 115-132.

Dittrich, W.H. (1999). Seeing biological motion: Is there a role for cognitive strategies? In A. Braffort, R. Gherbi, S. Gibet, J. Richardson, & D. Teil (Eds.), *Gesture-based communication in human-computer interaction* (pp. 3-22). Berlin: Springer-Verlag.

Ericsson, K.A., & Kintsch, W. (1995). Long-term working memory. *Psychological Review, 102,* 211-245.

Ericsson, K.A., Patel, V., & Kintsch, W. (2000). How experts' adaptations to representative task demands account for the expertise effect in memory recall: Comment on Vicente and Wang (1998). *Psychological Review, 107,* 578-592.

Ericsson, K.A., & Simon, H.A. (1993). *Protocol analysis: Verbal reports as data* (Rev. ed.). Cambridge, MA: Bradford Books/MIT Press.

Ericsson, K.A., & Williams, A.M. (2007). Capturing naturally occurring superior performance in the laboratory: Translational research on expert performance. *Journal of Experimental Psychology: Applied, 13*(3), 115-123.

Farrow, D., & Abernethy, B. (2003). Do expertise and the degree of perception-action coupling affect natural anticipatory performance? *Perception, 32,* 1127-1139.

Farrow, D., Abernethy, B., & Jackson, R.C. (2005). Probing expert anticipation with the temporal occlusion paradigm: Experimental investigations of some methodological issues. *Motor Control, 9,* 332-351.

Garland, D.J., & Barry, J.R. (1991). Cognitive advantage in sport: The nature of perceptual structures. *The American Journal of Psychology, 104,* 211-228.

Helsen, W.F., & Starkes, J.L. (1999). A multidimensional approach to skilled perception and performance in sport. *Applied Cognitive Psychology, 13,* 1-27.

Hodges, N.J., Huys, R., & Starkes, J.L. (2007). Methodological review and evaluation of research in expert performance in sport. In G. Tenenbaum & R.C. Eklund (Eds.), *Handbook of sport psychology* (pp. 161-183). Hoboken, NJ: Wiley.

Horn, R., Williams, A.M., & Scott, M.A. (2002). Learning from demonstrations: The role of visual search during observational learning from video and point-light models. *Journal of Sports Sciences, 20,* 253-269.

Howarth, C., Walsh, W.D. Abernethy, B., & Snyder, C.W., Jr. (1984). A field examination of anticipation in squash: Some preliminary data. *Australian Journal of Science and Medicine in Sport, 16,* 7-11.

Huys, R., Cañal-Bruland, R., Hagemann, N., & Williams, A.M. (2009). The effects of occlusion, neutralization, and deception of perceptual information on anticipation in tennis. *Journal of Motor Behavior, 41*(2), 158-171.

Huys, R., Smeeton, N.J., Hodges, N.J., Beek, P., & Williams, A.M. (2008). The dynamical information underlying anticipation skill in tennis. *Perception and Psychophysics, 18,* 1217-1234.

James, N., Caudrelier, T., & Murray, S. (2006). The use of anticipation by elite squash players. *Journal of Sports Sciences, 23*(11/12), 1249-1250.

Kording, K.P., & Wolpert, D.M. (2004). Bayesian integration in sensorimotor learning. *Nature, 427,* 244-247.

McMorris, T., & Graydon, J. (1996). Effect of exercise on the decision-making performance of experienced and inexperienced soccer players. *Research Quarterly for Exercise and Sport, 67,* 109-114.

McPherson, S.L., & Kernodle, M.W. (2003) Tactics, the neglected attribute of expertise: Problem representations and performance skill in tennis. In J.L. Starkes & K.A. Ericsson (Eds.), *Expert performance in sports: Advances in research on sport expertise* (pp. 137-168). Champaign, IL: Human Kinetics.

McRobert, A., Williams, A.M., Ward, P., & Eccles, D. (2009). Perceptual-cognitive mechanisms underpinning expertise: The effects of task constraints. *Ergonomics, 52*(4), 474-483.

McRobert, A., Ward, P., Eccles, D., & Williams, A.M. (2010). The effect of manipulating context-specific information on perceptual–cognitive processes during a simulated anticipation task. *British Journal of Psychology, 102.*

Milner, A.D., & Goodale, M.A. (1995). *The visual brain in action.* Oxford, UK: Oxford University Press.

Müller, S., & Abernethy, B. (2006). Batting with occluded vision: An in situ examination of the information pick-up and interceptive skills of high- and low-skilled cricket batsmen. *Journal of Science and Medicine in Sport, 9,* 446-458.

Müller, S., Abernethy, B., & Farrow, D. (2006). How do world-class cricket batsmen anticipate a bowler's intention? *The Quarterly Journal of Experimental Psychology, 59*(12), 2162-2186.

Nakagawa, A. (1982). A field experiment on recognition of game situations in ball games: In the case of static situations in rugby football. *Japanese Journal of Physical Education, 27,* 17-26.

Nisbett, R.E., & Wilson, T.D. (1977). Telling more than we can know: Verbal reports on mental processes. *Psychological Review, 84,* 231-259.

North, J.S., & Williams, A.M. (2009). Identifying the critical time period for information extraction when recognizing sequences of play. *Research Quarterly for Exercise and Sport, 79*(2), 268-273.

North, J., Williams, A.M., Ward, P., & Ericsson, A. (2010). Identifying the critical information sources to skilled anticipation and recognition using retrospective verbal reports. *Memory, 19*(2), 155.

North, J.S., Williams, A.M., Ward, P., Hodges, N.J., & Ericsson, K.A. (2009). Perceiving patterns in dynamic action sequences: The relationship between anticipation and pattern recognition skill. *Applied Cognitive Psychology, 23,* 1-17.

Oudejans, R.R.D., & Coolen, H. (2003). Human kinematics and event control: On-line movement registration as a means for experimental manipulation. *Journal of Sports Sciences, 21,* 567-576.

Roca, A., Ford, P.R., McRobert, A.P., & Williams, A.M. (2011). Identifying the processes underpinning anticipation and decision-making in a dynamic time-constrained task. *Cognitive Processing 12*(3), 301-10.

Savelsbergh, G.J.P., Williams, A.M., van der Kamp, J., & Ward, P. (2002). Visual search, anticipation and expertise in soccer goalkeepers. *Journal of Sports Sciences, 20,* 279-287.

Shim, J., Carlton, L.G., & Kwon, Y.H. (2006). Perception of kinematic characteristics of tennis strokes for anticipating stroke type and direction. *Research Quarterly for Exercise and Sport, 77,* 326-339.

Smeeton, N., Ward, P., & Williams, A.M. (2004). Transfer of perceptual skill in sport. *Journal of Sports Science, 19,* 3-9.

Starkes, J.L. (1987). Skill in field hockey: The nature of the cognitive advantage. *Journal of Sport Psychology, 9,* 146-160.

Starkes, J.L., & Deakin, J. (1984). Perception in sport: A cognitive approach to skilled performance. In W.F. Straub & J.M. Williams (Eds), *Cognitive sport psychology* (pp. 115-128). Lansing, NY: Sport Science Associates.

Starkes, J.L., Edwards, P., Dissanayake, P., & Dunn, T. (1995). A new technology and field test of advance cue usage in volleyball. *Research Quarterly for Exercise and Sport, 66*(2), 162-167.

Tenenbaum, G., Sar-El, T., & Bar-Eli, M. (2000). Anticipation of ball location in low and high-skill performers: A developmental perspective. *Psychology of Sport and Exercise, 1,* 117-128.

Troje, N.F. (2002). Decomposing biological motion: A framework for analysis and synthesis of human gait patterns. *Journal of Vision, 2,* 371-387.

Vaeyens, R., Lenoir, M., Williams, A.M., Mazyn, L., & Phillppaerts, R.M. (2007a). The effects of task constraints on visual search behaviour and decision-making skill in youth soccer players. *Journal of Sport and Exercise Psychology, 29,* 147-169.

Vaeyens, R., Lenoir, M., Williams, A.M., Mazyn, L., & Philippaerts, R.M. (2007b). Visual search behavior and decision-making skill in soccer. *Journal of Motor Behavior, 39*(5), 395-408.

van der Kamp, J., Rivas, F., van Doorn, H., & Savelsbergh, G.J.P. (2008). Ventral and dorsal contributions in visual anticipation in fast ball sports. *International Journal of Sport Psychology, 39*(2), 100-130.

Vickers, J.N. (2007). *Perception, cognition, and decision training: The quiet eye in action.* Champaign, IL: Human Kinetics.

Vickers, J., & Williams, A.M. (2007). Why some choke and others don't! *Journal of Motor Behavior, 39*(5), 381-394.

Wagg, C.J., Williams, A.M., Vogt, S., & Higuchi, S. (2009). The neural substrate of anticipation skill in tennis and soccer: An event-related fMRI study. *Journal of Sport and Exercise Psychology,* S31, 103.

Ward, P., & Williams, A.M. (2003). Perceptual and cognitive skill development in soccer: The multidimensional nature of expert performance. *Journal of Sport and Exercise Psychology, 25*(1), 93-111.

Ward, P., Williams, A.M., & Bennett, S.J. (2002). Visual search and biological motion perception in tennis. *Research Quarterly for Exercise and Sport, 73*(1), 107-112.

Weissensteiner, J., Abernethy, B., Farrow, D., & Müller, S. (2008). The development of anticipation: A cross-sectional examination of the practice experiences contributing to expertise in cricket batting. *Journal of Sport and Exercise Psychology, 30,* 663-684.

Williams, A.M. (2000). Perceptual skill in soccer: Implications for talent identification and development. *Journal of Sports Sciences, 18,* 737-740.

Williams, A.M. (2009). Perceiving the intentions of others: How do skilled performers make anticipation judgements? In M. Raab, J.G. Johnson, & H.R. Heekeren (Eds.), *Progress in brain research, Vol. 174, Mind and motion: The bidirectional link between thought and action* (pp. 73-83). The Netherlands: Elsevier.

Williams, A.M., & Burwitz, K. (1993). Advance cue utilization in soccer. In T.P. Reilly, J. Clarys, & A. Stibbe (Eds.), *Science and football II* (pp. 239-244). London: E & FN Spon.

Williams, A.M., & Davids, K. (1995). Declarative knowledge in sport: A byproduct of experience or a characteristic of expertise? *Journal of Sport and Exercise Psychology, 7*(3), 259-275.

Williams, A.M., & Davids, K. (1998). Visual search strategy, selective attention, and expertise in soccer. *Research Quarterly for Exercise and Sport, 69*(2), 111-128.

Williams, A.M., Davids, K., Burwitz, L., & Williams, J.G. (1993). Cognitive knowledge and soccer performance. *Perceptual and Motor Skills, 76,* 579-593.

Williams, A.M., Davids, K., Burwitz, L., & Williams, J.G. (1994). Visual search strategies of experienced and inexperienced soccer players. *Research Quarterly for Exercise and Sport, 5*(2), 127-135.

Williams, A.M., Davids, K., & Williams, J.G. (1999). *Visual perception and action in sport.* London: E & FN Spon.

Williams, A.M., & Elliott, D. (1999). Anxiety and visual search strategy in karate. *Journal of Sport and Exercise Psychology, 21,* 362-375.

Williams, A.M., & Ericsson, K.A. (2005). Some considerations when applying the expert performance approach in sport. *Human Movement Science, 24,* 283-307.

Williams, A.M., Hodges, N.J., North, J., & Barton, G. (2006) Perceiving patterns of play in dynamic sport tasks: Investigating the essential information underlying skilled performance. *Perception,* 35, 317-332.

Williams, A.M., Huys, R., Cañal-Bruland, R., & Hagemann, N. (2009). The dynamical information underpinning deception effects. *Human Movement Science, 28,* 362-370.

Williams, A.M., Janelle, C.M., & Davids, K. (2004). Constraints on the search for visual information in sport. *International Journal of Sport and Exercise Psychology, 2,* 301-318.

Williams, A.M., & North, J.S. (2009). Identifying the minimal essential information underlying pattern recognition. In D. Araujo, H. Ripoll, & M. Raab (eds.) *Perspectives on Cognition and Action in Sport* (pp. 95-107). Hauppauge, NY: Nova Science Publishing Inc.

Williams, A.M., & Reilly, T.P. (2000). Talent identification and development in soccer. *Journal of Sports Sciences, 18,* 657-667.

Williams, A.M., & Ward, P. (2007). Perceptual-cognitive expertise in sport: Exploring new horizons. In G. Tenenbaum & R. Eklund (Eds.), *Handbook of sport psychology* (3rd ed., pp. 203-223). New York: Wiley.

Williams, A.M., Ward, P., & Chapman, C. (2003). Training perceptual skill in field hockey: Is there transfer from the laboratory to the field? *Research Quarterly for Exercise and Sport, 74*(1), 98-103.

Williams, A.M., Ward, P., Knowles, J.M., & Smeeton, N.J. (2002). Perceptual skill in a real-world task: Training, instruction, and transfer in tennis. *Journal of Experimental Psychology: Applied, 8*(4), 259-270.

Williams, A.M., Ward, P., Smeeton, N.J., & Ward, J. (2008). Task specificity, role, and anticipation skill in soccer. *Research Quarterly for Exercise and Sport, 79*(3), 429-433.

Wright, M.J., & Jackson, R.C. (2007). Brain regions concerned with perceptual skills in tennis: An fMRI study. *International Journal of Psychophysiology, 63,* 214-220.

Wright, M.J., Bishop, D., Jackson, R.C., & Abernethy, B. (2010). Functional MRI reveals expert-novice differences during sport-related anticipation. *NeuroReport, 21*(2), 94-98.

Yarrow, K., Brown, P., & Krakauer, J.W. (2009). Inside the brain of an elite athlete: The neural processes that support high achievement in sports. *Nature Reviews Neuroscience, 10,* 585-596.

Chapter 19

Abernethy, B., Farrow, D., & Berry, J. (2003). Constraints and issues in the development of a general theory of expert perceptual-motor performance: A critique of the deliberate practice framework. In J.L. Starkes & K.A. Ericsson (Eds.), *Expert performance in sports: Advances in research on sport expertise* (pp. 349-369). Champaign, IL: Human Kinetics.

Allard, F., & Burnett, N. (1985). Skill in sport. *Canadian Journal of Psychology, 39,* 294-312.

Allard, F., Graham, S., & Paarsalu, M.E. (1980). Perception in sport: Basketball. *Journal of Sport Psychology, 2,* 14-21.

Anderson, J.R. (1982). Acquisition of cognitive skill. *Psychological Review, 89*, 369-406.

Bläsing, B. (2010). The dancers memory. In B. Bläsing, M. Puttke, & T. Schack (Eds.), *Neurocognition of dance* (pp. 75-98). London: Psychology Press.

Bläsing, B., Tenenbaum, G., & Schack, T. (2009). The cognitive structure of movements in classical dance. *Psychology of Sport and Exercise, 10*(1), 350-360.

Borgeaud, P., & Abernethy, B. (1987). Skilled perception in volleyball defense. *Journal of Sport Psychology, 9*, 400-406.

Braun, S.M., Beurskens, A.J.H.M., Schack, T., Marcellis, R.G., Oti, K.C., Schols, J.M., & Wade, D.T. (2007). Is it possible to use the SDA-M to investigate representations of motor actions in stroke patients? *Clinical Rehabilitation, 21*, 822-832.

Braun, S.M., Kleynen, M., Schols, J.M., Schack, T., Beurskens, A.J., & Wade, D.T. (2008). Using mental practice in stroke rehabilitation: A framework. *Clinical Rehabilitation, 7*, 579-591.

Champagne, A., & Klopfer, L. (1981) Structuring process skills and the solution of verbal problems involving science concepts. *Science Education, 65*, 493-411.

Chase, W.G., & Simon, H. (1973). The mind's eye in chess. In W.G. Chase (Ed.), *Visual information processing* (pp. 215-281). New York: Academic Press.

Chi, M.T.H. (1978). Knowledge structures and memory development. In R.S. Siegler (Ed.), *Children's thinking: What develops?* (pp. 73-105). Hillsdale, NJ: Erlbaum.

Chi, M.T.H., & Glaser, R. (1980). The measurement of expertise: Analysis of the development of knowledge and skill as a basic for assessing achievement. In E.L. Baker & E.S. Quellmalz (Eds.), *Educational testing and evaluation* (pp. 37-47). Beverly Hills, CA: Sage.

Chi, M.T.H., & Rees, E.A. (1983). A learning framework for development. In I.A. Meachan (Ed.), *Contributions to human development, 9* (pp. 71-107). Basel: Karger.

Decety, J., & Grèzes, J. (1999). Neural mechanisms subserving the perception of human actions. *Trends in Cognitive Sciences, 3*(5), 172-178.

De Groot, A.D. (1965). *Thought and choice in chess*. The Hague: Molton.

Ericsson, K.A. (2003). The challenge of studying the complex mechanisms mediating expertise. In J.L. Starkes & K.A. Ericsson (Eds.), *Expert performance in sports* (pp. 371-402). Champaign, IL: Human Kinetics.

Ericsson, K.A., & Starkes, J. L. (Eds.). (2003). *Expert performance in sports*. Champaign, IL: Human Kinetics.

French, K.E., & Thomas, J.R. (1987). The relation of knowledge development to children's basketball performance. *Journal of Sport Psychology, 9*, 15-32.

Friendly, M.L. (1977). In search of the M-gram: The structure of organization in free recall. *Cognitive Psychology, 9*, 188-249.

Geburzi, E., Engel, F., & Schack, T. (2004). Mental representation of basic movement in Latin dancing. In E. Van Praagh, J. Coudert, N. Fellmann, & P. Duché (Eds.), *Proceedings of the 9th Annual Congress of the European College of Sport Science* (p. 26). Clermont-Ferrand, France: European College of Sport Science.

Heinen, T., Schwaiger, J., & Schack, T. (2002). Optimising gymnastics training with cognitive methods. In M. Koskolou, N. Geladas, & V. Klissouras (Eds.), *Proceedings of the 7th Annual Congress of the European College of Sport Science* (p. 608). Athens: European College of Sport Science.

Hodges, N., Huys, R., & Starkes, J. (2007). Methodological review and evaluation of research in expert performance in sport. In G. Tenenbaum & R.C. Eklund (Eds.), *Handbook of sport psychology* (3rd ed., pp. 161-183). New York: Wiley.

Hommel, B., Müsseler, J., Aschersleben, G., & Prinz, W. (2001). The theory of event coding (TEC): A framework for perception and action planning. *Behavioral and Brain Sciences, 24*(5), 849-937.

Huber, J. (1997). Differences in problem representation and procedural knowledge between elite and nonelite springboard divers. *The Sport Psychologist, 11*, 142-159.

Jeannerod, M. (1997). *The cognitive neuroscience of action*. Oxford, UK: Blackwell.

Jeannerod, M. (2004). Actions from within. *Journal of Sport and Exercise Psychology, 2*(4), 376-401.

Kluwe, R.H. (1988), Methoden der Psychologie zur Gewinnung von Daten über menschliches Wissen (Psychological methods to examine data about human knowledge). In H. Mandl & H. Spada (Eds.), *Wissenspsychologie* (pp. 359-385). München: Psychologie Verlags Union.

Koch, I., & Hoffmann, J. (2000). The role of stimulus-based and response-based spatial information in sequence and learning. *Journal of Experimental Psychology: Learning, Memory, and Cognition, 26*(4), 863-882.

Koch, I., Keller, P., & Prinz, W. (2004). The ideomotor approach to action control: Implications for skilled performance. *International Journal of Sport and Exercise, 2*, 362-375.

Krause, W. (2000). *Denken und Gedächtnis aus naturwissenschaftlicher Sich (Thinking and memory from a natual science perspective)*. Göttingen, Germany: Hogrefe.

Lander, H.-J. (1991). Ein methodischer Ansatz zur Ermittlung der Struktur und der Dimensionierung einer intern-repräsentierten Begriffsmenge (A methodological approach to examine the structure and feature-dimensions of internal represented concepts). *Zeitschrift für Psychologie, 199*, 167-176.

Lander, H.-J., & Lange, K. (1992). Eine differentialpsychologische Analyse begrifflich-strukturierten Wissens (A differential analysis of conceptual represented knowledge). *Zeitschrift für Psychologie, 200*, 181-197.

McPherson, S.L., & Kernodle, M.W. (2003). Tactics, the neglected attribute of expertise: Problem representations and performance skills in tennis. In J.L. Starkes & K.A. Ericsson (Eds.), *Expert performance in sports: Advances in research on sport expertise* (pp. 137-167). Champaign, IL: Human Kinetics.

McPherson, S.L., & Thomas, J.R. (1989). Relation of knowledge and performance in boy's tennis: Age and expertise. *Journal of Experimental Child Psychology, 48*, 190-211.

McPherson, S.L., & Vickers, J.N. (2004). Cognitive control in motor expertise. *Journal of Sport and Exercise Psychology, 2*, 274-300.

Mechsner, F., Kerzel, D., Knoblich, G., & Prinz, W. (2001). Perceptual basis of bimanual coordination. *Nature, 414*, 69-72.

Olson, J.R., & Biolsi, K.J. (1991). Techniques for representing expert knowledge. In K.A. Ericsson & J. Smith (Eds.), *Towards a general theory of expertise* (pp. 240-285). Cambridge: Cambridge University Press.

Rosch, E. (1978). Principles of categorization. In E. Rosch & B.B. Loyd (Eds.), *Cognition and categorization* (pp. 27-48). Hillsdale, NJ: Erlbaum.

Rosenbaum, D.A., Cohen, R.G., Jax, S.A., Van Der Wel, R., & Weiss, D.J. (2007). The problem of serial order in behavior: Lashley's legacy. *Human Movement Science, 26*, 525-554.

Rosenbaum, D.A., Meulenbroek, R.G., Vaughan, J., & Jansen, C. (2001). Posture-based motion planning: Applications to grasping. *Psychological Review, 108,* 709-734.

Russell, S.J. (1990). Athletes knowledge in task perception, definition and classification. *International Journal of Psychology, 21,* 85-101.

Russell, S.J., & Salmela, J.H. (1992). Quantifying expert athlete knowledge. *Journal of Applied Sport Psychology, 4,* 10-26.

Schack, T. (2003). The relationship between motor representation and biomechanical parameters in complex movements—towards an integrative perspective of movement science. *European Journal of Sportscience, 2,* 1-13.

Schack, T. (2004a). Knowledge and performance in action. *Journal of Knowledge Management, 8*(4), 38-53.

Schack, T. (2004b). The cognitive architecture of complex movement. *International Journal of Sport and Exercise Psychology, 2*(4), 403-438.

Schack, T. (2010a). Do your senses tingle? Building blocks and architecture of dance. In B. Bläsing, M. Puttke, & T. Schack (Eds.), *Neurocognition of dance* (pp. 11-40). New York: Psychology Press.

Schack, T. (2010b). *Die kognitive Architektur menschlicher Bewegungen—innovative Zugänge für Psychologie, Sportwissenschaft und Robotik* (The cognitive architecture of human movements: Innovative approaches for psychology, sport science, and robotics). Reihe „Sportforum". Aachen, Germany: Meyer & Meyer.

Schack, T., & Bar-Eli, M. (2007). *Psychological factors of technical preparation.* In B. Blumenstein, R. Lidor, & G. Tenenbaum (Eds.), Psychology of sport training. Perspectives on sport and exercise psychology (Vol. 2, pp. 62-103). Oxford, UK: Meyer & Meyer Sport.

Schack, T., & Hackfort, D. (2007). *Action-theory approach to applied sport psychology.* In G. Tenenbaum & R.C. Ecklund (Eds.), Handbook of sport psychology (3rd ed., pp. 332-351). New Jersey: Wiley.

Schack, T., & Heinen, T. (2000). Mental training based on mental representation. In B.A. Carlsson, U. Johnson, & F. Wetterstrand (Eds.), *Sport psychology conference in the new millennium—a dynamic research-practise perspective* (pp. 333-337). Sweden: Halmstad University.

Schack, T., & Mechsner, F. (2006). Representation of motor skills in human long-term memory. *Neuroscience Letters, 391,* 77-81.

Schack, T., & Ritter, H. (2009). The cognitive nature of action—functional links between cognitive psychology, movement science and robotics. *Progress in Brain Research, 174,* 231-252.

Starkes, J.L. (1987). Skill in field hockey: The nature of the cognitive advantage. *Journal of Sports Psychology, 9,* 146-160.

Tenenbaum, G., Hatfield, B., Eklund, R.C., Land, W.M., Calmeiro, L., Razon, S., & Schack, T. (2009). A conceptual framework for studying emotions-cognitions-performance linkage under conditions that vary in perceived pressure. *Progress in Brain Research, 174,* 159-178.

Tergan, S.-O. (1989). Psychologische Grundlagen der Erfassung individueller Wissensrepräsentation. Teil 1: Grundlagen der Wissensmodulierung (Foundations of knowledge modulation). *Sprache und Kognition, 8,* 152-165.

Thomas, K.T., & Thomas, J.R. (1994). Developing expertise in sport: The relation of knowledge and performance. *International Journal of Sport Psychology, 25,* 295-312.

Weigelt, M., Ahlmeyer, T., Lex, H., & Schack, T. (in press). Individual skill diagnostics in high performance sports: A study on the structure of cognitive representations of a throwing technique in judo experts. *Psychology of Sport and Exercise.*

Weigelt, M., Rieger, M., Mechsner, F., & Prinz, W. (2007). Target-related coupling in bimanual reaching movements. *Psychological Research, 71,* 438-447.

Chapter 20

Asci, F.H., Eklund, R.C., Whitehead, J.R., Kirazci, S., & Koca, C. (2005). Use of the CY-PSPP in other cultures: A preliminary investigation of its factorial validity for Turkish children and youth. *Psychology of Sport and Exercise, 6,* 33-50.

Bandura, A. (2006). Toward a psychology of human agency. *Perspectives on Psychological Science, 1,* 164-180.

Blascovich, J., & Tomaka, J. (1991). The self-esteem scale. In J.P. Robinson, P.R. Shaver, & L.S. Wrightsman (Eds.), *Measures of personality and social psychological attitudes* (Vol. I, pp. 115-160). San Diego: Academic Press.

Bong, M., & Skaalvik, E.M. (2003). Academic self-concept and self-efficacy: How different are they really? *Educational Psychology Review, 15,* 1-40.

Bracken, B.A. (1996). Clinical applications of a context-dependent, multidimensional model of self-concept. In B.A. Bracken (Ed.), *Handbook of self-concept: Developmental, social and clinical considerations* (pp. 463-503). New York: Wiley.

Byrne, B.M. (1984). The general/academic self-concept nomological network: A review of construct validation research. *Review of Educational Research, 54,* 427-456.

Byrne, B. (1996). *Measuring self-concept across the life span: Issues and instrumentation.* Washington, DC: American Psychological Association.

Calsyn, R.J., & Kenny, D.A. (1977). Self-concept of ability and perceived evaluation of others: Cause or effect of academic achievement? *Journal of Educational Psychology, 69,* 136-145.

Coopersmith, S. (1967). *The antecedents of self-esteem.* San Francisco: Freeman.

Eiser, C., Eiser, J.R., & Havermans, T. (1995). The measurement of self-esteem: Practical and theoretical considerations. *Personality and Individual Differences, 18,* 429-432.

Eklund, R.C., Whitehead, J.R., & Welk, G.J. (1997). Validity of the Children and Youth Physical Self-Perception Profile: A confirmatory factor analysis. *Research Quarterly for Exercise and Sport, 68,* 249-256.

Fitts, W.H. (1965). *Tennessee Self Concept Scale, manual.* Los Angeles: Western Psychological Services.

Fleishman, F.A. (1964). *The structure and measurement physical fitness.* Englewood Cliffs, NJ: Prentice Hall.

Fleming, J.S., & Courtney, B.E. (1984). The dimensionality of self-esteem: II: Hierarchical facet model for revised measurement scales. *Journal of Personality and Social Psychology, 46,* 404-421.

Fox, K.R. (1990). *The Physical Self-Perception Profile manual.* DeKalb, IL: Office for Health Promotion, Northern Illinois University.

Fox, K.R., & Corbin, C.B. (1989). The Physical Self-Perception Profile: Development and preliminary validation. *Journal of Sport and Exercise Psychology, 11,* 408-430.

Harter, S. (1985). *Manual for the Self-Perception Profile for Children.* Denver: University of Denver.

Hattie, J. (1992). *Self-concept.* Hillsdale, NJ: Erlbaum.

James, W. (1890/1963). *The principles of psychology.* New York: Holt, Reinhart & Winston.

Jones, R.J.A., Polman, R.C.J., & Peters, D.M. (2009). Physical self-perceptions of adolescents in years 8, 9, and 10 in independent schools, state comprehensive schools and specialist sport colleges in England. *Physical Education and Sport Pedagogy, 14,* 109-124.

Lindwall, M., Aşçi, F.H., Palmeira, A., Fox, K.R., & Hagger, M.S. (2011). The importance of importance in the physical self: Support for the theoretically appealing but empirically elusive model of James. *Journal of Personality, 79*(2), 303–334.

Maïano, C., Morin, A.J.S., Ninot, G., Monthuy-Blanc, J., Stephan, Florent, J-F., & Vallée, P. (2008). A short and very short form of the Physical Self-Inventory for adolescents: Development and factor validity. *Psychology of Sport and Exercise, 9,* 830-847.

Marsh, H.W. (1990). Causal ordering of academic self-concept and academic achievement: A multiwave, longitudinal panel analysis. *Journal of Educational Psychology, 82,* 646-656.

Marsh, H.W. (1993). The multidimensional structure of physical fitness: Invariance over gender and age. *Research Quarterly for Exercise and Sport, 64,* 256-273.

Marsh, H.W. (1994). Sport motivation orientations: Beware of the jingle-jangle fallacies. *Journal of Sport and Exercise Psychology, 16,* 365-380.

Marsh, H.W. (1996a). Construct validity of Physical Self-Description Questionnaire responses: Relations to external criteria. *Journal of Sport and Exercise Psychology, 18,*111-131.

Marsh, H.W. (1996b). Physical-Self Description Questionnaire: Stability and discriminant validity. *Research Quarterly for Exercise and Sport, 67,* 249-264.

Marsh, H.W. (1997). The measurement of physical self-concept: A construct validation approach. In K. Fox (Ed.), *The physical self-concept: From motivation to well-being* (pp. 27-58). Champaign, IL: Human Kinetics.

Marsh, H.W. (2002). A multidimensional physical self-concept: A construct validity approach to theory, measurement, and research. *Psychology: The Journal of the Hellenic Psychological Society, 9,* 459-493.

Marsh, H.W. (2007). *Self-concept theory, measurement and research into practice: The role of self-concept in educational psychology.* Leicester, UK: British Psychological Society.

Marsh, H.W., Bar-Eli, M., Zach, S., & Richards, G.E. (2006). Construct validation of Hebrew versions of three physical self-concept measures: An extended multitrait-multimethod analysis. *Journal of Sport and Exercise Psychology, 28,* 310-343.

Marsh, H.W., Chanal, J.P., Sarrazin, P.G., & Bois, J.E. (2006). Self-belief does make a difference: A reciprocal effects model of the causal ordering of physical self-concept and gymnastics performance *Journal of Sport Sciences, 24,* 101-111.

Marsh, H.W., & Craven, R.G. (2006). Reciprocal effects of self-concept and performance from a multidimensional perspective. Beyond seductive pleasure and unidimensional perspectives. *Perspectives on Psychological Science, 1,* 133-163.

Marsh, H.W., Ellis, L., Parada, L., Richards, G., & Heubeck, B.G. (2005). A short version of the Self-Description Questionnaire II: Operationalizing criteria for short-form evaluation with new applications of confirmatory factor analyses. *Psychological Assessment, 17,* 81-102.

Marsh, H.W., Gerlach, E., Trautwein, U., Lüdtke, U., Brettschneider, W.-D. (2007). Longitudinal study of preadolescent sport self-concept and performance: Reciprocal effects and causal ordering. *Child Development, 78,* 1640-1656.

Marsh, H.W., & Hattie, J. (1996). Theoretical perspectives on the structure of self-concept. In B.A. Bracken (Ed.), *Handbook of self-concept* (pp 38-90). New York: Wiley.

Marsh, H.W., Hey, J., Johnson, S., & Perry, C. (1997). Elite Athlete Self-Description Questionnaire: Hierarchical confirmatory factor analysis of responses by two distinct groups of elite athletes. *International Journal of Sport Psychology, 28,* 237-258.

Marsh, H.W., Hey, J., Roche, L.A., & Perry, C. (1997). The structure of physical self-concept: Elite athletes and physical education students. *Journal of Educational Psychology, 89,* 369-380.

Marsh, H.W., Martin, A.J., & Jackson, S. (2010). *Introducing a short version of the Physical Self-Description Questionnaire: New strategies, short-form evaluative criteria, and applications of factor analyses.* Oxford, UK: SELF Research Centre, Oxford University.

Marsh, H.W., Papaioannou, A., & Theodorakis, Y. (2004). *Causal ordering of physical self-concept and exercise behavior: Mediated, moderated, spurious effects and the influence of physical education teachers.* Australia: SELF Research Centre, University of Western Sydney.

Marsh, H.W., & Peart, N. (1988). Competitive and cooperative physical fitness training programs for girls: Effects on physical fitness and on multidimensional self-concepts. *Journal of Sport and Exercise Psychology, 10,* 390-407.

Marsh, H.W., & Perry, C. (2005). Does a positive self-concept contribute to winning gold medals in elite swimming? The causal ordering of elite athlete self-concept and championship performances. *Journal of Sport and Exercise Psychology, 27,* 71-91.

Marsh, H.W., Perry, C., Horsely, C., & Roche, L.A. (1995). Multidimensional self-concepts of elite athletes: How do they differ from the general population? *Sport and Exercise Psychology, 17,* 70-83.

Marsh, H.W., & Richards, G.E. (1988). The Tennessee Self-Concept Scales: Reliability, internal structure, and construct validity. *Journal of Personality and Social Psychology, 55,* 612-624.

Marsh, H.W., Richards, G.E., Johnson, S., Roche, L., & Tremayne, P. (1994). Physical Self-Description Questionnaire: Psychometric properties and a multitrait-multimethod analysis of relations to existing instruments. *Sport and Exercise Psychology, 16,* 270-305.

Marsh, H.W., Walker, R., & Debus, R. (1991). Subject-specific components of academic self-concept and self-efficacy. *Contemporary Educational Psychology, 16,* 1-345.

Masse, C., Jung, J., & Pfister, R. (2001). Agressivité, impulsivité et estime de soi (Aggression, impulsiveness, and self-esteem). *Sciences et Techniques des Activités Physiques et Sportives, 56,* 33-42.

Ninot, G., Delignières, D., & Fortes, M. (2000). L' évaluation de l'estime de soi dans le domaine corporel (Assessment of the physical self). *Sciences et Techniques des Activités Physiques et Sportives, 53,* 35-48.

Ostrow, A.C. (1990). *Directory of psychological tests in the sport and exercise sciences.* Morgantown, WV: Fitness Information Technology.

Ostrow, A.C. (1996). *Directory of psychological tests in the sport and exercise sciences* (2nd ed.). Morgantown, WV: Fitness Information Technology.

Page, A., Ashford, B., Fox, K., & Biddle, S. (1993). Evidence of cross-cultural validity for the Physical Self-Perception Profile. *Personality and Individual Differences, 14,* 585-590.

Raustorp, A., Mattsson, E., Svensson, K., & Ståhle, A. (2006). Physical activity, body composition and physical self-esteem:

A 3-year follow-up study among adolescents in Sweden. *Scandinavian Journal of Medicine and Science in Sports, 16,* 258-266.

Raustorp, A., Ståhle, A., Gudasic, H., Kinnunen, A., & Mattsson, E. (2005). Physical activity and self-perception in school children assessed with the Children and Youth Physical Self-Perception Profile. *Scandinavian Journal of Medicine and Science in Sports, 15,* 126-134.

Richards, G.E. (1988). *Physical Self-Concept Scale.* Sydney: Australian Outward Bound Foundation.

Richards, G.E. (2004). *We are born and we die. But what happens in-between? A study of the physical self-concept of males and females across the age span.* Presented at the 3rd International SELF Conference, Max Planck Institute, Berlin.

Richards, G.E., & Marsh, H.W. (2005, November). *Physical self-concept as an important outcome in physical education classes: Evaluation of the usefulness in physical education of three physical self concept measures utilising a database of Australian and Israeli Students.* Presented at the Australian Association for Research in Education Annual Conference 2005 Creative Dissent: Constructive solutions, Sydney, Australia.

Rosenberg, M. (1965). *Society and the adolescent self-image.* Princeton, NJ: Princeton University Press.

Seligman, M.E.P., & Csikszentmihalyi, M. (2000). Positive psychology: An introduction. *American Psychologist, 55,* 5-14.

Shavelson, R.J., Hubner, J.J., & Stanton, G.C. (1976). Validation of construct interpretations. *Review of Educational Research, 46,* 407-441.

Smith, G.T., McCarthy, D.M., & Anderson, K.G. (2000). On the sins of short-form development. *Psychological Assessment, 12,* 102-111.

Sonstroem, R.J. (1978). Physical estimation and attraction scales: Rationale and research. *Medicine and Science in Sport, 10,* 97-102.

Sonstroem, R.J. (1997). The physical self-system: A mediator of exercise and self-esteem. In K.R. Fox (Ed.), *The physical self* (pp. 3-26). Champaign, IL: Human Kinetics.

Sonstroem, R.J., Harlow, L.L., & Josephs, L. (1994). Exercise and self-esteem: Validity of model expansion and exercise associations. *Journal of Sport and Exercise Psychology, 16,* 29-42.

Sonstroem, R.J., & Potts, S.A. (1996). Life adjustment correlates of physical self-concepts. *Medicine and Science in Sport and Exercise, 28,* 619-625.

Sonstroem, R.J., Speliotis, E.D., & Fava, J.L. (1992). Perceived physical competence in adults: An examination of the Physical Self-Perception Profile. *Journal of Sport and Exercise Psychology, 4,* 207-221.

Stephan, Y., Bilard, J., Ninot, G., & Delignières, D. (2003). Bodily transition out of elite sport: A one-year study of physical self and global self-esteem among transitional athletes. *International Journal of Sport and Exercise Psychology, 1,* 192-207.

Stephan, Y., & Maïano, C. (2007). On the social nature of global self-esteem: A replication study. *Journal of Social Psychology, 147,* 573-575.

Valentine, J.C., DuBois, D.L., & Cooper, H. (2004). The relations between self-beliefs and academic achievement: A systematic review. *Educational Psychologist, 39,* 111-133.

Vallerand, R.J., Blanchard, C., Mageau, G.A., Koestner, R., Ratelle, C., Leonard, M., Gagne, M., & Marsolais, J. (2003). Les passions de l'ame: On obsessive and harmonious passion. *Journal of Personality and Social Psychology, 85,* 756-767.

Welk, G.J., Corbin, C.B., Dowell, M.N., & Harris, H. (1997). The validity and reliability of two different versions of the Chil-dren and Youth Physical Self-Perception Profile. *Measurement in Physical Education and Exercise Science, 1,* 163-177.

Welk, G.J., Corbin, C.B., & Lewis, L.A. (1995). Physical self-perceptions of high school athletes. *Pediatric Exercise Science, 7,* 152-161.

Welk, G.J., & Eklund, B. (2005). Validation of the Children and Youth Physical Self-Perceptions Profile for young children. *Psychology of Sport and Exercise, 6,* 51-65.

Wells, L.E., & Marwell, G. (1976). *Self-esteem: Its conceptualization and measurement.* Beverly Hills, CA: Sage.

Whitehead, J.R. (1995). A study of children's physical self-perceptions using an adapted Physical Self-Perception Profile questionnaire. *Pediatric Exercise Science, 7,* 132-151.

Wichstrom, L. (1995). Harter's Self-Perception Profile for adolescents: Reliability, validity, and evaluation of the question format. *Journal of Personality Assessment, 65,* 100-116.

Wylie, R.C. (1974). *The self-concept* (Vol. 1). Lincoln, NE: University of Nebraska Press.

Wylie, R.C. (1979). *The self-concept* (Vol. 2). Lincoln, NE: University of Nebraska Press.

Wylie, R.C. (1989). *Measures of self-concept.* Lincoln, NE: University of Nebraska Press.

Chapter 21

Aloise-Young, P.A., Hennigan, K.M., & Leong, C.W. (2001). Possible selves and negative health behaviors during early adolescence. *Journal of Early Adolescence, 21,* 158-181.

Anderson, D.F., & Cychosz, C.M. (1994). Development of an exercise identity scale. *Perceptual and Motor Skills, 78,* 747-751.

Anderson, D.F., & Cychosz, C.M. (1995). Exploration of the relationship between exercise behavior and exercise identity. *Journal of Sport Behavior, 18,* 159-166.

Anderson, D.F., Cychosz, C.M., & Franke, W.D. (1998). Association of exercise identity with measures of exercise commitment and physiological indicators of fitness in a law enforcement cohort. *Journal of Sport Behavior, 21,* 233-241.

Anderson, D.F., Cychosz, C.M., & Franke, W.D. (2001). Preliminary exercise identity scale (EIS) norms for three adult samples. *Journal of Sport Behavior, 24,* 1-9.

Asci, F.H., Eklund, R.C., Whitehead, J.R., Kirazci, S., & Koca, C. (2005). Use of the CY_PSPP in other cultures: A preliminary investigation of its factorial validity for Turkish children and youth. *Psychology of Sport and Exercise, 6,* 33-50.

Bandura, A. (1997). *Self-efficacy: The exercise of control.* New York: Freeman.

Bannister, D., & Fransella, F. (1971). *Inquiring Man.* Harmondsworth: Penguin.

Banting, L.K., Dimmock, J.A., & Lay, B.S. (2009). The role of implicit and explicit components of exerciser self-schema in the prediction of exercise behavior. *Psychology of Sport and Exercise, 10,* 80-86.

Bem, D.J. (1972). Self-perception theory. In L. Berkowitz (Ed.), *Advances in experimental social psychology* (pp. 1-62). New York: Academic Press.

Berry, T.R. (2006). Who's even interested in the exercise message? Attentional bias for exercise and sedentary-lifestyle related words. *Journal of Sport and Exercise Psychology, 28,* 4-17.

Bond, K.A., & Batey, J. (2005). Running for their lives: A qualitative analysis of the exercise experience of female recreational runners. *Women in Sport and Physical Activity Journal, 14,* 69-82.

Brettschneider, W., & Heim, R. (1997). Identity, sport, and youth development. In K. Fox (Ed.), *The physical self: From motivation to well-being* (pp. 205-227). Champaign, IL: Human Kinetics.

Brewer, B.W., Van Raalte, J.L., & Linder, D.E. (1993). Athletic identity: Hercules' muscles or Achilles heel? *International Journal of Sports Psychology, 24,* 237-254.

Burke, P.J. (2006). Identity change. *Social Psychology Quarterly, 69,* 81-96.

Cardinal, B.J., & Cardinal, M.K. (1997). Changes in exercise behavior and exercise identity associated with a 14-week aerobic exercise class. *Journal of Sport Behavior, 20,* 377-387.

Carver, C.S., & Scheier, M.F. (1982). Control theory: A useful conceptual framework for personality-social, clinical, and health psychology. *Journal of Personality and Social Psychology, 53,* 1178-1191.

Crocker, P.R.E., Eklund, R.C., & Kowalski, K.C. (2000). Children's physical activity and physical self-perceptions. *Journal of Sports Sciences, 18,* 383-394.

Crocker, P.R.E., Sabiston, C.M., Forrester, S., Kowalski, N., Kowalski, K.C., & McDonough, M.H. (2003). Examining change in physical activity, dietary restraint, BMI, social physique anxiety and physical self-perceptions in adolescent girls. *Canadian Journal of Public Health, 94,* 332-337.

Crocker, P.R.E., Sabiston, C.M., Kowalski, K.C., McDonough, M.H., & Kowalski, N.P. (2006). Longitudinal assessment of the relationship between physical self-concept and health-related behavior and emotion in adolescent girls. *Journal of Applied Sport Psychology, 18,* 185-200.

Cross, S.E., & Markus, H. (1991). Possible selves across the lifespan. *Human Development, 34,* 230-255.

Cross, S.E., & Markus, H. (1994). Self-schemas, possible selves, and component performance. *Journal of Educational Psychology, 86,* 423-438.

Deci, E.L., & Ryan, R.M. (1985). *Intrinsic motivation and self-determination in human behavior.* New York: Plenum Press.

Deci, E.L., & Ryan, R.M. (1995). Human autonomy: The basis for true self-esteem. In M. Kernis (Ed.), *Efficacy, agency, and self-esteem* (pp. 31-49). New York: Plenum Press.

Deci, E.L., & Ryan, R.M. (2008). Self-determination theory: A macrotheory of human motivation, development, and health. *Canadian Psychology, 49,* 182-185.

Dishman, R.K., Hales, D.P., Pfeiffer, K.A., Felton, G., Saunders, R., Ward, D., Dowda, M., & Pate, R.R. (2006). Physical self-concept and self-esteem mediate cross-sectional relations of physical activity and sport participation with depression symptoms among adolescent girls. *Health Psycholoy, 25,* 396-407.

Dunkel, C.S., Kelts, D., & Coon, B. (2006). Possible selves as mechanisms of change in therapy. In C. Dunkel & J. Kerpelman (Eds.), *Possible selves: Theory, research, and applications* (pp. 187-204). Hauppauge, NY: Nova Science.

Dunton, G.F., Jamner, M.S., & Cooper, D.M. (2003). Physical self-concept in adolescent girls: Behavioral and physiological correlates. *Research Quarterly for Exercise and Sport, 74,* 360-365.

Eccles, J.S., & Wigfield, A. (2002). Motivational beliefs, values, and goals. *Annual Review of Psychology, 53,* 109-132.

Eklund, R.C., Whitehead, J.R., & Welk, G. (1997). Validity of the children's Physical Self-Perception Profile: A confirmatory factor analysis. *Research Quarterly for Exercise and Sport, 68,* 249-256.

Estabrooks, P., & Courneya, K.S. (1997). Relationships among self-schema, intention, and exercise behavior. *Journal of Sport and Exercise Psychology, 19,* 156-168.

Fiske, S.T., & Taylor, S.E. (1984). *Social cognition.* New York: Random House.

Fox, K.R. (1990). The Physical Self-Perception manual. DeKalb, IL: Northern Illinois University, Office of Health Promotion.

Fox, K.R. (Ed.). (1997). *The physical self: From motivation to well-being.* Champaign, IL: Human Kinetics.

Fox, K.R., & Corbin, C.B. (1989). The physical self-perception profile: Development and preliminary validation. *Journal of Sport and Exercise Psychology, 11,* 408-430.

Greenwald, A.G., & Banaji, M.R. (1995). Implicit social cognition: Attitudes, self-esteem, and stereotypes. *Psychological Review, 102,* 4-27.

Hagger, M.S., Biddle, S.H., & Wang, C.K. (2005). Physical self-concept in adolescence: Generalizability of a multidimensional, hierarchical model across gender and grade. *Educational and Psychological Measurement, 65,* 297-322.

Hardcastle, S., & Taylor, A.H. (2005). Finding an exercise identity in an older body: "It's redefining yourself and working out who you are." *Psychology of Sport and Exercise, 6,* 173-188.

Harter, S. (1978). Effectance motivation reconsidered. *Human Development, 21,* 34-64.

Harter, S. (1985). *Manual for the Self-Perception Profile for Children.* Denver: University of Denver.

Harter, S. (1990). Causes, correlates, and the functional role of global self-worth: A lifespan perspective. In R.J. Sternberg & J. Kolligan (Eds.), *Competence considered* (pp. 67-97). New York: Vail-Ballou Press.

Harter, S. (1999). *The construction of the self: A developmental perspective.* New York: Guilford Press.

James, W. (1892). *Psychology: The briefer course.* New York: Henry Holt.

Kendzierski, D. (1988). Self-schemata and exercise. *Basic and Applied Social Psychology, 9,* 45-59.

Kendzierski, D. (1990). Exercise self-schemata: Cognitive and behavioral correlates. *Health Psychology, 9*(1), 69-82.

Kendzierski, D. (1994). Schema theory: An information processing focus. In R.K. Dishman (Ed.), *Advances in exercise adherence* (pp. 137-159). Champaign, IL: Human Kinetics.

Kendzierski, D., Furr, R.M., & Schiavoni, J. (1998). Physical activity self-definitions: Correlates and perceived criteria. *Journal of Sport and Exercise Psychology, 20,* 176-193.

Kendzierski, D., & Morganstein, M.S. (2009). Test, revision, and cross-validation of the physical activity self-defintion model. *Journal of Sport and Exercise Psychology, 31,* 484-504.

Kendzierski, D., & Sheffield, A. (2000). Self-schema and attributions for an exercise lapse. *Basic and Applied Social Psychology, 22,* 1-8.

Kendzierski, D., Sheffield, A., & Morganstein, M.S. (2002). The role of self-schema in attributions for own versus other's exercise lapse. *Basic and Applied Social Psychology, 24,* 251-260.

Kowalski, K.C., Crocker, P.R.E., Kowalski, N.P., Chad, K.E., & Humbert, M.L. (2003). Examining the physical self in adolesent girls over time: Further evidence against the hierarchical model. *Journal of Sport and Exercise Psychology, 25,* 5-18.

Lantz, C.D., Rhea, D.J., & Mesnier, K. (2004). Eating attitudes, exercise identity, and body alienation in competitive ultramarathoners. *International Journal of Sport Nutrition and Exercise Metabolism, 14,* 406-418.

Leary, M.R., & Tangney, J.P. (2003). The self as an organizing construct in the behavioral and social sciences. In M.R. Leary

& J.P. Tangney (Eds.), *Handbook of self and identity* (pp. 3-14). New York: Guilford Press.

Long, B.C., & Flood, K.R. (1993). Coping with work stress: Psychological benefits of exercise. *Work & Stress, 7,* 109-119.

Magnus, C.M.R., Kowalski, K.C., & McHugh, T.F. (2009). The role of self-compassion in women's self-determined motives to exercise and exercise-related outcomes. *Self and Identity, 9,* 363-382.

Marcus, H. (1977). Self-schemata and processing information about the self. *Journal of Personality and Social Psychology, 35,* 63-78.

Marcus, H., & Nurius, P.S. (1987). Possible selves: The interface between motivation and the self-concept. In K. Yardley & T. Honess (Eds.), *Self and identity: Psychosocial perspectives* (pp. 159-172). New York: Wiley.

Markus, H., & Nurius, P.S. (1986). Possible selves. *American Psychologist, 41,* 954-969.

Marsh, H.W. (1989). Age and sex effects in multiple dimensions of self-concept: Preadolescence to early-childhood. *Journal of Educational Psychology, 81,* 417-430.

Marsh, H.W. (1994a). Sport motivation orientations: Beware of the jingle-jangle fallacies. *Journal of Sport and Exercise Psychology, 16,* 365-380.

Marsh, H.W. (1994b). The importance of being important: Theoretical models of relations between specific and global components of physical self-concept. *Journal of Sport and Exercise Psychology, 16,* 306-325.

Marsh, H.W. (1997). The measurement of physical self-concept: A construct validation approach. In K.R. Fox (Ed.), *The physical self: From motivation to well-being* (pp. 27-58). Champaign, IL: Human Kinetics.

Marsh, H.W., Marco, I.T., & Asci, F.H. (2002). Cross cultiral validity of the Physical Self-Description Questionnaire: Comparison of factor structures in Australia, Spain and Turkey. *Research Quarterly for Exercise and Sport, 73,* 257-270.

Marsh, H.W., Richards, G.E., Johnson, S., Roche, L., & Tremayne, P. (1994). Physical Self-Description Questionnaire: Psychometric properties and a multitrait-multimethod analysis of relations to existing instruments. *Journal of Sport and Exercise Psychology, 16,* 270-305.

Marsh, H.W., & Sonstroem, R.J. (1995). Importance ratings and specific components of physical self-concept: Relevance to predicting global components of physical self-concept and exercise. *Journal of Sport and Exercise Psychology, 17,* 84-104.

Marsh, H.W., & Yeung, A.S. (1998). Top-down, bottom-up, and horizontal models: The direction of causality in multidimensional, hierarchical self-concept models. *Journal of Personality and Social Psychology, 75,* 509-527.

McDonough, M.H., Sabiston, C.M., & Crocker, P.R.E. (2008). An interpretive phenomenological examination of psychosocial changes among breast cancer survivors in their first season of dragon boating. *Journal of Applied Sport Psychology, 20,* 445-440.

Messick, S. (1995). Validity of psychological assessment: Validation of inferences from persons' responses and performances as scientific inquiry into score meaning. *American Psychologist, 50,* 741-749.

Miller, K.H., Ogletree, R.J., & Welshimer, K. (2002). Impact of activity behaviors on physical activity identity and self-efficacy. *American Journal of Health Behavior, 26*(5), 323-330.

Moreno, R.W., & Cervello, E. (2005). Physical self-perception in Spanish adolescents: Gender and involvement in physical activity. *Journal of Human Movement Studies, 48,* 291-311.

Neff, K.D. (2003). Self-compassion: An alternative conceptualization of a healthy attitude toward oneself. *Self and Identity, 2,* 85-101.

Neff, K.D. (2004). Self-compassion and psychological well-being. *Constructivism in the Human Sciences, 9,* 27-37.

Nurius, P.S. (1991). Possible selves and social support: Social cognitive resources for coping and striving. In J.A. Howard & P.L. Callero (Eds.), *The self-society dynamic: Cognition, emotion, and action* (pp. 239-258). Cambridge: Cambridge University Press.

Ouellette, J.A., Hessling, R., Gibbons, F.X., Reis-Bergan, M., & Gerrard, M. (2005). Using images to increase exercise behavior: Prototypes versus possible selves. *Personality and Social Psychology Bulletin, 31,* 610-620.

Oyserman, D., & Fryberg, S. (2006). Possible selves of diverse adolescents: Content and function across gender, race, and national origin. In C. Dunkel & J. Kerpelman (Eds.), *Possible selves: Theory, research and application* (pp. 17-40). Hauppauge, NY: Nova Science.

Oyserman, D., & Markus, H. (1990). Possible selves and delinquency. *Journal of Personality and Social Psychology, 59,* 112-125.

Page, A., Ashford, B., Fox, K.R., & Biddle, S. (1993). Evidence of cross-cultural validity for the Physical Self-Perception Profile. *Personality and Individual Differences, 14,* 585-590.

Robbins, L.B., Pis, M.B., Pender, N.J., & Kazanis, A.S. (2004). Physical activity self-definition among adolescents. *Research and Theory for Nursing Practice, 18,* 317-330.

Ryan, R.M., & Brown, K.W. (2003). Why we don't need self-esteem: On fundamental needs, contingent love, and mindfulness. *Psychological Inquiry, 14,* 71-76.

Ryan, R.M., & Deci, E.L. (2000). Self-determination theory and the facilitation of intrinsic motivation, social development, and well-being. *American Psychologist, 55,* 68-78.

Sabiston, C.M., McDonough, M.H., & Crocker, P.R.E. (2007). Psychosocial experiences of breast cancer survivors involved in a dragon boat program: Exploring links to positive psychological growth. *Journal of Sport and Exercise Psychology, 29,* 419-438.

Shavelson, R.J., Hubner, J.J., & Stanton, G.C. (1976). Self-concept: Validation of construct interpretations. *Review of Educational Research, 46,* 407-411.

Sheeran, P., & Orbell, S. (2000). Self-schemas and the theory of planned behavior. *European Journal of Social Psychology, 30,* 533-550.

Sonstroem, R.J. (1997). The physical self-system: A mediator of exercise and self-esteem. In K.R. Fox (Ed.), *The physical self: From motivation to well-being* (pp. 3-26). Champaign, IL: Human Kinetics.

Sonstroem, R.J., Harlow, L.L., & Josephs, L. (1994). Exercise and self-esteem: Validity of model expansion and exercise associations. *Journal of Sport and Exercise Psychology, 16,* 29-42.

Sonstroem, R.J., & Morgan, W.P. (1989). Exercise and self-esteem: Rationale and model. *Medicine and Science in Sport and Exercise, 21,* 329-337.

Sonstroem, R.J., & Potts, S.A. (1996). Life adjustment correlates of physical self-concepts. *Medicine and Science in Sport and Exercise, 28,* 619-625.

Storer, J.H., Cychosz, C.M., & Anderson, D.F. (1997). Wellness behaviors, social identities, and health promotion. *American Journal of Health Behavior, 21,* 260-269.

Strachan, S.M., & Brawley, L.R. (2008). Reactions to a perceived challenge to identity: A focus on exercise and healthy eating. *Journal of Health Psychology, 13,* 575-588.

Strachan, S.M., Woodgate, J., Brawley, L.R., & Tse, A. (2005). The relationship of self-efficacy and self-identity to long-term maintenance of vigorous physical activity. *Journal of Applied Biobehavioral Research, 10*(2), 98-112.

Stryker, S. (1987). Identity theory: Developments and extensions. In K. Yardley & T. Honess (Eds.), *Self and identity: Psychosocial perspectives* (pp. 89-103). New York: Wiley.

Stryker, S., & Burke, P.J. (2000). The past, present, and future of an identity theory. *Social Psychology Quarterly, 63*(4), 284-297.

Whaley, D.E. (2003). Future-oriented self-perceptions and exercise behavior in middle-aged women. *Journal of Aging and Physical Activity, 11*, 1-17.

Waterman, A.S. (1985). *Identity in adolescence: Process and contents.* San Fracisco: Jossey-Bass.

Welk, G.J., & Eklund, R.C. (2005). Validation of the Children and Youth Physical Self-Perceptions Profile for young children. *Psychology of Sport and Exercise, 6*, 51-65.

Whaley, D.E., & Ebbeck, V. (2002). Self-schemata and exercise identity in older adults. *Journal of Aging and Physical Activity, 10*, 245-259.

Whaley, D.E., & Redding, T. (2001). Turning want to into will do. *Melpomene Journal, 20*, 22-26.

Whitehead, J.R. (1995). A study of children's physical self-perceptions using an adapted physical self-perception questionnaire. *Pediatric Exercise Science, 7*, 133-152.

Wylie, R. (1974). *The self-concept: A review of methodological considerations and measuring instruments* (Vol. 1). Lincoln, NE: University of Nebraska.

Yin, Z., & Boyd, M.P. (2000). Behavioral and cognitive correlates of exercise self-schemata. *The Journal of Psychology, 134*, 269-282.

Chapter 22

Ajzen, I. (1985). From intentions to actions: A theory of planned behavior. In J. Kuhi & J. Beckmann (Eds.), *Action control: From cognition to behavior* (pp. 11-39). New York: Springer.

Ajzen, I., & Madden, T.J. (1986). Prediction of goal-directed behavior: Attitudes, intentions, and perceived behavioral control. *Journal of Experimental Social Psychology, 22*(5), 453-474.

Allison, K.R., Dwyer, J.J.M., & Makin, S. (1999). Perceived barriers to physical activity among high school students. *Preventive Medicine, 28*(6), 608-615.

Anderson, E.S., Wojcik, J.R., Winett, R.A., & Williams, D.M. (2006). Social-cognitive determinants of physical activity: The influence of social support, self-efficacy, outcome expectations, and self-regulation among participants in a church-based health promotion study. *Health Psychology, 25*(4), 510-520.

Annesi, J.J. (2007). Relations of changes in exercise self-efficacy, physical self-concept, and body satisfaction with weight changes in obese white and African American women initiating a physical activity program. *Ethnicity and Disease, 17*(1), 19-22.

Armitage, C.J., & Conner, M. (1999). Distinguishing perceptions of control from self-efficacy: Predicting consumption of a low-fat diet using the theory of planned behavior. *Journal of Applied Social Psychology, 29*(1), 72-90.

Armitage, C.J., & Conner, M. (2001). Efficacy of the theory of planned behaviour: A meta-analytic review. *British Journal of Social Psychology, 40*, 471-499.

Armstrong, C.A., Sallis, J.F., Hovell, M.F., & Hofstetter, C.R. (1993). Stages of change, self efficacy, and the adoption of vigorous exercise: A prospective analysis. *Journal of Sport and Exercise Psychology, 15*, 390-402.

Bandura, A. (1977). Self-efficacy: Toward a unifying theory of behavioral change. *Psychological Review, 84*(2), 191-215.

Bandura, A. (1986). *Social foundations of thought and action: A social cognitive theory.* Englewood Cliffs, NJ: Prentice Hall.

Bandura, A. (1992). Self-efficacy mechanism in psychobiologic functioning. In R. Schwarzer (Ed.), *Self-efficacy: Thought control of action* (pp. 355-394). Washington DC: Hemisphere.

Bandura, A. (1997). *Self-efficacy: The exercise of control.* New York: Freeman.

Bandura, A. (2000). Health promotion from the perspective of social cognitive theory. In P. Norman, C. Abraham, & M. Conner (Eds.), *Understanding and changing health behaviour* (pp. 299-339). Reading, UK: Harwood.

Bandura, A. (2004). Health promotion by social cognitive means. *Health Education and Behavior, 31*, 143-164.

Bandura, A. (2006). Guide for constructing self-efficacy scales. In F. Pajares & T. Urdan (Eds.),

Adolescence and education: Vol. 5. Self-efficacy beliefs of adolescents (pp. 307-337). Greenwich, CT: Information Age.

Biddle, S.J.H. (2000). Emotion, mood and physical activity. In S.J.H. Biddle, K.R. Fox, & S.H. Boutcher (Eds.), *Physical activity and psychological well-being* (pp. 63-87). New York: Routledge.

Blanchard, C.M., Rodgers, W.M., Courneya, K.S., Daub, B., & Knapik, G. (2002). Does barrier efficacy mediate the gender-exercise adherence relationship during Phase II cardiac rehabilitation? *Rehabilitation Psychology, 47*(1), 106-120.

Bozoian, S., Rejeski, W.J., & McAuley, E. (1994). Self-efficacy influences feeling states associated with acute exercise. *Journal of Sport and Exercise Psychology, 16*, 326-333.

Brown, D.W., Balluz, L.S., Heath, G.W., Moriarty, D.G., Ford, E.S., Giles, W.H., & Mokdad, A.H. (2003). Associations between recommended levels of physical activity and health-related quality of life findings from the 2001 Behavioral Risk Factor Surveillance System (BRFSS) survey. *Preventive Medicine, 37*(5), 520-528.

Chen, G., Gully, S.M., & Eden, D. (2001). Validation of a new general self-efficacy scale. *Organizational Research Methods, 4*, 62-83.

Clark, D.O., Patrick, D.L., Grembowski, D., & Durham, M.L. (1995). Socioeconomic status and exercise self-efficacy in late life. *Journal of Behavioral Medicine, 18*(4), 355-376.

Craft, L.L., & Landers, D.M. (1998). The effect of exercise on clinical depression: A meta-analysis. *Medicine and Science in Sports and Exercise, 30*(5), 117.

Demark-Wahnefried, W., Peterson, B., McBride, C., Lipkus, I., & Clipp, E. (2000). Current health behaviors and readiness to pursue life-style changes among men and women diagnosed with early stage prostate and breast carcinomas. *Cancer, 88*(3), 674-684.

DuCharme, K.A., & Brawley, L.R. (1995). Predicting the intentions and behavior of exercise initiates using two forms of self-efficacy. *Journal of Behavioral Medicine, 18*(5), 479-497.

Duncan, T.E., & McAuley, E. (1993). Social support and efficacy cognitions in exercise adherence: A latent growth curve analysis. *Journal of Behavioral Medicine, 16*(2), 199-218.

Dwyer, J.J.M., Allison, K.R., & Makin, S. (1998). Internal structure of a measure of self-efficacy in physical activity among high school students. *Social Science and Medicine, 46*(9), 1175-1182.

Edmundson, E., Parcel, G.S., Feldman, H.A., Elder, J., Perry, C.L., Johnson, C.C., Williston, B.J., Stone, E.J., Yang, M., Lytel, L., & Webber, L. (1996). The effects of the Child and Adolescent Trial for Cardiovascular Health upon psychological determinants of diet and physical activity behavior. *Preventive Medicine, 25,* 442-454.

Elavsky, S., & McAuley, E. (2007). Exercise and self-esteem in menopausal women: A randomized controlled trial involving walking and yoga. *American Journal of Health Promotion, 22*(2), 83-92.

Elavsky, S., McAuley, E., Motl, R.W., Konopack, J.F., Marquez, D.X., Hu, L., Jerome, G.J., & Diener, E. (2005). Physical activity enhances long-term quality of life in older adults: Efficacy, esteem, and affective influences. *Annals of Behavioral Medicine, 30*(2), 138-145.

Ewart, C.K., & Taylor, C.B. (1985). The effects of early postmyocardial infarction exercise testing on subsequent quality of life. *Quality of Life and Cardiovascular Care, 1,* 162-175.

Feltz, D.L. (1994). Self-confidence and performance. In D. Druckman & R.A. Bjork (Eds.), *Learning, remembering, believing: Enhancing human performance* (pp. 173-206). Washington, DC: National Academy Press.

Fox, K.R. (1999). The influence of physical activity on mental well-being. *Public Health Nutrition, 2*(3A), 411-418.

Garcia, A.W., & King, A.C. (1991). Predicting long-term adherence to aerobic exercise: A comparison of two models. *Journal of Sport and Exercise Psychology, 13,* 394-410.

Grembowski, D., Patrick, D., Diehr, P., Durham, M., Beresford, S., Kay, E., & Hecht, J. (1993). Self-efficacy and health behavior among older adults. *Journal of Health and Social Behavior, 34,* 89-104.

Haskell, W.L., & Lee, I. (2007). Physical activity and public health: Updated recommendation for adults from the American College of Sports Medicine and the American Heart Association. *Circulation, 116.*

Hickey, M.L., Owen, S.V., & Froman, R.D. (1992). Instrument development: Cardiac diet and exercise self-efficacy. *Nursing Research, 41*(6), 347-351.

Hu, L., McAuley, E., & Elavsky, S. (2005). Does the Physical Self-Efficacy Scale assess self-efficacy or self-esteem? *Journal of Sport and Exercise Psychology, 27*(2), 152-170.

Jerome, G.J., Marquez, D.X., McAuley, E., Canaklisova, S., Snook, E., & Vickers, M. (2002). Self-efficacy effects on feeling states in women. *International Journal of Behavioral Medicine, 9*(2), 139-154.

Keysor, J.J. (2003). Does late-life physical activity or exercise prevent or minimize disablement? A critical review of the scientific evidence. *American Journal of Preventive Medicine, 25,* 129-136.

Konopack, J.F., Marquez, D.X., Hu, L., Elavsky, S., McAuley, E., & Kramer, A.F. (2008). Correlates of functional fitness in older adults. *International Journal of Behavioral Medicine, 15*(4), 311-318.

Laaksonen, D.E., Lindstrom, J., Lakka, T.A., Eriksson, J.G., Niskanen, L., Wikstrom, K., Aunola, S., Keinanen-Kiukaanniemi, S., Laakso, M., & Valle, T.T. (2005). Physical activity in the prevention of type 2 diabetes: The Finnish diabetes prevention study. *American Diabetes Association, 54,* 158-165.

Lee, I. (2003). Physical activity and cancer prevention—data from epidemiologic studies. *Medicine and Science in Sports and Exercise, 35*(11), 1823.

Li, F., Harmer, P., McAuley, E., Fisher, K.J., Duncan, T.E., & Duncan, S.C. (2002). Tai chi, self-efficacy, and physical function in the elderly. *Prevention Science, 2*(4), 229-239.

Maddux, J.E. (1995). Self-efficacy: An introduction. In J.E. Maddux (Ed.), *Self-efficacy, adaptation, and adjustment: Theory, research and application.* New York: Plenum Press.

Marcus, B.H., Selby, V.C., Niaura, R.S., & Rossi, J.S. (1992). Self-efficacy and the stages of exercise behavior change. *Research Quarterly for Exercise and Sport, 63,* 60-66.

Marquez, D.X., Jerome, G.J., McAuley, E., Snook, E.M., & Canaklisova, S. (2002). Self-efficacy manipulation and state anxiety responses to exercise in low active women. *Psychology & Health, 17*(6), 783-791.

Marquez, D.X., & McAuley, E. (2006). Social cognitive correlates of leisure time physical activity among Latinos. *Journal of Behavioral Medicine, 29*(3), 281-289.

McAuley, E. (1992). The role of efficacy cognitions in the prediction of exercise behavior in middle-aged adults. *Journal of Behavioral Medicine, 15*(1), 65-88.

McAuley, E. (1993). Self-efficacy and the maintenance of exercise participation in older adults. *Journal of Behavioral Medicine, 16*(1), 103-113.

McAuley, E., & Blissmer, B. (2000). Self-efficacy determinants and consequences of physical activity. *Exercise and Sports Science Reviews, 28*(2), 85-88.

McAuley, E., Courneya, K.S., & Lettunich, J. (1991). Effects of acute and long-term exercise on self-efficacy responses in sedentary, middle-aged males and females. *The Gerontologist, 31*(4), 534.

McAuley, E., Courneya, K.S., Rudolph, D.L., & Lox, C.L. (1994). Enhancing exercise adherence in middle-aged males and females. *Preventive Medicine, 23*(4), 498.

McAuley, E., Doerksen, S.E., Morris, K.S., Motl, R.W., Hu, L., Wojcicki, T.R., White, S.M., & Rosengren, K.R. (2008). Pathways from physical activity to quality of life in older women. *Annals of Behavioral Medicine, 36*(1), 13-20.

McAuley, E., Elavsky, S., Jerome, G.J., Konopack, J.F., & Marquez, D.X. (2005). Physical activity-related well-being in older adults: Social cognitive influences. *Psychology and Aging, 20*(2), 295-302.

McAuley, E., Elavsky, S., Motl, R.W., Konopack, J.F., Hu, L., & Marquez, D.X. (2005). Physical activity, self-efficacy, and self-esteem: Longitudinal relationships in older adults. *Journals of Gerontology Series B: Psychological Sciences and Social Sciences, 60*(5), P268-P275.

McAuley, E., Jerome, G.J., Elavsky, S., Marquez, D.X., & Ramsey, S.N. (2003). Predicting long-term maintenance of physical activity in older adults. *Preventive Medicine, 37*(2), 110-118.

McAuley, E., Jerome, G.J., Marquez, D.X., Elavsky, S., & Blissmer, B. (2003). Exercise self-efficacy in older adults: Social, affective, and behavioral influences. *Annals of Behavioral Medicine, 25*(1), 1-7.

McAuley, E., Konopack, J.F., Morris, K.S., Motl, R.W., Hu, L.A., Doerksen, S.E., & Rosengren, K. (2006). Physical activity and functional limitations in older women: Influence of self-efficacy. *Journals of Gerontology Series B: Psychological Sciences and Social Sciences, 61*(5), P270-P277.

McAuley, E., Konopack, J.F., Motl, R.W., Morris, K.S., Doerksen, S.E., & Rosengren, K.R. (2006). Physical activity and quality of life in older adults: Influence of health status and self-efficacy. *Annals of Behavioral Medicine, 31*(1), 99-103.

McAuley, E., Mailey, E.L., Mullen, S.P., Szabo, A.N., Wojcicki, T.R., White, S.M., Gothe, N., Olson, E.A., & Kramer, A.F. (2011). Growth trajectories of exercise self-efficacy in older adults: Influence of measures and initial status. *Health Psychology, 30,* 75-83.

McAuley, E., & Mihalko, S.L. (1998). Measuring exercise-related self-efficacy. In J.L. Duda (Ed.), *Advances in sport and exercise psychology measurement* (pp. 371-390). Morgantown, WV: Fitness Information Technology.

McAuley, E., & Morris, K.S. (2007). State of the art review: Advances in physical activity and mental health: Quality of life. *American Journal of Lifestyle Medicine, 1*(5), 389-396.

McAuley, E., Morris, K.S., Doerksen, S.E., Motl, R.W., Hu, L., White, S.M., Wojcicki, T.R., & Rosengren, K. (2007). Effects of change in physical activity on physical function limitations in older women: Mediating roles of physical function performance and self-efficacy. *Journal of the American Geriatrics Society, 55*(12), 1967.

McAuley, E., Morris, K.S., Motl, R.W., Hu, L., Konopack, J.F., & Elavsky, S. (2007). Long-term follow-up of physical activity behavior in older adults. *Health Psychology, 26*(3), 375-380.

McAuley, E., Motl, R.W., Morris, K.S., Hu, L., Doerksen, S.E., Elavsky, S., & Konopack, J.F. (2007). Enhancing physical activity adherence and well-being in multiple sclerosis: A randomised controlled trial. *Multiple Sclerosis, 13*(5), 652-659.

McAuley, E., Talbot, H.M., & Martinez, S. (1999). Manipulating self-efficacy in the exercise environment in women: Influences on affective responses. *Health Psychology, 18*(3), 288-294.

Morris, K.S., McAuley, E., & Motl, R.W. (2008). Self-efficacy and environmental correlates of physical activity among older women and women with multiple sclerosis. *Health Education Research, 23*(4), 744-752.

Motl, R.W., Dishman, R.K., Trost, S.G., Saunders, R.P., Dowda, M., Felton, G., Ward, D.S., & Pate, R.R. (2000). Factorial validity and invariance of questionnaires measuring social-cognitive determinants of physical activity among adolescent girls. *Preventive Medicine, 31*, 584-594.

Motl, R.W., & McAuley, E. (2009a). Longitudinal analysis of physical activity and symptoms as predictors of change in functional limitations and disability in multiple sclerosis. *Rehabilitation Psychology, 54*(2), 204-210.

Motl, R.W., & McAuley, E. (2009b). Symptom cluster as a predictor of physical activity in multiple sclerosis: Preliminary evidence. *Journal of Pain and Symptom Management, 38*, 270-280.

Motl, R.W., McAuley, E., & Snook, E.M. (2007). Physical activity and quality of life in multiple sclerosis: Possible roles of social support, self-efficacy, and functional limitations. *Rehabilitation Psychology, 52*(2), 143.

Motl, R.W., & Snook, E.M. (2008). Physical activity, self-efficacy, and quality of life in multiple sclerosis. *Annals of Behavioral Medicine, 35*(1), 111-115.

Motl, R.W., Snook, E.M., McAuley, E., & Gliottoni, R.C. (2006). Symptoms, self-efficacy, and physical activity among individuals with multiple sclerosis. *Research in Nursing and Health, 29*(6), 597-606.

Motl, R.W., Snook, E.M., McAuley, E., Scott, J.A., & Gliottoni, R.C. (2007). Are physical activity and symptoms correlates of functional limitations and disability in multiple sclerosis? *Rehabilitation Psychology, 52*(4), 463.

Oliver, K., & Cronan, T.A. (2005). Correlates of physical activity among women with fibromyalgia syndrome. *Annals of Behavioral Medicine, 29*(1), 44-53.

Plotnikoff, R.C., & Higginbotham, N. (2002). Protection motivation theory and exercise behaviour change for the prevention of coronary heart disease in a high-risk, Australian representative community sample of adults. *Psychology, Health, and Medicine, 7*(1), 87-98.

Rejeski, W.J., Ettinger, W.H., Martin, K., & Morgan, T. (1998). Treating disability in knee osteoarthritis with exercise therapy: A central role for self-efficacy and pain. *Arthritis Care and Research, 11*(2), 94-101.

Rejeski, W.J., & Mihalko, S.L. (2001). Physical activity and quality of life in older adults. *Journals of Gerontology Series A: Biological Sciences and Medical Sciences, 56*, 23-35.

Resnick, B., & Jenkins, L.S. (2000). Testing the reliability and validity of the Self-Efficacy for Exercise Scale. *Nursing Research, 49*(3), 154-159.

Resnick, B., & Nigg, C. (2003). Testing a theoretical model of exercise behavior for older adults. *Nursing Research, 52*(2), 80-88.

Rogers, L., Courneya, K.S., Verhulst, S., Markwell, S., Lanzotti, V., & Shah, P. (2006). Exercise barrier and task self-efficacy in breast cancer patients during treatment. *Supportive Care in Cancer, 14*(1), 84-90.

Rogers, L.Q., McAuley, E., Courneya, K.S., & Verhulst, S.J. (2008). Correlates of physical activity self-efficacy among breast cancer survivors. *American Journal of Health Behavior, 32*(6), 594-603.

Rovniak, L.S., Anderson, E.S., Winett, R.A., & Stephens, R.S. (2002). Social cognitive determinants of physical activity in young adults: A prospective structural equation analysis. *Annals of Behavioral Medicine, 24*(2), 149-156.

Rudolph, D.L., & McAuley, E. (1996). Self-efficacy and perceptions of effort: A reciprocal relationship. *Journal of Sport and Exercise Psychology, 18*, 216-223.

Ryckman, R.M., Robbins, M.A., Thornton, B., & Cantrell, P. (1982). Development and validation of a physical self-efficacy scale. *Journal of Personality and Social Psychology, 42*(5), 891-900.

Sallis, J.F., Pinski, R.B., Grossman, R.M., Patterson, T.L., & Nader, P.R. (1988). The development of self-efficacy scales for health-related diet and exercise behaviors. *Health Education Research, 3*(3), 283-292.

Saunders, R.P., Pate, R.R., Felton, G., Dowda, M., Weinrich, M.C., Ward, D.S., Parsons, M.A., & Baranowski, T. (1997). Development of questionnaires to measure psychosocial influences on children's physical activity. *Preventive Medicine, 26*, 241-247.

Schwarzer, R., & Jerusalem, M. (1995). Generalized self-efficacy scale. In J. Weinman, S. Wright, & M. Johnston (Eds.), *Measures in health psychology: A user's portfolio, causal and control beliefs* (pp. 35-37). Windsor, UK: NFER-Nelson.

Seeman, T., & Chen, X. (2002). Risk and protective factors for physical functioning in older adults with and without chronic conditions: MacArthur studies of successful aging. *Journals of Gerontology Series B: Psychological Sciences and Social Sciences, 57B*(3), S135-S144.

Seeman, T.E., Unger, J.B., McAvay, G., & Mendes de Leon, C.F. (1999). Self-efficacy beliefs and perceived declines in functional ability: MacArthur studies of successful aging. *Journals of Gerontology Series: Psychological Sciences and Social Sciences, 54*(4), P214-P222.

Sesso, H.D., Paffenbarger, R.S., & Lee, I.M. (2000). Physical activity and coronary heart disease in men in the Harvard Alumni Health Study. *American Heart Association, 102*, 975-980.

Sherer, M., Maddux, J.E., Mercadante, B., Prentice-Dunn, S., Jacobs, B., & Rogers, R.W. (1982). The self-efficacy scale: Construction and validation. *Psychological Reports, 51*, 663-671.

Shin, Y.H., Jang, H.J., & Pender, N.J. (2001). Psychometric evaluation of the Exercise Self-Efficacy Scale among Korean adults with chronic diseases. *Research in Nursing and Health, 24*, 68-76.

Sonstroem, R.J., Harlow, L.L., & Josephs, L. (1994). Exercise and self-esteem: Validity of model expansion and exercise associations. *Journal of Sport and Exercise Psychology, 16,* 29-29.

Stewart, A.L. (2003). Conceptual challenges in linking physical activity and disability research. *American Journal of Preventive Medicine, 25,* 137-140.

Taylor, A.H. (2000). Physical activity, anxiety and stress. In S.J.H. Biddle, K.R. Fox, & S.H. Boutcher (Eds.), *Physical activity and psychological well-being* (pp. 10-45). New York: Routledge.

Taylor-Piliae, R.E., & Froelicher, E.S. (2004). Measurement properties of tai chi exercise self-efficacy among ethnic Chinese with coronary heart disease risk factors: A pilot study. *European Journal of Cardiovascular Nursing, 3,* 287-294.

Treasure, D.C., Newbery, D.M., Helsen, W.F., Hodges, N.J., Starkes, J.L., Hung, T.M., Hatfield, B.D., Lawton, G.W., Saarela, P., & Hayashi, S.W. (1998). Relationship between self-efficacy, exercise intensity, and feeling states in a sedentary population during and following an acute bout of exercise. *Journal of Sport and Exercise Psychology, 20,* 1-11.

Trost, S.G., Sallis, J.F., Pate, R.R., Freedson, P.S., Taylor, W.C., & Dowda, M. (2003). Evaluating a model of parental influence on youth physical activity. *American Journal of Preventive Medicine, 25*(4), 277-282.

U.S. Department of Health and Human Services. (2008). *2008 Physical activity guidelines for Americans.* www.health.gov/paguidelines/guidelines/default.aspx.

White, S.M., Wójcicki, T.R., & McAuley, E. (2009). Physical activity and quality of life in community dwelling older adults. *Health and Quality of Life Outcomes, 7*(1), 10.

Wójcicki, T.R., White, S.M., & McAuley, E. (2009). Assessing outcome expectations in older adults: The Multidimensional Outcome Expectations for Exercise Scale. *Journals of Gerontology Series B: Psychological Sciences and Social Sciences, 64*(1), 33-40.

Chapter 23

Bandura, A. (1977). Self-efficacy: Toward a unifying theory of behavioral change. *Psychological Review, 84,* 191-215.

Bandura, A. (1986). *Social foundations of thought and action: A social cognitive theory.* Englewood Cliffs, NJ: Prentice Hall.

Bandura, A. (1990). Perceived self-efficacy in the exercise of personal agency. *Journal of Applied Sport Psychology, 2,* 128-163.

Bandura, A. (1997). *Self-efficacy: The exercise of control.* New York: Freeman.

Bandura, A. (2006). Guide for creating self-efficacy scales. In F. Pajares & T. Urdan (Eds.), *Self-efficacy beliefs of adolescents* (pp. 307-337). Greenwich, CT: Information Age.

Bandura, A., Adams, N.E., & Beyer, J. (1977). Cognitive processes mediating behavioral change. *Journal of Personality and Social Psychology, 35,* 125-139.

Bandura, A., & Locke, E.A. (2003). Negative self-efficacy and goal effects revisited. *Journal of Applied Psychology, 88,* 87-99.

Bray, S.R. (2004). Collective efficacy, group goals, and group performance of a muscular endurance task. *Small Group Research, 35,* 230-238.

Bray, S.R., & Widmeyer, W.N. (2000). Athletes' perceptions of the home advantage: An investigation of perceived causal factors. *Journal of Sport Behavior, 23,* 1-10.

Cervone, D. (1985). Randomization tests to determine significance levels for microanalytic congruences between self-efficacy and behavior. *Cognitive Therapy and Research, 9,* 357-365.

Chow, G.M., & Feltz, D.L. (2008). Exploring new directions in collective efficacy and sport. In

M. Beauchamp & M. Eys (Eds.), *Group dynamics advances in sport and exercise psychology: Contemporary themes.* London: Routledge.

Dithurbide, L., Sullivan, P.J., & Chow, G.M. (2009). Examining the influence of team-referent causal attributions and team performance on collective efficacy: A multilevel analysis. *Small Group Research, 40,* 491-507.

Edmonds, W.A., Tenenbaum, G., Kamata, A., & Johnson, M.B. (2009). The role of collective efficacy in adventure racing teams. *Small Group Research, 40,* 163-180.

Feltz, D.L. (1982). A path analysis of the causal elements in Bandura's theory of self-efficacy and an anxiety-based model of avoidance behavior. *Journal of Personality and Social Psychology, 42,* 764-781.

Feltz, D.L. (1988). Self-confidence and sports performance. In K.B. Pandolf (Ed.), *Exercise and sport sciences reviews* (pp. 423-457). New York: Macmillan.

Feltz, D.L., & Chase, M.A. (1998). The measurement of self-efficacy and confidence in sport. In J. Duda (Ed.), *Advancements in sport and exercise psychology measurement* (pp. 63-78). Morgantown, WV: Fitness Information Technology.

Feltz, D.L., Chase, M.A., Moritz, S.A., & Sullivan, P.J. (1999). A conceptual model of coaching efficacy: Preliminary investigation and instrument development. *Journal of Educational Psychology, 91,* 765-776.

Feltz, D.L., Chow, G.M., & Hepler, T.J. (2008). Path analysis of self-efficacy and performance revisited. *Journal of Sport and Exercise Psychology, 30,* 401-411.

Feltz, D.L., & Lirgg, C.D. (1998). Perceived team and player efficacy in hockey. *Journal of Applied Psychology, 83,* 557-564.

Feltz, D.L., & Lirgg, C.D. (2001). Self-efficacy beliefs of athletes, teams and coaches. In R.N. Singer, H.A. Hausenblas, & C.M. Janelle (Eds.), *Handbook of sport psychology* (2nd ed., pp. 340-361). New York: Wiley.

Feltz, D.L., & Riessinger, D.A. (1990). Effects on in vivo emotive imagery and performance feedback on self-efficacy and muscular endurance. *Journal of Sport and Exercise Psychology, 12,* 132-143.

Feltz, D.L., Short, S.E., & Sullivan, P.J. (2008). *Self-efficacy in sport: Research and strategies for working with athletes, teams, and coaches.* Champaign, IL: Human Kinetics.

Feltz, D.L., & Wood, J.M. (2009). Can self-doubt be beneficial to performance? Exploring the concept of preparatory efficacy. *The Open Sports Sciences Journal, 2,* 65-70.

Frank, J.D. (1935). Individual differences in certain aspects of the level of aspiration. *American Journal of Psychology, 47,* 119-128.

George, T.R., & Feltz, D.L. (1995). Motivation in sport from a collective efficacy perspective. *International Journal of Sport Psychology, 26,* 98-116.

Greenlees, I.A., Nunn, R.L., Graydon, J.K., & Maynard, I.A. (1999). The relationship between collective efficacy and precompetitive affect in rugby players: Testing Bandura's model of collective efficacy. *Perceptual and Motor Skills, 89,* 431-440.

Gully, S.M., Incalcaterra, K.A., Joshi, A., & Beaubien, J.M. (2002). A meta-analysis of team-efficacy, potency, and performance: Interdependence and level of analysis as moderators of observed relationships. *Journal of Applied Psychology, 87,* 819-832.

Harter, S. (1981). The development of competence motivation in the master of cognitive and physical skills: Is there still a place for joy? In G.C. Roberts & D.M. Landers (Eds.), *Psychology of motor behavior and sport, 1980* (pp. 3-29). Champaign, IL: Human Kinetics.

Heuze, J.P., Raimbault, N., & Fontayne, P. (2006). Relationships between cohesion, collective efficacy, and performance in professional basketball teams: Investigating mediating effects. *Journal of Sports Sciences, 24,* 59-68.

Hu. L., McAuley, E., & Elavsky, E. (2005). Does the Physical Self-Efficacy Scale assess self-efficacy or self-esteem? *Journal of Sport and Exercise Psychology, 27,* 152-170.

James, L.R. (1982). Aggregation bias in estimates of perceptual agreement. *Journal of Applied Psychology, 67,* 219-229.

Kozub, S.A., & McDonnell, J.F. (2000). Exploring the relationship between cohesion and collective efficacy in rugby teams. *Journal of Sport Behavior, 23,* 120-129.

Maddux, J.E. (1995). Self-efficacy theory: An introduction. In J.E. Maddux (Ed.), *Self-efficacy, adaptation, and adjustment: Theory, research, and application* (pp. 3-33). New York: Plenum Press.

Magyar, T.M., Feltz, D.L., & Simpson, I.P. (2004). Individual and crew level determinants of collective efficacy in rowing. *Journal of Sport and Exercise Psychology, 26,* 136-153.

Manzo, L.G., Silva, J.M., & Mink, R. (2001). The Caroline Sport Confidence Inventory. *Journal of Applied Sport Psychology, 13,* 260-274.

Martens, R., Vealey, R.S., & Burton, D. (1990). *Competitive anxiety in sport.* Champaign, IL: Human Kinetics.

Moritz, S.E. (1998). *The effect of task type on the relationship between efficacy beliefs and performance.* Unpublished doctoral dissertation, Michigan State University, East Lansing.

Moritz, S.E., Feltz, D.L., Fahrbach, K.R., & Mack, D.E. (2000). The relation of self-efficacy measures to sport performance: A meta-analytic review. *Research Quarterly for Exercise and Sport, 71,* 280-294.

Moritz, S.E., & Watson, C.B. (1998). Levels of analysis issues in group psychology. Using efficacy as an example of a multi-level model. *Group Dynamics: Theory, Research, and Practice, 2,* 285-298.

Myers, N.D., & Feltz, D.L. (2007). From self-efficacy to collective efficacy in sport: Transitional issues. In G. Tenenbaum & R.C. Eklund (Eds.), *Handbook of sport psychology* (3rd ed., pp. 799-819). New York: Wiley.

Myers, N.D., Feltz, D.L., & Short, S.E. (2004). Collective efficacy and team performance: A longitudinal study of collegiate football teams. *Group Dynamics: Theory, Research, and Practice, 8,* 126-138.

Myers, N.D., Payment, C.A., & Feltz, D.L. (2004). Reciprocal relationships between collective efficacy and team performance in women's ice hockey. *Group Dynamics: Theory, Research, and Practice, 8,* 182-195.

Nicholls, J.G. (1984). Achievement motivation: Conception of ability, subjective experience, task choice, and performance. *Psychological Review, 91,* 328-346.

Paskevich, D.M., Brawley, L.R., Dorsch, K.D., & Widmeyer, W.N. (1999). Relationship between collective efficacy and team cohesion: Conceptual and measurement issues. *Group Dynamics: Theory, Research, and Practice, 3,* 210-222.

Prussia, G.E., & Kinicki, A.J. (1996). A motivational investigation of group effectiveness using social cognitive theory. *Journal of Applied Psychology, 81,* 187-198.

Raudenbush, S.W., & Bryk, A.S. (2002). *Hierarchical linear models: Applications and data analysis methods.* Newbury Park, CA: Sage.

Rosenberg, M. (1965). *Society and the adolescent self-image.* Princeton, NJ: Princeton University Press.

Rousseau, D.M. (1985). Issues of level in organizational research: Multi-level and cross-level perspectives. *Research in Organizational Behavior, 7,* 1-37.

Ryckman, R., Robbins, M., Thornton, B., & Cantrell, P. (1982). Development and validation of a physical self-efficacy scale. *Journal of Personality and Social Psychology, 42,* 891-900.

Samuels, S.M., & Gibb, R.W. (2002). Self-efficacy assessment and generalization in physical education courses. *Journal of Applied Social Psychology 32,* 1314-1327.

Shea, G.P., & Guzzo, R.A. (1987). Groups as human resources. In K.M. Rowland & G.R. Ferris (Eds.), *Research in personnel and human resources management* (Vol. 5, pp. 323-356). Greenwich, CT: JAI Press.

Short, S.E., Apostal, K., Harris, C., Poltavski, D., Young, J., Zostautas, N., Sullivan, P., & Feltz, D.L. (2002). Assessing collective efficacy: A comparison of two approaches. *Journal of Sport and Exercise Psychology, 24,* S115-S116.

Short, S.E., Sullivan, P.J., & Feltz, D.L. (2005). Development and preliminary validation of the Collective Efficacy Questionnaire for Sports. *Measurement in Physical Education and Exercise Science, 9,* 181-202.

Stajkovic, A.D., Lee, D., & Nyberg, A.J. (2009). Collective efficacy, group potency, and group performance: Meta-analyses of their relationship, and test of a mediation model. *Journal of Applied Psychology, 94,* 814-828.

Steiner, I.D. (1972). *Group processes and group productivity.* New York: Academic.

Treasure, D.C., Monson, J., & Lox, C.L. (1996). Relationship between self-efficacy, wrestling performance, and affect prior to competition. *The Sport Psychologist, 10,* 73-83.

Vealey, R.S. (1986). Conceptualization of sport-confidence and competitive orientation: Preliminary investigation and instrument development. *Journal of Sport Psychology, 8,* 221-246.

Zaccaro, S.J., Blair, V., Peterson, C., & Zazanis, M. (1995). Collective efficacy. In J.E. Maddux (Ed.), *Self-efficacy, adaptation, and adjustment: Theory, research, and application* (pp. 308-330). New York: Plenum Press.

Zimmerman, B.J., & Cleary, T.J. (2006). Adolescents' development of personal agency: The role of self-efficacy beliefs and self-regulatory skill. In F. Pajares & T. Urdan (Ed.), *Self-efficacy beliefs of adolescents* (pp. 45-69). Greenwich, CT: Information Age.

Chapter 24

American College of Sports Medicine. (1998). Position stand: The recommended quantity and quality of exercise for developing and maintaining cardiorespiratory and muscular fitness in healthy adults. *Medicine and Science in Sports and Exercise, 30,* 975-991.

Andreacci, J.L., Robertson, R.J., Goss, F.L., Randall, C.R., & Tessmer, K.A. (2004). Frequency of verbal encouragement effects sub-maximal exertional perceptions during exercise testing in young adult women. *Medicine and Science in Sports and Exercise, 36,* S133.

Baden, D.A., McLean, T.L., Tucker, R., Noakes, T.D., & St. Clair Gibson, A. (2005). Effect of anticipation during unknown or unexpected exercise duration on rating of perceived exertion, affect, and physiological function. *British Journal of Sports Medicine, 39,* 742-746.

Barkley, J.E., & Roemmich, J.N. (2008). Validity of the CALER and OMNI-bike ratings of perceived exertion. *Medicine and Science in Sports and Exercise, 40,* 760-766.

Bar-Or, O. (1977). Age related changes in exercise prescription. In G. Borg (Ed.), *Physical work and effort* (pp. 101-102). Oxford, UK: Pergamon Press.

Baumeister, R.F. (1982). A self-presentational view of social phenomena. *Psychological Bulletin, 91,* 3-26.

Beedie, C.J., Coleman, D.A., & Foad, A.J. (2007) Positive and negative placebo effects resulting from the deceptive administration of an ergogenic aid. *International Journal of Sports Nutrition and Exercise Metabolism, 17,* 259-269.

Borg, E. (2007). *On perceived exertion and its measurement.* Unpublished doctoral dissertation, University of Stockholm, Sweden.

Borg, G. (1961a). Perceived exertion in relation to physical work load and pulse-rate. *Kungliga Fysiografiska Sallskapets I Lund Forhandlingar, 31,* 105-115.

Borg, G. (1961b). Interindividual scaling and perception of muscular force. *Kungliga Fysiografiska Sallskapets I Lund Forhandlingar, 31,* 117-125.

Borg, G. (1962). Physical performance and perceived exertion. *Studia Psychologia et Pedagogica, 11,* 1-35.

Borg, G. (1971). The perception of physical performance. In R.J. Shephard (Ed.), *Frontiers of fitness* (pp. 280-294). Springfield, IL: Charles C Thomas.

Borg, G. (1973a). *A note on category scale with ratio properties for estimating perceived exertion* (Reports From the Institute of Applied Psychology, No. 36). Stockholm: University of Stockholm.

Borg, G. (1973b). Perceived exertion: A note on "history" and methods. *Medicine and Science in Sports, 5,* 90-93.

Borg, G. (1978). Psychological assessment of physical effort. In *Proceedings of the 1978 International Symposium on Psychological Assessment in Sport* (pp. 49-57). Netanya, Israel: Wingate Institute for Physical Education and Sport.

Borg, G. (1982). Psychophysiological bases of perceived exertion. *Medicine and Science in Sports and Exercise, 14,* 377-381.

Borg, G. (1998). *Borg's perceived exertion and pain scales.* Champaign, IL: Human Kinetics.

Borg, G. (2004). *The Borg CR10 Scale folder. A method for measuring intensity of experience.* Hasselby, Sweden: Borg Perception.

Boutcher, S.H., Fleischer-Curtian, L.A., & Gines, S.D. (1988). The effects of self-presentation on perceived exertion. *Journal of Sport and Exercise Psychology, 10,* 270-280.

British Association of Sport and Exercise Sciences. (1997). *Sport and exercise physiology testing guidelines* (3rd ed.). Leeds, UK: British Association of Sport and Exercise Sciences.

Buckley, J., Eston, R., & Sim, J. (2000). Ratings of perceived exertion in braille: Validity and reliability in production mode. *British Journal of Sports Medicine, 34,* 297-302.

Chen, M.J., Fan, X., & Moe, S.T. (2002). Criterion-related validity of the Borg ratings of perceived exertion scale in healthy individuals: A meta-analysis. *Journal of Sport Sciences, 20,* 873-899.

Clark, V.R., Hopkins, W.G., Hawley, J.A., & Burke, L.M. (2000). Placebo effect of carbohydrate feeding during a 40-km cycling time trial. *Medicine and Science in Sports and Exercise, 32,* 1642-1647.

Corbett, J., Vance, S., Lomax, M., Martin, M., & Barwood, J. (2009). Measurement frequency influences the rating of perceived exertion during sub-maximal treadmill running. *European Journal of Applied Physiology, 106,* 311-313.

Demura, S., & Nagasawa, Y. (2003). Relations between perceptual and physiological response during incremental exercise followed by an extended bout of submaximal exercise on a cycle ergometer. *Perceptual and Motor Skills, 96,* 653-663.

Dunbar, C.C., Robertson, R.J., Baun, R., Blandin, M.F., Metz, K., Burdett, R., & Goss, F.L. (1992). The validity of regulating exercise intensity by ratings of perceived exertion. *Medicine and Science in Sports and Exercise, 24,* 94-99.

Ekkekakis, P. (2003). Pleasure and displeasure from the body: Perspectives from exercise. *Cognition and Emotion, 17,* 213-239.

Ekkekakis, P. (2005). The study of affective responses to acute exercise: The dual-mode model. In R. Stelter & K.K. Roessler (Eds.), *New approaches to sport and exercise psychology* (pp. 119-146). Oxford, UK: Meyer & Meyer Sport.

Ekkekakis, P., **Hall, E.E.**, & Petruzzello, S.J. (2005). Variation and universality in affective responses to physical activity of varying intensities: An alternative perspective on dose-response based on evolutionary considerations. *Journal of Sport Sciences, 23*(5), 477-500.

Ekkekakis, P., & Lind, E. (2005). The dual-mode model of affective responses to exercise of varying intensities: A new perspective on the dose-response relationship. In T. Morris (Ed.), *Proceedings of the 11th World Congress of Sport Psychology.* Sydney, Australia: International Society of Sport Psychology.

Esteve-Lanao, J., Lucia, A., deKoning, J.J., & Foster, C. (2008). How do humans control physiological strain during strenuous endurance exercise? *PLoS One, 3*(8), e2943. doi:10.1371/journal.pone.0002943.

Eston, R.G., Davies, B.L., & Williams, J.G. (1987). Use of perceived effort ratings to control exercise intensity in young healthy adults. *European Journal of Applied Physiology and Occupational Physiology, 56*(2), 222-224.

Eston, R.G., Lamb, K.L., Bain, A., Williams, A.M, & Williams, J.G. (1994). Validity of a perceived exertion scale for children: A pilot study. *Perceptual and Motor Skills, 78,* 691-697.

Eston, R.G., & Parfitt, C.G. (2006). Effort perception. In N. Armstrong (Ed.), *Paediatric exercise physiology* (pp. 275-298). London: Elsevier.

Eston, R.G., Parfitt, G., Campbell, L., & Lamb, K.L. (2000). Reliability of effort perception for regulating exercise intensity in children using the Cart and Load Effort Rating (CALER) scale. *Pediatric Exercise Science, 12,* 388-397.

Eston, R.G., & Williams, J.G. (1988). Reliability of ratings of perceived effort regulation of exercise intensity. *British Journal of Sports Medicine, 22*(4), 153-155.

Faulkner, J., & Eston, R.G. (2008). Perceived exertion research in the 21st century: Developments, reflections and questions for the future. *Journal of Exercise Science and Fitness, 6*(1), 1-14.

Fechner, G.T. (1860). *Elemente der Psychophysik* [Elements of Psychophysics] (D. Howes & E.G. Borin, Eds.). New York: Holt, Reinhart & Winston.

Finsen, L., Søgaard, K., Jensen, C., Borg, V., & Christensen, H. (2001). Muscle activity and cardiovascular response during computer-mouse work with and without memory demands. *Ergonomics, 44,* 1312-1329.

Focht, B.C., & Koltyn, K.F. (1999). Influence of resistance exercise of different intensities on state anxiety and blood pressure. *Medicine and Science in Sports and Exercise, 31,* 456-463.

Gamberale, F. (1985). Perception of exertion. *Ergonomics, 26,* 299-308.

Garcin, M., Vautier, J., Vandewalle, H., Wolff, M., & Monod, H. (1998). Ratings of perceived exertion (RPE) during cycling exercises at constant power output. *Ergonomics, 41,* 1500-1509.

Green, J.M., Crews, T.R., Bosak, A.M., & Peveler, W.W. (2003). Overall and differentiated ratings of perceived exertion at the respiratory compensation threshold: Effects of gender and mode. *European Journal of Applied Physiology, 89,* 445-450.

Groslambert, A., & Mahon, A.D. (2006). Perceived exertion: Influence of age and cognitive development. *Sports Medicine, 36,* 911-928.

Hall, E.E., Ekkekakis, P., & Petruzzello, S.J. (2005). Is the relationship of RPE to psychological factors intensity-dependent? *Medicine and Science in Sports and Exercise, 37,* 1365-1373.

Hardy, C.J., Hall, E.G., & Prestholdt, P.H. (1986). The mediational role of social influence in the perception of exertion. *Journal of Sport Psychology, 8,* 88-104.

Hardy, C.J., & Rejeski, W.J. (1989). Not what, but how one feels: The measurement of affect during exercise. *Journal of Sport and Exercise Psychology, 11,* 304-317.

Hochstetler, S.A., Rejeski, W.J., & Best, D.L. (1985). The influence of sex-role orientation on ratings of perceived exertion. *Sex Roles, 12,* 825-835.

Hutchinson, J.C., Sherman, T., Martinovic, N., & Tenenbaum, G. (2008). The effect of manipulated self-efficacy on perceived and sustained effort. *Journal of Applied Sport Psychology, 4,* 457-472.

Hutchinson, J.C., & Tenenbaum, G. (2006). Perceived effort—can it be considered Gestalt? *Psychology of Sport and Exercise, 7,* 463-476.

Hutchinson, J.C., & Tenenbaum, G. (2007). Attention focus during physical effort: The mediating role of task intensity. *Psychology of Sport and Exercise, 8,* 233-245.

Irving, B.A., Rutkowski, J., Brock, D.W., Davis, C.K., Barrett, E.J., Gaesser, G.A., & Weltman, A. (2006). Comparison of Borg- and OMNI-RPE as markers of the blood lactate response to exercise. *Medicine and Science in Sports and Exercise, 38,* 1348-1352.

Jones, L.A. (1986). Perception of force and weight: Theory and research. *Psychological Bulletin, 100,* 29-42.

Karageorghis, C.I., & Terry, P.C. (1997). The psychophysical effects of music in sport and exercise: A review. *Journal of Sport Behavior, 20,* 54-68.

Kang, J., Hoffman, J.R., Walker, H., Chaloupka, E.C., & Utter, A.C. (2003). Regulating intensity using perceived exertion during extended exercise periods. *European Journal of Applied Physiology, 89,* 475-482.

King, P.M., & Finet, M. (1994). Determining the accuracy of the psychophysical approach to grip force measurement. *Journal of Hand Therapy, 17,* 412-416.

Kinsman, R.A., & Weiser, P.C. (1976). Subjective symptomatology during work and fatigue. In E. Simonson & P.L. Weises (Eds.), *Psychological aspects of fatigue* (pp. 336-405). Springfield, IL: Charles C Thomas.

Lagally, K.M., & Robertson, R.J. (2006). Construct validity of the OMNI resistance exercise scale. *Journal of Strength and Conditioning Research, 20,* 252-256.

Lamb, K.L. (1995). Children's ratings of effort during cycle ergometry: An examination of the validity of the two effort rating scales. *Pediatric Exercise Science, 7,* 407-421.

Lamb, K.L., & Eston, R.G. (1997). Effort perception in children. *Sports Medicine, 23,* 139-148.

Lamb, K.L., Eston, R.G., & Corns, D. (1999). Reliability of ratings of perceived exertion during progressive treadmill exercise. *British Journal of Sports Medicine, 33,* 336-339.

Leung, M.L., Chung, P.K., & Leung, R.W. (2002). An assessment of the validity and reliability of two perceived exertion rating scales among Hong Kong children. *Perceptual and Motor Skills, 95,* 1047-1062.

Litt, M.D. (1988). Self-efficacy and perceived control: Cognitive mediators of pain tolerance. *Journal of Personality and Social Psychology, 54,* 149-160.

Lowe, B.D. (1995). Repeatability of magnitude production in isometric, hand-grip force estimation: A working-memory approach. *Perceptual and Motor Skills, 80,* 659-667.

Mahon, A.D., Gay, J.A., & Stolen, K.Q. (1998). Differentiated ratings of perceived exertion at ventilatory threshold in children and adults. *European Journal of Applied Physiology, 18,* 115-120.

Maresh, C., & Noble, B.J. (1984). Utilization of perceived exertion ratings during exercise testing and training. In L.K. Hall (Ed.), *Cardiac rehabilitation: Exercise testing and prescription* (pp. 155-173). Great Neck, NY: Spectrum.

Marino, F.E., Lambert, M.I., & Noakes, T.D. (2004). Superior performance of African runners in warm humid but not in cool environmental conditions. *Journal of Applied Physiology, 96,* 124-130.

Marinov, B., Mandadjieva, S., & Kostianev, S. (2008). Pictorial and verbal category-ratio scales for effort estimation in children. *Child: Care, Health and Development, 34,* 35-43.

Marcora, S.M. (2008). Do we really need a central governor to explain brain regulation of exercise performance? *European Journal of Applied Physiology, 104,* 929-933.

Marks, L.E. (1974). *Sensory processes: The new psychophysics.* New York: Academic Press.

Marriott, H.E., & Lamb, K.L. (1996). The use of ratings of perceived exertion for regulating exercise levels in rowing ergometry. *European Journal of Applied Physiology and Occupational Physiology, 72(3),* 267-271.

Marsh, A.P., & Martin, P.E. (1998). Perceived exertion and the preferred cycling cadence. *Medicine and Science in Sports and Exercise, 30,* 942-948.

Marshall, M.M., Armstrong, T.J., & Ebersole, M.L. (2004). Verbal estimation of peak exertion intensity. *Human Factors, 46,* 697-710.

McAuley, E., & Courneya, K.S. (1992). Self-efficacy relationships with affective and exertion responses to exercise. *Journal of Applied Social Psychology, 22,* 312-326.

Melzack, R. (1973). *The puzzle of pain.* New York: Basic Books.

Melzack, R., & Casey, K.L. (1968). Sensory motivational and central control determinants of pain: A new conceptual model. In D. Kenshalo (Ed.), *The skin senses* (pp. 423-443). Springfield, IL: Charles C Thomas.

Melzack, R., & Wall, P.D. (1965). Pain mechanisms: A new theory. *Science, 150,* 971-979.

Melzack, R., & Wall, P.D. (1996). *The challenge of pain* (2nd ed.). London: Penguin Books.

Merskey, H.M., & Bogduk, N. (1994). *Classification of chronic pain* (2nd ed.). Seattle: IASP Press.

Moray, N. (1979). *Mental workload: Its theory and measurement.* New York: Plenum Press.

Morgan, W.P. (1994). Psychological components of effort sense. *Medicine and Science in Sports and Exercise, 26,* 1071-1077.

Morgan, W.P., Hortsman, D.H., Cymerman, A., & Stokes, J. (1993). Facilitation of physical performance by means of a cognitive strategy. *Cognitive Therapy and Research, 7,* 251-264.

Morgan, W.P., & Pollock, M.L. (1977). Psychological characteristics of elite cyclers. *Annals of New York Academy of Science, 301,* 382-403.

Nethery, V.M. (2002). Competition between internal and external sources of information during exercise: Influence on RPE and the impact of the exercise load. *Journal of Sports Medicine and Physical Fitness, 42,* 172-178.

Noakes, T.D. (2004). Linear relationship between the perception of effort and the duration of constant load exercise that remains. *Journal of Applied Physiology, 96,* 1571-1572.

Noakes, T.D., & St. Clair Gibson, A. (2004). Logical limitations to the "catastrophe" models of fatigue during exercise in humans *British Journal of Sports Medicine, 38,* 648-649.

Noakes, T.D., St. Clair Gibson, A., & Lambert, E.V. (2005). From catastrophe to complexity: A novel model of integrative central neural regulation of effort and fatigue during exercise in humans. *British Journal of Sports Medicine, 39,* 120-124.

Noble, B.J., & Noble, J.M. (1998). Perceived exertion: The measurement. In J.L. Duda (Ed.), *Advances in sport and exercise psychology measurement* (pp. 351-360). Morgantown, WV: Fitness Information Technology.

Noble, B.J., & Robertson, R.J. (1996). *Perceived exertion.* Champaign, IL: Human Kinetics.

Nussbaum, M.A., & Lang, A. (2005). Relationships between static load acceptability, ratings of perceived exertion, and biomechanical demands. *International Journal of Industrial Ergonomics, 35,* 547-557.

Pandolf, K.B. (1982). Differentiated ratings of perceived exertion during physical exercise. *Medicine and Science in Sports and Exercise, 14,* 397-405.

Parfitt, G., Markland, D., & Holmes, C. (1994). Response to physical exertion in active and inactive males and females. *Journal of Sport and Exercise Psychology, 16,* 178-186.

Parfitt, G., Shepherd, P., & Eston, R. (2007). Reliability of effort production using the children's CALER and BABE perceived exertion scales. *Journal of Exercise Science and Fitness, 5,* 49-55.

Pender, N.J., Bar-Or, O., Wilk, B., & Mitchell, S. (2002). Self-efficacy and perceived exertion of girls during exercise. *Nursing Research, 51,* 86-91.

Rejeski, W.J. (1981). The perception of exertion: A social psychophysiological integration. *Journal of Sport Psychology, 4,* 305-320.

Rejeski, W.J. (1985). Perceived exertion: An active or passive process. *Journal of Sport Psychology, 7,* 371-378.

Robertson, R.J. (2004). *Perceived exertion for practitioners: Rating effort with the OMNI picture system.* Champaign, IL: Human Kinetics.

Robertson, R.J., Goss, F.L., Andreacci, J.L., Dubé, J.J., Rutkowski, J.J., Frazee, K.M., Aaron, D.J., Metz, K.F., Kowallis, R.A., & Snee, B.M. (2005). Validation of the children's OMNI-resistance exercise scale of perceived exertion. *Medicine and Science in Sports and Exercise, 37*(5), 2819-2826.

Robertson, R.J., Goss, F.L., Andreacci, J.L., Dubé, J.J., Rutkowski, J.J., Snee, B.M., Kowallis, R.A., Crawford, K., Aaron, D.J., & Metz, K.F. (2005). Validation of the children's OMNI RPE scale for stepping exercise. *Medicine and Science in Sports and Exercise, 37*(2), 290-298.

Robertson, R.J., Goss, F.L., Bell, J.A., Dixon, C.B., Gallagher, K.I., Lagally, K.M., Timmer, J.M., Abt, K.L., Gallagher, J.D., & Thompkins, T. (2002). Self-regulated cycling using the Children's OMNI Scale of Perceived Exertion. *Medicine and Science in Sports and Exercise, 34,* 1168-1175.

Robertson, R.J., Goss, F.L., Boer, N., Gallagher, J., Thompkins, T., Bufalino, K., Balasekaran, G., Meckes, C., Pintar, J., & Williams, A. (2001). OMNI scale perceived exertion at ventilatory breakpoint in children: Response normalized. *Medicine and Science in Sports and Exercise, 33,* 1946-1952.

Robertson, R.J., Goss, F.L., Boer, N.F., Peoples, J.A., Foreman, A.J., Dabayebeh, I.M., Millich, N.B., Balasekaran, G., Riechman, S.E., Gallagher, J.D., & Thompkins, T. (2000). Children's OMNI Scale Of Perceived Exertion: Mixed gender and race validation. *Medicine and Science in Sports and Exercise, 32*(2), 452-458.

Robertson, R.J., Goss, F.L., Dubé, J., Rutkowski, J., Dupain, M., Brennan, C., & Andreacci, J. (2004). Validation of the Adult OMNI Scale of Perceived Exertion for cycle ergometer. *Medicine and Science in Sports and Exercise, 36*(1), 102-108.

Robertson, R.J., Goss, F.L., Rutkowski, J., Lenz, B., Dixon, C., Timmer, J., Frazee, K., Dubé J., & Andreacci, J. (2003). Concurrent validation of the OMNI Perceived Exertion Scale for Resistance Exercise. *Medicine and Science in Sports and Exercise, 35,* 333-341.

Robertson, R.J., & Noble, B.J. (1997). Perception of physical exertion: Methods, mediators, and applications. *Exercise and Sport Sciences Reviews, 25,* 407-452.

Roemmich, J.N., Barkley, J.E., Epstein, L.H., Lobarinas, C.L., White, T.M., & Foster, J.H. (2006). Validity of PCERT and OMNI walk/run ratings of perceived exertion. *Medicine and Science in Sports and Exercise, 38,* 1014-1019.

Scott, L.M., Scott, D., Bedic, S.P., & Dowd, J. (1999). The effect of associative and dissociative strategies on rowing ergometer performance. *The Sport Psychologist, 13,* 57-68.

Spielholz, P. (2006). Calibrating Borg scale ratings of hand force exertion. *Applied Ergonomics, 37,* 615-618.

Stanley, C.T, Pargman, D., & Tenenbaum, G. (2007). The effect of attentional coping strategies on perceived exertion in a cycling task. *Journal of Applied Sport Psychology, 19,* 352-363.

Stevens, S.S. (1957). On the psychophysical law. *Psychological Review, 64,* 153-181.

Stevens, J.C. (1974). Psychophysical invariances in proprioception. In F.A. Geldard (Ed.), *Cutaneous communications systems and devices* (pp. 73-77). Austin, TX: Psychonomic Society.

Stevens, J.C. (1989). Static and dynamic exertion: A psychophysical similarity and dissimilarity. In G. Ljunggren & S. Dornic (Eds.), *Psychophysics in action* (pp. 81-93). Berlin: Springer-Verlag.

Stevens, J.C, & Mack, J.D. (1959). Scales of apparent force. *Journal of Experimental Psychology, 58,* 405-413.

Suminski, R.R., Robertson, R.J., Goss, F.L., & Olvera, N. (2008). Validation of the OMNI scale of perceived exertion in a sample of Spanish-speaking youth from the USA. *Perceptual and Motor Skills, 107,* 181-188.Swart, J., Lamberts, R.P., Lambert, M.I., St. Clair Gibson, A., Lambert, E.V., Skowno, J., & Noakes, T.D. (2009). Exercising with reserve: Evidence that the central nervous system regulates prolonged exercise performance. *British Journal of Sports Medicine, 43,* 782-788.

Sylva, M., Byrd, R., & Mangum, M. (1990). Effects of social influence and sex on rating of perceived exertion in exercising elite athletes. *Perceptual and Motor Skills, 70,* 591-594.

Tenenbaum, G. (2001). A social-cognitive perspective of perceived exertion and exertion tolerance. In R.N. Singer, H.A. Hausenblas, & C. Janelle (Eds.), *Handbook of sport psychology* (pp. 810-822), New York: Wiley.

Tenenbaum, G. (2005). The study of perceived and sustained effort: Concepts, research findings and new directions. In D. Hackfort, J.S. Duda, & R. Lidor (Eds.), *Handbook of research in applied sport psychology: International perspectives.* Morgantown, WV: Fitness Information Technology.

Tenenbaum, G., Falk, B., & Bar-Or, O. (2002). A note on the measurement and accumulation of perceived exertion in progressive cycling maximal power test in children and adolescents. *International Journal of Sport Psychology, 33,* 337-348.

Tenenbaum, G., Fogarty, G., Stewart, E., Calcagnini, N., Kirker, B., Thorne, G., & Christensen, S. (1999). Perceived discomfort in running: Scale development and theoretical considerations. *Journal of Sport Sciences, 17,* 183-196.

Tenenbaum, G., Lidor, R., Lavyan, N., Morrow, K., Tonnel, S., Gershgoren, A., Meis, J., & Johnson, M. (2004). The effect of music type on running perseverance and coping with effort sensations. *Psychology of Sport and Exercise, 5,* 89-109.

Tucker, R. (2009). The anticipatory regulation of performance: The physiological basis for pacing strategies and the development of a perception-based model for exercise performance. *British Journal of Sports Medicine, 43,* 392-400.

Van Doren, C.L. (1996). Halving and doubling isometric force: Evidence for a decelerating psychophysical function consistent with an equilibrium-point model of motor control. *Perception and Psychophysics, 58,* 636-647.

Ueda, T., & Kurokawa, T. (1991). Validity of heart rate and ratings of perceived exertion as indices of exercise intensity in a group of children while swimming. *European Journal of Applied Physiology and Occupational Physiology, 63,* 200-204.

Ueda, T., & Kurokawa, T. (1995). Relationships between perceived exertion and physiological variables during swimming. *International Journal of Sports Medicine, 16*(6), 385-389.

Utter, A.C., Robertson, R.J., Green, J.M., Suminski, R.R., McAnulty, S.R, & Nieman, D.C. (2004). Validation of the Adult OMNI Scale of Perceived Exertion for walking/running exercise. *Medicine and Science in Sports and Exercise, 36*(10), 1776-1780.

Utter, A.C., Robertson, R.J., Nieman, D.C., & Kang, J. (2002). Children's OMNI Scale of Perceived Exertion: Walking/running evaluation. *Medicine and Science in Sports and Exercise, 34*(1), 139-144.

Walker, C.A.H., Lamb, K.L., & Marriott, H.E. (1996). The validity of using ratings of perceived exertion to estimate and regulate exercise intensity during stepping ergometry. *Journal of Sports Science, 14,* 102-103.

Weber, E.H. (1834). *De pulsu, resorptione, auditu et tactu. Annotationes anatomicae et physiologicae.* Leipzig, Germany: Koehler.

Weir, J.P., Beck, T.W., Cramer, J.T., & Housh, T.J. (2006). Is fatigue all in your head? A critical review of the central governor model. *British Journal of Sports Medicine, 40,* 573-586.

Williams, J., Eston, R.G., & Furlong, B. (1994). CERT: A perceived exertion scale for young children. *Perceptual and Motor Skills, 79,* 1451-1458.

Yelling, M., Lamb, K., & Swaine, I. (2002). Validity of a pictorial perceived exertion scale for effort estimation and effort production during stepping exercise in adolescent children. *European Physical Education Review, 8,* 157-175.

Chapter 25

Abramson, L.Y., Seligman, M.E.P., & Teasdale, J.D. (1978). Learned helplessness in humans: Critique and reformulation. *Journal of Abnormal Psychology, 87,* 49-74.

Anderson, D.F., & Cychosz, C.M. (1994). Development of an exercise identity scale. *Perceptual and Motor Skills, 78,* 747-751.

Blais, M.R., Brière N.M., Lachance, L., Riddle, A.S., & Vallerand, R.J. (1993). L'inventaire des motivations au travail de Blais [The Blais work motivation inventory]. *Revue québécoise de psychologie, 14,* 185-215.

Blanchard, C.M., Mask, L., Vallerand, R.J., de la Sablonnière, R., & Provencher, P. (2007). Reciprocal relationships between contextual and situational motivation in a sport setting. *Psychology of Sport and Exercise, 8,* 854-873.

Bolles, R.C. (1967). *Theory of motivation.* New York: Harper & Row.

Brière, N.M., Vallerand, R.J., Blais, M.R., & Pelletier, L.G. (1995). Développement et validation d'une mesure de motivation intrinsèque, extrinsèque et d'amotivation en contexte sportif: L'Échelle de Motivation dans les Sports (EMS) [Development and validation of the French form of the Sport Motivation Scale]. *International Journal of Sport Psychology, 26,* 465-489.

Burton, K.D., Lydon, J.E., D'Alessandro, D., & Koestner, R. (2006). The differential effects of intrinsic and identified motivation on well-being and performance: Prospective, experimental, and implicit approaches to self-determination theory. *Journal of Personality and Social Psychology, 4,* 750-762.

Carbonneau, N., & Vallerand, R.J. (2011, February). *Toward a multidimensional taxonomy of intrinsic motivation.* Poster session presented at the 9th Annual Meeting of the Society for Personality and Social Psychology (SPSP), Tampa Bay, FL.

Chantal, Y., Guay, F., Dobreva-Martina, T., & Vallerand, R.J. (1996). Motivation and elite performance: An exploratory investigation with Bulgarian athletes. *International Journal of Sport Psychology, 27,* 173-182.

Chatzisarantis, N.L., Hagger, M.S., Biddle, S.J.H., Smith, B., & Wang, J.C.K. (2003). A metaanalysis of perceived locus of causality in exercise, sport, and physical education contexts. *Journal of Sport and Exercise Psychology, 25,* 284-306.

Conroy, D.E., Coatsworth, J.D., & Kaye, M.P. (2007). Consistency of fear of failure score meanings among 8- to 18-year-old female athletes. *Educational and Psychological Measurement, 67,* 300-310.

Conway, M.A., & Ross, M. (1984). Getting what you want by revising what you had. *Journal of Personality and Social Psychology, 47,* 738-748.

Cronbach, L.J. (1951). Coefficient alpha and the internal structrure of tests. *Psychometrika, 16,* 297-334.

Csikszentmihalyi, M., & Nakamura, J. (1989). The dynamics of intrinsic motivation: A study of adolescents. In C. Ames & R. Ames (Eds.), *Motivation in education: Vol. 3. Goals and cognitions* (pp. 45-71). New York: Academic Press.

Deci, E.L. (1975). *Intrinsic motivation.* New York: Plenum Press.

Deci, E.L., & Ryan, R.M. (1985). *Intrinsic motivation and self-determination in human behavior.* New York: Plenum Press.

Deci, E.L., & Ryan, R.M. (1991). A motivational approach to self: Integration in personality. In R. Dientsbier (Ed.), *Nebraska Symposium on Motivation: Vol. 38. Perspectives on motivation* (pp. 237-288). Lincoln, NE: University of Nebraska Press.

Deci, E.L., & Ryan, R.M. (2000). The 'what' and 'why' of goal pursuits: Human needs and the self-determination of behavior. *Psychological Inquiry, 11,* 227-268.

Doganis, G. (2000). Development of a Greek version of the Sport Motivation Scale. *Perceptual and Motor Skills, 90,* 505-512.

Edmunds, J., Ntoumanis, N., & Duda, J.L. (2006). A test of self-determination theory in the exercise domain. *Journal of Applied Social Psychology, 36,* 2240-2265.

Fairchild, A.J., Horst, S.J., Finney, S.J., & Barron, K.E. (2005). Evaluating existing and new validity evidence for the Academic Motivation Scale. *Contemporary Educational Psychology, 30,* 331-358.

Gillet, N., Vallerand, R.J., & Rosnet, E. (2009). Motivational clusters and performance in a real-life setting. *Motivation Emotion, 33,* 49-62.

Gillet, N., Berjot, S., & Paty, B. (2009). Profil motivationnel et performance sportive [Motivational profile and sport performance]. *Psychologie française, 54,* 173-190.

Greenwald, A.G., McGhee, D.E., & Schwartz, J.L.K. (1998). Measuring individual differences in implicit cognition: The implicit association test. *Journal of Personality and Social Psychology, 74,* 1464-1480.

Guay, F., Mageau, G., & Vallerand, R.J. (2003). On the hierarchical structure of self-determined motivation: A test of top-down and bottom-up effects. *Personality and Social Psychology Bulletin, 29,* 992-1004.

Guay, F., Vallerand, R.J., & Blanchard, C.M. (2000). On the assessment of situational intrinsic and extrinsic motivation: The Situational Motivational Scale (SIMS). *Motivation and Emotion, 24,* 175-213.

Hagger, M.S., & Chatzisarantis, N.L.D. (Eds.). (2007). *Intrinsic motivation and self-determination in exercise and sport.* Leeds, UK: Human Kinetics Europe.

Hagger, M.S., Charzisarantis, N.L.D., Barkoukis, V., Wang, C.K.J., & Baranowski, J. (2005). Perceived autonomy support in physical education and leisure-time physical activity: A cross-cultural evaluation of the trans-contextual model. *Journal of Educational Psychology, 97,* 376-390.

Harter, S. (1981). A model of mastery motivation in children: Individual differences and developmental change. In A. Collins (Ed.), *Minnesota Symposium on child psychology: Vol. 14* (pp. 215-255). Hillsdale, NJ: Erlbaum.

Hein, V., Müür, M., & Koka, A. (2004). Intention to be physically active after school graduation and its relationship to three types of intrinsic motivation. *European Physical Education Review, 10,* 5-19.

Hodge, K., Allen, J.B., & Smellie, L. (2008). Motivation in masters sport: Achievement and social goals. *Psychology of Sport and Exercise, 9,* 157-176.

Hu, L., & Bentler, P.M. (1999). Cutoff criteria for fit indexes in covariance structure analysis: Conventional criteria versus new alternatives. *Structural Equation Modeling, 6,* 1-55.

Jaakkola, T., Liukkonen, J., Laakso, T., & Ommundsen, Y. (2008). The relationship between situational and contextual self-determined motivation and physical activity intensity as measured by heart rates during ninth grade students' physical education classes. *European Physical Education Review, 14,* 13-31.

Jackson, S.A., & Eklund, R.C. (2002). Assessing flow in physical activity: The Flow State Scale-2 and Dispositional Flow Scale-2. *Journal of Sport and Exercise Psychology, 24,* 133-150.

Kingston, K.M., Horrocks, C.S., & Hanton, S. (2006). Do multidimensional intrinsic and extrinsic motivation profiles discriminate between athlete scholarship status and gender? *European Journal of Sport Science, 6,* 53-63.

Koestner, R. (2008). Reaching one's personal goals: A motivational perspective focused on autonomy. *Canadian Psychology, 49,* 60-67.

Koestner, R., Losier, G.F., Vallerand, R.J., & Carducci, D. (1996). Identified and introjected forms of political internalization:

Extending self-determination theory. *Journal of Personality and Social Psychology, 70,* 1025-1036.

Kruglanski, A.W. (1978). Endogenous attribution and intrinsic motivation. In M.R. Lepper & D. Green (Eds.), *The hidden costs of reward: New perspectives on the psychology of human motivation* (pp. 85-107). Hillsdale, NJ: Erlbaum.

Landry, J.B., & Solomon, M.A. (2004). African American women's self-determination across the Stages of Change for Exercise. *Journal of Sport and Exercise Psychology, 26,* 457-469.

Law, B., & Ste-Marie, D.M. (2005). Effects of self-modeling on figure skating jump performance and psychological variables. *European Journal of Sport Science, 5,* 143-152.

Lemyre, N.P., Treasure, D.C., & Roberts, G.C. (2006). Influence of variability in motivation and affect on elite athlete burnout susceptibility. *Journal of Sport and Exercise Psychology, 28,* 32-48.

Lepper, M.R., & Hodell, M. (1989). Intrinsic motivation in the classroom. In C. Ames & R. Ames (Eds.), *Research on motivation in education: Vol. 3. Goals and cognitions* (pp. 73-105). New York: Academic Press.

Levesque, C., & Brown, K.W. (2007). Mindfulness as a moderator of the effect of implicit motivational self-concept on day-to-day behavioral motivation. *Motivation and Emotion, 31,* 284-299.

Levesque, C., & Pelletier, L.G. (2003). On the investigation of primed and chronic autonomous and heteronomous motivational orientations. *Personality and Social Psychology Bulletin, 29,* 1570-1584.

Li, F. (1999). The Exercise Motivation Scale: Its multifaceted structure and construct validity. *Journal of Applied Sport Psychology, 11,* 97-115.

Li, F., & Harmer, P. (1996). Testing the simplex assumption underlying the Sport Motivation Scale: A structural equation modeling analysis. *Research Quarterly for Exercise and Sport, 4,* 396-405.

Lonsdale, C., Hodge, K., & Rose, E.A. (2008). The Behavioral Regulation in Sport Questionnaire (BRSQ): Instrument development and initial validity evidence. *Journal of Sport and Exercise Psychology, 30,* 323-355.

Lonsdale, C., Hodge, K., & Rose, E.A. (2009). Athlete burnout in elite sport: A self-determination perspective. *Journal of Sports Sciences, 27,* 785-795.

Mallett, C.J., & Hanrahan, S.J. (2004). Elite athletes: Why does the 'fire' burn so brightly? *Psychology of Sport and Exercise, 5,* 183-200.

Mallett, C.J., Kawabata, M., & Newcombe, P. (2007). Progressing measurement in sport motivation: A response to Pelletier, Vallerand, and Sarrazin. *Psychology of Sport and Exercise, 8,* 622-631.

Mallett, C.J., Kawabata, M., Newcombe, P., Otero-Rorero, A., & Jackson, S. (2007). Sport Motivation Scale-6: A revised six-factor sport motivation scale. *Psychology of Sport and Exercise, 8,* 600-614.

Markland, D., & Tobin, V. (2004). A modification to the Behavioural Regulation in Exercise Questionnaire to include an assessment of amotivation. *Journal of Sport and Exercise Psychology, 26,* 191-196.

Martens, M.P., & Webber, S.N. (2002). Psychometric properties of the Sport Motivation Scale: An evaluation with college varsity athletes from the U.S. *Journal of Sport and Exercise Psychology, 24,* 254-270.

McNeill, M.C., & Wang, C.K.J. (2005). Psychological profiles of elite school sports players in Singapore. *Psychology of Sport and Exercise, 6,* 117-128.

Mullan, E., Markland, D., & Ingledew, D.K. (1997). A graded conceptualization of self-determination in the regulation of exercise behavior: Development of a measure using confirmatory factor analytic procedures. *Personality and Individual Differences, 23*, 745-752.

Ntoumanis, N., & Blaymires, G. (2003). Contextual and situational motivation in education: A test of the specificity hypothesis. *European Physical Education Review, 9*, 5-21.

Pelletier, L.G., & Dion, S. (2007). An examination of general and specific motivational mechanisms for the relationships between body dissatisfaction and eating behaviors. *Journal of Social and Clinical Psychology, 26*, 303-333.

Pelletier, L.G., Dion, S., Tuson, K.M., & Green-Demers, I. (1999). Why do people fail to adopt environmental protective behaviors? Toward a taxonomy of environmental amotivation. *Journal of Applied Social Psychology, 29*, 2481-2504.

Pelletier, G.L., Fortier, M.S., Vallerand, R.J., & Brière, N.M. (2001). Associations between perceived autonomy support, forms of self regulation, and persistence: A prospective study. *Motivation and Emotion, 25*, 279-306.

Pelletier, L.G., Fortier, M.S., Vallerand, R.J., Tuson, K.M., Brière, N.M., & Blais, M.R. (1995). Toward a new measure of intrinsic motivation, extrinsic motivation, and amotivation in sports: The Sport Motivation Scale (SMS). *Journal of Sport and Exercise Psychology, 17*, 35-53.

Pelletier, L.G., & Sarrazin, P. (2007). Measurement issues in self-determination theory and sport. In M.S. Hagger & N. Chatzisarantis (Eds.), *Self-determination theory in exercise and sport* (pp. 143-152). Champaign, IL: Human Kinetics.

Pelletier, L.G., Vallerand, R.J., Green-Demers, I., Blais, M.R., & Brière, N.M. (1996). Construction et validation d'une mesure de motivation intrinsèque, de motivation extrinsèque et d'amotivation vis-à-vis les activités de loisir: L'Échelle de Motivation vis-à-vis les Loisirs (EML) [Construction and validation of the Leisure Motivation Scale]. *Loisir et Société, 19*, 559-585.

Pelletier, L.G., Vallerand, R.J., & Sarrazin, P. (2007). The revised six-factor Sport Motivation Scale (Mallett, Kawabata, Newcombe, Otero-Forero, and Jackson): Something old, something new, and something borrowed. *Psychology of Sport and Exercise, 8*, 615-621.

Perreault, S., & Vallerand, R.J. (2007). A test of self-determination theory with wheelchair basketball players with and without disability. *Adapted Physical Activity Quarterly, 24*, 305-316.

Radel, R., Sarrazin, P., & Pelletier, L.G. (2009). Evidence of subliminally primed motivational orientations: The effects of unconscious motivational processes on the performance of a new motor task. *Journal of Sport and Exercise Psychology, 31*, 657-674.

Raedeke, T.D., & Smith, A.L. (2001). Development and preliminary validation of an athlete burnout measure. *Journal of Sport and Exercise Psychology, 23*, 281-306.

Ratelle, C.F., Baldwin, M., & Vallerand, R.J. (2005). On the cued activation of situational motivation. *Journal of Experimental Social Psychology, 41*, 482-487.

Reid, G., Poulin, C., & Vallerand, R.J. (1994, June). *A pictorial motivation scale in physical activity for people with a mental disability: Development and initial validation.* Paper presented at the annual conference of the North American Society for the psychology of Sport and Physical Activity in Clearwater, FL.

Reid, G., Vallerand, R.J., Poulin, C., Crocker, P., & Farrell, R. (2009). The development and validation of the Pictorial Motivation Scale in physical activity. *Motivation and Emotion, 33, 161-172.*

Reiss, S., & Havercamp, S.M. (1998). Toward a comprehensive assessment of fundamental motivation: Factor structure of the Reiss Profile. *Psychological Assessment, 10*, 97-106.

Riemer, H., Fink, J.S., & Fitzgerald, M.P. (2002). External validity of the Sport Motivation Scale. *Avante, 8*, 57-66.

Ryan, R.M., & Connell, J.P. (1989). Perceived locus of causality and internalization: Examining reasons for acting in two domains. *Journal of Personality and Social Psychology, 57*, 749-761.

Shaw, K.L., Ostrow, A., & Beckstead, J. (2005). Motivation and the senior athlete: An examination of the psychometric properties of the Sport Motivation Scale. *Topics in Geriatric Rehabilitation. Motivation and the Older Adult, 21*, 206-214.

Standage, M., Duda, J.L.; & Ntoumanis, N. (2003). A model of contextual motivation in physical education: Using constructs from self-determination and achievement goal theories to predict physical activity intentions. *Journal of Educational Psychology, 95*, 97-110.

Standage, M., Sebire, S.J., & Loney, T. (2008). Does exercise motivation predict engagement in objective assessed bouts of moderate-intensity exercise?: A self-determination theory perspective. *Journal of Sport and Exercise Psychology, 30*, 337-352.

Standage, M., Treasure, D.C., Duda, J.L., & Prusak, K.A. (2003). Validity, reliability, and invariance of the Situational Motivation Scale (SIMS) across diverse physical activity contexts. *Sport Psychology, 25*, 19-43.

Thogersen-Ntoumani, C., & Ntoumanis, N. (2006). The role of self-determined motivation in the understanding of exercise-related behaviours, cognitions and physical-evaluations. *Journal of Sports Sciences, 24*, 393-404.

Vallerand, R.J. (1989). Vers une méthodologie de validation trans-culturelle de questionnaires psychologiques: Implications pour la recherche en langue française [Toward a cross-cultural methology to validate psychological instrument: Implication for research in the French language]. *Psychologie canadienne, 30*, 662-678.

Vallerand, R.J. (1997). Toward a hierarchical model of intrinsic and extrinsic motivation. In M.P. Zanna (Ed), *Advances in experimental social psychology* (pp. 271-360). New York: Academic Press.

Vallerand, R.J. (2001). A hierarchical model of intrinsic and extrinsic motivation in sport and exercise. In G. Roberts (Ed.), *Advances in motivation in sport and exercise* (pp. 263-319). Champaign, IL: Human Kinetics.

Vallerand, R.J. (2007). A hierarchical model of intrinsic and extrinsic motivation for sport and physical activity. *In* M.S.D. Hagger & N.L.D. Chatzisarantis (Eds.), *Self-determination theory in exercise and sport*. Champaign, IL: Human Kinetics.

Vallerand, R.J., Blais, M.R., Brière, N.M., & Pelletier, L.G. (1989). Construction et validation de l'Échelle de Motivation en Éducation (EME) (Construction and validation of the Academic Motivation Scale). *Revue canadienne des sciences du comportement, 21*, 323-349.

Vallerand, R.J., & Fortier, M.S. (1998). Measures of intrinsic and extrinsic motivation in sport and physical activity: A review and critique. In J. Duda (Ed.), *Advances in sport and exercise psychology measurement* (pp. 81-101). Morgantown, WV: Fitness Information Technology.

Vallerand, R.J., Pelletier, L.G., Blais, M.R., Brière, N.M., Senécal, C.B., & Vallières, E.F. (1992). The Academic Motivation Scale: A measure of intrinsic, extrinsic, and amotivation in education. *Educational and Psychological Measurement, 52*, 1003-1017.

Vallerand, R.J., & Thill, E. (Eds.). (1993). *Introduction à la psychologie de la motivation* (Introduction to the psychology of motivation). Laval, PQ: Études Vivantes.

White, R.W. (1959). Motivation reconsidered: The concept of competence. *Psychological Review, 66,* 297-333.

Wilson, P.M., Mack, D.E., & Grattan, K.P. (2008). Understanding motivation for exercise: A self-determination theory perspective. *Canadian Psychology, 49,* 250-256.

Wilson, P.M., Rodgers, W.M., & Fraser, S.N. (2002). Examining the psychometric properties of the Behavioral Regulation in Exercise Questionnaire. *Measurement in Physical Education and Exercise Science, 6,* 1-21.

Wilson, P.M., Rodgers, W.M., Loitz, C.C., & Scime, G. (2006). It's who I am . . . Really! The importance of integrated regulation in exercise contexts. *Journal of Applied Biobehavioral Research, 11,* 79-104.

Winninger, S.R. (2007). Self-determination theory and exercise behavior: An examination of the psychometric properties of the Exercise Motivation Scale. *Journal of Applied Sport Psychology, 19,* 471-486.

Chapter 26

Crocker, L., & Algina, J. (1986). *Introduction to classical and modern test theory.* New York: Harcourt Brace Jovanovich.

Cronbach, L.J. (1951). Coefficient alpha and the internal structure of tests. *Psychometrika, 16,* 297-334.

Cronbach, L.J., & Meehl, P.E. (1955). Construct validity in psychological tests. *Psychological Bulletin, 52,* 281-302.

Dacey, M., Baltzell, A., & Ziachkowsky, L. (2008). Older adults' intrinsic and extrinsic motivation towards physical activity. *American Journal of Health Behavior, 32,* 570-582.

Deci, E.L. (1992). On the nature and function of motivation theories. *Psychological Science, 3,* 167-171.

Deci, E.L., & Ryan, R.M. (2000). The 'what' and 'why' of goal pursuits: Human needs and the self-determination of behavior. *Psychological Inquiry, 11,* 227-268.

Deci, E.L., & Ryan, R.M. (2002). *Handbook of self-determination research.* Rochester, NY: University of Rochester.

Deci, E.L., & Ryan, R.M. (2008). Facilitating optimal motivation and well-being across life's domains. *Canadian Psychology, 49,* 14-23.

Duda, J.L., & Tappe, M.K. (1989). The Personal Incentives for Exercise Questionnaire: Preliminary development. *Perceptual and Motor Skills, 68,* 1122.

Edmunds, J., Ntouamnis, N., & Duda, J.L. (2007). Adherence and well-being in overweight and obese patients referred to an exercise on prescription scheme: A self-determination theory perspective. *Psychology of Sport and Exercise, 8,* 722-740.

Edmunds, J., Ntoumanis, N., & Duda, J.L. (2008). Testing a self-determination theory-based teaching style intervention in the exercise domain. *European Journal of Social Psychology, 38,* 375-388.

Frederick-Recascino, C.M. (2002). Self-determination theory and participation motivation research in the sport and exercise domain. In E.L. Deci & R.M. Ryan (Eds.), *Handbook of self-determination research* (pp. 277-294). Rochester, NY: University Of Rochester.

Frederick, C.M., & Ryan, R.M. (1993). Differences in motivation for sport and exercise and their relations with participation and mental health. *Journal of Sport Behavior, 16,* 124-146.

Frederick-Recascino, C.M., & Schuster-Smith, H. (2003). Competition and intrinsic motivation in physical activity: A comparison of two groups. *Journal of Sport Behavior, 26,* 240-254.

Ingeldew, D.K., Markland, D., & Medley, A. (1998). Exercise motives and stages of change. *Journal of Health Psychology, 3,* 477-489.

Ingeldew, D.K., & Sullivan, G. (2002). Effects of body mass and body image on exercise motives in adolescence. *Psychology of Exercise and Sport, 3,* 323-338.

Li, F. (1999). The exercise motivation scale: Its multifaceted structure and construct validity. *Journal of Applied Sport Psychology, 11,* 97-115.

Loevinger, J. (1957). Objective tests as instruments of psychological theory. *Psychological Reports, 3,* 635-694.

Loze, G.M., & Collins, D.J. (1998). Muscular development motives for exercise participation: The missing variable in current questionnaire analysis? *Journal of Sports Sciences, 16,* 761-767.

Lutz, R., Karoly, P., & Okun, M.A. (2008). The why and the how of goal pursuit: Self-determination, goal process cognition, and participation in physical exercise. *Psychology of Sport and Exercise, 9,* 559-575.

Lutz, R., Lochbaum, M., & Turnbow, K. (2003). The role of relative autonomy in post-exercise affect responding. *Journal of Sport Behavior, 26,* 137-154.

Maltby, J., & Day, L. (2001). The relationship between exercise motives and well-being. *The Journal of Psychology, 135,* 651-660.

Markland, D., & Hardy, L. (1993). The Exercise Motivations Inventory: Preliminary development and validity of a measure of individuals' reasons for participation in regular physical exercise. *Personality and Individual Differences, 15,* 289-296.

Markland, D., & Ingeldew, D.K. (1997). The measurement of exercise motives: Factorial validity and invariance across gender of a revised Exercise Motivations Inventory. *British Journal of Health Psychology, 2,* 361-376.

Markland, D. & Tobin, V. (2004). A modification of the Behavioral Regulation in Exercise Questionnaire to include an assessment of amotivation. *Journal of Sport and Exercise Psychology, 26,* 191-196.

Markland, D., & Vansteenkiste, M. (2007). Self-determination theory and motivational interviewing. In M.S. Hagger & N.L.D. Chatzisarantis (Eds.), *Intrinsic motivation and self-determination in exercise and sport* (pp. 87-99). Champaign, IL: Human Kinetics.

Messick, S. (1995). Validity of psychological assessment: Validation of inferences from persons' responses and performances as scientific inquiry into score meaning. *American Psychologist, 50,* 741-749.

Moreno, J.A.M., Galindo, C.M., & Pardo, P.M. (2008). Motivations and reasons for exercising in water: Gender and age differences in a sample of Spanish exercisers. *International Journal of Aquatics Research, 2,* 237-246.

Mullan, E., & Markland, D. (1997). Variations in self-determination across the stages of change for exercise in adults. *Motivation and Emotion, 21,* 349-362.

Mullan, E., Markland, D., & Ingledew, D.K. (1997). A graded conceptualisation of self-determination in the regulation of exercise behaviour: Development of a measure using confirmatory factor analytic procedures. *Personality and Individual Differences, 23,* 745-752.

Ortís, L.C., Mayamí, J.N., Feliu, J.C., Vidal, J.M. L., Romero, E.P., Bassets, M.P., Herreros, M.V., & Brosa, J.V. (2007). Exercise motivation in university community members: A behavioural intervention. *Psicothema, 19,* 250-255.

Pelletier, L.G., Dion, S.C., Slovinec-D'Angelo, M., & Reid, R. (2004). Why do you regulate what you eat? Relationships between forms of regulation, eating behaviours, sustained dietary behaviour change, and psychological adjustment. *Motivation and Emotion, 28,* 245-277.

Ryan, R.M., & Deci, E.L. (2007). Active human nature: Self-determination theory and the promotion and maintenance of sport, exercise, and health. In M.S. Hagger & N.L.D. Chatzisarantis (Eds.), *Intrinsic motivation and self-determination in exercise and sport* (pp. 1-19). Champaign, IL: Human Kinetics.

Ryan, R.M., Frederick, C.M., Lepes, D., Rubio, N., & Sheldon, K.M. (1997). Intrinsic motivation and exercise adherence. *International Journal of Sport Psychology, 28,* 335-354.

Sebire, S.J., Standage, M., & Vansteenkiste, M. (2008). Development and validation of the goal content for exercise questionnaire. *Journal of Sport and Exercise Psychology, 30,* 353-337.

Sheldon, K.M., & Filak, V. (2008). Manipulating autonomy, competence and relatedness support in a game-learning context: New evidence that all three needs matter. *British Journal of Social Psychology, 47,* 267-283.

Sit, C.H.P., Kerr, J.H., & Wong, I.T.F. (2008). Motives for and barriers to physical activity participation in middle-aged Chinese women. *Psychology of Sport and Exercise, 9,* 266-283.

Standage, M., Sebire, S.J., & Loney, T. (2008). Does exercise motivation predict engagement in objectively assessed bouts of moderate-intensity exercise?: A self-determination theory perspective. *Journal of Sport and Exercise Psychology, 30,* 337-352.

Stevenson, S.J., & Lochbaum, M.R. (2008). Understanding exercise motivation: Examining the revised social-cognitive model of achievement motivation. *Journal of Sport Behavior, 31,* 389-412.

Vallerand, R.J. (1997). Toward a hierarchical model of intrinsic and extrinsic motivation. In M.P. Zanna (Ed.), *Advances in experimental social psychology* (pp. 271-360). San Diego: Academic Press.

Vallerand, R.J. (2007). A hierarchical model of intrinsic and extrinsic motivation for sport and physical activity. In M.S. Hagger & N.L.D. Chatzisarantis (Eds.), *Intrinsic motivation and self-determination in exercise and sport* (pp. 255-280). Champaign, IL: Human Kinetics.

Vallerand, R.J., & Fortier, M.S. (1997). Measures of intrinsic and extrinsic motivation in sport and physical activity: A review and critique. In J.L. Duda (Ed.), *Advances in sport and exercise psychology measurement* (pp. 81-101). Morgantown, WV: Fitness Information Technology.

Vallerand, R.J., Pelletier, L.G., & Koestner, R. (2008). Reflections on self-determination theory: A Canadian contribution. *Canadian Psychology, 49,* 257-262.

Wilson, P.M., Mack, D.E., & Grattan, K.P. (2008). Understanding motivation for exercise: A self-determination theory perspective. *Canadian Psychology, 49,* 250-256.

Wilson, P.M., Rodgers, W.M., & Fraser, S.N. (2002). Cross-validation of the revised motivation for physical activity measure in active women. *Research Quarterly for Exercise and Sport, 73,* 471-477.

Wilson, P.M., Rodgers, W.M., Fraser, S.N., & Murray, T.C. (2004). Relationships between exercise regulations and motivational consequences in university students. *Research Quarterly for Exercise and Sport, 75,* 81-91.

Wilson, P.M., Rodgers, W.M., Loitz, C., & Scime, G. (2006). It's who I am . . . really! The importance of integrated regulation in exercise contexts. *Journal of Applied Biobehavioral Research, 11,* 79-104.

Wilson, P.M., & Rogers, W.T. (2008). Examining relationship between perceived psychological need satisfaction and behavioural regulations in exercise. *Journal of Applied Biobehavioral Research, 13,* 119-142.

Wininger, S.R. (2007). Self-determination theory and exercise behaviour: An examination of the psychometric properties of the Exercise Motivation Scale. *Journal of Applied Sport Psychology, 19,* 471-486.

Chapter 27

Abrahamsen, F.E., Roberts, G.C., & Pensgaard, A.M. (2008). Achievement goals and gender effects on multidimensional anxiety in national elite sport. *Psychology of Sport and Exercise, 9,* 449-464.

Abrahamsen, F.E., Roberts, G.C., Pensgaard, A.M., & Ronglan, L.T. (2008). Perceived ability and social support as mediators of achievement motivation and performance anxiety. *Scandinavian Journal of Medicine and Science in Sports, 18,* 810-821.

Adie, J.W., Duda, J.L., & Ntoumanis, N.T. (2008). Achievement goals, competition appraisals, and the psychological and emotional welfare of sport participants. *Journal of Sport and Exercise Psychology, 30,* 302-322.

Allen, J.B. (2003). Social motivation in youth sport. *Journal of Sport and Exercise Psychology, 25,* 551-567.

Alpert, R., & Haber, R.N. (1960). Anxiety in academic achievement situations. *Journal of Abnormal and Social Psychology, 61,* 207-215.

Appleton, P.R., Hall, H.K., & Hill, A.P. (2009). Relations between multidimensional perfectionism and burnout in junior-elite male athletes. *Psychology of Sport and Exercise, 10,* 457-465.

Balaguer, I., Duda, J.L., Atienza, F.L., & Mayo, C. (2002). Situational and dispositional goals as predictors of perceptions of individual and team improvement, satisfaction and coach ratings among elite female handball teams. *Psychology of Sport and Exercise, 3,* 293-308.

Balaguer, I., Duda, J.L., & Crespo, M. (1999). Motivational climate and goal orientations as predictors of perceptions of improvement, satisfaction and coach ratings among tennis players. *Scandinavian Journal of Medicine and Science in Sports, 9,* 381-388.

Bargh, J.A. (1997). The automaticity of everyday life. In R.S. Wyer (Ed.), *Advances in social cognition* (Vol. X, pp. 1-61). Mahwah, NJ: Erlbaum.

Barić, R., & Horga, S. (2006). Psychometric properties of the Croatian version of Task and Ego Orientation in Sport Questionnaire (CTEOSQ). *Kinesiology, 38,* 135-142.

Barkoukis, V., Ntoumanis, N., & Nikitaras, N. (2007). Comparing dichotomous and trichotomous approaches to achievement goal theory: An example using motivational regulations as outcome variables. *British Journal of Educational Psychology, 77,* 683-702.

Barkoukis, V., Tsorbatzoudis, H., & Grouios, G. (2008). Manipulation of motivational climate in physical education: Effects of a seven-month intervention. *European Physical Education Review, 14,* 367-387.

Bergin, D.A., & Habusta, S.E. (2004). Goal orientations of young male ice hockey players and their parents. *Journal of Genetic Psychology, 165,* 383-397.

Bois, J.E., Sarrazin, P., Southon, J., & Boiché, J.C.S. (2009). Psychological characteristics and their relation to performance in professional golfers. *The Sport Psychologist, 23,* 252-270.

Bortoli, L., Bertollo, M., & Robazza, C. (2009). Dispositional goal orientations, motivational climate, and psychobiosocial states in youth sport. *Personality and Individual Differences, 47,* 18-24.

Brannan, M.E., & Petrie, T.A. (2008). Moderators of the body dissatisfaction-eating disorder symptomatology relationship: Replication and extension. *Journal of Counseling Psychology, 55,* 263-275.

Brunstein, J.C., & Schmitt, C.H. (2004). Assessing individual differences in achievement motivation with the Implicit Association Test. *Journal of Research in Personality, 38,* 536-555.

Cattell, R.B. (1952). The three basic factor-analytic research designs—their interrelations and derivatives. *Psychological Bulletin, 49,* 499-502.

Collins, L.M. (2006). Analysis of longitudinal data: The integration of theoretical model, temporal design, and statistical model. *Annual Review of Psychology, 57,* 505-528.

Conroy, D.E. (2001). Progress in the development of a multidimensional measure of fear of failure: The Performance Failure Appraisal Inventory (PFAI). *Anxiety, Stress and Coping, 14,* 431-452.

Conroy, D.E. (2003). Representational models associated with fear of failure in adolescents and young adults. *Journal of Personality, 71,* 757-783.

Conroy, D.E. (2004). The unique psychological meanings of multidimensional fears of failing. *Journal of Sport and Exercise Psychology, 26,* 484-491.

Conroy, D.E., Cassidy, C.M., & Elliot, A.J. (2008). Prospective relations between 2 × 2 achievement goals and the quality of sport training. *International Review of Social Psychology, 21,* 109-134.

Conroy, D.E., & Coatsworth, J.D. (2004). The effects of coach training on fear of failure in youth swimmers: A latent growth curve analysis from a randomized, controlled trial. *Journal of Applied Developmental Psychology, 25,* 193-214.

Conroy, D.E., Coatsworth, J.D., & Fifer, A.M. (2005). Testing dynamic relations between perceived competence and fear of failure in young athletes. *European Review of Applied Psychology, 55,* 99-110.

Conroy, D.E., Coatsworth, J.D., & Kaye, M.P. (2007). Consistency of fear of failure score meanings among 8- to 18-year old female athletes. *Educational and Psychological Measurement, 67,* 300-310.

Conroy, D.E., & Elliot, A.J. (2004). Fear of failure and achievement goals in sport: Addressing the issue of the chicken and the egg. *Anxiety, Stress and Coping, 17,* 271-285.

Conroy, D.E., Elliot, A.J., & Hofer, S.M. (2003). A 2 × 2 Achievement Goals Questionnaire for Sport: Evidence for factorial invariance, temporal stability, and external validity. *Journal of Sport and Exercise Psychology, 25,* 456-476.

Conroy, D.E., Elliot, A.J., & Pincus, A.L. (2009). The expression of achievement motives in interpersonal problems. *Journal of Personality, 77,* 495-526.

Conroy, D.E., Elliot, A.J., & Thrash, T.M. (2009). Achievement motivation. In M.R. Leary & R.H. Hoyle (Eds.), *Handbook of individual differences in social behavior* (pp. 382-399). New York: Guilford Press.

Conroy, D.E., Kaye, M.P., & Coatsworth, J.D. (2006). Coaching climates and the destructive effects of mastery-avoidance goals on situational motivation. *Journal of Sport and Exercise Psychology, 28,* 69-92.

Conroy, D.E., Kaye, M.P., & Fifer, A.M. (2007). Cognitive links between fear of failure and perfectionism. *Journal of Rational-Emotive and Cognitive Behavior Therapy, 25,* 237-253.

Conroy, D.E., Metzler, J.N., & Hofer, S.M. (2003). Factorial invariance and latent mean stability of performance failure appraisals. *Structural Equation Modeling, 10,* 401-422.

Conroy, D.E., Poczwardowski, A., & Henschen, K.P. (2001). Evaluative criteria and consequences associated with failure and success for elite athletes and performing artists. *Journal of Applied Sport Psychology, 13,* 300-322.

Conroy, D.E., Willow, J.P., & Metzler, J.N. (2002). Multidimensional fear of failure measurement: The Performance Failure Appraisal Inventory. *Journal of Applied Sport Psychology, 14,* 76-90.

Courville, T., & Thompson, B. (2001). Use of structure coefficients in published multiple regression articles: β is not enough. *Educational and Psychological Measurement, 61,* 229-248.

Cumming, S.P., Smith, R.E., Smoll, F.L., Standage, M., & Grossbard, J.R. (2008). Development and validation of the Achievement Goal Scale for Youth Sports. *Psychology of Sport and Exercise, 9,* 686-703.

Cury, F., Elliot, A., Sarrazin, P., Da Fonseca, D., & Rufo, M. (2002). The trichotomous achievement goal model and intrinsic motivation: A sequential meditational analysis. *Journal of Experimental Social Psychology, 38,* 473-481.

De Bruin, A.P., Bakker, F.C., & Oudejans, R.R.D. (2009). Achievement goal theory and disordered eating: Relationships of disordered eating with goal orientations and motivational climate in female gymnastics and dancers. *Psychology of Sport and Exercise, 10,* 72-79.

Diener, C.I., & Dweck, C.S. (1978). An analysis of learned helplessness: Continuous changes in performance, strategy, and achievement cognitions following failure. *Journal of Personality and Social Psychology, 36,* 451-462.

Diener, C.I., & Dweck, C.S. (1980). An analysis of learned helplessness: II. The processing of success. *Journal of Personality and Social Psychology, 39,* 940-952.

Dru, V. (2003). Relationships between an ego orientation scale and a hypercompetitive scale: Their correlates with dogmatism and authoritarianism factors. *Personality and Individual Differences, 35,* 1509-1524.

Duda, J.L., & Nicholls, J.G. (1992). Dimensions of achievement motivation in schoolwork and sport. *Journal of Educational Psychology, 84,* 290-299.

Duda, J.L., & Whitehead, J. (1998). Measurement of goal perspectives in the physical domain. In J.L. Duda (Ed.), *Advances in sport and exercise psychology measurement* (pp. 21-48). Morgantown, WV: Fitness Information Technology.

Duley, A.R., Conroy, D.E., Morris, K., Wiley, J., & Janelle, C.M. (2005). Fear of failure biases affective and attentional responses to lexical and pictorial stimuli. *Motivation and Emotion, 29,* 1-17.

Dweck, C.S. (1975). The role of expectations and attributions in the alleviation of learned helplessness. *Journal of Personality and Social Psychology, 31,* 674-685.

Dweck, C.S. (1986). Motivational processes affecting learning. *American Psychologist, 41,* 1040-1048.

Dweck, C.S., & Elliott, E.S. (1983). Achievement motivation. In P.H. Mussen (Gen. Ed.) & E.M. Hetherington (Vol. Ed.),

Handbook of child psychology: Vol. IV. Socialization, personality, and social development (4th ed., pp. 643-691). New York: Wiley.

Eccles, J.S., & Wigfield, A. (2002). Motivational beliefs, values, and goals. *Annual Review of Psychology, 53,* 109-132.

Elliot, A.J. (1997). Integrating the "classic" and "contemporary" approaches to achievement motivation: A hierarchical model of approach and avoidance achievement motivation. In M. Maehr & P. Pintrich (Eds.), *Advances in motivation and achievement* (Vol. 10, pp. 143-179). Greenwich, CT: Jai Press.

Elliot, A.J. (1999). Approach and avoidance motivation and achievement goals. *Educational Psychologist, 34,* 169-189.

Elliot, A.J., & Church, M.A. (1997). A hierarchical model of approach and avoidance achievement motivation. *Journal of Personality and Social Psychology, 72,* 218-232.

Elliot, A.J., & Conroy, D.E. (2005). Beyond the dichotomous model of achievement goals in sport and exercise psychology. *Sport and Exercise Psychology Review, 1,* 17-25.

Elliot, A.J., Conroy, D.E., Barron, K., & Murayama, K. (2010). Achievement motives and goals: A developmental analysis. In R. Lerner, M. Lamb, & A. Freund (Eds.), *Handbook of lifespan development, Vol. 2: Social and emotional development* (pp. 474-510). New York: Wiley.

Elliot, A.J., & Dweck, C.S. (2005). *Handbook of competence and motivation.* New York: Guilford Press.

Elliot, A.J., & McGregor, H.A. (2001). A 2 × 2 achievement goal framework. *Journal of Personality and Social Psychology, 80,* 501-519.

Elliot, A.J., & Murayama, K. (2008). On the measurement of achievement goals: Critique, illustration, and application. *Journal of Educational Psychology, 100,* 613-628.

Elliott, E.S., & Dweck, C.S. (1988). Goals: An approach to motivation and achievement. *Journal of Personality and Social Psychology, 54,* 5-12.

Flores, J., Salguero, A., & Marquez, S. (2007). Goal orientations and perceptions of the motivational climate in physical education classes among Colombian students. *Teaching and Teacher Education, 24,* 1441-1449.

Fonseca, A.M. (2001). Estudo exploratório e confirmatório à estrutura factorial da versão portuguesa do Perception of Success Questionnaire (POSQ) (Exploratory and confirmatory factor analysis of the Portuguese version of the Perception of Success Questionnaire [POSQ]). *Revisita Portuguesa de Ciências do Desporto, 1,* 61-69.

Fryer, J.W., & Elliot, A.J. (2007). Stability and change in achievement goals. *Journal of Educational Psychology, 99,* 700-714.

Gelbort, K.R., & Winer, J.L. (1985). Fear of success and fear of failure: A multitrait-multimethod validation study. *Journal of Personality and Social Psychology, 48,* 1009-1014.

Gernigon, C., d'Arripe-Longueville, F., Delignières, D., & Ninot, G. (2004). A dynamical systems perspective on goal involvement states in sport. *Journal of Sport and Exercise Psychology, 26,* 572-596.

Grossbard, J.R., Cumming, S.P., Standage, M., Smith, R.E., & Smoll, F.L. (2007). Social desirability and relations between goal orientations and competitive trait anxiety in young athletes. *Psychology of Sport and Exercise, 8,* 491-505.

Guan, J., McBride, R., & Xiang, P. (2007). Reliability and validity evidence for achievement goal models in high school physical education settings. *Measurement in Physical Education and Exercise Science, 11,* 109-129.

Guan, J., Xiang, P., McBride, R., & Bruene, A. (2006). Achievement goals, social goals, and students' reported persistence and effort in high school physical education. *Journal of Teaching in Physical Education, 25,* 58-74.

Hall, H.K., & Kerr, A.W. (1997). Motivational antecedents of precompetitive anxiety in youth sport. *The Sport Psychologist, 11,* 24-42.

Hall, H.K., Kerr, A.W., Kozub, A., & Finnie, S.B. (2007). Motivational antecedents of obligatory exercise: The influence of achievement goals and multidimensional perfectionism. *Psychology of Sport and Exercise, 8,* 297-316.

Harwood, C., Cumming, J., & Hall, C. (2003). Imagery use in elite youth sport participants: Reinforcing the applied significance of achievement goal theory. *Research Quarterly for Exercise and Sport, 74,* 292-300.

Harwood, C., & Hardy, L. (2001). Persistence and effort in moving achievement goal research forward: A response to Treasure and colleagues. *Journal of Sport and Exercise Psychology, 23,* 330-345.

Harwood, C., Hardy, L., & Swain, A. (2000). Achievement goals in sport: A critique of conceptual and measurement issues. *Journal of Sport and Exercise Psychology, 22,* 235-255.

Harwood, C.G., & Swain, A.B.J. (1998). Antecedents of precompetition achievement goals in elite junior tennis players. *Journal of Sports Sciences, 16,* 357-371.

Hatzigeorgiadis, A. (2002). Thoughts of escape during competition: Relationships with goal orientations and self-consciousness. *Psychology of Sport and Exercise, 3,* 195-207.

Helmreich, R., and Spence, J. (1978). Work and Family Orientation Questionnaire: An objective instrument to assess components of achievement motivation and attitudes toward family and career [Abstract]. *JSAS Catalog of Selected Documents in Psychology, 8*(2), 35, 1-27.

Hermans, W.E. (1990). Fear of failure as a distinctive personality trait measure of test anxiety. *Journal of Research and Development in Education, 23,* 180-185.

Hodge, K., Allen, J.B., & Smellie, L. (2008). Motivation in masters sport: Achievement and social goals. *Psychology of Sport and Exercise, 9,* 157-176.

Hoppe, F. (1930). Untersuchungen zur Handlungs- und Affektpsychologie. IX. Erfolg und Mißerfolg [Psychological studies of action and affect. IX. Success and failure]. *Psychologische Forschung, 14,* 1-63.

Jackaway, R., & Teevan, R. (1976). Fear of failure and fear of success: Two dimensions of the same motive. *Sex Roles, 2,* 283-293.

Jackson, D.N. (1994). *Jackson Personality Research Inventory manual—revised.* Goshen, NY: Research Psychologists Press.

Jackson, D.N., Ahmed, S.A., & Heapy, N.A. (1976). Is achievement motivation a unitary construct? *Journal of Research in Personality, 10,* 1-21.

Jackson, D.N., Paunonen, S.V., Fraboni, M., & Goffin, R.D. (1996). A five-factor versus six-factor model of personality structure. *Personality and Individual Differences, 20,* 33-45.

Kavussanu, M., & Boardley, I.D. (2009). The Prosocial and Antisocial Behavior in Sport Scale. *Journal of Sport and Exercise Psychology, 31,* 97-117.

Kavussanu, M., & Ntoumanis, N. (2003). Participation in sport and moral functioning: Does ego orientation mediate their relationship? *Journal of Sport and Exercise Psychology, 25,* 501-518.

Kaye, M.P., Conroy, D.E., & Fifer, A.M. (2008). Individual differences in incompetence avoidance. *Journal of Sport and Exercise Psychology, 30,* 110-132.

Kouli, O., & Papaioannou, A.G. (2009). Ethnic/cultural identity salience, achievement goals and motivational climate in multicultural physical education classes. *Psychology of Sport and Exercise, 10,* 45-51.

Kristiansen, E., Roberts, G.C., & Abrahamsen, F.E. (2008). Achievement involvement and stress coping in elite wrestling. *Scandinavian Journal of Medicine and Science in Sports, 18,* 526-538.

Kuan, G., & Roy, J. (2007). Goal profiles, mental toughness and its influences on performance outcomes among Wushu athletes. *Journal of Sports Science and Medicine, 6,* 28-33.

Lavoi, N.M., & Stellino, M.B. (2008). The relation between perceived parent-created sport climate and competitive male youth hockey players' good and poor sport behaviors. *The Journal of Psychology, 142,* 471-495.

Lemyre, P.-N., Hall, H.K., & Roberts, G.C. (2008). A social cognitive approach to burnout in elite athletes. *Scandinavian Journal of Medicine and Science in Sports, 18,* 221-234.

Li, F., Harmer, P., Duncan, T.E., Duncan, S.C., Acock, A., & Yamamoto, T. (1998). Confirmatory factor analysis of the Task and Ego Orientation in Sport Questionnaire with cross-validation. *Research Quarterly for Exercise and Sport, 69,* 276-283.

Lochbaum, M., Stevenson, S., & Hilario, D. (2009). Achievement goals, thoughts about intense physical activity, and exerted effort: A meditational analysis. *Journal of Sport Behavior, 32,* 53-68.

Lyle, J. (2003). Stimulated recall: A report on its use in naturalistic research. *British Educational Research Journal, 29,* 861-878.

MacDonald, N.E., & Hyde, J.S. (1980). Fear of success, need achievement, and fear of failure: A factor analytic study. *Sex Roles, 6,* 695-711.

Magyar, T.M., & Feltz, D.L. (2003). The influence of dispositional and situational tendencies on adolescent girls' sport confidence sources. *Psychology of Sport and Exercise, 4,* 175-190.

Magyar, T.M., Feltz, D.L., & Simpson, I.P. (2004). Individual and crew level determinants of collective efficacy in rowing. *Journal of Sport and Exercise Psychology, 26,* 136-153.

McClelland, D.C. (1951). *Personality.* New York: William Sloane.

McClelland, D.C., Atkinson, J.W., Clark, R.A., & Lowell, E.L. (1953). *The achievement motive.* East Norwalk, CT: Appleton-Century-Crofts.

McClelland, D.C., Koestner, R., & Weinberger, J. (1989). How do self-attributed and implicit motives differ? *Psychological Review, 96,* 690-702.

Merriam-Webster Online Dictionary. (2009). Process. www.merriam-webster.com/dictionary/process.

Messick, S. (1995). Validity of psychological assessment: Validation of inferences from persons' responses and performances as scientific inquiry into score meaning. *American Psychologist, 50,* 741-749.

Mohsen, S. (2007). The study of validity and reliability in the participation motivation questionnaire and task and ego orientation in sport questionnaire among the secondary and high school students of Tehran. *Research on Sport Science, 4,* 15-31.

Morris, R.L., & Kavussanu, M. (2008). Antecedents of approach-avoidance goals in sport. *Journal of Sports Sciences, 26,* 465-476.

Mouratidis, A., Vansteenkiste, M., Lens, W., & Auweele, Y.V. (2009). Beyond positive and negative affect: Achievement goals and discrete emotions in the elementary physical education classroom. *Psychology of Sport and Exercise, 10,* 336-343.

Mulig, J.C., Haggerty, M.E., Carballosa, A.B., Cinnick, W.J., & Madden, J.M. (1985). Relationships among fear of success, fear of failure, and androgyny. *Psychology of Women Quarterly, 9,* 284-287.

Murray, H.A. (1938). *Explorations in personality.* New York: Oxford University Press.

Newton, M., Watson, D.L., Kim, M.-S., & Beacham, A.O. (2006). Understanding motivation of underserved youth in physical activity settings. *Youth and Society, 37,* 348-371.

Nicholls, J.G. (1976). Effort is virtuous, but it's better to have ability: Evaluative responses to perceptions of effort and ability. *Journal of Personality and Social Psychology, 31,* 306-315.

Nicholls, J.G. (1978). The development of concepts of effort and ability, perception of own attainment, and the understanding that difficult tasks require more ability. *Child Development, 49,* 800-814.

Nicholls, J.G. (1984a). Achievement motivation: Conceptions of ability, subjective experience, task choice, and performance. *Psychological Review, 91,* 328-346.

Nicholls, J.G. (1984b). Conceptions of ability and achievement motivation. In R. Ames & C. Ames (Eds.), *Research on motivation in education: Vol. 1. Student motivation.* New York: Academic Press.

Nicholls, J.G. (1989). *The competitive ethos and democratic education.* Cambridge, MA: Harvard University Press.

Nien, C.-L., & Duda, J.L. (2008). Antecedents and consequences of approach and avoidance achievement goals: A test of gender invariance. *Psychology of Sport and Exercise, 9,* 352-372.

Ntoumanis, N., & Biddle, S. (1998a). The relationship between competitive anxiety, achievement goals, and motivational climates. *Research Quarterly for Exercise and Sport, 69,* 176-187.

Ntoumanis, N., & Biddle, S. (1998b). The relationship between achievement goal profile groups and perceptions of motivational climates in sport. *Scandinavian Journal of Medicine and Science in Sports, 8,* 1210-1124.

Nunnally, J.C. (1994). *Psychometric theory* (3rd ed.). New York: McGraw-Hill.

Papaioannou, A. (1998). Goal perspectives, reasons for being disciplined, and self-reported discipline in physical education lessons. *Journal of Teaching in Physical Education, 17,* 421-441.

Passer, M.W. (1983). Fear of failure, fear of evaluation, perceived competence, and self-esteem in competitive trait anxious children. *Journal of Sport Psychology, 5,* 172-188.

Poulsen, A.A., Ziviani, J.M., & Cuskelly, M. (2006). General self-concept and life satisfaction for boys with differing levels of physical coordination: The role of goal orientations and leisure participation. *Human Movement Science, 25,* 839-860.

Ram, N., & Gerstorf, D. (2009). Methods for the study of development-developing methods. *Research in Human Development, 6,* 61-73.

Rawsthorne, L.J., & Elliot, A.J. (1999). Achievement goals and intrinsic motivation: A meta-analytic review. *Personality and Social Psychology Review, 3,* 326-344.

Roberts, G.C., Treasure, D.C., & Balague, G. (1998). Achievement goals in sport: The development and validation of the Perception of Success Questionnaire. *Journal of Sports Sciences, 16,* 337-347.

Roberts, G.C., Treasure, D.C., & Conroy, D.E. (2007). Understanding the dynamics of motivation in sport and physical activity: An achievement goal interpretation. In G. Tenenbaum & R.C. Eklund (Eds.), *Handbook of sport psychology* (3rd ed., pp. 3-30). Hoboken, NJ: Wiley.

Ryska, T.A. (2003). Sportsmanship in young athletes: The role of competitiveness, motivational orientation, and perceived purposes of sport. *The Journal of Psychology, 137,* 237-293.

Sage, L., & Kavussanu, M. (2007). Multiple goal orientations as predictors of moral behavior in youth soccer. *The Sport Psychologist, 21,* 417-437.

Schantz, L.H., & Conroy, D.E. (2009). Achievement motivation and intraindividual affective variability during competence pursuits: A round of golf as a multilevel data structure. *Journal of Research in Personality, 43,* 472-481.

Schiano-Lomoriello, S., Cury, F., & Da Fonseca, D. (2005). Development and validation of the Approach and Avoidance Questionnaire for Sport and Physical Education setting (AAQSPE). *European Review of Applied Psychology, 55,* 85-98.

Schmalt, H.-D. (1999). Assessing the achievement motive using the grid technique. *Journal of Research in Personality, 33,* 109-130.

Schmalt, H.-D. (2005). Validity of a short form of the Achievement Motive Grid (AMG-S): Evidence for the three factor structure emphasizing active and passive forms of fear of failure. *Journal of Personality Assessment, 84,* 172-184.

Schultheiss, O.C. (2007). A memory-systems approach to the classification of personality tests: Comment on Meyer and Kurtz (2006). *Journal of Personality Assessment, 89,* 197-202.

Schultheiss, O.C., & Pang, J.S. (2007). Measuring implicit motives. In R.W. Robins, R.C. Fraley, & R. Krueger (Eds.), *Handbook of research methods in personality psychology* (pp. 322-344). New York: Guilford Press.

Simons, J., Dewitte, S., & Lens, W. (2003). "Don't do it for me. Do it for yourself!" Stressing the personal relevance enhances motivation in physical education. *Journal of Sport and Exercise Psychology, 25,* 145-160.

Smith, J.M.J., & Harwood, C.G. (2001). The transiency of goal involvement within match-play: A case study of an elite player. *Journal of Sports Sciences, 20,* 71-72.

Smith, R.E., Smoll, F.L., Cumming, S.P., & Grossbard, J.R. (2006). Measurement of multidimensional sport performance anxiety in children and adults: The Sport Anxiety Scale-2. *Journal of Sport and Exercise Psychology, 28,* 479-501.

Smith, R.E., Smoll, F.L., & Schutz, R.W. (1990). Measurement and correlates of sport-specific cognitive and somatic trait anxiety: The Sport Anxiety Scale. *Anxiety Research, 2,* 263-280.

Sokolowski, K., Schmalt, H.-D., Langens, T.A., & Puca, R.M. (2000). Assessing achievement, affiliation, and power motives all at once: The Multi-Motive Grid (MMG). *Journal of Personality Assessment, 74,* 126-145.

Spangler, W.D. (1992). Validity of questionnaire and TAT measures of need for achievement: Two meta-analyses. *Psychological Bulletin, 112,* 140-154.

Spence, J.T., & Helmreich, R.L. (1983). Achievement-related motives and behaviors. In J.T. Spence (Ed.), *Achievement and achievement motives: Psychological and sociological approaches* (pp. 7-74). San Francisco: Freeman.

Standage, M., & Treasure, D.C. (2002). Relationships among achievement goal orientations and multidimensional situational motivation in physical education. *British Journal of Educational Psychology, 72,* 87-103.

Stoeber, J., Stoll, O., Pescheck, E., & Otto, K. (2008). Perfectionism and achievement goals in athletes: Relations with approach and avoidance orientations in mastery and performance goals. *Psychology of Sport and Exercise, 9,* 102-121.

Stoeber, J., Stoll, O., Salkmi, O., & Tiikkaja, J. (2009). Perfectionism and achievement goals in young Finnish ice-hockey players aspiring to make the Under-16 national team. *Journal of Sports Sciences, 27,* 85-94.

Stoeber, J., Uphill, M.A., & Hotham, S. (2009). Predicting race performance in triathlon: The role of perfectionism, achievement goals, and personal goal setting. *Journal of Sport and Exercise Psychology, 31,* 211-245.

Stuntz, C.P., & Weiss, M.R. (2009). Achievement goal orientations and motivational outcomes in youth sport: The role of social orientations. *Psychology of Sport and Exercise, 10,* 255-262.

Swain, A.B.J., & Harwood, C.G. (1996). Antecedents of state goals in age-group swimmers: An interactionist perspective. *Journal of Sports Sciences, 14,* 111-124.

Thrash, T.M., & Hurst, A.L. (2008). Approach and avoidance motivation in the achievement domain: Integrating the achievement motivation and achievement goal traditions. In A.J. Elliot (Ed.), *Handbook of approach and avoidance motivation* (pp. 217-233). New York: Guilford Press.

Treasure, D.C., Duda, J.L., Hall, H.K., Roberts, G.C., Ames, C., & Maehr, M.L. (2001). Clarifying misconceptions and misrepresentations in achievement goal research in sport: A response to Harwood, Hardy, and Swain. *Journal of Sport and Exercise Psychology, 23,* 317-329.

Vallacher, R.R., Nowak, A., Froehlich, M., & Rockloff, M. (2002). The dynamics of self-evaluation. *Personality and Social Psychology Review, 6,* 370-379.

Van Yperen, N.W., & Duda, J.L. (1999). Goal orientations, beliefs about success, and performance improvement among young elite Dutch soccer players. *Scandinavian Journal of Medicine and Science in Sports, 9,* 358-364.

Wang, C.K.J., Biddle, S.J.H., & Elliot, A.J. (2007). The 2 × 2 achievement goal framework in a physical education context. *Psychology of Sport and Exercise, 8,* 147-168.

Wang, C.K.J., Chatzisarantis, N.L.D., Spray, C.S., & Biddle, S.J.H. (2002). Achievement goal profiles in school physical education: Differences in self-determination, sport ability beliefs, and physical activity. *British Journal of Educational Psychology, 72,* 433-445.

Wang, C.K.J., & Liu, W.C. (2007). Promoting enjoyment in girls' physical education: The impact of goals, beliefs, and self-determination. *European Physical Education Review, 13,* 145-164.

Wanous, J.P., Reichers, A.E., & Hudy, M.J. (1997). Overall job satisfaction: How good are single-item measures? *Journal of Applied Psychology, 82,* 247-252.

Warburton, V.E., & Spray, C.M. (2009). Antecedents of approach-avoidance achievement goal adoption in physical education: A longitudinal perspective. *Journal of Teaching in Physical Education, 28,* 214-232.

Williams, L. (1998). Contextual influences and goal perspectives among female youth sport participants. *Research Quarterly for Sport and Exercise, 69,* 47-57.

Winter, D.G. (1994). *Manual for scoring motive imagery in running text* (4th ed.). Unpublished manuscript, University of Michigan, Department of Psychology, Ann Arbor, MI.

Wright, A.G.C., Pincus, A.L., Conroy, D.E., & Elliot, A.J. (2009). The pathoplastic relationship between interpersonal problems and fear of failure. *Journal of Personality, 77,* 997-1024.

Xiang, P., & Lee, A. (1998). The development of self-perceptions of ability and achievement goals and their relations in physical education. *Research Quarterly for Exercise and Sport, 69,* 231-241.

Chapter 28

Alpert, M., & Rosen, A. (1990). A semantic analysis of the various ways that the terms "affect," "emotion," and "mood" are used. *Journal of Communication Disorders, 23,* 237-246.

American College of Sports Medicine. (2010). *ACSM's guidelines for exercise testing and prescription* (8th ed.). Philadelphia: Lippincott Williams & Wilkins.

Annesi, J.J. (2006). Preliminary testing of a brief inventory for assessing changes in exercise-induced feeling states. *Perceptual and Motor Skills, 102,* 776-780.

Bandura, A. (1988). Self-efficacy conception of anxiety. *Anxiety Research, 1,* 77-98.

Bagby, R.M., Ryder, A.G., Schuller, D.R., & Marshall, M.B. (2004). The Hamilton Depression Rating Scale: Has the gold standard become a lead weight? *American Journal of Psychiatry, 161,* 2163-2177.

Batson, C.D., Shaw, L.L., & Oleson, K.C. (1992). Differentiating affect, mood, and emotion: Toward functionally based conceptual distinctions. In M.S. Clark (Ed.), *Review of personality and social psychology* (Vol. 13, pp. 294-326). Newbury Park, CA: Sage.

Beck, A.T., Steer, R.A., & Brown, G.K. (1996). *Beck Depression Inventory—Second Edition manual.* San Antonio: The Psychological Corporation.

Beck, A.T., Steer, R.A., & Garbin, M.G. (1988). Psychometric properties of the Beck Depression Inventory: Twenty-five years of evaluation. *Clinical Psychology Review, 8,* 77-100.

Beedie, C.J., Terry, P.C., & Lane, A.M. (2005). Distinctions between emotion and mood. *Cognition and Emotion, 19,* 847-878.

Bixby, W.R., Spalding, T.W., & Hatfield, B.D. (2001). Temporal dynamics and dimensional specificity of the affective response to exercise of varying intensity: Differing pathways to a common outcome. *Journal of Sport and Exercise Psychology, 23,* 171-190.

Blumenthal, J.A., Babyak, M.A., Doraiswamy, P.M., Watkins, L., Hoffman, B.M., Barbour, K.A., Herman, S., Craighead, W.E., Brosse, A.L., Waugh, R., Hinderliter, A., & Sherwood, A. (2007). Exercise and pharmacotherapy in the treatment of major depressive disorder. *Psychosomatic Medicine, 69,* 587-596.

Blumenthal, J.A., Babyak, M.A., Moore, K.A., Craighead, W.E., Herman, S., Khatri, P., Waugh, R., Napolitano, M.A., Forman, L.M., Appelbaum, M., Doraiswamy, M., & Krishnan, R. (1999). Effects of exercise training on older patients with major depression. *Archives of Internal Medicine, 159,* 2349-2356.

Bodin, T., & Martinsen, E.W. (2004). Mood and self-efficacy during acute exercise in clinical depression: A randomized controlled study. *Journal of Sport and Exercise Psychology, 26,* 623-633.

Bradley, M.M., & Lang, P.J. (1994). Measuring emotion: The Self-Assessment Manikin and the Semantic Differential. *Journal of Behavioral Therapy and Experimental Psychiatry, 25,* 49-59.

Crocker, P.R.E. (1997). A confirmatory factor analysis of the Positive Affect Negative Affect Schedule (PANAS) with a youth sport sample. *Journal of Sport and Exercise Psychology, 19,* 91-97.

DiLorenzo, T.M., Bargman, E.P., Stucky-Ropp, R., Brassington, G.S., Frensch, P.A., & LaFontaine, T. (1999). Long-term effects of aerobic exercise on psychological outcomes. *Preventive Medicine, 28,* 75-85.

Dunn, A.L., Trivedi, M.H., Kampert, J.B., Clark, C.G., & Chambliss, H.O. (2005). Exercise treatment for depression: Efficacy and dose-response. *American Journal of Preventive Medicine, 28,* 1-8.

Ekkekakis, P. (2008). Affect circumplex redux: The discussion on its utility as a measurement framework in exercise psychology continues. *International Review of Sport and Exercise Psychology, 1,* 139-159.

Ekkekakis, P., Hall, E.E., & Petruzzello, S.J. (1999). Measuring state anxiety in the context of acute exercise using the State Anxiety Inventory: An attempt to resolve the brouhaha. *Journal of Sport and Exercise Psychology, 21,* 205-229.

Ekkekakis, P., Hall, E.E., & Petruzzello, S.J. (2005). Evaluation of the circumplex structure of the Activation Deactivation Adjective Check List before and after a short walk. *Psychology of Sport and Exercise, 6,* 83-101.

Ekkekakis, P., Hall, E.E., Van Landuyt, L.M., & Petruzzello, S.J. (2000). Walking in (affective) circles: Can short walks enhance affect? *Journal of Behavioral Medicine, 23,* 245-275.

Ekkekakis, P., & Petruzzello, S.J. (2000). Analysis of the affect measurement conundrum in exercise psychology: I. Fundamental issues. *Psychology of Sport and Exercise, 1,* 71-88.

Ekkekakis, P., & Petruzzello, S.J. (2001a). Analysis of the affect measurement conundrum in exercise psychology: II. A conceptual and methodological critique of the Exercise-Induced Feeling Inventory. *Psychology of Sport and Exercise, 2,* 1-26.

Ekkekakis, P., & Petruzzello, S.J. (2001b). Analysis of the affect measurement conundrum in exercise psychology: III. A conceptual and methodological critique of the Subjective Exercise Experiences Scale. *Psychology of Sport and Exercise, 2,* 205-232.

Ekkekakis, P., & Petruzzello, S.J. (2002). Analysis of the affect measurement conundrum in exercise psychology: IV. A conceptual case for the affect circumplex. *Psychology of Sport and Exercise, 3,* 35-63.

Frijda, N.H. (2009). Mood. In D. Sander & K.R. Scherer (Eds.), *The Oxford companion to emotion and the affective sciences* (pp. 258-259). New York: Oxford University Press.

Gauvin, L., & Rejeski, W.J. (1993). The Exercise-Induced Feeling Inventory: Development and initial validation. *Journal of Sport and Exercise Psychology, 15,* 403-423.

Goldfarb, A.H., Hatfield, B.D., Sforzo, G.A., & Flynn, M.G. (1987). Serum β-endorphin levels during a graded exercise test to exhaustion. *Medicine and Science in Sports and Exercise, 19,* 78-82.

Gregg, V.H., & Shepherd, A.J. (2009). Factor structure of scores on the state version of the Four Dimension Mood Scale. *Educational and Psychological Measurement, 69,* 146-156.

Hamilton, M. (1960). A rating scale for depression. *Journal of Neurology, Neurosurgery, and Psychiatry, 23,* 56-62.

Hardy, C.J., & Rejeski, W.J. (1989). Not what, but how one feels: The measurement of affect during exercise. *Journal of Sport and Exercise Psychology, 11,* 304-317.

Hulley, A., Bentley, N., Clough, C., Fishlock, A., Morrell, F., O'Brien, J., & Radmore, J. (2008). Active and passive commuting to school: Influences on affect in primary school children. *Research Quarterly for Exercise and Sport, 79,* 525-534.

Jerome, G.J., Marquez, D.X., McAuley, E., Canaklisova, S., Snook, E., & Vickers, M. (2002). Self-efficacy effects of feeling states in women. *International Journal of Behavioral Medicine, 9,* 139-154.

Kwan, B.M., & Bryan, A.D. (2010). Affective response to exercise as a component of exercise motivation: Attitudes, norms, self-efficacy, and temporal stability of intentions. *Psychology of Sport and Exercise, 11,* 71-79.

Lang, P.J. (1980). Behavioral treatment and bio-behavioral assessment: Computer applications. In J.B. Sodowski, J.H. Johnson, & T.A. Williams (Eds.), *Technology in mental health care delivery systems* (pp. 119-137). Norwood, NJ: Ablex.

Larsen, R.J., & Diener, E. (1992). Promises and problems with the circumplex model of emotion. In M.S. Clark (Ed.), *Review of personality and social psychology* (Vol. 13, pp. 25-59). Newbury Park, CA: Sage.

Lox, C.L., Jackson, S., Tuholski, S.W., Wasley, D., & Treasure, D.C. (2000). Revisiting the measurement of exercise-induced feeling states: The Physical Activity Affect Scale (PAAS). *Measurement in Physical Education and Exercise Science, 4*, 79-95.

Lubin, B., Zuckerman, M., Hanson, P.G., Armstrong, T., Rinck, C.M., & Seever, M. (1986). Reliability and validity of the Multiple Affect Adjective Check List-Revised. *Journal of Psychopathology and Behavioral Assessment, 8*, 103-117.

McAuley, E., & Courneya, K.S. (1994). The Subjective Exercise Experiences Scale (SEES): Development and preliminary validation. *Journal of Sport and Exercise Psychology, 16*, 163-177.

McNair, D.M., & Lorr, M. (1964). An analysis of mood in neurotics. *Journal of Abnormal and Social Psychology, 69*, 620-627.

McNair, D.M., Lorr, M., & Droppleman, L.F. (1971). *Manual for the Profile of Mood States.* San Diego: Educational and Industrial Testing Service.

Miller, B.M., Bartholomew, J.B., & Springer, B.A. (2005). Post-exercise affect: The effect of mode preference. *Journal of Applied Sport Psychology, 17*, 263-272.

Morris, W.M. (1992). A functional analysis of the role of mood in affective systems. In M.S. Clark (Ed.), *Review of personality and social psychology* (Vol. 13, pp. 256-293). Newbury Park, CA: Sage.

Nemanick, R.C., & Munz, D.C. (1994). Measuring the poles of positive and negative mood using the Positive Affect Negative Affect Schedule and Activation Deactivation Adjective Check List. *Psychological Reports, 74*, 195-199.

Puetz, T.W., O'Connor, P.J., & Dishman, R.K. (2006). Effects of chronic exercise on feelings of energy and fatigue: A quantitative synthesis. *Psychological Bulletin, 132*, 866-876.

Reed, J., & Buck, S. (2009). The effect of regular aerobic exercise on positive activated affect: A meta-analysis. *Psychology of Sport and Exercise, 10*, 581-594.

Reed, J., & Ones, D.S. (2006). The effect of acute aerobic exercise on positive activated affect: A meta-analysis. *Psychology of Sport and Exercise, 7*, 477-514.

Rejeski, W.J., Hardy, C.J., & Shaw, J. (1991). Psychometric confounds of assessing state anxiety in conjunction with acute bouts of vigorous exercise. *Journal of Sport and Exercise Psychology, 13*, 65-74.

Rejeski, W.J., Reboussin, B.A., Dunn, A.L., King, A.C., & Sallis, J.F. (1999). A modified Exercise-Induced Feeling Inventory for chronic training and baseline profiles of participants in the Activity Counseling Trial. *Journal of Health Psychology, 4*, 97-108.

Richter, P., Werner, J., Heerlein, A., Kraus, A., & Sauer, H. (1998). On the validity of the Beck Depression Inventory: A review. *Psychopathology, 31*, 160-168.

Russell, J.A. (1980). A circumplex model of affect. *Journal of Personality and Social Psychology, 39*, 1161-1178.

Russell, J.A. (2003). Core affect and the psychological construction of emotion. *Psychological Review, 110*, 145-172.

Russell, J.A. (2005). Emotion in human consciousness is built on core affect. *Journal of Consciousness Studies, 12*, 26-42.

Russell, J.A., & Feldman Barrett, L. (1999). Core affect, prototypical emotional episodes, and other things called emotion: Dissecting the elephant. *Journal of Personality and Social Psychology, 76*, 805-819.

Russell, J.A., & Feldman Barrett, L. (2009). Core affect. In D. Sander & K.R. Scherer (Eds.), *The Oxford companion to emotion and the affective sciences* (p. 104). New York: Oxford University Press.

Russell, J.A., Weiss, A., & Mendelsohn, G.A. (1989). Affect Grid: A single item scale of pleasure and arousal. *Journal of Personality and Social Psychology, 57*, 493-502.

Smith, J.C., O'Connor, P.J., Crabbe, J.B., & Dishman, R.K. (2002). Emotional responsiveness after low- and moderate-intensity exercise and seated rest. *Medicine and Science in Sports and Exercise, 34*, 1158-1167.

Spielberger, C.D. (1972). Anxiety as an emotional state. In C.D. Spielberger (Ed.), *Anxiety: Current trends in theory and research* (Vol. 1, pp. 23-49). New York: Academic Press.

Spielberger, C.D. (1983). *Manual for the State-Trait Anxiety Inventory (Form Y).* Palo Alto, CA: Consulting Psychologists.

Spielberger, C.D., Gorsuch, R.L., & Lushene, R.E. (1970). *Manual for the State-Trait Anxiety Inventory.* Palo Alto, CA: Consulting Psychologists.

Spielberger, C.D., Lushene, R.E., & McAdoo, W.G. (1977). Theory and measurement of anxiety states. In R.B. Cattell & R.M. Dreger (Eds.), *Handbook of modern personality theory* (pp. 239-253). New York: Wiley.

Spielberger, C.D., & Reheiser, E.C. (2004). Measuring anxiety, anger, depression, and curiosity as emotional states and personality traits with the STAI, STAXI, and STPI. In M.J. Hilsenroth & D.L. Segal (Eds.), *Comprehensive handbook of psychological assessment* (Vol. 2, pp. 70-86). Hoboken, NJ: Wiley.

Svebak, S., & Murgatroyd, S. (1985). Metamotivational dominance: A multimethod validation of reversal theory constructs. *Journal of Personality and Social Psychology, 48*, 107-116.

Thayer, R.E. (1989). *The biopsychology of mood and arousal.* New York: Oxford University Press.

Watson, D., & Clark, L.A. (1997). Measurement and mismeasurement of mood: Recurrent and emergent issues. *Journal of Personality Assessment, 68*, 267-296.

Watson, D., Clark, L.A., & Tellegen, A. (1988). Development and validation of brief measures of positive and negative affect: The PANAS scales. *Journal of Personality and Social Psychology, 54*, 1063-1070.

Watson, D., & Tellegen, A. (1985). Toward a consensual structure of mood. *Psychological Bulletin, 98*, 219-235.

Weiner, B. (1985). An attributional theory of achievement motivation and emotion. *Psychological Review, 92*, 548-573.

Williams, D.M., Dunsiger, S., Ciccolo, J.T., Lewis, B.A., Albrecht, A.E., & Marcus, B.H. (2008). Acute affective response to a moderate-intensity exercise stimulus predicts physical activity participation 6 and 12 months later. *Psychology of Sport and Exercise, 9*, 231-245.

Yik, M.S.M., Russell, J.A., & Feldman-Barrett, L. (1999). Structure of self-reported current affect: Integration and beyond. *Journal of Personality and Social Psychology, 77*, 600-619.

Zevon, M.A., & Tellegen, A. (1982). The structure of mood change: An idiographic/nomothetic analysis. *Journal of Personality and Social Psychology, 43*, 111-122.

Zuckerman, M., & Lubin, B. (1965). *Manual for the Multiple Affect Adjective Check List.* San Diego: Educational and Industrial Testing Service.

Zuckerman, M., & Lubin, B. (1985). *Manual for the MAACL-R: The Multiple Affect Adjective Check List-Revised*. San Diego: Educational and Industrial Testing Service.

Zuckerman, M., Lubin, B., & Rinck, C.M. (1983). Construction of new scales for the Multiple Affect Adjective Check List. *Journal of Behavioral Assessment, 5*, 119-129.

Zuckerman, M., Lubin, B., Vogel, L., & Valerius, E. (1964). Measurement of experimentally induced affects. *Journal of Consulting Psychology, 28*, 418-425.

Chapter 29

American Psychiatric Association. (2000). *Diagnostic and statistical manual of mental disorders: DSM-IV-TR*. Washington, DC: American Psychiatric Association.

Apter, M.J. (1983). *The experience of motivation: The theory of psychological reversals*. London: Academic Press.

Arent, S.M., & Landers, D.M. (2003). Arousal, anxiety, and performance: A reexamination of the inverted-U hypothesis. *Research Quarterly for Exercise and Sport, 74*, 436-444.

Aubert, A.E., Seps, B., & Beckers, F. (2003). Heart rate variability in athletes. *Sports Medicine, 33*, 889-919.

Bar-Eli, M., & Blumenstein, B. (2004). Performance enhancement in swimming: The effect of mental training with biofeedback. *Journal of Science and Medicine in Sport, 7*, 454-464.

Bar-Eli, M., Dreshman, R., Blumenstein, B., & Weinstein, Y. (2001). The effect of mental training with biofeedback on the performance of young swimmers. *Applied Psychology: An International Review, 51*, 567-581.

Bar-Haim, Y., Lamy, D., Pergamin, L., Bakermans-Kranenburg, M.J., & van Ijzendoorn, M.H. (2007). Threat-related attentional bias in anxious and nonanxious individuals: A meta-analytic study. *Psychological Bulletin, 133*, 1-24.

Baumeister, R.F. (1984). Choking under pressure: Self-consciousness and paradoxical effects of incentives on skillful performance. *Journal of Personality and Social Psychology, 46*, 610-620.

Baumeister, R.F., & Showers, C.J. (1986). A review of paradoxical performance effect: Choking under pressure in sports and mental tests. *European Journal of Social Psychology, 16*, 361-383.

Behan, M., & Wilson, M. (2008). State anxiety and visual attention: The role of the quiet eye period in aiming to a far target. *Journal of Sport Sciences, 26*, 207-215.

Beilock, S.L., & Carr, T.H. (2001). On the fragility of skilled performance: What governs choking under pressure? *Journal of Experimental Psychology: General, 130*, 701-725.

Berntson, G.G., Quigley, K.S., & Lozano, D. (2007). Cardiovascular psychophysiology. In J.T. Cacioppo, L.G. Tassinary, & G.G. Berntson (Eds.), *Handbook of psychophysiology* (3rd ed., pp. 182-210). New York: Cambridge University Press.

Blumenstein, B., & Bar-Eli, M. (2004). The effect of extra-curricular mental training incorporating biofeedback on short running performance of adolescent physical education pupils. *European Physical Education Review, 10*, 123-134.

Blumenstein, B., Bar-Eli, M., & Tenenbaum, G. (1997). A five-step approach to mental training incorporating biofeedback. *The Sport Psychologist, 11*, 440-453.

Blumenstein, B., Bar-Haim, Y., & Tenenbaum, G. (1995). The augmenting role of biofeedback: Effects of autogenic, imagery, and music training on physiological indices and athletic performance. *Journal of Sports Sciences, 13*, 343-354.

Buchheit, M., Simon, C., Viola, A.U., Coutreleau, S., Piquard, F., & Brandenberger, T. (2004). Heart rate variability in sportive elderly: Relationship with daily physical activity. *Medicine and Science in Sports and Exercise, 36*, 601-605.

Burton, D. (1988). Do anxious swimmers swim slower? Re-examining the elusive anxiety-performance relationship. *Journal of Sport Psychology, 10*, 45-61.

Cacioppo, J.T., Martzke, J.S., Petty, R.E., & Tassinary, L.G. (1988). Specific forms of facial EMG response index emotions during an interview: From Darwin to the continuous flow hypothesis affect-laden information processing. *Journal of Personality and Social Psychology, 54*, 592-604.

Cacioppo, J.T., Tassinary, L.G., & Berntson, G. (Eds.). (2007). *The handbook of psychophysiology*. Cambridge, NY: Cambridge University Press.

Cerin, E. (2003). Anxiety versus fundamental emotions as predictors of perceived functionality of pre-competitive emotional states, threat, and challenge in individual sports. *Journal of Applied Sport Psychology, 15*, 223-238.

Cerin, E., & Barnett, A. (2006). A processual analysis of basic emotions and sources of concerns as they are lived before and after a competition. *Psychology of Sport and Exercise, 7*, 287-307.

Coan, J.A., & Allen, J.J.B. (Eds.). (2007). *Handbook of emotion elicitation and assessment*. New York: Oxford University Press.

Cohen, A., Pargman, D., & Tenenbaum, G. (2003). Critical elaboration and empirical investigation of the cusp catastrophe model: A lesson for practitioners. *Journal of Applied Sport Psychology, 15*, 144-159.

Cohen, S., Kessler, R.C., & Gordon, L.U. (1995). *Measuring stress: A guide for health and social scientists*. New York: Oxford University Press.

Coombes, S.A., Cauraugh, J.H., & Janelle, C.M. (2007). Dissociating motivational direction and affective valence: Specific emotions alter central motor processes. *Psychological Science, 18*, 938-942.

Coombes, S.A., Gamble, K.G., Cauraugh, J.H., & Janelle, C.M. (2008). Emotional states alter force control during a feedback occluded motor task. *Emotion, 8*, 104-113.

Cottyn, J., Clercq, D.D., Pannier, J., Crombez, G., & Lenoir, M. (2006). The measurement of competitive anxiety during balance beam performance in gymnasts. *Journal of Sport Sciences, 24*, 157-164.

Cox, R.H., Martens, M.P., & Russell, W.D. (2003). Measuring anxiety in athletics: The Revised Competitive State Anxiety Inventory-2. *Journal of Sport and Exercise Psychology, 25*, 519-533.

Cox, T., & Kerr, J.H. (1989). Arousal effects during tournament play in squash. *Perceptual and Motor Skills, 69*, 1275-1280.

Craft, L.L., Magyar, T.M., Becker, B.J., & Feltz, D.L. (2003). The relationship between the Competitive State Anxiety Inventory-2 and sport performance: A meta-analysis. *Journal of Sport and Exercise Psychology, 25*, 44-65.

Crocker, P.R.E. (1997). A confirmatory factor analysis of the Positive and Affect Negative Affect Schedule (PANAS) with a youth sport sample. *Journal of Sport and Exercise Psychology, 19*, 91-97.

Crocker, P., Kowalski, K., Hoar, S., & McDonough, M. (2004). Emotions in sport across adulthood. In M. Weiss (Ed.), *Developmental sport and exercise psychology: A lifespan perspective* (pp. 333-356). Morgantown, WV: Fitness Information Technology.

Davidson, R.J. (1995). Cerebral asymmetry, emotion, and affective style. In R.J. Davidson & K. Hugdahl (Eds.), *Brain asymmetry* (pp. 361-387). Cambridge, MA: MIT Press.

Davidson, R.J. (2004). Well-being and affective style: Neural substrates and biobehavioral correlates. *Philosophical Transactions of the Royal Society of London B, 359,* 1395-1411.

Davidson, R.J., Scherer, K.R., & Goldsmith, H.H. (Eds.). (2002). *Handbook of affective sciences.* Oxford: Oxford University Press.

Davis, J.E., & Cox, R.H. (2002). Interpreting direction of anxiety within Hanin's individual zone of optimal functioning. *Journal of Applied Sport Psychology, 14,* 43-52.

Dawson, M.E., Schell, A.M., & Filion, D.L. (2007). The electrodermal system. In J.T. Cacioppo, L.G. Tassinary, & G.G. Berntson (Eds.), *Handbook of psychophysiology* (3rd ed., pp. 159-181). New York: Cambridge University Press.

Dunn, J.G.H., Dunn, J.C., Wilson, P., & Syrotuik, D.G. (2000). Reexamining the factorial composition and factor structure of the Sport Anxiety Scale. *Journal of Sport and Exercise Psychology, 22,* 183-193.

Easterbrook, J.A. (1959). The effect of emotion on cue utilization and the organization of behavior. *Psychological Review, 66,* 183-201.

Edmonds, W.A., Tenenbaum, G., Mann, D.T.Y., Johnson, M., & Kamata, A. (2008). The effect of biofeedback training on affective regulation and simulated car-racing performance: A multiple case study analysis. *Journal of Sport Sciences, 26,* 761-773.

Edwards, T., & Hardy, L. (1996). The interactive effects of intensity and direction of cognitive and somatic anxiety and self-confidence upon performance. *Journal of Sport and Exercise Psychology, 18,* 296-312.

Ekman, P. (1984). Expression and the nature of emotion. In K.R. Scherer & P. Ekman (Eds.), *Approaches to emotion* (pp. 319-343). Hillsdale, NJ: Erlbaum.

Ekman, P., & Davidson, R.J. (1994). *The nature of emotion: Fundamental questions.* New York: Oxford University Press.

Eysenck, M.W., & Calvo, M.G. (1992). Anxiety and performance: The processing efficiency theory. *Cognition and Emotion, 6,* 409-434.

Eysenck, M.W., Derakshan, N., Santos, R., & Calvo, M.G. (2007). Anxiety and cognitive performance: Attentional control theory. *Emotion, 7,* 336-353.

Gehricke, J.G., & Shapiro, D. (2001). Facial and autonomic activity in depression: Social context differences during imagery. *International Journal of Psychophysiology, 41,* 53-64.

Gould, D., & Tuffey, S. (1996). Zones of optimal functioning research: A review and critique. *Anxiety, Stress and Coping, 9,* 53-68.

Gray, E.K., & Watson, D. (2007). Assessing positive and negative affect via self-report. In J. Coan & J.J.B. Allen (Eds.), *Handbook of emotion elicitation and assessment.* New York: Oxford University Press.

Grossman, P. (1992). Respiratory and cardiac rhythms as windows to central and autonomous bio-behavioral regulation selections of window frames, keeping the panes clean, and view the neural topography. *Biological Psychology, 34,* 131-161.

Gucciardi, D.F., & Dimmock, J.A. (2008). Choking under pressure in sensorimotor skills: Conscious processing or depleted attentional resources? *Psychology of Sport and Exercise, 9,* 45-59.

Hadd, V.N., & Crocker, P.R.E. (2007). The effect of stress-related factors on post-performance affects in competitive adolescent swimmers. *The International Journal of Sport and Exercise Psychology, 2,* 142-157.

Halberstadt, J. Winkielman, P., Niedenthal, P.M., & Dalle, N. (2009). Emotional conception: How embodied emotion concepts guide perception and facial action. *Psychological Science, 20,* 1254-1261.

Hancock, P.A., & Warm, J.S. (1989). A dynamic model of stress and sustained attention. *Human Factors, 31,* 519-537.

Hanin, Y.L. (1997). Emotions and athletic performance: Individual zones of optimal functioning model. *European Yearbook of Sport Psychology, 11,* 29-72.

Hanin, Y.L. (2000). Successful and poor performance and emotions. In Y. Hanin (Ed.), *Emotions in Sport* (pp. 157-188). Champaign, IL: Human Kinetics.

Hardy, L. (1990). A catastrophe model of anxiety and performance. In J.G. Jones & L. Hardy (Eds.), *Stress and performance in sport* (pp. 81-106). Chichester, UK: Wiley.

Hardy, L. (1996). Testing the predictions of the cusp catastrophe model of anxiety and performance. *The Sport Psychologist, 10,* 140-156.

Hariri, A.R. (2009). The neurobiology of individual differences in complex behavioral traits. *Annual Review of Neuroscience, 32,* 225-247.

Hatfield, B.D., & Hillman, C.H. (2001). The psychophysiology of sport: A mechanistic understanding of the psychology of superior performance. In R.N. Singer, H.A. Hausenblas, & C.M. Janelle (Eds.), *Handbook of sport psychology* (2nd ed., pp. 362-386). New York: Wiley.

Hillman, C.H., Apparies, R.J., Janelle, C.M., & Hatfield, B.D. (2000). An electrocortical comparison of executed and rejected shots in skilled marksmen. *Biological Psychology, 52,* 71-83.

Hillman, C.H., Cuthbert, B.N., Bradley, M.M., & Lang, P.J. (2004). Motivated engagement to appetitive and aversive fanship cues: Psychophysiological responses of rival sport fans. *Journal of Sport and Exercise Psychology, 26,* 338-351.

Hillman, C.H., Cuthbert, B.N., Cauraugh, J.H., Schupp, H.T., Bradley, M.M., & Lang, P.J. (2000). Psychophysiological responses of sport fans. *Motivation and Emotion, 24,* 13-28.

Houtman, I.L.D., & Bakker, F.C. (1989). The anxiety thermometer: A validation study. *Journal of Personality Assessment, 53,* 575-582.

Hull, C.L. (1943). *Principles of behavior.* New York: Appleton-Century-Crofts.

Izard, C.E. (1991). *The psychology of emotions.* New York: Plenum Press.

Janelle, C.M. (2002). Anxiety, arousal, and visual attention: A mechanistic account of performance variability. *Journal of Sport Sciences, 20,* 237-251.

Janelle, C.M., & Hatfield, B.D. (2008). Visual attention and brain processes that underlie expert performance: Implications for sport and military psychology. *Military Psychology, 20,* S39-S69.

Janelle, C.M., Hillman, C.H., Apparies, R.J., Murray, N.P., Meili, L., Fallon, E.A., & Hatfield, B.D. (2000). Expertise differences in cortical activation and gaze behavior during rifle shooting. *Journal of Sport and Exercise Psychology, 22,* 167-182.

Janelle, C.M., Singer, R.N., & Williams, A.M. (1999). External distraction and attentional narrowing: Visual search evidence. *Journal of Sport and Exercise Psychology, 21,* 70-91.

Jones, G., & Hanton, S. (2001). Pre-competitive feeling states and directional anxiety interpretations. *Journal of Sports Sciences, 19,* 385-395.

Jones, G., & Swain, A.B.J. (1992). Intensity and direction dimensions of competitive state anxiety and relationships with competitiveness. *Perceptual and Motor Skills, 74,* 467-472.

Jones, M.V., Lane, A.M., Bray, S.R., Uphill, M., & Catlin, J. (2005). Development and validation of the Sport Emotion Questionnaire. *Journal of Sport and Exercise Psychology, 27,* 407-431.

Kerick, S.E., Hatfield, B.D., & Allendar, L.E. (2007). Event-related cortical dynamics of soldiers during shooting as a function of varied task demand. *Aviation, Space, and Environmental Medicine, 78*(5), B-153-164.

Kerick, S.E., Iso-Ahola, S.E., & Hatfield, B.D. (2000). Psychomotor momentum in target shooting: Cortical, cognitive, affective, and behavioral responses. *Journal of Sport and Exercise Psychology, 22,* 1-20.

Kerr, J.H. (1985). The experience of arousal: A new basis for studying arousal effects in sport. *Journal of Sport Sciences, 3,* 169-179.

Kerr, J.H. (1990). Stress and sport: Reversal theory. In J.G. Jones (Ed.), *Stress and performance in sport* (pp. 107-131). New York: Wiley.

Koerner, N., & Dugas, M.J. (2006). A cognitive-affective model of generalized anxiety disorder: The role of intolerance of uncertainty. In G.C.L. Davey & A. Wells (Eds.), *Worry and psychological disorders: Theory, assessment, and treatment* (pp. 201-216). Chichester, UK: Wiley.

Konorski, J. (1967). *Integrative activity of the brain: An interdisciplinary approach.* Chicago: University of Chicago Press.

Krane, V. (1994). The Mental Readiness Form as a measure of competitive state anxiety. *The Sport Psychologist, 8,* 189-202.

Landers, D.M., Han, M., Salazar, W., Petruzzello, S.J., Kubitz, K.A., & Gannon, T.L. (1994). Effects of learning on electroencephalographic and electrocardiographic patterns in novice archers. *International Journal of Sport Psychology, 25,* 313-330.

Lane, A.M., Sewell, D.F., Terry, P.C., Bartram, D., & Nesti, M.S. (1999). Confirmatory factor analysis of the Competitive State Anxiety Inventory-2. *Journal of Sport Sciences, 17,* 505-512.

Lang, P.J. (2000). Emotion and motivation: Attention, perception, and action. *Journal of Sport amd Exercise Psychology, 20,* S122-S140.

Lang, P.J., Bradley, M.M., & Cuthbert, B.N. (2008). *International Affective Picture System (IAPS): Affective ratings of pictures and instruction manual* (Tech. Rep. No. A-8). Gainesville, FL: University of Florida.

Lang, P.J., Cuthbert, B.N., & Bradley, M.M. (1998). Measuring emotion in therapy: Imagery, activation, and feeling. *Behavior Therapy, 29,* 655-674.

Lang, P.J., Greenwald, M.K., Bradley, M.M., & Hamm, A.O. (1993). Looking at pictures: Affective, facial, visceral, and behavioral reactions. *Psychophysiology, 30,* 261-273.

Lang, P.J., McTeague, L.M., & Cuthbert, B.N. (2006). Fearful imagery and the anxiety disorder spectrum. In B. Rothbaum (Ed.), *Pathological anxiety: Emotional processing in etiology and treatment.* New York: Guilford Press.

Lazarus, R.S. (2000). How emotions influence performance in competitive sports. *The Sport Psychologist, 14,* 229-252.

Males, J., & Kerr, J.H. (1996). Stress, emotion, and performance in elite slalom canoeists. *The Sport Psychologist, 10,* 17-43.

Mann, D.T.Y., Williams, A.M., Ward, P., & Janelle, C.M. (2007). Perceptual-cognitive expertise in sport: A meta-analysis. *Journal of Sport and Exercise Psychology, 29,* 457-478.

Martens, R. (1977). *Sport Competition Anxiety Test.* Champaign, IL: Human Kinetics.

Martens, R., Burton, D., Vealey, R., Bump, L.A., & Smith, D.E. (1990). Reliability and validity of the Competitive State Anxiety Inventory-2. In R. Martens, R.S. Vealey, & D. Burton (Eds.), *Competitive anxiety in sport* (pp. 127-140). Champaign, IL: Human Kinetics.

Martens, R., Vealey, R.S., & Burton, D. (1990). *Competitive anxiety in sport.* Champaign, IL: Human Kinetics.

Masters, R.S.W. (1992). Knowledge, knerves, and know-how. *British Journal of Psychology, 83,* 343-358.

Maxwell, J.P., Masters, R.S.W., & Poolton, J.M. (2006). Performance breakdowns in sport: The roles of reinvestment and verbal knowledge. *Research Quarterly for Exercise and Sport, 77,* 271-276.

Mellalieu, S.D., Hanton, S., & Jones, G. (2003). Emotional labeling and competitive anxiety in preparation and competition. *The Sport Psychologist, 17,* 157-174.

Milton, J.G., Small, S.S., & Solodkin, A. (2004). On the road to automatic: Dynamic aspects in the development of expertise. *Journal of Clinical Neurophysiology, 21,* 134-143.

Moran, A., Byrne, A., & McGlade, N. (2002). The effects of anxiety and strategic planning on visual search behavior. *Journal of Sports Sciences, 20,* 225-236.

Morris, L.W., Davis, M.A., & Hutchings, C.H. (1981). Cognitive and emotional components of anxiety: Literature review and a revised worry-emotionality scale. *Journal of Educational Psychology, 73*(4), 541-555.

Mullen, R., & Hardy, L. (2000). State anxiety and motor performance: Testing the conscious processing hypothesis. *Journal of Sports Sciences, 18,* 785-799.

Mullen, R., Hardy, L., & Tattersall, A. (2005). The effects of anxiety on motor performance: A test of the conscious processing hypothesis. *Journal of Sport and Exercise Psychology, 27,* 212-225.

Murray, N.P., & Janelle, C.M. (2003). Anxiety and performance: A visual search examination of the processing efficiency theory. *Journal of Sport and Exercise Psychology, 25,* 171-187.

Murray, N.P., & Janelle, C.M. (2007). Event-related potential evidence for the processing efficiency theory. *Journal of Sport Sciences, 25,* 161-171.

Murray, N.P., & Raedeke, T.D. (2008). Heart rate variability as an indicator of pre-competitive arousal. *International Journal of Sport Psychology, 39,* 346-355.

Naugle, K.M, Joyner, J., Coombes, S.A., Hass, C.J., & Janelle, C.M. (2011). Emotional state affects the initiation of forward gait. *Emotion, 11,* 267-277.

Naugle, K.M., Joyner, J., Hass, C.J., & Janelle, C.M. (2010). Emotional influences on locomotor behavior. *Journal of Biomechanics, 43,* 3099-3103..

Nieuwenhuys, A., Pijpers, J.R., Oudejans, R.D., & Bakker, F.C. (2008). The influence of anxiety on visual attention in climbing. *Journal of Sport and Exercise Psychology, 30,* 171-185.

Perkins, D., Wilson, G.V., & Kerr, J.H. (2001). The effects of elevated arousal and mood on maximal strength performance in athletes. *Journal of Applied Sport Psychology, 13,* 239-259.

Pijpers, J.R., Oudejans, R.D., Holsheimer, F., & Bakker, F.C. (2003). Anxiety-performance relationships in climbing: A process-oriented approach. *Psychology of Sport and Exercise, 4,* 283-304.

Poolton, J.M., Maxwell, J.P., Masters, R.S.W., & Raab, M. (2006). Benefits of an external focus of attention: Common coding or conscious processing? *Journal of Sport Sciences, 24,* 89-99.

Posner, M.I., & Gilbert, C.D. (1999). Attention and primary visual cortex. *Proceedings of the National Academy of Sciences of the United States of America, 96,* 2585-2587.

Prapavessis, H., Maddison, R., & Fletcher, R. (2005). Further examination of the factor integrity of the Sport Anxiety Scale. *Journal of Sport and Exercise Psychology, 27,* 253-260.

Ramaekers, D., Ector, H., Aubert, A.E., Rubens, A., & Van de Werf, F. (1998). Heart rate and heart rate variability in healthy volunteers: Is the female autonomic nervous system cardio-protective? *European Heart Journal, 19*, 1334-1341.

Robazza, C., Bortoli, L., & Hanin, Y. (2006). Perceived effects of emotion intensity on athletic performance: A contingency-based individualized approach. *Research Quarterly for Exercise and Sport, 77*, 372-385.

Robazza, C., Bortoli, L, Nocini, F., Moser, G., & Arslan, C. (2000). Normative and idiosyncratic measures of positive and negative affect in sport. *Psychology of Sport and Exercise, 1*, 103-116.

Robazza, C., Pellizzari, M., Bertollo, M., & Hanin, Y.L. (2008). Functional impact of emotions on athletic performance: Comparing the IZOF model and the directional perception approach. *Journal of Sports Sciences, 26*, 1033-1047.

Rodrigues, S., Vickers, J., & Williams, A.M. (2002). Head, eye and arm coordination in table tennis. *Journal of Sport Sciences, 20*, 187-200.

Russell, J.A. (1980). A circumplex model of affect. *Journal of Personality and Social Psychology, 39*, 1161-1178.

Russell, W.D., & Cox, R.H. (2000). A laboratory investigation of positive and negative affect within individual zones of optimal functioning theory. *Journal of Sport Behavior, 23*, 164-180.

Saarela, R. (1999). *The effects of mental stress on cerebral hemispheric asymmetry and psychomotor performance in skilled marksmen.* Unpublished doctoral dissertation, University of Maryland.

Schneirla, T. (1959). An evolutionary and developmental theory of biphasic processes underlying approach and withdrawal. In M. Jones (Ed.), *Nebraska Symposium on Motivation* (pp. 1-42). Lincoln, NE: University of Nebraska Press.

Selye, H. (1955). Stress and disease. *Science, 122*, 625-631.

Smith, N.C., Bellamy, M., Collins, D.J., & Newell, D. (2001). A test of processing efficiency theory in a team sport context. *Journal of Sports Sciences, 19*, 321-332.

Smith, R., Smoll, F., & Schultz, R.W. (1990). Measurement and correlates of sport specific cognitive and somatic trait anxiety: The Sport Anxiety Scale. *Anxiety Research, 2*, 263-280.

Smith, R.E., Smoll, F.L., & Cumming, S.P. (2007). Effects of a motivational climate intervention for coaches on young athletes' sport performance anxiety. *Journal of Sport and Exercise Psychology, 29*, 39-59.

Smith, R.E., Smoll, F.L., Cumming, S.P., & Grossbard, J.R. (2006). Measurement of multidimensional sport performance anxiety in children and adults: The Sport Anxiety Scale-2. *Journal of Sport and Exercise Psychology, 28*, 479-501.

Spielberger, C.D. (1983). *State-Trait Anxiety Inventory for adults sampler set: Manual, test, scoring key.* Redwood City, CA: Mind Garden.

Steinhaur, S.R., Siegle, G.J., Condray, J., & Pless, M. (2004). Sympathetic and parasympathetic innervation of pupillary dilation during sustained processing. *International Journal of Psychophysiology, 53*, 77-86.

Tellegen, A. (1985). Structures of mood and personality and their relevance to assessing anxiety with an emphasis on self-report. In A.H. Tuma & J.D. Maser (Eds.), *Anxiety and the anxiety disorders.* Hillsdale, NJ: Erlbaum.

Tsorbatzoudis, H., Varkoukis, V., Kaissidis-Rodafinos, A., & Grouios, G. (1998). A test of the reliability and factorial validity of the Greek version of the CSAI-2. *Research Quarterly for Exercise and Sport, 69*, 416-419.

Vallerand, R.J., & Blanchard, C.M. (2000). The study of emotion in sport and exercise. In Y.L. Hanin (Ed.), *Emotions in sport* (pp. 3-37). Champaign, IL: Human Kinetics.

Vickers, J. (1996). Visual control when aiming at a far target. *Journal of Experimental Psychology: Human Perception and Performance, 22*, 342-354.

Vickers, J., & Williams, A.M. (2007). Performing under pressure: The effects of physiological arousal, cognitive anxiety, and gaze control in biathlon. *Journal of Motor Behavior, 39*, 381-394.

Watson, D., & Clark, L. (1994). Personality and psychopathology [Special issue]. *Journal of Abnormal Psychology, 103*(1).

Watson, D., Clark, L., & Tellegen, A. (1988). Development and validation of brief measures of positive and negative affect: The PANAS Scales. *Journal of Personality and Social Psychology, 54*(6), 1063-1070.

Webster, M. (2005). *The Merriam-Webster Dictionary* (5th ed.). Springfield, MA: Merriam-Webster.

Williams, A.M., & Elliot, D. (1999). Anxiety, expertise, and visual search strategy in karate. *Journal of Sport and Exercise Psychology, 21*, 362-375.

Williams, A.M., Singer, R.N., & Frehlich, S.G. (2002). Quiet eye duration, expertise, and task complexity in near and far aiming tasks. *Journal of Motor Behavior, 34*, 197-207.

Williams, A.M., Vickers, J., & Rodrigues, S. (2002). The effects of anxiety on visual search, movement kinematics, and performance in table tennis: A test of Eysenck and Calvo's processing efficiency theory. *Journal of Sport and Exercise Psychology, 24*, 438-455.

Wilson, M., Smith, N.C., Chattington, M., Ford, M., & Marple-Horvat, D.E. (2006). The role of effort in moderating the anxiety-performance relationship: Testing the prediction of processing efficiency theory in simulated rally driving. *Journal of Sports Sciences, 24*, 1223-1233.

Wilson, M., Vine, S.J., & Wood, G. (2009). The influence of anxiety on visual attentional control in basketball free throw shooting. *Journal of Sport and Exercise Psychology, 31*, 152-168.

Woodman, T., Albinson, J.G., & Hardy, L. (1997). An investigation of the zone of optimal functioning hypothesis within a multidimensional framework. *Journal of Sport and Exercise Psychology, 19*, 131-141.

Woodman, T., & Davis, P.A. (2008). The role of repression in the incidence of ironic errors. *The Sport Psychologist, 22*, 183-196.

Woodman, T., & Hardy, L. (2001). Stress and anxiety. In R.N. Singer, H.A. Hausenblas, & C.M. Janelle (Eds.), *Handbook of sport psychology* (pp. 290-218). New York: Wiley.

Yarrow, K., Brown, P., & Krakauer, J.W. (2009). Inside the brain of an elite athlete: The neural processes that support high achievement in sports. *Nature Reviews Neuroscience, 10*, 585-596.

Yerkes, R.M., & Dodson, J.D. (1908). The relation of strength of stimulus to rapidity of habit formation. *Journal of Comparative Neurology and Psychology, 18*, 459-482.

Zaichkowsky, L.D., & Baltzell, A. (2001). Arousal and performance. In R.N. Singer, H.A. Hausenblas, & C.M. Janelle (Eds.), *Handbook of sport psychology* (2nd ed., pp. 319-339). New York: Wiley.

Zelinsky, G.J., Rao, R.P.N., Hayhoe, M.M., & Ballard, D.H. (1997). Eye movements reveal the spatiotemporal dynamics of visual search. *Psychological Science, 8*, 448-453.

Chapter 30

Chan, T.S., & Repman, J. (1999). Flow in web based instructional activity: An exploratory research project. *International Journal of Educational Telecommunications, 5*, 225-237.

Cronbach, L.J., Schönemann, P., & McKie, D. (1965). Alpha coefficients for stratified-parallel tests. *Educational and Psychological Measurement, 25,* 291-312.

Csikszentmihalyi, M. (1975). *Beyond boredom and anxiety.* San Francisco: Jossey-Bass.

Csikszentmihalyi, M. (1990). *Flow: The psychology of optimal experience.* New York: Harper & Row.

Csikszentmihalyi, M. (1996). *Creativity: Flow and the psychology of discovery and invention.* New York: HarperCollins.

Csikszentmihalyi, M. (1997). *Finding flow: The psychology of engagement with everyday life.* New York: HarperCollins.

Csikszentmihalyi, M. (2003). *Good business: Leadership, flow, and the making of meaning.* London: Hodder & Stoughton.

Csikszentmihalyi, M., & Csikszentmihalyi, I. (Eds.). (1988). *Optimal experience: Psychological studies of flow in consciousness.* New York: Cambridge University Press.

Eklund, R.C. (1994). A season long investigation of competitive cognition in collegiate wrestlers. *Research Quarterly for Exercise and Sport, 65,* 169-183.

Fournier, J., Gaudreau, P., Demontrond-Behr, P., Visioli, J., Forrest, J., & Jackson, S.A. (2007). French translation of the Flow State Scale-2: Factor structure, cross-cultural invariance, and associations with goal attainment. *Psychology of Sport and Exercise, 8,* 897-916.

Garfield, C.A., & Bennett, H.Z. (1984). *Peak performance: Mental training techniques of the world's greatest athletes.* Los Angeles: Tarcher.

Jackson, S.A. (1992). Athletes in flow: A qualitative investigation of flow states in elite figure skaters. *Journal of Applied Sport Psychology, 4*(2), 161-180.

Jackson, S.A. (1995). Factors influencing the occurrence of flow states in elite athletes. *Journal of Applied Sport Psychology, 7,* 135-163.

Jackson, S.A. (1996). Toward a conceptual understanding of the flow experience in elite athletes. *Research Quarterly for Exercise and Sport, 67,* 76-90.

Jackson, S.A. (2000). Joy, fun, and flow state in sport. In Y. Hanin (Ed.), *Emotions in sport* (pp.135-156). Champaign, IL: Human Kinetics.

Jackson, S.A., & Csikszentmihalyi, M. (1999). *Flow in sports: The keys to optimal experiences and performances.* Champaign, IL: Human Kinetics.

Jackson, S.A., & Eklund, R.C. (2002). Assessing flow in physical activity: The FSS-2 and DFS-2. *Journal of Sport and Exercise Psychology, 24,* 133-150.

Jackson, S.A., Eklund, R.C., & Martin, A.J. (2010). *The FLOW Manual.* Mind Garden, Inc. www.mindgarden.com.

Jackson, S.A., Kimiecik, J., Ford, S., & Marsh, H.W. (1998). Psychological correlates of flow in sport. *Journal of Sport and Exercise Psychology, 20,* 358-378.

Jackson, S.A., & Marsh, H.W. (1996). Development and validation of a scale to measure optimal experience: The flow state scale. *Journal of Sport and Exercise Psychology, 18,* 17-35.

Jackson, S.A., Martin, A.J., & Eklund, R.C. (2008). Long and short measures of flow: Examining construct validity of the FSS-2, DFS-2, and new brief counterparts. *Journal of Sport and Exercise Psychology, 30,* 561-587.

Jackson, S.A., & Roberts, G.C. (1992). Positive performance states of athletes: Toward a conceptual understanding of peak performance. *The Sport Psychologist, 6,* 156-171.

Jackson, S.A., Thomas, P.R., Marsh, H.W., & Smethurst, C.J. (2001). Relationships between flow, self-concept, psychological skills, and performance. *Journal of Applied Sport Psychology, 13,* 154-178.

Karageorghis, C.I., Vlachopoulos, S.P., & Terry, P.C. (2000). Latent variable modelling of the relationship between flow and exercise-induced feelings: An intuitive appraisal perspective. *European Physical Education, 6,* 230-248.

Kawabata, M., Mallett, C., & Jackson, S.A. (2007). The Flow State Scale-2 and Dispositional Flow Scale-2: Examination of factorial validity and reliability for Japanese adults. *Psychology of Sport and Exercise, 9,* 465-485.

Kowal, J., & Fortier, M. (1999). Motivational determinants of flow: Contributions from self-determination theory. *Journal of Social Psychology, 139,* 355-368.

Martin, A.J., & Jackson, S.A. (2008). Brief approaches to assessing task absorption and enhanced subjective experience: Examining 'short' and 'core' flow in diverse performance domains. *Motivation and Emotion, 32,* 141-157.

Maslow, A.H. (1968). *Toward a psychology of being* (2nd ed.). New York: Van Nostrand.

Muzio, M. (Ed.). (2004). *Sport: Flow e prestazione eccellente* (Sport: Flow and excellent performance). Milano, Italy: FrancoAngeli.

Osbourn, H.G. (2000). Coefficient alpha and related internal consistency reliability coefficients. *Psychological Methods, 5,* 343-355.

Penman, S., Cohen, M., Stephens, P., & Jackson, S.A. (2006, April). *Results of the 'Yoga in Australia' Survey.* Presented at the International Ayurveda and Yoga Conference, Sydney, Australia. www.yogainaustralia.com.

Privette, G. (1983). Peak experience, peak performance, and flow: A comparative analysis of positive human experiences. *Journal of Personality and Social Psychology, 45,* 1361-1368.

Ravizza, K. (1984). Qualities of the peak experience in sport. In J. Silva and R. Weinberg (Eds.), *Psychological foundations of sport* (pp. 452-461). Champaign, IL: Human Kinetics.

Russell, W.D. (2001). An examination of flow state occurrence in college athletes. *Journal of Sport Behavior, 24,* 83-99.

Seligman, M.E. (2002). Positive psychology, positive prevention, and positive therapy. In C.R. Snyder and S.J. Lopez (Eds.), *Handbook on positive psychology* (pp. 3-9). Oxford, UK: Oxford University Press.

Seligman, M.E., & Csikszentmihalyi, M. (2000). Positive psychology: An introduction. *American Psychologist, 55,* 5-14.

Stavrou, N.A., & Zervas, Y. (2004). Confirmatory factor analysis of Flow State Scale in sports. *International Journal of Sport and Exercise Psychology, 2,* 161-181.

Tenenbaum, G., Fogarty, G.J., & Jackson, S.A. (1999). The flow experience: A Rasch analysis of Jackson's Flow State Scale. *Journal of Outcome Measurement, 3,* 278-294.

Vea, S., & Pensgaard, A.M. (2004, September). *The relationship between perfectionism and flow among young elite athletes.* Paper presented at the Advancement of Applied Sport Psychology Annual Conference, Minneapolis.

Vlachopoulos, S.P., Karageorghis, C.I., & Terry, P.C. (2000). Hierarchical confirmatory factor analysis of the Flow State Scale in exercise. *Journal of Sport Sciences, 18,* 815-823.

Wagenaar, W.A. (1986). My memory: A study of autobiographical memory over six years. *Cognitive Psychology, 18,* 225-252.

Wiggins, M.S., & Freeman, P. (2000). Anxiety and flow: An examination of anxiety direction and the flow experience. *International Sports Journal, 4,* 78-87.

Wrigley, W.J. (2005). *An examination of ecological factors in music performance assessment.* Unpublished doctoral thesis, Griffith University, Brisbane.

Chapter 31

American Psychiatric Association. (1994). *Diagnostic and statistical manual of mental disorders* (4th ed.). Washington, DC: Author.

Appleton, P.R., Hall, H.K., & Hill, A.P. (2009). Relations between multidimensional perfectionism and burnout in junior-elite male athletes. *Psychology of Sport and Exercise, 10,* 457-465.

Black, J.M., & Smith, A.L. (2007). An examination of Coakley's perspective on identity, control, and burnout among adolescent athletes. *International Journal of Sport Psychology, 38,* 417-436.

Chen, L.H., Kee, Y.H., Chen, M., & Tsai, Y.M. (2008). Relation of perfectionism with athletes' burnout: Further examination. *Perceptual and Motor Skills, 106,* 811-820.

Chen, L.H., Kee, Y.H., & Tsai, Y.M. (2009). An examination of the dual model of perfectionism and adolescent athlete burnout: A short-term longitudinal research. *Social Indicators Research, 91,* **189-201.**

Coakley, J. (1992). Burnout among adolescent athletes: A personal failure or social problem? *Sociology of Sport Journal, 9,* 271-285.

Cohn, P.J. (1990). An exploratory study on sources of stress and athlete burnout in youth golf. *The Sport Psychologist, 4,* 95-106.

Cresswell, S.L., & Eklund, R.C. (2004). The athlete burnout syndrome: Proposed early signs. *Journal of Science and Medicine in Sport, 7,* 481-487.

Cresswell, S.L., & Eklund, R.C. (2005a). Changes in athlete burnout and motivation over a 12-week league tournament. *Medicine and Science in Sports and Exercise, 37,* 1957-1966.

Cresswell, S.L., & Eklund, R.C. (2005b). Motivation and burnout among top amateur rugby players. *Medicine and Science in Sports and Exercise, 37,* 469-477.

Cresswell, S.L., & Eklund, R.C. (2005c). Motivation and burnout in professional rugby players. *Research Quarterly for Exercise and Sport, 76,* 370-376.

Cresswell, S.L., & Eklund, R.C. (2006a). Changes in athlete burnout over a 30-wk "rugby year." *Journal of Science and Medicine in Sport, 9,* 125-134.

Cresswell, S.L., & Eklund, R.C. (2006b). The convergent and discriminant validity of burnout measures in sport: A multi-method multi-trait analysis. *Journal of Sport Sciences, 24,* 209-220.

Cresswell, S.L., & Eklund, R.C. (2006c). The nature of player burnout in rugby. *Journal of Applied Sport Psychology, 18,* 219-239.

Cresswell, S.L., & Eklund, R.C. (2007a). Athlete burnout: A longitudinal qualitative study. *The Sport Psychologist, 21,* 1-20.

Cresswell, S.L., & Eklund, R.C. (2007b). Athlete burnout and organizational culture: An English rugby replication. *International Journal of Sport Psychology, 38,* 365-387.

Dale, J., & Weinberg, R.S. (1989). The relationship between coaches' leadership style and burnout. *The Sport Psychologist, 3,* 1-13.

Deci, E.L., & Ryan, R.M. (1985). *Intrinsic motivation and self-determination in human behavior.* New York: Plenum Press.

De Francisco, C., Arce, C., Andrade, E., Arce, I., & Raedeke, T. (2009). Propiedades psicométricas preliminares de la versión española del Athlete Burnout Questionnaire en una muestra de jóvenes futbolistas (Preliminary psychometric properties of the spanish version of the athlete burnout questionnaire in a sample of young soccer players). *Cuadernos de Psicología del Deporte, 9*(2), 45-56.

Eades, A.M. (1990). *An investigation of burnout of intercollegiate athletes: The development of the Eades Athletic Burnout Inventory.* Unpublished master's thesis, University of California, Berkeley.

Eklund, R.C., & Cresswell, S.L. (2007). Athlete burnout. In G. Tenenbaum & R.C. Eklund (Eds.), *Handbook of sport psychology* (3rd ed., pp. 621-641). Hoboken, NJ: Wiley.

Eklund, R.C., & Gould, D. (2008). Emotional stress and anxiety in the child and adolescent athlete. In H. Hebestreit & O. Bar-Or (Eds.), *The encyclopaedia of sports medicine: XIII. The young athlete* (pp. 319-334). London: Blackwell Scientific.

Feigley, D.A. (1984). Psychological burnout in high-level athletics. *The Physician and Sportsmedicine, 12,* 109-119.

Fender, L.K. (1988). *Athlete burnout: A sport adaptation of the Maslach Burnout Inventory.* Unpublished master's thesis, Kent State University, Ohio.

Firth, H., McIntee, J., McKeown, P., & Britton, P.G. (1986). Interpersonal support and nurses at work. *Journal of Advanced Nursing, 11,* 273-282.

Freudenberger, H.J. (1974). Staff burn-out. *Journal of Social Issues, 30,* 159-165.

Freudenberger, H.J. (1975). The staff burn-out syndrome in alternative institutions. *Psychotherapy: Theory, Research and Practice, 12,* 73-82.

Garden, A.M. (1987). Depersonalization: A valid dimension of burnout? *Human Relations, 40,* 545-560.

Giacobbi, P.R. (2009). Low burnout and high engagement levels in athletic trainers: Results of a nationwide random sample. *Journal of Athletic Training, 44,* 370-377.

Glass, D.C., & McKnight, J.D. (1996). Perceived control, depressive symptomatology, and professional burnout: A review of evidence. *Psychology and Health, 11,* 23-48.

Glass, D.C., McKnight, J.D., & Valdimarsdottir, H. (1993). Depression, burnout, and perceptions of control in hospital nurses. *Journal of Consulting and Clinical Psychology, 61,* 147-155.

Golembiewski, R.T., Munzenrider, R., & Carter, D. (1983). Phases of progressive burnout and their work site covariants: Critical issues in OD research and praxis. *Journal of Applied Behavioural Science, 19,* 461-481.

Goodger, K., Gorely, T., Lavallee, D., & Harwood, C. (2007). Burnout in sport: A systematic review. *The Sport Psychologist, 21,* 127-151.

Goodger, K., Wolfenden, L., & Lavallee, D. (2007). Symptoms and consequences associated with three dimensions of burnout in junior tennis players. *International Journal of Sport Psychology, 38,* 342-364.

Gould, D. (1993). Intensive sport participation and the prepubescent athlete: Competitive stress and burnout. In B.R. Cahil & A.J. Pearl (Eds.), *Intensive participation in children's sport* (pp. 19-38). Champaign, IL: Human Kinetics.

Gould, D., & Dieffenbach, K. (2002). Overtraining, underrecovery, and burnout in sport. In M. Kellmann (Ed.), *Enhancing recovery: Preventing underperformance in athletes* (p. 25-35). Champaign, IL: Human Kinetics.

Gould, D., Tuffey, S., Udry, E., & Loehr, J. (1996). Burnout in competitive junior tennis players: II. Qualitative analysis. *The Sport Psychologist, 10,* 341-366.

Gould, D., Tuffey, S., Udry, E., & Loehr, J. (1997). Burnout in competitive junior tennis players: III. Individual differences in the burnout experience. *The Sport Psychologist, 11,* 257-276.

Gould, D., Udry, E., Tuffey, S., & Loehr, J. (1996). Burnout in competitive junior tennis players: I. A quantitative psychological assessment. *The Sport Psychologist, 10,* 322-340.

Gould, D., & Whitley, M.A. (2009). Sources and consequences of athletic burnout among college athletes. *Journal of Intercollegiate Sports, 2,* 16-30.

Gustafsson, H., Hassmén, P., Kenttä, G., & Johansson, M. (2008). A qualitative analysis of burnout in elite Swedish athletes. *Psychology of Sport and Exercise, 9,* 800-816.

Gustafsson, H., Kenttä, G., Hassmén, P., & Lundqvist, C. (2007). Prevalence of burnout in competitive adolescent athletes. *The Sport Psychologist, 21,* 21-37.

Gustafsson, H., Kenttä, G., Hassmén, P., Lundqvist, C., & Durand-Bush, N. (2007). The process of burnout: A multiple case study of three elite endurance athletes. *International Journal of Sport Psychology, 38,* 388-416.

Hendrix, A.E., Acevedo, E.O., & Hebert, E. (2000). An examination of stress and burnout in certified athletic trainers at division I-a universities. *Journal of Athletic Training, 35,* 139-144.

Henschen, K. (1990). Prevention and treatment of athletic staleness and burnout. *Science Periodical on Research and Technology in Sport, 10,* 1-8.

Hill, A.P, Hall, H.K., Appleton, P.R., & Kozub, S.A. (2008). Perfectionism and burnout in junior elite soccer players: The mediating influence of unconditional self-acceptance. *Psychology of Sport and Exercise, 9,* 630-644.

Kelley, B.C., Eklund, R.C., & Ritter-Taylor, M. (1999). Stress and burnout among collegiate tennis coaches. *Journal of Sport and Exercise Psychology, 21,* 113-130.

Kellmann, M. (2002a). Psychological assessment of underrecovery. In M. Kellmann (Ed.), *Enhancing recovery: Preventing underperformance in athletes* (p. 37-55). Champaign, IL: Human Kinetics.

Kellmann, M. (2002b). Underrecovery and overtraining: Different concepts—Similar impact? In M. Kellmann (Ed.), *Enhancing recovery: Preventing underperformance in athletes* (p. 3-24). Champaign, IL: Human Kinetics.

Kentta, G., Hassmen, P., & Raglin, J.S. (2001). Training practices and overtraining syndrome in Swedish age-group athletes. *International Journal of Sports Medicine, 22,* 460-465.

Leiter, M.P., & Durup, J. (1994). The discriminant validity of burnout and depression: A confirmatory factor analytic study. *Anxiety, Stress and Coping, 7,* 357-373.

Lemyre, N.-P., Hall, H.K., & Roberts, G.C. (2008). A social cognitive approach to burnout in elite athletes. *Scandinavian Journal of Medicine and Science in Sports, 18,* 221-234.

Lemyre, N.-P., Treasure, D.C., & Roberts, G.C. (2006). Influence of variability in motivation and affect on elite athlete burnout. *Journal of Sport and Exercise Psychology, 28,* 32-48.

Lonsdale, C., Hodge, K., & Rose, E.A. (2006). Pixels vs. paper: Comparing online and traditional survey methods in sport psychology. *Journal of Sport and Exercise Psychology, 28,* 100-108.

Lonsdale, C., Hodge, K., & Rose, E. (2009). Athlete burnout in elite sport: A self-determination perspective. *Journal of Sports Sciences, 27,* 785-795.

Lovibond, S.H., & Lovibond, P.F. (1995). *Manual for the Depression Anxiety Stress Scales* (2nd ed.). Sydney, Australia: Psychology Foundation Monograph.

Main, L.C., & Grove, J.R. (2009). A multi-component assessment model for monitoring training distress among athletes. *European Journal of Sport Sciences, 9,* 191-198.

Marsh, H.W. (1998). Foreword. In J.L. Duda (Ed.), *Advances in sport and exercise psychology measurement* (pp. xv-xix). Champaign, IL: Human Kinetics.

Martin, J.J., Kelley, B., & Eklund, R.C. (1999). A model of stress and burnout in male high school athletic directors. *Journal of Sport and Exercise Psychology, 21,* 280-294.

Maslach, C. (1976). Burned-out. *Human Behavior, 5,* 16-22.

Maslach, C. (1982). *Burnout: The cost of caring.* London: Prentice Hall.

Maslach, C. (2003). Job burnout: New directions in research intervention. *Current Directions in Psychological Science, 12,* 189-192.

Maslach, C., & Goldberg, J. (1998). Prevention of burnout: New perspectives. *Applied and Preventative Psychology, 7,* 63-74.

Maslach, C., & Jackson, S.E. (1981). The measurement of experienced burnout. *Journal of Occupational Psychology, 2,* 99-113.

Maslach, C., & Jackson, S.E. (1986). *Maslach Burnout Inventory manual* (2nd ed.). Palo Alto, CA: Consulting Psychologists Press.

Maslach, C., Jackson, S.E., & Leiter, M.P. (1996). *Maslach Burnout Inventory manual* (3rd ed.). Palo Alto, CA: Consulting Psychologists Press.

Maslach, C., Jackson, S.E., & Leiter, M.P. (1997). Maslach Burnout Inventory, 3rd edition. In C.P. Zalaquett & R.J. Wood (Eds.), *Evaluating stress: A book of resources* (pp. 191-218). London: Scarecrow Press.

Maslach, C., Schaufeli, W.B., & Leiter, M.P. (2001). Job burnout. *Annual Review of Psychology, 52,* 397-422.

Perreault, S., Gaudreau, P., Lapoint, M.C., & Lacroix, C. (2007). Does it take three to tango? Psychological need satisfaction and athlete burnout. *International Journal of Sport Psychology, 38,* 437-450.

Plana, A.B., Fabregat, A.A., & Gassió, J.B. (2003). Burnout syndrome and coping strategies: A structural relations model. *Psychology in Spain, 7,* 46-55.

Raedeke, T.D. (1997). Is athlete burnout more than just stress? A sport commitment perspective. *Journal of Sport and Exercise Psychology, 19,* 396-417.

Raedeke, T.D. (2004). Coach commitment and burnout: A one-year follow-up. *Journal of Applied Sport Psychology, 16,* 333-350.

Raedeke, T.D., Granzyk, T.L., & Warren, A. (2000). Why coaches experience burnout: A commitment perspective. *Journal of Sport and Exercise Psychology, 22,* 85-105.

Raedeke, T.D., Lunney, K., & Venables, K. (2002). Understanding athlete burnout: Coach perspectives. *Journal of Sport Behavior, 25,* 181-206.

Raedeke, T.D., & Smith, A.L. (2001). Development and preliminary validation of an athlete burnout measure. *Journal of Sport and Exercise Psychology, 23,* 281-306.

Raedeke, T.D., & Smith, A.L. (2004). Coping resources and athlete burnout: An examination of stress mediated and moderation hypotheses. *Journal of Sport and Exercise Psychology, 26,* 525-541.

Raedeke, T.D., & Smith, A.L. (2009). *The Athlete Burnout Questionnaire manual.* Morgantown, WV: Fitness Information Technology.

Raglin, J.S. (1993). Overtraining and staleness: Psychometric monitoring of endurance athletes. In R.B. Singer, M. Murphey, & L.K. Tennant (Eds.), *Handbook of research on sport psychology* (pp. 840-850). New York: Macmillan.

Raglin, J.S., & Wilson, G.S. (2000). Overtraining in athletes. In Y.L. Hanin (Ed.), *Emotions in sport* (pp. 191-207). Champaign, IL: Human Kinetics.

Rowe, D.A., & Mahar, M.T. (2006). Validity. In T.M. Wood & W. Zhu (Eds.), *Measurement theory and practice in kinesiology* (pp. 9-26). Champaign, IL: Human Kinetics.

Rowland, T.W. (1986). Exercise fatigue in adolescents: Diagnosis of athlete burnout. *The Physician and Sportsmedicine, 14,* 69-77.

Schaufeli, W.B., & Enzmann, D. (1998). *The burnout companion to study and practice: A critical analysis.* Washington, DC: Taylor & Francis.

Schaufeli, W.B., Enzmann, D., & Girault, N. (1993). Measurement of burnout. In W.B. Schaufeli, C. Maslach, & T. Marek (Eds.), *Professional burnout: Recent developments in theory and research* (pp. 199-215). Washington, DC: Taylor & Francis.

Schaufeli, W.B., Salanova, M., Gonzalez-Roma, V., & Bakker, A.B. (2002). The measurement of engagement and burnout: A two sample confirmatory factor analytic approach. *Journal of Happiness Studies, 3,* 71-92.

Schmidt, G.W., & Stein, G.L. (1991). Sport commitment: A model integrating enjoyment, dropout, and burnout. *Journal of Sport and Exercise Psychology, 8,* 254-265.

Schutte, N., Toppinen, S., Kalimo, R., & Schaufeli, W. (2000). The factorial validity of the Maslach Burnout Inventory-General Survey (MBI-GS) across occupational groups and nations. *Journal of Occupational and Organizational Psychology, 73,* 53-65.

Silva, J.M. (1990). An analysis of the training stress syndrome in competitive athletics. *Journal of Applied Sport Psychology, 2,* 5-20.

Smith, R.E. (1986). Toward a cognitive-affective model of athletic burnout. *Journal of Sport Psychology, 8,* 36-50.

Tenenbaum, G., Jones, C.M., Kistantas, A., Sacks, D., & Berwick, J. (2003a). Failure adaptation: An investigation of the stress response process in sport. *International Journal of Sport Psychology, 34,* 27-62.

Tenenbaum, G., Jones, C.M., Kistantas, A., Sacks, D., & Berwick, J. (2003b). Failure adaptation: Conceptualisation of the stress response in sport. *International Journal of Sport Psychology, 34,* 1-26.

Van Dierendonck, D., Schaufeli, W.B., & Buunk, B.P. (2001). Towards a process model of burnout: Results from a secondary analysis. *European Journal of Work and Organizational Psychology, 10,* 41-52.

Vealey, R.S., Armstrong, L., Comar, W., & Greenleaf, C.A. (1998). Influence of perceived coaching behaviors on burnout and competitive anxiety in female college athletes. *Journal of Applied Sport Psychology, 10,* 297-318.

Yukelson, D. (1990). Psychological burnout in sport participants. *Sports Medicine Digest, 12,* 4.

Ziemainz, H., Abu-Omar, K., Raedeke, T., & Krause, K. (2004). Burn out im sport (Burnout in sport). *Leistungssport, 34,* 12-17.

Chapter 32

Armstrong, J.S., Denniston, W.B., & Gordon, M.M. (1975). The use of the decomposition principle in making judgments. *Organizational Behavior and Human Performance, 14,* 257-263.

Bar-Eli, M. (1984). Zur Diagnostik individueller psychischer Krisen im sportlichen Wettkampf: Eine wahrscheinlich-keitsorientierte, theoretische und empirische Studie unter besonderer Beruecksichtigung des Basketballspiels [The diagnosis of individual psychological crises in sports competition: A probabilistically oriented, theoretical and empirical study giving special attention to the game of basketball]. Unpublished doctoral dissertation, Deutsche Sporthochscule, Köln, Germany.

Bar-Eli, M. (1997). Psychological performance crisis in competition, 1984-1996: A review. *European Yearbook of Sport Psychology, 1,* 73-112.

Bar-Eli, M. (2002a). Athletes' perception of performance crisis: Descriptive and differentiating characteristics. *Sportwissenschaft, 32,* 415-428.

Bar-Eli, M. (2002b). Biofeedback as applied psychophysiology in sport and exercise: Conceptual principles for research and practice. In B. Blumenstein, M. Bar-Eli, & G. Tenenbaum (Eds.), *Brain and body in sport and exercise: Biofeedback applications in performance enhancement* (pp. 1-14). New York: Wiley.

Bar-Eli, M., Levy-Kolker, N., Pie, J.S., & Tenenbaum, G. (1995). A crisis-related analysis of perceived referees' behavior in competition. *Journal of Applied Sport Psychology, 7,* 63-80.

Bar-Eli, M., Sachs, S., Tenenbaum, G., Pie, J.S., & Falk, B. (1996). Crisis-related observations in competition: A case study in basketball. *Scandinavian Journal of Medicine and Science in Sports, 6,* 313-321.

Bar-Eli, M., Taoz, E., Levy-Kolker, N., & Tenenbaum, G. (1992). Performance quality and behavioral violations as crisis indicators in competition. *International Journal of Sport Psychology, 23,* 325-342.

Bar-Eli, M., & Tenenbaum, G. (1988a). Rule- and norm-related behavior and the individual psychological crisis in competitive situations: Theory and research findings. *Social Behavior and Personality, 16,* 187-195.

Bar-Eli, M., & Tenenbaum, G. (1988b). The interaction of individual psychological crisis and time phases in basketball. *Perceptual and Motor Skills, 66,* 523-530.

Bar-Eli, M., & Tenenbaum, G. (1988c). Time phases and the individual psychological crisis in sports competition: Theory and research findings. *Journal of Sports Sciences, 6,* 141-149.

Bar-Eli, M., & Tenenbaum, G. (1989a). A theory of individual psychological crisis in competitive sport. *Applied Psychology, 38,* 107-120.

Bar-Eli, M., & Tenenbaum, G. (1989b). Coach-psychologist relations in competitive sport. In A.D. LeUnes, J.S. Picou, & W.K. Simpson (Eds.), *Applied research in coaching and athletics, annual* (pp. 150-156). Boston: American Press. (Previously: *Journal of Applied Research in Coaching and Athletics, 4,* 150-156).

Bar-Eli, M., & Tenenbaum, G. (1989c). Game standings and psychological crisis in sport: Theory and research. *Canadian Journal of Sport Sciences, 14,* 31-37.

Bar-Eli, M., & Tenenbaum, G. (1989d). Observations of behavioral violations as crisis indicators in competition. *The Sport Psychologist, 3,* 237-244.

Bar-Eli, M., Tenenbaum, G., & Elbaz, G. (1989). Pre-start susceptibility to psychological crises in competitive sport: Theory and research. *International Journal of Sport Psychology, 20,* 13-30.

Bar-Eli, M., Tenenbaum, G., & Elbaz, G. (1990a). Psychological performance crisis in high arousal situations—diagnosticity of rule violations and performance in competitive team-handball. *Anxiety Research, 2,* 281-292.

Bar-Eli, M., Tenenbaum, G., & Elbaz, G. (1990b). Psychological strain in competition: The role of time phases. *Sportwissenschaft, 20,* 182-191.

Bar-Eli, M., Tenenbaum, G., & Elbaz, G. (1991). A three-dimensional crisis-related analysis of perceived team performance. *Journal of Applied Sport Psychology, 3,* 160-175.

Bar-Eli, M., Tenenbaum, G., & Geister, S. (2006). Consequences of players' dismissal in professional soccer: A crisis-related analysis of group-size effects. *Journal of Sports Sciences, 24,* 1083-1094.

Bar-Eli, M., Tenenbaum, G., & Levy-Kolker, N. (1992a). A crisis related analysis of perceived spectators' behavior in competition. *Canadian Journal of Sport Sciences, 17,* 288-298.

Bar-Eli, M., Tenenbaum, G., & Levy-Kolker, N. (1992b). A three-dimensional crisis-related analysis of perceived teammates' behavior in competition. *Journal of Sport Behavior, 15,* 179-200.

Bar-Eli, M., Tenenbaum, G., & Levy-Kolker, N. (1993). A three-dimensional crisis-related analysis of perceived coach's behavior in competition. *Scandinavian Journal of Medicine and Science in Sports, 3,* 134-141.

Bar-Eli, M., & Tractinsky, N. (2000). Criticality of game situations and decision-making in basketball: An application of performance crisis perspective. *Psychology of Sport and Exercise, 1,* 27-39.

Baumeister, R.F. (1984). Choking under pressure: Self-consciousness and paradoxical effects of incentives on skillful performance. *Journal of personality and Social Psychology, 46,* 610-620.

Baumeister, R.F., & Showers, C.J. (1986). A review of paradoxical performance effects: Choking under pressure in sports and mental tests. *European Journal of Social Psychology, 16,* 361-383.

Baumeister, R.F., & Steinhilber, A. (1984). Paradoxical effects of supportive audiences on performance under pressure: The home field disadvantage in sports championships. *Journal of Personality and Social psychology, 47,* 85-93.

Beilock, S.L., & Gray, R. (2007). Why do athletes choke under pressure? In G. Tenenbaum & R.C. Eklund (Eds.), *Handbook of sport psychology* (3rd ed., pp. 425-444). Hoboken, NJ: Wiley.

Bellhouse, D.R. (2004). The Reverend Thomas Bayes, FRS: A biography to celebrate the tercentenary of his birth. *Statistical Sciences, 19,* 3-43.

Collins, D. (2002). Psychophysiology and athletic performance. In B. Blumenstein, M. Bar-Eli, & G. Tenenbaum (Eds.), *Brain and body in sport and exercise: Biofeedback applications in performance enhancement* (pp. 15-35). Chichester, UK: Wiley.

Courneya, K.S., & Carron, A.V. (1992). The home advantage in sport competitions: A literature review. *Journal of Sport and Exercise Psychology, 14,* 13-27.

De Finetti, B. (1980). La prévision: Ses louis logiques, ses sources subjectives [Foresight: Its logical laws, its subjective sources]. In H.E. Kyburg, Jr., & H.E. Smokler (Eds.), *Studies in subjective probability* (pp. 1-68). Melbourne, FL: Krieger.

Edwards, W. (1962a). Dynamic decision theory and probabilistic information processing. *Human Factors, 4,* 59-73.

Edwards, W. (1962b). Subjective probabilities inferred from decisions. *Psychological Review, 69,* 109-135.

Edwards, W. (1968). Conservatism in human information processing. In B. Kleinmuntz (Ed.), *Formal representation of human judgment* (pp. 17-52). New York: Wiley.

Edwards, W., Lindman, H., & Savage, L.J. (1963). Bayesian statistical inference for psychological research. *Psychological Review, 70,* 193-242.

Edwards, W., Phillips, L.D., Hays, W.L., & Goodman, B.C. (1968). Probabilistic information processing systems: Design and evaluation. *IEEE Transactions on Systems Science and Cybernetics, 4,* 248-265.

Gabler, H. (1976). *Aggressive Handungen im Sport* [Aggressive actions in sport]. Schorndorf, Germany: Hofmann.

Geron, E. (1975). *Methoden und Mittel zur psychischen Vorbreitung des Sportlers* [Methods and means of athletes' psychological preparation]. Schorndorf, Germany: Hofmann.

Gettys, C.F., & Manley, C.W. (1968). The probability of an event and estimates of posterior probability based upon its occurrence. *Psychonomic Science, 11,* 47-48.

Gettys, C.F., Michel, C., Steiger, J.H., Kelly, C.W., & Peterson, C.R. (1973). Multiple-stage probabilistic information processing. *Organizational Behavior and Human Performance, 10,* 374-387.

Gould, D., Greenleaf, C., & Krane, V. (2002). Arousal-anxiety and sport behavior. In T. Horn (Ed.), *Advances in sport psychology* (2nd ed., pp. 207-241). Champaign, IL: Human Kinetics.

Guttman, L. (1954). An outline of some new methodology for social research. *Public Opinion Quarterly, 18,* 395-404.

Guttman, L. (1959). A structural theory of intergroup beliefs and action. *American Sociological Review, 24,* 318-328.

Guttman, R., & Greenbaum, C.W. (1998). Facet theory: Its development and current status. *European Psychologist, 3,* 13-36.

Hackfort, D., Duda, J.L., & Lidor, R. (Eds.). (2005). *Handbook of research in applied sport and exercise psychology: International perspectives.* Morgantown, WV: Fitness Information Technology.

Hammond, K.R., Kelly, K.J., Schneider, R.J., & Vancini, M. (1967). Clinical inference in nursing: Revising judgments. *Nursing Research, 16,* 36-45.

Kaplan, K.J., & Newman, J.R. (1966). Studies in probabilistic information processing. *IEEE Transactions on Human Factors in Electronics, 7,* 49-63.

McGrath, J.E. (1976). Stress and behavior in organizations. In M.D. Dunnette (Ed.), *Handbook of industrial and organizational psychology* (pp. 1351-1395). Chicago, IL: Rand McNally.

Nevill, A.M., & Holder, R.L. (1999). Home advantage in sport: An overview of studies on the advantage of playing at home. *Sports Medicine, 28,* 221-236.

Nitsch, J.R. (1976). *Zur Theorie der sportlichen Beanspruchung* [A theory of athletic strain]. In J.R. Nitsch & I. Udris (Eds.), *Beanspruchung im Sport* (pp. 15-41). Bad Homburg, Germany: Limpert.

Nitsch, J.R. (1982). Analysis of action and functionalistic approaches in sport psychology. In E. Geron (Ed.), *Handbook of sport psychology, Vol. 1: Introduction to sport psychology* (pp. 58-75). Netanya, Israel: Wingate Institute.

Nitsch, J.R., & Allmer, H. (1979). Naïve psychoregulative Techniken der Selbstbeeinflussung im Sport [Naïve psychoregulative techniques of self-influence in sport]. *Sportwissenschaft, 9,* 143-163.

Nitsch, J.R., & Hackfort, D. (1979). Naïve Techniken der Psychoregulation im Sport [Naïve techniques of psychoregulation in sport]. In H. Gabler, H. Eberspaecher, E. Hahn, J. Kern, & Schilling, G. (Eds.), *Praxis der Psychologie im Leistungssport* (pp. 299-311). Berlin: Bartels & Wernitz.

Phillips, L.D., & Edwards, W. (1966). Conservatism in a simple probability inference task. *Journal of Experimental Psychology, 72,* 346-355.

Phillips, L.D., Hays, W.L., & Edwards, W. (1966). Conservatism in complex probabilistic inference. *IEEE Transactions on Human Factors in Electronics, HFE-7,* 7-18.

Pollard, R. (2006). Worldwide regional variations in home advantage in association football. *Journal of Sports Sciences, 24,* 231-240.

Price, R. (1767). *Four dissertations. I. On providence. II. On prayer. III. On the reasons for expecting that virtuous men shall meet after death in a state of happiness. IV. On the importance of Christianity, the nature of historical evidence, and miracles.* London: Millar & Cadell.

Ramsey, F.P. (1990). Truth and probability. In D.H. Mellor (Ed.), *Philosophical papers* (pp. 40-58). Cambridge, UK: Cambridge University Press. (Reprinted from *Foundations of mathematics and other essays*, pp. 156-198, by R.B. Braithwaite, Ed., 1931, Abingdon, UK: Routledge & Kegan; and *Studies in subjective probability*, 2nd ed., pp. 23-52, by H.E. Kyburg, Jr. & H.E. Smokler, Eds., 1980, Melbourne, FL: Krieger).

Rapoport, A., & Wallsten, T.S. (1972). Individual decision behavior. *Annual Review of Psychology, 23,* 131-176.

Reichenbach, H. (1949). *The theory of probability.* Berkeley, CA: University of California Press.

Schum, D.A., Goldstein, I.L., Howell, W.C., & Southard, J.F. (1967). Subjective probability revisions under several cost-payoff arrangements. *Organizational Behavior and Human Performance, 2,* 84-104.

Schutz, R.W. (1994). Methodological issues and measurement problems in sport psychology. In S. Serpa, J. Alves, & U. Pataco (Eds.), *International perspectives on sport and exercise psychology* (pp. 35-56). Morgantown, WV: Fitness Information Technology.

Slovic, P., Fischhoff, B., & Lichtenstein, S. (1977). Behavioral decision theory. *Annual Review of Psychology, 28,* 1-39.

Slovic, P., & Lichtenstein, S. (1971). Comparison of Bayesian and regression approaches to the study of information processing in judgment. *Organizational Behavior and Human Performance, 6,* 649-744.

Smirnow, K.M. (1974). Der Vorstartzustand und die Bedeutung der Emotionen [The pre-start state and the meaning of emotions]. In K.M. Smirnow (Ed.), *Sportpsychologie* (pp. 303-316). Berlin: Volk und Gesundheit.

Upadhyay, S.K., Singh, U., & Dey, D.K. (Eds.). (2007). *Bayesian statistics and its applications.* Turnbridge Wells, UK: Anshan.

Vealey, R.S., & Garner-Holman, M. (1998). Applied sport psychology: Measurement issues. In J.L. Duda (Ed.), *Advances in sport and exercise psychology measurement* (pp. 431-446). Morgantown, WV: Fitness Information Technology.

Venn, J. (1962). *The logic of chance* (2nd ed.). New York: Macmillan. (Original work published 1876).

Von Mises, R. (1957). *Probability, statistics and truth.* New York: Macmillan. (Original work published 1928 in German).

Williams, J.M. (Ed.). (2005). *Applied sport psychology: Personal growth to peak performance* (5th ed.). New York: McGraw-Hill.

Wine, J.D. (1980). Cognitive-attentional theory of test anxiety. In L.G. Sarason (Ed.), *Test anxiety: Theory, research and application* (pp. 349-385). Hillsdale, NJ: Erlbaum.

Wine, J.D. (1982). Evaluation anxiety: A cognitive-attentional construct. In H.W. Krohne & L. Laux (Eds.), *Achievement, stress, and anxiety* (pp. 207-219). Washington, DC: Hemisphere.

Yerkes, R., & Dodson, J. (1908). The relation of strength of stimulus to rapidity of habit formation. *Journal of Comparative Neurological Psychology, 18,* 459-482.

Chapter 33

Abernethy, B., Summers, J., & Ford, S. (1998). Issues in the measurement of attention. In J. Duda (Ed.). *Advances in sport and exercise psychology measurement* (pp. 173-193). Morgantown, WV: Fitness Information Technology.

Atkinson, J. (1974). The mainstream of achievement-oriented activity. In J. Atkinson & J. Raynor (Eds.), *Motivation and achievement* (pp. 13-41). New York: Halstead.

Auweele, Y., Cuyper, B., Van Mele, V., & Rzewnicki, R. (1993). Elite performance and personality: From description and prediction to diagnosis and intervention. In R. Singer, M. Murphey, & L. Tennant (Eds.), *Handbook of sport psychology* (pp. 257-289). New York: Macmillan.

Bandura, A. (1977). Self-efficacy: Toward a unifying theory of behavioral change. *Psychological Review, 84,* 191-215.

Bond, J., & Sargent, G. (1995). Concentration skills in sport: An applied perspective. In T. Morris & J. Summers (Eds.). *Sport psychology: Theory, applications and issues* (pp. 386-419). Brisbane, Australia: Wiley.

Butler, R., & Hardy, L. (1992). The performance profile: Theory and application. *The Sport Psychologist, 6,* 253-226.

Clough, P., Earle, K., & Sewell, D. (2002). Mental toughness: The concept and its measurement. In I. Cockerill (Ed.), *Solutions in sport psychology* (pp. 32-45). London: Thomson.

Connaughton, D., Wadey, R., Hanton, S., & Jones, G. (2008). The development and maintenance of mental toughness: Perceptions of elite performers. *Journal of Sport Sciences, 26,* 83-95.

Cremades, J., & Pease, D. (2007). Concurrent validity and reliability of lower and upper alpha activities as measures of visual and kinesthetic imagery ability. *The International Journal of Sport and Exercise Psychology, 5,* 187-202.

Crocker, P., Kowalski, K., & Graham, T. (1998). Measurement of coping strategies in sport. In J. Duda (Ed.), *Advances in sport and exercise psychology measurement* (pp.149-161). Morgantown, WV: Fitness Information Technology.

Daw, J., & Burton, D. (1994). Evaluation of a comprehensive psychological skills training program for collegiate tennis players. *The Sport Psychologist, 8,* 37-57.

Dewey, D., Brawley, L., & Allard, F. (1989). Do the TAIS attentional style scales predict how visual information is processed? *Journal of Sport and Exercise Psychology, 11,* 171-186.

Duda, J. (1989). Relationship between task and ego orientation and the perceived purpose of sport among high school athletes. *Journal of Sport and Exercise Psychology, 11*(3), 318-335.

Duda, J., & Nicholls, J. (1992). Dimensions of achievement motivation in schoolwork and sport. *Journal of Educational Psychology, 84,* 290-299.

Duda, J., & Whitehead, J. (1998). Measurement of goal perspectives in the physical domain. In J. Duda (Ed.), *Advances in sport and exercise psychology measurement* (pp. 21-48). Morgantown, WV: Fitness Information Technology.

Durand-Bush, N., Salmela, J., & Green-Demers, I. (2001). The Ottawa Mental Skills Assessment Tool. *The Sport Psychologist, 15,* 1-19.

Fletcher, D., & Hanton, S. (2001). The relationship between psychological skills usage and competitive anxiety responses. *Psychology of Sport and Exercise, 2,* 89-101.

Ford, S., & Summers, J. (1992). The factorial validity of the TAIS attentional style subscales. *Journal of Sport and Exercise Psychology, 14,* 283-297.

Frey, M., Laguna, M., & Ravizza, K. (2003). Collegiate athletes' use of mental skill use and perceptions of success: An exploration of the practice and competition settings. *Journal of Applied Sport Psychology, 15,* 115-128.

Fournier, J., Calmels, C., Durand-Bush, N., & Salmela, J. (2005). Effects of a season-long PST program on gymnastic performance and on psychological skill development. *International Journal of Sport and Exercise Psychology, 3,* 59-78.

Gill, D., & Deeter, T. (1988). Development of the Sport Orientation Questionnaire. *Research Quarterly for Exercise and Sport, 59,* 191-202.

Gould, D., Guinan, D., Greenleaf, C., Medberry, R., & Peterson, K. (1999). Factors affecting Olympic performance: Perceptions of athletes and coaches from more and less successful teams. *The Sport Psychologist, 13,* 371-394.

Gould, D., Weiss, M., & Weinberg, R. (1981). Psychological characteristics of successful and non-successful Big Ten wrestlers. *Journal of Sport Psychology, 3,* 69-81.

Greenspan, M., & Feltz, D. (1989). Psychological interventions with athletes in competitive situations: A review. *The Sport Psychologist, 3,* 219-236.

Gucciardi, D., Gordon, S., & Dimmock, J. (2008). Towards an understanding of mental toughness in Australian football. *Journal of Applied Sport Psychology, 20,* 261-281.

Hall, C., Mack, D., Paivio, A., & Hausenblas, H. (1998). Imagery use by athletes: Development of the Sport Imagery Questionnaire. *International Journal of Sport Psychology, 28,* 1-17.

Hall, C., & Martin, K. (1997). Measuring movement imagery abilities: A revision of the Movement Imagery Questionnaire. *Journal of Mental Imagery, 21,* 143-154.

Hall, C., Pongrac, J., & Buckholz, E. (1985). The measurement of imagery ability. *Human Movement Science, 4,* 107-118.

Hardy, J., Gammage, K., & Hall, G. (2001). A descriptive study of athlete self-talk. *The Sport Psychologist, 15,* 306-318.

Hardy, J., & Hall, C. (2005). A comparison of test-re-test reliabilities using the Self-Talk Use Questionnaire. *Journal of Sport Behavior, 28,* 201-215.

Hardy, J., Hall, C., & Hardy, L. (2005). Quantifying athletes' self-talk. *Journal of Sport Sciences, 23,* 905-917.

Hart, S., & Staveland, L. (1988). Development of NASA-TLX (Task Load Index): Results of empirical and theoretical research. In P. Hancock & N. Meshkati (Eds.), *Human mental workload* (pp. 139-183). Amsterdam: North Holland.

Hatzigeorgiadis, A., Zourbanos, N., & Theodorakis, Y. (2007). The moderating effect of self-talk content on self-talk functions. *Journal of Applied Sport Psychology, 19,* 240-251.

Highlen, P., & Bennett, B. (1979). Psychological characteristics of successful and non-successful elite wrestlers: An exploratory study. *Journal of Sport Psychology, 1,* 123-127.

Isaac, A., Marks, D., & Russell, E. (1986). An instrument for assessing imagery of movement: The Vividness of Movement Imagery Questionnaire (VMIQ). *Journal of Mental Imagery, 10,* 23-30.

Jackson, S., & Csikszentmihalyi, M. (1999). *Flow in sport.* Champaign, IL: Human Kinetics.

Jones, G., Hanton, S., & Connaughton, D. (2002). What is this thing called mental toughness? An investigation of elite sport performers. *Journal of Applied Sport Psychology, 14,* 205-218.

Krane, V., & Williams, J. (2006). Psychological characteristics of peak performance. In J. Williams (Ed.), *Applied sport psychology: Personal growth to peak performance* (5th ed., pp. 207-227). New York: McGraw-Hill.

Lowther, J., Lane, A., & Lane, H. (2002). Self-efficacy and psychological skills use during the Amputee Soccer World Cup. *Athletic Insight: The Online Journal of Sport Psychology* [Online], 4. www.athleticinsight.com/Vol4Iss2/SoccerSelfEfficacy.htm.

Maehr, M., & Nicholls, J. (1980). Culture and achievement motivation: A second look. In N. Warren (Ed.). *Studies in cross-cultural psychology* (pp. 221-267). New York: Academic Press.

Mahoney, M. (1979). Cognitive skills and athletic performance. In P. Kendall & S. Hollen (Eds.), *Cognitive-behavioral intervention: Theory, research, and procedures* (pp. 423-443). New York: Academic Press.

Mahoney, M. (1989). Psychological predictors of elite and non-elite performance in Olympic weightlifting. *International Journal of Sport Psychology, 20,* 1-12.

Mahoney, M., & Avener, M. (1977). Psychology of the elite athlete: An exploratory study. *Cognitive Therapy and Research, 1,* 135-141.

Mahoney, M., Gabriel, T., & Perkins, T. (1987). Psychological skills and exceptional athletic performance. *The Sport Psychologist, 1,* 181-199.

Martens, R. (1987). *Coaches guide to sport psychology.* Champaign, IL: Human Kinetics.

Meichenbaum, D. (1985). *Stress inoculation training.* New York: Pergamon Press.

Morris, T., & Thomas, P. (1995). Approaches to applied sport psychology. In T. Morris & J. Summers (Eds.), *Sport psychology: Theories, applications and issues* (pp. 215-258). Milton, Australia: Wiley.

Meyers, A., Whelan, J., & Murphy, S. (1996). Cognitive behavioral strategies in athletic performance enhancement. In M. Hersen, R. Eisler, & P. Millr (Eds.), *Progress in behavioral modification* (Vol. 30, pp. 137-164). Pacific Grove, CA: Brooks/Cole.

Murphy, S., & Tammen, V. (1998). In search of psychological skills. In J. Duda (Ed.), *Measurement in sport and exercise psychology* (pp.195-209). Morgantown, WV: Fitness Information Technology.

Nideffer, R. (1976). Test of attentional and interpersonal style. *Journal of Personality and Social Psychology, 34,* 394-404.

Nideffer, R. (1987). Issues in the use of psychological tests in applied settings. *The Sport Psychologist, 1,* 18-28.

Nideffer, R. (1990). Use of the Test of Attentional and Interpersonal Style (TAIS) in sport. *The Sport Psychologist, 4,* 285-300.

Nideffer, R. (2007). Reliability and validity of the attentional and interpersonal style (TAIS) inventory concentration scales. In D. Smith & M. Bar-Eli (Eds.), *Essential readings in sport and exercise psychology* (pp. 265-277). Champaign, IL: Human Kinetics.

Orlick, T., & Partington, J. (1988). Mental links to excellence. *The Sport Psychologist, 2,* 105-130.

Ravizza, K. (1984). Peak experiences in sport. In J. Silva & R. Weinberg (Eds.), *Psychological foundations of sport* (pp. 452-462). Champaign, IL: Human Kinetics.

Reid, G., & Nygren, T. (1988). The subjective workload assessment technique: A scaling procedure for measuring mental workload. In P. Hancock & N. Meshkati (Eds.), *Human mental workload* (pp. 185-218). Amsterdam: North Holland.

Roberts, G.C., Treasure, D.C., & Balague, G. (1998). Achievement goals in sport: The development and validation of the Perceptions of Success Questionnaire. *Journal of Sport Sciences, 16*(4), 337-347.

Roberts, R., Callow, N., Hardy, L., Markland, D., & Bringer, J. (2008). Movement imagery ability: Development and assessment of a revised version of the Vividness of Movement Questionnaire. *Journal of Sport and Exercise Psychology, 30,* 200-221.

Salmela, J. (1992). *The Ottawa Mental Skills Assessment Tool (OMSAT).* Unpublished manuscript, University of Ottawa, Canada.

Seligman, M., & Csikszentimalyi, M. (2000). Positive psychology: An introduction. *American Psychologist, 55*, 5-14.

Shelton, T., & Mahoney, M. (1978). The content and effect of "psyching up" strategies in weightlifters. *Cognitive Therapy and Research, 2*, 275-284.

Smith, R., & Christensen, D. (1995). Psychological skills as predictors of performance and survival in professional baseball. *Journal of Sport and Exercise Psychology, 17*, 399-415.

Smith, R., Schutz, R., Smoll, F., & Ptacek, J. (1995). Development and validation of a multidimensional measure of sport-specific psychological skills: The Athletic Coping Skills Inventory-28. *Journal of Sport and Exercise Psychology, 17*, 379-398.

Smith, R., Smoll, F., & Ptacek, J. (1990). Conjunctive moderator variables in vulnerability and resiliency research: Life stress, social support, and coping skills, and adolescent sport injuries. *Journal of Personality and Social Psychology, 58*, 360-370.

Smith, R., Smoll, F., & Schutz, R. (1990). Measurement and correlates of sport-specific cognitive and somatic trait anxiety: The Sport Anxiety Scale. *Anxiety Research, 2*, 263-280.

Smoll, F., Smith, R., Barnett, N., & Everett, J. (1993). Enhancement of children's self esteem through social support training for youth sport coaches. *Journal of Applied Psychology, 78*, 602-610.

Spielberger, C. (1966). *Anxiety and behavior.* New York: Academic Press.

Swain, A., & Harwood, C. (1996). Antecedents of state goals in age-group swimmers: An interactionist perspective. *Journal of Sport Sciences, 14*, 111-124.

Taylor, M., Gould, D., & Rolo, C. (2008). Performance strategies of US Olympians in practice and competition. *High Ability Studies, 19*, 19-36.

Theodorakis, Y., Hatzigeorgiadis, A., & Chroni, S. (2008). Self-talk: It works, but how? Development and preliminary validation of the Functions of Self-Talk Questionnaire. *Measurement in Physical Education and Exercise Science, 12*, 10-30.

Thomas, P., Murphy, S., & Hardy, L. (1999). Test of Performance Strategies: Development and preliminary validation of a comprehensive measure of athletes' psychological skills. *Journal of Sport Sciences, 17*, 691-711.

Tutko, T., Lyon, L., & Ogilvie, B. (1969*). Athletic Motivation Inventory.* San Jose, CA: Institute for the Study of Athletic Motivation.

Van Schoyck, S., & Grasha, A. (1981). Attentional style variations and athletic ability: The advantage of a sports-specific test. *Journal of Sport Psychology, 3*, 149-165.

Vealey, R. (2002). Personality and sport behavior. In T. Horn (Ed.), *Advances in sport psychology* (pp. 43-82). Champaign, IL: Human Kinetics.

Vealey, R. (2007). *Coaching for the inner edge.* Morgantown, WV: Fitness Information Technology.

Vitalino, P., Russo, J., Carr, J., Miuro, R., & Becker, J. (1985). The Ways of Coping Checklist: Revision and psychometric properties. *Multivariate Behavioral Research, 20*, 3-26.

Weinberg, R., & Comar, W. (1994). The effectiveness of psychological interventions in competitive sport: A review and critique. *Sports Medicine Journal, 18*, 406-418.

Weinberg, R., & Gould, D. (2007). *Foundations of sport and exercise psychology* (4th ed.). Champaign, IL: Human Kinetics.

Williams, M., & Ericsson, A. (2008). How do experts learn. *Journal of Applied Sport Psychology, 30*, 653-662.

Zervas, Y., Stavrou, N., & Psychountaki, M. (2007). Development and validation of the Self-Talk Questionnaire (S-TQ) for sports. *Journal of Applied Sport Psychology, 19*, 142-159.

Chapter 34

Aldwin, C.M. (2007). *Stress, coping, and development: An integrative approach* (2nd ed.). New York: Guilford Press.

Amiot, C.E., Gaudreau, P., & Blanchard, C.M. (2004). Self-determination, coping, and goal attainment in sport. *Journal of Sport and Exercise Psychology, 26*, 396-411.

Anshel, M.H. (2001). Qualitative validation of a model for coping with acute stress in sport. *Journal of Sport Behavior, 24*, 223-246.

Anshel, M.H., & Anderson, D.I. (2002). Coping with acute stress in sport: Linking athletes' coping style, coping strategies, affect, and motor performance. *Anxiety, Stress and Coping, 15*, 193-209.

Anshel, M.H., Williams, L.R., & Williams, S.M. (2000). Coping style following acute stress in competitive sport. *The Journal of Social Psychology, 140*, 751-773.

Blumenstein, B. (2002). Biofeedback applications in sport and exercise: Research findings. In B. Blumenstein, M. Bar-Eli, & G. Tenenbaum (Eds.), *Brain and body in sport and exercise—biofeedback applications in performance enhancement* (pp. 38-54). New York: Wiley.

Blumenstein, B., Bar-Eli, M., & Tenenbaum, G. (1997). A five-step approach to mental training incorporating biofeedback. *The Sport Psychologist, 11*, 440-453.

Bolgar, M.R., Janelle, C., & Giacobbi, P.R. (2008). Trait anger, appraisal, and coping differences among adolescent tennis players. *Journal of Applied Sport Psychology, 20*, 73-87.

Boutcher, S.H., & Crews, D.J. (1987). The effect of a pre-shot attentional routine on a well-learned skill. *International Journal of Sport Psychology, 18*, 30-39.

Carver, C.S., Scheier, M.F., & Weintraub, J.K. (1989). Assessing coping strategies: A theoretically based approach. *Journal of Personality and Social Psychology, 56*, 267-283.

Cohn, P.J. (1990). Preperformance routines in sport: Theoretical support and practical implications. *The Sport Psychologist, 4*, 301-312.

Cohn, P.J., Rotella, R.J., & Lloyd, J.W. (1990). Effects of a cognitive-behavioral intervention on the pre-shot routine and performance in golf. *The Sport Psychologist, 4*, 33-47.

Creswell, J.W. (2007). *Qualitative inquiry and research design: Choosing among five approaches* (2nd ed.). Thousand Oaks, CA: Sage.

Crews, D.J., & Landers, D. (1993). Electroencephalographic measures of attentional patterns prior to the golf putt. *Medicine and Science in Sports and Exercise, 25*, 116-126.

Crocker, P.R.E. (1992). Managing stress by competitive athletes: Ways of coping. *International Journal of Sport Psychology, 23*, 161-175.

Crocker, P.R.E., Alderman, R.B., & Smith, F.M .R. (1988). Cognitive-affective stress management training with high performance youth volleyball players: Effects on affect, cognition, and performance. *Journal of Sport and Exercise Psychology, 10*, 448-460.

Crocker, P.R.E., & Graham, T.R. (1995). Coping by competitive athletes with performance stress: Gender differences and relationships with affect. *The Sport Psychologist, 9*, 325-338.

Crocker, P.R.E., & Isaak, K. (1997). Coping during competitions and training sessions: Are youth swimmers consistent? *International Journal of Sport Psychology, 228*, 355-369.

Crocker, P.R.E., Kowalski, K.C., & Graham, T.R. (1998). Measurement of coping strategies in sport. In J.L. Duda (Ed.), *Advances in sport and exercise psychology measurement* (pp. 149-161). Morgantown, WV: Fitness Information Technology.

Crocker, P.R.E., Mosewich, A.D., Kowalski, K.C., & Besenski, L.J. (2010). Coping: Research design and analysis issues. In A.R. Nicholls (Ed.), *Coping in sport: Theory, methods, and related constructs* (pp.35-52). Hauppauge, NY: Nova Science.

Eklund, R.C., Grove, J.R., & Heard, N.P. (1998). The measurement of slump-related coping: Factorial validity of the COPE and modified-COPE inventories. *Journal of Sport and Exercise Psychology, 20,* 157-175.

Endler, N.S., & Parker, J.D. (1990). The multidimensional assessment of coping: A critical evaluation. *Journal of Personality and Social Psychology, 58,* 844-854.

Endler, N.S., Parker, J.D.A., & Summerfeldt, L.J. (1998). Coping with health problems: Developing a reliable and valid multidimensional measure. *Psychological Assessment, 10,* 195-205.

Gaudreau, P., & Antl, S. (2008). Athletes' broad dimensions of perfectionism: Examining change in life-satisfaction and the mediating role of motivation and coping. *Journal of Sport and Exercise Psychology, 30,* 356-382.

Gaudreau, P., & Blondin, J.P. (2002). Development of a questionnaire for the assessment of coping strategies employed by athletes in competitive sport settings. *Psychology of Sport and Exercise, 3,* 1-34.

Gaudreau, P., & Blondin, J.P. (2004). Different athletes cope differently during a sport competition: A cluster analysis of coping. *Personality and Individual Differences, 36,* 1865-1877.

Gaudreau, P., Blondin, J.P., & Lapierre, A.M. (2002). Athletes' coping during a competition: Relationship of coping strategies with positive affect, negative affect, and performance-goal discrepancy. *Psychology of Sport and Exercise, 3,* 125-150.

Gaudreau, P., El Ali, M., & Marivain, T. (2005). Factor structure of the Coping Inventory for Competitive Sport with a sample of participants at the 2001 New York Marathon. *Psychology of Sport and Exercise, 6,* 271-288.

Gaudreau, P., Lapierre, A.M., & Blondin, J.P. (2001). Coping at three phases of a competition: Comparison between precompetitive, competitive, and post-competitive utilization of the same strategy. *International Journal of Sport Psychology, 32,* 369-385.

Goudas, M., Theodorakis, Y., & Karamousalidis, G. (1998). Psychological skills in basketball: Preliminary study for development of a Greek form of the Athletic Coping Skills Inventory-28. *Perceptual and Motor Skills, 86,* 59-65.

Gould, D., Eklund, R.C., & Jackson, S.A. (1993). Coping strategies used by US Olympic wrestlers. *Research Quarterly for Exercise and Sport, 64,* 453-468.

Hall, E.G., & Erffmeyer, E.S. (1983). The effect of visuo-motor behavior rehearsal with videotaped modeling on free throw accuracy of intercollegiate female basketball players. *Journal of Sport Psychology, 5,* 343-346.

Hanton, S., & Fletcher, D. (2005). Organizational stress in competitive sport: More than we bargained for? *International Journal of Sport Psychology, 36,* 273-283.

Hanton, S., Neil, R., Mellalieu, S.D., & Fletcher, D. (2008). Competitive experience and performance status: An investigation into multidimensional anxiety and coping. *European Journal of Sport Science, 8,* 143-152.

Hoar, S.D., Crocker, P.R.E., Holt, N.L., & Tamminen, K.A. (2010). Gender differences in adolescent athletes—coping differences with interpersonal stressors in sport: More similarities than differences? *Journal of Applied Sport Psychology, 22,* 134-149.

Hoar, S.D., Kowalski, K.C., Gaudreau, P., & Crocker, P.R.E. (2006). A review of coping in sport. In S. Hanton & S. Mellalieu (Eds.), *Literature reviews in sport psychology* (pp. 47-90). Hauppauge, NY: Nova Science.

Holt, N.L., Berg, K.-J., & Tamminen, K.A. (2007). Tales of the unexpected: Coping among female collegiate volleyball players. *Research Quarterly for Exercise and Sport, 78,* 117-132.

Holtzman, S., & DeLongis, A. (2007). Coping in context: The role of stress, social support, and personality in coping. *Journal of Personality, 73,* 1633-1656.

Jackson, R.C. (2003). Pre-performance routine consistency: Temporal analysis of goal kicking in the Rugby Union World Cup. *Journal of Sports Sciences, 21,* 803-814.

Kaissidis-Rodafinos, A., & Anshel, M.H. (2000). Psychological predictors of coping responses among Greek basketball referees. *The Journal of Social Psychology, 140,* 329-344.

Kim, J., Singer, R.N., & Radlo, S.J. (1996). Degree of cognitive demands in psychomotor tasks and the effects of the five-step strategy on achievement. *Journal of Human Performance, 2,* 155-169.

Kowalski, K.C., & Crocker, P.R.E. (2001). The development and validation of the Coping Function Questionnaire for adolescents in sport. *Journal of Sport and Exercise Psychology, 23,* 136-155.

Kowalski, K.C., Crocker, P.R.E., Hoar, S.D., & Niefer, C.B. (2005). Adolescents' control beliefs and coping with stress in sport. *International Journal of Sport Psychology, 36,* 257-272.

Kowalski, K.C., Mack, D.E., Crocker, P.R.E., Niefer, C.B., & Fleming, T.-L. (2006). Coping with social physique anxiety in adolescence. *Journal of Adolescent Health, 39,* 275.e9-275.e16.

Krohne, H.W. (1993). Vigilance and cognitive avoidance as concepts in coping research. In H.W. Krohne (Ed.), *Attention and avoidance* (pp. 51-69). Seattle: Hogrefe & Huber.

Kyrejto, J.W., Mosewich, A.D., Kowalski, K.C., Mack, D.E., & Crocker, P.R.E. (2008). Men's and women's drive for muscularity: Gender differences and cognitive and behavioural correlates. *International Journal of Sport and Exercise Psychology, 6,* 69-84.

Lally, P. (2007). Identity and athletic retirement: A prospective study. *Psychology of Sport and Exercise, 8,* 85-99.

Lazarus, R.S. (1990). Theory-based stress measurement: With commentaries. *Psychological Inquiry, 1,* 3-51.

Lazarus, R.S. (1991). *Emotion and adaptation.* New York: Oxford University Press.

Lazarus, R.S. (1999). *Stress and emotion: A new synthesis.* New York: Springer.

Lazarus, R.S. (2000). How emotions influence performance in competitive sports. *The Sport Psychologist, 14,* 229-252.

Lazarus, R.S., & Folkman, S. (1984). *Stress, appraisal, and coping.* New York: Springer.

Lidor, R. (2004). Developing metacognitive behavior in physical education classes: The use of task-pertinent learning strategies. *Physical Education and Sport Pedagogy, 1,* 55-71.

Lidor, R. (2007). Preparatory routines in self-paced events: Do they benefit the skilled athletes? Can they help the beginners? In G. Tenenbaum & R.C. Eklund (Eds.), *Handbook of sport psychology* (3rd ed., pp. 445-465). New York: Wiley.

Lidor, R. (2009). Free throw shots in basketball: Physical and psychological routines. In E. Tsung-Min Hung, R. Lidor, & D. Hackfort (Eds.), *Psychology of sport excellence* (pp. 53-61). Morgantown, WV: Fitness Information Technology.

Lidor, R., & Mayan, Z. (2005). Can beginning learners benefit from preperformance routines when serving in volleyball? *The Sport Psychologist, 19,* 343-362.

Lidor, R., & Singer, R.N. (2005). Learning strategies in motor skill acquisition: From the laboratory to the field. In D. Hackfort, J. Duda, & R. Lidor (Eds.), *Handbook of research in applied sport and exercise psychology: International perspectives* (pp. 109-126). Morgantown, WV: Fitness Information Technology.

Lobmeyer, D.L., & Wasserman, E.A. (1986). Preliminaries to free throw shooting: Superstitious behavior? *Journal of Sport Behavior, 9,* 70-78.

Louvet, B., Gaudreau, P., Menaut, A., Genty, J., & Deneuve, P. (2007). Longitudinal patterns of stability and change in coping across three competitions: A latent class growth analysis. *Journal of Sport and Exercise Psychology, 29,* 100-117.

Louvet, B., Gaudreau, P., Menaut, A., Genty, J., & Deneuve, P. (2009). Revisiting the changing and stable properties of coping utilization using latent class growth analysis: A longitudinal investigation with soccer referees. *Psychology of Sport and Exercise, 10,* 124-135.

Madden, C.C., Kirkby, R.J., & McDonald, D. (1989). Coping styles of competitive middle distance runners. *International Journal of Sport Psychology, 20,* 287-296.

Moran, A.P. (1996). *The psychology of concentration in sport performers: A cognitive analysis.* East Sussex, UK: Psychology Press.

Nicholls, A.R., & Polman, R.C.J. (2007). Coping in sport: A systematic review. *Journal of Sports Sciences, 25,* 11-31.

Nicholls, A.R., & Polman, R.C.J. (2008). Think aloud: Acute stress and coping strategies during golf performances. *Anxiety, Stress and Coping, 21,* 283-294.

Nicholls, A.R., Polman, R.C.J., Levy, A.R., & Backhouse, S.H. (2008). Mental toughness, optimism, pessimism, and coping among athletes. *Personality and Individual Differences, 44,* 1182-1192.

Ntoumanis, N., Biddle, S.J.H., & Haddock, G. (1999). The mediating role of coping strategies on the relationship between achievement motivation and affect in sport. *Anxiety, Stress and Coping: An International Journal, 12,* 299-327.

Radlo, S.J., Steinberg, G.M., Singer, R.N., Barba, D.A., & Melnikov, A. (2002). The influence of an attentional focus strategy on alpha brain wave activity, heart rate, and dart-throwing performance. *International Journal of Sport Psychology, 33,* 205-217.

Roth, S., & Cohen, L.J. (1986). Approach, avoidance, and coping with stress. *American Psychologist, 41,* 813-819.

Sabiston, C.M., Sedgwick, W.A., Crocker, P.R.E., Kowalski, K.C., & Stevens, D. (2007). Social physique anxiety in adolescents: An examination of influences, coping strategies and health behaviours. *Journal of Adolescent Research, 22,* 78-101.

Salazar, W., Landers, D., Petruzzello, S., Crews, D., Kubitz, K., & Han, M. (1990). Hemispheric asymmetry, cardiac response and performance in elite archers. *Research Quarterly for Exercise and Sport, 61,* 351-359.

Singer, R.N., Flora, L.A., & Abourezk, T. (1989). The effect of a five-step approach learning strategy on the acquisition of a complex motor task. *Journal of Applied Sport Psychology, 1,* 98-108.

Skinner, E.A., & Zimmer-Gembeck, M.J. (2007). The development of coping. *Annual Review of Psychology, 58,* 119-144.

Smith, B., & Sparkes, A.C. (2009). Narrative inquiry in sport and exercise psychology: What can it mean, and why might we do it? *Psychology of Sport and Exercise, 10,* 1-11.

Smith, R.E. (1980). A cognitive-affective approach to stress management training for athletes. In C. Nadeau, W. Halliwell, K. Newell, & G. Roberts (Eds.), *Psychology of motor behavior and sport—1979* (pp. 54-73). Champaign, IL: Human Kinetics.

Smith, R.E., & Christensen, D.S. (1995). Psychological skills as predictors of performance and survival in professional baseball. *Journal of Sport and Exercise Psychology, 17,* 399-415.

Smith, R.E., Schultz, R.W., Smoll, F.L., & Ptacek, J.T. (1995). Development and validation of a multidimensional measure of sport-specific psychological skills: The Athletic Coping Skills Inventory-28. *Journal of Sport and Exercise Psychology, 17,* 379-398.

Thelwell, R.C., Weston, N.J.V., & Greenlees, I.A. (2007). Batting on a sticky wicket: Identifying sources of stress and associated coping strategies for professional cricket batsmen. *Psychology of Sport and Exercise, 8,* 219-232.

Thing, L.F. (2006). "Voices of the broken body." The resumption of non-professional female players' sports careers after anterior cruciate ligament injury. The female player's dilemma: Is she willing to run the risk? *Scandinavian Journal of Medicine and Science in Sports, 16,* 364-375.

Totsika, V., & Wulf, G. (2003). The influence of external and internal foci of attention on transfer to novel situations and skills. *Research Quarterly for Exercise and Sport, 74,* 220-225.

Udry, E. (1997). Coping and social support among injured athletes following surgery. *Journal of Sport and Exercise Psychology, 19,* 71-90.

Vance, J., Wulf, G., Töllner, T., McNevin, N., & Mercer, J. (2004). EMG activity as a function of the performer⊠s focus of attention. Journal of Motor Behavior, 36, 450-459.

Wrisberg, C.A., & Anshel, M.H. (1989). The effect of cognitive strategies on free throw shooting performance of young athletes. *The Sport Psychologist, 3,* 95-104.

Wulf, G. (2007). *Attention and motor skill learning.* Champaign, IL: Human Kinetics.

Wulf, G., Hoss, M., & Prinz, W. (1998). Instructions for motor learning: Differential effects of internal versus external focus of attention. *Journal of Motor Behavior, 30,* 169-179.

Wulf, G., Shea, C., & Park, J.H. (2001). Attention and motor performance: Preference for and advantage of an external focus. *Research Quarterly for Exercise and Sport, 72,* 335-344.

Yoo, J. (2001). Coping profile of Korean competitive athletes. *International Journal of Sport Psychology, 32,* 290-303.

Zachry, T., Wulf, G., Mercer, J., & Bezodis, N. (2005). Increased movement accuracy and reduced EMG activity as the result of adopting an external focus of attention. *Brain Research Bulletin, 67,* 304-309.

Zaichkowsky, L.D. (1983). The use of biofeedback for self-regulation of performance states. In L.E. Unestahl (Ed.), The mental aspects of gymnastics (pp. 95-105). Örebro, Sweden: Veje.

Chapter 35

Annesi, J.J. (1999). Effects of minimal group promotion on cohesion and exercise adherence. *Small Group Research, 30,* 542-557.

Bandura, A. (1986). *Social foundations of thought and action: A social cognitive theory.* Englewood Cliffs, NJ: Prentice Hall.

Bovard, E.W. (1951). Group structure and perception. *Journal of Abnormal and Social Psychology, 46,* 389-405.

Brawley, L.R., Carron, A.V., & Widmeyer, W.N. (1987). Assessing the cohesion of teams: Validity of the Group Environment Questionnaire. *Journal of Sport Psychology, 9,* 275-294.

Burke, S.M., Carron, A.V., Eys, M.A., Ntoumanis, N., & Estabrooks, P.A. (2006). Group versus individual approach? A meta-analysis of the effectiveness of interventions to promote physical activity. *Sport and Exercise Psychology Review, 2,* 19-35.

Burke, S.M., Carron, A.V., Patterson, M.M., Estabrooks, P.A., Hill, J.L., Loughead, T.M., Rosenkranz, S.R., & Spink, K.S. (2005). Cohesion as shared beliefs in exercise classes. *Small Group Research, 36,* 267-288.

Buton, F., Fontayne, P., Heuzé, J., Bosselut, G., & Raimbault, N. (2007). The QAG-a: An analog version of the Questionnaire sur l'Ambiance du Groupe for measuring the dynamic nature of group cohesion. *Small Group Research, 38,* 235-264.

Carron, A.V. (1980). *Social psychology of sport.* Ithaca, NY: Mouvement.

Carron, A.V. (1982). Cohesiveness in sport groups: Interpretations and considerations. *Journal of Sport Psychology, 4,* 123-138.

Carron, A.V. (1993). The Coleman Roberts Griffith Address: Toward the integration of theory, research, and practice in sport psychology. *Journal of Applied Sport Psychology, 5,* 95-109.

Carron, A.V., Brawley, L.R., & Widmeyer, W.N. (1998). The measurement of cohesiveness in sport groups. In J.L. Duda (Ed.), *Advances in sport and exercise psychology measurement* (pp. 213-226). Morgantown, WV: Fitness Information Technology.

Carron, A.V., Brawley, L.R., & Widmeyer, W.N. (2002). The Group Environment Questionnaire: Test manual. Morgantown, WV: Fitness Information Technology.

Carron, A.V., & Chelladurai, P. (1981). The dynamics of group cohesion in sport. *Journal of Sport Psychology, 3,* 123-139.

Carron, A.V., Colman, M.M., Wheeler, J., & Stevens, D. (2002). Cohesion and performance in sport: A meta-analysis. *Journal of Sport and Exercise Psychology, 24,* 168-188.

Carron, A.V., Hausenblas, H.A., & Eys, M.A. (2005). *Group dynamics in sport* (3rd ed.). Morgantown, WV: Fitness Information Technology.

Carron, A.V., & Ramsay, M.C. (1994). Internal consistency of the Group Environment Questionnaire modified for a university residence setting. *Perceptual and Motor Skills, 79,* 141-142.

Carron, A.V., & Spink, K.S. (1993). Team building in an exercise setting. *The Sport Psychologist, 7,* 8-18.

Carron, A.V., Widmeyer, W.N., & Brawley, L.R. (1985). The development of an instrument to assess cohesion in sport teams: The Group Environment Questionnaire. *Journal of Sport Psychology, 7,* 244-266.

Carron, A.V., Widmeyer, W.N., & Brawley, L.R. (1988). Group cohesion and individual adherence to physical activity. *Journal of Sport and Exercise Psychology, 10,* 119-126.

Courneya, K.S., & McAuley, E. (1995). Cognitive mediators of the social influence-exercise adherence relationship: A test of the theory of planned behaviour. *Journal of Behavioral Medicine, 18,* 499-515.

Cronbach, L. (1951). Coefficient alpha and the internal structure of tests. *Psychometrika, 16,* 297-334.

Cumming, S.P., Smith, R.E., Smoll, F.L., Standage, M., & Grossbard, J.R. (2008). Development and validation of the Achievement Goal Scale for Youth Sports. *Psychology of Sport and Exercise, 9,* 686-703.

Dimock, H. (1941). *Rediscovering the adolescent.* New York: Association Press.

Dion, K.L. (2000). Group cohesion: From "field of forces" to multidimensional construct. *Group Dynamics: Theory, Research and Practice, 4,* 7-26.

Estabrooks, P.A., & Carron, A.V. (1997). The association among social support, subjective norm, and group cohesion in elderly exercisers. *Journal of Applied Sport Psychology, 9*(Suppl.), S90.

Estabrooks, P.A., & Carron, A.V. (1999). Group cohesion in older adult exercisers: Prediction and intervention effects. *Journal of Behavioral Medicine, 22,* 575-588.

Estabrooks, P.A., & Carron, A.V. (2000). The Physical Activity Group Environment Questionnaire: An instrument for the assessment of cohesion in exercise classes. *Group Dynamics: Theory, Research and Practice, 4,* 230-243.

Eys, M.A., Carron, A.V., Bray, S.R., & Brawley, L.R. (2007). Item wording and internal consistency of a measure of cohesion: The Group Environment Questionnaire. *Journal of Sport and Exercise Psychology, 29,* 395-402.

Eys, M.A., Hardy, J., Carron, A.V., & Beauchamp, M.R. (2003). The relationship between task cohesion and competitive state anxiety. *Journal of Sport and Exercise Psychology, 25,* 66-76.

Eys, M.A., Loughead, T.M., Bray, S.R., & Carron, A.V. (2009). Development of a cohesion questionnaire for youth: The Youth Sport Environment Questionnaire. *Journal of Sport and Exercise Psychology, 31,* 390-408.

Festinger, L., Schachter, S., & Back, K. (1950). *Social pressures in informal groups.* New York: Harper & Brothers.

Fiedler, F.E. (1954). Assumed similarity measures as predictors of team effectiveness. *Journal of Abnormal and Social Psychology, 49,* 381-388.

Gill, D.L. (1977). Cohesiveness and performance in sport groups. *Exercise and Sport Sciences Reviews, 5,* 131-155.

Golembiewski, R. (1962). *The small group.* Chicago: University of Chicago Press.

Goodman, P.S., Ravlin, E., & Schminke, M. (1987). Understanding groups in organizations. In L.L. Cummings & B.M. Staw (Eds.), *Research in organizational behavior* (pp. 121-173). Greenwich, CT: Jai Press.

Gould, S.J. (1996). *The mismeasure of man.* New York: Norton.

Granito, V.J., & Rainey, D.W. (1988). Differences in cohesion between high school and college football teams and starters and nonstarters. *Perceptual and Motor Skills, 66,* 471-477.

Gross, N., & Martin, W. (1952). On group cohesiveness. *American Journal of Sociology, 57,* 533-546.

Hager, T. (1995). *Force of nature.* New York: Simon & Schuster.

Henderson, J., Bougeois, A.E., LeUnes, A., & Meyers, M.C. (1998). Group cohesion, mood disturbance, and stress in female basketball players. *Small Group Research, 29,* 212-225.

Heuzé, J., & Fontayne, P. (2002). Questionnaire sur l'Ambiance du Groupe: A French-language instrument for measuring group cohesion. *Journal of Sport and Exercise Psychology, 24,* 42-67.

Heuzé, J.P., Raimbault, N., & Fontayne, P. (2006). Relationships between cohesion, collective efficacy, and performance in professional basketball teams: An examination of mediating effects. *Journal of Sport Sciences, 24,* 59-68.

Heuzé, J.P., Sarrazin, P., Masiero, M., Raimbault, N., & Thomas, J.P. (2006). The relationship of perceived motivational climate to cohesion and collective efficacy in elite female teams. *Journal of Applied Sport Psychology, 18,* 201-218.

Hoigaard, R., Safvenbom, R., & Tonnessen, F.E. (2006). The relationship between group cohesion, group norms, and perceived social loafing in soccer teams. *Small Group Research, 37,* 217-232.

Hoigaard, R., Tofteland, I., & Ommundsen, Y. (2006). The effect of team cohesion on social loafing in relay teams. *International Journal of Applied Sports Sciences, 18,* 59-73.

Kincaid J.P., Fishburne, R.P., Rogers, R.L., & Chissom, B.S. (1975). *Derivation of new readability formulas (Automated Readability Index, Fog Count and Flesch Reading Ease Formula) for navy enlisted personnel.* Millington, TN: Naval Air Station Memphis.

Klein, M., & Christiansen, G. (1969). Group composition, group structure and group effectiveness of basketball teams. In J.W. Loy & G.S. Kenyon (Eds.), *Sport, culture and society* (pp. 397-408). New York: Macmillan.

Landers, D.M., & Lueschen, G. (1974). Team performance outcome and cohesiveness of competitive co-acting groups. *International Review of Sport Sociology, 9,* 57-69.

Landers, D.M., Wilkinson, M.O., Hatfield, B.D., & Barber, H. (1982). Causality and the cohesion-performance relationship. *Journal of Sport Psychology, 4,* 170-183.

Lenk, H. (1969). Top performance despite internal conflict: An antithesis to a functional proposition. In J. Loy & G. Kenyon (Eds.), *Sport, culture and society: A reader on the sociology of sport.* Toronto: Macmillan.

Lott, A.J., & Lott, B.D. (1965). Group cohesiveness as interpersonal attraction: A review of relationships with antecedent and consequent variables. *Psychological Bulletin, 64,* 259-309.

Martens, R., Landers, D.M., & Loy, J.W. (1972). *Sport Cohesiveness Questionnaire.* Washington, DC: American Alliance for Health, Physical Education, Recreation and Dance Publications.

McGrath, J.E. (1962). The influence of positive interpersonal relations on adjustment and effectiveness in rifle teams. *Journal of Abnormal and Social Psychology, 65,* 365-375.

Melnick, M.J., & Chemers, M. (1974). Effects of group social structure on the success of basketball teams. *Research Quarterly, 45,* 1-8.

Mudrack, P.E. (1989a). Defining group cohesiveness: A legacy of confusion? *Small Group Behavior, 20,* 37-49.

Mudrack, P.E. (1989b). Group cohesiveness and productivity: A closer look. *Human Relations, 42,* 771-785.

Rubin, K.H., Bukowski, W., & Parker, J. (2006). Peer interactions, relationships, and groups. In N. Eisenberg (Ed.), *Handbook of child psychology: Social, emotional, and personality development* (6th ed., pp. 571-645). New York: Wiley.

Schachter, S. (1951). Deviation, rejection, and communication. *Journal of Abnormal and Social Psychology, 46,* 190-207.

Schutz, R.W., Eom, H.J., Smoll, F.L., & Smith, R.E. (1994). Examination of the factorial validity of the Group Environment Questionnaire. *Research Quarterly for Exercise and Sport, 65,* 226-236.

Smith, R.E., Smoll, F.L., & Barnett, N.P. (1995). Reduction of children's sport performance anxiety through social support and stress-reduction training for coaches. *Journal of Applied Developmental Psychology, 16,* 125-142.

Spink, K.S., & Carron, A.V. (1993). The effects of team building on the adherence patterns of female exercise participants. *Journal of Sport and Exercise Psychology, 15,* 39-49.

Spink, K.S., & Carron, A.V. (1994). Group cohesion effects in exercise classes. *Small Group Research, 25,* 26-42.

Stogdill, R.M. (1964). *Team achievement under high motivation.* Columbus, OH: Ohio State University, College of Commerce and Administration, The Bureau of Business Research.

Sullivan, P.J., Short, S.E., & Cramer, K.M. (2002). Confirmatory factor analysis of the group environment questionnaire with coaching sports. *Perceptual and Motor Skills, 94,* 341-347.

Terry, P.C., Carron, A.V., Pink, M.J., Lane, A.M., Jones, G.J.W., & Hall, M.P. (2000). Perceptions of group cohesion and mood in sport teams. *Group Dynamics, 4,* 244-253.

Turman, P.D. (2003). Coaches and cohesion: The impact of coaching techniques on team cohesion in the small group sport setting. *Journal of Sport Behavior, 26,* 86-104.

Vallerand, R.J. (1989). Vers une méthodologie de validation transculturelle de questionnaires psychologiques: Implications pour la recherche en langue française [Toward a methodology for cross-cultural validation of psychological questionnaires: Implications for research in the French language]. *Psychologie Canadienne, 30,* 662-680.

Vallerand, R.J., & Halliwell, W.R. (1983). Vers une méthodologie de validation transculturelle de questionnaires psychologiques : Implications pour la psychologie du sport [Toward a methodology for cross-cultural validation of psychological questionnaires : Implications for sport psychology]. *Canadian Journal of Applied Sport Science, 8,* 9-18.

Watson, J.D., Martin Ginis, K.A., & Spink, K.S. (2004). Team building in an exercise class for the elderly. *Activities, Adaptations and Aging, 28,* 35-47.

Westre, K.R., & Weiss, M.R. (1991). The relationship between perceived coaching behaviors and group cohesion in high school football teams. *Sport Psychologist, 5,* 41-54.

Widmeyer, W.N., Brawley, L.R., & Carron, A.V. (1990). The effects of group size in sport. *Journal of Sport and Exercise Psychology, 12,* 177-190.

Yukelson, D., Weinberg, R., & Jackson, A. (1984). A multidimensional group cohesion instrument for intercollegiate basketball. *Journal of Sport Psychology, 6,* 103-117.

Chapter 36

Bakeman, R., & Gottman, J. (1997). *Observing interaction: An introduction to sequential analysis.* New York: Cambridge University Press.

Bakeman, R., & Quera, V. (1995). *Analyzing interaction: Sequential analysis with SDIS and GSEQ.* New York: Cambridge University Press.

Baker, M. (1999). Argumentation and constructive interaction. In P. Courier & J.E.B. Andriessen (Eds.), *Foundations of argumentative text processing* (pp. 179-202). Amsterdam: Amsterdam University Press.

Bakhtin, M. (1981). *The dialogic imagination* (M. Holquist, Ed.). Austin, TX: University of Texas Press.

Beers, P.J., Boshuizen, E., & Kirschner, P. (2004). *Computer support for knowledge construction in collaborative learning environments.* Paper presented at the American Educational Research Association Conference, San Diego.

Calmeiro, L. (2006). *The dynamic nature of the emotion-cognition link in trapshooting performance.* (Doctoral dissertation, Florida State University, 2006). http://etd.lib.fsu.edu/theses/available/etd-08112006-172106.

Carr, C., & Anderson, A. (2001). *Computer-supported collaborative argumentation: Supporting problem-based learning in legal education.* Paper presented at the Computer Support for Collaborative Learning (CSCL) 2001 Conference, Maastricht,

Netherlands. http://citeseerx.ist.psu.edu/viewdoc/download?doi=10.1.1.3.8080&rep=rep1&type=pdf.

Cho, K., & Jonassen, D. (2002). The effects of argumentation scaffolds on argumentation and problem solving. *Educational Technology Research and Development, 50*(3), 5-22.

Dick, W., Carey, L., & Carey, J. (2005). *The systematic design of instruction* (6th ed.). Boston: Allyn & Bacon.

Domagoj, L., Tenenbaum, G., Eccles, D., Jeong, A., & Johnson, T. (2009). Intra-team communication and performance in doubles tennis. *Research Quarterly for Exercise and Sport, 80*(2), 281-290.

England, E. (1985). Interactional analysis: The missing factor in computer-aided learning design and evaluation. *Educational Technology, 25*(9), 24-28.

Fiore, S.M., Salas, E., Cuevas, H.M., & Bowers, C.A. (2003). Distributed coordination space: Toward a theory of distributed team process and performance. *Theoretical Issues in Ergonomic Science, 4*, 340-364.

Garrison, R. (2000). Theoretical challenges for distance education in the 21st century: A shift from structural to transactional issues. *International Review of Research in Open and Distance Learning, 1*(1), 1-17.

Gottman, J.M. (1979). *Marital interactions: Experimental investigations.* New York: Academic Press.

Guerlain, S., Shin, T., Guo, H., Adams, R., & Calland, J.F. (2002). A team performance data collection and analysis system. In S. Hughes & M. Lewis (Eds.), *Proceedings of the Human Factors and Ergonomics Society 46th Annual Meeting* (pp. 1443-1447). Santa Monica, CA: Human Factors and Ergonomics Society.

Gunawardena, C., Lowe, C., & Anderson, T. (1997). Analysis of global on-line debate and the development of an interaction analysis model for examining social construction of knowledge in computer conferencing. *Journal of Educational Computing Research, 17*, 397-431.

Jeong, A. (2003a). The sequential analysis of group interaction and critical thinking in online threaded discussions. *The American Journal of Distance Education, 17*(1), 25-43.

Jeong, A. (2003b). *The effects of message-reply and time-based structures on group interactions and critical thinking in asynchronous online discussions.* Paper presented at the Association of Educational Communication and Technology Conference, Anaheim, CA.

Jeong, A. (2004). The combined effects of response time and message content on group interactions in computer-supported collaborative argumentation. *Journal of Distance Education, 19*(1), 36-53.

Jeong, A. (2005). The effects of linguistic qualifiers on group interaction patterns in computer-supported collaborative argumentation. *International Review of Research in Open and Distance Learning, 6*(3).

Jeong, A. (2006). The effects of conversational styles of communication on group interaction patterns and argumentation in online discussions. *Instructional Science, 34*(5), 367-397.

Jeong, A. (2007). The effects of intellectual openness and gender on critical thinking processes in computer-supported collaborative argumentation. *Journal of Distance Education, 22*(1), 1-18.

Jeong, A. (2009). Discussion analysis tool (DAT). http://garnet.fsu.edu/~ajeong/DAT.

Jeong, A., & Davidson-Shivers, G. (2006). The effects of gender interaction patterns on student participation in computer-supported collaborative argumentation. *Educational Technology, Research, and Development, 54*(6), 543-568.

Jeong, A., & Juong, S. (2007). Scaffolding collaborative argumentation in asynchronous discussions with message constraints and message labels. *Computers and Education, 48*, 427-445.

Johnson, D., & Johnson, R. (1992). *Creative controversy: Intellectual challenge in the classroom.* Edina, MN: Interaction Book.

King, F., & Roblyer, M. (1984). Alternative designs for evaluating computer-based instruction. *Journal of Instructional Development, 7*(3), 23-29.

Koschmann, T. (1999). Toward a dialogic theory of learning: Bakhtin's contribution to understanding learning in settings of collaboration. In C. Hoadley & J. Roschelle (Eds.), *Proceedings of the Computer Support for Collaborative Learning (CSCL) 1999 Conference* (pp. 308-313), Palo Alto, California: Stanford University.

Lemus, D., Seibold, D., Flanagin, A., & Metzger, M. (2004). Argument and decision making in computer-mediated groups. *Journal of Communication, 54*(2), 302-320.

Mandl, H., & Renkl, A. (1992). A plea for "more local" theories of cooperative learning. *Learning and Instruction, 2*, 281-285.

McAlister, S. (2003). Assessing good educational argumentation. Paper submitted to the 2003 CSCL conference, Bergen, Norway.

Newman, D., Johnson, C., Cochrane, C., & Webb, B. (1996). An experiment in group learning technology: Evaluating critical thinking in face-to-face and computer supported seminars. *Interpersonal Computing and Technology: An Electronic Journal for the 21st Century, 4*(1), 57-74.

Olson, G., Herbsleb, J., & Rueter, H. (1994). Characterizing the sequential structure of interactive behaviors through statistical and grammatical techniques. *Human-Computer Interaction, 9*(3/4), 427-472.

Rourke, L., Anderson, T., Garrison, D.R., & Archer, W. (2001). Methodological issues in the content analysis of computer conference transcripts. *International Journal of Artificial Intelligence in Education, 12*, 8-22.

Salas, E., & Cannon-Bowers, J.A. (2000). The anatomy of team training. In S. Tobias & J.D. Fletcher (Eds.), *Training and retraining: A handbook for business, industry, government, and the military* (pp. 312-335). New York: Macmillan.

Sloffer, S., Dueber, B., & Duffy, T. (1999). Using asynchronous conferencing to promote critical thinking: Two implementations in higher education. http://crlt.indiana.edu/publications/crlt99-8.pdf.

Soller, A. (2004). Computational modeling and analysis of knowledge sharing in collaborative distance learning. *The Journal of Personalization Research, 14*(4), 351-381.

Strijbos, J.W., Martens, R.L., Jochems, W., & Kirschner, P.A. (2004). *The effect of functional roles on perceived group efficiency and communication during computer-supported collaborative learning.* Paper presented at the American Educational Research Association, San Diego.

Veerman, A., Andriessen, J., & Kanselaar, G. (1999). Collaborative learning through computer-mediated argumentation. In C.M. Hoadley & J. Roschelle (Eds.), *Proceedings of the Computer Support for Collaborative Learning (CSCL) 1999 Conference* (pp. 640-650). Palo Alto, CA: Stanford University.

Wiley, J., & Voss, J. (1999). Constructing arguments from multiple sources: Tasks that promote understanding and not just memory for text. *Journal of Educational Psychology, 91*, 301-311.

Yukelson, D. (1993). Communicating effectively. In J.M. Williams (Ed.), *Applied sport psychology: Personal growth to peak performance* (2nd ed., pp. 122-136). Mountain View, CA: Mayfield.

Chapter 37

Amorose, A.J., & Anderson-Butcher, D. (2007). Autonomy-supportive coaching and self-determined motivation in high school and college athletes: A test of self-determination theory. *Psychology of Sport and Exercise, 8,* 654-670.

Amorose, A.J., & Horn, T.S. (2000). Intrinsic motivation: Relationships with collegiate athletes' gender, scholarship status, and perceptions of their coaches' behavior. *Journal of Sport and Exercise Psychology, 22,* 63-84.

Amorose, A.J., & Horn, T.S. (2001). Pre- to post-season changes in the intrinsic motivation of first year college athletes: Relationships with coaching behavior and scholarship status. *Journal of Applied Sport Psychology, 13,* 355-373.

Barnett, N.P., Smoll, F.L., & Smith, R.E. (1992). Effects of enhancing coach-athlete relationships on youth sport attrition. *Sport Psychologist, 6,* 111-127.

Barrow, J.E. (1977). The variables of leadership: A review and conceptual framework. *Academy of Management Review, 1,* 231-251.

Bass, B.M. (1985). *Leadership and performance beyond expectations.* New York: Free Press.

Chaumeton, N.R., & Duda, J.L. (1988). Is it how you play the game or whether you win or lose? The effect of competitive level and situation on coaching behaviors. *Journal of Sport Behavior, 11*(3), 157-174.

Chelladurai, P. (1978). *A contingency model of leadership in athletics.* Unpublished doctoral dissertation, University of Waterloo, Department of Management Sciences, Canada.

Chelladurai, P. (1993). Leadership. In R.N. Singer, M. Murphy, & K. Tennant (Eds.), *The handbook on research in sport psychology* (pp. 647-671). New York: Macmillan.

Chelladurai, P. (2007). Leadership in sports. In G. Tenenbaum & R.C. Eklund (Eds.), *Handbook of sport psychology* (3rd ed., pp. 113-135). Hoboken, NJ: Wiley.

Chelladurai, P., & Arnott, M. (1985). Decision styles in coaching: Preferences of basketball players. *Research Quarterly for Exercise and Sport, 56*(1), 15-24.

Chelladurai, P., & Haggerty, T.R. (1978). A normative model of decision-styles in coaching. *Athletic Administration, 13*(1), 6-9.

Chelladurai, P., Haggerty, T.R., & Baxter, P.R. (1989). Decision styles choices of university basketball coaches and players. *Journal of Sport and Exercise Psychology, 11,* 201-215.

Chelladurai, P., & Quek, C.B. (1995). Decision style choices of high school coaches: The effects of situational and coach characteristics. *Journal of Sport Behavior, 18*(2), 91-108.

Chelladurai, P., & Riemer, H. (1998). Measurement of leadership in sports. In J.L. Duda (Ed.), *Advancements in sport and exercise psychology measurement* (pp. 227-253). Morgantown, WV: Fitness Information Technology.

Chelladurai, P., & Saleh, S.D. (1980). Dimensions of leader behavior in sports: Development of a leadership scale. *Journal of Sport Psychology, 2,* 34-45.

Cumming, S.P., Smith, R.E., & Smoll, F.L. (2006). Athlete-perceived coaching behaviors: Relating two measurement traditions. *Journal of Sport and Exercise Psychology, 28,* 205-213.

Deci, E.L., & Ryan, R.M. (1985). Intrinsic motivation and self-determination in human behavior. New York: Plenum Press.

Hollembeak, J., & Amorose, A.J. (2005). Perceived coaching behaviors and college athletes' intrinsic motivation: A test of self-determination theory. *Journal of Applied Sport Psychology, 17,* 20-36.

Horn, T.S. (1985). Coaches' feedback and changes in children's perceptions of their physical competence. *Journal of Educational Psychology, 77,* 174-186.

Horn, T.S. (2002). Coaching effectiveness in the sport domain. In T.S. Horn (Ed.), *Advances in sport psychology* (2nd ed., pp. 319-354). Champaign, IL: Human Kinetics.

Iordanoglou, D. (1990). *Perceived leadership in Greek soccer: A preliminary investigation.* Unpublished manuscript, University of Manchester, Department of Education, Manchester, UK.

Isberg, L., & Chelladurai, P. (1990). *The Leadership Scale for Sports: Its applicability to the Swedish context.* Unpublished manuscript, Dalarna University College in Falun/Borlänge, Sweden.

Jambor, E.A., & Zhang, J.I.(1997). Investigating leadership, gender, and coaching level using the Revised Leadership for Sport Scale. *Journal of Sport Behavior, 20*(3),313-321.

Kenow, L., & Williams, J.M. (1992). Relationship between anxiety, self-confidence, and the evaluation of coaching behaviors. *Sport Psychologist, 6,* 344-357.

Kenow, L., & Williams, J.M. (1993). *Factor structure of the Coaching Behavior Questionnaire and its relationship to anxiety and self-confidence.* Unpublished manuscript, University of Arizona, Tucson.

Kim, B.-H., Lee, H.-K., & Lee, J.-Y. (1990). *A study on the coaches' leadership behavior in sports.* Unpublished manuscript, Korea Sport Science Institute, Seoul.

Lacoste, P.L., & Laurencelle, L. (1989). *The French validation of the Leadership Scale for Sports.* Unpublished manuscript, Université du Quebec at Trois-Rivieres, PQ.

Mageau, G.A., & Vallerand, R.J. (2003). The coach–athlete relationship: A motivational model. *Journal of Sports Sciences, 21,* 883-904.

Price, M.S., & Weiss, M.R. (2000). Relationships among coach burnout, coach behaviors, and athletes' psychological responses. *Sport Psychologist, 14,* 391-409.

Ryan, R.M., & Deci, E.L. (2000). Self determination theory and the facilitation of intrinsic motivation, social development, and well being. *American Psychologist, 55,* 68-78.

Ryan, R.M., & Deci, E.L. (2002). An overview of self-determination theory: An organismic-dialectical perspective. In E.L. Deci, & R.M. Ryan (Eds.), *Handbook of self-determination research* (pp. 3-33). Rochester, NY: University of Rochester Press.

Serpa, S., Lacoste, P., Pataco, V., & Santos, F. (1988). *Methodology of translation and adaptation of a specific sport test: A Leadership Scale for Sports.* Paper presented at the 2nd National Symposium on Psychology Research, Lisbon, Portugal.

Smith, L.S., Fry, M.D., Ethington, C.A., & Li, Y. (2005). The effect of female athletes' perceptions of their coaches' behaviors on their perceptions of the motivational climate. *Journal of Applied Sport Psychology, 17,* 170-177.

Smith, R.E., Nolan, W.S., Zane, F.L., Smoll, F.L., & Coppel, D.B. (1983). Behavioral assessment in youth sports: Coaching behaviors and children's attitudes. *Medicine and Science in Sports and Exercise, 15*(3), 208-214.

Smith, R.E., & Smoll, F.L. (1990). Self-esteem and children's reactions to youth sport coaching behaviors: A field study of self-enhancement processes. *Developmental Psychology, 26*(6), 987-993.

Smith, R.E., Smoll, F.L., & Christensen, D.L. (1996). Behavioral assessment and interventions in youth sports. *Behavior Modification, 20*(1), 3-44.

Smith, R.E., Smoll, F.L., & Curtis, B. (1978). Coaching behaviors in Little League Baseball. In F.L. Smoll & R.E. Smith (Eds.), *Psychological perspectives on youth sports* (pp. 173-201). Washington, DC: Hemisphere.

Smith, R.E., Smoll, F.L., & Hunt, E.B. (1977). A system for the behavioral assessment of athletic coaches. *Research Quarterly, 48*, 401-407.

Smith, R.E., Zane, N.W.S., Smoll, F.L., & Coppel, D.B. (1983). Behavioral assessment in youth sports: Coaching bejaviors and children's attitudes. *Medicine and Science in Sport and Exercise, 15*, 208-214.

Smoll, F.L., & Smith, R.E. (1989). Leadership behaviors in sport: A theoretical model and research paradigm. *Journal of Applied Social Psychology, 19*, 1522-1551.

Smoll, F.L., Smith, R.E., Barnett, N.P., & Everett, J.J. (1993). Enhancement of children's self-esteem through social support training for youth sport coaches. *Journal of Applied Psychology, 78*(4), 602-610.

Smoll, F.L., Smith, R.E., Curtis, B., & Hunt, E. (1978). Toward a mediational model of coach-player relationships. *Research Quarterly, 49*, 528-541.

Trail, G.T. (2004). Leadership, cohesion, and outcomes in scholastic sports. *International Journal of Sport Management, 5*(2), 111-132.

Tutko, T.A., & Richards, J.W. (1971). *Psychology of coaching.* Boston: Allyn & Bacon.

Vallerand, R.J. (2007). Intrinsic and extrinsic motivation in sport and physical activity. In G. Tenenbaum & R.C. Eklund (Eds.), *Handbook of sport psychology* (pp. 59-83). Hoboken, NJ: Wiley.

Williams, L.M., Jerome, G.L., Kenow, L.J., Rogers, T., Sartain, T.A., & Darland, G. (2003). Factor structure of the Coaching Behavior Questionnaire and its relationship to athlete variables. *Sport Psychologist, 17*(1), 16-34.

Zhang, J., Jensen, B.E., & Mann, B.L. (1997). Modification and revision of the Leadership Scale for Sport. *Journal of Sport Behavior, 20*(1), 105-121.

Chapter 38

Bandura, A. (1977). *Social learning theory.* Englewood Cliffs, NJ: Prentice Hall.

Bandura, A. (1991). Social cognitive theory of moral thought and action. In W.M. Kurtines & J.L. Gewirtz (Eds.), *Handbook of moral behavior and development: Theory, research, and applications* (Vol. 1, pp. 71-129). Hillsdale, NJ: Erlbaum.

Bandura, A. (1999). Moral disengagement in the perpetration of inhumanities. *Personality and Social Psychology Review, 3*, 193-209.

Blasi, A. (1980). Bridging moral cognition and moral action: A critical review of the literature. *Psychological Bulletin, 88*, 1-45.

Blasi, A. (1987). Comment: The psychological definitions of morality. In J. Kegan and S. Lamb (Eds.), *The emergence of morality in young children* (pp. 83-90). Chicago: University of Chicago Press.

Boardley, I.D., & Kavussanu, M. (2009). The influence of social variables and moral disengagement on prosocial and antisocial behaviors in field hockey and netball. *Journal of Sports Sciences, 27*, 843-854.

Boardley, I.D., & Kavussanu, M. (2010). Effects of goal orientation and perceived value of toughness on antisocial behavior: The mediating role of moral disengagement. *Journal of Sport & Exercise Psychology, 33*, 176-192.

Bredemeier, B.L., & Shields, D.L. (1984). The utility of moral stage analysis in the investigation of athletic aggression. *Sociology of Sport Journal, 1*, 138-149.

Bredemeier, B.J.L., & Shields, D.L. (1998). Moral assessment in sport psychology. In J.L. Duda (Ed.), *Advances in sport and exercise psychology measurement* (pp. 257-276). Morgantown, WV: Fitness Information Technology Press.

Carlo, G. (2006). Care-based and altruistically based morality. In M. Killen & J. Smetana (Eds.), *Handbook of moral development* (551-579). Mahwah, NJ: Erlbaum.

Cortina, J.M. (1993). What is coefficient alpha? An examination of theory and applications. *Journal of Applied Psychology, 78*, 98-104.

Coulomb, G., & Pfister, R. (1998). Aggressive behaviors in soccer as related to competitive level and time: A field study. *Journal of Sport Behavior, 21*, 222-231.

Coulomb-Cabagno, G., & Rascle, O. (2006). Team sports players' observed aggression as a function of sex, competitive level, and sport type. *Journal of Applied Social Psychology, 36*, 1980-2000.

Eisenberg, N. (2000). Emotion, regulation, and moral development. *Annual Review of Psychology, 51*, 665-697.

Eisenberg, N., & Fabes, R.A. (1998). Prosocial development. In N. Eisenberg (Ed.), *Handbook of child psychology, Vol. 3: Social, emotional, and personality development* (pp. 701-778). New York: Wiley.

Gee, C.J., & Leith, L.M. (2007). Aggressive behavior in professional ice hockey: A cross-cultural comparison of North American and European born NHL players. *Psychology of Sport and Exercise, 8*, 567-583.

Gibbons, S.L., & Ebbeck, V. (1997). The effect of different teaching strategies on the moral development of physical education students. *Journal of Teaching in Physical Education, 17*, 85-98.

Gibbons, S., Ebbeck, V., & Weiss, M. (1995). Fair play for kids: Effects on the moral development of children in physical education. *Research Quarterly for Exercise and Sport, 66*, 245-255.

Haan, N. (1991). Moral development and action from a social constructivist perspective. In W.M. Kurtines & J.L. Gerwitz (Eds.), *Handbook of moral behavior and development: Vol. 1. Theory* (pp. 251-273). Hillsdale, NJ: Erlbaum.

Hanegby, R., & Tenenbaum, G. (2001). Blame it on the racket: Norm-breaking behaviors among junior tennis players. *Psychology of Sport and Exercise, 2*, 117-134.

Hassandra, M., Goudas, M., Hatzigeorgiadis, A., & Theodorakis, Y. (2007). A fair play intervention program in school Olympic education. *European Journal of Psychology of Education, 22*, 99-114.

Hassandra, M., Hatzigeorgiadis, A., & Goudas, M. (2005). Confirmatory factor analysis of the Fair Play in Physical Education Questionnaire. In *Proceedings of the 8th European Conference of Psychological Assessment* (pp. 82-83), Budapest: Hungarian Psychological Association.

Horrocks, R. (1979). The relationship of selected prosocial play behaviors in children to moral reasoning, youth sports, participation, and perception of sportsmanship. *Dissertation Abstracts International, 40*(04-A).

Husman, B., & Silva, J. (1984). Aggression: Definitional considerations. In J.M. Silva, & R.S. Weinberg (Eds.), *Psychological foundations of sport* (pp. 246-260). Champaign, IL: Human Kinetics.

Jones, M.V., Bray, S.R., & Olivier, S. (2005). Game location and aggression in rugby league. *Journal of Sports Sciences, 23*, 387-393.

Kavussanu, M. (2006). Motivational predictors of prosocial and antisocial behaviour in football. *Journal of Sports Sciences, 24*(6), 575-588.

Kavussanu, M. (2008). Moral behaviour in sport: A critical review of the literature. *International Review of Sport and Exercise Psychology, 1*, 124-138.

Kavussanu, M., & Boardley, I.D. (2009). The Prosocial and Antisocial Behavior in Sport Scale. *Journal of Sport & Exercise Psychology, 31*, 1-23.

Kavussanu, M., & Roberts, G.C. (2001). Moral functioning in sport: An achievement goal perspective. *Journal of Sport & Exercise Psychology, 23*, 37-54.

Kavussanu, M., Roberts, G.C., & Ntoumanis, N. (2002). Contextual influences on moral functioning of college basketball players. *The Sport Psychologist, 16*, 347-367.

Kavussanu, M., Stamp, R., Slade, G., & Ring, C. (2009). Observed prosocial and antisocial behaviors in male and female soccer players. *Journal of Applied Sport Psychology, 21*(Suppl. 1), S62-S76.

Kirker, B., Tenenbaum, G., & Mattson, J. (2000). An investigation of the dynamics of aggression: Direct observations in ice hockey and basketball. *Research Quarterly for Exercise and Sport, 71*, 373-386.

Kohlberg, L. (1984). *Essays on moral development: Vol. 2. The psychology of moral development.* San Francisco: Harper & Row.

LaVoi, N.M., & Babkes Stellino, M. (2008). The relation between perceived parent-created sport climate and competitive male youth hockey players' good and poor sport behaviors. *The Journal of Psychology, 142*, 471-495.

Lee, M.J., Whitehead, J., & Ntoumanis, N. (2007). Development of the Attitudes to Moral Decision-Making in Youth Sport Questionnaire (AMDYSQ). *Psychology of Sport and Exercise, 8*, 369-392.

Lee, M.J., Whitehead, J., Ntoumanis, N., & Hatzigeorgiadis, A. (2008). Relationships among values, achievement orientations, and attitudes in youth sport. *Journal of Sport & Exercise Psychology, 30*, 588-610.

McGuire, E.J., Courneya, K.S., Widmeyer, W.N., & Carron, A.V. (1992). Aggression as a potential mediator of the home advantage in professional ice hockey. *Journal of Sport & Exercise Psychology, 14*, 148-158.

Miller, B.W., Roberts, G.C., & Ommundsen, Y. (2005). Effect of perceived motivational climate on moral functioning, team moral atmosphere perceptions, and the legitimacy of intentionally injurious acts among competitive youth football players. *Psychology of Sport and Exercise, 6*, 461-477.

Rascle, O., Coulomb, G., & Pfister, R. (1998). Aggression and goal orientations in handball: Influence of institutional sport context. *Perceptual and Motor Skills, 86*, 1347-1360.

Rest, J.R. (1984). The major components of morality. In W. Kurtines & J. Gewirtz (Eds.), *Morality, moral behavior, and moral development* (pp. 556-629). New York: Wiley.

Rutten, E.A., Dekovic, M., Stams, G.J.J.M., Schuengel, C., Hoeksmad, J.B., & Biesta, G.J.J. (2008). On- and off-field antisocial and prosocial behavior in adolescent soccer players: A multilevel study. *Journal of Youth and Adolescence, 31*, 371-387.

Sage, L., & Kavussanu, M. (2007). Multiple goal orientations as predictors of moral behavior in youth soccer. *The Sport Psychologist, 21*, 417-437.

Sage, L., & Kavussanu, M. (2008). An exploration of temporal stability and reciprocal relationships between goal orientations, motivational climate and prosocial and antisocial behaviour in youth football. *Journal of Sports Sciences, 26*, 717-732.

Sage, L., Kavussanu, M., & Duda, J.L. (2006). Goal orientations and moral identity as predictors of prosocial and antisocial functioning in male association football players. *Journal of Sports Sciences, 24*, 455-466.

Sheldon, J.P., & Aimar, C.M. (2001). The role aggression plays in successful and unsuccessful ice hockey behaviors. *Research Quarterly for Exercise and Sport, 72*, 304-309.

Shields, D.L., & Bredemeier, B.J.L. (1995). *Character development and physical activity.* Champaign, IL: Human Kinetics.

Shields, D.L., & Bredemeier, B.J.L. (2007). Advances in sport morality research. In G. Tenenbaum & R.C. Eklund (Eds.), *Handbook of sport psychology* (3rd. ed., pp. 662-683). Indianapolis: Wiley.

Shields, D.L., Bredemeier, B.L., LaVoi, N.M., & Power, F.C. (2005). The sport behavior of youth, parents, and coaches: The good, the bad, and the ugly. *Journal of Research in Character Education, 3*, 43-59.

Shields, D.L., LaVoi, N.M., Bredemeier, B.L., & Power, F.C. (2007). Predictors of poor sportspersonship in youth sports: Personal attitudes and social influences. *Journal of Sport & Exercise Psychology, 29*, 747-762.

Stephens, D.E. (1998). Aggression. In J.L. Duda (Ed.), *Advances in sport and exercise psychology measurement* (pp. 277-292). Morgantown, WV: Fitness Information Technology Press.

Stephens, D.E., Bredemeier, B.J.L., & Shields, D.L. (1997). Construction of a measure designed to assess players' descriptions and prescriptions for moral behavior in youth sport soccer. *International Journal of Sport Psychology, 28*, 370-390.

Stuart, M.E., & Ebbeck, V. (1995). The influence of perceived social approval on moral development in youth sport. *International Journal of Sport Psychology, 28*, 370-390.

Tisak, M.S., Tisak, J., & Goldstein, S.E. (2006). Aggression, delinquency, and morality: A social-cognitive perspective. In M. Killen & J. Smetana (Eds.), *Handbook of moral development* (pp. 611-632). Mahwah, NJ: Erlbaum.

Turiel, E. (1983). *The development of social knowledge: Morality and convention.* Cambridge, UK: Cambridge University Press.

Vallerand, R.J., Briere, N.M., Blanchard, C., & Provencher, P. (1997). Development and validation of the Multidimensional Sportspersonship Orientations Scale. *Journal of Sport & Exercise Psychology, 19*(2), 197-206.

Weiss, M.R., Smith, A.L., & Stuntz, C.P. (2008). Moral development in sport and physical activity. In T.S. Horn (Ed.), *Advances in sport psychology* (pp. 187-210). Champaign, IL: Human Kinetics.

Chapter 39

ActiGraph. (2009). *Accelerometers.* Retrieved from http://www.theactigraph.com

Accusplit Inc. (2009). *Pedometers.* Retrieved from http://www.accusplit.com

Ainsworth, B. E., Jacobs Jr., D. R., & Leon, A. S. (1993). Validity and reliability of self reported activity status: The lipid research clinics questionnaire. *Medicine and Science in Sports and Exercise, 25*, 92-98.

American College of Sports Medicine. (1998). ACSM position stand on exercise and physical activity for older adults. *Medicine and Science in Sports and Exercise, 30*(6), 992-1008.

Astrand, P.O., & Rodahl, K. (1970). *Textbook of work physiology.* New York: McGrawHill.

Badenhop, D. T., Cleary, P. A., Schaal, S. F., Fox, E. L., & Bartels, R. L. (1983). Physiological adjustments to higher or lower intensity exercise in elders. *Medicine and Science in Sports and Exercise, 15*, 496-502.

Ballard-Barbash, R., & Swanson, C.A. (1996). Body weight: Estimation of risk for breast and endometrial cancers. *American Journal of Clinical Nutrition, 63n*, 437S-441S.

Barry, A. J., Daly, J. W., Pruett, E. D. R., Steinmetz, J. R., Page, H. F., Birkhead, H. C., et al. (1966). The effects of physical conditioning on older individuals: Work capacity, circulatory respiratory function, and work electrocardiogram. *Journal of Gerontology, 21*, 182-191.

Baquet, G., Stratton, G., Van Praagh, E., & Berthoin, S. (2007). Improving physical activity assessment in prepubertal children with high-frequency accelerometry monitoring: A methodological issue. *Preventive Medicine. 46*, 317-324.

BioTrainerUSA. (2009). *Accelerometers.* Retrieved from http://www.biotrainerusa.com

Blair, S. N., Goodyear, L. W., Gibbons, L. W., & Cooper, K. H. (1984). Physical fitness and incidence of hypertension in healthy normotensive men and women. *Journal of the American Medical Association, 252*, 487-490.

BodyMedia, Inc. (2009). *Multichannel Activity Monitors.* Retrieved from http://www.sensewear.com

Borkan, G. A., Hults, D. E., Gerzof, S. G., Robbins, A. H., & Silbert, C. K. (1983). Age changes in body composition revealed by computed tomography. *Journal of Gerontology, 38*, 673-677.

Brozek, J. (1952). Changes of body composition in man during maturity and their nutritional implications. *Federation Proceedings, 11*, 784-793.

Bouchard, C., Shephard, R. J., & Stephens T. (Eds.). (1994). *Physical activity, fitness, and health: International proceedings and consensus statement.* Champaign, IL: Human Kinetics Publishers.

Bouchard, C., An, P., Rice, T., Skinner, J. S., Wilmore, J. H., Gagnon, J., . . . Rao, D. C. (1999). familial aggregation of VO(2max) response to exercise training: Results from the heritage family study. *Journal of Applied Physiology, 87*(3), 1003-1008.

Buckworth, J., & Dishman R. K. (2002). *Exercise psychology.* Champaign, IL: Human Kinetics.

CamNtech. (2008). *Actiheart.* Retrieved from www.metrisense.com/docs/actiheart_brochure.pdf

Cardinal, B. J., & Sachs, M. L. (1996). Effects of mail mediated, stage matched exercise Behavior change strategies on female adults' leisure time exercise behavior. *Journal of Sports Medicine and Physical Fitness, 36*, 100-107.

Carron, A. V. Hausenblas. H. A., & Estabrooks, P. A. (2003). *The psychology of physical education.* New York: McGrawHill.

Caspersen, C. J. (1989). Physical activity epidemiology: Concepts, methods, and applications to exercise science. *Exercise Sport Science Review, 17*, 423-473.

Casperson, C. J., Bloemburg, W. H., Sarris, W. H. M., Merritt, R. K., & Kromhout, D. (1991). The prevalence of selected physical activity and their relation with coronary heart disease risk factors in elderly men: The Zutphen study. *American Journal of Epidemiology, 1078-1092.

Cauley, J. A., Kriska, A. M., LaPorte, R. E., Sandler, R. B., & Pambianco, G. (1987). A two year randomized exercise trial in older women: Effects on HDL cholesterol. *Atherosclerosis, 66*, 247-258.

Ceesay, S. M., Prentice, A. M., Day, K. C., Murgatroyd, P. R., Goldberg, G. R., Scott, W., & Spurr, G. B. (1989). The use of heart hate monitoring in the estimation of energy expenditure: A validation study using indirect whole-body calorimetry. *British Journal of Nutrition, 61*(2), 175-186.

Centers for Disease Control and Prevention (CDC). (1996). Factors associated with prevalent self reported arthritis and other rheumatic conditions – United States 1989-1991. *Morbidity and Mortality Weekly Report, 45*, 487-491.

Colditz, G. A., Willet, W. C., Rotnitzky, A., & Manson, J. E. (1995). Weight gain as a risk factor for clinical diabetes mellitus in women. *Annals of Internal Medicine, 122*, 481-486.

ConsumerSearch Inc. (2009). *Heart rate monitors: reviews.* Retrieved from http://www.consumersearch.com/heart-ratemonitor

Dauncey, M. J., & James, W. P. (1979). Assessment of the heart rate method for determining energy expenditure in man, using a whole-body calorimeter. *British Journal of Nutrition, 42*(1), 113.

Daniel, Sizer, & Latman. (2005). Evaluation of *body composition* methods for accuracy. *Biomedical Instrumentation and Technology, 39*(5), 397-405.

Davidson, L., McNeill, G., Haggarty, P., Smith, J. S., & Franklin, M. F. (1997). Free living energy expenditure of adult men assessed by continuous heart rate monitoring and doubly labeled water. *British Journal of Nutrition, 78*(5), 695-708.

Di Pietro, L. C., Caspersen, A. M., Ostfeld, A. M., & Nadel, E. M. (1993). A survey for assessing physical activity among older adults. *Medicine and Science in Sports and Exercise, 25*, 628-642.

Drinkwater, B.L., Horvath. S. M., & Wells, C. L. (1975). Aerobic power of females, ages 10 to 68. *Journal of Gerontology, 30*, 385-394.

Fehling, P. C., Smith, D. L., Warner, S. E., & Dalsky, G. P. (1999). Comparison of accelerometers with oxygen uptake in older adults during exercise. *Medicine and Science in Sports and Exercise, 31*(1), 171-175.

Fiatarone, M. A., Marks E. C., Ryan, N. D., Meredith, C. N., Lipsitz, L. A., & Evans, W. J. (1990). High intensity strength training in nonagenarians. *Journal of the American Medical Association, 26*(30), 3029-3034.

Fiatarone, M. A., O'Neill, E. F., Ryan, N. D., Clements, K. M., Solares, G. R., Nelson, M. E., . . . Evans, W. J. (1994). Exercise training and nutritional supplementation for physical frailty in very elderly people. *New England Journal of Medicine, 330*, 1769-1775.

Felson, D. T. (1996). Weight and Osteoarthritis. *American Journal of Clinical Nutrition, 63*, 430S-432S.

Freedson, P., Pober, D., & Janz, K. F. (2005). Calibration of accelerometer output for children. *Medicine and Science Sports and Exercise, 7*, S523-530.

Frontera, W. R., Meredith, C. N., O'Reilly, K. P., Knuttgen, H. G., & Evans. W. J. (1988). Strength conditioning in older men: Skeletal muscle hypertrophy and improved function. *Journal of Applied Physiology, 64*, 1038-1044.

Gilders, R. M., Voner, C., & Dudley, G. A. (1989). Endurance training and blood pressure in normotensive and hypertensive Adults. *Medicine and Science in Sports and Exercise, 21*, 629-636.

Godin, G., & Shepard, R. J. (1985). A simple method to assess exercise behavior in the community. *Canadian Journal of Applied Sports Sciences, 10*, 141-146.

Hagberg, J. M., Graves, J. E., Limacher, M., Woods, D. R., Leggett, S. H., Cononie, C., . . . Pollock, M. L. (1989). Cardiovascular responses of 70-79 year old men and women to exercise training. *Journal of Applied Physiology, 66*, 2589-2594.

Hartley, L. H., Grimby, G., Kilbom, A., Nilsson, N. J., Åstrand, I., Bjure, J., . . . Saltin, B. (1969). Physical training in sedentary middle aged and older men. *Scandinavian Journal of Clinical and Laboratory Investigation, 24*, 335-344.

Heath, G. W., Hagberg, J. M., Ehsani, A. A., & Holloszy, J. O. (1981). A Physiological comparison of young and older endurance athletes. *Journal of Applied Physiology, 51,* 634-640.

Heyward, V. H., & Wagner, D. R. (2004). *Applied body composition assessment* (2ⁿᵈ ed.). Champaign, IL: Human Kinetics.

Heyward, V. H. (2006). *Advanced fitness assessment and exercise prescription* (5ᵗʰ ed.). Champaign, IL: Human Kinetics.

Horan, M. J. & Lenfant, C. (1990). Epidemiology of blood pressure and predictors of hypertension. *Hypertension, 15*(Suppl I), I20-I24.

Huang, Y., Macera, C. A., Blair, S. N., Brill, P. A., Kohl, H. W., 3rd, & Kronenfeld, J. J. (1998). Physical fitness, physical activity, and functional limitation in adults aged 40 and older. *Medicine and Science in Sports and Exercise, 30,* 1430-1435.

Jacobs Jr., D. R., Ainsworth, B. E., Hartman, T. J., & Leon, A. S. (1993). A simultaneous evaluation of 10 commonly used physical activity questionnaires. *Medicine and Science in Sports and Exercise, 25,* 81-91.

Jago, R., Watson, K., Baranowski, T., Zakeri, Yoo, S., Baranowski, J., & Conry, K. (2006). Pedometer reliability, validity and daily activity targets among 10 to 15 year old boys. *Journal of Sports Sciences, 24*(3), 241-251.

Jette, A. M. & Branch, L. G. (1981). The Framingham disability study: II – physical disability among the aging. *American Journal of Public Health, 71,* 1211-1216.

Kalkwarf, H. J., Haas, J. D., Belko, A. Z., Roach, R. C., & Roe, D. A. (1989). Accuracy of heart rate monitoring and activity diaries for estimating energy expenditure. *American Journal of Clinical Nutrition, 49*(1) 37-43.

Kang, J. (2008). *Primer for exercise science.* Champaign, IL: Human Kinetics.

Kasch, F. W., Phillips W. H., Carter J. E. L., & Boyer, J. L. (1972). Cardiovascular changes in middle-aged men during two years of training. *Journal of Applied Physiology, 314,* 53-57.

Kasch, F.W., & Wallace, J. P. (1976). Physiological variables during 10 years of endurance exercise. *Medicine and Science in Sports, 8,* 58.

Kasch F. W., Boyer J. L., Van Camp, S. P., Verity L. S., & Wallace J. P. (1993). Effect of exercise on cardiovascular aging. *Age and Aging, 22,* 510.

Kashiwazaki, H. (1999). Heart rate monitoring as a field method for estimating energy expenditure as evaluated by the doubly labeled water method. *Journal of Nutritional Science and Vitaminology, 45*(1), 79-94.

King, A. C., Haskell,W. L., Taylor, C. B., Kraemer, H. C., & DeBusk, R. F. (1991). Group vs. home based exercise training in healthy older men and women: A community based clinical trial. *Journal of the American Medical Association, 266*(11), 1535-1542.

Kohrt, W. M., Malley, M. T., Coggan, A. R., Spina, R. J., Ogawa, T., Ehsani, A. A., . . . Holloszy, J. O. (1991). Effects of gender, age and fitness level on response of VO₂max to training in 60-71 year olds. *Journal of Applied Physiology, 71,* 2004-2011.

Kriska, A. M., & Casperson, C. J. (1997). Introduction to a collection of physical activity questionnaires. *Medicine and Science in Sports and Exercise, 29*(6, suppl), S5-S9.

Lasco, R. A., Curry, R. H., Dickson,V. J., Powers, J., Menes, S., & Merritt, R. K. (1989). Participation rates, weight loss, and blood pressure changes among obese women in a nutrition exercise program. *Public Health Reports, 104*(6), 641-646.

Lew, E. A. (1985). Mortality and weight: Insured lives and the American Cancer Society studies. *Annals of Internal Medicine, 103,* 1024-1029.

Li, R., Deurenberg, P., & Hautvast, J. G. (1993). A critical evaluation of heart rate monitoring to assess energy expenditure in individuals. *American Journal of Clinical Nutrition, 58*(5), 602-607.

Livingstone, M. B., Prentice, A. M., Coward, W.A., Ceesay, S. M., Strain, J. J., McKenna, P. G.,. . . Hickey, R. J. (1990). Simultaneous measurement of free-living energy expenditure by the doubly labeled water method and heart rate monitoring. *American Journal of Clinical Nutrition, 52*(1), 59-65.

Marcus, B. H., Banspach, S.W., Lafebvre, R. C., Rossi, J. S., Carleton, R. A., & Abrams, D. B. (1992). Using the stages of change model to increase the adoption of physical activity among community participants. *American Journal of Health Promotion, 6*(6), 424-429.

Marcus, B. H., & Stanton, A. L. (1993). Evaluation of relapse prevention and reinforcement interventions to promote exercise adherence in sedentary females. *Research Quarterly for Exercise and Sport, 64,* 447-452.

Manson, J. E., Nathan, D. M., Krolewski, A. S., Stampfer, M. J., Willett, W. C., Hennekens, C. H. (1992). A prospective study of exercise and incidence of diabetes among U.S. male physicians. *Journal of the American Medical Association, 268*(1), 63-67.

McArdle, W. D., Katch, F. I., & Katch, V. L. (2007). Exercise physiology: Energy, nutrition, & human performance (6ᵗʰ ed.). Philidelphia: Lippincott Williams & Wilkins.

McAuley, E., & Jacobson, L. (1991). Self-efficacy and exercise participation in sedentary adult females. *American Journal Health Promotion, 5*(3), 185-191.

McCaron, D. A., & Reusser, M. E. (1996). Body weight and blood pressure regulations. *American Journal of Clinical Nutrition, 63,* 423S-425S.

McCrory, M. A., Mole, P. A., Nommsen-Rivers, L. A., & Dewey, K. G. (1997). Between day and within day variability in the relation between heart rate and oxygen consumption: Effect on the estimation of energy expenditure by heart rate monitoring. *Journal of the American Medical Association, 66*(1), 18-25.

McKenzie, T. L., Marshall, S. J., Sallis, J. F., & Conway, T. L. (2000). Student activity levels, lesson context, and teacher behavior during middle school physical education. *Research Quarterly for Exercise and Sport, 71,* 249-259.

McKenzie, T. L., Sallis, J. F., & Nader, P. R. (1991). SOFIT: System for observing fitness instruction time. *Journal of Teaching in Physical Education, 11,* 195-205.

McKenzie, T. L., Sallis, J. F., Prochaska, J. J., Conway, T. L., Marshall, S. J., & Rosengard, P. (2004). Evaluation of a two year middle school physical education intervention: MSPAN. *Medicine and Science in Sports and Exercise, 36*(8), 1382-1388.

Meredith, C. N., Frontera, W. R., Fisher, E. C., Hughes, V. A., Herland, J. C., Edwards, J., & Evans, W. J. (1989). Peripheral effects of endurance training in young and old subjects. *Journal of Applied Physiology, 66,* 2844-2849.

MetriSense Inc. (2009). Actiheart. Retrieved from http://www.metrisense.com/products/9.html

Mitchell, J., Tate, C., Raven, P., Cobb, F., Kraus, W., Moreadith, R., . . . Wenger, N. (1992). Acute response and chronic adaptation to exercise in women. *Medicine and Science in Sports and Exercise, 24,* S258-265.

Montoye, H. J., Kemper, H. C. G., Saris, W. H. M., & Washburn, R. A. (1996). *Measuring physical activity and energy expenditure.* Champaign, IL: Human Kinetics.

Morio, B., Ritz, P., Verdier,. E, Montaurier, C., Beaufrere, B., & Vermorel, M. (1997). Critical evaluation of the factorial and heart rate recording methods for the determination of energy expenditure of free living elderly people. *British Journal of Nutrition, 78*(5), 709-722.

National Association for Sport and Physical Education. (2005). *Physical education for lifelong fitness: The physical best teacher's guide* (2nd ed.). Champaign, IL: Human Kinetics.

National Institutes of Health, National Heart, Lung, and Blood Institute. (1997). *The sixth report of the joint national committee on detection, evaluation and treatment of High Blood Pressure.* Washington, DC: NIH Publication No. 984080.

New Lifestyles Inc. (2007). *Pedometers and accelerometers.* Retrieved from: http://www.thepedometercompany.com

Nilsson, A., Ekelund, U., Yngve, A., & Sjostrom, M. (2002). Assessing physical activity among children with accelerometers using different time sampling intervals and placements. *Pediatric Exercise Science, 14*, 87-96.

Nigg, C. R. (2001). Explaining adolescent exercise behavior change: A longitudinal application of the transtheoretical model. *Annals of Behavioral Medicine, 23*, 11-20.

Noldus Information Technology. (2009).*Human behavior research.* Retrieved from http://www.noldus.com/humanbehavior-research

Ogawa, T., Spina, R. J., Martin, W. H., Kohrt, W. M., Schectman, K. B., Holloszy, J. O., & Ehsani, A. A. (1992). Effects of aging, sex, and physical training on cardiovascular responses to exercise. *Circulation, 86*, 494-503.

Paffenbarger, R. S., Wing, A. L., Hyde, R. T., & Jung, D. L. (1983). Physical activity and the risk of hypertension in college alumni. *American Journal of Epidemiology, 64*, 748-752.

Pambianco, G., Wing, R. R., & Robertson, R. (1990). Accuracy and reliability of the Caltrac accelerometer for estimating energy expenditure. *Medicine and Science in Sports and Exercise, 22*(3), 858-862.

Polar Electro. (2009). *Heart rate monitors.* Retrieved from http://www.polarusa.com/usen

Pollock, M. L. (1973). The quantification of endurance training programs. *Exercise and Sport Science Reviews, 1*, 155-189.

Pollock, M. L., Dawson, G. A., Miller H. S., Ward Jr., A., Cooper, D., Headley, W., et al. (1976). Physiologic response of men 49 to 65 years of age to endurance training. *Journal of the American Geriatrics Society, 24*, 97-104.

Pollock, M. L., Mengelkoh, L. S., Graves, J. E., Lowenthal, D. T., Limacher, M. C., Foster, C., & Wilmore, J. H. (1997). Twenty year follow-up of aerobic power and body composition of older track athletes. *Journal of Applied Physiology, 82*, 1508-1516.

Ready, A. E., Naimark, B., Ducas, J., Sawatsky, J. V., Boreskie, S. L., Drinkwater, D.T., & Oosterveen, S. (1996). Influence of walking volume on health benefits in women post-menopause. *Medicine and Science in Sports and Exercise, 28*, 1097-1105.

Reiser, L. M., & Schlenk, E. A. (2009). Clinical use of physical activity measures. *Journal of the American Academy of Nurse Practitioners, 21*(2), 87-94.

Richardson, M. T., Leon, A. S., Jacobs Jr., D. R., Ainsworth, B. E., & Serfass, R. (1994). Comprehensive evaluation of the Minnesota leisure time physical activity questionnaire. *Journal of Clinical Epidemiology, 47*, 271-281.

Richardson, M. T, Leon, A. S., Jacobs, D. R., Ainsworth, B. E., & Serfass, R. (1995). Ability of the Caltrac accelerometer to assess daily physical activity. *Journal of Cardiopulmonary Rehabilitation, 15*(2), 107-113.

Ritz, P., & Coward, W. A. (1995). Doubly labeled water measurement of total energy expenditure. *Diabetes Metabolism, 21*(4), 241-251.

Roberts, S. B., Dietz, W., Sharp, T., Dallal, G. E., & Hill, J. O. (1995). Multiple laboratory comparison of the doubly labeled water technique. *Obesity Research, 3*(1), 313.

Rogers, M. A., Hagberg, J. M., Martin, W. H., Ehsani, A. A., & Holloszy, J. O. (1990). Decline in VO2Max with aging in master athletes and sedentary men. *Journal of Applied Physiology, 68*, 2185-2199.

Rogers, M. A., & Evans, W. J. (1993). Changes in skeletal muscle with aging: Effects of exercise training. *Exercise and Sports Science Reviews, 21*, 65-102.

Rothenberg, E., Bosaeus, I., Lernfelt, B., Landahl, S., & Steen, B. (1998). Energy intake and expenditure: Validation of a diet history by heart rate monitoring, activity diary and doubly labeled water. *European Journal of Clinical Nutrition, 52*(11), 832-838.

Rowell, L. B. (1986). *Human circulation: Regulation during physical stress.* New York: Oxford University Press.

Rutgers, C. J., Klijn, M. J., & Deurenberg, P. (1997). The assessment of 24 hour energy expenditure in elderly women by minute by minute heart rate monitoring. *Annals of Nutrition and Metabolism, 41*(2), 83-88.

Sawaya, A. L., Tucker, K., Tsay, R., Willett, W., Saltzman, E., Dallal, G. E., & Roberts, S. B. (1996). Evaluation of four methods for determining energy intake in young and older women: Comparison with doubly labeled water measurements of total energy expenditure. *Journal of the American Medical Association, 63*(4), 491-499.

Sharpe, T., & Koperwas, J. (2003). Behavioral and sequential analysis: principals and practice. California: Sage Publications.

Sharpe, T. (n.d.). Software assist for education and social science settings: Behavior evaluation strategies and taxonomies (BEST) and accompanying qualitative applications. Retrieved from http://www.skware.com/softwaredata/BestCD.pdf

Schoeller, D. A., & Hnilicka, J.M. (1996). Reliability of the doubly labeled water method for the measurement of total daily energy expenditure in free-living subjects. *Journal of Nutrition, 126*, 348S-354S.

Schwartz, R. S., Shuman, W. P., Larson, V., Cain, K. C., Fellingham, . . . Abrass, I. B. (1991). The effect of intensive endurance training on body fat distribution in young and older men. *Metabolism, 40*, 545-551.

Schmidt, M. D., Blizzard, L., Venn, A., Cochrane, J., & Dwyer, T. (2007). Practical considerations when using pedometers to assess physical activity in population studies: Lessons from the Burnie Take Heart Study. *American Alliance for Health, Physical Education, Recreation and Dance, 78*(3), 162–170.

Sharkey, B. J., & Gaskill, S. E. (2007). *Fitness and health.* (6th ed.). Champaign, IL: Human Kinetics.

Siconolfi, S. F., Lasater, T. M., Snow, R. C. K., & Carleton, R. A. (1985). Self-reported physical activity compared with maximal oxygen uptake. *American Journal of Epidemiology, 122*, 101-105.

Sidney, K. H., Shephard, R. J., & Harrison, J. (1977). Endurance training and body composition of the elderly. *American Journal of Clinical Nutrition, 30*, 326-333.

Sidney, K. H. & Shephard, R. J. (1978). Frequency and intensity of exercise training for elderly subjects. *Medicine and Science in Sports, 10*, 125-131.

Smith, A. L., & Biddle, S. J. H. (2008). *Youth physical activity and sedentary behavior: Challenges and solutions.* Champaign, IL: Human Kinetics.

Sportline. (n.d.). *Products/Technology.* Retrieved from http://www.sportline.com

Spurr, G. B., Prentice, A. M., Murgatroyd, P. R., Goldberg, G. R., Reina, J. C., & Christman, N. T. (1988). Energy expenditure from minute by minute heart rate recording: Comparison with indirect calorimetry. *American Journal of Clinical Nutrition, 48*(3), 552-559.

Starling, R. D., Matthews, D. E., Ades, P. A., & Poehlman, E. T. (1999). Assessment of physical activity in older individuals: A doubly labeled water study. *Journal of Applied Physiology, 86*(6), 2090-2096.

Stewart, A. L., Sepsis, P. G., King, A. C., McLellan, B. Y., & Ritter, P. L. (1997). Evaluation of CHAMPS, a physical activity promotion program for older adults. *Annals of Behavioral Medicine, 19*(4), 353-361.

Svendsen, O., Hassager, C., & Christiansen, C. (1994). Six months' follow-up on exercise added to a short-term diet in overweight postmenopausal women: Effects on body composition, resting metabolic rate, cardiovascular risk factors and bone. *International Journal of Obesity, 18,* 692-698.

Tipton, C. M. (1984). Exercise, training, and hypertension. *Exercise Sport Science Review, 12,* 447-505.

Tipton, C. M. (1991). Exercise, training, and hypertension: An update. *Exercise Sport Science Review, 19,* 447-505.

Tipton, M. (2006). *Advanced exercise physiology.* American College of Sports Medicine.

Trappe, S. W., Costill, D. L., Vukovich, M. D., Jones, J., & Melham, T. (1996). Aging among elite distance runners: A 22 year longitudinal study. *Journal of Applied Physiology, 80,* 285-290.

Treuth, M. S., (2002). Applying multiple methods to improve the accuracy of activity assessments. In G. J. Welk (Ed). *Physical activity assessments for health related research.* Champaign, IL: Human Kinetics (pp. 213-226).

Trost, S. G., Pate, R. R., Freedson, P.S., Sallis, J. F., & Taylor, W. C. (2000). Using objective physical activity measures with youth: How many days of monitoring are needed? *Medicine and Science Sports and Exercise, 32,* 426-431.

Tudor-Locke, C. (2002). Taking steps towards increased physical activity: Using pedometers to measure and motivate. *President's Council on Physical Fitness and Sports, 3*(17).

United States Department of Health and Human Services. (2008). *2008 Physical activity guidelines for Americans: Be active, healthy, and happy.* Retrieved from http://www.health.gov/paguidelines/pdf/paguide.pdf

Voorips, L. E., Ravelli, C. J., Dongelmans, C. A., Deurenberg, P., & Van Staveren, W. A. (1991). A physical activity questionnaire for the elderly. *Medicine and Science in Sports and Exercise, 23,* 974-979.

Wallace. (1995). Cardiovascular changes with age and exercise: A 28 year longitudinal study. *Scandinavian Journal of Medicine and Science in Sports, 5,* 147-151.

Washburn, R. A., Smith, K. W., Jette, A. M., & Janney, C.A. (1993). The physical activity scale for the elderly. *Journal of Clinical Epidemiology,* 153-162.

Weber, J., &Wertheim, E. (1989). Relationships of self-monitoring, special attention, body fat percent, and self-motivation to attendance at a community gymnasium. *Journal of Sport and Exercise Psychology, 11,* 105-114.

Welk G. J., & Blair, S. N. (2000) Physical activity protects against the health risks of obesity. *President's Council on Physical Fitness and Sports: Research Digest, 3,* 12.

Welk, G. J. (2002). *Physical activity assessments for health related research.* Champaign, IL: Human Kinetics.

Westerterp, K. R., Brouns, F., Saris, W. H., & Hoor, F. (1988). Comparison of doubly labeled water with respirometry at low and high activity levels. *Journal of Applied Physiology, 65*(1), 53-56.

Willet, W. C., Manson, J. E., Stampfer, M. J., Colditz, G. A., Rosner, B., Speizer, F. E., & Hennekens, C. H. (1995). Weight, weight change, and coronary heart disease in women: Risk within the "normal" weight range. *Journal of the American Medical Association, 273,* 461-465.

Wing, R. R., Matthews, K. A., Kuller, L. H., Smith, D., Becker, D., Plantinga, P. L., & Meilahn, E. N. (1992). Environmental and familial contributions to insulin levels and change in insulin levels in middle aged women. *Journal of the American Medical Association, 268,* 1980-1985.

Wood, P. D., Stefanick, M. L., Williams, P. T., & Haskell, W. L. (1991). The effects on plasma lipoproteins of a prudent weight reducing diet, with or without exercise, in overweight men and women. *New England Journal of Medicine,* 325(7), 461-466.

Woods, S., Sivarajan Froelicher, E., Underhill Motzer, S., & Bridges, E. (2005). *Cardiac nursing* (5th ed.). Philidelphia: Lippincott Williams & Wilkins.

INDEX

Note: The italicized *f* and *t* following page numbers refer to figures and tables, respectively.

ABOUT THE EDITORS

Gershon Tenenbaum, PhD, is a professor of educational psychology at Florida State University in Tallahassee, where he teaches courses on measurement in sport and exercise. He previously served as the director of the Center of Research and Sport Medicine at the Wingate Institute in Israel and was the coordinator of the sport psychology program at the University of Southern Queensland in Australia.

Tenenbaum's research on measurement and statistical methods in the domain of sport and exercise psychology has been widely published, and he has published over 300 articles in peer-refereed journals and book chapters in leading journals in psychology, sport and exercise psychology, sports medicine, and sport sciences. In addition, he has edited and written several handbooks and books, including the *Handbook of Sport and Exercise Psychology, Third Edition* (with Robert Eklund), *Case Studies in Applied Psychophysiology: Neurofeedback and Biofeedback Treatments for Advances in Human Performance* (with William Edmonds), *The Cultural Turn in Sport and Exercise Psychology* (with Tatiana Ryba and Robert Schinke), *Brain and Body in Sport and Exercise: Biofeedback Applications in Performance Enhancement* (with Boris Blumenstein and Michael Bar-Eli), *The Practice of Sport Psychology*, and *Research Methodology in Sport and Exercise Sciences: Quantitative and Qualitative Methods* (with Marcy Driscoll).

Gershon Tenenbaum

Tenenbaum was the president of the International Society of Sport Psychology (ISSP) and a fellow of both the National Academy of Kinesiology (NAK) and the Association for Applied Sport Psychology (AASP). Tenenbaum was the editor of the *International Journal of Sport Psychology* and the *International Journal of Sport and Exercise Psychology*. Each year, he organizes several sessions and symposia on measurement issues at conferences in the United States and abroad.

In 2011, Tenenbaum received the Scientific Award for Scientific Achievement from the American Psychological Association (APA) Division 47 (Sport and Exercise Psychology division). In 2005, he was awarded the Benjamin S. Bloom Professorship from Florida State University and the Presidential Award from the International Society of Sport Psychology. In 2002, he was named a Distinguished Sport Science Scholar Lecturer in sport and exercise psychology for the University of Utah. He was also the recipient of the International Society of Sport Psychology Honor Award in 1997.

Tenenbaum holds a doctorate in measurement and statistics from the University of Chicago. He resides in Tallahassee and enjoys traveling to conferences throughout the world, visiting his homeland of Israel, and watching competitive sport.

Robert C. Eklund, PhD, is a professor of sport psychology in the department of educational psychology and learning systems at Florida State University in Tallahassee, where he was recently named the Mode L. Stone Distinguished Professor of Sport Psychology. He earned his doctoral degree in exercise and sport science with a specialization in sport and exercise psychology from the University of North Carolina at Greensboro. He is a fellow of both the American College of Sports Medicine (ACSM) and the National Academy of Kinesiology (NAK).

Eklund has published over 60 articles in referred journals; coedited (with Gershon Tenenbaum) the prestigious *Handbook of Sport Psychology, Third Edition;* coauthored two measurement manuals; and authored or coauthored

Robert C. Eklund

12 book chapters in the area of sport and exercise psychology. Eklund has presented his research and participated as a keynote lecturer and invited colloquia participant at numerous conferences worldwide.

Eklund is the current editor in chief of the *Journal of Sport and Exercise Psychology* and has served in that capacity since January 2003. He has also served as associate editor for the *Journal of Applied Sport Psychology* and psychology section editor for *Research Quarterly for Exercise and Sport*. In addition to providing editorial review services for a range of scholarly journals, Eklund currently serves as an editorial board member for *The Sport Psychologist; Sport, Exercise, and Performance Psychology; Pamukkale Journal of Sport Sciences; and Hacettepe Journal of Sport Sciences*. In the past, he has served on the editorial boards for the *Journal of Sport and Exercise Psychology* and the *Journal of Applied Sport Psychology*.

Eklund resides in Tallahassee with his wife, Colleen, and two sons, Garth and Kieran. He enjoys their sport involvement immensely as well as their interest in spending sunny afternoons fishing at the beach.

Akihito Kamata

Akihito Kamata, PhD, is a professor of psychometrics and educational measurement in the department of educational methodology, policy, and leadership at the University of Oregon. Before joining the University of Oregon in 2009, he was on faculty at Florida State University for 11 years, where he also served as the chair of the department of educational psychology and learning systems.

Kamata's primary research interest is implementation of item-level test data analysis methodology through item response theory modeling, multilevel modeling, and structural equation modeling. Kamata has done pioneering work on multilevel item response theory modeling, which is represented by his 2001 publication in the *Journal of Educational Measurement*, a special issue on multilevel measurement modeling in the *Journal of Applied Measurement* in 2005, and several book chapters on the topic, including a chapter in the *Handbook of Advanced Multilevel Analysis* (2011). He has other publications on psychometrics, measurement theory, and applied measurement, including articles in the *Journal of Educational Measurement, Applied Psychological Measurement, Structural Equation Modeling,* and *Psychometrika*.